The Literary Digest, Volume 71

Isaac Kaufman Funk, Edward Jewitt Wheeler, William Seaver Woods

THE
LITERARY DIGEST

VOLUME LXXI

OCTOBER, 1921—DECEMBER, 1921

FUNK & WAGNALLS COMPANY, PUBLISHERS
354 TO 360 FOURTH AVENUE, NEW YORK

October 1, 1921

The Literary Digest

(Trade-Mark Reg U.S. Pat. Off.)

New York FUNK & WAGNALLS COMPANY London

PUBLIC OPINION New York combined with The LITERARY DIGEST

The Literary Digest

VOLUME LXXI

(FOR THREE MONTHS ENDING DECEMBER 31, 1921)

INDEX OF SUBJECTS

A

Subject	Date	Page
Accidents due to fatigue	Dec. 24	22
Photographs to prevent	Nov. 26	24
Study of fatal	Nov. 26	58
Acosta, Bert	Nov. 19	58
Actors forsaking Shakespeare	Nov. 5	23
Advertising, "Buy Now"	Nov. 12	72
Aerial wireless torpedo	Nov. 26	13
Aeroplane, Who invented the	Dec. 17	21
Air and ventilation	Oct. 8	64
flights, Keeping fit in	Dec. 3	39
gliders, German	Oct. 15	44
lines, European	Oct. 15	34
navies	Nov. 12	28
Airmen hunting seals	Nov. 5	20
Air-photography, Real estate	Oct. 29	25
Maps by	Nov. 19	22
Airplane race, Pulitzer	Nov. 19	58
Air-tight butter	Nov. 19	21
Alaska's glacier highway	Dec. 31	22
Allies' budget balances	Dec. 24	44
American art, Defending	Oct. 15	24
capital in Europe	Oct. 1	13
A. E. F., Senator Watson attacks	Nov. 26	16
American letters, J.L.Ford on	Dec. 3	25
troops in Germany	Oct. 1	44
America's debtors	Nov. 5	13
lack of criticism	Oct. 29	29
triumph, Press on	Dec. 24	16
Anarchist attack on Herrick	Nov. 5	9
Antiseptics, Varying	Dec. 3	22
Arithmetic, Electrical	Dec. 24	20
Armenia, Distress in	Oct. 22	30
Armies of the world	Nov. 12	14
Arms Conference		
Association of Nations	Dec. 10	5
Asia's Christians and	Dec. 3	28
British-American relations	Nov. 26	14
Canada and	Nov. 19	48
Catechism of	Nov. 12	25
China at	Oct. 15	9
"	Nov. 26	11
"	Dec. 17	13
Christmas and	Dec. 24	28
Delegates to	Nov. 12	37
Disarmament issue	Nov. 12	
ends Anglo-Jap treaty	Dec. 17	16
French attitude	Oct. 22	5
Governors on	Dec. 3	12
Japan at	Dec. 3	5
Japanese comment on	Oct. 1	17
League of Nations and	Oct. 1	7
" " "	Oct. 8	12
Naval agreement	Dec. 31	9
program, Hughes	Nov. 26	7
Submarines in	Dec. 3	16
Russia and	Nov. 19	17
H. G. Wells at	Dec. 17	26
Women at	Nov. 26	48
World press on	Nov. 12	20
See also Disarmament		
Army discipline censured	Nov. 12	29
Physically unfit in	Dec. 24	41
Senator Watson attacks	Nov. 26	16
Art, Defending American	Oct. 15	24
for all the country	Dec. 10	23
Art for America, British	Nov. 5	22
Association of Nations plan	Dec. 10	5
Astronomers vs. biologists	Nov. 5	18
Austria seeks financial aid	Oct. 22	16
Australia, "Empty"	Nov. 5	15
Australian loan from New York	Dec. 17	18
Authors, Older and younger	Dec. 17	26
Automobile bootlegging	Oct. 22	45
distribution, Limits of	Oct. 8	70
tire prices	Dec. 10	58
"hoboes"	Dec. 31	36
transportation, Private	Dec. 31	21
Automobiles, Old	Oct. 15	52
Automobiling across America	Oct. 15	48
and typhoid	Oct. 22	22

B

Subject	Date	Page
Bacteria and antiseptics	Dec. 3	22
Baltic union	Oct. 8	20
Bahaism	Dec. 24	30
Bank leadership	Oct. 15	54
rate normal	Oct. 22	48
Banking in New York, Branch	Nov. 12	73
Beer bills in Congress	Nov. 19	13
Benson, John G.	Oct. 8	31
Bible in schools	Oct. 29	32
Biologists vs. astronomers	Nov. 5	18
Bird and negro, Missionary	Dec. 10	50
Can a snake charm a	Dec. 10	52
Birds, Banded	Dec. 10	51
Bispham, David	Oct. 22	27
Blood pressure	Oct. 1	23
Boat, At sea in a life-	Oct. 22	41
race, Fishermen's	Nov. 19	38
Bombs for police, Tear	Oct. 15	22
Bonds, Warning against foreign	Dec. 3	58
Books, Children's	Nov. 5	42
for France	Oct. 29	27
Books, Recent:		
Adele Doring at Boarding School (North)	Nov. 5	52
Aesop's Fables	Nov. 5	46
Alice's Adventures in Wonderland and Through the Looking Glass (Carroll)	Nov. 5	50
Animal Life in Field and Garden (Fabre)	Dec. 10	52
Arabian Nights Entertainments	Nov. 5	49
At Greenacres (Taggart)	Nov. 5	53
Beggar's Opera (Gay)	Dec. 24	41
Black Diamond, The (Young)	Dec. 3	40
Bolivar Brown (Dudley)	Nov. 5	50
Book of Insects (Fabre)	Dec. 24	39
Book of Jack London (London)	Nov. 5	37
Borough Treasurer, The (Fletcher)	Dec. 3	40
Bottle Imp, The (Taggart)	Nov. 5	53

Subject	Date	Page
Books, Recent:		
Boy Explorers in Darkest New Guinea (Miller)	Nov. 5	46
Boy Hunters in Demerara (Hartley)	Nov. 5	50
Boy Scouts of Campfire Stories (Mathiews)	Nov. 5	45
Brass (Norris)	Oct. 29	46
Breezes (Morse)	Nov. 5	46
Brother Eskimo (Sullivan)	Nov. 5	53
Carrots: Just a Little Boy (Molesworth)	Nov. 5	52
Castaways of Banda Sea (Miller)	Nov. 5	52
Catty Atkins: Riverman (Kelland)	Nov. 5	52
Children's Garland of Verse (Rhys)	Nov. 5	49
Circus Comes to Town, The (Mitchell)	Nov. 5	46
Cuckoo Clock, The (Molesworth)	Nov. 5	52
Days of the Discoverers (Lamprey)	Nov. 5	45
Dodo Wonders (Benson)	Oct. 8	54
Donovan Chance, The (Lynde)	Nov. 5	52
Dragon's Secret, The (Seaman)	Nov. 5	53
Dutch Boy Fifty Years After (Bok)	Nov. 5	42
Education of Eric Lane (McKenna)	Oct. 8	56
Elephant God, The (Casserly)	Nov. 5	50
Everychild (Dodge)	Nov. 5	42
Fairy-Tales and Stories (Anderson)	Nov. 5	42
Fern Seed (Rideout)	Oct. 8	51
Fifty Years a Journalist (Stone)	Dec. 24	36
Folly of Nations (Palmer)	Dec. 3	42
Forty-odd Years in the Literary Shop (Ford)	Dec. 3	24
From Private to Field Marshall (Robertson)	Dec. 24	36
Girls of Highland Hall (Rankin)	Nov. 5	49
Golden West Boys: Injun and Whitey (Hart)	Nov. 5	44
Grim (Flouron)	Dec. 10	48
Hero Tales of Ireland (Curtin)	Nov. 5	42
How It Came About Stories (Linderman)	Nov. 5	45
If Winter Comes (Hutchinson)	Dec. 3	46
In the Tiger's Lair (Miller)	Nov. 5	52
Jim and Peggy at Meadowbrook Farm (O'Kane)	Nov. 5	46
Laramie Holds the Range (Spearman)	Nov. 5	53
Lazy Matilda and Other Tales (Pyle)	Nov. 5	48
Life and Work of Edwin Austin Abbey (Lucas)	Dec. 24	36

Books, Recent: Date Page
Little Back Room, The (Chamberlayne) Oct. 8 52
Little Man with One Shoe (Bailey) Nov. 5 50
London, Book of Jack (London) Nov. 5 37
Master of Man, The (Caine) Oct. 29 48
Memories and Notes of Persons and Places (Colvin) Dec. 24 41
Metipome's Hostage (Barbour) Nov. 5 42
Mind in the Making, The (Robinson) Dec. 24 38
More That Must Be Told (Gibbs) Dec. 24 36
Mountain Memories (Conway) Oct. 22 38
Mr. Waddington of Wyck (Sinclair) Dec. 3 44
Must We Fight Japan? (Pitkin) Nov. 26 29
My Brother, Theodore Roosevelt (Robinson) Nov. 5 32
Dec. 24 38
My Memories (Windischgraetz) Nov. 19 44
One-Third Off (Cobb) Oct. 22 38
Orphan Dinah (Phillpotts) Dec. 3 48
Our Dog Friends Nov. 5 50
Passing of the Old West, The (Evarts) Dec. 24 36
Peeps at Many Lands Nov. 5 48
Physical Growth of Children (Baldwin) Oct. 15 22
Picture Stories from Great Artists (Cody and Dewey) Nov. 5 42
Plays of Edmond Rostand (Norman) Dec. 24 38
Poppy's Pluck (Taggart) Nov. 5 53
Potomac Landings (Wilstach) Dec. 24 36
Public Opinion and the Steel Strike of 1919 Nov. 19 30
Puritan Twins, The (Perkins) Nov. 5 48
Puss-in-Boots, Jr. and the Good Gray Horse (Cory) Nov. 5 50
Queer Little Man (Taggart) Nov. 5 53
Quentin Roosevelt (Roosevelt) Dec. 24 39
Reflection (Coatsworth) Oct. 8 38
Requiescat in Pace (Calgett) Nov. 26 38
Revolutionary, The (Lawrence) Oct. 29 34
Robinson's Collected Poems, Edwin Arlington Dec. 24 38
Romance of Business, The (Forbes) Dec. 24 38
Roosevelt in the Bad Lands (Hagedorn) Dec. 24 38
Roosevelt the Happy Warrior (Gilman) Nov. 5 32; Dec. 24 37
Scottish Chiefs (Porter) Nov. 5 50
Sport of Our Ancestors, The (DeBooke) Dec. 24 39
Star People, The (Johnson) Nov. 5 44
Stories of American Inventions (McFee) Nov. 5 45
Strange Adventures of a Pebble (Hawksworth) Nov. 5 44
Street of Faces, The (Vince) Dec. 24 39
Swiss Family Robinson Nov. 5 50
Tale of Two Cities (Dickens) Nov. 5 42
Thankful Spicers, The (Brownell) Nov. 5 50
Their Friendly Enemy (Hunting) Nov. 5 52
Three Soldiers (Dos Passos) Nov. 12 29

Books, Recent: Date Page
To Let (Galsworthy) Oct. 29 43
Tony Sarg Marionette Book (McIsaac) Dec. 24 37
Treasury of Flower Stories (McFee) Nov. 5 52
Treasury of Plays for Children (Moses) Nov. 5 46
True Account of the Battle of Jutland (Frothingham) Oct. 8 33
Uncollected Poetry and Prose of Walt Whitman (Halloway) Dec. 24 41
Variations (Huneker) Dec. 24 37
War Government of British Dominions (Keith) Oct. 8 20
War Trail, The (Gregor) Nov. 5 42
Wasted Generation, The (Johnson) Dec. 3 49
Welsh Fairy-Tales (Griffis) Nov. 5 50
Westward Hoboes (Dixon) Dec. 31 36
What Happened at Jutland (Gill) Oct. 8 33
What Japan Thinks (Sato) Nov. 12 52
With Beatty in the North Sea (Young) Dec. 24 36
Woodrow Wilson as I Know Him (Tumulty) Dec. 24 36
Bootlegging by automobile Oct. 22 44
Boys fewer, Bad Dec. 31 28
Brazil's economic troubles Nov. 26 21
Bridge built in ten days Oct. 15 21
Britain's colonial revolution Oct. 8 20
dangerous poor Oct. 15 15
temperance reform Nov. 19 20
British-American doctrine, Harding's Nov. 5 5
gold conference Nov. 12 72
relations Nov. 26 14
Harvey on Nov. 26 14
Shaw on Nov. 19 27
Dominions, Women for Nov. 19 19
-French team work needed Nov. 19 18
-Irish negotiations Oct. 1 10
minister warns France Dec. 10 14
on Irish reluctance Oct. 8 21
pictures sold Nov. 5 22
Railway Bill Oct. 8 75
School histories pro- Dec. 31 26
tariff making Oct. 1 56
wealth for unemployed Nov. 5 16
Budget balances, Allies' Dec. 24 44
Federal Dec. 17 9
Building boom and business Dec. 17 58
exteriors, Cleaning Dec. 3 21
trust, Prison for Dec. 10 11
Bus, Railroad motor Nov. 12 73
Buses, Trackless trolley Nov. 26 25
Business below normal Oct. 8 75
Christianizing Oct. 1 31
conditions improving Oct. 15 11
Butter, Carbon-dioxide for Nov. 19 20
"Buy Now" advertising Nov. 12 72

C

Cafeteria, Moving-platform Dec. 24 21
Canada and Arms Conference Nov. 19 48
-United States peace celebration Oct. 8 40
Canada's Americanization Nov. 26 20
Liberal victory Dec. 31 16
soldier farmers Oct. 15 40
Canadian Importer's adventure Oct. 22 41
Canal, New York barge Nov. 19 64
Carbon dioxide for dairy products Nov. 19 20
Caruso's last song Oct. 8 44
Catholic nations at Vatican Oct. 29 30
priests, Investments of Oct. 8 31
revival in France Dec. 31 29
youth, Recruiting Nov. 5 28
Catholics leave Rome, Czech Oct. 22 29
Census: gain and loss Dec. 3 11
density of population Oct. 29 11
Central America, Republic of Oct. 22 11
Europe's reading Oct. 15 25
Chaliapin Dec. 31 24

Date Page
Chaplin's art, Charlie Oct. 8 26
Charcoal for gas masks Oct. 1 48
Charities, Faults of Nov. 19 31
Chautauqua, Briton on Oct. 8 27
Chemical "fruit products" Dec. 10 56
warfare Nov. 12 28
" Dec. 24 8
Chicago, Free press upheld in Oct. 29 13
Chicago's unlettered state Dec. 24 25
Chickens in graphic formations Dec. 10 21
Children grow, How Oct. 15 22
Homes for orphan Dec. 17 29
Punishing Oct. 15 29
Sleep of Dec. 10 21
wage-earners Nov. 26 32
Children's humor Oct. 22 26
China and Shantung Dec. 3 17
" the conference Oct. 15 9
" " " Dec. 17 13
Cooking in Oct. 1 24
Medical education in Nov. 5 57
Slavery of children in Dec. 10 28
China's "declaration of independence" Nov. 26 11
Ten Points Nov. 26 11
Chinese Christians and Conference Dec. 3 28
labor organizing Nov. 5 14
politics, Geography of Oct. 29 21
Christianity in Japan Oct. 22 30
Christmas and disarmament Dec. 24 28
Christianizing business Oct. 1 31
Church and labor Dec. 10 27
and unemployment Oct. 15 29
" workingmen Nov. 26 30
Dramas for the Oct. 29 31
insurance of preachers Nov. 26 31
ministers need critics Nov. 19 32
neglect of the sick Oct. 15 30
press on Ku Klux Klan Oct. 1 30
pulpit dialog Oct. 1 32
pulpits, Empty Oct. 22 28
report on steel strike Nov. 19 30
sectarianism Dec. 31 29
Sensationalism in Oct. 29 32
union still a dream Nov. 26 32
unity in Vermont Oct. 1 32
windows, Lighting Nov. 26 31
Churches, Peace crusade and Nov. 12 32
Church's "social clinic" Oct. 8 31
Clemenceau statue at Ste. Hermine Oct. 22 24
Cobb on reducing, Irving Oct. 22 38
College enrollment high Oct. 8 29
exams, Abolishing Dec. 3 27
Colleges for disarmament Nov. 19 29
Colorado's colored gems Oct. 8 69
Comprest air in Mesopotamia Nov. 19 61
Concrete road upheavals Dec. 10 21
Conference, *See* Arms Conference
Conferences, Former peace Nov. 12 44
Congress, Farm bloc in Dec. 24 10
Constantinople as free city Dec. 3 19
Conversation, Evolution of Nov. 26 29
Corn and pork Dec. 31 42
Burning Nov. 26 12
cob, Uses of Dec. 17 21
from Indian mounds Oct. 8 67
New uses for Dec. 17 20
Warehousing Nov. 19 64
Corsets, Good and bad Nov. 5 20
Cost of living increasing Oct. 8 9
Cotton mills, "Murder" in Nov. 19 32
Court of International Justice Oct. 8 16
Cricket, Why British like Nov. 19 56
Crime decreasing in England Dec. 24 30
Criminal detection by pores Nov. 5 19
Criminals betrayed by skin Dec. 17 40
Curzon warns France, Lord Dec. 10 14
Czecho-Slovakia and Poland Dec. 17 19
Czecho-Slovakia's new church Oct. 22 29

D

Dante, America and Oct. 29 26
DeLipsky's lighting, Nicholas Dec. 10 23
Debtors, America's Nov. 5 13
Delegates to Arms Conference Nov. 12 36
Department stores' business Dec. 17 58
Devils, Modern belief in Dec. 3 30

	Date	Page
Diamond cutting by machine	Dec. 3	22
'*Die Tote Stadt*'	Dec. 17	24
D'Indy, Vincent	Dec. 24	25
Disarmament and League of Nations	Oct. 1	7
	Oct. 8	12
and steel	Dec. 3	14
Colleges for	Nov. 19	29
in dollars	Nov. 12	16
Land	Dec. 3	8
not to be overdone	Oct. 29	12
problems	Nov. 12	7
World leaders on	Nov. 12	24
See also Arms Conference		
Drama vs. novel, Modern	Dec. 31	25
Drinkwater vs. Walpole	Dec. 31	25
DuPont munitions makers	Nov. 19	48
Dyer anti-lynching bill	Dec. 31	11
E		
Earth move, Seeing the	Oct. 29	24
Earth's water drying up	Nov. 5	21
Edison defends questionnaire	Nov. 26	47
Electric fish-stop	Nov. 26	23
power at million volts	Oct. 22	21
signs	Oct. 8	24
Electrical arithmetic	Dec. 24	20
test of emotion	Dec. 17	40
work, Dangers in	Oct. 29	23
Emotion, Electrical test of	Dec. 17	40
Employees fix salaries	Oct. 22	50
England, Crime decreasing in	Dec. 24	30
English week, Better	Oct. 29	36
Europe, American capital in	Oct. 1	13
Plans for financing	Dec. 10	10
European air lines	Oct. 15	34
bandits, Outwitting	Oct. 8	46
budget balances	Dec. 24	44
Europe's reading, Central	Oct. 15	25
Eye glasses, Becoming	Oct. 1	21
Warning against	Dec. 24	20
F		
Families, Shrinking	Nov. 19	22
Family fallacy, Five-in-a-	Oct. 15	56
Farm bloc in Congress	Dec. 24	10
Fatigue, Accidents due to	Dec. 24	22
Financial leadership	Oct. 15	54
Financing Europe	Dec. 10	10
Finger-print "poroscopy"	Nov. 5	19
Finger-prints in art dispute	Oct. 15	26
Firemen, Gas-masks for	Oct. 8	66
Fisher on free press, Judge	Oct. 29	13
Fishermen's race	Nov. 19	38
Fish-stop, Electric	Nov. 26	23
Fishways for salmon	Oct. 15	20
Floods, Protection from	Oct. 29	24
Flys die, How	Nov. 5	21
Foch in America	Dec. 24	32
Foil covers for gum	Nov. 19	23
Food for vegetarians	Oct. 8	69
prospect for winter	Oct. 22	48
Football as a fighting game	Nov. 19	52
Ford and history, Henry	Nov. 26	27
Ford on writing, James L.	Dec. 3	24
Ford's railway wages, Henry	Oct. 15	38
Foreign debtors, America's	Nov. 5	13
Forgery, Detection of	Oct. 1	25
France, America on defense of	Dec. 31	5
and German mark	Nov. 26	18
and land armament	Dec. 3	8
Cost of living in	Nov. 26	57
Germans aid to rebuild	Oct. 29	18
Lord Curzon warns	Dec. 10	14
More books for	Oct. 29	27
Nobel prize for Anatole	Dec. 3	25
Poll on attitude toward	Dec. 31	5
Protestant growth in	Nov. 5	27
retires paper currency	Oct. 22	49
France's Catholic revival	Dec. 31	29
new financial policy	Dec. 17	58
Free press upheld in Chicago	Oct. 29	13
French-British teamwork needed	Nov. 19	18
French feeling on disarmament	Oct. 22	5
Fruit products, Chemistry and	Dec. 10	54
G		
Gadski's German concert	Nov. 19	26
Gainsborough's "Blue Boy" sold	Nov. 5	22
Galvanic reflex and emotion	Dec. 17	40
Gas masks, Charcoal for	Oct. 1	48
for firemen	Oct. 8	66
warfare	Dec. 24	8
Gasoline, Molasses test for	Dec. 3	21
Gems, Colored	Oct. 8	69
Geology and liquor-making	Nov. 26	59
and mountains	Dec. 3	23
German gliders	Oct. 15	44
mark, France and	Nov. 26	18
value	Oct. 15	16
"	Oct. 22	8
marks, Gambling in	Oct. 29	50
militarism	Dec. 10	16
music, Return of	Nov. 19	26
poets in politics	Oct. 1	27
-Poland settlement	Oct. 29	16
reparations payments	Dec. 17	11
Republic's third year	Dec. 31	19
Germans aid to rebuild France	Oct. 29	18
Germany after Russian trade	Oct. 15	18
American troops in	Oct. 1	44
pays in goods	Oct. 1	59
Germany's postage stamps	Dec. 10	58
Germ-laden money	Nov. 26	22
Germs and antiseptics	Dec. 3	22
Poisoning with disease	Dec. 31	21
Girls' Community Club	Dec. 17	30
Glacier highway, Mendenhall	Dec. 31	22
Glasses, *See* Eye-Glasses		
Gliders, German	Oct. 15	44
Gold booms	Oct. 1	58
conference, Anglo-American	Nov. 12	72
output, World's	Nov. 19	66
Gorilla, John Daniel	Dec. 10	44
Governors on Arms Conference	Dec. 3	12
Grape-seed, Oil from	Dec. 10	57
Grapes for raisins	Oct. 8	73
Grasso, Giovanni	Oct. 8	28
Greco-Turk war	Oct. 29	20
Greece's gloomy outlook	Dec. 24	18
Greek war and discontent	Nov. 19	20
Gum, Metal foil covers for	Nov. 19	23
H		
Halifax, Rebuilding	Nov. 19	62
Handwriting test by camera	Oct. 1	25
Hapsburg, Hungary rejects	Nov. 5	7
Tragedy of Charles	Nov. 19	44
Hara assassinated, Premier	Nov. 19	11
Harding on negro, President	Nov. 19	7
Harding's appeal for Russians	Dec. 17	5
British-American doctrine	Nov. 5	5
message to Congress	Dec. 17	9
Yorktown speech	Nov. 5	5
Harvey's "no alliance" speech	Nov. 26	14
Heifetz plays for Helen Keller	Dec. 31	25
Helium for dirigibles	Oct. 1	22
Hens in graphic formation	Dec. 10	21
Herrick, Attack on Ambassador	Nov. 5	9
Histories, Pro-British	Dec. 31	26
History and Henry Ford	Nov. 26	27
teaching, Dull	Nov. 5	24
Holland and Pacific problems	Dec. 3	18
Homes for orphan children	Dec. 17	29
Homicide statistics	Dec. 17	29
Hospital without wards	Oct. 15	20
Houses of straw	Dec. 31	20
Hughes and diplomats, Secretary	Dec. 17	38
Human tropisms	Oct. 1	54
Humor of children	Oct. 22	26
Hungary again rejects Charles	Nov. 5	7
Charles Hapsburg and	Nov. 19	44
Hylan's hold on New York, Mayor	Nov. 19	12
I		
Ice-cream, "Air-tight"	Nov. 19	21
"*Il Piccolo Marat*"	Oct. 1	26
Immigration law, Faults of	Oct. 1	14
India wants self-rule	Oct. 15	17
Indian mounds, Corn from	Oct. 8	67
Inge on Christianity, Dean	Nov. 5	28
Insanity, Danger signals of	Nov. 19	60
Insuring the minister	Nov. 26	31
Interchurch World Movement	Nov. 19	30
Interest, rent, wages, prices	Dec. 3	58
Investors, Government warns	Dec. 3	58
Ireland's secret government	Dec. 24	34
Irish-British negotiations	Oct. 1	10
"	Oct. 1	19
"	Oct. 8	21
Irish Free State	Dec. 17	5
Italian political parties	Dec. 31	18
Socialists and Laborites	Dec. 10	17
theater	Oct. 8	28
J		
Japan and "empty" Australia	Nov. 5	15
Christianity in	Oct. 22	30
Democracy in	Oct. 29	38
on Arms Conference	Oct. 1	17
on Shantung	Dec. 3	17
Japanese Christians and Arms Conference	Dec. 3	28
navalism, Admiral on	Nov. 12	52
plea for publicity	Nov. 26	20
Premier assassinated	Nov. 19	11
treaty scrapped, Anglo-	Dec. 17	16
Japan's needs and pledges	Dec. 3	5
official propaganda	Nov. 5	16
"Jazz" art	Oct. 1	29
Jeritza, Marie	Dec. 17	24
Jobs to fit mental levels	Nov. 5	17
Jones-Wells controversy	Oct. 1	28
Jutland, Real story of	Oct. 8	33
K		
Kansas Industrial Court	Dec. 31	14
Kato, Admiral Tomosaburo	Dec. 17	34
Keller hears Heifetz, Helen	Dec. 31	25
Kitchener's death in movies	Dec. 24	27
Knickerbockers for women	Nov. 5	41
Korngold, Erich	Dec. 17	25
Ku Klux Klan, Church press on	Oct. 1	30
L		
Labor and the packers	Dec. 24	13
Labor Board, Railroad	Dec. 24	11
wage statistics	Nov. 5	8
Child	Nov. 26	32
Church and	Dec. 10	27
editors on unemployment	Nov. 5	10
Living standards of	Dec. 10	58
organizing, Chinese	Nov. 5	14
wages, Railroad	Oct. 29	7
see also Unemployment		
Laborers, Protestants and	Nov. 26	30
Lawless age, Our	Oct. 8	30
Laziness, Mental	Nov. 5	54
League of Nations and "Association" plan	Dec. 10	5
Disarmament and	Oct. 1	7
" "	Oct. 8	12
Court	Oct. 8	16
Leonardo's Madonna of the Rocks	Oct. 15	26
Leverhulme portrait, Price of	Oct. 29	28
Liberia, Religious sects in	Oct. 15	30
Life, Medical science prolonging	Dec. 3	23
on the planets	Nov. 5	18
Light, Changing scenes by	Dec. 10	23
Liquor-making and geology	Nov. 26	59
Literary criticism, American	Oct. 29	29
Literary generations	Dec. 17	26
Living standard, Wage-earners'	Dec. 10	58
London, Jack	Nov. 5	37
Longfellow, Englishman on	Oct. 22	25
Luminous watch dials	Dec. 3	57
Lynching, Bill to halt	Dec. 31	9
M		
Macbeth in one scene	Dec. 31	27
MacReady eight miles in air	Dec. 3	39
Mails, Marines to protect	Dec. 3	34
Manhattan, To extend	Dec. 10	18
Maps:		
China	Oct. 29	21
Czecho-Slovakia	Dec. 17	19
Europe, air lines	Oct. 15	34
Europe and Americas	Dec. 10	10
Japan	Dec. 3	6
Manhattan addition	Dec. 10	18
Mt. Everest	Oct. 22	36

Maps: Date Page
Pacific Nov. 12 10
Poland Dec. 17 19
Sacco-Vanzetti agitation Dec. 10 36
United States Census Oct. 29 10
" " Dec. 3 10
" " Dec. 3 11
United States oil and trees Nov. 10 25
Upper Silesia Oct. 29 16
Maps by air photography Nov. 19 22
Marinetti's Surprise Theater Dec. 3 27
Marines protect railway mail Dec. 3 34
Mascagni's new opera Oct. 1 26
Meatless diet Oct. 8 69
Medical education in China Nov. 5 57
science prolonging life Dec. 3 23
superstitions Dec. 24 22
Mental laziness Nov. 5 54
levels, Jobs to fit Nov. 5 17
Mesopotamia to be restored Nov. 19 61
Mexico, Opera in Oct. 1 29
Protestantism in Dec. 3 30
Mexico's economic prospects Oct. 15 58
reconstruction Dec. 24 17
Milk from rice Dec. 17 23
Mine statistics, 1919 Nov. 19 67
Mineral oils, Refining Oct. 8 60
Molasses test for gasoline Dec. 3 21
Money, Germ-laden Nov. 26 22
Rise in sterling Dec. 31 42
Moon's irregularities Dec. 31 21
Motor buses on railroad Nov. 12 73
Mt. Everest expedition Oct. 22 34
Mountains and geology Dec. 3 23
Movie censor, Mother as Oct. 1 31
morals, Cleaning up Oct. 15 28
music Nov. 5 23
volcano and earthquake Nov. 19 23
Movies, Kitchener's death in Dec. 24 27
misrepresent America Nov. 26 28
recreational defects Oct. 22 20
Talking Dec. 3 20
Munitions, Makers of Nov. 19 48
Murder statistics Dec. 17 29
Music, American Nov. 19 29
Movie Nov. 5 23
Return of German Nov. 19 26

N

Naval agreement Dec. 31 9
Navies of the world Nov. 12 12
Negro's status, President on Nov. 19 7
New Mexico's election Oct. 1 12
New York barge canal Nov. 19 64
Hylan's hold on Nov. 19 12
Plan to extend Dec. 10 18
transit plan Oct. 15 8
Nilsson, Christine Dec. 10 22
Nobel prize-winners Dec. 3 25
Non-Partizan League Governor { Oct. 22 12 / Nov. 19 10 }
North Dakota recall election Oct. 22 12
" " " Nov. 19 10
Norway, Prohibition in Dec. 10 17
Novel vs. play, Modern Dec. 31 25

O

Obregon, Alvaro Oct. 1 36
Oil camps, Cleaning up the Oct. 22 20
fields, Trees and Nov. 19 25
from grape-seed Dec. 10 57
Plant indications of Dec. 24 21
Oils, Refining mineral Oct. 8 60
Oleomargarin, Defense of Oct. 15 19
Opera, *Die Tote Stadt* Dec. 17 24
in Mexico Oct. 1 29
Operatic star, Marie Jeritza Dec. 17 24
Oranges, Coloring Oct. 29 25
Orpen's Lord Leverhulme Oct. 29 28

P

Pacific problems Dec. 3 5
Holland on Dec. 3 18
treaty Dec. 24 5
Foreign press on Dec. 24 16
see also Arms Conference
Packers, Labor and the Dec. 24 13
Palestine, Dispute over Nov. 5 26
Panama Canal tolls Oct. 22 9
too small Oct. 29 22
Usefulness of Dec. 31 43
Pavements, Shock-absorbing Oct. 1 48
"Peace Portal" Oct. 8 40
Pejibaye palm Oct. 8 22
Pepys street Oct. 15 27
Philanthropy, Faults of Nov. 19 31
Philippine independence postponed Dec. 10 7
report, Wood's Dec. 10 7
Photographs, Air real estate Oct. 29 25
to teach safety Nov. 26 24
Photography, Maps by air Nov. 19 22
to detect forgery Oct. 1 25
Physically unfit, The Dec. 24 41
Piano, Untuned Dec. 10 19
Pike against otter Dec. 10 48
Pitoeff's Macbeth Dec. 31 27
Plague menace Oct. 22 22
Planets, Life on the Nov. 5 18
Poetry, Current:
Après la Guerre (Lucio) Oct. 1 34
Armistice (Going) Nov. 26 36
Armistice Day 1918–1921 (Jordan) Nov. 12 35
Artist's Signature (Thomas) Dec. 24 31
Atonement (Kilmer) Dec. 17 32
Autumn Sadness (Sanetomo) Nov. 5 30
Ballade of the Last Night, A (Dunsany) Dec. 3 32
Balm (Piper) Oct. 15 32
Blessing, A (Dearmer) Oct. 1 34
Children and the Shadow, The (Thomas) Oct. 8 38
Christmas (Ruffner) Dec. 31 31
Complex (Redman) Oct. 22 32
Conqueror, The (Boyer) Dec. 10 31
Cry of the Mother to the Indian Youth (Nivedita) Nov. 19 34
Doll, The (Lowell) Oct. 22 32
Drummond in the Subway (Armstrong) Oct. 29 34
Epitaph for the Unknown Soldier (Kohn) Nov. 26 36
Evening Hour, The (Gokyoku) Nov. 5 30
Flying-Fish Sailor, The (C. F. S.) Dec. 3 32
From the Line (Kerr) Nov. 12 35
Giardino Pubblico (Sitwell) Oct. 29 34
Golden Step, The (Robinson) Dec. 10 31
Gondoliers, The (Seaman) Nov. 19 34
Hero and Leander (Macleod) Nov 5 30
Holy Stall, The (Johnson) Dec. 24 31
Home-keepers, The (Le-Cron) Oct. 1 34
Hoping Against Hope (Sanetomo) Nov. 5 30
Hora Novissima (Benson) Nov. 19 34
I Want to Go Home (Bishop) Nov. 12 35
I Would Give Gold (Jastrow) Dec. 3 32
Illusions of War, The (Le-Gallienne) Dec. 30 31
In a Warm Corner (Campbell) Dec. 10 31
In After Days (Dobson) Oct. 8 38
In Arlington (Mead) Nov. 26 38
In Dublin Town (Stephens) Nov. 19 34
In the Tender Irish Weather (Middleton) Nov. 5 30
Japanese Lyrics (Ozaki) Nov. 5 30
Jilt, The (Lee) Dec. 10 31
Journey, The (Le Mesurier) Oct. 3 34
La Danseuse (Cranmer) Dec. 10 31
Leads of the Golden Star (Chaffee) Nov. 26 38
Lawyer's Tale, The (Graves) Oct. 8 38
Le Petit Manoir (Garvin) Nov. 5 30
Little Road, The (Mills) Oct. 8 38
Lotus Song (B. L. S.) Nov. 5 30
Lover Since Childhood, A (Graves) Oct. 29 34
Poetry, Current: Date Page
Marvels of Arizona, The (Bond) Oct. 1 34
Morning and Night (Anderson) Oct. 15 32
Mother Manhattan (Siegrist) Dec. 24 31
Narrow Door, The (Mew) Oct. 1 34
Noël (Johnson) Dec. 24 31
November 11th (Campbell) Nov. 26 35
October (Kenyon) Oct. 15 32
October (McGee) Oct. 15 32
October (Percy) Oct. 15 32
Old Man Winter (Piper) Oct. 15 32
Old Wives' Tales (Graves) Oct. 22 32
On the Coming of Our Unknown Hero (Hennessy) Nov. 26 35
One Shall Prevail (Montgomery) Dec. 17 32
Our Unknown Soldier (Cloyne) Nov. 19 34
Our Unknown Soldier (Palmer) Nov. 26 38
Panther! Panther! (Wheelock) Oct. 15 32
Passamaquoddy Love Song (Prince) Oct. 8 38
Passing of the Unknown Soldier (Owens) Nov. 26 35
Phantom Fleet, The (Jarrett) Dec. 17 32
Philosopher, The (Braley) Dec. 31 31
Pixies' Plot, The (Phillpotts) Dec. 24 31
Poet to His Muse, The (Fairweather) Oct. 22 32
Sand Dunes (Moreland) Dec. 31 31
Sea Quatrains (Code) Oct. 15 32
Sighs (Manyoshu) Nov. 5 30
Sight and Sound (Percy) Dec. 31 31
Soliloquy for a Third Act (Morley) Dec. 17 32
Solitary, The (Teasdale) Oct. 1 34
Song against Children (Kilmer) Dec. 17 32
Sunk Lyonesse (De la Mare) Oct. 8 38
Supreme Sacrifice Hymn (Anon.) Nov. 26 38
They (Sassoon) Nov. 12 35
Those Who Sleep in France (Achorn) Dec. 3 32
To Michael (Gibson) Nov. 12 35
To Peace (W. W. M.) Dec. 31 31
To Shelley (Loomis) Dec. 24 31
To the Recruitin' Sergeant (Dawson) Nov. 12 35
To the Younger Generation (Dodd) Dec. 31 31
Trails (Stork) Dec. 24 31
Tramp Songs (Piper) Oct. 15 32
Turn in the Road, The (Dorset) Oct. 22 32
Under Roof (Piper) Oct. 15 32
Underground River, The (Sanetomo) Nov. 5 30
Unemployed! (VanCleve) Nov. 5 30
Unknown (Cardoze) Nov. 26 38
Unknown? (Chapman) Nov. 26 35
Unknown, The (Kemp) Nov. 26 35
Unknown Dead, The (Rathom) Nov. 26 35
Unknown Soldier Armistice Day at Arlington, The (Rice) Nov. 26 36
Unknown Soldier, The (Thomson) Nov. 26 38
Unknown Soldier Speaks, The (Ruffner) Nov. 26 38
Voice of the Unknown Dead (Stotesbury) Dec. 10 31
Wall Street (Fraser) Nov. 19 34
Wanderlust (Nevin) Nov. 19 34
Who Is This That Cometh with Bloodstained Garments? (MacFarland) Nov. 26 38
Poland and Czecho-Slovakia Dec. 17 19
gets Silesian mines Oct. 29 16
Population, Density of Oct. 29 11
Gain and loss in Dec. 3 11

	Date	Page
Pork and corn	Dec. 31	42
"Portal of Peace," Blaine.	Oct. 8	40
Porto Rico denounces Gov-		
ernor	Dec. 10	12
Potash in Texas	Oct. 8	73
Power at a million volts	Oct. 22	21
Volcano steam	Oct. 22	19
Preacher, Insuring the	Nov. 26	31
Preachers' need of critics	Nov. 19	32
Training	Oct. 8	32
Price deflation, Inequality of	Nov. 26	54
Prices higher	Oct. 8	9
wages, interest, rent	Dec. 3	58
Prohibition and bootlegging	Oct. 22	45
"medical beer"	Nov. 19	13
enforcement failures	Oct. 15	12
Prohibition in Norway	Dec. 10	17
Salvation Army on	Oct. 8	32
under ridicule	Dec. 17	28
Protestant neglect of sick	Oct. 15	30
Protestants and laborers	Nov. 26	30
Pueblo's flood protection	Oct. 29	24
Pulitzer airplane race	Nov. 19	58
Punishment passing, Corporal	Oct. 15	29
R		
Race, Fishermen's	Nov. 19	38
Radio station, Largest	Dec. 10	20
Railroad freight cars rebuilt	Oct. 22	23
Labor Board adjustments	Dec. 24	11
mergers	Oct. 22	10
motor bus	Nov. 12	73
rates and wages	Oct. 29	7
Smallest	Dec. 17	22
wage statistics	Nov. 5	8
Railroads, Transcontinental	Nov. 5	58
Railway bandits, Marines vs.	Dec. 3	34
bill, British	Oct. 8	75
cars, Rough use of	Oct. 29	23
plan, New York street	Oct. 15	8
Rainmakers	Dec. 10	19
Raisin industry	Oct. 8	73
Read, Forgetting how to.	Nov. 5	25
Red Cross, After-war work of	Nov. 12	31
Reducing, Irvin Cobb on	Oct. 22	38
Reindeer, Raising	Oct. 8	25
Religion and science	Nov. 5	28
sports	Dec. 3	29
Dean Inge on	Nov. 5	28
in France, Protestant	Nov. 5	27
See also Church		
Religious sectarianism	Dec. 31	29
Rent, interest, wages, prices	Dec. 3	58
Republican weather	Oct. 8	12
Republicans win in New Mex-		
ico	Oct. 1	12
Restaurant, Moving platform	Dec. 24	21
Reynolds' "Tragic Muse" sold	Nov. 5	22
Rice, Milk from	Dec. 17	23
Rivers flowing underground	Nov. 5	21
Road upheavals, Concrete	Dec. 10	21
Rock and rye	Nov. 26	59
Rogers groups, John	Nov. 19	28
Roosevelt, Intimate books on	Nov. 5	32
Russia and Arms Conference	Nov. 19	17
and Baltic Union	Oct. 8	20
Famine truce in	Oct. 1	20
fatal to science	Dec. 10	25
in transformation	Oct. 22	18
President's appeal for	Dec. 17	5
Prison life in	Dec. 10	42
Russian cooperatives	Dec. 17	17
debt offer	Nov. 19	14
famine and Bolshevism	Dec. 31	17
fund appeal	Dec. 10	27
" "	Dec. 31	13
tests Lenine	Oct. 29	19

	Date	Page
Russian famine victims	Dec. 10	26
gold gone	Oct. 1	56
relief and Soviets	Oct. 8	18
trade, Germany after.	Oct. 15	18
Russia's communistic religion	Dec. 3	29
new bourgeoisie	Dec. 24	19
Ruth, Babe	Oct. 1	40
Ruth at the bat, Babe	Oct. 1	43
S		
Sacco and Vanzetti case	Nov. 5	9
" " "	Dec. 10	34
Safety, Photographs to teach	Nov. 26	24
Sailors, Home for	Dec. 31	30
Salmon cannery, Largest	Oct. 1	51
Fishways for	Oct. 15	20
Salvation Army on prohibition	Oct. 8	32
Sargent's Boston paintings	Nov. 26	26
Saving increases	Nov. 26	56
School abolishes exams	Dec. 3	27
histories, Pro-British	Dec. 31	26
Schools and Arms Conference	Dec. 3	12
Bible in	Oct. 29	32
Science, Bolshevism fatal to	Dec. 10	25
Seal-hunting from the air	Nov. 5	20
Seaman's Church Institute	Dec. 31	30
Shakespeare, A play about	Dec. 24	24
Shakespearean players passing	Nov. 5	23
Shantung controversy	Dec. 3	17
Shaw's political pessimism	Nov. 19	27
Sherman law violators	Dec. 10	11
Shipping in 1920, World	Oct. 29	51
Shops painted white	Dec. 24	22
Sick, Protestant neglect of	Oct. 15	30
Signs, Electric	Oct. 8	24
Silesian settlement	Oct. 29	16
Skin and galvanic reflex	Dec. 17	40
Slavery of Chinese children	Dec. 10	28
Sleep of children	Dec. 10	21
Smuts on Conference, J. C.	Dec. 17	19
Snake charm a bird? Can a	Dec. 10	52
Soaps that fade dyes	Dec. 17	22
"Social Clinic"	Oct. 8	31
Soldier Hero, Samuel Woodfill	Nov. 26	40
Speech week, Better	Oct. 29	36
Spirits, Belief in evil	Dec. 3	30
Sports and religion	Dec. 3	29
Stammerers, Curing	Oct. 8	62
Star-Spangled Banner, Last		
verse of	Dec. 3	26
Stars, Life on the	Nov. 5	18
Steel and disarmament	Dec. 3	14
strike, Church report on	Nov. 19	30
wages reduced	Oct. 1	58
Sterling, Rise in	Dec. 31	42
Stores, Department	Dec. 17	58
Strauss in America, Richard	Nov. 19	26
Straw fuel	Oct. 1	24
houses	Dec. 31	20
Street car vs. automobile	Dec. 31	21
Submarines in the Conference	Dec. 3	16
Lost and saved	Dec. 31	32
Suicide increase	Oct. 22	23
Sun's heat, Mystery of	Dec. 31	23
Syria, French democratizing.	Oct. 1	18
T		
Talking, Evolution of	Nov. 26	29
movies	Dec. 3	20
Tariff making, British	Oct. 1	56
Tax bill, Penrose	Oct. 8	14
law, New	Dec. 10	8
Tear bombs for police	Oct. 15	22
Theater, Marinetti's Surprise	Dec. 3	27
Tin foil covers for gum	Nov. 19	23
Tire prices	Dec. 10	58
Torpedo, Aerial wireless	Nov. 26	13

	Date	Page
Trackless trolley	Nov. 26	25
Travel, Winter	Dec. 17	42
Trees and oil-fields	Nov. 19	25
Trolley plan, New York	Oct. 15	8
Trackless	Nov. 26	25
Tropisms, Human	Oct. 1	54
Trust, Prison for building	Dec. 10	11
Tunnel-building machine	Nov. 19	24
Turco-Greek war	Oct. 29	20
Typhoid and motoring	Oct. 22	22
U		
Unemployed, British wealth		
for	Nov. 5	16
Unemployment, Church and	Oct. 15	29
Conference	Oct. 15	5
results	Oct. 29	14
decreasing	Oct. 29	14
Labor editors on	Nov. 5	10
in Britain	Oct. 15	15
Unemployment, World	Oct. 1	14
" "	Oct. 22	17
V		
Vanderbilt's motor trip,		
Cornelius, Jr.	Oct. 15	48
Vanderlip's European plans,		
F. A.	Dec. 10	10
Vanzetti and Sacco case	Nov. 5	9
" "	Dec. 10	34
Vatican, Diplomats to the	Oct. 29	30
Vermont, Church unity in	Oct. 1	32
Volcano, Movie	Nov. 19	23
Steam power from	Oct. 22	19
W		
Wages, prices, interest, rent	Dec. 3	58
Walpole vs. Drinkwater	Dec. 31	25
War costs	Nov. 12	16
"	Nov. 12	18
debts and family income.	Oct. 15	57
Ward, Briton defends Artemus	Dec. 17	25
Warehousing corn	Nov. 19	64
Warfare, Chemical	Nov. 12	28
" "	Dec. 24	8
Watch dials, Luminous	Dec. 3	57
springs, Breaking of	Dec. 24	23
Water drying up, Earth's.	Nov. 5	21
Watson attacks A.E.F., Senator	Nov. 26	16
Wells at Conference, H. G.	Dec. 17	26
-Jones controversy	Oct. 1	28
White paint for shops	Dec. 24	22
Who's who at the Conference	Nov. 12	37
Winter, How to keep young in	Dec. 17	41
travel	Dec. 10	42
Wives, Healthy and happy	Oct. 8	23
Woman's advance in Far East	Dec. 24	29
Women at the Arms Confer-		
ence	Nov. 26	48
Britain's surplus	Oct. 22	15
Knickerbockers for	Nov. 5	41
Married	Oct. 8	23
Women's chances in Domin-		
ions	Nov. 19	19
Wood preservation, Hypoder-		
mic	Dec. 31	22
Woodfill, Samuel	Nov. 26	40
Wood's Philippines report	Dec. 10	7
World armies	Nov. 12	14
navies	Nov. 12	12
shipping, 1920	Oct. 29	51
X		
X-Rays more powerful	Oct. 15	23
Z		
ZR-2, Helium and the	Oct. 1	22

INDEX OF AUTHORS

A

Author	Date	Page
Achorn, Erik	Dec. 3	32
Adachi Kinnosuke	Dec. 17	34
Alden, Carroll Storrs	Dec. 31	34
Allen, Henry J	Oct. 29	36
" "	Dec. 3	13
" "	Dec. 31	14
Andersen, Hans Christian	Nov. 5	42
Anderson, Maxwell	Oct. 15	32
Anderson, William H	Oct. 15	13
Armstrong, Hamilton Fish	Oct. 29	34
Atkinson, Mary Irene	Dec. 17	29
Austin, O. P.	Nov. 12	17

B

Author	Date	Page
B. L. S.	Nov. 5	30
Bailey, Margery	Nov. 5	50
Bainville, Jacques	Dec. 17	27
Baldwin, B. T.	Oct. 15	22
Balfour, Arthur J	Nov. 5	4
" "	Nov. 26	9
Barbour, Ralph Henry	Nov. 5	42
Barry, Robert	Dec. 10	6
Bastin, S. Leonard	Oct. 29	24
Baxter, Percival P	Dec. 3	12
Beaux, Cecilia	Oct. 15	24
Beck, James M.	Oct. 8	30
Bell, Clive	Oct. 1	29
Benes, Eduard	Dec. 17	19
Benét, Laura	Dec. 17	32
Bennett, Henry H.	Oct. 8	68
Benson, Arthur H. T.	Nov. 19	34
Benson, E. F.	Oct. 8	54
Bianchi, Julio	Oct. 22	11
Bishop, C. M.	Nov. 12	9
Bishop, Charles B.	Nov. 12	35
Bishop, Warren	Oct. 22	19
Blaine, John J.	Dec. 3	12
Bliss, Tasker H.	Nov. 12	32
Blythe, Samuel G.	Nov. 12	9
Bodman, Harold C.	Oct. 1	38
Bogart, E. L.	Nov. 12	18
Bok, Edward	Nov. 5	42
Bond, Josiah	Oct. 1	34
Booth, Evangeline	Oct. 8	32
Borah, Senator W. E.	Nov. 12	24
" "	Nov. 26	7
" "	Dec. 10	7
Borden, Sir Robert L.	Nov. 12	24
Borissoff, A.	Dec. 24	19
Bowes, Julian	Oct. 15	24
Bowie, C. P.	Oct. 22	20
Bowie, William	Dec. 3	23
Boyer, Jacques	Nov. 26	22
Boyer, Lucien	Dec. 10	31
Boyle, Emmet D.	Dec. 3	55
Braley, Berton	Dec. 31	31
Briand, Aristide	Oct. 22	5
" "	Nov. 12	24
" "	Dec. 3	16
Bridge, Sir Cyprian A. G.	Nov. 26	10
Briggs, Cyril V.	Nov. 19	9
Brisbane, Arthur	Nov. 19	14
" "	Nov. 26	7
Brooks, Benjamin T.	Oct. 8	60
Broun, Heywood	Nov. 12	29
Brownell, Agnes May	Nov. 5	50
Bruce, H. Addington	Oct. 29	36
Bury, Howard	Oct. 22	34

C

Author	Date	Page
C. F. S.	Dec. 3	32
Cahen, G. M.	Oct. 15	18
Caine, Hall	Oct. 29	48
Calder, Senator W. M.	Oct. 22	10
Calgett, W. H.	Nov. 26	38
Campbell, Archibald Y.	Dec. 10	31
Campbell, Frank E.	Nov. 26	35
Campbell, Thomas E.	Dec. 3	55
Canby, Henry Seidel	Nov. 12	29
Candler, Martha	Oct. 29	31
Cannon, Cornelia J.	Nov. 19	31
Capper, Senator Arthur	Nov. 26	12
" " "	Dec. 24	10
Cardoze, Frederic T.	Nov. 26	38
Carey, Robert D.	Dec. 3	55
Carroll, Lewis	Nov. 5	50
Carson, Jessie	Oct. 29	27
Caruso, Enrico	Oct. 8	44
Casserly, Gordon	Nov. 5	50
Cecil, Lord Robert	Oct. 8	12
Chaffee, Lorena Davison	Nov. 26	38
Chamberlayne, E. S.	Oct. 8	52
Chapman, Arthur	Nov. 26	35
Chenery, William L.	Oct. 29	15
Childers, Erskine	Dec. 17	8
Claudy, C. H.	Oct. 22	44
Clemenceau, Georges	Oct. 22	24
Cloyne, Arthur Newberry	Nov. 19	34
Clynes, J. R.	Dec. 31	17
Coale, James J.	Nov. 26	30
Coatsworth, Elizabeth J.	Oct. 8	38
Cobb, Irvin	Oct. 22	38
Code, Grant H.	Oct. 15	32
Cody, Mary R.	Nov. 5	42
Cohalan, Daniel F.	Dec. 17	5
Colby, Frank Moore	Nov. 26	29
Colvin, Sidney	Dec. 24	41
Connolly, James B.	Nov. 19	38
Contremoulins, G.	Oct. 15	23
Conway, Sir Martin	Oct. 22	36
Cooper, Robert A.	Dec. 3	13
Cory, David	Nov. 5	50
Courtney, W. L.	Oct. 22	25
Cousins, W. S.	Dec. 31	42
Cox, Channing H.	Dec. 3	12
Crane, Jacob L., Jr.	Nov. 19	62
Cranmer, Elsie Paterson	Dec. 10	31
Cunningham, Alyse	Dec. 10	44
Curtin, Jeremiah	Nov. 5	42
Curtis, H. D.	Dec. 31	23
Curzon, Lord	Dec. 10	14

D

Author	Date	Page
Daly, Charles D.	Nov. 19	52
Dane, Clemence	Dec. 24	24
Darst, James E.	Dec. 24	32
D'Avenel, Viscount	Dec. 31	29
Davidson, E. W.	Oct. 15	21
Davis, D. W.	Dec. 3	54
Davison, E. L.	Dec. 31	25
Dawes, Charles G.	Dec. 17	10
Dawson, Coningsby	Nov. 12	30
Dawson, George C.	Nov. 12	35
Dearmer, Geoffrey	Oct. 1	34
De Booke, Lord Willoughby	Dec. 24	39
De la Mare, Walter	Oct. 8	38
De Lipsky, Nicholas	Dec. 10	23
Dernburg, Bernhard	Nov. 26	18
D'Estournelles, Baron	Nov. 12	24
Devine, Edward T.	Nov. 19	32
Dewar, Arthur C.	Dec. 24	27
Dewey, Julia M.	Nov. 5	42
Dickens, Charles	Nov. 5	42
Dillon, E. J.	Oct. 1	36
" "	Dec. 24	17
Dixon, Joseph M.	Dec. 3	54
Dixon, Winifred H.	Dec. 31	36
Dobson, Austin	Oct. 8	38
Dodd, Lee Wilson	Dec. 31	31
Dodge, Louis	Nov. 5	42
Dorset, E.	Oct. 22	32
Dos Passos, John	Nov. 12	29
Downes, William Howe	Nov. 26	26
Drach, George	Oct. 22	30
Drexel, Constance	Nov. 26	48
Drinkwater, John	Dec. 31	26
DuBois, W. E. B.	Nov. 19	9
Dudley, Bide	Nov. 5	50
Dunlap, Laura C.	Oct. 8	31
Dunn, Arthur Wallace	Nov. 12	9
Dunn, D. M.	Nov. 5	20
Dunsany, Lord	Dec. 3	32
Du Pont, Pierre S.	Nov. 19	48
Dupuy, Paul	Dec. 17	27
Duranty, Walter	Dec. 3	29

E

Author	Date	Page
Eaton, Walter Prichard	Nov. 19	28
Edison, Thomas A.	Nov. 26	47
Einaudi, Luigi	Dec. 10	17
Evarts, Hal G.	Dec. 24	36

F

Author	Date	Page
Fabre, Jean Henri	Dec. 10	52
" "	Dec. 24	39
Fairweather, E. Lyndon	Oct. 22	32
Felton, Samuel E.	Dec. 24	12
Fernald, James C.	Oct. 29	36
Fischer, Martin H.	Dec. 17	22
Fisher, Harry M.	Oct. 29	14
Fiske, Bradley A.	Nov. 12	24
Fletcher, J. S.	Dec. 3	42
Fleuron, Svend	Dec. 10	48
Foch, Marshal Ferdinand	Dec. 24	32
Forbes, W. Cameron	Dec. 10	7
" "	Dec. 12	38
Ford, James L.	Dec. 3	24
Fosdick, Harry Emerson	Dec. 3	28
Fowle, A. A.	Nov. 19	41
Fowle, Leonard M.	Nov. 19	42
Frame, Mrs.	Dec. 24	29
Frampton, A. Ellis	Nov. 26	24
Francis, Philip	Nov. 26	7
Frank, Glenn	Oct. 22	28
Fraser, Jack	Nov. 19	34
Frothingham, Thomas G.	Oct. 8	33
Fuller, Henry B.	Dec. 24	25
Fullerton, Hugh S.	Oct. 1	40

G

Author	Date	Page
Gabriel, Gilbert W.	Oct. 1	26
Galsworthy, John	Oct. 29	43
Gardner, Roy	Dec. 3	36
Garvin, Viola	Nov. 5	30
Gay, John	Dec. 24	41
Gibbs, Sir Philip	Dec. 24	36
Gibson, Wilfrid Wilson	Nov. 12	35
Gilbreth, Frank B.	Dec. 24	22
Gilbreth, Lillian M.	Dec. 24	22
Gilman, Bradley	Nov. 5	32
" "	Dec. 24	37
Goddard, Henry Herbert	Nov. 5	17
Going, Charles Buxton	Nov. 26	36
Gokyoku	Nov. 5	30
Goldberg, Isaac	Dec. 3	25
Golla, Dr.	Dec. 17	40
Gorman, Herbert S.	Dec. 3	26
Gorovtzeff, A.	Oct. 29	19
Gould, George M.	Dec. 24	20
Gounaris, Premier	Nov. 19	20
Grasty, Charles H.	Dec. 17	12
Graves, Robert	Oct. 8	38
" "	Oct. 22	32
" "	Oct. 29	34
Greenwood, Ernest	Oct. 1	14
Gregor, Elmer Russell	Nov. 5	42
Griffis, William Elliot	Nov. 5	50
Groesbeck, Alex. J.	Dec. 3	12
Guthrie, John D.	Dec. 31	22

H

Author	Date	Page
Haas, Walter Stanley	Dec. 31	32
Hackett, Frances	Nov. 12	29
Hagedorn, Hermann	Dec. 24	38
Halloway, Emory	Dec. 24	41
Hamilton, J. G.	Nov. 26	12
Hannay, David	Oct. 8	36
Hapsburg, Charles	Nov. 19	44
Hara, Takashi	Nov. 12	24
Hard, William	Nov. 12	26
Hardee, Cary A.	Dec. 3	13
Harding, President W. G.	Nov. 5	6
" "	Nov. 12	9
" "	Nov. 12	24
" "	Nov. 19	7
" "	Dec. 17	5
" "	Dec. 17	9
Hardwicke, Thomas W.	Dec. 3	13
Harper, Roland M.	Nov. 19	25
Hart, Louis F.	Dec. 3	56
Hart, William S.	Nov. 5	44
Hartley, George Inness	Nov. 5	50
Harvey, George	Nov. 26	14
Hatton, Richard	Nov. 12	7
Hawksworth, Hallam	Nov. 5	44
Hawley, L. F.	Oct. 1	48
Heath, W. P.	Nov. 19	21
Hellwig, E. W.	Dec. 17	20

Name	Date	Page
Henderson, Arthur	Nov. 12	24
Hennessy, Roland Burke	Nov. 26	35
Hibben, John Grier	Nov. 12	24
Hichens, W. L.	Oct. 22	17
Hill, David Jayne	Nov. 26	15
Hobson, J. H.	Dec. 17	12
Hoffman, Frederick L.	Dec. 17	29
Hogue, Richard W.	Oct. 1	31
Hooper, Ben W.	Dec. 24	11
Hoover, Herbert C.	Nov. 12	24
" "	Dec. 31	13
Huddleston, Sisley	Oct. 22	16
Hughes, Secretary C. E.	Nov. 26	8
" "	Dec. 3	9
Huneker, James	Dec. 24	37
Hunt, Frazier	Oct. 29	38
Hunting, Gardner	Nov. 5	52
Huntington, Henry S.	Oct. 22	29
Hutchinson, A. S. M.	Dec. 3	46
Hyde, Arthur M.	Dec. 3	12
Hylan, John F.	Oct. 15	9
" "	Nov. 19	12
I		
Iden, V. G.	Oct. 29	22
Inge, W. R.	Nov. 5	28
Ireland, Merritte W.	Nov. 12	31
Irwin, Will	Nov. 12	18
" "	Nov. 12	30
J		
James, Edwin L.	Oct. 1	7
James, William	Nov. 12	15
Jarrett, Cora Hardy	Dec. 17	32
Jastrow, Stash	Dec. 3	32
Jeffers, LeRoy	Nov. 5	36
Jeffreys, Harold	Dec. 10	19
Jermane, W. W.	Oct. 15	12
Johnson, Gaylord	Nov. 5	44
Johnson, Owen	Dec. 3	49
Johnson, M. M.	Dec. 24	31
Jones, Edgar DeWitt	Dec. 31	29
Jones, H. A.	Oct. 1	28
Jordan, Ethel Blair	Nov. 12	35
Jusserand, Jules J.	Nov. 12	24
K		
Kaltenborn, H. V.	Oct. 22	5
Kato, Admiral Tomosaburo	Nov. 12	24
" " "	Nov. 26	9
" " "	Dec. 3	6
Kelland, Clarence B.	Nov. 5	52
Kellogg, Vernon	Dec. 10	26
Kelly, Fred C.	Oct. 8	70
Kemal, Ali	Oct. 29	20
Kemp, Harry	Nov. 26	35
Kennedy, John B.	Dec. 31	27
Kennedy, John S.	Dec. 31	28
Kenworthy, Lieut.-Commander	Nov. 12	24
Kenyon, Bernice Lesbia	Oct. 15	32
Kerr, R. Watson	Nov. 12	35
Kilby, Thomas E.	Dec. 3	13
Kilmer, Aline	Dec. 17	32
Kimmins, C. W.	Oct. 22	26
Kloeckner, Privy Councilor	Oct. 15	17
Knappen, Theodore M.	Nov. 12	28
Knopf, Alfred A.	Oct. 15	25
Kohn, Annette	Nov. 26	36
Korngold, Erich	Dec. 17	24
Krehbiel, H. E.	Nov. 19	26
"	Dec. 17	24
"	Dec. 24	25
"	Dec. 31	24
Kruttschnitt, Julius	Oct. 29	8
L		
LaFollette, Senator R. M.	Dec. 24	5
Lake, Everett J.	Dec. 3	12
Lamache, Gustave	Dec. 31	20
Lamb, David C.	Oct. 22	15
Lamprey, L.	Nov. 5	45
Lange, Louis Christian	Oct. 8	13
Langley, S. P.	Dec. 17	22
Lauck, W. Jett	Nov. 5	8
Lauzanne, Stephane	Dec. 3	16
Lawrence, D. H.	Oct. 29	34
LeCron, Helen Cowles	Oct. 1	34
Lee, Agnes	Dec. 10	31
Lees, G. F. Frederick	Nov. 5	19
LeGallienne, Richard	Dec. 10	31
Le Mesurier, L.	Oct. 1	34
Lempp, Herr	Dec. 31	21
Lennox-Simpson, B.	Nov. 12	62
Lensky, Z.	Dec. 17	17
Lewis, Isabel M.	Dec. 31	21
Lewis, W. Lee	Dec. 24	9
Linderman, Frank B.	Nov. 5	45
Lloyd George, David	Oct. 15	15
" " "	Oct. 22	17
" " "	Nov. 12	24
" " "	Dec. 17	17
Locard, Edmond	Nov. 5	19
Lomax, Montague	Dec. 3	30
Loomis, Charles Grant	Dec. 24	31
Lord, F. Townley	Dec. 3	29
Loucheur, Louis	Oct. 29	18
London, Charmian	Nov. 5	37
Lovejoy, Owen R.	Nov. 26	32
Lovett, Robert S.	Oct. 22	11
Lowell, Amy	Oct. 22	32
Lucas, E. V.	Dec. 24	36
Lucio	Oct. 1	34
Lunarcharsky	Dec. 10	25
Lynde, Francis	Nov. 5	52
M		
McAdoo, W. G.	Nov. 26	7
McAll, Reginald L.	Nov. 5	27
McCartney, Maxwell H. H.	Oct. 22	7
McCoy, Samuel	Dec. 24	34
McCray, Warren T.	Dec. 3	12
McFee, Inez	Nov. 5	45
" "	Nov. 5	52
McGarry, William A.	Oct. 15	22
McGee, Margaret	Oct. 15	32
McGovern, Chauncey	Oct. 1	25
McIsaac, F. J.	Dec. 24	37
McKelvie, Samuel R.	Dec. 3	13
McKenna, Stephen	Oct. 8	56
McMaster, W. H.	Dec. 3	12
McNutt, William Slavens	Oct. 15	40
" " "	Nov. 19	48
McRae, Thomas C.	Dec. 3	13
Mabey, Charles R.	Dec. 3	55
MacFarland, Mary L. D.	Nov. 26	38
Macfie, Ronald Campbell	Dec. 17	40
Macleod, J. T. G.	Nov. 5	30
Manyoshu	Nov. 5	30
Martel, E. A.	Nov. 5	21
Martin, Edward S.	Dec. 24	28
Martin, Frederick	Oct. 8	62
Mathiews, Franklin K.	Nov. 5	45
Matthew, W. D.	Nov. 5	18
Maurice, Sir Frederick	Nov. 12	24
Mead, Edna	Nov. 26	38
Mechem, Merritt C.	Dec. 3	55
Meighen, Arthur	Nov. 19	51
Merz, Charles	Nov. 26	12
" "	Dec. 3	7
Mew, Charlotte	Oct. 1	34
Middleton, Edgar C.	Nov. 5	20
Middleton, Lillian	Nov. 5	30
Miller, Arthur M.	Nov. 26	59
Miller, Leo E.	Nov. 5	52
Miller, Nathan L.	Dec. 3	12
Miller, Warren H.	Nov. 5	46
" "	Nov. 5	52
Mills, Ellen Morrill	Oct. 8	38
Mitchell, Lebbeus	Nov. 5	46
Molesworth, Mary L.	Nov. 5	52
Monroe, James	Nov. 12	46
Montgomery, Roselle M.	Dec. 17	32
Moore, I. Foster	Nov. 5	21
Moore, R. B.	Oct. 1	22
Moreland, John R.	Dec. 31	31
Moresco, E.	Dec. 3	18
Morgan, Ephraim F.	Dec. 3	13
Morley, Christopher	Dec. 17	32
Morrow, Edwin P.	Dec. 3	13
Morse, Lucy Gibbons	Nov. 5	46
Moses, Montrose J.	Nov. 5	46
Moulton, Robert H.	Oct. 1	23
Mowrer, Paul Scott	Oct. 1	7
" " "	Oct. 22	6
" " "	Dec. 3	9
Muhse, A. C.	Oct. 1	24
Muhse, F. F.	Oct. 1	24
Murphy, Charles	Nov. 19	12
Murphy, Frank G.	Oct. 1	21
Muskowvitz, Henry	Nov. 19	64
Myers, D. S.	Nov. 26	31
N		
Neff, Pat M.	Dec. 3	54
Nevin, Hardwicke	Nov. 19	34
Newman, Ernest	Dec. 31	24
Nilsson, Hjalmus	Dec. 3	21
Nivedita, Sister	Nov. 19	34
Norman, Henderson D.	Dec. 24	38
Norris, Charles G.	Oct. 29	46
Norris, George W.	Oct. 15	57
" "	Nov. 12	16
North, Grace May	Nov. 5	52
Noyes, M. S.	Dec. 10	54
O		
Obregon, Alvaro	Oct. 1	36
Ochakovsky, I.	Dec. 10	42
O'Connell, Cardinal W. H.	Dec. 10	28
O'Kane, Walter Collins	Nov. 5	46
Olcott, Ben W.	Dec. 3	56
O'Leary, Grattan	Nov. 19	51
Owens, Vilda Sauvage	Nov. 26	35
P		
Packard, Winthrop	Dec. 10	50
Pal, Bepin Chandra	Oct. 15	17
Palmer, Mitchell	Nov. 19	13
Palmer, Frederick	Dec. 3	42
Parker, John M.	Dec. 3	13
Parmer, Virginia Nelson	Nov. 26	38
Patrick, G. T. W.	Oct. 22	20
Patterson, Ada	Dec. 17	30
Peabody, Mrs. Henry W.	Dec. 24	29
Peffer, Nathaniel	Oct. 29	38
Percy, William Alexander	Oct. 15	32
" " "	Dec. 31	31
Perkins, Lucy Fitch	Nov. 5	48
Pershing, John J.	Nov. 12	24
" "	Nov. 26	40
Phillpotts, Eden	Dec. 3	48
" "	Dec. 24	31
Pinthus, Kurt	Oct. 1	27
Piper, Edwin Ford	Oct. 15	32
Pitkin, Walter B.	Nov. 26	29
Pope Benedict XV	Nov. 12	24
Popenoe, Paul	Nov. 5	17
Popenoe, Wilson	Oct. 8	22
Porter, Jane	Nov. 5	50
Pratt, Thomas B.	Oct. 29	50
Preus, J. A. O.	Dec. 3	12
Price, B. K.	Dec. 3	22
Price, Theodore H.	Oct. 15	6
Prince, John D.	Oct. 8	38
Pyle, Katharine	Nov. 5	48
Q		
Queen, W. M.	Dec. 17	23
R		
Rabak, Frank	Dec. 10	57
Radek, Karl	Oct. 8	18
Rankin, Carroll Watson	Nov. 5	49
Rankine, A. O.	Dec. 3	20
Rathenau, Walter	Oct. 29	18
Rathom, John F.	Nov. 26	35
Raymond, E. T.	Oct. 8	26
Redman, Ben Ray	Oct. 22	32
Reed, John H.	Oct. 15	30
Reed, Paul S.	Dec. 24	21
Reily, E. M.	Dec. 10	12
Reinsch, Paul S.	Oct. 15	9
Restortziff, M.	Dec. 10	25
Rhys, Grace	Nov. 5	49
Rice, Grantland	Nov. 26	36
Richardson, William D.	Oct. 15	19
Richet, Charles	Dec. 3	22
Ridder, Bernard H.	Dec. 31	41
Rideout, Henry M.	Oct. 8	51
Riis, Roger William	Oct. 8	46
Ritchie, Albert C.	Dec. 3	13
Rizer, Edward F.	Oct. 29	24
Robertson, J. B. A.	Dec. 3	54
Robertson, Sir William	Dec. 24	36
Robinson, Anne Johnson	Dec. 10	31
Robinson, Corinne Roosevelt	Nov. 5	32
" " "	Dec. 24	38
Robinson, Edwin Arlington	Dec. 24	38
Robinson, James Harvey	Dec. 24	38
Roosevelt, Kermit	Dec. 24	39
Roosevelt, Theodore	Nov. 5	32
Rostand, Edmond	Dec. 24	38
Ruffner, Joseph, Jr.	Nov. 26	38

Name	Date	Page
Ruffner, Joseph, Jr.	Dec. 31	31
Russell, George W.	Dec. 17	7
Russell, L e M.	Dec. 3	13
S		
Sadero, Geni	Oct. 8	44
Samoiloff	Dec. 10	24
Samuel, Sir Herbert	Nov. 5	26
Sanetomo	Nov. 5	30
San Souci, Emery J.	Dec. 3	12
Sassoon, Siegfried	Nov. 12	35
Sato, Tetsutaro	Nov. 12	52
Schapiro, J. S.	Nov. 5	25
Schurman, Jacob Gould	Nov. 12	9
Scott, C. B.	Oct. 29	23
Seaman, Augusta H.	Nov. 5	53
Seaman, Sir Owen	Nov. 19	34
Shaw, George Bernard	Nov. 19	27
Shepherd, William G.	Oct. 1	44
"	Dec. 17	28
Shoup, Oliver H.	Dec. 3	55
Siegrist, Mary	Dec. 24	31
Simonds, Frank H.	Nov. 12	8
Sinclair, May	Dec. 3	44
Sitwell, Osbert	Oct. 29	34
Slater, R. L.	Dec. 31	25
Small, Len	Dec. 3	12
Smith-Gordon, Lionel	Dec. 17	8
Smith, Max	Dec. 17	25
Smuts, Jan Christiaan	Dec. 17	19
Sothern, Edward H.	Nov. 5	23
Spearman, Frank H.	Nov. 5	53
Spencer, Warren	Dec. 3	21
Spewack, Samuel	Dec. 10	34
Sproul, William C.	Dec. 3	12
Spurr, Frederic C.	Oct. 1	32
Steed, Wickham	Dec. 10	6
Steele, Willis	Dec. 31	28
Stephens, James	Nov. 19	34
Stephens, William D.	Dec. 3	56
Stokes, Harold Phelps	Dec. 17	38
Stone, Melville E.	Dec. 24	36
Stork, Charles Wharton	Dec. 24	31
Stotesbury, Herbert	Dec. 10	31
Straton, John Roach	Oct. 15	28
Sullivan, Alan	Nov. 5	53
Sullivan, Mark	Oct. 22	9
"	Dec. 17	27
Swaffer, Hanner	Oct. 8	26
Sze, Alfred S.	Nov. 26	11
T		
Taggart, Marion Ames	Nov. 5	53
Taylor, Alf A.	Dec. 3	13
Taylor, Deems	Dec. 17	25
Teasdale, Sara	Oct. 1	34
Thayer, Robert E.	Oct. 29	9
Thomas, M. Carey	Nov. 5	24
Thomas, Edith M.	Oct. 8	38
"	Dec. 24	31
Thomas, Lillian Beynon	Dec. 31	30
Thompson, O. R. Howard	Nov. 26	38
Tippy, Worth M.	Oct. 15	29
Tong, Hollington K.	Nov. 12	64
Towse, J. Rankin	Nov. 5	23
Trevor, Philip	Nov. 19	56
Tumulty, Joseph P.	Dec. 24	36
Tuohy, Ferdinand	Dec. 17	27
U		
Ulm, Aaron Hardy	Nov. 26	28
Underwood, W. E.	Oct. 8	24
Usher, H. B.	Nov. 12	8
V		
Van Cleve, Florence	Nov. 5	30
Vanderbilt, Cornelius, Jr.	Oct. 15	48
Vanderlip, Frank A.	Dec. 10	10
Van Fleet, William C.	Dec. 10	11
Vickrey, Charles V.	Oct. 22	30
Vince, Charles	Dec. 24	39
Vogt, Paul L.	Oct. 1	32
W		
W. W. M.	Dec. 31	31
Waite, Helen Elmira	Dec. 3	26
Walker, J. Bernard	Nov. 12	12
Walker, Leslie J.	Oct. 22	30
Walpole, Hugh	Dec. 31	26
Walters, Angus	Nov. 19	41
Wang, K. P.	Dec. 3	6
Watson, Senator T. E.	Nov. 26	16
Wead, C. K.	Dec. 10	19
Weizmann, Chaim	Nov. 5	26
Wells, H. G.	Oct. 1	28
"	Dec. 3	5
"	Dec. 3	9
"	Dec. 17	27
Whalen, Grover A.	Nov. 26	25
Wheelock, John Hall	Oct. 15	32
Willet, Grace Williamson	Oct. 29	36
Williams, S. R.	Dec. 24	23
Wilson, P. W.	Dec. 3	9
Wilstach, Paul	Dec. 24	36
Windischgraetz, Prince Ludwig	Nov. 19	44
Winters, S. R.	Oct. 29	25
Wood, Junius	Dec. 17	36
Wood, Leonard	Dec. 10	7
Woodfill, Samuel	Nov. 26	40
Woods, Arthur	Oct. 29	14
Wright, Adam H.	Oct. 8	64
Wright, Orville	Dec. 17	22
Y		
Yajima, Kaji	Nov. 26	53
Young, Francis Brett	Dec. 3	40
Young, Filson	Dec. 24	36
Young, Owen D.	Dec. 10	20
Yule, Emma Sarepta	Oct. 29	41

Dramatized Facts out of The Day's Work

No. 9

Where the facts came from

The great Carolina Flood of 1916 wrought havoc for 30 miles, leaving towns and factories desolate and helpless. Grinnell Company played an important part in the work of restoration. All consulting engineers realize that in such disasters the Grinnell Company can mobilize its field forces, backed by its factories and engineers, to meet the immediate needs of stricken communities.

MAYOR CITY ENGINEER SUPERINTENDENT OF WATERWORKS CONSULTING ENGINEER

Coming!—in the hour of desperate need

The Mayor, haggard from loss of sleep since the dreadful night when the flood broke, eagerly scanned the drawn faces about him for reassurance. "With the Power House swept away, the situation is appalling. I tell you we've got to move faster. The city's industries are without lights, or water, or power. The Fire Chief has given official warning that the danger of a conflagration is imminent."

"What more can the public expect?" wavered the City Engineer. "We are salvaging the big pumps from the river bed. I've drafted every mason in town, commandeered all the brick. The walls are going up five feet a day!"

"Hang the walls!" snapped the Superintendent of Waterworks. "We've got more than mere building to worry us. Think of that mammoth piping job! Bends, welded nozzles, hangers—ton upon ton of piping to be put up and fitted—"

"Wait a minute," interjected the Consulting Engineer, one of the biggest in the country.

"What do you gentlemen think I'm here for?—To rush this work through without delay—and that's just what I'm doing. Complete blueprints of the piping job went to the piping people days ago."

"—And just what does that mean?" barked the Superintendent.

"Mean? It means *service*—I guess you don't know what Grinnell Company does in such emergencies as this. It means that four of their plants—Providence, Warren, Atlanta, and North Charlotte—are working together to turn out the piping we need, in record time—condensers, valves, hangers, and all the accessories."

"It means piping hundreds of miles away!" said the Mayor despairingly. "That means weeks."

"No, the pipe is coming! Four cars will arrive tomorrow," was the prompt reply.

"But where'll we get the men to put it up?" inquired the City Engineer.

"Grinnell Company has a road force of 1300 men. They are sending us as many as we need. If the piping job's not complete by the time the roof is on the Power House, I miss my guess."

The Mayor looked his astonishment. "That *will* be service," he said. Then the old frown returned. Almost pleadingly he asked, "Will you stay right here and see that the city's interests are protected?" He was thinking that excuses for big bills won't go at election time, even if the work was properly authorized.

The Consulting Engineer laughed his assurance. "Don't worry. When Grinnell does a job, haste means *service*—not *waste*. Grinnell *guarantees* this piping work and does it in this case on a cost plus basis."

The Mayor for the first time in days smiled a little. "The best news is that cars and men are coming. I want to be on hand myself to see those cars come in."

GRINNELL GUARANTY

The value of Grinnell Company's Service does not stop at the rapidity with which its large and highly-specialized organization executes difficult jobs. Engineers and architects know that Grinnell Company maintains one of the world's greatest industrial laboratories on piping, and that its road force can be depended upon to do erecting work on a par with the finest engineering. They know the value to business men of *a courageous guaranty behind ideas, men and materials.*

GRINNELL

INDUSTRIAL PIPING

Automatic Sprinkler Systems, Heating, Power and Process Piping

Send for your copy of the "Grinnell

Volume 70
No. 14

TABLE • OF • CONTENTS

October 1, 1921

TOPICS OF THE DAY: Page

The Arms Parley and the League as Rivals 7
Talking Ireland into Peace 10
New Mexico as a Straw 12
Yankee Capital Invading Europe 13
The World's Unemployed 14
Our "3 per cent." Immigration Snarl 14
Topics in Brief 16

FOREIGN COMMENT:

Japanese Doubts of the Washington Conference 17
France Democratizing Syria 18
Grounds for an Irish-English Compromise 19
The Famine-Truce in Russia 20

SCIENCE AND INVENTION:

How to Look Well in Glasses 21
Would Helium Have Saved the ZR-2? 22
About Blood Pressure 23
Cookery in the Land of Straw Fuel 24
A New Way to Trap Forgers 25

[Continued on page 48]

LETTERS AND ART: Page

Mascagni's New Democratic Opera 26
German Poets Turning to Politics 27
An Authors' Battle 28
The Best of Jazz 29
Opera in Mexico 29

RELIGION AND SOCIAL SERVICE:

Ku Klux Condemned by the Religious Press 30
To Christianize Business in England 31
Mother as a Movie Censor 31
Using the "Devil's Advocate" 32
Church Unity Progress in Vermont 32

MISCELLANEOUS:

Current Poetry 34
Personal Glimpses 36-47
Investments and Finance 56-59
Current Events 60-61
The Spice of Life 62

TERMS: $4.00 a year, in advance; six months, $2.25; three months, $1.50; single copy, 10 cents; postage to Canada, 85 cents a year; other foreign postage, $2.00 a year. BACK NUMBERS, not over three months old, 25 cents each; over three months old, $1.00 each. QUARTERLY INDEXES will be sent free to subscribers who apply for them. RECEIPT of payment is shown in about two weeks by date on address-label; date of expiration includes the month named on the label. CAUTION: If date is not properly extended after each payment, notify publishers promptly. Instructions for RENEWAL, DISCONTINUANCE, or CHANGE OF ADDRESS should be sent *two weeks* before the date they are to go into effect. *Both old and new addresses* must always be given. PRESENTATION COPIES: Many persons subscribe for friends. Those who desire to renew such subscriptions must do so before expiration.

THE LITERARY DIGEST is published weekly by the Funk & Wagnalls Company, 354-360 Fourth Avenue, New York, and Salisbury Square, London, E. C.

Entered as second-class matter, March 24, 1890, at the Post-office at New York, N. Y., under the act of March 3, 1879.

Entered as second-class matter at the Post-office Department, Ottawa, Canada.

Personally Endorsed

ONLY a work well done deserves the name of its maker as a mark of pride in the accomplishment.

The name Firestone embossed on a tire carries the stamp of approval from the man who first built the product for the few, and heads the organization which now produces it for the millions.

It is more than that. It is the endorsement of the 100% stockholding force of Firestone workers—individuals who have personally pledged themselves to see that you get "Most Miles per Dollar."

It is not surprising that now, after twenty years of experience and comparison, a vast following accepts this name as authentic proof of highest quality.

MOST MILES PER DOLLAR

Home Study
BusinessCourses

The urgent need of business today is for high-salaried executives, managers and departmental specialists. Under the LaSalle Problem Method you can get, in your spare time at home by mail, under expert guidance, training which parallels actual business practice. The University's staff of 1750 people includes 450 business authorities, educators and assistants ready at all times to give prompt counsel and advice to enrolled members on any business question or problem. This is a service not obtainable from any other educational institution.

Write your name and address at the bottom and mail today. We will send full information and book of remarkable records of advancement made by LaSalle trained men; also our interesting book, "Ten Years' Promotion in One." Low cost and convenient monthly terms which anyone can afford. Money refunded if dissatisfied upon completion of course. Nearly 300,000 have enrolled. Find out what LaSalle training can do for you. Check and mail the coupon NOW.

LaSALLE EXTENSION UNIVERSITY
The Largest Business Training Institution in the World
Dept. 1052-R Chicago, Ill.

Gentlemen: Send without obligation to me information regarding course indicated below, also a copy of your interesting book, "Ten Years' Promotion in One."

- ☐ Business Management
- ☐ Higher Accountancy
- ☐ Traffic Management—Foreign and Domestic
- ☐ Railway Accounting and Station Management
- ☐ Law—Degree of LL.B.
- ☐ Commercial Law
- ☐ Industrial Management Efficiency
- ☐ Business Letter-Writing
- ☐ Banking and Finance
- ☐ C. P. A. Coaching for Advanced Accountants
- ☐ Modern Foremanship
- ☐ Personnel and Employment Management
- ☐ Business English
- ☐ Commercial Spanish
- ☐ Effective Speaking
- ☐ Expert Bookkeeping

Name..

Present Position..

Address..

NATIONAL SPORTSMAN

is a monthly magazine, crammed full of Hunting, Fishing, Camping, Trapping stories, and pictures valuable information about guns, rifles, revolvers, fishing tackle, camp outfits, best places to go for fish and game, fish and game laws, and a thousand and one helpful hints for sportsmen. National Sportsman tells you what to do in the woods, how to cook grub, how to build camps and blinds, how to train your hunting dog, how to preserve trophies, how to start a gun club: how to build a rifle range. No book or set of books you can buy will give you the amount of up-to-date information about life in the open that you get from a year's subscription to the National Sportsman.

Special Offer

On receipt of $1.00 we will send you the National Sportsman for a whole year together with one of our handsome Ormolu Gold Watch Fobs shown herewith. Mail your order today. Your money back if not fully satisfied.

NATIONAL SPORTSMAN
265 Newbury Street
BOSTON, MASS.

The Technical Book You Need

YOU'LL FIND just the book you need in our free 96-page catalog, the most complete on scientific and practical subjects. Supplements for 1919 and 1920, and 32-page 1921 book list also sent. Prices are not stabilized but we notify of any change before filling orders. Write for catalog and lists to-day and keep it for reference.

Scientific American Publishing Company,
234 Broadway, New York City

The Boy's Life of Christ

The story of Jesus, his boyhood and his ministry, told in simple yet vivid language that will hold and interest

HOW FAR DOES the MIND INFLUENCE the BODY?

The answer to this absorbingly interesting question will be found in the books of **Paul Dubois, M.D.**, Professor of Neuropathology at the University of Berne, Switzerland, who has made a lifelong study of the subject. This eminent authority approaches the problem both as a psychologist and a physician, yet in a style so clear that it presents no difficulties to the layman. All six books are sane, well-balanced, and instinct with an optimism that will be found contagious.

THE PSYCHIC TREATMENT OF NERVOUS DISORDERS

Translated by Smith Ely Jelliffe, M.D., and William A. White, M.D. In this strong, optimistic book Dr. Dubois discusses the philosophy underlying the position he holds and describes clearly and charmingly the exact methods by which he has achieved such notable success. 8vo, Cloth, 471 pp. Copious Index. $3.50; half leather, $4.50. By mail, 25 cents extra.

NERVOUS STATES—THEIR NATURE AND CAUSES

Authorized translation by Edward G. Richards. Points out that neurasthenia is not a new disease created by the conditions of modern life, but is due to fatigue brought on by psychic debilities and can be cured by the education of the mind and strengthening of the will. 12mo, Cloth. 75 cents; by mail, 80 cents.

THE PSYCHOLOGICAL ORIGIN OF MENTAL DISORDERS

Authorized translation by Edward G. Richards. A sympathetic and intensely human book, showing how mental disorders are caused by commonplace factors of everyday life, which precipitate the individual into an abnormal state, and how just as these conditions are formed, they can be reformed and normal health regained. 12mo, Cloth. 75 cents; by mail, 83 cents.

THE EDUCATION OF SELF

Translated from the latest French edition by Edward G. Richards. Charming essays that shed new light on the question of self-control and show that the only true road to happiness lies in moral development. 12mo, Cloth. $1.75; by mail, $1.85.

REASON AND SENTIMENT

Authorized translation by Edward G. Richards. A delightful and charmingly written essay, setting forth when sentiment and when reason should determine our line of conduct. Will be found specially helpful in directing the minds of parents toward the proper molding of their children's intellectual life. 12mo, Cloth. 75 cents; by mail, 81 cents.

THE INFLUENCE OF THE MIND ON THE BODY

Translated by L. B. Gallatin. An intimate and clearly expressed talk on this much discussed subject that every physician, nurse, or layman who is interested in the mutual reactions of mind and matter, should read with care. It contains a wealth of inspiration and help, and points the way to a healthier and happier life. 12mo, Cloth, 75 cents; by mail, 81 cents.

FUNK & WAGNALLS COMPANY, 354-360 FOURTH AVENUE, NEW YORK

A Fascinating New Book of Natural History

The interesting life of the insect world is portrayed vividly in this new book. The appearance, habits, characteristics, etc., of all kinds of insects, including Butterflies, Beetles, Grasshoppers, Ants, Bees, and many other varieties, are described in a pleasingly simple style, and yet with careful accuracy on the scientific side. The book is not only most entertaining, it is also instructive, identifying all the insects, showing which are beneficial and which are injurious. This is a simple course in Natural History, arranged in an unusual and fascinating form.

Knowing Insects Through Stories

By FLOYD BRALLIAR

Amazing Glimpses Into Insect Life

The most remarkable facts about the lives of various insects are revealed here. How the Hornet makes paper; how the Spider binds its victims, how the Ant milks its cows; how the Queen Bee starts a colony; and many other things of the greatest interest are told. And all is presented in delightful story form. The book is profusely illustrated, many of the plates being in the actual colors of the insects represented. The book is bound in decorative cloth.

Price $1.75 net; by mail $1.87

FUNK & WAGNALLS COMPANY 354-360 Fourth Avenue, New York

Thousands of Inspirations for Sermons

—up-to-date Sermons throbbing with human interest—Sermons which set forth invincible proofs, carry positive conviction, arouse the half-hearted, vanquish doubt, and win renewed and complete faith from the semi-cynic and the critic. This positively NEW and ONLY book of its kind will place in your hands over 700 large pages of the most remarkable and gripping literature bearing upon the Bible that has ever been published, together with 113 photographs of antiquities in the form of statues, papyri, instruments, tools, paintings, buildings, ruins, coins, inscriptions, etc.

THE NEW ARCHEOLOGICAL DISCOVERIES

AND THEIR BEARING UPON THE NEW TESTAMENT AND UPON THE LIFE AND TIMES OF THE PRIMITIVE CHURCH

By CAMDEN M. COBERN, D.D., Litt.D.; James M. Thoburn Chair of English Bible and Philosophy of Religion, Allegheny College; Honorary Secretary for Pennsylvania and Member of the General Executive Committee (American Branch) of the Egypt Exploration Fund, etc., etc. Introduction by Edouard Naville, D.C.L., LL.D., F.S.A.; Foreign Associate of the Institut de France; Professor of Archeology in the University of Geneva, Switzerland.

Do You Know That Thirteen New Sayings of Jesus Have Been Found in an Oasis in the Libyan Desert?

Recently Discovered MSS. Confirm the Historical Accuracy of the New Testament?

Thousands of Autographed Letters Written In and Before the First Century Are Now at Our Disposal?

The New Testament Was Written in the Language of the Common People?

A Wonderful New Manuscript of the Four Gospels with Fragments of the Pauline Epistles was Recently Found by an American in Egypt?

Excavations Recently Made Throw an Illuminating Light on the Cities Visited by St. Paul?

Suffragists, Millionaire Tax Dodgers, High Cost of Living, Shorthand, Elevators, Hot Air Heating, Grafting Politicians, Pipe Organs, Trusts and Trade Unions, "Preparedness," etc., were common things in Apostolic times?

Here is Meat for Hundreds of Sermons and Sermon Illustrations!

This is a scholarly pioneer work, without a competitor. It has just been published. It summarizes all discoveries of the past few decades in all lands, right up to the present, which have any important bearing upon the New Testament writings or the Primitive Church. It is withal a thrilling, readable Chronicle of intense human interest. Large Octavo, bound in cloth. Many illustrations; intensively and thoroughly indexed.

Only $1.00 Now

Pin a $1.00 bill to this coupon and sign and send it. We will immediately send the book, carriage paid, for your approval. The full price is $3.16. Examine it for ten days and then send us $2.16 to pay the balance, or return the book, and in this event we will immediately refund all you have paid. You run positively NO Risk.

Funk & Wagnalls Company, 354-360 Fourth Ave., New York

Gentlemen: Please send me one copy of **The New Archeological Discoveries.** I enclose $1.00. If not satisfied, I may return the book at your expense, within ten days, and you will refund the money paid. If I decide to keep the volume, I will send $2.16 within ten days, completing the purchase. (Price in full, $3.16 postpaid.)

Name..

Address..

Re-roof for the last time

Just starting to re-roof for the last time the residence of Mr. George C. St. John, New Rochelle, N. Y.

NO muss or litter or confusion; no cluttered lawns and broken shrubbery. Any good carpenter or roofer can do the job.

Economical

Not only do you save the cost of tearing off the old shingles and the risk of rain getting into the house during the progress of the job, but once you have applied Johns-Manville shingles you have a roof that should last as long as the structure it protects. Furthermore the old shingles form a valuable insulating blanket which renders the house warmer in winter and cuts your coal bill. This also means that in summer the house is cooler.

So it is for more than economy that we urge you to re-roof right over the old one. You actually get a better, stronger and more serviceable roof.

Fireproof

Johns-Manville Asbestos shingles are composed of Asbestos fibre and Portland Cement united under tremendous hydraulic pressure. There is nothing in them to rot or burn or disintegrate. The Underwriters' Laboratories Inc., have given their approval to the Johns-Manville Asbestos shingle and to this modern method of re-roofing, originated and perfected by Johns-Manville.

Beautiful

A roof of Johns-Manville Asbestos shingles is indeed handsome, and not only when new. After it has begun to age it becomes more and more attractive, taking on softer shades which gradually merge harmoniously with the surroundings. There is a variety to choose from, too; soft shades of brown, red and gray; rough, artistic edges or sharp, smooth ones; two shapes also so that they can be laid by the hexagonal method shown above, or the straight shingle method, as you prefer.

Send for the book

Get the whole story of the origin, development and perfecting of this new method of re-roofing which enables you to get a permanent, beautiful, fireproof roofing job for least cost.

The famous blow-torch test

Johns-Manville Asbestos Shingles can resist the fierce heat of the Blow Torch. Make this test on any roofing material you may be considering.

JOHNS-MANVILLE, Incorporated
294 Madison Ave., N. Y. City
Branches in 63 Large Cities
For Canada:
CANADIAN JOHNS-MANVILLE CO., Ltd., Toronto

Johns-Manville Service Covers the Continent

Through—

Asbestos

and its allied products

JOHNS-MANVILLE
Serves in Conservation

Heat Insulations, High Temperature Cements, Asbestos Roofings, Packings, Brake Linings, Fire Prevention Products

JOHNS-MANVILLE
Asbestos Roofing

Twenty Miles Each Way and *worth it!*

THERE are still places in America where the audience arrives in the saddle and the hitching post does more than support the figure of a loafer.

The Paramount dramas of luxurious life in the mansions of Fifth Avenue, the castles of old England and the chateaux of the Riviera are as wonderful to these tanned horsemen as photoplays of *their* lives are to the metropolitan fans.

Paramount Pictures draw people from longer distances than any other photoplays.

"Twenty miles each way *and worth it!*" for the folks of the open country might be translated: "Twenty blocks each way *and worth it!*" to the city dweller, who may pass three or four ordinary theatres enroute.

Unremitting devotion to the ideal of better entertainment, better motion pictures, has not gone unrewarded.

You people with an ounce of discrimination know that Paramount Pictures are everlastingly *there*.

You know by your own business gumption and experience that more than 11,200 theatres are not showing Paramount Pictures regularly merely because someone *said* they were better.

And you know that the greatest organization in the screen industry—with magnificent studios in England and America and with a reputation for success so magnetic as to draw the greatest talent in directing, acting, authorship and screen technique—did not just happen, like the mushroom, overnight, but was laboriously cut and polished, like the diamond.

And like the diamond, the brilliance of Paramount Pictures is indestructible, making men and women tireless in quest of them, knowing as they do that if it's a Paramount Picture it's the best show in town.

Paramount Pictures

PARAMOUNT PICTURES

listed in order of release

Sept. 1, 1921, to Dec. 1, 1921

Ask your theatre manager when he will show them

Wallace Reid in "The Hell Diggers"
By Byron Morgan.

Gloria Swanson in Elinor Glyn's
"The Great Moment"
Specially written for the star by the author of "Three Weeks."

Betty Compson in
"At the End of the World"
By Ernst Klein
Directed by Penrhyn Stanlaws.

"The Golem"
A unique presentation of the famous story of ancient Prague.

"Dangerous Lies"
With David Powell
By E. Phillips Oppenheim
A Paul Powell Production.

Cecil B. deMille's
"The Affairs of Anatol"
By Jeanie MacPherson
Suggested by Schnitzler's play
With Wallace Reid, Gloria Swanson, Elliott Dexter, Bebe Daniels, Monte Blue, Wanda Hawley, Theodore Roberts, Agnes Ayres, Theodore Kosloff, Polly Moran, Raymond Hatton and Julia Faye.

Elsie Ferguson in "Footlights"
By Rita Weiman, directed by John S. Robertson.

Thomas Meighan in "Cappy Ricks"
By Peter B. Kyne.

George Melford's
"The Great Impersonation"
By E. Phillips Oppenheim
Cast includes
James Kirkwood and Ann Forrest.

A George Fitzmaurize production
"Experience"
with Richard Barthelmess as "Youth"
By George Hobart.

William deMille's "After the Show"
By Rita Weiman; cast includes
Jack Holt, Lila Lee and Charles Ogle.

Ethel Clayton in William D. Taylor's
Production "Beyond"
By Henry Arthur Jones.

William S. Hart in
"Three Word Brand,"
A William S. Hart Production.

George Loane Tucker's
"Ladies Must Live,"
with Betty Compson;
by Alice Duer Miller.

"The Bonnie Briar Bush,"
by Ian MacLaren.
A Donald Crisp Production.

George Melford's Production
"The Sheik"
With Agnes Ayres and
Rudolph Valentino
From the novel by
Edith M. Hull

Jack Holt in "The Call of the North,"
adapted from "Conjuror's House"
by Stewart Edward White.

THE LITERARY DIGEST

PUBLIC OPINION (New York) combined with THE LITERARY DIGEST

Published by Funk & Wagnalls Company (Adam W. Wagnalls, Pres.; Wilfred J. Funk, Vice-Pres.; Robert J. Cuddihy, Treas.; William Neisel, Sec'y) 354-360 Fourth Ave., New York

Vol. LXX, No. 14 — New York, October 1, 1921 — Whole Number 1641

TOPICS - OF - THE - DAY

(Title registered in U S Patent Office for use in this publication and on moving picture films)

THE ARMS PARLEY AND THE LEAGUE AS RIVALS

WITH TWO RIVAL BODIES trying to save the world from war and ruin, one working from Geneva and the other from Washington, fear is beginning to be felt that their efforts may interfere with and weaken each other and prevent the highest success that might be hoped for. Thus the Springfield *Republican* is imprest by the fact that it is the correspondent of the pro-Harding Chicago *Daily News*, Paul Scott Mowrer, who reports that anti-American feeling is now running strong among the League delegates because they suspect our Government of a "silent struggle" to kill the League. According to Mr. Mowrer it is felt in Geneva that the coming conference at Washington was designed to steal the League's disarmament thunder, and also to lay the foundation for a new association of nations that would put the existing League underground. "The people of forty nations are being told by their correspondents that the League can not make disarmament progress because America will not work with it," cables Edwin L. James from Geneva to the New York *Times*, and he adds: "All the countries of the League are being told that America is killing the League because she wants her own league." The League and the Washington Conference "cannot both live," affirms the Fresno *Republican*, which goes on to say:

"The existence of either of these assemblages is inconsistent with that of the other.

"If the assembly of the League of Nations were really a functioning body, there would be no need for a disarmament conference. The calling of the conference is in some sense an aspersion on the League of Nations, or of the way it was formed or constituted. The disarmament conference is the vital body, at least for the present. The League of Nations is marking time."

Already, the correspondents report, the League of Nations Assembly has found it expedient to "shelve" the question of disarmament until after the Washington Conference; and a dispatch from Buenos Ayres suggests that South American countries would be willing to withdraw from the League and join an association of nations to be sponsored by President Harding.

LOSING CONFIDENCE IN THE OLD NOSTRUM

"I've taken a lot of that medicine without getting rid of my troubles."

—Brown in the Chicago *Daily News*.

But the League itself, and a majority of our editors, seem to take a more optimistic view of the situation. As the Topeka *Capital* expresses it, "There is a certain rivalry between the two efforts, yet neither is necessarily obstructive of the other, and the cooperation of both is not impossible." And it adds:

"These two distinct attacks on the problem of armament rivalry of great Powers deserve popular support in every part of the world. The success of either or both should be universally desired. Failure in a matter of such dire importance should not be accepted by the peoples who pay the bills of armament rivalry and of the wars thereby inflicted upon them."

Some months ago Mr. Viviani, the president of the League's Temporary Mixed Commission on the Reduction of Armaments, publicly exprest his own great satisfaction at President Harding's initiative, and declared his belief that the work of his commission would be of use to the Washington conference. In its report to the League Assembly, published on September 19, Mr. Viviani's commission finds that the Washington conference can better deal with the question of naval disarmament than the League. On this point it says: "The limitation of naval armaments, which presumably will be one of the principal problems discust in Washington, can indeed be most effectively secured by common agreement among the Powers." But meanwhile, the report adds, "a field of useful work remains open to the League of Nations. The financial position of the European states imperiously demands further reductions of military expenditures and indeed it is not too much to say that the economic revival of Europe depends largely upon such reductions being

From "Collier's," reproduced by permission.

TAKING MOST OF THE BEDCLOTHES. —Darling in *Collier's Weekly*.

effected." The report states in passing that America's failure to ratify the arms convention, which she signed at St. Germain, has prevented world-wide application of the principle, since Great Britain, France, Japan and Italy, altho willing to ratify, are holding off because of the attitude of the United States. In its discussion of the question of the private manufacture of arms, the report enumerates the following grave charges against arms manufacturers:

"First—That the armament firms have been active in fomenting war scares and in persuading their own countries to adopt warlike policies and increase their armaments.

"Second—That the armament firms have attempted to bribe Government officials, both at home and abroad.

"Third—That the armament firms have disseminated false reports concerning the military and naval programs of countries in order to stimulate armament expenditure.

"Fourth—That the armament firms have sought to influence public opinion through the control of newspapers in their own and foreign countries.

"Fifth—That armament firms have organized international armament rings through which the armament race has been accentuated by playing off one country against another.

"Sixth—That the armament firms have organized international armament trusts which have increased the price of armament sold to governments."

The document ends as follows:

"The inevitable conclusion to be drawn from the present report is that mankind at the present time is still too far removed from the ideal of peace towards which, however, all the efforts of the League of Nations, whose supreme object it is, must lead it.

"The delays, difficulties and cruel anxieties which beset us arise from the fact that while the League of Nations aims above all at maintaining peace, the fires of war are still smoldering in, alas! too many quarters of the globe.

"Nevertheless, the commission feels justified in the confidence that its labors will not have been without value in furthering the realization of this splendid ideal. It would be cruel injustice to reproach it with not having completed its task. The League of Nations after two brief years of existence could scarcely be expected to have solved all the problems which have perplexed the world for so many centuries.

"But even in this vital question of disarmament it may pride itself on having opened up to men of good-will a road which will lead them to realization of a less primitive ideal than that which has guided them since the dawn of history."

Of the five great Powers that will meet in Washington on Armistice Day to discuss the limitation of armament, four are members of the League of Nations. Will they be conscious of a divided loyalty? No, thinks the St. Louis *Globe-Democrat*, which goes on to say:

"The covenant of the League declares that 'The members of the League recognize that the maintenance of a peace requires the reduction of national armaments to the lowest point consistent with national safety and the enforcement by common action of international obligations,' and it prescribes that 'The Council, taking account of the geographical situation and circumstances of each state, shall formulate plans for such reduction for the consideration and action of the several governments.' In accordance with that provision the Council appointed, a year ago, a permanent Advisory Armaments Commission to study the problem, and in December the United States was invited to name a representative with advisory powers to sit with this commission, an invitation which President Wilson declined, inasmuch as the United States had refused to enter the League.

"It was generally conceded that an effective program for the limitation of armament could not be agreed upon unless the United States was a party to it. The richest and most powerful country in the world, with the largest navy save one, and with a navy-building program that would soon give it first rank in naval power, no government of the first class felt free to contemplate a material reduction of its military equipment without some definite knowledge of the attitude and purposes of the United States in this matter. Our Government not only refused to enter the League, but refused to have any communication with the League, thus making it impossible to reach any understanding through League agencies upon which a program of disarmament could be established. This country, in short, stood in the way of the most important step toward permanent peace that it was possible for the nations to take. That obstacle has been removed by President Harding in the call for a disarmament conference, to which the nations most vitally concerned, and no others, are invited, have responded with alacrity.

These nations could not bring America into active cooperation with them, because of the political circumstances that had prevented us from becoming a party to the League in which they are associated, but this Government could bring them into co-operation with it, by means of a conference outside of and independent of the League, for the accomplishment of the same purposes. In this matter the aim of the League and the aim of the conference are identical. It should make no great difference to the League, how or by what agencies the thing is done if it be done. Any action by the nations for the promotion of peace is in accord with the principles of the League and a furtherance of its designs."

Nor will successful action by the Washington Conference weaken the League or lesson its usefulness as an agency for peace, declares this St. Louis paper:

"On the contrary, we are inclined to believe that effective accomplishment at the Washington meeting will remove the greatest obstacle that now exists to the achievement of the League's purposes. It was from the beginning plainly recognized that limitation of armaments was one of the most important and at the same time one of the most difficult tasks intrusted to that organization. Even if the United States had been an active member it would have been hard for the League, with its powers limited to inquiry and recommendation, to have established an agreement among the nations on this matter. It will be exceedingly difficult for the coming conference to do this, but composed as it will be of special representatives acting directly on behalf of their respective governments, with these governments deeply concerned in the success of the conference and prepared to accept its conclusions, it is reasonable to expect that the difficulties will be cleared away and agreement accomplished. That being done the way would seem to be open to a larger field of usefulness for the League than would be possible to it so long as the armament problem remained unsolved. The American Government may continue to ignore this great organization, but none the less it exists, and it is operating to carry out the purposes of its creation. With the establishment of the International Court of Justice it will have completed its equipment for the promotion and application of principles of international law that are founded upon justice, and will have set up the machinery for the impartial consideration of international dispute as a means to the maintenance of international right and international peace. It may be that somehow we shall absorb the League, it may be that willy nilly it will absorb us, but one thing is sure, the essential principles upon which it is founded are American principles, and in it or out of it we shall have to walk in step with it or be untrue to ourselves."

"Lamentable as it is that the League of Nations has been crippled by the antagonism of the United States and hampered by the continued functioning of the Allied Supreme Council," says the New York *Times*, "the fact remains that to-day the center of hope for limiting armaments lies not at Geneva, but at Washington." "The principal reason why the conference offers better prospects for immediate results than the League's commission is that the United States will be represented in the conference, and under the present Administration the United States will not even receive or reply to communications from the League," remarks the Philadelphia *Record*, which adds:

"The United States has succeeded, so far as this matter is concerned, in thwarting the League of Nations. It is not creditable to the United States that it has done this, but as it has called the limitations conference the end may be attained by a different process.

"There is no indication that the limitation of armies will be considered at the limitations conference. This subject which is hardly second to the limitation of navies, will remain for the League's commission to deal with. The League is still the only organization that can deal with the causes of war and means to avert war. The International Court of Justice has been selected, and will soon organize, and will have a powerful influence, even without us, in moving nations to settle their controversies by negotiation or litigation or arbitration. In case these methods are refused, or fail, the League remains the only '*posse comitatus* of nations' to prevent war, which Mr. Roosevelt insisted upon repeatedly between 1910 and 1915, and for which Mr. Taft created his League to Enforce Peace."

As the Newark *Evening News* sees it, the League "does not expect much from the Harding conference," but "will await the outcome with impatience and, if it fails of substantial results, resume its own efforts more vigorously than ever." "America," says the Boston *Herald*, "is at one with the League of Nations in its aims, while differing in its methods." And in the New York *Journal of Commerce* we read:

"There would have been no need to hold a special conference on disarmament had the United States subscribed to the Covenant of the League of Nations. That instrument provides fully for the main purpose of the Washington Conference, inasmuch as the members of the League formally recognize that the maintenance of peace requires the reduction of national armaments to the lowest point consistent with national safety, and the enforcement by common action of international obligations.

AND WE MIGHT HAVE HAD SEATS WITH ALL THE REST OF THE FOLK.

—Williams in the Indianapolis *News*.

"But, with the United States standing outside of the circle of the League, it would be folly to attempt to formulate an international rule of armaments. Hence, President Harding's proposal comes in most opportunely to enable the League to function in a matter which constitutes one of the determining reasons for its existence. In regard to the problems of the Pacific, with which it is specifically charged to deal, the conference will have an obvious advantage over any mechanism that could be provided by the League of Nations. That is to say, it can act promptly, and with a degree of authority inherent in the limitation of its membership to the Powers immediately concerned."

Meanwhile, the popular demand for a solution of the disarmament problem is growing, particularly in the United States. When ninety-six United States Senators and four hundred and thirty-five Congressmen returned to Washington after a month's recess spent in renewing contact with their home communities, a Washington correspondent tells us, they were nearly unanimous in reporting disarmament the most popular issue "back home." Among the electorate of the country as a whole "the concern about reducing armaments is even greater than the concern about unemployment," we are told; because "to the sentiment based on the old League of Nations idealism is added a hard practical sentiment in favor of disarmament, based on the wish for lower taxes."

TALKING IRELAND INTO PEACE

ALL SUMMER LONG the Irish people, relieved by the truce from the terror of noonday riots and midnight assassinations, have been soothed into security by the almost daily interchange of statements between their representatives and the eloquent Welshman who speaks for the British empire. So grateful is the peace that editors and correspondents, while perplexed by successive deadlocks and ultimata, do not see how any sane leader will dare break the soporific charm of the cross-channel conversations by renewing the clash of arms. But whatever the final outcome, the diplomatic correspondence that has been going on these three months between the British Prime Minister and the Sinn Fein President has, as viewed objectively by our press, "all the fascination of a brilliant and dramatic matching of wits." "What a weaving of words and what a correspondence!" exclaims the Philadelphia *Public Ledger*. "The epistolary gladiators wield words as rapiers with a subtlety and skill that can be admired. No sooner do the spectators applaud the thrust of the Welshman than they are compelled to give plaudits to the parry and reposte of the Irishman." So remarks the Pittsburg *Dispatch*, noting that in the meanwhile, "as a witty cartoonist has depicted it, the door of Irish negotiations is left open because it is revolving." We have all of us learned not to take the notes of the negotiators at face value, the Chicago *Evening Post* observes, for "when the letters sound most hostile Dublin and London are most hopeful." The New York *Evening Post* finds "as much tragedy as comedy" in the situation, and comes to the conclusion that the fundamental of it "is apparently the need of a minute's recess in which Ireland shall declare herself independent and taste of her independence and then proceed to apply for admission into the British Empire."

When Celt meets Celt the verbal tug-of-war is likely to be

THEY ALWAYS LEAVE THE DOOR OPEN.

—De Mar in the Philadelphia *Record*.

interesting and long-drawn-out. At least our newspaper writers are sure it's so in the present case. Here it is October and the debate which has been substituted for murders and reprisals and counter-reprisals has been going on since July 8. In fact, it really began two weeks earlier. The New York *Tribune* presents this brief résumé of the negotiations between Premier Lloyd George and Mr. De Valera:

"June 24—Premier Lloyd George invited Eamon de Valera, 'president of the Irish republic,' and Sir James Craig, premier of Ulster, to a conference in London, looking toward peace in Ireland.

Photograph by International.

WITH A DUKE AT HIS BRIDLE REIN.

David Lloyd George, who has been called "the most remarkable Prime Minister of England since the time of the elder Pitt," thinking about his next note to De Valera as he rides over the Scottish moors attended by his host, the Duke of Atholl.

"July 8—De Valera accepts the invitation and a truce is declared.

"July 10—Lloyd George asks De Valera to set a date.

"July 11—De Valera sets July 14.

"Aug. 11—De Valera, after conferences with Lloyd George in London, resulting in Great Britain offering dominion home rule, sends note to Lloyd George refusing the proposals on the ground that British reservations in them offset the advantages, and arguing for full independence and absolute separation. De Valera also suggests referring the issues to an arbitration committee composed of one representative on each side and the President of the United States.

"Aug. 14—Lloyd George in a note to De Valera refuses to compromise on the question of the right to secede, or to submit to foreign arbitration, but expresses the hope that Ireland will accept the terms, the best England can offer.

"Aug. 24—De Valera informs Lloyd George that the Dail Eireann has rejected the terms unanimously, but is ready to appoint representatives to negotiate peace on the principle of government by the consent of the governed. He adds that Ireland is ready to defend herself by force.

"Aug. 26—Lloyd George replies that further negotiations would be futile and dangerous until the Sinn Fein can comprehend the extent of the government's concessions. He offers to meet De Valera again, but is not willing to discuss the principle of government by the consent of the governed.

"Aug. 31—Ireland again rejects Lloyd George's terms, but offers to meet the Premier once more if he will discuss government by the consent of the governed. It declares that the people of Ireland acknowledge no voluntary union with Great Britain.

"Sept. 8—British Cabinet invites De Valera to send delegates to a conference at Inverness, Scotland, September 20, with the sole condition that Ireland must remain within the Empire.

"Sept. 16—De Valera's reply is made public in Dublin, accepting the invitation, but insisting that Sinn Fein delegates can sit only as representatives of an independent state.

"Sept. 16—Lloyd George cancels Inverness conference, declaring this would amount to recognition of the Irish republic, but says he will consult with Ministers as to his future course.

"Sept. 16—De Valera telegraphs his surprize at Lloyd George's decision, and explains that if Ireland did not make clear the status of her representatives her position would be prejudiced.

"Sept. 17—Lloyd George reiterates and amplifies his refusal to confer on the basis of an independent Ireland.

"Sept. 17—De Valera telegraphs that he accepted the invitation without calling on Great Britain to abandon any principles, and adds that 'we can only recognize ourselves for what we are.'

"Sept. 18—Lloyd George telegraphs De Valera that he is ready to meet Sinn Fein delegates as the representatives of their people, but that the claim to represent a sovereign state must be withdrawn."

In this interchange "Lloyd George, master of Old World diplomacy, has been vanquished by De Valera," so Frank P. Walsh thinks. This zealous American upholder of the Sinn Fein position adds, in a statement made for the Universal Service after a visit to Ireland and printed in the New York *American:*

"The Talleyrand-Metternich style of slippery indirectness and craftiness was met by forthright truth and naked statement, and went down in defeat before them.

"The notes of Lloyd George have been wordy and vague, while those of De Valera have been models of terseness and lucidity."

"The Irish unquestionably have the best of the verbal argument," agrees the Socialist New York *Call*, and the Irish insistence upon entering into negotiations as a sovereign state does not seem to the *Minnesota Daily Star* any mere technicality. Americans find something bold and fine in Patrick Henry's "Give me liberty or give me death," and it is difficult for the Minneapolis labor journal "to discover any reason why the words do not as well become an Irish Republican leader as they did our own Patrick Henry."

Taking "a merely sporting view of the wordy duel," most

FED UP.

—Gale in the Los Angeles *Times*.

thinking readers would, however, in the opinion of the New York *World*, "adjudge the honors to the shrewd Welsh attorney." That is,

"Lloyd George has accomplished his main purpose of uniting behind him practically all shades of English opinion. Not even the English Labor Party can as a whole accept the De Valera premise of a sovereign Ireland, including Ulster. On the other hand, Mr. De Valera, urged on by fanatical Sinn Feiners, chiefly in the United States, out of the dust and heat of conflict, has been maneuvered into a position where it is doubtful if he can command a united Irish support."

HARMONY OR BUST.

—Morris for the George Mathew Adams Service.

That "Lloyd George has shown himself a shrewder controversialist than De Valera and has pushed the Irish leader from one position to another until at last the Premier has got all that he need ask," is also the opinion of the New York *Times*. "Mr. De Valera and the Irish republic have been put in the wrong," flatly declares the Boston *Transcript*. De Valera's apparent belief that Irish independence can be won by rhetorical subtlety "would be amusing if it were not so damaging," says the New York *Evening Post*. Such tactics, it believes, have harmed his case and "when a journal which has fought for Irish freedom, as *The New Statesman* has fought for it, can speak of 'the impossible Irish' it is time for level-headed Irishmen to ask themselves whether De Valera has not been suffered to go too far." The trouble with the Irish, according to the London weekly, is that they are "an intensely 'political' race; they love caucuses and secret societies and shibboleths; but they have almost no capacity at all for 'getting to business.'" As the British editor further discourses on Irish "impossibility":

"In politics, the English habitually think in terms of realities. We employ all sorts of resounding phrases, and political abstractions and pretenses, but we do not think in them—whereas the Irish do. They care more for a phrase than for a fact, more for a verbal admission of their 'independence' than for the realities of freedom. . . How are we to conduct serious negotiations with such a people? Inevitably we must get at cross-purposes."

But *The New Statesman* does not believe that there can be an absolute deadlock, for the Irishmen "do not want to go on fighting us any more than we want to go on fighting them." But English opinion, it concludes, is an extremely important factor, and "if Mr. Lloyd George should appeal to the country on the basis of the published correspondence between Mr. De Valera and himself and General Smuts, he will win hands down. And he will gain a new mandate."

The diplomacy over Ireland, observes the Dallas *News*, has

certainly been open enough." The British and the Irish leader each feels obliged to keep his own extremists in line. Thus the discussion "becomes a sort of contest in shouting from the housetops that the mountains will level with the plains and snails will run over pedestrians before either side will give in an inch." While "this sort of parley is good for the lungs, unfortunately, it doesn't seem to get anywhere." And the Texas editor finds it a valuable index of the value of "open covenants openly arrived at":

"WELL, I CAN ALWAYS CHANGE DOCTORS."
—Knott in the Dallas *News*.

"We speak of open covenants openly arrived at—and there is an interpretation of the phrase which can be made to stand the test of common sense. But taken literally and applied as many seem to desire, the method defeats its own ends, assuming that it were enforceable. Manifestly, the holding of caucuses and conferences from which the nimbus of public clamor and prejudice is shut out must be possible if an agreement is to be reached which can be formulated into a covenant at all. The Irish situation thus far seems to illustrate this."

But right here another Texas paper begs to differ. It does not agree with those who say that a quiet talk behind closed doors would wind the business up more quickly. It has the idea that "these secret agreements which satisfy because of the speed by which they can be arranged only serve to postpone the real issue." For, observes this daily, the Houston *Chronicle:*

"If the Irish and English people are not brought together in spirit, a contract entered into by two men or by 200 men will not count for much in the long run.

"We think the publicity of this correspondence, tho it seems to retard the immediate result, serves a good purpose.

"It will certainly define and clarify the various issues involved.

"It will permit people on both sides to understand each other's position in a more thorough manner.

"It will remove the possibility of snap judgment, as well, as any misapprehension of the consequences.

"Undoubtedly the British premier and Mr. De Valera could have concocted some kind of a makeshift by pussyfooting around in secret.

"Would it have stuck? Would it have removed the fundamentals of the conflict?

"Of course, it takes more time for millions to come to an agreement than it does tens, or even hundreds, but isn't an agreement so made apt to last longer?"

NEW MEXICO'S ELECTION AS A STRAW

THE "SHOW-DOWN" IN NEW MEXICO, as the Savannah *News* (Dem.) calls the special election which resulted in the victory of a Republican Senator last week, is interpreted as "a conditional O. K. of the Harding Administration," by the Albuquerque *Journal*, an independent Republican paper of New Mexico, which is in a position to size up State sentiment. That the special election was a "referendum" is, in fact, generally conceded by both Democratic and Republican editors; as Mark Sullivan, Washington political correspondent of the New York *Evening Post*, writes, "it was the first election of a national official since the Republicans came into power, and because of this, politicians of both parties look forward to proclaiming the result as an index of any change or lack of change in public sentiment."

Nationwide interest in what ordinarily would have been a purely local affair was first aroused by President Harding's letter reviewing the accomplishments of the first six months under the Republican régime. This, complained several Democratic papers, was clearly a campaign document to aid in the New Mexico election, and thereupon, says *The Post's* correspondent, the Democratic and Republican National Committees made the election an important matter. Senators and Congressmen from surrounding States, and well-known women speakers were prest into service.

Running against Senator Bursum, Republican, who won, were a Democrat, Judge Hanna, who aspired to the governorship in the last election, a Socialist, and an Independent Republican. The election was to choose a Senator to serve out the unexpired term of Albert B. Fall, now Secretary of the Interior, who, as the New York *World* points out, was not in New Mexico aiding in the election of his Republican successor, but "rounding up cattle and buffalo in Montana." As the Democratic Roswell (N. M.) *Record* sums up the results of September 20:

"The election was won by the Republicans for two main reasons. First, the majority of the voters of the State felt that the National Administration as represented by Mr. Bursum should be given further time to develop its plans. Second, New Mexico normally has a Republican plurality and there were no outstanding reasons why any large defection should go to Mr. Hanna. The vote that might have elected Mr. Hanna to the Senate went to Senator Bursum largely because of the disposition to give the party represented by Senator Bursum a fair opportunity to make good.

"The great lesson that must be drawn from Tuesday's election is that the voters are waiting to see how the Republican party handles the situation that confronts the country. If the New Mexico election means anything, it means that further time will be given the Republicans. On the other hand *The Record* is firmly convinced that the voters will demand some material results by the time of the Congressional elections next fall."

The New York *World* (Ind. Dem.), the Springfield *Republican*, and other papers of similar political belief, find it hard to forgive President Harding for inditing the aforementioned "campaign document." President Wilson was furiously denounced for "dragging the Presidential office into politics," as *The Republican* puts it, while President Harding now congratulates the new Republican Senator from New Mexico and looks upon his election as "heartening." Which causes *The World* to remark in sarcastic vein:

"During the Senatorial campaign in New Mexico the Republicans took great pains to explain that the campaign was only a local issue. Merely for form's sake President Harding appealed for mercy for Bursum in a letter to Senator McCormick.

"But now that the election in New Mexico is over and Senator Bursum has been elected, a wave of enthusiasm sweeps the Republican Party. After all, it seems that the election of an obscure candidate in the Southwest was a great national issue. The Harding Administration has won a great victory. Its policies have been triumphantly vindicated at the polls."

YANKEE CAPITAL INVADING EUROPE

OF FAR-REACHING SIGNIFICANCE, thinks the Springfield *Union*, is the acquisition by an American syndicate of a one-third share in the vast properties of Archduke Frederick of Austria. These consist of part of the Teschen iron mines and steel works, employing 20,000 workers; hundreds of thousands of acres of valuable forest lands, many fertile farms, the dairies that supply Vienna with milk, lumber mills, beet-sugar plantations and mills, chateaux, villas and historic castles scattered throughout Italy, Austria, Roumania, Czecho-Slovakia, Poland, Hungary and Jugo-Slavia. In addition, many Vienna apartment buildings and a museum containing approximately a million art objects were acquired. On the very day that this singular information was published, William M. Wood, head of the American Woolen Company, announced that a subsidiary concern had obtained options on the output of thirty-five worsted, woolen, and yarn mills in Germany, Czecho-Slovakia and Austria. The plan of the American concern, we are told, is to provide credit, and furnish raw materials and semi-finished products to some of the mills for a percentage of their output, according to the New York *News Record*, an authority in the textile trade. Thus a large amount of American capital is placed behind foreign resources and labor. As the Philadelphia *Public Ledger* remarks, "It is all very dramatic and unusual. For a century European capital crossed the Atlantic to develop the New World; now the New World's capital flows back across the sea to rehabilitate a broken Europe."

The investment of American money in foreign enterprises, and the employment of American brains in the economic restoration of Europe will be "for the great advantage of this country, as well as of Europe," believes the Baltimore *Evening Sun*, for "every such investment will do its part toward relieving the present unstable conditions of world business." And surely we can afford to make such investments, point out other editors, for at the present time we have about half the gold of the world.

The action of the American Woolen Company's subsidiary concern will make the United States a formidable rival of Great Britain as an investor in the textile enterprises of other nations, declares the *News Record*. Whether the company will import foreign-made woolens into the United States remains to be seen, however. It is well known that Germany, for instance, is making goods at prices far below ours, and it is only a question of time, thinks the head of the American Woolen Company, when "these goods are going to come into this country, anyhow." Why should not American business men reap the profits, asks Mr. Wood. As *The News Record* tells us:

"Why American textile men should have withheld so long from mill investments abroad was a question that puzzled even those American textile men who were in a position to make such investments. There were examples right in their own mill communities of foreigners owning and operating mills in direct competition with their own. Yet there was no effort made to depart from their defensive attitude and carry the competition right into the foreigners' own lands.

"The weaving industry, next to pottery perhaps the oldest in civilization, had lent itself peculiarly to the talents of American organization, and in its allied branches America had long ago taken the lead of all other nations. But American enterprise was confined within American territorial limits and no inducement abroad was sufficient to interest American capital.

"It was said that American capital had all it could do to erect plants and furnish the operating expenses for the rapidly growing industry at home, and this, in a measure, was true. But it is now realized that the war has changed conditions and that American textile interests enjoy unequaled opportunities to expand abroad."

Now, explains the Boston *News Bureau*, gold "has become with us a veritable embarrassment of riches, but the flow remains insignificant compared with the debit balance against the rest of the world." Continues this financial daily:

"Under a war-transformed relation, we already hold a paper or security stake in Europe generally estimated around $16,000,000,000—with predictions common that it will exceed $20,000,000,000 before the peak is reached. We are quite disinclined to increase the governmental accommodations, but we may have to extend further the commercial credits before the trade tide has definitely turned.

"Already a good many mills and foundries in the Old World are reputed to have passed into hands of such American buyers, just as a good many more are understood to have arranged to operate practically as agents for American or English principals, supplying them with raw material. The outright sales of such properties mean a transfer of American principal on a large scale that, in respective exchange terms, means a big dent in the collective European debit account."

SAME OLD WAGE SLAVES, BUT A NEW KING.

Hapsburg holdings acquired by a U. S. syndicate.—News Item.

—Walker in the New York *Call*.

"Business is proverbially unsentimental," as the Kansas City *Journal* reminds us, "therefore mere sentiment will not retard the expansion of commercial relations between the United States and her late enemy nations." Transactions of the kind already noted "indicate the way in which events naturally turn when a country long a debtor suddenly becomes the chief creditor nation of the world," notes the Springfield *Union*. It adds:

"It may be said that this is transferring to Europe capital that could be used in our own industries, but it is not a transfer of capital now at the disposal of this country. The money used is money that we can not at present collect in other ways; the whole American payment can be completed in the exchange market without the movement of a dollar. It may also be said that such a process, if carried out to any great extent, would result in the employment of foreign labor to the exclusion of our own. But the situation is such that the needs of Europe can be supplied only by increased production based on the depreciated currencies in which purchases must be made. A large part of Europe has nothing with which to buy goods on the present American basis of wages and costs. But American capital can employ foreign labor on its own soil with its own currency for the supply of its own needs, and at the same time establish a more workable relation with American industry and markets.

"This American syndicate's purchase is not an isolated or unique instance. Others less dramatic are taking place, without attracting special attention, and the tendency is likely to become more and more apparent. It should have a remarkable expansion whenever Russia with her vast resources regains a workable political and economic connection with the rest of the world."

THE WORLD'S UNEMPLOYED

WITH THE EXCEPTION OF GREAT BRITAIN and the United States, both of which are faced with critical unemployment problems, other nations throughout the world are comparatively well off, according to the figures of Ernest Greenwood, American representative of the International Labor Organization of the League of Nations, in a New York *Times* article. In fact, Spain does not seem to have felt the unemployment crisis to any extent, he says, while in Italy, where conditions are improving slowly but surely, the number of workers out of employment in May of this year was estimated to be only about 250,000. Japan also is rapidly recovering from her wide-spread depression of last year. But "unemployment has been increasing rapidly in Great Britain," Mr. Greenwood tells us, "and that country is facing a crisis as serious, if not more serious, than our own." Of 12,000,000 registered workers, there were in June 2,127,400 unemployed, despite the British Government's extensive program for the organization of public works. In France conditions seem to have improved. In one industry, however (the textile industry), there was a falling off of production last summer ranging all the way from 15 per cent. to 75 per cent. in some districts. And while this year's figures of the Ministry of Labor are not available, the central employment offices of that body placed 1,078,000 workers last year in transient and comparatively permanent positions.

The principal measures which have been taken by the various countries to alleviate unemployment are unemployment insurance, a national system of free employment exchanges, the organization of public works to furnish employment, and the coordination of all three of these systems. It is perhaps in the latter that the ultimate solution of the unemployment problem will eventually be found, thinks Mr. Greenwood. In Italy, for instance—

"The present measures for dealing with unemployment are compulsory insurance against unemployment and the establishment of free public employment exchanges. The Italian law for unemployment insurance does not stop at a mere organization of insurance nor confine its activities to the collection of contributions and the payment of benefits. It goes further, recognizing the principle that any wisely conceived plan of insurance ought not only to provide for the repair of the loss, but also to prevent or at least reduce the risk of its recurrence."

Early in 1919 there were more than a million workers in Germany out of employment, but at the present time their number is estimated to be only about 300,000. In 1920, 400,-000,000 marks were spent by the German Government for productive work for the unemployed. Belgian trade unions reported in February of this year that 22.7 per cent. of their membership of 621,000 were unemployed, the textile trades suffering more heavily than all other trades combined. The Belgian Government is endeavoring to meet the crisis by entering upon a number of public works.

In Denmark the unemployment figures in February were 23.2 per cent., and in the Netherlands the total number of workers out of employment last January was 81,743, while Czecho-Slovakia now reports only 50,000. In Poland there were about 88,000 unemployed on April 1, while in February 20.8 per cent. of Sweden's trade unionists were out of work. Although the total population of the Austrian Republic is 6,667,430, according to Mr. Greenwood's figures, only 19,000 were without employment in May of this year. The ninety free employment agencies throughout Canada placed 600,000 persons in positions during the first fifteen months following March, 1919, but early in this year the percentage of unemployed reported by trade unions had increased to over 13.0 per cent.

It is Mr. Greenwood's conclusion that "the judicious release of public contracts in such times as these would have a tonic effect upon the whole labor market," and that "the tendency to unemployment would therefore be considerably lessened." However, he considers it unlikely that there will ever be a return to the economic conditions which existed prior to July, 1914:

"The relation of countries has been altered materially. Some industrial nations have fewer exports than in 1914. Transportation systems are changing. There are enormous public works to be undertaken, large government loans, a large amount of paper money and fluctuating exchanges. Rates of wages and prices of the war period show indications of surviving for many years in all countries. These are totally diverse from those of the pre-war period. The casualties due to the war, partial cessation of immigration, the decrease in birth rates, and conditions of military service will all certainly affect employment in many countries for years to come."

OUR "3 PER CENT." IMMIGRATION SNARL

THE FIRST TWO MINUTES OF AUGUST found two ships lying quietly off New York, just outside the three-mile limit. And these particular ships were not "boot-leggers," either; they were carrying immigrants from Europe. The reason for hovering outside the jurisdiction of the United States—with steam up—was that the July quotas allowed several European nationalities had been exceeded. When the new month was ushered in, however, a race for shore began, with the result that the winner (by two minutes) filled the quotas, and nothing but deportation remained for scores of immigrants on the losing vessel. In the wee sma' hours of September 1 a similar race occurred, in which six ships participated, and it is predicted that the same thing will happen around midnight of September 30.

Happenings of this sort—"attempts to evade the law," the Cleveland *News* calls them—throw the searchlight on the "3 per cent." Emergency Immigration Act, which limits immigration to 3 per cent. of each nationality already in the United States, as determined by the census of 1910. Many editors declare that it is "unworkable," and that it visits hardships on those who come here expecting to find a home, even in some instances separating families of a certain nationality when the quota of that nationality is filled. The New York *Globe* finds the new act "stupid"; *The World*, "asinine" and "idiotic"; *The Evening World*, "oppressive, absurd and illogical." "We have had foolish experiments in immigration control, but none to compare to this," avers the last-named paper. "Stupidity in framing and administering this restrictive immigration act seems to have gone the limit," agrees the Philadelphia *Bulletin*, while the Syracuse *Herald* informs us that "it is the testimony of all who know that the new law for regulating immigration is working badly."

President Harding, however, in replying to representations by a New York Congressman of cruelties in the enforcement of the new law, declares that, if the case has been correctly presented to him, "the difficulty must be charged to dishonest steamship agents who have brought to this country innocent immigrants in spite of our continued warnings." "And Mr. Harding was not far wrong," believes the Washington *Herald*, which remarks that "it is hard to teach an old dog new tricks." "These steamship companies," adds Mr. Hoover's paper, "have sinned so long in immigration transportation that it is hard for them to reform."

"There is no fault to be found with the method of admitting a specified number of aliens of any one nationality each month, but Congress left the method to be applied in a blundering and inhumane way," maintains the Troy *Record*. As the Syracuse *Herald* explains:

"The majority of Congress evidently believed that the plan of opening our gates to 3 per cent. per annum, averaged by months, of the total number of aliens from any given country enumerated by the census of 1910 would be a happy way out of our immigration difficulty. But it has not proved to be happy; and we have reason to doubt whether it is sensible or just.

"The longer the new expedient is tried, we believe, the more clearly it will appear that a rationing yardstick is not the best gage for measuring the inflow of immigration."

"The spirit of the law, not the letter, is violated in the way it is enforced," complains the Indianapolis *Star*. Moreover, says the Minneapolis *Journal*, "it works injustice and hardship." But the net effect of the new immigration policy, thinks the editor of the bulletin of the Associated General Contractors, will be to "prevent the immigration to this country of the most useful class of immigrants—the common laborers who come here to work in the construction industry."

But in the opinion of the Los Angeles *Times*, all this "clamor about the iniquities of the new immigration law is assuming such proportions as to lead one to suspect that propagandists are back of it." As this paper sees it, "undesirables are kept away from our shores at a time when the number of unemployed is probably as great as at any time in our history." It is no secret, says *The Times*, that "representatives of the trans-Atlantic steamship companies have been busy in Washington, calling for conferences and buttonholing Congressmen, with the intent of securing modification of the present restrictions." The Cincinnati *Times-Star* even declares that recent incidents "have been seized upon by people who oppose any restriction of immigration as part of their campaign to discredit the new immigration law." "Who pays for this effort to depopularize the new law," asks *The Times-Star*. And it goes on:

"The fact is that the new immigration law, from the date of its enactment, has been subjected to organized attack by individuals, racial groups and newspapers who are intent upon bringing about its repeal and who, at the bottom of things, are against any action by the American Government to protect this country from practically unlimited immigration."

While a portion of the surplus immigrants may be permitted to enter the United States under personal bond, and be charged to the year's totals, it is pointed out that at the end of this year "the day of reckoning must come." Under the provisions of the new act, the quota divisions of the 71,163 immigrants which may be accepted in any one month are as follows:

Albania	57	Portugal	454
Austria	1,480	Roumania	1,483
Belgium	311	Russia	6,349
Bulgaria	60	Spain	133
Czecho-Slovakia	2,854	Sweden	3,991
Danzig	57	Switzerland	749
Denmark	1,129	United Kingdom	15,441
Finland	778	Other Europe	17
Fiume	14	Armenia	318
France	1,138	Palestine	11
Germany	13,608	Smyrna district	88
Greece	657	Syria	181
Hungary	1,127	Other Turkey	43
Italy	8,404	Other Asia	16
Jugo-Slavia	1,281	Africa	24
Luxemburg	18	Australia	54
Netherlands	720	New Zealand	10
Norway	2,423	Atlantic Islands	12
Poland	4,004	Pacific Islands	4
Eastern Galicia	1,156		

After the steamship companies have been compelled to carry back (at their own expense) a few hundreds of the surplus, "they will begin to cooperate with each other and the law will be found entirely workable," thinks the Washington *Herald*. At present, points out the New York *Tribune*, "the new law provides no fine or punishment for steamship companies which disregard its provisions." Nor is the company required to refund the returned immigrant's passage money, adds the Commissioner General of Immigration in a New York *World* interview. The only recourse left to immigration officials is to obey the law, explains the Detroit *Free Press*, which believes the law was enacted "because this country now has more workers than it can employ." At any rate, argues the Philadelphia *Inquirer*, "immigration officials should not be allowed to strain

IN THE LAND OF LIBERTY.
—Morris for the George Matthew Adams Service.

the law and admit surplus immigrants. There is too much law enforcement already at the discretion of the enforcing authorities."

What, then, is the remedy for the situation? Whatever the merits of the law, and however it is being enforced, "it is plain that if we are not to have a constant process of 'quota' congestion at this end, the flow of immigration must be regulated in Europe," declares the New York *Evening Post*. "There are both humane and economic reasons" why this should be done, agrees the New York *Tribune*, and the Philadelphia *Record* is authority for the statement that "it not only would be more efficient, but cheaper in the long run than our present system." Canada eliminates the unsuitable immigrant at the source, points out a writer in *The Outlook* (New York) and "this is much to be preferred over rejection upon arrival at a Canadian port, which may involve hardship to this immigrant, unnecessary transportation expenses, and vexatious delays." Our consuls abroad could visé the immigrant's passports after thorough medical and other examination, maintains the New York *Tribune*. In the belief of this paper:

"That there should be such examination goes without saying. We are now practising it, in difficult and unsatisfactory circumstances, at Ellis Island. Certainly it would seem to be to the advantage of all concerned to have it done on the other side. It would cost our Government less. It would be better for the immigrants. It would be better for the steamship companies, for it would mean fewer to be taken back at the companies' expense.

"With a competent consular service nine-tenths of those who are now rejected and excluded at Ellis Island would be rejected on the other side, and would thus be saved a fruitless journey."

TOPICS IN BRIEF

Alleged prohibition is the cause of alleged liquor.—*Fresno Herald.*

Liquor is hard on the constitution and vice versa.—*Nashville Tennessean.*

Political gas is not of the illuminating variety.—*Columbia (S. C.) Record.*

Niagara isn't the only roaring flood on our northern border.—*Columbia (S. C) Record.*

There are some German marks which can never be wiped out.—*Wall Street Journal.*

In West Virginia it took armament to force disarmament—and the world is just an enlarged West Virginia.—*Greenville (S. C.) Piedmont.*

These are anti-bellum days.—*Newspaper Enterprise Association.*

Some representatives in Congress are only fairly so.—*Charleston Gazette.*

Human nature can't be altered by being haltered.—*Columbia (S. C.) Record.*

Limitation of armament should have no limitation downward—*Norfolk Virginian-Pilot.*

Is the legacy of national prohibition to be bootlegacy?—*Chicago Journal of Commerce.*

Samson had the right idea about advertising. He took two columns and brought down the house.—*Charleston Gazette.*

Tariff tinkerers usually have a high conception of duty.—*Rochester Times-Union.*

Prohibition has a hard time trying to compete with an inventive people.—*Charleston Gazette.*

The disarmament conference is to establish non-communication with Mars.—*Nashville Tennessean.*

The only time the Spanish cabinet breaks into the news is when it resigns.—*Honolulu Star-Bulletin.*

In 1916 Germany planned on making America pay for the war. Well, we are.—*Marquette Tribune.*

Football will be popular this year because it has so much kick in it.—*Boston Shoe and Leather Reporter.*

One American book is supremely popular in Europe—Uncle Sam's Pocket-book.—*Greenville (S. C.) Piedmont.*

We always thought the Irish wanted freedom until they began to insist on having a republic.—*Columbia (S. C.) Record.*

We wonder if Ireland does form an independent republic whether it will include New York City.—*Charleston Gazette.*

THE NOSE-BAG.

—Ireland in the Columbus *Dispatch.*

Dove of peace hovering over Ireland is taking awful chances. —*Wall Street Journal.*

Every time Hoover takes his eye off it, the cost of living goes up again.—*New York World.*

When we feed Russia, we can omit the soup. She's already in that.—*Nashville Tennessean.*

The Greeks are pushing the Turk hard, but have not yet got his Angora.—*Boston Herald.*

The new heads of Alaska and the Philippines are Bone and Wood, respectively.—*Nashville Tennessean.*

News item: "Ford cars have taken another drop." Where'd they get it?—*Greenville (S. C.) Piedmont.*

If the nations ever bill and coo it will be because thought of the bill teaches them to coo.—*Tacoma Ledger.*

The German cry has been changed from "Hoch, der Kaiser!" to "God save the mark."—*Columbus Dispatch.*

Mr. Gompers can boast that the union workers who proclaimed "No beer, no work!" had both demands conceded.—*Wall Street Journal.*

Money goes a little farther now, but it is still unable to go quite as far as next payday.—*Indianapolis Star.*

The man who first called it the "easy" payment plan was mighty careless with his adjectives.—*Roanoke World News.*

Madame Curie says the earth is not cooling off. Certainly not where the Irish question is discussed.—*Greenville (S. C.) Piedmont.*

The Bolshevists may not be strong on providing food for Russia, but they are experts at making a hash of things.—*Columbia (S. C.) Record.*

The difference between an Irishman and an American is that the Irishman thinks he isn't free and the American thinks he is.—*Minnesota Star.*

"Pike's Peak or Bust!" said the pioneers.
"Price Peak and Bust!" say the profiteers.
—*Brooklyn Eagle.*

Astronomers can explain almost everything except the odd circumstances that moonshine is more abundant on dark nights.—*Indianapolis Star.*

The Chicago telegraph messenger recently arrested for speeding shouldn't be punished—he should be sent to Congress.—*Columbia (S. C.) Record.*

George Harvey and Charlie Chaplin Vie for News Space in London.—Headline. Who says the Londoner has no sense of humor? — *Little Rock Arkansas Gazette.*

A British psychologist says that one way to avoid apoplexy is to tell the truth. But if we told the whole truth it might give some other people apoplexy.—*Philadelphia Record.*

"Prosperity," says Brother Williams, "makes us all feel like dancin' a jig, an' w'en we gits done dancin' and payin' de fiddler, we ain't got no prosperity!"—*The Atlanta Constitution.*

We are tickled most to death with a government that can build forty-million-dollar battleships for the junkman and can't afford to buy a home for its Ambassador to France.—*Columbia (S. C.) Record.*

Reduction of navies should proceed on the theory that the Dove of Peace is not a fleet bird.—*Norfolk Virginian Pilot.*

The premier of Britain is willing to turn the policing power over to the Irish. Most American cities did that long ago.—*Manila Bulletin.*

There is a growing suspicion that an underselling Germany is about as much of a menace as an overbearing Germany.—*Canton Repository.*

What this country needs from the miners and operators is more underground operation and fewer field operations.—*Little Rock Arkansas Gazette.*

American sportsmen have taken the other cups from Europe. It only remains for the Anti-Saloon League to take the hiccup.—*Richmond News Leader.*

The kickers forget that the only liberties that have been taken from the American people have been taken by the American people.—*Akron Beacon-Journal.*

The Germans are planning a new offensive against the world; they are talking about exiling all the Hohenzollerns from Germany.—*Columbia (S. C.) Record.*

It strikes us those Greeks would make much better headway against the Turks if they charged as they do in some of their fruit stores over here.—*Philadelphia Enquirer.*

Once again Mars is reported to be trying to communicate with us. If the Martians knew more about us they wouldn't be so curious.—*Boston Shoe and Leather Reporter.*

In the heart of the New York financial district there is an animal hospital. —News Item. We didn't know New York's financial district had a heart. —*Little Rock Arkansas Gazette.*

Relief workers say that if Russia pulls through the coming winter it will be by a close shave, but it will be hard to make the world think Russia will resort to this.—*Manila Bulletin.*

"League of Nations Takes Slap at U. S." says a headline. Uncle Sam is in a good-natured mood, and probably would turn the other cheek if he knew which one he had been slapped on.—*Kansas City Star.*

FOREIGN - COMMENT

JAPANESE DOUBTS OF THE WASHINGTON CONFERENCE

THE SPECTACLE OF JAPAN accepting the invitation of the United States to confer at Washington inspires many Japanese editors with suspicions resembling those which the fly may have felt when invited into the spider's parlor. "The Paris conference threw the world into great complications," doubtfully observes the *Yorodzu* of Tokyo, one of the most strongly nationalistic of Japanese journals. "We do not know whether the forthcoming Washington conference is auspicious or inauspicious. We only hope that it may turn out auspicious." One of the difficulties, the *Yorodzu* believes, is the fact that Great Britain and the United States "are as unfriendly as a dog and a monkey over oil concessions and other interests," and, this Japanese authority suspects, if any agreement is possible between them, "it will be confined to cases where the two countries are jointly to obtain interests from a third country." The editor hints that this "third country" may be China or Japan. Finally—

"To ensure that all the countries make only just claims, it is necessary that the proceedings should be opened to the public. At Paris the General Conference was open, but the conferences of Big Five and Big Three were all secret. With regard to the Washington Conference, the American Government does not intend to open it to the public. This causes in our minds doubts concerning the objects of the conference. If the American Government is really solicitous for the peace of the world, why not arrange for the discussion of all questions in broad daylight? Can we hope for the success of the conference without doing so? We venture to ask this of the American Government."

This fear lest the conference will devolve into a star chamber proceeding where Japan will be quietly but thoroughly "trimmed" by America, with British connivance, is not uncommon among the Japanese editors. Small reliance is placed upon the friendship of Great Britain. "For fear of offending America, Great Britain has sacrificed the Anglo-Japanese alliance," says the *Kokumin* (Tokyo), which believes that, due to the labor troubles in England and the "bad statesmen" in Japan, "America alone" is allowed to be "wayward and selfish." The present state of affairs, believes this journal, "is calculated to make America a second Germany." On the other hand, the *Jiji*, possibly the largest and most influential of the Japanese dailies, finds reason to hope that "America may be sincere and courageous enough to remove any obstacle to the realization of a reduction of naval armaments." Japan, should, of course, it asserts, "consent to restrict or abolish her defense work which in American eyes may appear to be a menace, or appear to be unnecessary." At the same time—

"Japan may advise America to restrict or reduce her naval bases in the Pacific so that an agreement to this effect may be reached in the interest of peace. From Japan's point of view, Pearl Bay, Guam, and Manila constitute bases of offensive operations, and if equipment in these islands is further extended, with increased accommodation for warships and increased capacity for supplies, it will mean a great menace to Japan. In this case, it will be clear that Japan should not be content with an agreement merely concerning the number of major ships."

The *Asahi* of Osaka pleads for compromise even while expressing doubts of the legality of America's attitude in the Yap case. "It

A GERMAN VIEW.

"To keep his balance against England and Japan, Uncle Sam must have this make-weight." —*Wahre Jacob* (Stuttgart).

JAPANESE SKEPTICISM.

"Is Sam attempting the impossible?" —*Asahi* (Tokio).

AMERICA'S DISARMAMENT PROJECT UNDER SUSPICION.

should be considered whether it is advisable from the view-point of actual interests for Japan roundly to repudiate America's contention on the ground of legal reasons," argues this daily, and concludes:

"Diplomacy does not go beyond the rule of give and take. Japan's policy should be to carry her point in reason, to assume a generous attitude in fact, and thus to remedy the whole situation with a view to attaining the real object of the reduction of armaments."

The Tokyo *Nichi Nichi*, agreeing that the important end to be sought is the reduction of armaments, adds that it is doubtful how far this object can be achieved, if other matters, such as the question of the international control of China, are introduced. This journal, like the *Jiji* of Tokyo and *Asahi* of Osaka, rejoices that America has disclaimed any intention of putting China under international control.

China is considered as both a danger spot and a possible solution of the conference by the *Yomiuri* of Tokyo. The regulation of Chinese commerce is closely bound up, in the view of this paper, with the Japanese density of population. Further immigration to the United States and Australia, whether possible or not, "can not actually solve the problem." The only remedy is said to be "to develop home industries and sustain our surplus population by exporting our products." "As to the opening of the Chinese continent," we read:

"Japan stands in the same position as the United States and their interests are identical. The only point of difference between the two refers to Shantung and Manchuria. Apart from the question of Shantung, it is to our interest to open Manchuria as much as possible from the above-mentioned point of view. The only question is where the line should be drawn. Up to this limit we should take the initiative in declaring the new policy and endeavor to realize it, and beyond that point, we should sincerely try to reach an understanding with America and the other Powers as well as China. So far as our policy relating to the Chinese continent and Manchuria is concerned, we believe that if Japan attends the Pacific Conference with the above-mentioned determination, it will convert the so-called national peril into a national boon."

Nobody seems to remember that Mexico has a coast in the Pacific, remarks the *Yorodzu*, which suggests that as China has been invited to the Pacific conference, "there can be no reason why Mexico should not be invited" and it continues:

"American action in the past toward Mexico has been characterized by much unscrupulousness, and Japan may call America sufficiently to task. Let us make it brought home to America that before criticizing Japan's action in China and Korea, she should reflect on her action in Mexico. There are also problems relating to South and Central America, nor are materials in Europe for censuring America scanty. America should be held to accountability as frequently, as strongly, and as persistently as possible so that she may be practically silenced. This is the only policy which Japan can take at the Washington Conference. If the Japanese delegates attend it with this determination, they may be able to avoid such humiliation as was experienced in the past."

FRANCE DEMOCRATIZING SYRIA

A FEDERALIZED REPUBLIC on the Swiss model is being made out of Syria, and it seems that some of the Syrians don't like it, to judge from the harsh criticism of French policy in sections of the Syrian press, where it is felt that France purposes by the division of the country into autonomous states to insure French domination. But the French insist that this arrangement is entirely in the best interest of the Syrians themselves, and the Paris *l'Europe Nouvelle* declares that the policy of France in the Levant is "incarnated of clear and just ideas." The attempted assassination of General Gouraud, the French High Commissioner in Syria, stirs the Arabic press there and in the United States to a lively discussion of what France has "accomplished so far in Syria." The attempt on the French High Commissioner's life was made during one of his frequent inspection tours, when he was on his way to visit a certain Arab chieftain, near Damascus, who in the early days of French occupation had proved a thorn in the flesh. But after the fall of Prince Faysal, this chieftain was "chastised and forgiven" by the French.

THE FRENCH FOUNDER OF INDEPENDENT SYRIA.

General Gouraud, French High Commissioner in Syria, who is forming an independent Syria on the model of the republic of Switzerland and of the United States.

According to the Syrian papers, the assassins were not Syrians but Bedouin Arabs from the province of Eastern Jordan, which is under the jurisdiction of Prince Abdullah, brother of Prince Faysal.

Everywhere the French General went after that fateful event, in which one officer was killed and the Governor of Damascus, Hakki Bey al-Azm, was wounded, people hurried to meet him and impress upon him their loyalty to his person and their devotion to France with monstrous public celebrations of joy and elaborate and ornate speeches. At one of those occasions, in Beirut, it is reported by *al-Bashir* that a certain Bishop addrest the General thus: "You have come with your glory as your guide and pole-star to finish the mission of the material and moral civilization of Syria, a civilization which has attained such a high mark in France." To this the sarcastic columnist of *al-Bayan*, Mr. Ibn Malek, retorts with the remark: "Has not his reverence heard, if he has not seen with his own eyes, of the degradation of morals in Syria since the French occupation?"

The suppression of the Syrian press is another favorite subject of the immune Syrian Nationalist papers in the United States and South America. Four papers in Syria have been discontinued for varying lengths of time and their editors confined to prison either for "embarrassing" the French Government by their criticism or for printing news which harasses the French mandate in the Near East. On the occasion of suppressing *al-Ahwal* for printing a "false report" that Kamal Pasha was preparing to attack Aleppo, *Mirat-ul-Gharb* rages against the French authority in Syria. Thus it says in its defense of the editor of *al-Ahwal*:

"The Government itself indulges in lying, for it has never ceased announcing, through its officials and through its reports in the papers, that security and peace have returned to the land, whereas terrorism and insecurity are rife from the one end of the country to the other; and the greatest proof of that is the continuance of the French expeditionary force, which numbers eighty thousand warriors! The Government forgets, when it declares that peace and safety have been established, that General Gouraud himself came near being a victim of assailants."

A more constructive note is sounded by *al-Sayeh*, a liberal Syrian paper in New York supporting the French mandatory in Syria, for it says:

"The hopeful is ever fond of his hope, looking in the direction from which his sun shall rise. So are we in our fondness of Syria, and our hope in its brilliant future."

This paper does not exonerate the French authorities of every fault, and frankly admits that they have committed certain mistakes, but adds that man is never aright except after trials. The editorial goes on to compare France to a wise teacher who entices his little pupil by petty cajolery and bribes and says the French Government was only conceding to local popular prejudice when it dissected Syria into small semi-independent provinces, contrary to the aspirations of all patriotic Syrians. But just as General Gouraud was the first to denounce this policy of decentralization, he was also the first to proclaim his desire for a unified Syria.

In the same spirit the *Syrian Eagle* (Brooklyn) approaches the perplexing and vague question, "What has France done in Syria?" It contrasts the present French rule in Syria with the old Turkish régime and finds much in the new to commend as an earnest of future progress in the line of the democratization of Syria. It asks significantly:

"When was it possible, before, for the papers to write even one word of criticism against the government, or mention the news of a revolution, or the founding of a republic, or the assassination of a king, or like events which were current in the world? Can any one deny that Syria to-day is by far better than it was in the time of the Turks; that it has now a representative government, and a Council which discusses national affairs and determines what is good for the country?"

For an official assurance about the purposes of France, we have the words of General Gouraud, in a speech delivered at Damascus, which is published in *l'Europe Nouvelle*. It runs in part:

"Consider Switzerland, where populations of different religion and language work fraternally in the support of a federation based on the common mind. In centuries past new cantons entered freely into the state; because the federal form permitted them to join the association without abandoning their individual character, and thus they enlarged the Helvetic Confederation. Consider also the United States. Reflection on these examples and their justification in fact led me last year to create the autonomous states of Syria. I may add that in these states of moderate size, where each can more easily govern its own public interests and action, I foresaw the best apprenticeship for the self-government of the nation. But I never have stopped believing that a union should be given to these states by which they would together form that independent Syria which France has always wished to organize."

GROUNDS FOR AN IRISH-ENGLISH COMPROMISE

ARGUMENTS ABOUT IT AND ABOUT, with the emphasis on technical points that suggest political strategy rather than an honest desire to reach an understanding, have disgusted that highly considered defender of liberalism, the Manchester *Guardian*. The English and Irish negotiators remind it of the two Greek armies which met but never fought, "for the man on the extreme flank on both armies kept edging more and more to his right, to secure their unprotected side, and as the movement became general, the two armies gradually faded away out of sight of each other." Taking up the attitude of Ireland, which it has long championed against British aggression, the editor argues:

"THE HARP THAT ONCE . . ."

THE SHOWMAN: "It's now or never, boys! Let's patch up the poor old Harp and have some harmony at last!"

—*The Passing Show* (London)

"Mr. De Valera and his colleagues say that Ireland is not treated as a free and equal nation if she is told that England cannot afford to acquiesce in her separation from the British Commonwealth. Let us suppose that a British Government had said: 'Do what you like; but as a perfectly free people, able to choose its own course, will you come to some arrangement with us to secure our joint safety?' What would Mr. De Valera have answered? Would he have said, 'No; I refuse to enter into any relations with you.' Clearly not, for at the end of this letter he says that his Parliament is prepared to negotiate a peace 'on the basis of the broad guiding principle of government by the consent of the governed,' a peace that will be just and honorable to all and 'fruitful of concord and enduring amity.' Now Mr. De Valera knows perfectly well that, rightly or wrongly, the British people are afraid of the consequences of leaving the Irish harbors undefended, and therefore when he talks of negotiating a peace that will be fruitful of enduring amity he must mean that he is prepared to make some concession to British strategic interests. In other words, Mr. De Valera recognizes that 'geographical propinquity' creates a problem. His letter rather suggests that if the discussion had begun at the other end, if England, instead of stating her view of her strategical necessities, had left it to Ireland to begin, the discussion might have gone rather farther by this time. As a perfectly free nation the Irish people would perhaps accept what it rejects when England has seemed to use the language of superior power."

Too much importance, believes this editor, is attached by De Valera to "formal independence," and he says:

"Anybody who knows the circumstances of the new small nations on the Continent, the extent to which they are overshadowed by foreign economic and political interests, must realize that it is possible to have complete sovereign indepedence and to be very far from controlling your own life. . . . And we would suggest to those who are conducting negotiations on behalf of Ireland that they should remember that proposals made for securing our safety are not meant to carry with them the implications that are read into them; they are not made in the spirit of empire or for the sake of asserting rights. Cannot Irishmen consider such proposals on their merits, and put forward alternative suggestions? The interests of Ireland, no less than those of England, demand that discussion. Does her dignity forbid it?"

THE FAMINE-TRUCE IN RUSSIA

BOLSHEVIKS, SOCIAL DEMOCRATS, and conservatives in Russia, their mutual animosities softened by the ravages of famine, are now said to be cooperating for the first time since 1917. There is at least a "temporary reconciliation," we are told, between the various political and social factions, which have formed a public committee for

THE TRAGEDY OF SELF-SERVICE IN PETROGRAD.
Russian girls waiting their turn in the line at a food depot.

the relief of the millions of sufferers from famine and disease. The Russian papers published in Russia, all of them of Bolshevik sympathies since the government suppresses the others, take a somewhat dubious view of the present truce, one of them even declaring that the Allies are taking advantage of the Russian difficulties to prepare a new blow against the Soviet government. The *Posledniya Novosti*, however, a conservative Russian daily published in Paris, putting aside its demand that the Bolsheviks be routed, root and branch, suggests that a coalition government, including representatives of all the present Russian parties, may grow out of the famine relief committee. "The quarrel is not yet settled," admits the editor, but—

"As to the question of a coalition, there have now appeared, not exactly new considerations, but new facts, and facts of great significance. In Russia a coalition has come into being, although in a limited form. The public committee for the relief of famine sufferers attests to that in a manifest manner.

"It may be the report that this committee will serve as the nucleus of the future government is premature and exaggerated. But those forces which impelled people of different parties to unite for public work will impel them to unite also for government work. The Moscow committee for the relief of famine sufferers united, on the plank of averting Russian ruin, the Cadets (Constitutional Democrats), the Social Democrats, the Social Revolutionaries and a number of non-party men.

"The thing which has united Russian people of most diverse views into a committee with a single purpose, is the consciousness of the catastrophe which has overtaken Russia. When the political workers felt that a great danger was threatening Russia, they found in themselves strength enough to overcome the traditional barriers which divided them, in order to undertake the common task."

This willingness to compromise, almost "to forget and forgive," is not shared by the *Krasnaya Gazeta* of Petrograd, an organ of the extreme Bolshevik faction. The *Gazeta*, presenting the viewpoint of the faction which is in power and intends to stay there, asserts editorially:

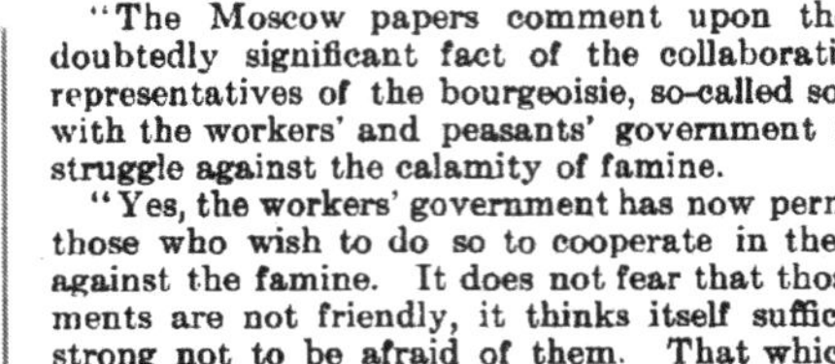

"The Moscow papers comment upon the undoubtedly significant fact of the collaboration of representatives of the bourgeoisie, so-called society, with the workers' and peasants' government in the struggle against the calamity of famine.

"Yes, the workers' government has now permitted those who wish to do so to cooperate in the fight against the famine. It does not fear that those elements are not friendly, it thinks itself sufficiently strong not to be afraid of them. That which the White Guards abroad consider a sign of weakness, is a sign of strength. We are sure that we shall be able to cope with this calamity, in spite of all our enemies abroad, who are drinking champagne on the occasion of famine in a great country."

In a somewhat milder vein the editor of the *Kommunistichesky Trood* (Petrograd), also a defender of the Soviets, calls attention to the mixture of radicals and conservatives brought about by famine conditions. The editor observes:

"We do not shut our eyes to the situation, and we know these representatives of the propertied and intellectual classes, who have not changed their orientation, have not become adherents of the Soviet government. They understand that the Soviet government is the only force which can save the country and organize relief to overcome the famine and the disorganization."

"We can only welcome those representatives of the bourgeois class who, without politics," announces the *Krestyanskaya Gazeta* (Moscow), "have decided to join in the relief of a class which, from their point of view, has 'outraged' and 'robbed' the bourgeois class." This Soviet organ proceeds:

"The Soviet government promises all kinds of assistance to those elements of so-called bourgeois society who wish to work for the relief of the famine sufferers. For the first time since the civil war, members of a hostile class consent to work and offer their services, at a difficult moment, to a government which has overthrown the government of their class. Their coming without political demands, is the beginning of their sobering up."

Wide World Photos

FAMINE REFUGEES RESTING BY THE ROADSIDE.
The problem of feeding eight children is not easy in the best of countries and conditions, but famine-stricken parents in Russia find the only solution in flight.

SCIENCE - AND - INVENTION

HOW TO LOOK WELL IN GLASSES

TO SEE WELL and to look well in glasses are two very different things. One depends on the lenses. But whether the glasses add to the natural beauty of his features or make him "ugly enough to stop a clock," depends not on the lenses, but on the frame that holds them and the device used for fastening both lens and frame to the face. In a pamphlet entitled "Be Beautiful in Glasses," Dr. Frank G. Murphy, who describes himself as an oculist of twenty-five years standing, offers what he calls "a treatise on the art of utilizing optical illusions produced by spectacles and eyeglasses to beautify the face." The illusions to which he refers are chiefly two—that which causes light-colored objects to appear larger than dark ones, and that by which a figure bearing straight lines appears stretched out in the direction of these lines. Glasses, Dr. Murphy reminds us, are primarily worn to obtain better vision, and usually little or no attention is paid to what he calls their "cosmetic effect." To those with an eye for beauty in color and figure it is evident, he thinks, that the glasses worn by most people are not suitable for them. He continues:

PROBLEM OF THE ROUND FACE.

Horizontal lines, as in the spectacles in the first figure, make the face seem broader. The up-and-down lines in the second figure make it seem narrower.

"It frequently happens that neither the patient nor the refractionist is sufficiently familiar with the natural laws governing the effect of color and lines to determine the most suitable frames to be selected and some refractionists even consider it an intrusion on their dignity for the patient to suggest the kind of frame he should wear and are in the habit of prescribing a certain kind of frame for every one regardless of the fact that by so doing many become almost caricatures of their former selves.

"To those whose glasses become them there is a comfort which to some extent is shared by their friends and all who look upon them. The writer feels that a consideration of the subject of optical illusions produced by eyeglasses and spectacles is timely.

"Frames when once purchased practically become a part of the facial anatomy, thereby altering the personality, as they are usually worn for several years and sometimes to the end of life. We seek the knowledge of artists to beautify our gardens, houses and barns, but do not seek expert advice on the ornamentation of our own physiognomies. A comely face surely contributes to the happiness of a community quite as much as does a mansion with all its architectural beauty.

THE LONG, NARROW FACE, WITH WIDE TEMPLE.

Here the curves in the loop spring and ribbon add harmony to the facial lines, while the horizontal lines in the third figure increase the defect.

"A distinct line drawn through an object always makes that object appear longer and larger in the direction of the line. This is why spectacles with temples over the ears and low nosepieces makes a face look broader. Light-rimmed or rimless glasses make the face look wider and those with dark rims make it appear narrower than it is. There is no face so nearly perfect that its weakest lines can not be emphasized by the caricaturist and but few are so handsome that artistically selected glasses will not improve their appearance. The facial features that concern most people are their round or narrow faces and the length and size of their noses. And it is these features of the face that are most modified for the better by frames when a proper selection is made. Even the shadow of frames has more effect on the face than one at first thought might suppose and this is one objection to the very large shell frames."

Cheering news for the elderly, and for all who have doubts about their own pulchritude, in fact, is then given in the following paragraphs, along with the advice on selecting glasses:

"Most gray-haired people are better looking than they were when their hair was of a darker color, because the hair when gray, being more nearly the color of the skin, the outline of the face is softened, is more obscure, and then we imagine the thin face to be more round than it really is and the full face to be not nearly so round. This occasionally enables some gray-haired people to ignore the broadening and narrowing effect of frames. If the skin is white and quite devoid of color it may be remembered that a very light-colored frame adds whiteness to the face and also that dark frames emphasize whiteness by contrast. Gold or light wine-colored frames are more appropriate as they reflect color and the appearance of youth.

"Most people are better looking than they think they are. Commendable efforts to improve the facial appearance are frequently made and, in the attempt, glasses are often secured that defeat the object in view or, if the face is large, cosmetics may be used to whiten it, which makes it appear larger than before; or if the face is short and too round, the brows and eyelashes may be darkened, which makes the face appear shorter and wider.

"It is not always lack of information or bad taste that causes some to select conspicuous shoes for ill-shaped feet, purchase hats and clothing that do not become them, paint their faces unseemly and select glasses that emphasize their defective features, for often it is defective sight that limits their faculty for discerning beauty. It is not possible to be hard of hearing and not know it, but many have defective vision and are unconscious of their own visual imperfections. Most people are more concerned about their noses than they are about their other features. They are too large or too small, too short or too long, and yet these seldom are the qualities that determine the beauty of the nose. Whether its lines are in harmony with other lines of the head, the place and manner in which the lip leaves the nose and the curve of the nostrils are the lines that determine the beauty of most noses, and yet it is not at all from these qualities that judgment is commonly passed upon them. If folk could place upon their faces the kind of noses they imagine they would like to possess we would be a sorry looking people.

"Nature is much more kind to us than we give her credit for being. She knew what she was about when she made the typical negro black and gave him a small nose to harmonize with his receding forehead and protruding lips. His black skin makes his face look smaller and emphasizes his eyes and teeth. He would not be better looking if he had a large nose or was white."

The illustrations, Dr. Murphy tells us, are purposely overdrawn to show the effect of the differently constructed frames. Spectacles always make the wearer look older than eyeglasses do, side-pieces that hook over the ears being responsible. One of the earliest indications of age is the small creases in the skin (crow's-feet) that start just below the outer corners of the eyes and find their way toward the temples. The side pieces of spectacles parallel these and are as effective in producing the appearance of age. He proceeds:

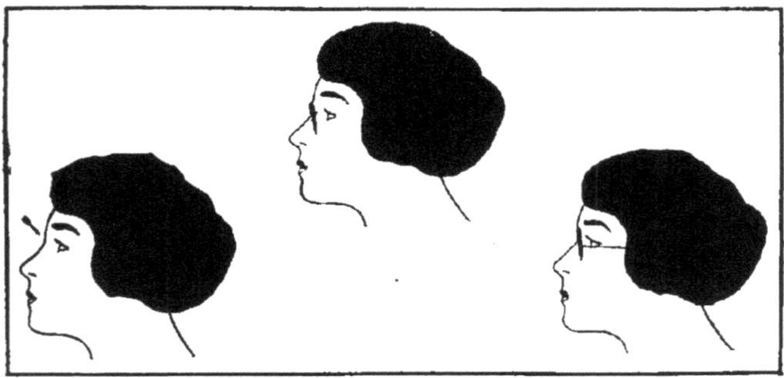

IF YOU HAVE A SHORT NOSE.

The slight defect seen in the first figure is corrected by the eyeglass in the second. The spectacle in the third figure improves the appearance, but may give the end of the nose a seeming upward tilt.

"The drop-eye or leaf-shaped lens possesses no qualities that commend it from a cosmetic standpoint, as its outline is not beautiful and is at variance with the other lines of the face. It may sometimes be advisable to use it when the eyebrows are heavy and the eye sets deep in the socket, that the glass may be sufficiently close to the eye. A skillful operator usually has no difficulty in placing the oval or round lens low enough for desk work.

"Glasses, for their cosmetic effect, as well as for the comfort of the wearer, should be set high or low according to the height of the wearer. They who are tall should wear their glasses low as they look up less and down more than other people do and children should wear their glasses high for they are constantly looking up at people and objects about them.

"Dark-rimmed glasses always make a face look smaller than it really is and light-colored rims larger. This effect is not because black objects look smaller and white ones larger than they are, but because of the perpendicular and longitudinal lines that are added or made less pronounced. If the eyebrows and eyelashes on any face were entirely removed that face would look much longer than it previously did. The brows and eyelashes are horizontal lines that shorten and broaden the face. Of two faces, a brunette and a blond of equal dimensions, the face of the brunette will appear to be the shortest and widest unless the blonde has dark brows and eyelashes. In general, the lighter the hair the less attention need be paid to the widening effect of frames as the outline of the face becomes less definitely defined. When light-rimmed glasses are worn, the brows, lines above the eyeballs, and the lashes are less in evidence and consequently the face appears larger in every direction but increased more in length than in width which effect is in proportion to the elimination of the dark lines. One who has a long thin face with the eyebrows and eyelashes light in color, might wear light-rimmed glasses with a conspicuous horizontal nosepiece and also darken the brows and possibly the eyelashes, all of which will tend to shorten and broaden the face.

"Usually the large face should wear dark-rimmed glasses and the small face light ones. The brunette with a short, round face in which it is desirable to enlarge the face as much as possible, might wear the light-rimmed eyeglasses with loop spring and, in addition, trim the dark eyebrows so that the face will be lengthened by less conspicuous horizontal lines of the brows. The perpendicular sections of the dark rims narrow the appearance of the face tho the horizontal sections of the rims around the glasses do not shorten the face to the same extent as they parallel the other horizontal lines of the face, namely the eyebrows and rows of lashes which already have affected an apparent shortening of the face.

"The very large dark shell frames have been popular with some people in spite of the fact that they are conspicuous. However, they are fairly comfortable and look best on large faces. Those with short noses do not look well in them and those who wish to shorten the appearance of their noses could do so as effectively with the low, dark nosepiece and lighter and less conspicuous rims; the extremely large rims distract the attention from the other features of the face and in this respect they are a boon to those who have been 'cheated of feature by dissembling nature' or think they have. They are comfortable for office and library use and because of the large frame they are not easily broken.

"Whatever size of glasses or style of frame may be in use, their cosmetic effect will ever depend upon the accuracy with which the natural laws governing visual illusion produced by color and lines have been regarded."

WOULD HELIUM HAVE SAVED THE *ZR-2?*

WHAT WOULD HAVE HAPPENED if the airship *ZR-2*, which broke and burst and fell in flames at Hull, England, had been filled with helium, which is incombustible, instead of with hydrogen, which is highly inflammable? If the trouble was started by ignition of the hydrogen, the use of helium might have saved vessel and crew. If the breakage and buckling of the frame came first, the use of helium would not have prevented the disaster, but the airship would not have become all at once a blazing wreck, and more lives might have been saved. An editorial writer in *Chemical and Metallurgical Engineering* (New York), who asks the question stated in our title, says that however the question is answered, anyone who knows the facts must admit that there has never been enough helium produced to have filled the ship, even if all of it could have been assembled for use in the fatal trial flight. He continues:

"Helium is a typically American resource. Numerous natural gas fields are known by the Bureau of Mines where recoverable quantities of helium could be obtained by a process which is already a demonstrated success in the plant at Fort Worth, Tex. No other nation has such helium reserves. Therefore, so long as helium production does not result in export, America will have exclusive advantage of this non-flammable balloon gas."

While officials reserve judgment on the airship wreck until we can learn more of the causes and the significance of the catastrophe, certain fundamental facts are strikingly given by R. B. Moore, chief chemist of the Bureau of Mines, who has been intimately associated with the development of the helium resources and is still in charge of much Government work in this field. He says in effect:

"For the price of one battleship it would easily be possible to maintain and operate permanently six of the most modern helium-filled dirigibles which the best talent of America could design. Included in this program would be adequate provision for reserves of helium-bearing natural gas, adequate facilities for generation of the needed helium, its recovery and repurification, and generous allowance for needed fundamental research in physics, chemistry and engineering. The question therefore is, 'Which will contribute most to American security and defense, one additional modern first-line battleship or an elaborate program in the field of non-flammable, lighter-than-air craft of wide-cruising radius, tremendous powers of offense and almost unrivaled ability in defensive observation?'"

ABOUT BLOOD PRESSURE

HAVE YOU "A BLOOD PRESSURE"? You certainly have, if you are alive—as certainly as you have a pulse or a temperature. But just as a man who says "I have a temperature" really means to tell us that it is above normal, so the man who "has blood pressure" intends to convey the idea that it is abnormally high. Temperature and blood pressure may both be too low, also; but then the complainant says exactly what he means. The importance of blood pressure as a symptom has been understood by physicians only within recent years, and there has been no device to measure it accurately until very lately. The apparatus now generally used ranks, we are told by Robert H. Moulton, in *The Forecast* (New York, September), as one of the most important surgical instruments devised in years, taking a place with the stethoscope, the pulmotor and the clinical thermometer. Says this writer:

"No matter if a man has been pronounced in perfect health by the best of physicians after the customary examination, he cannot be honestly assured by such an opinion unless his blood pressure has been accurately measured. The dictum holds good for all individuals, but particularly for those over forty. In life insurance, blood pressure cuts a very important figure—in fact, a few of the more progressive companies will not accept a 'risk' above the age of forty until the new applicant's blood pressure has been taken by competent physicians.

"It should not be understood by this that blood pressure itself is necessarily something harmful, because every person, normal or otherwise, has it. Only when it is found to be unusually 'high' or 'low' is it to be taken as evidence of something wrong. A comparison, which illustrates the point very clearly, is the pressure exerted by water when passing through an ordinary garden hose. In our bodies the hose is represented by an artery, and the pressure is caused by the heart forcing the blood through this artery.

"Pressure is less where fluid is passing through a flexible tube, because the walls, owing to their elasticity, offer little resistance. But with the same force behind, the pressure is increased if the walls of the tube are unyielding. Tubes of rubber and glass are excellent illustrations of such contrasts. Where hardening of the arteries—due to old age, gout, alcoholism, or other excesses—has set in, the blood pressure, as a consequence, is high. Too much pressure, 'high pressure,' is very apt to break the artery. If this occurs in the brain, apoplexy results.

"A device for taking the measure of blood pressure, an ingenious instrument called the manometer, has recently been perfected and is rapidly coming into general use. The instrument records the pressure of the blood on a diaphragm dial very similar in appearance to a steam gage dial.

"The apparatus, which is the invention of Dr. Thomas Rogers of Rochester, New York, consists of three parts, a small metal case containing several sensitive diaphragms, a dial and an air bag. The air bag is first strapped on the subject's arm over the femoral artery, and is inflated with a bulb attached to it. The operator then adjusts a stethoscope to his ears and finds the pulse, after which he is ready to take his records. The pulse throbbing against the air bag is communicated through a rubber tube to the case containing the diaphragms upon which a vibration is set up. These vibrations, which are simultaneous with the pulse, are translated into millimeters by the delicate needle on the dial.

AVERAGE BLOOD PRESSURE AT GIVEN AGES.

Ages	Average Blood Pressure
15-20	119.85 mm.
21-25	122.75 "
26-30	123.63 "
31-40	126.96 "
41-45	128.56 "
46-50	130.57 "
51-55	132.13 "
56-60	134.78 "

An allowance of either 15 above or 20 below should be made as such variations occur in perfectly healthy persons.

"In order to make a thorough record both the systolic and diastolic, or maximum and minimum, pressures must be taken. The former is produced by the forward and the latter by the backward stroke of the heart. It is well established that the normal maximum, or systolic blood pressure in adults ranges from 105 to 145 millimeters. Suppose the manometer is applied over the artery of a man still in his twenties. The hand on the dial goes up to about 122. What's the verdict? That young fellow's blood pressure is perfectly normal, and the chances are, even if any other examination by other methods is made, nothing will be found wrong with his heart or kidneys. This test should always be made before any one takes up athletic work of any kind.

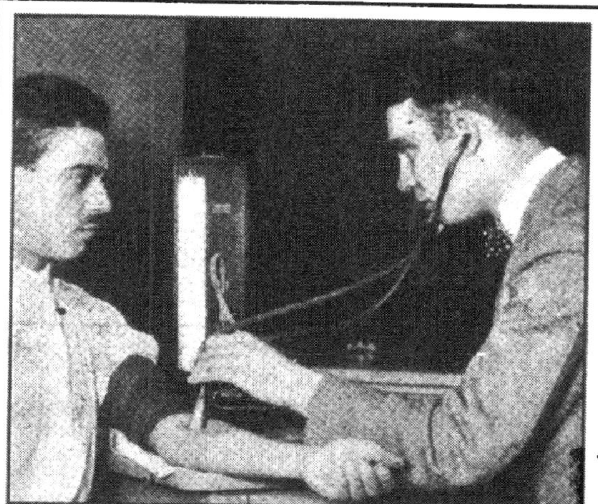

Courtesy of the Life Extension Institute.

TESTING THE BLOOD PRESSURE.

"Suppose, on the other hand, that a man a little over forty has his blood pressure taken, and the hand on the dial turns as high as 155 or 160, then the probabilities are that there is some disease hidden away in his system, though he may never have complained of ill health in his life. At the best guess, his state of health would not be above suspicion, and would require a further search by other means.

"Suppose again that some third individual around the age of fifty undergoes examination for his physical condition, and after the usual 'pounding and sounding' in every possible way, nothing is found wrong with him. He beams with satisfaction; so far all is well.

"Then the manometer is brought forth and carefully applied, and the hand moves up to 185. What then? Even with no other manifestation of trouble, the chances are about even that unless he adopts some means to combat this high pressure—which it is possible to do—he will develop in the next year or two either 'hardening' of the arteries, a trouble known as 'heart murmur,' or an actual enlargement of the heart; or, if not one of these, then some kidney trouble, like Bright's disease, or some of the many nervous affections and even, possibly, diabetes. He will also run a more than usual risk of dying sooner or later from either apoplexy or kidney trouble. It is not positive that he will, but certainly his chances of doing so are too great for him not to heed the warning of the little instrument used in ascertaining his blood pressure."

It is interesting and important to note, Mr. Moulton goes on, that in healthy persons the blood pressure will rise under certain circumstances. Those of a nervous, anxious temperament, with worry or nerve strain, have a tendency to increased pressure in their arteries. Exercise and muscular action of any kind will also raise the pressure, especially in the veins. Even posture has an influence, pressure being highest while standing, and lowest when sitting or lying down. He goes on:

"In those between the ages of thirty-five or forty to sixty-five, blood pressure is most frequently caused by nervous reaction from overwork, worry, extreme mental activity with lack of physical exercise, or a too heavy diet and lack of exercise. Between the ages of forty and sixty-five the mind is usually more active than at any other period. The average successful American business man of this age is constantly living at high pressure. His entire working day is apt to be just one blood-raising pressure after another.

"The fact that mental excitement and perturbation cause increased pressure of the blood has been taken advantage of lately in connection with a series of interesting experiments conducted by Prof. W. H. Cowing of Harvard University to determine the practicability of using blood pressure machines in detecting crime.

"Professor Cowing's idea is that the machines would not only record the heart-beats, but, to a certain extent, the emotions, of the subject. No matter how stolid a transgressor may appear on the exterior while undergoing the 'sweating' process or cross-examination, Professor Cowing explains, the use of the machine in the court-room will reveal his slightest emotion. The agitation thus disclosed in his mind, which otherwise would be unobserved, may constitute circumstantial evidence which will have a strong bearing on the disposal of his case.

THE RICE OBLIGINGLY PROVIDES THE FUEL TO COOK IT.

Boatloads of rice-straw on a river in China.

"During the experiments conducted by Professor Cowing, the emotions of sorrow, joy, hatred, love, pain and pleasure were all recorded by the machine before they were displayed by the face.

"While considering the evil effects of high blood pressure, it is necessary also to sound a warning against low blood pressure. Dr. W. A. Evans of Chicago in his talks on 'How to Keep Well' states he has no advice to give to old people suffering from low blood pressure, but that he does have much to say to young people suffering from the same malady.

"'There are two great causes of low blood pressure,' he continues. 'It may be due to weakening glands. For instance, a person who is just recovering from an attack of typhoid fever will have a low blood pressure. This can be looked upon as a compensation process, and nothing should be done about it. The heart muscle is weak and a low blood pressure relieves it of some strain. The rule is, in all this group of secondary blood pressures, most of which are temporary, to let them alone. Stimulants of various sorts might prove effective, but they do enough harm to offset any good. Nature is disposed to sing a slender tune for the time being, and why not abide by nature's decision?

"'The other great cause of low blood pressure is more important. It is due to lack of dynamic force. A part of this is due to inheritance and a part to bad training. This group of people includes the whiners, those who drag around, those who lie in bed, and those who never get anywhere because of imaginary semi-invalidism. Most of them are lazy, many are slow mentally and physically, many are under-nourished, and many are given to self-pity. Medical opinion is that they are deficient in some ductless gland secretion. What they need is pep, snap, energy, willingness to forget themselves and to face the world. The cure is training. There is no other. But the training cannot be effected in a few days or by half-hearted effort. The disposition of this group is to do everything half-heartedly.'

"Thus it will be seen that by taking measure of our blood pressure we can measure our life. If our blood pressure registers normal we can postpone old age by avoiding as far as possible those things which cause blood pressure. If it does not register normal we must then look for the cause, and still postpone old age, or avert early death by eliminating the cause."

COOKERY IN THE LAND OF STRAW FUEL

FUEL IS DIFFICULT to obtain in China. How the necessity for strict conservation, and the utilization of every bit that comes to hand, is reflected in the cookery customs of the country, is explained in an article entitled "Influence of Fuel Scarcity on Chinese Cookery," contributed to *Good Health* (Battle Creek, Mich.), by A. C. and F. F. Muhse. In the great deforested areas of China, where the population is densest, wood is so scarce, these writers tell us, that it is practically out of the question as fuel. In winter the people depend chiefly upon padded or additional garments, rather than upon artificial heat.

The problem of fuel in central and southern China is, therefore, to obtain enough for cooking purposes. Lack of transportation makes the cost of coal prohibitive for millions of families, and straw and stubble supply the cooking fuel for the majority of the people, charcoal, coal, wood, and coal-dust balls being used by the remainder. We read:

"In these thickly populated areas, rice is very generally grown, usually as the second crop of the year. In certain parts wheat, too, is grown, especially during the cooler season, but is out of the way in time for the planting of rice during the summer months. The constant supply of green grass meets the needs of the few domestic animals kept in these parts, and only a limited amount of straw goes into the compost heaps to be used as fertilizer. Consequently, when the grain is garnered, most of the straw is bound up into bundles for fuel, and is carried by boat to the cities. Huge bamboo frames are built around the living quarters and out over the sides of the boats, so that when loaded, they appear like floating haystacks.

"Stoves of brick, mortar, and clay, built in as part of the house, are the ones in which straw is used. Such a stove is usually more or less semicircular in the floor plan, and so located in the room that the smoke flue can connect with an outer wall. But it is so placed that the straw can be fed into the straight side—fed in 'behind' we would say—and in such a position, too, that the semicircular or cooking surface projects into the room. Restaurant stoves of this type may have three or four, or even more, holes, each a large opening surrounded by a raised clay collar, over which the cooking utensil closely fits. Such a stove in the ordinary home kitchen has two holes, one for the rice utensil and one for the mixed food utensil, and sometimes an additional tiny hole for a water kettle.

"Straw, of course, makes a quick, intense heat which is soon spent. Accordingly, the stoves are so constructed as to prevent the escape of heat from crevices, and in such a manner as to concentrate a small amount of heat where needed and so distributed as to be completely absorbed. The circular or convex metal cooking utensil universally used is a big factor in fuel conservation. The flange of the utensil that rests closely over the clay collar of the stove is thicker than the perfectly rounded bowl and absorbs the heat in a uniform manner. Water for rice, for example, boils very quickly. The washed rice is then thrown in, and within a few minutes a little straw has brought it to such a stage that the boiling rice can be covered, and within a short time water, heat, and fire are all used up together, with a big fluffy mound of rice as the result.

"The covers used for such cooking are unique, thick wooden

ones, that are excellent nonconductors of heat. They are flat and rest sometimes directly on the metal cooking utensils. But for steaming, a circular wooden frame, similar to a section of barrel six or eight inches in depth, may be placed directly on the flange of the metal vessel, and this in turn covered with the wooden lid.

"In passing, it might be said that smoke flues open as a rule somewhere along the surface of an outer wall, since a strong draft is evidently neither essential nor desirable for a fuel which burns so readily as does straw in these brick and mortar stoves. A bird's-eye view over the roofs of a Chinese city shows very few, if any, projecting chimneys."

Three methods of cooking only are generally employed in home kitchens—stewing, steaming, and frying in oils. Practically all pastry, for instance, is steamed rather than baked. And rarely is any provision ever made in homes for the roasting of meats. Foods of this type are purchased from restaurants. The writers proceed to add these interesting particulars:

"The kind of stove described above is very commonly used throughout China. In a cosmopolitan city like Shanghai, one sees, however, many kinds of stoves or cooking outfits. The Ningpoese, for instance, seem to prefer charcoal braziers, tin-lined clay pots very similar to those used in our Southern States by negro laundry-women. Charcoal is brought by boats to coast and river cities and provides a very satisfactory cooking fuel. Very, very little wood is used, and serves mostly as kindling for the charcoal and coal.

"Coal is used in a flueless type of stove. These are usually plain rectangular masses of masonry, on the upper surface of which are two or more openings with clay rims like those on the stoves before described. The coal is fed into the fire-box through the openings mentioned, and then beneath the fire-box is a grate, and beneath it an ash-box. Such a stove is in use where continuous heat is maintained, particularly in restaurants where water is kept hot throughout the day. It is a common practise for housewives to buy hot water from such restaurants. Very little raw water is drunk by the Chinese; instead, a large quantity of weak tea is made up daily and set aside to be used cold between meals just as we use water from the tap or from wells.

"Coal-dust balls consist of coal dust mixed with camel dung, dried in the sun. A cheap fuel is thus furnished, common especially in the most northern provinces.

"A sort of 'fireless cooker' arrangement used in cheap restaurants, consists of barrel, or tub-like, containers, partially filled with non-conducting material, into which is shaped in clay a thick-walled cavity reaching down about sixteen inches. Burning charcoal is placed in the clay cavity and left there long enough to thoroughly heat the clay walls. After removing the coals, bits of shaped dough are attached to the heated clay and allowed to 'bake.'

"The practise of cutting into shreds most of the food materials before cooking is doubtless due in large part to the desire to conserve fuel. That this method of preparation is not entirely to facilitate the use of chop-sticks is evident at big feasts, where certain dishes are always served in which squab, fish, even small hams, come to the table cooked whole, but so very tender as to be readily pulled apart by one's chop-sticks.

"Practically all cooked dishes exposed for sale in the cheaper eating-places, and many of those served at feasts, are mixed foods which were cut into shreds before cooking. Materials cut into shreds cook much more quickly, thus saving heat, and moreover, it does away with the need for reheating left-over foods, thereby consuming additional fuel.

"Still one other fuel-conserving practise in Chinese cookery should be mentioned. Nearly all feasts—formal dinners or banquets as we say—are served by the large restaurants. Either the host invites his guests directly to the restaurant, or he will invite them to his home and arrange with some famous restaurant to do the catering. Feasts given by women for their women friends are invariably served in the home, and usually by a caterer.

"All that has been here said refers particularly to the inhabitants of cities. In the villages, however, similar cooking practises obtain, the fuel used being of the kind most easily procurable around their homes. Much that would in this country be a total waste is there gathered and stored for cooking fuel by the rural people."

A NEW WAY TO TRAP FORGERS

PRESS DISPATCHES from California tell of the confession of a forger after he had been confronted with photographic evidence of his crime obtained by Chauncy McGovern, a San Francisco handwriting expert, by a method said to have been employed for the first time on this case. In this method transparent photographs of the forged signature are superimposed over the real one, and the deviations, which thus become apparent, are shown to be in the direction of the forger's own peculiarities of handwriting. A dispatch from Martinez, Cal., to *The Chronicle* (San Francisco, Aug. 23) reads as follows:

"Probation was denied Lester J. Bradshaw, former paying teller of the First National Bank, Richmond, to-day by Judge R. H. Latimer, and he was given an indeterminate sentence of from one to ten years in San Quentin Prison.

"Bradshaw, recently brought back from Australia to face a charge of absconding with $10,000 of the bank's funds, confessed taking the money and threw himself on the clemency of the court.

FALSE AND TRUE WRITING PHOTOGRAPHED TOGETHER.

The faint lines show how the forgery departs from the true signature, revealing the habitual handwriting of the forger.

"Bradshaw's confession came, it was said, after he was confronted with photographic evidence of forgery prepared by Chauncy McGovern, San Francisco handwriting expert.

"In his confession Bradshaw told the police that he took small amounts at first and found it so easy to 'get away with' that he expanded his speculations until he forged five drafts of $2,000 each late in November.

"Two days after obtaining the money Bradshaw resigned his position and married Miss Leone Anderson, pretty Oakland girl, and sailed for Australia on his honeymoon.

"Radio advices to the captain of the steamer *Ventura* resulted in his detention aboard the vessel when it docked in Sydney. He was later brought back by Sheriff R. R. Veale.

"Bradshaw stoutly protested his innocence for more than eight months after being extradited from Australia. Finally he was confronted with the camera-made evidence."

In a letter to The Digest, Mr. McGovern asserts that his method is "a new way to utilize the camera to catch criminals who commit forgeries of the 'traced' variety," and that any ordinary police photographer can duplicate the work done in this case, so simple is the plan. He goes on:

"It consists of making separate negatives of each of the forged tracings—pencil, green ink, red ink, and black, on thick ledger paper. Then a 'film positive' is made from each negative. Next is overlapped or superimposed over the positive of the genuine 'model' signature used by the forger any single one of the positives or transparencies; after which a new negative is made from any two superimposed positives—ending with the making of a 'contact' print from the combination new negative.

"The resultant contact print will furnish a well-defined indication of every tiny point at which the traced forgery deviates from the genuine model. And, finally, a close comparison between each of these combination negative contact prints, and a contact print of any negative of the forger's known writing of letters of the kind, will show, strikingly, that where each of the traced forgeries deviates from the genuine model, the deviation is exactly along the lines of the characteristic way in which the forger shapes such letters in his normal writing."

LETTERS - AND - ART

LITERATURE DRAMA MUSIC FINE-ARTS EDUCATION CULTURE

MASCAGNI'S NEW DEMOCRATIC OPERA

THAT the war has not entirely killed artistic invention seems to be proven in Italy. Mascagni has repeated the triumph of thirty-one years ago when Italy went mad over "Cavalleria Rusticana," and now his new work, "Il Piccolo Marat," has set the populace into frenzies. They speak of 'fenomeno-Mascagni," and the king is about to bestow Italy's highest honor upon the composer in appointing him to the Senate.

Courtesy of "Leslie's Illustrated Weekly"

MASCAGNI, THE MUSICAL POLITICIAN.

"One look at the big, broad-shouldered, leonine old fellow that he is to-day convinces you of his absolute independence of spirit."

Mascagni is reported to have said that "should he ever be granted any such legislative opportunities, he will introduce a measure calling upon every Italian composer of note to produce one opera every two years." Then, reflects Gilbert W. Gabriel, writing in *Leslie's Illustrated Weekly*, "every six years, say, there would surely be one great masterpiece for the public to single out and cheer in the parade." This would be turning Italy's musical world into a forcing house, though Mascagni has observed that pace for the last thirty-one years, having produced fifteen major works in that time. Compared to him, "Puccini is a dilettante; Leoncavallo was a mere idler." The latest work of Mascagni is said to be "aimed at the public's conscience as well as at its ear":

"That is one of the elements which have heightened its opportunity. Great operas have always had a way of mixing into national affairs. Many an innocent libretto has helped to overthrow a dynasty. The 'Piccolo Marat' may not be a great opera, but it comes at a great moment. It is set in the French Revolution, but the thunder of that warfare is too connotative to be missed. This is Italy of Socialisti and Fascisti, and it rings with rough-and-tumble choruses, hard-breathing perorations, defiances of Death, Despot and Devil. Toward the end it all goes up in operatics. There are killings all around, and lovers melodious to the end. The revolutionary element capitulates to the purely romantic. But for at least two acts Mascagni has addrest the Italian people openly and hotly through the Italian people's favorite means of grand opera. In only two of his operas has he ever truly had that chance—in his first and his latest.

"Here, in briefest form, is the story of the 'Piccolo Marat': In a little French city on the Loire, in the days of the Reign of Terror, a local old *Tyrant* rules with bloody hand. But the people discover his little niece *Mariella* in the act of carrying food to him of such a luxurious sort that they pursue her revengefully. She is saved by a strange young man who, in shielding her, addresses the crowd so stirringly that it dubs him the '*little Marat*.' Her uncle, equally pleased with the youth, sets him to guarding the prison where unfortunate nobility are incarcerated. This is the youth's great chance: he is in reality the princely son of a noble house, and is only waiting to rescue his mother from behind the bars. Left alone on his rounds he can disclose himself and his plan to his mother.

"The next act is in the fearful sanctum of the *Tyrant*. *Mqriella* is falling in love with her '*Piccolo Marat*.' He confesses to her his real identity and assures her, in the famous love duet (the one which causes the ten-minute ovations and the upturned lights) that rank will make no difference in their equality; that his mama shall be her mama, and she shall be his bride. They commence then to plot the princess's release and their own escape. The *Tyrant* sits in judgment on a number of victims —a scene which, like several others in the opera, must remind the listener of a similar one, quite differently conceived, in Giordano's 'Andrea Chenier,' now a favorite work in the Metropolitan repertory. A deputy from the chief council in Paris arrives with orders, only to be seized and pummeled by the people in a fury of choral invectives. A crazy carpenter arrives, maddened by the fact that the *Tyrant* will not accept his new patent for a Boat of Death—a rowboat which could carry condemned prisoners out into midstream, then scuttle itself and drown the prisoners with a pretty efficacy. The *Tyrant* laughs it all to scorn.

"In the last act the young lovers are putting their plot into action. They have succeeded in making the *Tyrant* drunk. They can truss him up, release the noble mother and fly off. But the *Tyrant* breaks away to his weapons and mortally wounds the *little Marat* just at the end of the sortie. He himself is finished off by the mad carpenter who comes in and crushes his skull in revenge for not accepting the patent rowboat. The *little Marat* begs *Mariella* to fly with his mother, and the opera ends with a tableau which shows the 'boat of death' sailing down the Loire, deeply laden with catastrophe."

One comes away from the "Piccolo Marat," says Mr. Gabriel, with a "sense of stormy times stormily described." It is called "as direct an expression of Italian democracy of today as 'Boris Godounoff,' a much greater opera, was of the Russian people of Moussorgsky's time." To understand this element in the "Piccolo Marat," we are told, it is necessary to understand Mascagni himself. We read:

"He has preserved the best Wagnerian traditions in casting in his lot with the revolutionists. He did not hesitate to address the Socialistic workmen about a year ago and tell them that their cause was right. He publicly promised them that he would write them a hymn of their own—and you can take your choice of at least two of them which would do Socialistic service if lifted from 'Il Piccolo Marat.' This all happened in the troublous north of Italy. It caused a tremendous sensation southwards, toward official Rome. But Mascagni did not mind. One look at the big, broad-shouldered, leonine old fellow that he is today convinces you of his absolute independence of spirit. He has a burning eye; his hair is grayer than it may have been ten years ago but it still lifts away from his huge forehead in a wave of anger. And he has wit, a ready, droll, rememberable wit, and a tongue to speak it with. Whether he makes music or speeches, Italy listens. He says what he pleases, writes what he pleases. He makes his audience wait almost two full acts until he gives it that panacea for all operatic ills, the love duet; they appreciate it the more for the waiting. He launches his première of a ticklishly revolutionary libretto in Rome itself—Rome, the stronghold of Nationalism; and royalty vies with rowdies to crowd the house. Bluntly, courageously, he has seized the Italian heart once again. His picture is in every shop-window. His opera is in every music-store. He tours the country with a 'Piccolo Marat' company under his own direction and fills big amphitheaters and arenas. For the first time since 'Iris' he is the master of operatic Italy."

GERMAN POETS TURNING TO POLITICS

GERMAN POETRY IS REVELING in politics now that no longer the menace and blight of *lèse majesté* hangs over the makers of it. "It is as if a reaction had come," says *The Nation and The Athenaeum*, (London) "after so many years of repression, when the excursions of poets, novelists, and dramatists, if their sentiments were at all unfavorable to the Imperial régime, were liable to be visited—in Prussia, at least—with severe reproof or actual legal penalties." Moral and religious heterodoxy, before the war, was far commoner in Germany than anywhere else in Europe, but politics was a land tabu. Now they have obtained their right of entry, the poets are exercising the privilege with remarkable thoroughness. A recent volume with the formidable title of "Menschheitsdämmerung" (Twilight of Humanity) has recently appeared in Berlin, containing a collection of poems by most of the younger German poets, "particularly of those whose political inclinations are to the Left." In an editorial paragraph the editor, Kurt Pinthus, "explains and justifies the method of these poets":

"Never was the esthetic principle, the principle of *l'art pour l'art*, so despised as in this poetry, which is called the 'youngest,' or the 'expressionist,' because it represents eruption, explosion, intensity—qualities it must possess to break through the hostile barriers opposing it. It avoids the naturalistic representation of reality, and . . . is produced by the powerful means of expression it is able to draw from the spirit. . . . Social conditions are not reproduced in realistic detail, as was the case with the literature of the 'nineties, but are transferred entirely into universal human ideals. Even the Great War, which crusht out the existence of many of these younger artists, is not rendered realistically. It is—and was long before its actual outbreak—constantly before their minds as a vision of universal terror, as the most inhuman of evils, which can only be driven from the world by the triumph of the ideals of brotherhood among men."

Thus the younger poets are "not esthetic, still less are they naturalistic writers after the style of Arno Holz, Johannes Schlaf, or the earliest Hauptmann." On the other hand:

"They generalize the social problem, endeavor to take it into their imagination and there transform it, making of their work not a mere picture of evil political or social conditions, but a kind of spiritual delineation and protest.

"The result, one must confess, is scarcely more inspiring than that achieved by the naturalists of the old school. It is pessimism in both cases: with the Hauptmanns an objective pessimism—so we might distinguish one from the other—and with these younger men of our own day a subjective pessimism. The ulta-realistic dramatists and poets of the 'nineties made their audience depress by actual concrete cases of social misery and injustice; the new men make their audience equally deprest, but rather at the sight of the poet's own depression and despair. Thus

IN THE FIRST HEYDAY OF FAME

Mascagni as he looked when the world was singing "Cavalleria."

Paul Zech, in a short poem entitled 'Fabrikstrasse,' gives a vivid but fleeting impression of what a road leading to a factory looks like, and then crushes the reader with the spiritual weight it has placed on his own mind. The achievement may be salutary in its effect, the means by which it is produced may be employed with considerable talent. What can not, surely, be admitted is the claim that this constitutes a tremendous advance over the art of, say, 'Die Weber.' There is a difference of method, that is all, and imaginative exaltation is scarcely more in evidence in the one case than in the other. A worse case is Walter Hasenclever, who seems to be more under the hopeless influence of actualities than any of his colleagues. During the war this young writer wrote a kind of modernized 'Antigone,' which, although an ill-disguised dramatic sermon against the war and the German Emperor, nevertheless contained several beautiful passages. In 'Der politische Dichter' he has got together a number of his political poems—among them 'Jaures Tod—Jaures Auferstehung,' a poem on the suppression of the Spartacist revolt, dedicated to the memory of Karl Liebknecht. They have emphasis, a certain melodramatic energy—as has his symbolist dramatic poem 'Der Retter'—but scarcely any other element of greater vitality than is possest by a newspaper article. There is, one feels, the stuff of true poetry in Hasenclever, but it will hardly find expression so long as he confines his attention to or draws his inspiration exclusively from current German politics."

Exceptions are to be found in "poets who do not withdraw from the events and emotions of the time—on the contrary, plunge right into them—and yet preserve imagination, which is timeless." We find that—

"It is all a question of comparative values. With Hasenclever and so many of his colleagues it is, first of all, a matter of producing a political effect—the means employed are beside the point. With Werfel, and now and then with other poets of the same group—Johannes R. Becher, for example—the transformation of political or social sentiments into imaginative experience is complete, the indefinable and infinitely deep abyss between propaganda and poetry is bridged. Several of the poems of Werfel printed in the "Menschheitsdämmerung" collection stand out from among the others by reason of this quality. Poems such as 'Wir sind,' 'Herz, frohlock,' even 'Der Krieg,' written on August 4, 1914, can be detached from their age and its strivings with greater ease than the work of any of the other poets. A few of the best will hardly appear old-fashioned when the German Revolution, with the motives behind it, has passed into the mists of history. The next generation of readers of poetry will not turn to even the 'political' poems of Werfel—as, on the whole, it will turn to those of such poets as Ludwig Rubiner, Wilhelm Klemm, René Schickele, Alfred Wolfenstein—merely for historical guidance as to what the younger men thought and said during the Great War and on its catastrophic culmination. It will turn to them for their poetry, and nothing but their poetry."

AN AUTHORS' BATTLE

MR. HENRY ARTHUR JONES has been hitting Mr. H. G. Wells on the raw, and the result is a literary quarrel worthy of the best vituperative pamphleteering days of the eighteenth century. With the safe distance of an ocean between, the New York *Times* looks on and observes that "when Mr. H. G. Wells likens the controversial Mr. Henry Arthur Jones to a mud volcano, a sewing machine and three pennyworth of cat's meat, the cisatlantic reader, unaccustomed to the delights of such argument, would have him write so always." But Mr. Wells doesn't do quite this, even though Mr. Jones persists in taking him in such a light. Mr. Wells is annoyed because Mr. Jones lines him up among the "haters of England," as shown in the Wells book called "Russia in the Shadow" and the already famous "Outline of History." Mr. Jones has addrest to his compatriot what in its author's words is "a carefully reasoned analysis of your collectivist and international theories and of your social philosophy generally, together with some playful coaxings which I hope may lead you to examine the political doctrines you are advocating so profusely." This book, to have been called "My Dear Wells," is held up on the threat of a libel suit. To Mr. Wells the "playful coaxings" are otherwise described in his letter to the Chicago *Tribune:*

"MY DEAR WELLS,"

Who does not relish the overtures to controversy forced on him by Mr. H. A. Jones.

"His campaign is a great nuisance to me, for these articles not only crop up here, there and everywhere where there is a paper in need of cheap copy, but, also, he supplements it by a stream of private letters to me. The thing is as tiresome as being shouted after in the streets or having some one without rhyme or reason perpetually banging at one's door knocker.

"The stuff he writes about my opinions is too incoherent and extravagant for notice. . . .

"But he has one or two weaknesses that call for a word or so from me. He has a curious inability to understand what is honest quotation. For example, I wrote that Lenin was beloved by the energetic people in Russia. He has seized upon the word 'beloved,' and for the last year, whenever he could get it into print, he has tried to persuade his readers that I have written of Lenin in terms of personal endearment; he has twitted me again and again with my 'beloved Lenin.' This is out and out lying. But he is mentally and morally incapable of understanding that, and so this nuisance goes on. It is a petty point, but it puts me wrong with the public.

"Another thing he does is rather more amusing.

"Like Dogberry, he has a passion for abusive terms. He clothes himself with cursing as with a garment. He desires me to call him names. It would be a very natural thing if I did so, but I don't, and so he is forced to say that I do. . . .

"He has now quite a garland of more or less appropriate phrases, which I have never applied to him, but which he has, as it were, distilled out of this business and applied to himself. For example, I said I would as soon engage in serious controversy with a barking cur as with Mr. Jones. He is now filling the London papers—it is our 'silly season' here—and no doubt he is trying to fill the American papers with the important news that I have called him a 'barking cur.' One might as soon expect reason from a mud volcano or a sewing machine or three pennyworth of cat's meat as from a mind of this sort. This last, you will note, is rather an odd sentence, but I have put it in this form so that later on we may have Mr. Jones dashing about with the announcement that I have called him a 'mud volcano,' a 'sewing machine' and 'three pennyworth of cat's meat'."

Mr. Jones, given the occasion, retorts in the New York *Times:*

"Mr. Wells's letter gives the American public an entirely false account of the facts in the case. He represents me as inflamed by the petty motive of personal malice. He says that I am carrying on a campaign 'here, there and everywhere where there is a paper in need of cheap copy.' He further says that I supplement this public campaign by writing private letters to him in so persistent a way that he feels as if I were shouting after him in the streets or perpetually banging his door knocker. He declares that I am filling the London papers in the 'silly season,' and that I am trying to fill American papers with the important news that he has called me 'a barking cur.' Mark how my plain tale shall set him down.

"I have written no letter about him whatsoever to any paper other than The New York *Times*, The London *Evening Standard* and The London *Morning Post*. Will he say that these are papers which are 'in need of cheap copy'?

"I have written no private letter to Mr. Wells since this discussion began. I thought it courteous to send him, before publication, a copy of each letter before it appeared. I have done this through my secretary, who has enclosed quite a short polite note explaining the circumstances. There has been no other communication whatever between us."

The serious side of Mr. Jones's charge is contained in the following paragraphs from the same letter:

"My object in writing 'My Dear Wells' is a very simple one. We have a busy group of thinkers and writers whom I call the Haters of England. They always think and write against their own country. If there is sedition and revolt in any part of the British Empire, they stir it up. If there is trouble and unrest at home, they foment it. During the war they were worth many army corps to Germany. Now that the war has left us a legacy of new insecurities and perils, these Haters of England are busy spreading disaffection and disunion both in our internal and foreign affairs.

"Mr. Wells is one of the most popular of these thinkers and writers, who always think and write against England. For years in our most widely circulated journals he has been spreading theories that tend to promote sedition at home, to break in pieces the British Empire, and to shake the foundations of civil order throughout the world. In the present treacherous condition of British industries and finances, imperiled as we are in all parts of the world, I count Mr. Wells as a more dangerous enemy of England than any German who four years ago bombed our women and children.

"For this reason, I have written 'My Dear Wells' and have carefully dissected his main doctrines and theories. But I am not conscious of any personal malice against him. Again and again I have challenged him to meet me in argument upon these matters of deepest concern to hundreds of millions of

Healthy, happy boys and girls,
Sparkling eyes and flying curls,
Showing by their dashing play
They eat Campbell's every day!

Campbell's
CONDENSED
TOMATO
SOUP
JOSEPH CAMPBELL COMPANY
CAMDEN, N.J. U.S.A.

Bounding health

How much it depends on the food we eat! One simple rule will add as much downright pleasure to your eating as it will bring unfailing benefit. Eat good soup every day! Do it yourself and insist that your children gain the strength and vigor that soup gives.

Campbell's Tomato Soup

is a shining example of how good soup stimulates appetite, energizes digestion, nourishes and constructs the body tissues. Pure tomato juices, creamery butter and granulated sugar are skillfully spiced and blended with the other ingredients to produce this tonic, healthful, delightful dish. You never tire of it.

21 kinds 12c a can

Campbell's SOUPS

LOOK FOR THE RED AND WHITE LABEL

CURRENT - POETRY

Unsolicited contributions to this department cannot be returned.

SAN FRANCISCO never mentions the earthquake; Arizona mentions everything and seems to expect you to take her for what she's worth. *Arizona Lyrics* (Alto) publishes every other month and lately had this:

THE MARVELS OF ARIZONA

By Josiah Bond

I

The tarantula and vinagaron,
Matasiete, scorpion,
The centipede so queerly grown,
All crawl in Arizona!

II.

The Gila Monster, venting spleen,
The campomoche, slick and green,
The hydrophobia skunk, so mean,
All kill in Arizona!

III.

The horned toads and the rattlesnakes,
Cactus spikes and pointed stakes,
The plains and the imagined lakes,
All bed in Arizona!

IV.

Sahuaro, datil and mescal,
The ocotillo, chaparral,
Sotol, viznaga and nopal,
All grow in Arizona!

V.

The enchiladas, night and morn,
Tortillas poured from plenty's horn,
Tomales made of meat and corn,
All cloy in Arizona!

VI.

The olden houses built of mud,
Plains steeped in prehistoric blood,
Now garbed with blossom and with bud,
All merge in Arizona!!

The cult of the garden has not reached quite the pitch with us that our English cousins boast. But here in the London *Outlook* we see a garden that must be rare even over there. Yet how fascinating is just the roll-call of the denizens thereof:

A BLESSING

By Geoffrey Dearmer

May your home all blessed be,
A home and wild flower sanctuary.
May still crocus candles glow
With hanging drops of driven snow
With celandine and spiking squills
And wide-awoken daffodils;
Closed and tattered tulips creaking
Stalk to stalk; mimosa seeking
Levels where her sulphur springs
May powder faintly whirring wings;
And sudden-green your garden stay
From front of March till fall of May.

When your Spring to Summer grows
May the puffed and rampant rose
Mingle scent with scent of stocks.
May sweet peas in fluttering flocks
More your heart than twigs entwine.
May the dancing columbine
In her frock of frailest blue
Hold your heart entangled too.
May Jacob's bells below you chime
Whilst you his light ladder climb.
May Solomon's seal, white row on row,
Chime above you, and below
May lilies of the valley chime
And tell the time below the lime.

So, when rich Autumn fills your figs
And breathes bloom on your grapes. May grigs
With gills of pink and domes of cream
Amid your dewy meadows gleam.
And when winged dragons, horned and blue,
With oozy, hidden haunts in view,
Vie with the last bees booming by—
When late birds ride the racing sky—
May soon your fasting garden sing
The coming Festival of Spring.

Death moves many moods, but this one is all of the zest of future living. It is a fine document of the personal conviction of immortality. The *Westminster Gazette* (London) prints it.

THE JOURNEY

By L. Le Mesurier

It's a wild night for a soul to go.
Stars shine, but winds blow
And the flood tides flow.

It's a long road to the nearest star
Where the band of well-beloved are,
But I shall reach it, near or far.

A wild night for a naked soul
To cast aside the broken bowl
And start for the distant goal.

A wild night and a lonely way,
And Death is terrible, they say,
Yet methinks I like his looks today.

And glad I'll lay my garments by
And fling me forth to the windy sky
When Death rides by.

A long road to the nearest star,
Where the band of well-beloved are,
But I shall reach it, near or far.

The complaint behind the scorn of these words is unspoken; perhaps it is merely the exasperation of age. Printed in the *Yale Review:*

THE SOLITARY

By Sara Teasdale

Let them think I love them more than I do,
Let them think I care, though I go alone,
If it lifts their pride, what is it to me
Who am self-complete as a flower or a stone?

It is one to me that they come or go
If I have myself and the drive of my will,
And strength to climb on a summer night
And watch the stars swarm over the hill.

My heart has grown rich with the passing of years
I have less need now than when I was young
To share myself with every comer,
Or shape my thoughts into words with my tongue.

The signing of our peace treaty with Germany seemed to leave our poets dumb. "Bored indifference" is what a correspondent of the *Freeman* sees in populace as well as poets. The same attitude was observed in England when her turn came and the Manchester *Guardian* was the only paper practically to signalize it in verses like these which the *Freeman* quotes as apropos for us:

APRÈS LA GUERRE

By Lucio

And will there be bands and bonfires?
And will there be guns and milk?
Will all the ex-sodgers assemble,
All privately thanking their stars
That this calculation was not 'the duration'
As reckoned by Tommies and Tars?

No, nothing like that will be noted—
The day will have moments of joy,
But joy that's official and rather judicial
And not for the vulgar *polloi*.

Discreet and genteel the rejoicing,
With jests of a dignified shape—
The pundits who tell 'em will write them on vellum
And bind them all up with red tape.

Away in some office in Whitehall
The pundits will gravely await
The due presentation of some proclamation,
The which they will witness and date;

And then they'll lean back on their divans
(Nay, even self-righteously sprawl),
And ejaculate, "Ah! To us the éclat—
We finished the war after all!"

"Sir, a whole history," said *Hamlet*, and here is life and death compresst in a nutshell. It is a poem from "Saturday Market" (Macmillan Company), and the writer is one of the significant members of the modern English school.

THE NARROW DOOR

By Charlotte Mew

The narrow door, the narrow door
On the three steps of which the café children play
Mostly at shop with pebbles from the shore,
It is always shut this narrow door
But open for a little while today.

And round it, each with pebbles in his hand,
A silenced crowd the café children stand
To see the long box jerking down the bend
Of twisted stair; then set on end,
Quite filling up the narrow door
Till it comes out and does not go in any more.

Along the quay you see it wind,
The slow black line. Some one pulls up the blind
Of the small window just above the narrow door—
"*Tiens! que veux-tu acheter?*" Rénée cries,
"*Mais, pour quat'sous, des cignons,*" Jean replies
And one pays down with pebbles from the shore.

We end with a quotation from *Contemporary Verse* that all our modernists will cry "pish!" to, but what of that? They preach discontent:

THE HOME-KEEPERS

By Helen Cowles Le Cron

A little dream keeps house with me—
Outside, the surge and flow
Of city throngs, of wind, of sea—'
The world the great ones know.

But we—we wash the cups and spoons
And make the copper shine,
And knit, on sunny afternoons,
Beside the trumpet-vine.

We smile at many a secret joke;
We weed the lettuce-bed;
We sweep the hearth, and pause to stroke
The snow-white kitten's head.

The neighbors hear our songs, and say,
"How queer some folks can be!"
They wonder what can keep us gay,
My little dream and me.

But I am wise, and therefore know,
For sewing up a seam

WAGNER
& LISZT
painted for the
Steinway
Collection
BY N. C. WYETH

STEINWAY

THE INSTRUMENT OF THE IMMORTALS

OCCASIONALLY the genius of man produces some masterpiece of art—a symphony, a book, a painting—of such surpassing greatness that for generation upon generation it stands as an ideal, unequaled and supreme. For more than three score years the position of the Steinway Piano has been comparable to such a masterpiece—with this difference: A symphony, a book, a painting, once given to the world, stands forever as it is. Its creator cannot bequeath to future generations the task of carrying it to still higher perfection. But the Steinway, great as it was in Richard Wagner's day, has grown greater still with each generation of the Steinway family. From Wagner, Liszt and Rubinstein down through the years to Paderewski, Rachmaninoff and Hofmann, the Steinway has come to be "The Instrument of the Immortals." He who owns a Steinway is in company with the great. And he who owns a Steinway possesses an unmistakable token of musical culture and distinction, recognized the world over.

Steinway & Sons and their dealers have made it conveniently possible for music lovers to own a Steinway.
Prices: $875 and up, plus freight at points distant from New York.

PERSONAL ▾ GLIMPSES

OBREGON AS HERO AND BUSINESS MAN

A GREAT MAN, one of the greatest in history, is doing his work practically unrecognized by the world in general and America in particular, if we may trust the judgment of E. J. Dillon, one of the oldest and best known of British journalists. The new hero, whom Mr. Dillon places above Bismarck and Roosevelt, among others, for certain qualities of leadership, "and that elusive quality which occasionally goes by the name of grandeur," is Alvaro Obregon, President of Mexico. He is also, which may be more to the point in the eyes of a great many Americans, an organizer of industry, "a man of action, simple in his tastes, unpretentious in his manner, and sincere," asserts a representative of *System* (Chicago), and he is quoted in the pages of that magazine for October as unequivocally inviting the United States to assist in Mexico's commercial development. To the *System* representative he gave a two-hour exclusive interview, in which he promised that there would be no confiscation, deplored that a small group of "special interests" in the United States "in their desire to keep everything to themselves, have frightened away other investors, and through their world-wide propaganda have deprived Mexico of its good name in order to monopolize her riches." The government has made "marvelous" progress, declares this writer, and, as soon as recognition comes, this country will waken to the fact that a new and better Mexico has arisen, under the guidance of its one-armed, plain-speaking President.

By Courtesy of "System" Chicago — From the "Revista de Revistas," Mexico City

MEXICO'S "MAN OF ACTION."

President Obregon, as pictured by photographer and by cartoonist.

Obregon, it may be remembered, recently survived another attempt on his life, a very common achievement with him if most of his biographers are to be believed. Both Agnes C. Laut in *The Forum* and Sophie Treadwell in the New York *Tribune* have testified to the Mexican President's "magnetism," democratic instincts and genius for commanding the sort of people it is necessary to command in present-day Mexico. Other interviewers have shown him lounging in coffee-houses, gossiping and telling "funny stories." Characteristic of his attitude toward himself is said to be the story he tells of the loss of his arm. The arm was lost on the battlefield, and could not be identified among the other arms scattered about, he relates, until somebody dropped a piece of money, which the Obregon fingers, true to their master's instincts even in separation and death, immediately grasped. Tho many observers have testified that the President is *sympatico*, as the Spanish word meaning genial, friendly, and sympathetic goes, Mr. Dillon is the first who has found Obregon worthy of a place among the great ones of the earth. "In the course of a varied experience in most parts of the globe, during the long span of time between the close of the

Mr. Dillon in *The Nation* (New York), "I have come into contact with most of the statesmen, rulers, and leaders of men whose deeds and endeavors have made contemporary history. The list includes Bismarck, Gambetta, Gladstone, Crispi, Chamberlain, President Kruger, the Marquis Ito, Disraeli, Roosevelt and Venizelos, and most of the prominent public workers of the present day." Of all the world characters named on this formidable list, Mr. Dillon goes on:

> I can honestly say that none impress me so powerfully or so favorably from the point of view of leadership, single-mindedness, and that elusive quality which occasionally goes by the name of grandeur as the Mexican reformer of whose existence and aims the people of the United States are only now beginning to have a vague inkling.
>
> Alvaro Obregon is a born leader with whom love of justice is a consuming passion, and duty the highest law. A man of sterling character and of a humane and sympathetic temper, he combines the fervor of the idealist with the capacity of the organizer, and his solicitude for the well-being of the masses is the driving force of his public and private activities. His words are acts and his promise the beginning of achievement. His respect for truth in all its Protean shapes and singular surroundings is almost tantamount to worship.
>
> Before I had the advantage of meeting Obregon I had heard much about him from eminent Americans—experts all of them on Mexican affairs—to whom the principal sources of information, public and private, were easily accessible. And the portrait which I drew from the data thus liberally supplied was the reverse of attractive. Later on when I came to know him as he is I perceived that the data were fabrications and the portrait a sorry caricature.
>
> I should like, were it possible, to ascribe the circumstantial and false information volunteered to me by my informants to what Goethe termed the dangerous ease with which a great man's contemporaries usually go astray about him. "That which is uncommon in the individual bewilders them," the poet adds, "life's headstrong current distorts their angle of vision and keeps them from knowing such men and appreciating them." But it is to be feared that the true explanation lies elsewhere.
>
> My first visit to Obregon took place while I still believed that he was one of the least reputable types of the class ridiculed in the United States as the Mexican bandit general. Primed with this idea I called on him one afternoon at his hotel in Mexico City. His ante-chamber was filled with typical representatives of the despised poverty-stricken masses with whom he was hail-fellow-well-met. He inquired what he could do for me. I answered, "I merely wish to know how you intend to deal with the problems of recognition, of Mexico's debts, of foreign claims for losses, and kindred matters, when, as now appears certain, you will have entered upon the duties of President." "My answer is simple," he replied laughingly. "Mexico will pay all her debts and satisfy all the just claims of foreigners. As for recognition, I can not admit that that is a Mexican problem. Foreign states will recognize the lawful government of the Republic in accord- ... with the law of nations. That is all. You would not sug-

GOODYEAR

In rural communities, as on city boulevards, "more people ride on Goodyear Tires than on any other kind"

THE very finest indorsement of Goodyear Tires for passenger cars is the steadfast preference shown for them by the American people. This preference has never been so great nor so intense as now. It is the natural result of the good service that Goodyear Tires have given over a long period of years. Today they are better tires than they have ever been. They are bigger, heavier, stronger. Whether you drive a large or a small car, you should use Goodyear Tires. More people ride on Goodyear Tires than on any other kind gest, would you, that any of them will make a new departure?" I arose, said that I would not trespass further on his time, thanked him for his reply, wished him good afternoon, and left.

Next day a friend of his informed me that the General would be pleased to see me again, to have a more satisfactory talk with him, adding that he had been under the impression that I was one of the numerous callers whose aim was to ply him with futile questions and then to comment adversely on his answers. He intended to start in two days for his home in Nogales and would gladly receive me any time before his departure. I said that I would not trouble the General further now but might possibly be in Nogales myself in a few weeks when I would take the liberty to call on him. The next day I received an invitation to accompany him on his journey to Nogales, and after a few hours' deliberation I accepted it.

On that journey and on our many subsequent travels the writer had a rare opportunity to study General Obregon in the various lights shed by adventures pleasant and unpleasant, exhilarating and depressing. He testified:

I saw him in his native place surrounded by his family and his kindred. I conversed with his earliest teachers and his schoolmates. I observed him as a candidate for the Presidency and listened to over a hundred of his electoral addresses, always with a keen sense of esthetic enjoyment and at times with admiration for his fairness and generosity as an antagonist. To my knowledge he possest documents which if published would have debarred certain of his adversaries from ever again appearing on the public stage. But he declines to make use of them during the elections or indeed later unless the behavior of the authors should oblige him to make known their misdeeds.

Obregon is a man of the people, a proletarian of the proletariate, a lack-all who worked his way up from the lowest rung of the social ladder to the highest by dint of intense painstaking while preserving his 'scutcheon from blot or stain. Whatever he set his hand to, that he persevered in until he accomplished the task. As a simple workman he labored with might and main to the satisfaction of his employers, who soon gave him a post of trust and responsibility. As a farm hand and farmer he acquainted himself with agriculture in most of its branches until his qualifications enabled him to render a lasting service to the whole state in which he was born. Combining mechanics with agricultural industry, he invented a sowing machine which is employed today in various states of the Republic. Political conditions constraining him to abandon his peaceful existence and his ideal family life, he became a soldier and applied himself so intensely to the requirements of his new profession that he finally ended this uncongenial career with the triumph of the popular cause and the well-deserved reputation of a genial military strategist as well as a most successful organizer.

Obregon is one of the very few men I have met—Venizelos is another—on whom power and rank have no further effect than that of sharpening their sense of responsibility. In all other respects he is as he was. Kerensky, the Russian lawyer whom the turn of fortune's wheel raised to the highest post in Russia, had his head turned dizzy and his estimate of values upset by the all too sudden change. In the Czar's luxurious apartments he is said to have attired himself in magnificent costumes and to have striven to add a cubit to his mental and moral stature by the aid of the cast-off finery of the former autocrat. Obregon is a man of a wholly different cast of mind and type of character. He owes everything to himself, nothing to artifice. In virtue of his unbroken military successes, his moral rectitude, and his transparent sincerity he wields an extraordinary sway over the spirits of his countrymen; and he uses this for the purpose of inculcating among them faith in the great emancipating principles of right and wrong, respect for law and individual right, and a striving after freedom with order and administration with integrity.

Obregon's presence is the embodiment of unaggressive strength and quiet natural dignity. His glance is searching and is often accompanied by a mental, almost perceptible, effort to complete the impression which he is receiving from the words of his interlocutor by inspection of his motives. Optimism is usually depicted in his mien, tone, and language, but it is the optimism of the man who having struggled against vast odds and won feels himself specially favored by circumstance and inspirited by past experience. He is cautious withal by temperament, enthusiastic by reflection, persevering on principle. While preaching high ideals he rates at its just value the poverty of the soil in which he is sowing them and is prepared to content himself with a proportionate harvest. In his theories there is no room for staggering misgiving, and from his action he banishes hesitation. "Vacillation spells failure," is one of his every-day sayings. While guided by experience, he is not self-opinionated; his inquiries are broad, his mind open, and his prejudices are neither many nor insuperable.

Obregon's moral code, like that of the Japanese, is interlaced with what is known in Spanish lands as the *punto d'honor*, and for this as for that he is ready to make the supreme sacrifice. He is neither vain nor conventionally modest, simply proud with that legitimate pride which springs from consciousness of duty performed and his rôle well played.

As an orator he deserves high rank for qualities which are innate and are therefore often belittled by those who lack them. He discards the usual artificial aids and speaks briefly, simply, and to the point. His every discourse is a message. He has the knack of imparting to his hearers a direct interest in the matter dealt with. And however homely the subject, he views it with a mind permeated with a sense of the larger issues of which it is an integral part. Obregon knows the crowd much better than the individual. None the less he is often strikingly right in his judgment of individuals, which is mostly intuitive, but when dealing with personal friends his intuition is sometimes paralyzed. He is then blind to defects that are almost obvious.

One afternoon in Tehuacan General Obregon talked about his plans of reconstruction and the principles that would govern them. "And here," says Mr. Dillon, "is a concise note of the conversation which I jotted down immediately after for future reference":

He is resolved to substitute morality for politics. Recognizes power only as a means to an end—the end to be the good of the community. The making of laws is easy and the belief is common that by statutes you can right every wrong. But what counts more than the wording of an act of Congress is the integrity of those who interpret and administer it. Never hesitate in a crisis. If you take a resolution carry it out with might and main. If you are dubious give it up altogether, and if convinced that it is the right thing to do tackle it even though you have no hope of achieving it and persevere even though failure should stare you in the face, for it is not only what you have actually done but also what you would do that counts.

Mexico will find her right position, not through aloofness from world affairs, but rather by recognizing the essential unity of humankind and the need of developing the resources of each country for the benefit not only of the nation that owns them but also of humanity. Hatred of foreigners is a curse to the people who indulge in it, as history shows. Foreigners are the needed cooperators of Mexicans and should therefore be cordially welcomed.

Such in brief is the man who is striving to reconstruct the southern Republic to-day. During the few months that have elapsed since he entered upon his official duties he has accomplished much and has prepared the ground for much more. For the first time in history Mexico is now on the right road. Revolution has ceased and peace is firmly established. The factions that for years kept the country plunged in chaos are appeased. The outlook is most promising. The only lever by which the Republic can at present be thrust back into the quagmire of meaningless strife is of foreign origin. And the only apparent motive for using this fatal lever is a crazy infatuation for a hollow form.

General Obregon can not purchase recognition by a treaty. He can and will discuss a treaty when he is recognized. To sign a political compact would be to violate the constitution and his oath, and to insist that he shall be a law-breaker and a perjurer in order to qualify himself for recognition is hardly in accordance with President Harding's public professions.

Some sort of diplomatic arrangement with the United States will be necessary, agrees Harold C. Bodman, the *System* interviewer, before the United States and Mexico can really settle down to a friendly and businesslike basis. It is suggested that the Mexican administration, according to some of the men with whom Mr. Bodman talked in Mexico City, "may swallow its pride and replace its verbal assurances by written guarantees, thus satisfying the United States diplomatically, and giving unbounded encouragement to all who have been struggling with the unsatisfactory business conditions of the past seven to ten years." There is peace now in Mexico, says the writer:

The President jokingly asked me if I had taken out additional insurance before coming to Mexico. There are no signs of banditry on the railroads or in the interior; one can move about the country freely, and as for any considerable revolutionary movement, the people are sick and tired of war. In fact, the lands have been so wasted and neglected, and the live stock so depleted during the past ten years that it is quite unlikely that the country could support another revolution of any proportion.

To cite two graphic examples, the State of Guadalajara, for-

merly one of the richest wheat sections of the world, is now importing wheat from the United States, and the largest shoe factory in Mexico gets its supply of cowhides from the United States.

I asked the President whether to his large and well-organized army should be attributed the present peace and stability of the country.

"The feeling of quiet and security in the Republic," he replied, "is due only in part to the protection which our army affords. The real and primary cause for our present feeling of rest is the fact that the people of Mexico realize that their Government is handling affairs justly, honestly and without force. A people voices its approval of a government by obeying its laws and respecting peace. Disapproval is voiced by revolution.

"One of the chief aims of this Government is to reduce the army as soon as possible, our belief being that a reduction of our armed forces will build up morale and establish the full confidence of the people in the stability of the administration. Our plan is to make agricultural colonies of the reserves, thus reducing the forces which increase consumption, and at the same time increasing those forces that stimulate the productivity of the country."

Considering the fact that the Obregon government has not been able to borrow so much as a single peso for the reconstruction of the country, it is little short of marvelous that so much has been accomplished.

"A ruthless fight has been waged and is still being waged with increasing vigor by the Mexican Government," said the President, "for the moralization of Government administration. The result has been that the sources of revenues have not only been sufficient to meet all budget disbursements, but also to permit many public improvements and enterprises.

"During the Carranza administration, the Government paid 75 per cent. of its wages to employees in gold. The balance was paid in paper money. Now the Government pays all of its debts in gold, and almost all salaries have been raised. Every Government employee is paid on the day his salary is due. Ten million pesos ($5,000,000) have been spent on rolling-stock for the railways; twenty ships of various specifications have been purchased; large amounts of money have been expended on education and public works such as irrigation, and great sums have been paid to the banks on indebtednesses of former administrations. In spite of this enormous overhead expense which the Government is under, still there is a surplus of money in the treasury.

"The fact that the Mexican Government wishes to pay its debts is not a dream. The Government authorities have given assurance to the representatives of all holders of Mexico's debt that they will not resort to any subterfuges or evasions, but that they will try to reach a settlement with a spirit of equity, until the creditors are entirely satisfied.

"I do not claim to be a worker of miracles—I am not a superman—but I am doing all that is within my power to close the channels of graft and to moralize the administration, and those who work with me have the same desire. I wish to stress this point with all emphasis, in order that the business men of the United States may regard this administration not with suspicion, but with confidence. I wish to have these men realize that my words have been, and always will be, backed up by deeds.

"I fully appreciate that the fate of this administration depends upon building the stable foundations of a new Mexico—new in spirit, conception and plan. It would be criminal to erect the foundations of this beautiful structure without respect to international law and justice, when our clear conscience tells us that if the foundations are not secure, the entire fabric will fall and bury us beneath its ruins."

To these statements made to newspaper and magazine interviewers, may be added an official declaration of Obregon's purposes as President of Mexico. In his recent message to the Mexican Senate he said, as quoted in the New York *Tribune:*

"Our government is as much preoccupied with protection of the interests of Americans in Mexico as is the government of the United States. It considers such protection one of its most imperious obligations to that great country, not only because of material bonds on account of its neighborhood, but also because of the moral ones, greater yet, rising out of our sympathy for its democratic institutions and the high quality of its people. Both governments, therefore, are in accord on this purpose, and the Mexican government, with the object of cooperating more efficiently in its realization—that is, desiring to take a stand which will strengthen the prestige of said government, and thus enable it best to fulfill its obligations and at the same time bring about closer future relations between the two countries—has preferred to eliminate any chance of making promises which might humiliate it through the natural carrying out of its political and administrative plans."

And *The Tribune* is moved by the settlement reached by President Obregon and the American oil men to remark that the Mexican

BABE RUTH IS SUPERNORMAL, HENCE THE "HOMERS"

"BETTER EYES, a quicker nerve system, and higher intelligence"—these are the scientific reasons, whatever others may be adduced by some tens of thousands of interested fans, for the ability of Babe Ruth to set new hitting records in baseball. The home-run champion is above normal in many ways, say two scientists who have been putting the "Bambino" through a series of tests at Columbia University. The tests were performed at the University's Psychological Research Laboratory by Albert Johanson and Joseph Holmes, and Ruth stood very high in the score, although he had just finished a hard game at the Polo Grounds. "The tests prove," writes Hugh S. Fullerton, sporting editor of *The Evening Mail*, in the October issue of *The Popular Science Monthly*, "that the coordination of Ruth's eye-brain-nerve system and muscles is practically perfect, and that the reason he did not acquire his great batting power before the sudden burst at the beginning of the baseball season in 1920 was because, prior to that time, pitching and studying batters disturbed his almost perfect coordination." Mr. Fullerton goes on:

The tests revealed the fact that Ruth is 90 per cent. efficient, compared with a human average of 60 per cent. That his eyes are about 12 per cent. faster than those of the average human being. That his ears function at least 10 per cent. faster than those of the ordinary man. That his nerves are steadier than those of 499 out of 500 persons. That in attention and quickness of perception he rates one and a half times above the human average. That in intelligence, as demonstrated by quickness and accuracy of understanding, he is approximately 10 per cent. above normal.

The investigation lasted more than three hours, during which Ruth stood most of the time, walked up and down stairs five times, and underwent the tests in a close, warm room. The tests used were ones that primarily test motor functions and give a measure of the integrity of the psycho-physical organism. Babe Ruth was posed first in an apparatus created to determine his strength, quickness, and approximate power of the swing of his bat against his ball. A plane covered with electrically charged wires, strung horizontally, was placed behind him and a ball was hung over the theoretical plate, so that it could be suspended at any desired height.

The bat, weighing fifty-four ounces (exactly the weight of the bats Ruth uses on the diamond), was swung as directed, touched the ball, and the secret of his power—or, rather, the amount of force with which he strikes the ball—was calculated. At least, the basis of the problem was secured: The bat, weighing fifty-four ounces, swinging at the rate of 110 feet a second, hits a ball traveling at the rate of say, sixty feet a second, the ball weighing four and a quarter ounces and striking the bat at a point four inches from the end. How far will the ball travel?

There are other elements entering into the problem, such as the resilience of the ball, the "English" placed on it by the pitcher's hand, and a few minor details. But the answer, as proved by the measurements, is somewhere between 450 and 500 feet. This problem can not be worked down to exact figures because of the unknown quantities.

Before proceeding to the psychological tests, however, we tried another in physics to satisfy my curiosity. A harness composed of rubber tubing was strapped around Ruth's chest and shoulders and attached by hollow tubes to a recording cylinder. By this means his breathing was recorded on a revolving disk. He was then placed in position to bat, an imaginary pitcher pitched an imaginary ball, and he went through the motions of hitting a home-run. The test proved and the needle recorded the fact that as a ball is pitched to him Babe draws in his breath sharply as he makes the back-swing with his bat, and really "holds his breath" or suspends the operation of breathing until after the ball is hit. But for that fact he would hit the ball much harder and more effectively than he now does.

The first test to discover the efficiency of his psycho-physical organism was one designed to try his coordination—a simple little test. The scientists set up a triangular board, looking something like a ouija board, with a small round hole at each angle. At the bottom of each hole was an electrified plate that registered every time it was touched. Ruth was presented with a little instrument that looked like a doll-sized curling iron, the end of which just fitted into the holes. Then he was told to take the

Friction—
the unseen enemy of production
in your plant

D. T. E.

Why Oils that lubricate most are Cheapest in the end

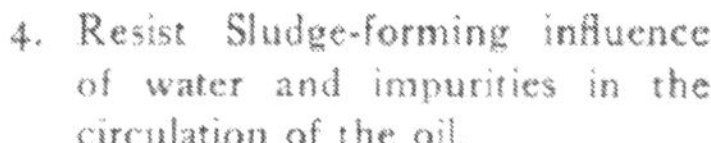

EVERY NEW INVENTION in machinery, every new mechanical improvement, comes in answer to Industry's constant call:

"Reduce operating costs. Increase production."

If you operate a turbine you do so for the economy of its high speed and compact power.

To reap the full benefit of this high speed and power, you *must* provide correct lubrication.

High speeds involve heat. To correctly lubricate you must have an oil that carries away heat. Your oil must also separate readily from water and other impurities so that your turbine lubricating system will not clog with Sludge—the bane of turbine operation. Gargoyle D. T. E. Oils are manufactured specifically to—

1. Form and maintain a lubricating film on bearing surfaces at high speeds.
2. Flow rapidly, carrying off heat.
3. Separate readily from water and impurities.
4. Resist Sludge-forming influence of water and impurities in the circulation of the oil.
5. Stand up under continuous service, retaining their quality and their characteristics when re-used after filtering.

If you wish to secure the full benefits of correct lubrication measured by long-lasting oil qualities, increased power and increased production, our nearest branch stands ready to make specific lubricating recommendations.

These recommendations are the outcome of more than 50 years' experience in the manufacture and application of high-grade lubricating oils together with accurate knowledge of operating conditions in all types of machinery, and constant engineering field experience.

Send to our nearest branch for paper on Turbines—their construction, operation and lubrication.

GARGOYLE

Lubricating Oils

A grade for each type of service

For Lower Production Costs

Steam Cylinders

Gargoyle Steam Cylinder Oils minimize power losses and undue wear in steam cylinders the world over. No other steam cylinder oils are so widely endorsed by engine builders.

The well-known Gargoyle Cylinder Oil 600-W and several other Gargoyle Lubricating Oils are specially manufactured for cylinder and valve lubrication to meet conditions in all types of Steam Engines, Steam Pumps, Steam-driven Compressors, Locomotives, etc.

Turbines

A worry of every turbine operator is sludge. Gargoyle D. T. E. Oils are manufactured and especially treated to meet the exacting requirements of turbine lubrication. These oils separate readily from moisture and impurities and thus provide remarkable freedom from sludge.

Internal Combustion Engines

The severe lubricating requirements of gas engines, Diesel engines and oil engines are scientifically met by Gargoyle D. T. E. Oils.

Compressors and Vacuum Pumps

Correct lubrication is of unusual importance in compressor work. Carbon in the air cylinder has sometimes caused explosion. Gargoyle D. T. E. Oil Heavy Medium is made especially to minimize carbonization. It is correct for air or gas compressors and vacuum pumps.

Bearings

A wide range of Gargoyle Bearing Oils is provided to meet all specific operating conditions of engines and machines involving sizes, speed, pressure, temperature and lubricating methods.

* * *

THROUGH our nearest branch or distributor, we shall be glad to assist you in selecting the correct Gargoyle Lubricating Oils for use throughout your entire plant.

Stocks are carried in principal cities throughout the country.

Domestic Branches:

New York (*Main Office*)	Chicago
Boston	Detroit
Philadelphia	Indianapolis
Pittsburgh	Minneapolis
Buffalo	Des Moines
Rochester	Kansas City, Kan.
Albany	Dallas

VACUUM OIL COMPANY

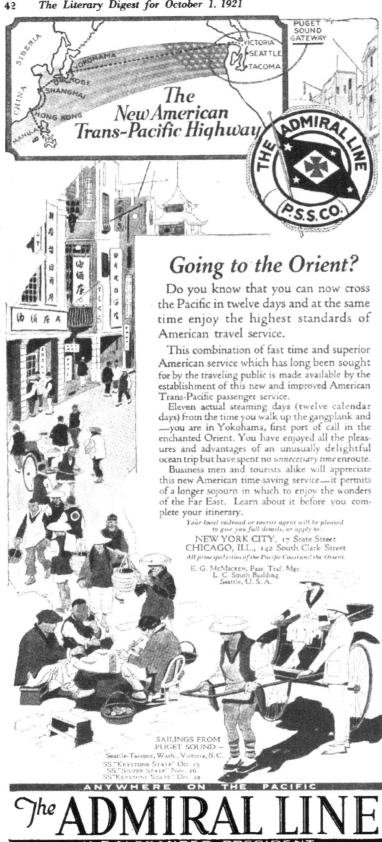

PERSONAL GLIMPSES
Continued

as often as he could in one minute, going around the board from left to right.

He grew interested at once. Here was something at which he could play. With his right hand he made a score of 122. Not unnaturally, his wrist was tired and Babe shook it and grinned ruefully.

Then he tried it with his left hand, scored 132 with it, proving himself a trifle more left than right handed—at least in some activities. The significance of the experiment, however, lies in the fact that the average of hundreds of persons who have taken that test is 82 to the minute.

The scientists discovered exactly how quickly Ruth's eye functions by placing him in a dark cabinet, setting into operation a series of rapidly flashing bulbs and listening to the tick of an electric key by which he acknowledged the flashes.

The average man responds to the stimulus of light in 180 one-thousandths of a second. Babe Ruth needs only 160 one-thousandths of a second. There is the same significance in the fact that Babe's response to the stimulus of sound comes in 140 one-thousandths of a second as against the average man's 150 one-thousandths.

Translate the findings of the sight test into baseball if you want to see what they mean in Babe Ruth's case.

They mean that a pitcher must throw a ball 20 one-thousandths of a second faster to "fool" Babe than to "fool" the average person.

All this theorizing interests an editorial writer on the Syracuse *Post-Standard*. He looks into the matter in this somewhat skeptical fashion:

> Give a child a watch and before many hours have passed the works will be scattered from one end of the house to the other. Give a psychologist the case of Babe Ruth and immediately he disintegrates the mental and physical structure and proves without question that the home-run ability of the great batsman is due to supernormality.
>
> Ruth is 30 per cent. above normal in his physical and mental functionings, these psychologists have found. His eyes, brain, nerves and muscles are almost perfectly coordinated, and thus when he and his mighty bat meet a pitched ball squarely, something happens that has put Ruth in a class by himself. His physical and mental entities act in unison, and that is why he is supernormal.
>
> Perhaps it is interesting and valuable to know why Babe hits so many home-runs; that his mind and muscles coordinate. The fans are interested principally in having him break his record. There is little psychology in the throng of spectators breathlessly awaiting the conjunction of the bat of the Babe and the ball of the pitcher.

Now that we know what the scientists think of Babe Ruth's exploits, it is interesting to note Ruth's own sensations when he broke his own—and the world's—record of 54 home runs in a single season. That was the Yankee slugger's mark last year. The 55th for 1921 came on September 17th at the Polo Grounds. Whatever he does in the future Babe Ruth will never forget the thrill his achievement gave him, at least that is what he says in a signed statement appearing on the sporting page of the New York *American*. It was like this:

The minute Bill Bayne let go of the ball, I said to myself, "Here comes No. 55." It was the funniest home-run feeling I ever experienced. My arms and eyes and legs all seemed to sense what was going to happen. Even Elmer Miller, at third, seemed to catch the spell and started for home as though he had a guarantee I would come across.

Then, the big thump, and the fans cut loose. Take it from me—that was the thrill that counted.

Of course the fans were thrilled, too, and their feelings have been set down by a New York *American* sports writer in the following verses:

BABE RUTH AT THE BAT

AFTER THE FAMOUS POEM, "CASEY AT THE BAT"

There was ease in Babe Ruth's manner as he stepped into his place;
There was pride in Babe Ruth's bearing and a smile on Babe Ruth's face.
And when, responding to the cheers, he lightly doffed his hat,
No stranger in the crowd could doubt 'twas Babe Ruth at the bat.
Ten thousand eyes were on him as he rubbed his hands with dirt.
Five thousand tongues applauded when he wiped them on his shirt.

Then, while the writhing pitcher ground the ball into his hip,
Defiance gleamed in Babe Ruth's eye, a sneer curled Babe Ruth's lip.
And now the leather-covered sphere came hurtling through the air,
And Babe Ruth stood a-watching it in haughty grandeur there.
Close by the sturdy batsman the ball unheeded sped—
"That's not my style," said Babe Ruth. "Strike one!" the umpire said.
From the benches, black with people, there went up a muffled roar,
Like the beating of the storm waves on a stern and rockbound shore.

"Kill him! Kill the umpire!" shouted some one in the stand;
And it's likely they'd have killed him, had not Babe Ruth raised his hand.
With a smile of Christian charity great Babe Ruth's visage shone.
He stilled the rising tumult; he bade the game go on.
He signaled to the pitcher, and once more the spheroid flew,
But Babe Ruth still ignored it, and the umpire said "Strike two."
"Fraud!" cried the maddened thousands, and the echo answered fraud,
But one scornful look from Babe Ruth, and the audience was awed.

They saw his face grow stern and cold, they saw his muscles strain,
And they knew Babe Ruth would not let that ball go by again.
The sneer is gone from Babe Ruth's lip, his teeth are clinched in hate,
He pounds with cruel violence his bat upon the plate.
And now the pitcher holds the ball, and now he lets it go.
And now the fence is shattered with the force of Babe Ruth's blow.

Oh, somewhere in this favored land the sun is shining bright;
The band is playing somewhere, and somewhere hearts are light.
And somewhere men are laughing and somewhere children shout;
But there is no joy in St. Louis—
MIGHTY BABE RUTH HAS KNOCKED HIS RECORD - BREAKING FIFTY-FIFTH

PERSONAL GLIMPSES
Continued

HAPPY DAYS FOR THE AMERICAN TROOPS ON THE RHINE

THE ordinary doughboy's salary in Coblenz is equivalent to 3500 marks a month, "which is the salary of a highly paid bank president." The American Army of Occupation there has succeeded in turning the German town into a fairly good American one. One-third of the doughboys there have German wives, German children—and American households. In short, the American troops on the Rhine find that the country agrees with them, and the Germans thereabouts seem to be agreed that the doughboys are good for the country. So at least reports William G. Shepherd, lately a visitor among these American troops, whom he calls "the lotus eaters of the Rhine." Like the original lotus eaters, very few of the Americans want to go home. As for the German attitude toward them, Mr. Shepherd says that he tried to get a certain Prussian officer of his acquaintance to criticize the Americans. The Prussian was willing enough to discuss the causes of the war, the execution of Nurse Cavell, and "he took no pains to hide the fact that he is still a Prussian at heart, and that one day France had better look out." But when it came to criticizing the American Army on the Rhine, writes Mr. Shepherd, in *Leslie's Weekly*—

"They are good soldiers," he said. "They are not mean-minded. They have no hate. They are orderly. They marry our girls. They spend their money. And if they stay here very much longer, I think we shall make good Germans out of them."

At several stations I noticed French sentries on duty.

"What are the French doing here?" I asked. "I thought the Americans were covering the Rhine territory."

"Yes," laughed the German officer. "Have you seen the plan of the American occupation drawn out on paper? It looks like a fan, doesn't it, with the handle at Coblenz? Well, the outer edge of that fan is all French. It is an American fan with an edging of French lace."

"Do you mean to tell me," I insisted, "that there are French troops between the Americans and Germany? French troops in front of the American troops?"

"*Ach*, sure!" He laughed at my indignation. "The French moved up in front of the Americans over a year ago."

And he was right. It was only another of those European tricks that were played on Americans at every turn during the war, both in military and diplomatic matters. At Coblenz I found out from American officials that he was dead right. The French troops had been moved in ahead of the Americans many months before, and no American officer could get into Germany without passing through the French lines.

However, if any one fears that the Americans on the Rhine are likely to be turned into Germans if they remain long enough in Coblenz, says Mr. Shepherd, "he has only

correspondent discovered "that incredible thing—a European German with 'pep.'" In fact, we are told:

If Coblenz doesn't turn American, it will be surprizing. At almost any stated time during the past eighteen months one-third of the doughboys in Coblenz had German wives, German children—and American households; with American papers, American books, American news about Big League ball scores, American candy, American chewing-gum, and letters and news from the folks in some American home across the water. I went into the homes of American soldiers in Coblenz, and they were not German homes. The food was American, the talk and the thought were American—and the wife and children were happy.

"At least four thousand German girls have emigrated to the United States," said an officer at Coblenz, "without ever stepping a foot out of this town."

The troops I found at Coblenz this time were very different from the soldiers I had seen there two years before. Those men of two years before had gone to Europe to fight; these men that I saw now had come to Europe to "occupy." The other men were impatient to get home; these men want to remain. They came to Germany to remain, and they want to stay as long as possible. They are the happiest, most contented men in the American Army, or, perhaps, in any army in the world for that matter, and they don't want to go home.

And why shouldn't they be happy? In the first place, in a military way they know they are doing something. The average military unit at a post in the United States is like an engine in a round-house waiting to be taken out for a purpose. It doesn't know when it will be used; possibly it may never be used again; but the men in the unit spend their time in keeping the wheels greased, the brasswork polished and steam up. It's different in Coblenz. Here every one knows that the big engine of which he is a part is doing a job; it isn't in the roundhouse. This gives military life at Coblenz a purpose.

The American soldier at Coblenz receives thirty-five American dollars a month. This has brought him as high as 3,500 marks a month, which is the salary of a highly paid bank president. If he goes to the army stores to buy food supplies brought from America, it is true that his $35 will not go far. But fresh German candy is better than stale American candy, and it costs forty marks a pound instead of a hundred. Bread, if he is a householder, will cost him five marks a loaf; meat, of good quality, will cost him half the price of candy. Butter—fresh German butter, not butter imported in tins—will cost him twenty marks a pound. Thirty-five hundred marks a month, some officers have estimated, is the equivalent of $3,000 a year in the United States.

And the Coblenz doughboys are savers, too. There is the example of the great department store, for instance. The Tietz Company owns great stores in several German towns. The Coblenz store is a good one. Some time ago, the officers at Coblenz say, the word went around among the doughboys that stock in the Coblenz Tietz Company was for sale. They made a rush for it. They dug into their savings and invested in Tietz. Everybody who could find any shares loose bought them. Tietz kept going up, but the doughboy was undaunted. Tietz was the tip. The result

The spare minutes which other young men wasted, he INVESTED in the one thing which pays larger dividends than anything else in the world. Send for the free booklet in which Dr. Eliot of Harvard tells how even 15 minutes a day can give a man this great asset—"The essentials of a liberal education."

The newsboy who has made a hundred millionaires

THOUSANDS of men are on his payrolls, many of them college graduates. To his achievements at least a hundred millionaires owe the foundation of their fortunes.

Yet his own schooling ended while he was still in his 'teens; as a mere boy he earned his living selling newspapers on the trains.

What was it that lifted him beyond other young men whose opportunities were so much greater? Genius? Yes; but he did not depend upon his genius.

Every Spare Hour He Read and Read

Between trains you always knew where to find young Edison, says his biographer. He would bury himself in the Detroit Public Library, and grapple "bravely with a certain section trying to read it through shelf by shelf, regardless of subject."

Much of his reading of course was wasted, for he had no guide. There was no man of broad knowledge or practical experience to select for him the few great books that are most worth while, and arrange them with notes and reading courses, so that even a few minutes a day would give "the essentials of a liberal education."

How eagerly young Edison, groping earnestly, aimlessly through a great mass of books would have welcomed the information which is contained in the free book offered below. It gives the plan, scope and purpose of Dr. Eliot's Five-Foot Shelf of Books.

Every well-informed man and woman should at least know something about this famous library. To grope aimlessly among 4,000,000 books—so many of them worthless—is an almost tragic waste of time.

DR. ELIOT'S FIVE-FOOT SHELF OF BOOKS

The ESSENTIALS in Fifteen Minutes a Day

The free book offered below tells how to eliminate groping; it explains how Dr. Eliot from his lifetime of reading and study, forty years of it as president of Harvard, has selected a *wasteless* library for busy men and women. How he has put into his Five-Foot Shelf the "essentials of a liberal education," and so arranged it with notes and reading courses that even fifteen minutes a day are enough.

How, in a word, any thoughtful man or woman can now get through pleasant reading, the knowledge of literature and life, the culture, the broad viewpoint which every university strives to give.

"For me," wrote one man who had sent in the coupon, "your little free book meant a big step forward, and it showed me besides the way to a vast new world of pleasure."

Every reader of this page is invited to have a copy of this handsome and entertaining little book. It is free, will be sent by mail, and involves no obligation of any sort. Merely clip the coupon and mail it to-day.

P. F. COLLIER & SON COMPANY
Publishers of Good Books Since 1875
NEW YORK

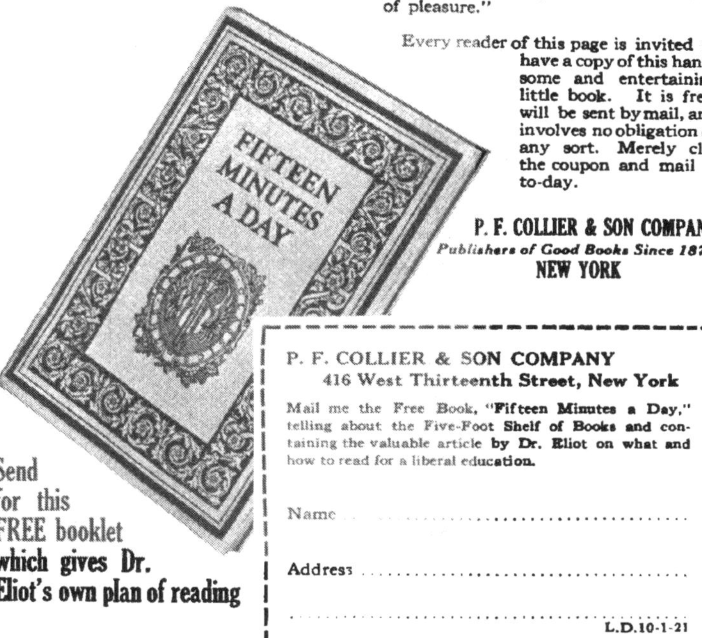

Send for this FREE booklet which gives Dr. Eliot's own plan of reading

P. F. COLLIER & SON COMPANY
416 West Thirteenth Street, New York

Mail me the Free Book, "**Fifteen Minutes a Day,**" telling about the Five-Foot **Shelf of Books** and containing the valuable article **by Dr. Eliot** on what and how to read for a liberal education.

Name ....

Address ....

....

L.D.10-1-21

PERSONAL GLIMPSES
Continued

action to prevent the control of the store falling into the hands of American soldiers. They issued a new stock, the story goes, which gives the directors control of the company. But the Tietz dividends which find their way into the pockets of the doughboys on the Rhine are large and luscious, as German dividends go, and Tietz Coblenz stocks are high-priced and sound. Many a boy or girl, born in Coblenz on the Rhine, will have a legacy of stock in this Rhine department store. The 8,000 men who have found their way, through army red tape, to Coblenz are long-headed young fellows.

But the money lure is not all. There is the matter of education for one thing, says Mr. Shepherd, for—

Every doughboy who reaches Coblenz must say whether or not he wants to go to school. If he hasn't sense enough to say "yes," there's no harm done; he just goes on being a bonehead. If he expresses a desire to go to school—and not more than one out of a hundred declines—he has the choice of three schools. He may go to a grade school, where he is taught all the elementary subjects that he would have in a good grade-school at home. Or, if he is sufficiently advanced, he may go to a high school, where he will decide to receive instruction in commercial education, including typewriting, stenography, bookkeeping, filing, and so forth. Or he may elect to take only high-school studies. If he is of sufficient caliber, he may go to a school that will fit him for West Point. In addition to these schools there are manual training schools, where in time he will receive a diploma in carpentering, machinery work, horseshoeing, telegraph, shoemaking, or one of several other trades and occupations. And, if he finds that these schools are unattractive, he may enter the agricultural college, where he will have training in stock-breeding, cattle-raising and agriculture—incidentally furnishing a large part of the army at Coblenz with fresh vegetables and quantities of excellent milk and butter.

Not one young man in a hundred who has left Coblenz has gone home without an education which he would have missed in private life. For three hours a day and five days a week almost everybody in Coblenz is in a schoolroom. Almost everywhere you go you will see some khaki-clad class emerging from some schoolroom.

We have considered the monetary and educational advantages of life at Coblenz. Now for pleasure. It exists abundantly. There are army dances somewhere every night. Not a day goes by that a doughboy with nothing else to do can not hear a band concert. In this same park there are boxing matches once or twice a week. Any youth who takes it into his head to make a try at boxing has only to declare his desires and hopes and his career as an army boxer is either opened to him or closed in the Coblenz ring very shortly. There are steamboat rides on the river and picnics at the castle of Ehrenbreitstein; which, standing directly across the river from American army headquarters on a challenging hill, invites every newcomer to climb to it. And, in addition to all this, there is that vast amount of lovemaking to be done which every American doughboy seems to accept as a sacred duty.

No; the doughboy that I found on the

Rhine this time doesn't want to go home.

This very desire to remain on the Rhine is wisely used by the officers to direct their troops toward orderliness and self-improvement. The soldier who "goes wrong" in Coblenz is punished by being sent home. By this I do not mean to say that every soldier or officer who comes back to the United States from Coblenz has been sent home for misconduct. There are scores of other reasons why he may have gone back to America. But the "bad ones" go home, and that is punishment enough. I learned that courts martial are not held oftener than is absolutely necessary. A soldier who shows the wrong spirit at Coblenz—who overdrinks or openly misbehaves in public places—is not likely to hear much censure. But he goes home on the next boat; and that's the end of it. When I was in Coblenz last spring the "bad ones" had been pretty well weeded out.

They may be lotus-eaters, these doughboys of ours on the Rhine, but they are wise ones.

Among the officers the desire to remain in Coblenz is even more pronounced than among the doughboys. Over four hundred wives of officers were in Coblenz last spring. An officer, with his family, is entitled to have a residence in Coblenz. The army secures it for him. The rental is nominal. The officer has his own car. Moreover, his American money enables him to keep up a standard of living that he could not possibly maintain on less than $15,000 a year in the United States.

"We're all spoiled and we know it," the wife of a prominent officer said to me last spring. "Life here is glorious, but we never could afford such things at home. The servants are cheap and wonderful. My husband and I and the children have a perfectly wonderful house, good enough for Fifth Avenue. There's the car, and the dances twice a week at the officers' club, and the excursions on the Rhine and the wonderful automobile roads along the river—oh, we don't ever want to go home again in our family. Besides," she added, "we're piling up a bank account."

There are figures that go to show that men in the army on the Rhine have saved as high as $1,000,000 a year.

In Coblenz, in truth, lies the kernel of the American Army. And because the American Army is so small the kernel ought to be kept very good. For every 10,000 citizens France has 185 men under arms; for every 10,000 citizens Great Britain has 93 men under arms; Japan, by the same ratio, has 36 men under arms. The United States stands at the very bottom of the list—or, perhaps, it might be called the very top of the list—with only 21 men under arms for every 10,000 of us.

"Do you think we ought to be called home?" they asked me at Coblenz.

I couldn't say anything else but "no"—even if they were having a good time. . . .

When I went down to the station to take the train for Paris I got into conversation with the conductor of the Pullman car, which is set aside for American officers by the French on the daily train for Paris.

"Any room?" I asked him.

"Not a berth taken," he said dolefully.

And I rode all night to Paris in that car—alone.

"I never get any tips on this car," lamented the porter. "I don't have a dozen passengers a week."

And so I had to give him a giant's tip, for Old Glory's sake, just because Paris has lost its lure for American officers on the Rhine.

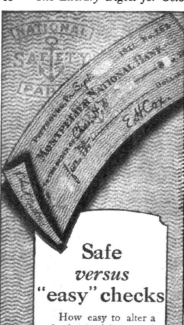

SCIENCE • AND • INVENTION • CONTINUED

SHOCK-ABSORBING PAVEMENTS

MATERIAL intended to withstand shock should have a certain amount of elasticity. This is true of fortifications, intended to bear the shock of projectiles; it is true also, says a writer in *The American City* (New York), of pavements, built to bear the impact of heavy traffic. The first few days of Germany's rush upon Belgium, he reminds us, taught that forts of stone and concrete could not withstand the terrible impact of giant explosives. But trenches in the earth and parapets of sand-bags absorb the impact of shells and reduce their shattering effect to a minimum. He proceeds:

"General Jackson applied the same principle in the War of 1812, only instead of using sand-bags, he employed bales of cotton to withstand the shells from the British men-of-war. The cotton-bales absorbed the impact and withstood the shattering effect of the explosives better than rigid forts!

"The great service given by sand-bags to the Belgians and by cotton-bales to General Jackson was rendered through their ability to absorb impact. It might be said, too, that their quality of resiliency, while not so pronounced as those of a material like rubber, was of considerable significance in withstanding the shattering effect of the explosives. All materials that are compressible have qualities of resiliency, and the ability of the sand-bags and cotton-bales to resume their original form after sudden and terrific impact was of no little consequence in their great service.

"From war-time necessity for shock-absorbing and resilient materials we may turn readily to commercial and civilian demand for materials having these same qualities. For instance, materials having resilient and shock-absorbing qualities must be used in the following: rubber tires—either solid or pneumatic—for automobiles and motor-trucks; rubber heels for shoes; golf-balls that withstand incessant banging; and roads and pavements that undergo terrific traffic.

"Toughness in a rubber tire is a necessary means to its longevity of service, but its quality of resiliency is just as important, the same as it is in a pavement. A rubber tire upon striking obstacles, whether in the form of a rut in a road or a rock or stone, must be able to resume its original form and shape after the impact.

"The manufacturers emphasize the idea that zinc oxid in rubber tires helps perfect the all-important feature of resiliency in the tires. They do this knowing the significance of the tire's ability to return to its original form after encountering obstacles.

"The manufacturers of rubber heels emphasize the same quality of resiliency in their product, and of necessity must apply the same principle as do the manufacturers of rubber tires.

"And does not the same hold good in the production of golf-balls? Think how long a piece of stone or concrete would last under the incessant pounding which a golf-ball must endure. A very short time, to be sure! The reason why the golf-ball lasts is that in addition to being tough, it is also resilient. The stone or concrete, too, may be tough, but its lack of resiliency results in its breaking.

"Eminent engineers consider resiliency of prime importance and infinite value in the construction of roads and pavements. The same principle holds good with these as with the shock-absorbing and resilient sand-bags and cotton-bales of war-time, and the resilient and shock-absorbing tires, rubber heels, and golf-balls of peace-time commercial life. The inability of too rigid, non-resilient pavements to 'iron themselves out' under terrific modern traffic is the reason for this general belief among engineers.

"Experiments begun by Government experts to determine the destructive effect of impact on pavements and to find a remedy show some striking results. Results now announced show that a weight of 7,750 pounds on the wheel of a truck moving at a speed of fifteen miles per hour becomes 43,000 pounds in its destructive effect if the wheel has a drop of one inch. Such a drop is very readily caused by any small obstruction or crack in the pavement. In solving the impact problem engineers use an asphalt cushion course. The cushion will absorb the shock so as to reduce the shattering effect of impact on the foundation.

"Expenditure for construction and maintenance of highways outside of cities is now averaging some $500,000,000 a year."

CHEAP CHARCOAL FOR GAS-MASKS

FOR GAS-MASKS a very dense charcoal with high absorptive power is required. We all remember collecting peach-pits for this purpose during the war. Coconut-shell is the material generally used. Such materials as these can evidently not be had in great quantity, but it has now been found by experiments made at the United States Forest Products Laboratory, Madison, Wis., that, instead of a dense woody substance, soft-wood sawdust may be employed and the necessary density arrived at by pressure. In this way, we are told by L. F. Hawley, writing in *The Journal of Industrial and Engineering Chemistry*, a charcoal was made of about the same density as coconut-shell charcoal and more rapidly absorptive of poisonous gases, chloro-picrin being taken as the standard. The best results were obtained in the laboratory, but good ones were reached in production on a commercial scale. Writes Mr. Hawley:

"Late in 1917 it was called to the attention of the Forest Products Laboratory that coconut-shell for making gas-mask charcoal was becoming scarce and that a dense charcoal manufactured from a plentiful domestic material would be desirable. The writer was acquainted with the process in which the distillation of briquetted hardwood sawdust was carried out under slight mechanical pressure for the purpose of preventing the briquets from falling to pieces during the process, and it was thought that by both making and distilling the briquets at much higher pressures an artificially dense charcoal could be produced.

"A small 'home-made' apparatus was used to try out this idea. It was soon

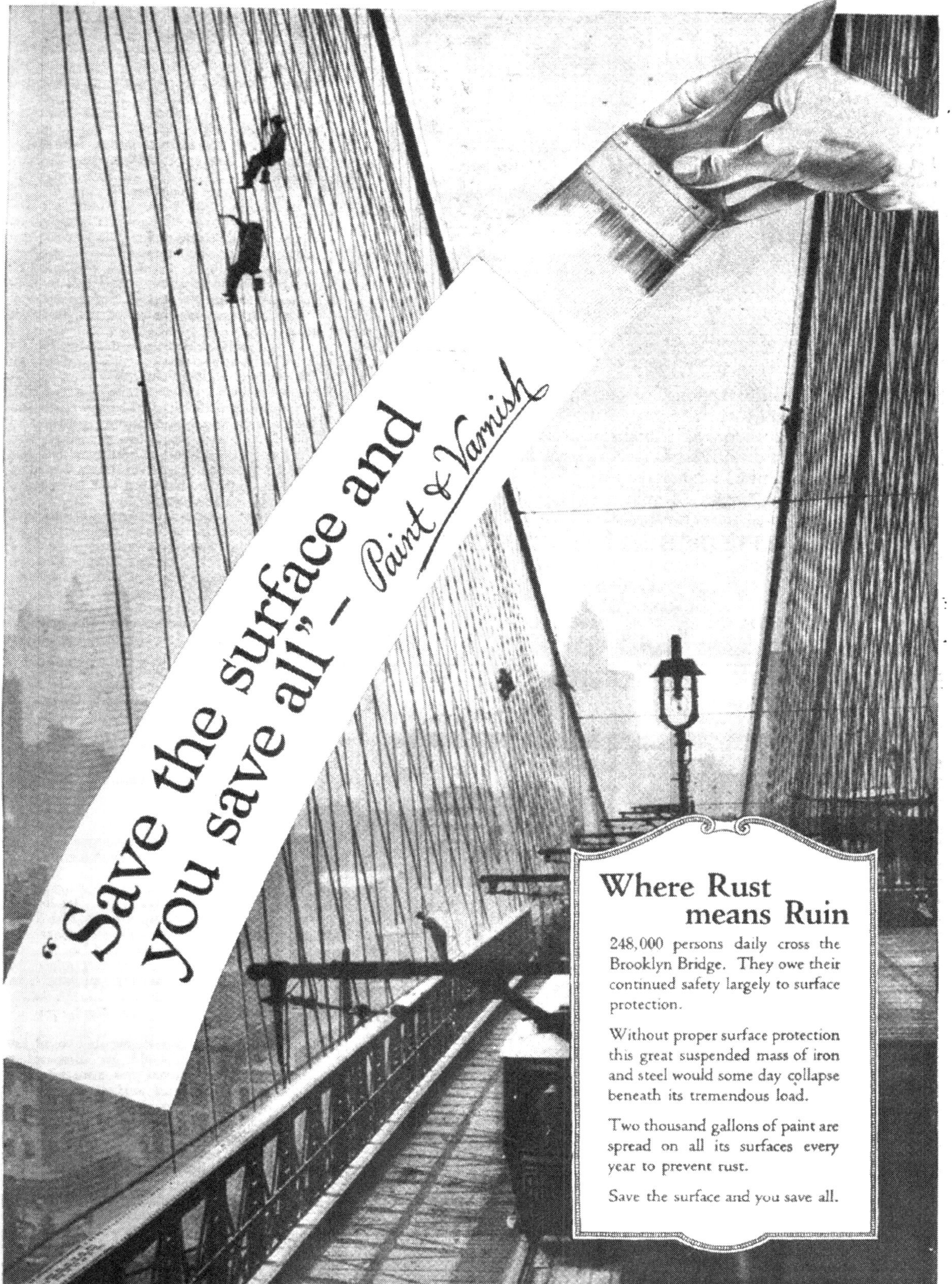
"Save the surface and you save all" — Paint & Varnish
Where Rust means Ruin
248,000 persons daily cross the Brooklyn Bridge. They owe their continued safety largely to surface protection.
Without proper surface protection this great suspended mass of iron and steel would some day collapse beneath its tremendous load.
Two thousand gallons of paint are spread on all its surfaces every year to prevent rust.
Save the surface and you save all.

SCIENCE AND INVENTION
Continued

found that fine sawdust was required for best results, and that the briquetting pressures should be at least fifteen tons per square inch.

"Several species of wood were tried under varying conditions of pressure before and during distillation, and a charcoal with maximum apparent density of 0.57 was made from maple-wood sawdust briquetted at 50,000 pounds per square inch, and distilled under 300 pounds per square inch. Apparently there is a stage during the distillation when the wood or charcoal is slightly plastic and the application of the proper amount of pressure at this time increases the density of the final charcoal.

"Not only a high apparent density was required but also an absorption value after activation, which value, however, varied in general with the density of the charcoal. Pine-woods with natural resin binders and hardwoods with binders of resin, hardwood pitch, asphalt, etc., were found to give higher gravity briquets and charcoal, but the absorption of these charcoals was in no case so high as that obtained from wood briquetted without a binder.

"Further work on untreated woods with or without binders was stopt by the discovery of a material which was very much more promising. It was found that the insoluble residue obtained by hydrolyzing sawdust with dilute acid and leaching out the sugar gave a denser briquet, and a higher yield of a denser charcoal, and that the charcoal was more absorbent after activation.

"When distilled under a pressure of 300 pounds per square inch, this charcoal resembled anthracite coal more than ordinary charcoal; it had a conchoidal fracture, was hard and shiny, and showed no trace of the structure of the wood from which it was made. In fact, thin pieces under the microscope were slightly translucent.

"These results were so promising that further small-scale work was considered unnecessary, and attempts were made to confirm the results in semicommercial apparatus.

"It was soon found that the optimum pressures as estimated from the results with the small apparatus were too high and that only about 125 pounds per square inch were required for the best results.

"It was also found that, as might be expected, a much more careful regulation of conditions was required in the larger apparatus to obtain a satisfactory product.

"Even with the best regulation of the temperature that could be obtained a portion of the charcoal was unsatisfactory in density. The end surfaces of all the briquets next to the plate were hard and dense, but the center portion of some of them was porous and soft.

"Since it seemed that it was only the pressure conditions of the small-scale work which were not reproduced very closely in the large-scale work, an attempt was made to reproduce the pressure conditions also. The pressure in the small-scale work was known to have been very uneven. This effect was simulated in the larger apparatus by adjusting the pressure control apparatus so that the pressure varied over a wide range. With these conditions it was possible to make a

WORLD'S LARGEST SALMON CANNERY

IN the United States, of course! It is situated at South Bellingham, Wash., and is the property of the Pacific-American Fisheries. In the height of the season this one cannery turns out 756,000 one-pound cans of salmon daily. This figure suggests that quite a number of people must be eating canned salmon pretty regularly, and would like to know how it is prepared. The machinery for cleaning the fish, cutting them up, filling the cans, exhausting the air, sealing them, and finally cooking the contents, is all electrically operated. The fish are caught in all sorts of ways—by trolling, gill-nets, seines, reef-nets, and traps. Indians troll from their canoes, but the use of the high-powered motor-boat is the favorite modern method, we are told by a writer in *The Journal of Electricity and Western Industry* (San Francisco, June 1). The purse seine boats range from 48 to 50 feet in length and have engines running from 20 to 85 horse-power. Eight fishermen compose a crew and carry their seines on a turn-table on the after-deck. On Puget Sound the seines are enormous, being as much as 300 fathoms long. We read:

"With the cooperation of a small launch or tender, the nets are paid out until they entirely surround a school of fish. Then the engine on the seiner operates and the winch does the rest, gradually hauling in the net and pulling in the purse line.

"Out on the water the purse-seiners, gill-netters, and others, deliver their fish to scows belonging to the cannery, taking a receipt for the same. These scows, and scows containing the fish direct from the traps, finally reach the wharf of the cannery. In unloading the scow several men stand therein and pitch the fish with a pew, which is a one-tined fork, throwing them on to a chain-conveyor, through which they drop onto an elevator conveyor provided with strips of wood placed crosswise to catch the fish as they drop. This elevator conveyor leads to another elevator running at right angles the length of the butchering-room in the cannery and is provided with chutes through which the salmon drop so as to be conveniently placed on the floor.

"In the course of their ascent on the elevator conveyor above referred to, a man stands near-by with a little adding machine by means of which he records, by species, the number of the salmon delivered.

"Salmon used to be butchered by Chinamen, but a machine has been invented which takes the place of the Chinamen and which has therefore been given the name of 'the iron Chink.' This machine is a marvelous piece of mechanism and butchers the salmon at the rate of sixty per minute. It cuts the head and tail off; divests the salmon of its fins; slits open the belly and sweeps out the entrails which drop through a hole in the floor and are carried on chain-conveyors to scows and transported to the fertilizer. After being thus butchered, the salmon is automatically released from the iron chink and passed to a belt-conveyor which carries it to a trough of running water where a Chinaman has still a chance to demonstrate his skill. And this he does to perfection, for he scours until not a trace of viscera or objectionable tissue remains.

Making Sales at Lowest Cost

THE SHADED PART *of this penny represents what it costs the full page advertiser to get you to read this message.*

—the addressing and mailing and delivery into your hands; all for 3/10ths of a cent;

—$4,000 for a full page advertisement that is delivered to 1,300,000 families;

—if the advertiser mailed a postal card to 1,300,000 separate addresses it would cost 6½ times as much or about $26,000;

—circular matter under one cent postage cannot be manufactured for less than $25.00 per thousand;

—in proper letter form with a two cent stamp the postage alone is $26,000 and the finished job (at the lowest of prices) $45,500 or eleven times what this page costs the advertiser.

WHILE you are reading this, so hundreds this very minute are reading it, too. Ever think how many of these hundreds need what *you* make? How many of them *want* what you make?

Unless you tell them about what you make, their needs lie dormant, unexpressed. Or else they are met by some other making something like what you make,

but costing more than your potential customer feels he would like to pay, or being less carefully made than your product, too poorly constructed, to really meet your potential customer's needs.

The reason businesses like Campbell's Soup and Victor and Arrow Collars and Oneida Community and The Literary Digest keep going up and up and up is because they tell the 110,000,000 more—and more often—about their product than other concerns in their same lines.

These concerns think in terms of fractions of a cent. They know there is no way to reach every one so quickly and at so low a cost as just sitting down and talking to people like this, through national advertising.

There is no mystery about it. It is just as natural as the way you develop friendships. Among your friends there are a lot of people you didn't like when you were sizing them up. And there are those other people—ex-friends—that you liked once, those who didn't measure up somehow.

Businesses that think well enough of themselves to try to win your friendship by talking to you this way, are not likely to disappoint you—at first or any time after.

Advertisers like those mentioned add to their reputation for making good goods and selling them right, the inestimable value of having millions of friends. The relation is positive, instead of nameless and negative. So the good advertising does lives after it.

The Literary Digest

354 FOURTH AVE., NEW YORK — 122 SO. MICHIGAN AVE., CHICAGO

Bankers, heads of industrial enterprises, lawyers whose clients discuss advertising with them are invited to send for a DIGEST *representative. We are frequently able to give good advice leading toward a proper solution of the possible application of advertising to business enterprises.*

SCIENCE AND INVENTION
Continued

"The salmon are now trucked in large h bins to an elevator conveyor where ey pass crosswise beneath circular gang ıives, set at such intervals that they cut e fish into pieces suitable for talls, flats, half-flats, as the case may be. From ıese elevators the fish drop into the bins ady for the filling machine. Cans flowg in a continuous stream from a loft ›ove on an inclined chute pass the filling achine, and in passing each receives from ıe plunger its quota of salmon.

"There is a device connected with the ling machine which furnishes the requisite nount of salt, about a quarter of an ınce to each can. If the machine is not equipped, the salt is in the can before it aches the filler. This is the only foreign ıbstance that enters a can of salmon."

As the cans move along two young omen stationed on either side of the line, niformed and wearing cotton gloves, ıpply any deficiency from pieces of salıon ready to hand. The cans then pass ırough jets of water and an ingenious eighing-machine rejects automatically ıy can that does not come up to standard. till on the belt conveyor, they then pass › the clincher where the cap is clinched ghtly to the can so as to permit the exausting of the air after it enters the acuum machine. To quote further:

"From the clincher the cans pass to the ealing machine which for the most part ›nsists of a revolving disk with six indiıdual chambers. The doors of these ıambers open automatically to receive ıe can and each chamber is furnished with sealing mechanism. When the can enters ıe chamber the door automatically closes nd exhaustion immediately commences. 'his is effected by pumps some distance way. As soon as the air is exhausted, ouble seaming takes place; that is, the dge of the top of the can and the flange n the side are hooked together and turned n with such force that with the aid of the ement gasket, used in seaming, it makes a ıermetic closure. This completed, the ıir is admitted automatically to the hamber by a release valve and the can is lischarged.

"There are eighteen lines of machinery n this cannery, each capable of sealing ı2,000 cans per ten-hour day. The canıery at the height of the season can, herefore, turn out daily 756,000 cans or .5,750 cases of salmon, each containing 48 ›ne-pound cans.

"From the vacuum machine the cans ılip down an inclined plane called 'the oader' onto iron trays called coolers. The ›oolers are piled on trucks and the trucks ıre wheeled on rails to the retorts, which s the name of the big horizontal steel ›ylinders where the processing or cooking takes place. The processing is by steam and lasts one hour and thirty minutes, in a temperature of 240 F.

"After processing, the coolers with their burdens of cans are trucked to the washing tank, and then pass to the warehouse.

"The rendering plant of the company is located on Eliza Island, six miles from the cannery. For each 1,000 cases of salmon packed two barrels of oil and one ton of fish meal are produced.

"The oil is used in paints, in tanning, in

SCIENCE AND INVENTION
Continued

making soaps, tree sprays, etc. Fish meal is used in poultry food. It is rich in protein and bone phosphates and is combined with grain meals and mill feeds in the preparation of the poultry food. Fish meal is highly recommended also as food for dairy cows.

"Electricity is employed throughout the plants, about 350 kilowatts being the present figure for the Bellingham cannery."

HUMAN TROPISMS

WHEN a plant sends its shoot upward and its root downward; when a moth flies toward the light—they are exhibiting what the biologists call tropisms. They are reacting to certain physical influences as surely as when they fall to the ground under the influence of gravity. An editorial writer in *Chemical and Metallurgical Engineering* (New York) pictures such organisms as under the illusion of voluntary action, and he wonders whether human beings, too, when doing something for a fancied reason that seems to them logical, are not also hurried along by influences that have nothing to do with brain action. Men and women, he thinks, have their tropisms as well as insects, fish, or plants. Pure constructive thought is rare. Says the editor:

"Dr. Jacques Loeb, of the Rockefeller Institute, has made many and profound studies of tropisms, and published several books on the subject. A tropism is a non-volitional act. Perhaps we can best explain it in the example of a species of fish with which Dr. Loeb was at one time experimenting. The fish were heliotropic—that is, the presence of light in a dark place compelled them to turn toward it. Thus if such fish are placed in a globe and if the globe be taken to a dark room into which a lighted candle or other light is brought they will forsake everything and keep their noses prest against the side of the globe nearest the light. Move the light and all the fish will move to face it and stay right there as long as the light does; stay there until they float, belly up, on the surface with the life gone out of them. Disagreements, the search for food, love-making, and all the other joys and sorrows of fish life are forgotten or abandoned against what seems a grand passion of curiosity. Take the light away or make the whole room generally light again and the fish will swim about as before just as tho nothing extraordinary had happened.

"But if, while they are engaged in what seems like pop-eyed and perpetual wonder at the burning candle, we secretly lead into the water in which they swim a tube conducting carbon dioxid, we shall soon meet an amazing phenomenon. As the saturation of the water with CO_2 reaches a given point the apparent curiosity of the fish ceases, and one by one they give up their posts of observation and swim around and back and forth with no more reference to the burning candle or the single bright light than a society goldfish. The little extra carbonic acid made them just like others. The phenomenon is an instructive example of photochemistry, and a demonstration of the theory of mass action in life."

Now suppose, the writer says, that these fish were people and could talk. And suppose we should ask the biggest one why he looked at the candle. He goes on:

"'Why,' he would reply, 'I observed a new element in our world, and I didn't know what it was. So I made up my mind that I would not leave my post until I learned what it was, or at least what it would do. 'Here,' I said, 'is danger, and only death itself can drag me from my vigil until I know what it signifies'!

"Then we might ask him why he quit looking at it and gave up his quest. In reply he would declare that he finally reached the conclusion that the light was not dangerous; that it was a thing that did not concern the life of the colony. At this point he dismissed the subject from his mind and went about his business, or he might offer any other reason *ex post facto*. An intimation as to the influence of carbon dioxid upon his opinions would offend him. He would want us to understand that he knew what he was about, that he was a fish of character, and not to be swayed in his opinions by carbon dioxid or anything else. If we were to ask him why the other fish also began to swim about freely at the same time as he, he would distend his chest and inform us with a dignified swish of his tail that he was probably not wholly without influence among his neighbors. Other fish would claim similar originality, fishy books would be written on the claims of the various leaders who brought the community back to 'normalcy,' and the history of the great light disturbance would become a subject of academic dispute, and later a standard means of training the minds of young fish.

"Now we're like that; very like it. For the past few years this country has been very prosperous and money has been easy to make. Thinking has hardly been necessary. We know of a young engineer who knew his business moderately well, but found it more profitable to work as a journeyman carpenter. Work has been very well paid. Hundreds of thousands of persons—men being scarce—have consequently declared that labor is the true source of all wealth; and there are tons of so-called literature to prove it. This means that, given a man, a horse, and a cart, the cart and its earnings belong to the horse.

"Gradually conditions are changing. The impossible has happened. American dollars have become so precious in comparison with foreign money that the foreigner refuses to buy of us. Ten dollars a day and bankers' hours—which are the hours banks are open rather than the hours bankers work—are still standards of payment for certain kinds of labor, but the jobs are getting scarce. Labor is beginning to underbid, and while we insist that labor is not a commodity and that every man and woman who works in an organization is part of its human staff, the fact remains that a little competition is a wholesome thing. There are limits to the earning power of a husky shoulder carrying a hod, especially in comparison with the earning power of thinking. Tropisms are less valuable than thoughts.

"Now if our good dollars have got to be so valuable that the poor foreigner can't use them, then we must do something besides strut about and explain our glory and our might and our wisdom in making our dollars so valuable. When we do that we are merely displaying tropisms."

INVESTMENTS AND FINANCE

TARIFF MAKING BY JURY

HOW would it do, instead of spending many weary months devising a tariff bill in Congressional committee rooms, to leave it to Secretary Hoover to appoint a jury of representative American business-men to put a protective tariff on any individual commodity which is winning its way in our markets on account of cheap production abroad? An exactly similar scheme goes in force in England this month. There is a new Safeguarding of Industries Act which is technically a revenue measure but is really high tariff protection, having been passed chiefly through fear of German competition. So the editor of *The American Exporter* (New York) informs us. As he describes the British plan:

Under this law, whenever complaint is made to the Board of Trade, which corresponds to our Department of Commerce, that a commodity is being sold in Great Britain at less than the actual cost of production in the country in which it is manufactured, or at prices which, by reason of depreciation of the currency of the country in which it is manufactured, are below the prices at which the same goods could be made profitably in Great Britain, then the Board of Trade is to call upon a committee or jury of five business men to ascertain and report upon the facts. This jury is to be selected from a large, permanent panel appointed by the president of the Board of Trade.

If the jury finds that the case is proved, its verdict to that effect will be followed by an order from the Board of Trade, approved by the House of Commons, placing the guilty commodity under a duty of 33⅓ per cent. But to warrant such a verdict the jury or committee must not only find that the facts with regard to the foreign prices are proven, but that the British industry making the same class of commodity is being conducted with reasonable efficiency and economy.

American products will not be affected for the reason that there is a treaty or convention existing between the United States and Great Britain which forbids the levying of discriminatory duties. The law specifically exempts from its provisions the commodities of any country with which such an agreement is in force.

The most important countries to whose commodities the law will apply are Germany, Austria, France and Czecho-Slovakia, with none of which countries Great Britain has any agreement limiting her freedom of action in the matter of discriminatory duties, and in addition all their currencies are heavily depreciated in terms of the pound sterling. The law states that no action is to be taken with regard to commodities whose prices are affected by currency depreciation, unless the currency of the country in question is depreciated not less than 33⅓ per cent.

Under another section of the new law a comparatively few commodities are placed under a 33⅓ per cent. duty, from whatever country they come. The commodities specified are lines in which Germany has been conspicuous.

SOVIET GOLD ALL GONE

ALTHO the Bolsheviki controlled an enormous stock of gold when they came into power in Russia, this has practically vanished, and according to reports received by Secretary of Commerce Hoover, Soviet Russia is now bankrupt, as far as its gold supply is concerned. It has been estimated by the Department of Commerce, which has been receiving reports regularly from Washington, that the Soviet government held $19,040,200 in gold on August first. The total value of gold exported from August 2 to August 10 was $17,775,889, leaving an estimated balance of $1,264,311. This last-named sum of gold must have vanished by the end of August at the rate at which the Soviet government has been disposing of its gold by shipment abroad. Further information is given in a Washington dispatch to the New York *Times:*

The Soviet government has disposed of about $175,000,000 worth of gold since February of the present year. The Russian Government gold reserve at the beginning of the World War in 1914 was $801,500,000. The Russian Government sold $330,000,000 of this gold to England for Russian credit abroad, with the important agreement that the gold should be returned to Russian use after the war. The old Russian Government also shipped $2,500,000 of its gold reserve stock to Sweden for credit during the war. Consequently the balance of Russian national gold reserve on hand at the time of the outbreak of the Bolshevik revolution was $469,000,000, all that was left of the original stock of $801,500,000.

Starting with this balance of $469,000,000, the Bolsheviki received from other sources, mainly through confiscations, additional gold valued at $177,000,000, so that the total amount of gold in the State Bank in Petrograd in November, 1918, was about $646,000,000. Out of this the Bolsheviki paid to Germany under the terms of the Brest-Litovsk Treaty as the first instalment of contribution the sum of $160,000,000. The Siberians also managed to capture $330,000,000 worth of Russian gold. This left a balance of $156,000,000 on hand in the possession of the Soviet government in the summer of 1919.

The Soviet managed to increase this amount by the recapture from Siberia, after the collapse of Kolchak, the sum of $233,998,519 out of the $330,000,000 which the Siberians had captured.

The Russian Soviet government also came into possession of $215,000,000 of Rumanian gold which had been sent into Russia for safekeeping.

The Soviet authorities, according to information in possession of the State and Commerce Departments, early in February of 1921 themselves reported that the balance then on hand amounted to approximately 350,000,000 rubles, or $175,000,000. This was not accounted for by the Soviet leaders, but it is known to American officials that a certain amount of the Soviet gold had been paid for these ceded terri-

Goldwyn
Presents

Dangerous Curve Ahead

A comedy drama of American married life — with Helene Chadwick and Richard Dix

by

Rupert Hughes

Directed by
E. Mason Hopper

THE DAILY DIVORCE:
Every morning Harley had to tear himself away from her in order to get to the office—late!

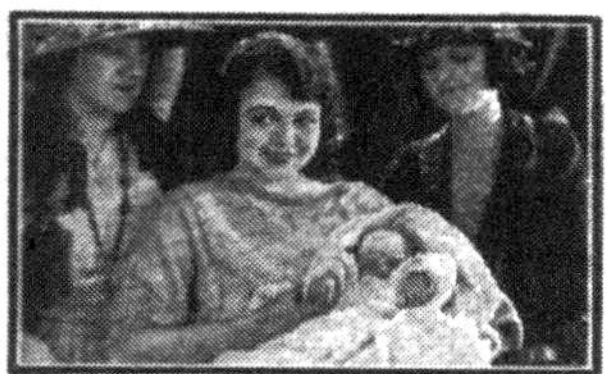

THE FIRST BABY:
Phoebe learns that there is a lot besides poetry about bringing up babies.

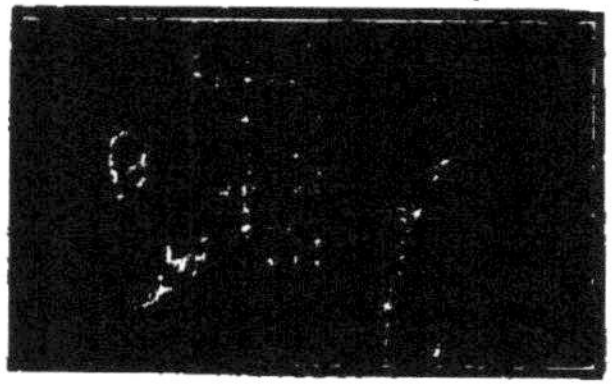

THE OLD LOVER:
The long business trip means for Harley the big chance; but for

MOST motion pictures end with a marriage. But here's one that begins with a marriage—a marriage of just two such young people as started their great adventure next door to you this summer.

Any wife will laugh a lot and cry a lot—when she sees it. Husbands will come away from this picture with a deeper understanding of what their young wives have to cope with. Fathers and mothers will chuckle and weep over it.

There are dangerous curves that every married couple must take. What are they? How can they be rounded without a crash?—Perhaps you think you know.

"Dangerous Curve Ahead" shows them to you cleverly, lightly, yet with a deep insight into human hearts.

Author and director worked together for one year on this picture. Such close co-operation is the result of Goldwyn's plan of bringing American authors into direct contact with picture production.

This picture *lives*. It is something refreshingly new in the art of the screen.

A Goldwyn Picture

beginning
Oct. 2nd Nation-wide showing
Watch your theatre

INVESTMENTS AND FINANCE
Continued

tories of Russia, other amounts were used for the maintenance of Soviet agencies abroad, as well as for political propaganda, and that the balance had been distributed abroad as an attraction for trade and political relations with Russia.

STEEL WAGES BACK TO 1917 LEVEL

A THIRD successive cut in wages by the United States Steel Corporation took effect on August 20. This cut, as the New York *Evening Post* notes, brings the wages of unskilled laborers down to $3 for a ten-hour day, which was the scale in force on May 1, 1917. As we read:

The last cut previous to the one announced for August 29 occurred on July 16 of this year and was in the form of a cessation of payment of time and a half for time over eight hours. It amounted to a reduction of about 9.5 per cent. With the present cut, wages will remain 60 per cent. higher than they were in 1915.

The following is a table showing changes in wages from 1915 to the present for unskilled labor.

	Wages 10-hour day	*Per cent. advance*	*Per cent. advance over 1915 rate.*
1915	$2.00	——	——
Feb. 1, 1916	2 20	10 0	10.0
May 1, 1916	2.50	13 6	25.0
Dec. 15, 1916	2 75	10.0	37.5
May 1, 1917	3 00	9.0	50 0
Oct. 1, 1917	3.30	10 0	65.0
April 16, 1918	3.80	15.0	90.0
Aug. 1, 1918	4 20	10.5	110 0
Oct. 1, 1918	4 62	10.0	131.0
Feb. 1, 1920	5 06	10.0	153 0
May 16, 1921	4.05	[1]20.0	102.5
July 16, 1921	3.70	[2]9.5	85.0
Aug. 29, 1921	3 00	[1]18.9	50.0

[1] Reduction. [2] Elimination of time and a half for overtime work over eight hours.

THERE IS ONE INDUSTRY WHICH ALWAYS EXPANDS IN TIMES OF DEFLATION

WHEN the world has more gold than it needs to back its currency and regulate exchanges, then industrial development booms, and when the reverse is the case conservative, safe and efficient business is the order of the day. In the latter case all industrial development is restricted with one exception, and that exception *The Wall Street Journal* goes on to say, is obviously gold. "Gold development booms and other development is at a minimum." The writer explains these statements by making a brief reference to modern financial history:

After our panic in 1893, felt all over the world, and during the long dull years which followed it there was an unprecedented gold boom. This was the Transvaal boom of 1895. That activity spread to little else. The new Kaffir market alone was active in the London Stock Exchange and our own stock market was as dull as dishwater.

This is no mere coincidence. Gold was

discovered in Australia in 1857, another panic year. The world experienced the usual after-effects of the panic, but the Australian gold boom went on.

Gold discovery in California in 1849 developed right through a period of dulness, and there had been a panic in Europe in 1847. So far as our business was concerned, although we were not much influenced by Europe at that time, the only effect of the gold was to check the outflow of specie. Curiously and significantly, it did not make up for the familiar aftermath of uncertainty following the Mexican War.

Reports from the Porcupine district in the Province of Ontario show that gold miners are coming back to work and finding it, but at moderate wages. How many people know that the Hollinger mine there is now considered the second largest gold mine in the world?

As the purchasing power of gold must necessarily increase, the inducement to develop gold deposits anywhere they can be found grows steadily more attractive. The world during the war limited gold production for that of the baser but more useful metals. With the demand for the latter falling off and the decline in commodities and wages, adventure inevitably turns to gold.

Gold is history's significant exception—significant because it is the exception which proves the economic rule.

HOW GERMANY WILL PAY FRANCE IN MATERIALS

A MUTUALLY agreeable arrangement has recently been reached whereby the Germans will be enabled to pay their reparations to a considerable extent by means of goods rather than cash, while the French will get a large supply of materials quickly. As *Bradstreet's* informs its readers:

This agreement provides for the delivery by the German Government of building materials valued at 7,000,000,000 gold marks to France by May 1, 1926, beginning on October 1 next. In return France is to credit Germany with 1,000,000,000 marks annually on the reparations account in case the deliveries reach that amount, and to reimburse Germany for any sum in excess of the former's share of the reparations payments within the period. In working out the agreement in practise two companies are to function, one organized in Germany and the other in France. Both are to be under government control, but participation of private capital is to be permitted to a certain extent. The German company, according to report, is to take care of the assembling, transportation and delivery of the material at suitable points, payment being made to the producers or manufacturers out of bonds of the German Government specially issued for the purpose. The French company, it is understood, is to sell the material thus provided in the open market exclusively for the rebuilding of northern France, while the French Government will arrange that prices shall not be cut below a figure allowing of a reasonable competition with private French producers or manufacturers. Some opposition to the plan may be encountered in the legislative bodies, but it is expected that it will be overcome. The project is one that should commend itself to the Germans because it enables them to pay the reparations to a considerable extent by means of goods rather than cash, while the French

CURRENT EVENTS

FOREIGN

September 15.—Premier Lloyd George calls off the proposed peace parley between Sinn Fein and British representatives because of Eamon De Valera's insistence that Ireland must enter the conference as a sovereign state.

Rioting is renewed in Belfast, and two women are injured.

Bolivia withdraws her demand for the inclusion of her dispute with Chile in the business of the Assembly of the League of Nations.

September 16.—Eamon De Valera replies to Premier Lloyd George that the peace negotiators must meet without prejudice and be untrammeled by any conditions except those imposed by facts.

Lord Robert Cecil, of England, launches a campaign to require the League of Nations to conduct open sessions.

An insurrection is reported in Bosnia, now a part of Jugo-Slavia.

September 17.—Premier Lloyd George and Eamon De Valera exchange more telegrams looking to the proposed peace conference.

The German Reichsrat ratifies the treaty of peace between Germany and the United States.

Sir Ernest Shackleton, the British explorer, starts on his quest into the uncharted regions of the Antarctic, South Atlantic and Pacific Oceans.

September 18.—Premier Lloyd George notifies Eamon De Valera that he can not meet the Sinn Fein delegates as representatives of a sovereign and independent tate.

A demonstration and parade are held in Vienna under pan-German auspices to protest against "the ignominous peace" and to demand immediate union with Germany.

Greek forces operating against the Turkish nationalists in Asia Minor are reported in retreat to previous positions.

Maintenance cost of the United States forces of occupation in the Rhineland is $278,067,000, according to figures made public by the Reparations Commission in Paris; of France 230,485,470 French francs; of England, £52,881,298; of Belgium, 378,731,390 Belgian francs; and of Italy, 15,207,717 French francs.

September 19.—Eamon De Valera suggests in a note to Lloyd George that a "treaty of accommodation and association" be concluded between the peoples of Ireland and Great Britain and the British Dominions in order to "end the dispute forever."

All Russia is being warned of impending war with Poland and Roumania, according to dispatches from Riga.

September 20.—The British Government formally accuses the Russian Soviet government of flagrant violations of Russia's undertaking under the trade agreement with Great Britain to cease anti-British propaganda.

A revolt is reported in the Russian Baltic fleet, and 400 officers are said to have been arrested and taken to Moscow.

The Peking Union Medical College, erected by the China Medical Board of the Rockefeller Foundation at a cost of $8,000,000, is dedicated.

DOMESTIC

September 14.—John Bassett Moore, an authority on international law and formerly a member of the Permanent elected to be one of the eleven Judges of the League of Nations' International Court of Justice.

September 15.—President Harding felicitates the five Republics of Central America on the celebration of the centenary of their independence.

The four packing houses of Chicago announce a return to the open-shop plan at the expiration of their agreement entered into before Federal Judge Alschuler.

September 16.—Major-General Charles T. Menoher, Chief of the Army Air Service since 1918, asks Secretary of War Weeks to relieve him of that office and assign him to a command in the field.

The Senate Finance Committee decides to exempt incomes between $5,000 and $6,000 from 1 per cent. surtax provided for in the Fordney bill and in existing law, and to shade down the surtax on incomes up to $66,000.

Savings of small investors throughout the country total approximately $27,000,000,000, of which $21,000,000,000 is invested in Government securities and $6,000,000,000 is represented by the deposits of more than 30,000 savings banks, according to figures issued by the Treasury. The savings average $250 to every man, woman and child in the country.

The bodies of the American victims of the dirigible *ZR-2*, wrecked in England, reach New York on board the British cruiser *Dauntless*.

September 17.—The Senate Finance Committee votes to impose a tax of $6.40 a gallon on all distilled spirits withdrawn for any purpose other than manufacture.

The New Jersey American Legion Convention adopts a resolution condemning the Ku Klux Klan and warning all non-Legion men to serve their country without race or creed prejudice.

Municipal authorities of Louisville, Kentucky, ban a meeting of organizers of the Ku Klux Klan.

The United States Railroad Labor Board establishes a precedent that employees may not be discharged without cause, in a decision requiring the Butler County Railroad to reinstate two foremen released because they belonged to the same union as the men working under them.

September 18.—Railroad shopmen have voted to strike against the general railroad wage reduction of July 1, according to President B. M. Jewell, but will defer action until the promulgation of working rules now pending before the United States Railroad Labor Board.

Senators Kenyon and Shortridge, of the Congressional investigation committee, visit the tent colony of the Mingo County coal-mine strikers to hear their side of the causes of the industrial troubles in that region.

The National Legislative Committee of the American Legion appeals to employers to help the unemployed.

September 19.—The State Department announces that all legitimate Russian interests will be protected at the conference on armament limitation.

Thousands of unemployed world-war veterans parade in Boston, and petition Governor Cox to take immediate steps to relieve the unemployment situation.

The City Council and the Baptist Ministers Conference of Chicago take steps to check the growth of the Ku Klux Klan.

William T. Tilden defeats Wallace F. Johnson, and retains the national lawn tennis championship.

September 20.—Dr. J. D. Prince, professor of Slavonic languages at Columbia University, is selected by President

THE SPICE OF LIFE

Naturally.—The hand that used to rock the cradle never saw the inside of a $20 pair of shoes.—*The Trades Unionist (Washington, D. C.).*

An Expensive Luxury.—"Are they unhappily married?"

"Oh! I hardly think they're rich enough for that."—*London Mail.*

The Moneymoon.—"Mr. ——, the popular rugger player, is joining the ranks of the Benedicts this week, his finance being due out from home."—*Malay Paper,* quoted in *Punch.*

It Might Be Discouraging.—A female salmon yields about 3,500 eggs per year. This is the sort of thing we hush up for fear our Wyandottes should give up trying.—*London Opinion.*

When it Matters.—There isn't much difference between sight and vision, except when you make the mistake of calling a woman one when you mean the other.—*Fayette (Mo.) Advertiser.*

Remarkable.—"It is simply rotten. The people here treat us as if they knew we were not accustomed to much money—and yet I am always talking about money."—*Meggenderfer Blaetter (Munich).*

The Only Question.—"I wonder how many men will be made unhappy when I marry?"

"It all depends upon how many times you marry."—*Kasper (Stockholm).*

Not Exactly Gallant.—The General Assembly of the Presbyterian Church of England has resolved to admit women to be elders. Even behind their backs it sounds unchivalrous.—*Punch (London).*

The Silver Lining.—"Good Heavens, man; pretty badly smashed up, ain't you? Anybody with you?"

"Yes, the chap who was trying to sell me this used car."—*Harper's Magazine.*

A Futurist Worker.—"You look tired!"

"Well, it's hard work carrying a hod of bricks up to the third story."

"Have you been doing it long?"

"No—I start to-morrow!"—*Simplicissimus (Munich).*

Have an Object in Life.—THE OLD 'UN—"Pluck, my boy, pluck: that is the one essential to success in business."

THE YOUNG 'UN—"Yes, of course, I know that. The trouble is finding some one to pluck."—*London Opinion.*

A Timid Ditty.—MOTHER—"Do you feel timid about asking Jack for money, dear?"

DAUGHTER (a quite new bride)—"No, mother, but he seems very timid about giving it to me."—*London Mail.*

It Sounds Like Trouble Very Early.—"The home of Mr. and Mrs. John M—— was the scene of a beautiful wedding yesterday when their daughter Margaret was joined in holy deadlock to Mr. David P——."—*Calgary Herald,* quoted in *Lon-*

Bound to Be a Happy Marriage.—YOUNG BRIDE—"I wish I'd married a man who could paint the beauty of nature."

TACTFUL HUSBAND—"My dearest, you'd soon get tired of posing!"—*London Mail.*

A Fine Point.—"What are you doin' of, James?"

"Sharpenin' a bit o' pencil."

"You'll 'ave the union after you, me lad. That's a carpenter's job."—*Punch (London).*

The Finale.—MRS. BROWN—"I hear the vicar thinks your daughter has a real genius for reciting, Mrs. Smith."

MRS. SMITH—"Yes. All she wants, he says to me, is a course of electrocution, just to finish 'er off, like."—*London Opinion.*

Auto-Attraction. — DAUGHTER — "He's frightfully attractive, I think."

MOTHER—"I can't see it."

DAUGHTER—"Good Heavens, do you mean to say you can't see that big yellow car?"—*The Passing Show (London).*

Perfectly Unspeakable.—"Dr. Stratton constantly tells how disgusting these things are which he is -asi m rdleu upeupeuptupu mons. They are disgusting, and no preacher should discuss disgusting things in public in this way."—*New York Times.*

The Correct Announcement. — NEW COOK—"What do I say, Ma'am, 'Dinner is served' or 'Dinner is ready'?"

MISTRESS—"Well, if it is anything like it was yesterday, it would be simpler to say 'Dinner is spoiled.'"—*Karikaturen, Christiania.*

Good for Nerve, Anyway.—FIRST INVALID—"Is this a good place for the nerves?"

SECOND INVALID—"Oh, yes! When the proprietor of this hotel first came here he charged ten shillings a day—now he has the nerve to charge twenty-five!"—*The Passing Show (London).*

The Etiquette of the Road.—Even if it is a good deal of trouble, motorists usually can avoid some additional trouble by stopping as soon as possible after hitting a pedestrian. And, besides, ordinary manners demand that he stop; the pedestrian nearly always does.—*Kansas City Star.*

Not a Pose.—"How long have you been indisposed, my poor fellow?" asked a fair visitor at a hospital of a big negro who was strapped up in bed with an injured back.

"Dis ain't no pose 'tall, miss," answered the patient in tones of disgust. "Dis am merely de careless manner in which dem forgetful doctors went away and lef' me yestiddy."—*The American Legion Weekly.*

A Temptation.—One of the hardest things in the world for a colyumist to do is keep his hands off society items when they come in sequence like this:

"Mrs. Q. S. Jones and daughters of Little River, Neb., arrived yesterday for a two weeks' visit with Mr. and Mrs. K. I. Smith of Locust street.

"Mr. K. I. Smith of Locust street left for New York last night on a two or possibly three weeks' business trip."—*Kansas*

Did *you* answer this ad?

The Literary Digest for July 9, 1921

A New Floor On Your Old
without stopping production

You can put Genasco Vulcanite Mastic floors in your factory without disturbing the machinery or stopping production. Think of the time, trouble and expense saved!

Genasco Mastic is laid in a continuous sheet over your old, worn-out floors—whether wood, concrete, tile or brick. One hour later it is ready for use.

Genasco Mastic floors are acid-proof, moisture-proof, noiseless and dustless. They are free from cracks and crevices and can be kept faultlessly clean and sanitary with ease.

Unlike concrete, tile or brick floors, Genasco Mastic floors are shock-absorbing, do not generate cold and do not tire the feet of your workers.

Water cannot penetrate Genasco Mastic. Acid does not faze it. Neither do temperature changes or vibrations. The heaviest kind of trucking and foot traffic have little or no effect on it.

Genasco Mastic is made of Trinidad Lake Asphalt—a world-old product tempered in the fires of creation—the most element and wear-resisting material known to science.

Millions of square feet of Genasco Mastic floors are now giving splendid service in factories, railway terminals, hospitals, schools, post offices, stores, packing houses, etc., in all parts of the world.

Write at once for our illustrated booklet describing the various uses and methods of applying Genasco Vulcanite Mastic. Also ask us for information regarding any other product of the Genasco Line.

THE BARBER ASPHALT PAVING COMPANY

New York Chicago Pittsburgh PHILADELPHIA St. Louis Kansas City Atlanta

GENASCO LINE

Trinidad Lake Asphalt (For streets and roofs)
Standard Trinidad Built-Up Roofing
Bermudez Road Asphalt (For Road building)
Genasco Roll Roofing
Genasco Seal-bac Shingles
Genasco Latite Shingles
Genasco Vulcanite Mastic Flooring
Genasco Acid-Proof Paint
Genasco Industrial Paint
Genasco Boiler Paint
Genasco Asphalt Putty
Genasco Asphalt Pipe Coating
Genasco Asphalt Fibre Coating
Genasco Tile Cement
Genasco Waterproofing Asphalts
Genasco Waterproofing Felts and Fabrics
Genasco Battery Seal Compound
Genasco Mineral Rubber
Genasco Mineral Spirits
Genasco Base Oils
Genasco Flotation Oils
Genasco Motor Oils
Genasco Soluble Oils
Iroquois Road-building Machinery

Genasco

Asphaltic Roofing, Flooring, Paints and Allied Protective Products

Thousands, after reading the above ad, said: "That's the floor I want!"

A veritable deluge of orders and inquiries from all parts of the United States and Canada have kept pouring in since this advertisement appeared in July. Such a tremendous response — the great number and diversity of replies — is indicative of three things: the extraordinary demand for an industrial and institutional flooring such as Genasco Mastic, public faith in the name GENASCO, and a definite upward swing in building construction. *If you did not answer this ad,* or if you are interested in any other of the Genasco products, fill out the adjoining coupon and mail at once.

The Barber Asphalt Paving Company, Philadelphia

Sirs—Without obligation, please send me illustrated booklet on Genasco Vulcanite Mastic.

Name ....

Address ....

I am also interested in ....

PEBECO
TOOTH PASTE
TOOTH ★ PEBECO
Leaves
the Mouth
Cool and
Fresh
PEBECO TOOTH PASTE
COUNTERACTS "ACID-MOUTH"
Lehn & Fink
New York

October 8, 1921

The Literary Digest

(Title Reg. U.S. Pat. Off.)

THE INTERNATIONAL FISHERMEN'S CUP RACE

New York FUNK & WAGNALLS COMPANY London

PUBLIC OPINION New York combined with The LITERARY DIGEST

Vol. ~~70.~~ 71 No. ~~15.~~ 2 Whole No. 1642 October 8, 1921 Price 10 Cen

Barrett Everlastic Roofings

HERE and there through the countryside you see a home that stands out as exceptionally attractive and artistic. You mention it as "the house with the beautiful roof." For it is usually the roof that first inspires your admiration.

Roofs of such distinction are not high in cost. The rich red or green color of Everlastic Multi- or Single Shingles and their natural finish of finely crushed slate add immeasurable charm to any house. Yet with their moderate price and remarkable durability these roofings are decidedly economical in cost per year of service.

There is a form of Everlastic for every type of steep roofed building—for your home, for schools, churches, factories, farm buildings, etc.

When you buy, be sure you get Everlastic.

Your Choice of Four Styles

***Everlastic Multi-Shingles**—four shingles in one.* Made of high grade waterproofing materials and surfaced with crushed slate, red or green. When laid they look exactly like individual shingles.

Everlastic Single Shingles. Same material and art-finish (red or green) as the Multi-Shingles, but made in single shingles; size 8 x 12¾ inches A finished roof of Everlastic Single Shingles is far more beautiful than an ordinary shingle roof and costs less per year of service.

Everlastic Slate-Surfaced Roofing. The most beautiful and enduring roll roofing made. Surfaced with crushed slate in art-shades of red or green. Very durable; requires no painting. Nails and cement in each roll.

Everlastic "Rubber" Roofing. This is one of our most popular roofings. It is tough, pliable, elastic, durable and very low in price. It is easy to lay; no skilled labor required. Nails and cement included in each roll.

Illustrated booklets of the four styles free on request.

Volume 71
No. 2

TABLE ▾ OF ▾ CONTENTS

October 8, 1921

TOPICS OF THE DAY: Page

- Cost of Living Going Up Again . . . 9
- Still Republican Weather . . . 12
- Why the League Marks Time . . . 12
- The Tax Bill as a Bitter Pill . . . 14
- The League's Court Started . . . 16
- Topics in Brief . . . 17

FOREIGN COMMENT:

- Soviet Skeptics and "Capitalist" Relief . . . 18
- Britain's "Colonial Revolution" . . . 20
- Russia Faced by a Baltic Union . . . 20
- British View of Irish Reluctance . . . 21

SCIENCE AND INVENTION:

- A Neglected Fruit Tree . . . 22
- Are Our Wives Healthy and Happy? . . . 23
- New Wrinkles in Electric Signs . . . 24
- Uncle Sam's Success with Reindeer . . . 25

[Continued on page 60]

LETTERS AND ART: Page

- Charlie Chaplin's Art Dissected . . . 26
- Chautauqua in a Nutshell . . . 27
- Grasso and the Italian Theater . . . 28
- Colleges for Silk Shirts . . . 29

RELIGION AND SOCIAL SERVICE:

- Our Lawless Age . . . 30
- The Shepherd and the Wolves . . . 31
- "A House of Happiness" for the Great White Way . . . 31
- How Not to Train Preachers . . . 32
- A Salvation Army Report on Prohibition . . . 32

MISCELLANEOUS:

- Review of New Books . . . 33-36, 50-59
- Current Poetry . . . 38
- Personal Glimpses . . . 40-49
- Investments and Finance . . . 70-75
- Current Events . . . 76-77
- The Spice of Life . . . 78
- The Lexicographer's Easy Chair . . . 78

TERMS: $4.00 a year, in advance; six months, $2.25; three months, $1.50; single copy, 10 cents; postage to Canada, 85 cents a year; other foreign postage, $2.00 a year. **BACK NUMBERS,** not over three months old, 25 cents each; over three months old, $1.00 each. **QUARTERLY INDEXES** will be sent free to subscribers who apply for them. **RECEIPT** of payment is shown in about two weeks by date on address-label: date of expiration includes the month named on the label. **CAUTION:** If date is not properly extended after each payment, notify publishers promptly. Instructions for **RENEWAL, DISCONTINUANCE,** or **CHANGE OF ADDRESS** should be sent *two weeks* before the date they are to go into effect. *Both old and new addresses* must always be given. **PRESENTATION COPIES:** Many persons subscribe for friends. Those who desire to renew such subscriptions must do so before expiration.

The Literary Digest is published weekly by the Funk & Wagnalls Company, 354-360 Fourth Avenue, New York, and Salisbury Square, London, E. C.

Entered as second-class matter, March 24, 1890, at the Post-office at New York, N. Y., under the act of March 3, 1879.

Entered as second-class matter at the Post-office Department, Ottawa, Canada.

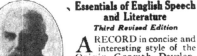

Last Chance to Get the World's Greatest Books — ONLY 10c EACH

Big Sale Closes November 1

Since announcing our introductory sale two weeks ago we have sold over two million books. It is imperative that we close our unheard-of low price offer sharply at midnight, Nov. 1. After Nov. 1 you will be obliged to pay the regular price of 25c each for the world's great sellers. Your chance to get as many or as few as you want of the world's greatest books at only 10c each will be gone after Nov. 1. If you are a lover of good fiction, philosophy, and the most intriguing books that have ever been published—do not wait a single minute but simply scan through the titles below—set down the numbers you want—for instance if you want Carmen, write down "21"—that makes it easier for you, and insures more prompt delivery, as we handle all book orders by number.

Take Your Pick at Only 10c a Book

Order by Number

1 Rubaiyat of Omar Khayyam
2 Oscar Wilde's Ballad of Reading Jail.
3 Eighteen Little Essays. Voltaire
6 De Maupassant's Stories.
7 A Liberal Education Thomas Huxley
10 Shelley. Francis Thompson
11 Debate on Religion between John Haynes Holmes and G. Bowne
12 Poe's Tales
13 Is Free Will a Fact or a Fallacy? Debate
14 What Every Girl Should Know Mrs. Sanger
15 Balzac's Stories.
17 On Walking. Thoreau.
18 Idle Thoughts of an Idle Fellow Jerome.
19 Nietzsche: Who He Was and What He Stood For
20 Let's Laugh. Nasby.
21 Carmen. Merimee
25 Rhyming Dictionary
26 On Going to Church Bernard Shaw.
27 Last Days of a Condemned Man Hugo.
28 Toleration Voltaire
29 Dreams Schreiner.
30 What Life Means to Me Jack London
31 Pelleas and Melisande. Maeterlinck.
32 Poe's Poems
33 Brann Smasher of Shams
35 Maxims of La Rochefoucauld
36 Soul of Man Under Socialism. Wilde.
37 Dream of John Ball. William Morris.
38 Dr. Jekyll and Mr Hyde. Stevenson.
40 House and the Brain Bulwer Lytton
41 Christmas Carol Dickens.
42 From Monkey to Man.
43 Marriage and Divorce. Debate by Horace Greeley and Robt. Owen.
44 Aesop's Fables
45 Tolstoi's Stories.
46 Salome Wilde.
47 He Renounced the Faith. Jack London.
48 Bacon's Essays.
49 Three Lectures on Evolution. Haeckel
50 Common Sense. Paine
51 Bruno: His Life and Martyrdom.
52 Voltaire. Victor Hugo.
53 Insects and Men: Instinct and Reason Clarence Darrow.
54 Importance of Being Earnest O. Wilde.
56 Wisdom of Ingersoll.
57 Rip Van Winkle.
58 Boccaccio's Stories
59 Epigrams of Wit.
60 Emerson's Essay on Love
61 Tolstoi's Essays.
62 Schopenhauer's Essays.
65 Meditations of Marcus Aurelius.
68 Shakespeare's Sonnets.
70 Lamb's Essays.
71 Poems of Evolution. Anthology.
72 Color of Life. E. Haldeman-Julius.
74 On The Treshold of Sex.
75 The Choice of Books. Carlyle
76 The Prince of Peace. Bryan.
78 How to Be an Orator. John T. Altgeld.
79 Enoch Arden.
80 Pillars of Society. Ibsen.
81 Care of the Baby.
82 Common Faults in Writing English.
83 Marriage: Its Past, Present and Future Annie Besant
85 The Attack on the Mill. Emile Zola
86 On Reading. Georg Brandes.
87 Love: An Essay. Montaigne.
88 Vindication of Thomas Paine. Ingersoll.
89 Love Letters of Men and Women of Genius
91 Manhood: The Facts of Life Presented to Man
92 Hypnotism Made Plain.
93 How to Live 100 Years. Cornaro.
94 Trial and Death of Socrates
95 Confessions of an Opium Eater De Quincey.
96 Dialogues of Plato
98 How to Love
99 Tartuffe. Moliere
100 The Red Laugh Andreyev
101 Thoughts of Pascal
102 Tales of Sherlock Holmes.
103 Pocket Theology Voltaire.
104 Battle of Waterloo Hugo
105 Seven That Were Hanged. Andreyev.
106 Thoughts and Aphorisms. Geo Sand.
107 How to Strengthen Mind and Memory.
108 How to Develop a Healthy Mind
109 How to Develop a Strong Will.
110 How to Develop a Magnetic Personality
111 How to Attract Friends
112 How to Be a Leader of Others
113 Proverbs of England
114 Proverbs of France.
115 Proverbs of Japan
116 Proverbs of China
117 Proverbs of Italy.
118 Proverbs of Russia
119 Proverbs of Ireland
120 Proverbs of Spain.
121 Proverbs of Arabia.
122 Debate on Spiritualism Conan Doyle and Jos. McCabe
123 Vegetarianism Debate
125 War Speeches of Woodrow Wilson
126 History of Rome. A. F. Giles.
127 What Expectant Mothers Should know.
128 Julius Caesar. Who He Was and What He Accomplished
129 Rome or Reason Debate. Ingersoll and Manning.
130 Controversy on Christianity Debate. Ingersoll and Gladstone.
131 Redemption. Tolstoi
132 Foundations of Religion.
133 Principles of Electricity.

Special Bargain

We have a special proposition for those who order a complete set—218 volumes. The regular price after Nov. 1 will be $54.50 figured at 25 cents each. If you order the entire set before Nov. 1 we will let you have the 218 volumes for $16.90

135 Socialism for Millionaires. G. B. Shaw.
136 Child Training.
137 Home Nursing.
138 Studies in Pessimism. Schopenhauer
141 Would Practice of Christ's Teachings Make for Social Progress? Debate.
142 Bismarck and the German Empire.
143 Pope Leo's Encyclical on Socialism.

Order by Number

144 Was Poe Immoral? Sarah H. Whitman
145 Great Ghost Stories.
147 Cromwell and His Times.
148 Strength of the Strong London.
151 Man Who Would Be King. Kipling.
152 Foundations of Labor Movement. Wendell Phillips.
154 Epigrams of Ibsen.
155 Maxims. Napoleon
156 Andersen's Fairy Tales.
157 Marx vs. Tolstoi.
158 Alice in Wonderland.
159 Lincoln and the Working Class.
160 Ingersoll's Lecture on Shakespeare.
161 Country of the Blind H. G. Wells.
162 Karl Marx and the American Civil War
164 Michael Angelo's Sonnets.
165 Discovery of the Future. H. G. Wells.
166 English as She Is Spoke Mark Twain.
167 Rules of Health Plutarch
168 Epigrams of Wilde
169 Church Property Be Taxed? Debate.
171 Has Life Any Meaning? Debate.
172 Evolution of Love. Ellen Key
173 Vision of Sir Launfal. Lowell
174 Free Speech Trial of Wm. Penn
175 Science of History Froude.
176 Four Essays Havelock Ellis.
177 Subjection of Women. John Stuart Mill.
179 Constitution of League of Nations.
180 Epigrams of Shaw.
181 Epigrams of Thoreau
183 Realism in Art and Literature. Darrow.
184 Primitive Beliefs H. M. Tichenor.
185 History of Printing. Disraeli
186 How I Wrote "The Raven." Poe.
187 Whistler's Humor
188 How Voltaire Fooled Priest and King Darrow.
189 Eugenics H Ellis.
190 Psycho-Analysis—The Key to Human Behavior Fielding
191 Evolution vs. Religion. Balmforth.
192 Book of Synonyms.
195 How to Keep Well.
196 The Marquise Geo Sand
197 Witticisms and Reflections of Mme. De Sevigne.
198 Majesty of Justice Anatole France.
200 Ignorant Philosopher Voltaire
201 Satan and the Saints. H. M Tichenor.
202 Survival of the Fittest. H. M. Tichenor.
203 Rights of Woman Havelock Ellis.
204 Sun Worship and Later Beliefs. Tichenor.
205 Artemus Ward, His Book.
206 Debate on Capitalism vs. Socialism. Seligman and Nearing.
207 Olympian Gods. H. M Tichenor
210 The Stoic Philosophy. Prof. Gilbert Murray.
211 Idea of God in Nature. John Stuart Mill.
212 Life and Character. Goethe
213 Lecture on Lincoln. Robt. G Ingersoll
214 Speeches of Lincoln
215 The Miraculous Revenge. Bernard Shaw.
216 Wit of Heinrich Heine. George Eliot.
218 Four Essays. Jean Jaures.

RUSH YOUR ORDER TODAY

Sale Ends November 1 *Sale Ends November 1*

Your order will be accepted if it bears a postmark of your town of on or before midnight, Nov. 1, even though it is a few days late in reaching us. But as it is better to be on time than to be sorry, you had best make your selection right now before you have a chance to forget. All books are guaranteed—order as many as you wish—if you don't like them after a 3-day examination send them back and we'll return your money. All books clearly printed on good book paper, 64 to 160 pages. Pocket size. Bound in heavy card cover paper. Don't wait—don't hesitate—the sale will be over Nov. 1—send your order now. If you want 20 books send $2—if 50 send $5 and so on. Check, money order or registered cash. We pay postage on cash orders Carriage charges collect on C. O. D. orders Add 10c to checks for exchange

Appeal Publishing Company

E. H. Julius, *President* 780 Appeal Building, Girard, Kansas

---

ABINGDON

Vital BOOKS

TRANSCENDING the thousand writings of a day are those rare, enduring works which mark in the progress of man another step to greater things. Such works hold within their covers a vital force eternal as the fire in a flawless diamond.

To people who discriminate, who seek the pure metal and discard the dross, the name Abingdon is a guarantee of this vital force.

Abingdon Books are sold at all good Book Shops.

UNITED STATES CITIZENSHIP

By George Preston Mains

The author discusses "fundamentally and informingly some of the larger relations of the citizen to his government," with due emphasis upon "the supreme need and imperative importance of an intelligent and loyal suffrage." It is the kind of book that will improve the quality of American citizenship wherever it is read and studied.

Price, net, $2.00, postpaid

THE UNITED STATES AND CANADA

A Political Study

By George M. Wrong

"A discussion of the common interests of the two countries with a view to a better understanding."—Indianapolis News.

Price, net, $1.25, postpaid.

JOHN RUSKIN, PREACHER

And Other Essays

By Lewis H. Chrisman

In this book we have a presentation of Ruskin as an interpreter of the things of God, but there are ten other essays of breadth, beauty, virility, keen analysis and marked interpretive value in the book.

Price, net, $1.25, postpaid.

THE MEANING OF EDUCATION

By James H. Snowden

Prof. Snowden presents here a scholarly and valuable study of the psychology of education.

Price, net, 75 cents, postpaid.

THE OPINIONS OF JOHN CLEARFIELD

By Lynn Harold Hough

John Clearfield is a person of unusual intellectual virility, vivacity and vision. He has much to say about books, but there are many other items of interest and value upon which he renders "opinions" that are worthy of careful consideration.

Price, net, $1.25, postpaid.

LINCOLN AND PROHIBITION

By Charles T. White

The author's purpose in writing this book is "to set forth in connected and logical form a brief but comprehensive record of Abraham Lincoln's efforts for the suppression of intemperance."

In Press.

(Prices are subject to change without notice)

THE ABINGDON PRESS
NEW YORK CINCINNATI

Suppose You Were a Caveman

Suppose your ancestors had only very recently climbed down from the trees and stopped running on all fours—

Suppose you were in that particular stage of evolution in which man had just discovered the use of the club—that extended arm which enabled him, with very little increase of effort, to make the blow of his fist so many times more powerful—.

And suppose some man came to you and showed you a bow and arrow and demonstrated how you could use it against your enemies or against wild beasts to strike a deadly blow without endangering yourself from the clubs or claws of your opponents—

And suppose you had adopted his bow and arrow and had by virtue of it achieved a dominant place in your tribe—

And that your prestige and power were now slipping away from you because every one else had copied your bow and arrow and learned to use them as well as you did—

And now suppose that the man who had told you about the bow and arrow came to you and described a rifle—

Wouldn't you believe him, and wouldn't you go to considerable trouble to get the new and better arm?

Of course you would.

Well, to-day an understanding of the laws of Efficiency will give you as much dominance over the rank and file of humanity as the possession of a repeating rifle would have given your cave dwelling ancestor over his fellows.

Surely you will want to take advantage of this new step forward?

Or will you turn a deaf ear and let others get the rifle while you still struggle to bend the bow?

How to Achieve Your Ambition

THERE are certain qualities that every man must exercise if he would win promotion, more pay, more influence and power. You possess these qualities to a greater or lesser extent. Develop them—use them—profit by them! In the majority of men these qualifications are dormant. A great psychologist recently said that the average man did not develop one-tenth of his natural forces. In the stirring pages of these ten great books, you can find the inspiration necessary to carry your own individuality up to its highest point of development. They create the characteristics that win power, position, and happiness for all who will master them. More than one hundred thousand men and women own these unusual volumes, and it is safe to say that to them they have brought new hope, rekindled the fires of ambition, and lifted them joyously to higher and more influential places in the world.

These Books Show You How to

Win by force of character	Banish fear and worry
Create opportunities and make the most of them	Overcome foolish sentiment
Analyze and solve the problems of your daily life	Avoid all kinds of excesses
Organize all your faculties and use them to your greatest advantage	Banish indecision
Speak with greater power	Overcome nervousness and lack of balance
Be always self-confident and at ease	Judge and use advice
Impress and influence those you associate with	Arouse enthusiasm in yourself and others
Develop executive ability	"Size up" an audience and determine upon the right appeal
Understand and overcome your weak points	Develop business instinct
Appreciate, develop, and use your strong points	Weigh the practicality of any plan
	And hundreds of other equally important subjects

Poise: How To Attain It

Volume I. Poise is that quality which gives us the strength of mind to analyze the possibilities that are dormant within us, to cultivate them, and to strengthen them in every possible way. It is open to all the world to acquire this gift, to cultivate it as the germ of every sort of success, the happy issue of which depends upon a thorough realization of one's own merits. This volume shows how to be at ease under all circumstances, even the most trying.

Character: How To Strengthen It

Volume II. Character is what one is, reputation is what one is thought to be. The great difference between men—between the weak and the strong, the mean and the mighty—is in character. One can build up and develop character, and every phase of life is thereby improved and enlarged. This volume explains the best methods of development. How to make the most of your strong points and strengthen your weak ones. How to conquer fear and foolish sentiment; how to see things clearly and make wise decisions.

Timidity: How To Overcome It

Volume III. This volume shows you how to get rid of doubt of yourself which is the cause of all timidity—mental, moral, and physical. Timidity is a disease that disqualifies a man for success of any kind. In the face of such a temperament, the doors of opportunity are constantly closing. This book indicates the cure. It describes the way to attain thorough self-confidence; how to develop moral courage of your convictions; how to develop physical courage; how to gain the power that will give you mastery of yourself and others.

Influence: How To Exert It

Volume IV. This book, like all the others in the series, is intensely practical. It explains how to develop your influence to its highest degree of power, and how to exert it to the fullest extent upon all with whom you come in contact, to your own best advantage. It is not based upon untried theories, but upon actual achievements along these lines. For the author was an eminent man who exercised a dominant influence over his associates; and he shows how others may acquire, enlarge, and exert a like dominance. To influence others! what a marvelous power, and what assured success to him that possesses it!

Common Sense: How To Exercise It

Volume V. Common Sense is one of Nature's priceless gifts, as valuable as it is rare. The one attribute that will carry a man successfully through the perplexities of life. This volume shows how to develop Common Sense to the utmost and how to get the fullest advantage from it in daily life—utilizing it most profitably in business. How to see all sides and then take the wisest course; how to weigh advice and judge its value; how to dispel illusions and overcome unwise impulses; how to analyze evidence and make intelligent deductions.

Practicality: How To Acquire It

Volume VI. "Practicality is an inexhaustible wonder-working currency accepted everywhere." It is not dull or commonplace, but one of the attributes of greatness. This volume shows you how to organize your whole mind on a practical basis, so that all of its operations work to your greatest advantage. How to arrive at immediate decisions, which shall also be the best ones for your interests. Practicality is the sense of seeing things as they are and of doing things as they ought to be done. This book shows you how to acquire both these faculties.

Opportunities: How To Make the Most of Them

Volume VII. The mold of every man's fortune is in his own hands. This book shows you how to eliminate the elements of chance, luck, hazard from all your undertakings; how to achieve your goal by taking full advantage of the opportunities that come to every one; and how to create other favorable opportunities for yourself and get the most out of these.

Perseverance: How To Develop It

Volume VIII. Of all the modern "Keys to Fortune," none more easily turns the lock than Perseverance. Napoleon said: "Victory belongs to him who has the most perseverance." And he demonstrated the truth of these words by his acts. Equally true is this statement: "Success attends him who determines to persevere." No matter what other qualities one possesses, without perseverance they count for little. This volume shows you how to acquire this *indispensable* faculty, if not already yours; and how to develop it to the highest degree if you already possess it.

Speech: How To Use It Effectively

Volume IX. The man who presents what he has to say in a clear, concise, and forceful manner commands attention and gains his point. But failure is almost inevitable when ideas, wishes, thoughts are inadequately expressed. This volume shows you how to talk to win in every phase of life—whether in a dinner speech, in a social conversation, on a platform, in a business interview, or anywhere else. It gives you the secrets of appealing to the fundamental instincts of human nature; it shows how to present your facts and opinions to the best advantage; it explains how and when to arouse the different emotions, etc.

Personality: How To Build It

Volume X. Personality is what distinguishes one individual from another—makes him liked or disliked—contributes to his success or failure. This volume shows you how to build a strong and winning personality, that carries everything before it. "Man is not the creature but the architect of circumstance," says Carlyle. "It is character that builds an existence out of circumstance." And personality is the dominating element of character.

"The volume on 'Practicality' alone is worth many times the price paid for the ten books."—*Joseph I. Cantarow, Ph.G.*, Hartford, Conn.

"They are really indispensable. A real student is bound to take his place in the first rank of constructive, efficient, and consequently successful business men."—*Elmer H. Dearth*, Pres. Manufacturers and Traders Casualty Co., Detroit, Mich.

"If it were so that I couldn't obtain another set, the one I have wouldn't be on sale for five times the price paid for it."—*Dr. Edward F. Fisher*, Alton, Ill.

10 Books Sent for Only $1 FOR EXAMINATION

You need not write a letter to order these books. Just sign and mail the coupon below with $1.00 stamps, cash, money order or check. If the volumes do not please you, you can send them back at our expense, we will refund the $1.00, and you will owe us nothing. If you keep them, you pay only $2.00 per month for seven months—$15.00 in all. Don't delay—because of the uncertain manufacturing costs the next edition may be priced higher. They are big value at the present figure. ***Bound in Beautiful Dark Brown "LUXART"—Semi-Flexible and Richly Embossed in high-relief.***

FUNK & WAGNALLS COMPANY D. 10-8-21
354-360 Fourth Avenue, New York

Enclosed find $1.00 Send me, carriage prepaid, the new ten-volume MENTAL EFFICIENCY LIBRARY bound in semi-flexible "Luxart," richly embossed. If the books are unsatisfactory, I will send them back to you, at your expense, within ten days after receipt; you will refund my money and I shall owe you nothing. If I keep them, I will send $2.00 a month for seven months.

NAME ....

STREET ADDRESS ....

CITY .... STATE ....

Let RAND McNALLY Help You Interpret The Day's News—

A Medium-Priced ATLAS

for the home or office

The whole world is completely mapped, indexed and described in this compact, handsomely printed and durably bound new International Atlas.

All new countries and new boundaries.

Beautifully tinted maps in great detail.

Up-to-date statistical data on reverse of each map.

An index of over 100,000 places in alphabetical order.

Charts and diagrams of great practical value.

This atlas is the finest compendium of geographical information ever gathered between the covers of a medium-priced book.

Size 11x14 inches
384 pages

Send for descriptive circular with sample map. Free on request.

We are living in a wonderful age. The day's news is a kaleidoscopic record of history in the making. The newspapers and magazines are crowded full of strange and wonderful names.

The Europe of today is far different from the Europe of our school-days. New nations have come into being—the boundaries of the old have been moulded anew by the heavy hand of war.

To some people the events of the last seven years have been a liberal education. To others, a meaningless jumble of queer sounding names and places—somewhere in Europe. "To simply read is but a waste of hours. To read and remember and understand—that is education."

Keep your RAND McNALLY Atlas beside you as you read. Consult it freely. You will find it incomparably helpful in interpreting the day's news. Czecho-Slovakia, Danzig, Saarbrucken, and the Aland Islands will come out of the haze of their newness and become as familiar as Mexico, Boston, Alaska or the Hawaiian Islands.

Every map or atlas bearing the name RAND McNALLY is as accurate and as up-to-the-minute as it is possible for human hands to make it. RAND McNALLY maps and atlases are not only accurate when first made, but hundreds of thousands of dollars are spent yearly to keep them accurate. More than 65,000 changes are made yearly in just one atlas.

This year, particularly in view of the many changes brought about by recent events, you will find it to your advantage to look for the name RAND McNALLY when purchasing maps or atlases.

RAND McNALLY & COMPANY

Map Headquarters

536 S. CLARK STREET, CHICAGO — 42 E. 22ND STREET, NEW YORK

RAND McNALLY ATLASES ARE FOR SALE AT ALL BOOK SHOP[S]

CAREFUL buying favors White Trucks. More of them in relation to all other makes are being purchased every month. The recent reductions in White prices represent better truck values than it has been possible to offer since 1914.

5-ton	$4,500	3½-ton	$4,200
2-ton	3,250	¾-ton	2,400

f. o. b. Factory

THE WHITE COMPANY, *Cleveland*

White Trucks

THE LITERARY DIGEST

PUBLIC OPINION (New York) combined with THE LITERARY DIGEST

Published by Funk & Wagnalls Company (Adam W. Wagnalls, Pres.; Wilfred J. Funk, Vice-Pres.; Robert J. Cuddihy, Treas.; William Neisel, Sec'y) 354-360 Fourth Ave., New York

Vol. LXXI, No 2 | New York, October 8, 1921 | Whole Number 1642

TOPICS - OF - THE - DAY

COST OF LIVING GOING UP AGAIN

THE TREND OF LIVING COSTS, as the Baltimore *Sun* observes, "is the most important issue in the average household of America to-day." When, therefore, this trend is upward, especially in foodstuffs, as during the past few weeks, father and mother naturally wonder a bit anxiously if this upward trend indicates the end of price reductions in many lines and the beginning of a new era of increasing costs. If prosperity is waiting for prices to come down where people can buy, then the reverse movement has a meaning to every one, banker, merchant, or toiler, and if the toiler happens to be among our millions of unemployed, his interest in this subject is apt to be especially acute. Government figures for August tell us that wholesale prices of such important foodstuffs as butter, cheese, eggs, rice, milk, sugar, fruits and potatoes showed decided advances; and that food articles in the aggregate were thirteen per cent. higher than in the month before. Wholesale prices have also begun to increase in England, France, Japan, Norway and Germany we are told. At the same time, say Department of Labor figures, 27 of the 43 articles on which monthly retail prices are obtained increased from one per cent., in the case of certain meats, to 24 per cent., for potatoes. "All this," notes the Seattle *Union Record*, "in the face of the fact that the price to the producer has either gone down or is stationary." To offset these advances, there are, however, as Charles Cason points out in *Forbes Magazine* (New York), five commodities now selling at less than their pre-war prices—copper, coffee, hides, cattle and corn. But three of these, he adds, are produced by the farmer.

HE CAN'T SEE WHAT HOLDS 'EM UP.

—Williams in the Philadelphia *Retail Public Ledger.*

It is true that in a year there has been a decrease of 25 per cent. in food prices from the peak of 1920, notes the Philadelphia *Public Ledger*, but "we are still paying 53 per cent. more for staples than we paid in 1913." Both the New York *Globe* and *The American Agriculturist* (New York), however, maintain that pre-war prices never again will be the standard. "There seems to be little doubt that the decline in prices has come to an end," agrees the New York *Commercial*, while the Seattle *Post-Intelligencer* declares that "it is folly to hope for pre-war price levels."

"Whatever the causes or whose the responsibility for maladjustment of prices, the fact is universally admitted that retail values have not fallen in keeping with wholesale prices," avers the New York *Journal of Commerce*. Yet, asserts New York's Commissioner of Markets, in speaking of the local situation, "if dealers were not seeking excessive profits, prices to consumers would be lower than at any time since the beginning of the war." As the Providence *Bulletin* remarks:

"Just at this time any price reaction toward higher levels is to be deplored. The economic life of the country is in sore need of a sane and reasonable readjustment, and a conservative relief from unconscionable living costs is imperative. The antagonism to lower prices must in time give way to inexorable conditions. With a great wave of unemployment in evidence and with lower wage scales for those who are working, prices eventually must decline for the simple reason that the public will be unable to pay high prices. It may be disagreeable to 'business,' but it is one of the fundamental economic facts that the maintenance of high prices depends in the end upon the public's purchasing ability.

"In the matter of food costs it does not appear that the reported increases have in any way benefited the producers. They are not receiving any more for their products, altho the consumers are compelled to pay more. In any event, the general downward trend has been interrupted, and the fact may reasonably be regarded with dismay by the general public. In various items there had been no downward trend whatever. This is conspicuously the case with rents, which in general remain about double the figures that prevailed five years ago."

But "it is not likely that the recent upward trend in prices means any general return to high price levels," thinks the Cincinnati *Times-Star*. "The end of August," we are reminded by the Baltimore *American*, "always brings to a close the period of

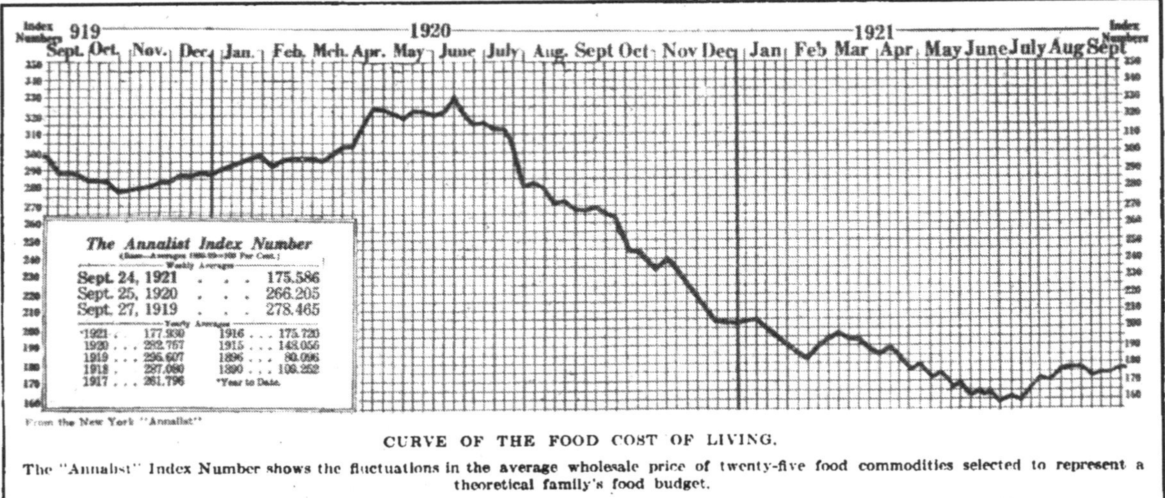

CURVE OF THE FOOD COST OF LIVING.

The "Annalist" Index Number shows the fluctuations in the average wholesale price of twenty-five food commodities selected to represent a theoretical family's food budget.

summer cheapness for many kinds of farmer produce, therefore a seasonal rise in food costs starts in this part of the year." Eggs always go up in price at this time, notes another editor. "The recent upward trend should be regarded as a recovery, rather than an advance," believes *The Ohio Farmer* (Cleveland), "for it undoubtedly is influenced by a slight general recovery in farm products." The last year's decline also carried some food prices down "too far," in the opinion of the *National Stockman and Farmer*, "and these are merely seeking their proper level." The Norfolk *Virginian-Pilot*, too, is sure that the upward trend in the foodstuff market is "impermanent," mainly because "the heavy staples, instead of rising in price, are either stationary or show a slow drift toward still lower levels." "Eventually, prices all round must decline, because the public will be unable to pay them unless there is a revival of industry," concludes the Pittsburgh *Gazette-Times*. "Many influences, however, are working against a return to old prices and conditions," declares the New York *Globe*, which reminds us that:

"Retail prices are so obviously out of harmony with wholesale prices that it is fairly plain that some of the items composing the cost of living will continue to be readjusted downward. That is about as much as can be safely forecast.

"The fallacy in much of the present discussion comes from the false memory that prices were stable in 1914. That was not true. Since the McKinley Administration prices had been steadily rising in the United States. The Department of Labor index number for retail prices of the principal articles of food was 100 in 1913. But in 1907 it was only 82, and year by year the increases were almost uninterrupted. About a year ago the high point was reached, when the index number was 219 and the dollar of 1913 was worth distinctly less than 50 cents. By February last the index had gone down to 158, or 61 points. But for well on to a quarter of a century prices have moved upward. It is not more valid, therefore, to argue that they will now rebound to the level of 1914 than it would be to hold that the figure of 1907 or of 1900 will again be reached."

Reasons for the recent advance, from profiteers to short crops, come from all sides. The 70-per cent. increase in the price of cotton, thus giving Southern farmers more money to spend, is also advanced as a reason by *Wallace's Farmer* (Des Moines). "Labor costs, coal costs, high interest rates and high freight rates"—each has contributed to the rise in food costs, maintains the Memphis *Commercial Appeal*, which further declares that "war profiteers are seizing upon a natural demand to advance prices." At any rate, thinks *The Financial World* (New York), "a rise in commodity prices for some months seems inevitable." This is accounted for by the New Orleans *Times-Picayune* by "the sensational rise in price of lumber, cotton and rice in the South and a better feeling in the Northern grain markets." Continues this paper:

"A merchant can not observe the buoyancy of his neighbor, the cotton planter, without experiencing some of the latter's new enthusiasm, and enthusiasm in business unfailingly becomes translated into stiffer prices. Recent industrial betterment has led to a considerable increase in employment, and that in turn to an increased buying power which, continuing the chain from cause to effect, means an encouragement to the merchant to mark up, be it ever so little, the charges he makes for his goods."

But the National Bank of Commerce (New York), in an analysis of business conditions, warns against any advance in prices because of the betterment of business. As the Rochester *Post-Express* remarks editorially, using the bank's warning as a guide:

"There is no justification for any world-wide rise in prices at this time. Producers of raw materials have taken their losses, as have many classes of labor. Other classes have taken losses as a result of unemployment. Prices cannot go up without curtailing buying, and thus halting the progress already made. The only far-sighted policy is expansion of sales on a small margin of profits.

"Periods of genuine as contrasted with artificial prosperity are never characterized by rising prices. Approximate stabilization is their prerequisite. The reason is simple. Sound business can not operate on a basis of speculative profits. Excessive speculation in prices is what ails the country just now. We sell more raw material and manufactures in international markets than any other nation. We must sell at prices at least equal to, if not lower than, those of other countries if we are to retain these markets.

"Workers who are holding out for higher prices for their labor are foolish. Workers pay their own wages. Wages are only goods in another form. If workers hold their own wages at a higher rate than the goods which they manufacture are worth, they are taking more than is just from other workers that must buy the goods. These will retaliate by raising their own wages, and the first will in turn have to pay the advanced wages of the others."

Not only are food prices up, and likely to remain so, we are told, but the Springfield *Republican* further reminds us that retail clothiers have been advised that "they could not look for lower prices on woolen goods for the spring season of 1922." The price increase in ginghams, bleached goods, and other fabrics in the first week of September is given as 30 per cent. by a bulletin of the Cleveland Trust Company, and the bulletin adds that, "because of the lack of an accumulation of stocks by manufacturers, jobbers or retailers, rising prices are possible for some months." In several parts of New England marked reductions in shoes are reported, but this, it is said, is to make room for a new stock for the fall trade. Notwithstanding these reductions, "the price of shoes is still too high," asserts the New York *Evening World.*

Excessive costs of distribution, too, are said to account for the present high costs of many things. According to Representative Sidney Anderson (Rep. Minn.) this particularly applies to agricultural products. Mr. Anderson is chairman of the Joint Congressional Committee of Agricultural Inquiry, and he has found that of every dollar the consumer pays for goods and commodities, 37 cents represents the cost of producing the article, 14 cents represents all the profits, and 49 cents represents the cost of service." As the Omaha *Bee* remarks, "we are becoming organized most beautifully—but we are paying for it."

"Take milk, for instance. No longer does the farmer drive up to our door with his product. Business practise requires that he hire a trucking concern to carry his product to town, that he sell it to a milk producers' association, which in turn sells it to a creamery which cleans it, purifies it and mixes it and which then sells it to dealers who peddle it about the city. Nor do the men who handle the milk work twelve or fourteen hours a day for board and $20 a month as they used to. Labor has advanced and now insists upon eight hours a day, with one half holiday and a wage more commensurate with adequate standards of living. Again, the public through health officials, demands sanitary handling and careful inspection of the milk, that we may be saved from the spread of disease.

"Naturally, it all costs money. Naturally, the consumer pays more. Mayhap he pays too much; even so, that question is and will continue to be argued at length. But there can be no doubt that a part of the increased cost is rightly charged to the new frills required by advancing civilization.

"As with milk, so with other things. Business and labor have gone hand in hand in lessening the scope of each activity; in increasing the number of middlemen."

Then there is "the one food that people must have—bread," which the New York *News* tells us, is selling at ten cents a loaf—

LEANING ON THE SCALES AGAIN.

—Thomas in the Detroit *News.*

"despite the fact that the cost of the wheat in a loaf is less than two cents." In New York, notes the Brooklyn *Eagle*, white eggs sell at fancy prices, while in Boston the contrary prevails and brown eggs command the highest price. So the price of eggs is kept up, we are told, by this "food prejudice," and New England poultrymen sort out the white eggs and ship them to New York, and send the brown ones to Boston, thus getting the highest price in both markets.

"Prices are still seriously out of line with each other," the Cleveland Trust Company's bulletin points out. "This is true within each country and in some measure as between different countries all over the world. There is lack of balance between wholesale prices and retail ones, between prices and wages, between the costs of commodities and those of transportation, and a very serious lack of balance between the costs of raw materials and those of finished products."

NONE SO BLIND AS THOSE WHO WILL NOT SEE.

—Brown in the Chicago *Daily News.*

As the Cleveland *Plain Dealer* appraises the situation:

"People who would know the facts regarding the business situation to-day need to be on their guard alike against the professional crape hanger and the professional sunshine spreader. The country is not on the brink of disaster, as some would lead us to believe who point to the unemployment situation at home and retarded recovery abroad. Neither is business now nor is it likely to be for many months 'better than ever.' Slowly but surely the process of readjustment is working itself out. That process will be facilitated and the upward movement will gain momentum just to the degree that the financial and industrial community recognizes the true situation in which it finds itself—much better than it was a year ago; not nearly so good as the majority had hoped for by early autumn."

The United States, in fact, appears to have reached the slack between the ebb and flow," thinks the Boston *Herald*. Or, to paraphrase a Salvation Army saying, "business may be down, but it is not out." And even at that, we aren't so badly off maintains *The Herald:*

"Shall we grumble or bewail our lot? Let us be thankful. We have lower prices and lighter taxes than the people of any other country that took part in the World War. See what the British consumer and taxpayer has to bear. The cost of living in Great Britain at the beginning of the present month was 120 per cent. above the cost in the year before the war. And a year ago it was 189 per cent. above. Our 53 per cent. looks small beside these figures. As to British taxation and debt, our commercial attaché at London reports that the heaviness of the taxation is the greatest obstacle to a revival of business. The revenue raised last year, he says, was more than twice as much as the 'deadweight national debt' in 1914. Interest on the existing debt exceeds the entire pre-war revenue of the British government, and the per capita debt has leaped from $75 in 1914 to $810 in 1921. It is within the mark to say that American conditions are about four times better."

STILL REPUBLICAN WEATHER

POLITICAL WEATHER PROPHETS who looked for the recent special elections in New Mexico and Massachusetts to furnish barometric confirmation of their predictions of notable changes in the political drift have been doomed to disappointment, agree Republican, Democratic and independent journals. The victory of the Republican candidate in the Sixth Congressional District of Massachusetts, by about the normal Republican majority, makes it clear enough to the New York *Times* that "the Democrats had been filled with false hopes and the Republicans were needlessly alarmed." All it shows, in the opinion of the politically wise Springfield *Republican* (Ind.) in the State where the election took place, is "that Essex County is just about as Republican as it always has been." The people of Essex County have shown, says the Republican Boston *Herald*, that they "are willing to accord the Republican Administration plenty of time to make good its campaign promises. They did not expect that all the ills to which President Harding fell heir last March were to disappear within six months." The rest of the country had been looking upon the election to throw some light on Eastern sentiment on national issues. Vice-President Coolidge had spoken in the District on behalf of the Republican nominee, and Senator David I. Walsh (Dem. Mass.) had come to the assistance of the Democratic candidate. On Election Day about half the voters stayed home, but those that did come out gave Col. A. Platt Andrew (Rep.) about three votes to every one for Charles I. Pettingell (Dem.)—practically the same ratio that held in the regular election last November. In respect to the Harding policies this result, observes the Springfield *Union* (Rep.), "bears the same kind of testimonial as the recent special Senatorial election in New Mexico." And here the most widely read Democratic paper in New England agrees. As the Boston *Post* observes:

"The result indicates that the Harding Administration retains the confidence of the voters, and that Democratic criticism has so far failed to make an impression.

"It must be admitted that President Harding has done well, handicapped as he has been by Republican leaders in Congress. The average voter feels in the mood to help him out with his support.

"There are no clouds so far on the horizon for the Administration."

While the Massachusetts election "proves that the people who voted for President Harding still have confidence in him" it does not, in the opinion of the Philadelphia *Inquirer* (Rep.) mean that they are "satisfied with everything that has been done at Washington." Perhaps, we read, "many citizens are dissatisfied with the failure of Congress to measure up to the possibilities of the hour, but even if that be true they feel that they have a safe helmsman at the wheel, and that in the end most of our difficulties will be settled to the satisfaction of the people."

WHY THE LEAGUE MARKS TIME

IF THE LEAGUE OF NATIONS is to lead the world to new plateaus of peace and brotherhood, its friends and foes alike are asking, why does it not demonstrate its leadership in the matter of disarmament, instead of waiting for the outcome of the Harding conference. "Reduction of armaments is a test case for us," declared Lord Robert Cecil, urging the Assembly of the League of Nations to make some definite move in the direction of disarmament, instead of "postponing everything." "All that has been heretofore proposed is that we gather some statistics," he exclaimed; and by his insistence he carried through the League's committee on disarmament a resolution "that the temporary mixed commission be asked to make general proposals for the reduction of armaments, which, in order to secure precision, should be in the form of a draft treaty or other equally definite plan to be presented to the Council if possible before the Assembly of next year." Previously the mixed commission had delivered its formal report (quoted in part in these pages last week) which ended with the pessimistic statement that "mankind still is too far removed from the ideals of peace to make possible at present the solution of the question of disarmament." In support of this conclusion the report points out that when the League Assembly asked the member nations to limit their expenditures for the purpose of armaments for two years to the amount of this year's budget, only three—China, Bolivia, and Guatemala—gave unconditional pledges.

LET UNCLE SAM PULL THEIR TEETH.

—Morris for the George Matthew Adams Service.

In the face of this record foes of the League declare exultantly that it is impotent, and its friends are driven to explanations and excuses. "The League is simply not an instrument for accomplishing that sort of work," avers the Baltimore *American*, which is not surprized that its disarmament commission "passes the matter gracefully on to a different type of organization [the Washington Conference] which is less directly calculated to defeat its own ends"; and the San Francisco *Chronicle* finds evidence in the recent proceedings at Geneva that the League's organization "is fundamentally unsound," and that any attempt to enforce its authority "would disrupt the concern at once." "I do not disguise from myself that the League is, so far, a weak and impotent affair," cables Sir Philip Gibbs to the Springfield *Republican*, a pro-League paper; but, he adds, "I am one of those who still believe in the League of Nations as an international machine which in future years may be used and made an instrument of reconstruction and power." And the New York *Times*, another friendly journal, while admitting that "in its first years the League has suffered a rather unusual infliction of infantile maladies," goes on to say:

"But the deeper currents of world thought are steadily turning toward it, acknowledging the righteousness of its spirit, the wisdom of many or most of its provisions. In the long run that is what will determine its fate, not a blind and impractical devotion to the letter. In establishing the World Court the League has already to its credit an achievement of the very first order, destined to mark an epoch in the history of the cause of peace."

BIGGEST SHOW ON EARTH

—Yardley in the San Francisco *Bulletin*.

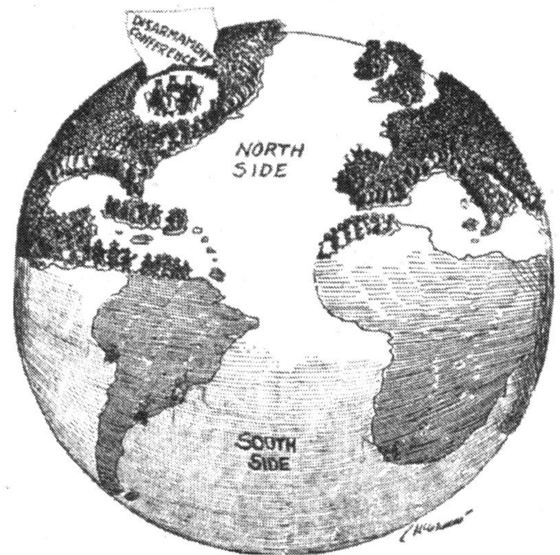

Copyrighted, 1921, by the Chicago "Tribune"

WHERE THE HOPES OF EVERY NORTH-SIDE TAXPAYER ARE CENTERED.

—McCutcheon in the Chicago *Tribune*.

CARTOON VISIONS OF THE COMING WASHINGTON ARMS PARLEY.

Article VIII of the League Covenant says: "The members of the League recognize that the maintenance of peace requires the reduction of national armaments to the lowest point consistent with national safety and the enforcement by common action of international obligations." And elsewhere the same document declares: "The Council, taking account of the geographical situation and circumstances of each state, shall formulate plans for such reduction (of armaments) for the consideration and action of the several governments." Why, editorial observers ask, has this not been done? What are the obstacles that loom in the League's path when it turns its face toward the goal of reduced armaments? International fear and international suspicion, answers Lord Robert Cecil, South Africa's representative in the League Assembly. To use his own words, "the nations of the world are hacking themselves to pieces for fear some one else will hack them to pieces instead." Another answer, embodied in the report of the League's mixed commission on disarmament, is that the League is made ineffectual in this matter by the absence from its membership of the United States, Germany and Russia. But the most sensational explanation was offered in the League Assembly by Louis Christian Lange, delegate from Norway, who charged the big powers in the League with blocking disarmament against the wishes of a majority of the nations of the earth. These big powers, he said, dominate the League by their control of the League Council. Mr. Lange's argument is thus summarized editorially by the New York *Commercial:*

"The great obstacle, he said, lay in the make-up of the permanent advisory committee on disarmament which, he maintains, is composed of representatives of the War Ministries. These representatives, he said, had instructions from their Cabinets. War Ministries, he insisted, had not been, and never would be, in favor of disarmament. Because a conference on the limitations of armaments is to take place in the United States was no reason why the League's plans for lifting the military burden from the shoulders of Europe should be disregarded. Mr. Lange readily admitted the correctness of Mr. Balfour's argument that the world is not ready to take up the question of disarmament. But accepting the three stages in the process given by Mr. Fisher, one of Mr. Balfour's associates—1, an exact report on all armaments; 2, progressive reductions, and, 3, real disarmament, Mr. Lange said that Mr. Balfour talks of a third stage when what should be done is to take up the first stage. Not until such beginning has been made is it possible to even advance in the direction of the millennium."

Mr. Lange also told the Assembly that the League's lack of results in the regulation of the private manufacture of arms, one "great cause of war," was largely due to the failure of the United States to ratify the Treaty of St. Germaine, which, he said, she signed in 1919 and then appeared to forget. On this point we read in a Geneva dispatch to the New York *World:*

"As if to satisfy Lord Robert Cecil and other disarmament enthusiasts, H. A. L. Fisher of Great Britain announced that he would ask the Assembly to pass a resolution urging the Washington conference to consider the St. Germaine protocol designed to restrict private traffic in arms. This is taken to mean that the British delegation at Washington will press for ratification of this instrument by the United States."

Commenting rather pessimistically on the charges of insincerity on the part of the great Powers, the New York *Journal of Commerce* remarks:

"The truth is that the disarmament issue has been unfairly and hypocritically treated from the very beginning of the League of Nations discussion. No definite or satisfactory provision was made for it. Those who now deplore the lack of progress are apparently the very nations that have the largest forces either on land or sea or both and which are disposed to use disarmament merely as a means of calling a halt on competition while they themselves hold to the lead they have already established.

"To expect the smaller powers not to see through so transparent a pretext as is thus offered would be to assume that they have been hopelessly hoaxed by the pretentious talk of world reduction of forces that has gone on during the past two years. While European nations have been asking postponement of their interest payments, and practically repudiating responsibility for their debt to this country they have been building and arming as fast, in various cases, as ever.

"President Harding's meeting to be held in Washington will have to be organized along distinctly new lines if it is to accomplish any material results. The chief requisite is honesty and sincerity of intention on the part of the delegates of the European powers. Without these no agreement is likely to be reached."

THE TAX BILL AS A BITTER PILL

THERE HAVE BEEN EVANGELISTS who could stir a congregation into ecstasy while the collection was being taken. Talent of this rare variety might be welcomed by the Republican leaders in Congress who are trying to fulfil platform pledges of tax reduction and at the same time secure enough revenue to pay the Government's bills without incurring the displeasure of either big business or organized farmers. The Fordney tax bill, passed by the House of Representatives, was not received by the taxpayers with any great burst of jubilation, and the difficulty of sweetening the very necessary dose of taxation has been further illustrated by the coolness with which the press of the country seem to greet Senator Penrose's revision of the House measure. Leading independent and financial journals are severely critical, and in Senator Penrose's own State and city the regularly Republican Philadelphia *Inquirer* denounces the Senate bill as a "most disappointing" measure which "does not keep faith with the party platform." And when a leading Republican Senator like Mr. Smoot of Utah frankly admits that the bill is bound to be "unpopular" and "disastrous," the New York *World* (Dem.) feels justified in saying that there will be some Republican opposition in Congress as well as a united Democratic opposition to the House revenue bill as revised by the Senate Finance Committee. What the Democrats think of the Penrose bill may be indicated by Senator Simmons's (Dem. N. C.) description of it as "the most horrible and unjust proposition of taxation that has ever been presented in this chamber," W. J. Bryan's characterization of it in his *Commoner* as "the most unblushing piece of piracy ever proposed in Congress," and the calm observation of the Democratic New York *Times*, "that it is a tax bill for politics, not for revenue."

One of the reasons for the disappointment manifested by journals in the financial and business centers is that the Senate Finance Committee, instead of practically re-writing the Fordney bill as the correspondents had predicted, made few and slight changes in the measure passed by the House. According to *Bradstreet's*, there were two reasons for this:

"One is the desire to pass a tax revision bill speedily, and with this end in view anything like a wide divergence between the two Houses is regarded by the leaders as a condition to be avoided. Another is the position of the so-called farmer-labor group in the Senate, which has been steadily against the retroactive repeal of the excess profits tax and of the higher surtax rates on the larger individual incomes."

NOW WHY DOESN'T BUSINESS COME BACK?

—Morris for the George Matthew Adams Service.

The basic principles of the Penrose bill follow those laid down by the framers of the House measure, writes the Washington correspondent of the New York *Times*. Indeed, he says, "aside from repealing the capital stock tax next January, increasing the tax on net incomes of corporations to 15 per cent. and cutting the freight and passenger transportation rates in half in 1922 instead of repealing them, the Senate measure may be described as identical with the bill which was acceptable to the House." According to Senator Penrose, the principal departures made from the existing revenue law are:

"The repeal of the excess profits tax, which would reduce the revenue about $400,000,000 annually; the repeal of the surtaxes in excess of 32 per cent., involving an immediate loss of $80,000,000 to $90,000,000 a year; the repeal of the capital stock tax, involving an annual loss of about $75,000,000; the reduction of the transportation taxes by one-half on January 1, 1922, and their final repeal as of December 31, 1922, involving a reduction of $131,000,000 during the calendar year 1922, and an eventual loss of $262,000,000 per year, and the adoption in lieu of the excess profits and capital stock taxes of an additional income tax upon corporations of 5 per cent., which would increase the revenue about $260,000,000 annually."

The framers of the bill before the Senate believe that it will yield $84,000,000 more this fiscal year than the measure passed by the House, but $136,000,000, less than the Treasury experts

GOSH, HOW WE DREAD IT!

—Donahey in the Cleveland *Plain Dealer*.

expect to receive this year if the present law continues in effect. It is the intention of the Senate Finance Committee that their bill shall produce enough revenue to meet all ordinary expenses, "but not enough to create a current surplus and thus encourage unnecessary spending." According to a table accompanying the bill, collections for this year will be divided as follows:

Individual incomes taxes	$850,000,000
Corporation income taxes	430,000,000
Profits tax	600,000,000
Back taxes	230,000,000
Miscellaneous	1,214,000,000

Additional revenue to pay Government expenses will be provided as follows:

Public land sales	$1,500,000
Federal Reserve Bank	60,000,000
Interest on foreign obligations	25,000,000
Repayment of foreign obligations	30,000,000
Sale surplus war supplies	200,000,000
Panama Canal receipts	14,500,000
Other miscellaneous	156,000,000

Senator Penrose thinks that his bill will be passed by the Senate by the last of October, and that it "should meet with the approval of the House, as it follows closely along the lines of the House bill." But the Democrats will try to force changes, and Senator Smoot's sales tax amendment and Senator Calder's liquor levy are to be reckoned with, say the correspondents. So the bill in its final form may be very different from that introduced in the Senate at the end of the summer recess.

A LOT OF DIFFERENCE IT MAKES TO THE BIRD!

—Thomas in the Detroit *News*.

The chief talking point of the bill drawn up by Senator Penrose, is, according to the Omaha *Bee* (Rep.), that it "takes good care of the family man of small income and lays no undue pressure on those whose means are limited."

The New York *Tribune* (Rep.) seems to regret that Secretary Mellon's "many sensible suggestions" were rejected and that "the Senate committee yielded to prejudices left over from the Kitchin era by trying to collect once more what revenue from the income rates exceeding 32 per cent. remains collectible." Nevertheless it believes that "the Senate bill distributes the reductions in income-tax payments better than the House bill did," and it comes to the conclusion that the pending measure will "lift materially the tax burden on the transactions of the calendar year 1922, and at the same time will give the Treasury a margin of safety for refunding financing."

But another Republican daily, the Philadelphia *Inquirer*, as already noted, confesses to grievous disappointment over the work of Senator Penrose and his colleagues. It does not mince words in telling what it thinks of the bill:

"Some effort has been made to accomplish a 'real reduction of the tax burden,' but taken as a whole, the bill now before the Senate does not keep faith. Instead of 'promptly' removing the deadly excess profits taxes they are continued until next January. These taxes 'excessively mulct the consumer' and

GETTING SOAKED.

—Kirby in the New York *World*.

'needlessly repress enterprise.' The reduction of the confiscatory income taxes is likewise postponed to the destruction of industrial expansion. . . .

"There is no use in mincing words about this important matter. All through it are evidences of surrender to the ignorance or demagogism of the leaders of organized labor and of farmers' alliances of the Middle West. The petitions of nearly every chamber of commerce in the United States have gone unheeded. There is no substitution of 'simple for complex tax laws'; no change in the 'character' of taxes. A few bones are thrown to the taxpayer. Scarcely that. Rather let it be said that the public was promised bread and has been given a stone."

The real reason for postponing the repeal of the excess profits tax and the higher income surtaxes until next January is, in the opinion of the independent Springfield *Republican*, "nothing but the fear of the Congressional politicians that the party in power would suffer reprisals at the polls; neither the Senate leadership nor the President dares to force an immediate issue over the taxation of wealth in view of the use the opposition could make of the issue in political campaigning."

"That Botched Revenue Bill," is the headline which sufficiently conveys the opinion of the pro-Harding independent Chicago *Daily News*, and the New York *Herald*, also independent, but a strong supporter of the present Administration, says: "The taxation job as it stands to-day is a thoroughly bad job."

The taxpayer has not received what the politicians promised him in the way of tax reform. Yet it seems to *The Wall Street Journal* that he should be thankful that he has at least been given "something on account":

"Progress is possible only through compromise. The House revenue bill is a compromise and the Senate Finance Committee bill is merely a variation on that compromise. The difference between the bills is that of minor details. Both bills are a timid step toward rectification of the economically absurd revenue legislation adopted in time of war stress.

"It is proposed now to repeal all corporation excess profits taxes and to reduce to a maximum of 32 per cent. all surtaxes on individual income. This is some return to sanity in taxation. Both the House by enactment, and the Senate Finance Committee by recommendation, agree on this step. It is the one outstanding feature of the pending revenue bill that seems sure of enactment. It is something tangible 'on account' which the taxpayer will acknowledge."

THE LEAGUE'S COURT STARTED

JUST HOW IMPORTANT the new Permanent Court of International Justice will be remains of course for the future to say, but at its birth, at any rate, nearly everyone has a good word for it.

At last "the sword is put in the hands of justice," exclaims G. N. Barnes, former British Minister of Labor, as he hails the recent election by the League of Nations of the eleven judges. The formation of the new Court represents "one of the greatest triumphs for peace," agrees the Brooklyn *Eagle*, and in the opinion of the Richmond *Times-Dispatch*, this body of international jurists "will make war practically indefensible by passing on the justiciable issues in all controversies brought before it by nations anxious to have their cause justified before the court of public opinion." It will be to the world, in time, believes the Troy *Record*, "what the Supreme Court is to this country."

Right here, however, it is pointed out that the Supreme Court has power to enforce its decisions, while, as the Canton *News* remarks, "the Court can only advise; it has no power to enforce." "This is a rather unfortunate feature of the organization, and one which Elihu Root strenuously objected to at the time representatives of Great Britain, in particular, succeeded in eliminating the compulsory feature of the Court's status," declares Governor Cox's paper, the Dayton *News*. The *News* even suggests that Mr. Root eliminated himself from the list of possible judges because of his aversion to this phase of the Court's structure. "For," it reminds us, "a court hardly seems to be a court at all unless its rulings and decisions are accepted by the parties concerned as binding."

According to Article XIV of the Covenant of the League—

"The Council shall formulate and submit to the members of the League for adoption plans for the formulation of a Permanent Court of International Justice. The Court shall be competent to hear and determine any dispute of an international character which the parties thereto submit to it. The Court may also give an advisory opinion upon any dispute or question referred to it by the Council or by the Assembly."

In July of last year a committee of ten representatives of the greater Powers drew up, with the aid of Mr. Root, the scheme of organization for the Court. A majority of twenty-four members of the League ratified the draft of the plan, and it was declared adopted. The question of recognizing the Court's compulsory jurisdiction was left to the individual choice of the nations, and to date thirteen have accepted the principle. The Court, explains the Philadelphia *North American*, will deal only with issues of law, fact, and right, rendering judgments strictly on the law, regardless of political considerations; for questions capable of settlement by arbitration there remains the tribunal established several years ago at The Hague. As *The North American* points out:

"The Court has jurisdiction 'to hear and determine suits between States' relating to interpretation of treaties, any question of international law, or breach of international obligation and reparation therefor. It is to deal wholly with legal and justiciable issues, settling them according to the principles of established international law, customs and conventions. The judges are to act in a judicial capacity and not as representatives of the nations to which they belong.

"Elected for nine years, the members of the Court will sit permanently at The Hague, and are to engage in no other occupation. The Court is to be open 'of right' to nations members of the League; other States 'may have access to it' under conditions determined by the League Council."

OUR REPRESENTATIVE IN THE WORLD COURT.

Dr. John Bassett Moore, elected by the League of Nations as a judge of the International Court of Justice.

As a non-member of the League, what will be the relationship of the United States to the new World Court? Not a few observers, notes *The North American*, "hold that the Court will have a position as equivocal as that of the League." "We are not part or parcel of the League, which ordains this new Court, nor are we responsible for Judge Moore's selection," explains the Grand Rapids *Herald*; "we had nothing to do with the new Court, and we are under no obligation to it; we are bound neither to plead before it nor to accept its verdicts." Article XVII of the Covenant, however, states that "in the event of a dispute between a member of of the League and a State which is not a member," the State not a member shall be invited to "accept the obligations of membership in the League for the purposes of such dispute." If it refuses, and resorts to war against a member of the League, then it comes under Article 16, and shall "be deemed to have committed an act of war against all other members of the League."

The new World Court, however, "is open to every State on earth, regardless of League status, and will function with about the same independence as the Hague Tribunal," asserts the Philadelphia *Public Ledger*. At present, say Geneva dispatches, there are only two cases on the docket. Since the constitution of the Court—largely the handiwork of Mr. Root, we are told—provides that the judges shall be selected "regardless of their nationality," an American experienced in diplomacy and international law, John Bassett Moore, was one of those elected. The other ten are: Viscount Robert Finlay, of Great Britain; Dr. Yorozu Oda, of Japan; Dr. Andre Weiss, of France; Commendatore Dionisio Anzilotti, of Italy; Dr. Ruy Barbosa, of Brazil; Dr. B. T. C. Loder, of Holland; Dr. Antonio S. de Bustamente, of Cuba; Judge L. Nyholm, of Denmark; Dr. Max Huber, of Switzerland; and Rafael Altamira y Crevea, of Spain.

Six of the eleven judges chosen are members of the Hague Court, observes the New York *Evening Post*. The Springfield *Republican* sees in their election "a long step forward in the League of Nations," and the New York *World* looks upon the new Court as "the greatest court ever organized in the history of international jurisprudence."

TOPICS IN BRIEF

Disarm or disburse.—*Greenville (S. C.) Piedmont.*

Normalcy is evidently the land of promise.—*Columbia Record.*

The South is "cottoning" to Prosperity.—*Greenville (S. C.) Piedmont.*

The only nation that can lower taxes is indignation.—*Richmond News Leader.*

Even in soaking the consumer there ought to be a saturation point.—*Dallas News.*

Germany is busy because she is willing to work for less to get more.—*Boston Herald.*

The "rib-roast," we surmise, originated in the Garden of Eden.—*Columbia Record.*

The joke will be on Signor Marconi if Mars reverses the charges on him.—*Minneapolis Tribune.*

Lloyd George insists that De Valera accept the English sovereign at par.—*New York Herald.*

De Valera seems to be sparing no effort to write all of Ireland's wrongs.—*Norfolk Virginian-Pilot.*

The politicians are skilled at creating every sort of debt but a debt of gratitude.—*Columbia Record.*

Anything can be made out of cotton except a good price for a full crop.—*Greenville (S. C.) Piedmont.*

General Dawes finds it easier to damn the spenders than it is to dam the spending.—*Columbia Record.*

So many people are busy being unemployed that it is extremely hard to get any work done.—*Boston Transcript.*

However, the report that the League of Nations is dying comes from those who once said it was dead.—*Detroit News.*

Lenin and Trotzky would like to try their methods on a country where the people don't have to eat.—*Detroit Journal.*

Eventually the politicians may discover that they cannot negotiate the rocky road back to normalcy shod in gum-shoes.—*Columbia Record.*

A rumor that King George has exprest an opinion upon some subject was promptly denied. Britannia, at the latest bulletin, was resting easier, but still feverish.—*Liberator (New York).*

A Chicago man who stole an airplane will be employed by the owner of the stolen property, but, unfortunately, there are not enough airplanes for all the unemployed to steal.—*Indianapolis News.*

Chewing the rag fills no empty stomachs.—*Columbia Record.*

A Flivver must be mighty disgusting to a horsefly.—*Detroit Journal.*

Normalcy in cost tags is what people are looking for.—*Detroit Journal.*

The price of soft coal suggests that it will be a hard winter.—*Detroit News.*

To attain real peace the world must work its arms off.—*Norfolk Virginian-Pilot.*

Many people want jobs, but not as many want work.—*Boston Shoe and Leather Reporter.*

Business is turning the corner, but not on two wheels.—*Boston Shoe and Leather Reporter.*

The man with money to burn has no trouble making a match.—*Greenville (S. C.) Piedmont.*

By comparison with the rest of the world, Mexico seems peaceful these days.—*Honolulu Star-Bulletin.*

A railroad pool is never made by squeezing the water out of the stock.—*Greenville (S. C.) Piedmont.*

A good motto for our federal officers: When in Washington, do as Washington did.—*Asheville Times.*

The problem of Congress seems to be to place the taxes where they will affect the fewest votes.—*Canton News.*

Since a dry wave brought in Prohibition, it isn't surprizing to find the drouth a little wet.—*Rochester Times-Union.*

The young man's crop of wild oats would be lessened by more efficient threshing.—*Minneapolis Nonpartisan Leader.*

As reformers see it, there's too much latitude in woman's dress and not enough longitude.—*Norfolk Virginian-Pilot.*

The problem of unemployment could be solved by purchasing a second-hand Ford for every fellow out of a job.—*Charleston Gazette.*

You see, coal is high because of the freight rate. And the freight rate is high because locomotives must burn high-priced coal.—*Tacoma Ledger.*

The tariff bill puts skeletons on the free list. This is gratifying evidence that our domestic skeleton industry is able to compete with the pauper skeletons of Europe.—*Liberator (New York).*

According to Treasury Department figures, every man, woman and child in the country has $250 saved. Strange that our banker never mentioned it to us.—*St. Paul Pioneer Press.*

The earth has fourteen movements, say scientists. This evidently omits reform movements.—*Norfolk Virginian-Pilot.*

One method of curbing the national unrest would be to abolish a few thousand of the political berths in Washington. — *Columbia Record.*

Well, we never did know why a disarmament conference had to drag in the Asiatic question when we thought Hiram Johnson had settled that.—*Charleston Gazette.*

A movie actress says she's looking for a perfect man to marry him. She can locate quite a number by reading tombstones, but she can't marry them. — *Greenville (S. C.) Piedmont.*

An Irish correspondent writes us: "Lloyd George, Welshman tho he be, ought to have sense enough to understand that an Irishman does not want peace by agreement." Work it out for yourself.—*Charleston Gazette.*

It is said that Charlie Chaplin deeply loves both his native country and the land of his adoption. Perhaps, in the interest of both, he might be induced to pay off England's little debt to America. It is only $4,500,000,000. — *Boston Transcript.*

WONDERS OF AMERICA—THE GRAND CANYON.

—Brown in the Chicago *Daily News.*

The biggest corner ever known in the market must be the corner that business is reported to be turning.—*Boston Herald.*

These fellows who are so opposed to disarmament must have all their investments in tax-free securities.—*Nashville Southern Lumberman.*

An English dancer says sleeping outdoors makes one beautiful. At last we are able to account for the charming appearance of the average hobo.—*Seattle Times.*

A Scotch professor estimates the age of the earth at 8,000,000,000 years, and yet it isn't old enough to invent an effective substitute for war.—*Boston Shoe and Leather Reporter.*

We learn from the esteemed *Lit. Dige.* that an artificial silk purse has actually been made from a sow's ear. Now let these same clever chemists make a sow's ear out of a silk purse, and we'll all sit up and take notice. —*Weston (Ore.) Leader.*

Wayne B. Wheeler says that if England would drink nothing but water she could pay us what she owes us. According to which logic as Uncle Sam drinks nothing but water he has so much money he doesn't need to collect any debts. —*Louisville Courier-Journal.*

AMERICAN FOOD INVASION OF RUSSIA.

Famine refugees in Moscow waiting their turn for daily rations at the American Relief Administration.

SOVIET SKEPTICS AND "CAPITALIST" RELIEF.

RUSSIAN SOVIET NEWSPAPERS assail the "capitalist forces" behind relief measures taken in Russia, altho they do not attempt to deny how much the famine-stricken country needs help. To their mind, the famine offers the Allied countries the opportunity they were unable to secure by supporting anti-Soviet military movements, either morally or materially. France particularly is labeled as the most iniquitous among the Allied group, and it is charged that she plans "a new intervention" to overthrow the Soviet régime. An authoritative voice of such Russian suspicions is that of Karl Radek, known as one of the Soviet government's most active agents in foreign propaganda. Writing in the Soviet organ *Izvestia*, under the significant heading of "A Stone Instead of Bread" he says:

"The famine in the Volga region occupies the attention of capitalistic Europe and the 'White' Russian press abroad. But he would be profoundly mistaken who imagined that the news of the dreadful national calamity struck the conscience of the capitalistic press, that it evoked human feelings in it. The capitalistic press regards the famine in Russia merely from this standpoint: Will it not help it at last to dispose of Soviet Russia, will it not help it to remove from the body of world capitalism 'the Soviet splinter'?

"We are on the eve of the preparation of a new intervention. France is the initiator; she is preparing a military base in Poland and simultaneously attempting to draw into military combinations the Baltic states and Rumania. But not a single statesman in Reval, Riga and Helsingfors, who has not lost his mind, believes that Soviet Russia is scheming against these countries. But as France pays with gold for participation in such preparations, they are not averse to taking part in them.

"In this way or that way, by one method or another, the Allies are preparing for Soviet Russia a new blow, taking advantage of the famine."

That Mr. Radek may be preparing a safety exit in case of what may happen, would seem not wholly improbable, in view of the disclosures of a Russian letter published by the London *Daily Telegraph*. This letter is furnished to the London daily "from a trustworthy source in Germany," and is "evidently addrest to Lutovinoff, a prominent Soviet official abroad, by a very near relation." It is dated from Moscow, July 15th, and in connection with the statements of Mr. Radek, contains the following interesting paragraph:

"The necessity of inviting the cooperation of representatives of the bourgeoisie and the old intelligentsia is regarded by many as the beginning of the end, and it is useless to try and disillusion any one of the fact that the first consignment of corn from abroad, brought in without the participation of the Soviet Government, and distributed by some Red Cross other than the Soviet Red Cross—Quakers or any one you like—will cause a revolution in the whole outlook of the people, and transform it from being an obedient executor of the Central Government into its hated and deadly foe. They are always talking among us of the impossibility of accepting the American conditions and of the impossibility of allowing interference by foreign charitable organizations in the work of combating the famine. Those who oppose this do so purely for consideration of their own skins, for the inevitable collapse is clear to all, besides the inevitable bloody retribution for all our failure to create a system which would have been able to help the people to save themselves from the horror of this unparalleled famine. But one must be honest even in this question. Even now we could forget the petty interests of this Utopian folly on which we have lived for the past three years, and could make a choice either to sacrifice 20,000,000 starving people to the Utopian folly of a world revolution, and on the bones of a dying people continue to wave our party standard, or to stand together with the people, to bear its burden in order to save from starvation millions of those who are now faced with death. I have made the choice, and I am now going with the people."

This Soviet letter-writer wrote after "an official journey through the famine-stricken areas along the Volga" which was undertaken "by order of the Central Committee in company with members of the Petrograd Soviet and delegates of Kameneff's Commission," and he further relates:

"Our terms of reference were to ascertain how far the local committees were doing effective work, how far the instructions of the central authorities were being carried out, and how far the resources at the disposal of local authorities were sufficient to mitigate in some degree the unparalleled disaster which has affected almost all Russia. In Samara we found ourselves in the heart of the famine area. There is absolutely nothing there. Three months' blazing drought had burnt up everything. There had been no rain, and now the locusts, which have come from the south, are themselves perishing for lack of food, being unable to feed themselves off the half-burnt shoots of the corn. You can not imagine what is going on in the towns. I made a very careful study of the famine in 1891, but the extent of the disaster which has overtaken us now surpasses by many times everything which took place then, and it must be remembered that this is only the beginning. What, then, will happen in the autumn, when the question of sowing will have to be faced, when there will be no berries, no foliage, no root crops, with which the majority of the peasants are at present feeding themselves, and on the approach of winter, when the human organism demands additional nourishment?

"When one recollects our disorganized transport, the shallowness of our rivers during the present year, and, finally, our clownish administration, then it is awful, both for the people and for one's self. Russia has been fated to undergo a great trial, but fate is preparing an even greater trial for all of us, who are responsible to the people for our powerlessness to help them at this critical moment. It must not be forgotten that in the famine of 1891 we had a well-organized administrative machine, properly functioning railways, and there was finally a government with authority in which the moujik had confidence, and which the intelligentsia were prepared to obey. Now there is nothing of this. The people will have to look to themselves throughout the long cold winter, and will have to support by themselves the struggle against hunger, and cold, disease, and universal chaos."

This Soviet investigator goes on to say that in Saratoff the local Provincial Extraordinary Commission gave information of a new form of speculation, namely, "the sale of children into slavery by their parents, and the entering of whole families into servitude for a few poods of flour." These facts were true even in former famines, he says, but then it was the Kalmyks, Tartars, and Bashkirs, half-savage nomads, among whom the selling occurred:

"Now our Russian peasants are asking to be taken into slavery, seeing in that the only salvation from unavoidable death by starvation. Where are the people gone out of the villages? Men point to the East in the direction of Orenburg Steppes. We met two or three such hordes on our way. Of course, there was no possibility of having any talk with them; if they had only known who we were it would have fared ill with us. It seemed to me that I had been carried back into history and that Russia was again passing through the time of the great migration which entirely recast the map of Europe.

REPAYING GOOD FOR EVIL.

—*News of the World* (London.)

"I have not enough courage to venture a solution. I know there is no solution. The government has none, and even the immediate future seems bound to me to be appallingly miserable. What can the government do against the peasantry? How will it defend itself against the reproaches of this million-headed monster? Who will stand up in their defense? You see it is impossible to depend upon the Red Army. The fact is that all are peasants themselves, and will soon be starving just as the villages are starving. And what of the workmen? Well it can not be said that many of them remain. I feel myself now like a man in a house which has been burnt down, where at any moment part of a wall may give way, or a cornice crush everything which lies beneath it. I can not get this feeling off my mind, either now when I am in Moscow, or when I traveled along the dead steppes and the abandoned villages of the dying Volga country. Others in Moscow have the same feeling. Nervousness, confusion, uncertainty of the immediate future are noticeable both in the talk and work of comrades who were formerly among the most staunch."

AMERICAN LIFE-SAVERS IN RUSSIA.

The first train of workers of the American Relief Administration entering Soviet Russia across the Latvian frontier.

None of the doubt that encompasses the Soviet mind, according to the foregoing letter, is discernible by such French observers as the Paris *Temps* and the *Journal des Débats*, which maintain that the Soviet government is exploiting the famine to strengthen their position at the expense of the Western powers. Says the *Journal des Débats:*

"Supposing that part of the food reaches its true destination, the people who will have received succor will only know that the food comes to them from a committee controlled by the Soviets, and the latter will certainly not miss the opportunity of posing as Providence in the eyes of the population. . . .

"Already Tchitcherin believes he has got America and Europe in his hand. Speculating on the very natural pity of Westerners, he has undertaken to force the foreign governments to give permission for supplies of every sort to be sent to Russia. He calculates on thus proving to the Russian people the prestige and power of the Soviets.

"Krassin at Petrograd boasts of his success over foreign diplomacy. Encouraged by past results, he carries his impudence so far as to demand our money. He declares that he is now concentrating his efforts on the flotation of an international loan, 'without which,' he says, 'we can never put Russia on her feet again,' and it is French money which comes first to his mind."

BRITAIN'S "COLONIAL REVOLUTION"

THE BRITISH COMMONWEALTH has passed through a revolution, as may be plainly seen if we compare the position of Australia or Canada as they were ten years ago with their position to-day, remarks the Manchester *Guardian*, which tells us that this colonial revolution resembles other British revolutions in the sense that "it has not been the deliberate application of a set of ideas or the definite expression of a new temper." The new relationship between the colonies and the motherland has long been implicit in the old, we are reminded, but "if there had been no war it might have developed much more gradually and perhaps more reluctantly." The war brought the Dominions from the position in which, according to General Smuts, they were still "subject provinces of Great Britain" into the position they occupy to-day of "absolute equality and freedom with the other nations of the world." Whatever it has done with democracy elsewhere, the war has "in this definite and limited sense" made democracy safe in the Dominions, according to this famous Manchester newspaper, which adds:

"It was the final act of the war, the making of the peace, that really set the seal on the new position of the Dominions. In 1897 and 1902 they had declined to take any share in the control of British foreign policy or the burdens of the defense of the Empire. In 1899 and 1907 they were not consulted about the Peace Conferences at The Hague. At the Colonial Conference of 1907 Australia had protested against British policy in the New Hebrides, and Newfoundland against British policy in the matter of fishing rights, and in 1909 the Commonwealth of Australia made a formal protest against the conclusion of the Declaration of London without consultation with the Dominions. In 1911 the British Government was anxious to arrange for cooperation and mutual consultation, but the Dominions were lukewarm, and difficulties arose. Then came the war. The Dominions had nothing to do with the declaration of war, tho that declaration involved them in a state of war with a great Power. They might have withheld their cooperation, but they threw themselves into the struggle, and were more and more consulted as time went on. From 1917 their representatives took part in the deliberations of the War Cabinet, and at the Peace Conference they had a position indistinguishable from that of a sovereign State."

The history of these developments is taken from the "War Government of the British Dominions" published by the Carnegie Endowment for International Peace and the author of the volume, Dr. A. B. Keith, is described by *The Guardian* as "a well-known authority on his subject." In commercial conventions the right of the Dominions to separate representation had been recognized before the war, this newspaper reminds us, and after some discussion it was decided that the Dominions should send their own representatives to Paris. Canada was specially anxious to do this, but Australia was less eager, tho we are told she had protested against the conduct of the British Government in assenting to the armistice terms without consulting her. We read then:

"It was agreed finally that Canada, Australia, and South Africa should each have two representatives, and New Zealand one. Colonial delegates took a part in all the chief Commissions, and the Prime Minister of Canada was appointed chairman of the British Empire delegates in the absence of Mr. Lloyd George. Moreover, a Dominion representative acted from time to time as one of the five British delegates. Each of the Dominions ratified the Treaty through its own Parliament, and the ratification of the British Empire was not effected until each Parliament had approved. The government had made the tactless suggestion that the ratification need not be delayed for Parliamentary sanction in the Dominions, but Sir Robert Borden made a prompt and vigorous protest against this view. The peace gave the Dominions a recognized position as nations. As members of the League of Nations they send delegates to that Assembly who are quite independent of British influence; and the Assembly, which elects four members of the Council, may elect a Dominion representative if it desires. Moreover, three Dominions hold mandates under the League of Nations."

But the most striking feature of "self-determination" in the new status of the Dominions is the principle laid down in a debate on the Peace Treaty in September, 1919, by General Smuts when he said the United Kingdom "has no right to legislate for the Union and that the Royal Veto is obsolete with regard to Dominion legislation." Altho the right to secede from the Empire would seem to be implied, nevertheless, as *The Guardian* points out:

"General Smuts made one exception of the highest importance in the case of a law proposing the secession of the Union from the British Empire: such a law must be refused the royal assent, as the Crown could not divorce itself from the Union. Dr. Keith discusses this view and the famous unconsidered declaration of Mr. Bonar Law about the right of secession. Dr. Keith points out that all that Mr. Bonar Law could have meant was that if a Dominion wished to leave the Commonwealth the British Government would as a matter of policy not resist it. There is clearly no right of secession in the sense that a Dominion may remove itself from the British Commonwealth by a simple act of its Parliament, to be ratified as a matter of course like any acts of a purely domestic nature. A good deal of confusion in other controversies would have been avoided if this had been understood. The British Commonwealth is now a federation of nations, united by the Crown. It rests on common tradition and common convenience, and it can never rest permanently on any other basis. Force could not keep any member within the circle, but separation would not be one single impulsive act; it would be the result of a considered resolution following on a careful discussion of all the consequences to the State proposing it and to the other members of the Commonwealth."

RUSSIA FACED BY A BALTIC UNION

FREE FROM RUSSIA'S HEAVY HAND, the Baltic states are working towards a union among themselves to safeguard their new-found liberties and stabilize their economic existence. Thus we are informed by the *Danziger Zeitung*, which points out that the economic adjustment of Europe as a whole can not be managed until the chaos of Eastern Europe is cleared up. Poland, Esthonia, Latvia and Finland seem destined to be the pillars of the economic edifice of new Eastern Europe, according to this journal, "providing of course that all thought of dominance by any one of these states is banished, and that all mutual mistrust among them is removed." Poland is distrusted "because of her incontestable superiority," it seems, and there is no question that she is the strongest among these countries, politically and also economically "despite present conditions."

Lithuania in particular is said to have her doubts about Poland, and these doubts constitute a serious obstacle to the quick formation of the Baltic Union. We are told also that an alliance between these states would not be satisfactory, for what is needed is a union much more intimate and solid, "something similar to the former union of North Germany and perhaps even a new form of closer contact." Altho this union should have in view only economic aims, the *Danziger Zeitung* notifies us that "on the political side also it would be of high importance." As long as the Baltic states, and especially Poland, are not soundly guaranteed against all danger, whether from Bolshevik Russia or from "a Russia that should endeavor to recover the Baltic heritage of the Tsars," the state of the union would be "only ephemeral and illusory." It is indispensable, therefore, according to this journal, that Poland be stalwart and strong, in order to secure stability in Eastern Europe.

Diplomatic conversations on the subject of the union have been renewed between Lithuania, Esthonia and Latvia, we are informed, and the prediction is made that Poland and Finland will undoubtedly join in the discussions. Finally, we are notified of the great importance the Baltic Union will have on the Russian state "of to-morrow" and herein the matter "becomes of profound interest not only to Eastern Europe but to the peace and prosperity of Europe as a whole."

BRITISH VIEW OF IRISH RELUCTANCE

HAD REJECTION BEEN MEANT in the Irish replies, it could have been conveyed in a phrase, for De Valera had only to say: "We stand for a republic; you merely offer us a form of the British connection." Then the parley would have been ended, remarks the London *Nation and Atheneum*, which points out that De Valera considered there was "debatable ground within the offer" of the British Government, and admits that "it is the business of statesmanship to explore" such territory. Broadly speaking, Sinn Fein Ireland fears three things as a result of the new constitution, according to this weekly, which explains:

CHASING THE SHADOW AND MISSING THE SUBSTANCE.
—*The Daily Express* (London).

"The first is the loss of Irish unity, a feeling strongly entertained by the fighting leaders. Ireland apprehends that unless the new instrument contains, as it most certainly should contain, a provision for a Central Federal Council, it would seem merely to create two ineffectual Parliaments, most unfairly and unequally dowered with powers, and unable to speak for the country as a whole. I imagine that this finish is essential to the structure, and that it must be provided.

"Secondly, Sinn Fein fears that the Bill will contain a free right of entry for British militarism, *e.g.*, that British regiments will be fixt on her soil for the double purpose of guarding the aerodromes and maintaining the recruiting stations. I submit that here, again, the distrust is easily removable. Naturally the military do not want to lose their Irish recruits. But for that purpose it is not necessary to place the stations in Ireland. England will serve just as well. And if there is a treaty of amity, the guarding of the aerodromes (need they all be military?) could safely be left to the Irish militia.

"Thirdly, there is the sore point of Fermanagh and Tyrone. These counties, with the spectacle of Orange barbarism before them, are already demonstrating their desire to amalgamate with the South. From that hour the Northern connection, set purely as political tactics, becomes palpably unjust. There, doubtless, lies a difficulty, and a need for British courage in the handling of it."

Moreover, there is a fourth line of possible divergence from the British terms, in the judgment of this periodical, which thinks the Irish "may revert to an old conception, never quite abandoned, by their advanced thinkers." Allusion is made to the revival of the notion of "a Dual Monarchy as an alternative to a Republic," and *The Nation* says this is Mr. Arthur Griffith's plan, a variant of which was proposed in *The Nation* some time ago. We read then:

"The Prime Minister is the least pedantic of men, and if a monarchical solution should once more become a definite and powerful slant of Irish opinion—well, the British Constitution is an elastic thing, and it can be adapted to that particular need as to others."

Reference to the Dual Monarchy is suspected by some in a speech made at Dundee, Scotland, by Secretary for the Colonies Winston Spencer Churchill, who said that the British Government would insist upon allegiance to the King whether as "King of Great Britain or of Ireland," and press dispatches report that this declaration was "considered by many of his hearers virtually to hold out the prospect to Ireland of a separate kingdom along the lines suggested by Lord Hugh Cecil last May, when he brought forward a scheme by which Ireland would be made an independent kingdom, the king to be a member of the Windsor family, probably the Prince of Wales, to be appointed by the King of England."

As to the potency of religion as an issue in the Irish problem, this weekly supplies interesting information communicated by "an English traveler for a well-known firm of publishers," who lately returned from Ireland, "strongly imprest with the popularity of the truce." This English informant writes:

"Altho I found everything quiet in accordance with the truce, yet one could feel an undercurrent of unrest and uncertainty. The North and South are affected in quite different ways. In the North, Belfast, etc., there is a religious war on, the Catholics are persecuted publicly by the Protestants, and this has the effect of the Catholics returning this hatred, very often leading to bloodshed. I might say that the only part of Ireland that at present is under martial law and has a curfew is loyal Belfast.

"In the South there is not, and never has been, any religious war, Catholics and Protestants living peaceably side by side; in fact, the Sinn Fein party comprises both religions. The whole question in the South is a national one, and after what the soldiers, etc., of the I. R. A. have suffered, one can clearly see that whether they accept the present settlement or not, it will take years for the hatred of British rule to die down. I did not notice any particular personal bitterness, but customers and others I met did not attempt to hide the bitterness against the government. I am certain that it would have been dangerous for De Valera to do anything but refuse the government terms. But I believe the people will accept them, and thus relieve De Valera from climbing down from the Republican platform."

THE MAGIC CIRCLE.

JOHN BULL: "I don't mind what step you dance, my friends, as long as you keep inside the circle."
—*News of the World* (London).

SCIENCE - AND - INVENTION

A NEGLECTED FRUIT TREE

WITHOUT SPECIAL CARE, three to four hundred pounds of delicious and nourishing food may be obtained from a dooryard group of three or four pejibaye palms, now well known in Costa Rica. Its fruits, whose substance resembles that of the chestnut or the cocoanut, are a staple food in the limited region between Ecuador and Lake Nicaragua. It is strange, then, thinks Wilson Popenoe, explorer for the U. S. Department of Agriculture, that it is not more widely known and distributed. Writing in *The Journal of Heredity* (Washington), Mr. Popenoe characterizes the tree as a tropical American counterpart of the Oriental date palm. Both species are capable, almost unaided, of supporting life. There is, however, this noteworthy difference: sugar is the principal constituent of the date, while starch is the most important nutritive element in the pejibaye. We read on:

"In Costa Rica the pejibaye has been cultivated by the Indians since remote antiquity. In the lowlands of Colombia, Venezuela, and Ecuador it forms a staple foodstuff of numerous aboriginal tribes. The Jibara Indians of Ecuador hold the fruit in such esteem that the ripening season is celebrated annually by a feast.

"It seems remarkable, therefore, that this palm should not have become widely distributed. Its cultivation, as an economic plant, is now limited to that region between the Lake of Nicaragua and Ecuador.

"The pejibaye palm is a pinnate-leaved species, reaching a maximum height of about sixty feet. Its straight, slender stem, commonly about six inches thick, is armed from the ground upward with stiff, very sharp, black spines about two inches long. These are arranged in circular zones of varying width, those near the base of the stem being four to six inches wide, while higher up the width decreases to one or two inches; there is about an inch of smooth trunk between the zones.

"The leaves, which are graceful in appearance, especially when the palm is young, are commonly eight to twelve feet in length, and deep green in color. The racemes, which are produced from the trunk of the palm immediately below or among the lower leaves, and are protected by erect spathes, are stout, and 18 to 24 inches long. The first fruits mature in September. From this month until March or April there are usually ripe fruits on the plant, provided the racemes are not cut when the first fruits reach maturity. The long time which the fruits will remain on the palm in good condition is a noteworthy feature.

"Racemes of mature fruits sometimes weigh twenty-five pounds or more, and five or six such racemes are often produced by the palm in a single crop. The maximum production of one palm (or, more properly speaking, one stem, since four or five stems are often allowed to grow from a common base) is about 150 pounds of fruit. It is seen, therefore, that the productiveness of the pejibaye is similar to that of the date palm.

"The individual fruits are top-shaped conical, or ovoid in form, and vary from one to two inches in length. There is a wide range of variation in the color of the surface, that of some varieties being clear light yellow, while in others the color is deep orange or reddish orange, sometimes shading to brown. The outer integument or skin is thin; in some varieties it adheres closely to the flesh, even after the fruit has been boiled, while in others it can be peeled readily from the boiled fruit. The character of the flesh is not easily described; it is dry, mealy, yet firm in texture, and pale orange to yellow in color. The single seed, from which the flesh separates very readily after the fruit has been boiled, is conical, somewhat angular in outline, about three-quarters of an inch long, black, with a thin but hard shell enclosing a white kernel resembling that of the cocoanut in character.

"In food-value as expressed in calories, the pejibaye and the avocado stand first among the tropical fruits of economic value; some varieties of the latter have a higher value than the pejibaye but the average is about the same."

FOOD IN THE FRONT YARD.

The pejibaye palm will yield a hundred pounds or more of nourishing food every year with little care or expense.

A list of the most noteworthy tropical fruits would have to include the pejibaye, Mr. Popenoe says, because of the relatively small proportion of water contained in the fruit; the large amount of carbohydrates (mainly starch), the considerable quantity of fat and the small size of the seed. And it is not only of high food-value, but it is delicious as well. Mr. Popenoe believes that it is destined to become of great importance in many tropical countries, and it is in this belief that he writes the present paper, in order to bring it to the attention of tropical horticulturists and to place on record the available data regarding its culture. He goes on:

"The pejibayes sold in the markets of Costa Rica have usually been boiled in salted water for about three hours. In this condition they are ready for eating without further preparation, except to remove the skin. They are so palatable in this form, that very few efforts seem to have been made by Costa Ricans to devise more elaborate methods of preparation, though enough has been done to show that this fruit lends itself to various uses.

"After it has been boiled, the fruit cannot be kept in good condition more than five or six days. Before cooking, however, it has excellent keeping qualities. If placed in a dry room, where the air will have free access to it, the fruit will not decay, but will gradually dry up.

"It should be a simple matter to ship pejibayes to distant markets. If properly packed, they should keep ten days to two weeks, at least, without suffering materially either in appearance or flavor. It may be mentioned, in this connection, that it seems feasible to dry the boiled fruit and store it for an indefinite period.

"Like the chestnut, which the boiled fruit strikingly resembles in texture and flavor, the pejibaye is used as a stuffing for turkey and chicken. Dried, it might be reduced to a flour which would serve various culinary uses. But to one who has eaten the freshly boiled pejibaye, there is no incentive for seeking new ways of preparing the fruit for the table.

"In addition to the fleshy portion of the fruit, the hard white kernel of the seed is eaten. It resembles the cocoanut in flavor, and contains a large quantity of oil. The *palmito* or terminal bud of the palm may be used as a vegetable, but its consumption necessitates the destruction of the palm. It cannot, therefore, be considered of much economic importance. The wood, which is dark brown in color, nearly as hard as bone, and takes a fine polish, was used by the Indians in pre-Columbian days to make spears, and for pointing their arrows. It is now employed for walking-sticks.

"It is doubtful if the species will grow successfully in a cool subtropical climate such as that of southern California. In extreme southern Florida, however, there are probably regions where it will succeed. In Cuba, Porto Rico, and the other West Indian islands it should find itself entirely at home, and we recommend it as a culture for these islands. In many parts of Brazil it should also succeed, while the Asiatic tropics undoubtedly offer immense regions where it could be cultivated.

"Three or four palms, grown in the dooryard with practically no expense, would mean the production of three or four hundred pounds of excellent food every year. And this would be a food of delicious character, available during six to eight months.

"In conclusion, we wish to urge upon horticulturists in tropical regions where this palm is not yet cultivated, the desirability of its introduction and establishment as a common dooryard tree; with a view, later, to the extension of its culture, so as to place the pejibaye upon the substantial basis of a profitable commercial fruit, a position which it will achieve if the necessary initiative is supplied to effect its preliminary planting and study."

ARE OUR WIVES HEALTHY AND HAPPY?

MOST OF THEM ARE, if we are to credit the results of an investigation made by the Bureau of Social Hygiene upon a group of one thousand married women. In this research, the problems of marriage and married life have been attacked in an unusually broad manner, we are told by the writer of a leading editorial in *American Medicine* (New York). A preliminary statement of results appeared in *The Social Hygiene Bulletin* in June. Admitting the inherent difficulties and the limitations of the questionnaire method, says the editorial writer, there is no reason to doubt the statements that have been submitted by the thousand women who filled out the various questions which covered childhood, adolescence, and marriage. The questions were formulated carefully and their content and form were established after a consultation with competent advisers in psychology, psychiatry, and sociology. We read:

Photos by courtesy of "The Journal of Heredity," Washington, D. C.

AS THE BUNCH COMES FROM THE TREE.

It is boiled in salt water before eating and is neither sweet nor sour, but resembles the chestnut in flavor and form.

"PEJIBAYES! PEJIBAYES!"

A common street scene in Costa Rica, where the fruit is popular with all classes and fetches a good price.

"The results naturally came from a selected group—in a sense, a self-selected group possessing more than the average ability. From an educational standpoint the queries demanded a higher order of intelligence than is represented in a cross section of the female mind of the country, hence it is not surprising to find that 66.9 per cent. of the answers came from graduates of colleges or universities. Thirty per cent. of the answers came from women between the ages of 28 and 33 years, tho the age variations extended from 21 years to 83.

"Had one asked previous to the beginning of the study, from what type of women most of the replies would have emanated, one would have been tempted to suggest that neurotic and unhappy women would have rejoiced in the opportunity to unburden themselves and thus achieve temporary relief in relating their experiences. The facts did not justify this pessimistic attitude. According to their own statements, approximately 74 per cent. stated that their health up to marriage was good or better, while 16.3 per cent. said that their health was fair, and, furthermore, 63 per cent. admitted that their health after marriage was the same as before, while 19 per cent. testified that their health was better than before marriage, as compared with 14.4 per cent. who regarded their health as worse than before marriage. Thus it is patent that the highly intelligent group that reported did not partake of the nature of unhappy, neurotic, disgruntled malcontents whose answers were dictated by an ulterior desire to escape discomfort or to warn others to avoid matrimony by reason of their experiences.

"Some importance must be attached to the experience of the individuals in the work of the world. Approximately 59 per cent. of the women had been gainfully employed before marriage, while, after marriage, only 23.5 per cent. were in gainful employment outside the home. These figures are not evidences of economic status tho they may reflect the increase in economic freedom which woman has attained. Employment after marriage no longer can be construed to be the result of the inability of the husband to give adequate support, because in any group

Photo by Brown Brothers

WHAT MAKES THE "GREAT WHITE WAY" WHITE: SO MANY ELECTRIC SIGNS THEY ARE IN EACH OTHER'S WAY.

it may represent the personal preference of the woman to continue her active interests or to maintain her economic independence."

It is interesting to consider the statements of the writers with reference to their own happiness. Fully 87 per cent. attest happiness in marriage. The general divorce rate, even tho an inaccurate figure, is placed at about 8 per cent. of all marriages. Among the thousand women the divorce rate was only one-half of one per cent. The fact that only 4.4 per cent. of the women answering the questions stated themselves to be unhappy is reassuring. The writer continues:

"The real worth of a study of this character is to be found in the analysis of the elements entering into ill health or unhappiness in so far as marriage is responsible for their development. It is patent that the study of a group of women so high above the general average of the feminine population can give comparatively little data generally applicable to all women. The conditions of education, the contacts of employment, the independence of opinion, the willingness to participate in a study of this character all serve to isolate these thousand women as unusual. Nor is it unfair to believe that their capabilities of adjustment to married life are on a higher plane than those who have not had their advantages. It is probable, likewise, that their mental status gave them a higher degree of protection in the matter of mating, and therefore lessened the likelihood of their health being undermined by reason of physically poor matings.

"One might even ask the question whether the high rate of happiness was in any way related to the low birth rate within the group, but this question is unfair because thus far there has been no correlation worked out between the reporting of happiness or unhappiness and the number of children living or dead. Many of the women are sufficiently young to make it certain that the full complement of children has not been secured, and in consequence the present average of 1.77 children per woman is not to be considered as the potential child-bearing index of the women in the group.

"Whatever makes for familial happiness promotes social welfare and incidentally conduces to a higher standard of communal health. The health of families as a unit possesses more than a fictitious value, and there are distinct advantages in recognizing that the health and happiness of families are so interwoven that both must be considered in the management of their general problems. The physician is thoroughly cognizant of the meaning of happy families in his ordinary routine of caring for the sick and endeavoring to protect and conserve the well."

NEW WRINKLES IN ELECTRIC SIGNS

EIGHT MILLION ELECTRIC LAMPS are used to-day in illuminated signs throughout the United States. That is only eight to a store. If half the stores in the country displayed signs requiring a hundred bulbs each, fifty million would be necessary. The conclusion of W. E. Underwood, who writes in *The Electrical Review* (Chicago) on "Developments in Electric-Sign Lighting Practise," is that two to four times as many lamps may soon be required for this purpose, and he is probably conservative.

Electric-sign advertising, Mr. Underwood believes, has shown little if any decrease during the past year, altho many other forms of advertising have been pared to the bone. His conclusion is that electric-sign advertising must be considered intensely profitable by the average buyer of electric display space. He proceeds:

"Under the present conditions of keenest sales competition there is a strenuous struggle for the potential buyer's attention. Two merchants, side by side, competing for trade, will certainly not overlook the electric sign as an immediately effective way of compelling attention. The contest is to see whose sign can be made to gain the greater share of interest.

"It used to be, when electric signs were few and far between, that 'any old electric sign' got its full quota of attention. Even with low candle-power lamps, and without motion or color, it had a 100 per cent. attention value because it was silhouetted against the surrounding velvet darkness. Nowadays, there are few locations where the lone electric sign has the field all to itself. Every 'Main Street' is a miniature Broadway.

"There are three ways in which the electric sign may gain added attention value without increased size. The first to be thought of and utilized was color. The next step was motion, by means of flasher effects; and, finally, within the last year or two, there has been a nation-wide movement on the part of electric display advertisers to make their signs more effective by means of greater brightness.

"Before the war there was a quite popular movement among merchants towards store-front lighting, accomplished by means of one or several high wattage lamps suspended over the front of the store. At that time many tiny hole-in-the-wall merchants bought this equipment, installed it and then found it too expensive to operate continuously night after night. This experience, together with the fuel-conservation program entailed by the war, was adverse to the growth of this type of lighting demand. The demand is again growing rapidly and more conservatively, and such lighting is gaining headway among the more prosperous merchants who can easily afford it, as well as among the more aggressive but small merchants who realize its advantages in attracting trade which might otherwise overlook their humble places of business.

"Even before the tide set in for brighter electric signs there was a decided tendency towards better lighted store-windows—a tendency which has been constantly augmented. It is odd in a way that progress in sign lighting has been from light, to colored light, to motion and then to more light, while store-window lighting early turned to motion and to greater brilliancy, but is just now turning to the practical application of color in lighting.

"It is estimated that there are something like 8,000,000 electric sign sockets in use in the United States, requiring about the same number of lamps each year. It requires no wide stretch of imagination to picture an increase of two, three or even four times in the lamp wattage required for these sign sockets if the present higher wattage tendency continues, as seems likely. Nor does it require great imagination to foresee a considerably increased revenue to the whole electrical industry as a result. This includes electrical retailers, contractors, jobbers, sign people, central stations and manufacturers of lighting equipment.

"Of stores there is a round 1,000,000 in the country, so that each bit of progress in the lighting art, whether it be a step towards higher intensity, a step in the direction of color lighting or a trend towards store-front lighting, is immediately reflected as new lighting business in every town and city the country over. And the really encouraging part is that instead of suffering a depression and handicap because of a general slackness in business this particular demand is, if anything, augmented by the keener competition among merchants and manufacturers which goes hand in hand with dull times."

UNCLE SAM'S SUCCESS WITH REINDEER

THE announcement that a shipment of thirty thousand pounds of Alaskan reindeer meat has just been received at San Francisco calls attention, says *The Trade Record* issued by The National City Bank of New York, to the remarkable success of our reindeer experiment in Alaska, where the value of the reindeer herds, established a few years ago, is now counted by millions of dollars. In the early part of our ownership of Alaska, it seems, the Eskimos were chiefly dependent upon the whale, walrus, caribou and seal for their animal food, but with rapid destruction of these by the white man's rifle, the supply of animal food, an absolute essential in that climate, was greatly reduced, and the existence of the natives thus threatened. This condition was brought to the attention of the public in the United States in the early nineties by Dr. Sheldon Jackson, who had been sent to Alaska by the Government to establish schools among the natives, and he conceived the idea of introducing the reindeer, then unknown in Alaska, but proving extremely useful in Siberia and Lapland. We read further:

"Personal appeals by Dr. Jackson to the public in the United States resulted in contributions of $2,148, and sixteen head of reindeer from Siberia were landed in Alaska in 1891, followed by about one hundred and fifty in later shipments during the year. Congress then made several small contributions, and by 1900 the total number of reindeer imported into Alaska from Siberia had aggregated about twelve hundred. Importation was then suspended and a colony of 'reindeer masters' was brought from Lapland to instruct the Eskimos in the care of the twelve hundred animals thus supplied to them.

"As a consequence of this establishment of the reindeer industry in Alaska a quarter century ago, the number of reindeer now scattered through that territory is about 140,000 and their value between three and four million dollars. So liberally are the reindeer herds now supplying the natives, their owners, with meats, milk, butter and cheese, that their owners are now able to spare large quantities for the white population of Alaska and limited quantities for shipment to the Pacific Coast cities and thence to the great trade centers of the country, so that 'reindeer steaks' may be had in the markets of the great cities as far east as the Atlantic coast.

"The special value of this reindeer enterprise in Alaska was found in the fact that it turned into food form a natural growth formerly unutilized, and at the same time encouraged a fixed habitation and a domestication of industry on the part of a population formerly nomadic through its dependence upon the ocean's frontage for its supply of animal food. The reindeer, which thrives upon the formerly unutilized mosses and lichens of the Arctic 'tundra,' which he digs from beneath the snow in winter, serves not only as a food supply but also a draft and pack animal in transporting mails and merchandise, while his skins furnish clothing and shelter for the natives.

"The Alaskan reindeer herds, the descendants of the twelve hundred reindeer imported from Siberia a quarter century ago, are not only thriving upon a formerly unutilized domestic product, but supplying meat, milk, butter and cheese to the natives of Alaska and also the white population of 'Seward's Ice Box,' as Alaska was designated at the time of its purchase from Russia. Alaska has sent us since its purchase nearly a billion dollars' worth of precious metals and merchandise, including gold, silver, copper, furs, fish and meats, and taken in exchange nearly a half billion dollars' worth of the product of our farms and factories. The shipments from Alaska to the United States in the fiscal year just ended amounted to over sixty million dollars, and her takings of our domestic products, nearly thirty million dollars. The total value of gold, silver, and merchandise sent from Alaska to the United States in the eighteen years since an official record of this movement was established aggregates 805 million dollars, and our shipments to Alaska in the same period, 425 million dollars, making it quite apparent that our total trade with Alaska since its purchase for $7,200,000 in 1867 has aggregated more than $1,500,000,000, of which over $1,000,000,000 was the products of Alaska sent to our own ports, and about $500,000,000 of merchandise sent for use in that area."

Photo by Lomen Brothers, Nome.

AS TAME AS CATTLE: REINDEER IN ALASKA.

LETTERS - AND - ART

LITERATURE DRAMA MUSIC FINE-ARTS EDUCATION CULTURE

CHARLIE CHAPLIN'S ART DISSECTED

POPULARITY HAS ITS GREATEST EXPONENT at the moment in Charlie Chaplin. "The best-known and the best-liked, if not the most respected figure in the world to-day is undoubtedly Charlie Chaplin," says the by no means frivolous Manchester *Guardian*, accustomed to weighing its words. And this tribute is only one of the many that greet the comedian of the films as he returns for a visit to his native city. Charlie's reception in London equaled or outdid the one accorded in the same place last year to Mary Pickford, and the outbreak is noted as a symptom in the gathering "afternoon of the British Empire." All the British papers are full not only of his doings on his holiday, but of analysis of his art. The London *Graphic* has a sort of pæan from the pen of one named Hanner Swaffer. Thus:

"If, by the chance of somebody else's invention, you can, if you know how to walk clumsily—every time more clumsily—you can put, even into the meanest Far-Eastern, non-speaking language, a smile and the memory of something funny—if, when the whole world of war is upside down, you can make everybody in the world laugh, when everybody else is crying, you have done what the Kaiser couldn't do and what Kitchener couldn't do. You have saved, even the next world, when the last one is dead.

"Poor Charlie Chaplin! 'A land of heroes,' we call it now. He was born in a London slum. He was kicked around, when he was a boy, and made ridiculous. All through his little silly boyish years he cried; and when you have seen 'The Kid,' his last, and best, film you know that Charlie Chaplin has put into that picture a thing that makes Gladstone's speeches on Bulgarian atrocities merely ponderous nothings. The whole social fabric is wrong, and Charlie Chaplin knows it. He is the only man in the picture business who does. He was kicked around, even on the stage; he was knocked about on every stage on which he appeared. He learned there the details of an artistry which is being discovered, nowadays, by people who realize that, if you can show the same thing to the whole world at the same time wherever you wish to do it—well, Charlie Chaplin doesn't show to Chinamen and Indians, as some Americans do, white grafters and white slum-owners and white dope fiends. His gospel, screened, is like Mary Pickford's—the screened gospel of humanity, the hope of a little child."

Photograph by Underwood & Underwood

CHARLIE ARRIVES IN LONDON.

"The ovations of the crowd," says the London *Outlook*, "are in essence similar to the plaudits of the people over the artistic victory of Cimabue."

While the actor is at hand all the Chaplin films, even those that had gone to the lumber room, are brought out again, and at the sight of these samples of his life-work, says the Manchester *Guardian*, "one is imprest again with the idea that he was inspired by the study of cats," for—

"His instantaneous expression of likes and dislikes, his speed in action and sudden change to demureness, his complete unreasonableness, his intense seriousness—all these are the traits of good cats. When he suddenly notices the face of the lady next to him in the stalls he acts exactly like a cat that has had milk put before it. No expostulation or exclamation—just instant departure. When he sees a man he does not like, he instantly gets to work on him with feet and hands. The cinema is man robbed of speech, and Chaplin goes to the best dumb performer in the world—the cat. The dog is too much an imitator of man to be a master of pantomime. Charlie, I think, has gone to the cats."

It is not Mr. Chaplin's financial success that mainly impresses Mr. E. T. Raymond, who writes in the London *Outlook*. It is "the noteworthy part" he has played in perfecting the art of the screen—"something as distinct from any other art as painting is from sculpture, or literature from music."

"His earlier manner, marked as it was by a singular but not easily definable genius, was mainly dictated by the conditions of his employment. As the inspired buffoon of the film, he was expected to confine himself to buffoonery. The crudely commercial instincts which dominated the 'movie' business recked little of art. They thought in simple terms of 'sob-stuff,' 'cowboy drama,' and 'knockabouts.' Mr. Chaplin was the strength of the knockabout business, and the more extravagant he could make it the better he pleased his employers. Nevertheless it was the art of the thing, and not the mere agile imbecility of it, which counted. In this, as in other matters, all the people are not fooled all the time; there must be something more than the effervescence of animal spirits to account for an ascendency lasting over years.

"That there was something more was seen when Mr. Chaplin, emancipated from control, began to do his business in exact accordance with his own ideas. The humor was refined without loss of strength. An unsuspected emotional range was revealed in the pieces in which the humorous blended with the pathetic. It could no longer be denied, by the most superior, that the thing was art, and art of a most subtle kind. It is, indeed, not too much to say that Mr. Chaplin has been the first to demonstrate the possibilities of the cinema as the vehicle of a humor incommunicable by any other means. He is the Columbus of the new film world. . . .

"But there is another point of view, and that is that the most syndicated and mechanized of all entertainment businesses has still to depend, not on its mechanical resources, but on the force of the human brain and human soul. It is seen that no 'talent for organization' can supersede the creative impulse. The cinema world will have its Charlie Chaplin, and nothing 'just as good.' The triumph of Mr. Chaplin is, in a very real sense, a human triumph, and any incidental absurdities of his visit to London should not blind us to the fact that the ovations of the crowd will be in essence similar to the plaudits of the people over the artistic victory of Cimabue. It may seem absurd to compare the Italian painter with the Americanized Cockney. But the one, like the other, was the pioneer of a new art. The only difference—and it is a mournful one—is that the very greatest art was once a popular affair, and the vulgarest felt some share in its conquests. But we must take such comfort as we can, and it is something to the good that, whatever we may think of Mr. Chaplin in the *rôle* of a popular hero, it is he, and not the chairman of some great picture syndicate, that the crowd turns out to honor."

As if such praise were not enough, *The Guardian* is, on another occasion, moved by the immense ovations of the welcoming crowd to ruminate:

"What will history, one wonders, have to say about these overwrought transports of public emotion, frequent now, almost unknown in England before the South African War? That in the afternoon of our day of empire we, too, like Greeks and Romans, became for the first time excitable to excess, a prey to 'stunts,' hysterical responders to the current suggestion? We hope not, tho the change does give matter for thought. At any rate the public opinion which chose this latest idol has chosen the best man of all that it had to choose in his own kind. If such popular homage as Garrick never received goes now to an actor whose voice has never been heard, at least he is surely the best cinema actor who ever was seen; his comedy, so far as pantomime can show, is of the great tradition; it springs from that genius for childlike wonder, in presence of life, which makes all the great comedians our brothers, as lovable as secret recollections of our own simpler, outworn selves."

CHARLIE IS COMING!

This is how the London *Daily Express* foresaw his reception.

A French writer in *Le Figaro*, sighing: "Ah, if Molière had known Charlot," adds: "To be able to give wit to a table, proves him an indisputable as well as exceptional master, and justifies the triumphal arches that Europe will surely build to honor Mr. Chaplin. So he can leave Molière content with his different gifts and not dispute his mastery in the art of penetrating the hearts of men."

CHAUTAUQUA IN A NUTSHELL

SUCH AN AMERICAN INSTITUTION as "Chautauqua" is still news to the British public, tho it is somewhat venerable with us. The size of this country explains its flourishing condition, since it supplies so many people remote from cultural centers with mental occupation. England doubtless has the same "dullness and stagnation which is the lot of little towns," but the railway takes you from one end of their country to another in twenty-four hours. The writer of the following for the Manchester *Guardian* does not recommend a new institution to his readers, but views it as one of the curiosities of his American travels:

FRANCE, TOO, WAS EXPECTANT.

"If you don't eat all your soup at once, I'll keep Charlot away from Paris." (In France he is affectionately, "Charlot.")

—Cave in *Le Matin* (Paris).

"The Chautauqua season has been in full blast here. Motoring through hundreds of little towns, you will see a prominent sign upon which is written the name of the town and, after it, the word 'Chautauqua.' Behind it is one huge tent and perhaps a number of others. A little town of 500 inhabitants will gather together as many as 5,000 people at its local Chautauqua, and as something like ten thousand Chautauquas are being held at the same time, it is estimated that perhaps 20,000,000 people take part in them during the course of the summer.

"The superior smile at Chautauqua. In truth it has a little of the element of the correspondence college and nothing at all in common with the British Association. The first gathering together was more or less religious in character and was held on the shores of Lake Chautauqua, about half a century ago, amid nearly virgin forest. With the religious element were gradually combined instruction and recreation. Perhaps it is more like the Y. M. C. A. than any other institution, but even that does not describe it exactly. From that original gathering it has spread all over the country. It is essentially an institution for a big country.

"Americans have a positive hunger for 'getting together' and, having got together, for receiving instruction upon not too arduous terms. Chautauqua meets this need so successfully that it is a household word.

"At the central gathering together still on Lake Chautauqua, arrangements are made for lectures and instruction of every possible kind. Months beforehand terms have been arranged with some of the best musicians, painters, historians, and so forth to organize a course of study for the two summer months. Thus a pianist arranges for a series of pupils whose studies he overlooks during that time, both in the form of actual practise and of theory together. Many people find in Chautauqua stimulus for the whole year, especially those who, by reason of such circumstances as distance or shortage of funds, are very much thrown back upon their own resources. The life is most of the time in the open air, rowing, swimming; riding—all of which are easily available here—being among the recreations. People meet their friends year after year, and some of them lay emphasis on study, some on recreation, some on religion. It is designed with extraordinary aptitude to meet all needs.

"The local Chautauqua is the event of the year, and it saves many a little town from that dullness and stagnation which is the lot of little towns in whatever continent."

GRASSO AND THE ITALIAN THEATER

MUSIC AND THE DRAMA divide things Italian in New York on a strange basis. Instead of going "fifty-fifty," as the phrase is, they split something like ninety-ten, and the results in both cases are quite satisfactory to the elements interested. The Metropolitan Opera House reflects so much glory on Italian art, points out the New York

GIOVANNI GRASSO

Who comes for his first visit with the reputation of being the greatest melodramatic tragedian of Italy.

Herald, that "the Italian Government abandoned an idea once suggested of establishing an Italian theater in this city." The houses devoted to Italian theatrical art are humble enough. "Theaters abandoned by the inexorable decrees of the burlesque wheel, unsuited to the cinema, and too old-fashioned for the use of the Yiddish actors, usually serve as her temples." But when the stars of the Italian stage visit the city, "nothing could be more creditable to Italian stage art than the enthusiastic support accorded them in the humble theaters of this city." So the *Herald* reviews the situation on the occasion of the first American visit of the famous Sicilian actor, Giovanni Grasso. We read:

"It was Mimi Aguglia who first added the prestige of a distinguished name to these troupes. Ever since her first engagements at the playhouses on Broadway she has paid frequent visits to the Italian theaters of this and other large cities. So prosperous has her experience proved that Giovanni Grasso, long associated with this actress abroad in the performance of the Sicilian folk pieces, has come to New York and selected a theater in the Bowery as the scene of his appearances.

"There is no reason why the local Italian colony should feel any mortification that the distinguished foreigner is inviting this country to witness his art under such modest circumstances. Ermete Novelli and some of his predecessors made but little appeal to the English-speaking public. Nor did their own countrymen seem anxious to witness their appearances here when the scene was one of the theaters up-town. It did not seem to be a question of the prices; seats in the galleries were as cheap as any to be had down-town. The Italian colony could not for some reason be attracted to its favorites up-town, generous as it may be in its support of the opera.

"So there is greater glory in the presence of large audiences at the theaters in the Bowery than in the meager gatherings that greeted the eminent Signor Novelli at the Lyric Theater or Signora Aguglia at the Broadway Theater on her first visit here. The applause of crowding compatriots, even if it echo under the shabby ceilings of a Bowery playhouse, has the sound of genuine appreciation more stimulating to art and more encouraging than the polite approval of a few, ignorant of the language which the actors are speaking."

If a stray visitor of alien tongue goes here he is greeted with smiling interest. The bill changes every night and the prodigious work involved in such an effort is helped out by a prompter whose whispering is an accompaniment like a rustling breeze to the entire course of the play. "The repertory is catholic. From the 'Year of the Plague in Naples' down to Sem Benelli and D'Annunzio, they put the drama of all periods before their compatriots." The present visitor is described by the Brooklyn *Eagle*:

"Giovanni Grasso, who is playing at the Royal Theatre in the Bowery, comes to this country with the reputation of being the greatest melodramatic tragedian of Italy. But he is anxious to be more than an actor—a man with a mission, in fact. That mission is through his dramatic art to nurture, to inspire, to develop the better qualities of his own Sicilian race, for every play in which he appears, he says, teaches a lesson. Here, that mission is to inspire these qualities so that the Sicilians in New York may be better Americans, for, he says, as the pigeons in Europe flock around the man who feeds them, his countrymen flock to hear him play because they are always seeking something that will help them, that will do them good, and they know they can find something in the plays. That is the reason, he says, why he has made the Sicilian drama his specialty; why, in these later years, he has confined himself to it. Sicilians often are misunderstood, he says; they are credited chiefly with being vindictive, while they have many good and great characteristics. So it is his mission to reveal the true Sicilian nature to other races as well as to keep before his countrymen the higher qualities of manhood.

"Some persons, for example, Grasso said, think the Sicilian is not chivalrous. That is false. The Sicilian has high regard for women. He tells a story of his own experience. He was fourteen years old and was playing Shakespeare's 'Othello' in Italian in the theater in Catania, Sicily, which had been his father's. His father, by the way, had died previously and the support of the family had devolved upon him. Near the stage sat a man and his wife. The man was bullying the woman quite audibly. Grasso after a time, in an aside, warned him to stop. The bully persisted. Again Grasso interrupted his lines to say in Sicilian, 'If you don't cut it out, I'll smash you.' The warning went unheeded. Finally Grasso stopt in the middle of a phrase, sprang from the stage, grabbed the man, punched his head and threw him into the aisle. Then he went back to the stage and resumed his speech.

"The applause of the audience stopt the performance, Grasso says, but he explained that the applause was not because he had introduced something exciting into the play, but because he had taken the part of a woman. That he says, was evidence of Sicilian chivalry.

"Speaking of himself and his early life, Grasso says his first experience with the stage was with marionettes. His father had a Punch and Judy theater in Catania. Grasso himself had his part in a play when he was seven years old. Since that time he has been an actor.

"While 'Othello' is the only play by Shakespeare in which he has appeared, the Sicilian is intimate with all the Shakespearean works. One characteristic of their heroes, he says, is that they are chivalrous, and this he greatly admires. He explained that one reason why he had not essayed more Shakespearean rôles is that he grew too large early. When he thrashed the nagging husband at fourteen, he was no stripling, but a man in build. He stands at least six feet in height, but looks almost squat because of his bulk. His strength seems to be prodigious, for when he strikes his clenched fist into the open palm of his other hand, it is with the force of a pile-driver."

COLLEGES FOR SILK SHIRTS

NOT ALL THE WAR WAGES went for silk shirts, thinks the Detroit *Free Press*, else there would not be the crowding into college that this autumn is witnessing. Something must have been held back from the swollen wages of that time to pay for the expensive education of to-day, especially now that unemployment has become so wide-spread. The two conditions appear irreconcilable and newspapers are trying to fathom the mystery. "Usually a business depression results in small entering classes," points out the Decatur *Herald*. But at some institutions the doors have to be closed before all the applicants are enrolled. The situation would seem to afford ample material for answer to the questions raised by a play current in New York which sets out to exhibit the worthlessness of the modern system of college education. One of the characters in "The Man in the Making" says there's a great difference between going to college and being sent there. As he was *sent* without the proper preliminary training, he fell among the wasters and brought chagrin to his father and disasters to himself. The play's message may have plenty of confirmation if some of the comment on the present situation realizes itself in results. The Decatur daily for example, observes:

"Why this rush to the campuses at a time when incomes are supposed to be reduced and household economies are essential?

"One reason may be found in the general lack of jobs at high wages rather common two and three years ago, which enabled a youngster just out of high school to gratify his whim for shirts of vari-colored shades and fine texture, and to dress in clothes possessing that dash and swagger popularly supposed to characterize the habiliments of college men. Why go to college if you can draw down the mazuma in an office and still dress like a collegian?

"Not many youngsters are being kidnaped for high-paying positions these days. In fact a good many of these same young men have found to their sorrow how slender is the hold on the ladder of success when a man enters life work with his education still incomplete. Years like 1918, 1919, and 1920 seem to refute the old fogy notion that the grinding drudgery of hard work is essential for success, but the last year has rather tended to prove that the man without special training is under a heavy handicap. So young men are returning to school.

"The 5,000,000 unemployed represent that part of the population that would not be interested in higher education under any circumstances. The families of only moderate means who put a boy or girl into college will manage somehow, for any father or mother worth the name will gladly make sacrifices in behalf of their children's education."

The Troy *Record* finds some comfort in the possibility that the facts argue an overdoing of the prediction of a hard winter. Banks report larger savings deposits than ever before. Then,

"Certainly the young men and women who are enrolling for the college year because they are out of work have the wherewithal to finance themselves; otherwise they would not enroll.

"If the opinion that interest in higher learning is being taken up at the point where it stopt when we went to war is true, that is one of the most encouraging signs of the times. There is an inclination in some quarters to deprecate the time spent in college and university. The criticism is not warranted, for knowledge never hurt anybody. A self-educated man may be more successful than a college graduate, but that is not the fault of the college or of the education.

"It is possible for a young man to waste his time in college, just as it is possible for him to waste his time anywhere else. Everything else equal, the college man will be better equipped to grapple the problems of life than the man who is deprived of such an education.

"That, however, is not so much to the point as the fact that if there is popular interest in higher learning, the general level of intelligence is raised. That is desirable, for besides increasing efficiency, it adds to a people's ability to enjoy a thousand and one facts of life of which they would otherwise be ignorant."

Harvard reports 1000 applicants for entrance; Dartmouth has found itself compelled to decline 1500 applications; other New England colleges are similarly affected in a somewhat less degree. "Capacity" signs will likely be hung out all along the way, facts which lead the Manchester (N. H.) *Union* to recall an overmodest prophesy. It even forces the suggestion that education may be overdone, or at least that certain institutions might grow beyond the limits of manageable size:

GRASSO, AS CARUSO SAW HIM.

This cartoon was drawn by Caruso in Sorrento three weeks before his death, and was sent by him to *La Follia*, the Italian paper published here. It shows the enormous Grasso as he appears in "Malia," the stormy Sicilian play which served for his London début in 1908, and for Mimi-Aguglia's New York début later in the same year.

"Some striking calculations of probable college attendance twenty-five and fifty years hence were published a couple of years ago, based on statistics obtainable at that time. It was made clear that a tremendous impetus had been given to the movement toward higher institutions of learning, and it was shown that with a continuance and growth of the movement the universities of the future promised to dwarf in comparison the largest of those at the present. As a matter of fact, some of the universities to-day are so huge that grave question has arisen in some quarters if they have not passed the point of maximum vantage in the training of students, and there has been a distinct increase of activity by advocates of the small college as opposed to the vast university. The statement of conditions at the beginning of the new academic year promises to heighten general interest in this question.

"It has long been admitted that education is one of the nation's greatest businesses, and we now have evidence that it is a business which is continuing to develop through hard times just as it developed in times of popular affluence. The immediate problem of making the supply equal the demand for educational facilities is likely to be sufficiently absorbing to concentrate attention upon the needs of the present, to the temporary exclusion of worry about the similar, if still more extensive, difficulties of the generations to come."

OUR LAWLESS AGE

CONTEMPT FOR LAW and the present revolt against the spirit of authority make this age eminently "one of sham and counterfeit," said James M. Beck, Solicitor-General of the United States, in an address before the recent convention of the American Bar Association at Cincinnati, the speaker rejecting the easy theory that these symptoms of a grave malady are merely a reaction of the World War. His portrayal of the lawlessness which now seems to be characteristic of the whole world and which is said to be so much evidenced in our own criminal statistics, evokes sympathetic response from some of the religious press, and George F. Foster declares in *America* (Catholic) that "the citizens of this country should be grateful to Mr. Beck for his timely warning of the perils of the immediate future." Far from causing the moral sickness of the age, says the Solicitor-General in his address as published in the daily press, the World War was in itself, perhaps, but one of its many symptoms. Some of the contributory causes of the world's disorder listed by this legal authority are reluctance to obey laws regarded as unreasonable or vexatious, the law's delays and laxity in administration which have bred a spirit of contempt, and the rampant individualism which began in the eighteenth century, with its excessive emphasis on the rights of man and small stress on man's duties. In proof of his contention, Mr. Beck instances the records of the criminal courts and police dockets, frequently mentioned in the press; violations of the sumptuary laws, which in the case of the prohibition statute have resulted in fines aggregating an estimate of $300,000,000; and "an increase in nine years of nearly 400 per cent in the comparatively narrow sphere of the Federal criminal jurisdiction." Nor is the spirit of revolt limited to secular laws, thinks Mr. Beck, for

"In the greater sphere of social life we find the same revolt against the institutions which have the sanction of the past. Laws which mark the decent restraints of print, speech and dress have in recent decades been increasingly disregarded. The very foundations of the great and primitive institutions of mankind—like the family, the Church and the State—have been shaken. Nature itself is defied. Thus, the fundamental difference of sex is disregarded by social and political movements which ignore the permanent differentiation of social function ordained by God himself."

Five plagues are afflicting humanity, said the Pope last year in a public utterance before the College of Cardinals. The first, Mr. Beck recalls, is the unprecedented challenge to authority; second, hatred between man and man; third, abnormal aversion to work; fourth, the excessive thirst for pleasure; fifth, a gross materialism which denies the reality of the spiritual in human life. All these charges, says the lawyer, are proved in recent experience. It is, however, to a wide-spread change in social conditions rather than to any change of man's essential nature that the Solicitor-General attributes the malady of our time. It seems to him that "the morale of our industrial civilization has been shattered. Work for work's sake, as the most glorious privilege of human faculties, has gone, both as an ideal and as a potent spirit. The conception of work as a degrading servitude to be done with reluctance and grudging inefficiency, seems to be the ideal of millions of men of all classes and in all countries." The great enigma, then, which this situation propounds to us, and which, "like the riddle of the Sphinx, we will solve or be destroyed," is this: "Has the increase in the potential of human power, through thermodynamics, been accomplished by a corresponding increase in the potential of human character?" Unfortunately,

"A mass morality has been substituted for individual morality, and group morality generally intensifies the vices more than the virtues of man. What was true of Germany was true—although in lesser degree—of all civilized nations. In all of them, the individual had been submerged in group formations, and the effect upon the character of man has not been beneficial. . . .

"There are many palliatives for the evils which I have discussed. To rekindle in men the love of work for work's sake and the spirit of discipline, which the lost sense of human solidarity once inspired, would do much to solve the problem, for work is the greatest moral force in the world. If we of this generation can only recognize that the evil exists, then the situation is not past remedy.

"I have faith in the inextinguishable spark of the Divine which is in the human soul and which our complex mechanical civilization has not extinguished. Of this, the World War was in itself a proof. All the horrible resources of mechanics and chemistry were utilized to coerce the human soul, and all proved ineffectual."

"This thoughtful and philosophical address can not fail to exert considerable influence," believes *The Reformed Church Messenger*, and it asks:

"Is the Church doing all that is within her power to bring her children back to 'the law and the testimony,' and to inspire them with the vision which alone can bring guidance and restraint and make life decent, tolerant and brotherly? Of all men in the world, *Christian pastors have the largest responsibility to-day in emphasizing the truth that 'the duty of everyone consists in respecting the rights of others.'* The peril of the hour is that classes and individuals are trying to diminish other people's rights and then enlarge their own. And the wages of lawlessness is chaos and death."

It is a gloomy picture Mr. Beck has drawn, says *The Catholic Vigil* (Grand Rapids)—"a picture that is all shadow." He sees tradition swept aside by a generation which "in its wild debauch of freedom has thrown its heritage to the winds and turned its drunken steps into the darkness." Then,

"What is to be the outcome of it all? The supreme test of man's building came in the World War which focused the manifold weaknesses of that building; the strain was too great. It is no longer a crisis that confronts the world, but a failure, the same failure that confronted the race at the dawn of things, the failure of humanity to get along without God. Were every invention of the mechanical era wiped out to-day at a single stroke, humanity would be the richer; there would be less poverty, less discontent, less maddening money fever than there is to-day. We have simply taken the wrong road and we have about reached the journey's end."

However, *The Churchman* (Episcopal) thinks that if Mr. Beck were to look beneath the surface, "he would find many hopeful signs in our day and generation." To be sure, there is much evil, but there is something good too, and, says this journal:

"We venture to think that Mr. Beck does not know his generation at all. We doubt whether he knows what most of the young minds and souls are thinking about or dreaming. A good many of our young men and women could paint about as pessimistic a picture of the generation which Mr. Beck probably holds in veneration as the one which he painted in Cincinnati of our present day. It would be well for men like Mr. Beck to take time to ask questions. Perhaps he has asked questions and does not understand the answers received."

THE SHEPHERD AND THE WOLVES

ON THE FRONT DOOR of every rectory should be placed a placard like this one which an Iowa bank has posted above the teller's window: "Stock Salesmen, Bird-Dogs, Oil-Well Men, Blue-Sky Artists, Porch Climbers, Confidence Men and Thieves Not Wanted—Stay Out." The writer who makes this remark in the current *Ecclesiastical Review* (Catholic, Philadelphia) is so gravely concerned over the "notorious fact that priests as a class fall easy victims to investment salesmen," that he advises the theological seminaries of his Church to add to their courses on pastoral theology a few lectures on the subject of a priest and his personal investments. If young aspirants for priesthood "were asked to take notes of such lectures for future reference and were told to read those notes before making any investments, they would be in a position to escape many a pitfall," we are told. One of the reasons why Catholic priests are so likely to be victimized is the fact that they are in a somewhat different position from other men. That is—

"Business men have a logical place for their earnings. They buy a store of their own, or use the surplus for necessary improvements, or increase their stock. Laboring men have a desire to own a home of their own, and making payments on that home gives them a place for their savings. A priest is not so situated. He has no family that induces him to save for future needs, and there is no particular endeavor that calls for his savings. His money is loose and he becomes a prey to the wily investment salesman. Back of all this, tho, there is something else that leads many men of the cloth to spend their money foolishly, and lose it. There are any number of safe investments that net a very fair rate of interest. Many men are not satisfied with 6 or even 8 per cent.; they want extraordinary returns, anywhere from 25 to 100 per cent., and with this object in view, they make investments and fall easy victims to those who offer large dividends, and end by losing their money, capital as well as interest. So it is covetousness, greed for dollars, that makes many a man invest heavily and lose all."

Another aspect of the investment game that is not a credit to the clergy and which has given rise to bitter feeling and a great deal of scandal, according to the Catholic writer, is the fact that some priests who "are not satisfied to make fools of themselves in money matters try to get others into the same class." In particular, "when priests urge laymen, often their own parishioners, to get in on investments that turn out badly, they are injuring their cause more than they imagine." For we are asked to think of "the humiliation a pastor must feel when his own people ask him about a venture into which he led them and he must give them an evasive answer, because he knows the money is lost and the victims know, too, that it is gone never more to return."

Young priests are warned against propositions guaranteeing to double or triple their money, and are advised to place their money in safe bonds and mortgages with a fair rate of interest, or in insurance policies or building-and-loan shares. A parting admonition is offered, which perhaps might be taken to heart by Protestants as well as Catholics, laymen as well as priests:

"Fathers, beware of friends, college chums, and ex-seminarians. These men are pests when it comes to working priests. Investments are not matters of friendship or sympathy. When a friend offers to let you in on the ground floor, be very cautious, because most of their floors are built upon a tottering foundation."

"A HOUSE OF HAPPINESS" FOR THE GREAT WHITE WAY

"BENSONIZING THE CHURCH is a mighty good thing," recently wrote a Broadway actor after a visit to Union Methodist Church, which embraces in its program music teaching, free shower-baths, a cheap luncheon, a "social clinic" for the discouraged and inept, homes for boys and girls, and a children's playground, everything being open to all, "regardless of creed, nationality, or social standing in New York's 'White Light' district." As briefly mentioned in these pages last November, Union Church advertises itself to Broadway by means of a blazing cross over the entrance, and it makes an especial appeal to strangers by arranging personal conveniences for them and caring for those in need. As the actor is further quoted in the New York *Christian Advocate* (Methodist), he was much surprized that "all other people in the church are not alike, but that if one goes far enough into it, he will find a lot of straight-forward, decent-living, clean-thinking folks that any red-blooded man would love to associate with." The church is known as "a House of Happiness" because of the cheer it has brought to many unfortunates. "One of the first things Dr. John G. Benson did after coming to Union Church," writes Laura Comstock Dunlap in the New York *Globe*, "was to open to the public without charge the shower-baths which had been installed for the benefit of the soldiers who were welcomed at the church during the war. Then he utilized the culinary arrangements which had been a canteen feature to furnish luncheon to the public at the moderate price of 35 cents." Now "about 200 persons are fed every day, seated in a pleasant dining-room with regular waiters." More important, perhaps, is that—

DR. JOHN G. BENSON,
Who operates a "social clinic" for the discouraged and the unfortunate.

"Next, Dr. Benson formed what he calls his 'social clinic.' Every afternoon he devotes two hours to listening to those in need of help or advice and often ends by turning them over to his specialists, a lawyer, a business adviser, a doctor, or a dentist, who form his cabinet. While these local plans were being worked out, Dr. Benson was quietly forming a group of associate members all over the United States, now numbering a thousand. They are those who by the payment of $5.00 a year or more became identified with the movement. In return they have a church home when they come to the city. They may send their baggage to the parish house, to be held pending their choice of a location. The office staff will hold mail, receipt for telegrams, secure tickets for places of amusement and map out an itinerary for shopping or sightseeing. On the other hand the associates may be very useful to the church. No fewer than fifty runaway girls have been returned to their friends or suitably located in New York in the year since Dr. Benson came to the work, most of them from the West. In communicating with their friends the good pastor often makes use of the nearest associate to reassure the frightened parents or call them to the rescue. The lure of Broadway brings many young people to this particular part of New York, and Dr. Benson has made known his desire to be of service to the stranded and distrest to all the traffic officers for blocks around. The result is the kindly 'cops' turn the footsteps of wanderers to this church of the open door, where they receive a warm welcome.

"It is in fact for the benefit of boys and girls out of work or alone in the city that the Union Church is putting forth its most strenuous efforts at present. Two houses next the church have been purchased, thrown together, and fitted up for the use of girls. The parlor of one house has been made a memorial by Oscar J. Dennis, and under the name of the Dennis Parlor will be used as a reception-room where girls may receive their callers.

It will have wicker furniture, a library, little desks, a telephone, and every convenience. In the basement the old-fashioned kitchen will be supplied with an electric laundry machine where the girls may do their washing, and on the capacious range they may cook their breakfasts or indulge in candy-making to their hearts' content. The back parlor of this house will be used for Dr. Benson's clinic. Both houses are now practically full, but rooms are always reserved for 'transients,' meaning the stranger or girl out of work. To her no charge is made for the room except the performance of such duties as may be assigned her until she has the position which Dr. Benson is wonderfully successful in obtaining for her. It is desired to extend this feature of the work and next winter vocational classes, including printing, will be started to fit the girl for earning her living. At present a good many are placed in families as domestic help. Meantime the boys are not forgotten. For them several floors of the parish house have been fitted up into dormitories, and the boy, like the girl, is not charged till he gets a job. During the summer a slanting roof of the house is to be raised so that in all about 100 young men may be accommodated in the four floors of the building. The front rooms are to be devoted to vocational work."

These, we are told, are only a few of the plans of "this wizard in modern church activities," which has so imprest Broadway and won for him a testimonial from men "of every religion and none." While he believes in salvation in "the good old Methodist way," Dr. Benson has also a word for "salvation through music, the arts, or whatever arouses the best and holiest instincts of man."

HOW NOT TO TRAIN PREACHERS

PULPIT POWER is one of the most pressing needs of the clergyman to-day, yet, complains the Boston *Transcript*, the university summer schools open to ministers make no reference to preaching in their courses. One summer school, for instance, which the Boston paper takes to illustrate its argument, offers lectures on the Ethics of Law, the Ethics of Medicine, of Journalism, on the relation between Capital and Labor, "Religion in Life," and on many other interesting topics; but "one is struck by the fact that not in the entire list of studies is to be found the one most important study of all. . . . No attempt is made to teach the minister how to send home his message from the pulpit." It is presumed that most of the clergymen-students have a message they would like to deliver, "but probably not one in ten of them is presenting that message, in his regular work, as effectively as he might." *The Transcript* thinks that—

"Knowledge of history and sociology and exegesis and general literature are valuable to any preacher, but pulpit power is far more valuable. And most preachers, after they have been in active work for a half dozen years, and have learned that they are not endowed with the genius of Chalmers or Whitefield or Brooks, are in a more receptive state of mind toward the practise of homiletics toward developing whatever moderate power they have than they were when they left the theological school. Whether we like it or not, the pulpit to-day is in a severer competition with rivals than ever before in Christian history. Concerts, magazines, newspapers, automobiles, outdoor sports, moving-pictures and many other attractions decimate the church congregations. And the preacher, while he may urge duty as the ground of church attendance, owes it to his people and to his own ordination vows to learn how to present his message in the most attractive and persuasive and compelling way of which he is capable.

"The teaching of pulpit address and homiletical power is far more difficult than instruction in ecclesiastical history or applied ethics. But it should be taught. Somehow, probably by the most practical and detailed kind of 'laboratory method,' of actual demonstration sessions, should the best methods of preaching be imparted and the efficacy of our preachers be increased. The sermon, in its preparation and delivery, is far the most important instrument at the minister's command. Therefore any summer school or winter school or divinity school which aims at preparing devout young men to enter the ministry or helping working-ministers to greater efficiency should give a large place to the instruction, the development, of the minister as preacher."

A SALVATION ARMY REPORT ON PROHIBITION

THE SALVATION ARMY is in a peculiarly advantageous position for appraising the results of prohibition in our great cities, a matter which has been the subject of much dispute. In a recent number of *The War Cry*, Commander Evangeline Booth of the Army in this country makes what may be considered an official report on the early fruits of nation-wide prohibition. "Boozer's Day" has been an established Army institution in New York City for a long time. Year by year, writes Commander Booth, "we have celebrated the Thanksgiving holiday from six in the morning collecting the drunks from the park benches, feeding them, and sobering them up, and saving them with huge and lasting results. But last year they were not there, and so we gave the day to the poorest children of the great city." And here Commander Booth finds "one of the most significant of the early results of prohibition" as far as the Salvation Army is concerned:

"It means that in the future we shall have less to do with the grave, and more to do with the cradle; less binding up of life's broken plants, and more training of life's untrammeled vines; that more of our energy, our ingenious methods, will be thrown into the work of prevention, which in the final analysis must be so much more valuable to the home, the nation and the Kingdom of God than even the most worthy work of cure.

Who better than the Salvation Army, it is asked, can speak of the results of the banishment from the streets and hovels of the poor of "this liquid fire and distilled damnation?" She answers that the Army's social secretaries report that drunkenness among the men frequenting the Army hotels and Industrial Homes has almost entirely disappeared, that men who formerly could hardly support themselves from day to day now possess savings accounts. In one hotel twenty-five men, who before prohibition could muster only a dime among them, now have deposits ranging from $100 to $500.

Above all in importance are the benefits which Commander Booth finds have accrued to the children. "Better pre-natal care for the mother, more food, improved clothing, more money, and, above everything else, the absence of inebriation's brutalities, are all in evidence, telling in the life's chances of these infants." Commander Booth has been asked "if it is true that the law is being violated." Her answer is:

"Yes, as the laws against arson, theft and murder have been violated; but these laws and their penalties remain, and so will the Eighteenth Amendment stand. . . .

"We recognize that the task of banishing all intoxicating liquor from the land is a stupendous, a lengthy one; but the same strong forces of moral sentiment, scientific education, and business prudence which made outlaw of its sale and manufacture are equal to the undertaking. And, behind such efforts, there must also be reckoned with the dynamics of divine inspiration."

But will prohibition stand? "Without hesitation," the Salvationist leader replies "Yes!"

"The edifice of prohibition has been well and substantially built, its labor has not been spasmodic nor its material cheap, and what it has taken so many years to raise up would surely take as many years to pull down. Therefore, for the future, we are unafraid. The coming generation, growing up without alcohol, educated in the history of its abuses against hygi ne, commerce, and morality, will muster so vast an army against their fathers' greatest foe as to protect from any and every jeopardy the legislation which safeguards their national life.

"By the Constitutional Amendment of Prohibition a measure has been enacted that will do more to bring the Kingdom of God upon earth than any other single piece of legislation, for the rum demon is the foundation and the bolsterer-up of almost all evils. Therefore history for righteousness has been made history that will live, for activities have been set in motion for civic and national betterment that will never stop until all evil is dead."

REVIEWS - OF - NEW - BOOKS

JELLICOE

BEATTY

HIPPER

VON SCHEER

BRITISH AND GERMAN ADMIRALS WHO FOUGHT THE BATTLE OF JUTLAND.

THE REAL STORY OF JUTLAND

FIVE years and more have now passed since the British Grand Fleet under Admiral Jellicoe, and the German High Sea Fleet, under Admiral von Scheer, met off the Skagerak, that broad sheet of water between the north coast of Denmark and the south coast of Norway, in what is known as the Battle of Jutland. The loss in shipping of that action was more than 172,000 tons, and the loss, killed and wounded, was approximately 10,000 men. These five years have given the experts time to study and analyze this action, which in size of armaments has been declared the most tremendous naval battle in history. In particular the reports and accounts written by the commanders on both sides have been minutely examined, and we now have several studies of the engagement written by American naval authorities,* who are free from the strong feelings displayed by writers in Great Britain, where the battle of the pens has almost equaled the big sea fight in uproar, in fury, and in indecisive result.

Many of the great naval engagements of history have been perpetuated and made more clear by certain phrases or utterances with which the lay mind instantly associates them. Thus, mention the Battle of Lake Erie and to the lips leap Perry's familiar "We have met the enemy and they are ours!" Trafalgar at once suggests Nelson's message, "England expects every man to do his duty." The forcing of the Mississippi is linked with Farragut's "Damn the torpedoes; full steam ahead"; and the action in Manila Bay with Dewey's "You may fire when you're ready, Gridley." These were all comparatively simple sea battles; fought to a definite decision; easy for the mind to grasp and to understand. The obscurity associated with the Jutland fight is appropriately matched with the fact that it is likely to go down into history associated with the words "low visibility," and just as those words are obscure and baffling to the lay mind, the battle itself is still somewhat of a conundrum. Why?

The Battle of Jutland may be compared to a gigantic, bloody, and destructive game of hide and seek, in which each side, tho both sides displayed marked valor, played the game coyly and cautiously. To Admiral von Scheer is attributed the recent statement that had Admiral Beatty, in command of the British cruiser forces, turned full to the westward upon making contact with the German light forces, the German Main Fleet would have followed Beatty and Hipper in the belief that Beatty was running for home. Jellicoe could have put the British Main Fleet between the Germans and their bases, and instead of the indecisive result, the entire German sea power might have been annihilated. In other words, Beatty lost the great opportunity when he failed to pretend to run away and hide at the right time. But had Beatty laid the trap, would Hipper have fallen into it? Von Scheer asked Hipper that question after the battle and Hipper's reply was that he would probably have followed Beatty, and doubted seriously that he would have given the order to break off the engagement. What might have happened is always pure supposition, in which the situation at a particular hour is molded to fit a partizan theory. What actually did happen, to sum up the action as an American critic, Captain Thomas G. Frothingham, U. S. R., sees it, was that: "As a matter of fact the Battle of Jutland did not have any actual effect on the situation on the seas. The British Fleet still controlled the North Sea. The Entente Allies were still able to move their troops and supplies over waterways which were barred to Germans. Not a German ship was released from port, and there was no effect upon the blockade. After Jutland, as before, the German Fleet was confined to its bases, except for occasional sorties into the North Sea. . . . The Jutland action had cheered the German people, but it had not given to Germany even a fragment of sea power."

It has been contended that Great Britain by her North Sea blockade enjoyed all the advantages that would have been gained by the destruction of the German High Sea Fleet. That, maintains Commander Gill, in his "What Happened at Jutland," is not correct. Germany's fleet was an important factor throughout the war. It was the power of this fleet that made the Baltic practically a German lake, kept open the trade routes between Germany and the North European neutrals, closed Russia's chief ports, and protected the German frontiers from the Gulf of Riga to Holland. It would be difficult to overestimate the influence, both direct and indirect, which the German High Sea Fleet exerted in bringing about the collapse of Russia. And, finally, it was the cover of the High Sea Battle Fleet that permitted the U-boats freedom to come and go in the prosecution of their campaign against commerce. In estimating the tactical situation in the North Sea there should be no misunderstanding as to the essential task of the German battleship fleet and the great influence a decisive British victory at Jutland would have had on the course of the war.

The Battle of Jutland was not a battle that may be given in a nutshell. But sifting, weighing and comparing the conflicting

*FOOTNOTE. The facts for this article are drawn from:

"What Happened at Jutland." By C. C. Gill, Commander U. S. Navy. With a foreword by Admiral H. B. Wilson, U. S. Navy New York. (George H. Doran Company.)

"A True Account of the Battle of Jutland." By Thomas G. Frothingham, U. S. Navy. (Bacon & Brown, Cambridge, Mass.)

"The High Sea Fleet at Jutland." By H. H. Frost, Lieut. Commander U. S. Navy. United States Naval Institute Proceedings.

"The Battle of Jutland." By David Hannay. *Edinburgh Review*. January, 1921.

An article in the New York *Herald* for August 14, 1921, based upon an interview between Admiral von Scheer of the German High Sea Fleet and another naval officer.

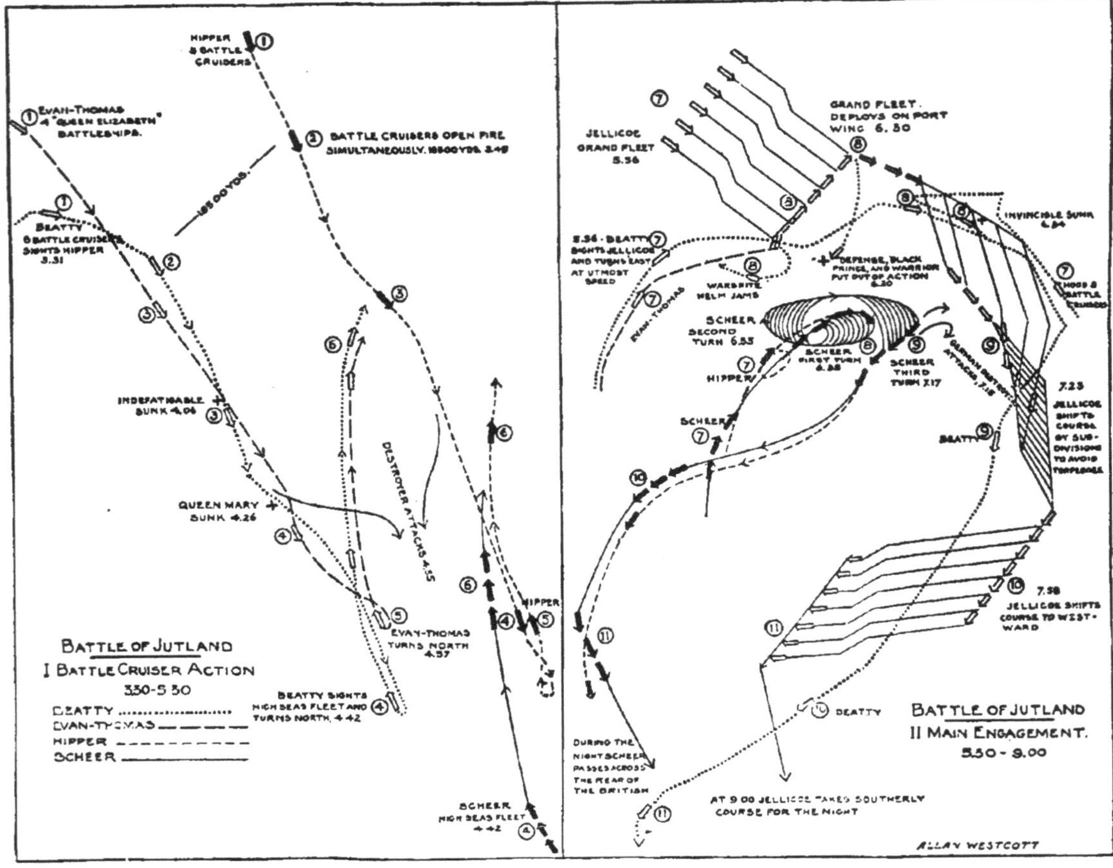

I. BATTLE CRUISER ACTION.

1. 3:30 p. m.—**Beatty sights Hipper.**
2. 3:48 p. m.—**Battle cruisers engage at 18,500 yds., "both forces opening fire practically simultaneously."**
3. 4:06 p. m.—***Indefatigable* sunk.**
4. 4:42 p. m.—**Beatty sights High Sea Fleet, and turns north (column right about).**
5. 4:57 p. m.—**Evan-Thomas turns north, covering Beatty.**
6. 5:35 p. m.—**Beatty's force, pursued by German battle cruisers and High Seas Fleet, on northerly course at long range.**

II. MAIN ENGAGEMENT.

7. 5:56 p. m.—**Beatty sights Jellicoe and shifts to easterly course at utmost speed.**
8. 6:20—7:00 p.m.—**Jellicoe deploys on port wing column (deployment complete at 6:38). Beatty takes position ahead of Grand Fleet. Hood takes station ahead of Beatty. Evan-Thomas falls in astern of Grand Fleet. Scheer turns whole German fleet to west (ships right about) at 6:35, covered by smoke screens. Scheer repeats the turn of the whole fleet (ships right about) to east at 6.55.**
9. 7:17 p. m.—**Scheer for the third time makes "swing-around" of whole German Fleet (ships right about) to southwest, under cover of smoke screens and destroyer attacks. Jellicoe turns away to avoid torpedoes (7:23).**

10—11. 8:00—8:30 p. m.—**Jellicoe disposes for the night.**

Most of the published narratives have used many charts to trace the events of the action. It has been found possible to indicate all the essentials upon this one chart. It should be noted that superimposed indications have been avoided, where ships have passed over the same areas (especially in the three German ships-right-about maneuvers). Consequently this chart is diagrammatic only.

THE BATTLE OF JUTLAND.

From "A Guide to the Military History of the World War," by Thomas G. Frothingham, Captain, U. S. R.

---

evidence, the story may now be told with reasonable clarity. First, how did the fleets compare in fighting strength? That is not a matter of serious dispute. The force under Jellicoe was superior in numbers, and in some ways in quality. Jellicoe had 41 capital ships, made up of 28 battle-ships, 9 battle-cruisers, and 4 armored cruisers. It had also 103 "ancillary craft," made up of 25 light cruisers, and 78 destroyers. Von Scheer's fleet consisted of 27 capital ships; 22 battle-ships, and 5 battle-cruisers; and 11 light cruisers, and 88 destroyers. The armament of the British fleet amounted to 362 great guns as compared to 244 in the German fleet; also, of the British guns 142 were 13.3-inch caliber, and 48 were of 15 inches. None was less than 12 inches; whereas in the German ships there were 20 guns of 10-inch caliber and the others were all of 11 or 12 inches. Summed up, the total weight of projectiles in the British fleet was 420,600 lbs. to 216,264 in the German; while British tonnage superiority was 1,139,000 to 590,000. Also Jellicoe had an important speed advantage, not because none of the German ships could steam as fast as the swiftest of the British, but because 6 of the 22 German battle-ships were pre-dreadnoughts, and were slow, which of course slowed down the entire fleet movement.

On the other hand, there were certain German advantages. David Hannay, writing in *The Edinburgh Review* for January, 1921, pointed out that the German destroyers were fitted out with more torpedo tubes, and the German battle-ships were constructed with more beam and therefore could be better protected to withstand hammering. The American Captain Frothingham has emphasized the German superiority in signaling. The Ger-

Shopping in Cantilever Shoes is a Joy

THE pleasure of shopping can be spoiled by wearing uncomfortable shoes. But in comfortable Cantilever Shoes, shopping is a real delight.

Many of the fresh, happy faces you see in the stores nowadays are due to comfortable shoes. One can be on one's feet all day in smart Cantilevers and then feel like dancing "half the night."

The arch of Cantilever Shoes is flexible, like the foot. It is not made rigid by a metal "shank-piece" such as is concealed in the arch of all ordinary shoes. The shape follows the natural lines of the foot. When you walk, your feet feel light and free; the flexible, snug-fitting shank supports the foot without restraining its natural action. Good circulation is permitted and the arch muscles exercise, which keeps the foot strong and well. Thus are weak arches benefited.

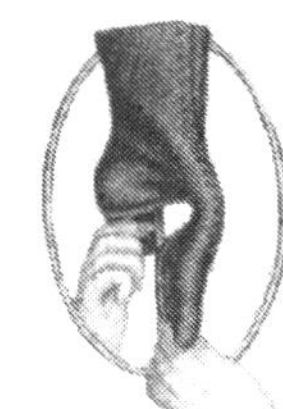

Cantilever heels of the right height permit correct posture. High French heels tilt the body out of balance, causing harmful pressure on some of the internal organs, which often results in headache, backache and other unhappy conditions.

Cantilever Shoes are not only good-looking but they encourage better health and a happier spirit—both of which improve a woman's appearance and add to her natural charm. You will be fitted carefully at the nearest Cantilever store.

If no dealer listed at the right is near you, the Manufacturers, Morse & Burt Co., 1 Carlton Avenue, Brooklyn, N. Y., will mail you the Cantilever Shoe Booklet and the address of a nearby dealer.

Cantilever
Shoe
like the foot
it has a
flexible arch

Cantilever Dealers

Akron—11 Orpheum Arcade
Altoona—Bendheim's, 1302—11th Ave.
Asbury Park—Best Shoe Co.
Asheville—Anthony Bros.
Atlanta—Carlton Shoe & Clo. Co.
Austin—Carl H. Mueller
Baltimore—325 No. Charles St.
Battle Creek—Bahlman's Bootery
Bay City—D. Bendall Co.
Birmingham—219 North 19th St.
Boston—Jordan Marsh Co.
Bridgeport—W. K. Mollan
Brooklyn—424 Fulton St.
Buffalo—639 Main St.
Butte—Hubert Shoe Co.
Charleston—J. F. Condon & Sons
Chicago—30 E. Randolph St. (Room 502)
Cincinnati—The McAlpin Co.
Cleveland—Graner-Powers, 1274 Euclid Av.
Colorado Springs—M. B. Rich Shoe Co.
Columbia, S. C.—Watson Shoe Co.
Columbus, Miss.—Simon Loeb's
Columbus, O.—The Union
Dallas—Leon Kahn Shoe Co.
Davenport—R. M. Neustadt & Sons
Dayton—The Rike-Kumler Co.
Denver—A. T. Lewis & Son
Des Moines—W. L. White Shoe Co.
Detroit—T. J. Jackson, 41 E. Adams Ave.
Easton—H. Mayer, 427 Northampton St.
Elizabeth—Gigl's, 1053 Elizabeth Ave.
Elmira—C. W. O'Shea
El Paso—Popular Dry Goods Co.
Erie—Weschler Co., 910 State St.
Evanston—North Shore Bootery
Fitchburg—Wm. C. Goodwin
Fort Dodge—Schill & Habenicht
Galveston—Fellman's
Grand Rapids—Herpolsheimer Co.
Greenville, S. C.—Pollock's
Harrisburg—Orner's, 24 No. 3rd St.
Hartford—86 Pratt St.
Houston—Clayton's, 803 Main St.
Huntington, W. Va.—McMahon-Diehl
Indianapolis—L. S. Ayres & Co.
Jackson, Mich.—Palmer Co.
Jacksonville—Golden's Bootery
Jersey City—Bennett's, 411 Central Ave.
Johnstown, Pa.—Zang's
Kansas City, Kan.—Nelson Shoe Co.
Kansas City, Mo.—Jones Store Co.
Knoxville—Spence Shoe Co.
Lancaster—Frey's, 3 E. King St.
Lansing—F. N. Arbaugh Co.
Lawrence, Mass.—G. H. Woodman
Lincoln—Mayer Bros. Co.
Little Rock—Poe Shoe Co., 302 Main St.
Los Angeles—505 New Pantages Bldg.
Louisville—Boston Shoe Co.
Lowell—The Bon Marche
Macon—The Dannenberg Co.
McKeesport—Wm. F. Sullivan
Meridian—Winner, Klein & Co.
Milwaukee—Brouwer Shoe Co.
Minneapolis—21 Eighth St., South
Missoula—Missoula Merc. Co.
Mobile—Level Best Shoe Store
Montgomery—Campbell Shoe Co.
Morristown—G. W. Melick
Muncie—Miller's, 311 So. Walnut St.
Nashville—J. A. Meadors & Sons
Newark—807 Broad St. (Opp. City Hall)
New Britain—Sloan Bros.
New Haven—153 Court St. (2nd floor)
New Rochelle—Ware's
New York—22 West 39th St.
Norfolk—Ames & Brownley
Oklahoma City—The Boot Shop
Omaha—1708 Howard St.
Pasadena—Morse-Heckman Co.
Passaic—Kroll's, 37 Lexington Ave.
Pawtucket—Evans & Young
Philadelphia—1300 Walnut St.
Pittsburgh—The Rosenbaum Co.
Pittsfield—Fahey's, 234 North St.
Plainfield—M. C. Van Arsdale
Portland, Me.—Palmer Shoe Co.
Portland, Ore.—353 Alder St.
Poughkeepsie—Louis Schonberger
Providence—The Boston Store
Raleigh—Walk-Over Boot Shop
Reading—S. S. Schweriner
Richmond, Va.—S. Sycle, 11 W. Broad
Rochester—148 East Ave.
Rockford—D. J. Stewart & Co.
Rock Island—Boston Shoe Co.
Saginaw—Goeschel-Brater Co.
St. Louis—516 Arcade Bldg., (Opp. P. O.)
Salt Lake City—Walker Bros. Co.
San Antonio—Guarantee Shoe Co.
San Diego—The Marston Co.
San Francisco—Phelan Bldg. (Arcade)
San Jose—Hoff & Kayser
Santa Barbara—Smith's Bootery
Savannah—Globe Shoe Co.
Schenectady—Patton & Hall
Seattle—Baxter & Baxter
Shreveport—Phelps Shoe Co.
Sioux City—The Pelletier Co.
Sioux Falls—The Bee Hive
South Bend—Ellsworth Store
Spokane—The Crescent
Springfield, Ill.—A. W. Klaholt
Springfield, Mass.—Forbes & Wallace
Stamford—L. Spelke & Son
Syracuse—136 S. Salina St.
Tacoma—Fidelity Building (8th floor)
Tampa—Glenn's, 507 Franklin St.
Terre Haute—Otto C. Hornung
Toledo—LaSalle & Koch Co.
Trenton—H. M. Voorhees & Bro.
Troy—W. H. Frear & Co.
Tulsa—Lyons' Shoe Store
Vancouver—Hudson's Bay Co.
Waco—Davis-Smith Booterie
Walla Walla—Gardner & Co.
Washington—1319 F Street
Waterbury—Reid & Hughes Co.
Wheeling—Geo. R. Taylor Co.
Wichita—Rorabaugh's
Wilkes-Barre—M. F. Murray
Winston-Salem—Clark-Westbroo.. Co.
Worcester—J. C. MacInnes Co.
Yakima—Kohls Shoe Co.
Yonkers—Louis Klein, 22 Main St.
York—The Bon Ton
Youngstown—B. McManus Co.

mans prepared their maneuvers carefully in advance, with the result that while the British Commander-in-Chief was obliged to keep up a constant succession of instructions by signal, the German Admiral was able to perform his surprizing maneuvers with comparatively few master signals. Rear-Admiral Caspar Goodrich is thus quoted: "Jellicoe was sending out radio instructions at the rate of two a minute, while von Scheer made only *nine* such signals during the entire battle." In his story of the battle, Lord Jellicoe has also emphasized the great advantage possest by the Germans in their recognition signals at night. Admiral Sir Percy Scott, who last March contended that if Germany had had one hundred more submarines she would have won the war, has said of Jutland: "The British Fleet was not properly equipped for fighting at night. The German Fleet was." To which Captain Frothingham adds: "The British Fleet was not prepared in methods in advance to cope with the conditions of the afternoon of May 31. The German fleet was. Herein lay the chief cause for failure to gain a decision, when the one great opportunity of the war was offered to the British Fleet. In the three decades before the World War great strides had been made in naval development, with only the unequal fighting in the American war with Spain and in the Far East to give the tests of warfare. In this period it is probable that at different times first one navy would be in the lead and then another. It was the misfortune of the British in the Battle of Jutland that the Germans, at that time, were better prepared in equipment and rehearsed methods for an action under existing conditions. This should be recognized as an important factor—and the failure to win a decision should not be wholly charged against the men who fought the battle."

As to the battle itself. For ten months a state of war had held. It had become the custom of the British Fleet to leave its safeguarded bases in the north of the British Isles and make periodical sweeps through the North Sea. The Admiralty ordered the Grand Fleet to make such a sweep on May 30, 1915. At the same time the German High Fleet was also in the North Sea. There had been an insistent demand on the part of the German people for activity on the part of their fleet. In response, von Scheer, who had lately become Commander-in-Chief, had taken his ships to sea at times. Altho it was primarily a policy of demonstration for effect in Germany, Scheer had improved the efficiency of his command and had with him all the strength he could muster, including the pre-dreadnoughts. Thus, provided conditions proved favorable, he was ready to fight. In the early afternoon of Wednesday, May 31, the fleets met. There was a smooth sea, little wind, and in the early stages of the action visibility was good. The first phase of the battle lasted from 2 P. M. to 4.55 P. M., and was confined to the British Advance Force under Beatty and the German Advance Force under Hipper. In a word, it was an action of battle cruisers. At 2 o'clock, when the fleets were fifty miles apart, each fleet learned of the other's presence. They zigzagged towards each other, and at 3.48, at a range of 18,500 yards, commenced action, both sides opening fire practically simultaneously. Coming to Beatty's aid was Admiral Evan-Thomas, with his slower squadron of four battle-ships. But he was too far away to be a factor in the battle's flict between Beatty's six cruisers and Hipper's five. The British fought on a course curving to the southeast, and then on a south-southeast course, and the Germans fought them on a parallel course instead of edging away from a superior British force. "It is now easy to see," so comments Captain Frothingham, "that the trend of the action was absolutely in the direction of the approaching main body of the German High Sea Fleet, but this, very naturally, was not apparent at the time to Vice-Admiral Beatty." Beatty evidently thought that the force immediately under his command was sufficient for the task, and the odds were unquestionably with him. Yet it was his squadron that suffered, losing one-third of its ships, the *Indefatigable* sinking at "about 4.06," and the *Queen Mary* at "about 4.28." The destroyers engaged in this first phase did no material damage to the capital ships.

When Beatty became aware of the proximity of the main body of the German High Sea Fleet the game of hide and seek was reversed. Beatty's ships turned right about and the German battle cruisers turned to follow them. On a northwest course the battle was continued at a range of 14,000 yards. Meanwhile, from the north, the British Grand Fleet had been closing in at the utmost speed. This marks the beginning of the second phase of the action. The situation was this: Jellicoe was groping for a junction, and not moving from definite information from Beatty. Scheer, following up Hipper's pursuit, was handicapped in speed by his slow-moving pre-dreadnoughts. One advantage the British had derived from the change in course was that Evan-Thomas's ships were drawn into effective range, at one point of the battle covering what was practically Beatty's hurried retreat. In an increasing mist the main bodies of the two fleets were drawing closer together. "To understand the course of the action at this critical stage," writes Captain Frothingham, "the reader should realize that the Germans possest a fleet maneuver which had been carefully rehearsed for such a contingency, in sudden contact with a superior enemy force. This was a simultaneous 'swing-around' of all the ships of the fleet, to turn the line and bring it into an opposite course."

Again the game of hide and seek. Almost at the moment of contact, under cover of a smoke screen, Scheer swung about, veering off to the southwest. The British had no idea that the Germans would be able to carry out this change of direction of the German line. They were even less prepared for the subsequent "swing around" which again turned the tide of hide and seek, converting the Germans once more to the attacking rôle. This was the third phase of the battle, lasting from 6.40 to 7.17 P.M. In the course of it Scheer turned back and attacked the British center with guns and torpedoes. Ahead of the fleet there was sent forward a determined attack by the German torpedo flotillas. While this maneuver subjected the van of the German fleet to heavy damage, the attack had the effect of making the Grand Fleet turn away and open the range.

Then, successfully for the third time, Admiral Scheer executed the same maneuver of ships-right-about, and again his fleet was on a westerly course screened by dense smoke, and freed from the gun-fire of the British fleet. "One reason for the failure of the British to understand these maneuvers of Admiral Scheer," writes Captain Frothingham, "was the fixed conous turn of all the ships of a fleet was impracticable in action—consequently they did not expect it to be used by their enemies." But for the third time Scheer had done it, and from that moment his fleet was not in great danger, nor even seriously engaged. As the twilight advanced he could prepare for the night. He found all his battle-ships in condition to do 16 knots, "the speed requisite for night work, and thus keep their places in line." The fourth phase of the action from 7.17 P.M. to 9 P.M., summed up by Commander Gill, is that in the gathering twilight Scheer, avoiding action, hauled around from west to southeast and sought to draw closer to Horn Reef. Jellicoe tried to regain touch on westerly courses, then turned to the southwest, and finally to south. As a result of Scheer's tactics, according to Captain Frothingham, the British Admiral was always groping for his enemy in mist and smoke, with only occasional glimpses of the German ships. The fifth and closing phase of the action, extending from 9 P.M. to 3 the next morning, brought no further shock of battle on a grand scale. There were isolated fights between disabled vessels of both fleets, with much shooting, with explosions and fire lighting up the darkness. The Germans proceeded to their bases undisturbed, and, according to Admiral Scheer, the fleet was repaired and fit to go to sea again by the middle of August.

What was the effect of the Battle of Jutland upon the *morale* of the nations engaged and their allies? David Hannay, in his article in the *Edinburgh*, pictured England's disappointment. He wrote:

"No one who read his paper on the morning of June 3, 1916, with the least attention, can forget that he was stung by a most unpleasant twinge. The Admiralty report had a disturbing air of being artfully worded to prepare him for worse news. So the first seeds of doubt, of dissatisfaction, of disappointment, were planted. They took root and began to grow beneath the surface. The removal of the censorship gave the growth free access to the air, and they have borne a large crop. One of the minor (but not wholly unimportant) questions left for the minute historian in the future is: Who were the official gentlemen of some importance at the time whose nerves were badly 'rattled' during those early June days; and who blabbed their fears? Nothing was more natural than that the country should be made to feel disenchanted and anxious by what it was told. For twenty months the Germans had not sought battle. The graver kind of authorities who addrest the public had repeated, day after day, the welcome assurance that the irresistible superiority of the British fleet was proved to demonstration by the manifest reluctance of the enemy to risk a trial of strength. Other teachers of a less magisterial, but more popular order, were telling all who would listen that the Germans were cowards who fought with babies only. Comic journalists had been pouring out pictures of absurd creatures, addle-headed, blear-eyed, pot-bellied, knock-kneed. These were Germans. If these wretched objects dared to face British tars they would be cleared off the surface of the earth in one 'hurricane sweep.' People would not, of course, have confessed that they took all this loud heehawing and guffawing seriously—but it told. And now, all at once, a public carefully prepared to expect only unqualified triumph was compelled to learn that the two fleets had met; that the British fleet had suffered heavy loss; that the German fleet was not destroyed;

CURRENT - POETRY

Unsolicited contributions to this department cannot be returned.

THE Buffalo *Evening News* selects the following poem of Austin Dobson, who lately died at a ripe old age, as one most "Appropriate for quotation at this hour." It will not need a further commentary to tell why:

IN AFTER DAYS

By Austin Dobson

In after days when grasses high
O'ertop the stones where I shall lie,
Though ill or well the world adjust
My slender claim to honour'd dust,
I shall not question nor reply.

I shall not see the morning sky;
I shall not hear the night-wind sigh;
I shall be mute, as all men must
In after days!

But yet, now living, fain would I
That some one then should testify,
Saying—"He held his pen in trust
To Art, not serving shame or lust."
Will none? Then let my memory die
In after days!

If we are to escape a settled gloom as the heritage of the war it will not be through putting by thoughts of its inevitable consequence. Mrs. Thomas in her poem in the New York *Times* proves this impossibility:

THE CHILDREN AND THE SHADOW

By Edith M. Thomas

I

There are some thoughts that so the mind appall,
One would not be alone with them . . . One such
There is that, reaching with an Afrite's clutch,
Can make me for the time its frozen thrall:
What if behind that blackest War of all
Were Powers who this world but for evil touch,
Whom War's iniquity did pleasure much—
As if therein they hailed Man's second fall?
This shadow from my thoughts would not away;
It was as though it reached beyond our age,
With worse to come . . . Were it not well to go
And watch awhile the children at their play?
For their unclouded looks should make me know,
'Tis of our time—and not their heritage.

II

The children at their play have no more care
For seasons that have rocked this world in wrath
Than have this year's sweet flowers for Winter's scath,
When sleeted storms did plow their thoroughfare.
Let it suffice—this Summer's light and air!
They have no part in last year's aftermath;
And since such comfort kindly Nature hath,
Let me, too, in the sportive moment share!
This was the thought that did my heart upstay,
When, suddenly, before my spirit's eyes,
Though distant far, defiled a ghostly train—
Children! The children who no more shall play,
Russia's starved little ones . . . Now, once again
The War's long shadow on my pathway lies.

This British poem which *The Century* prints with a decoration that we would like to include shows that the magic of old themes still lives. De la Mare is not of today's ephemera:

SUNK LYONESSE

By Walter de la Mare

In sea-cold Lyonesse,
When the Sabbath eve shafts down
On the roofs, walls, belfries
Of the foundered town,
The Nereids pluck their lyres
Where the green translucency beats,
And, with motionless eyes at gaze,
Make minstrelsy in the streets.

The ocean water stirs
In salt-worn casemate and porch,
Plies the blunt-snouted fish
With fire in his skull for torch.
And the ringing wires resound,
And the unearthly lovely weep
In lament of the music they make
In the sullen courts of sleep,

Whose marble flowers bloom for ay,
And, lapped by the moon-guiled tide,
Mock their carver with heart of stone,
Caged in his stone-ribbed side.

The fascination of little roads is felt by many. This is from *The Lyric West* and we print it in place of one sent in by a reader who liked the one by "G. S. B." in our issue of July 30, and offered his as "by a real Westerner." There is no gainsaying the devotion of this author to the object of his affection, as we see in his last four lines:

Could I but blow some magic horn,
And call to Life again those joyous days,
I should lie me down along this road somewhere,
And blow, from morn to morn!

Turn we now to the other:

THE LITTLE ROAD

By Ellen Morrill Mills

Did you ever notice a little road
That you didn't wonder where it led?
Whether—after the cool, green wood—
It chanced on the dell where your dream-house stood?
Maybe—beginning dusty and rough,
It keeps up the pretense just long enough
To tire those who haven't the clew,
And leave the adventure—and end—to you?
Maybe it leaves the highway to follow
Up, swooping up like the flight of a swallow—
Till valley and town lie dim below,
And Time flies far on the winds that blow,
There you may find a nook for your dreaming,
Seeming,
Just planned for you from the Edenglow.

So the little road cries to me: "Follow, follow,
Maybe you'll find that your dreams are hollow,
Maybe you'll see—but follow, follow,
Come with the faith of the homing swallow,
Or, to your death, you will never know."

Here is cynicism relieved by wit. So artificial is the conceit that it seems a leaf out of the seventeenth century. Yet its deftness, doubtless, commends it to *The New Republic*, and on that score may gain other admirers.

THE LAWYER'S TALE

By Robert Graves

Richard Roe wished himself Solomon,
Made cuckold you should know by one John Doe:
Solomon's neck was firm enough to bear
Some score of antlers more than Roe could wear.

Richard Roe wished himself Alexander,
Being robbed of house and land by the same hand
Ten thousand acres or a principal town
Would have cost Alexander scarce a frown.

Richard Roe wished himself Job the prophet,
Sunk past reclaim in stinking rags and shame;
Job's plight was utterly bad, his own even worse,
He found no God to call on or to curse.

He wished himself Job, Solomon, Alexander,
For cunning, patience, power to overthrow
His tyrant, but with heart gone so far rotten
That most of all he wished himself John Doe.

To reflect all sides of to-day's verse something must go to our readers from such purveyors of the modern spirit as *The Dial*. The following has realism and humor, and makes us think that perhaps geraniums are merely handicapped by their name:

REFLECTION

By Elizabeth J. Coatsworth

Geraniums . . .
Who ever heard that Sappho put
Geraniums in her hair?

Or thought that Cleopatra brushed
Her long Greek face against their petals?

Did Beatrice carry them?
Or any bird sigh out his wild-fire heart
In passion for them?

Yet sparrows, far outnumbering nightingales,
Have gossiped under their tomato cans,
And lonely spinsters loved them more than cats

And living girls have felt quite festive, going
Down vulgar streets
With such unsubtle gaiety at their belts.

As a specimen of the work of our latest literary ambassador we quote one of the Algonquin love songs from "Kulóskap the Master" (Funk & Wagnalls Co.), by Dr. J. D. Prince, professor of Slavonic languages at Columbia, selected by President Harding as Minister to Denmark:

PASSAMAQUODDY LOVE SONG

Translated by Prof. John Dyneley Prince

Anigowanotenu!
Oft these lonely days thou look'st
On beauteous river and down shining stream.
Oft thou look'st and sighest deep,
Anigowanotenu!

With me thy lover by thy side
How fair that stream did bubble on!
How lovely was the silver moon!
Thy heart now tells thee of that joy.
E'en unto death I think of thee.
Anigowanotenu!

Oft these lonely days thou look'st
On beauteous river and down shining stream.
Oft thou look'st and sighest deep.
Anigowanotenu!

When we in birch canoe did glide
Together on that glistening lake,
How fair the hills and how we watched
The *red* leaves whirling in the breeze.
Anigowanotenu!

Anigowanotenu!
We'll rove once more in bark canoe
And watch the *green* leaves swirl on high
When spring smiles on the mountain tops
Anigowanotenu!
Oft these lonely days thou look'st
On beauteous river and down shining stream.
Oft thou look'st and sighest deep.
Anigowanotenu!

GULBRANSEN

(*Pronounced Gul-BRAN-sen*)

Player-Piano

"Jack, you don't look like much of a musician but you certainly can make that player-piano sing." "You're behind the times, Frank. A fellow doesn't need long hair to play a Gulbransen well. Learned it in a couple of weeks."

Any Man Can Get Real Music Out of a Gulbransen

Why do men hunt, fish, swim, skate—play ball, golf, tennis, pool, cards? Something to do. Why do they smoke when quiet? Something to do. It's part of the secret of Gulbransen success—something interesting for men to do at home.

Thousands of men, who wouldn't willingly *listen* to music 15 minutes, will play the Gulbransen for hours. Something to do. A few just pedal, and let it go at that; there are poor players at all games. But most men try to play the Gulbransen well—and succeed with astonishing satisfaction.

It's certainly the best single handed indoor Game. Something new every minute. Real skill to develop. Pleasure in entertaining friends. Solace for the soul when things go wrong. The Gulbransen comes to you with instruction rolls that teach you how to play.

Nationally Priced

Gulbransen Player-Pianos, three models all playable by hand or by roll, are sold at the same prices to everybody, everywhere in the United States, freight and war tax paid. Price, branded in the back of each instrument at the factory, includes six Gulbransen instruction rolls and our authoritative book on home entertaining and music study with the Gulbransen. 1921 reduced prices:

White House Model $700. Country Seat Model $600. Suburban Model $495

GULBRANSEN-DICKINSON CO., CHICAGO

Get Our New Book of Player Music — Free

The only book ever published showing the complete range of player-piano music of all kinds. This book is so classified and arranged that it is a guide to musical education for any player-piano owner. Sent free, if you mail us the coupon at the right.

Did you know the wonderful Gulbransen Player action can be installed in any piano (or old player-piano)? Yes, grand or upright. Check coupon for details.

To Gulbransen Owners: Keep your Gulbransen in tune—at least two tunings a year. You'll enjoy it more.

Try the Gulbransen Only Ten Minutes

At our dealer's store you can prove to yourself in ten minutes that the Gulbransen is easy for you to play well—a marvelous instrument—positively fascinating. The coupon below brings you dealer's address and full information.

Check here if you do not own any piano or player-piano. ☐

Check here if you want information about having a new Gulbransen player action installed in your present piano (or player-piano). ☐

Write your name and address i the margin below and mail this Gulbransen-Dickinson Co., 3230 V Chicago Ave., Chicago.

CELEBRATING A 3000-MILE VICTORY OF PEACE

IF THE DOVE OF PEACE has a permanent home it is probably somewhere along the three-thousand-mile line of lake and river and imaginary fence that separates the Dominion of Canada from the United States. No other boundary of such length has been free from war for so long a time since the fall of the Roman Empire. And the Pax Romana was an armed peace maintained by the legions of the Cæsars, whereas for a full century the people of the United States and the Dominion have left their common border unguarded by forts or ships or guns or garrisons. The recent celebration of this century of peace and disarmament is seized by editors on both sides of the border as an extremely significant and valuable lesson for the delegates who are to meet in Washington next month to consider limitation of armament on the part of the great military and naval powers. It is true that the century of peace really ended six years ago and a flag was, indeed, raised on the boundary in 1915. But at that time Canadians were too busy fighting the Great War to waste their energies in peace celebrations, and the dedication of a permanent memorial was postponed until this year. And so press dispatches from the Pacific coast inform us, ten thousand Americans and Canadians met on September 5 to dedicate by impressive ceremonies a massive concrete "Portal of Peace." The date was the anniversary of the first Battle of the Marne and also of the boarding of the *Mayflower* by the Pilgrim Fathers; and incidentally it coincided with the completion of the appropriately named Pacific Highway stretching from Vancouver, B. C., to San Diego, Cal. The place was Blaine, Washington, and the arch stands one hundred yards from where the 49th parallel—the international boundary line—meets Boundary Bay. Along with mementoes of pioneer days, wood from the *Mayflower*, and fragments from the first steamboat to ply the Pacific have been built into the arch for permanent preservation. The ceremonies, including music, the unfurling of flags and speechmaking were in charge of an international committee. Speakers emphasized the enduring friendship between the two countries and the appropriateness of the fact that the first international Peace Portal should be built on the shores of the Pacific Ocean. One American drew a comparison between the warlike motive which prompted the erection of the Arc de Triomphe in Paris and the century-old amity which the new arch celebrates.

NOT AN "ARCH OF TRIUMPH," BUT A "PORTAL OF PEACE."

The $40,000 gateway at Blaine, Wash., dedicated on September 5. Across the plinth on the United States front is inscribed, "Children of a Common Mother," and on the Canadian front, "Brethren Dwelling Together in Unity." On the doors will be the inscriptions, "Open for One Hundred Years" and "May These Doors Never Be Closed."

But the great significance of the occasion, agree the newspapers in both the Dominion and the Republic, is the example which has been set for a world seeking relief from the burdens of armament and the horrors of war. For a hundred years this border, unlike the steel-lined frontiers of Europe, has been quite unguarded, and the two peoples, though sometimes differing, have neighbored without serious friction. The whole business, says the Lincoln (Neb.) *State Journal* in the United States, "is about the best exhibition of international common sense an addle-pated human race has given," and "the disarmament conference can not have its attention attracted too strongly to the Canadian boundary and its new Peace Portal." The outpouring of the people at Blaine is characterized by the Portland *Oregon Journal* as "a sample of the pent-up-tide of human sentiment that will some day burst its dam and flood the world with its spirit of resentment against wholesale massacre, debt, death and devastation, which war is and always will be." The town of Blaine, says the Cincinnati *Times-Star*, has preached an eloquent sermon to a warlike world, "it is a sermon on disarmament, on the practical every-day operation, of international friendship, and the successful avoidance of suspicion." The celebration, says the Canadian Montreal *Gazette*, "opens up the most enticing possibilities, for what has been done by the United States and the Dominion can be done by other nations. If the European Central Empires had followed the signal example thus set, instead of expressing might and arrogance and power by rings of steel, the Great War need not have taken place." The Montreal daily points out that:

> The public men, both in the United States and Canada, have had the intelligence and common sense to see that if either nation made the slightest movement toward the setting up of any instrument of force, the provocation would be replied to in kind. There would be angry feelings; there would be mutual suspicion; and the boundary line, which has never been profaned by the smallest instrument of violence, would bristle with guns, suggesting the notion of violence—precisely what is to be avoided at all costs in human relations.

The world has erected many a memorial to its warmakers and few, almost none, to its peacemakers, the Vancouver *Province* is moved to remark:

BUNGALOW DESIGN NO. 610

Designed for the Service Department, American Face Brick Association

This six-room bungalow is one of the sixty-four designs in our "Face Brick Bungalow and Small House Plans." Note how it nestles close to the ground, its hospitable entrance, its pleasing roof lines, and its exceptionally compact, convenient interior arrangements.

Face Brick for Bungalows

FOR beauty, for durability, and for economy, Face Brick is unequalled as a facing material for bungalows and small houses.

The wide variety of colors and textures, and the artistic possibilities in bonding, mortar joints and panel work, give an infinite scope to the owner's individual taste.

Savings in repairs, in painting, in fuel costs and insurance rates, its long life and slow depreciation, make the Face Brick house the most economical you can build.

You will find these matters fully discussed in "The Story of Brick," an artistic booklet with numerous illustrations and helpful information for all who intend to build. A copy will be sent free to prospective builders.

"Face Brick Bungalow and Small House Plans" are issued in four booklets, showing 3 to 4-room houses, 5-room houses, 6-room houses, and 7 to 8-room houses, in all sixty-four, each reversible with a different exterior design. These designs are unusual and distinctive, combined with convenient interiors and economical construction. The entire set for one dollar. Any one of the booklets, 25 cents, preferably in stamps.

We have the complete working drawings, specifications and masonry quantity estimates at nominal prices. Select from the booklets the designs you like best and order the plans even if you are not going to build now, for their study will be not only interesting and instructive, but helpful in forming your future plans for your home.

You may want "The Home of Beauty," fifty designs, mostly two stories, representing a wide variety of architectural styles and floor plans. Sent for 50 cents in stamps. We also distribute complete working drawings, specifications and quantity estimates for these houses at nominal prices.

Address, American Face Brick Association, 1134 Westminster Building, Chicago, Illinois.

War monuments have been erected in many cities, towns and country places in Canada and the United States to commemorate the heroism of those who fought and fell in the late war and in other wars. To-day one monument stands on the border between the English-speaking nations on this continent as a testimony of gratitude and satisfaction for a century of peace. All the war monuments pay honor to an idea as well as to the men and women who died for it. The peace memorial represents an idea, but also commemorates the lives and deeds of all who in these three generations of human life wrought for peace. It is a memorial to every ruler who in times of stress refrained from provocative language or found the soft answer which turns away wrath; to every statesman and diplomat who had the good-will to seek and the gifts to devise a peaceful method of settling an exasperating dispute; to every public man of both nations who cultivated the habit of friendly speech and action toward the other; to every writer for the press and every author whose printed word was free from offense; to all preachers, teachers and persons of light and leading who helped the old and young people about them to know the best rather than the worst of their foreign neighbors; to the men of business who dealt honorably and in a spirit of cooperation with alien nations; to captains and sailors of both nations who have for a hundred years fraternized in all the ports and harbors of the world; to students and scholars who have studied and taught together in the great schools of both countries, and to the tens of millions of undistinguished men and women, dwelling on each side of the frontier, who lived in kindly fellowship with foreign fellow men.

No monument could preserve the names of all whose life and deeds are recognized by this peace memorial. But, as the church festival of All Saints commemorates the innumerable and nameless faithful of all time, so the memorial dedicated to-day recognizes the merits of all who have helped to keep the peace between Britain and the United States.

LEADING THE WORLD IN THE PATHWAY OF PEACE.

If Britannia and Columbia, here represented by their daughters at the Peace Portal celebration, can keep peace along an unguarded boundary, why cannot the whole world do likewise?

That the peace should have been kept along this three-thousand-mile line for a full century is the more significant because this peace was preceded by two centuries of intermittent warfare. Again and again French colonists in Canada with the help of Indians and French soldiers fought British colonists from the south cooperating with regiments of Red Coats and following British officers. There were conflicts early in the seventeenth century. Then came the series of wars, known successively in our Colonial history as King William's War, Queen Anne's War, King George's War, and the French and Indian War. The pages of our school histories are full of stories of the raids and sieges that took place. The capture of Quebec by Wolf in 1759 ended the Franco-British phase of warfare across the Canadian border, for by the treaty of 1763 Canada became a British possession. Then in 1775 the American Revolution began. The historians tell us how the leaders of the revolting colonies tried to make their movement continent-wide and invaded Canada, hoping that the conquered French would rise and join them in throwing off the British yoke. Montreal was taken and occupied for months by the Continental Army. Benedict Arnold, then one of the most gallant figures in the Colonial army, was wounded at the unsuccessful siege of Quebec, and the Revolutionary Army finally withdrew from Canada. Later Canada was the base of Burgoyne's ill-fated attempt to split the colonies in two. After the War the emigration of 40,000 American Tories—the United Empire Loyalists—to Canada added an element to the population which was identical in culture with that of the States, but which remained for a generation or two bitterly anti-American. When the War of 1812 broke out, the Canadian border saw the last flare-up of two centuries of fighting. Spectacular naval campaigns were fought on Lake Champlain and Lake Erie. A force from Canada took Detroit, and along the Niagara boundary the noise of the guns at Chippewa and Lundy's Lane drowned out the roar of the great cataract. But since the signing of the Treaty of Ghent between Great Britain and the United States on December 24, 1814, there has been peace along the border, and by the terms of the treaty that border has been left unguarded by sentinel or armament or fortification. "English forces and American troops have not faced each other in anger since the guns of Lundy's Lane, Lake Erie and New Orleans were stilled." Here, continues the Philadelphia *Public Ledger*, "is a border where the boundary posts are so many marks of good faith, good-will and understanding, instead of so many sign-posts of hatreds, suspicion and clashing interests," and "time has shown that there was no more need of arms and armed men on the border and armed ships on the Great Lakes than there was for Illinois and Michigan, Indiana and Wisconsin to maintain armed guards on their boundaries and fighting ships on the lakes to guard against each other."

Indeed, there has been hardly more thought of armed conflict between the two countries than there is between two neighbors living side by side in a quiet suburb. Yet even in the best regulated village or suburb there are occasionally misunderstandings over the rights of a neighbor's children, or dogs, or chickens, or over the precise location of a fence post. And so Canada and the United States, though remaining at peace, have indulged in more than one serious controversy. In fact, as the *The Boston Globe* points out in a leading editorial:

We have had as many disputes during the past 100 years with our friendly neighbor to the northward as most European nations have had with one another. The difference has been in method of settlement. Where two European nations have almost invariably called out the reserves to settle things (thereby settling nothing at all), in our disputes with Canada we have each hired a lawyer.

It was the "godlike Daniel" who took up the job for the States in 1841, when our long-standing boundary dispute with England over Canada came to a crisis. Feeling ran at fever pitch on both sides. Many folks up in Maine were for calling the police. Canadians yelled exasperating epithets across the stone wall. But Webster and Ashburton threshed out the dispute in verbal pyrotechnics quite successfully, within a year. And Aroostook went back to hoe its potatoes.

Two years later there was another squall, this time on the Oregon boundary. British Columbians and American homesteaders rubbed elbows of wrath once more. "If we can't have the boundary laid at 54′ 40″, we'll punch the daylights

People Don't Regret Buying Closed Cars

THERE is something about the snug click of the door latch and the clean, windless interior of a closed car that makes you feel at home and comfortable in there.

The deep-cushioned seats, the curtains, the glass, the conversation in low tones—all these things make getting somewhere as pleasant as being there. Getting home is never a problem, and the weather is an incident.

In the Standard Eight Coupé, Sedan, or Sedanette the powerful motor carries the extra burden of a closed body with an effortless ease.

Any good closed car is a source of great satisfaction to the owner. The makers of the Standard Eight have built their closed cars exceptionally well, as part of their plan to make the Standard Eight a permanent and respected factor in the automotive field.

Vestibule Sedan, $5000 *Sedan, $4800* *Sedanette, $4500* *Coupé, $4500*
Touring Car, $3400 *Roadster, $3400* *Sport, $3400* *Chassis, $3150*
Above prices f. o. b. Butler, Pa.

STANDARD EIGHT

A POWERFUL CAR

STANDARD STEEL CAR COMPANY

Automotive Dept. *Pittsburgh, Pa.*

PERSONAL GLIMPSES
Continued

out of somebody," howled the gentlemen from the Mississippi country. But they didn't. The quarrel was reduced to its lowest terms in a case for the lawyers, and peace resulted from mutual concession in 1846.

A few years ago, when that hoary old trumpet for the munitions owners, the London *Post*, discovered four more small guns in an American revenue boat on the Great Lakes than in the corresponding Canadian cutter, it rose in a frenzy of indignation and shouted from Fleet Street to Heaven. But the only echo from either Canada or the United States was a gale of laughter.

The whole story of our relations with Canada has, of course, not yet ended, but evidence of 100 years is splendid indication of one fact recognized here by peoples, though not, as yet, in Europe by diplomats: to effect real disarmament, not treaties, secret or otherwise, but mutual understanding is needed.

That fact, brought out in Blaine today, is worth pondering, especia ly by the class assembling for the November conference in Washington. The lesson of the Canadian boundary has taught Canada and the United States "where they're at." If, as President Harding intimates, mankind yearns to follow this example, then his disarmament conference might do far worse than study that lesson.

CARUSO'S LAST SONG

CARUSO, it is said, often helped those who were as ambitious as himself, but less gifted, and there comes now a story of an Italian woman opera singer who went to him for an opinion and received a singing lesson instead. The great tenor was apparently unsympathetic at first, but he mellowed under the inspiration of his own memories of hard work and achievement, and gave his visitor an insight into his method. Geni Sadero, the opera singer who called on Caruso shortly before his death, writes in the *Tribuna* of Rome an article describing her visit which is reprinted in the New York *Tribune*, from which we take it:

"'And you really came right down to Sorrento to hear my opinion,' asked the great tenor, crossing his arms and looking at me in any but a pleasant way. I felt rather mortified at this reception and could only answer 'yes,' with an inclination of my head. He kept looking at me in a surprized and irritated manner, and I felt so unhappy that I could have jumped over the bannisters of the terrace where we stood, right into the blue sea, even if I had been forced to swim to Naples so as to catch the return train to Rome.

"Caruso looked at me once more, and prest his lips together as though he were preparing for an important speech. Then he turned his head and contemplated with loving eye the sunlit gulf. But he soon resumed his imperious attitude and went on:

"'Let us reason together. You are a singer. Yes, I know, a special kind of singer; one who has been on the stage for several years, who has had important judgments passed on her singing and who will think herself to be some one. Do not be agitated; this is the truth.

"'I, Enrico Caruso, am never satisfied with myself. It seems to me that I have not reached that technical perfection for which I have been seeking for years. You saw me yesterday on this terrace while the gramophone was executing some songs of mine. While I was listening to them I was criticizing the tenor Caruso. I hope you heard me? I was noticing, year after year, the progress made toward that equality of voice, that intensity of vibration, that equilibrium of the respiratory dynamic, and finally that spontaneity for which I wish; all those things which are necessary when you really want to sing properly. And I do not think that I have reached the limit of my desire. How, then, can I be satisfied with you, even should you be a phenomenon?'

"I attempted to open my lips so as to utter a word, but I could not, and he proceeded:

"'I understand. You want a sincere opinion, even if it be drastic. That is a kind of madness. How often have I had this very same wish manifested to me by people who afterward turned into enemies! Why should we not remain friends? I do not intend to say the truth any more, but I have also the right not to tell lies. Therefore, I do not wish to hear any more singing, nor to pass an opinion about singers. You understand? "The day will come when you will say that I am right. My opinion has very often been misinterpreted; newspapers have said things which never crossed my mind. And now I am silent so that I shall have peace.'

"Then I got up, trying to be as collected as possible, and said to him: 'Listen, M. Caruso, I do not wish to appear to you as one of the so-called celebrities. You are quite right, and I respect your reasons. I shall go back to my room and pack, and this evening I leave.'

"The great tenor looked at me, and a broad smile, nearly a childish one, brightened his expressive, swarthy face. 'Sit down,' he said, 'and do not be so full of pride. I do not wish you to go like that; also I am curious to hear those famous songs of yours. Please return at 5:30, and I will give you half an hour of my time. But I shall just listen, and not speak.'

"Punctually at 5:30 I returned to his sitting-room. Caruso entered, dropt into an armchair, and taking my music told me to go to the piano and proceed with my singing.

"I sat at the piano and ran through a few of my songs. But when I came to the Neapolitan song 'Michelamma,' I felt as though I could not continue. 'Go on,' he said, 'I want to hear it.' Suddenly, when I was half way through the song, he got up, full of fervor, and gently began to sing 'Michelamma' himself in an undertone. But what an undertone! It was like a cello with the mute on. He thus proceeded, improving the interpretation, the accent, the cadences, the accentuato, and so on; and when he had finished he said, 'Now repeat it yourself, please, but at once.' Three and four times he made me repeat it, until I have the right accent, and he, satisfied, said, 'So you must sing it.'

"Then, music in hand, he went on with his remarks. He pointed out the songs which he fancied most, saying that he would sing them at his concerts. He asked me how, and for how long, I studied; he showed me a few cadences to repeat, and

PERSONAL GLIMPSES
Continued

thus ended by giving me a marvelous singing lesson.

"I felt as though in a dream, and tried to follow him, frightened that by a misplaced word I might break the spell and enchantment of the moment. I felt before Caruso as a humble instrument which he found suitable to his touch. In an outburst of generous sincerity he unraveled the treasures relating to his studies and labors to a poor mite who thought that she knew how to sing!

"He accompanied me to the door, took both my hands and said: 'Listen; I have not told you my opinion of your singing, but when you go to New York you must come to see me.'

"I went down the stairs as though dazed. I heard a gong sound—it was 8 o'clock. So I left the great artist, hopeful of a complete recovery, happy with the thought that in November he would restart his engagement at the Metropolitan. . . . But destiny decided otherwise in the midst of his happiness. . . . A little woman places at his feet a bunch of field flowers, her gratitude, and the expression of her deep sorrow."

OUTWITTING EUROPEAN BANDITS

LESS bloody, perhaps, but no less bitterly fought than the battles of the Meuse and the Argonne Forest are the pecuniary encounters between American tourists and Europeans looking for an "easy mark," or franc, as the case may be. American tourists, it seems from the observations of a late traveler in foreign parts, are regarded as "legitimate" game by the European "hold-up men," the efficient shock troops of which, we are told, consist of waiters and taxicab drivers whose discernment of possibilities was sharpened in deadlier affrays. So anyone going from America to Europe, writes Roger William Riis in the Kansas City *Star*, must either take what is offered him, or gird up his loins and fight. The writer and a friend, who recently "took in" the important places, girded up their loins and fought, not without success. If the waiters didn't add up the date on the bills, they did add up figures which didn't belong in the total, and there followed lively and refreshing tilts in which the two travelers did not always come out second best. With their wits sharpened by constant contact with the wiles of mercenary waiters and hardened taxicab drivers, these two tourists managed to reduce their expenses considerably, tho, in the process, confesses the chronicler, they were changed from inoffensive, peace-loving individuals into argumentative and belligerent men. The first encounter with a modernized Robin Hood went against the Americans. They had met a pretty girl on the boat going over, and decided to take her out to lunch. She, wisely, had her lunch privately beforehand, and exprest a wish for nothing more than one order of the filet of sole that looked so alluring over the little alcohol lamp on which it was keeping warm. The writer and his friend, however, ran down fancy items in the corners of the menu, and ate with great gusto. It was a good meal, we are informed, but the fine after effects were modified by a bill for 100 francs. Because of the presence of the pretty girl, the men paid without a murmur. The blow was sufficient, and plans were laid to outwit the enemy. There were some mistakes at first in tactics and strategy; but the Americans profited by each encounter, and, says the writer:

"The opening victory, July 7, was exceedingly interesting from the point of view of technique. We were preparing to leave the Frankfurter Hof in Frankfurt-am-Main, and we asked for the bill. Scrutinizing it in every detail, we noted 12½ marks (all of 19 cents) charged for the morning's breakfast. We had paid for that at the time, and said so.

"No," answered the cashier. "How could you have paid for it if it is here shown as unpaid?"

We suggested delicately that mistakes have been known to occur, and we were met with a stare of cold scorn.

"The breakfast was twelve marks fifty," said the scorner. He sounded like an ultimatum running full speed ahead.

Now, the progress of these battles is often interesting because of the manner of fighting of the different combatants. There are waiters and taxi men who throw down the gage to you in so polite and pleasant a way that you, too, remain polite and pleasant, and the struggle to the end is well-mannered and delightful. There are others, again, who throw the gage into your face and then pick it up and slap your eye with it. Harwood and I always made a practise of starting slowly and gently, but when the slap in the eye came, we unleashed all the dogs of war.

So when this guerrilla stated in a cold and final tone that the breakfast would cost us twelve fifty, he committed the final assault. We hoisted the red flag.

"Whom does the breakfast cost twelve fifty?" we demanded.

The cashier turned away to his books.

"It costs you gentlemen, since you ate it," he retorted, and promptly lost further interest in the conversation.

We held a brief council of war, and then went in search of the waiter who had served us the disputed breakfast. We put the case up to him. He listened carefully.

"But certainly," he said. "Wait a moment."

And in the moment he returned, bearing in his hand the bill for the breakfast, receipted by the restaurant cashier. That waiter was a freak. Or else the god of war was fighting actively for us that day. We carried the receipted bill back and called loudly on the insulting cashier.

"Here you see that we paid the bill, as we said."

He eyed it.

"There has been some mistake," he mumbled.

"Then," we said, malignantly pushing our advantage, "perhaps next time you won't be so sure of your system. You see we were right, and you were wrong."

Luscious word, that, "wrong." We became very adept at rolling it richly over the tongue in several languages. So

Pocketbook Interest and the Road to Success

Pocketbook interest is the sales-lever of the world. In most cases it is moved by the eye flashing acceptance to the mind. Buying is largely visual. It is made natural and easy by attractive, forceful labels and packages. But they must be correct in design and made luminous by colors rightly chosen for the work they should do.

We make beautiful, forceful labels and folding boxes for every kind of merchandise. They are done in the proper color scheme for any given purpose. They invite ownership of goods and they tell a picture story of quality, because they are conceived and printed with selling success, over the counter, fully in mind.

This is Color-Printing Headquarters. In color inserts for the finest catalogs, we show merchandise with graphic exactness. And we design and execute delightful covers for magazines and catalogs—so say our friends. Our equipment for this work is complete, modern and reinforced by most competent craftsmanship, knowledge and watchfulness.

For many advertisers, we create ideas for window trims, cutouts, hangers and posters, individual, powerful and appropriate. We reproduce textiles so accurately that fabric and print are accepted as one. One plant alone uses annually 1,000,000 pounds of ink ground on the premises—and 23,000,000 pounds of paper and cardboard.

We print, too, calendars of characteristic charm, for particular buyers. Any of these pieces looks as if the entire care and interest of our organization were concentrated on it alone. Here is magnitude in printing—with full appreciation of small orders as well. They have always been the seed for business growth and meet cordial welcome here.

Our trade-mark bureau, without charge, creates trade-names and devises trade-marks, searches titles to existing ones. In this department are filed 730,000 such devices, registered and unregistered. So at a great saving of money and time, and probably avoiding costly litigation, by comparison we quickly establish whether or not a design is entitled to registration.

THE UNITED STATES PRINTING & LITHOGRAPH CO.

PERSONAL GLIMPSES
Continued

would you, under the provocation we suffered.

Taxi drivers, as I said, are the shock troops of the attack. Shifting prices in Germany have caused laws to be passed permitting the taxi drivers to multiply by a certain sum the figure shown on the taximeter. Thus, in Frankfurt, the meter figure is multiplied by six; in Berlin, by seven or eight, according to whether you take a gasoline or an electric car, and in Hamburg, by eight or nine. This complicated defense repulsed us once and caused the defeat of July 7 with a loss of 14 marks. But once we had caught the idea, we fought it to a standstill at every turn."

Taxicab drivers should be treated as a race unto themselves, says the writer, who believes that they are as distinct in racial lineage as are the Caucasians, the Mongols and the Indians. He found those in Paris to be big, red-faced, fierce-whiskered giants, easily kings of the race. Then there are smaller, rat-faced drivers, who plan, as they drive, incredible plots of free-booting and villainy. How this class fights we may learn from the following account:

The last one I crossed arms with in Europe gave me the battle of the summer. It was in Antwerp. He had driven me, in his horse carriage, some ten minutes' drive to the door of the American Express office. Then he demanded 10 francs.

"Ten francs! What does the meter say?" I asked.

"I have no meter. I make my own prices."

Then I knew that I was up against a veteran warrior. Well, I would show him.

"Ten francs is too much. I'll give you three," I stated.

"Three francs!" he shouted. "I want nine!"

"Three," I said, firmly, and handed him a five-franc note. "Give me change."

"Instead, he pocketed the bill, mounted his seat and picked up the reins. It was a critical moment. Snatching his whip from its holder, I shouted, ferociously as he had done:

"Give me change, or I keep your new whip!"

Fuming, he jumped off the seat. In his rage he slipped into Flemish, his native tongue, and I don't know what wonderful things he was saying to me when I spied the five-franc note in his hand. Seizing him by the wrist, I pried open his fingers and recovered the money. It was a neat struggle, won only on points.

"Now," I said, "you come along into the American Express office and see what they say."

He came. We surrounded the doorkeeper, I brandishing the whip in one hand and the bill in the other, he shaking both fists before him, most vituperatively. I asked the doorkeeper how much I ought to pay him. The doorkeeper spoke English, which was a keen relief, for foreign languages always cramp the full flow of one's indignation, but for all his English he betrayed me.

"I don't know," he said, with one eye on the sputtering enemy. "You should have arranged a price with him first."

rejoiced in Flemish and reached for the bill. Holding the bill high in the air, I fired shell for shell and bomb for bomb in English. We revolved around one another like two prize-fighters. It was not a gentlemanly scene, but it was spirited. The doorkeeper being French became enthusiastic over the waving of hands and plunged in for himself. So the three of us revolved around and around again, while the clatter of the battle rose in the office like machine-gun fire on the front.

With the aid of a sorrowful clerk who came forward exclaiming in Oxford English, "Gentlemen! Gentlemen! Not in the office!" the doorkeeper at length pushed us out on the sidewalk. I think he hated to see us go. The outcome of it was that I gave the driver the five francs and the whip and thanked him for a game fight; and he drove off, beaming. It was a draw, with much honor accruing to both sides.

The final and crowning victory came when the writer was in the pink of condition from a long summer of fighting. He had calculated his trip so well that he had just $45 left to pay his way from Montreal, where he was to land, to New York. He found that the steamer had been canceled, in which emergency the company agreed to support him in Antwerp till the sailing of the next steamer, eight days later. That didn't suit, as the writer wanted to be in New York in ten days. After persuading the company to give him passage to Liverpool, he goes on:

I was uncertain whether or not the company would reimburse me, so I lived economically. But in Liverpool I became weary of economy and went to the best hotel and ate a twelve-shilling dinner and lived in luxury. Next day I rallied for the struggle again. I had kept all hotel and restaurant bills, and I marched with them into the steamship office and threw them on the counter. The total was four pounds.

"So! Will you pay these?" I asked politely, after explaining my case. Oh, no! Not at all! Such things weren't done. Besides, in great emergencies the company allowed twelve shillings a day for such cases, and here I had spent twelve shillings for one dinner. No, no!

"When I travel for my own firm in America," I said, "they allow me $25 a day for expenses." I said the $25 in italics.

"That's far too much," retorted the enemy briskly.

The last phase of the battle was the bitterest. It lasted forty-five minutes and ended with complete victory for me. They paid me the four pounds, and not only that, but they paid me nearly a pound extra. I haven't yet figured that out, unless they were dazed by my assault and gave more ground than I asked.

So I found myself with $50 in my pocket, five more than I had had in Antwerp when the first gun was fired. And in the meantime I had had two unexpected days in England, without spending a cent.

It's a great game for the veterans. Only the fittest survive. If the account makes us sound like professional cranks and kickers, all I have to say is, try it yourself. We only wanted our rights, and the fact that the enemy yielded in almost every case is conclusive proof that they knew we were right, for never in the world would those hardy fighters surrender anything that was theirs. Oh, no, it's just a case of necessity. You must fight or be skinned alive.

REVIEWS OF NEW BOOKS
Continued

(*Continued from page 36*)

but that our own naval authorities could only affirm, with no convincing appearance of confidence, that the enemy had suffered about as much loss as he had inflicted."

Mr. Hannay contrasts with this the impression that the battle made in Germany. How came it to pass that the result of the encounter could be interpreted in such a manner as to leave a cheering effect on the German public? He replies:

"The explanation that they were deceived by lies really won't do. Not even the German Admiralty and censorship could have persuaded their docile people that Admiral von Scheer's ships were still in existence, with a few exceptions, if they were not. Moreover, it was a matter of fact that the German fleet was out again in August, and that the bulk of ours was still not thought too much to keep watch on it. The Germans had cause to be pleased when it was known that their outnumbered and outclassed navy could meet the Grand Fleet in battle, and could not only escape the annihilation which on a comparison of forces seemed to be the inevitable result of an encounter, but could inflict more loss than it suffered."

To this add the opinion of Captain Frothingham:

"There is no question of the fact that the withdrawal of the British fleet had a great moral effect on Germany. Morale was all-important and the announcement to the people and the Reichstag had a heartening effect on the Germans at just the time they needed some such stimulant, with an unfavorable military situation for the Central Powers. It also smoothed over the irritation of the German people against the German Navy, at this time when Germany had been obliged to modify her use of the U-boats upon the demand of the United States. For months after the battle the esteem of the German people for the German Navy remained high, and this helped to strengthen the German Government."

The losses in the battle were as follows:

	BRITISH	TONS
Queen Mary	(Battle Cruiser)	26,350
Indefatigable	(Battle Cruiser)	18,800
Invincible	(Battle Cruiser)	17,250
Defence	(Armored Cruiser)	14,600
Warrior	(Armored Cruiser)	13,550
Black Prince	(Armored Cruiser)	13,350
Tipperary	(Destroyer)	1,430
Nestor	(Destroyer)	890
Nomad	(Destroyer)	890
Turbulent	(Destroyer)	1,100
Fortune	(Destroyer)	965
Ardent	(Destroyer)	935
Shark	(Destroyer)	935
Sparrowhawk	(Destroyer)	935
	Total tonnage	111,980

	GERMAN	TONS
Lutzow	(Battle Cruiser)	26,180
Pommern	(Pre-dreadnought)	13,200
Wiesbaden	(Cruiser)	5,400
Elbing	(Cruiser)	4,500
Rostock	(Cruiser)	4,900
Frauenlob	(Cruiser)	2,700
V-4	(Destroyer)	570
V-48	(Destroyer)	750
V-27	(Destroyer)	640
V-29	(Destroyer)	640
S-33	(Destroyer)	700
	Total Tonnage	60,180

KILLED AND WOUNDED:

British (approximately)	6,600
German	3,076

MEETING ONE'S DOUBLE

IT was a surprize to Leonard Corsant when the girl in the office of the steamship company on the dock at Alexandria recognized him, laughingly signed an official paper for him and, when he exprest amazement at her powers of recollection, complimented him on his improved appearance. He was on his way home to America after some years spent in the Far East, and his path led through Italy, France and England. Landing in Naples he finds Italy less delightful than he had expected, but before leaving Rome he has a curious experience. A stranger addresses him in a humble little café, refers to a former meeting and, with an unpleasant air of condescension, informs him that "they" are after him. But this incident is wiped from his memory by an illness in Paris, and as soon as he is well enough to travel he starts for a little village in England, the cradle of his race, which his father had told him to be sure to visit whenever he should be in that country. Here he establishes himself at a little inn where he is the only guest, and in a fortnight he is well, spending his time in walks about the beautiful country and in making friends with the people.

So is the stage set for Mr. Henry M. Rideout's story of "Fern Seed" (Duffield, $1.75), a delightful book, for the interest is held up to the last moment while the descriptions of English rural life, the thatched cottages, the fields and the villagers are charming indeed.

But soon Corsant is aware of a curious attitude towards him on the part of the people; it is not in the least unfriendly, but rather a sort of repressed recognition, and he has one or two singular encounters with some of the older inhabitants of the place. His inquiries concerning certain people and places are met with a sort of surprize at first and then with a kind of polite tolerance. One day, while walking in the fields, he has an encounter with a young man who is playing golf. They enter into conversation and each seems pleased with the other, when a chance remark on the part of Corsant causes the stranger to stiffen up and leave without a word. On returning to the inn Corsant finds that he has taken the stranger's jacket by mistake and, searching the pockets for something that may enlighten him as to the name and address of the owner, he finds an open envelop directed to himself. Thinking it might be a letter of introduction he opens it and finds a receipted bill showing that in London two days ago L. Corsant had slept and breakfasted at a little out-of-the-way hotel. At first he thinks the man must have been using his name, but rejects that theory when he recalls the stranger's face and manner.

The first clearance in this atmosphere of mystery comes through George Grayland, a handsome man, part gipsy, who gets Corsant into the church tower with him, demands his real name, and threateningly asks why he is masquerading in the village under that of Corsant. This leads to an explanation and the air begins to clear. The golf-playing young man is Laurence Corsant, the English representative of the name, just back from the East where he has been doing some work for the Government, unrecognized officially, but nevertheless of the greatest importance. He had been captured and tortured by some of the natives at the instigation of a German, at work for his government in the same part of the country, and it was no thanks to him that Corsant had escaped with his life.

REVIEWS OF NEW BOOKS
Continued

Corsant for a part of the time, at once recognizes this man in Leonard's description of the stranger who had spoken to him in the Italian wine-shop. Young Corsant has come down to his old home wishing to live quietly for a time, only to find his distant relative there before him and mistaken for him by all the villagers, for there is a strong resemblance between the two kinsmen. This is a pity, for Laurence has some papers in his possession which his enemy is anxious to obtain, and the news spread through the countryside of his return.

A few days later Leonard, needing some money, repairs on foot to a nearby town and there discovers that the man who had spoken to him in Rome is on his track, and the rest of the book is taken up with the arrival of the German with a friend to aid him in obtaining the papers, and the manner of his circumventing by Leonard, aided by George Grayland. Laurence goes to town and asks Leonard to stay at his house during his absence, a plan which suits the two conspirators extremely well. The foreigners arrive, and there is a good scene where they are routed. The book is very well written and bears the indescribable *cachet*, so rare in much of the recent fiction, of being the work of a cultivated man.

HATE AND POLITICS IN THE LITTLE BACK ROOM

WE are having plenty of small town books, and why not? Is not America a nation of small towns, scattered all over her broad miles, each different and yet each basically akin? From them come the young men who reach their stature in the great cities, from them comes the opinion that rules in legislatures and at Washington. They are us and we are them, and it is the province of our writers to describe and interpret them. There can be ill-natured studies, like those by Lewis or Dell, funny ones like H. L. Wilson's, sympathetic and beautiful ones like Tarkington's. And to this latter class belongs the latest to come to hand, a study of a boy, later a man, who works his way up from being a mill-worker to a commanding position as a lawyer, and of his gradual development into a fighter for clean politics, after a long intimacy with the methods of the little back room of the saloon and the men who frequent it. It is called "The Little Back Room," by E. S. Chamberlayne (Stokes & Co.)

The book is written in the first person, in a leisurely and intimate manner. It puts men and women before you. Many of the men at least are absolutely lacking in what might be called social conscience; that is, they are ready to sacrifice their community for themselves and their friends. Aside from this they are generally reputable, kindly and affectionate creatures, clever as to worldly affairs, uncultivated perhaps, but not uneducated. We meet them all over America, where they have been a force whose power it is difficult to estimate.

The hero of this novel was born into the spirit and environment of these men, into their notions of honor and responsibility. But he belongs to the new generation. He does not remain where he arrives.

We have in this hero a boy, grave, clear-sighted and yet imaginative; a boy who has ad a rough experience of life which makes im cognizant of many things at seventeen iat are usually not come by till much iter; a boy instinctively straightforward, ompletely honest, quick of mind and slow f speech. By an accident he is flung into itimacy with the inner circle that rules the own, taken in hand as he is seen to be lever and discreet, and given the training e is fit for and which he longs for—training s a lawyer.

This accident, as I have called it, is some- that bizarre. The boy is not yet seven- een, but he has lain in wait with an old evolver, determined to kill a man high in he social life of the town and favored by he politicians for Congress, a man of little bility but considerable appearance, a use- ul stalking horse for party purposes. This man has brought about the ruin of a oung girl, a cheap little person, but coming f a family that would rather see her dead han see her disgraced. When she dies under an operation her betrayer, Troxell, s able to have matters properly arranged; ier family thinks she is dead from appendi- itis, and there is no scandal whatever. But the girl had confided in young Peter, who fancied himself in love with her. And n his blind boyish devotion and sense of chivalry he had decided to kill Troxell.

He waits for him in a certain alley leading to the door of the little back room where the political talks take place, but is discov- ered just as he is about to shoot, and his wrist broken by a stick in the hands of Este, one of the politicians, who further beats him up till he is unconscious and a good deal of a wreck. Troxell remains unaware of the attempt upon his life. Este then has him taken to the rooms of a young fellow who is a protégé of one of the big men of the party, where he is nursed back to health. It is necessary to get his story and to protect Troxell, of course, and the young iron-worker can hardly be murdered and thrust away. So it is that he is approached man to man, made to see the idiocy of such proceedings, offered a fair chance at an education, and provided with a good friend in the shape of Mac- gruder, the protégé whose rooms he is living in as part prisoner, part invalid.

The shock of what he has been through has made a man of Peter Cadogan. Mac- gruder puts facts before him clearly, and he likes Macgruder at once. Troxell is old Porter Marshall's nephew, and Marshall owns the Guaranty Trust Company, the iron works, and "runs this little old town of Colchester." To drag the girl's name through the papers is the last thing that Peter wants. He has never really cared for her, and he determines to put the whole affair aside and to turn to work. Marshall gives him a law-school training, he begins to meet new people, girls, other men, to think new thoughts, to grow and develop. He has Troxell always in the back of his mind, certainly, but he sees that shooting him dead is not the way to settle matters, and that to tell the girl's father and make a miserable thing of his tender memory of his daughter, and probably a murderer out of the old man, is also impossible. For the time the matter is closed.

It is not only the political adventures of Peter that we follow, it is his love affairs and his friendships. Peter is a big man, tall and well made, a quick and clever boxer, and with a countenance good to look upon. His amazing honesty and the directness of his speech make him seem odd and sound strange. Women fall in love with him rather easily. But Peter himself moves slowly there, too. Peter is really moving along a road of his own, a road that is

REVIEWS OF NEW BOOKS
Continued

hedged about with his ideals, and colored with a light whose radiance is partly of the imagination. When he does fall in love it is with a girl of immense charm and cleverness, but who is looking for money and position rather than love. She is ready to sacrifice her heart for her material advantage, and to sacrifice Peter along with it. He relinquishes her, but he continues to adore her, though he never lets himself, or rather his love, be exploited. The whole affair between these two is drawn with a curiously subtle insight into shadowy impulses and youthful emotions. Its ending, long after the young woman's marriage to another man, marks one of the great forward steps in Peter's development. He has reached the end of a dream. Presently he turns to reality.

The book is too long to describe in detail, and the method of its writing makes quotation difficult. There is a trace of Henry James in the conversations, in the delicacy and detail of character transcription. It moves too slowly for hurried reading, but it never lags, and it is always alive. You feel the sincerity of the author even as he makes you feel the sincerity of his Peter. He neither praises nor blames, but he paints in the calm words of truth the practises of the little back room. He shows the vote-buying tactics, the swaps, the compromises that go on. He reveals the mingling of contempt and liking which inspires most of the men, the rotten contracts, the manipulations of public funds, reveals it through the men themselves, who regard it all as commonplace, proper and inevitable. And up against all this he places the growing figure of Peter Cadogan, with his gradual realization of the crookedness in the midst of which he is working, his developing determination to clean things up.

And with this runs Peter's difficult understanding of what love really is and who it is that he loves, an understanding reached after much pain and many mistakes.

In the last portion of the story Cadogan gets his revenge over Troxell. The thing is dramatically done, and it is also convincing. Troxell is precisely the sort of man to have made the sort of criminal blunders he is guilty of, and to have left just the traces needed for the young district attorney to fasten upon him the necessary evidence. He is also the sort of man who would commit suicide. So he slips through Cadogan's fingers, and escapes prison. But in doing it he sets Cadogan himself free. And this is how Cadogan sizes up the effect on himself. He is talking to his friend, Macgruder:

"Do you know, I believe that man Troxell has been a weight on my mind ever since I first encountered him."

He seemed imprest. "A subconscious influence they call that, don't they? It might very well be."

"I don't know what they call it, but I know it's so. Wasn't I always as grave as a deacon? A prig, that Boykin person called me; and, my God, Mack, it's so! Worse than that, I've been more or less of a brute. And all, really, because I insisted on taking life with such damnable solemnity. After all, I was only a boy, and I'm not much more now. I feel as though that cur had robbed me of my youth. . . . I don't know how to explain it, but I know now I've been carrying that man like a weight on my mind all these years, and never knew it. I ran into him when I was too young. It can't be a good thing for a boy to grow up before his time. . . . After all, I'm glad I haven't got to think of him in the penitentiary. I want to forget him . . ."

Hate is not good meat. Hate made the darker shadows in young Peter's life, but after all it was the hate of a clean, honest spirit for a low and vile one, and it did him no real harm. It matured him, it saddened him, it snatched away his youth, but it helped him to build too. Peter is worth knowing, and the background against which he is thrown is worth understanding.

There is nothing of the sort of limitations we are used to expecting in a small town book about this novel. Several of its characters are quite of the world. Mrs. Redlander is a woman of unusual orginality and varied experiencé, a woman of the large cities who does to some extent rule Colchester society, but who finds plenty of interest in the occupation. There is no sighing for larger opportunities from anyone involved, and no sensation that the ground is not fit for any type of human development. There is no Chinese wall about Colchester, in fact. It merges into outside thought and action without losing its own identity or force. The book will certainly be widely read, and merits wide reading.

THE IRREPRESSIBLE DODO

TWO literary enigmas have greatly puzzled the reading public of late. The first is why Mrs. Asquith, beloved as she tells us she has been by princes, peers, potentates and philosophers, should have so little of interest to tell us about any of them, and the other is why Mr. E. F. Benson, instead of giving us a sequel to his satirical masterpiece "Queen Lucia" should be so enamored of his character Dodo, Lady Chesterford, that he is unable to let her subside into oblivion. We have had "Dodo," "Dodo's Daughter," and now this elderly rattle is once more brought to our notice in a book called "Dodo Wonders" (Doran, $1.90 net).

Dodo is now fifty-five years of age. She has had three husbands, three children, and has three grandchildren. But she has changed very little and developed less. Her talk is just what it used to be, something that Mr. Benson calls witty. At her own ball, which of course is going off with wonderful éclat, she says: "Jumbo, dear, why can't we double as one does at bridge, and then somehow it would be eleven o'clock last night, and we should have it all over again? Jumbo, it seems, is her pet name for an Oriental potentate whom she had known in his Oxford days and whom she describes as having been " . . . absolutely at my feet. . . . My dear, he used to send me large pearls, which I was obliged to send back to him, and then he sent them again. What they cost in registered parcel post baffles conjecture."

London just before 1914 is the scene of the opening of the story and some of Dodo's old friends are still to the fore. Edith Arbuthnot, the musician, is one. She has just returned from a successful professional tour in Germany, where she has been decorated by the King of Bavaria. Miss Grantham is another, and both of these ladies have some words of common sense to address to Lady Chesterford as to her frivolous way of life, her shallowness and her egoism. But Dodo is unmoved by these criticisms and goes on entertaining her friends, minor royalties in the shape of Prince and Princess Albert Allerstein, and such tiresome members of the aristoc-

From Any Dealer Or Any Owner

Get the Truth About the Chalmers

Everywhere, Chalmers owners are testifying to the low costs and high value, the power and performance, of their car.

Everywhere, Chalmers dealers are demonstrating Chalmers superiorities in all points of good performance, fine riding and driving.

Get the truth about the Chalmers—*from the car itself*, and from its owners.

Dealers Will Show You—Owners Will Tell You—

How little it costs to run and keep the Chalmers. How free from trouble it is. How long it lasts.

How wonderfully well it rides. How easily it is steered. How effectively its brakes work.

How silent its motor is, and how it produces splendid performance without labor or strain.

How powerful it is on the grades and in all kinds of heavy going.

How easily it throttles down, and how smoothly and swiftly it picks up again.

All Models Equipped With Cord Tires

Chalmers Motor Car Company, Detroit, Michigan

Chalmers Motor Company of Canada, Limited, Windsor, Ontario

CHALMERS

REVIEWS OF NEW BOOKS
Continued

racy as Lord Cookham, whose pomposity and sense of his own importance bring him perilously near what in ordinary mortals would be ill-breeding.

And then, upon this noisy, extravagant, pleasure-seeking society suddenly breaks the war, and in a moment everything is changed. We are accustomed to praise highly, and with justice, the fine work done by Englishwomen during the war, but Mr. Benson shows us what the luxuriously bred had to learn before they could be of any use. Dodo finds her society accomplishments entirely futile, nor can she even look after the wants of her own child of ten in the absence of his nurse. She can't even learn to knit a sock or sew on a button. Lord Chesterford gives his country-house for a hospital and Dodo spends much energy and more money in fitting up a corner of it for herself and family. This she considers war-work. Edith Arbuthnot can not believe that the nation which has given the world so much good music can be guilty of the atrocities laid to it, but when a bomb falls in front of her house, wrecking two front rooms, she is at once converted to a more patriotic state of mind. Dodo's war work resolves itself into entertaining convalescent soldiers, varied by visits to town in search of the amusements of previous years. But, strange as it may seem, the flavor of that time escapes her and even to her picayune soul the magnitude of the struggle is made apparent. The book closes after the armistice. Edith and the Chesterfords are talking together and Edith declares that the war has made no change in any of them. Dodo denies this and points out that she now has a parlormaid instead of a butler, at the same time admitting that she is on the point of engaging (at vast expense) a man for that position.

Mr. Benson has now brought his heroine nearly to her sixtieth year and it would seem a good time to bid her farewell. But there is a haunting possibility that we may yet hear more of her. What is to prevent a book of her Personal Reminiscences?

LADY BARBARA NEAVE CARRIES ON

IT seems likely that anyone who read Stephen McKenna's "Lady Lilith" will want to read this second portion of the trio "The Sensationalists," the third part of which is still to appear. The last book left Lady Lilith, the nickname given to Lady Barbara Neave because some one had said that she was older than good and evil, on the point of meeting the successful playwright, Eric Lane, whose name was on every tongue in London, even tho the war was still on. Lady Barbara has been seriously ill because of overwork in a hospital for the wounded, and lacerated nerves over a love affair in which she had behaved outrageously; as a romance she had sworn to accept Jack Waring whenever he chose to ask her. But Jack has been missing for months, and before he was missing he had returned her letters unopened and refused any opportunity to see her. Yet she continued to consider herself as his until she knew definitely that he would never claim her; this, it may be remarked, she never dreamed possible, for Lady Barbara is possest of a vanity immense and corroding, a vanity to which she will sacrifice not alone anyone else, but even herself.

This second book takes up the story at the moment where it was dropt; it is rather a second volume of a three-volume novel than a part of a trilogy, tho it makes a complete novel in itself—and a novel difficult to lay aside, in spite of the fact that the extraordinary cleverness and mercilessness with which McKenna has drawn the portrait of Barbara makes her so real that she awakens in the reader a feeling of repulsion, almost of horror. Young, beautiful, rich, full of intelligence as she is, she is poisonous—here is, indeed, the portrayal of the true vampire woman, not the one who takes a man's money and leaves him when he is broke, but of her who sucks his very soul dry, and who clings desperately to her victim as long as the remotest chance that she can extract one more thrill, one more satisfaction to her aching vanity remains. But let us get to the story.

Eric Lane is one of the small group of Oxford students who had made a sort of clique in the university, and of whom Jack Waring was the leader. He and Eric had been intimate friends, tho Jack had never revealed to him the disastrous affair with Babs Neave. Of course he knows Babs by name and reputation. A girl of twenty-two or three who had shocked all London society with her self-will and her escapades, whose pictures were always to be found in the public prints, whose name had already been associated with one man's death, was hardly likely to be unknown to a man like Eric, even though he mixed not at all in society, having consistently worked for the position he had at length reached through toilsome and boring years as a journalist and hack writer for money to live on while he should get a footing in the theater.

Now society runs after Eric, and it is at a dinner given by Lady Poynter that the two meet. Lady Babs, who has been distinctly bored by the confinement of her long illness, and who has bordered insanity in her neurotic agonies over Jack Waring, is ready for a new sensation. She marks Eric as the man capable of giving it to her. Here is a picture of her as she enters the drawing-room, late of course:

"After pausing on the threshold to see who was present, Lady Barbara Neave entered the room falteringly, and with a suggestion that she was belatedly repenting a too venturesome effect in dress. The men, she knew, were only watching her eyes and waiting for the surprized smile of recognition which always made them feel they had been missed; but Mrs. Shelley, she would wager, was privately noting that a dove-colored silk dress and a scarlet shawl embroidered with birds in flight made a white face look ashen; Sonia O'Rane was probably wondering why her maid had not told her that a band of black tulle with a red rose at one side simply emphasized her hollow cheeks and sunken eyes. . . She moved listlessly and smiled mysteriously to herself as though unconscious that every one was silent and watchful; then the surprized smile transfigured her, she kissed the other women with childlike abandon, leaving the men to watch and envy."

But Lane was not there to see this entry. He was later even than Babs, and for a few moments she decided that she was predestined never to meet him. He had rescued her in a faint in a railway train, not knowing who she was, months ago, and handed her over to a first-aid station, leaving his flask with his initials in her possession. She had not seen him, but as she was recovering just as he left her, had

REVIEWS OF NEW BOOKS
Continued

marked the deep notes of his voice, and this voice had haunted her in her dreams. It was chance only that had made her acquainted with his identity, and it was because of all this that she waited the meeting with a feverish intensity. Here was Fate patently at work. And evidently Fate has ruled against the meeting.

Eric comes, however. And all the evening Barbara plays her finest game for him, a game all the finer because it is desperately sincere. Barbara must have her sensations, her experiments in emotion. To get them she will go to extremes, equaling those of a drug addict who must get his poison or die for lack of it.

Towards the end of the evening the girl asks Eric to see her home, and by a ruse at once clever and unscrupulous she actually forces Lane to take her to his own apartment. There she makes love to him. He is at once attracted and disgusted, but more than all he is interested and bewildered. Barbara is safe with him, and she knew she was safe. At length he persuades her to let him take her home:

"As Eric struggled with the sleeves of his coat, she twined her arms around his neck. The scent of carnations was now faintly blended with the deeper fragrance of the single rose behind her ear.

"'And you'd never kissed anyone before,' she whispered."

And so it was that what Barbara calls the "Education of Eric Lane," began.

For some months it is she who does the pursuing, who calls him up, who invites herself to luncheon with him, who gets him invited to the same country houses where she is to go. But by degrees she begins to be indispensable to the young man. Her fire and originality, her endless changes, her coldness, her abandon, the teasing spirit of her and the abject remorse she shows if she has hurt him too deeply, these things come to be the meat and drink of life to him. Always she tells him she loves him. But if he presses her to marry him, to allow an engagement between them, she falls back on her vow to Jack Waring. She is his promised bride unless he decides to throw her over.

Finally news comes of Jack, who has been detained in a German prison, wounded, ill, and not allowed, because of an early attempt to escape, to communicate with the outside world. News comes, but not to Babs. Jack finally writes from Switzerland, where he has been sent, as no longer capable of soldiering. He is better, he is full of eagerness for home, but for Barbara he shows neither thought nor memory.

Upon this a terrific struggle takes place between Eric and Babs. She wishes to hold her capture without promising anything, but is at last forced to allow a secret engagement or lose him. But Eric, after five weeks of this, releases the girl until Jack has had a chance to see her and release her in his turn. Or perhaps claim her.

Jack reaches England, and writes at once to Eric, whom he is longing to see. He has gone through London to his home. But he has not communicated with Barbara. And then Eric calls her up:

"'Babs—Jack's in England. . . I thought you'd like to know.'

"'Thank you, Eric,' she answered quietly.

There was a pause neither of them liked to break. At last Eric said:

"'He didn't come to see you. Why don't you recognize that it's all over, Babs? You say your soul belongs to Jack-well, he's had the chance to come and claim it.'

"There was a second pause, followed by a sigh.

"'It's hard to explain, Eric. You see, only he and I know how much he was in love with me before. I was the only person he'd ever cared for. Even I didn't understand how much he loved me until that night.' She sighed again. 'I don't believe that, after loving me, he could suddenly cease to love me.'

"'You gave him pretty good provocation,' Eric suggested.

"'But you don't cease loving people because they behave badly to you. I've behaved abominably to *you*. You've given me everything, and all I've done in return is to make you ill and miserable. I've ruined your work, your life—you've told me so, Eric. I've been utterly selfish and heartless. You know I'm vain, you know I'm spoiled, you admit I've behaved atrociously. But you want to marry me in spite of all.'

"'I love you in spite of all.'

"Barbara said nothing, and her silence was a confession and answer. There were a hundred reasons why Jack had not come to see her; his future was uncertain, he must wait for a final verdict from his doctor, he was perhaps still chewing the cud of his resentment. And, when the first reasons were exhausted, her vanity wove a hundred more in stout, impregnable protection against the fantastic thought that any man could tire of her.

"'Oh, I wish you *didn't!*' cried Barbara, at last. 'Why don't you go away and forget all about me?'

"She had trapped him neatly, as he had no doubt she knew.

"'I can't forget you,' he answered, savagely conscious that he was presenting her with new weapons. 'Whatever you did, you'd be the biggest thing in my life; I should always need you.'

"This time she put her triumph into words.

"'Don't you think that Jack may need me as badly?'"

And Eric, unable to break loose, allowed neither to hope nor yet utterly to despair, hangs on, ill and miserable indeed. Hangs on until suddenly he reaches the decision to leave England for good. He is threatened with a serious, a complete breakdown; an opportunity to go to America at the most flattering terms comes to him. Barbara has lately cut all communications with him, and he has seen her meet Jack for a moment in a theater—a meeting which seems to effect Jack not at all. So he makes all his preparations and is to sail next day when he once more meets Barbara, at the same house, Lady Poynter's, where they first met.

The last scene between the two is a consummate piece of writing. It ends finally by Eric leaving the girl running after his taxi as he returns, from her door, where he had left her, to his own rooms. He enters them to hear the telephone madly ringing, and knows who it is that is calling:

"There was nothing for it but to tie a handkerchief over the slapper of the bell . . . then he threw himself in shirt and trousers on the bed, and buried his face in his hands."

It is the end.

The reader lays down the book wondering what the third of the series is to relate, and whether perhaps it will be Barbara at last who is taught, who is trained, who is punished. (The Education of Eric Lane. By Stephen McKenna. George H. Doran

DOCTORING MINERAL OILS

REFINING an oil is simply "doctoring" it so that it will sell, we are told by Benjamin T. Brooks, writing in *Chemical and Metallurgical Engineering* (New York). The alterations that make it salable may be such as to have no perceptible effect in increasing its actual value for use, as when objectionable odors are removed or agreeable color imparted. In fact, these processes may actually remove useful elements. Mr. Brooks believes that additional study of the refining problem by chemists will result in large savings. In "doctoring" an oil, we should have in mind, of course, the use that is to be made of it, and so manage the process that all the constituents that contribute to this use are retained. Mr. Brooks believes that inaccurate tradition, rather than scientific knowledge, guides most refiners at present, and he instances the case of the "olefines" or unsaturated hydrocarbons, actually valuable parts of the oil, which are usually removed and so wasted. Writes Mr. Brooks:

"What does refining really consist in? Opinions may differ, and usually do, as to what constitutes refining and whether or not a given oil is 'refined,' 'well refined,' 'poorly refined,' 'properly refined,' or 'suitably refined' for a given purpose and what not, but I believe the only answer or definition of refining which can at present be given is substantially this: Doctoring it so it will sell. Petroleum products are 'refined' according to the dictates of the salesmen and the standards to which the public has become accustomed. People outside of petroleum refineries object to offensive odors, and therefore, one of the first requirements of a refined oil is that its odor shall not be unduly offensive. People generally like pretty colors and the public has become accustomed to insist upon water-white oils in certain cases, light yellow or amber oils in others, pretty red ones, in other cases, or oils with a pretty green, bronze, or blue fluorescence, as the case may be. The public has become accustomed to and expects these properties in certain oils, but does not expect petroleum oils to be perfumed or colored pink. These physical properties, odor, and color are mentioned in the first place as they are most conspicuous and have considerable to do with the salability of these products, but have little or nothing to do with their suitability or relative excellence in their usual applications.

"One class of hydrocarbons which has been considerably discust is the class known as olefines or unsaturated hydrocarbons. Previously the general notion has been that refining consists essentially in removing these unsaturated hydrocarbons, and practically everything in the calendar which could be considered objectionable in an oil, including odor, was attributed to the presence of unsaturated hydrocarbons. But in the case of gasoline or motor fuel it has been shown by Hall and others that ordinary simple olefines behave just as well in internal combustion engines as saturated hydrocarbons; perhaps a little Mellon Institute, Dr. Harry Essex made very satisfactory block tests on an automobile engine running entirely on unsaturated hydrocarbons, even turpentine doing very well considering its boiling point and volatility, once the engine had become warm. Offensive odors in motor-fuels are due to relatively very small proportions of derivatives containing sulfur, nitrogen, and naphthenic acids, and these malodorous constituents can be completely removed independently of the unsaturated hydrocarbons and the resulting motor-fuel may be quite superior in odor, and keeping qualities as regards color, to most of the gasoline marketed to-day."

The economic importance of an adequate supply of motor-fuel is such, Mr. Brooks believes, that the unsaturated hydrocarbons, which in the aggregate represent many millions of gallons, should not be removed unless it can be conclusively shown that there is good reason to do so. It would undoubtedly be better, he thinks, to leave them in the motor fuel than to partly remove and partly alter them, as is done in ordinary refining, resulting in loss and in introducing heavy oily residues into the refined product. He continues:

"When we consider the refining of lubricating oils we encounter another set of trade customs and prejudices, together with a series of unsolved scientific problems, the most important of which is naturally the subject of viscosity. Every one knows that when an unrefined lubricating oil distillate is allowed to stand it darkens rapidly in color, and this proceeds from the exposed surface gradually downward until the whole oil has become very dark in color. This phenomenon is evidently one of air oxidation. As usual, following the old formula, the blame is put upon olefines. However, viscous oily, unsaturated hydrocarbons do not show this behavior. The substances which cause this development of color may easily be minor constituents constituting less than 1 per cent. of the crude lubricating distillate, but just what they are we do not know.

"Is it worth while, from a practical standpoint, to study this question? Personally, I am convinced that it is. Dunstan in England has suggested that it is desirable to retain olefines in lubricating oils and that they may have lubricating qualities superior to the saturated hydrocarbons. Every possible means of reducing the present large refining losses must be carefully considered. The refining of lubricating oils should, therefore, be carefully studied with the object of discovering methods of refining which will accomplish the particular results desired, and no more. When the days of 'slaughtering' crude petroleum are over—and they are rapidly passing—research on such problems will be imperative. A study of our production statistics indicates that if the refining losses of lubricating oils could be halved many millions of gallons would be added annually to our supply of lubricating oils.

"It may be pointed out that none of the testing methods now employed are any measure of the film strength of a lubricating oil. During the war the value of castor-oil or additions of 1 or 2 per cent. of

Pennsylvania VACUUM CUP CORD TIRES

On Every Boulevard, Street, and Highway

—wherever cars are driven—you hear the *sound of safety*—

A steady, even purr, the *gripping, holding, letting go* of the thick-lipped Vacuum Cups on the wet, oily pavements as your car glides along safely, holding true to the course ahead.

Priced on a parity with ordinary makes of tires and *guaranteed* —per warranty tag attached to each casing—for *9,000 miles,* Vacuum Cup Cord Tires set the highest individual standard of *safety, service,* and *economy.*

PENNSYLVANIA RUBBER COMPANY
of AMERICA, Inc., Jeannette, Pa.
Direct Factory Branches and Service Agencies Throughout the World

Custom Built Car of H. R. H. Queen Mother Emma of Holland, Vacuum Cup Equipped by Royal Request.

SCIENCE AND INVENTION
Continued

clearly shown, this benefit chiefly consisting in greater tenacity or wetting power of the oil for the metal. So far as I am aware there is no term which expresses precisely this property, altho the terms 'oiliness' and 'body' connote something of this behavior. In a moving bearing, under heavy duty, the tendency is for the oil to be squeezed from between the moving surfaces, and if the oil film has not sufficient tenacity or adhering power the film will be broken and metal to metal friction will result. Given this analysis of the problem, any reasonably competent mechanism could devise an instrument which would measure this property of oils in a way which would constitute a much more rational means of determining the lubricating value of different oils.

"It is not too much to expect that economies which can be effected through better refining methods will more than cover the sum total of the cost of all petroleum investigations, even should these investigations be undertaken on a very large scale indeed. Other possible results of research might, therefore, be reckoned as pure gain, and it is worth pointing out in this connection that the actual experience of manufacturers who maintain research is that the big difficult problems yield by far the greatest financial returns in the long run, as compared with the benefits of solving a multitude of easy little problems."

CURING STAMMERERS IN THE SCHOOL

IN the city of New York there are 30,000 stammerers, of whom 8,000 are of school age. The Board of Education has instituted a department under a Director of Speech Improvement to cope with the situation, and has just issued an appeal to teachers to cooperate in a national movement for better phonation. Statistics compiled by the Adjutant-General of the United States Army show the vital necessity for this work. Ignorance of this subject is appalling, we are told, among those who have the care of children. This is due to the paucity of efficient literature. Teachers and parents have been compelled to depend upon the misleading advice of friends who suggest innumerable panaceas, the majority of which but serve to aggravate the condition. We quote from a leaflet by Dr. Frederick Martin, Director of Speech Improvement, issued by the Department of Health, as follows:

"Many cities have already adopted a definite program for the pedagogical correction of stammerers and there is little doubt that, before many years, the universal school curriculum will adequately provide for these sufferers and all those with cognate defects of speech.

"It is almost impossible to approximate the economic cost of stammering. It impairs the mental growth of the sufferer, causing self-repression. The defect interferes with the expression of ideas as well as the utilization of potential energy in the business or social world. With the lack opportunity for the development of intellectual capacity, but there is a tendency to a lowering of the moral stamina. The Government has recognized this menace by refusing to permit immigrants who stammer to enter the country, because of the great probability of their becoming public charges. The many stammerers who leave school early in life, and begin at once to retrograde because of their defect, could easily be influenced to continue their education if hope of its cure were held out to them. The child handicapped with a defect of phonation often appears mentally inferior because of his peculiar hesitancy and timidity in speech. Where he is able to keep up with his class, it is at a cost of so much mental and physical suffering that the nervous system and mental disposition are often harmfully affected.

"It is vitally important that stammering be corrected in the schools, not only on account of those so afflicted, but for the good of normal pupils who may, through association or mimicry, acquire the habit.

"Stammering, according to its universally accepted meaning in English, is a halting, defective utterance. The sufferer has difficulty in starting a word or in passing from one letter to another. It is a momentary lack of control of the muscles of articulation in the effort to speak. Often the stammerer will come to an absolute halt, being unable to produce voice. The defect is sometimes accompanied by irregular spasmodic movements of the face, tongue, neck, or body, caused by the effort made to produce a sound or articulate speech. One form of stammering is commonly known as stuttering. It is the unnecessary repetition of a letter or word before passing to the next—as 'd-d-dog,' or 'They-they-they went-went out.'

"Stammering is, at bottom, a mental fault which eventuates in a physical disability. It is often caused by fear, imitation, or improper speech training, and is really an acquired affection. Most children who stammer begin to show the defect after their school-life has begun. Children are sometimes made to read and use words much too difficult for them to articulate, pronounce, or even understand. The result is the formation of a habit of stumbling, hesitancy, then stuttering—which may become confirmed when the child is oversensitive, or is made conscious of his habit through improper correction. He then prefers silence to ridicule or destructive criticism.

"One great difficulty in meeting the requirements of this problem, is the attitude of parents in calmly waiting for the child to outgrow the defect. A child thus treated usually continues stammering for years, driving in deeper his false habits of speech, which would never exist were the cause known and the defect corrected in its incipiency.

"The class teacher can prove the greatest factor in solving the problem of the stammering child, by preventing the defect or eliminating it during its first stages. If properly corrected in the lower grades, each case will respond readily to treatment. When first noticing any stumbling, stuttering or hesitancy in recitations, one should gently check the child, without attracting the attention of other members of the class, and lead him into a more confident, deliberate, and better articulated mode of expression.

"A common fallacy in attempting to correct a case is to ask the stammerer to take a breath before speaking each word or words that he may fear. The fear that

SCIENCE AND INVENTION
Continued

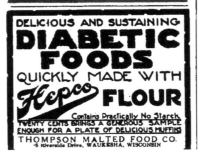

he is made to realize that he must stop, and unnaturally take a breath, recalls to his mind his inability to speak as others do. He even forms a mental picture of his past sufferings, and fear predominates to such a degree that all coordination of the nerve centers controlling speech is temporarily destroyed. The disturbance is not caused by a lack of breath, but by interference with the normal subconscious control. There is always enough residual air in the lungs to produce voice. Stammerers can sing without difficulty, and singing requires greater lung-power than speaking.

"Irrespective of the primal cause, it will be found that 90 per cent. of our cases have not their vocal organs fixt in the correct position for producing the sound which they are attempting to make. A boy may try to say 'mother' with his mouth wide open; an impossible position for the letter 'm,' which requires that the lips be prest together. The conscious control of the organs makes for perfect speech.

"The main factor is the teacher's knowledge of the proper workings of the mechanism of speech and how to develop in the mind of the sufferer a new subconscious control of his vocal organs."

THE RIGHT KIND OF AIR

PLENTY of air, with plenty of moisture in it, is the corner-stone of health, thinks Dr. Adam H. Wright, of Toronto, chairman of the Ontario Provincial Board of Health. These are matters, especially the item of humidity, on which all medical men do not agree; but Dr. Wright certainly has a good proportion on his side, altho he is fair enough to quote high British authority on the other. He cites a common question—"Is night air bad?" and quotes the reply of one physician to the effect that he did not see how one was to get away from it. The inquirer, of course, he goes on to explain, meant outside air as compared with house air. Dr. Wright admits that outside air at night is not in some ways as good as that of the day, especially during sunlight, but it is certainly the best available. He continues:

"In considering ventilation arithmetical computations are not altogether satisfactory, as mathematical correctness is generally impossible; but we may start with one estimate frequently made by hygienic authorities. Each adult is supposed to require an 'hourly supply of 3,000 cubic feet of air for the removal of his own *effete* matters.'

"If there is not a constant inflow of fresh air and outflow of used air, some vitiation occurs in a very short time. To get enough of a continuous current is difficult in very cold weather in our climate. We must consider that ventilation goes hand in hand with heating, and the question of expense, especially with present prices of fuel, becomes a very serious one.

"We expect much from diffusion and gravity, but they are not sufficient in inhabited rooms. Under ordinary circumstances there are inlets and outlets in

windows and doors—even through bricks, plaster, and mortar; so there is always some ventilation even when we try to prevent it by double windows, papering the walls, and closing up cracks.

"The simplest and most common method, and perhaps the most effective, is to open a window. This brings up the important question of the draft, which is considered so dangerous. We are told in that admirable text-book on 'Practical Hygiene,' by Harrington and Richardson, that drafts which are productive of discomforts are more dangerous than the ordinary vitiation of the air. As I sleep in a draft with comfort and benefit during the greater part of the year—always when the temperature is not at or below zero—I have not that dread of a healthy draft which so commonly prevails. That precious draft of 'God's pure air' is much maligned.

"However, it must be admitted that drafts are not always harmless. You can not expose yourself inside or outside in cold weather with comfort and safety, clad in pajamas or a bathing costume. If not properly protected by bed-clothing or suitable wearing-apparel you will get unduly chilled and suffer evil consequences therefrom.

"To come back to our bedroom, one may properly ask, how much air should be introduced during our sleeping hours, or how large should the opening be? No fixt or definite directions can be given, but the following figures may furnish a rough guide. In the colder months raise or lower (or both, as I generally prefer) the window from one to twelve inches, or less than one inch in zero weather.

"The chief requirement in the ventilation of a room at night is a regular income of air with a constant current, called by architects, 'thorough ventilation.' Keep drafts away from the bed so far as possible. If this is impossible, let the drafts come and go as they like, and sleep where you like. If you fear drafts it is a very simple matter to deflect the current by some of the many devices which are well known and used."

Dr. Wright advises that the temperature of the bedroom during sleeping hours should be about 50 degrees in cold weather. If at bedtime the average temperature of the house is about 70 degrees, it is not prudent, he says, to retire with the air at that temperature when cooling takes place during the night, and get up in the morning on a shiver-producing atmosphere of 45 to 50 degrees. It is well to open the window an hour or two before going to bed, closing the door at the same time to avoid cooling the living-room before retiring. He proceeds:

"If, when getting into bed, you have sufficient covering to keep the body and extremities warm, you will be in a good, hygienic condition, and you can breathe the comparatively cool air quite as safely as you can respire even cooler air outside when you are walking or motoring along the streets.

"The simple rules proposed apply only to an ordinary normal inhabited dwelling and are not suited for a sick-room, the proper ventilation of which will not be discust in this paper.

"There is one important matter so intimately connected with ventilation that

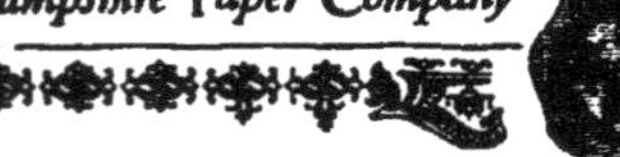

SCIENCE AND INVENTION
Continued

of providing moisture in the air of our dwellings during cold weather.

"Sir Hermann Weber, one of England's most distinguished physicians, insisted on keeping the air in the house pure and dry. Our opinion on this continent is that we should keep it pure and moist during the cold season. The relative humidity should be about 50 per cent. If less than that, say 35 to 40, the dry air has a great absorbing power and it will take up moisture from persons and things—from the skin, the mucous membranes, especially of the respiratory tract, from the lips and nostrils down to the bronchial tubes, from wood furniture, from leather binding of books, causing them to crack and fall to pieces. It causes undue dryness of the skin, irritation of the throat with a cough sometimes bronchial, sometimes a laryngeal cough of a peculiar character, ending in a 'squeal.' The so-called 'winter cough' is very common in Canada and the United States. Some of us found it very obstinate in the past, but we now think that the proper remedy in at least a large proportion of cases is the provision of moisture in the air we breathe.

"The most common methods of inducing this moisture are by heating water in water-holders attached to our furnaces, humidifying pans fastened to our radiators, and various forms of humidifiers planned by architects and sanitary engineers. About two to four (or perhaps more) gallons should be evaporated per day in a fairly large house. Dr. H. J. Barnes, of Boston, has devised a humidifier which he uses in his office. It evaporates a gallon of water a day which produces about 35 per cent. humidity."

GAS-MASKS FOR FIREMEN

THAT a fireman's mask which will protect against all forms of smoke and chemical fumes will soon be commercially available as the result of the work of Government chemists is indicated in a recent paper entitled "Gas-masks for gases met in fighting fires," just issued by the United States Bureau of Mines. The army gas-mask gives protection against smoke and products of combustion, but not against carbon monoxid or ammonia gas, the authors assert. City firemen have been overcome while wearing army gas-masks. Masks of the army type should not be used in mines after fires and explosions, but self-contained oxygen breathing apparatus should be employed. To quote an abstract furnished by the Bureau:

"The Bureau of Mines has tested and used many types of self-contained oxygen breathing apparatus in fighting mine-fires and in rescuing miners trapt in poisonous gases resulting from fires or from explosions in mines. Similar devices have been used by city fire-fighters but have never been considered entirely satisfactory owing, largely, to their weight, to the time necessary for adjusting them to wearers, and the constant care required to maintain the apparatus in good working condition. Hence there has long been need for a light, easily adjusted, and dependable breathing apparatus for protecting fire-fighters from irritating and poisonous gases and smokes.

"The dangers from gases that city firemen face and the need of standardized methods of protection against them have been emphasized by overconfidence in the capacity of the army type of gas-mask to protect the wearer against industrial gases, an assurance that has probably arisen because soldiers were taught that the United States Army gas-mask would protect them against all the gases they might encounter. This statement, true for the battle-field, but not true for all industrial gases, including products of combustion, has been brought back by soldiers and spread generally among workers. Furthermore, city firemen and mine operators have been circularized with letters and advertisements of army gas-masks offered for sale by certain persons who made unreserved statements, probably through ignorance, that the masks would protect wearers in mines and burning buildings. The falsity of these statements was evident to the Bureau of Mines, which took steps immediately to notify the public that Army gas-masks had serious limitations, especially when used in fire-fighting or in any place where unusually heavy amounts of poisonous gas are present.

"The work described in this paper was undertaken to obtain information regarding the use of the Army type of mask for fighting fires and for doing rescue work in mines and the mineral industries. Incidentally, the results may be of interest to city firemen, insurance underwriters, State officials, property owners, and others who are interested in protection of property from fire.

"The investigations of chemists working under the direction of the Bureau of Mines and subsequently in the Chemical Warfare Service promise the early development of an absorbent for carbon monoxid which will admit of the manufacture of a combination canister which will protect against smoke, ammonia, carbon monoxid, and practically all chemical fumes. When this is accomplished the firemen can be protected in any atmosphere where a safety lamp will burn. The Bureau of Mines will cooperate with city fire departments in determining the nature of gases found in fires and with manufacturers in approving suitable gas-masks for fire-fighting."

PRIMITIVE CORN FROM INDIAN MOUNDS

COMMENTING on the article quoted in our issue for July 9, telling of the development of Indian corn from wild teosinte grass by Luther Burbank, *The News-Advertiser* (Chillicothe, Ohio) asserts that corn in a stage of development, similar to one passed through by Burbank's plants, during his breeding experiments, has been found in the Indian Mounds of Ohio, thus confirming Burbank's belief that the Indians developed their corn in the course of cultivation, occupying probably centuries instead of years. Writes the editor of the paper just named:

"At one stage in the development of the plant [by Burbank] it grew in the form of corn as it is to-day, on a cob, in rows, but each grain was enclosed in a separate, thin husk, with the whole ear enclosed in husk also.

SCIENCE AND INVENTION
Continued

"It is at this point where the connection between Burbank and the Moundbuilders is made.

"In the issue of *The News-Advertiser* for September 2, 1920, appeared a story of some peculiar corn raised by Albert Wachenschwanz, of 343 North High Street. This corn was practically like modern maize except that each grain was enclosed in an individual 'husk' exactly as it is at one stage in the Burbank experiment.

"The seed which was planted by Mr. Wachenschwanz came from a mound near, or of the famous Harness group, along the Scioto River, below this city. It was found in an earthen vessel, with a cover hermetically sealed, either purposely or through the action of time. The seeds had not been parched or cooked and had never decayed or germinated. Mr. Wachenschwanz was given ten grains by the late William B. Mills, local archeologist, the mound excavation then being made under direction of the State Archeological Society.

"This was some four years ago. Mr. Wachenschwanz planted the seed, which germinated and the corn matured, some of the ears were mere 'nubbins,' only four or five inches long, but others were from eight to ten inches. He repeated the experiment and has always succeeded in raising corn. This year again, he has some growing. Every year has seen the same individual husks on the grains.

"He has sent specimen ears of the corn to the various agricultural colleges, but never got much information or enlightenment until he read the article in the DIGEST. This shows that at the time the Moundbuilders, whatever their race, were erecting their earthworks and cultivating the soil here in the Scioto Valley, their maize had reached only to the point where each grain still retained its own husk. With the slow rate of development under crude methods it may have been centuries before maize reached the stage it was in when the first white men settled in America, when the individual grain-husks had disappeared, and only the main ear-husk remained."

Henry H. Bennett, Secretary of the Chillicothe Park Commission, who calls our attention to the article quoted above, says in a letter to THE LITERARY DIGEST;

"This section of the Scioto Valley, about midway between Columbus and the Ohio River, was probably the most densely settled section of the entire country in the time of the race commonly known as the Moundbuilders, more than four thousand mounds and other earthworks having been listed within the limits of this county, Ross, alone. Many valuable discoveries have been made in these earthworks, but none seems to me more interesting than the finding of this seed-corn and its subsequent planting and growth. It is especially interesting in connection with the experiments of Mr. Burbank. I have seen this corn myself, and know that it is as described. The grower of it has promised me several ears when his present crop matures, one of which I intend to send to Mr. Burbank, who may be interested in seeing that the corn of the Moundbuilders was apparently midway in development from the wild grass to the maize as found by the first white settlers in America."

ODERATION IN A MEATLESS DIET

OOD may be efficient without meat, concludes a reviewer in *The British Med- l Journal* (London) of a pamphlet on vege- ian athletics issued by the Vegetarian ciety of Manchester, from the pen of nry Light, captain for twenty years of e Vegetarian Cycling and Athletic Club. ys this paper:

"We are glad to see that he is no ex- emist, but one who recognizes the value moderation both in opinions and in eir expression. He presents first a rmidable list of eminent athletes who ve given up a meat dietary, and if we n trust the statements about their food take (and non-scientific people are apt take but scant account of accuracy ithout any intention to deceive) there good testimony as to the value of their esent system. But this does not mean at they were strict vegetarians. We lieve it is usual to dub their dietary 'em' (vegetables, eggs, milk, including ilk products, for example, cheese). There no physiological reason why such a et should be inefficient if taken in prop- ly balanced proportions. Toward the ose of the pamphlet the question, 'What onstitutes overfeeding and underfeeding?' raised. To answer such a poser we ould have to explain the whole of the rinciples of nutrition, and that is be- ond the scope of this note. Suffice it to y that the amount must depend on the ge, size, and activities of each individual. he main factor that causes variation in n average adult is the amount of work e does. The energy-supplying food (fat nd carbohydrate) must be proportioned o this. The supply of the protein food hich builds tissues and repairs waste a much more constant figure unless ctual growth is in progress. There is no eason why all this should not be supplied y the vegetable world. The usefulness f meat in a dietary depends on what ubner called the specific dynamic action f protein, and of all proteins those of nimal flesh are most efficacious in this irection. But if meat has a specific ction, the vegetarians can claim that lants have also a specific usefulness in upplying to animals those accessory actors known as vitamins, which are in- lispensable to health and even to life tself."

COLORED GEMS—If experiments now being carried on at the Reno station of the Bureau of Mines are successful, says *The Mining Congress Journal* (Washington, D. C.), it will be possible to give color to colorless gems which exist in abundance in the West. We read:

"The experiments so far have produced results which are considered promising. The penetrating radiation of radium is the agency through which gems are being colored. In a preliminary experiment, a colorless Colorado topaz was tinted yellow. The coloring when exposed to light was found to be not permanent, and the experi- mentation continues with a view to making the color light-proof. Successful termina- tion of the experiments would add mate- rially to the value of Western gem stones, whose market value is low on account of their lack of the tint qualities deemed essential by gem manufacturers."

INVESTMENTS AND FINANCE

HOW MANY AUTOS CAN WE OWN?

VERY nearly all the Americans who can afford to buy automobiles have them already, according to computations made by Leonard P. Ayres, vice-president of the Cleveland Trust Co. As there are 105 million of us, and only nine million cars, this opinion seems surprizing at first blush. But Mr. Ayres reminds us that great deductions must be made from the total population before we arrive at the number of possible car-owners. To begin with, few families, no matter how wealthy, want a car for each member. A large part of the population is below car-owning age. A very large part have not the incomes to buy or keep a car. Taking everything into account, Mr. Ayres believes that we are nearer the limit than most persons realize, and that the manufacture of cars in future will be chiefly for replacements. In other words, the motor-car, as an industrial product, must hereafter be looked upon as a necessity of life, like hats, for instance, or shoes. We quote an article contributed by Fred C. Kelly to *The Times* (New York), which reads:

"Everybody who drives an automobile, or has tried to find a vacant space in which to park one, and every pedestrian who is daily obliged to dodge automobiles, or to wait for the endless stream of them to pass, so that he may cross a busy street—every one of these persons, or nearly everybody—must have asked himself at some time:

"'What is going to happen when there are several times as many automobiles as there are now? How many automobiles are there going to be in this country, anyhow? Where are we going to put them all?'

"The presumption always seems to be that there is practically no end to the increase in the use of automobiles. About 9,000,000 are now in use, but there are something like 105,000,000 people in the United States, so that there are still many millions who do not own their own cars. How many of these 105,000,000 are eventually going to buy? Not nearly so many as might be expected. Indeed, it appears doubtful if there will ever be even twice as many cars in use as there are today. The point of saturation is probably only a few years ahead.

"Mr. Ayres found that the capacity of the automobile factories in this country was more than 1,000,000 cars a year in excess of the present demand. If these factories were run at their full capacity for a few years they would soon supply every potential buyer in the United States. There would be so many automobiles in use that the gasoline supply would be inadequate, and some other kind of motive power would have to be developed.

"The greatest number of possible automobile buyers, even by a liberal estimate, is less than 20,000,000—about the number of white American families. Not every man who has the price of an automobile will buy one. For example, there are fishermen, lumbermen, sailors, soldiers, lighthouse keepers and others who would have scant opportunity to drive a car after they got it. Then there are thousands of people living in cities whose earnings might permit them to keep automobiles if they were in a smaller place, where garage rents are less, and also where there is less traffic.

"Mr. Ayres finds that at the end of 1920 there were about forty-two cars in use for each 100 white men of voting age. In several States the entire population might crowd into the automobiles there registered and all go riding at once. Each car lasts, on the average, about six seasons.

"It seems altogether doubtful if the sale of the higher-priced cars will ever be much more than it is now. Ayres believes that for several years new users of cars will be confined largely to people of limited means who will buy less costly machines.

"Fairly reliable figures for the registration of automobiles in each State are available, beginning with the year 1912. After making allowance for imports and exports, it is found that the total number of new cars put into use in this country since the beginning has been 11,075,813. Since the number registered last year was somewhat in excess of 9,000,000 and the number in use at the end of the year undoubtedly rather less than that number, it follows that about 2,000,000 cars have been eliminated.

"Some cars, of course, are destroyed almost as soon as they are put into service, while others, that were first registered ten years or more ago, are still running; but the outstanding fact about the registration figures is that they have been for the past nine years about equal each year to the sum of the cars produced in that year and the five previous years. This means that the average length of life of the cars has been about six registrations."

Estimates of the ability of the country to purchase and use cars have varied enormously, Mr. Kelly tells us. On the one hand, States such as South Dakota, are so well supplied that the entire population could probably go riding simultaneously. On the other hand, it may be argued that great possible markets may still exist. This may be investigated by studying the composition of the population with reference to its probable purchasing power. The census data for 1920 are not available, but those of 1910 give us a fairly reliable basis for discovering the proportions of the whole population found in certain great groups. The results, says Mr. Kelly, do not bear out the idea that the remaining new market is large. He continues:

"The automobile has been adopted by the American people with great rapidity. So short a time ago as in 1912 there were 114 people for each car in use, while eight years later there was one car for each twelve people. The extremes are found in the States of the Pacific division, with one car for every seven persons, and those

YOUR Printer

Do you make him your partner or your victim?

BRAINY men—men whose abilities would net them greater profits in other industries—spend their lives as printers because each day they learn something new about the work they love.

These printers, just as other notable men in other professions, are sometimes very timid. This may be because of their complicated subject, which they fear the buyer of printing does not clearly understand. Whatever the reason is, many buyers of printing construe it as an opportunity to force their opinions on the printer.

What is the result? Very often it is poor printing, a dissatisfied buyer, and a disliked printer. Why should the printer, of all persons, be the craftsman whom everybody feels qualified to tell how to run his business?

Why will many buyers of printing continue to think that printing is philanthropy? "You can't get something for nothing" is as true in printing as in any other business. And it is more evident, because nothing shows its cheapness quicker than cheap printing.

But if a printer does turn out a good job, even in face of difficulties, what is his reward? Isn't it often only an opportunity to hand in a competitive bid on the next job?

Why is the printer so seldom allowed to feel a spirit of partnership with the buyer—to feel that he is working *with* him instead of *for* him? Why is the spectre of a lost account hung ever before his eyes?

Buyers of printing, remember this: The first step toward better printing is to make your printer your partner.

We can make this plea for the printer because of our intimate knowledge of the situation. Just a step away, we get a true viewpoint on both the printer and you.

We do our share for the printer and you by providing better paper. You can do yours by placing greater confidence in your printer.

MANY jobs of printing cost as much as a small house. No house is built without a blue print. No printing can be properly planned without a dummy.

To aid printers and buyers of printing toward a better understanding of the job at the outset, we have prepared books of dummy material. These books contain specimens of type, borders, initials, engravings, page arrangements, rules, and decorations.

This month the book issued is printed on Warren's Lustro, and we recommend it as helpful to anyone planning printing that will be executed on glossy-coated paper.

These books are distributed to printers, buyers of printing, artists, and designers by paper merchants who sell Warren's Standard Printing Papers. If you do not know the merchant to whom you should apply, write to us and we will send you his name.

better paper — better printing

S. D. WARREN COMPANY, BOSTON, MASS.

INVESTMENTS AND FINANCE
Continued

of the East South Central division, with one car for each twenty-seven persons.

Great deductions must be made from the total population of the country as soon as we begin the attempt to estimate the possible purchasers of automobiles. To begin with, some 44 out of each 100 are less than 21 years of age, while 4 in each 100 are over 65 years of age.

This leaves 52 per cent. of the people from whom most of the purchasers must clearly come. Seventeen of these 52 are immigrants and colored people. While there are in the aggregate many motor owners in these groups, it seems entirely probable that no very large number among them who do not already own cars will be able to purchase them during the next few years.

The remaining possible purchasers are the remaining 35 per cent. About half of them are women who are, in the main, the wives of the men. It seems to be a fair conclusion that the purchasers of automobiles will in their very great majority come from the 18 per cent. of the population who are native white men between the ages of 21 and 65. This group comprises about 19,000,000. Probably about half of them already own cars.

The important fact is that the number of potential purchasers in this country who are still unsupplied with cars is much smaller than has generally been supposed. Nearly every family would doubtless like to own a passenger automobile. But the facts seem to show that no such universal use of automobiles is possible at present or in the near future because a large proportion of the people cannot afford to purchase or to run them. Many more than half of all the income receivers get less than $1,000 a year.

It is sometimes suggested that the number of cars in use may actually decrease now that the abnormal wages of the war period are past. Mr. Ayers believes it improbable that anything short of a prolonged era of serious business depression can force many people who now have cars to give them up.

The productive capacity of the automobile industry in this country has been stated to be 2,660,000 cars a year at the close of 1920. If all plants should produce at their full capacity and if the cars should last on the average long enough to be registered during six seasons, the annual registration would soon be from 15,000,000 to 16,500,000.

The use in the near future of anything like twice the present number of motor vehicles seems most unlikely. Another consideration of no small importance, as already mentioned, is that if the number of automobiles should be doubled in the near future, some other motive power than gasoline would probably have to be developed to propel them.

The answer appears to be, then, that competition between these manufacturing establishments will be sharper than ever, and prices of automobiles will eventually be much lower.

As part of the trend toward lower automobile prices, comments the Springfield *Republican*, "there may be considerable demand for 'sub-flivers' if the experimental cars of this diminutive type make good."

THE CALIFORNIA GRAPE SURVIVES PROHIBITION

A GOOD many people must have been puzzled, the Springfield *Republican* observes, when the President of the California Grape Growers Association recently stated in his annual address that the California grape industry had been more prosperous since prohibition went into effect. "Prohibition destroyed the California wine industry, and the wine is made from the grapes." The Massachusetts paper solves the puzzle by calling attention to the California raisin industry:

Raisins are made from grapes, and California's production of raisins has greatly increased in recent years. Indeed, that State is now the chief American raisin producer, the total production for the United States being 264,000,000 pounds in 1916, 300,000,000 pounds in 1918 and 380,000,000 pounds in 1920. This year there is a short crop amounting to only 220,000,000 pounds, but prices for California producers are high.

With the United States also dominating the export trade in raisins more and more—the shipments abroad in 1920 amounting to 110,000,000 pounds—the future can not seem dark to the California grape grower even under prohibition.

A WARNING TO PROSPECTIVE INVESTORS IN POTASH

TO protect the public from misrepresentation and fraud on the part of unscrupulous promoters and sellers of stocks based on potash deposits in western Texas, the United States Geological Survey states that the potash deposits there, instead of being eleven hundred or even three hundred feet thick, as represented by the promoters, have not yet been proved to be of workable thickness or of commercial value. As the Survey continues in a recent bulletin:

Rich potash salts, comprising the mineral polyhalite, which were deposited in association with great thicknesses of rock salt and gypsum in "red beds," as in Germany, and, in fact, at the same time as the German deposits, have been discovered by representatives of the United States Geological Survey and the Texas University Bureau of Geology and Technology in a coöperative search, but tho this discovery, which was made public early in June, is encouraging and interesting, the practical question whether the deposits are thick enough to mine—that is, whether they are worth anything—is yet to be answered.

The signs of potash which constituted the recent discovery came from drill cuttings from three wells in Midland, Dawson, and Ward counties, that have been drilled for oil near the Staked Plains region, which the geologists, on scientific grounds, have considered the most promising region for the occurrence of potash salts in connection with the great thickness in common rock salt covering the "red beds" region of western Texas, eastern New Mexico, western Oklahoma, and southern Kansas. The results of the tests of the borings from these three wells, of which those that are farthest apart are distant from each other about 125 miles, are certainly encouraging, but the United

FISHING, with advertising is seine fishing—deep-sea fishing—for industrial Captains Courageous.

In this issue of *The Digest* orders for inestimable dollars worth of business will be gathered by the hundred advertisers fishing here in this sea of 1,300,000 subscribers.

It is not uncommon for a single advertisement to open an account which all other methods have failed to uncover. Such an account may open with a few hundred dollars or a few thousand, and go on and on for years, yielding tens of thousands, hundreds of thousands—every cent of which was earned by that single advertisement.

—A full-page advertisement in The Digest costs 3/10 of a cent per home;
—addressing and mailing and delivery of each complete copy of The Digest; all for 3/10 of a cent;
—$4,000 for 1,300,000 copies of this full page advertisement;
—if the advertiser mailed a postal card to 1,300,000 separate addresses it would cost 6½ times as much or about $26,000;
—circular matter under one cent postage cannot be manufactured for less than $25.00 per thousand;
—in proper letter form with a two-cent stamp the postage alone is $26,000, and the finished job (at the lowest prices) $45,500, or eleven times what this page costs the advertiser.

Great national magazines make it possible for the advertiser to go deep-sea fishing for business in every important community stimulating sales in cities and towns everywhere.

Magazine circulations follow population and it amazes some advertisers when they learn that *The Literary Digest*, for instance, sells in

	Copies		Copies		Copies
Madison, Wisc. - - -	1,305	Takoma, Wash. - -	2,080	Lima, Ohio - - - -	1,052
Parkersburg, W. Va.	676	Greensboro, N. C. -	777	Shreveport, La. - -	1,434
Wilkensburg, Pa. -	1,112	Shawnee, Okla. - -	521	Watertown, N. Y. -	592
Sherman, Texas - -	668	Holyoke, Mass. - -	638	Fresno, Calif. - -	1,301

Bait your hooks and load your lines. Have your copy in New York on or before October 19th. Complete copies of *The Digest* will be in the mails October 22nd and the entire edition (of the October 29th issue) distributed within five days.

Immediate National Publicity

The Literary Digest

354 FOURTH AVENUE
NEW YORK

122 SOUTH MICHIGAN AVE.
CHICAGO

INVESTMENTS AND FINANCE
Continued

that the conditions of drilling and sampling at all three points are so unsatisfactory that it still remains to be seen whether the beds that are rich in potash are thick enough to justify their commercial exploitation. For the accurate tests of such deposits necessary for a sound commercial conclusion drill cores are needed instead of the unsatisfactory samples brought up by the bailer, or, worse yet, washed up by the rotary rig without means of determining accurately either the thickness of the layer of potash or its depth from the surface. Thorough tests with the core drill are justified by the tremendous importance to the whole United States of the discovery of commercial deposits of potash in this region—a discovery of far greater value than that of an oil pool.

THE NEW DEAL FOR ENGLISH RAILROADS

LIKE our own roads, the British railroads were taken over by the government during the war. Direct government control lasted until it was superseded by the resumption of private operation under a regulative Act of Parliament, not unlike the existing Esch-Cummins law in this country. Government control in England ended August 15. The new Railways Act gives the British roads a new deal, observes the New York *Herald*, which asserts that in England "government control revealed itself as destructive instead of constructive," and "wrecked the railways both physically and financially." Stockholders in the roads, says one of our commercial attachés in London, writing to *Commerce Reports*, published by the Department of Commerce, have complained that they were at a disadvantage in earning power as compared with other great industries. According to this authority:

The financial sheets of the British railroads show that while their net income has been doubled during the past seven years expenditures have been tripled. The deficit between income and expenditures has, roughly speaking, been equalized by Treasury grants in the form of subsidies.

It is noted by the writer in *Commerce Reports* that under the new British Railway Bill

Charges are not to be determined by the operating companies, but by "Rates Tribunals" and are to be so fixt as to yield an annual revenue equivalent to that of 1913. The rates of pay and conditions of service are to be settled by the Central Wages Board. The companies are to receive a subvention of £60,000,000 for the restoration of the roads to the physical condition they were in when the Government assumed control.

Satisfaction over the terms of the new railway bill is exprest throughout the United Kingdom, as it is felt that both the railway companies and the trade-unions have gotten what they asked for, and at the same time the general public is protected by the tribunal which establishes maximum traffic charges. This Act, coming immediately after de-control, substitutes forms of regulation which are more far-reaching than anything known to the experience of the country, since it takes from the various companies the prerogative to make their own rates and settle differences with their own workmen.

For purposes of administration and to secure greater economies as to personnel, improvement in traffic, and general coordination in service, the railway systems in the United Kingdom—composed of 27 great constituent and 96 subsidiary companies—are to be amalgamated into four main groups.

Other features of the law are set down as follows by the New York *Herald:*

The Ministry of Transport, shorn of everything but supervisory power, is retained. A rates tribunal along the lines of our Interstate Commerce Commission is erected. The wage adjustment boards are to continue. A bureau of statistics will gather data for the revision of tariffs and reclassification of goods. In short, rule of thumb methods are to be discarded in favor of accuracy and economy. The chief end of of railways, so it is hoped, will be transportation and not politics.

BUSINESS FIFTEEN PER CENT. BELOW NORMAL

EVERYONE realizes that business is below par, but few of us have been able to estimate just how much it is deprest below what might be called a normal condition. A public utility company in New York has, according to *The American Banker*, come to the conclusion that "measured not by money values but by actual volume of commodities produced, manufactured, transported, and sold through wholesale and retail channels, business of all kinds throughout the United States is at the present time only about 15 per cent. below normal," altho 30 per cent. below the abnormal level of war times. Of course this is an average, some lines of business being more than 15 per cent. below normal while others are deprest less than 15 per cent. As *The American Banker* summarizes the situation in the light of these figures:

General business has fallen approximately 30 per cent. from the highest peak of activity reached during the war period. Just now we appear to be "dredging bottom" of a depression period, yet few if any communities have had to open soup kitchens, and the consuming public—which means the people as a whole—are buying goods in quantity and variety sufficient to keep the retail trade fairly active almost everywhere. There are considerably more than 100,000,000 Americans to be provided with food, clothing, fuel, shelter, transportation and innumerable "necessities" which in other countries would be deemed costly comforts, with innumerable articles considered by Americans as merely ordinary conveniences, yet which people of foreign lands would deem veritable luxuries obtainable by none but the wealthy. According to past business history in the United States, a regular series of well recognized characteristics have developed during a period of depression and, when they have fully developed, a revival has set in.

CURRENT EVENTS

FOREIGN

September 21—While the British Cabinet meets at Gairloch, Scotland, to discuss the unemployment problem, serious disorders fomented by mobs of unemployed men break out in several parts of England.

An explosion in a chemical plant at Oppau, on the Rhine, wrecks the town, kills more than 1,000, and injures more than 4,000 people.

France gives an enthusiastic welcome to General Pershing, visiting that country to bestow the Congressional Medal of Honor on the unknown poilu buried beneath the Arc de Triomphe.

The Russian Soviet government rejects the Polish ultimatum demanding that it comply with the terms of the Riga treaty by October 1.

Altho not invited, the Russian constituent assembly in Paris, representing nearly all the anti-Bolshevik groups, appoints a mission to attend the Washington disarmament conference.

September 22—Seethikoya Tangal, of Kumaramputhur, British India, proclaims a Mohammedan kingdom and appoints himself governor. A British column inflicts a severe defeat on rebellious Indians near Karavarakundu.

The value of the ships surrendered by Germany is fixed at 745,000,000 gold marks, in an official communication issued by the Reparations Commission.

The Assembly of the League of Nations admits to membership Latvia, Esthonia and Lithuania.

September 23—The Council of Ambassadors notifies Hungary that she must withdraw from Burgenland, or West Hungary, awarded to Austria by the Treaty of Trianon, or be forcibly expelled by the Allies.

Belfast shopkeepers begin a boycott of goods from Southern Ireland in reprisal for the Sinn Fein boycott of Ulster products.

September 24—The Assembly of the League of Nations adopts a resolution giving its moral support to the Council of the League in the latter's efforts to settle the dispute between Poland and Lithuania over Vilna.

September 25—Three persons are killed and 36 wounded in rioting in Belfast.

September 26—The Riot Act is read in Belfast and the special constabulary is reestablished.

September 27—The Assembly of the League of Nations adopts a resolution asking the League's committee on disarmament to make proposals for the reduction of armaments, to be presented next year.

The cost of maintaining the Allied troops on the Rhine up to the end of March, 1921, was more than one hundred billion paper marks, according to figures published in Berlin. The whole expense must be borne by Germany, under the Versailles Treaty.

The Anhwei province of China has been flooded with the loss of thousands of res and property damage estimated at ,0,000,000, according to a dispatch om Shanghai.

flicts between Fascisti and Socialists Ortanova, Italy, result in two persons eing killed. A general strike is reorted declared in virtually all of south aly.

Inter-Allied Control Commission in ermany expresses satisfaction with the rogress of the surrender and destrucon of German armaments, according reports received in London.

DOMESTIC

ember 21.—Colonel Mason M. Patrick, n engineer officer, is nominated as Director of the Army Air Service.

sident Harding submits to the Senate he German, Austrian, and Hungarian peace treaties.

ember 22.—Major-General Leonard Wood is formally nominated by President Harding as Governor-General of he Philippine Islands.

tember 23.—The Senate Foreign Relations Committee reports favorably the German, Austrian, and Hungarian treaties, with reservations requiring the sanction of Congress for representation of the United States in foreign agencies, and protection of the property rights of American citizens.

muel Gompers, President of the American Federation of Labor, asks labor organizations in Great Britain, France, Italy and Japan to join in demonstrations for disarmament on Armistice Day.

arry Kimball, of New York City, is selected by the United States Shipping Board as financial vice-president, at a salary of $30,000 a year.

ptember 24.—A letter from President Harding to Senator Lodge urging early ratification of the peace treaties with Germany, Austria, and Hungary is read in the Senate.

ptember 26.—The commission appointed by President Harding to investigate the unemployment situation begins its meetings in Washington, and hears a warning from President Harding against relief "which seeks tonic from the public treasury."

ptember 27.—One seaman is drowned and another imprisoned, either dead or alive, in the United States naval submarine *R-6* which sinks in San Pedro Harbor, near Los Angeles.

President Harding issues a proclamation to State Governors requesting them to designate October 10 as fire-prevention day.

A Candidate for the Next Peace Conference.—The wife of a Western Congressman is sensitive on the subject of her deficient orthography, and her demands for information as to correct spelling sometimes place her peace-loving husband in a delicate position.

One day, as she was writing a letter at her desk, she glanced up to ask:

"Henry, do you spell 'graphic' with one 'f' or two?"

"My dear," was the diplomatic reply, "if you're going to use any, you might as well use two."—*Harper's Magazine.*

THE SPICE OF LIFE

Honest Confession.—An honest landlord advertises, "Moderate Apartment at Modern Rent."—*Arkansas Gazette.*

Their Pictures Remain.—Rural photographers are packing away their wooden fish for the winter.—*Flint Journal.*

Long and Hard.—Germany calls reparations "Wiedergutmachungsleistungen." Naturally it comes hard.—*Knoxville Journal and Tribune.*

The Real Terror.—"What is this 'white terror' in Bavaria?"

"White sausage at 50 marks a pound."—*Simplicissimus* (*Munich*).

Shows His Standing.—ETHEL—"You can't judge a man by the way he dresses."

MARY—"Oh, I don't know! I can tell a gentleman by his get-up in a crowded car!"—*Judge* (*New York*).

Helpful.—English is to be the official language at the Washington Disarmament Conference, but interpreters will be provided for those who can only speak American.—*Eve* (*London*).

Feeble with Age?—A colloquialism that should be banished is "springing a joke." Most jokes of to-day do not spring; they are pushed and fall helpless a few feet away.—*Chicago Journal of Commerce.*

Providential.—He was more religious than educated and so not to be too greatly censured for this "testimony" at prayer meeting: "I thank the Lord that I have three wives in heaven."—*The Epworth Herald.*

Inconsiderate.—"Now look here, Johnson, this man is doing double the work you do."

"That's what I've been telling him, sir; but he won't stop."—*The Christian Register* (*Boston*).

They Agreed.—VISITOR, in early morning, after week-end, to chauffeur—"Don't let me miss my train."

CHAUFFEUR—"No danger, sir. The Mistress said if I did, it'd cost me my job."—*London Opinion.*

Their Turn.—GLORIA—"Where are those wonderful servants of fifty years ago, that mother talks of?"

FLAVIA—"Oh, my dear! Don't you *know?* Why! They're having servant troubles of their own!"—*London Mail.*

Government Instruction.—"How do you manage to make both ends meet," we said to the happy little housekeeper.

"Oh, but I don't make both ends meet," she corrected. "I keep house like the United States, and never make ends meet."

"Like the United States?" we queried, puzzled.

"Yes; I get what I want whether I can afford it or not, and then at the end of the year I give my husband a deficiency bill. You know; just like Congress does every session, to make the public think it has lived within its income." Whereat we were lost in admiration.—*Leslie's.*

Exactly So.—"Yessir, eighty-two, I be, an' every tooth in my 'ead same as th' day I were born."—*London Mail.*

How to Treat Sharks.—"Sharks are not dangerous if kept amused or interested," states a weekly journal. Great care should be taken, however, when one of these creatures is invited to take part in a game of "snap."—*The Passing Show* (*London*).

Nothing to Fear.—IRATE GOLFER—"You must take your children away from here, Madam—this is no place for them."

MOTHER—"Now don't you worry—they can't 'ear nothin' new—their father was a sergeant-major, 'e was!"—*London Opinion.*

The Carborundum Degree.—SAMBO—"Looky heah, big boy, don' yo-all mess wid me, 'cause Ah's hard! Las' week Ah falls on a buzz saw an' Ah busts it—com-plete-ly."

RAMBO—"Call dat hard? Listen, man, Ah scratches de bath tub."—*The American Legion Weekly.*

Safety First.—"When do you intend to make another speech?"

"Not before the holidays," replied Senator Sorghum. "Things out home are getting into such a state of agitation that about the only really discreet remark a statesman can make to his constituents is 'Merry Christmas.'"—*Washington Star.*

Just Made Over.—After Mr. Brown had raked his yard he took the accumulated rubbish into the street to burn. A number of neighbors' children came flocking about the bonfire, among them a little girl whom Mr. Brown did not remember having seen before. Wishing, with his usual kindliness, to make the stranger feel at ease, he beamed upon her and said, heartily:

"Hello! Isn't this a new face?"

A deep red suffused her freckles. "No," she stammered, "it ain't new. It's just been washed."—*Harper's Magazine.*

Limited Liability.—Among the witnesses called in a trial in a Southern court was an old darky.

"Do you swear that what you tell shall be the truth, the whole truth and nothing but the truth?" intoned the clerk.

"Well, sah," returned the witness, shifting uneasily. "Dis lawyer gemmun kin make it a pow'ful lot easier on hisself an' relieve me of a mighty big strain ef he'll leave out anything about gin an' chickens. 'Ceptin' fo' dose, Ah guess Ah kin stick to de truth."—*The American Legion Weekly.*

Within Bounds.—While making a visit to New York, a man unmistakably of country origin was knocked down in the street by an automobile. A crowd instantly surrounded him with condolences and questions.

"Are you hurt, my friend?" kindly asked a gentleman, who was first among the rescuers, as he helped the stranger to his feet and brushed the mud and dust from his clothes.

"Well," came the cautious reply of one evidently given to non-committal brevity of speech, "it ain't done me no good."—*Harper's.*

THE LEXICOGRAPHER'S EASY CHAIR

In this column, to decide questions concerning the current use of words, the Funk & Wagnalls New Standard Dictionary is consulted as arbiter.

Readers will please bear in mind that no notice will be taken of anonymous communications.

"D. O. C.," Jersey City, N. J.—"Who is credited with being the discoverer of the blond Eskimo? Also, please favor me with the title of a book on these people."

The *blond Eskimos* were discovered by Stefansson in 1910. Consult Stefansson's "My Life with the Eskimo," New York, 1912; H Rink's "Tales and Traditions of the Eskimo," London, 1875; R. E. Peary's "Northward Over the Great Ice," 1898, Volume I, Appendix ii.

"B. C. H.," Erath, La.—"Kindly tell me where the words 'I am from Missouri' originated."

The dictionary gives the following:—"*I'm from Missouri; you've got to show me* (Colloq., U. S.), I am not easily taken in; I am on the alert against deception: first used by W. D. Vandiver, Representative from Missouri in Congress, and in consequence the State has become known to some extent as the 'Show me' State."

"A. D. C.," Weaverville, N. C.—"Is the 's' pronounced in the names *St. Louis* and *Louisville?* Or is the 's' silent, and the 'i' pronounced as it is in 'police'?"

St Louis is pronounced *sent lu'is* (*e* as in *prey*, *u* as in *rule*, *i* as in *habit*), or *lu'i* (*u* as in rule, *i* as in *habit*), or French, *san lu'i* (*a* as in *fat*, *n* with a nasal sound, *u* as in *rule*, *i* as in *police*). *Louisville* is pronounced *lu'is-vil* (*u* as in *rule*, first *i* as in *habit*, second *i* as in *hit*), or *lu'i-vil* (*u* as in *rule*, first *i* as *habit*, second *i* as in *hit*).

"E. B.," Hammond, Ind.—"Kindly tell me if Italy had an alliance with any European country at the beginning of the World War. Also, what alliances were entered into by Italy after the beginning of the World War?"

At the outbreak of the World War, Italy was a member of the Triple Alliance, the other members being Austria-Hungary and the German Empire. Italy became a party to this alliance in May, 1882, and it was renewed on December 8, 1912.

By this treaty, Italy bound herself in certain circumstances to go to the aid of her allies in the event of their being attacked without direct provocation on their part. Before she entered the War on the side of the Allies in May, 1915, the Italian Government declared that the Austro-Hungarian Government had violated Article VII of the treaty by failing to communicate to the Italian Government the terms of the demands made upon Serbia in July, 1914, prior to the declaration of war against that country. Italy contended that the treaty did not bind her as it stipulated that she should only lend assistance to the other signatories in the case of a defensive war.

Italy has since the War ratified the treaties with Germany and Austria, tho for a time her delegates withdrew from Paris in consequence of the dispute over the future of Fiume.

"J. D. J.," Jamestown, Kan.—"What is the correct pronunciation of the word *interesting?*"

The word *interesting* is correctly pronounced *in'ter-est-ing*—first *i* as in *hit*, first *e* as in *moment*, second *e* as in *get*, second *i* as in *habit*.

"E. B. H.," Birmingham, Ala.—"Please tell me which is more correct to say, 'He will *take* her to church,' or 'He will *carry* her to church.'"

The use of the verb *carry* in the sense of "escort," "conduct," or "accompany," is archaic to-day. In the general uses of this term, it means actually to convey or bear, either in the mind or upon or about one's person, that to which reference is made.

Altho formerly used with the meaning of "conduct," "guide," or "escort," the term in this sense is not now permissible. Do not say, "Mr. A. *carried* Miss B. to the church," but say rather, ". . . *escorted* Miss B. to the church."

"B. E. C.," Chicago, Ill.—"Please give the correct pronunciation of the word *anastigmat* as applied to photographic lenses."

The word *anastigmat* is correctly pronounced *an'a-stig'mat*—first and third *a's* as in *fat*, second *a* as in *final*, *i* as in *hit*.

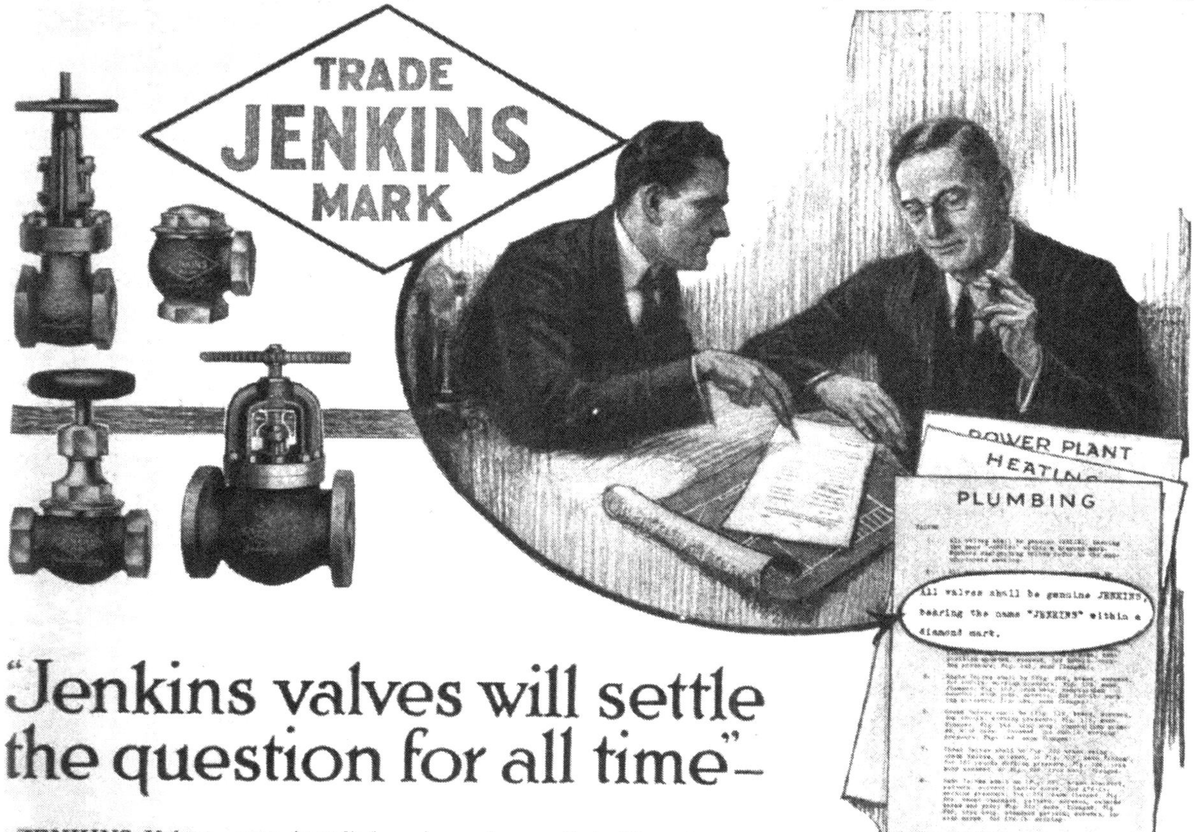

TRADE JENKINS MARK

"Jenkins valves will settle the question for all time"—

JENKINS Valves, once installed, are in service to stay. Architects and Engineers know that, in specifying and installing Jenkins Valves, they are providing a valve that will satisfactorily and permanently perform every function.

Being men who possess a thorough knowledge of valves and their requirements, they know Jenkins Valves stand up in continuous use. Jenkins Valves after 30 years, and many much longer, are still performing the service for which they were installed.

Jenkins method of manufacture, the care exercised, and the high standard set and maintained must necessarily produce a superior valve. Every Jenkins Valve is cast of the best metal and in a proportion that secures a heavier and stronger valve—one that is safe and dependable in severe as well as in average service. All castings are perfect and accurately machined, to assure an exact unity of parts. Parts are interchangeable—"veteran" valves can always be supplied with replacement parts that "fit." Every valve before leaving the factory must prove itself in rigid tests.

Jenkins Valves are made in brass, iron, and steel, in types and sizes for all requirements of power plant, plumbing, and heating service. In fact, there is a "Jenkins" for every valve purpose. They are obtainable at supply houses everywhere, and are known by the Jenkins "Diamond Mark" and signature cast on the body.

Engineers, Architects, Plumbing and Heating Contractors, home builders, and others interested in valves are invited to write for descriptive literature on Jenkins Valves for the service in which they are interested.

JENKINS BROS.

80 White Street .... New York
524 Atlantic Avenue .... Boston
133 No. Seventh Street .... Philadelphia
646 Washington Boulevard .... Chicago

Jenkins Bros., Limited
Montreal, Canada. London, England.
FACTORIES: Bridgeport, Conn.; Elizabeth, N. J.; Montreal, Canada.

MANUFACTURERS OF MACHINES

who seek to carry efficiency and dependability to every point in their products, use Jenkins Valves wherever valves are required. Illustration above shows tire mould made by Western Rubber Mould Co., Chicago, which uses Jenkins Valves exclusively on its tire moulds, vulcanizers, and steam generators.

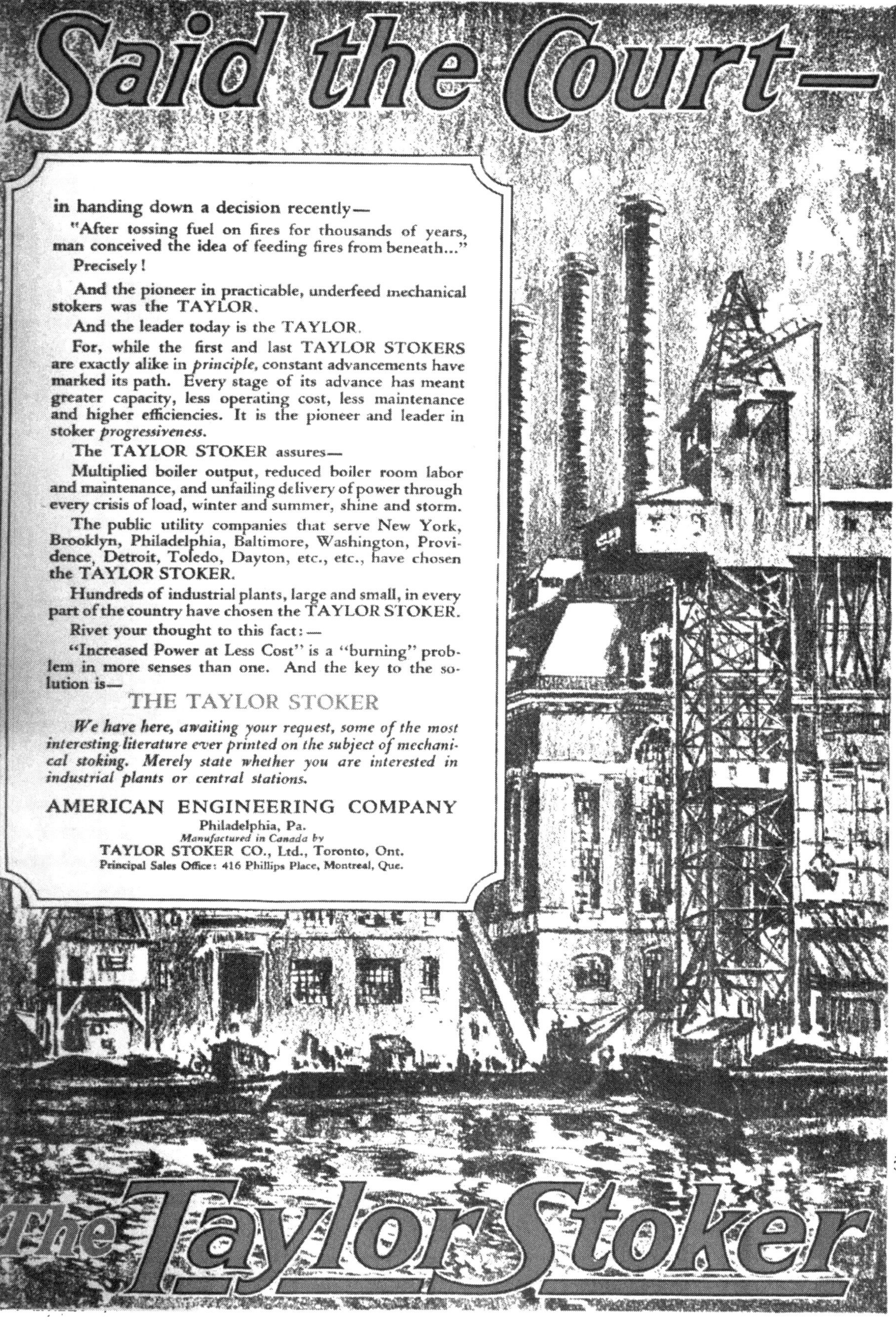

Said the Court—
in handing down a decision recently—
"After tossing fuel on fires for thousands of years, man conceived the idea of feeding fires from beneath..."
Precisely!
And the pioneer in practicable, underfeed mechanical stokers was the TAYLOR.
And the leader today is the TAYLOR.
For, while the first and last TAYLOR STOKERS are exactly alike in principle, constant advancements have marked its path. Every stage of its advance has meant greater capacity, less operating cost, less maintenance and higher efficiencies. It is the pioneer and leader in stoker progressiveness.
The TAYLOR STOKER assures—
Multiplied boiler output, reduced boiler room labor and maintenance, and unfailing delivery of power through every crisis of load, winter and summer, shine and storm.
The public utility companies that serve New York, Brooklyn, Philadelphia, Baltimore, Washington, Providence, Detroit, Toledo, Dayton, etc., etc., have chosen the TAYLOR STOKER.
Hundreds of industrial plants, large and small, in every part of the country have chosen the TAYLOR STOKER.
Rivet your thought to this fact:—
"Increased Power at Less Cost" is a "burning" problem in more senses than one. And the key to the solution is—
THE TAYLOR STOKER
We have here, awaiting your request, some of the most interesting literature ever printed on the subject of mechanical stoking. Merely state whether you are interested in industrial plants or central stations.
AMERICAN ENGINEERING COMPANY
Philadelphia, Pa.
Manufactured in Canada by
TAYLOR STOKER CO., Ltd., Toronto, Ont.
Principal Sales Office: 416 Phillips Place, Montreal, Que.
The Taylor Stoker

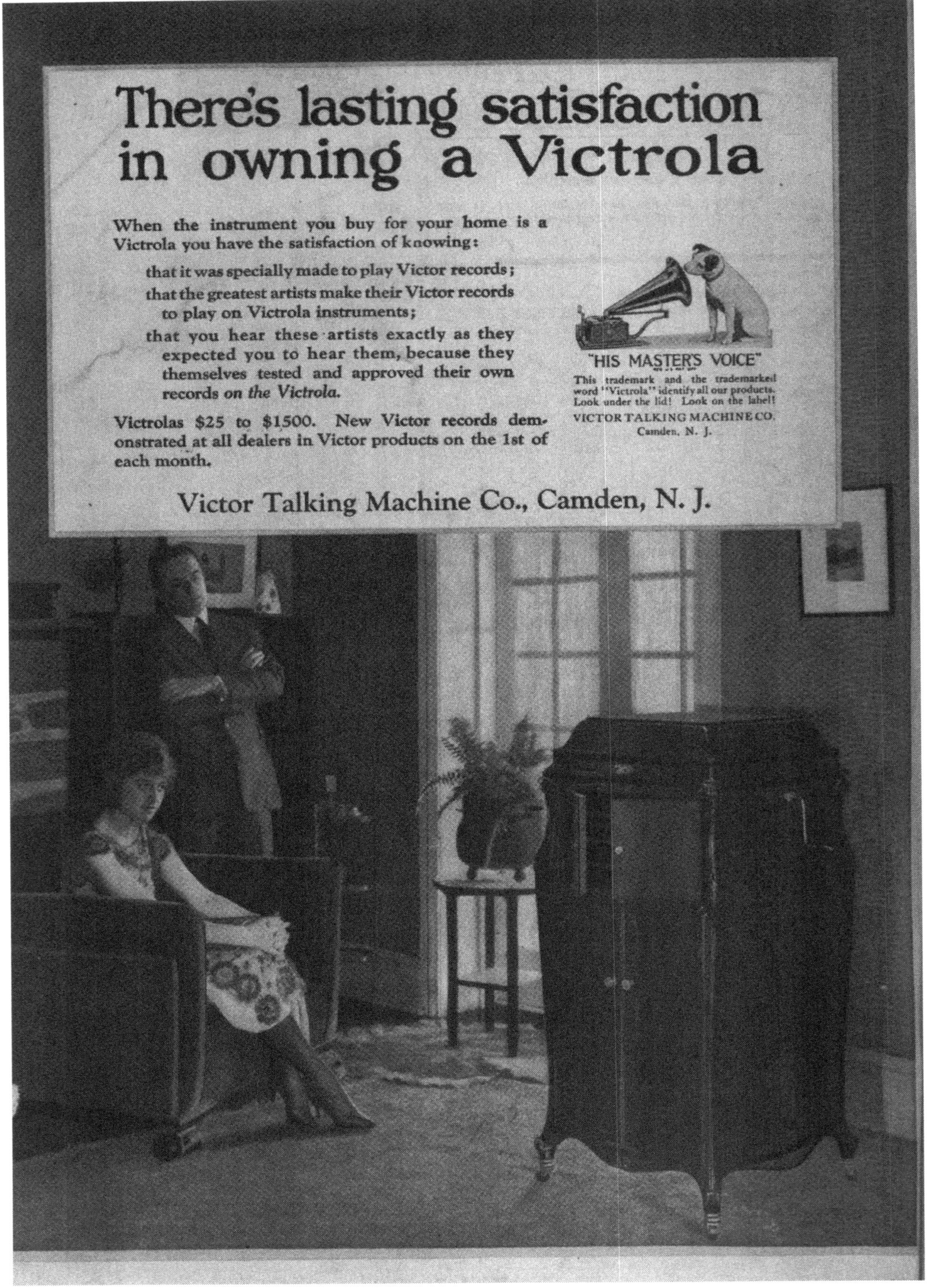

There's lasting satisfaction in owning a Victrola

When the instrument you buy for your home is a Victrola you have the satisfaction of knowing:

- that it was specially made to play Victor records;
- that the greatest artists make their Victor records to play on Victrola instruments;
- that you hear these artists exactly as they expected you to hear them, because they themselves tested and approved their own records *on the Victrola.*

Victrolas $25 to $1500. New Victor records demonstrated at all dealers in Victor products on the 1st of each month.

"HIS MASTER'S VOICE"

This trademark and the trademarked word "Victrola" identify all our products. Look under the lid! Look on the label!

VICTOR TALKING MACHINE CO.
Camden, N. J.

Victor Talking Machine Co., Camden, N. J.

October 15, 1921

The Literary Digest

(Title Reg. U.S. Pat. Off.)

THE HOMECOMING

New York FUNK & WAGNALLS COMPANY *London*

PUBLIC OPINION *New York* combined with *The* LITERARY DIGEST

MICHELIN TIRES

Always in the lead—Now better than ever

EVERY motorist owes it to himself to test Michelin Tires in comparison with other makes.

The new and improved tread compound; the extra width and thickness of tread; the sturdy oversize body; the recognized easy riding qualities; the superior protection against skidding—all these advantages are yours in the truly wonderful Michelin Cord.

And Michelin's moderate prices are not the least of Michelin advantages.

MICHELIN TIRE COMPANY, MILLTOWN, N. J.

Other factories: Clermont-Ferrand, France; London, England; Turin, Italy—Dealers everywhere

21•9

Why Some People Are Never At Ease Among Strangers

PEOPLE of culture can be recognized at once. They are calm, well-poised. They have a certain dignity about them, a certain calm assurance which makes people respect them. It is because they know exactly what to do and say on every occasion that they are able to mingle with the most highly cultivated people and yet be entirely at ease.

But there are some people who are never at ease among strangers. Because they do not know the right thing to do at the right time, they are awkward, self-conscious. They are afraid to accept invitations because they do not know what to wear, how to acknowledge introductions, how to make people like them. They are timid in the presence of celebrated people because they do not know when to rise and when to remain seated, when to speak and when to remain silent, when to offer one's chair and when not to. They are always uncomfortable and embarrassed when they are in the company of cultured men and women.

It is only by knowing definitely, without the slightest doubt, what to do, say, write and wear on all occasions under all conditions, that one is able to be dignified, charming and well-poised at all times.

How Etiquette Gives Charm and Poise

Etiquette means good manners. It means knowing what to do at the right time, what to say at the right time. It consists of certain important little laws of good conduct that have been adopted by the best circles in Europe and America and which serve as a barrier to keep the uncultured and ill-bred out of the circles where they would be uncomfortable and embarrassed.

People with good manners, therefore, are people whose poise and dignity impress you immediately with a certain awe, a certain respect. Etiquette makes them graceful, confident. It enables them to mingle with the most cultured people and be perfectly at ease. It takes away their self-consciousness, their timidity. By knowing what is expected of them, what is the correct thing to do and say they become calm, dignified and well poised—and they are welcomed and admired in the highest circles of business and society.

Here's the Way People Judge Us

Let us pretend that we are in the drawing room and the hostess is serving tea. Numerous little questions of conduct confront us. If we know what do to we are happy, at ease. But if we do not know the correct and cultured thing traying ourselves. We know that those who are with us can tell immediately, simply by watching us and talking to us, if we are not cultured.

For instance, one must know how to eat cake correctly. Should it be taken up in the fingers or eaten with a fork? Should the napkin be entirely unfolded or should the center crease be allowed to remain? May lump sugar be taken up with the fingers?

There are other problems, too—many of them. Should the man rise when he accepts a cup of tea from the hostess? Should he thank her? Who should be served first? What should the guest do with the cup when he or she has finished the tea? Is it good form to accept a second cup? What is the secret of creating conversation and making people find you pleasant and agreeable?

It is so easy to commit embarrassing blunders, so easy to do what is wrong. But etiquette tells us just what is expected of us and guards us from all humiliation and discomfort.

Many embarrassing blunders can be made in the public restaurant. Should the young lady in the picture pick up the fork or leave it for the waiter to attend to? Or should one of the men pick it up?

Etiquette in Public

Here are some questions which will help you find out just how much *you* know about the etiquette that must be observed among strangers. See how many of them you can answer:

When a man and woman enter the theatre together, who walks first down the aisle? When the usher points out the seats, does the man enter first or the woman? May a man leave a woman alone during intermission?

There is nothing that so quickly reveals one's true station and breeding than awkward, poor manners at the table. Should the knife be held in the left hand or the right? Should olives be eaten with the finger or with a fork? How is lettuce eaten? What is the correct and cultured way to eat corn on the cob? Are the finger-tips of both hands placed into the finger-bowl at once, or just one at a time?

When a man walks in the street with two women does he walk between them or next to the curb? Who enters the street car first, the man or the woman? When does a man tip his hat? On what occasions is it considered bad form for him to pay a woman's fare? May a man on any occasion hold a woman's arm when they are walking together?

Some people learn all about etiquette and correct conduct by associating with cultured people and learning what to do and say at the expense of many embarrassing blunders. But most people are now learning quickly and easily through the famous Book of Etiquette—a splendid, carefully compiled, authentic guide towards correct manners on all occasions.

Do You Know

- ***how*** to introduce men and women correctly?
- ***how*** to word invitations, announcements, acknowledgements?
- ***how*** to register at a hotel?
- ***how*** to take leave of the hostess after an entertainment?
- ***how*** to plan home and church weddings?
- ***how*** to use table silver in the proper way?
- ***how*** to do at all times, under all conditions, the cultured, correct thing?

The Book of Etiquette

The Book of Etiquette makes it possible for you to do, say, write and wear what is absolutely correct and in accord with the best form on every occasion—whether you are to be bridesmaid at a wedding or usher at a friend's private theatre phases. There are chapters on the etiquette of engagements, weddings, dances, parties and all social entertainments. There are interesting chapters on correspondence, invitations, calls and calling cards. New chapters on the etiquette in foreign countries have been added, and there are many helpful hints to the man or woman who travels.

With the Book of Etiquette to refer to, there can be no mistakes, no embarrassment. One knows exactly what is correct and what is incorrect. And by knowing so definitely that one is perfect in the art of etiquette, a confident poise is developed which enables one to appear in the most elaborate drawing-room, among the most brilliant and highly cultured people, without feeling the least bit ill at ease.

Send No Money

To enable everyone, everywhere, to examine the famous Book of Etiquette without obligation, we make this special offer to send the complete two-volume set free for 5 days to anyone requesting it. Entirely free—no money in advance. All that is necessary is your name and address on the coupon below and the Book of Etiquette will be sent to you at once at our expense. You have the privilege of examining it, reading it, and deciding for yourself whether or not you want to keep it.

Send for the Book of Etiquette today. Read some of the interesting chapters. Surprise your friends and acquaintances with your knowledge of what to do, say, write and wear on all occasions. And when you have been fully convinced that etiquette widens your circle of friends, makes you admired and respected, increases your knowledge of society and its requirements, gives you poise, self-confidence and charm—keep the set and send us $3.50 in full payment. But if you are not utterly delighted after the 5-day free trial, simply return books and you won't be out a cent.

The Book of Etiquette is published in handsome cloth binding decorated in gold. Send for your set today. Just the coupon, remember—no money. But get your coupon off NOW. Nelson Doubleday, Inc., Dept. 3910, Oyster Bay, N. Y.

NELSON DOUBLEDAY, Inc.
Dept. 3910, Oyster Bay, New York

Without money in advance, or obligation on my part, send me the Two Volume set of the Book of Etiquette. Within 5 days I will either return the books or send you $3.50 in full payment. It is understood that I am not obliged to keep the books if I am not delighted with them.

Name . . . .
(Please write plainly)

Address . . . .

☐ Check this square if you want these books with the

Volume 71
No. 3

TABLE ▾ OF ▾ CONTENTS

October 15, 1921

TOPICS OF THE DAY: Page

Nation-Wide "First-Aid" for the Jobless 5
New York's Answer to the Transit Puzzle 8
Chief Problem of the Conference 9
Early Tints of the Business Dawn 11
Porosity of Prohibition 12
Topics in Brief 14

FOREIGN COMMENT:

Britain's "Dangerous Poor" 15
German Mark "Frightfulness" 16
Does India Know What It Wants? 17
Germany After Russian Trade 18

SCIENCE AND INVENTION:

A Defense of Oleomargarin 19
Fishways for Salmon 20
A New Sort of Hospital 20
Building a Bridge in Ten Days 21
Tear Bombs for Mobs and Bandits 22
How Children Grow 22
X-Rays Growing More Powerful 23

LETTERS AND ART: Page

Standing Up for American Art 24
What Central Europe Reads 25
Finger-Prints to Settle Art Disputes 26
Pepys Street 27

RELIGION AND SOCIAL SERVICE:

Time to Clean Up Movie Morals 28
The Passing of the Birch 29
The Church's Big Chance 29
Squabbling Sects in Liberia 30
Protestant Neglect of the Sick 30

MISCELLANEOUS:

Current Poetry 32
Personal Glimpses 34-43
Motoring and Aviation 44-53
Investments and Finance 54-58
Current Events 59-60
The Lexicographer's Easy Chair 61
The Spice of Life 63

TERMS: $4.00 a year, in advance; six months, $2.25; three months, $1.50; single copy, 10 cents; postage to Canada, 85 cents a year; other foreign postage, $2.00 a year. **BACK NUMBERS**, not over three months old, 25 cents each; over three months old, $1.00 each. **QUARTERLY INDEXES** will be sent free to subscribers who apply for them. **RECEIPT** of payment is shown in about two weeks by date on address-label; date of expiration includes the month named on the label. **CAUTION:** If date is not properly extended after each payment, notify publishers promptly. Instructions for **RENEWAL, DISCONTINUANCE,** or **CHANGE OF ADDRESS** should be sent *two weeks* before the date they are to go into effect.

Both old and new addresses must always be given. **PRESENTATION COPIES:** Many persons subscribe for friends. Those who desire to renew such subscriptions must do so before expiration.

THE LITERARY DIGEST is published weekly by the **Funk & Wagnalls Company, 354-360 Fourth Avenue, New York, and Salisbury Square, London, E. C.**

Entered as second-class matter, March 24, 1890, at the Post-office at New York, N. Y., under the act of March 3, 1879.

Entered as second-class matter at the Post-office Department, Ottawa, Canada.

These 7 Simple Paper Tests Will Make You a Judge of Good Business Paper

UNLESS you are a paper expert you undoubtedly have found it quite difficult to judge good business paper.

When you have had to decide between two makes of letter or ledger papers—papers that looked alike and seemed alike—you have had no accurate method of determining a choice. Price probably swayed you. Yet price is the one test *not* to use in judging the quality of a paper.

What business men have been looking for is a series of simple, homely tests that any one can make. Tests that will tell you immediately the true character and quality of the business paper you buy.

Our 68 years of experience in making good business papers enables us to offer you the "Parsons Tests"—simple, accurate, easy to make. They are good enough for us to use at our own mills in judging the quality of our own manufacture.

To assist you in making these tests, as illustrated here, we will send a liberal sample book of Parsons Defendum Ledger Paper in white and also in buff that is becoming so popular because of its ease on the eyes.

Test the quality of Defendum Ledger with the ledger paper you are now using. Test the lighter weights with the letter paper you are now using. These tests will show you why Parsons Defendum Ledger is the largest selling ledger paper in the world.

PARSONS PAPER Co., Holyoke, Mass.

Preserve this page for ready reference. Write for the Parsons Defendum Sample Book, and additional copies of the "Parsons Tests."

PARSONS MADE IN U.S.A.

PARSONS

Makers of Good Business Paper Since 1853

PARSONS PRODUCTS: *Defendum Ledger, Algonquin Bond, Parsons Bond, Gothic Bond, Mercantile Record, Old Hampden Bond, Parsons Linen, Mercantile Bond, Scotch Linen Ledger, Parchment Bristol*

THE LITERARY DIGEST

PUBLIC OPINION (New York) combined with THE LITERARY DIGEST

ished by Funk & Wagnalls Company (Adam W. Wagnalls, Pres.; Wilfred J. Funk, Vice-Pres.; Robert J. Cuddihy, Treas.; William Neisel, Sec'y) 354-360 Fourth Ave., New York

l. LXXI, No. 3 New York, October 15, 1921 Whole Number 1643

TOPICS - OF - THE - DAY

(Title registered in U S Patent Office for use in this publication and on moving picture films)

Copyright by Kadel and Herbert News Service, New York.

MEMBERS OF THE NATIONAL CONFERENCE ON UNEMPLOYMENT.

The reader will recognize Secretary Davis, Secretary Hoover, Samuel Gompers and Charles M. Schwab.

NATION-WIDE "FIRST-AID" FOR THE JOBLESS.

THERE IS ENOUGH MENACE in the unemployment situation, as cold weather sets in, whether the jobless army is a few thousand larger or smaller, to call for nation-wide emergency treatment. This, at least, is the conclusion reached by President Harding's National Conference on Unemployment and generally confirmed by the daily newspapers who know the local conditions throughout the country. In its emergency report the conference places the number of our unemployed to-day at "between 3,500,000 and 5,500,000"—the Department of Labor conceding a reduction of 200,000 since its earlier figures were given out. Normal unemployment in this country, one of the witnesses before the conference stated, is "about 1,500,000." In England, as shown on another page, an unemployed army of 1,500,000 is considered alarming. Another expert told the conferees that involuntary idleness in the United States between July, 1920, and August, 1921, had meant a loss in wages amounting to $6,500,000,000. For purposes of comparison it is interesting to note the report in Berlin dispatches that the number of unemployed in Germany is "less than 400,000," and that this number is "decreasing steadily."

The problem of meeting the emergency of unemployment "is primarily a community problem," declares the conference's steering committee; and it therefore calls upon municipal authorities in all parts of the country to organize emergency committees to grapple with it. These committees are urged to see that local public construction work is begun, that factory and store repairs are undertaken now, and that, where necessary, work is distributed on the part-time employment basis, thus taking care of as many jobless as possible. Its further recommendations are thus summarized in a Washington dispatch to the New York *Herald:*

"That the Federal, State and municipal governments proceed at once with the expansion of their school, sewerage and repair work and with public buildings and road construction.

"That manufacturers and wholesalers readjust the prices of their commodities to replacement values in terms of efficient producing and distributing cost plus reasonable profit, and that retailers follow this lead in price reduction so that the confidence of the buying public may be restored.

"That the construction industry be revived to reduce the shortage of homes and to cut down unemployment in the building trades by concerted action in the States against those factors, such as 'undue costs' and 'malignant combinations,' which have been making proper expansion impossible."

In the building industry, "which has been artificially restricted during and since the war" the conference sees "the greatest area for immediate relief of unemployment." On this point its report says:

"We are short more than a million homes; all kinds of building and construction are far behind national necessity. The Senate Committee on Reconstruction and Production, in March of this year, estimated the total construction shortage in the country at between ten and twenty billion dollars. Considering all branches of the constructed industries, more than two million people could be employed if construction were resumed. Undue cost and malignant combinations have made proper expansion impossible and contributed largely to this unemployment situation. In some places these matters have been cleaned up. In other places they have not and are an affront to public decency. In some places these things have not existed. In others costs have been adjusted. Some materials have been reduced in price as much as can be expected. Where conditions have been righted, construction should proceed, but there is still a need of community action in provision of capital on terms that will encourage home building. Where the costs are still above the other economic levels of the community, there should be searching inquiry and action in the situation. We recommend that the Governors summon representative committees, with the cooperation of the Mayors or otherwise, as they may determine (a) to determine facts; (b) to organize community action in securing adjustments in cost, including removal of freight discriminations and clean out campaigns against combinations, restrictions of effort, and unsound practises where they exist to the end that building may be fully resumed."

Included in the steering committee's report is the program of

THE CONNECTING BELT.

—Thurlby in the Seattle *Times*.

the manufacturers' committee, which offers the following recommendations:

"Part-time work, through reduced time or rotation of jobs.

"As far as possible, manufacturing for stock.

"Taking advantage of the present opportunity to do as much plant construction, repairs and cleaning up as is possible, with the consequent transfer of many employees to other than their regular work.

"Reduction of the number of hours of labor per day.

"The reduction of the work week to a lower number of days during the present period of industrial depression."

Editorial approval of the Conference's emergency program is intermingled with expressions of disappointment because it doesn't go deeper into the problem. "It was appropriate," remarks the Socialist (New York) *Call*, "that fifty jobless ex-soldiers stood on the sidewalk and sang, while the report was being read, 'Wait Till the Clouds Roll By'." It is "admirable as far as it goes," but "inadequate," thinks the New York *Globe*, which says that "the Administration can not wash its hands of responsibility for the unemployed and piously ask the States and the cities to carry the full load." The Conference has "put the cart before the horse" in treating unemployment as a local matter, in the opinion of the New York *Journal of Commerce*. Its proposals offer nothing for the betterment of underlying conditions, adds this New York paper, which goes on to ask:

"Why regard unemployment as a casual or incidental feature of economic disturbance and as such to be cared or provided for on a sporadic basis? Why not regard its existence as calling for the most thorough probing of our tax, tariff, and railway problems with a view to establishing the cause and applying the remedies for present evils?"

"The President, after gathering up the problem from the localities and taking it on to Washington for examination, is now passing it back to the localities just as it was," remarks the New York *World;* and the Minneapolis *Minnesota Star*, after perusing the report, remarks cynically that "nothing is either settled or unsettled" by it. Theodore H. Price, writing in the New York *News Record*, predicts little result from the emergency program because "the real trouble is the overgrowth of our city population, and unemployment will probably be a recurring phenomenon until people are driven back to the country."

But "no one expected the Unemployment Conference to abolish unemployment with a wave of a Federal wand," avers the New York *Evening Post*, which continues:

"It is ill-natured for critics to jeer because this national gathering comes to the conclusion that the problem is primarily one for the local communities. The important consideration is that it accompanies its statement of this fundamental fact with a thoughtful, promising program of attack, and that it creates a national mechanism for coordinating and guiding local effort. The nation can itself provide large-scale employment only in two ways: by appropriating millions, as in the past, for Federal-State road construction, and by expediting public building already covered by appropriations. The Conference is for these steps. But much more is to be expected from the galvanization of private and public effort in our municipalities by a chain of local committees, advised and guided by the national committee, to head which Secretary Hoover has just appointed Mr. Arthur Woods."

THE UNEMPLOYED: "GIVE ME A CHANCE AT IT."

—Morris for the George Matthew Adams Service.

"It will not be claimed that this program will work miracles," says the New York *Tribune*, "but it will do some good." "The measures recommended are intended only to suggest ways of meeting a swift emergency, and upon that narrow basis the program should be judged," notes the New York *Globe*. And in the Washington *Post*, which is sometimes spoken of as "semi-official," we read:

"*The Post* has previously stated that the unemployment problem can not be solved by Congressional enactment or by executive order. To that statement it may be added that no formula devised by the conference will automatically cure the situation. Only an internal remedy will prove effective.

"The practical question which presents itself to the country is to find employment for 2,000,000 people who are idle and want to work. There are now, according to the statistics of the Department of Labor, about 12,000,000 persons engaged in what are known as productive industries. Thus the problem narrows down to this: Put another man or woman at work for every six persons now on the payroll.

"It can be done if the influences in the nation are coordinated to that end. When each community strives to excel in reducing its idle contingent, the results will quickly show."

Turning to Mr. Hoover's Washington *Herald*, we find the problem presented from a somewhat different angle:

"The bald fact is that there are the 4,000,000 idle. That to treat this as some one's fault, or as a problem for charity, or as a local condition to be met by localities as individuals, is unworthy our Amercanism and in direct contravention of our governmental and social system, and of all that is distinctly American. The one fundamental American right is to work, to be self-supporting, to have an economic chance and equal industrial opportunity. Political opportunity and economic opportunity are correlatives. Neither can long exist without the other without leading to social upheaval, or social collapse. Where either is denied property rights are in jeopardy. . . .

"It is suggested that manufacturers, wholesalers and retailers reduce prices. Why should prices have advanced in the last month? Certainly raw materials and labor charges can not be held responsible for this; and probably nothing would bring a greater measure of relief than reduced prices to induce broader buying. Every item in all this shows the national character of the situation and that it can be adequately met only by concerted, national, cooperative action involving every element of our economic life.

"*The Herald* takes issue that Congress should not be appealed to in the emergency. There is much Congress can do and should do, not as a bonus, but as the opposite of a dole. If ever there was a call for real statesmanship in America, it is now to bring a wise, constructive, economic program, not a hodgepodge of favor or privilege, but a policy which will put substance under equal economic opportunity and assure a man's right to be able to support his own family in his own home."

The most conspicuous defect of the emergency report, in the opinion of many editors, is that it ignores the question of wage reduction. "The basic need is that the prices of all essential commodities shall be reduced, and the major factor in prices is wages," says the New York *Times*; and the New York *Herald* declares that "the wage question is the very heart of the unemployment question." If the conference is to get anywhere it must face the truth regarding the need of wage cuts, avers the Newark *News*, which continues:

Copyrighted 1921, by The Star Company.

A NIAGARA GOING TO WASTE.

—Williams in the New York *American*.

"If Mr. Gompers or anybody else thinks that it is within the power of any thirty-eight conferees at Washington to put all union employees back at regular work at union wages in times like these, he is an optimist indeed. Organized labor clings tenaciously to the idea that in the liquidation period it alone can escape the deflation process. But it clings in vain. On the other hand, it must be admitted that there are plenty of employers eager to make this the occasion for pounding wages down. Between the two there is a golden mean of readjustment, and an unwillingness by either side to seek it obstructs the major object of the conference.

"Perhaps the conference as a whole will go into this question of creating employment by lowered wages, irrespective of the attitude of the committee Mr. Gompers seems to have dominated. It can not do otherwise and be true to its trust."

"Capital, as represented by business and industry in the National Unemployment Conference, is making a far better showing than labor in getting at the problem," declares the Philadelphia *Public Ledger*, which points out that while business and industry admit that "it is time to take more losses and get back to normal," labor "lags, waiting for some advantage." It is now labor's turn to offer its contribution to the solution of the problem, thinks this Philadelphia paper, which concludes an editorial headed "What Will Labor Do?" with the following challenging paragraphs:

"Senator Nelson declares that workmen are themselves responsible for much unemployment, because they will not consent to a readjustment in wages. He mentions the rail workers; but he might have included the building trades and a dozen others. There is an impression abroad that thousands out of work might be working if they would accept the class of work offered and the wages that can be paid.

"No matter how hard the nation may try, it can not give back the war-time jobs at the war-time wages. The emergency measures are temporary stimulants; 'shoots in the arm' to rally a weak patient. If the patient goes back to his old ways and excesses, he will again collapse. With the best will in the world, industry can not pay war-time wages or anything like war-time wages. If the unemployed are waiting for this, they are likely to be 'unemployed' for a long time.

"What will labor do about it? Business has recognized an emergency and admits its share of the responsibility."

"Will labor recognize and admit its share of the emergency and the responsibility, consider and accept the necessary reductions and take the road to meet emergency half way? If not, the success of the conference and its plans, temporary and permanent, can be no more than half-success at best."

NO HELP WANTED.

(Cover for *The American Legion Weekly* of October 14)

NEW YORK'S ANSWER TO THE TRANSIT PUZZLE

THOUSANDS OF DECREPIT "trolley" systems throughout the country, and hundreds of thousands of citizens suffering by the disorganization of city transit, may find help for their troubles in New York's ambitious attempt to devise a permanent traction program. Two points in particular catch the journalistic eyes of the country in the report of the city's transit commission: it recommends municipal ownership and consolidation of all the lines, and it provides that the five-cent fare shall be retained for at least a year, with probabilities that it will be continued or even reduced at the end of that time. Speaking for the District of Columbia, Mr. Hoover's Washington *Herald* argues for a similar solution of traction difficulties in the District, "which also has maintained a five-cent fare, tho it has put several lines in the hands of a receiver." There is no possible solution other than "consolidation at earning values," this editor concludes. "Paper values, book values, stocks on which the railways do not earn a dividend, must be written off." The Springfield *Republican* believes that the commission's report "contains the promise of a really satisfactory program for the first time since travel about the city began to be complicated and congested, which was a good many years ago." The New Haven *Journal-Courier*, taking a similarly favorable view, concludes that "if the plan succeeds, we shall be prepared to see the principle upon which it turns attract the attention of all American municipalities. It must, unless all sight is lost of its character as a community problem." It must be remembered, too, the Newark *Evening News* warns its readers, that New York's drastic program is prepared for roads, a number of which are bankrupt or threatened with bankruptcy. However, concedes this journal, "success with a five-cent fare under the new plan may prove in degree the extent of which stock manipulation is responsible for the roads' financial condition, if due allowance is made for the necessary waste created by revolutions in the system of transportation." Looking at the report from the largest of the neighboring cities, where transit difficulties have become almost as serious as in New York, the Philadelphia *Public Ledger* observes that, bad as Manhattan may be—

"They have five-cent trolley fares on their surprizingly efficient lines. They have always had them—even while the rest of the country has had to dig painfully for more. They propose to keep nickel fares and, with that purpose in view, they have formulated a plan for the merger and future municipal ownership of all street-car systems on their island.

"They believe that they can buy all subway, overhead and surface lines and reorder them in one system for the good of the city, and then retire their purchase bonds with future profits from five-cent fares! They have redefined the issues at stake in a hundred controversies and formulated a simple principle that sooner or later must be universally acceptable.

"They hold, by inference, that in every large city trolley service is a necessity of life and that it should be free forever from the depressing influence of political and financial opportunism.

"The cliff-dwellers are indubitably right in that assumption. So large have American cities grown that you cannot get to work without the trolley. You cannot get home without them. You cannot hold a job or earn a living or do the day's shopping without the incidental help of the street cars.

"Street-car systems ought to be as free from deliberate exploitation by profit-takers as the water supply is. Ordinarily there is no substitute—no alternative."

Much of the trouble with transit systems all over the country, believes this journal, is due to absentee ownership. "A group of financiers sitting in Buffalo and in New York naturally can know little or nothing about the transit requirements of Camden, New Jersey. But, as matters are going nowadays, they may have full power to dictate the rate of fare and the operating policy of the Camden car line." As for the greatest danger of municipal control, political graft, the proponents of the principle believe that—

"The practise of municipal ownership would be fatal to 'the rotten politicians' whose sins are forever being recounted in defense of the private ownership of basic public utilities. Men who support the New York plan insist that the public tolerates rotten politics only so long as it feels no direct injury from the system.

"The public will not realize that it is being hurt every day indirectly. But translate Tammanyism or Vareism in terms of street car fares or service and, the New Yorkers believe, you will have the public on the warpath in no time."

WHAT THE TRANSIT BOARD PROPOSES

(Essential features of the plan for the reorganization and operation of New York's transit system as summarized by the New York Evening Mail*)*

MUNICIPAL OWNERSHIP—Through surrender by the companies of all existing franchises, including "perpetual franchises," in return for securities based on actual value of lines for operating purposes.

FIVE-CENT FARES—Provided for a period of one year from the inauguration of the system, after which a rate fixed automatically to meet actual cost of operation.

UNIFIED SYSTEM—By the consolidation of all necessary lines under the direction of a single ownership and authority.

PUBLIC CONTROL—Through a board of seven members, three to be appointed by the mayor, one each by three operating companies and a chairman to be selected by the other six, or in case of failure to agree, to be named by the Transit Commission or whatever body may succeed it.

PRIVATE OPERATION—Through the organization of three companies designated for the purpose of operating the respective groups under the supervision of a fourth company, whose managing directorate is the board of control.

UNIVERSAL TRANSFERS—To be established at proper points on all the lines of the three operating systems as rapidly as financial conditions will permit.

PROFIT SHARING—After payment of all obligations and maintenance of a "barometer' fund (reserve), a fund to be used for the joint benefit of the operating personnel.

PAYING OFF DEBT—Provision for the amortization within the period of the leases of the valuations fixed by the Transit Commission.

A summary of the chief proposals, given in the central "box" on this page, shows briefly what the commission proposes to do. This drastic-looking program is reenforced by the language which is used in dealing with some of the changes recommended. The commission says, for instance, regarding the present financial conditions of the companies which it is proposed to merge under municipal ownership:

"There is, of course, no doubt that their plight is attributable in no small degree to incidents of their own selfish and often unsavory history. Revenues that in the past should have gone into better facilities, or into the maintenance of reserves that conservative business practise required, have been paid into private pockets through swollen or forced dividends. Beyond question, many millions of dollars realized from nickel fares have thus been diverted from the purposes to which morally they belonged. This was true ten years or more ago in the case of most of the surface lines, almost none of which has paid any dividends since. It has been exemplified strikingly in the recent policy of the Interborough Company."

Here is certainly no attempt to let the transit corporations down easy, argue the defenders of the report. Nor, in proposing to get rid of all false valuations, burdensome inter-leases, and, in general, "to clean out the separate special private interests with their persistent friction and conflicting policies," does the commission anywhere suggest that municipal ownership "shall mean showers of plums for private holders of transit securities." On the contrary, the report says:

"In readjusting securities on the basis of honest value the commission has in view, and will insist upon, the elimination of 'water' of every description and the frank recognition of a depreciation that investors have long since discounted. In requiring that existing 'preferentials' be given up, as a part return for the stability the plan would give to real investment, the commission again seeks to cut out whatever has become unstable or artificial in transit finance. Preferential allowances held to be fair and necessary when the dual contracts were negotiated ten years ago are not fair under the conditions of to-day. If the subway operators argue that their preferentials should be continued, and that a fare should be fixed sufficient to cover them, they would claim in effect that they alone are entitled to 100 per cent. protection against the losses and shrinkages of the war, while the city, the private investors and every other party to the old agreements have been required to carry very substantial losses, direct and indirect."

"The commission makes the right approach to its task when it acknowledges that ground exists for public anger over the past history of traction in this city," declares the New York *Evening Post*, putting itself on record in favor of the report. Public attention, it goes on, "will no doubt center about the commission's stand on the five-cent fare," and in this particular "the basic consideration is that, when fare readjustments do become necessary, they will leave the public with the sense that it is not being 'gouged' by the 'interests' but that it is being asked to pay a fair return for efficient and honest service." The New York *Times*, *Herald*, *Tribune*, and *World*, without regard to political complexion, have joined in enthusiastic support of the commission's recommendations. A more reserved opinion is exprest by *The Globe*, which concludes that "the promise" of the report is excellent, but the details may require a good deal of tinkering. "Excellent," sums up the verdict of *The Evening World*, *The Evening Mail*, and *The Sun*.

This almost unanimous judgment of approval, both within and outside the city, is tempered in a few instances by regret that the report, by being issued shortly before New York's municipal election—seemingly in order to take the wind out of Mayor Hylan's campaign issues of a five-cent fare and municipal ownership—acquires a taint of political partizanship. The Hearst papers, supporting the Mayor, charge that the admittedly "preliminary plan" is issued merely as a vote-catcher, and that a sufficient number of "jokers" will be incorporated, after election, to permit an eight or ten cent fare, with the city's backing of "the same private interests that now operate and control the lines." It is notable, however, that Mayor Hylan's own plan aims at much the same ends, through the use of much the same means, advocated by the commission. His "recommendation," as quoted by the New York *American*, is that—

"The private operators turn the city-owned subways back to the city for municipal operation at a five-cent fare. These lines carry more than two-thirds of all the passengers in the city. The remainder can be better accommodated by the operation of modern automobile buses. Surface lines that have become obsolete can and should be taken off the streets of our city. The city will not buy them."

CHIEF PROBLEM OF THE CONFERENCE

THE CENTRAL PROBLEM of the Conference soon to be held at Washington is China. "The declared purpose is to bring the Powers into conference to discuss every problem affecting China's relations with foreign nations, with the object of reaching a common understanding deemed essential to the avoidance of friction and the perilous clashing of interests," explains the New York *Journal of Commerce*. And in the opinion of Mark Sullivan, Washington correspondent of the New York *Evening Post*, "of all the discussion at the coming Conference which is comprehended under the phrase 'Far Eastern questions,' 90 per cent. has to do with China." At the present moment, he adds, the vitality of China is especially weakened by factionalism. "China has for years been carrying on a civil war comparable in magnitude and importance to our own," notes the Springfield *Republican*, "tho very different in character. In fact, it resembles our own in that the southern part of China has been trying to secede." Mainly on this account we find that pacifist China stands first among the nations of the world in the number of soldiers actually under arms, being credited with 1,370,000, while France's strength is placed at 1,034,000 men. The government at Peking, we are told, is the one which represented China at the Peace Conference, signed Japan's twenty-one demands and borrowed quite recently $30,000,000 from Japan, making a grand total of $300,000,000. The government of southern China, established at Canton and representing, according to dispatches, more than half of China's total population, resents this propensity to borrow, particularly from Japan, and disapproves of the Peking Government's action regarding Japan's famous "twenty-one demands." It is, furthermore, afraid that the Peking delegation to the Conference will be dominated by Japanese intrigue, according to the New York *Times*. Therefore, thinks this paper, "if President Harding wants all China represented at the Conference, it must invite the Canton Government to send delegates." Dr. Wu Ting Fang, former Chinese Minister to the United States, is Minister of Foreign Affairs in Dr. Sun Yat Sen's Canton Government, and in his opinion "Peking is too far committed to Japan to make a strong case in the Washington Conference."

As a part of her fundamental policy at the Conference "Japan will not permit the 'scrapping' of the 'twenty-one demands' agreement with the Peking Government," cables the Tokyo correspondent of The Associated Press, "nor will it tolerate interference in the Shantung question." But, points out the New York *Evening Post* editorially, "it is China's contention that there is nothing to discuss with Japan; that the latter holds no legal rights in Shantung; that Japan is bound by her explicit promise at the Paris Peace Conference to get out of Shantung. In the face of that broken pledge, what use is there in negotiating with Japan?" As Dr. Paul S. Reinsch,

SAY, POP, WHAT IS PACIFIC ABOUT THIS OCEAN?

SEARCH ME, SONNY.

—Thomas in the Detroit *News*.

former United States Minister to China, explains in a New York *Times* article:

"The Japanese maintain persistently that they have no designs upon the political sovereignty of Shantung Province or of China. Their argument, therefore, is much the same as tho a foreign Power, having occupied the State of Pennsylvania, should assert its willingness to relinquish all claim to political control of the State, asking in return merely the city of Philadelphia and the Pennsylvania Railroad system. For China to negotiate with Japan in regard to Shantung is equivalent to the surrender of her claim to the railroad. All discussion of the sovereignty of Shantung is beside the point. Japan could only have secured a sovereignty over that province by capturing it from China and even the Japanese make no such claim. The troops along the railroad are there for military occupation."

CHINA THINKS IT'S A LAUNDRY PARTY.

—Reynolds in the Tacoma *Ledger*.

"There can be no assurance of permanent peace in the Pacific so long as the forces which make for war are allowed to continue at work in China," concludes Dr. Reinsch. "It is the weakness and disorganization of China which has brought about all the questions at issue in the Far East," maintains the Baltimore *News*. "The United States wants nothing in the Pacific except what it has," declares the Kansas City *Star*. But, as the Washington *Post* explains:

"Political ascendency over China by Japan is intolerable to the Western Powers, including the United States. They will resort to war rather than submit to the extinguishment of Chinese sovereignty. The reason for this fixt attitude is quite simple. It is a question of self-defense. The Western nations have nothing to fear from China in the hands of the Chinese; they have much to fear from China in the hands of the Japanese."

The Philadelphia *Record*, on the other hand reminds us that "Japan's friendship is important; she is the only Asiatic Power that is strong and progressive, and her enmity would be serious." The United States wants Japan to yield something of its Asiatic claims and curtail its naval expansion, notes *The Record*:

"We want it to limit its ambitions to dominate Asia, to reduce its navy, and to give Shantung to us so that we can give it to China. And if Japan, shall do all this, is it likely that she will do it without extorting a good round price from us?

"China is very anxious to get back the port she leased to Germany for 99 years, but she will not take it from Japan. The rest of the world must take it from Japan and present it to China on a tray. The Paris Peace Conference refused to do this, and the Chinese delegates would not sign the Treaty. The League of Nations has so far declined to do it. But America having shown its antagonism to Japan, and having espoused the cause of China, which is helpless and which pleads irresponsibility for its own acts, its lease to Germany and its treaty with Japan, China is now relying upon the United States to compromise itself still further in Asia by taking Kiao Chau away from Japan and presenting it to China."

"Having protested at the time of the Paris Peace Conference against the award of all Germany's 'rights, title and privileges' in Shantung to Japan, China persists in maintaining that the award is illegal and can not be recognized," says the New York *World*. In this paper's opinion—

"By adopting this highly legalistic attitude China has barred to herself the only means by which she could recover Shantung. Japan is in possession there, and, wrongly or rightly, the title was confirmed by the Treaty of Versailles. She is solemnly pledged to restore the province to China, but so long as China on no terms will consider receiving it at Japan's hands, Japan stays where she is and China is the poorer.

"Nominally China's grievance, in which she seeks sympathy and support, is against Japan, but actually it is directed against all the Powers that in signing the Treaty of Versailles awarded Shantung to Japan. In bringing her case to the attention of the Washington conference she will be insisting that the leading nations which overruled her previous protest at Versailles revoke their own decision and dispossess Japan. If that were practicable, nothing is less likely to happen. By entering into direct negotiations with Japan, China can obtain for herself without great delay the actual benefits to which she is entitled by regaining Shantung, but she prefers the rôle of an uncompromising litigant with diminishing chances of substantial success."

JAPAN HAS NO OBJECTION TO CHINA SITTING AT THE CONFERENCE TABLE, PROVIDING——

—Morris for the George Matthew Adams Service.

EARLY TINTS OF THE BUSINESS DAWN

BUSINESS IS LIKE AN OPERA SINGER—temperamental, sensitive to environment, and responsive to the attitude of the public—thinks the Boston *Herald*. "Is Business Turning the Corner?" was the title of our last article on this important subject, and since that time (September 24th) the New York *Journal of Commerce* has replied that "business has passed the turning point and has started upon the upgrade; the indications of such a trend are unmistakable." But what are these indications? First, perhaps, comes the net operating income of the country's largest railroads for August, which marked the best showing that they have made in more than a year. The total is estimated to be $90,000,000, as against $69,000,000 in July. In July of last year, it is pointed out, there was a deficit of $11,000,000. Railroad business is barometric because it consists in hauling the products of other businesses. "This showing is considered a hopeful sign in the period of general industrial depression," writes the New York *Times's* Washington correspondent; "already many of the railroads have begun to increase their working forces in the repair and maintenance departments." Another item which encourages the railroads is the prospective gain of 40 per cent. in the amount of perishable freight during the next three months over the corresponding period of 1920.

HIT 'IM AGAIN.

—Donahey in the Cleveland *Plain Dealer*.

"The significance of the latest cheer-up news on the general business situation is that it presents facts rather than opinions," notes the Pittsburgh *Chronicle-Telegraph*. One of the most important of these, reports the New York *Evening Post*, is the reduction in unemployment, and the stiffening in iron and steel prices. Another very encouraging feature of the business situation, writes B. C. Forbes in the Philadelphia *Public Ledger*, is that "idle money is piling up so steadily that the banks now have to seek out borrowers in order to find work for the funds." Business conditions in South America show unmistakable signs of recovery, says the Department of Commerce. In the woolen industries, we are told by the Springfield *Union*, "the increase in the number of employed over a year ago is 114 per cent." Virtually all Liberty Bond issues advanced late in September to the highest price quoted in more than a year, the gains amounting to $4 and $5 on each $100 for most issues, observes the New York *World*. In the opinion of this paper—

"This is a highly encouraging symptom for the general business outlook. Some of the strength in these bonds is no doubt due to Treasury buying for the sinking fund, but the major causes are larger and deeper. As the low prices had resulted from the forced liquidation of individuals and corporations in more or less distress for want of cash, so the present sharp turnabout in the market indicates that liquidation in that quarter is well over.

"Money is cheaper all around. This is another cause of the strength in Liberty Bonds. Even at the present higher prices for the best security in the world the yield on these bonds of maturities five years or so away, if held to maturity, is above 6 per cent., while railroad equipment notes are being easily floated to yield less than 6 per cent.

"But money is cheaper all around for the reason that liquidation has been extending all around. And if liquidation is over in Liberty Bonds it is inferable that it is about over in other markets."

True, the number of business failures stands at an unusually high figure, points out the Cleveland *Plain Dealer*—almost twice as many as a year ago, notes the *Wall Street Journal*. But the Manchester *Union* interprets what seems at first glance an "alarming business death-rate" to be "a very healthy mortality; the elimination of the parasitical middleman." In fact, says the Federal Reserve Board in its September report, "the month has been in the main a period of distinct encouragement, and gives promise of better conditions as autumn advances." There are further decided improvements in the credit situation, and manufacturing continues to show a wholesome improvement in many lines, adds the Board. "With excellent harvests, the West has recovered from deflation more rapidly than any other part of the country," believes the Seattle *Times*.

"The New York and Boston Federal Reserve banks having reduced their rediscount rates to 5 per cent., the expectation is that it will eventually be followed by other banks in the system," remarks the New York *Commercial*. The reduction already made, thinks the New York *Globe*, "is an invitation to returning business," for "these banks have concluded, apparently, that the period of liquidation is over, and that new business should be encouraged." We read on:

"The greatest test of the Federal Reserve System came last autumn, when by raising its discount rate the Reserve Bank hastened liquidation.

"The important matter, however, is that the nation abandoned the policy of drift and sought to steer a course. That policy is again emphasized in the new lower discount rate. Prophecy in the economic sphere is as dangerous as it is elsewhere, but it is plain that, other factors being favorable, a lower discount rate will of itself accelerate business."

"One of the favorable indications of returning prosperity is that exports in August increased $54,000,000 and reached the highest point since March," notes the Philadelphia *Record*. Imports were only $16,000,000 more than in July, adds this paper. "The export demand for corn continued throughout September, and is still in evidence," reports *Financial America* (New York). It is admitted by the New York *Journal of Commerce* that the total of exports during the last year or so has shrunk noticeably. But, it points out, "the fact is not generally known that the amount of goods exported in the last year compares favorably with any year during the war, and shows a marked increase over the total of export trade in pre-war years."

While the railroad earnings quoted earlier are said to be "encouraging," experts say that the carriers, under present conditions of business, will not be able to reduce rates materially and still earn 6 per cent. on the tentative valuation, unless operating expenses are further reduced. Operating expenses for July of this year were 29.4 per cent. less than for July, 1920. As we are told by the Pittsburgh *Gazette Times:*

"The railroads of the country represent a capitalized enterprise of approximately $20,000,000,000. For the past several years this enterprise has been on the road to bankruptcy. In this year 1921 it financial plight was such that it was compelled to neglect ordinary repair and upkeep of equipment and maintenance of way and structures. Its purchases of steel and other materials were reduced to a minimum. To-day the outlook for the industry appears brighter than in several years past. Because of this fact the roads have felt justified in increasing the number of men employed on roadway. This has been quite noticeable of late in this district. As their financial prospects improve they will feel justified in placing orders for rails, cars and structural material, and this will furnish tonnage for idle mills and furnaces. The effect will be increased traffic and general business will grow by what it feeds on. . . .

"The outlook at the opening of the last quarter of 1921 is brighter than at any previous time this year. The time will be too short for the development of anything resembling a 'boom' in business during the ensuing three months. On the contrary, some authorities are still talking of a 'hard winter' ahead; but fundamental conditions are expected to make progress toward normal, and with the opening of next spring the outlook will be clearer than at any time since the signing of the armistice. Meanwhile the Administration will proceed with well-laid plans for encouraging business."

"But," warns the Chicago *Journal of Commerce,* "prosperity cannot and will not come back overnight; the way to recovery will be just as long as the road to false war prosperity proved—and possibly longer." "We are getting along fairly well," admits the Philadelphia *Inquirer,* "but no progress of any value will be made unless it be on broad economic lines which take into consideration the entire state of society and its workings." "Better not cheer until you are out of the wood," advises the conservative *Wall Street Journal* in another editorial; "we are in for a bad winter, and ought to recognize it now. Intensifying the present unemployment there will be palpable necessity and positive want." "The leaders of finance and industry know that the future is still guesswork, and they do not hesitate to say so in private conversation," asserts the Boston financial correspondent of the New York *Evening Post,* who, however, admits that "the optimism of the moment probably is better than a feeling of avowed depression." Yet, points out the Philadelphia financial correspondent of the same paper, "there is no export business except in grain and cotton." A captain of industry of Denmark, where the steel industry is practically closed down because of the dislocation of trade with Russia, even believes that substantial improvement in world business conditions must await the reopening of business relations with Russia.

The Peoria *Transcript* is of the opinion that these "prosperity just around the corner" interviews that appear in metropolitan dailies are to be taken with the proverbial grain of salt. Says this paper:

"If 'big business' would eliminate 'bunk' and give the public, including organized labor, economic facts, the return to normalcy would be facilitated. Prosperity 'around the corner' is a grim mockery in a situation which is palpably anti-economic. There will be no prosperity until there is a resumption of productive industry on a basis which will give manufacturers a chance to enter the world markets and retailers a chance to reduce prices without incurring losses.

"Faith cures in business are played out. What is needed is a major operation on war wages."

POROSITY OF PROHIBITION

"WHEN DOES IT BEGIN?" a foreign visitor countered, when asked his opinion of prohibition during the first year of its enforcement. Then, along about the first of this month two Labor members of the British Parliament who visited the United States last summer to investigate and report on the results of prohibition, stated in their joint report that "prohibition, as we in England were led to believe it prevailed, does not exist; America has been described to us as 'a bootleggers' paradise.'" The non-enforcement of prohibition in the United States, they aver, "and the resultant consequences on the morals of the people bode ill for the future, particularly as regards the rising generation."

Coincident with this official report comes the news from Chicago that, according to the Chief of Police, "fifty per cent. of Chicago's police force are identified with the bootlegging industry"; that "prohibition enforcement in Chicago is a joke"; that "there is more drunkenness than ever before, more deaths from liquor than before prohibition, and more of every evil attributable to the use of liquor." It is even declared in a Chicago dispatch to the New York *Times* that "one police station was the home of a nest of bootleggers, who delivered whisky in the patrol wagon," and that uniformed policemen would rob whisky shipments in the freight yards, under pretense of confiscating the liquor, and sell the booty in case lots. Thereupon a policeman would appear and demand a substantial amount for protection, and after the amount had been paid still another policeman would "raid" the place—and collect another fee for protection. Yet another policeman, it is said, would confiscate the liquor and eventually sell it to some saloonkeeper.

A nationwide prohibition survey conducted by the New York *Tribune,* with the aid of its correspondents in many of the large cities, finds that "smoothly running bottlegging machines" are operating in a dozen large centers, and that "the Eighteenth Amendment is being flouted almost as openly in every other large city as in New York," where the greatest degree of wetness is supposed to prevail. "Bootlegging has never been so prevalent throughout New England, with the exception of the first few months of prohibition enforcement," reports one *Tribune* correspondent. "People drink more than they ever did," we hear from Baltimore, while it is estimated that in the vicinity of Detroit "a thousand cases of Canadian liquor come across the border every twenty-four hours." Altogether, say United States customs authorities, international bootleggers smuggle into this country about 9,000,000 gallons of liquor a month. "More Scotch whisky has been imported into the Province of Quebec in the last year than in the entire ten years that went before," avers the Providence *News,* which further declares that this enormous surplus comes into the United States. Added to all these, says the New York *Evening Post,* are the 180,000 gallons of whisky and the 362,532 quarts of champagne that were legally imported during the first eight months of 1921.

Other cities covered by *The Tribune's* survey are Philadelphia, St. Louis, Cincinnati, New Orleans, Cleveland, Denver and San Francisco. In all these cities, we are told, the Volstead Law is being violated everywhere. New York receives six train-loads of liquor a day, asserts the New York *World,* "but how this stuff gets in or where it comes from no one has officially found out." "The enforcement of the law," maintains the Seattle *Post-Intelligencer,* has become "complicated and impossible, mainly because bootlegging is in the hands of 'big business.'" The enforcing of prohibition "threatens to demoralize completely the police departments of American cities," agrees the Philadelphia *Public Ledger.* As W. W. Jermane writes from Washington to the Seattle *Times:*

"It is not too much to say that prohibition seems to be nearing a crisis, and that the question of whether it is to break down under general non-enforcement, as the Fourteenth Amendment has done, may be determined in the next twelve months.

"I write this not as indicating a desire to take the 'wet' side, but to express the sentiment of a large number of public men in this city (Washington) who believe in prohibition, but are becoming convinced that radical leadership is more responsible than everything else combined for the difficulties that beset the prohibition movement at every turn. The 'wets,' they point out, want nothing better than to have a national referendum, and the intolerant attitude of prohibition leadership is playing directly into their hands. If such a campaign were brought on while reaction against that leadership was at a high point, the 'wet' vote might be large enough to show sentiment so nearly equally divided as to make prohibition a major political issue for an indefinite time.

"There is no doubt that a test at the polls showing the country pretty evenly divided would encourage the 'wets,' dishearten the 'drys,' and tremendously increase the difficulties of law enforcement."

"The men who 'put across' prohibition have succeeded in making a nation of home-brewers and in creating contempt for law," asserts the Providence *News*, which believes that, instead of "appropriating millions of the peoples' money for an army of prohibition agents, the Volstead Law should be amended so as to make it an agent for temperance and not a sham proposition for prohibition." At present, contends the Albany *Knickerbocker Press*, the law plays into the hands of "the bootlegger, the moonshiner and the liquor dealer; they do not want the law changed any more than the Anti-Saloon League does." "Either repeal a law or enforce it," is the terse admonition of the Boston *Globe*. In New York, intimates *The World*, it will either be necessary to "install three enforcement agents to a family, so that they can stand guard in three eight-hour shifts, or hire the entire population of the city as special enforcement agents and set every man to watch himself." Continues *The World* in one of its many editorials on the subject:

"The Eighteenth Amendment and the Volstead Act have proved once more in the United States that people will not obey an unpopular law. They have proved also that Government can not enforce an unpopular law. Just as the citizens of a country are corrupted by the existence of a statute which nobody obeys unless he wants to, the officials in a Government are corrupted by the existence of a statute which nobody enforces unless he feels like it. The Volstead law is sometimes enforced, but in the communities in which public sentiment is hostile it receives only perfunctory and superficial attention.

"When the most spectacular law on the statute books is ignored by the public and treated by the guardians of the law as a source of income it is small wonder that all law fails somewhat of the respect in which it was once held. A country can not possess two codes—one to be broken, the other to be obeyed."

A BIG JOB
—McCay in the New York *American*.

But, asks the New York *Evening Post*, if New York is the "wettest spot in the country," and "the authorities can not count upon assistance from the public in enforcing the laws," "how does it happen that the 'wet' candidate for Mayor did not receive more votes at the primaries?" Continues *The Post:*

"Prohibition has no place in a municipal campaign, but Judge Haskell insisted on giving it a place. His platform, for all its technical mitigations, was a 'wet' platform. If an overwhelming tide of resentment against the prohibition laws is really sweeping through the city, here was the chance for an unmistakable protest. But Haskell received only one vote in every six cast in the primaries, and two-thirds of his votes came from Brooklyn and represented local pride and not 'wet' sentiment. As in the case of the much-advertised anti-prohibition parade on July 4, the 'wet' public hesitates to come out into the open; and the suspicion arises whether that public is as large as is commonly supposed.

"It may be argued, and with a good deal of force, that men are against prohibition who will not speak out openly against it. It might be said, cynically but with much truth, that there are men who are not opposed to the prohibition laws so long as the laws remain a dead letter. This habit of passing laws for printing in the statute books, and not for enforcement, is a common American vice. But if this is true of local sentiment on prohibition, then the answer is that prohibition enforcement takes on even more importance than is involved in the specific problem. It becomes a test of the operation of democracy."

At the present moment, declares William H. Anderson, New York State Superintendent of the Anti-Saloon League, "there is a wide-spread conspiracy, backed up by most of the newspapers in the larger cities, to discredit prohibition and its enforcement." In a Burlington, Vermont, dispatch to the New York *Times*, Mr. Anderson is quoted further:

"They object, first, that it can not be enforced—then, when we proceed to real enforcement business, they charge that the measures employed are fanatical violations of personal rights.

"Most of the newspapers in New York City are dishonest on this question. By dishonest I do not mean they take money in return for so many square inches of misrepresentation, but they apparently are 'wet' enough to work for an outlaw and criminal liquor traffic for nothing—and board themselves. . . .

"But the significant and disturbing thing is that it has been possible for this traffic, with the aid of 'wet' Congressmen and Senators and others to block for a half a year in a Congress elected overwhelmingly 'dry,' enforcement legislation vitally needed to uphold the Constitution.

"This fight has been made by the 'wets' to get a running start for their effort to elect a 'wet' Congress and 'wet' National House of Representatives and one-third of the United States Senate next year. They can not do it if the moral forces are awake and do their duty."

TOPICS IN BRIEF.

DISARM or disburse.—*Greenville (S. C.) Piedmont.*

HOME brew is responsible for some of the home bruisers.—*Dallas News.*

WHATEVER Americanism may be, it isn't pessimism.—*Richmond News Leader.*

WHY not set the army of unemployed at the job of cutting down prices?—*New York World.*

VACATIONS are now over, except for the unemployed and public officials.—*Brooklyn Eagle.*

ANDY VOLSTEAD says that his life has been threatened, but we'll wager no bootlegger did it.—*Columbia Record.*

IT is our idea that a picture that has to be examined with an X-ray to tell whether it is worth $100,000, isn't worth examining.—*Dallas News.*

THOSE infant republics are up in arms.—*Washington Post.*

APPARENTLY you can't keep a good price down.—*Rochester Times-Union.*

BRIEF explanation of the hatred of aliens: "My folks came over first."—*Minnesota Star.*

IF we don't hurry and build more battleships, we won't be ready for disarmament.—*Brooklyn Eagle.*

MEXICAN GOVERNMENT machinery might run better without quite so much oil.—*Wall Street Journal.*

ACCORDING to the Federation of Woman's Clubs, who are carrying on an anti-cockpit campaign, cock fighting is fowl play.—*Manila Bulletin.*

IT is said that we are after what Russia raises, and, without using the four-letter word, Lenine would like to see us get it.—*Wall Street Journal.*

IN reply to "What is the world coming to?" we say "America." —*Wichita Beacon.*

ONE good way to curtail armament would be to hire plumbers to build the battleships. — *Tacoma Ledger.*

JOHN BARLEYCORN has had more obituaries written about him than any other living person.—*Columbia Record.*

IF the Ku Kluxers wish to prove their Americanism, they might try stamping out race prejudice.—*Baltimore Sun.*

THE International Court would have brighter prospects if there was also an international sheriff.—*Roanoke World News.*

THERE is something peculiarly touching about a bald-headed man's condemnation of bobbed hair.—*Akron Beacon-Journal.*

"GOOD times are just around the corner." But it is hard to negotiate the corner on four flat tires.—*New York Morning Telegraph.*

THE world is learning that, if it is to have permanent peace, it must rely on its hands rather than its arms.—*Norfolk Virginian-Pilot.*

THE League of Nations is beginning to look like a bill after the enacting clause has been stricken out. —*Boston Shoe and Leather Reporter.*

IN BAD.

—Spencer in the Omaha *World-Herald.*

WEATHER sharps are predicting a hard winter for everybody except coal dealers.—*Brooklyn Eagle.*

"BABE" RUTH, we surmise, is a graduate of the well-known university of hard knocks. — *Columbia Record.*

NOW all we'll have to do in order to enjoy the proposed income tax reductions is to reduce our incomes. —*Brooklyn Eagle.*

A PORTION of the army of unemployed wouldn't be in the state it is if it were not so badly officered.—*Philadelphia Inquirer.*

BUSINESS having "turned the corner" is now wondering what will happen in the next block.—*Boston Shoe and Leather Reporter.*

WITH the mark worth less than a cent, the pfennig must be what scientists are breaking atoms into. —*Little Rock Arkansas Gazette.*

PERHAPS the greatest industrial deterrent to-day is that so many persons spell utility with an F.—*Boston Shoe and Leather Reporter.*

MAYBE if we disarm, Henry Ford will offer us a couple of hundred dollars for our battleships and arms and ammunition.—*New York World.*

ONE of our friends wants to know why we are so down on politicians. Well, it is mainly because we are so up on politicians.—*Columbia Record.*

REPUBLICAN institutions cannot long endure where there is enforced labor; or, for that matter, where there is enforced idleness.—*Roanoke World News.*

THERE are two sides to profiteering in food, remarks the Philadelphia *Record*, but the side that the consumer gets is the rough side.—*Charleston News and Courier.*

SPEAKING of children outshining their parents, there is the Eighteenth Amendment, which is better known than all the rest of the Constitution.—*Chicago Journal of Commerce.*

IT is unfortunate that a country like Ireland which finds government so irksome should have to have two governments at one and the same time. —*Nashville Southern Lumberman.*

IT seems likely that the Yap problem may be adjusted before the disarmament conference, which will, at least, settle the status of about ten acres of the earth's surface.—*Columbia Record.*

DESPITE the unemployment, the savings banks of the country are holding their deposits well, which proves that on the average the thrifty workers are holding their jobs.—*Boston Shoe and Leather Reporter.*

PROHIBITION, says a California authority, has caused the price of grapes to advance from $10 to $75 per ton. Wonder if we couldn't get Mr. Volstead to pass a law prohibiting the use of lumber.—*Nashville Southern Lumberman.*

THE comparative numbers of males and females in the United States is 53,899,451 of the former, and 51,809,319 of the latter. But, as somebody has observed in words to the same effect, the ruling powers lie not in numbers.—*Chicago Journal of Commerce.*

A REFORMER says he will move heaven and earth to enforce prohibition. The real problem, however, is to find some way to move the Bahamas.—*Baltimore Sun.*

A SMALL-TOWN telephone manager protests against the accusation that his operators read novels on duty. They don't. They don't have to.—*Chicago Journal of Commerce.*

THE first thing some people want when they get a little money is a car; and then the first thing they want when they get a car is a little money.—*Chicago American Lumberman.*

SENATOR FRANCE accuses Major Ryan, head of the American Red Cross, of fomenting the Kronstadt mutiny. That would be more than enough to make a Red cross.—*Liberator.*

"GAMBLING blamed for fall of mark." And the gambler most responsible is an exile in Holland who convinced himself that he was betting on an absolutely sure thing.—*Providence Journal.*

THE only difference between the positions of De Valera and Lloyd George is that one contends that Ireland is a sovereign state and the other that it is a state of the sovereign.—*Nashville Southern Lumberman.*

NAVAL Cut Up to Disarmament Conference.—*Headline.* This is bound to make trouble, no matter who is meant by the "naval cut-up." If it's Sims, the Democrats will howl, and if it's Daniels, the Republican delegates will walk out.—*Kansas City Star.*

WAYNE B. WHEELER says that if England would drink nothing but water, she could pay us what she owes us. According to which logic as Uncle Sam drinks nothing but water he has so much money he doesn't need to collect any debts.—*Louisville Courier-Journal.*

FOREIGN - COMMENT

BRITAIN'S "DANGEROUS POOR"

A MILLION AND A HALF PERSONS are living on public and private charity, English newspapers exclaim in consternation as they ponder the "unemployment lague" which constitutes a menace to the peace of the country. Jnemployment demonstrations are reported from various ections and it is darkly significant that a warning to the workers gainst a social upheaval as a remedy for unemployment was ttered in a speech at Sunderland by James Henry Thomas, ieneral Secretary of the National Union of Railwaymen and abor Member of Parliament. He pleaded that "the next ew months will be the most difficult period for the leaders," nd admitted that "at no time during the war did the situation ook so black and dangerous as now." Meanwhile, London ispatches inform us that the British cabinet has a relief plan, f which a huge credit scheme and immediate help for the estitute are the chief features. The credit scheme involves n agreement by manufacturers, bankers, and labor organzations on the establishment of credits endorsed by the banks. he government, we are told, has not the funds; and this rivate provision of capital will make it possible for the manfacturers to extend long-time credit to customers, and thus, t is hoped, to induce many manufacturers to reopen their lants and absorb a goodly percentage of England's 1,500,000

THE NEUTRAL.
—*Evening News* (London).

inemployed. An official report of the conference at Gairloch Scot'and) between Premier Lloyd George and the eight London Labor Mayors on the dangers implicit in the unemployment sitation throughout the kingdom quotes the Mayor of Hackney s saying "there is a bitter feeling and a sheer lack of faith in he whole institution of the State which is growing among those bands of hungry and desperate men"; and "it is important to note that it is not only the extremists who tend that way, but our best people." This mayor said further that while he and his colleagues had been able to "preserve a great amount of

THE HORNETS' NEST.
—*The Irish Weekly Independent* (Dublin)

order in London," they "have arrived at a point where passion and despair will get the upper hand" and he added:

"The taxpayer of London also is suffering financial burdens which are becoming intolerable. The burden automatically comes on the shoulders of the working and lower middle classes in the shape of taxes. The wages and salaries of these people are going down, and it is vital that their burdens of taxation be relieved."

Lloyd George's reply, given in the official report of the conference, reads as follows:

"The situation is of an appalling character, and it calls for serious reflection. It is not only a London problem, but it is a problem for the whole country. First of all I am considering what can be done to improve the supply of normal labor on lines of the ordinary work of the country. We need real cooperation by all the interests concerned.

"Starvation for the man who is willing to work and who is deprived of work through no fault of his own brings a situation which no civilized community can tolerate.

"I have pride in the fact that we have done more for the unemployed than has ever been done before. We have a debt of £8,000,000,000 (roughly $30,000,000,000) and a gigantic burden of local and national taxation, yet we have done much for the unemployed.

"In America there are 6,000,000 out of work. There is no unemployment fund. The States are doing nothing. The whole thing is left to the shift of circumstances.

"Since the war we have provided £106,000,000 ($400,000,000) in one or another form for unemployment. But it is no use to come to the state only for aid. You must, somehow or other, find a scheme where the state will do its part, the local authority its part, and the employer, banker, foreign trader, manufacturer and trade unionist all do their share. We must get everybody in it. We are discussing things along this line, and I am seeing representative men from both sides during the next few weeks to see if it cannot be done.

"At the present moment we are considering a government loan to tide you over your difficulties. In order to enable you to go to the banks, we shall put the whole weight of the government behind you for these loans."

When the Mayors asked whether he considered $3 weekly doles enough to live on, Lloyd George replied:

"I want you to put yourself in my position. I have got to find every year over £1,000,000,000 ($4,000,000,000) in a country where the biggest pre-war budget was £200,000,000 ($800,000,000), and in a country impoverished by war. One thing I am afraid of is exactly what you said—that 'can't' one day will be converted into 'won't.' If that happens you will be just where Russia is to-day."

While the unemployed must be helped, the London *Spectator* says care must be taken not to injure those who are at work. For, if the poor rates were increased without limit, in order to give every unemployed person a full week's wages at trade union rates, "many employers would have to close their works and the number of unemployed would rapidly increase, until most rate payers were in receipt of poor relief." Then of course the whole social fabric would collapse, and we are told that—

"It is easy to draw up schemes of public works that might be carried out and that would be beneficial to the community, and to suggest that the unemployed—regarded in theory as a mass of navvies—should be set to work on these schemes forthwith. . . . But the question is by no means so simple as all that. Many of the unemployed town-dwellers are wholly unfit for rough manual labor on reclamation works, even if it were possible to take them to the coastal districts or the moorlands where the work has to be done, and to house them when they arrived. A fourth of the unemployed are women."

Nevertheless, *The Spectator* thinks it should be possible for the state and local authorities to find work for some of the unemployed on the roads, which have many of them become "positively unsafe to the development of motor traffic." But it does not expect such relief to be "economically profitable," tho the nation will benefit by getting better roads "as well as by restoring self-respect to a number of men who are idle through no fault of their own." For the true remedy of unemployment conditions, *The Spectator* bids us look elsewhere, and points out that "the reduction of prices by a general lowering of the cost of production is the main condition precedent to the revival of our foreign trade, which will quickly create employment in all industries." On this point a financial authority, the London *Statist*, observes:

"Government policy should aim at the economic restoration of Europe and the reopening of trade relations even with former and present enemies. To this end diplomatic and financial assistance should be accorded to the Succession States, especially to those friendly to British interests, and to Germany and Russia."

GERMAN MARK "FRIGHTFULNESS"

GERMAN MARK SPECULATION surprizes some British observers of the foreign exchange market, but if the English are puzzled by the dizzy antics of the mark, German press observers are almost overcome. Only front page headlines are equal to the story which the *Berliner Tageblatt* calls the "mark catastrophe" as it proclaims that one dollar equals 127 marks. The *Vossische Zeitung* at the top of its type cries out "The Collapse of the Mark" and says "the depreciation of the mark ever assumes more catastrophic form. From quarter hour to quarter hour foreign exchange rates rise by leaps and bounds." The stability of the mark is possible, according to this newspaper, when continental debts are consolidated, and it adds:

"The stabilizing of the mark can only follow a flow of gold from countries where there is a surplus of trade into lands which are sick in consequence of an absence of gold. Unless this occurs the World War will have left only defeated and ruined nations behind it."

GERMANY'S FLOOD OF PAPER MONEY

—*Simplicissimus* (Munich.)

An American correspondent at Berlin points out as a symptom of "mark hysteria" that "no two papers this evening quote the dollar at the same figure, tho the official Reichsbank quotation fixed the dollar as equal to 124.87 marks." The *Deutsche Zeitung* headlined the mark value on the date of September 27th as 126 to one dollar, and added:

"Those circles which maintain that the dollar would go above 150 marks appear to be right. The reasons for the rapid upward movement are not clear, but are explained by the precipitant exchange purchases by German industry and extensive reparation purchases by the Reichsbank."

Heavy speculation in connection with the German mark has gone on practically since the quotation of the Berlin Exchange was resumed in the London market, we learn from the London *Statist*, which advises us that—

"Speculators in this exchange may be divided into two classes: those who buy in the expectation of making a quick sale with a narrow margin of profit, and those who buy as a lock-up investment in the hope of a recovery to at or near the pre-war sterling value in the course of some years. The former class operate from experience of the very wide limits within which the mark has fluctuated in the past, for after a sharp fall in value the currency has frequently shown an equally sharp recovery. The latter class, which is perhaps the more numerous, appear to be animated by confidence in the ultimate economic recovery of Germany, which, they assume, will entail a simultaneous recovery in the value of Germany's currency unit."

This view is "altogether erroneous," in the judgment of *The Statist*, which says that even if Germany recovers her former economic strength during the course of a few years, it is absurd to think that the German Government will undertake the enormous sacrifices involved in deflating the mark, and *The Statist* proceeds:

"On the contrary, there is little reason why the external depreciation of the mark should not continue till a much higher quotation in sterling is reached. The collapse in the values of the Polish mark and the Russian rouble afford striking examples of the extremities to which a paper currency may depreciate in a short space of time under a profligate financial policy. The present trend of Germany's finances points, in fact, to a still lower value for the mark, for the printing-press is being constantly used in order to cover revenue deficits. It is true that some improvements have been effected in recent months in the direction of increasing tax revenue and reducing expenditure, but these have not been reflected in the movements in the note circulation, being more than offset by the necessity for providing for reparation payments. These latter will long continue to put a very severe strain on Germany's public finances and there is, indeed, little prospect of the State expenditure for some years to come being met otherwise than by large fresh issues of notes to supplement tax revenue."

According to some Berlin dispatches, the view in Allied circles is that the precipitous decline of the mark is due to the failure of the Reichsbank to support exchange as it has previously done, and this course is said to be "deliberate, as the government is averse to artificial support, making the financial position seem better than it really is, with big reparation payments ahead." What is more, one Berlin correspondent writes that "in some Allied quarters the fall of the mark is construed as forecasting an effort for delay in reparation payments" and intimations are freely heard of "an imminent financial catastrophe."

Berlin dispatches also cite the statement of Privy Councilor Kloeckner that "the rapid rise of the mark would be even worse" than its descent and "would spell certain disaster." Mr. Kloeckner is described as one of Germany's most powerful captains of industry and, through his alliance with the great Thyssen interests, the most formidable rival of Hugo Stinnes. He is quoted as speaking at a stockholders' meeting in this wise:

"The present boom stands or falls with the movement of the mark. The rapid rise of the mark would entail a catastrophe of unprecedented magnitude and scope. But we are still far from that point of time. So long as the London ultimatum is not revoked and Germany is not freed from the huge occupation burden, the mark is bound to remain bad. The only way to improve conditions is more work."

Mr. Kloeckner takes an optimistic view of the present industrial situation, not only in Germany, but in the world at large, and says:

"Unlike many of my fellow-industrialists, I am of the opinion that the present movement is not a quickly passing pseudo boom. Gradually the international wave of mounting economic life is affecting production as well. Reports from France and Belgium sound more hopeful. From neutral countries, particularly South America, Germany's industries are receiving as large orders as before the war. Between England and Germany, too, important exchange trade deals could now be negotiated."

INDIA'S SPINNING-WHEEL SLOGAN.

Mr. Gandhi, the Indian Self-Rule (Swaraj) leader, argues that one means towards the goal is the use of the native spinning-wheel (charkha) and the wearing of coarse hand-spun cloth exclusively. In demonstrations in the large towns of the country on August first, bonfires were made of garments fashioned in foreign cloth. In Bombay Mr. Gandhi himself started such a fire in the presence of more than a hundred thousand supporters. The spinning-wheel shown above is nine yards by seven, and was drawn in a parade through the streets of Delhi by two big bulls, while white-clad men on the cart showed the wheel in operation.

"DOES INDIA KNOW WHAT IT WANTS?"

INDIAN NATIVES want something, and apparently want it badly, but until they know clearly just what they want, how is it properly to be striven for? This is the question put by Mr. Bepin Chandra Pal in the Bengali magazine *Nabya Bharat*, as he examines the attitude of various Indian groups towards the Gandhi crusade for Swaraj, which, translated, means "self-rule." He tells us of Hindu patriots who under this slogan hope for "a new era, a Hindu kingdom in India," and think of the day when the Hindus will become "masters of India," for—

"By *Swaraj*, they understand Hindu Raj. A Hindu will be the President of the *Swaraj* republic and the people of this *Swaraj* will follow Hinduism.

"Religion according to race will be established in the Hindu republic. Hindu customs will again be introduced. India will again occupy a high place among the countries of the world under Hindu influence."

Similarly, he tells us, there are many Mussulmans who want to see their lost glory and destroyed supremacy restored in India, and in consequence—

"By *Swaraj* these people understand Mussulman Raj. The Moslem community still extends over all the countries from Turkey to China, but these Mussulmans are weak and confused. It is not impossible by uniting the whole Mussulman community to build a pan-Islamic federation if the Moslem power becomes supreme in India. This feeling is predominant in the minds of Mussulmans educated on modern lines. It is, therefore, not inconceivable that these Mussulmans are yearning for a Moslem kingdom in India and these Mussulmans always assert that they are Moslems first and Indians next."

This Indian writer avers that he has known many men who want to establish a Hindu kingdom in India. On the other hand, by the words and behavior of the Moslem leaders he is convinced that, if not all, at least some of them desire to see a Moslem empire, but he adds:

"Putting aside the case of Hindus and Mussulmans, it cannot, on taking the native Princes into consideration, be said that a new nation composed of Hindus and Mussulmans is being built in India. In these Native States, the British people are the real rulers and the Princes are more or less puppets. If these Princes understand anything by *Swaraj*, they understand only the arbitrary rule of themselves and nothing else. Then, last of all, the Sikhs in the West and the Mahrattas on the South, from whom the English people have taken the kingdom by force and established British rule, have not altogether forgotten the past. To judge from human nature it cannot be said that these races will not think of regaining the past if opportunities are afforded. Under these circumstances, then naturally crosses the mind the question: This *Swaraj* for which we are crying so much—whose Raj will it be? Is it possible to gain the object if that object is not known?"

GERMANY AFTER RUSSIAN TRADE

GERMANY, NOT ENGLAND, is playing the leading rôle in Russian trade for the present, according to neutral and American observers in the Baltic states, who say that the race for Russian business is now in full cry, with representatives heading for Moscow on every train. There is special rejoicing among the Germans at this new stage, for they started as long ago as the Treaty of Brest-Litovsk. At that time, we learn from a German journalist, the German industrial experts saw their opportunity in Russia and decided to get it down to a working basis. The Germans divided their commercial projects with the Soviet organizations into three fields: First, they were to supply Russia with agricultural implements, of which the peasants were utterly in want. Secondly, they were to reorganize the Russian transport system, especially in technical matters, and to supply rails, rolling stock, and locomotives. Thirdly, they purposed to furnish chemical and pharmaceutical products, of which there was no stock whatever in the old empire of the Tsars.

THE HERR AND THE HARE

—*The Daily Express* (London).

There is no doubt that the German industrial and commercial leaders took the question of trade possibilities with Russia much more seriously than did the Russian extremists, writes this German journalist, Mr. G. M. Cahen, in the Paris *l'Europe Nouvelle*, for he humorously tells us that in the autumn of 1917 a Bolshevik, one Sobelson-Radek, confided to him at Stockholm, that "in order to show their gratitude to the Germans for the help extended by the industrials of the Reich, the Soviets were sending them back some hundreds of thousands of German prisoners who had been successfully inoculated with the Bolshevik virus!" This German journalist goes on to speak of a proposed joint effort in Russia between the Germans and an Anglo-American group of capitalists, and he avers that there is no doubt "such an association exists in the Baltic countries." So we ought not to be surprized if a similar arrangement were concluded in Soviet Russia, for there are many reasons in favor of such cooperation. This German informant then proceeds:

"In the first place, is it not quite natural that in this new and revolutionary Russia, business interests should take guarantees against any objections which might be made to the concessions granted them and the contracts made with them by one government that might be replaced by another? Again, is not the best guarantee to form a defense force against such eventualities by grouping these business interests into a syndicate of cooperation and common action? What is more, the need of the German groups on the one hand is for capital, and of the Anglo-American groups for experts. Now Germany has the experts and the Anglo-Americans have the money."

This German journalist goes on to say that there are many people at Berlin who feel sure that such a development of commercial relations could have only the happiest results for the entire body of German interests; but he himself believes that in view of present conditions there are more drawbacks than advantages. To turn the major part of German industrial activity toward Russia is from a political standpoint a mistake, for the close alliance between German financiers and industrials and the Americans, English and Russians, who have very little concern in the biggest burden on Germany's mind, namely, the reparations, would permit the loss in values of capital which would be exploited solely for the profit of a little group of great lords of industry and finance in Germany, to the detriment of the major mass of workers. We read then:

"I have good reasons for believing that my opinion is gradually growing in Berlin, and that these commercial relations are only admitted as a last resource because in the world paralysis of trade the Germans despair of finding anywhere a field for their activities, except in Russia. If French commerce were engaged actively in the Russian and Baltic markets, all German producers would take new confidence. The Pan-German press has supported the theory that Germany is interested in having Russia refuse to recognize its debt to France. In my opinion such an attitude is both deplorable and absurd. In point of fact Germany can only acquire the strength to quit herself of the reparations and the debts that weigh upon her shoulders so heavily if France is restored in her former financial power. As long as the Russian debt is not liquidated there can be no sound structure reared in eastern Europe. Yet after all, there is no reason to be alarmed about all these mysterious financial and industrial combinations of which we have been speaking. What would be really disturbing were to see France continue always to refrain from interesting herself in the economic problems of Russia. For the future evolution of Europe is bound up in this."

WHO WON THE WAR?

The Man who Thinks he did. The Man who Guesses he did. The Man who Knows he did.

—*London Opinion.*

SCIENCE - AND - INVENTION

A DEFENSE OF OLEOMARGARIN

EVEN A WORM WILL TURN; and the oleomargarin industry has now reared up and is defending itself with some spirit against what it conceives to be the unjust attacks of the dairymen, getting in a few offensive movements too, on its own account. Its latest grievance is that certain dietitians have been featuring the richness of butter and butter products in the fat-soluble vitamin, stated to be absolutely necessary to the preservation of life and health. That butter has almost a monopoly of this substance, and that, closely as oleomargarin may imitate it in other respects, it is wofully deficient in this, are conclusions to which, apparently, many authorities have come. They are, however, combated as unwarranted by Dr. William D. Richardson, chief chemist of Swift & Company, Chicago, in a paper read before the Institute of Independent Margarin Manufacturers and printed in *The American Food Journal*. Dr. Richardson asserts that, while oleomargarin in its genesis and early history was to be considered a substitute for butter, it may now be looked upon as an established separate product, functioning as a spread for bread following a rather early custom developed in northwestern European countries. He continues:

"It should be remembered that butter as a spread for bread is used in a comparatively small area of the earth, chiefly in North Europe and America and that in many other parts of the globe it is not used at all. In some places olive oil is the chief fatty product used both for cooking and as such for ordinary consumption; in others tallow drippings; and in the greater part of the world's area, namely, the great rice producing sections, which cereal furnishes the principal grain for more than half the population of the earth, various fats and oils are used in admixture. The use of butter may be looked upon as a local custom altho we who have grown up with the custom are apt to consider it a universal and necessary one. However, the use of the product is a custom with us and the majority in North Europe and America has cultivated a taste for a fat with the so-called lactic flavor instead of for olive oil or tallow drippings or cocoanut oil without the lactic flavor. Hence it is quite natural and desirable that the lactic flavor should be given to the fat designed for table use.

"The necessary food substances now generally known as vitamins eluded detection for many years owing to the fact that they are contained in practically all natural foodstuffs.

"When the first announcements were made of the hypothesis that the growth of children and of animals in general depended upon the presence of a substance which was designated as fat soluble A, which was stated to be present in butter-fat more than in other foods, and these announcements were seized upon by certain extremists, some of them disinterested but more of them interested in a commercial way in exploiting the discovery, to state that the human race was dependent upon dairy products for its continued healthy existence, it might have been foreseen that any such narrow deduction from the premises would not stand the test of time. As a matter of fact many chemists and others, including the writer of this paper, predicted that fat soluble A would be found in a great variety of other foods in sufficient quantity for animal and human needs. This was a foregone conclusion from well-known facts of natural history. Those facts are in brief that milk is supplied by nature only for the nourishment of the young of mammals and the supply is cut off automatically after a time which varies for different species from about one month to about a year. Thereafter none of the species in a state of nature is furnished with milk and milk therefore can not be considered in any sense a natural food for adults.

"In the light of all these well-known facts which have been fully realized by naturalists for years, it seems strange that any one could have been persuaded that vitamins or any other essential food constituent could have a solitary or limited source or be of such limited origin that the welfare of any species and of the human race, in particular, would be dependent upon a sole source of supply. It is not difficult for any one to admit that milk, species for species, is the ideal food for mammalian young, but this admission does not by any means carry with it the corollary that milk and dairy products are the ideal or the necessary food for mammalian adults. If it were so, then nature must have erred grievously in not providing some source of supply for all her mammalian adult family, men and animals. The general facts of natural history indicate conclusively that there is no intention in the scheme of nature to have adult mammals or mankind dependent in any degree for growth, health or general welfare on milk or dairy products. If rats, the experimental animals most used in the past for dietetic experiments, are fed a mixed ration of moderate variety, consisting of the food commonly used on the ordinary table, meat, vegetables, grains and fruits, but without milk or dairy products, they get along very well indeed, without developing dietary or deficiency diseases, showing normal growth and health, except for an occasional ailment or infection to which such laboratory animals are always subject. Such rats reproduce unto the *n*th generation in spite of the absence of their per diem of milk. When to such a diet either oleomargarin or butter is added no noteworthy change results as might have been foreseen and expected. Rabbits and guinea pigs grow to maturity, flourish and reproduce on green things as do the large herbivorous animals, while the carnivorous kinds eschewing vegetable products subsist entirely on meat. These would commonly be considered to be most unbalanced diets, but the addition of dairy products does not change the course of nature."

Not content, however, with setting forth the claims of oleomargarin, Dr. Richardson next proceeds to carry the war into Africa by attacking the dairy industry as indefensibly wasteful in its methods. He writes:

"What would you think of an industry, and particularly a food industry, which to a large extent allows its raw material to decompose and spoil before working it up into the manufactured or finished product, and then, what would you think of the same industry if after manufacturing its principal product, it deliberately threw away, wasted, or only partly utilized, by-products of as great intrinsic value as the principal product and in quantity two to three times as great?

"Yet the dairy industry, considered as a whole, does allow a large portion of its raw material to spoil before beginning to manufacture its product. In one direction it only recovers from 30 to 35 per cent. of the total solids available in the milk. The remainder, amounting from 65 to 70 per cent., is either thrown away altogether, thrown away all but the casein, or degraded into an animal feed instead of being properly conserved for human food. I do not hesitate to say that the dairy industry to-day is the most wasteful example of a food industry in civilized countries. That it should be allowed to continue on its present uneconomic basis is an astonishing example of public indifference, prejudice and failure to understand.

"Economically the butter industry is indefensible on account of the enormous wastes entailed in the nation's human food supply. To a less extent the cheese industry is indefensible although it wastes or debases only milk sugar, salts and vitamins, whereas the butter industry in addition to sugar, salts and vitamins also wastes or debases the most valuable constitutent of all from a dietary standpoint, the casein."

He says, in conclusion:

"The early statements of the vitamin enthusiasts about the indispensability of milk in the adult diet have been refuted by later experiments as could easily have been foreseen, and was foreseen by broad-minded dietitians with some knowledge of natural history. The extreme statements of six or eight years have been modified and modified again until to-day they would be laughed at in their original form."

FISHWAYS FOR SALMON

THE ENGINEER who is planning hydroelectric developments in the Northwest should not forget that his dams must be provided with fishways for the salmon that are to furnish the raw material for one of the region's most important industries. Substantial progress, we are told by a writer in *Engineering and Contracting* (Chicago), has been made in salmon fishway design for overcoming high obstructions in the streams of Oregon and Washington, but the problems presented by the construction of a great dam (such as that proposed in the Klamath River in California) in a river supporting a commercial run of salmon has not been previously attacked. We read:

"As a salmon is a large active fish several feet long and sometimes attaining the weight of 90 pounds, necessarily fishways for his accommodation must be of substantial size. One type of fishway that has been used consists of a deep flume six feet wide divided into six-foot boxes by partitions which have a two-foot notch arranged for spilling water from each box to the next. From eight to ten second-feet of water is required. A better way, however, is to construct the fishway as a series of pools, water spilling from one pool to the next; as thereby, when the physical conditions permit, pools of large dimensions may be obtained with moderate expense. The secret of success with fishways for salmon is to make them of ample size with plenty of water, and to provide frequent extra large pools for resting purposes.

"Fly-fishing, for which an innumerable variety of lures is available, is considered sport; but it is nothing to the sport the fishway engineer has in devising his fishway entrance to entice the salmon to enter, for which purpose he has three lures. One of these is the salmon's migrating instinct; another is his instinct to return to his parent stream, and the third is the salmon's instinct or liking for aerated water, which as a French scientist has pointed out is one of the strong impulses which actuates the salmon in his migration.

"The great dam to be located just above the confluence of the Salmon River on the Klamath River has several natural advantages favorable for the location of a fishway, principally because there is a saddle a short distance away from the dam which will be used for spillway purposes, and where the fishway can be built on a long, easy grade from the water. By taking advantage of the natural slope the engineers may, by building small dams or walls, form large resting pools at frequent intervals. To entice the salmon into the fishway, a big basin adjoining the river is to be the entrance to the fishway. Into it will tumble all the waters from the spillway, and several cascades will be arranged to aerate the water highway."

Courtesy of "Engineering and Contracting," Chicago.

A "FISHWAY" TO HELP SALMON CLIMB THE DAM

East approach on fishway over the Portland Light & Power Co.'s Dam on the Willamette River, at Oregon City, Ore. The large pools where the salmon can rest are from 15 to 20 feet wide.

A NEW SORT OF HOSPITAL

IT NEVER OCCURRED to our hospital builders before, seemingly, that the poor patients in the open wards might be affected by mental comfort and discomfort just as much as by bodily welfare. In fact, "we have behaved as though the patient had a body, but no mind or soul," said Dr. Hugh Cabot, professor of surgery at the University of Michigan, in an address before the Michigan Hospital Association that is reported in *The Modern Hospital* (Chicago). The depressing surroundings in a hospital ward are nothing less than a "psychic insult to the patient," Dr Cabot roundly declares, and *The Modern Hospital* frankly admits that it would be hard to defend the open ward from this charge. But at the very time when Dr. Cabot was thus denouncing the open-ward system, New York newspapers were announcing the approach of the completion of the Fifth Avenue Hospital, called "the only wardless hospital in the world." This new institution, it is claimed, will meet all the requirements specified by Dr. Cabot. It will be nine stories high and will contain 300 private rooms and no wards. It is on Fifth Avenue, facing one of the most beautiful parts of Central Park. Says *The World* (New York):

"The construction plan is unique. In order that every room shall be an outside room, with plenty of light and air, the building will be in the shape of a great X, with semi-square structures at the ends of the cross-bars. There will be no wards, not even any two-patient rooms. Each patient in the institution will have a room to himself, also a bath. Yet in spite of this exclusiveness, and in spite of the fact that everything in connection with the institution is to be of the best quality and most modern nature, one-half of the bed capacity is to be for the free, or semi-free, use of the public. The rates are to be 'from nothing up' and particular attention is to be paid to that class of patients who are not extremely poor, who do not desire to accept the charity of a free ward in a public hospital, but to whom the rates of an ordinary high-class hospital would be prohibitive."

The new hospital's rates are to be based on the patient's ability to pay, and an endowment of $1,500,000 has been provided to maintain the hospital as planned. Going deeper into the idea of an escape from depressing surroundings, *The Architectural Review* says:

"The anesthesia rooms are so placed that the patients will not come in contact with anything that suggests a surgical operation from the time of their arrival until they are placed under the ether. These rooms will look like small parlors, with curtains, wooden furniture, etc., and will have buff painted walls, instead of the usual white marble or tile. They will be especially ventilated to remove any fumes of ether that might annoy patients."

The walls will be equipped with deadeners, so that the sounds of the delirious will not reach other ears. Each room in the hospital will be regulated separately as to temperature. One room may be warm enough to induce perspiration, while that adjoining it may have a zero temperature.

The New York *Evening Telegram* says:

"Another feature of the hospital is the entire floor devoted to the care of children, from the new-born babe to the boy or girl of fifteen. Glass partitions instead of solid walls will be placed in this department. These will provide the necessary isolation, but will permit the patients the pleasure of seeing the other little ones. On this floor will also be one outside and four inside playrooms, which will be liberally supplied with toys, games and picture books."

The hospital will contain a complete nurses' home, according to the New York *Tribune*, and each nurse will have a furnished room; and the New York *Herald* adds that no nurse of fewer than two years' experience will be permitted to attend a patient at a bedside, a plan which will insure competent ministration to every patient. But the crowning glory of this twentieth century hospital, says the New York *Times*, "will be the entire absence of those long, awful looking, bed-lined apartments known as wards, reeking of disinfectants and filled with the sight of suffering."

It is something of a revelation to know that the new hospital will be operated at practically the same cost as those having the ward system, which was believed to be justified by the saving. The Fifth Avenue Hospital is the dream of Dr. Wiley Woodbury, a former lieutenant-colonel in charge of the base hospital at Camp Upton, Long Island. He has planned hospitals in Belgium, Siam, Australia, China and the Philippines.

Illustrations by courtesy of "The Scientific American" New York.

AFTER THE FIRE, EARLY ON THE MORNING OF JUNE 17.

BUILDING A BRIDGE IN TEN DAYS

ALL BRIDGE-CONSTRUCTION records are said to have been broken by the replacement of the Point of Pines bridge over the Saugus River, between Lynn and Revere, Mass., early in July. The new bridge, a wooden structure 400 feet long and 33 feet wide, was put up in ten days and cost $33,000. Counting the clearing away of burnt parts before reconstruction could begin, the whole job took exactly 13 days, one hour and twenty minutes. A bare 31 days elapsed between the burning of the old bridge and the throwing back of the gates on July 18 to permit a parade of automobiles across the new structure. Traffic on the main highway to the north shore of the Saugus was thus resumed in a minimum of time. Says E. W. Davidson, in an account contributed to *The Scientific American*:

ON JULY 12, ALL BURNED PILES REPLACED OR SPLICED.

"The train of events leading up to this remarkable undertaking started with the fire on June 17, partly destroying the original structure across the Saugus River. That fire broke a vital traffic artery. On the following day the Metropolitan District Commission announced that a new bridge would cost between $60,000 and $150,000 and no funds were available. But in view of the fact that a $50,000 State emergency fund existed, the Commission's engineers started specifications, anyway. On the 21st Lynn, Revere, and the town of Swampscott asked the Commission for a temporary bridge. A hearing was announced on the 23rd and held on the 30th. In the interim the Commission's engineer had reported that to build a bridge costing $150,000 would mean shutting off travel for six months.

"This suggestion of delay, with the summer's heavy automobile travel just starting, worried Lynn and Revere not a little. But on the 29th, the day before the Commission's hearing, the big electric company, with works near the Lynn end of the bridge, offered to rebuild the bridge in temporary form at cost within 15 days.

"Engineers scoffed, but H. S. Baldwin, department engineer of the General Electric, was sure it could be done. That afternoon Mr. Baldwin went out in a rowboat and inspected the ruins. That night complete tentative plans and estimates were made.

"The next day after the hearing the Commission decided to let the electric company go ahead. The city of Lynn appropriated $40,000 to finance the work and Governor Cox gave assurance that the State would reimburse the city next winter when the Legislature meets.

"Detail plans were drawn July 2, the engineers finishing them in the small hours of the next morning, so that they could be given to contractors for bids. The contract was let at $14,200, and the electric company agreed to furnish the materials and supervision for $20,000.

"On the morning of July 4 steam derricks appeared at the bridge and work started tearing off the damaged deck and weakened piles. Three days later new construction began.

"Storms and heart-breaking obstacles interfered from the start. At first it looked like a month's job. Flood-lights were put up and the work drove ahead night and day. As days passed, the outlook grew brighter.

"By July 12 all the caps except on six spliced joints at the Lynn end of the bridge were in position. On the 14th it was possible to cross the bridge on the loose planking while the cross bracing went ahead swiftly.

"When the job of laying the wearing surface of 2-inch spruce planks began, the workmen were sure that sawing would take ten days to two weeks. An individually motor-driven circular saw table with mitering arrangements operated by two experts was rushed out from the Lynn Works. The planks were cut at the proper angle as fast as they could be fed. The laying of the planks was so swift that Mayor Creamer was able to drive the last spike on the 18th, and the bridge was done.

"Only the best materials have been put into the structure. The new piles are of oak; the stringers, caps, deck, fence, post and hand-rails are of long leaf hard pine, and the wearing surface of spruce; 270,000 board feet of lumber have been used. Instead of a temporary bridge, it is made as well as, if not better than, the original structure and is guaranteed for ten years."

COMPLETED BRIDGE ON JULY 18, TEN DAYS AFTER WORK BEGAN.

TEAR-BOMBS FOR MOBS AND BANDITS

THE PHILADELPHIA POLICE think that they now have the means of stopping a charging mob or a fleeing bandit, putting either out of commission and yet inflicting no permanent injury. This is to be done by grenades throwing out a gas similar to the "tear-gas" used in the late war. Experiments with such bombs in South Philadelphia are said to have been eminently successful. William A. McGarry, writing in *The Scientific American* (New York,) says that the bombs are "quite as effective as rifle or revolver fire, and far less deadly." Two types shortly will be on the market for use by the police and also by banks, storekeepers and paymasters. One contains the familiar lachrymose gas, the other what is known as "stunic" gas, which stuns one who inhales it, leaving him virtually unconscious and utterly helpless for some minutes. Writes Mr. McGarry:

"The effect of the tear-bombs shown to the police in that city is identical with that caused by the lachrymose gas used by the Germans. The gas causes irritation of the lining of the eyelids and of part of the eye itself, so intense and painful that it is impossible for the victim to keep his eyes open, and he is rendered helpless for from five to twenty minutes. In no case is there any permanent ill effect.

"Knowing that the results would be exceedingly painful, the rookie squad nevertheless volunteered to be the victims of the demonstration. They formed themselves into a 'mob' about one hundreds yards away from the police, and charged. They were permitted to cover about half the distance before the bomb-throwing started.

'Four bombs then were hurled in the path of the charging men. The seven-inch rubber containers bounced once or twice and then exploded one after another, with sharp reports. Dense clouds of white vapor rose, spreading slowly in all directions to almost unbelievable volume. This soft, white vapor, shifting before the light breeze, might have been a stone wall. It brought the 'mob' to a dead stop within fifteen feet.

"The mechanism of the bombs is extremely simple, and this is the feature that is expected to make them popular with the police and with paymasters who must travel lonely roads. They are exploded by a spring detonator that is generally set for five seconds, altho this may be regulated to suit. It is claimed that with a little practise a bank teller, for instance, could learn to snatch up one of the bombs with either hand and set the spring with a slight pull of his thumb. A demonstration of the stunic gas within a building was given at the same time as the tear-gas exhibition, four bluecoats offering themselves up for sacrifice. They were unconscious from five to ten minutes each, as only sufficient chemical was used to show its effectiveness.

"The police are particularly hopeful that the bombs will be of value in chasing motor bandits.

"Some months ago a Trenton motorcycle policeman was shot and killed by a boy automobile thief fleeing from that city. He had overtaken the car and rode alongside, or within a few lengths, for nearly a mile before he was struck with the fatal bullet. It is contended that had he been equipped with a tear bomb his life would have been saved, in all probability, as he had plenty of opportunity to throw it into the car. Another advantage of the bomb for this kind of work is that it makes a stain on motor varnish by which the car may be recognized by police elsewhere, if the driver escapes his first pursuers.

"'These bombs will not be used against every crowd that creates trouble,' says Superintendent Mills. 'They are for use only against mobs bent on destruction; mobs that assume dangerous proportions and that can not be dispersed by ordinary methods. A bomb squad is being formed for each police division, and these men will be trained in the use of the new weapons. Only men who can keep their heads in emergencies will be appointed to these squads.'"

Courtesy of "The Scientific American."

POLICE TEAR-BOMB.

Showing its size in relation to the human hand.

HOW CHILDREN GROW

TALL CHILDREN reach their full growth sooner than short ones, but growth in height is so regular that a child's height in subsequent years may be foretold with some accuracy. One child may be four or five years older, physiologically, than another whose age is the same in years. Country girls mature earlier than city girls. Children pick out as playmates those of the same degree of maturity, not those of the same age chronologically. Physiological age, or degree of maturity, should be taken into account in educational work and in child-labor legislation, instead of actual years. Growth in weight is more variable than growth in height, and depends more on season and environment. These and other interesting conclusions are drawn by Prof. B. T. Baldwin, director of the Iowa Child Welfare Research Station, in a recent book on "The Physical Growth of Children." We quote as follows from a review in *The University of Iowa Service Bulletin* (Iowa City):

"The height of children doubles during the first six years after birth and the weight increases four times. The greatest increase is during the first year in both height and weight.

"The most significant conclusion for Iowa boys and girls lies in the fact that they are above the average of the United States in height. They begin soon after birth to lose weight in proportion to their height. This becomes more evident as the ages increase. Here is probably a nutritional and health education problem, showing the need for physical examinations, medical inspection and directed play. Rural Iowa children from birth to six years of age are above urban Iowa children in stature and weight.

"As a rule, tall boys and tall girls reach their period of maximum adolescent stature earlier than do short ones.

"Tall children at any age remain relatively tall under normal conditions. Growth in height is comparatively so uniform that one can prophesy with a relatively high degree of accuracy how tall a young child will be at subsequent years.

"The application of mathematical formulæ reveals a great probability that a tall boy or girl at six years of age will be a tall boy or girl at twelve years of age; a tall boy or girl at nine or ten will be tall at fifteen or sixteen years of age. Under the conditions obtaining the height of the boys or girls may be predicted within three or four centimeters for periods of six or eight years.

"Among children who are best developed from a physical point of view there is no fixed age for physiological development. Physiologically speaking, adolescence does not begin at the same chronological age for all normal boys or for all normal girls. Boys or girls of the same chronological age may differ in physiological age from one to four or five years and still be normal in physical development.

"Girls from the country and from the smaller cities (under 11,000 population) mature earlier than those from Chicago and New York, the median ages being respectively thirteen years, seven months, and thirteen years, nine months. This conclusion substantiates the similar conditions found for boys. These results are supplemented by 200 X-ray photographs on normal and superior children, which furnish additional criteria of physiological age.

"Boys not only grow very differently from girls, but their development is decidedly more highly correlated in its varied aspects. There is a biological difference between the growth of boys and girls during these ages from seven to seventeen.

"A few applications of the concept of physiological age to child development may be cited.

"Physiological age has a direct bearing on *physical training* and *directed play*. Not only do children naturally play with boys and girls of their same physiological age, but the types of games in

Photos copyrighted by Kadel & Herbert. Courtesy of "The Popular Science Monthly."

X-RAYS STRONG ENOUGH TO TRAVEL 262 FEET, AS INDICATED, AND PRODUCE RADIOGRAMS SHOWN BELOW

which they participate are dependent upon the stage of physiological maturity.

"Physiological age is directly related to *stages of mental maturation*. The physiologically more mature child has different attitudes, different types of emotions, different interests, than the child who is physically younger tho of the same chronological age. While a child may be precocious intellectually, and have a higher intelligence quotient and pass beyond its chronological age in the development of certain mental traits, other type traits indicative of mental maturity may be undeveloped.

"Another study shows that at each chronological age the physiologically accelerated boys and girls have a higher mental age than those of the average or below the average physiological age.

"The larger and physiologically more mature child may be able to do certain types of school work better, altho of inferior ability in specific traits which have been greatly emphasized by school curricula. No child should be promoted or demoted without taking into consideration his or her physiological age. Girls may be expected to progress more rapidly than boys.

"Child labor legislation should take into consideration the physiological development as well as chronological age and school standing. Some children are sufficiently mature physically to meet the requirements of an age limit of fourteen or sixteen, while others are immature and in a stage of physiological growth where more school training, more physical training and more opportunity for physical development are essential."

X-RAYS GROWING MORE POWERFUL

THE cheering conclusion, recently quoted in these columns, that X-rays are no longer dangerous, owing to improved methods, is not accepted by G. Contremoulins, chief of the principal radiographic laboratories in Paris hospitals, who writes on the subject in *Popular Science Monthly* (New York, October). They may be safe for the operators, and for the patients, but the rays now in use are so powerful that they may do damage to innocent persons at a distance; and Mr. Contremoulins is not so sure that the precautions taken to protect operators are perfectly satisfactory.

Five months after the discovery of X-rays, he says, an exposure of eight hours was required for a radiograph of a profile head, the tube being placed ten inches from the sensitive plate. In April, 1921, a similar image was obtained in four hours at a distance of ninety yards. This means that the radiation is more than twenty thousand times stronger than in 1896. He goes on:

"With the very weak radiation that I have used for my experiments, corresponding to the ordinary radiographic and radioscopic work, it has been easy for me to obtain images of metallic objects and human bones placed on a sensitive plate fifteen feet from the radiating source, altho the rays passed directly through a slab of marble an inch thick, a sheet of lead one-tenth of an inch thick, and a flooring eight inches deep, built of oak boards and rough plaster.

"Fifty feet from this same source I have been able in four hours to fog a photographic plate placed behind a wall of brick and stone twenty inches thick. Also in the same time I have obtained a correct radiograph of a skull and a crab, two hundred and sixty-two feet from the X-ray machine. All these experiments were made with a seventeen-centimeter spark and two milliamperes of current.

"If photographic plates are so readily affected by these rays, we must admit that animal cells also are affected to an appreciable degree. The X-rays that are being used to cure a patient may at the same time inflict radiodermatitis on other persons exposed to their influence in adjoining rooms or buildings. Nothing will suffice for safety but to cover the walls and floors of X-ray rooms with sheets of lead from a quarter to half an inch thick, according to the power of the source and its distance from the lining.

"As an experimenter from the very first discovery of the X-rays, beginning in February, 1896, I shall probably end in the manner of my late associates, but at least my own experience may benefit others. I was able, up to the war, to direct my laboratory at the Necker Hospital without having received injury. Research work with foreign bodies carried on during the war with army material, which allowed no efficacious protection, has given me inflammation of the skin of my hands, justifying my fears.

"Biologic reactions from X-rays take two forms. The first is a skin lesion known as radiodermatitis, caused by the skin absorbing a large quantity of radiations. The second results from the improvements in X-ray tubes and the use of filters absorbing the radiations of long wave length, currently named 'soft radiation.' This reaction takes place deep beneath the skin upon the active cells that are the most vulnerable. It is principally the internal secretion glands that are affected. Among those who continually receive even weak doses, a gradual lessening of vitality takes place, leading slowly to a physiological impoverishment that inevitably carries them off sooner or later.

PHOTOS MADE 262 FEET AWAY

By X-rays traversing the path indicated above by the dotted lines.

"The problem of suitable protection is becoming a serious one. It is no longer a question of 70,000 to 90,000 volts in action, but of 200,000 volts under three milliamperes. And when we reflect that recent investigations in the treatment of cancer show the necessity of twelve to fifteen hour radiations with extremely penetrating rays, we must ask with anxiety what will happen to innocent people in neighboring parts of the building.

"Use of such X-ray energies should be regulated by the authorities along with other 'dangerous occupations.'"

LETTERS - AND - ART

LITERATURE DRAMA MUSIC FINE-ARTS EDUCATION CULTURE

STANDING UP FOR AMERICAN ART

A DECLARATION OF DEPENDENCE is something new for American ears and seemingly something too much for American nerves. So when an eminent portrait painter like Miss Cecilia Beaux told the International Art Congress assembled in Paris that "America has no national art and must continue for many years to come to look to France for inspiration," she spoke words that are meeting repudiation. It was perhaps a desire to hear the eagle in terms of a cooing dove rather than its frequent screaming that led Miss Beaux to say "America is constantly striving for its own national art, and in time it will come, but for many years we shall have to find our chief inspiration in Holland and Italy, and especially in France." Twenty-four countries were represented at the Congress and since, as the Associated Press dispatch informs us, "the delegates were unanimous in agreeing that art should be given the opportunity to promote international amity and prevent future wars," Miss Beaux may have wished to escape any charge of chauvinism. Comfort for wounded feelings may be found in that part of the dispatch declaring that "in the course of informal discussions after the first session some of the delegates said specimens of American art they had seen indicated a national school already had been established in its preliminary stages." One of the earliest aggrieved voices sounds in the Philadelphia *Ledger* which refers to Miss Beaux as a "native of Philadelphia, many times medalist at the Pennsylvania Academy and a Doctor of our University, an artist whom her own community is delighted to honor as her conspicuous attainment has deserved," but doubtless here deserving a rebuke:

"No foolish chauvinism will keep our painters from learning what they can in Europe. But some of them—as is seen each year at the annual exhibition of the Pennsylvania Academy—have found already in this country plenty of material that lends itself to imaginative description with the brush, and have treated it with vigorous individuality of method. If our painters have as a rule eschewed the sensational vagaries of those who defy all conventional ideas of form, proportion and perspective, that very tendency to common sense and self-restraint is, we like to believe, characteristic of the life of America which it is the effort of our own art to depict."

PAINTED BY CECILIA BEAUX.

A Philadelphia artist, who thinks American art must for many years yet look abroad for "inspiration." The opinion is unpopular.

Through its secretary, Julian Bowes, the League of New York Artists, Inc., a society composed of more than 3000 American painters and sculptors, also takes exception to Miss Beaux's words. In his letter to the New York *Tribune*, Mr. Bowes observes:

"In view of this particular artist's remarks it is pleasing to American ears to hear that the French and other nationalities represented at the conference had agreed that the specimens of American art they have seen indicated a national school already established in this country.

"This is not only true, but the American people have now begun a movement to clear the way and make free the exposition of all developments in the arts and crafts. They are demanding the new notes as soon as they can get them and the absolute freedom of the artist in exhibiting his work, that nothing may be lost to the honor and glory of their Republic.

"To-day our oncoming artists are technically as proficient in almost all departments of arts and crafts as were the men of any period of design history.

"America is now turning her attention to the recording of her achievements in art. Architecture has taken a new lien on life, and no longer relies upon the design of the past. American engineers, true artists, have surmounted the highest plane in human achievement, and have long since placed America foremost in civilization.

"American artists are and should be thankful for the traditions of European countries, but it must not be forgotten that we have our own traditions as well. Such men as Robert Fulton, Samuel F. B. Morse, and many others, were artists and gave to the world the steamboat, the submarine and the telegraph. Others of lesser distinction have contributed their share to the civilization in which America leads.

"From the cloud of the World War just concluded America emerges with head erect and with face toward the future. The great spirit of adventure is still in the veins of American artists, and the urge to create has now manifested itself in full force."

Treating the subject of a "national art" broadly, an editorial in *The Tribune* tries to offset the cabled remarks in pointing out that "the quasi-official status of a body of this sort sometimes gives to the pronouncements of its members a sanction and a reverberating effect they do not invariably deserve." Then going on it asks and answers:

"What is a national art? The critic who conclusively defined it would work a miracle, for different nations give it a different significance. In Italy, during the Renaissance, it meant a wide-spread burst of artistic energy, strongly influenced by the patronage of the Church. In Spain art was an imported luxury, only nationalized, rather late in the day, by a handful of brilliant painters, Zurburan, Murillo, El Greco, Velasquez. And, paradoxically, the greatest of these, who might almost be said to constitute the Spanish school, Velasquez, dowered his nation by realizing his own ideas. He points to the core of the whole problem.

"Personality is the central source of every national school. Italian art is the art of a Bellini or a Titian, a Raphael or a Michael Angelo; German art is the art of a Dürer or a Holbein. In the Low Countries it is a Rembrandt or a Hals, a Rubens or a Van Dyck, who stands for the national background. In England it is Hogarth or Reynolds. France is the only country whose art has been nationalized through alliance with the state, and if academic solidarity and discipline have occasionally been justified of their children it is nevertheless true that the outstanding masters of the school have triumphed through sheer personal power, from Claude and Poussin down through Watteau to Ingres, the Romanticists, the Barbizon men and the Impressionists. Briefly, a national art connotes the ministrations of intensely individualized men, and there our very youth, perhaps, has caused us to develop an impressive number of remarkable artists.

"Stuart and Copley affirm the fact, despite their allegiance to eighteenth-century English tradition. Once we come down into the modern era, pausing on admirable painters like Sully and Morse, we encounter some of the highest types to be found anywhere. Inness, Wyant and Homer Martin are among them, pioneers in a landscape school that has never lost its vitality and distinction. Winslow Homer appears, as racy a painter as ever lived. John La Farge enters the field, painter of landscape, flowers and the figure, mural decorator, designer of stained glass, a kind of universal genius. American art produces men of imaginative power like Elihu Vedder, Albert P. Ryder and Abbot Thayer. It adds to the painters of Venice the greatest since Turner, William Gedney Bunce. In creative originality it can claim Whistler, in technical virtuosity Sargent. It has had a Saint-Gaudens in sculpture; in architecture men like Hunt, Richardson and McKim. But we need not multiply names. We have cited as many as are necessary to enforce the point that in our own time, as in the past, a national art is indicated in the emergence of gifted men from a nation's loins."

In matters of form and composition, this writer points out, "our school, as a school, can still profit by discreet contact with French art." But—

"Even the weakness of our rank and file runs the risk of falling into a deeper pit if it leans too confidently on the arid, cut-and-dried formulas into which the Salon has lapsed. Moreover, with all our deficiencies on our heads, it remains true that almost any exhibition of miscellaneous American art to-day will exhale an atmosphere of energy, freshness and sincerity not to be surpassed abroad. We are second to none in abundance of mediocrity. There are quite as many dull and stupid painters in the United States as there are in Paris or London. But the proportion of men of talent is just as encouraging here as there. In landscape painting we are magnificently in the van. This is not a matter of patriotic sentiment; it is a matter of demonstrable fact.

"Nowhere do we meet more frequently than among commentators on American art 'a certain condescension in foreigners.' The English and the French are fond of patronizing us. Before the American meekly kisses the rod he ought to run through a Salon or a Royal Academy. Then let him ask himself if we are really so far behind in the making of a national art. If he considers the only relevant test, the one which we have outlined above, he will admit that an American accent in painting exists; that it is unmistakable, and that it gives us a place among the nations not to be lightly denied."

WHAT CENTRAL EUROPE READS

WITH TAGORE A BEST SELLER in Germany one ought to look for a more peaceful frame of mind among the people of the new republic. But our favorite phrase hardly describes the poet's vogue. "Terrifically popular" is the way Mr. Alfred A. Knopf, the New York bookseller, describes it to an interviewer for the New York *Evening Post*. Our paltry one or two hundred thousand for the most widely read popular novel is not to be mentioned alongside the record of the Indian Seer. Mr. Knopf says:

"When I was in Berlin, Tagore's publisher placed an order for 1,000,000 kilograms—more than 2,000,000 pounds—of paper for his books. That is enough for 3,000,000 volumes."

PEOPLE OF EUROPE, KEEP YOUR "BLESSINGS" TO YOURSELVES.

Thus the *Nebelspalter* (Zurich) represents Tagore's attitude toward European missions in Asia.

Germany is serious minded in its other reading as we learn from the same source:

"Germany has turned to the reading of works on philosophy, art, and religion, and such books are far outselling works of fiction. Such works, for instance, as Keyserling's 'Das Reisetagebuch eines Philosophen' (the Travel Diary of a Philosopher), which is a bulky book in two volumes having more than 1,000 pages, has sold upwards of 50,000 copies in Germany. In addition to Tagore's works, Spengler's 'Das Untergang des Abendlandes' (The Downfall of the Eastern Countries) is having a phenomenal success.

"The adverse exchange has practically cut off the supply of foreign books from Germany. They simply can't afford them. I saw for sale in Munich French books that had been printed in Vienna and English books printed in Berlin."

Mr. Knopf's recent journeyings took him into Scandinavian countries also. His mission was to interest the Continental publishers in the younger American authors, especially novelists, who are almost unknown outside of England. He got a curious side-light on a recent Nobel Prize author, one time a Chicago street-car conductor:

"It was his plan to call on Knut Hamsun. The story runs in Norway that Hamsun is perhaps one of the most difficult men in the world to see, and he has not been interviewed within the memory of man. He is too nervous to meet people, he says, and lives in isolation on his farm near Grimstad, Norway, where he raises stock and writes books.

"'He will not have a single animal on his farm die any other than a natural death,' said Mr. Knopf. 'Nevertheless, he raises stock for profit, and so whenever he has occasion to sell any animals the purchaser must sign a contract not to kill or hurt them.'

"Mr. Knopf learned that to reach Hamsun at Grimstad, he would have to take a steamer at 11 o'clock at night, get off at 4 o'clock in the morning, go to a little hotel near by and wait, catch a boat back at 4:30 o'clock the next morning, to reach his starting point again at 10:30 o'clock that night. Nevertheless, he was undaunted, and asked Hamsun's publisher to try to arrange the *rencontre*.

"But, alas! when the publisher sent a note to Hamsun, he received an emphatic reply. Mr. Hamsun's nerves simply wouldn't stand the ordeal. It upset him to an inconceivable degree to meet any one, any one at all. It couldn't be done. The other day a French colonel, motoring through the country, had stopped at his door, had bowed seven times and said seven words, and the nerve-shattered Hamsun had had to bow seven times and say seven words! It was terrible! He was just now recovering. And then he ended the letter by saying plaintively: 'Isn't it too bad, Mimi has died?' Mimi was a cow, it seems, and he had just had finished for her a lovely new cowshed, but before the last stone was laid, poor Mimi herself lay down and died. Poor Mimi! Her beautiful byre wasted!

"According to Mr. Knopf, Hamsun has never seen even his publisher. All business is transacted by mail, and the writer flatly refuses to talk or meet in person the man who makes his writings into books.

"While Hamsun is the great literary figure of Norway, he is not the most popular. A woman, Sigrid Undset, is the Norwegian Zane Grey or Edgar Rice Burroughs, or Gene Stratton-Porter. Books are not cheap in Norway as they were in the days before the war. Hergesheimer's 'Java Head,' published in paper covers, sold for 9½ kroner, he said, which is little known in Scandinavia. Willa Cather is probably best known. The Scandinavian reader likes 'O Pioneers' and her other works of this flavor.

"Practically the only American books which are published in Germany and the Scandinavian countries are adventure stories, Western and mystery tales, and in general the cheapest of our fiction.

"Believe it or not, 'Main Street' hasn't yet penetrated to Germany. Several hundred copies have been sold in England."

FINGER-PRINTS TO SETTLE ART DISPUTES

ENGLAND'S MINIONS OF THE LAW settle her art problems where her critics fail. The law courts, a few years ago, proved almost the whole tribe of critics at fault over the genuineness of a painting attributed to Romney. Now Scotland Yard has settled an even more difficult problem involving the work of Leonardo da Vinci. The pseudo-Romney was reputed to be a group-portrait of Mrs. Siddons and her sisters, which one famous critic declared he would hold to be Romney's work if God Almighty maintained the opposite. The litigation was ended by the chance discovery of the original sketch signed by Ozias Humphreys. The National Gallery has a "Virgin of the Rocks" similar in essentials to the same subject by Leonardo da Vinci in the Louvre. The British Gallery had paid $45,000 for it, but art connoisseurs were nowise unanimous on the matter of its coming from the same hand. Scotland Yard by its finger-print process proved literally that it did, and the art world is afforded a sensation. In the Boston *Post* occurs the interesting story:

THE LOUVRES LEONARDO

"The Madonna of the Rocks," whose genuineness is unquestioned.

"Modern criminology has given the answer. The police made reply where art critics could not. An expert inspector in the criminal identification department of the Scotland Yard pointed to the finger-prints and said: 'This is the work of Leonardo da Vinci.'

"Sir Charles Holmes, an eminent art critic, one day not long ago determined that it was time, once and for all, to decide if the National Gallery had been tricked out of $45,000 and a claim to a treasure. He knew that much of the exquisite modeling of the oil painting had been done by softening the still wet paint with finger and thumb tips. The prints of these fingers remained clearly defined, no matter who the painter was or how long ago he did his work.

"He did not have to sign his name. On the canvas, in the whorls, arches, loops and dots of his finger-prints he wrote his identity. A half a thousand years ago, perhaps, he never thought of it. It took Holmes to realize it and a modern police criminologist to read that unintentional signature. Great painters in the past were often subject to strange whimsicalities, to odd little tricks of marking a masterpiece so that it could be known, with signature or without, as theirs. But no trick ever was as successful as that of finger-traced hieroglyphic. "It was easy work for Sir Charles Holmes.

"First of all, he selected half a dozen examples of Leonardo's works, about which there was no possible dispute as to authenticity. Then he obtained the collaboration of the police.

"Scotland Yard's expert examined all the finger-prints on the six sure examples. Then he was taken to the Louvre, where he examined the painting there, declaring it undoubtedly genuine. Last of all, he examined the National Gallery painting—and announced also that it was genuine.

"One wonders whether the shadow of Leonardo is happy, now that his trick of making a copy of his own painting has been discovered, and his name has been connected in the papers with the police.

"Leonardo was a man of strange fancies, anyway. The world knows him as one of the greatest of universal geniuses time has ever seen. Not only was he a painter without a superior—to use Gautier's phrase—in the history of art, but also an inventor, architect, engineer, sculptor, naturalist, philosopher and man of science.

"But he was more than all this. Michelangelo was profound, definite, persevering, overwhelming. But Leonardo was, in John Addington Symonds's words, 'the wizard or diviner; to him the Renaissance offers her mystery and lends her magic. Art and science were never separated in his work; and both were not infrequently subservient to some fanciful caprice, some bizarre freak of originality. Curiosity and love of the uncommon ruled his nature.'"

Having settled the question of Leonardo's imitation of himself the next that follows is, "Why should he do it?"

"Leonardo cannot answer. But he did it, for his finger-prints tell the story. One 'Virgin of the Rocks' was a unique masterpiece. But a second 'Virgin of the Rocks' is—what?

"'How mysterious, how charming and how strange,' writes a French critic of the painting at the Louvre, 'is this "Virgin of the Rocks." A kind of basaltic cave, in which flows a stream that through its limpid water shows the pebbles of its bed, shelters the holy group, while beyond, through the arched entrance to the grotto, lies a rocky landscape, sparsely set with trees, wherein a river runs; and all of this is of such an indefinable color that it seems like those faint wonderlands through which we wander in our dreams. And the adorable Madonna, with the pure oval of her cheeks, her exquisite chin, her downcast eyes circled by a shadowy penumbra, on her lips that vague and enigmatic smile which Da Vinci loved to give the faces of his women —she is a type all Leonardo's own, and recalls nothing of Perugino's Virgins, or of Raphael's.'

THE NATIONAL GALLERY EXAMPLE.

Whose genuineness has been established by finger-print tests.

"Tho very similar in general effect 'The Virgin of the Rocks' in the National Gallery differs from that in the Louvre in one important particular. In the former the angel does not look directly out of the picture nor point to the infant Baptist. The gilt nimbuses over the heads of the three principal figures, as well as the reed cross which rests on St. John's shoulder, are additions of a comparatively late period, and the right hand of the Virgin has been repainted. In general, the National Gallery picture is softer in outline and less severe.

"The weight of criticism in recent years was in favor of the hypothesis that the Louvre picture was the original, and that the 'Virgin of the Rocks' in the National Gallery was a replica, probably painted under the master's supervision and perhaps in his studio. It was imagined that the English-owned painting had been executed by Ambrogio de Predis.

"However, the affair is settled now. A whim of the whimsical Leonardo started it. The love of art critics for argument and the mystery of the two copies continued it. But it took a police inspector to end it."

Leonardo was the foremost scientist of his age, but the Cincinnati *Times-Star* thinks he would have "scoffed had he been told by medieval savants that five hundred years after he had painted certain of his virgins, the authenticity of his work would be proven by the thumb-prints which he unconsciously had left upon his immortal canvases."

"But we of to-day look upon this latest and most novel use of finger-print science almost as a matter of routine. Nature never made two thumbs precisely alike. From the day of Adam each human being has had his own private pattern of whorls and loops upon fingers and thumbs. Leonardo da Vinci, then, left upon his pictures an autograph which never could be forged, never altered. When with his thumb he rubbed the colors on his famous 'Virgin,' which now hangs in the Louvre, and when eleven years later he did the unprecedented thing of reproducing an original work he laid the groundwork of a dispute which was to last for centuries. . . . After five centuries an art mystery of the first order has been solved by deciphering the mysterious copyright and certificate of identity with which nature endows each of her children. Such a solution would have been impossible even a generation or two ago."

"PEPYS STREET."—Samuel Pepys is a familiar name in British and American journalism, tho the man lived so long ago. His style lends itself to gossiping columnists. Now it appears that a London street is to be named for him, as we learn from *The Daily Telegraph:*

"A happy thought has come to the City Corporation. It is going to name one of its ways Samuel Pepys street (possibly plain Pepys street), and that a way which is intimately associated with the diarist. That is as it should be. If there is a typical Londoner, surely it is old Pepys. What stone of London did he not know? A man of affairs before all things, a man of middle-class origin, as we should say to-day, though thrown into constant contact with the great—and, as his not inconsiderable 'gettings' accumulated, with some pretentions himself to be of 'the quality'—Pepys was quite unlike his contemporary diarist, John Evelyn. The last-named traveled the world, and delighted to tell us about it, with some grandiloquence. Pepys had traveled London, no man who has done that thoroughly can be said to be ill-equipped. Both were egoists, but there is a naïveté about Samuel Pepys' egoism which has more charm, is much more alluring than Evelyn's cold correctness. Evelyn was, I fear, a prig, and to his companions, I feel sure, a bore. He never forgot his birth and station, having no reason to do so. Perhaps Pepys, whose vanity in himself is an enduring delight, thought that he had such reason."

TIME TO CLEAN UP MOVIE MORALS

DEBAUCHERIES in the moving-picture world, as recently exposed in the daily papers, have aroused indignant denunciations both in the pulpit and in secular quarters, and the Detroit *Free Press* perhaps expresses a common opinion when it says that the time has come for a general "cleaning-up" of the motion-picture industry. What the demand for censorship has been unable to accomplish, thinks *The News*, of the same city, "promises to be most thoroughly accomplished through the revelations of the Arbuckle case." The recent tragedy in San Francisco has served to throw again an unwelcome spotlight on the motion-picture industry as a whole, and to reveal, as we are told in effect, that many of the popular idols have feet of clay.

In more than one instance the "stars" are solemnly warned against the easy assumption accredited to them that the "eccentricities of genius," as their moral lapses have been rather euphemistically termed, will excuse them from accountability to ordinary law and custom. On the other hand, there is a disposition among most of the papers not to condemn all members of the movie world because of the faults of a few. More and more often, however, the mirror of its vices is being held up to the motion-picture industry by religious leaders of all denominations.

THE GOOD THAT COMES FROM EVIL

—Thomas in the Detroit *News*.

"The motion-picture business to-day is rotten," said the Rev. Dr. John Roach Straton, pastor of Calvary Baptist Church, in New York, who is one of several ministers who have publicly denounced the movie people. As quoted in the New York papers, Dr. Straton charged that the industry "is rotten in its management, as some of the more reputable producers themselves have been saying recently in magazine articles. It is rotten in its ideals. The dollar-mark is over it all, and because those who mainly control it have found out that an appeal to the salacious and the sensuous increases their dividends, they are dragging all the people, including the youth of the nation, through a silly, sordid, sensuous stream of moral infamy." Other critics have not been less sparing, and the Springfield *Republican* believes that "the public will regard the conditions revealed in the Arbuckle case as characteristic of the industry as a whole. It will associate this picture of depravity with the depravity of the film."

"What the screen persons do with their souls is their own business," says *Columbia*, official organ of the Knights of Columbus; "but there is abounding evidence that the motion-picture has been anything but a moral force in the life of the nation." A few more scandals, "and public opinion, decent public opinion, will demand that some steps be taken to curb people who are paid, and paid well, to entertain, from assuming that they are privileged to outrage even such notions of Christian decency as survive in this imperfect age of the 'screen.'" Without passing on the guilt or innocence of the comedian, says *The Catholic Bulletin* (Cleveland), "the champions of clean movies declare that the revelations attending the case are of themselves sufficient to show that the source of the moving pictures in many cases is so low morally that their productions can not escape the taint." Yet *The Baltimore Catholic Review* declares that "for months movie-producers have called those who have protested against some of our nauseating pictures prudes and illiterates, while these producers were pampering uneducated, shallow-minded, good-looking, empty-pated 'swell-heads.'" False standards are created by the movie hero, declares *The Catholic Standard and Times* (Philadelphia):

"He is idolized and worshiped by the public, especially by the young. His moral shortcomings are readily condoned and even glorified. A glamor surrounds him, which even transfigures his ethical defects. . . . In this way the standards of morality are perverted and much harm is done to the young generation that learns to look up to men and women who show but scant respect for virtue and defy the law of God and man.

"The atmosphere of the movie colony appears to be thoroughly unwholesome. The Ten Commandments seem to be unknown or entirely forgotten in those quarters. Men live as if they had no responsibilities. The main reason for this condition is the total commercialization of the film industry. Mammon has stamped upon it his degrading seal. So it has happened that fabulous fortunes have come into the hands of men and women that were devoid of moral discipline and to whom the sudden acquisition of wealth could not but be disastrous.

"If things are so, it stands to reason that no elevating influences can come from the movies. A commercially exploited enterprise never has a beneficent effect. Insidious and evil influences will reach out from the screen as long as moral corruption holds sway behind the camera. Good and evil influences are personal irradiations and can never be dissociated from the person itself."

"Such things should be no surprize to us," says *The Presbyterian Advocate*. When people with little character "are made rich beyond the dreams of avarice we should not be surprized at their exhibiting a lack of self-control at which decency must shudder." Somewhat similarly, *The Churchman* (Episcopal) believes that "there is too much money in the moving-picture business, not only for the good of the actor's art, but for the morals of the film artists." Of some of the celebrities this journal says "their morals, or immorals, invade our households; their charms and their vices assault us at every turn; their names are household words. Where is this to end?" However, "attacking the movies in general, in the hope of diminishing the effect on the public mind of some of their abuses, is bad policy on the part of clergymen or other custodians of public morals," declares the Boston *Transcript*. "The movies can not be displaced from their position as the cheapest and most popular of amusements" and "the chance which they afford for instruction and a readily available means of moral guidance is so great that it would be folly to attack them as a demoralizing agency." In fact,

"To say that the whole tendency of the business is demoralizing is to say that mankind is totally bad and hopeless. And as a matter of fact, the major tendency in the business is just the other way. The people as a rule not only insist upon having vice punished and virtue rewarded on the films, but they often rise up in wrath against such film atrocities as are attempted by unscrupulous parties. And always there are available the services of national and local censorship, which are easily and effectively applied.

"To crusade against the movies in general, and spread abroad wholesale denunciations, is exactly on a parallel with the old-time pulpit denunciation of the whole acting stage as the work of the devil. Three-quarters of a century ago there were pulpit orators who demanded the suppression of the theaters altogether. We may see what became of that agitation. The theater won out because the people wanted it, and on the whole it has been an agency of public culture and morality. The same fate will overtake any wholesale protest against the movies. The film world will be purged of its evils by the sure process of time and a bettering public judgment."

THE PASSING OF THE BIRCH

CORPORAL PUNISHMENT is not conducive to moral discipline, says the Austin *Statesman*, taking issue with the theory that the "absence of the birch behind the door" is responsible for so many graduates into crime. As quoted in these pages on August 27, Judge Alfred J. Talley, of the Court of General Sessions, New York, said that corporal punishment is the only sure kind of discipline and that the parents are to blame for much of the moral laxity now existing. This claim "is untrue," says *The Statesman*, arguing that "juvenile delinquency proved that the old restraints had become ineffective and could not be kept up." And the assumption that early correction by corporal punishment will obviate any necessity of correction later ignores, we are told, "the fact that there was a time when this form of punishment extended over the entire term of life," and that "it has been progressively reduced with the advance of civilization and the coming into operation of social influences." As a matter of fact, it is argued further, "the removal of former restraints is likely to cause one to become the victim of those very impulses whose purpose they were to suppress. This is the most probable cause of the crime wave among the youth of the nation, and yet the judge advises a return to the ineffectual methods which were partially abandoned as a result of the increase in delinquency." As it is now,

"The social life which has begun to dawn for children has created a public interest in childhood which is opposed to the old restraints, and the enjoyment of general interests by children makes them no longer amenable to physical correction. They have acquired the faculty of reason and, though outwardly yielding, maintain a moral dissent and continue to concentrate on their own aims and purposes regardless of their parents' wishes. This is the most distressing and significant of all indications that the old restraints cannot possibly be made effective. It seems inevitable that we must eventually adopt the positive method with children, as we have with adults, by drawing them into an association and cultivating general interests out of which may arise common rights and common duties and the development of a sentiment which will express the force of such associations and be adequate to the discharge of any necessary obligations. This we can do by thinking and acting with them, and not for them; by respecting their feelings and treating their faults as real tho venial, and granting them some freedom of action. Necessary restraints there must be, but such as are imposed by experience—not such as are arbitrarily inflicted."

THE CHURCH'S BIG CHANCE

SKIN-DEEP RELIGION will not help relieve the unemployment situation which looms up as the big problem which Church and Government must tackle together. The crisis demands all our efforts, and offers, moreover, "a great opportunity to the Church of Christ to express the Christian spirit in quick and generous action." President Harding called his conference of national figures to discuss ways and means of alleviating the unemployment conditions, and the churches, we are told with some emphasis, should not hesitate to act. The picture, while dark, is not without its hopeful aspects, writes Dr. Worth M. Tippy in *The Christian Herald*. Dr. Tippy, who is Secretary of the Commission on the Church and Social Service, has made an investigation of the situation, and finds some improvement in the agricultural States and in a few industrial centers. Workers are displaying the proper spirit in helping each other, but what is, perhaps, more cheering and significant is that "employers very generally are trying to hold their employees together, distributing work so as to make it possible for families to live." They have found it pays to keep their men together, but "they are strongly influenced also by human consideration. Instead of taking advantage of the situation, thousands of firms are jeopardizing their capital to keep men at work." In spite of all the alleviating circumstances, however, the situation is perilous, and the writer is convinced that we shall need all our strength in the coming months to meet it.

Neighborliness, friendliness, charity, he urges, must be exprest in full measure. Money must be provided for local charity organizations. The offering "must be big-visioned and generous, or it will miserably fail of the opportunity." For neither the structure of civilized society nor the practical value of Christianity in human relations, says *The Continent* (Presbyterian), "can be put to any severer test than when men ready to work can find no means of livelihood for themselves or those depending on them. A religion indifferent to the pain and strain inflicted on self-reliant men under such circumstances would deserve the scorn of humanity." As it is, the man who is unable to get work is the figure, we are told, before whom the modern industrial organization stands worse abashed than before any other of its accusers. Socialism would never appeal to half the number who now advocate it, if it were not for the oft-recurring specter of hunger.

"Those therefore who are convinced that there is another way to solve this problem without cutting the great nerve of individual responsibility which now energizes civilization are placed this autumn where they need to bestir themselves if their opinion is to be vindicated. The unemployed must receive this winter a brotherly care lifted far above condescending charity. It must be a care that will set an example for future workless periods (if they cannot be avoided) and it must be demonstrative proof that society knows how to take over the burdens of the weak on the shoulders of the strong, prosperous and fortunate. That the American soul is feeling all this and means to realize it is encouragingly signified both by the impulses at Washington which have brought about President Harding's conference on unemployment and by the popular sympathy already in lively evidence for the purposes of that gathering. The churches should be foremost in upholding any policy it adopts.

"The churches, too, should remember that experiments in Christian communism attempted by the Disciples of the Lord in apostolic times were prompted by no economic theory but solely by fellow-feeling for brothers and sisters in need. The method did not prove a permanent working method, but its spirit was perfectly Christian. And still to-day a thorough Christian confronting want will find it impossible to say that 'aught of the things he possesses is his own.' While any soul willing to labor and serve lacks the elemental human necessities, private hoarding, however legal, cannot be morally tolerable to any one who has walked with Christ."

The one encouraging feature of the situation, thinks the Boston *Pilot* (Catholic), has been the absence of acute suffering

But we must remember that savings accounts are nearly exhausted, and that conditions are becoming more critical. Hope remains, however, for—

"God is still in the Heavens and the world is making heroic efforts to recover from the lesions of war and materialism. In the present dark outlook caused by the shadow of unemployment, the two virtues most needed are courage and encouragement. Those who find themselves like Dante in the dark and somber wood will emerge like him to the Empyrean of light and happiness if they have his hardihood and faith."

SQUABBLING SECTS IN LIBERIA

DENOMINATIONAL BIGOTS and conflicting creeds, says a writer in the field, should have no place in the program to Christianize Liberia, but rather should be considered "a menace and a handicap to the highest welfare of both the Christian Church and the Nation." The negro republic, writes John H. Reed in *The Liberia Methodist*, a recently founded journal of which he is the editor, is the chief gateway to the "Dark Continent," and its population must be the leaven for the whole mass of Africa. Therefore "it behooves the wise ecclesiastical leaders of all the various denominations to catch the significance of this world vision and situation, and accordingly form zones of influence in their present missionary operations in the Republic of Liberia." Here, we are told, a nation is in formation, and conflicting religious forces "must only tend to disrupt and disorganize the governmental agencies at work in the building of the State." In the second place,

"Such a missionary propaganda becomes a waste of men and means when the chief aim of these ecclesiastical leaders in the field is the making of Baptists, Methodists, Episcopalians, Presbyterians, Lutherans, or any other denominational cult, based upon the dead husks of worn-out tenets, dogmas, creeds and antiquated doctrines, foisted upon the heathen mind for the mere sake of numbers, thereby mobilizing the forces of baptized heathenism, which becomes a more potent foe to Christian civilization than if the heathen population were left alone to work out its own eternal destiny. The overlapping of these denominations for the past three-quarters of a century has been, and is now, a fruitless effort at so-called African redemption within this Republic. Altar against altar, five struggling churches and congregations where there should be one, is the sad story of missionary operations of the denominations along the seacoast of Liberia, where one is piled on the other with the din and confusion of church bells, calling together the remnant of a shattered civilized population in the struggling attempt to perpetuate the denominational unit, while the extensive heathen population, numbering fully ninety-seven per cent. of the whole population of the Republic, still stalks the hinterlands in the aimless and hopeless quest for the UNKNOWN GOD."

Another trouble encountered is the constant influx of "the self-appointed, independent missionary, whose sole stock in trade is to claim a complete monopoly of the oracles of God and gift of the Holy Spirit to the exclusion of the other denominational bodies." These independent propagandists find a fruitful source of income in the American public, we are told, and thus divert much money from authentic channels. So the hour has struck when the benevolent agencies of foreign mission boards must begin forming a Christian solidarity for the salvation of the African republic. And—

"Finally, the most significant fact in connection with such a movement is that Liberia stands as the only open door into which the various denominational benevolent boards can enter without let or hindrance on part of the government. Europe is in Africa, as already indicated, carrying forward the mightiest industrial and commercial propaganda, possibly, in the history of civilized nations. Liberia is the last expression of self-government and self-determination on part of the darker, backward peoples, and therefore demands, not ecclesiastical and denominational segregation, but instead complete unification for the successful outcome of the Black Man at nation-building. Anything else becomes a fearful travesty upon the Church of Jesus Christ, which stands as the fountain-head of the world's highest and best civilization. Let there be concord, peace, harmony, not discord, war, separation Where the Church leads, the Nation must follow."

PROTESTANT NEGLECT OF THE SICK

IN NEGLECTING CARE OF THE SICK and allowing this form of Christian fellowship to become almost entirely commercialized, "Protestantism has sold one of its most precious birthrights for a mess of denominational pottage," complains a Protestant organ, *The Herald of Gospel Liberty* (Christian), which believes that if Protestantism continues the neglect it will never regain the leadership in this field of ministry. Once in every community, we are told, the Church endeared itself to the people because of its devotion to the homes of the sick, regardless of whether they were of its own membership or not. "Good old mothers of some church were always at every childbirth, and men and women of some church were always prompt and profuse in their offers to 'sit up with the sick' and generous with fruits and dainties and sick-room comforts." It was a great opportunity for the Church, and "a satisfying and spiritual exercise for those who rendered the service." Now, however, many pastors and churches have not awakened to how rapidly this field is being taken from them. The visiting nurse, sent out by the city or by the Red Cross, is taking the place of the kindly neighbor; the care of the sick has become a science, and there is no longer much room for amateur service. "In the real and vital and life-saving ministry of the sick, the Church is not represented any more at all in the average home during the hours of most severe sickness, at the very time when hearts are most anxious and distrest and most susceptible to the rightly exprest tenderness and comfort of Jesus Christ."

Set in strong contrast to this, says this Protestant paper, is the record of the Catholic Church, which, since early times, "has had its hospitals, its brotherhoods and sisterhoods devoted to the most loving and unselfish care of the poor and afflicted," and whose young women have entered its orders of nursing "with a consecration and a self-abnegation that is unequaled in Protestantism, even on the mission field itself." As for Protestantism:

"In its churches, hospital service and the care of the sick receive such an incidental and minor attention as to be negligible indeed as a spiritual quickening or a motive of Christian devotion and consecration. Only a few, and those of the larger denominations, make any pretense of building hospitals and developing a passionate loyalty and consecration to this service in the hearts of the people. In literally thousands of Protestant churches, there is not one single invitation given from year's end to year's end for offerings for the care of the sick and the afflicted—even in their own membership. Comparatively few help the great hospitals of the city, with the crying need in all of them for more free service for the poor. And not only, even in the denominations which maintain hospitals, is it rare indeed for any pastor to present the claims of nursing to his young womanhood as a field of marvelous opportunity for Christ's service; but in most Protestant churches both pastors and parents rather discourage young women from becoming nurses—because of the hard and slavish work. . . . An appeal to Protestant girls to become nurses for the sake of Christ and in the spirit of Christ, with the same motive and the same consecration with which they would become foreign missionaries, is a thing almost unknown among our churches—as is also any generous and sufficient plan among local Protestant churches to help take care of the sick and the afflicted. . . .

"In every community, the churches ought to unite in an intelligently planned and comprehensive effort to furnish visiting nurses and sick-room comforts and equipment for every home where there is sickness; and, in the name of the church of Jesus Christ, to have a vital participating part in ministering to the diseased and maimed and physically unfortunate in every community."

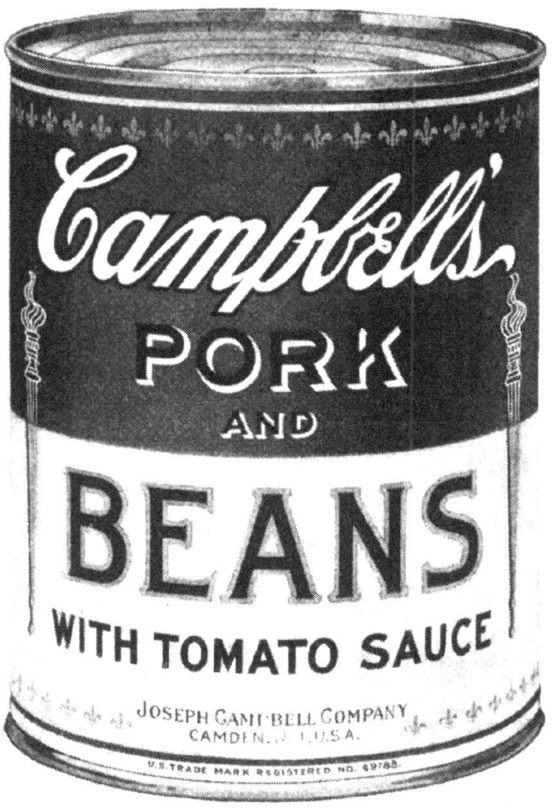

You can eat them plentifully!

Campbell's Beans are slow-cooked. This means that they are thoroughly cooked. Indeed, they are so wholesome and so easily digested that parents find them ideal food for the children. These beans may be eaten with the full assurance that they will be readily assimilated and will yield rich, substantial nourishment. Wonderful tomato sauce!

12 cents a can

Except in Rocky Mountain States and in Canada

Campbell's

THE BEANS THAT ARE SLOW-COOKED AND DIGESTIBLE

CURRENT - POETRY

Unsolicited contributions to this department cannot be returned.

TRIBUTE to the month is ample in *Contemporary Verse* (October), and the power of nature to induce varying moods is freely illustrated. One may choose from the three samples we give here as one's own reactions impel, only Mr. Percy bears much resemblance to the author of "Thanatopsis":

OCTOBER

By William Alexander Percy

These are the days, too few, that I would hold,
Of birds that pause before they seek the south,
Of leaves that rustle not, but, dying, fall
In richer beauty than they ever lived.

Of light that is too merciful at last
To be all gold, but aureoles with blue
Or such dim purple as the moon exhales,
The wasted brambles and the wounded trees.

Now are untended ways made beautiful
By cobweb flowers, the wistfullest I know,
Rememberers of all forgotten dead—
Wild asters in my country they are called.

At last it is too late for all regret,
Too late for deeds, and dreams hold no reproach,
And might have been is vague as what may be
And all is well tho much has never been.

OCTOBER

By Bernice Lesbia Kenyon

Come out, Playfellow! Do you hear me sing
And beat against the door? Come out! Come out!
Let us put all the settling leaves to rout,
And breathe out silver frost at everything!
Let us match swiftness with the sea-bird's wing,
And laugh into the sunlight, laugh and shout
That day is up, the great gods are about!
Let our loud calling make the hillsides ring!
What if we know that winter is supreme,
That autumn fades, that all this life must die—
That in the end our love is only dream,
And sometime in dead brightness all will lie?
We have to-day, with the whole earth agleam,
The sun to flaunt in, and the voice to cry!

OCTOBER

By Margaret McGee

I must stretch, I must drag at myself,
I must tug up, and run,
I must fall, I must twist, I must leap—
For the summer is done.
I must whirl with the ruddy brown dust in the road
Round and round,
Tumbling over and flying and falling
Like leaves on the ground.
I must crimson my cheek like the sumac
With blood that's astir,
And grow firm like the jolly sweet nut
In the ripening burr.
I must shine, I must shimmer and sing like the sun,
Marching by.
I must tag-heel the wind of this joy to its lair
In the sky.

BANTERING the ocean has not been the frequent way with poets, so the whimsical familiarity of some of these phrases supplies a fresh note. There is always a way of seeing the wave's majesty:

SEA QUATRAINS

By Grant H. Code

I

Too fast the silly white-caps run
Their helter-skelter races;
They stumble when the goal is won
And fall upon their faces.

II

A purple light is shaken over
The greener ocean shadows,
Like clover on the cooler depths
Of grass in upland meadows.

III

The sea hangs kelp upon the sand
Like garlands on a grave,
Mourning the dead and silent land
With every living wave.

IV

The breakers thunder in the night
With which the sea is drenched
Only one plunging line is white;
Even the stars are quenched.

V

The fairest ship ever a wreck
Had not so white a sail
As this fair wave cast up to break,
Driven before the gale.

SINCE the days of Josiah Flint the romance of tramp life, as the tramp from our streets, has grown rarer in our literature. These songs in *The Measure* (New York) seem to catch the pathos as well as the romance of the tramp's lot:

TRAMP SONGS

By Edwin Ford Piper

UNDER ROOF

The road is long, it has no end,
Weary traveler,
A hard, hard road if you got no friend—
Rain—rain on the roof.

A fearful road on a pitch dark night,
Lonely traveler,
For the wind and the rain they growl and bite—
Rain—rain on the roof.

The nightbirds wail, the wild beasts cry,
Lonely traveler
And ghosts on the moaning wind go by—
Rain—rain on the roof.

Tell your tale while the storm is loud,
Weary traveler,
Pipe smoke for an incense cloud—
Rain—rain on the roof.

BALM

The balm is lush, the soil is rich,
And purple asters blow
Between the hedge and the roadside ditch
To watch men come and go.
And it's fare you well,
I am left alone.

The wind is loud and the wind is low,
And the leaves say, "hush and hush,"
To the ripening hours of afternoon
When a warbler sings or a thrush.
And it's fare you well,
I am left alone.

They saw where the traveler laid him down—
The dove and the cuckoo,
The balm and the feverfew—
To slumber deep in a long, long sleep—
Balm in the moonlit dew,
Balm in the moonlit dew!
And it's fare you well,
I am left alone.

OLD MAN WINTER

Go down the road, and down the road
By leafless hedge and willow;
And stretch your bones on the frosty ground
With shoes to make a pillow.
But it's south, boys, south!
Run away from old man winter.

"O rain come wet me, sun come dry me,
Wind o' winter don't come a-nigh me!"

It's late to limp by hill and plain
In rag o' coat and breeches;
The dogs they chase me out of the road
And hunt me down the ditches.
But it's south, boys, south!
And run from old man winter.

"O rain come wet me, sun come dry m
Sleet o' winter don't come a-nigh m

I follow the duck and the mourning dove,
I'm headed south for winter;
I'll throw my feet on a Dixie street
Or lie in jail for the winter.
And it's south, boys, south!
Away from old man winter.

"Rain come wet me, sun come dry me
Moonlit snow, O don't come a-nigh m

THE tang of autumn is in this p from the September *Measure* in a s on "Judith of Minnewaukan," an id Dakota.

MORNING AND NIGHT

By Maxwell Anderson

The cloud-bank lies in a red-gold ring;
The wind-break thins of leaves;
From the red-gold fields
They have carried the sheaves.

It will be night again. The lights
Come out above the piers,
Come out again in the wind-searched dark
And the earth turns heavily down the years.

After the night it will again be morning;
Alone between the lake and sky
Judith remembers night and morning,
And morning and night pass by.

Spring, and the unknown farm-hands
Sow the gray land to the north with grain;
Autumn, and unknown harvesters
Come back for the grain again.

When a north wind blows she has heard th
voices
On the wind blown and torn;
They pass in a mask of shadows;
Life passes; noon and night and morn.

Slit the thin cobweb, let the thread burn throug
Why should it hold her longer to the play
Who has found only morning answering an
night—
Only dark answering day?

A CORRESPONDENT speaks of the follow ing from *Scribner's* (October) that "it s nicely describes a universal experience." How universal it is may be a question. We give the poem as a test:

PANTHER! PANTHER!

By John Hall Wheelock

There is a panther caged within my breast,
But what his name there is no breast shall know
Save mine, nor what it is that drives him so,
Backward and forward, in relentless quest:
That silent rage, baffled but unsuppressed,
The soft pad of those stealthy feet that go
Over my body's prison to and fro,
Trying the walls forever without rest.

All day I feed him with my living heart,
But when the night puts forth her dreams and stars
The inexorable Frenzy reawakes;
His wrath is hurled upon the trembling bars,
The eternal passion stretches me apart—
And I lie silent, but my body shakes.

GOODYEAR BELTS

100% Goodyear Belt Equipment

Installed according to G.T.M. recommendation at REEVES PLANT

Cleveland Builders' Supply and Brick Company, Cleveland, Ohio.

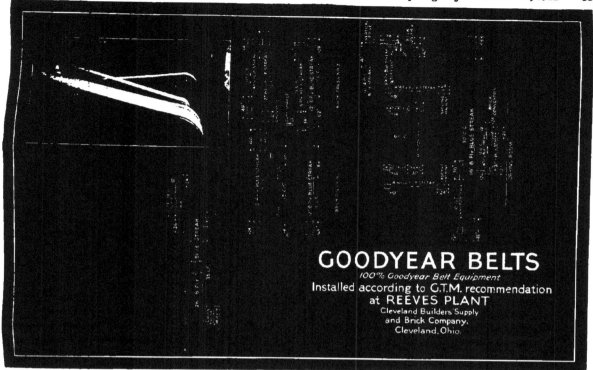

Blueprint sketch of the 100%-Goodyear-belted Reeves plant of the Cleveland Builders' Supply and Brick Company, Cleveland, Ohio, with insert photograph of the mud-drag drive

Thirty-one Plants—and the G.T.M.

They thought that belt woes were a necessary evil, in the plants and warehouses of the Cleveland Builders' Supply and Brick Company, Cleveland, Ohio. So they were putting up with a lot of grief from many kinds of belting—slippage, loss of valuable power, production time lost through shutdowns for repairs to belts, and continual, expensive replacement of belting.

They were keenly interested when the G.T.M.—Goodyear Technical Man—told them he had a plan for the ending of belt troubles and the increasing of belt service. They agreed that a belt exactly designed and scientifically specified to the conditions of service should work more efficiently and economically, and last a longer time.

"We'll test your Analysis Plan," said E. W. Farr, Director in Charge of Production. And he led the G.T.M. to the champion belt-eater in the Reeves plant—the notorious mud drag. "Every day throughout the winter," he said, "this belt must pull tons of frozen clay, sometimes mixed with rock. The best belts we have had on this drive lasted from three weeks to six months."

The G.T.M. studied that drive, and recommended a Goodyear Blue Streak Belt, 8-inch, 6-ply. That belt is on the mud-drag job today, after four years of continuous, trouble-free service.

Eventually, the entire plant was equipped with Goodyear Belts, and the G.T.M. analysis extended, drive by drive, to the Company's 31 plants and warehouses.

Goodyear Belts hold records for economy, efficiency and long life in every one of the Company's plants today. In one of the warehouses, a Goodyear Wyoga Conveyor doubled the number of cars unloaded per hour. On the tile machine at the Brookside plant, a Goodyear Blue Streak already has equaled the run of the best previous belting, and looks good for months to come. Another, in the Vernon plant, has lasted two years in first-class condition, as against 15 months for its predecessor. Since the Reeves plant has been 100% Goodyear belted, the production has doubled.

You can get the same service from the G.T.M. For further information about the Goodyear Analysis Plan or about Goodyear Belts for Transmission and Conveying, write to The Goodyear Tire & Rubber Company, Akron, Ohio, or Los Angeles, California.

PERSONAL · GLIMPSES

THE WIDENING AIR-WEB OVER EUROPE

A NEW WEB OF TRANSPORTATION is beginning to cover the world, an air-web high above the earth-going systems already in existence. It is growing "slowly and with as much precision and method as a spider weaves her home between two towering stalks," observes one of the many journalists whose attention has been attracted by this new conquest of the air. The center of the web, the place where the greatest activity is to be seen, "from where all the slender threads are sent out to ever increasing spans," is not in the birth-place of aviation, the United States. The countries of continental Europe, particularly France and Germany, are leading in the development, with England and Italy close seconds. Almost every capital in Europe, except Berlin, is now linked with Paris, or about to be, by regular air lines, many with daily service. In Germany, the air lanes are shorter, being mostly confined to the nation's own territory, but, it appears, they are hardly less thoroughly developed and they connect with lines that lead nearly everywhere, except to Paris. It was in Germany that a New York *Times* correspondent, in response to a telephone call, received an aerial time table, "the first complete publication of its sort in history," in the correspondent's belief.

"Its mere existence," he comments, "not to speak of its contents, is surely a striking witness to Germany's development of aerial transport. A substantial booklet of nearly 100 pages, it is as matter-of-fact and substantial as Bradshaw's European Railway Time Table." *Aerial Age* (London) quotes him further:

> Fourteen pages alone are filled with the details of regular daily or twice daily services to places within the borders of Germany. They give to the minute the times of departures and arrivals. There is not even a saving clause about wind and weather permitting, so that it requires quite a mental effort to realize that before one are the pathless tracks of the air and not steel railroads.
>
> By arrangements with Holland and other neighboring countries long distance services are linked up with England and Scandinavia. There is a map which shows at a glance the principal daily services inside Germany and their communications with overseas routes.
>
> To this regular passenger transportation all sorts of subsidiary services are being added. The flying post, for instance, is rapidly developing, especially as it is not burdened with any

one has to do to insure this speedy delivery is to mark the letter "by flying post," and drop it into any letter box in the ordinary way. In this matter, too, international arrangements have been made so that a letter posted in Berlin at 7:30 o'clock in the morning reaches London, for example, at 5:30 the same evening.

One interesting use of the aeroplane, to which special attention is directed, is for keeping the rest of Germany in swift touch with the lost territories, such as Danzig, or areas like Memel, whose fate is not yet determined, so that the populations of these districts shall not cease to imbibe the true gospel of Deutschtum.

Aeroplanes leave Berlin early every morning loaded with newspapers. Hydroplanes serve the same purpose for the Island of Sylt, off the coast of Schleswig, leaving Hamburg immediately on the arrival of the Berlin journals by train.

Reverting to the aerial *Bradshaw*, a glance at the advertisements reveals still further enterprise. Here, for example, is the Hamburg-American line offering its own services to any town in Germany. It will send passengers or goods by special aeroplanes available to start at the shortest of notice. Another firm supplies aerial photographs, suggesting their particular desirability for enterprising financiers on the lookout for suitable sites for establishing new settlements and spas.

LINES OF COMMUNICATION THAT RUN "AS THE CROW FLIES"

The widening air-web above Europe, the main French and German lines of which are here shown, permits transportation for the first time in history to take the shortest route between two points, a straight line. Both French and German lines connect, either directly or through other systems, with most of the capitals of Europe, but it is notable that there is as yet no route between Berlin and Paris.

One of the German lines referred to above as planned to keep Germany in touch with her lost areas, or at least her separated areas, is the Lloyd Ostflug, between Germany and the part of Prussia still left of her. According to *The Aeroplane* of London:

> It was incorporated in November last with a capital of 4,000,000 marks. The well-known Junkers Works at Dessau, the Ostdeutscher Landwerkstatten at Seerappen, the Norddeutscher Lloyd and the Albatross Airplane factory at Johannisthal, near Berlin, are all interested in this new company, whose main office is at the capital. It was formed to insure rapid transport primarily between Germany and that part of Prussia separated from Germany now by the new Polish territory, and named Ostpreussen (East Prussia). It is intended soon to extend the service farther East, particularly to Kovno in Lithuania and Moscow in Russia. The Berlin-Schneidemuhl-Danzig-Königsberg service began last December. A great deal of information and experience is being gained for the eventual intended extension to the East, but at the moment many difficulties have to be surmounted, especially those of a political character. The Polish Government refuses to allow the machines to fly over Polish territory between Danzig and Germany, with the result that they are compelled to fly over the sea between Danzig and Schneidemuhl, and latterly also between Stettin and Danzig. Recently a change of route was required, so that it is now Berlin-Stettin-Danzig-Königs-

STOP PAYING *these needless expenses*

Do you know that an average of one dollar out of every three spent in running a car goes for repairs?

Do you realize that one-fifth of the investment in the average motor car is lost each year through rapid depreciation?

These are tolls—needless expenses—that motorists are paying *largely because of faulty lubrication*—the use of oils poor in quality or wrong in type.

Think of this tremendous waste—especially when need for greater economy is urgent—when you want a dollar's worth for every dollar you spend!

How can you eliminate faulty lubrication with all its evils and wastes? The only answer is—buy lubrication instead of just "oil", by making certain the oil you use is the right lubricant for your particular engine.

Motorists who use SUNOCO, the six-type non-compounded motor oil, take no chances. The use of Sunoco guarantees proper lubrication for any design of engine—winter or summer.

Sunoco is the highest quality and most scientifically accurate motor lubricant possible to manufacture—entirely different from ordinary oil. It is made in six types but *only one quality*—no "seconds" to confuse you.

Sunoco eliminates the trouble and expense of carbon—gives greater power and mileage on less gasoline and oil—reduces repair bills and adds greatly to the life of your car.

Put Sunoco to the test. Have your crankcase drained, cleaned and filled with the type of Sunoco specified for your particular car by the dealer's "Sunoco Lubrication Guide."

Make certain, also, that you get *genuine* Sunoco. Examine the container from which Sunoco is drawn, or better still, buy it in sealed cans or drums.

Every motorist should have a copy of "Accurate Lubrication"—a booklet that tells how to operate your car with greater economy and efficiency. It is free. Ask your dealer or write us for a copy at once and give the name and address of your dealer.

SUN COMPANY

Producer and Refiner of Lubricating Oils, Fuel Oil, Gas Oil, Gasoline and other Petroleum Products

More than 1,500,000 gallons of lubricating oils per week **Philadelphia** *Branch Offices and Warehouses in 32 Principal Cities*

SUNOCO

MOTOR OIL

TO THE TRADE—A wonderful sales opportunity is open to dealers. Write for the Sunoco Sales Plan.

were made, but in March, as a result of the experience gained, from 90 to 95 per cent. were accomplished, and now 97 to 98 per cent. of all flights are regularly carried out. The Lloyd Ostflug, by arrangement with the Danzig Air Mail, has been carrying the official mails on this service, and the Post-Office is quite satisfied with the results obtained. Passengers were not carried until March 15th last. The railway time of 14 hours between Berlin and Königsberg was cut to 5½ hours by the air service. Flights have been made with great regularity, and during one 12-day period, 80 passengers were carried. Frequently all the seats are spoken for in advance. The time-table is as follows: Leave Berlin 8.45 A. M., arrive Stettin 9.45; leave Stettin 9.55, arrive Danzig 1.50 P. M.; leave Danzig 2.05, arrive Königsberg 3.15 P. M. Returning, leave Königsberg at 9.45 A. M.; arrive Danzig 10.55; leave Danzig 11.10, arrive Stettin 3.05 P. M.; leave Stettin 3.15, arrive Berlin 4.15 P. M.

The fares for the trip, comparable to that from New York to Buffalo, are quite low (especially when we remember that the mark is worth less than a cent in American money), as follows:

Berlin-Königsberg	975	marks
Stettin-Königsberg	890	"
Berlin-Danzig	300	"
Berlin-Stettin	225	"
Stettin-Danzig	690	"
Danzig-Königsberg	290	"

Since the first of August flights have been made regularly to Kovno in Lithuania. The Königsberg-Danzig line is now used a great deal by Lithuanians, and the same is the case with the new Kovno-Königsberg-Danzig line, as it will overcome the Polish official difficulties that have been put in the way of transporting passengers from Lithuania to Danzig and Germany.

During June the machines of the Lloyd Ostflug flew 41,480 kilometers without a single accident since the start of the service. Junker all-metal cantilever-wing limousines are used on the service, and are of a type suitable for it in that, owing to the possibilities of forced landings in open country which lacks accommodation, the metallic construction renders the machines almost weather-proof.

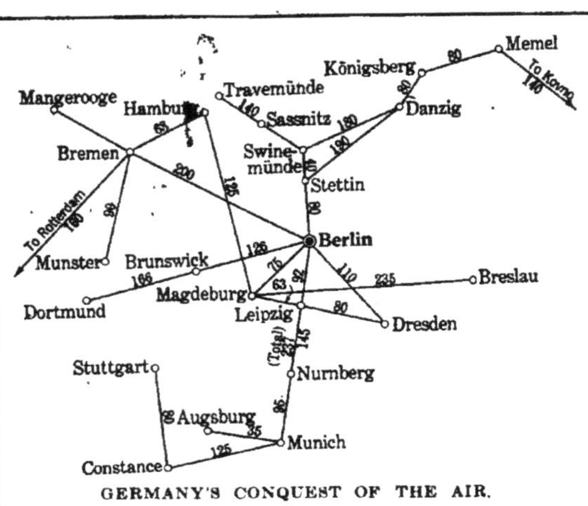

GERMANY'S CONQUEST OF THE AIR.

With characteristic method, the Germans now issue a complete air time-table, said to be the first publication of its sort in the history of the world. Times of arriving and departing planes are given to the minute, and it is reported that the schedules are being maintained practically without variation.

It is in France, however, untrammeled by the troublesome air restrictions forced upon Germany by the Allies, says another writer, the Paris correspondent of the New York *Herald*, that civil aviation and air transport have received their greatest impetus. Working quietly over the space of the three years since hostilities ended, we are told:

France has accomplished records that are perhaps less imposing than the crossing of an ocean or the scaling of mountain peaks, but which nevertheless have placed her to the fore as a leader of the world's aeronautic development.

The year 1920 was spent in the successful remodeling of the whole system of aviation. Under a new branch of the national government, an Under Secretariat for Aeronautics, the principle of unity of technical control has been reconciled with autonomy in the administration of the commercial, military and naval branches.

This department, nursed by the parent government through a separate budget, has assisted financially in the establishment of a prodigious net of commercial airways across the land. It is responsible for the preparation of efficient training centers, has instituted pilots' schools, created a national office of meteorology, and is at present seeking not only the betterment of commercial aviation but the encouragement of scientists and inventors who have turned their attention to aeronautics by offering substantial bonuses for improvements to the motor, control of the planes and everything that goes to make up the ship of the air.

It is the ambition of the French enthusiasts to permit one to breakfast in any part of France and lunch the same day in the most distant corner. Travel that requires more than twenty-four hours on the fastest express trains, from the Channel to the Riviera, has already been accomplished between lunch and dinner time. The whole program of international airways now being worked up by the French department would permit breakfast in Warsaw and dinner the same day in Morocco, ordinarily a voyage by train and boat of four or five days.

A fraction of the progress made in the development of air travel is indicated in statistics compiled by this government department, showing that during 1920 close on to a thousand aeroplanes were turned out by French shops. The number of passengers carried in twelve months was 7,000, against 960 in 1919. Traffic in merchandise followed the same rate of progression, increasing 850 per cent. within a year—although the period was really supposed to be one devoted to special study and reconstruction. The figures have been eclipsed this year.

The present air map contains the following French lines in actual operation.

Paris-London.
Paris-Brussels-Amsterdam-Copenhagen.
Paris-Strasbourg-Prague-Warsaw.
Paris-Bordeaux-Bayonne-Spain.
Paris-Le Havre.
Toulouse-Barcelona-Valencia-Rabat-Casablanca (Morocco).
Bordeaux-Montpelier-Nîmes-Nice.

In addition to those airways which are actually in operation and have proved their worth by ever increasing patronage and receipts, the program for the coming year shows the following lines projected, which are intended to link up, further, the visionary web which the Air Department is seeking:

Paris-Geneva-Milan-Rome.
Paris-Bucharest-Constantinople.
Casablanca-Oran-Algiers-Tunis.
Marseilles-Nice-Ajaccio (Corsica)-Tunis.
Casablanca-Dakar.
St. Nazaire-Tours-Macon-Geneva.
Dijon-Mulhouse.
Paris-Liege.

Brief as it is, this list of main airways—to which the weekly flight across the Mediterranean of a surrendered German dirigible in the interest of French colonial commerce is shortly to be added—represents all that is most vigorous in the world's attempt to subjugate the air to its daily needs.

Not only passengers are carried on these air lanes, which French planes have extended over most of Europe. Strange cargoes pass through the air these days. For instance, says the writer:

Flying pigs have now become an actuality, although they did not take kindly to the air. A crate of porkers was sent from the French capital to Croydon recently, where the distinguished travelers, the first of their race to realize the ambition to fly, were bustled into a taxicab and rolled to the national British stock show.

Millinery, a cargo of lobsters, boxes of early strawberries, trays of jewels and watches, and even cases of rare wines and champagne have been included at times among the freight shipments handled by air, for in addition to the fact that the fragile goods are less roughly handled in their flight by air than by train, there is also far less danger of theft than in the open baggage rooms of the railway station.

In the operation of all her airways, we are told, France uses every precaution of safety. While in December, 1918, the government controlled only four flying centers, and each one very incomplete—

There are now dozens of these air ports scattered over the country. Where formerly the pilot had to trust to luck when attempting a landing, he can now circle down over a field as level as a table, where he can be sure of landing his passengers and freight in absolute safety.

A large number of main air ports, fitted with hangars and

Other protections

Modern science also urges certain aids to Nature, and Pepsodent contains them.

Each use of Pepsodent multiplies the salivary flow. That is Nature's great tooth-protecting agent. It multiplies the starch digestant in the saliva. That to digest the starch deposits which may otherwise cling and form acid.

It multiplies the alkalinity of the saliva. That is Nature's agent for neutralizing acids—the cause of tooth decay.

All these results come from every application. All are now considered essential, in view of modern diet. None of them have been accomplished by the ordinary tooth paste.

Like New Teeth

The teeth that people see sometimes after film removal

This offers you a ten-day test of a new teeth-cleaning method. Millions now employ it. Leading dentists everywhere advise it. The results are seen in whiter teeth on every side today.

See the results on your own teeth. Learn how much those pleasing effects may mean. For your sake and your family's sake, ask for this 10-Day Tube.

One must fight film

That viscous film which you feel on your teeth is their chief enemy. It not only dims them, but it destroys them. Most tooth troubles are now traced to film.

It clings to teeth, gets between the teeth and stays. It often forms the basis of a cloudy coat. It is the film-coat that discolors, not the teeth. And film is the basis of tartar.

Film also holds food substance which ferments and forms acid. It holds the acid in contact with the teeth to cause decay. Millions of germs breed in it. They, with tartar, are the chief cause of pyorrhea.

Old methods of brushing did not effectively combat it. Much film remained, often to do ceaseless damage. Despite the tooth brush, therefore, tooth troubles have been constantly increasing. Very few people escaped.

A change has come

Now dental science, after long research, has found effective film combatants. Many careful tests, under able authorities, have proved them.

These two methods are combined in a dentifrice called Pepsodent. And millions of people have come to employ it, largely by dental advice.

The results are quickly seen and felt. One cannot doubt them. We urge you to prove them for yourself and judge what they mean to you.

Watch the change in a week

Send the coupon for a 10-Day Tube. Note how clean the teeth feel after using. Mark the absence of the viscous film. See how teeth whiten as the film-coats disappear. Watch the other good effects.

The results will be new to you, the benefits apparent. A book we send explains the purpose of each new effect. Ten days will enable you to decide between the new way and the old. And you should do that. Whiter, cleaner, safer teeth mean much to you and yours. Cut out the coupon now.

Pepsodent REG. U.S. PAT. OFF.

The New-Day Dentifrice

The scientific film combatant, each use of which brings five effects authorities now desire. Advised by leading dentists everywhere today. All druggists supply the large tubes.

10-Day Tube Free 614

THE PEPSODENT COMPANY,
Dept. 205, 1104 S. Wabash Ave., Chicago, Ill.
Mail 10-Day Tube of Pepsodent to

. . . .

. . . .

. . . .

Only one tube to a family

workshops, control their chain of intermediate posts and aid stations. Flares visible at a distance of 25 miles are in use on the principal landing grounds, and two flames for which visibility at a distance of 94 miles is claimed, are being installed this year to guide airmen across the waters of the Mediterranean. A score of weather stations, located at these air ports, exchange reports four times daily, and a pilot before taking off knows well the weather to expect before effecting his next landing. In this way planes can be routed around, above or below storms that are known to exist along "the right of way."

As a result of these precautions fatal accidents have been few.

Wireless equipment is placed on practically every passenger plane, and within a short time every plane flying over the routes out of French air ports will be required to have wireless, so that they can keep in constant touch with land stations along their routes and thus be assured of constant warnings regarding approaching storms. Storms need have no effect on the voyagers, however, for they are put away snugly in a luxurious cabin, fitted with movable chairs, tables for card-playing, magazines and a toilet room. On some airways tea and cakes are obtainable on board, while in all of them is a supply of iced water. Only smoking is prohibited, for the danger of fire is too great to permit of this relaxation.

With all its many advantages it is not surprizing that air travel has grown by leaps and bounds. In 1919, from July to December, 1,173 passenger flights were made over French airways. This number grew during 1920 to 4,428, while during the first three months of the present year the number increased to 1,625. The number of passengers carried grew from 729 for the last half year of 1919 to 5,968 for 1920, and 1,884 for the first quarter of 1921—an approximation of over 7,500 for this entire year.

The number of passengers carried on the Paris-London airway doubled during the last year, while the traffic on the Paris-Roumania line increased six times, Paris-Brussels-Amsterdam three times, and Nimes-Nice ten times. As an example, the Compagnie des Grands Express Aeriens carried between Paris and London and Paris and Amsterdam 27 voyagers in January, 28 in February, 185 in March, 231 in April, 270 in May, 407 in June, and will have passed 500 this month.

In some instances there are strap-hangers even in these air expresses, for the demand for reservations far exceeds the supply. In May 27 prospective passengers were refused transportation on the Paris-Roumania airway, and 40 at the other air ports.

The Air Department is making active preparations for the inauguration of dirigible service across the Mediterranean. The former German airship *Nordstern* has been refitted so as to carry as many as fifty voyagers in its two passenger cabins in addition to its crew of five men.

It is expected that while passengers in number will be carried by these ships the principal bulk of their earnings will come from the handling of freight. They will open up to France her African colonies.

While the proposed line from Bordeaux to Genoa, via Montpellier and Marseilles, will be inaugurated by a freight-carrying plane, it is eventually proposed to use a dirigible over this route. This airway is primarily for freight also, for it will lessen delivery time by five days.

In addition to planning its new airways the Air Department is at present most occupied with the problem of developing a stronger motor capable of propelling a heavier type of passenger and freight plane. For the most part the motors used at present remain from the stock manufactured for war purposes. While they were ample to drive the light reconnaissance planes, the fighters, and even the slow-moving but heavily weighted bombers they are not exactly the type required for passenger service, which demands both speed with lifting power.

While in 1914 an aeroplane engine weighing 120 pounds furnished 60 horse-power this strength had been increased by the time of armistice to 200 horse-power for the same weight motor. Higher and faster were the requirements of an army plane, and these motors served their purpose, and served it well, as the air supremacy of the Allies proved during the war, but now with commercial aviation coming to the fore there is a need for a heavier, safer, equally strong motor, but built along more robust lines, which will permit longer continuous flights.

The government, as an incentive to private companies operating the airways, offers a substantial subsidy, in return for which it maintains a control over all machines used, and over the pilots. In this way France has always in hand a formidable air fleet always at the call of the government, which within a space of a few hours could be put into fighting trim to repel any invader.

Civil firms are given by the government half of the cost of all planes used on purely French lines. In addition, a premium amount of freight carried. For all firms other than French the government offers fuel at cost, so that there are no firms operating airways which are not in every sense of the word a financial success.

The French have every reason to be proud of their air program and the progress they are making. Their air policy has been neatly framed with a view to making the most of aeronautics as a commercial asset. Aeronautics, like any other transport system, must have a special character combining private industry with public service. In France the State has intervened with exemplary discretion. It has promoted tests and experiments. It encourages. It has lent legal force and ample funds. It has given the new branch a discipline and a code "similar to that of the merchant marine."

HOW THE FORD RAILROAD MAN EARNS MORE PAY

ON THE DAY when general railroad wage rates were reduced 12 per cent., Henry Ford put into effect a 40 per cent. increase on his own line. "A masterpiece of strategy," *The Wall Street Journal* called it, and the newspapers of the country mentioned it in passing, along with the other astonishing facts that Henry Ford had cut freight rates, and at the same time added materially to the earning power of his railroad. The advance in wages, it now appears, was made in such a way that Mr. Ford profited by it along with his employees. "With doubled wage rates," reports a correspondent of *The Wall Street Journal*, "he gets triple or quadruple returns in service." Here is a concrete example of a Ford railroad man "on the job," compared with a railroad worker of the same class on another road:

"An inspection of a Ford's watchman's shanty showed that the man was not only a watchman but a crossing carpenter, a track inspector and a part-time clerk. He had a set of track tools, a shovel and several brooms. In each direction the track was swept up clean and bore much evidence of the watchman's efforts.

"In a nearby Wabash shanty sat two idlers. A board was out of the crosswalk and one wing of the crossing gate was broken. There was much débris. Asked why he did not fix things up a bit, this watchman replied: "First, because the walk is a carpenter's job and the gate a signalman's job, and, second, because I am not being paid for tinkering." Here again Ford pays twice the rate, $6 against $3.30, but gets nearly three times the service."

The railway unions, which Ford ignored, are said to have numerous rules regulating the exact sort of work a man may do, and what he shall be paid for it, all directed to the end of raising wages and cutting down hours of labor. Ford, says the writer, "beat the unions at their chief pastime, increasing pay, but at the same time he so arranged his rules that he gained by the increase over the union schedules. For instance:

"Passenger engineers, who with overtime formerly received $300 a month under the national agreement 'rules,' now receive $375 a month. But to earn this they must put in 208 hours of actual service in a month. This may mean 16 hours the first day, four hours the second, or any combination within the law, but only actual service is paid for.

"An engineer on the Ford road may cover three or four times as many miles for the same amount of pay as an engineer on, say, the Michigan Central or the Wabash. Assume a passenger run of 75 miles. The 'rules' regard this a day's work of eight hours and prescribe $6.08 as the pay, notwithstanding that the trip takes two hours' actual running time.

"Under the Ford plan the engineer would receive $3.60 and Ford may order him to turn around and start back. Ford could also order another round trip within eight hours but under the 'rules' the Michigan Central or the Wabash would have to call four engineers for the same amount of service, giving each a day's pay for about two hours' work and one hour getting ready. Collectively the four engineers would cover 286 miles for $24.32. The Ford engineer would cover an equal distance for $14.40.

"'Rules' prevent cutting down the number of crews on the second terminal without reducing service a proportionate amount. Hence, most roads are denied the opportunity of realizing any return for the five or six hours' pay unearned by

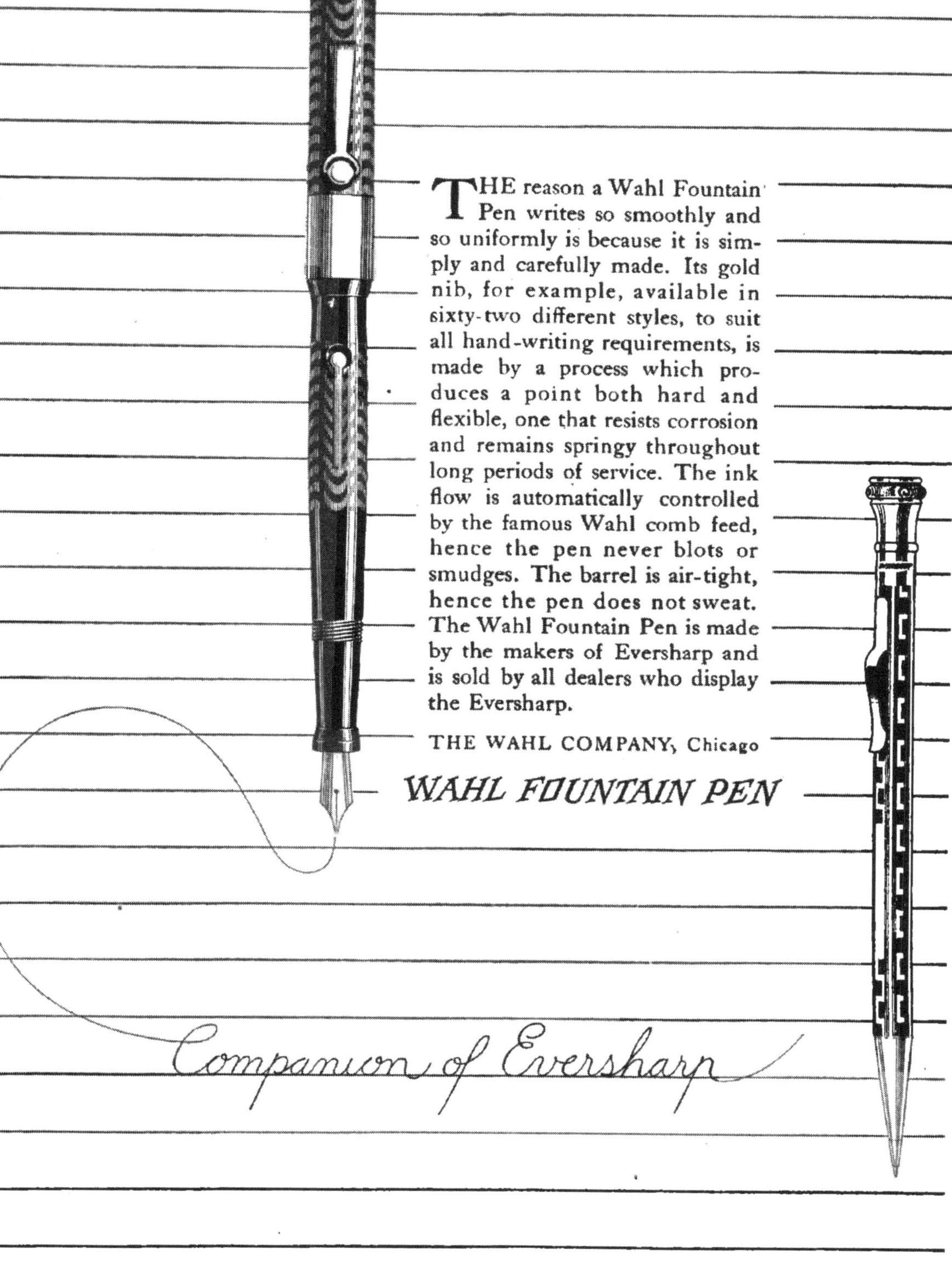

THE reason a Wahl Fountain Pen writes so smoothly and so uniformly is because it is simply and carefully made. Its gold nib, for example, available in sixty-two different styles, to suit all hand-writing requirements, is made by a process which produces a point both hard and flexible, one that resists corrosion and remains springy throughout long periods of service. The ink flow is automatically controlled by the famous Wahl comb feed, hence the pen never blots or smudges. The barrel is air-tight, hence the pen does not sweat. The Wahl Fountain Pen is made by the makers of Eversharp and is sold by all dealers who display the Eversharp.
THE WAHL COMPANY, Chicago
WAHL FOUNTAIN PEN
Companion of Eversharp

Yet Ford's employees are said to be "satisfied and efficient" under his system, which gives them more pay in return for keeping on the job. The writer presents some further incidents, each with its little economic moral:

"Ford's road has three switch engine crews working in the Detroit yards. The engines are being worked 24 hours a day. Recently one broke down and it was found a cotter-pin had to be replaced. Instead of sitting idle while repairs were going on the conductor and brakemen trotted off to lunches, and instead of laying up the engine until an exact duplicate of the cotter-pin could be obtained, the engineer picked up a bolt and with the fireman's help had the engine running within 12 minutes.

"Ford can call on his enginemen for any kind of service without penalty. But should a road operating under the 'rules' stop a freight train more than three times between terminals to pick up or set out cars, extra fees must be paid the crew notwithstanding that eight hours have not yet elapsed. How Ford beats the unions in this respect is shown by a recent incident on a nearby division of another railroad.

"A freight train was started out for a 65-mile run which was commonly covered in three hours. Four stops were made within the first five miles to pick up cars which added, because of the 'rules,' 69 cents to the engineer's pay and 54 cents to the fireman's. At the last stop instructions were received to go back to the starting point to pick up three cars of perishable freight which came in from a connecting railroad after the train in question had left.

"It took about half an hour to go back and pick up those cars and the run was finally completed within about five hours' total time.

"But it cost the railroad a total of $26.35 for the enginemen's pay because under the 'rules' they received the following:—

	Engineer	Fireman
One day's pay	$7.20	$5.36
Picking up or dropping cars at 3 or more points extra	.69	.54
Extra day's pay because going back to terminal	7.20	5.36
Total	$15.09	$11.26

"Ford on the other hand can back his engines up as often as he pleases and stop them as often as he cares to without penalty. For similar service consuming five hours' time he would pay his engineer $9 and his fireman $6.50.

"A story is related of an engineer on the Ford road who earned $225 during the first two weeks of September, which included pay for overtime, but at regular hourly rate of $1.80.

"To earn $225 in 15 days means he must have put in approximately 124 hours. Omitting Sundays, on which the Ford engineers do not work, there were 12 working days, or an average of 12.4 hours per day, which paid about $12.60 per day.

"On the passenger mileage basis of other roads this engineer could have covered with certain fast trains about 450 miles per day. Altho passenger engineers do not make runs of this distance, it is noteworthy for comparison purposes that this mileage on the Ford basis, whether performed by one engineer or four, would have cost no more than 12 hours' pay, or $21.60. But under the 'rules' a like amount of service or mileage would cost 36 hours' pay, or $27, though only 12 hours' actual service was rendered. Ford thus beats the unions on mileage as well as services rendered.

"The major part of the reduction of Ford's railway forces, from 2700 to 1650, has come in the maintenance of way department, where the force was cut from 1291 in August, 1920, to 646 in July, 1921. Mechanical department was cut down from 628 to 466 and station forces from 276 to 200 between the same dates, but the number of enginemen has been reduced only by four, and the trainmen by 17.

"Railroad men view the lack of increase in engine and train forces as particularly remarkable because daily car handlings have increased from 200 to around 800, running at times to 1200.

"In St. Thomas, Ont., the Michigan Central has a roundhouse foreman who receives $225 per month and is on duty from 7 a. m. to 6 p. m. One day the foreman was sick and a mechanic was substituted. When payday arrived the latter made the following claim for pay according to the 'rules':—

	Hours
For the extra hour before 8 o'clock	5
For regular hours, 8 to 4	8
For extra hour, 4 to 5, overtime	1½
For time, 5 to 6	5

Mechanic's rate is $ .77 an hour, making total pay..... $15.01

A Ford mechanic's rate is $ .90 an hour, for same actual performance he would receive 9.00

The Michigan Central mechanic without the rules would have received 7.77

"Ford can handle six and eight times as many freight cars with the same number of men who formerly handled 200 per day, because when there are cars to move everybody within reach is a trainman; when there is a switch to turn the fireman becomes a switchman; when the fireman is busy elsewhere the engineer fills the coal tank. The company pays a flat overtime rate, but gets a service for every hour of employment. The men are satisfied and efficient."

FARMERS FROM VETERANS, AS CANADA DOES IT

HAMMERING swords into ploughshares is all very well, but Canada is improving upon the idea by turning the completed ploughshares over to her war veterans together with farms where the ploughshares may appropriately be put to use. Canada is leading the world, reports a visiting American newspaper man, "in the manner in which she has turned over her land to be farmed by the men who fought to preserve it." By comparison with the policy of the United States, this journalist, William Slavens McNutt, points out in *Leslie's Weekly*, our northern neighbor's well worked-out plan looks not so much like generosity as a good bargain. The Dominion is likely to profit financially by its venture, which is not precisely in the nature of a "bonus." Even the few veteran farmers who have "failed" have returned to the Canadian treasury more than they took out.

Canada sent 418,000 men to France out of a population of approximately 8,000,000. Of these men about 60,000, the same number lost by the United States from a population of 110,000,000, were killed. In facing the problem of what to do with the 338,000 of her sons who were brought back from France, it must be remembered, writes Mr. McNutt, that:

"Canada paid her own way in the war without help from Great Britain. The interest charges on Canada's national debt in 1920 were nine times greater than the country's total revenue in 1914. Remember that 155,000 of the 338,000 men who came back were more or less weakened by wounds. Remember also that many of those men had been away from their homes and their jobs for five years or more. Remember further that 50 per cent. of those returned were married men and that their average age was about thirty-five years. They were by no means all single men who could spare a few years from their lives to no great hurt. It is a matter of record that one Canadian soldier who saw active service overseas was seventy-two years old.

"Canada went at the problem of aiding these men in reestablishment with a fortunate degree of the spirit that had moved her while the job was one of getting them into the army, getting the army to France and maintaining it in the fighting line there."

Many of the men who came back wanted to go on the land, and it was greatly to the benefit of the nation that they should go there. The government took up the matter of giving its veterans a chance to become first-class farmers if they wanted to. As a first move in this direction—

"Canada formed what is known as The Soldier Settlement Board, a government organization, empowered to loan money—actually loan money!—to returned soldiers who were found fit to become farmers, and aid them in buying farms, stock and equipment.

"Of the details of the scheme more later. Let us first have a look at the result of the experiment to date.

"Of 59,331 applicants 43,063 were granted qualification certificates by the board. These 43,063 returned soldiers are to-day farming a total area of 4,854,799 acres. Digest that—4,854,799 acres! When one takes into account that in all Canada there are only 50,000,000 acres under crop out of a potential arable acreage amounting to 300,000,000 the comparable magnitude of the soldier settlement movement can be best appreciated. Another comparison: In the entire province of Manitoba there are 50,000 farms. The returned soldiers added to Canada almost as

Suppose I had said "No, I don't play Auction"

"HERE was the very man I had been trying to see for a year; on the same train, for an eighteen-hour journey, and a mutual friend right at hand to introduce me. Here was the opportunity not only to meet him but to see his real self revealed in a game of cards; also to show him my own mental capacity and incidentally my grasp of his business and certain requirements of that business which my concern was prepared to fill. Suppose I had said, 'No I don't play Auction.'"

How often do similar opportunities present themselves to you! Follow this suggestion—

Play cards for wholesome recreation

and you will find the accomplishment a continual help in business and social life. Play cards often—you will improve your mind and you will become the alert kind of player that worth-while people like to play with.

Send for a copy of "The Official Rules of Card Games" giving complete rules for 300 games and hints for better playing. Check this and other books wanted on coupon. Write name and address in margin below and mail with required postage stamps to

The U. S. Playing Card Company, Dept. B-1, Cincinnati, U. S. A.

Manufacturers of

BICYCLE

PLAYING CARDS

(Also Congress Playing Cards. Art Backs. Gold Edges.)

Auction at a Glance

PARTNERS AND DEAL—4 players, 2 against 2, using 2 packs. Remove jokers; shuffle one pack and draw for partners. 2 lowest cards play 2 highest. Lowest deals first. His partner shuffles the other pack, and places it at his right, ready for next deal. Player on dealer's right cuts, and 13 cards are dealt to each player, one at a time. If a misdeal, same player deals again. Deal passes to left.

BIDDING—There are 5 bids: clubs lowest, then diamonds, hearts, spades, no-trumps. Dealer must bid at least "one" in a suit, or no-trump, or he may pass. Each player in turn to the left may pass, or bid the same number in a higher suit, or more in a lower suit. Highest bid allowed is seven. The bidding goes round until three players in succession pass.

DOUBLING—Any player may double opponents' bid, and either opponent may redouble or bid something else. Only one redouble is allowed. The double increases value of tricks and penalties in scoring but not in bidding; 2 spades will overbid 2 hearts doubled.

THE PLAY—The declarer is the player who *first* named the winning suit. His partner is "dummy." The one at the left of declarer leads any card; then dummy's cards are laid face up on table, sorted into suits. Dummy takes no further part in play. Each player must follow suit if he can, otherwise trump or discard. Cards rank from A down to deuce, and trumps always win. Highest card played wins the trick; winner leads for next trick. First 6 tricks taken by declarer are his "book." All over the book count toward game. If declarer has bid 3 he *must* win 3 over his book, or 9 tricks.

SCORING—Only the declarer's side can score toward game. (Opponents score only honors and penalties.) Declarer scores for each trick over his book, 10 points at no-trumps, 9 at spades, 8 at hearts, 7 at diamonds, or 6 at clubs. These trick scores are all put "below the line" on score pad. 30 points is game, but all over 30 is scored. Draw a line under a game won. Partners winning two games ends the rubber.

HONORS AND PENALTIES—Besides scores toward game, there are honor scores and penalties, which go "above the line" on pad. Honors are A K Q J 10 of the trump suit, or the 4 aces at no-trump. Credit goes to original holders of these cards, on either side. 3 between partners have the value of 2 tricks, so that 3 in spades would be worth 18; 4 honors same as 4 tricks; 5 honors same as 5 tricks; but 4 or 5 in one hand count double; and 4 in one hand, 5th in partner's are the same as 9 tricks. (In spades, this would be 81 points.) At no-trumps, 3 aces count 30, 4 aces 40, and 4 in one hand, 100. For winning 12 tricks, add 50; for grand slam, 13 tricks, 100. For winning rubber, add 250. If contract is doubled, trick scores have a double value, or quadruple if redoubled. Spades doubled count 18 a trick to declarer if he makes his contract; if redoubled, 36. He also gets 50 in honors for fulfilling doubled contract, and 50 for each trick over contract. If redoubled, this figure is 100. If he made 5 over book on contract to make 5, doubled, he would score 5 times 18 below the line and 150 above, plus honors.

PENALTIES—If declarer fails to make contract, he scores only honors as held; the adversaries score 50 in honors for each trick he falls short; 100 if doubled; 200 if redoubled. Penalty for a revoke by declarer is 50 in honors. If his adversaries revoke, he can take 50 points, or 2 of their tricks, which he scores. The revoking side can score nothing but honors as held.

At the end of a rubber, everything is added, and lower score deducted from the higher; the difference is the number of points won. The side having most points technically wins rubber, regardless of which side won two games. Cards are then cut for a new rubber.

For full rules and hints on bidding and play see "The Official Rules of Card Games" or "Six Popular Games" offered below.

The U. S. Playing Card Co., Dept. B-1, Cincinnati, O. Send postpaid books checked below.

- ☐ **"Official Rules of Card Games"** 300 games, 250 pages, 20c.
- ☐ **"Six Popular Games"** Auction, Cribbage, Pitch, Five Hundred, Solitaire, Pinochle. 6c.
- ☐ **"How to Entertain with Cards."** Suggestions for parties and clubs. 6c.
- ☐ **"Card Tricks."** Mystifying tricks that can be done with a deck of cards. 6c.
- ☐ **"Fortune Telling with Playing Cards."** How to tell fortunes with a regular deck of cards. 6c.
- ☐ **"Card Stunts for Kiddies."** Amusing and instructive kindergarten lessons. Not card games but pasteboard stunts, using old cards as bits of board. 6c.

All 6 books 40c. Write Name and Address in margin below.

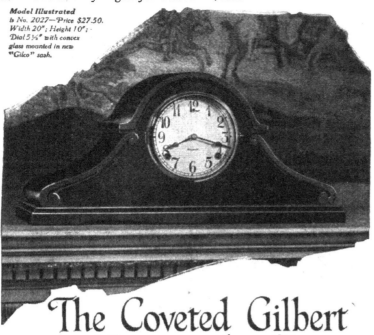

PERSONAL GLIMPSES
Continued

2,153,184 acres were bought; soldier grants accounted for 1,361,280. The rest was encumbered land amounting to 360,227 acres.

"Of the total number of returned soldiers who went on the land under the supervision of the Soldier Settlement Board, 19,771 received help in the form of loans at 5 per cent. The loans for stock and equipment were for five years; those for the purchase of land run for twenty-five years.

"The government, through the board, loaned these 19,771 men $80,371,750.48. These loans have been made since the establishment of the board in 1917. To date only 200 of the men who thus received financial assistance in getting started on farms have failed and been sold out. The government's original investment in these men, who have failed for some reason and been sold out, was $708,708.79. The return realized by the board on the resale of property of these failures was $711,335.89. Instead of losing the government has realized a small return even on its investment in those who were unable to succeed!

"No doubt many more of those who took advantage of the opportunity will fail and be sold out, but the great majority will stick and win through to ownership of their own homes and financial independence.

"In 1920 the soldier settlers who went on the land under supervision of the board produced crops to the value of between $14,000,000 and $15,000,000. Write that down in your memory—43,063 soldiers who in 1918 were fighting in the line in France or recovering from wounds received in action, were settled on the land in their home country in 1920, and produced crops to the value of between $14,000,000 and $15,000,000!

"The applicants for aid were required to pay down 20 per cent. of the cost of land, stock and equipment. They were then examined by experts as to their fitness to farm. If they lacked the necessary experience they were sent to a farm training center, of which the board at one time operated seven in various provinces. There they worked, as at the vocational training schools, until they were found fit to undertake the management of their own farms.

"Each applicant who wanted to purchase a farm made his own selection of a place and the best possible bargain with the owner. Then he reported to the board. The board then sent an inspector to appraise the farm desired by the applicant and complete the deal with the owner. In this way an amount aggregating $3,632,421.36 was cut from the prices stated as the lowest at which the vendors would sell. Those who sold land to returned soldiers got a fair price, but the board saw to it that that was all they did get. To cut out the rapacious real estate speculator it was stipulated that land sold to soldiers under the supervision of the board must not have been previously sold within the space of one year.

"No man in Canada," says the writer, "fattened his purse at the expense of the returned soldier who wanted to go on the land." Both stock and equipment were purchased under the supervision of settlement board experts and it is estimated that a saving of approximately one-third was effected. Loans were granted up to $7,500. Furthermore—

"No cash payment is required from the settler on the purchase of stock and equipment, as both stock and equipment are purchased by the board and sold to the soldier farmers on lien agreements. The board has bought for the settlers and holds title in this way to 38,363 horses, 62,201 cattle, and thousands each of sheep and swine. The government is apparently quite well protected in its investment, as the return of a profit on the 200 failures sold out would indicate; and more than 40,000 out of a total of 338,000 returned soldiers are on the land who would probably otherwise be adding materially to Canada's present unemployment problem, which is acute.

"I give here a few examples copied at random from thousands of reports: The first, a story from Manitoba, I write as a verbatim quote from the report: 'Altho somewhat handicapped by the effects of wounds which he sustained during the war, A. Lagimodierre of Lorette, was settled by the board on 240 acres of land in August, 1919. The greater portion of this—170 acres—was tractor broken, but the settler put in his crops and harvested with horses. In spite of the fact that by reason of war scars he is forced to wear leg supports he is a great worker and has developed his holding in a remarkable way. He has a good herd of cattle and a complete outfit of machinery. Lagimodierre was a private in the First Divisional Ammuniton Column. He secured a loan of $7,030 from the board for the following purposes: Land purchase, $4,030; permanent improvements, $1,000; stock and equipment $2,000. He had 100 acres in wheat, but unfortunately his yield was poor, owing to the drought and other causes, and he harvested only 700 bushels. He had 400 bushels of barley, 280 bushels of flax and 300 tons of hay, besides which he had returns amounting to $650 from his nine cows and $240 from the sale of pigs. His total revenue for his first year was $3,890, which placed him in excellent position to meet his obligations and carry him over until next harvest.'

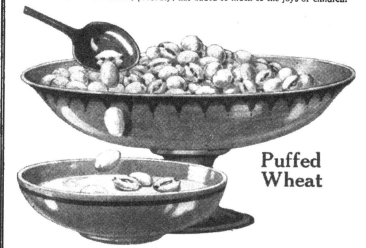

"The report neglects to state that Lagimodierre was one of the first men to enlist in 1914, he then being in his middle forties, and that he has a wife and family to support.

"Let us take the case of Capt. J. H. Times, of the prairie province of Saskatchewan. He borrowed $7,200 from the board and settled on 320 acres of improved land near Mortlach. In 1920 he seeded 200 acres and the value of the harvest he reaped was $3,400. He has 32 head of cattle.

"Then there is B. E. Fulton of the Calgary district in Alberta. Fulton was a sapper in the 89th Canadian Engineers. He borrowed $5,000 from the board and bought 150 acres. His first year sales amounted to $3,400, and he is doing fine, thank you!

"Here is the story of a man over sixty years old who fought in France and won first prize at a pumpkin show in British Columbia as a result. I quote from the report: 'A notably successful soldier-farmer in the Chilliwack District in British Columbia district is T. P. Wicks, who, although over sixty years of age, had a good war service and promises an exceptional career on the land. While in France he obtained some pumpkin seed from a poilu who had obtained them from Algeria while on service there. His pumpkins took first prize at the Chilliwack show this fall.'

"No doubt there are many ways of earning first prize at a pumpkin show, but for devious originality I cite the method

MOTORING • AND • AVIATION

NEW SOARING RECORDS IN GERMANY

WITHOUT an engine, with only air currents and his own skill to assist his frail, bird-like "glider," a German flyer lately succeeded in remaining in the air thirteen minutes, circling, turning and balancing like a soaring bird. He covered some six miles between start and finish, and "altogether," says *Flight* of London, which reports the achievement, "this is one of the most interesting flights ever made by man and is, in a small way, indication of what, with a little practise, we may hope to do in the way of powerless flight." Another flyer, a few days later succeeded in remaining in the air fifteen minutes and forty seconds, traveling a total distance of more than four miles, and achieving the remarkable gliding ratio of one in thirty-two, which means that he traveled thirty-two feet for every foot he descended. Still another glider, on September 6, managed to stay in the air twenty-two minutes, unfortunately "finishing with a dive and a crash." These record-making achievements, which far surpass any results obtained by our own Wright Brothers in their experiments with motorless flying machines, were the direct result of a large competition for gliders, held in the hills in the Rhön district in Germany. The flights were not made in the competition, but the practise which the birdmen obtained while endeavoring to win the prizes helped them to gain the control of their delicately balanced machines necessary to make the later record. The soaring competition itself was largely the result of the prohibition imposed by the Allies upon Germany against building power-driven airplanes. If Germany wished to make full scale experiments, this was the only way in which she could do it, the writer in *Flight* observes. He goes on:

That German experimentalists are fully alive to the possibilities of full-scale experiments of this nature is proved by the fact that no less than 45 machines were entered for the Soaring and Gliding Competition which has just been held in the hills of the Rhön district. Organized by the *Südwestgruppe des Deutschen Luftfahrer-Verbandes*, and the *Verband Deutscher Modell-und-Gleitflug-Vereine*, and under the patronage of no less an institution than the *Wissenschaftliche Gesellschaft für Luftfahrt*, the response has been extraordinary. Contrary to expectations, most of the machines entered turned up at Rhön, and a few late comers swelled the list still further.

The competition was divided into five different categories under the following heads: (1) Great Rhön Soaring Prize (30,000 Mks.) for the greatest duration, a minimum of five minutes being stipulated, and the machine not to alight at a point more than 50 meters (148 ft.) below the starting point; (2) Greatest total duration of flight obtained by any one machine piloted by the same pilot on each occasion, each flight in order to count for this prize having to be of at least 15 seconds' duration (1st Prize 5,000 Mks., 2nd 3,000 Mks. and 3rd 2,000 Mks.); (3) Smallest mean loss of height during a complete flight, each to be of at least one minute duration (1st Prize 5,000 Mks., 2nd 3,000 Mks. and 3rd 2,000 Mks.); (4) Greatest distance flown (Prize amounts same as previous); (5) Prizes to be distributed at discretion of the judges; 25,000 Mks.

There were several instances of machines reaching heights considerably above their starting point. Thus Klemperer, on the Aachen monoplane shown in the accompanying photograph, made a very long flight (after the close of the competition) during which he reached a height estimated as being at least 300 feet above his starting point. This extraordinary flight lasted for just over 13 minutes, and the approximate flight path is shown in the accompanying sketch map, which we reproduce by courtesy of *Flugsport*. It will be seen that he described figures-of-eight, did sharp turns, and generally behaved more as if upon a

Copyrighted by the American News Service

SOARING THROUGH THE SKY WITH NO ENGINE

The Klemperer-Aachen monoplane glider, here shown in flight on an even keel, is able to soar by taking advantage of air currents. It lately traveled a distance of more than six miles, rising, at one point, several hundred feet above the starting ground.

LINCOLN

M O T O R C A R S

The impression held by so many

LINCOLN owners that they are peculiarly favored in having a *special* car, is true only in the sense that *every* LINCOLN is a *special* car; special because each is the object of infinite care that every LINCOLN shall uphold the LINCOLN'S high repute.

Lincoln Eight Cylinder Motor Cars comprise a wide and varied range of open and closed Body Types, eleven in all—two and three-passenger Roadsters; four-passenger Phaeton; five and seven-passenger Touring Cars; four-passenger Coupe; four, five and seven-passenger Sedans; seven-passenger Town Car; seven-passenger Limousine.

Some are types of quiet, conservative mien while others are of more imposing aspect, yet all reflect the air of elegance and true refinement.

The impression that

they have a *special* car is a natural conclusion which comes from the fact that the LINCOLN handles so much *more easily*, runs so much *more smoothly*, is so much *more comfortable*, is so much *more capable;* and because nimbleness, and vim, and go, are so much *more in evidence* than in anything to which motordom had hitherto been accustomed.

LINCOLN MOTOR COMPANY
DETROIT, MICH.

LELAND-BUILT

MOTORING AND AVIATION
Continued

power-driven aeroplane than using a glider. His highest altitude was reached about six minutes after the start. Another thing which this map brings out very clearly is the manner in which Klemperer followed the valleys and took advantage of the gusts, up-currents, etc., which were caused by the nature of the country. It will be noticed that during the first part of the flight, when he had the wind against him, he made relatively small headway, altho attaining a good height. Then, as he turned across the wind, he gained speed,

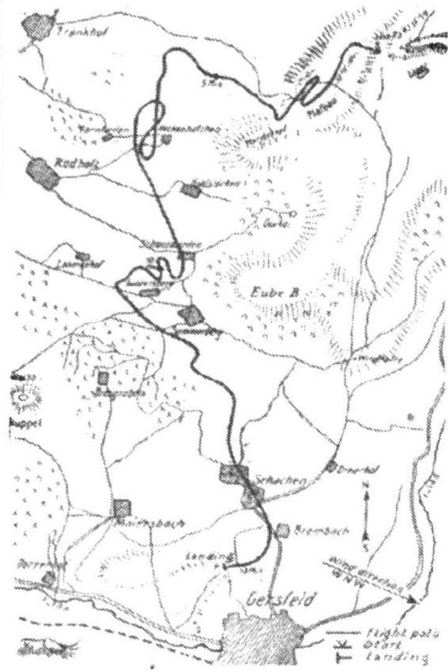

PATH OF THE MOTORLESS MONOPLANE

The Aachen glider's flight, as shown by this diagram, included turns and twists suggesting the flight of a power-driven machine. The start of the flight was against the wind, but the greater part of the record distance was made by flying across the air currents.

and the last half or so of the flight, which was down wind more or less, was covered in three minutes.

The manner of starting the gliders is described from the report of Handley-Page, one of the most prominent British aeroplane manufacturers, who paid a visit to the Rhön district during the competition. Two men, we are told, are posted at the wing tips of the machine—

Two others hold a long rope passing over notches in the undercarriage or some other suitable part of the machine. This long rope has incorporated in it long pieces of rubber shock absorbers. Before the start these two men walk forward and somewhat outwards, as far as the rope and rubber cords will allow. Then on the word "go" from the pilot the two men holding the wing tips let go and the two on the rope start running forward down the hill. In this manner a form of catapult is formed which accelerates the machine very quickly, and in a few yards it is up to flying speed and in the air, when, as it passes the two of the notches and is left behind. Owing to the light wing loading (according to Mr. Handley Page the average is somewhere about 1½ lb. per sq. ft.) the machines get off very quickly into the wind, and then comes the glide during which a skilful pilot takes advantage of every gust to keep the machine up or even to rise slightly. The method appears to be that the pilot, when a gust strikes the machine, elevates as much as he thinks the machine will stand, and then, when the gust is dying down, he flattens out and continues the glide.

As regards the competition itself, the writer goes on:

Many scores of flights were made, and there is only one serious accident to report. This happened to Willy Leusch, on the 'Weltensegler.' At the moment of writing we are not quite clear what happened, but it appears that, after an excellent start, and after having been in the air for slightly over a minute, the machine was seen to swerve to the right and it then got into a nose dive and crashed, the pilot dying from his injuries later. Apart from this regrettable mishap the competition was without serious accidents, although minor breakages were frequent enough, as was to be expected from machines so lightly built as these gliders must necessarily be.

The prizes in Class (1) (Great Rhön Soaring Prize) were not awarded.

The greatest total duration of flight obtained was that of Pelzner, who made no less than 62 flights, of which 57 were on the Pelzner biplane and the other 5 on the North-Bavarian Aviation Society (No. 40) biplane. Pelzner's aggregate on the two machines amounted to about 36 mins. 40 secs. and won for him the 1st prize of 5,000 Mks. in Class (2). Second prize in this class was won by Koller on the Bavarian Aero Club of Munich's monoplane machine. Koller's total time was 31 mins. 36 secs., but this total was obtained in 25 flights, so that on an average Koller's flights must have been close on twice the duration of Pelzner's. The longest of them was of slightly over five minutes' duration, and the distance covered was 4,080 meters (a little over 2½ miles). In this flight Koller made a complete circuit of 360 degrees. Third prize was awarded to Klemperer on the Aachen monoplanes for a total of 15 flights with a duration of 32 mins. 25 secs.

In Class (3) a slight rearrangement of the prizes was made, first and second being made up to an equal amount of 4,000 Mks. each, and third prize 2,000 Mks. First and second were awarded to Koller and Klemperer respectively it being thought that their performances were both of equal merit. Third prize was given to Martens for his performance on the Hannover monoplane.

In Class (4) (greatest distance) first price was won by Koller on the Munich Monoplane, second prize by Martens on the Hannover, and third prize by Klemperer on the Aachen. In this connection it should be pointed out that Klemperer's marvelous flight shown in the accompanying sketch map was made after the close of the competition and therefore does not count for the prizes. It would appear that in order to get the best possible results during the competition, the pilots should have an opportunity of practising for a month or so beforehand so as to get experience. The very fact that some of the best performances were put up after the close of the competition proves this. It is, of

MOTORING AND AVIATION
Continued

enters into the equation to a very great extent, and, as suitable country is not to be found everywhere, the problem of previous practise is often a matter of difficulty. There is little doubt that next year, if the competition is repeated, as we trust it will be, very much better results will be obtained. It has been a matter of some disappointment that the Great Rhön Prize was not awarded, and the opinion seems to prevail in "Soaring Circles" that the rules should be modified, not necessarily in order to make the competition easier, but so as to make it more useful.

Very little information is available as regards the details of the competing machines. Generally speaking, however, the designs were sound, altho, as was inevitable in a competition of this nature, some freaks were to be found among them. The "Weltensegler," on which Leusch met his death had no tail of any description; its stability being attained by a pronounced sweep-back and control by means of movable wing tips. It would appear that possibly one of these gave way and that this was the cause of the accident. As our illustrations will show, those machines which did best in the competition were of fairly orthodox design, one of the most interesting being the Hannover, in which there is an ordinary rectangular section *fuselage* with a monoplane cantilever wing and orthodox tail planes. One of the features of this machine is the use of footballs in place of wheels with pneumatic tires. We understand from Mr. Handley Page that these were a great success, giving ample shock-absorbing and having less frictional resistance on the grass than the skids with which the majority of machines were provided.

The Munich monoplane on which Koller did such good work would appear to be the essence of simplicity. There are three necessary elements in a glider: the wing, the tail, and the pilot's seat. In the Munich these three are of the simplest possible form and are connected by a few struts giving perfect triangulation. A feature of this machine is that there is no elevator. The tail consists of a fixt tail plane and a rudder. The wings have their entire trailing edge hinged, a side-to-side movement of the control stick giving a differential movement to the two halves of the trailing edge for *aileron* control, while a fore and aft movement pulls down or elevates the entire trailing edge, thus causing it to perform the function of an elevator. The system appears to have worked well and altogether this glider is very taking in its almost crudely elementary simplicity.

The Aachen monoplanes on which Klemperer did his excellent work are well shown in our photographs, and are similar to the machine which did so well in last year's competition. Some refinements have been incorporated, notably as regards the placing of the pilot. This year's models retain the "trousered" undercarriage which characterized the previous machine and the curved skids appear to have worked well. The problem of skids of suitable shape is less simple than one would imagine, and on this subject we may have something to say later. For the present we must confine ourselves to congratulating the Rhön competitors on their achievement and expressing the hope that next year

"WESTWARD HO!"—IN A CONTINENT-CROSSING CAR

WE need not worry too much because the work of the explorer and pioneer is nearly finished, argues one motor enthusiast, so long as it is possible to hold the wheel of a car and follow the highways into some of the less known parts of the continent. "For each of us there is a little private job of exploring left to do," writes this modern pioneer, Cornelius Vanderbilt, Jr., in *Motor* (New York), "and the motor car made this individualistic pioneering not only possible, but pleasant. Surely no man can have a desire more laudable than that of exploring and learning to know his own land. And in a far-flung country such as ours, intimate contact with distant sections is the only way in which the individual citizen can acquire a real understanding of his own land and people, and so can develop the reasoned patriotism that is essential to our consistent national development." Fired with such thoughts, Mr. Vanderbilt writes:

The early days of May, 1921, found us wending our motored way across the vast spaces which combine to make this dry but well-beloved United States. For years we had all longed to make such a trip, but never before had time and circumstances combined to make it possible.

We knew that transcontinental expresses make the overland trip in four and a half days, and that various stock cars have recently been crossing in five or six days. We had no desire to emulate these record-breaking exploits, but we did manage to complete the journey from New York to Seattle in one hundred and fifty-four hours, actual running time.

Altho we carried a tent for emergency use, we found good accommodations at practically every night stop. Almost always we were able to secure a room with bath, which latter is particularly acceptable on a trip of this kind. Twice during the long trek we had to put up at what the movies would have us believe is the typical Western hotel, comprising principally a barroom, still noisy in spite of the Eighteenth Amendment, and alcoves instead of real bedrooms. But these experiences only made us enjoy the more the conventional accommodations of the following nights.

On the whole the food that we secured was excellent, plain but cleanly served. One unhappy feature of the fare was a woful paucity of green vegetables, especially in the Far West. Figures I know are seldom palatable literary fare, but let me add that the daily average for room and three square meals was *four dollars and forty-seven cents* apiece.

Indeed the hotel keepers of the West are too thoroughly "sold" on the value of motor tourist traffic, to risk driving it away by overcharging. In one wide-awake community in North Dakota we were informed that 24,250 cars had passed through there last summer. Almost every city, town or hamlet in the Far West is now providing a camping ground, where motor tourists may find harbor for the night, and such conveniences as are possible under the circumstances. And every night these municipal camping grounds are crowded with all makes and manners of motor conveyances, tenanted by as motley an assemblage of human voyagers on the highway as it

Lysol Disinfectant

Reg. U. S. Pat. Off.

Kills the germs that dodge the cleaner

The cleaner that keeps your rooms free from dust and dirt is powerless to rid your floors of the unseen germ life that is tracked there. Such germ life is often a contributing cause of contagious sickness.

Before using your cleaner, sprinkle the rugs, mats, and floors with a few drops of Lysol Disinfectant diluted with water. That kills the germ life which otherwise would be stirred up and spread throughout the house.

Add a little Lysol Disinfectant to the scrubbing water, too. Being a soapy liquid, Lysol Disinfectant cleans as it disinfects.

Use it in solution according to directions. A 50c bottle makes 5 gallons of germ-killing solution. A 25c bottle makes 2 gallons.

Beta-Lysol is crude Lysol Disinfectant for farm and factory use put up in quart, gallon, and five-gallon cans. It is the most economical form for large users. Ask for Beta-Lysol.

Free Samples of Lysol Products

Lysol Shaving Cream in Tubes

Makes a quick, easy job for the razor. In addition, it renders the razor and shaving brush aseptically clean. Guards tiny cuts from infection. Sold by druggists everywhere.

A Postcard Brings Free Samples.

Learn why thousands of men use Lysol Shaving Cream regularly. A sample of Lysol Toilet Soap will be included for the family to try. Send name and address on a postcard.

Lysol Toilet Soap 25c a Cake

Produces a rich, creamy lather. Protects the health of the skin. Also refreshingly soothing, healing and helpful for improving the skin. At druggists everywhere.

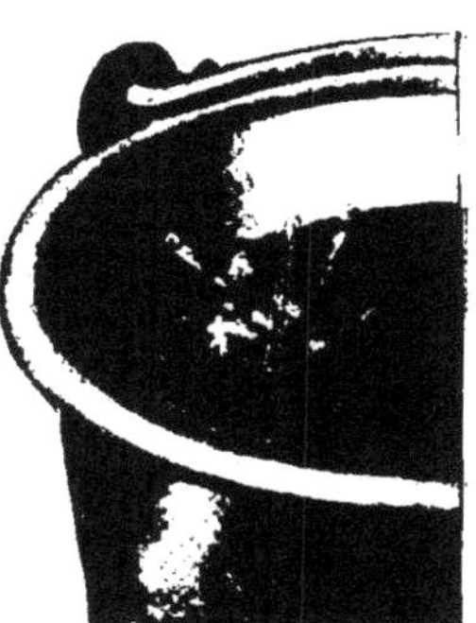

LEHN & FINK, Inc.
635 Greenwich Street, New York
Makers of Pebeco Tooth Paste

Harold F. Ritchie & Co., Selling Agents for the United States and Canada
171 Madison Avenue, New York City 10 McCaul St., Toronto

MOTORING AND AVIATION
Continued

excluding representatives of the black and yellow races.

"It was our nightly custom to go down to the motor camping-grounds and chat with the curious types that the chances of the open road had brought thither for a brief breathing spell. It gave us local color in large and assorted masses, and occasionally we stumbled on a good story. I remember one such in particular.

"We were resting, after a particularly hard night spent in fighting the mud of bottomless Montana roads, at a little hotel far up in the mountains. There was no village, but the hotel had set aside a tiny oasis, sheltered by towering cottonwoods, wherein the weary nomads of the highways could rest after their strenuous battles with the atrocious roads of the district. On this occasion there were some ten or twelve motor cars drawn up in this outdoor garage. One of them was a house on wheels, of which we had seen such numbers in the West that they no longer excited particular interest. The owner was a middle-aged man of obviously foreign origin. His traveling companion was also foreign in a sense, for he was a huge bull terrier, somewhere in whose tempestuous ancestry there had entered a dash of Russian wolfhound.

After a number of fruitless endeavors, says the writer, his party managed to engage the skipper of this menage in conversation. They learned that he was a titled Montenegrin, William R—— by name, an officer in the Czecho-Slovakian army, a nephew of the former King of Montenegro, and related to the Queen of Roumania. As for his other recommendation, writes Mr. Vanderbilt:

"He acknowledged that he was what we picturesquely term 'the black sheep of his family,' and that many years ago, when he was still a youngster, he had deserted kith and kin to follow Colonel Cody, better known as Buffalo Bill, to his ranch in Wyoming. To what must have been a natural aptitude, his life with Cody had added a lust for adventure that had carried him into almost every land under the sun and through a series of experiences that might give another Homer the material for a dozen epics.

"During his long life of adventuring Wilhelm had hunted in Africa, he had brought back blood-curdling stories from the Himalayas he had mushed in the Yukon and put in a year before the mast among the South Sea Islands. He knew intimately the most remote regions of Canada, and had been a member of an expedition up the Amazon. And now finally he has decided that the life of the open road, traveling where chance suggests or preference sends him, is the best life of all, and so he is a nomad of the highways in his ingeniously contrived motor bungalow.

"We spent an evening with 'Wild Bill,' going through his scrap-books, in which we saw signed letters from the crowned heads of Europe, from the nobility of Russia, from the potentates of Asia, and from the statesmen of the United States. Theodore Roosevelt wrote to him as 'Bill,' and his praise of the great American was never-ending.

"The following morning we took him with us on a fishing expedition over the

. We spent the day trying to land the y trout, but Wild Bill did more than and had a string of thirty-five beauties, ost before we had cast our lines. The ting incident of the day occurred about k when a huge rattler coiled up behind rear wheel of our car and commenced ling menacingly at our little Spitz py. Wilhelm saw it and announced his ntion of capturing the snake without g any weapon. First he drew its at- ion from the puppy to himself, and then an a chase between man and snake, the er striking repeatedly but always a few short of its wily hunter. In and out of orn field they ran, until the suspense ame too much for one of our party, who fully planted a couple of bullets in the ke's body. This only seemed to anger it more, but a moment later Wild Bill denly planted both his steel-shod heels the reptile's head. Even with its head shed, the snake still attempted to coil strike. After the battle we measured dead snake and found that it was four ., two inches long and five inches thick."

'aking up the practical side of his trip, . Vanderbilt gives his route as that of National Parks Highway. From New k he drove along the Lincoln Highway Maryland and thence through West ginia, Pennsylvania, Ohio, Indiana, and nois. The roads were paved most of the y. Even after leaving Chicago, the party no trouble until they reached the ders of Montana. North Dakota, home the Nonpartizan League, was especially d, he writes:

"We made our best time in crossing the iries from Fargo to Bismarck, where we tered the express train's time by four nutes. The roads in practically all the thwestern section are hard-buttomed l good in rain or fair weather. Occasional wers in Minnesota convert the gumbo o something resembling a mass of half- ted glue, far worse than the clays of ath Carolina and Georgia. We were tunate in being able to stop every time t a heavy rain threatened, and in this y we carried West with us a pleasant ough memory of Minnesota's roads.

'From the moment we entered Mon- a our troubles began, and we did not ake off the hoodoo until we had passed friendly portals of Washington. Our lcome to Montana took the form of a d-storm followed by a cloudburst. We d just crossed the State line when we ticed a portentously black cloud on the rizon. Being warned of what this enomenon meant, we put on all possible ed across the prairie and managed to ch the tiny village of Hysham just as the t grains of sand began to fly. Safe in the rage we watched the storm break, a nding vortex of flying sand that cut like whip, as it hurtled along on the wings of a ty-mile gale. About an hour later came rain. Rain, did I say? Not in the sense at we know it, for the water in this came wn as if it were the overflow from a servoir. Two hours after it started we uld not cross the village street and finally ter a couple of attempts to rush the rrent we were forced to put up for the ght in a funny little rooming house.

"We got under way at four o'clock the xt morning, but it was many days before escaped from the dire effects of that rrential storm. Trees had been uprooted, uses blown over, cattle drowned, bridges re down, and the mighty Yellowstone had

Residence at Plainfield, N. J. 10" Colonial Redwood Siding painted white.

Residence at Highland Park, Ill. Redwood sawn shingles.

California Redwood
the Western Wood for Eastern Homes

IN mansion or bungalow — wherever you build — California Redwood, used for exterior construction and finish, provides unusual protection against climatic extremes and freedom from wood-destructive elements.

Redwood Resists Rot

Every fibre of Redwood is impregnated during growth with a *natural* preservative which prevents the growth of decay-producing fungi. Properly seasoned, Redwood is practically immune from warping, shrinking and swelling. Climatic conditions and earth moisture do not weaken or rot Redwood.

The good appearance and soundness of your house are assured when you build with Redwood sidings, shingles, porch posts and columns, railings, roof boards, gutters, window and door frames—for these parts of the buildings are exposed to the weather, or in contact with the earth. For all these purposes Redwood is best.

Economical Too

In a Redwood house, repair and upkeep expenses are reduced to a minimum. Being unusually free from knots, splits, checks and other imperfections, there is little waste in Redwood lumber. The builder's time is saved in working with Redwood. Having a close grain smooth texture, and being free from resinous substances, Redwood takes and holds paint well.

Pergola and screen. Redwood painted white.

Residence at Oakland, California. Redwood Shakes

The Pacific Lumber Co.
OF ILLINOIS
REDWOOD

2085 McCormick Building, Chicago
New York City, N. Y. Kansas City, Mo.
THE PACIFIC LUMBER CO.
San Francisco, Cal. Los Angeles, Cal.
Export Company:
A. F. THANE & CO.
233 Broadway, New York City
311 California Street, San Francisco

The Largest Manufacturers and Distributors of California Redwood
Members of the California Redwood Association

Residence at Des Moines, Iowa. 8" Colonial Redwood Siding painted white.

Residence at Chetek, Wis. 1" Redwood Siding—Natural oiled finish.

Residence in Mission Hills of Country Club District, Kansas City, Mo. Redwood Siding painted white.

Every Home-Builder Should Have this free Redwood Booklet

If you are planning a home you should know more about Redwood—why and where it should be used in your new home. We will gladly send you this information. Write for Redwood Booklet No. 5, "Architectural and Building Uses." Address post card to our Chicago office today.

MOTORING AND AVIATION
Continued

overflowed its banks, so that east and west traffic had been practically discontinued. We were obliged to spend one night in the car and escaped more serious trouble only because we proceeded with the utmost caution.

"Indeed the transcontinental trip is one vast reel of scenic delight and inspirational happening. Whether the tourist is on the prairies of the northwest or crossing the Continental Divide at an altitude of 7,000 feet or negotiating the tremendous heights of Snoqualmie Pass over the backbone of the Cascades, the whole journey is a lesson in Americanism, in reduction of ego, and finally in pride of being an insignificant member of the great nation that calls this marvelous country its homestead."

THE WANDERINGS AND LATTER ENDS OF SOME OLD CARS

WHAT becomes of all the old automobiles? The greater part of them pass through a variety of existences before they are "junked," the number of changes depending principally upon the excellence of their construction in the first place. Some of them have many of their parts transferred to brothers of the same make. Some, following the precedent established by the once popular carriage horses of the city streets, are put out to spend the remainder of their lives on isolated farms. Up in one corner of Springfield, Massachusetts, there is an automobile exchange which receives a good many of the worn-out cars of the vicinity, and it was there that a reporter for the Springfield *Republican* looked into the matter of the latter ends of some of them. "A large acreage is needed for the burying ground of these motor cars," he writes:

Their remains are generously distributed over every available space, leaving here and there a few alleyways over which the prospective customer or curiosity seeker may find his way. He is sure to stumble over innumerable pieces of iron, rods and crank shafts that pierce their way from beneath the piles or from under some mutilated chassis. But the owner of this field of iron assured one that he has cleaning days, like any other respectable housekeeper.

Once upon a time one of the most expensive limousines that could be built was presented, in all its shining newness, to the daughter of a wealthy man. For two seasons it was the haughty bearer of family, friends and relatives on missions that were happy, and sometimes a bit sorrowful.

One day a tire blew out; soon after another, which had been showing signs of wear, gave up the ghost, too, and announced that it just wouldn't run more than twenty miles more at the very greatest concession. The engine decided to display a few temperamental tricks hitherto unsuspected by the fair owner, and these unexpected happenings were more than her good nature could tolerate. A conference with "dad," some advice from the chauffeur, and certain pleasantries from a salesman, ended in the car being turned in for a younger and more up-to-date brother.

The second-hand man took only a few

days to put the machine back into tip-top shape, and started out in search of another buyer. For some $4000 less than the original cost, the car became the property of a man whose money was a recent acquisition. In time the second owner acquired even more money and decided he must have the latest model of the make. So once again the machine found its way back to the service shop.

Here it stayed longer than on its first visit, eventually emerging from the paint and machine shop in satisfactory running condition. Its third owner proved to be a man comfortably well off, but not over-endowed with this world's goods. Three thousand dollars made the car his. His family of romping youngsters grew to love the big substantial machine, and practically lived in it. It never left the flower-trimmed driveway without its roomy seats literally overflowing with active children. It didn't take long for the upholstering to become threadbare, and constant washing and polishing could not efface the unmistakable signs of wear. Unquestionably the car was deteriorating in value, and reluctantly the genial third owner let it go.

Back in its old place in the garage, it became a patient waiter for another master. Weeks went by before the car, already repaired as neatly as possible, caught the wary eye of a large taxi-stand owner. It suited his need to a T and he bought it for $2,000. With a clicking meter to identify it with the trade, the car once more roamed in the outside world. But with what a difference! Now instead of bowling over smooth macadam roads, it was forced to rumble its way, always with all possible speed, over the checkered streets of a city. It ran off a profitable mileage for the taximan, before he relinquished it to another firm.

This smaller taxi company transported the machine to a large city where the paving was yet more uneven, and the cobbles far less securely placed. Under the none too careful driving, the machine gradually lost its prideful air, and when nearly every nut had been shaken loose, and the springs jumped at the slightest bump, it was once more relegated to the used-car shop. After a tedious siege in the repair department, it emerged a respectable shade, albeit a remnant, of its former self.

Along came a farmer who viewed the car with cunning eye, and decided to purchase it for a lesser price than a new machine, of the garden variety, would cost him. Back in the country the old machine gave of its fast failing best to the thrifty farmer and his family. Before many months had elapsed, the man used it less and less for pleasure riding, and made it earn its keep and fuel by hauling his vegetables and other produce into market. Eventually he and his mechanical son decided it would be an easy matter to transfer the big engine to a home-made truck body. This was speedily accomplished, and the bulky body was left alone by the side of a three-wheeled buggy, a discarded sleigh and broken-down farm implements.

It was not long before the domestic daughter of the house discovered that this shelter would make the finest kind of a playhouse. She, her sisters and the neighbors' children moved in with their dolls, cutlery, and house furnishings the very next day. And the truck? For two years it plied stolidly between farm and market, the engine protesting at first mildly, and gradually more emphatically, until, one day the farmer and his boy left it at the shack of an Italian laborer in exchange for a Jersey

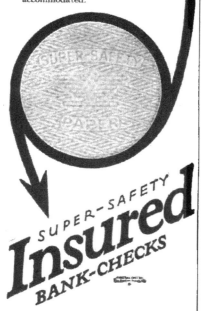

INVESTMENTS ▲ AND ▲ FINANCE

"NO FINANCIAL MOSES NEED APPLY"

OVER and over again some one tells us that the times are crying vainly for a financial Moses to lead the nation out of the wilderness of present-day business difficulties, and the question is somewhat despairingly asked: "Where is the man big enough to take the late J. Pierpont Morgan's place?" To which a writer in *The Annalist* answers under the caption used above, that there is to-day no need for any such financial Moses and that "the development of such a figure would be absolutely contrary to the trend of the times, and entirely out of keeping with the present structure of business and finance in the United States." It is just as impossible, we are told, "for a new Morgan to arise under conditions existing in the United States to-day, as it would be for a snow man to thrive in Wall Street in August." In the old days, "with thirty thousand banks utterly unorganized" something like the Morgan leadership was necessary, "and it was in Wall Street that steps were always taken to 'save the situation.'" For, if the immense banks and other great organizations under the elder Morgan's direction "engaged in the same internecine strife as occurred among banks outside of the ring, and between different parts of the country, the nation would have seen even worse panics than it did see." "There might have been better leadership, but definite leadership of some sort was essential." But, we are reminded, there has been a change in the financial structure of the country. "Under national auspices, and under the leadership of a public body, more than 70 per cent. of the nation's total banking resources are now marshaled in a great federation which is absolutely clear of private domination, which contains no inner ring, and which leaves every member free to run its own affairs." More important than the use of the nation's gold reserve and the many forms of technical coordination through the Federal Reserve system, is, in the opinion of the writer we are quoting, "the way in which the present-day unified banking reports make clear to the eyes of all bankers the exact condition of the financial seas":

In the dark ages a banker might know all about the position of his own institution, but there was a big element of guesswork as to what others were doing, particularly for those outside the Morgan empire. He might know that his own bank was in a sound position; that his credit was not overextended; that his reserves were ample; that his customers were meeting their obligations regularly, and that their business was justifying the amount of bank credit they were obtaining from him, but he could not gage accurately the position of banking as a whole. He could not watch carefully the expansion of credit in relation to business, and he could not take steps to cooperate with his fellow bankers to stop inflation. This blind condition has been succeeded by one in which, from week to week, the country's total banking position is made clear from the data issued by the Federal Reserve Board. Each week every banker can see how much gold reserve there is. Each week he can see how much total credit there is. Each week he can see the exact state of the currency. From week to week he can watch the expansion and contraction of credit and currency in keeping with the rise and fall of business, and, more than that, the means are placed in every individual banker's hands to play a part in expanding or contracting the currency in keeping with current business needs.

The point of which is this, that this making clear of the facts and requirements of the situation for all bankers to see has largely superseded the need for individualized personal leadership. An observance of the plain dictates of banking prudence by all bankers is now possible, and universal obedience to these sound principles will give the banking system of the country the necessary unity of action such as could not be achieved under any conceivable individual leadership. In other words, each banker, as is the pilot of a boat, is furnished with an open and plain chart to steer by.

Thus the need for individualized personal leadership has been eliminated and nowadays the bankers of the country "are each pilots of their own boats in accordance with their own reading of the chart and not in accordance with the dictation of some dominant super-pilot." While many of our bank presidents to-day are men of outstanding individual ability "there is none among them whose power in banking extends beyond the walls of his own bank. Their years of experience have taught them the requirements of sound banking; their years of authority have filled them with independence of spirit, and their years of responsibility have made them realize how essential it is to the welfare of the nation that banking as a whole be actuated by uniform principles of prudence and constructive business policies."

And so, concludes the writer:

It is a day of the leadership of principles rather than of an individual, which is more in keeping with the genius of America than was that type of financial leadership which was autocratic. No matter how beneficent dominant individual leadership might be, public antagonism against it would be inevitable.

No financial Moseses need apply, because they are not needed. They need not apply because they are not wanted. They need not apply because we have a much better way of doing things.

This new situation is good for the country, but it is bad for radicalism. It does not give soapbox oratory any great outstanding head to knock down.

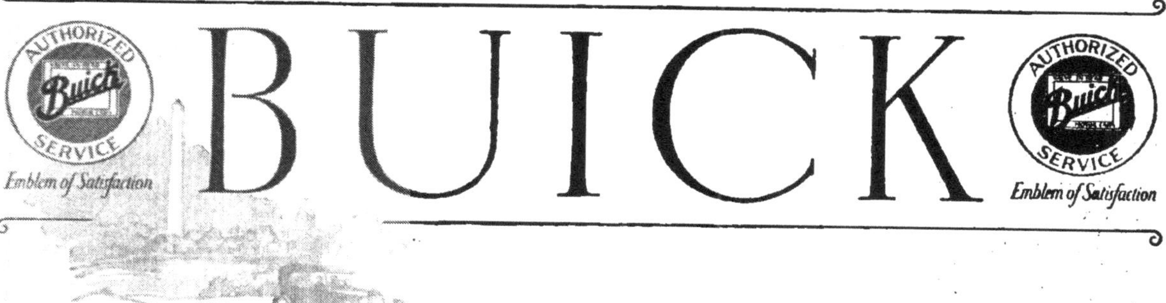

To go there and get back—to master road and distance—to stand up under the hardest daily service—that is what Buick motor cars are built for.

Seven Trans-continental Trips—and Buick Never Faltered

Every year since 1914, James A. Bell, aged 60, and Mrs. Bell have driven across the Continent. The first two trips were made in four-cylinder Buicks, the last five in the same 1916 Buick Six.

In all these fifty thousand miles but one small part was replaced, caused by an accident pulling another car out of a sand-hole.

A wonderful record, yes—yet typical of hundreds of thousands of other Buick cars you see every day whose stories never are told.

You know what you're getting when you buy a Buick!

BUICK MOTOR COMPANY, FLINT, MICHIGAN
Division of General Motors Corporation
Pioneer Builders of Valve-in-Head Motor Cars
Branches in all Principal Cities—Dealers Everywhere

Buick Sixes

22-Six-44 Three Pass. Roadster	$1495
22-Six-45 Five Pass. Touring -	1525
22-Six-46 Three Pass. Coupe -	2135
22-Six-47 Five Pass. Sedan - -	2435
22-Six-48 Four Pass. Coupe -	2325
22-Six-49 Seven Pass. Touring	1735
22-Six-50 Seven Pass. Sedan -	2635

Buick Fours

22-Four-34 Two Pass. Roadster	$ 935
22-Four-35 Five Pass. Touring	975
22-Four-36 Three Pass. Coupe	1475
22-Four-37 Five Pass. Sedan	1650

All Prices F. O. B. Flint, Michigan

WHEN BETTER AUTOMOBILES ARE BUILT, BUICK WILL BUILD THEM

INVESTMENTS AND FINANCE
Continued

THE FIVE-IN-A-FAMILY FALLACY

FOR years, the economists have been using the estimate of five persons in the average wage-earner's family—husband, wife, and three children under fourteen—in arriving at conclusions in regard to wages, budgets, and living costs. But under existing conditions it is a fallacy to use a family of five as a basis for determining a minimum or average wage, says the Philadelphia Chamber of Commerce's Committee on Industrial Relations. As reported in the New York *Tribune*, the committee holds that—

> The average person engaged in a gainful occupation in this country does not support a family of five, and those persons who have three or more children are, as a rule, only required for a limited period of their lives to support that number.
>
> It is impossible under existing conditions for all workers, skilled and unskilled, to receive a minimum annual pay equal to the living cost for a family of five.

According to estimates made for 1917, and adjusted to the population in 1920, it has been found, we read in *The Tribune*, that the average number of persons supported by one wage-earner is 2.46. With this in mind, the Philadelphia committee concludes that "each worker in the country need only earn an average of about three-fifths of the amount estimated as a minimum basis in order that every group of five may have the support called for on a basis of reasonable living standards." But this contention is questioned by the writer in *The Tribune* on the ground that the removal of two persons from a family of five does not reduce the expense by two-fifths. "Certain fixed charges remain the same, for the smaller family as for a larger one. This is obvious to any one familiar with overhead, either in business or household economy."

The real issue, we read, seems to be whether an attempt should be made to establish an ideal minimum wage, which industry might not be able to pay, "or whether those families having more than the average number of dependents must subsist on an adequate income." In the opinion of the Philadelphia committee, "a strict adherence to the family of five theory in wage decisions, if carried out extensively, would lead to general wage scales which industry as at present organized cannot afford to pay."

The committee is also imprest by the great variation in the different estimates of a proper worker's income, based on the family of five theory which has been established by the United States Bureau of Labor Statistics. For instance, the New York Factory Investigating Commission's 1914 figures, revised to May, 1920, the

$1,764.25 against $876.43 in 1914. But the Philadelphia Municipal Bureau of Research put the minimum at $1,992.40 in May, 1920, while Professor Osburn's budget for the War Labor Board, similarly revised, is said to place the minimum at $2,329.14.

HOW UNLIMITED ARMAMENT LIMITS ALL OUR INCOMES

As "a business man talking to business men" at a dinner in Philadelphia Mr. George W. Norris, Governor of the Federal Reserve Bank in that city, emphasized the financial necessity for disarmament. Before the war, he said, as reported in the New York *Evening Post*, "we congratulated ourselves that we were not as war-ridden Europe, overburdened with debt charges and obliged to give the time of our young men and the resources of tax-payers to great armies and navies." The Great War, however, "has not only added enormously to the burdens of the European nations, but has also radically altered our own position, and put us measurably on a par with them." According to Mr. Norris, "the combined pre-war expenditures of the United States, Great Britain, France and Italy for military purposes have been more than trebled, their debt charges have been increased nine-fold, and their total governmental expenditures are now about six and a half times what they were in the pre-war period." That is, he explained by pointing to a chart, the annual debt charges of these five Great Powers have risen from $497,000,000 before the war to $5,556,000,000 at the present time; their military expenditures from $1,321,000,000 to $4,092,000,000, and their total expenditures from $3,134,000,000 to $19,309,000,000. Mr. Norris then proceeds to show by the following tabulation just how these enormous expenditures for military purposes hit the average American, British, French, and Italian family:

GOVERNMENTAL EXPENDITURES PER FAMILY OF FIVE

Before War— Total expenditures.	Debt expenditures.	Military expenditures.	All other expenditures.
United States: $33.00	$1.15	$23.10	$8.75
Great Britain: $102.00	12.90	40.80	48.30
France: $122.80	31.75	44.20	46.85
Italy: 70.70	14.05	14.15	42.50
Average: $82.125	$14.96	$30.56	$36.00
After war—			
United States: $214.80	$43.25	$54.10	$117.45
Great Britain: $548.90	182.25	109.55	257.10
France: $633.30	238.80	131.60	262.90
Italy: $642.65	109.90	121.10	411.65
Average: $509.91	$143.55	$104.08	$262.27
Ratio of increase: (6.2)	(9.5)	(3.4)	(7.1)

INVESTMENTS AND FINANCE
Continued

MEXICO'S ECONOMIC BALANCE SHEET

PRESIDENT OBREGON'S apparent intention to put his country on its feet in a business way lends interest to a recent survey of economic conditions and prospects in Mexico which appeared in a September issue of *Commerce Reports*. Omitting the general comment, we reprint as follows its brief summing up of conditions under five heads:

(1) A refunding of perhaps $75,000,000 of defaulted bonds, plus some $3,000,000 of accrued interest, a funding of foreign damage claims of at least $50,000,000, and a substantial increase of the net revenues of the Government, to provide service on all this, are essential for the near future. The currency system is dangerous in its rigidity, but steps are being taken to reform it.

(2) A practically complete new banking system has to be built, and it is hoped to insert in it desirable features of the American Reserve system.

(3) Under existing currency and banking systems the question of foreign exchange enters little into commercial questions.

(4) The normalization of prices is proceeding more slowly and more irregularly than in the United States. Local manufacfacturers are prosperous.

(5) Labor is much cheaper in Mexico than in the United States, but readjustment is yet taking place in most lines. Unemployment is serious. There remains danger of disaster from radical agitation, but it is diminishing.

STATEMENT OF THE OWNERSHIP, MANAGEMENT, ETC.

Required by the Act of Congress of August 24, 1912, of "THE LITERARY DIGEST"

Published weekly at New York, N. Y.

For October 1, 1921

State of New York }
County of New York } ss.

Before me, a Notary Public in and for the State and county aforesaid, personally appeared Wm. Neisel, who, having been duly sworn according to law, deposes and says that he is the Secretary of the Funk & Wagnalls Company, Publishers of THE LITERARY DIGEST, and that the following is, to the best of his knowledge and belief, a true statement of the ownership, management (and if a daily paper, the circulation), etc., of the aforesaid publication for the date shown in the above caption required by the Act of August 24, 1912, embodied in Section 443, Postal Laws and Regulations, printed on the reverse of this form, to wit:

1. That the names and addresses of the publisher, editor, managing editor, and business managers are

Publisher, Funk & Wagnalls Co., 354 4th Ave., N. Y. C.
Editor, Wm. S. Woods, 354 4th Ave., N. Y. City.
Managing Editor, Wm. S. Woods, 354 4th Ave., New York City.
Business Managers, The Board of Directors of Funk & Wagnalls Co., 354 4th Ave., New York City.

2. That the owners are: (Give names and addresses of individual owners, or, if a corporation, give its name and the names and addresses of stockholders owning or holding 1 per cent. or more of the total amount of stock.)

Funk & Wagnalls Co., 354 4th Ave., New York City.
Cuddihy, Robert J., 354 4th Ave., New York City.
Cuddihy, E. F., 354 4th Ave., New York City.
Funk, E. M., 354 4th Ave., New York City.
Funk, Wilfred J., 354 4th Ave., New York City.
Funk, Wilfred J., and Scott, Lida F., as Trustees for themselves and B. F. Funk, 354 4th Ave., New York City.
Neisel, C. L., 354 4th Ave., New York City.
Scott, Lida F., 354 4th Ave., New York City.

3. That the known bondholders, mortgagees, and other security holders owning or holding 1 per cent, or more of total amount of bonds, mortgages or other securities are: None.

4 That the two paragraphs next above, giving the names of the owners, stockholders, and security holders, if any, contain not only the list of stockholders and security holders as they appear upon the books of the company, but also, in cases where the stockholder or security holder appears upon the books of the company as trustee or in any other fiduciary relation, the name of the person or corporation for whom such trustee is acting is given; also that the said two paragraphs contain statements embracing affiant's full knowledge and belief as to the circumstances and conditions under which stockholders and security holders who do not appear upon the books of the company as trustees hold stock and securities in a capacity other than that of a bona-fide owner; and this affiant has no reason to believe that any other person, association, or corporation has any interest direct or indirect in the said stock, bonds, or other securities than as so stated by him.

WILLIAM NEISEL, Secretary of FUNK & WAGNALLS COMPANY, Publisher and Owner.

Sworn to and subscribed before me this 1st day of October, 1921.

[Seal]

ROLLO CAMPBELL, Notary Public.

(My commission expires March 30, 1923.)

CURRENT EVENTS

FOREIGN

September 28.—The Independent Socialist Party introduces in the Reichstag a bill providing that all property of former Emperor William and the former German princes shall be confiscated by the state, and that all officials holding monarchist views shall be dismissed without pension.

September 29.—Premier Lloyd George invites Eamon De Valera, Sinn Fein leader, to London on October 11, for a personal discussion to settle the Irish problem.

The British India Office states that the military authorities in Madras, India, take a serious view of the rebellion in the Malabar district, where the Moplaks are conducting guerrilla warfare.

The peace treaty between Germany and the United States is reported favorably to the Reichstag by the Foreign Affairs Committee.

The Assembly of the League of Nations adopts a resolution requesting the delegates to solicit from their respective governments authority to sign the conventions for the repression of the white slave traffic.

Premier Ponikowski, of Poland, has telegraphed Premier Lloyd George that the Polish Government will make every effort to follow a policy of peace and economic rehabilitation, according to a dispatch from London.

September 30.—The Austrian Government officially confirms reports that former Premier Friederich of Hungary has issued a proclamation establishing West Hungary as an independent monarchy.

Eamon De Valera accepts Premier Lloyd George's invitation to a peace conference in London on October 11.

Chancellor Wirth charges the German Nationalist Party with fomenting a conspiracy for the overthrow of the German Republic and warns them that the government is thoroughly prepared to crush such a move.

Representatives of wireless interests in Great Britain, France, Germany and the United States begin organizing in Paris an international wireless company for the control and development of the greater part of the world's radio facilities.

The Chinese Government sends an identic note to the American and Japanese Legations at Pekin declaring that agreements between the United States and Japan regarding the future status of the Island of Yap constitute a violation of China's sovereignty and the principle of national equality.

October 1.—The Committee on Disarmament of the Assembly of the League of Nations proposes that the Council of the League report to the various governments its appeal that appropriations for armaments in the next two years be limited to the amount of the expenses this year.

October 2.—The Mohammedan rebels in Melattur, India, are reported to be offering the Hindus the alternative of death or Islam.

General Pershing bestows the Congressional Medal of Honor on France's unknown poilu buried beneath the Arc de Triomphe.

The Village of Loscheim, near Malmedy, is restored to Germany by the frontier commission.

Former King William II. of Wurtemburg, who abdicated in November, 1918, dies in his seventy-fourth year.

October 3.—The Assembly of the League

CURRENT EVENTS
Continued

unanimity for amendments by requiring only a three-fourths majority vote.

Spanish troops inflict heavy losses on Moorish tribesmen in an advance along a front of ten kilometers before Zeluan.

October 4.—Many police and unemployed are injured in what is said to have been the largest demonstration by unemployed known in London.

Hungary withdraws from Burgenland, or West Hungary, and the territory is formally taken over by Austria.

DOMESTIC

September 28.—The Interstate Commerce Commission reports a tentative plan for consolidation of all major American railroads into 19 systems. Hearings will be held to discuss the proposed consolidation.

Lieutenant John A. MacReady, United States Air Service, establishes a new world's record for altitude by climbing 40,800 feet above sea level, at Dayton, Ohio.

Twenty-two terra-cotta corporations are indicted under the Sherman Anti-Trust Law by a special Federal Grand Jury in New York.

September 29.—Senate Democrats adopt unanimously a resolution offered by Senator Harrison, of Mississippi, expressing the hope that the conference on the limitation of armament will succeed.

The convention of the United Mine Workers of America at Indianapolis votes disapproval of salary increases for approximately 60 per cent. of the union's officers.

The majority report of the Privileges and Elections Committee absolves Senator Newberry of the charges of having violated the corrupt practises act by undue expenditures.

The United States Shipping Board rejects the bid of the Ship Construction and Trading Company, Inc., of New York, for the Government's fleet of wooden ships. The bid was $2,100 for each ship.

September 30.—President Harding issues a proclamation asking the American people to honor their war dead on Armistice Day, November 11, by offering a two-minute silent prayer at noon, when the body of an unknown soldier killed in action will be buried in Arlington National Cemetery.

National officers of the American Legion in conference at Indianapolis announce that the 900,000 unemployed ex-service men will be cared for by the Legion.

October 2.—Figures obtained in Washington place the number of men in the active armies of the fourteen most important nations in the world at approximately 6,000,000.

October 3.—President Harding requests the Governors and Mayors throughout the country to organize in each community machinery for correction of economic conditions along lines worked out by the Washington unemployment conference.

Ex-President Taft takes the oath of office as Chief Justice of the Supreme Court of the United States.

October 4.—President Harding authorizes Secretary of State Hughes to invite Holland, Belgium and Portugal to discuss subjects affecting the Far East during the Washington disarmament conference.

Colonel Arthur Woods, former New York City Police Commissioner, is appointed by Secretary Hoover head of the emergency volunteer relief committees, organized by the national unemployment

THE LEXICOGRAPHER'S EASY CHAIR

In this column, to decide questions concerning the current use of words, the Funk & Wagnalls New Standard Dictionary is consulted as arbiter.

Readers will please bear in mind that no notice will be taken of anonymous communications.

"L. K.," Ft. D. A. Russell, Wyo.—"In speaking of time, 'A' says 'Ten minutes *of* twelve'; 'B' says 'Ten minutes *to* twelve.' 'A' insists that 'B' is wrong. Which is correct and why?"

"Ten minutes *to* twelve" is the only form that is heard in England, but general usage in America has sanctioned the idiomatic phrase " . . . *of* twelve."

"J. W.," Westmount, Can.—"Please give me the correct pronunciation of the word *impious*."

The correct pronunciation of the word *impious* is *im-pi-us*—first *i* as in *hit*, second *i* as in *habit*, *u* as in *but*. The pronunciation *im-pai'us*—*i* as in *hit*, *ai* as in *aisle*, *u* as in *but* is incorrect.

"M. B. H.," San Francisco, Cal.—"Is the following sentence grammatically correct: 'Mr. Anthony, he wanted them, Miss Keen, she wanted them and Mr. Brown, he wanted them'? One party says it is not correct, that the words 'he' and 'she' are superfluous. I say it is correct, the words being in apposition and used for emphasis. Please decide."

The pronoun of the *third person* is scarcely ever expressed if the noun is given. Such expressions as "The man *he* told me" are never used by correct writers or speakers. Therefore, your sentence should read, "Mr. Anthony wanted them, Miss Keen wanted them, and Mr. Brown wanted them."

"J. T.," Kingston, Jamaica.—"Which is correct, 'The public *are*,' or 'The Public *is*'; also 'The government *are*,' or 'The government *is*'?"

The words *public* and *government* are collective nouns. A collective noun, tho singular in form, may take a verb either in the singular or the plural number, according as it refers to the objects composing it as one aggregate or as separate individuals; as, "The audience *was* large"; "The audience *were* divided in opinion." Therefore, either *is* or *are* may be used with the words you cite, depending upon what is meant.

"S. W. S.," Syracuse, N. Y.—"Can you tell us or suggest where we can find out the letter which is most used in the alphabet; also the one least used?"

The letter *e*, the fifth in the alphabet, is the most frequently used in the English alphabet. The letter in the alphabet that is the least used is *z*. The following is a table of the relative proportions in which the various letters of the alphabet are used:

A	85	F	25	K	8	P	17	U	34		
B	16	G	17	L	40	Q	5	V	12		
C	30	H	64	M	30	R	62	W	20	Z	2
D	44	I	80	N	80	S	80	X	4		
E	120	J	4	O	80	T	90	Y	20		

"E. N.," Chicago, Ill.—"Please give me whatever information you can concerning the meaning and origin of the proper name *Nourse*."

The name *Nourse* is the same as *Nurse*, which is an Anglo-French-Latin name, from Middle English *norice*, *nurice*, Old French *norrice* (French *nourrice*), Latin *nutrix*, *-icis*, a nurse.

"J. E. B.," Warwick, N. Y.—"Kindly advise the names given the flotilla of three vessels of Columbus on his voyage of discovery, 1492."

The names of the three vessels to which you refer were the *Santa Maria*, *Pinta* and *Nina*.

"S. M. P.," Cleveland, O.—The correct pronunciation of *Arkansas* is *ar'kan-so*—first *a* as in *art*, second *a* as in *final*, *o* as in *or*.

"M. B.," Bridgeport, Conn.—"Kindly tell me whether *is* or *are* should be used in the following sentence, 'As a large number of gears of your manufacture *is* or *are* used by our Company, it would be of assistance to me, etc.'"

When the word *number* is used to express a unit of some sort, it is singular; as, "The number of men *was* small." "The number of members *is* increasing." Used in the sense of *several*, it is plural; as, "A large number of men *speak* in favor of single tax." In the sentence cited *are* and not *is* should be used—"As a large number of gears of your manufacture *are* used by our Company, etc."

Making Sales at Lowest Cost

THE SHADED PART *of this penny represents what it costs the full page advertiser to get you to read this message.*
*—the addressing and mailing and delivery into your hands; all for 3/10ths of **a cent**;*
*—$4,000 for a full page advertisement that is delivered to 1,300,000 **families**;*
—if the advertiser mailed a postal card to 1,300,000 separate addresses it would cost 6½ times as much or about $26,000;
—circular matter under 1 cent postage cannot be manufactured for less than $25.00 per thousand;
—in proper letter form with a two cent stamp the postage alone is $26,000 and the finished job (at the lowest of prices) $45,500 or eleven times what this page costs the advertiser.

WHILE you are reading this, so hundreds this very minute are reading it, too. Ever think how many of these hundreds need what *you* make? How many of them *want* what you make?

Unless you tell them about what you make, their needs lie dormant, unexpressed. Or else they are met by some other making something like what you make,

but costing more than your potential customer feels he would like to pay, or being less carefully made than your product, too poorly constructed, to really meet your potential customer's needs.

The reason businesses like Ivory Soap and Palmolive and Dodge Bros. and Hart, Schaffner and Marx and The Literary Digest keep going up and up and up is because they tell the 111,000,000 more—and more often—about their product than other concerns in their same lines.

These concerns think in terms of fractions of a cent. They know there is no way to reach every one so quickly and at so low a cost as just sitting down and talking to people like this, through national advertising.

There is no mystery about it. It is just as natural as the way you develop friendships. Among your friends there are a lot of people you didn't like when you were sizing them up. And there are those other people—ex-friends—that you liked once, those who didn't measure up somehow.

Businesses that think well enough of themselves to try to win your friendship by talking to you this way, are not likely to disappoint you—at first or any time after.

Advertisers like those mentioned add to their reputation for making good goods and selling them right, the inestimable value of having millions of friends. The relation is positive, instead of nameless and negative. So the good advertising does lives after it.

The Literary Digest

354 FOURTH AVE., NEW YORK **122 SO. MICHIGAN AVE., CHICAGO**

Bankers, heads of industrial enterprises, lawyers whose clients discuss advertising with them are invited to send for a DIGEST *representative. We are frequently able to give good advice leading toward a proper solution of the possible application of advertising to business enterprises.*

THE ▲ SPICE ▲ OF ▲ LIFE

And a Strong One, Too.—Cussing won't help the situation, perhaps; but what business needs is a good buy-word.—*Baltimore Sun.*

Keeping Her Cheerful.—"Do you think I can make her happy?"

"Well, she'll always have something to laugh at."—*London Opinion.*

His First Case.—ROOKIE SENTRY—"Halt, who's there?"

VOICE—"Private Stock, Company C."

ROOKIE SENTRY—"Advance, Private Stock, and be sampled."—*The American Legion Weekly.*

Something Doing.—FIRST SALESGIRL—"That man I just sold a five-pound box of candy to said it was for his wife."

SECOND DITTO—"Is he newly married?"

FIRST—"Either that or he's done something."—*Boston Transcript.*

Too Many Tooters.—MOTORIST (pulling up)—"What's the matter; didn't you hear me blow my horn?"

PEDESTRIAN—"Yes, but there's so much hay fever about, I didn't think it was an automobile."—*Boston Transcript.*

The Humanitarian.—"I use this horrible shriek horn on my automobile for humane reasons," explained Lieutenant Husted. "If I can paralyze a pedestrian with fear, he will stand still and I am less likely to run over him."—*The Arklight.*

Enough Is Enough.—SOLOIST SUNDAY MORNING—Mrs. N——— McE——— will sing at the First Congregational church Sunday morning the offertory solo, "A Thousand Ways," by Harkness. F——— W. W——— will be heard in the Mendelssohn aria, "It Is Enough."—From a news item in the *Tacoma Ledger.*

They Go Together.—"The rapidly increasing divorce rate," remarked the wit, "indicates that America is indeed becoming the land of the free."

"Yes," replied his prosaic friend, "but the continued marriage rate suggests that it is still the home of the brave."—*The American Legion Weekly.*

No Superficial Sorrow.—She was a rather elderly woman of dusky hue of the kind who looks upon all members of the white race in a friendly, confidential way. And she was arrayed in deepest mourning from head to foot. Also the look upon her face was entirely in keeping with her melancholy array. It certainly seemed that she was dressed up within the last inch of her mournful feelings. But such, alas! was not the case. For finally she halted before the counter she was seeking—the underwear counter. And this is the conversation that ensued:

"Honey," she addressed the young woman clerk, "is you got any black underwear?"

"No, auntie," replied the salesgirl, "but I have some very nice white ones. Won't they do?"

"No, honey," replied the woman with just a touch of sorrow. "No, they don't do. When I mourns, I mourns clean down to de skin."—*El Paso Times.*

The Peaceful Life.—It has just about gotten so in this country that the cook quits when the family tires of canned goods.—*Dallas News.*

We All Need It.—General Wood's suggestion that the Filipinos be taught law and order ought not to be limited to the Filipinos.—*Syracuse Herald.*

More Evidence Needed.—BLACKSTONE—"What made the jury disagree in that prohibition case?"

WEBSTER—"There wasn't enough evidence to go round, so all except the first four jurors voted for a reasonable doubt."—*The American Legion Weekly.*

Unto the End.—"How's this?" asked the lawyer. "You've named six bankers in your will to be pallbearers. Of course, it's all right, but wouldn't you rather choose some friends with whom you are on better terms?"

"No, Judge, that's all right. Those fellows have carried me for so long they might as well finish the job."—*The American Legion Weekly.*

Delicate Revenge.—"You must have made a few enemies in your long political career?"

"More than a few," answered Senator Sorghum. "I have forgiven them all."

"That is magnanimous."

"Not especially. By forgiving them I call their attention to the fact that they never succeeded in injuring me enough to earn my abiding resentment."—*Washington Star.*

Stunning Retort.—When the woman motorist was called upon to stop, she asked, indignantly, "What do you want with me?"

"You were traveling at forty miles an hour," answered the police officer.

"Forty miles an hour? Why, I haven't been out an hour," said the woman.

"Go ahead," said the officer. "That's a new one to me."—*Exchange.*

The Literary Lid Is Off.—Some of our story writers are running riot with their similes. Here are a few we gathered in our late reading:

"Her lips quivered like a light auto."

"He edged nearer to her until he was almost as close as the air in the subway."

"But his mind, like her face, was made up."

"Her hair dropped on her pallid cheek like seaweed on a clam."

"He gazed anxiously at her face, the way a person in a taxi gazes at the face of the meter."—*Boston Transcript.*

Getting Acquainted.—A new foreman took charge of the shop this particular morning, and many of the men had not as yet met him. About the middle of the forenoon he was making a tour of the buildings to familiarize himself with the layout, when on passing a small enclosure he saw two workmen inside who were sitting down smoking. Before he had the opportunity to speak one of the men said: "Hello, what are you doing, stranger?"

"I'm Dodgen, the new foreman," was the reply.

"So are we, come in and have a smoke."—*Forbes Magazine (N. Y.)*

October 22, 1921

The Literary Digest

(Title Reg. U.S. Pat. Off.)

One of Uncle Sam's Assets:
A GIRL SCOUT!

New York FUNK & WAGNALLS COMPANY London

PUBLIC OPINION New York combined with The LITERARY DIGEST

Vol. 71, No. 4. Whole No. 1644 October 22, 1921 Price 10 Cents

MOTOR
NASH
CARS

NASH SIX PRICES

All Nash passenger cars have cord tires as standard equipment

5-passenger touring .	$1545
2-passenger roadster . .	$1525
4-passenger sport model .	$1695
7-passenger touring . .	$1695
4-passenger coupe . .	$2395
7-passenger sedan . .	$2695

Prices f. o. b. Kenosha

NASH FOUR PRICES

All Nash passenger cars have cord tires as standard equipment

5-passenger touring .	$1195
2-passenger roadster . .	$1175
3-passenger coupe . .	$1735
5-passenger sedan . .	$1935

Prices f. o. b. Milwaukee

The determined aim of every man in the great Nash organization, executives, workmen, distributors and dealers, is to constantly raise Nash standards of value and service.

As we develop and improve Nash cars, adding new features and new equipment, and refining every detail that perfects Nash performance, we are also developing our service for Nash owners. Every Nash dealer maintains adequate facilities to give prompt and expert care to every Nash car in his territory.

THE NASH MOTORS COMPANY

KENOSHA, WISCONSIN

Manufacturers of Passenger Cars and Trucks, Including Famous Nash Quad

The Reason of Brunswick Dominancy Is No Secret

Perfect Rendition of So-Called "Difficult" Tones Sets *New* Standard in Musical World

In the homes of greatest musicians, both in Europe and America, you will find The Brunswick.

In the world-great conservatories, you will find it.

In every city and community, where there are shops devoted to that which is best in music, you will find Brunswick featured as the Standard of today.

Brunswick has established a new era. It is the criterion by which phonographic music now is judged.

Advanced Methods

This universal preference of the knowing is due to Brunswick's advanced methods of Reproduction and of Interpretation.

By means of them, perfect rendition of the so-called "difficult" tones is achieved—the piano, the harp, the human voice, and even soprano High "C" attained without "metallic suggestion," discord or vibration!

The Brunswick Method of Reproduction embodies the oval Tone Amplifier of moulded wood (built like a fine old violin) and the patented *Ultona*, which plays *all makes of records* at a turn of the hand.

The Brunswick Method of Interpretation results in sweeter and more beautiful records—tones almost unbelievably true, notes amazing in their fidelity.

Both methods are *exclusively* Brunswick—obtainable on no other make of phonographs or records.

Hence, those high in the musical world will tell you that buying any phonograph, without at least *hearing* The Brunswick, is a mistake. And that to be without Brunswick Records is to be without much of what is best in music.

Costs No More

Brunswick—the *accepted* instrument of the musical world—costs no more than an ordinary phonograph.

You can purchase a Brunswick for as little as $65. There are fourteen models, in all finishes, including a comprehensive showing of authentic period models.

Call on your nearest Brunswick dealer for a demonstration. The Brunswick plays all makes of records, and Brunswick records can be played on any phonograph. Hear, compare—then judge for yourself.

THE BRUNSWICK-BALKE-COLLENDER CO.
Established 1845—Chicago

Any Phonograph Can Play Brunswick Records
© B. B. C. Co., 1921
Brunswick

Hear These Brunswick Super-Feature Records

30013 12-in. $1.50 — *Un bel di vedremo* (Some Day He'll Come) from Madame Butterfly Act II, Scene I (Puccini) Soprano (in Italian) *Florence Easton*

10042 10-in. $1.00 — *O Sole Mio* (My Sunshine) (Capurro-di Capua) Tenor (in Italian) . . . . *Mario Chamlee*

10043 10-in $1.00. — *Serenade du Tsigane* (Gypsy Serenade) (Valdez) Pianoforte by Frederic Persson Violin Solo . . . . . . *Max Rosen*

Note: New Brunswick records will be on advance sale at all Brunswick dealers on the 20th of this month in the East, and West of Denver on the 26th.

BRUNSWICK
PHONOGRAPHS AND RECORDS

The musical sensation of the day—the world's

Volume 71
No. 4

TABLE · OF · CONTENTS

October 22, 1921

TOPICS OF THE DAY: Page

- France to Disarm, If— . . . 5
- How the Falling Mark Hits America . . . 8
- Favoring Our Ships at Panama . . . 9
- Nineteen Big Rail Systems . . . 10
- Central America's Three-in-One . . . 11
- North Dakota's Political Twister . . . 12
- Topics in Brief . . . 14

FOREIGN COMMENT:

- Britain's Two Million "Surplus Women" . . . 15
- "Must Austria Die?" . . . 16
- Unemployment a World Condition . . . 17
- Russia in Transformation . . . 18

SCIENCE AND INVENTION:

- Hitch Your Engine to a Volcano . . . 19
- Cleaning Up the Oil Camps . . . 20
- Recreational Defects of the Movies . . . 20
- Power at a Million Volts . . . 21
- Motoring and Typhoid . . . 22
- Time to Fight the Plague . . . 22

SCIENCE AND INVENTION: *(Continued)* Page

- To Resurrect the Old Wooden Car . . . 23
- More Suicides—Why? . . . 23

LETTERS AND ART:

- Clemenceau and His Poilus Eternalized in Stone . . . 24
- A Diminishing Poet . . . 25
- What Children Laugh At . . . 26
- David Bispham . . . 27

RELIGION AND SOCIAL SERVICE:

- Why so Many Pulpits Are Empty . . . 28
- The Czech Break from Rome . . . 29
- Christianity's Advance in Japan . . . 30
- Armenia a Vast Orphan Asylum . . . 30

MISCELLANEOUS:

- Current Poetry . . . 32
- Personal Glimpses . . . 34-47
- Investments and Finance . . . 48-50
- Current Events . . . 51-53
- The Spice of Life . . . 54
- The Lexicographer's Easy Chair . . . 55

TERMS: $4.00 a year, in advance; six months, $2.50; three months, $1.50; a single copy, 10 cents; postage to Canada, 85 cents a year; other foreign postage, $2.00 a year. BACK NUMBERS, not over three months old, 25 cents each; over three months old, $1.00 each. QUARTERLY INDEXES will be sent free to subscribers who apply for them. RECEIPT of payment is shown in about two weeks by date on address-label; date of expiration includes the month named on the label. CAUTION: If date is not properly extended after each payment, notify publishers promptly. Instructions for RENEWAL, DISCONTINUANCE, or CHANGE OF ADDRESS should be sent *two weeks* before the date they are to go into effect.

Both old and new addresses must always be given. PRESENTATION COPIES: Many persons subscribe for friends. Those who desire to renew such subscriptions must do so before expiration.

THE LITERARY DIGEST is published weekly by the Funk & Wagnalls Company, 354-360 Fourth Avenue, New York, and Salisbury Square, London, E. C.

Entered as second-class matter, March 24, 1890, at the Post-office at New York, N. Y., under the act of March 3, 1879.

Entered as second-class matter at the Post-office Department, Ottawa, Canada.

These Ten Mighty Minds
Could Study in Vain for Ten Lifetimes

—their collective intelligence would not be sufficient to fully master and assimilate all of the knowledge contained in this one amazing book. It is the world's greatest reference work. No book on earth contains so much knowledge compressed and ready for instant use—all in one plain alphabetical order, ready to answer your little child's simple question or your own perplexing and intricate one. One man can hardly even conceive the vastness of its contents; no ten men could ever master its sum total of knowledge. No subject of human interest is excluded from its scope—Literature, Art, Music, Electricity, Medicine, Law, Manufacturing, Grammar, Advertising, Shipbuilding, War, Peace, Politics, Religion, Statesmanship, Baseball, Automobiling, Engineering, Architecture, Science, Mathematics, Speech, Philosophy—anything—everything you can think of is included in its range. No one can ever *know it all*, but one can *have it all* at his elbow for instant use in this remarkable book. It has cost over $1,450,000 to produce it—you may have it now at only 10c per day for a short time.

In these days of intense specialization in one particular branch of a subject or art, it is often impracticable for a man to master much more than his own profession or business. But no man wants to be in ignorance regarding *any* of the other great branches of human knowledge, and here, in this modern compendium, may have the world's knowledge concentrated in a single volume. You may know in an instant—and know authoritatively—the exact "what, when and why" of any query which may arise in your business, professional or social life. You need it, your home needs it—your family, especially the children, will always benefit by its use.

Besides its exact scientific record of fundamental truths in various branches of knowledge, this surprizing volume will elicit the wonder and admiration of your children and family for its pictures and explanations of the wonders and marvels of the land, the sea, the sky, and of man's handiwork as witnessed in the world's progress. If your children could get the habit of referring to this volume, they would reach maturity liberally grounded in the world's knowledge. It is the world's greatest book of reference for the home, the office, the school.

Leaders in American Life and Institutions Praise It Unstintedly

Some Interesting Facts About this Wonder Book

Over 380 editors and specialists were employed in its compilation and it took almost four years to complete.

It cost over $1,450,000 to produce—most expensive book published.

It defines over 453,000 living vocabulary terms, thousands more than any other dictionary. Nearly 3000 pages.

It is the *only* Dictionary having all of the information within its pages in one alphabetical order—an immense time-saving feature.

The *only* Dictionary that gives exact information and dates of events under the heading of history, biography, and geography.

The *only* Dictionary that includes, wherever possible, specimens of celebrated paintings from the brushes of the world's greatest artists.

The *only* Dictionary that gives 7,500 separate Lists of Synonyms, and discussions of more than 23,500 synonymous terms.

The *only* Dictionary that gives Antonyms. Nearly 5,000 of these are given.

Contains 32,000 illustrative *quotations*, and is the *only* Dictionary giving the author, work, volume and page, for immediate reference to the author's spelling and use of the word.

The *only* Dictionary that presents a Consensus of Correct Pronunciation by the decisions of a Committee of Twenty-five Experts from the leading educational institutions of the English-speaking world.

Contains the Text-Book Key. Each word is respelled twice for pronunciation, *First*, in the New Scientific Alphabet; *second*, in the *text-book key*.

In its making the active cooperation of the United States Government was secured through authoritative assistance rendered by the Secretaries of its great Departments or by the Departments themselves.

The *only* Dictionary that contains rules governing grammatical and rhetorical construction.

The *only* Dictionary that makes a point of systematically correcting the common errors of speech.

Latest and most up to date vocabulary, including all war words. All universities and colleges located.

Contains over 7,000 definitive pictorial illustrations.

The New Standard contains exact dates of births and deaths of prominent persons.

The New Standard contains sixty full-page illustrations, some in over forty colors.

The STANDARD DICTIONARY has received the unqualified endorsement of hundreds of leaders of thought and action all over the globe. A great army of the nation's leading men have already expressed their highest respect and admiration for this wonderful book. Among hundreds who praise it and recommend its use are: Andrew Carnegie, Cardinal Gibbons, Hudson Maxim, Brander Matthews, U. S. Commissioner of Education P. P. Claxton, W. H. P. Faunce, S. Parkes Cadman, George Barr McCutcheon, George Ade, John Wanamaker, Elbert H. Gary, Jack London, Samuel Gompers, Archbishop Ireland, etc.

John Wanamaker, *Famous Merchant:*—"Artistic, complete, and of unrivaled excellence."

United States Commissioner of Education, Philander P. Claxton:—"This great work can not fail to be a distinct contribution to English scholarship."

Jack London, *the Popular American Author:*—"I am convinced that your new unabridged is the best kit of tools I possess in my library."

The Funk & Wagnall's
New Standard Dictionary

Over 3,000 Large Quarto Pages—over 60 Full-Page Illustrations—More Than 7,000 Text Illustrations—453,000 Vocabulary Terms, thousands more than any other dictionary—380 Editors and Specialists—533 Readers for Quotations—32,000 Illustrative Quotations—28,500 Synonyms and Antonyms—31,000 Historic Events Chronologically Arranged—65,000 Proper Names—One Vocabulary Order—Latest New Words.

Yours For Only 10c a Day

IT IS MORE THAN 100 DICTIONARIES IN 1

Covers the Following Subjects and Many More Besides

Agriculture, Anatomy, Anthropology, Bee-Keeping, Archeology, Architecture, Art, Astronomy, Aviation, Baseball, Bibliology, Biography, Biology, Botany, Ceramics, Chemistry, Chess, Commerce, Decoration, Engineering, Economics, Electricity, Entomology, Explosives, Finance, Football, Foreign Words and Phrases, Geography, Geology, Golf, Hebrew and Jewish Terms, History, Insurance, Irrigation, Labor, Law, Literature, Mathematics, Medicine, Militarism, Mining, Motor Boating, Motoring, Music, Naval and Nautical Terms, Numismatics, Optics, Osteopathy, Pedagogy, Philosophy, Psychology, Photography, Phrenology, Physical Culture, Poetry, Poultry, Printing, Railroading, Socialism, Sociology, Sports, Tennis, Theatrical Terms, Theosophy, Union Labor, War Words, Wireless Telegraphy, Yachting, Zoology

Most Authoritative Dictionary

Six months after publication 75,000 copies had been sold; it is the dependable authority in all branches of the United States Government, in Courts of Law, in the leading Universities and Colleges and in the Public Schools. In Commercial life the NEW Standard is popularly recognized as the *one* dictionary that never fails.

Only 10c per Day

$3.00 per month makes this De Luxe Volume yours. It cost us millions—you may have it, in its finest binding, for only 10c a day—$3.00 per month, $40.00 in all. See below.

A Necessary Work

to every home and office, because it is not merely a "word-book," but a repository of practically all human knowledge; there is scarcely a question that can be asked that this wonderful volume will not answer instantly, satisfyingly, authoritatively.

A Most Beautiful Gift Book

Magnificent, Limp Morocco, Leather Binding, full gold edges, beautiful colored illustrations, and many other features of excellence, combine to make this a superb gift book.

Superb Limp Morocco Binding. Bible Paper. For the price quoted above you will receive the finest edition of the STANDARD DICTIONARY published. It is printed on genuine Bible paper, and bound in full flexible levant morocco leather. Sign and send coupon at right and at least have the pleasure of examining this superb example of the bookmaker's art.

$2 Brings this Wonder Book

We will place this truly marvelous volume in your home or office for a ten-day examination upon receipt of only $2. We will pay all carriage charges. If it is not satisfactory for any reason, you may return it at our expense, we will refund your money, and you will be under no obligation whatever. If you find that it will be as great a help to you as it has already been to thousands of busy Americans and that you wish to retain it, you may send us $3.00 a month until $40.00 in all has been paid.

FUNK & WAGNALLS COMPANY
354-360 Fourth Avenue, New York

Herewith $2. Please send me for examination, charges prepaid, one copy of the Funk & Wagnalls New Standard Dictionary in one volume, Bible Paper, bound in Full Flexible Limp Levant Leather (acid free). If the book is unsatisfactory, I may return it within ten days. If I keep it, I agree to pay $3.00 each month thereafter until $40.00 in all has been paid. Dig. 10-22-21

Name . . . .

Street . . . .

City . . . . *State* . . . .

Know what you get

YOU'LL pay enough for an overcoat to get a good one Will you get it? Fine all-wool quality? The best style? The long service? Real economy?

You will if you find our label in the coat; it guarantees your complete satisfaction

Hart Schaffner & Marx

THE LITERARY DIGEST

PUBLIC OPINION (New York) combined with THE LITERARY DIGEST

[Pub]lished by Funk & Wagnalls Company (Adam W. Wagnalls, Pres.; Wilfred J. Funk, Vice-Pres.; Robert J. Cuddihy, Treas.; William Neisel, Sec'y) 354-360 Fourth Ave., New York

[V]ol. LXXI, No 4 New York, October 22, 1921 Whole Number 1644

TOPICS - OF - THE - DAY

FRANCE TO DISARM, IF—

HOW NAVAL DISARMAMENT can end war on land seems to puzzle the French, who recall that Belgium and France were not invaded by a navy in 1914, and who at this moment see the jealous nations of Europe facing each other within easy marching distance. Yet despite the fact that the World War was mainly a land war, President Harding's call to the Washington Conference says that the question of naval armament will "naturally have first place," altho "it has been thought best not to exclude questions pertaining to other armament." To France, however, the "other armament" is the main point, and if another European war is to be prevented, this sort of armament must be considered. France wishes "nothing but success" to the Washington Conference in its efforts to safeguard peace in the Pacific, says ex-Premier Clemenceau, breaking a silence of a year and a half. "But the Pacific Ocean is far away," he adds, "and the German frontier is very close to us." And he insists that "no one can refuse to consider the French question from the same point of view as the question of the Pacific." "France must remain armed as long as her security has not been assured," announces Premier Briand, who is expected to head the French delegation to the arms parley. "No country more than ours desires to limit military burdens," he declares; but he goes on to make it no less emphatically clear that any reduction of the size of the French Army must depend upon the elimination of the German menace—in other words, an Allied understanding for the protection of France.

"AM I IN FOR AN OPERATION OR A MANICURE?"
—Morris for the George Matthew Adams Service.

It was in his key-note speech at St. Nazaire, a few days before the reopening of the French Parliament, that Premier Briand thus defined France's attitude toward disarmament, in terms that win, the correspondent tells us, the virtually unanimous indorsement of the French press. To quote him at greater length on this point:

"I will say, and will express the sentiment of France in saying, that no country more than ours desires to limit military burdens and give to useful work the greatest possible number of young men; but no country more than France has the duty to remain armed so long as her security is not assured. If France, during the forty years in which, in spite of mutilation, she maintained peace, had not known how to arm herself, where would have been to-day the peace of the world? France withstood the first shock, because France was strong, and peace was saved.

"To-morrow France must not risk the same menace. All the guarantees of peace and of territorial integrity being given France, France stands ready to be the first to make the step which is asked. For the rest, when one looks at the beauty of her patience in her strength, how apparent is the work of calumny which attributes to her dreams of perpetual war and plans of imperialism! We have already answered these accusations. I hope that, thanks to our moderation, there is now no one in the world who would repeat such lies."

Says the Paris *Temps*, expressing a point of view echoed in dozen of its contemporaries:

"The security of France means the peace of Europe. It is a basic condition of economic and political solidarity in the world. That is why, as M. Briand says, France has an important rôle to play at Washington.

"She is pacifist more than any other nation, because she knows what war, even victorious war, costs. She is ready to lighten armaments costs which bear down on all peoples to-day. But France will not disarm so long as her security is not definitely assured. She will dispose of none of her means of defense until she has the assurance that she will not be menaced for her existence. That is where the solidarity of the Allied and Associated Powers can best assert itself, and that is the only means by which the problem of disarmament can be solved."

All the French editors emphasize Briand's declaration that disarmament and security are tied together, reports the Paris correspondent of the New York *Times*; and he adds: "What the French want, of course, is ratification of the treaty of military guarantee."

French reasoning with regard to disarmament is simple, writes H. V. Kaltenborn, Paris correspondent of the

Brooklyn *Eagle*, who represents the average Frenchman as saying:

"We have just managed to escape annihilation; at the cost of untold sacrifices we have chained the bloodthirsty giant across the Rhine. We are never going to release him until we are absolutely sure that he cannot harm us again."

"I have talked with representatives of every class of Frenchman, including pacifists, and this point of view is universal," reports Mr. Kaltenborn, who adds: "Any French ministry that took a different point of view would be overthrown, and the succeeding ministry would give increasing emphasis to the point of view." Turning to American comment on this French point of view, we are reminded by Paul Scott Mowrer in the October *Current Opinion* that—

IF PRESIDENT HARDING WANTS RESULTS.

—Thiele in the Sioux City *Tribune*.

"The reasonableness of the French demand for safety was so apparent to every one at the Peace Conference that three measures looking permanently to this end were finally adopted:

"(1) The disarmament of Germany.

"(2) A pledge by the League of Nations to make common cause with any one of its members which should be the victim of unprovoked aggression.

"(3) An additional specific pledge by Britain and the United States to aid France in case of a renewal of unprovoked German aggression.

"In consideration of these three things, France somewhat reluctantly agreed to abandon the idea of attempting to form an independent, unarmed, neutral 'buffer' state between the Rhine and the French frontier."

But what has happened, asks Mr. Mowrer. And he answers:

"The complete disarmament of Germany has proved extremely difficult. The Treaty was hardly signed before 'unofficial' military organizations began to spring up all over Germany. Only the other day a German deputy, Herr Gruber, declared in the Reichstag that in Bavaria alone over 112,000 rifles and 10,000 machine-guns have been hidden away. What will all this come to in a few years hence? There are still 60 million Germans to 40 million Frenchmen. Will the Germans be able to make up by force of numbers what they may lack in equipment? The question is the more painful, as both the other safety devices offered France have gone by the board. The League of Nations, by the refusal of the United States to join, is practically paralyzed; and the triple guarantee pact, by the refusal of the United States to sign it, has never come into effect, for Britain's acceptance of it was made conditional on that of the United States."

The ideal of every Frenchman, says Mr. Mowrer, remains an Anglo-French-American alliance. "But, alliance or no alliance," he concludes, "France has not the slightest intention of abandoning what she considers her just right to security. Unless France can be assured of the moral support of the Allies, "the French delegates will not discuss the reduction of land armament," declares Wilbur Forrest, Paris correspondent of the New York *Tribune;* "and she will show at the conference that Germany's adherence to the terms of the Versailles Treaty is mainly the result of the maintenance of a French army large and powerful enough to enforce the Treaty."

The uncompromising attitude of France in this instance finds considerable support among American editors, who are inclined to agree with Mr. Forrest's analysis. "In the present race for the biggest navies France is not a competitor," notes the President's Marion *Star*, which doubts if the United States, Japan, or Great Britain "can show that it needs a great navy more than France needs an adequate army." "France," concludes *The Star*, "will be one of the foremost problems of the disarmament conclave." The policy "so aptly stated by Premier Briand for his own country," remarks the New York *Globe*, "will probably be that of every other country from which the United States can rationally expect support in November." "To expect France to talk of reducing armaments without raising the question of how she is to be guaranteed in the future is beyond reason," declares the Newark *News;* and the New York *Tribune* agrees editorially that "so long as France lacks the support of the United States and England, she can not afford to weaken her defenses to such an extent that she will be at the mercy of Germany." According to *The Tribune:*

"The French feel that they are in measure under suspicion at the bar of American opinion. France will be the only European Power represented in the Washington Conference which hasn't yet had the opportunity to make large reductions in its post-war land forces. This failure to reduce was not due to any perverse ambition. From the French point of view it has been a misfortune, for a large army is expensive and the French budget is overweighted. The cost of the occupation of the Rhineland has to be met out of the French treasury, and in the division of the first billion of German reparations not a mark has been allotted to France.

"The French have accepted a huge burden in maintaining their military establishment. They are doing a work of benefit to all the Allied Powers and to civilization itself in guarding the German western frontier and compelling Germany to observe her treaty obligations. Without the French Army there would be no guaranty against a German repudiation of the peace and a return to chaos in central Europe. The French Army is not simply the agent of France. It is the agent of all the nations which helped to defeat Germany.

"The French have already disarmed as far as they can disarm within reason. They must do so for economy's sake. They remain the best judges of the force which they ought to employ in Europe, where they are the armed instrument of the Entente and of America."

Recent estimates of the number of men in the various armies to-day, issued from Washington, placed the strength of the French Army at 1,034,000. This estimate is challenged in an Associated Press dispatch from Paris, in which we read:

"Marshal Foch will be prepared to lay before the Conference every particular concerning the present land armaments of France.

"France is reducing her Army, it is said. The troops in active service to-day are about 60 per cent. of the number on May 1 of this year. France then had about 800,000 men under arms. She now has between 450,000 and 500,000, including the Army of the Rhine and colonial troops. Figures will be incorporated in the report of Marshal Foch showing France's position to be substantially as follows:

"France already has done a great deal toward land disarmament, having practically demobilized 40 per cent. of her Army in five months. The 300,000 odd men have not all been demobilized permanently. A large percentage remain subject to immediate call from the General Staff and could be mobilized in a few days should circumstances require it.

A later dispatch from Paris tells us that "the Army and Navy are costing France 4,500,000,000 francs annually, while the deficit in the budget is 2,500,000,000 francs, nearly all of which could be made up by economies in the military and naval sections if France should be guaranteed otherwise against surprizes from the East."

According to the same dispatch the French General Staff has information that "every regiment in the German Army as allowed under the Treaty has 300 non-commissioned officers to each regiment, 200 of whom are serving as privates." These, it is pointed out, can be automatically reinstated in the event of mobilization, thus bringing the number of non-commissioned officers to the pre-war figure. This would permit the mobilization of 1,000,000 men inside of a week, we are told, "as the former soldiers are well organized into gymnastic societies, war veteran camps, and other associations, and are subject to prompt concentration." In view of this condition of affairs among a people "superior in numbers and economic resources, unrepentant in defeat and burning for revenge," as the Los Angeles *Times* puts it, "the French people can not be expected to dispense with a powerful and thoroughly equipped standing army." There seems to be no doubt that, as the Washington *Post* notes, "intense hatred inspires the people of both France and Germany, and the commonest remark among them is that there will be another war at a favorable time." In *The Atlantic Monthly* Maxwell H. H. McCartney, who lived for several years in Germany before the war, tells us of the sentiment that now sways that country:

"If Great Britain was the most hated enemy during the war, France is now loathed with a deadly hatred of which no secret is made. Before the war Germany certainly did not hate France so much as France hated Germany; and even during the war the German press often exprest its admiration for the bravery of the French *poilus*. All such admiration has long vanished.

"People in railway-carriages speak quite openly about this hatred, and canvass the time—it may be twenty-five years, it may be longer—when the final reckoning with France is to come. 'We want,' the Germans say, 'no allies. We ask only to be left alone with the French, and we are sure that the next time France will not have England and America on her side.' Such remarks I have heard literally scores of times, and they undoubtedly represent the average German's views and wishes. Time will, of course, do something toward softening down these feelings; but it is an undeniable fact that many Germans of my personal acquaintance are systematically training up their children to hate France."

But while we find the general attitude of the American press toward France's position to be one of sympathy, in many instances this sympathy is mingled with misgiving. If Premier Briand adheres to his stand, avers the New York *World*, "then, so far at least as land armaments are concerned, the Washington Conference fails from the start." Equally pessimistic, but less sympathetic, is Mr. Hearst's New York *American*, which proclaims that "it may confidently be taken for granted that neither Japan, England nor France has the remotest intention of abandoning imperialism or militarism at the Washington Conference," and insists that "the United States should not make any sort of alliance with any other Power or Powers." There is "not a chance" of the United States entering into any such alliance, declares the Des Moines *Register*.

At the same time friends of France recall the recent words of United States Ambassador Myron T. Herrick at the Inter-Allied Club in Paris, when he assured a group of distinguished guests who had gathered in honor of General Pershing that "the whole American people" say through General Pershing that "we still remember, and if that be not enough, we can still act." And the Ambassador added significantly: "If there be those who cherish the hope that this purpose has been altered or will be changed, let them take fair warning."

SUGGESTED FOR DISARMAMENT HALL DECORATIONS.

—Knott in the Dallas *News*.

HOW THE FALLING MARK HITS AMERICA

GERMANY'S AIM—not to speak of marksmanship—may not be to force the mark down to where it is practically worthless, but some of our editors are inclined to think that whatever the policy, the continual dropping serves Germany's purposes. For one thing, Germany's financial plight helps to demonstrate her inability to keep up reparations payments. For another, she is enabled by the exchange situation to produce more cheaply and thus sell more cheaply than her competitors in foreign markets. And then, too, the extreme cheapof the mark has tempted many Americans to invest good American dollars in them, to the advantage of German bankers. The tremendous depreciation of the mark, caused largely by the continued issuance of paper money, holds a warning for us, contends the Philadelphia *Inquirer*, for it must "eventually result in a catastrophic collapse whose repercussions will be felt throughout the world." Unless something effective is done to stay the present rush toward financial chaos in Germany and Eastern Europe, similarly declares *Forbes*, a financial weekly, "the final upshot can not but hurt American commerce, American agriculture, and American pay envelopes." On the other hand, the Springfield *Republican*, is convinced that if a financial crash comes in Germany "its international effect may not be at all catastrophic, because Germany has been so far self-contained since 1914."

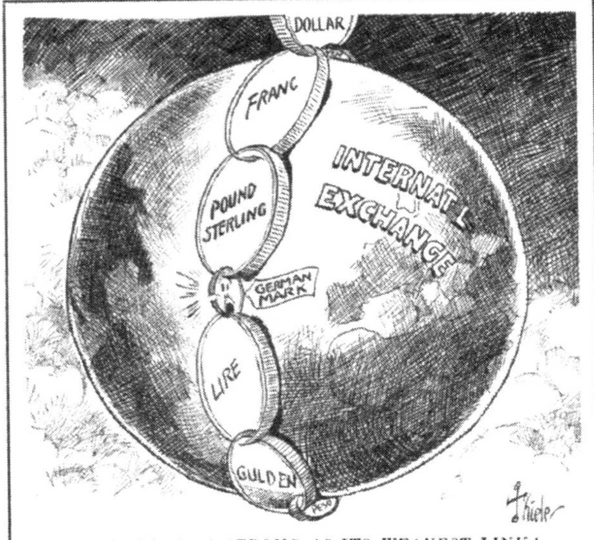

A CHAIN IS AS STRONG AS ITS WEAKEST LINK!
—Thiele in the Sioux City *Tribune*.

The German mark, normally worth 23.8 cents, dropt in value to less than ten cents after the close of the war and since then has continued to decline, falling during September to less than four-fifths of a cent. This decline has been paralleled by an increase in circulation of paper marks. To-day, as the editor of *The Financial World* notes, Germany possesses, roughly speaking, only one mark in gold to cover 90 marks in paper at present in circulation. Germany's currency position up to September 7, is set down as follows by this authority:

In 1911 Gold Reserve totaled	$251,750,000
On Aug. 27, 1920, Gold Reserve totaled (marks)	1,091,585,000
On Sept. 7, 1921, Gold Reserve totaled (marks)	1,023,708,000
July 25, 1912, German outstanding notes (marks)	1,044,260,000
July 25, 1914, German outstanding notes (marks)	1,890,893,000
Aug. 27, 1919, German outstanding notes (marks)	28,188,000,000
Sept. 7, German outstanding notes (marks)	80,727,526,000

By the end of September, several financial papers note, Germany's note circulation had reached 82,178,940,000 marks, and is now probably near ninety billions.

There is a strong belief in this country, France and Germany, "that by the activity of their printing presses, the rulers of Germany are deliberately hatching a scheme to embarrass their former enemies and victors and repudiate their indemnity promises." But tho reporting this belief, *The American Banker* does not share it, feeling that the mark is simply following the natural trend of the international money market. Whatever the explanation, comments theNew York *Herald*, "each depreciation works in favor of Germany industrially, but further threatens her cash payments to the Allies on reparations account." As the Baltimore *Evening Sun* explains how industrial Germany profits by the present plight of the mark:

"Suppose, for example Herr Klockner manufactures a machine which he can quote at 1,000 marks paper. This machine he can offer in the United States to-day at about $8. If the mark rose to one cent, he would have to charge $10; if it went to ten cents he would have to charge $100. Thus he can undersell his competitors. Ergo, he has his chance to edge in.

"Now, of course, this state of affairs cannot go on interminably. The value of the mark cannot approach zero so closely that, to all intents and purposes, it vanishes into thin air. When Herr Klockner, for instance, has to buy raw materials from other countries he will have to pay such prices that he will no longer be able to offer his machine for 1,000 marks.

"But, after all, if his main object was to regain his lost markets by putting his competitors out of them to a greater or less extent, he has succeeded. And the reason he is able to get back is because the exchange value of the mark is so unfavorable."

The recent "nose dive" of the German mark, as some one has called it, is taken by several editors as a demonstration of the way German financiers have fooled American investors and speculators. Germany financed its war "partly through fiat currency"; now, observes the Troy *Record*, "if a part of this debt could be shifted to fools in America by selling the paper to them and repudiating it later, no one could complain except the fools." At home in Germany, says *The Financial World*, "the true intrinsic value of the mark was understood," but—

"Among our large German population, to which must be added a considerable number of American speculators, there was discovered an immense buying power for marks. The German printing press was kept busy supplying the demand from nine cents, the price of the mark at the time the armistice was signed, to lower quotations recently. Now that the mark has dropt to under a cent this buying has stopt, and American holders are wondering what is coming, and fear the worst."

Germany has profited at the expense of Americans who, according to a writer in the New York *Times*, have invested perhaps $100,000,000 in German marks at an average price of two and a half cents. At the present price of the mark they have lost 60 cents on every dollar, and there "stand the German printing presses grinding away ceaselessly." Germany, comments *The Wall Street Journal*, has probably by now "repudiated the mark for the ninety billionth time at least"—

"And yet intelligent people are asking if the mark is a 'buy', on the theory that the mark will once more be worth par in American money at some time in the future. How many have stopt to think that Germany would have to raise $21,438,000,000 to redeem 90,000,000,000 marks at the old gold par?"

According to these papers and others, American holdings of German marks are practically worthless. But Mr. Hearst's New York *Evening Journal* advises:

"Be careful how you sell German money or anything else German. When they get raw materials and straighten out their affairs you might wish you had 'gone long' instead of 'short'!"

FAVORING OUR SHIPS AT PANAMA

A POOR PRELUDE to the approaching disarmament parley, in the judgment of many of our papers, was supplied by the United State Senate when it passed the Borah bill exempting our coastwise shipping from the payment of Panama Canal tolls. "Even without entering into the merits of the controversy, it is not easy to reconcile Mr. Borah's persistent advocacy of exemption with his original zeal for the Disarmament Conference—a project which, tho greatly expanded, is in part due to his initiative," remarks the Philadelphia *Evening Public Ledger*. For, explains this Philadelphia paper, "rightly or wrongly, Great Britain believes with Elihu Root, Walter Page, the late Joseph H. Choate and Woodrow Wilson that the wording of the Hay-Pauncefote Treaty is clear, and that it will not justify the arrogation by any nation to itself of special privileges for its vessels passing through the isthmus." Opposing the bill in the Senate, Senator McCumber, Republican, of North Dakota, charged that its passage would constitute an act of bad faith comparable to Germany's violation of Belgian neutrality. "Germany, with the exigency of a great war before her, declared that her treaty with Belgium was a scrap of paper," said the Senator, but in the Panama Tolls Bill, "without any such exigency before us, and without even an attempt being made to secure a modification of our solemn obligation, we are asked to declare that the Hay-Pauncefote Treaty shall be regarded as a mere scrap of paper." Having invited other great nations to join us in "a solemn compact to check the mad and exhausting race of the nations for naval supremacy," let us not, he pleaded, "enter the council chamber with soiled hands." Because "the peace of the world rests upon the sanctity of treaties," Senator Colt of Rhode Island, another Republican opponent of the bill, urged that the question be settled through diplomatic channels, or by arbitration, and not by legislation. Still another Republican, Senator Wadsworth of New York, said that the United States violated the Hay-Pauncefote Treaty when it ratified the Colombian Treaty last May and agreed to allow Colombian vessels free passage through the Canal. "We'll live to rue the day," he declared, "that we gave one nation privileges discriminatory against others." At the same time Senator Lodge, Republican leader in the Senate and one of our delegates to the Disarmament Conference, stated that while we have the "legal right" to give American coastwise ships free passage through the Canal, "there are compelling reasons why we should not exercise that right at this time." On the eve of the Conference, he added, these reasons "are especially potent"; and he urged that the question of free tolls be left to arbitration.

The Borah bill passed the Senate on October 10 by 47 to 37 vote. party lines breaking on the issue. Thence it went to the House, where it will probably remain in committee. Washington dispatches intimate, until after the Disarmament Conference. Washington rumors further have it that President Harding "will exert his full influence to that end." "It is no secret that the Administration regretted that the Panama Tolls Bill should be brought up at this time," writes Mark Sullivan in the New York *Evening Post*, and he goes on to say:

"From the point of view of the Administration, the slight balm in the situation lies in the fact that the Senate action amounts to nothing until the House acts also. Of course, now that everybody sees the situation as it is, the House will be prevented from taking action. Also, there is a small school of opinion which says that it is of advantage, rather than disadvantage, to bring up the Panama issue now. This is the school which persistently regards the coming conference as a trading affair. This school says that equal tolls for England is a thing which America can trade for Great Britain's assent to the things we want in the conference. It is this same school which now wants America to bring up a threat against Great Britain's mercantile shipping by a proposal to discriminate in favor of ships owned by the United States in the matter of freight rates and tariffs.

"Decidedly the better and larger view in Washington, however, is that the coming conference should be prevented from being a trading affair, and that each delegate should regard himself not as representing rigidly the interest of his own country and hostile to the interests of other countries, but rather as representing the interests of the world as a whole."

KEEP IT QUIET UNTIL THE COMPANY GOES.

—Morris for the George Matthew Adams Service.

"The Canal tolls question is a Pacific Ocean question, whether or not it is given a place in the agenda of the Conference," declares the Springfield *Republican*, which goes on to say:

"Even if the right to pass the Borah bill could not be seriously challenged, it would be offensive diplomacy to pass it under existing conditions.

"Add to these considerations one other—that the British interpretation of the Hay-Pauncefote treaty as guaranteeing the same treatment to the ships of all other nations that American ships receive in the Canal has been indorsed by Elihu Root, who has been made one of the American commissioners to the coming Conference. The question of our treaty right to discriminate in favor of American ships in the matter of Canal tolls is at least a highly debatable one, in view of Mr. Root's attitude, and therefore it might well be kept in the background during the Conference in order that the situation should not be needlessly complicated.

"Other reasons for opposing the Borah bill are disconnected with the Washington Conference, but they are worth noting. The Middle West objects to it because free tolls for our coastwise shipping would amount to a discrimination in transportation in favor of the Atlantic and Pacific coasts as against the Mississippi valley. The transcontinental railroads, too, have reason to complain if their maritime competitors are to be especially favored by the free use of a canal for the building of which the whole American people were taxed."

Altho the principle of free use of the Canal by American coastwise ships has been embodied in both Republican and Democratic platforms, and was actually enacted into law in 1912 and repealed in 1914, the Borah bill seems to arouse little enthusiasm in our press at this time. The New York *Tribune* in an editorial headed "Is Our Word Good?" cites that clause of the Hay-Pauncefote Treaty that says:

"The Canal shall be free and open to the vessels of all nations observing these rules, on terms of entire equality, so that there shall be no discrimination against any such nation or its citizens or subjects in respect of the conditions or charges of traffic or otherwise. Such conditions and charges of traffic shall be just and equitable."

"Shall we keep faith on the Panama Canal tolls?" asks the Kansas City *Star;* and the Chicago *Tribune* calls the Borah bill "dangerous" and a betrayal of the nation's honor. So, too, the San Francisco *Chronicle*, while "strongly in favor of making coastwise traffic toll-free," "can conceive of no action by Congress more likely to defeat the purposes of the coming conference on disarmament than the Borah bill." Any modification of the treaty, it avers, "should be sought by negotiation."

JUST AS IF HE CAN'T TREAT HIM WITHOUT INCLUDING THE NEIGHBORS' KIDS!

—Wahl in the Sacramento *Bee.*

On the other hand Senator Reed of Missouri attributes opposition to "free tolls" to "powerful pro-British influences in this country." Senator Borah says he conferred with those most responsible for the Disarmament Conference before he introduced his bill, and they raised no objection. Says Senator Calder, of New York:

"I am convinced the granting of free tolls to American ships could not be construed as a discrimination under the terms of the Hay-Pauncefote treaty. Coastwise trade is restricted by law to transportation exclusively in American ships, and ships of all other nations are prohibited from engaging therein. Therefore, it appears that coastwise commerce in the very nature of things cannot be affected by the terms of the treaty which relate to tolls."

"The right of the United States to grant preferential treatment to its coastwise shipping is questioned only by extremists," affirms the Philadelphia *Evening Bulletin;* and in the New York *Evening Mail* we read:

"If the President should sign the tolls bill, and if Britain should formally protest against our interpretation of the Hay-Pauncefote treaty, does anybody suppose that this country would not be willing to arbitrate the issue? Our passage of the bill simply records our interpretation of the pact. If Great Britain has a different one, the obvious course will be to refer the controversy to an unbiased court.

"Exemption of our coastwise vessels from tolls is not an act of aggression against any nation, but purely an act regulatory of our domestic trade.

"That is the American contention. It may be a fair subject for argument from the British point of view, but certainly there is nothing in it to embarrass the disarmament Conference."

NINETEEN BIG RAIL SYSTEMS

IN THE ERA OF ROOSEVELT, some one has remarked, the Government did its best to keep the railroads from merging. Now we behold Congress and the Interstate Commerce Commission asking the roads to combine and merge on a gigantic scale reminiscent of the most daring dreams of Hill and Harriman. But, say the editors who are inclined to approve the Interstate Commerce Commission plan for uniting our 200 principal railroads into 19 systems, the motive is quite different. The earlier generation of railroad magnates objected to being regulated and tried to make the strong roads stronger by combination. The Commission to-day is trying to smooth the way to efficient Federal regulation of rates and profits by persuading the "strong" roads to bear the burdens of the weak, and the weak to yield up their separate identities in order to share the profits of the richer lines.

So the Commission, obeying a clause in the new railroad law, "sketches a new railroad map of the United States," in the words of the Boston *News Bureau*, with "little regard for ancient alliances and ties of sentiment." Besides two somewhat localized systems, the plan, as the St. Louis *Star* notes, calls for "five more or less parallel systems from New York to Chicago and St. Louis; six from Chicago and St. Louis to the Pacific Coast; four from Chicago, St. Paul and St. Louis to the Gulf of Mexico; two from the South Atlantic States through the South to St. Louis."

There is no intention here to hinder competition, comments the New York *Tribune.* Indirect competition will be preserved between interpenetrating regional groups; "geographical areas are to compete for access to their markets and for improved railroad facilities." Yet to a Socialist daily like the New York *Call* "the suggestion that the railroads be permitted to merge into Nineteen Big Unions means the final collapse of the old idea of competition in transportation." And the Socialist vision sees the "Nineteen Big Unions" leading to "The One Big Union" of transportation, and beyond that to the "benevolent assimilation" of the railroads "by an industrial democracy mastered by the useful workers of the nation."

The Commission's tentative plan for voluntary railroad mergers which is based on a report by Professor W. Z. Ripley of Harvard, and is likely to be the subject of official hearings and public discussion for many months, meets with considerable press approval. The effect will be salutary, says the Brooklyn *Eagle.* Railroad consolidation, concludes the Manchester *Union*, "ought to work something like the removal of the tolls barriers that handicapped medieval commerce." Aside from the economies permitted, two distinct benefits ought to come from voluntary consolidation similar to the Commission's scheme, the Newark *News* tells its readers:

"The first is escape for a long time to come from the ghost of public ownership. The second is the ability to work out profitable combinations without interference by the anti-trust laws, including the absorption of lines not particularly strong in themselves, but which might develop amazingly under centralized management as feeders for great systems."

But all the Commission can hope to do, as the Baltimore *Evening Sun* remarks, "is to lead the railroad horse to water; it can not make him drink." The Maryland paper has noted no great enthusiasm for the consolidation plan among the managers of the larger railroads. The strong roads, writes Glenn Griswold in the Chicago *Journal of Commerce*, "do not want to be burdened with the weak lines except at a price that will make the gamble attractive, while the weak companies will insist on a price that will approach the official valuation rather than going value as an investment." "Is there not a possibility, speaking from the strictly business point of view," asks the Buffalo *Times*, "that the weak railroads would prove a burden to the strong ones without getting from them a sufficient amount of help to create compenation for the financial and transportation problem that would be leveloped under the proposed arrangement?"

The Wall Street Journal calls attention to the danger "that we may sacrifice the beneficent influence of competition in service and efficient management without securing the doubtful advantage of uniform earning power." Besides, it sees "a Supreme Court law-suit bristling in every line, every syllable, every letter of the plan." It quotes, too, with an approving word an article on railroad consolidation by Judge Robert S. Lovett in *The World's Work*. Judge Lovett, who is Chairman of the Union Pacific board, confesses to a doubt whether the process of merger "will merely lower the general average of railroad credit and service or whether it will result in wrecking the strong together with the weak lines." This experienced railroad executive also believes that the plan will be difficult to work out practically. Strong and weak lines do not always lie where they can be united into a continuous system. Then there are sections where all the roads are strong and all are weak. The problem of relative values will be extremely difficult to solve, also that of refinancing under consolidation. Judge Lovett says he has "no doubt that many consolidations ought to be effected in the public interest," but "they should be dictated by considerations of transportation alone and the needs of the particular case." Finally, this railroader's "own judgment is that if all the railroads shall be consolidated into a small number of large systems to compete with each other, it will be but a few years thereafter until we have 'strong' systems and 'weak' systems again, just as now, differing only perhaps in the size of the systems, which in case of failure will only add to the magnitude of the disaster."

CENTRAL AMERICA'S THREE-IN-ONE

A NEW STATE, about 100,000 square miles in area, with a population of 4,000,000, came into being on October 10th when the governments of Honduras, Guatemala, and Salvador were united under the Provisional Federal Council of the Central American Federation, and the hope is variously exprest in the press of the United States that the new republic "may fulfil the purpose and ambitions of its creators with harmony among its own inhabitants unvexed by attempts of aggression from abroad." Dr. Julio Bianchi, Minister of Guatemala to the United States, issues a signed statement in which he says that the constitution adopted by Guatemala, Honduras and Salvador "now is in effect and the work of administering the affairs of these three states as of one republic is being carried on by a provisional government." Furthermore:

"Elections will be held within a few days for the selection of officials who will take the oath of office in January, succeeding the present provisional government. The Constitution changes the name of the new nation from 'The Federation of Central America' to 'The Republic of Central America.' A study of the Constitution shows that it binds Guatemala, Honduras and El Salvador into a real union instead of joining these three nations in a loose federation. In the new republic, Guatemala, Honduras and El Salvador have the status of states and are united in much the same way as the states of the United States.

"In view of world-wide discussion of disarmament, the provisions for control of the military are of especial interest, as these provisions probably will result in disarming Central America. The Constitution provides that all of the armies and military supplies of the several states shall be under the control of the Federal Government of the Republic. The states will be allowed to maintain police forces only sufficient to maintain law and order, the size of these forces to be determined by the Federal Government. No state may purchase military supplies, this function and the right to proclaim martial law in any part of the Republic belonging exclusively to the Federal Government. It is my opinion that these provisions will have the effect of disbanding the armies of Guatemala, Honduras and El Salvador in a short time. The importance of such a step may be better understood when it is known that the cost of maintaining the small army of Guatemala last year was more than half of the total expenses of the Government of Guatemala."

The Spanish-American daily *La Prensa* (New York) points to the material as well as the moral benefit to be gained by the union of Central America and adds:

"To maintain this union and strengthen it to stand all tests of domestic and foreign friction, all Central Americans must be ready to cooperate. The work should be unselfish, patriotic, and sincere towards the accomplishment of this great ideal. In the heart of the youth of the country, who worked so enthusiastically to bring about the confederation, there must be vigilance and alertness in order that it may solidify and endure."

The Republic of Central America lies between Mexico and Nicaragua, with its capital at Tegucigalpa in Honduras. Dispatches from that city advise that the pact of the union was signed early in January of this year at San Jose, Costa Rica, by delegates of the three federated states and of Costa Rica. But the National Assembly of Costa Rica rejected the pact by a vote of 19 to 20; and Nicaragua refused to sign it because of differences with its neighbor states over the interpretation of the Bryan-Chamorro treaty, which gave to the United States special rights for the construction of a new interoceanic canal through its territory. In both Costa Rica and Nicaragua it is reported that public opinion is divided, and a Unionist party is "endeavoring to bring about union with the Federation." If this should happen the population of the new state would be increased by 1,000,000 inhabitants, and would be extended in boundary down to Panama. From Tegucigalpa dispatches we learn further that—

"The union of these sister republics has been a national aspiration since eighty years ago, when political troubles destroyed the Federal Republic of Central America. That republic, as a whole, liberated itself from Spanish power in 1821 and maintained its unity until the forties. The people speak the same language—Spanish, have the same religion—Roman Catholic, and are of the same race, mainly Indian, except in Costa Rica, where the white race predominates. Since the Spanish conquests they have had identical legislation and the same culture.

"The text of the treaty of union provides for a government modeled on the lines of the Constitution of the United States, with three separate branches, the executive, legislative, and judicial, altho the executive is modeled more on the Swiss system. A constitution embodying these provisions was finally approved by the Constituent Assembly which met in September at Tegucigalpa. Liberty of thought and religion are provided.

"In so far as it does not infringe on the Federal Constitution, each state will retain its autonomy and independence in the management and direction of its internal affairs and will carry on governmental functions not specifically delegated to the federation."

The New York *Herald* reminds us that it is evidence of the "sobriety and mature political judgment" of the citizens of the constituent states that the Federation has been formed "after free discussion, and that it enters upon its career backed by an authentic and unquestioned mandate from the people who have erected it." This New York daily declares it is the "hope of the people of the United States that their fellow freemen on the American continents will find it possible to maintain their liberty under democratic institutions in peace, and to prosper in freedom." Says the New York *Tribune*:

"The desire for union in external relations is economic as well as political. These small powers have found it a burden to maintain diplomatic staffs abroad and also representation in the League of Nations. They have suffered, too, from revolutionist activities directed at one state from within the boundaries of another. The federation will have a population of only 4,000,000. That is small enough for a small state, which has nowadays to face largely increased costs of government. Economic interest will have to contend, however, with the strong separatist tendencies which for nearly a hundred years have frustrated attempts at Central American union."

NORTH DAKOTA'S POLITICAL TWISTER

NORTH DAKOTA, CENTER of America's most radical political experiment, is facing the worst storm of its tempestuous career. In many ways, declare numerous editors both inside and outside the State, the recall election, to be held on October 28, is hardly less important to the country as a whole than to the State in which it occurs. For the first time an attempt will be made to remove the highest executives

Courtesy of "The Outlook," New York

A TROUBLE-MAKER FOR THE LEAGUE.

R. A. Nestos, candidate for Governor put forward by the Independent Voters' Association, has promised to carry out most of the Nonpartizan League policies, but with a different technique.

of a State through the recall, and the fate of the Nonpartizan League of North Dakota hangs in the balance with its leaders. North Dakota's present condition resembles "Soviet Russia on a small scale," believes the Philadelphia *Inquirer*, taking an attitude typical of the press of the country as a whole toward North Dakota's political experiment. Outside the State, only a few labor and Socialist papers support the League. The critics of the League charge that it has endeavored "to establish state Socialism to a degree never before attempted outside of Russia." It established banks, wheat elevators, flour mills, home-building associations, and the like, with, they charge, "uniformly disastrous results." The Leaguers reply that all these institutions are doing as well as could have been expected. The State group which is putting through the recall election, an organization called the Independent Voters' Association, however, is attacking not so much the principles involved as the manner in which they have been put into effect. The Independent Committee, as quoted by several supporters of the recall movement, announces that—

"In this recall election campaign the principal questions involved are whether or not public officials shall be required to render honest public service and not be permitted to appropriate public property for their personal gain. These are fundamental principles of public government and civilization itself."

There is a "strong minority" in the State, we are told, which believes the difference between the two factions now fighting for control is much the same as between Tweedledum and Tweedledee. Represented chiefly by one of the State's best-known papers, the Bismarck *Tribune*, this minority is "sitting pat," and will ultimately, predicts a small-town editor, put out of commission whichever faction wins in the present election.

In order to get at the conditions behind the present upheaval, THE DIGEST sent a letter to the editor of every newspaper and magazine in the State. "The whole country is interested in the Nonpartizan League and in what its effects have been in North Dakota," the editors were reminded, and they were asked kindly to clip and mail u[s] their editorials on the results of the League's control in North D[a]kota, and especially on the probable outcome of the recall vote next week. The nearly two-score replies received are approximately two to one against the present administration. The Independent Voters' Association, as quoted by the Denhoff *Voice*, presents these principal counts against the League, which of course are merely quoted here without prejudice for or against them:

"Taxes have been tripled in North Dakota by League laws.

"Marketing conditions, which were to be improved, are worse than they ever were.

"The Bank of North Dakota is insolvent.

"The program of State marketing has been scrapped in favor of a cooperative marketing plan.

"The State homebuilders' department has quit functioning.

"The State insurance department is more than a year behind in its payment of losses, and some of the 1920 claims will not be paid for two years.

"Virtually every enterprise sponsored by the inner circle of the Socialist leaders is bankrupt, the Consumers' United Stores company alone costing the farmers more than $1,000,000.

"State money was deposited in 'League banks' and re-loaned by them to the political gangsters for their private schemes. These schemes are now bankrupt, the League banks are bankrupt, and the Bank of North Dakota is whistling for its money.

"The State flour mill lost more in the first year of operation than it cost to buy the property."

The Tower City *Topics* and the Castleton *Reporter*, in particular, charge that the State has been "playing favorites" in allotting the loans of State money on farm land. Men and families close to the Nonpartizan leaders, it is said, got large sums of money "when hundreds of farmers were applying for small loans" that were actually needed to keep them going. "The chain stores are in the hands of a receiver," the Lamoure County *Chronicle* points out, taking up other State activities that did not succeed. "Nearly all of the League newspapers are on the rocks, and the farmer stockholders are holding the bag. Hell's to pay all around." However, "one thing has been demonstrated to the satisfaction of all fair-minded men," believes the Hannaford *Enterprise*, "and that is as soon as business is taken into politics, efficiency and economy are lost, and graft and favoritism take their places."

Looking at the operation of the League from the neighboring State of Minnesota, where an attempt is being made to put the same policies into force, the Minneapolis *Journal* observes that "the recall feature was placed in North Dakota's constitution by the Nonpartizan League in 1918. Now, by an irony of fate, the same weapon is turned against it, probably to its undoing." Admitting that "it is difficult to arrive at the exact situation in a State where every one is a partizan," the editor goes on:

"Incompetence and worse than incompetence are proved against the officials who have ruled North Dakota for nearly five years, with almost absolute powers. When country school districts have money in the Bank of North Dakota and are unable to draw on it to pay their bills, the facts come home to the farmers.

"That is tangible evidence. When the farmer, who has

sunk a hundred dollars in a 'cooperative store,' sees the store closed up with no assets, when the newspaper he helped to buy suspends publication, a financial wreck—the facts come home again.

"There ought not to be any question about the result October 28. Regardless of varying views as to the policy of State ownership, the situation demands a change of management, and Minnesota will be glad to see North Dakota clean house."

All these allegations are of course presented here without any endorsement and merely to inform our readers of the political situation in North Dakota. The pro-League editors have a short and simple reply to most of these accusations. They admit a certain amount of "costly experimentation," made costlier by financial interests, grain brokers, and numerous middlemen who have been hurt by the State's venture into business and finance. On the other hand, writes D. L. Campbell, publisher of the Northward *Leader*, "Our State is not run from St. Paul, Minnesota, and the real issue is still, shall the farmer set a fair price for his own product, shall he break the financial powers that control him and establish his own strongholds?" The Bank of North Dakota, which is attacked as the key to the situation by the League opponents, is defended by the League press. After weathering a storm largely produced by political opponents, says the Kidder County *Farmers Press*, Steele, N. D., "the bank has gained strength and confidence and is to-day practically the only financial institution in the State that can borrow outside money. The half million dollars recently borrowed, the selling of its bonds, the resumption of making farm loans, and the payment of all registered checks, are the worst pills the Independent Voters Association has yet had to swallow." Briefly, says the Griggs County *Sentinel Courier*, setting the accomplishments of the League against the shortcomings alleged by the other camp:

"The Nonpartizan League administration in North Dakota has been responsible for encouraging improvements and discouraging speculation; for a law saving farmers 60 per cent. or thereabouts in the cost of hail insurance; for giving assistance to workmen and their families through the Workmen's Compensation Law; for the law giving labor an eight-hour day and women a minimum wage law; for the stringent and most effective morality laws known in the world; for such progressive legislation as the Initiative Referendum and Recall law; for the saving of great sums of money through the efficient fight against railroad rate grabs and further grabs by public utility corporations; for the enactment of a Home Building law, that, when conditions will allow it to properly function, will provide a way for all worthy men to own their own homes; for the protection afforded the property owner through the law causing 30 days' notice before foreclosure of a mortgage; for a moratorium act that was effective until one year after the war; for a law guaranteeing bank deposits within the State; for a law which pays the farmer for dockage in his grain; for a grain-grading law that is based on milling and baking values; for a reduction in State costs through the law providing at cost for fire insurance on public buildings and bonding of public officials; for aid and encouragement to drouth sufferers and dairy associations; for the inauguration of a State-owned bank to handle and profit from the public monies; for the construction of a great State-owned elevator and mill; for a start in the direction of reducing the spread between the prices paid to producers and prices charged to the consumer; and for numerous other laws and features, among which could be named the soldiers compensation law, which was the first passed by any State in the Union. In addition to these things the people of the State have become intensely interested in their government. It is safe to say that no people have such good understanding of government as have the people of North Dakota."

The recent sale of the State bonds, long held up, according to the League defenders, through "the boycott by Wall Street," is declared by the *Courier-News* (Fargo) to make the recall election unnecessary:

"The sale of the bonds vindicates the Bank of North Dakota. While the I. V. A. are sending money out of the State, the Bank of North Dakota is bringing money into the State. All the so-called 'frozen assets' will now be released. And, best of all, the making of farm loads can be resumed. So why the recall? It can only add some $100,000 of expense to the already hard-up farmers. It can accomplish no possible good."

"The recall election is being brought on by a bunch of disgruntled politicians, who are on the outside trying to break in. That's really all I know for sure," writes Robert Norris, Manager of the Grant County *Leader* of Carson, N. D., and the editors of the Williams County *Farmers Press*, at Williston, of the Ward County *Farmers Press*, at Minot, and of the Mandan *News* agree with him. Several of the pro-League editors point to the attitude of the Bismarck *Tribune* as evidence that the present attack is not being made by men honestly desirous of changing the policies of the government, but merely by outsiders who want to get in. "It seems beyond the realm of reason that any fair-minded people would challenge a State administration on such a flimsy program" as the Independent Voters Association has put forward, says *The Tribune*. It opposes the whole "Socialistic" program of both the Independents and the Nonpartizans. "If there has been any dishonesty, any stealing of State funds," the editor goes on:

A GOVERNOR WHO FACES A "RECALL."

Lynn J. Frazier, executive head of North Dakota, is in danger of losing his place through the operation of a "recall" measure enacted by his own party.

"Why does not the I. V. A. come to Bismarck and file information with State's Attorney McCurdy and demand the arrest and removal from office of the offending officials through the courts?

"Why resort to a recall a few months ahead of a primary election to place in power another coterie which professes to believe in the same thing and which seeks to gain the reins of power under the disguise of salvage? The I. V. A. program spells anything but salvage however cleverly that intent is camouflaged.

"The Great State of North Dakota had better wait until the issues are properly joined and, in one mass action, repudiate Socialism in every form and restore government to its orderly and effective functions."

TOPICS IN BRIEF

HIGH rates drive freight traffic to the highway.—*Indianapolis Star.*

SOVIET Russia is figuring how to save its face and feed it, too.—*Brooklyn Eagle.*

THE U. S. A. is dry land surrounded by three miles of dry water.—*Nashville Tennessean.*

A JUDGE can make his meaning clearer to bootleggers if he will only use long sentences.—*Asheville Times.*

NAVAL disarmament, robbing the dogs of war of their barks, will eliminate much of their bites.—*Columbia (S. C.) Record.*

WHAT the nation asks of the Government is to cut out some of the gold tax and get down to brass tacks.—*Columbia (S. C.) Record.*

MANY men would avoid failure in business if their wives did not have such extravagant husbands.—*Boston Shoe and Leather Reporter.*

ONE of the principal defects in the governmental machine, it seems to us, is that there is a superfluity of nuts.—*Columbia (S. C.) Record.*

THE magazine writer who says a dog fills an empty space in a man's life must have been referring to a hot dog.—*Greenville (S. C.) Piedmont.*

THE thing that troubles the country is not only the unemployment of the idle, but the idleness of the employed.—*Chicago American Lumberman.*

HEINIE calls reparation "Wiebergutmachunsbleistungen," with emphasis on the next to the last syllable, which is "stung."—*Greenville (S.C.) Piedmont.*

"Is Professional Baseball Sport?" asks a headline in *The Literary Digest*. Yes, when the home team wins. In Portland it's agony.—*Weston (Ore.) Leader.*

AUTUMN is here, and the house shortage will soon become more acute as people resume the practise of starting fires with kerosene.—*Canton Repository.*

MAY not the Ku Klux Klan be a unique plan to rid the market of a lot of nightshirts which were relegated to shelves by the more popular pajamas?—*Pittsburgh Post.*

THE Zionist leader who asserts there is no such thing as a law of gravitation may have obtained the impression while looking for war prices to come down.—*Miami Metropolis.*

DE VALERA, it seems, can't take England's Ulster off.—*Washington Post.*

ODD that the blue law machine doesn't get under way; it's all cranked up.—*Brooklyn Eagle.*

THE record of the present Congress suggests that reaction equals inaction.—*Norfolk Virginian-Pilot.*

Now that Mexico has taken up baseball, we may expect the game to be revolutionized.—*Brooklyn Eagle.*

CHINA says she must fight Japan with words. Well, a Chinese word looks like a lethal weapon.—*Toronto Star.*

"DE VALERA Will Stand Pat," says a headline. Of course, but will Lloyd-George?—*Greenville (S. C.) Piedmont.*

WEST VIRGINIA will now have to get busy and mine and sell a little coal in order to lay in a supply of winter ammunition.—*Brooklyn Eagle.*

LINCOLN was right, of course; you can't fool all of the people all of the time; but you only have to fool a majority.—*Columbia (S. C.) Record.*

THE editor who spoke of a severe shake-up in Government offices evidently refers to the fact that bureau chiefs ride in flivvers now.—*Manila Bulletin.*

WILBUR GLENN VOLIVA protests that the world is flat; but he probably never will be convinced that it's on the level.—*Nashville Southern Lumberman.*

MR. HARDING'S best chance to uplift the Republican party in the South is to get jobs for them in the elevators in the North.—*Columbia (S. C.) Record.*

BEFORE long those German printing presses won't be able to print enough marks in twenty-four hours to pay for the oil and repairs.—*Boston Shoe and Leather Reporter.*

OFTEN the fellow who yells the loudest that the workingman should have saved his war wages is some profiteer who didn't give him a chance.—*Chicago American Lumberman.*

IRELAND wants to be admitted to the League of Nations at once. She wants a place in the League whether she is to be a republic or a dominion. It might be a good idea to seat an Irish delegate or two. If the League could hold together with Ireland on the inside it would demonstrate its cohesiveness and worth.—*Los Angeles Times.*

COVER DESIGN OF "THE SATURDAY EVENING POST," OCTOBER 8.

October 15, 1921
The Literary Digest
FUNK & WAGNALLS COMPANY

COVER DESIGN OF "THE LITERARY DIGEST," OCTOBER 15.

IT TOOK THE DOG JUST A WEEK TO GET BACK.

FOREIGN - COMMENT

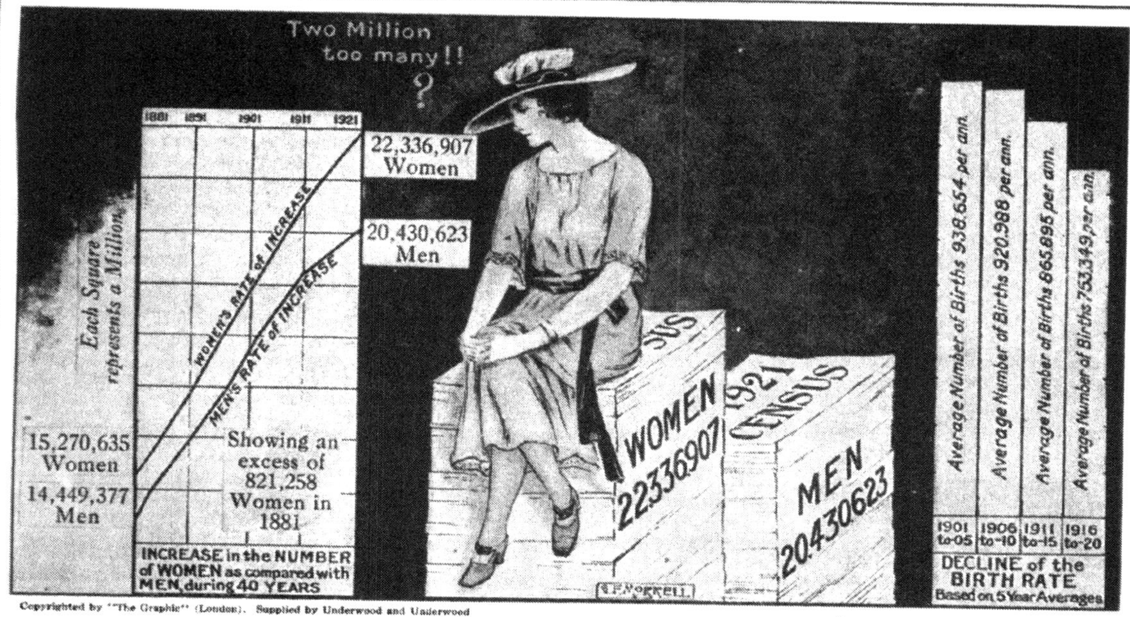

Copyrighted by "The Graphic" (London). Supplied by Underwood and Underwood

"FOR THE FEMALE OF THE SPECIES IS MORE NUMEROUS THAN THE MALE."

The increase of three-quarters of a million in the preponderance of women, as shown by the British census, is regarded as one of the direct legacies of the war, for before 1914 women outnumbered men in the United Kingdom by 1,250,000. The excess is said to be smallest in rural and mining areas.

BRITAIN'S TWO MILLION "SURPLUS WOMEN"

A MAJORITY OF TWO MILLION WOMEN is the startling revelation of the British census, and the press point out that the war cannot be held entirely responsible for this condition, because before 1914 there were a million and a quarter more women than men in the United Kingdom. Then one of the chief causes of the minority of males was their much greater inclination to emigrate. There are 22,336,907 women, and only 20,430,623 present and prospective mates for them, writes a contributor to the London *Graphic*, who adds that thus "there are two million women who have known the child's joy of pressing their dolls to their breast, and who will never get any farther towards the sweet reality to which this instinct points." Consequently more and more women are being sent into the competitive wage market with a resultant "serious bearing on business." This writer asks hopelessly how the "army of confirmed bachelors can be induced to abandon their state of 'singled blessedness' and to undertake the duties and responsibilities of wedlock," for while the British birth-rate is falling, the teeming populations of India, Japan, and China are "already overflowing into other lands in every direction they can." Some of them are highly intellectual peoples, and their influence on the future "may well make us uneasy, more especially since Britain has in the last thirty years increased by but nine and a half millions, of whom nearly five and a half millions were women." In India, China, and Japan the "reverse prevails as regards the relative increase of the sexes," for there the males are in the majority. England must find employment for these two million women, writes a contributor to the London *Times*, for most of them are dependent on their own work for support, and so "we naturally think of emigration." While it would seem to be very simple to redress the balance of population by distributing "our excess women over different parts of the Empire" still, it is not so simple as it seems, according to this writer, who proceeds:

"Not only must the newcomer be able to wash and work and sew, she must also be strong and willing to rough it and able to stand fatigue. The highly specialized town worker from this side of the water would, I fear, find herself terribly out of place in such an environment."

A more hopeful and more authoritative view is exprest in the same newspaper by Hon. John McEwan Hunter, Agent-General for Queensland, who advocates a great colonization scheme to exploit the immense possibilities of Australia. Mr. Hunter declares that the British Empire has no such thing as "surplus men and women" and confidently predicts that a liberal colonization plan in cooperation with the Dominion governments "might readily convert a national danger into a great and lasting blessing." Commissioner Lamb, head of the Emigration Department of the Salvation Army, is quoted as saying that in twenty years this organization has helped more than 100,000 to emigrate from the mother country and settle in the Dominions. What is more, "from the beginning women were so assisted and the increasing urgency of female emigration was realized before the figures of the recent census raised the question of the surplus women." *The Times* reports further that in Commissioner Lamb's opinion:

"It would be advantageous to distribute the excess of females somewhat more evenly over the whole Empire, and that many women are now well fitted to go out and prove suitable helpmeets to the men who are doing pioneer work in the Empire. Methods of easy transportation, group settlement, the supply of newspapers, the existence of postal and telegraphic facilities, leave life unshorn of those amenities, even if British women have come to regard them as essential. And what of the 50,000 widows and 150,000 children who are being cared for by the state here? The Salvation Army, he adds, has been particularly successful and happy in the transfer overseas of hundreds of such representatives of the best elements of British citizenship.

"Summing up some of the experiences of his department in arranging for the emigration of upwards of 15,000 women during 20 years, Commissioner Lamb said that not one-half of one per cent. of the number have failed to 'make good'; that over 90 per cent. of the money advanced to them for passages has been repaid, tho of similar advances made to single men less than 40 per cent. has been refunded; that in some groups which were watched particularly, 60 per cent. of the women became married within three years of their settlement in the Dominions; that there is a steady demand from the Dominions for women workers; that the 'white slave traffic' within the Empire is unknown; and that there are thousands of women in this country waiting to seize the opportunity which life in the Dominions offers. Of the total number of its emigrants about 80 per cent. have gone to Canada. 'During recent visits to the United States,' Mr. Lamb added, 'I have noticed something new—a loud, clear, and insistent demand there for Britishers, especially British women."

Editorially *The Times* points out the inadequacy of census figures as proofs of "surplus" in either sex. It remarks that the factors determining the possible source of inequality in the sexual ratio are "certainly variable" and adds:

"On the average, male infants are rather larger than female, which may lead to an inequality in the actual mortality of childbirth, with different results in the case of lower and higher races or even strata of the population. After birth, at each successive age, conditions of life press with different incidence on males and females. These later factors, such as food, education, games, apprenticeships, and choice of vocation, are obviously all under human control. But they must be estimated before they can be dealt with. The beginning must be made with calculation of the respective numbers of males and females at each successive age of life. Then only will it be possible to speak of 'surplus women' with accuracy, and to discuss the causes which have produced what inequalities may be revealed. The census figures are the raw material with which investigations have to be made."

The preliminary report of the census on which the above discussion is based gives the population of Great Britain on June 19 as 42,767,530, an increase of 1,936,134, or 4.7 per cent. over the figures of 1911. London dispatches further relate that:

"This is a smaller increase than any recorded in any decade for 100 years. That it is not smaller is mainly due to the fact that the normal flow of emigration was checked during the war. No Irish census was taken this year, so the figures given to-day relate to England, Scotland and Wales.

"In England there are 16,984,087 males and 18,694,443 females, and in Wales 1,098,133 males and 1,108,579 females, while Scotland has a surplus of more than 180,000 females. The excess of females in Great Britain in 1911 was 1,179,276, as against more than 1,900,000 this year.

"The increase in the preponderance of females is regarded as one of the direct legacies of the war. The preponderance corresponds to the ratio of 1,095 females to 1,000 males in England and Wales, the highest proportion of females ever recorded. The preponderance of females is smallest in rural and mining areas.

"The administrative County and City of London with a population of 4,483,249, shows a decrease of 0.9 per cent. from the 1911 figures; but Greater London—that is, the metropolitan police area—with 7,476,168, shows an increase of 3.1 per cent.

"Between 1915 and 1919 there was a notable decline in the birth-rate for England and Wales, the drop being from 20 to 25 per cent. below what might have been expected in normal circumstances. The lowest return was 662,661 for 1918, as against an average of 920,938 for several years up to 1910, and 957,782 last year.

"The census figures show that the population of British islands adjacent to the Kingdom is 299,704.

"The population of the Indian Empire is 319,075,132, an increase of 1.2 per cent.; of the Union of South Africa, Europeans only, 1,521 635, an increase of 19.2 per cent.; of Australia, excluding full-blooded aborigines, 5,426,008, an increase of 21.8 per cent., and of New Zealand, excluding the Maoris, 1,218,270, an increase of 20.8 per cent."

"MUST AUSTRIA DIE?"

UNLESS RESTORED FROM COMA by prompt and practical help from the Allied and other countries, Austria must cease to exist, is the cry of the Austrian press, which is echoed by correspondents far and wide. Appeals for help are aimed directly at America, and Vienna financiers and government officials are quoted in press dispatches as saying that "with securities and foreign currencies mounting sky-high, the problem is again up to America." In the words of one official, Austria, is "going to the dogs" and "if there is no speedy change, anything may happen." The *Neue Wiener Journal* publishes an appeal to the American Commissioner asking why Washington is waiting so long to suspend the lien on Austria, which has already been waived by other nations, and asking that the American people be told openly of their unconscious cruelty, as Austria is now standing with a knife at her throat. To the Entente the Vienna *Neue Freie Presse* states the case as follows:

"Despite all the difficulties with which it is confronted, the Entente must make up its mind to solve the Austrian crisis, which becomes more and more perilous. The catastrophic rise of foreign exchange is the best proof that confidence has ceased to exist, and, also, that somehow the situation must be cleared up. . . . If the Entente continues to act with the same mortal slowness, if again we are to pass through weeks and months and receive only communiqués, discourses, and official visits instead of real aid, then our economic ruin will be fatally precipitated. What is needed is prompt political and economic action, failing which, this country shall die."

While the anxiety of the people was temporarily calmed toward the end of September when Great Britain made a small credit advance, we learn from Paris dispatches, a week later a panic swept the Vienna Bourse with a new fall in the crown to more than 3000 to the dollar. The population, it is said, having lost faith in the government, were panic-stricken lest the country be unable to keep up its food reserve, and rushed to the stores to lay in supplies. Prices immediately jumped as goods disappeared from the markets. Many of the stores had the war-time aspect of long lines of would-be purchasers, while others closed because all their stocks had been sold.

Press dispatches inform us also that many American investors in Paris who have been buying Austrian crowns at the rate of 10,000 for 100 francs are alarmed, and are throwing their influence at Washington into the balance, not only because further drops are foreseen, with the possibility of Austria's total repudiation of her bank-notes, but also because "the report is current that the Paris Bourse and the Vienna government are contemplating stamping all issues to 60 per cent. of their face value in the hope of getting respite to tide over the winter purchases."

All asked of America is that she should forego her claims on Austria for twenty years, writes Mr. Sisley Huddleston in *Eastern Europe* (London), and assuming that America will forego her claims, for "it is not credible" that after the earnest plea of the Supreme Council America should not agree, then Austria "would have a clean slate, for the two outstanding European nations will offer no serious opposition." We read then:

"The new Bank of Issue should, according to the recommendations of the Financial Commission of the League of Nations, provide Austria with a money which shall be stable in value. This means that all the available property in Austria—state revenue, monopolies, forests, and real estate—must form in one way or another the basis on which the new issue, which will be equivalent to the pre-war French franc, should rest.

"With radical economies effected in state expenditure, and with credits which would undoubtedly be forthcoming, Austria would be given new heart and new hope, and the optimistic—perhaps too optimistic—reporters to the League believe that in six months Austria should again become practically self-supporting."

UNEMPLOYMENT A WORLD CONDITION.

"THE WORLD'S WORK has been brought to a standstill," is the finding of Professor Casel of Sweden, whom Premier Lloyd George calls "one of the most brilliant economists," and whose words he used in a speech at Inverness with reference to unemployment conditions in the United Kingdom. Professor Casel speaks of the unemployment figures throughout the world as "alarming" and declares it remarkable that "the two countries whose credit stands highest are those suffering the most severely, the United States and Great Britain." Mr. Lloyd George cited the fluctuations of the exchanges of the various countries as chief obstacles to trade, adding that—

"These conditions will stabilize first of all when nations learn that concord and cooperation with their neighbors constitute the only real firm basis for their own national prosperity. They will also improve when nations realize that they are not increasing their national wealth every time they turn out a new batch of treasury notes from the printing press, and that is a very important consideration. There are very able men who think we have gone too far in America and this country in the process of deflation, but there is absolutely no doubt in the minds of many that those other countries have gone much too far in the process of inflation, and the first real condition of stability in business is the stabilizing of exchanges. You will not stabilize until you stabilize both your foreign policy and your financial policy. . . .

"Our credit stands not merely higher than that of any of the belligerent countries in Europe, but infinitely higher. No one in this country will be allowed to starve so long as there is a crumb in the national cupboard. We can control our own finances, our own trade relations, our own foreign policy, but we can not control the trade and foreign policy of other nations. . . .

AUGUST 4TH, 1914; AUGUST 4TH, 1921.

"S'posin' WE hadn't afforded it in 1914, eh, Bill?"

—*The Star* (London).

"I am hopeful. I think things are improving. What is wanted is an atmosphere of peace throughout the world. Economy must also be a factor. There must be cooperation between all classes of a community, otherwise things will proceed from a crisis to disaster. The people must march side by side, but not in sections or tribes."

One of the business experts who met Mr. Lloyd George to confer on unemployment and its remedies is Mr. W. L. Hichens, Chairman of Cammell, Lasaid & Co., who is quoted as saying at a meeting of the London Iron and Steel Exchange that—

"There can be no real and permanent improvement in trade until the political conditions of Europe are more stable. The thing that matters, it seems to me as a business man, is stability.

"HE LAUGHS BEST WHO LAUGHS LAST."

—*The Bystander* (London).

I don't care how many marks go to the pound so long as it is stable and definite, and you know where you are. . . .

"Inflation is the root cause of this instability. It is a monster created for a certain purpose. It has proved too powerful for those who called it into existence, and in the end it is going to prove their destruction. . . . It is a mistake to suppose that you can first trade with a country and then by that means stabilize the political and financial situation.

"I can not see the use of trying to start trade with Poland and some of the other countries whose exchange has gone completely until they restore some sort of financial order. You can do a bit of bartering here and there, but that is not what we want. We want some definite medium of exchange, and if those countries where exchange has broken down can not restore it they should hand over their financial arrangements to the League of Nations in order to restore them to something like solvency."

An ironic contrast is presented in the unemployment conditions in "defeated Germany," according to Berlin press correspondents, who inform us that the unemployment wave which is sweeping the world has "left Germany in the best condition of any of the great industrial nations except France." A boom in industry, stimulated by the low value of the mark in other countries, absorbed the idle men and women until, late in September, the unemployed numbered only 383,000. This number is said to be decreasing steadily, and shows "a progressive decline in unemployment in Germany in the past twelve months." In France American correspondents report that while that country is the "greatest sufferer of all the Allies in the war" she stands, as far as unemployment is considered, in the best position of any of the Allied and associated nations. Against the millions out of work in Great Britain and the United States, and 500,000 in Italy and 100,000 in Switzerland, writes one correspondent, "careful research on unemployment in France shows it is not a problem here."

RUSSIA IN TRANSFORMATION

NEW ECONOMIC POLICY in Russia promises to bring as great a change as did the Bolshevik revolution, according to Riga dispatches, and the change is not from Communism to Capitalism but rather from State Socialism to Individualism—from bureaucracy to personal initiative. On the economic side the aim is to stimulate production of food and manufactured goods, we are told, and to reestablish a normal system of money. On the administrative side the intent is to abolish routine red tape and procrastination in order to make way for strictly business methods. In the beautiful perfection of Soviet theory no word has ever been uttered about that bane of reactionary systems, namely, "red tape." In fact, all the red in the Soviet system has been supposed to be used in flags and proclamations; but now the London *Daily Telegraph* discovers a sample of red tape at its reddest in the letter of a Russian woman refugee from Moscow, who experienced all the comic complexities of its winding in the very tragic circumstance of seeking a serum for her husband, who was desperately ill. Writing in *The Rul,* a Russian newspaper published in Berlin, she admits that her natural impetuosity under the conditions sent her straight to the bacteriological institute, where the serum is stored. She had a doctor's prescription, which availed her naught, however, and she was informed that she must have an order from the special bureau in the Commissariat for Health. She tells us then:

APOLOGIZING TO THE DEAD.

LENINE: "I beg your pardon—the mistake is mine!"

—*Le Matin* (Paris).

"Next morning about twelve (it is useless to go before) I hastened to the Commissariat. There they began by telling me that before coming to them I should have gone to the local sanitary authority. But my palpitations became so bad that they took mercy upon me. After having waited for two hours I received a document with three signatures. For this I was obliged to go into three different rooms and to sign in two large registers. After this I went with the paper to another institution, a sub-commissariat. The inquiry sent me to room No. 28. After a long walk through what had been large halls and spacious corridors, but now full of the usual filth and partitioned in all directions with coarse, unpainted boarding, I got at last to room No. 28. The place was full of angry female officials (nowadays we are all irritable). A long parley convinced me that No. 28 was the wrong room and that my real destination was No. 32. There I found a very nice gentleman, who immediately decided that I must go to room No. 37. Two oldish solemn men sitting there looked at my paper from both sides. They consulted gravely, and finally decided that I must go to No. 40. There another nice gentleman immediately discovered that my business was very pressing, and sent me into the next room to his secretary, who, having made several cabalistic pencil marks on my document, sent me on to No. 38. The young lady there decided that time was up and that I must return next day."

But the lady seeking the serum wheedled this woman official into entering her document in a register, and giving it to a messenger "to put on the desk of somebody in the next room," and what happened follows:

"I do not know how long the paper would have remained on the desk if the gentleman from No. 40 had not come in. He was very sympathetic and told the messenger to bring the paper back. The document was again entered into another fat register, I signed for it, and went to No. 28, where they made a mark. Then the same thing was repeated in No. 32. Then they sent me back to No. 28. There four people got busy on me at once. The document was entered into two other fat registers, and then it was quite taken away from me and another paper given to me instead. Then it really became late, and I was told to return next morning. I did so. In No. 28 I had to sign again in two registers, received two slips, signed again for these, and was at last free to go to the laboratory. There I had to sign only three times, waited only half an hour, and received a splendid German serum, of which, it appears, there is a great stock, but few people have the patience to go through the mill to obtain it."

Bolshevik admissions of Communism's failure are shown by the *Daily Telegraph* in an appeal by the Central Executive Committee of the Third Internationale in Moscow to its Bureau in Western Europe, in which we read that "at present the entire foundations of the Internationale are being undermined from within by the black elementary force of millions of starving people."

AND THE TSAR IS THE CAUSE OF IT ALL.

LENINE: "Let me explain: These people are victims of the Tsarist régime, which got them into the habit of eating every day!"

—*Le Figaro* (Paris).

Photo by U. S. Bureau of Mines. Courtesy of "The Nation's Business," Washington, D. C.

VOLCANIC SPRINGS YIELDING 6,600 TO 30,800 POUNDS OF STEAM AN HOUR, AT LARDERELLO, ITALY.

HITCH YOUR ENGINE TO A VOLCANO

HEAT FROM THE EARTH'S CENTRAL STORE might doubtless be made available by boring down to it. This has been more than once proposed, but the huge expense has prevented. The earth's internal heat, however, is not everywhere at great depths. In volcanic regions it comes near to the surface; when there is an eruption it overflows without any boring. In Italy, ready-made steam has been used for years as a power source, and this use has now been greatly expanded, as we learn from an article by Warren Bishop in *The Nation's Business* (Washington, October). Engineers have often advised us to harness the waterfalls, says this magazine in its sub-heading; but there is something novel in the idea of hitching your engine to a volcano and sitting back to watch it run. To reduce the cost of living, begins Mr. Bishop, we must reduce the cost of motion and the first step is the wiser use of our stored-up power. He goes on:

"But what of a country where water power is out of reach and coal and oil must be imported? Here's one answer:

"Hitch your engine to a volcano, not a live, active volcano, but one that has simmered down after a few hundred or a few thousand centuries and now contents itself with spouting up steam.

"That has been done with success in Italy, and in Hawaii a movement is on foot to puncture the outer slopes of Kilauea. The last territorial legislature had before it a bill appropriating $25,000 for experimental borings, but it failed to pass.

"The Italian use of latent steam of volcanic origin is in Tuscany, near the ancient Etruscan city of Volterra, one of the world's oldest centers of civilization. Here, distributed over an area of about forty square miles, are natural steam springs, the last breathings of a volcano extinct so long ago that every surface indication of it has been worn away.

"This ready-made supply of steam had been known to man for centuries, and for centuries man had kept away from it as an evil omen. Then about 130 years ago two Italian chemists discovered boric acid in the water that boiled out of the earth. Up to that time most of the world's supply of borax had been brought from Tibet.

"A century or more ago, Larderel, a Frenchman, started the first plant for the extraction of boric acid from these springs and soon was supplying a great part of the world's needs. As the demand increased it was found necessary to have more steam, and artificial 'steam wells' were driven around the natural springs.

"Unlike oil wells, Tuscany's steam springs give no signs of drying up. The springs around Larderello, the center of the boric acid industry, yield from 6,600 to 30,800 pounds of steam an hour. Just whence the steam comes let geologists argue. It can be had for the drilling at half a dozen places from five to twenty miles distant. Steam naturally suggested power. Some ten years before the war, Prince Ginori Conti, the head of the boric acid works, turned the natural steam directly into a piston engine. It worked, and a larger one was built to drive the dynamo that lit the boric acid works at Larderello. That engine has now been running fifteen years.

"Not long before the war a more ambitious plan was begun. It was decided to build a turbo-generator of 250 kilowatts. In this larger project natural steam is used as fuel rather than as direct motive power. There were fears as to the effect of the gases in the steam on turbine blades and difficulties in condensing these gases.

"With this equipment power was provided for various of the company's plants and sent to Volterra, more than thirty miles away. So this ancient Etruscan city, with a history that goes back to centuries before Christ, was the first to draw its electric power from the underground heat of the globe.

"Now the power plant has been greatly expanded. Three units of 2,500 kilowatts each were installed during the war and a fourth is under way. Volcanic steam is used as the heating principle, generating pure water steam somewhat as in the ordinary water tube boiler. Power is sent to Siena and on to Florence, some fifty miles away, to Leghorn, to Piombino and to Massa. A still larger power plant is being planned at Lago."

Other parts of Italy, we are told, are awake to the possibilities of volcanic heat as a source of power. Her fuel needs are well known. Experimental borings are being made near Naples at the Solfatara, a small extinct volcano. All over the world are regions of recent volcanic action where boiling springs and natural steam jets may yet turn factory wheels and light houses. Prince Conti's success led the scientists of the Geophysical Laboratory in Washington to suggest that Hawaii's sugar plantations might find a source of power in Kilauea. The problem is more difficult of approach than was that at Larderello, for boring would be vastly more difficult. Mr. Bishop continues:

"Japan is another example. The largest producer of coal in Asia, she has the smallest reserves, but she has hot springs with possibilities of power. In New Zealand are jets of natural steam, and most of her natural supply of coal is of low grade, so that she annually imports half a million tons. The west coast of South America presents the same situation, scanty coal supplies and obvious sources of volcanic heat.

"What of the continental United States? We are constantly being warned of our lessening coal reserves and our disappearing supply of oil, but here and there are scattered boiling springs and volcanoes whose surface activity is at a minimum. Wherever there are hot springs or spouts of steam of volcanic origin there are possibilities of usable power. Mt. Lassen and Mt. Hood are two places which come to mind. Out in Sonoma county, California, an enterprising resort proprietor is trying to find out if he can light and heat his hotel from his hot springs.

"We may not have to draw on Yellowstone Park to heat and light our Western Empire, but it is one of the things that could be done, and done, the scientists say, with a minimum of disfigurement to the scenic beauty of that wonderland."

CLEANING UP THE OIL CAMPS

SANITARY CONDITIONS in the average oil camp or in a "boom" oil town are so imperfect as practically to invite the visitation of a costly fire or epidemic, according to a recent report by C. P. Bowie, petroleum engineer, issued by the U. S. Bureau of Mines. Such communities usually have no water supply, or a wholly inadequate one. Garbage and decaying vegetable matter, tin cans, old rags and scrap paper lie in heaps about temporary structures or are strewn over vacant lots. Flies swarm and the atmosphere reeks with offensive odors. To quote further an abstract prepared by the Bureau:

"Many oil men employ the contract system of drilling, which almost eliminates the tendency of companies to build camps or small towns over which they may exercise personal supervision as to housing and sanitation. In the contract system, the company bargains for the development of its holdings with a contractor who provides, at a stipulated price, the material and labor for drilling the wells. The system relieves the company of all responsibility except its financial obligations to the contractor.

"The contractor engages his drillers, tool dressers, and laborers. Most of them are brought from outside districts, and if oil is found and the field gives promise of commercial production, the oil workers are followed by freighters, 'jitney' drivers, restaurant keepers, inn-keepers, and the innumerable small-trades people who, with their families, go to make up the population of such districts. So it is that a stretch of trackless prairie sometimes becomes, almost overnight, a community numbering thousands of people who establish themselves in temporary buildings, tents, dugouts, lean-to shelters, or even within four topless walls of burlap, or in the open. These mushroom communities have been aptly termed 'rag towns.' Ranger, Desdemona, and Burk-Burnett, Texas, were towns of this type in 1919. While it is admitted that the sanitation conditions in such communities are deplorable, it has been argued that they are the results of extraneous circumstances and will be remedied as soon as conditions become normal, but experience has shown that so-called 'normal' conditions are never attained until such a community has been visited by costly fires and epidemics. In fact, 'normal' conditions are not established until the field has been proved a success or failure, which often takes months or even years.

"The responsibility for the betterment of such conditions plainly belongs to the State governments; broadly speaking, all the States have legislation adequate to cope with those exigencies. The enforcement of the laws, however, too often is left to the community itself and rests in the hands of a few men, who either think that they can not afford to run the risk of antagonizing their neighbors by the enforcement of ordinances, or are so engrossed in business that they are indifferent to the responsibilities entrusted to them. Therefore, the neglect of those in authority to meet these responsibilities brings hardship and unnecessary misery to a class of migratory workers who may be especially susceptible to the influences of social unrest.

"The employer is also a sufferer. He meets a material loss through the 'soldiering' of discontented workers, petty strikes, and an enormous turnover in his force of laborers. Experience has shown that insanitary conditions may decrease the working efficiency of the men 25 per cent.

"In the older oil fields, the Bureau of Mines finds that the sanitary conditions about oil wells are practically the same as the sanitary conditions of the surrounding country. The oilworkers usually live at the farmhouses in the vicinity, and as production in the oil fields becomes settled, the pumping of the wells is carried on by farm laborers or by men who live in the neighboring towns. Sanitary conditions in these districts are seldom all that can be desired; they are, however, much superior to conditions in the new oil fields of less populated districts."

RECREATIONAL DEFECTS OF THE MOVIES.

WHILE THE EDUCATIONAL VALUE of the moving picture is under frequent discussion, its recreational value seems to have been taken for granted. Yet even this is sharply called in question by Prof. G. T. W. Patrick of the University of Iowa, in an article entitled "The Play of a Nation," contributed to *The Scientific Monthly* (Utica, N. Y.). Professor Patrick's article is somewhat general, but we quote only so much of it as refers to the play-value of the movies. One point in their favor, he begins, is that they are accessible and available. They satisfy vicariously the love of adventure, the roaming instinct, the delight in the new and the strange and the wonderful. They divert the weary soul and relieve the strain upon the will. They bring a glimpse of fairyland into lives that are drab and prosy. To those who have no beauty in their surroundings, beauty is brought in many forms upon the screen. But when this is said, he goes on, all is said:

"Good play is out of doors and involves the larger fundamental muscles of the trunk and legs, and for children this is primary and indispensable. They must be active in play and all sedentary people must be active in play. It is bad enough that children should be confined in a schoolroom five precious hours of the day. It is worse if they are penned in between a desk and a seat. For such children to spend still other hours of the day or evening or any hours of their holidays in confinement is serious, and especially in these days of universal reading, when old and young alike spend so many hours sitting, reading fascinating books of fiction, and interesting magazines and papers.

"In the moving-picture theater the bodily confinement is complete and uncompromising. In the schoolroom the child can at least wriggle. In the movies the attention is so wrapt as to result in a statue-like rigidity of the whole body for hours. For adults this is unfortunate; for children it is fatal. Many moving-picture theaters are stuffy. Most of them are crowded. The physical conditions are thus the worst possible from the standpoint of recreational needs.

"As regards the use of the sense-organs, the eye, overworked among our modern reading people, gains no rest from moving pictures, but is taxed to the very utmost and kept under strain for hours. To what extent the eyes will suffer from the movng pictures, I am not here discussing. I am only pointing out the failure of the movies to conform in this respect to recreational requirements. The relations of the eye and ear to our modern life are such that good music is of far greater value as recreation and relaxation than any appeal to the eye. If our play is to take the form of any entertainment on the stage, good music in any form, whether in concert, recital, folk songs, or opera, would seem to be deserving a very high place.

"Another aspect of the moving pictures in their relation to the human mind, which must be taken into account, is their effect upon the emotions. The emotional flooding of the mind which the spectator experiences probably has no recreational value in itself. In the legitimate drama this tumult of the emotions, tempered by the human voice and by all the settings of real art, may be for the adult a harmless accompaniment of esthetic enjoyment. In the moving pictures such frequent and excessive overflow of the emotional life can hardly fail to disturb the delicate balance between real life and its natural emotional response. Certain films widely exhibited to large audiences draw too heavily upon the emotions. Old-time revivalists have been censured for working upon the feelings of their hearers by appeals to the very intimate and personal experiences connected with birth, death and marriage. These tales were innocent compared with the harrowing scenes sometimes presented on the screen. Tears flow and the breast heaves, but the natural expression of emotional states through action is prohibited. In real life such emotional situations lead to action. In the movies nothing happens. The natural response is lacking.

"We must conclude therefore that from the standpoint of the psychology of play, the movies offer little of recreational value, while for children they may be the source of the most pernicious mischief. The physical decadence which is anyway threatening our people because of our modern life of comfort, ease, and inactivity, with its excessive demands upon the brain and its neglect of physical development, is likely to receive a considerable impetus from the moving pictures."

When society comes to its senses and sweeps bad pictures from the stage, then, says Professor Patrick, the question of the recreational and educational value of the movies will be more carefully raised. The recreational value, he is sure, is slight, while the educational value he considers greatly overestimated. The child learns by doing, not by seeing. What is important is that he himself should learn to contribute to human utilities. He continues:

"Mr. Chesterton says that our modern people do not know how to amuse themselves because they are not free men. Our amusements are mechanical, as our whole life is. We have to be amused by machinery, such as the cinema and the automobile. True recreation is that in which we ourselves participate. There must be action and self-expression.

"It will not do to lay all the evils of the present time—and they are very threatening—upon our institutions nor upon the war. To a considerable extent they have their source in the unstable brain of the individual. Our material and social environment is changing very rapidly, while the human brain and body are changing little or not at all.

"Nothing would do more towards the solution of our social problems than providing healthful and harmonizing recreations for the nation. The way to do this may be beset with difficulties but the true approach seems to be through the public schools. The cultivation of good taste in selecting our amusements would do something, but practical results will be more likely to follow the enlarged opportunities for good sports and healthful plays and a revision of our school program in the direction of the English system, in which sports and play are an integral part of public school curriculum."

In conclusion Professor Patrick says that the three recreations of the great body of the American people—the dance, the movies, the automobile—"do not rank high in real recreational value"; one has "a doubtful social value" and one "a pernicious influence."

POWER AT A MILLION VOLTS

SUCCESSFUL GENERATION OF ELECTRIC POWER at more than one million volts has just been accomplished at the high voltage engineering laboratory of the General Electric Company at Pittsfield, Mass., we are told by *The Railway Review* (Chicago,). The power, which was generated in the company's plant, was "stepped up" by transformer equipment until the electric pressure reached the enormous voltage of one million. An arc was formed across a gap nine feet wide. The actual transmission was for a short distance only, within the building, but it was sufficient to indicate the feasibility of sending electric energy for much greater distances than have heretofore been practicable. We read:

Courtesy of the General Electric Co., Schenectady, N. Y.

A MILLION VOLTS JUMPING A NEEDLE GAP OF NINE FEET.

Below is seen a sphere gap also used for testing high voltage.

"Physical laws applying to high voltage phenomena were found to hold good at these enormous potentials. Tests were made on strings of standard ten-inch suspension insulators up to 1,100,000 volts. The laws in relation to the loss through radiation from the conductor were checked and found to hold. A short transmission line was tested and results indicated that a line using four-inch diameter conductors or larger would be necessary at 1,000,000 volts.

"The successful conclusion of the tests is the result of more than thirty years of constant experimentation during which time transmission voltages have arisen steadily from the first 15,000-volt line built in Pittsfield in 1891. The voltage range and the distance for which electric current can be transmitted have been greatly increased since then. A power line is now under construction in California which will carry current for a distance of approximately 250 miles, and this plant will in itself establish a record. The apparatus for it was made in Pittsfield. The successful transmission of electric energy at a million volts points out the possibilities of covering much greater distances if necessary.

"The high voltage engineering laboratory and transformer testing plant at the Pittsfield works is unique among such establishments in the United States. The building contains complete power transformer testing facilities, and the high voltage laboratory where work requiring potentials well up into hundreds of thousands of volts is carried on. The high voltage laboratory is the only one of the kind capable of reproducing with any degree of similarity the high potential occurring in actual transmission practise. The General Electric Co. expended nearly a million dollars in building and equipping this feature of the Pittsfield plant. There are about one and one-half miles of bar copper and approximately 57 miles of cable in the testing equipment. The total weight of the copper in the installation is nearly 100 tons, and its cost was approximately $100,000. The high voltage transformer used there has the highest voltage rating of any in the United States with the exception of a duplicate at the Schenectady works of the same company."

MOTORING AND TYPHOID

THE CITY-DWELLER is apparently in greater danger of contracting disease when he is touring in the country than when he stays at home. He does not have to be particular about his drinking water at home, for the Board of Health sees to all that. So in the country he drinks everything watery that he runs across, and frequently is ill in consequence. For years, we are told by a writer in *Public Works* (New York), it has been common for health officials to expect a greater or less increase in the typhoid rate in the late summer and early fall, such cases having been contracted chiefly by drinking impure water at resorts, and being classified as "vacation typhoid." During the past few years the water supplies in popular resorts have been pretty well looked after, and most of the cases of "vacation typhoid" probably have been caused by impure well water at farmhouses and boarding-houses. We read:

"During the past two or three years the enormous increase in the amount of automobile touring has greatly augmented the danger of typhoid contracted on these pleasure trips. Not only are those touring through the country liable to drink from polluted wells or streams, but, in certain sections of the country especially, a great many of them camp out at points in more or less common use, generally on the outskirts of cities. Since in the majority of cases these camping places are under no supervision whatever, their condition from the point of view of sanitation soon becomes dangerous to campers, and there is great probability that many of them may become centers of typhoid dissemination.

"The United States Public Health Service is looking into this matter, paying especial attention to the national parks, endeavoring to make them safe and sanitary for the vast numbers who have recently taken to touring them. On May 15 the service sent its first sanitary engineers into Yellowstone, Mt. Rainier, Yosemite and Grand Canyon parks, while other engineers are being sent to the other parks as they become available. In the largest and most popular parks, such as Yellowstone, it will be necessary for a sanitarian to remain all summer. The work of the health service consists in examining and protecting health supplies, disposing of garbage and sewage, inspecting milk and food and the way they are handled, providing for camp policing and sanitation, and preventing malaria. Malaria-carrying mosquitoes have been found in Yosemite Park and special efforts are being made to eradicate them there and prevent them from obtaining a foothold in other parks.

"A number of cities, especially in the West, have provided special camping places near their boundaries where water and sanitary facilities are provided, and which are under a more or less continuous supervision. From a health view, if from no other, it is desirable that all such camping places be under strict supervision of some State, county or city authority.

"The State Highway Department of Pennsylvania has received hundreds of inquiries relative to possible camping sites on the highways of that State and finds that few, if any, municipalities provide such sites. It is reported that there are no suitable locations for camping in the vicinity of Philadelphia, but the automobile club of that city is endeavoring to provide camp grounds on Roosevelt Boulevard. On the Lincoln Highway there are scores of camp sites along the Juniata River, and there are numerous places between Philadelphia and Pittsburgh on this highway where private land owners permit tourists to occupy their ground. A number of local motor clubs throughout the State have arranged for free camping sites, but so far as can be learned no municipalities of the State have charge of any of these sites, nor does it appear that there are any special precautions taken towards insuring sanitary conditions. Even in the notice sent out by the State Highway Department 'it is urged upon all users of sites that they gather up waste paper and other debris upon leaving', but no warning is given of the danger of insanitary practises.

"It would seem as though all State health departments should take action in this matter, posting signs at all places used either with or without permission by numbers of touring parties, giving instructions as to where safe water may be obtained, advising the boiling of doubtful water, and giving instructions for sanitary use of the grounds. In addition, they should arrange to secure in some way an enforcement of sanitary regulations relative to the use of camping sites, either directly through their own agents or through the nearest local boards of health. It would seem probable that funds for the payment of at least a considerable part of the cost of this oversight might be obtained by contributions by State or local motor clubs, since it is the motorists themselves who would chiefly be benefited by the enforcement of such sanitary regulations."

TIME TO FIGHT THE PLAGUE

PLAGUE BELTED THE WORLD in 1914. The war gave it time to dig itself in, and it is now well established. If the nations of the earth desire to avoid a great outbreak they must take united action, says an editorial writer in *The Nation's Health* (Washington). Now is the time for international work; when the outbreak comes, the opportunity to ward it off will be past. Sanitary officers, the writer thinks, should feel apprehensive over the present plague situation. Prior to the war, bubonic plague had become established in China, India, the West Coast of Africa, and in the rural districts of central California. These acted as reservoirs from which plague flowed out from time to time to gain a foothold in new territory. He continues:

"If there was a concentrated rodent population and rats had free access to human habitations, the epidemic, in the absence of intelligent control operations, was large in proportion to the population. If, on the other hand, there was a sparseness of rodent or human population, or if human beings dwelt for the most part in a rat-free environment, only a few sporadic human cases occurred. If the city rat lived in fairly close proximity to the suburban and rural wild rodent, plague would be passed to the latter with a gradual lowering of virulence, the production of chronic plague, and the establishment of residual focus.

"While the experiences of the Public Health Service in California demonstrated how well nigh impossible is the eradication of such a focus, they also showed the practicability of delimiting the infected area and of preventing the spread of the disease into urban centers.

"Just prior to the war with Germany, plague was reported in Venezuela, Brazil, Chile, Ecuador, Peru, Cuba, Louisiana, and California, in the Western Hemisphere; in the Azores and Russia; in Turkey, Arabia, Persia, Ceylon, India, Siam, Indo-China, Dutch East Indies, the Straits Settlements, the Philippines, China and Japan; in Egypt, Morocco, Tripoli, Senegal, British East Africa, German East Africa, Zanzibar, and Mauritius; in Australia, Hawaii and New Caledonia. In other words, on June 30, 1914, plague belted the world.

"Then submarines and raiders began to infest the seas; in a moment the shipping of the world was diverted to the carriage of munitions; steamships moved in convoys; international maritime schedules were rearranged, and many hitherto busy ports were temporarily abandoned; the fleets of the globe were taken over by the Allies; production fell off enormously; world commerce underwent a complete metamorphosis. In spite of this tremendous change, the Armistice found plague distributed practically as it was at the beginning of the war five years before. In other words, while commerce had not spread the disease, civilization had been too busy in its fight for self-preservation to wage warfare against pestilence.

"In the period of readjustment which succeeded, the nations found themselves impoverished and for the most part that condition still prevails. People who are struggling for the barest necessities of life cannot appreciate the necessity for plague eradication, therefore plague has had seven years in which to dig itself in and to establish chronic enzootic foci.

"Just now ship movement is still below the pre-war average rate. World commerce will keep pace with the return of prosperity and correspondingly the potentialities of plague diffusion will increase. If plague is actively combated now while shipping is slack, those potentialities will not be realized. Plague can be more cheaply fought now than later and future losses from disastrous quarantine may be avoided.

"Some international agency should at once commence an organized campaign against plague. The world menace of the disease should be signalized to the nations, and infected ports should be stimulated and assisted to the end that plague repressive measures be immediately instituted. What has been done in stamping out yellow fever indicates how successful such movements could be. The energetic prosecution of a world-wide anti-plague campaign is to-day the crying sanitary need."

TO RESURRECT THE OLD WOODEN CAR

THE OLD WOODEN FREIGHT CARS that have been taking up track room by thousands, are to be furbished up, reinforced, given a new coat of paint and put to work again. Railroads are thinking up ways of saving an honest penny as well as of turning it. To the public, holding its breath and waiting expectantly for the rates to sag a little, the saving proposition looks like an eminently sensible one. So when you see the faithful old wooden "box" or "flat" trundling past your Pullman window, forbear to smile, and nod approval instead. During the war, we are told by a writer in *The Railway Review* (Chicago), many railroads found the cost of maintenance on these cars so high that they concluded it was cheaper to remove them from service and dismantle them than to repair and keep them in use. This attitude seems reasonable, when one takes into consideration the cost of switching, delay to traffic, damage to freight, and repairs. Yet many roads have found the cause of this great outlay and have removed it; thus keeping the old cars in service and earning from them a good revenue. He continues:

"It is poor economy to allow these cars to stand around, taking up track room, becoming more and more dilapidated, and not earning a penny. Just now seems to be the opportune time to make ready to take care of these cars when the order comes. If one road finds it economical to rebuild the majority, there is no good reason why others can not do likewise.

"No doubt many of the wooden cars have been useless so long that they are hopelessly decayed, but most of them have only a few weak parts, and these can be strengthened, making the car almost as good as new. Some roads have a large percentage of wooden cars, as they have not done much buying since the heavier engines were put into service. The idea of destroying all these cars is not to be thought of.

"A careful inspection should be made of every wooden car on hand, and those decayed or wrecked beyond repair should be dismantled at once. The necessary salvage to repair the remaining cars should be saved. A careful estimate should be made of the cost of rebuilding these cars and the program worked out so that everything will be ready to order the material and do the work when the time comes.

"There is no improvement on the new modern car that can not be applied to the old wooden car, and that at very little more expense. Parts now are made that strengthen every weak part of these cars, and it seems a mistake to destroy all of them. Many parts on the old car are standard on the modern car, and enough improvements can be put on the old car to make it really valuable."

All these betterments, we are told, can be applied to the old car for the same amount which they cost on the new one, and without disturbing the other parts of the car to any extent. To quote further:

"Although old cars have depreciated, many to-day are worth more than they cost when new, owing to the advances in material and labor. The prices of new equipment have increased, in some cases over 200 per cent. A car that cost $1,250 in 1912, costs $3,000 at the present time.

"The claim can not be substantiated that these cars are too small and, for that reason, are out of date, for there is still a demand for small cars. Many of the 100,000 capacity cars to-day are hauling less than one of these small cars will hold.

"Often when inspection is left to the car foreman, he is too rigid in his decisions, and a car that should be rebuilt will be recommended for dismantling. Perhaps his error is because he does not understand the value of the old car, or it may be that he is overburdened with work and does not have the facilities to handle anything in addition. Facilities must be provided to make the rehabilitation of these cars profitable.

"It costs money in these days to dismantle cars—money which could be used much more advantageously in building up. Every time a car is torn down, another must be built to take its place, if the same amount of business is to be handled; hence this is a serious question: 'What are you going to do with the old wooden cars?'"

MORE SUICIDES—WHY?

SUICIDE IS AGAIN on the increase, according to *The Statistical Bulletin* of the Metropolitan Life Insurance Co. (New York). There are indications, it says, that the downward trend in the suicide death-rate which has continued since 1915 has received a decided check this year. We read:

"During the first seven months of 1921, the rate from suicide among more than thirteen million industrial policyholders was 7.3 per 100,000, which is an increase of 26 per cent. over the rate for the corresponding period of 1920. Other observers have noted the same facts in their respective fields. The National Committee for Mental Hygiene has called attention to the marked increase in the number of suicides, especially among ex-soldiers and others

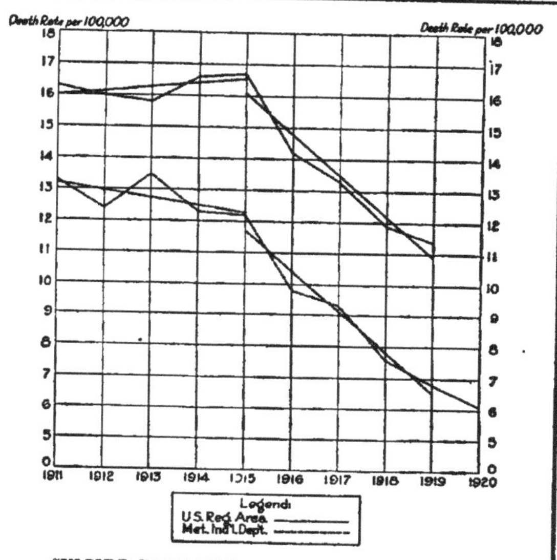

SUICIDE RATE PER 100,000 FOR TEN YEARS.

The unbroken lines above show the rate for the general population; the broken lines below show the rate for wage-earners in a large industrial insurance company. The decrease from 1915 to 1920 has halted, we are told, and the rate is now rising again.

in the general population. The suicide rates of the past ten years present some very interesting characteristics as shown on the accompanying graph. This graph points out that there have been two distinct periods within the last decade. First, there are the years 1911 to 1915, which preceded the intense industrial activity incident to the war. They were years of below-average economic prosperity, and we find only slight changes in the suicide death-rate during this period. Wage-earners show a slight decline; the general population of the Registration Area a slight increase. But in neither case are the changes of great significance. The second period, beginning with 1915, shows marked changes. These were the war years of great economic expansion and increased prosperity for the great body of the American people. Every year, both among the insured and the general population, recorded marked declines in the suicide rate. The straight lines in the graph show the sharp tendency toward reduction. In 1920, the rate among insured wage-earners was less than one-half what it had been in 1911. Yet, in the later months of 1920, a fundamental change seems to have set in which has continued throughout the first seven months of 1921. Month after month, the suicide rate is mounting over the corresponding figures for the months of 1920, and it is very likely that the rate for the whole year will be higher than for the preceding one. It is an interesting problem to know whether the unemployment situation of the last year is, in fact, responsible for the observed conditions as to suicide. Are suicide rates a very sensitive index of the prevailing economic well-being of the people? It would seem so."

LETTERS - AND - ART

LITERATURE DRAMA MUSIC FINE-ARTS EDUCATION CULTURE

CLEMENCEAU AND HIS POILUS ETERNALIZED IN STONE

MR. WILSON HAS NO STATUE erected to recognize his leadership of the nation in the war, tho he is to have a "Foundation" to perpetuate his ideals. Mr. Lloyd George has his; Clemenceau has his, and precedent even was created when the "Tiger" delivered the address at the unveiling of his replica in stone. Clemenceau could face himself, but not the photographers. He ordered them to go or he would quit the stand. When they demurred he ordered the Prefect "to throw them out by the neck if they wouldn't go otherwise." Along with Clemenceau are honored the soldiers of the Vendée, for it is at Sainte-Hermine, where the "Tiger," spent his youth, that this statue is now erected. His words cabled to American papers sound the old note:

"We know that the victory belongs to all the Allies. We should not be worthy of ourselves if we forgot it. It is not less apparent to-day that proof came for the need of alliance as soon as their arms fell from the hands of the enemy.

"I felt that on the first day, and prompt confirmation has not been lacking.

"The danger of falling back into old formations became at once apparent. Our war of the Entente would have been a derisive adventure if it had not forever slammed the door on such a worn-out policy.

"We have all need for each other on an equal footing. It is on the prosaic calculation of our interests in the full light of day that the future ought to be founded. We have all given too much of ourselves to the common cause not to keep our respect for it, and we feel profoundly the necessity for unity in times of difficulty.

"Does not the size of modern war forbid any one to think of militarism? Our conscience, our sentiments, our wishes are for peace, and we will never lose a chance of giving proof of that. Let there then be no hidden thoughts representing us as an eventual danger, and, above all, let none make the mistake of making a show which could be mistaken by Germany to be an advance of sympathy at compound interest.

"Germany sought domination by an extortionate race. As long as she has not abandoned this foolish dream, the alliance cannot weaken, except to the detriment of that one among us who gives way. Our watchword should be this: Neither to dominate nor to be dominated; peace of equity for all the world.

"At Versailles, we made Germany bow the knee. How, then, has she been allowed to forget it?"

His respects are paid to us also in "no measured terms" as the reporter reminds us:

"For the maintenance of peace, our allies felt the necessity of offering us their concurrence, without waiting for the French negotiator to ask for it. With this object, they made engagements which one day they will be reminded of. Thanks to the Treaty of Versailles, their acts at this moment are being decided by ours.

"I see that at this moment every one is magnificently busy about assuring the peace of the world in the Far East. We can wish only success for such a noble enterprise. But we are manifestly of the world, and the Pacific Ocean is a considerable way away, while our frontier is near to Germany. Why not, then, recognize that all just causes are rigorously bound together?

"The Washington Conference might find in the actual state of affairs a fine occasion to redress the faults of execution which are to-day apparent.

"More than ever the interests of peoples are intertwined. The appeal of France should be heard by all to assure a durable condition of peace in Europe, without which nothing can be established.

"America wishes universal peace as much as France and England. That was the meaning of her intervention on our side against Germany. What a strange epilog, then, if she had summoned the representatives of civilization only to tell them of her disinterestedness in the cause of humanity for which she had spilled so much blood. That could not be.

"No one, in truth, can refuse to consider the French question from the same point of view as the question of the Pacific. And, if any one should make the attempt, all peoples would not be long in disavowing him. For the circle of human solidarity never ceases to grow, and our contemporaries are beginning to learn to fear for themselves when they have given others cause for fear."

Illustrations from "L'Illustration," Paris

CITIZENS OF THE VENDÉE.

Clemenceau and his poilus in the trenches. The statue erected at Sainte-Hermine in honor of "the Tiger."

In The Associated Press dispatch some variants of the foregoing with some additional phrases are given of the speech whose keynote was "Remember":

"Let us remember and let us keep from substituting by vain words the acts which are expected of the country. Let us remember France's motto, 'Live in the Peace of Justice or Perish.'

"Victory was a victory by all the Allies. But as soon as the enemy was disarmed the trouble commenced in the Entente. At Versailles we bended Germany's knee. Why has she been permitted to forget it? We hold her signature to undertakings which count no longer. Yesterday we were the victors. Let no one place us in the situation where we ask whether we still are victors.

"I am not here to accuse any one. Evil came from the fact that chiefs with the powers of subordinates wielded control that had to be controlled.

"We showed supreme weakness—we lacked nothing, neither in right nor in power. It is not too late to say that reparations and securities are inseparable terms; that each Frenchman is

WHAT THE MOTORIST SEES BY A FRENCH WAYSIDE.

The sculptor, Sicard, tried to realize the "Tiger's" two phrases: "It is not I who am interesting, it is the poilus," and "I make war!"

worth one German, and that France renounces nothing of what is due her."

In *L'Illustration* (Paris) is this picturesque account of the statue:

"The excursionists who in recent weeks have been touring in the Vendée in the neighborhood of Sables-d'Olonne and of Roche-Sur-Yon, and who have followed the state road which goes from Chantonnay to Lucon, have no doubt met a surprize. For as they passed by Sainte-Hermine, a place of about eighteen hundred inhabitants in the Arrondissement of Fontenay-le-Comte, their eyes were suddenly confronted with a strange group of statuary whose white brilliance stands out against the sky and the verdure of the surrounding foliage. This group stands on a stretch of greensward between a little old house and a new building occupied by a hatter. The lower part of the group consists of some helmeted soldiers in a trench, their shoes heavy with mud. Dominating the group is a civilian, wearing a traveling cloak and a small soft hat. With tense face and grave eyes, he scans the horizon, while the rough faces of the fighting men are lifted towards him.

"This silhouette of a man with nervously clenched hands drooping mustache, and prominent cheek-bones, who would not recognize it? It is Georges Clemenceau. Mr. Lloyd George has his British monument in Wales, which has recently been unveiled. Mr. Clemenceau rightfully has his in the Vendée which honors itself in having given him birth. In truth, it was in the humble little community of Mouilleron-en-Pareds that Mr. Clemenceau was born in 1841. But his youth was passed at Sainte-Hermine, and Sainte-Hermine claims him for her own. What is more, when consulted by the monument committee, Mr. Clemenceau himself selected the place at which the monument should be erected.

"The commission to execute the statue was given to the sculptor Sicard, a personal friend of the former French Premier. He has been working at Sainte-Hermine for two years, where with his assistants he has quarried and carved the block of stone—the hard rock of Bouillenay in Burgundy, out of which he has brought forth these singularly expressive and vivid figures. The artist took his inspiration from a famous phrase of Mr. Clemenceau uttered in the Chamber of Deputies, which is: 'I make war!' And also from the other phrase that the former Premier often repeated: 'It is not I who am interesting, it is the poilus!' Mr. Sicard therefore has kept them together. What is more, how many there are who have thus seen Clemenceau standing erect on a trench, friendly and familiar among the men as a symbol of that hope which was to bring us victory."

A DIMINISHING POET

LONGFELLOW IS SO TAKEN FOR GRANTED by us that he is seldom mentioned outside of school. It might appear that he is becoming somewhat of a myth in England since a writer there only a week or so ago referred to him, not by name, but as "a rather obscure genius." And the occasion of it was to point to a refutation of one of his principal poems about "footprints," brought about by Charlie Chaplin, who had made his own indelible in cement at his California home. It is long since one has seen a reappraisal of Longfellow, but Mr. W. L. Courtney has contributed one to the London *Daily Telegraph*. We quote some parts of this as a reminder to some of our poetry editors of departed glories in the American Parnassus:

"We may smile at Longfellow's sentimentalisms, and we may remain unmoved by his frigid conceits; we may find it impossible to read 'The Spanish Student,' or 'Outremer,' or 'Hyperion,' or 'Kavanaugh,' and we may become as indignant as Poe was at the ever-insistent moral. Nevertheless, we have to admit that a great deal of Longfellow has been incorporated into our language and become a part of our literary stock-in-trade; and that when the poet is at his best he can give us unforgetable poems and lines of rare beauty. It is not necessary to think of his show-pieces, such as 'Evangeline' and 'Miles Standish' and 'Hiawatha.' Some of his minor poems are at once popular and deserve their popularity. If only they were not so terribly familiar, if we could come across them for the first time, we should be able to do them greater justice. Think, for instance, of 'The Wreck of the Hesperus,' 'The Bridge,' 'The Psalm of Life,' 'The Village Blacksmith,' 'Excelsior.' They are eminently the sincere, straightforward utterances of a good man, who had not a deep analytical mind, and, indeed, profest his disbelief in analytical poetry, who never desired to startle us by a paradox or annoy us by a crude sophism, but claimed to be a teacher and a simple-minded moralist, capable of wrapping up truisms in a garb of quite respectable poetry. It was not his business to walk along the heights; he is content to ramble in the valley. But he can bid us lift up our eyes to the hills whence, in his judgment, cometh help to the sons of man. And we are quite confident that he always says what he thinks, and says it with a clarity which is not always shared by his fellow-bards."

If Longfellow, like Whitman, had never gone abroad and

"come under a literary culture so different from that which he had first imbibed," something might have resulted which now only furnishes ground for speculation. Longfellow, who has had so great a public among the common people of England who take their poetry simply, might even have ingratiated himself with the 'superior classes who affect Whitman or leave us alone entirely. Mr. Courtney makes out a pretty good case for Longfellow even as it is:

"His earliest poems on Nature revealed a certain objectivity of treatment, as tho the poet were really trying to interpret for himself in his own language the impressions that the scenery made upon him. His later poems are—to use the ordinary jargon—not objective, but subjective, that is to say, they reflect the mood of the poet, and are bookish in their associations. The obvious reasons for this divergency of the later from the earlier method were the voyages he made to Europe in order to fit himself to be a professor. His purpose was to study modern languages, and it was a result of the first journey, and also of one which he undertook in similar fashion before assuming professorial duties at Harvard, that Longfellow steeped himself in the literatures of Europe, and lost all originality as a consequence. It is not for nothing that he has been hailed as one of the most successful translators who have ever lived. The work of translation is diametrically opposed to that of creation, and the hand is subdued to that in which it works. He translated Spanish, German, Italian, Scandinavian, Swedish, and other literatures, and based a good deal of his own subsequent work on what he had imbibed from abroad. Curious and significant also is the fact that from 1826 to 1837, that is, from the age of 19 to 30, he did not publish a single original poem. It required the impulse of a genuine and personal grief to reopen the fountain of poetry in his mind, and it was the death of his wife that made him teach in song what he had learned in sorrow. Indeed, in two respects Longfellow showed that he was not an artist of the very first rank—one, because he became so voluminous a translator, and apparently so loved his task that he devoted many of the later years of his life to Dante and the Divine Comedy. And the second and more subtle reason is that his eye was fixt not so much on the art-effect as on the moral effect, the didactic lesson, the ever-intrusive moral.

"Edgar Allan Poe criticized Longfellow with an asperity which was undeserved. He complained bitterly of the want of originality in Longfellow, the fatal tendency to plagiarize from others, and repeat what had already been said. There is nothing to be made out of this charge even if we accepted the fact that Longfellow imitated, very closely imitated, his originals. He confessed as much himself. Sometimes he explained the sources whence he derived his poems. Sometimes he left it to his public to find out how much of his inspiration was due to his own genius and how much to that of others. His first book of travel, 'Outre-mer,' was after the manner of Washington Irving; his second, 'Hyperion,' after the manner of Richter. 'Hiawatha' was closely modeled, so far as meter and treatment were concerned, on the great Finnish epic 'Kalevala.' His critics constantly alluded to this last fact, and his friends pointed out that there was no mystery about the matter, and that at least Longfellow ought to have the credit of adapting a foreign theme to an American romance. More fatal, perhaps, was the rush of German sentimentalism into America for which Longfellow was mainly responsible. Teutonic romanticism was one of the things earliest learnt, owing to European travel, and only towards the very end discarded. Its languors sicklied o'er the complexion of Longfellow's verse, lingered on in its maturer forms, and perhaps was only got rid of when the poet wrote the breezy, happy romance called 'The Courtship of Miles Standish.'

"The meter of this poem and also of its predecessor, 'Evangeline,' is decidedly unfortunate. It is written in hexameters, and do what we will, we can never make hexameters work as an English meter. Of course, there has been a good deal of controversy on the subject. Sir Philip Sidney is usually quoted as one of those who support the introduction of hexameters. So, too, Gabriel Harvey declared that if any epitaph was needed for him, it should be that he was 'the inventor of English hexameters.' Later experiments are to be found in Clough in his well-known 'Bothie.' The verses never run easily or smoothly, they always either gallop or stumble or drag themselves along, and the irritating dactyl in the last foot but one usually has a jarring effect on the nerves. The meter does not escape these defects even when handled by a Longfellow or a Southey, and there is little doubt that 'The Courtship of Miles Standish' would be even a better poem than it is if it had been written according to a different pattern."

WHAT CHILDREN LAUGH AT

PEOPLE TROUBLED WITH NERVES will perhaps say that children need no encouragement to laughter, but the matter is important enough to be analyzed and reported for the august British Association. One of the addresses at the recent session of this body, held in Edinburgh, was taken up with a consideration of the sense of humor in school children. Dr. C. W. Kimmins of London told the Psychology Section what he had found out, beginning with children of five, who evinced an extraordinary interest in Charlie Chaplin. The reason for it, he thinks, is because "there is not only continual movement and change of action, but also that Charlie is breaking all the conventions and doing the very things that children are forbidden to do." If parents have not been aware of this, the report from so high a source may curtail Charlie's future audiences. "Punch and Judy," however, has found no adequate competitor in interest for children. Dr. Kimmins, as reported in the London press, has been concerned to discover the nature of the material which at different ages causes amusement in children and provokes laughter. We read:

"As to the chief causes of laughter, experts are not in agreement. Bergson maintains that the comic is that side of a person which reveals his likeness to a thing and conveys the impression of pure mechanism. The corrective is laughter. Absent-mindedness he describes as one of the great watersheds of laughter, and says it is the part of laughter to reprove absent-mindedness. Freud in his 'Wit and the Unconscious' has elaborated the idea of pleasure being derived from the economy of psychic expenditure. Word pleasure and pleasure in nonsense, Freud says, are a relief from critical reasoning. Man is an untiring pleasure-seeker. Under the influence of alcohol a man becomes a child again, and is freed from logical inhibitions. Boris Sidis holds that laughter never comes from economy, but from superabundance of energy. Laughter, says another authority, binds us to the childhood of the race.

"There is no difference of opinion as to the great physiological value of laughter. In an analysis of the results he has obtained, Dr. Kimmins says that cases of puns perpetrated by children under seven years of age are very rare, while many of the reported stories are due to misunderstanding of the words used. As an illustration, he quotes the classic instance reported by Sir Joshua Fitch, who asked some small children to write the Lord's Prayer, and afterwards came across such mistakes as 'Harold be Thy name' and 'Lead us not into Thames Station.' The records of children of nine years of age show a very great change. Boys and girls at this period are particularly interested in funny stories and jokes; riddles and play upon words maintain their position at that age, but the popularity of the misfortunes of others as a source of merriment is ceasing to exist and soon disappears entirely. At ten years of age children are very keen on books of jokes and comic papers. The affairs of the classroom are found to afford suitable material for the gratification of the sense of humor, and the lecturer quotes a case in which the teacher wrote on the blackboard, 'Don't throw matches about; remember the Fire of London,' to which was added by a boy, 'Don't spit; remember the Flood.'"

The period between eleven and twelve years of age, we are told, "appears to mark quite clearly the parting of the ways, and a sense of humor seems to disappear entirely." Something rather alarming takes its place:

"The funny story is of a far more personal nature, the element of superiority runs riot, and children delight in extravagant stories of stupidity concerned with adults rather than themselves. Stories involving a smart but often rude retort appeal at this age, and to illustrate his point Dr. Kimmins mentions the teacher who told a stupid boy that when Lloyd George was his age he was top of his school, to which the boy replied that when Lloyd George was the teacher's age he was Prime Minister.

"In the period from fourteen to fifteen years of age it is more difficult to generalize. There appears to be, however, very clear evidence that the revival of humor at thirteen in the case of girls and fourteen in the case of boys is well maintained. In the selection of funny stories by the children a much larger percentage comes from the works of well-known writers; W. W. Jacobs and Ian Hay's stories are popular, and of individual stories 'Three Men in a Boat,' 'Daddy Longlegs,' 'Mrs. Wiggs of the Cabbage Patch,' 'The Young Visiters,' 'Tom Sawyer,' and 'Alice in Wonderland' are much quoted. The cultured home, says the lecturer, has a great influence on the choice and variety of stories, whereas the very poor child relies on the school and the comic papers for his selections.

"Children often laugh at stories which they do not understand because others laugh, and many instances occur of children repeating stories of which clearly they have not grasped the point. For instance, the story is told of a man who was boasting of his mountaineering experiences, and a friend said, 'I suppose you saw Ben Nevis?' 'No,' he said, 'I called on him, but he was not in.' A child told that as a funny story, but instead of Ben Nevis substituted the mountain of Snowdon, thus missing the whole point."

DAVID BISPHAM.

IN OUR WHOLE OPERATIC HISTORY it would be hard, perhaps impossible, to match the career of the late David Bispham. He was both American and international. He sang the rôles of the greatest European composers, but the purpose that was nearest his heart was to interpret music in the tongue of his native country. "The possessor of a fine barytone voice, he took pains to learn how to use it perfectly," says *The Musical Courier* (New York), "and this mastership once attained, he employed it only in presenting the best that there is in song and oratorio literature and in the operatic repertory." His fame, which was considerable abroad, was nationwide in his home country, and that from personal contact. *The Courier* continues in its estimate:

Copyrighted by Aime Dupont

THE AMERICAN BARYTONE.

"No singer of the last quarter century has been heard by so many Americans from Bangor to Los Angeles as our own American singer, David Bispham."

"His marked personality and sturdy artistic purpose colored all he did and made it outstanding. Perhaps what stands most to his credit is the fact that he devoted himself, heart, soul and voice, to proving that songs or opera can be presented in the English language with no loss of effect; and he did prove it—in his own case. The trouble is that there are so few artists who ever can (or, at least, ever do take the pains to attempt to) acquire the remarkable enunciation in the native tongue which was characteristic of Bispham. He was the friend of the young composer and the introducer of many songs in English which have become popular through his efforts. Every American musician owes him a debt of gratitude, for he was a pioneer in proving to the world at large that this country can produce artists who rank with the best in the world. His untimely death—he was only sixty-four and still very active, especially as a teacher—is mourned by thousands who knew the man both as friend and artist."

With our generous worship of the singer from foreign lands, here was one, as the New York *Evening Post* shows, who was not only worthy to stand beside the best of them, but was accorded recognition in such a place. Generous as nature has been in producing great singers among American women, Mr. Bispham had scarcely a peer among his countrymen. *The Post* says:

"No singer in the last quarter century has been heard by so many Americans from Bangor to Los Angeles as our own American singer, David Bispham—born of Quaker parents and graduate of a Quaker college. He had an excellent barytone voice of normal range; he had remarkable abilities as an actor; and his capacity for hard, unceasing work was the wonder of all who knew of his activities. His repertory included two-score operas, a hundred oratorios, and one is almost inclined to say myriads of songs. During the years he was at the Metropolitan Opera House he was indispensable for barytone parts. He sang all the operas of the 'Ring,' and his rendition of Wagnerian parts like *Kurvenal, Beckmesser, Telramund* and *Alberich* has been regarded as the best to which the Metropolitan audiences have been treated. His acting in these German operas was as admirable as is that of Scotti in the Italian and French operas today, and when he retired he was as much missed as Scotti would be in leaving the operatic stage.

"But it was not the Bispham of grand opera that American audiences of Topeka, Atlanta, Denver, and a thousand other cities and towns knew. They knew the Bispham of the oratorios and of Damrosch's 'Dannie Deever,' and other songs, both serious and humorous. His clear enunciation—he was an excellent dramatic reader—and his gift for mimicry and dramatic expression made him a recital singer whom it will take long to replace."

Mr. Bispham's public life began in 1891 when he sang in "La Basoche" at the Royal English Opera House in London. His career is thus sketched in the New York *World:*

"He made his initial appearance at the Metropolitan Opera House on November 27, 1896, singing *Telramund* in 'Lohengrin,' with Mme. Emma Eames as *Elsa*, Mme. Olitzka as *Ortrud*, Jean de Reszke as *Lohengrin* and Edouard de Reszke as the *King*. Mr. Bispham was heard frequently in all the Wagner dramas except 'Parsifal,' which was not produced while he remained in the company. He also sang in a wide Italian and French repertory.

"He was always a vigorous advocate of opera in English, but it was not till comparatively lately that he had opportunities to demonstrate the value of his theories. On October 26, 1916, the newly formed Society of American Singers produced two Mozart operettas, 'Bastien and Bastienne' and 'The Impresario,' at the Empire Theater. As the opera director Mr. Bispham, always a good actor, made one of the greatest comedy successes of his career. He reappeared in this and other rôles with English text in subsequent seasons of the same company.

"The distinguished barytone was not satisfied with musical triumphs alone. He appeared on several occasions in a short drama, entitled 'Beethoven,' giving a characteristic impersonation of the great composer. He also gained considerable approval as a public reader. . . . .

"Mr. Bispham was eminent also as an oratorio and recital singer. He was heard here in all the great oratorio works. In his earlier days his recitals were among the most important contributions to the musical seasons. He frequently sang most effectively such works as Schumann's 'Dichterliebe,' Schubert's 'Muellerlieder,' 'Die Schoene Magellone' of Brahms, and also his 'Four Serious Songs,' which Mr. Bispham introduced here. His delivery made known and popular Walter Damrosch's 'Danny Deever,' and he also sang the rôle of *Chillingworth* in Mr. Damrosch's first opera 'The Scarlet Letter' (1896).

"Mr. Bispham was successful not only in the most serious styles but also in humorous lyrics, to which his remarkably clear diction brought potent aids. He was at home in the principal operatic languages and his singing in English was regarded by students as a model. His Wagner impersonations, particularly *Telramund, Kurvenal, Beckmesser* and *Alberich*, will be remembered as among the best ever brought before Metropolitan audiences."

Comparing the fortunes of Caruso and Bispham, the Wilmington *Every Evening* says:,

"While one man was thrilling even the bored members of the Gold Crust with his gloriously beautiful art, the other was singing before hoi-polloi and making hoi-polloi dream dreams of loveliness. One was the darling of the Golden Horseshoe; the other was the idol of those souls whose drab lives were brightened by his voice.

"Both men were great in their fields. Both were beloved by their associates. Both were men—as well as artists. America can ill afford to lose two of its brightest stars."

WHY SO MANY PULPITS ARE EMPTY

MUCK-RAKING OF PULPIT AND PEW is the crying need of the times, writes Glenn Frank in *The Century Magazine*, of which he is the editor, after disentangling from various studies of the situation several reasons why 5,000 Protestant pulpits are vacant and why young men are less and less inclined to enter the Protestant ministry. Back of the statistics and interpretations of the situation recently published in the New York *Evening Post* and summarized in these pages on July 16, he believes, lies a story of profound human interest which some day a publicist interested in the problem of religious leadership in the United States will give us. In that book the statistical tables "will be translated into illuminating stories of communities of 'sheep without a shepherd,' stories of communities in which religious leadership has failed to challenge either the mind or the creative moral impulses of the people, tragic stories of great spirits broken by the economic slavery of the American ministry, stories of ignorant pulpits starving and insulting intelligent pews, and, contrariwise, of intelligent pulpits strangled by illiberal pews."

Among the reasons assigned for the lack of pulpit recruits are the decline in the economic status and social influence of the clergy, and the increased attractiveness of other professions. What has not been sufficiently emphasized, in connection with the last-named reason, believes Mr. Frank, is that much preaching has gone outside the churches, "slipt out of surplice and pulpit," and found expression in many new and secular avenues. "Novelists, dramatists, college professors, university presidents, judges, labor leaders, secretaries of state, governors, journalists, and other public men have in our day 'preached' with all the passionate emphasis of Puritan parsons on the moral ideals of the race." In this category of unwitting parsons Mr. Frank includes the late Theodore Roosevelt, William Jennings Bryan, Winston Churchill, because of his "The Inside of the Cup"; Charles Rann Kennedy, the playwright; Secretary Charles E. Hughes, who, when he was Governor of New York, "preached from the rostrums of county fairs and political mass meetings the same basic moralities his father preached for forty years from the pulpit," and Ex-President Woodrow Wilson, whose appeals to young men when he was president of Princeton "were as high appeals as any made by his clerical predecessors." Another reason given for the vacant pastorates is the lack of freedom of speech in the modern pulpit. Here—

"The danger lies in those pew-holders who insist upon the preacher's sticking exclusively to the 'old gospel,' by which they really mean sticking to a safely irrelevant doctrinal sermonizing which will not disturb their Sunday morning devotions in the way impertinent discussions of 'Christianizing the social order' do. The danger lies in those pew-holders who want the world of devotion and the world of dividends kept safely distinct in air-tight compartments. It is manifestly true that no young man of intellectual insight and sincerity can look forward with any degree of satisfaction to a limitation of his public utterances to pious exhortations to abstract moralities. He knows that under such limitations he can never be more than a seller of rhetoric. And whether it be noble or ignoble, religious or irreligious, the able young man of to-day is not interested in the exclusive task of 'labeling men and women for transportation to a realm unknown' and sedulously avoiding straightforward consideration of that reconstruction of human society which Jesus of Nazareth had in mind when he talked of the kingdom of God coming on earth."

Changes in religious emphasis, too, we are told, have had their effect. There would not be this critical situation "if the great scholars who have done so much to rescue Christianity from the fogs of myth and mysticism had matched the itinerant evangelist's ardent preachments with an equally effective presentation of their findings." And many men "would not feel, as they now do, that they would have to scrap their scientific training if they entered the ministry." Another thing to be considered is the "lack of a program" which challenges men's faith and courage. They will be interested in the ministry if it is stated in terms of concrete contemporary affairs as well as in terms of abstract principles. Then there is the feeling that ministers are made a class apart, shunted into "narrow channels of merely theological interests"; and the old cry against the materialism of the age, tho the writer believes "there has never been a time when as many young men of intellectual power and a sense of social responsibility were devoting themselves to poorly paid work because some program of achievement challenges their interest and their courage." The failure of the Interchurch World Movement is believed by certain leaders to have "shattered the faith of many young men in the power of the Church to effect genuine readjustments in human society." The decline of religious life in the home is also cited as a cause of vacant pulpits, tho the writer affirms that "in fundamental moral atmosphere and in wholesomeness of outlook upon life I believe that modern American family life is preferable to the stern ritualism of earlier days." The one bright ray, to many, "is that the majority of the more liberal seminaries and those having university connections are better attended than ever before, while many of the conservative seminaries are searching desperately for students to fill their halls."

The Presbyterian excludes some of Mr. Frank's conclusions, but agrees that the lack of freedom of speech in the pulpit, changes in religious emphasis, the failure of the Interchurch World Movement, and the decline of religion in the home have had an effect in depleting the ranks of recruits for the ministry. These four reasons, it says, have one root, and really constitute one and the same cause:

"The rationalistic seminaries have destroyed the faith of their students in Christ and the Bible, and they have left them without a divine message, and turned them over to every wind of the doctrines of men. They have wrong thoughts of God, and some of them have become atheists. When they enter the Evangelical pulpits, they find themselves in conflict with the people in faith, and they call this conflict the lack of freedom in the pulpit, when indeed it is the lack of faith in the preacher and his intruding upon the people teaching which they have intelligently repudiated. A rationalistic congregation would not allow such intrusion a second time. The change of emphasis in religion is the same thing: it simply means a change from the authority of the Bible to that of philosophy and religious consciousness. The Interchurch Movement was due to the same intrusive, presumptive, and reckless spirit, without authority and without principle. It diverted attention from the power of the gospel to the power of organization. The decline of religion from the home marks the appalling ignorance of the Bible and the carelessness of parents and their prayerless indifference to the ministry. These indeed are the things which have depleted the evangelical ministry and disturbed and injured the evangelical church. They have destroyed religion in the home and withered the coming crop of young preachers. They have robbed the present preachers of their message and sent them for occupation into the field of worldliness. The real evangelical ministry can be obtained only from the God of the church, who hurls them forth in answer to the prayer of his people. But when through teaching the people fail to believe in the Bible and its promise upon prayer and in the God of prayer, they will not pray for a ministry or anything else."

THE CZECH BREAK FROM ROME

CZECHO-SLOVAKIA'S NEW CHURCH, which has declared its independence of Rome and become aligned with the Eastern Orthodox Church, is making considerable progress in numbers and influence, according to a Protestant observer who writes from Serbia, and, as viewed by him, the

TWO LEADERS OF THE CZECH CHURCH.
Zahradnik-Brodsky, an ex-Roman Catholic priest, and his wife.

"reformation" may result in further startling changes in Central Europe. Of the 7,000,000 Czechs in Bohemia, Silesia and Moravia, 800,000 are said to have gone into the new church, and the example of their break from the old order has been suggested for imitation in Jugo-Slavia and Poland. Full of so many potentialities, this scheme of religious reorganization has attracted much attention in America, and is being watched with deep interest by leaders of all denominations. But, as told in these pages last December, the schism is largely discounted by Catholic observers here, and they point to the Catholic Congress held in Prague last summer, when messages of loyalty were sent to the Pope, as "outstanding testimony to the recovery of Catholic forces" in the new republic. However, "the spirit of John Huss continues to stir Bohemia," writes the Rev. Henry S. Huntington in *The Christian Work* (Undenominational), and the "liberalizing movement" is steadily gaining ground. The latest efforts to establish an independent church had their origin in a union of Czech Catholic clergy which was abolished in 1907 by a combination of Church and State, and which was revived in the "great wind of liberty" which passed over Central Europe after the armistice. Three men stand out as its leaders, says this writer—Zahradnik-Brodsky on the political side, Farsky and Dlouhy-Pokorny on the spiritual. Zahradnik-Brodsky, tho a Roman Catholic priest, believed that celibacy was wrong, and married in 1908. His wife, we read, "is a woman of character and ability," who by her articles explaining and stimulating the new church movement "has rendered great service to the cause." Of more recent history we are told that—

"Soon after the armistice Zahradnik sent out a letter to the 6,000 Czech Roman Catholic clergy of Bohemia, Silesia and Moravia, including the bishops, asking their opinions in regard to a progressive program which he outlined. That program demanded the democratization of the Church by the election of the bishops and priests; the abolition of patronage and of fees for the performance of ecclesiastical functions, such as baptisms, marriages, funerals, and so on; the removal of the requirement of celibacy; the establishment of a patriarchate for the Church in Czecho-Slovakia, so making it semi-independent; and the use of the vernacular, here the Czech language, in the services.

"Half of the priests answered the inquiry. Ninety per cent. of the 3,000 who replied endorsed the program. Half the rest approved part of it. Only five per cent. of those who answered had no sympathy with the movement. It was not only the young men who favored it. Among those who endorsed it was one monk-priest ninety years of age."

Delegates representing more than a thousand priests, we are told, conducted negotiations with the Vatican, and their demands were refused. Nothing daunted, 250 of the progressive clergy met on January 8, 1920—"a day to be remembered for centuries in Central Europe"—and organized the National Czech Church on the Hussite basis, that it should use the vernacular in the services, be democratic, with the laymen sharing in the conduct of the church business, and accept freedom of conscience. Regarding changes already effected, we are told that:

"The new Church has abolished the confessional, holding the common confession of the people in the service to be sufficient. It does not believe in purgatory; it holds commemorative services for the dead, but ascribes to them no magic merit. It takes no fees for its services. It abolishes the requirement of celibacy. Unlike the Roman Church, it gives the wine as well as the bread to the people at the communion or mass. Its service is like that of the Roman Church except that it is in Czech. As the people

Illustrations by courtesy of "The Christian Work," New York.

THOUSANDS TURNING TO THE NEW FAITH.
Bishop Dosity announcing the agreement with the Greek Church in a Moravian village.

are ready the Church will gradually change the forms to fit the new ideas.

"Theologically the Church takes the position of the Orthodox Church of the East. That is, it accepts the decisions of the seven Ecumenical Councils and the Symbolum Oecumenicum of Constantinople. The Symbolum Oecumenicum of Constantinople is the famous confession on which the Eastern and Western churches split. It omits the 'filioque,' that is, the assertion that the Holy Spirit proceeds from the Son as well as the Father."

Altho the government pays toward the support of all the old churches, both Roman Catholic and Protestant, it has not yet extended financial recognition to the new Church, because, we are told, it does not wish to offend the Vatican.

The movement into the new Czech Church is one of three present religious movements in Czecho-Slovakia, we are informed in a footnote to Mr. Huntington's article. Another is an exodus from the Roman Catholic to the Protestant Church. About 60,000 people are said to have turned from Roman Catholicism to the Reformed faith since Czecho-Slovakia became free. But—

"The third great movement is one out of the Church altogether. A million people have declared themselves without creed since 1918. Before that time small scattered groups of 'free thinkers' existed in Czech cities, but the total number of persons connected with them would have numbered at most only a very few thousands. Many of these churchless people are by no means irreligious. They have been so antagonized by their experiences in the Church that they temporarily react from it completely. Some of the groups have started Sunday schools for the ethical instruction of their children. They represent a great and hopeful mission field for the finest and freest type of Christianity."

Catholic observers hold, however, that the schism is not numerically great or of serious importance, and Leslie J. Walker, S. J., writes in the London *Tablet* (Catholic) that "there is plenty of life in the Church in Czecho-Slovakia," and that "its clergy for the most part are faithful and zealous." The real hope for Christianity here, he asserts, "lies with the old Church, which, in spite of a hostile government, a small schism, many apostasies, much indifference, a vigorous Serbian propaganda, and a still more influential propaganda emanating from wealthy Protestants in America, has in the space of two years become better organized and far more active than she was under the Austrian régime for three centuries."

CHRISTIANITY'S ADVANCE IN JAPAN—Before peers and plowmen are represented in the Christian Church in Japan, much work and patience will be required, for, as we are told by an observer on the ground, "the Christian religion in Japan is at present being preached to and believed in by only a part of the middle-class society." Despite this, there is said to be considerable justification for a feeling of satisfaction over the growth of Christianity in Nippon, writes George Drach in *The Lutheran*, tho attention is called to the fact that only one Japanese in 250 is a member of a Christian church. Mr. Drach, who acknowledges an article by D. R. McKenzie in the 1921 issue of *The Christian Movement in Japan* as the source of his information, tells us further that, as in Western communities, the tendency from the time the first church was established in Japan in 1872 has been in the direction of several independent churches. There have been, however, several group unions. Of these—

"Five churches of the Presbyterian group are united in the Church of Christ in Japan (33,000 members), four Anglican churches in the Japanese Anglican Church (20,000), three Methodist churches in the Japan Methodist Church (22,000), and the work of the American Board has resulted in one Congregational Church (25,000). The remaining 35,000 Christians belong to twenty other organizations. There are no visible signs of any further union."

These figures do not represent the full strength of Christianity in Japan, we are told, as there are many outside the church whose attitude is distinctly favorable. They have been influenced by the Sunday schools, Bible classes, Y. M. C. A., Y. W. C. A., Christian schools and institutional work. A favorable indication is that "the anti-Christian attitude of former days on the part of leading public men has given way to a pro-Christian attitude." Now the call is for men and women to go into the great unevangelized country districts. For this "tactful, consecrated men and women are wanted, who are willing to leave the rôle of leadership with the Japanese, where it belongs, and to supplement the work of the churches by doing country pioneer work."

ARMENIA A VAST ORPHAN ASYLUM

WAR HAS NOT CEASED for Armenia, says Charles V. Vickrey, Secretary of the Near East Relief Association, who reports that conditions in that country are actually worse now than they were at the signing of the armistice. Mr. Vickrey, who recently returned from a tour of the Levant, found famine conditions unparalleled even in the tragic history of the Near East. Such food as the Armenians had been able to obtain had been taken from them by the Turks, and at Erivan, the capital of Armenia, there was "nothing in the way of new and desirable merchandise, but only hopeless women and children wandering about, trying to exchange a second-hand garment or other personal property for food with which to satisfy hunger." This was in August, and "one's imagination recoils before the picture of what conditions will be in February and March, when the snow will lie deep on these high plateaus." The chief hope for these people, we are told, lies in the Near East Relief, which is working valiantly to assist them. But it is a black picture which Mr. Vickrey paints. According to his report as published in the press, the causes of the famine date back to and include the wholesale destruction of 1915, when hundreds of thousands of Turkish Armenians sought and found refuge in the Russian Caucasus. "Every year since that time the country has been more or less overrun and pillaged by contending or unfriendly military forces." Drought made conditions worse, and when the Turkish forces withdrew from Alexandropol in late April they took with them all transportable food supplies and other property that might be useful to them in fighting the Greeks on the western front. However,

"The Near East Relief now has more than fifty American experienced relief workers in this area, who, in the vicinity of Alexandropol alone are caring for 20,000 orphan children, constituting probably the greatest assemblage of orphan children that the world has ever known. The president of the local government of the Alexandropol district says that there are 20,000 more children in his district that will suffer and succumb during the coming winter if they are not added to this orphanage population. The total number of orphans in the Near East Relief territory exceeds 100,000.

"As we were coming out of Armenia to Batum, we passed on a railway, three trainloads of American relief supplies, every car bearing the 'Near East Relief' label and the entire train consigned direct from the docks at Batum to the warehouses in Alexandropol. Every pound of these food supplies remains under a thorough check and the immediate personal supervision of experienced American relief workers from the time it leaves the ship in Batum until it reaches the ultimate destination. Two ships were unloading in Batum while we were there, but they carried only a little more than 5,000 tons of the 100,000 tons that are needed to save the situation in this region alone, exclusive of the larger requirements farther north along the Volga."

It would be futile to attempt to minimize the gravity of this situation, says the *Christian Science Monitor* (Boston). But, serious as conditions are, "it is welcome to find that the Near East Relief is not allowing itself, in any sense, to be dismayed by the task which is laid upon it." Such frank statements are useful, "but they can not, for one moment, be accepted as arguments for pessimism. Their only effect must be a renewed effort and a renewed determination to supply the help needed."

On Hallowe'en when we are seen
We'll make a big sensation
And far and wide on every side
Spread Campbell's reputation!

The hit of the evening!

There, at the very beginning of the feast, it greets you with the sunny smiles of summer. It puts a sparkle in your appetite. Rich, spicy, delicious, served steaming hot, every spoonful invites to pleasure. Start the dinner with Campbell's Tomato Soup and every dish seems to gain a keener flavor!

Campbell's Tomato Soup

is one of the most popular of the famous soups which have made the name of Campbell's a household word. Pure tomato juices, velvety creamery butter, pure granulated sugar, dainty herbs and spices all go to make Campbell's Tomato Soup a leading favorite of the American dining table.

21 kinds **12c a can**

Campbell's SOUPS

LOOK FOR THE RED AND WHITE LABEL

CURRENT - POETRY

Unsolicited contributions to this department cannot be returned.

A LONG poem in the Mary Wilkins tradition with a few more modern implications appears in *The North American Review*. It reveals a cloistered New England interior with two aging spinsters ensconced amid their fading family splendors. Since the whole poem is too long to quote we must summarize parts, and with this explanation we get to the first scene of

THE DOLL

By Amy Lowell

For many years I've always ended up
With the two Misses Perkins. They were a whiff
Of eighteen-forty, and I rather liked
To talk to them and then come back and play
Debussy, and thank God I had read Freud;
The contrast was as genial as curry.
I only wish that I could make you see them.
Their garden path with spice-bushes and lilacs,
The scraper by the door, the polished knocker,
And then the hall with the model of a clipper
Upon a table in a square glass case.
She is a replica of the *Flying Dolphin*
And Captain Perkins made her on a voyage
Of eighteen months to China and Ceylon.
Miss Julia just remembers when he brought
The model home and put it where it stands.
I always laid my gloves upon the table
Just by the clipper's stern, and stood my sunshade
Against the corner, and tiptoed up the stairs.
Miss Perkins was an invalid, for years
She had not left her bed, so I was summoned
Up slippery stairs and over cool, long matting
Into her room, and there in a great four-poster
The little lady would greet me with effusion.
"Clara, Dear, how good of you to come!
Julia and I were wondering if you would.
You'll have a cake and a small glass of sherry.
Hannah will bring them in directly. Now,
How is the music getting on? To think
You play at concerts! Julia and I read
About your triumphs in the newspapers."
And all the time, behind the house, the sea
Was moving—moving—with a long slow sound . . .

The thing that always obsessed the visitor was a large wax doll—

Upright in a winged armchair by the bed.
She sat and gazed with an uneanny ardor
Straight at the andiron, her hands palm upward.

Before another summer brought the next visit the invalid "passed away" and the call of sympathy was finally paid, the visitor being entertained in the vacant room of the departed—

She begged me
To go upstairs. "I cannot bear to be
In any room but Jane's," she told me.
"I've sat there so much with her, quite ten years
It was she did not leave it." So we mounted
The broad old stairs, and softly trod the matting
Walking gently as in a house of mourning.
I was resentful, it was four full months
Since I had got that lonely little letter.
Was this a mausoleum? Was Miss Julia
To find her only company with ghosts?
The gaudy paper of the narrow hallway,
Flashing its minarets to a sapphire Heaven
Seemed to be mocking us with Eastern splendor,
With Eastern customs and an Eastern languor.
The conch shells roared a siren song of oceans,
Flanking the newel posts, as we passed by them.
Miss Jane's room was a lovely blaze of sunlight,
The empty bed was orderly and sane,
The Bay of Naples gladdened without hurting.
I shook myself free of the swarming stillness
And saw with satisfaction that the chair,
The doll chair, had been moved, it stood beside
The window with its back toward the room.
Why did I walk up to it? I don't know.
Some feeling that the usualness of streets
Comes kindly over a long spent emotion
Perhaps. At any rate, I did so, saying
How bright and gay the portulacas were,
Or something of the sort. And then I started
To sit down in the chair and saw the doll
With palms stretched out and little slippered feet
Pointing before her. There she sat, her eyes
Fixt glassily upon the window-pane.
I may have jumped, at any rate Miss Julia
Flushing a painful pink said steadily:
"It was so dull for her after Jane died,
I moved her here where she could see the street.
It's very comforting to watch the passing.
I think. I always find it so." That's all.
I don't know how the visit went, nor what
I said, nor where I sat. I only know
I took the train that evening back to town
And stayed up half the night playing Stravinski.
I dreamt wax doll for three weeks afterwards,
And I shall go to London this vacation.

Something bears the hint that the concrete picture presented in the foregoing is philosophized in this from the London *Mercury*. We hear so much to-day about complexes and inhibitions that all fairy-tales seem likely to go up in these phenix flames:

OLD WIVES' TALES

By Robert Graves

Were the tales they told absurd,
  Random tags for a child's ear?
Soon I mocked at all I heard,
  Though with cause indeed for fear.

Of the mermaids' doleful game
  In deep water I heard tell,
Of lofty dragons blowing flame,
  Of the horned fiend of Hell.

Now I have met the mermaid kin
  And find them bound by natural laws,
They have neither tail nor fin,
  But are the deadlier for that cause.

Dragons have no darting tongues,
  Teeth saw-edged nor rattling scales,
No flame issues from their lungs,
  Poison has not slimed their tails.

But they are creatures of dark air,
  Unsubstantial tossing forms,
Thunderclaps of man's despair
  In mid whirl of mental storms.

And there's a true and only fiend
  Worse than prophets prophesy,
Whose full powers to hurt are screened
  Lest the race of man should die.

Ever in vain may courage plot
  The dragon's death with shield and sword,
Or love abjure the mermaid grot,
  Or faith be fixt in one blessed word,

Mermaids will not be denied
  Of our last enduring shame,
The dragon flaunts his unpierced hide,
  The fiend makes laughter with God's name?

Poets may all be soon reduced to the state this one of the *Westminster Gazette* (London) complains of if relief doesn't come from some source:

THE POET TO HIS MUSE

By E. Lyndon Fairweather

Muse, why have you left me to govern my fancies alone?
Disorderly phantoms, they surge round the gate of my speech
And break down the barriers of reason and sense. I have flown
To my stronghold of silence: but there they are forcing a breach—
My stronghold is crumbling, my thoughts are too many and strong.
Scenes, faces, scents, sounds—they are whirling and plunging and churning;
The blue of a withered flower, a child's faint cry,
The smell of the earth, the creak of a cart-wheel turning,
Thin wisps of distant music that falter and die—
That falter and die ere I weave them and make them a song.
Muse, why have you left me thus? Come with your old domination
And marshal these rebels—the rainbow that jostles the moon,
The shouting that drowns a poor whisper, the fierce animation
That murders my stillness, December entangled with June.

Your voice will turn chaos to order, confusion to peace;
Moon—whisper—June—stillness shall mingle, and flame, and live:
They shall leap from my heart as one, and the strife will cease,
My soul will find rest in the joy that my song shall give.

Harper's has a poem which satisfies itself with a simpler psychosis.

THE TURN IN THE ROAD

By E. Dorset

My wife and I had quarreled; 'twas my books,
  My distant walks, my solitary chess,
  And all that nourished my "damned laziness."
I did not speak, of course; but then, black looks
Hurt more than blows. If men, one day, were cooks
  And drudges, like all women, they'd confess
  What brutes they'd been, and ease the loneliness
Of home, nor keep their wives on tenterbooks,
Wondering what they'd do next. *I* sat on burrs.
  My liberty then given—with the house
All paid for, and the half my income hers,
  I took my bag, as meek as any mouse.
At the road's turn, my tragedy grew laughter
To hear her cry, and mark her hurrying after.

Harper's also has a consideration of the disturbing theme in lighter vein, something that helps us to decide that the matter of the subconscious is not so fearfully important after all:

COMPLEX

By Ben Ray Redman

I have a Freudian complex,
A funny little complex,
That's lurking in the hinterland
  Of my subconscious brain;
It's frightfully perplexing,
And really rather vexing;
I half suspect, to tell the truth,
  It's driving me insane.

It's not an inhibition,
Nor yet a prohibition,
But be assured it's troublesome
  As either one could be.
Indeed it's so annoying
I know it is destroying
The very small intelligence
  The gods vouchsafed to me.

Why I'm so much annoyed
Is, before I studied Freud,
I never knew a thing about
  These complexes at all;
But since they are in season,
I'll have mine or know the reason,
Though the up-keep on a complex
  Is a figure to appal.

The Safe Antiseptic
A delightfully effective mouth wash and gargle; efficient in dozens of other ways as a household antiseptic.
LISTERINE
LAMBERT PHARMACAL COMPANY

Don't have sore throat again this winter

As you know, many illnesses start with sore throat. The mouth is an open door to disease germs.

So, particularly at this time of the year, it is a wise precaution to use, systematically, some safe and effective mouth wash.

Listerine, recognized for over forty years as the standard household antiseptic, will help you and the members of your family ward off throat troubles that so often anticipate more serious ills.

Listerine as a mouth wash and gargle is a pleasant, effective precaution. Thousands of families have made it a part of their morning and evening toilets—as regularly as using the tooth brush.

If you are not familiar with this delightful use of Listerine as a daily mouth wash, let us send you a generous sample—which you may try. Note how sweet, fresh and clean it leaves your mouth and teeth.

LAMBERT PHARMACAL COMPANY, SAINT LOUIS, U. S. A.

Lambert Pharmacal Co., 2104 Locust St., St. Louis, Mo.
Please send me a sample of Listerine as you suggest in this advertisement

Name .... *Address* ....
City .... *State* ....

Photo from the Wide World Photos, Copyrighted by the New York Times Company.

A DEFIANT MONARCH OF MOUNTAINS.

Mount Everest, shown as photographed from a point about seven miles distant, has thus far baffled the British expedition which is trying to climb it. Only one previous explorer has reached within forty miles of the base of the giant peak. The view shown is a part of the northern front, where the British explorers discovered a series of precipices from one thousand to two thousand feet high, and practically impossible of ascent.

MOUNT EVEREST'S DEFIANCE

ONLY ONE POSSIBLE ROUTE remains to be explored by the British expedition which has spent the summer fighting its way toward Mount Everest, literally "the top of the world." Heights of more than 20,000 feet have beer reached in exploring the surrounding country, and the expedition has penetrated nearer the base of the huge peak than any other white men have ever reached, but in spite of all the resources of seasoned and well-equipped climbers, the top of the mountain, 29,002 feet above sea level, seems likely to remain safe from invasion, at least until next year. The expedition reports that sheer precipices, from the top of which avalanches bombard the lower slopes, cut off most of the approaches, and the London *Times* warns that "in all probability the best that can be hoped for is that before the end of the present season a possible route for the ascent may have been mapped out. We must not expect that the final attempt will be made before next year." Sir Martin Conway, M. P., the British mountaineer who led the first expedition to the Himalayas, does not believe, says the Manchester *Guardian*, that the explorers will be able to reach the summit this year, and is dubious even of its final success. The London *Graphic* gives this general account of the expedition:

The point from which the Mount Everest reconnoitering expedition started was Darjeeling, a well-known health resort on the borders of Sikkim, Nepal and Bengal. The town is the nearest hill station to Calcutta, and it contains a large summer population of Europeans, mostly women and children, who cannot stand the heat of the plains of Bengal during the period from March to October.

The expedition, in charge of Colonel Howard Bury, and consisting of Mr. Harold Raeburn, Mr. Bullock, Mr. Woolaston, Mr. Mallory and Dr. Kellas, of the Alpine Club, Dr. Heron, of the Geological Survey of India, and Majors Morshead and Wheeler, of the Survey of India, left Darjeeling on May 18. Unfortunately, it had not gone far when Dr. Kellas, who had been mountaineering in Sikkim for two months before the start, fell ill, and suddenly died of heart failure while crossing a pass. Reports from the expedition state that Dr. Kellas was buried on a mountain slope within sight of Mount Everest, which he had hoped to climb.

The first part of the journey was performed by mule transport, about forty of these animals, each carrying something like 160 pounds of stores, being required for the purpose. The great trade route running north and east to Lhassa, the Tibetan capital, was followed.

While in the Chumbi Valley the ground, so to speak, is more or less familiar, beyond the Tibetan village of Kampa Dzong, which the expedition left behind early in June, very little is known of the country. Tho very circuitous, this route offers the least trouble with transport. There are more direct routes between Darjeeling and Kinchinjunga and towards Mount Everest, but for a party necessarily loaded with a large transport train they are impossible. Unfortunately, as we now know, the mules supplied by the government collapsed, owing to the difficulties of the roads, and the expedition would have been in a very serious predicament but for the fact that local mules and ponies were available.

The route traverses five distinct territories — Bengal, Bhutan, Tibet, Sikkim and Nepal, and this fact alone necessitated very careful preparatory work before the details of the expedition could be considered. Thanks, however, to the cordial relations between these states and the British Raj every facility for the expedition was willingly offered."

The latest dispatch from the leader of the expedition, Colonel Howard Bury, which appeared in the Philadelphia *Public Ledger*, records the work of the expedition in investigating and mapping the eastern valley approaches to Everest. Exploration in this quarter was undertaken after approach from the north, northeast and west had been found practically impossible. From Kharta, writes Colonel Bury, they went to the Khartasangpo Valley, about seven miles distant. They followed a large glacier

river, bordered by "many prosperous looking villages and monasteries." After turning into "a side valley a few miles further up," he goes on—

We camped overnight at 16,000 feet among the highest rhododendrons we have seen. Opposite was a glacier coming down from a rocky peak.

The following morning after a steep ascent and passing a turquoise blue lake we reached the summit of Langmala, 18,000 feet high. All the Tibetan coolies complained of headaches. The climb was most steep and they were not in the best training. The view from the pass was most extensive, with a fine prospect eastward far beyond and Arun valley to the distant snow ranges. Our immediate prospect to the west was, however, the most interesting and also the most tantalizing, as clouds came down low, covering up everything above 22,000 feet. Thus we were prevented from recognizing the highest mountains.

Below the clouds, however, was a wonderful panorama. Three great glaciers, each many miles long, swept down majestically in grand curves, almost meeting 4,000 feet below our feet. One glacier came from Mount Everest itself; another from Makalu, 27,800 feet high, and the third from high peaks to the northwest of Mount Everest.

After passing another charming turquoise lake called Shurimtho, we descended over pleasant, grassy uplands, covered with gentians and mauve asters, for about 3,000 feet. Finding a shepherd camped on a sheltered terrace some 1,000 feet above the valley, we decided to pitch our tents close to him, as fuel and water were plentiful and we should also get fresh milk and butter from him. Toward evening the mists lifted, giving wonderful and entrancing glimpses of immense snowy peaks, towering to incredible heights.

That night there was a slight frost and the morning broke absolutely cloudless. Never shall we forget the beauty of that sunrise on the marvelous cliffs of Makalu which, not four miles away, towered some 11,000 feet above us, or the first rosy hue on the more distant and retiring summits of Mount Everest. It was an indescribably beautiful scene and I doubt if anywhere in the world is there another valley to equal this in its overpowering grandeur.

This valley, subject to wet monsoon mists, is green with juniper, willows and mountain ash. Right down to the green vegetation came the ice and snow. Of the two mountains, Makalu is, from the valley, by far the more beautiful and striking, as Mount Everest stood back too far and did not show its great height. Gigantic cliffs, lightly powdered with snow, came straight down for 11,000 feet into the valley. On either side were perpendicular cliffs of black rock, so steep that snow and ice were unable to lodge on them. Below the cliffs started the Kangdoshang glacier which swept across the valley until it struck the other side and forced a glacial stream coming from the Kangshung glacier of Mount Everest to enter a great ice cavern in order to pass under it. Some ten or twelve miles higher up, Mount Everest filled the head of the valley in the shape of a great semicircle, with a precipitous southeastern ridge, more than 27,000 feet high, sweeping out toward Makalu. No Tibetans knew Makalu by that name, their name being Chomoloendo.

From our camp we descended into a valley crossing the Radker stream, coming down from the Radker glacier. We then ascended a green valley leading toward our objective, which was gleaming high and white in front of us. The Kangdoshung glacier formed a decided obstacle to our progress, and it was a steep climb to get above it. But after this we came to grassy pastures, extending some 80 miles up the valley, virtually to the foot of Mount Everest.

Here, at an elevation of 16,400 feet, they found shepherds with herds of yak. Here also, was "a delightful, sunny place in which to camp," only a mile from the peak of Makalu, almost as high as Everest, "with the towering cliffs and snows of Mount Everest filling the valley." In the morning, as his story runs—

I started early with a couple of coolies, to go up a spur some miles further up the valley and immediately opposite Mount Everest. The weather at first was unfavorable and the valley was filled with clouds, but getting about 19,500 feet up, we suddenly emerged into blue sky, with a most glorious panorama in front of us.

More than 90 miles away, to the east, could be seen the tops of Kinchingunga and Jannu appearing above a sea of clouds, while Mount Everest and other lofty ridges stood up straight in front of us across the valley, with their formidable black cliffs descending sheer for 2,000 feet on the glaciers, above which were hanging glaciers. All day one could hear the roar of great pieces of ice breaking off from them and crashing into the Kangshung glacier below.

From this side and from this amphitheater there seemed to be no way of directly attacking the great mountain. The lofty southeast ridge descended most precipitously to a high pass, beyond which was a very prominent conical peak, followed by another pass, then snow slopes finally merging into Makalu. To the northeast of Mount Everest were confused masses of snow peaks.

After a map in the London "Daily Telegraph."

ADVANCING ON "THE TOP OF WORLD."

The British Mount Everest expedition followed the indicated route in its preliminary survey of the country around the world's highest peak. Since then, further exploration has shown that practically impregnable precipices shut off approaches from the north, west, south, northeast, and east. The latest news from the expedition, reprinted herewith, tells of the exploration of the eastward side, beginning at Kharta, shown to the northeast of the summit. Only one possible approach remains, that from the southeast, which is now being explored.

Between this approach to Mount Everest and the Rognbuk valley there appeared to be another valley. Toward this our Alpine climbers were now turning their attention, trying to discover into which valley the glaciers came down. Therefore, after pronouncing that there were no possible means of getting up Mount Everest from the east, they went back direct to the Khartatsangpo valley, and now are following that river to its source.

We went back another way, to the east of Makalu, and were well rewarded by some magnificent views of its two great peaks. We went down the first valley to the Shinchuthoungkar, which has forests of silver fir and juniper, with long, gray lichens hanging down from every bough, wild roses and most luxuriant vegetation. From the east of Makalu, from between its twin peaks, a big glacier descends to 12,000 feet. It was very curious to see birch and fir trees growing on either side of the ice. Below this glacier the valley bottom was quite flat, with grassy meadows and patches of forest most unlike the ordinary narrow Himalayan valley.

We now turned up a side valley to the east to cross to Shaola and camped at 15,000 feet, opposite the twin peaks of Makalu. Here were masses of deep red meconoposis and several varieties of primulas new to me. That evening we had superb views of Makalu. From Shaola, 16,500 feet, on our way down toward Kharta, we saw many Himalayan snow cock and passed several fine lakes. It was singular that, altho lakes are so rare in this district. Arriving back at Kharta we found ourselves in a different climate, dry and fine."

Some of the difficulties which the expedition has to face in its attempt to scale Everest are explained by Sir Martin Conway, based on his own knowledge of the region. "In the first place," he said, as quoted in a dispatch to the Manchester *Guardian*—

We are in complete ignorance as to the nature of the mountain. It is only known by distant views of the upper part. Nobody before the present expedition has been within forty miles of the mountain, and only one person has been as near as that. The Himalayans are much younger than the Alps and the Welsh hills, and differ from the former in being much more precipitous and much less rounded-off by the action of the forces of denudation, inasmuch as they are in an earlier stage of disintegration. The result is that it is the exception to find a peak

Saving Buyers $900–$1000

SINCE June of this year, Templar has lowered its price on open cars $900 (now $1985) and on closed cars $1000 (now $2785). These reductions are big enough to tell their own story: a net cash saving of $900 or $1000 to car buyers makes Templar conspicuously attractive.

Also of unusual importance is the fact that, at a price which formerly bought cars of but medium grade, you can now own a famous Templar—known always and everywhere as the Superfine Car.

Lower than Before the War

FRANKLY, Templar's new prices are too low. Even before the war Templar sold higher than present prices. "A good buy" then, it is a most exceptional buy now.

Always rich in merit, Templar steadily improves. We are constantly making it better. So that today you can buy the best Templar ever built at the lowest price in Templar's entire history.

Next Prices Higher

HOWEVER, let us make it perfectly clear that Templar's new prices are too low for Templar's quality. And therefore, since we pledge ourselves to maintain and improve that quality, we reserve the right to increase our prices at any time without notice.

We make this statement in the utmost good faith, as man to man. Templar's next prices must surely be higher. Indeed, we had that fact fully in mind when we decided upon the astonishing low prices of $1985 and $2785.

Note These Facts

THE facts behind our present low prices are these. Thousands of men and women who should be happy owners of Templars haven't any real idea how splendidly Templar could serve them. The long way to show them would be to advertise Templar's points of strength, one after another.

The short way—the way we have taken—is to make Templar's prices so extremely low that thousands of new buyers will quickly find out for themselves, as Templar owners, that Templar is precisely the car they have long desired.

A Car "Just Right"

AND what a wonderfully desirable car Templar is! Graceful, fast, sturdy. Champion of coast-to-coast record cars. No waster of gas or tires. No profit-maker for repair shops. Easy to drive, steady on the road, of just the right size to get in and out of city traffic quickly. And in every item of equipment, as in every ounce of material and every stroke of workmanship—genuinely high grade.

Let's get acquainted. We shall be glad to send the name of the Templar dealer nearest you.

The Templar Motors Company, 2400 Halstead Street, Cleveland.

that is at all climbable. Many of the big mountains of the range are cut off all round by peaks below, and even if this is not so in the case of Everest and if it be proved that the mountain may be scaled from base to summit, the mere length of the ascent presents problems too complicated in character for any expedition to anticipate.

So far as it is possible to judge from photographs of the upper part of the mountain, its summit is reached from the north by a long and not very steep tho probably narrow ridge which at an Alpine level might not be difficult. But climbing at an altitude of 28,000 to 29,000 feet is a totally different proposition. The highest ascent thus far is that of the Bride, in the Himalayas, which the Duke of the Abruzzi climbed to a height of 24,500 feet.

It was not difficult, but on the last day the rate was only 150 feet an hour, and it was safe therefore to assume that beyond 26,000 feet experts could not proceed faster than 100 feet an hour with a maximum of 1000 feet in a day. To ensure this progress a series of camps would have to be established at exceedingly high altitudes, beginning at the lowest with one at 18,000 feet. Others would have to be placed at altitudes of 21,000, 23,000, 24,500, 26,000, 27,000, and 28,000 feet respectively, each higher camp being somewhat smaller than that immediately below. These camps would necessitate carrying considerable weights up to great heights; they would have to be strong enough to withstand the heavy storms which are more frequent than good weather at high altitudes; they would have to be victualled for several days, and would have to provide shelter for several sleepers, and for at least two in the highest of all.

Tent platforms are not likely to be provided by nature and would most probably have to be hewn out of the solid ice. This would be very slow work, because the primary effect of high altitudes on man is to induce sleep and fatigue rapidly when any work is done. The camps would also have to be fairly permanent structures to last at least two seasons.

In his recently issued volume, "Mountain Memories—A Pilgrimage of Romance," published in this country by the Funk & Wagnalls Company (New York), Sir Martin presents an enlargement of the statements here credited to him, and draws for illustration upon his own experiences in the Himalayas. "The Himalaya and mountains behind it are not like the Alps, a relatively settled range," he writes. "They are young ranges, jutting up in crude perpendicularity into the sky and rapidly disintegrating under the actions of hot sunshine, cold frost, and heavy snowfalls. In time the sharp peaks will be blunted, the cliffs sloped back, the valleys filled and a much lower and more rounded group of mountains will take their place. Now they are in the early and dramatic stage of their existence. That is why they are so very lofty and why the peaks are so precipitous. Every mountain in the Alps can be climbed. It is rare to find a high Himalayan peak which is even problematically climbable. This is hard doctrine for the ordinary Alpine climber who thinks the word inaccessible should be abolished in application to mountains." He started his own journey thus prejudiced, he admits, but experience soon changed his view. With an eye to the beauty and grandeur of the scene, as well as to the actual details of climbing, he describes a typical bit of Himalayan country, the Baltoro Glacier. They started from camp at a height of 18,000 feet, and "drove a flock of sheep and goats to the last grass." Continuing, he writes:

The journey to the foot of the glacier took four days and involved many difficulties. The sheep and goats and all the loads, 103 in number, had to be carried over a crazy rope-bridge—a very slow process when only one man could be allowed on it at a time. There were also several streams to be waded, rushing torrents with beds of rolling rocks. One was only just fordable by the aid of a rope stretched across for support against the weight of water. It was an insignificant brook when we camped near its banks one evening and might have been crossed with utmost ease, but during the night a glacier-lake must have burst and flooded it, for in the morning it was more than a hundred yards wide and in places over waist-deep. The crossing filled five hours with hard work. Not long after it had been safely accomplished the torrent ran dry!

I forgat during how many marches we toiled over the monstrous mo aine covering or along the right bank of the glacier. Nothing exceeds in to'lsomeness such ground. The rocks lying about were large and all were loose, they were piled into mounds or waves. We must always be going up or down. There were quantities of lakes on the ice to be circumvented, and glacier streams with vertical ice-banks to be crossed. You can not wade these streams, for their floor is smooth ice and the current would instantly sweep you away on such slippery footing. You must travel alongside till you find an overhanging place that can be jumped. This makes the route tantalizingly circuitous. You are frequently forced to go in an undesired direction, it may be a mile out of your way—a serious matter when a whole day's march for coolies over such ground may not be more than three miles.

About twenty miles from the foot of the glacier we made a couple of expeditions up its north bank to a peak and a saddle each over 18,000 feet high, relatively trifling elevations amid such surroundings. K.2's summit was still some 10,000 feet higher, rising as much above us as Monte Rosa above Zermatt. The purpose of these climbs was to reconnoiter K.2, but they revealed only its summit heaving above an intervening ridge. We were not, however, unrewarded, for we could at last look up and down the huge glacier and across it to the wide and splendid north face of Masherbrum. Thus displayed, that mountain is perhaps the finest I have ever seen and the most uncompromisingly inaccessible. Imagine a snow-draped pyramid like the Weisshorn lifted far aloft on a wide-spreading foundation of splintered buttresses fringed with rows of aiguilles, large and small, in countless multitude. The sides of the ridges are grooved like corduroy with avalanche tracks. Between the ridges are hanging glaciers and larger glacier arms deeply penetrate the mass. The ridges are all parallel and of like gracefully curved outline. One beyond another they sweep down to the Baltoro and form a perfect composition like the feathers of an eagle's extended wing. It is an exceptionally fine example of mountain architecture, a natural composition, almost resembling an artistic creation. The immense sweep of the glacier, hence visible from its foot to the monumental Golden Throne at its head, bound all the parts of half the panorama together.

ACQUIRING SNAPPY PORES WITH IRVIN COBB

"HOW TRUE IT IS," monologs Irvin Cobb, "that we who would pluck the mote from behind a fellow being's waistcoat so rarely take note of the beam which we have swallowed crosswise!" Even so, with the assistance of a penny-in-the-slot weighing machine and some opportunities for comparison with an "undoubtedly fat" friend, Mr. Cobb ultimately reached the conclusion that he weighed much too much. A splendid resolution sprouted within him shortly afterwards, he announces in his new book, "One-Third Off" (Doran). It was one of several resolutions which he entertained before he finally found a cure for too much size. This first resolution had to do with exercise. As for dieting, he admits—

It did not occur to me that cutting down my daily consumption of provender might prove helpful to the success of the proposed undertaking. Or if it did occur to me, I put the idea sternly from me, for I was by way of being a robust trencherman. I had joyed in the pleasures of the table, and I had written copiously of those joys, and I now declined to recant of my faith or to abate my indulgences.

All this talk which I had heard about balanced rations went in at one ear and out at the other. I knew what a balanced ration was. I stowed one aboard three times daily—at morn, again at noon, and once more at nightfall. A balanced ration was one which, being eaten, did not pull you over on your face; one which you could poise properly if only you leaned well back upon rising from the table, and placed the two hands, with a gentle lifting motion, just under the overhang of the main cargo hold.

Surely there must be some way of achieving the desired result other than by following dieting devices. There was—exercising was the answer. I would exercise and so become a veritable faun.

Now, as far as I recalled, I had never taken any indoor exercise, excepting once in a while to knock on wood. I abhorred the thought of ritualistic bedroom callisthenics such as were recommended by divers health experts. Climbing out of a warm bed and standing out in the middle of a cold room and giving an imitation of a demoniac semaphore had never appealed to me as a fascinating divertisement for a grown man. As I think I may have remarked once before, lying at full length on one's back on the floor immediately upon awakening of a morning, and raising the legs to full length twenty times struck me as a performance lacking in dignity, and utterly futile.

Besides, what sort of a way was that to greet the dewy morn?

So as an alternative I decided to enrol for membership at a gymnasium where I could have company at my exercising and make a sport of what otherwise would be in the nature of a punishment. This I did. With a group of fellow inmates for

PERSONAL GLIMPSES

Continued

my team mates, I tossed the medicine ball about. My score at this was perfect; that is to say, sometimes when it came my turn to catch I missed the ball, but the ball never once missed me. Always it landed on some tender portion of my anatomy, so that my average, written in black-and-blue spots, remained an even 1000.

Daily I cantered around and around and around a running track until my breathing was such probably as to cause people passing the building to think that the West Side Y. M. C. A. was harboring a pet porpoise inside. Once, doing this, I caught a glimpse of my own form in a looking-glass which for some reason was affixt to one of the pillars flanking the oval. A looking-glass properly did not belong there; distinctly it was out of place and could serve no worthy purpose. Very few of the sights presented in a gym which largely is patronized by city-bred fat men are deserving to be mirrored in a glass. They are not such visions as one would care to store in fond memory's album. Be that as it may, here was this mirror, and swinging down the course suddenly, I beheld myself in it. Clad in a chastely simple one-piece garment, with my face all a blistered crimson and my fingers interlaced together about where the third button of the waistcoat, counting from the bottom up, would have been had I been wearing any waistcoat, I reminded myself of a badly scorched citizen escaping in a scantily dressed condition from a burning homestead bringing with him the chief family treasure clasped in his arms. He had saved the pianola!

From the running track or the medicine ball court it was the devotee's custom to repair to the steam room and "simmer pleasantly in a temperature of 240 degrees Fahrenheit," more or less, until, he says—

All I needed before being served was to have the gravy slightly thickened with flour and a dash of watercress added here and there. Having remained in the steam cabinet until quite done, I next would jump into the swimming pool, which concluded the afternoon's entertainment.

Jumping into the cool water of the pool was supposed to reseal the pores which the treatment in the hot room had caused to open. In the best gymnasium circles it is held to be a fine thing to have these educated pores, but I am sure it can be overdone, and personally I can not say that I particularly enjoyed it. I kept it up largely for their sake. They became highly trained, but developed temperament. They were apt to get the signals mixed and open unexpectedly on the street, resulting in bad colds for me.

For six weeks, on every week day from three to five P. M., I maintained this schedule religiously—at least I used a good many religious words while so engaged—and then I went on the scales to find out what progress I had made toward attaining the desired result. I had kept off the scales until then because I was saving up, as it were, to give myself a nice jolly surprize party.

So I weighed. And I had picked up nine pounds and a half! That was what I had gained for all my sufferings and all my exertions—that, along with a set of snappy edge of how a New England boiled dinner feels just before it comes on the table.

"This," I said bitterly to myself—"this is sheer foolhardiness! Keep this up for six weeks more and I'll find myself fallen away to a perfect three-ton truck. Keep it up for three months and I'll be ready to rent myself out to the aquarium as a suitable playmate for the leviathan in the main tank. I shall stop this idiocy before it begins making me seasick merely to look down at myself as I walk. I may slosh about and billow somewhat, but I positively decline to heave up and down. I refuse to be known as the human tidal wave, with women and children being hurriedly removed to a place of safety at my approach. Right here and now is where I quit qualifying for the inundation stakes!"

Which accordingly I did. What I did not realize was that the unwonted exercise gave me such a magnificent appetite that, after a session at the gymnasium, I ate about three times as much as I usually did at dinner. . . . So, never associating the question of diet with the problem of attaining physical slightness, I swung back again into my old mode of life with the resigned conviction that since destiny had chosen me to be fat there was nothing for me to do in the premises excepting to go right on to the end of my mortal chapter being fat, fatter and, perhaps, fattest. I'd just make the best of it.

And I'd use care about crossing a county bridge at any gait faster than a walk.

ELEVEN MEN IN A LIFE-BOAT, FIFTEEN DAYS AT SEA.

"THE great traditions of the sea," says a report from Seattle, were preserved by eleven sailors who set out in an open boat to get help for a disabled steamer, were carried out of their course by a hurricane, and finally reached the sought-for help after fifteen days on the Pacific Ocean. The story of their voyage, pieced together from their statements after they had come through to safety "with unbroken nerve and courage," is told by a writer in the Seattle *Times*. It shows, he says, that they "fought dauntlessly against odds which threatened any moment to snuff out their lives," kept a stiff upper lip even when "they thought they had sighted land and then found it was only a cloud bank by the heaving waters," and finally won out, against both long odds and bad luck, by grim courage and determination. To begin the story at the beginning:

The *Canadian Importer* sailed from Vancouver, B. C., August 13, and from Nanaimo, August 15, bound for Australia with a full cargo of lumber. On Friday, August 19, the ship suddenly began filling with water. The inflow continued until there were 17 feet of water in her No. 2 hold and her engine room, extinguishing her fires and putting her wireless apparatus out of commission. After a desperate but vain fight of several hours to regain control of the ship, Capt. C. R. Bissett decided the only recourse lay in sending a life-boat in search of assistance, as he was out of the steamship track. His vessel was then 623 miles southwest of the Columbia River lightship. At that time the *Canadian Importer* was listing 30 degrees.

PERSONAL GLIMPSES
Continued

J. W. Watt, two bonnie Scots, who, Captain Bissett thought, would smell their way to land, if in no other way, were detailed for the boat and three seamen and three firemen volunteered to join the party. One engineer was also allowed to go. Just before the boat pushed off Cadet R. Newell rushed to the bridge and asked Captain Bissett if he could go along. The skipper warned him of what the consequences might be, but he still adhered to his request, which was granted.

Then Purser B. D. Soissons ran into Newell and he also began figuring on making the trip in the life-boat. Soissons and Newell believed they would reach San Francisco in five days and would "have a big time."

"It was a funny idea all right, because none of us had any money," remarked Newell after arriving in Victoria.

Anyway Soissons made his request to Captain Bissett and it was granted.

There was a great scene on the starboard side of the *Canadian Importer* as the little craft took aboard its four breakers of water, bully beef and hardtack, and the men who were to seek aid scampered aboard. There were mingled feelings. No one knew whether or not they would see one another again. The life-boat might be engulfed or the *Importer* might slip beneath the surface at any moment, as her fore and aft bulkheads were all that kept her afloat.

The "good-bys," "good voyage" and "good luck" swept back and forth in small barrages, and the hands waved the final farewells.

Then Mr. Laird ordered the "dipping lugg" set and the little life-boat rapidly passed out of sight of the *Importer* at four o'clock on Friday afternoon, August 10. The wind was favorable and a fine passage to San Francisco was expected.

On Saturday and Sunday the boat ran into calms and drifted about. The men celebrated the Sabbath by going over the side and enjoying a swim. This recreation suddenly came to a close when a ten-foot shark poked its nose above the surface and showed a beautiful row of pearly teeth.

The life-boat was skimming along on Monday at 2 a. m. when lights were sighted. Every man was roused and half the flares were fired and a bucketful of waste saturated in kerosene was burned, but altho the ship was but four miles off, the danger signals were not seen. As the bright lights of the passenger ship passed out of sight there were murmured imprecations on the head of the lookout of the ship.

The men laid down in their cramped quarters to sleep, with one officer and one man on watch. The night was spent with the officers doing six-hour watches and the men on for one hour each. The men slept in the bottom of the craft with their blankets fastened to the oars to form a cover.

One week passed and still there was no sight of land. Then signs of a cyclone approached. Early one morning the sky grew dark, and at noon a great heat wave struck the craft, followed by a terrific wind and a downpour which amounted almost to a cloud-burst. Only through skilful handling did the life-boat succeed in surviving the storm, which lasted for four days and three nights. Neither officer had a wink of sleep during the time. The course was altered and the life-boat ran before the wind with her sail well reefed.

The gale blew from the northeast and the craft was heading in the direction of San Pedro. During this awful ordeal some of the men nearly perished. Drenched to the skin, with the temperature very low, no sun, the cold spray continually slapping them and only cramped quarters to squat in, the crew endured many tortures. Finally, however, we are told:

> The gale blew itself out and with a favorable wind from the southeast, Mr. Laird decided to head for San Francisco, and such rapid progress was made that all hands one night thought they were off Cape Mendocino.
>
> In the fading light one of the crew remarked, "Looks like land ahead."
>
> Every one searched the horizon and sure enough it looked like Mendocino. Darkness came on and Mr. Laird decided to reef the sail so that they would not get too close to land before daybreak.
>
> There was little sleeping that night and Banks, a Liverpool fireman, kept all hands in good spirits by the yarns he spun of his trip across Canada on freight trains. He was the life of the boat and with one of the seamen, who couldn't help singing, many dreary hours were turned into sunshine.
>
> Every one strained his eyes at daybreak to see how far they were offshore. They searched, but no land was to be seen.
>
> "Only a cloudbank," informed Mr. Laird, and everyone's spirits went down like a rock in the ocean.
>
> No one despaired of ultimate success despite the fact that hardtack and bully beef are not likely to improve a man's tenacity to hang on. However, a subject which was never dry always came to the forefront in dull moments.
>
> "Wait till we get back to old British Columbia and hook 'longside a liquor permit," some one would chip in, and then would follow a general review of the best beverages.
>
> An albatross brought moments of sport and amusement and also a lot of thunder from Mr. Laird, who considered the bird the Jonah of the trip. The albatross picked up the boat and hung about for four days.
>
> "I'd shot the thing if I had had a rifle," said Mr. Laird.
>
> But Mr. Laird didn't have a rifle and his Jonah stayed with him.
>
> Various means were devised of catching the bird and ending its days. Mr. Laird, who hails from Melbourne and has had some experience on the plains, decided to lasso the bird, and on one shot put the noose over his victim's head, but he could not draw the line taut before the bird was away.
>
> Undaunted, Mr. Laird tried another ruse. He baited a line, which had been used for fishing, with a hope that the albatross would snap up the bait and take the hook. But the bird was wary and stood off.
>
> One of the crew tried to kayo the bird with a boat hook, but nearly went overboard.
>
> Then came the sporting instinct. It was decided that every man on board should contribute 50 cents to the first man who saw land. The pool amounted to $5.50.
>
> On the 15th night Cadet Newell was just going off watch when he thought he saw a light. He paused and concluded that it was the blinking light on the Farallones. He called every one and they all watched

The story of your foot troubles is told by *your shoes*

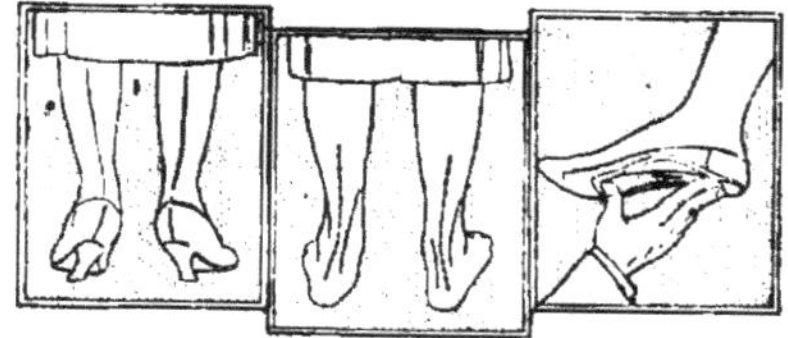

Do your heels wear down on the inside, feet tire quickly, ankles rotate inward and "turn" easily? This indicates "weak foot" and the beginning of the painful "flat foot."

Dr. Scholl's Foot-Eazer will give the needed support to the foot, straightening up the shoe

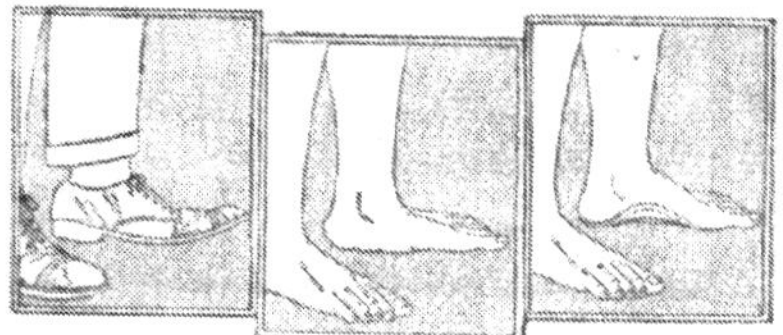

When the shank of this shoe is forced down and the sides are bulged and wrinkled, "flat foot" has developed.

Dr. Scholl's Tri-Spring Arch Support, of extra-strong construction, will support the foot, taking the weight off the instep of the shoe

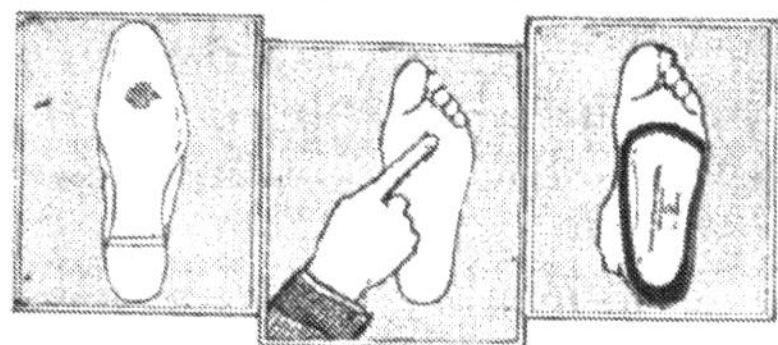

If the sole of your shoe shows undue wear at this point, the metatarsal arch, across the ball of the foot, is weakening.

Burning sensation and callouses on sole, cramp-like pains in the ball of the foot result. Dr. Scholl's Anterior Metatarsal Arch Support benefits this trouble by supporting this arch

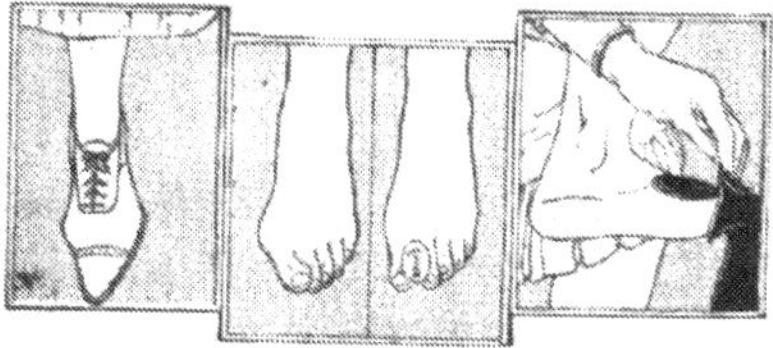

That unsightly bulge on the side of your shoe can be benefited by Dr. Scholl's Toe-Flex which gently straightens the great toe. Of fine, flexible rubber, 3 sizes, 75c each.

Dr. Scholl's Bunion Reducer relieves pressure; keeps shoe from bulging; reduces the growth by natural absorption. 75c each

Don't blame your shoes if they quickly lose their shape, if your feet tire and ache. First get at the real cause, then see how much better your shoes will wear, how fine your feet will feel

Oct. 22 to 29

Dr. Scholl's National Demonstration Week

This week, October 22 to 29, is the time to have your shoe trouble quickly and permanently corrected. It's Dr. Scholl's National Demonstration Week.

Step into the first store where you see Dr. Scholl's Foot Comfort Appliances displayed. There you will find someone thoroughly competent to tell you exactly what's causing your trouble. Then and there you can have exactly fitted to your foot, without removing your hose, the particular Dr. Scholl Appliance you need to remove that cause.

Developed and patented by the internationally-known foot specialist, Dr. Wm. M. Scholl, every Dr. Scholl Foot Comfort Appliance has been tested and its worth proven in actual use by hundreds of thousands of people in all parts of the world. Simple in construction, light and resilient, yet strong, as they must be, they can be worn comfortably in any shoe or slipper.

Determine to make this splendid opportunity yours for—remember!—so easily you can prevent those shoe troubles; so surely you can have active, shapely, comfortable feet.

The Scholl Mfg. Co., Dept. 810, 213 W. Schiller St., Chicago, Ill.; 339 Broadway, New York City; 112 Adelaide St., E., Toronto, Canada.

Branches in London, Paris, Melbourne, Sydney, Cape Town and Buenos Aires

---

Special Remedies from Dr. Scholl's Laboratories—obtainable at shoe, department, *and* drug stores

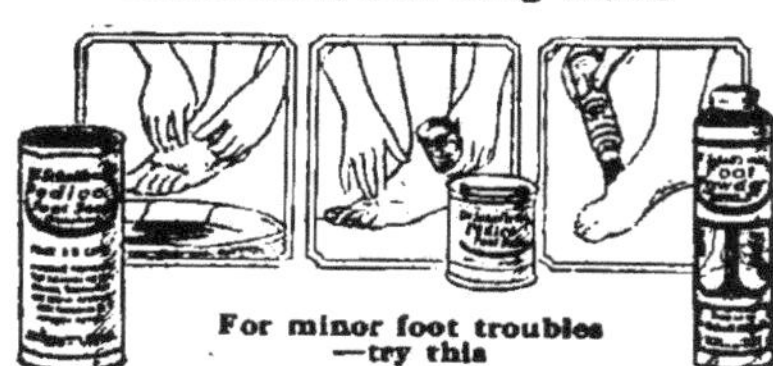

For minor foot troubles —try this

For hot, tired, aching, tender and perspiring feet, use Dr. Scholl's Home Treatment—a granulated, cleansing Foot Soap, a penetrating, healing Foot Balm, and a Foot Powder, antiseptic and deodorising. Makes the feet feel

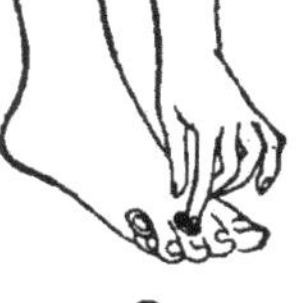

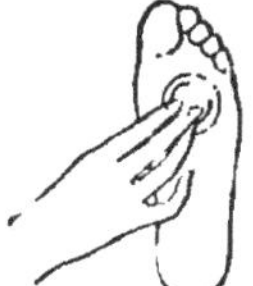

In one minute corns stop hurting

—and stop hurting for good. Dr. Scholl's Zino-pads protect while they work. Thin, adhesive, waterproof. Absolutely safe! Sizes for Corns, callouses, bunions. 35c a box.

Dr. Scholl's Zino-Pads

Put one on—the pain is gone!

FREE SAMPLE

USE THIS COUPON

THE SCHOLL MFG. CO., Dept. 810
213 West Schiller St., Chicago, Ill.

Please send me a free sample of Dr. Scholl's Zino-pads for corns ( ) callouses ( ) or bunions ( ) (check which kind is wanted), together with a copy of Dr. Scholl's booklet "The Feet and Their Care."

Name....................................

Street....................................

City....................................

PERSONAL GLIMPSES
Continued

There it was, a "blinker" all right, but it was not regular enough for a shore light.

Continuing for a while with the light always in view, other lights flashed into vision, and it was concluded that a ship was at hand.

Up went the flares and this time the signal was seen.

Using his only chart as a megaphone. Mr. Laird shouted, "How far to San Francisco?"

A short exchange of questions revealed that the rescue ship was the tug *Sea Lion*, bound for the *Canadian Importer*.

Mr. Laird summarizes the trip in these words:

"Our rations were kept in the bow and some of the seamen were usually complaining about hunger. Amidships two of the younger members of the boat crew had their quarters and one of them had a Bible and read it by the moonlight. Back aft there was Third officer Watt and myself and we were usually complaining in seafaring terms about the bad weather we were experiencing. You know we expected to reach land in five days, but we were buffeted around for fifteen days and then didn't get there, so there was some excuse for our objections."

DARK, AND OFTEN VAIN, WAYS OF THE AUTOMOBILIOUS BOOTLEGGER

THE innocent-looking motor car, coming down from a supposedly innocent excursion into Canada, has places for concealing liquor that makes the old-fashioned bootleg method seem contemporary with the ark. Even if it is true, as a recent investigator of automobile bootlegging concedes, that "Uncle Sam is sometimes slow but mighty sure," with the result that "the official life of an automobile whisky-runner may be merry, but it is inevitably short," nevertheless the fact remains that the automobile is the mainstay of the bootlegging industry in the United States. Without taking sides in the matter, in fact, after carefully declaring his neutrality, C. H. Claudy, writing in *Motor Life*, presents some of the methods used in concealing whisky in motor cars. The spare-tire, false-limousine-top, and double-gasoline-tank methods are illustrated by example. Incidentally, the writer points out, we do not hear much about the returns from the confiscated cars which are sold to the highest bidder. He mentions that:

The average second-hand value of cars seized for illicit transportation of liquor (for know, ye tempted, that if a prohibition enforcement agent finds "hip licker" in your car, he will not only confiscate the hootch, but will also take the car and sell it to the highest bidder) is more than a thousand dollars. Only high-priced, powerful, roomy and reliable cars are good enough for the bootlegger; it is a paying proposition for him to operate a Packmobile or a Caddifayyette, even if he loses a few.

The United States Government is cowering in a corner, trying to hide its sins of wasteful expenditure and misorganized effort from the eyes of a Congressional investigating committee and a budget outfit. Their attention is respectfully called to the fact that a waiting world is *not* informed how many automobiles have been seized by prohibition officers, or how much money has been realized from their sale. The Internal Revenue Bureau gives the cheering information that the value of property seized in law enforcement of the prohibition act during the fiscal year was in excess of $2,000,000, but how much of this was whisky, and how much automobiles, deponent sayeth not.

The United States is divided into prohibition districts, and each one is a little world unto itself, and if it reports at all to its creator and parent, does so sketchily. They *believe* in Washington that three-fourths of illegal liquor traffic is motor-car traffic and that "a great many" automobiles have been confiscated, but how they know they don't say.

As for the automobilious bootlegging methods in actual use, he writes, illustrating by examples:

One Harlow R. Dennison (at least that was the nice name he put on the police blotter) did mental arithmetic. Booze could be bought from a man, who had a friend, who was first cousin to a guard of a Government warehouse. The booze could be bought for $4.30 a quart in five-gallon lots. Ten gallons is forty quarts. Forty quarts retailing at $8 the quart is $320. Set against this forty quarts at $4.30, $172, add $10 for gasoline and incidental expenses, and a net profit of $138 was left for Mr. Dennison, IF he could get his forty quarts from the warehouse to the city.

Mr. Dennison thought of numerous clever schemes, of which the spare tire seemed the cleverest. A spare tire 34 by 4½ inches holds about twenty-five quarts of liquid. It isn't easy to get liquid into a tire, but it can be done. And Mr. Dennison did it and made at least four and perhaps five trips—the police are not quite sure—but he made his error. Mr. Dennison carried two spare tires, brazenly at the rear of his car. But forty quarts didn't fill them and sixty quarts more than filled them. So he bought sixty quarts, and filled each tire as full as it would hold. In doing so he spilled a little about the valve stem, sticking through the rim.

The prohibition authorities of the city to which Mr. Dennison was proceeding were quite cognizant that he brought in booze, and a lot of it. But in spite of careful inspection, they didn't know just how. There was none under the seat, the groceries in the tonneau were bona-fide potatoes and apples, the gasoline tank held gasoline. But one day an officer spied the place where the dust on a spare had obviously *been splashed off*. The officer unscrewed the valve cap and sniffed—and Mr. Dennison lost his car and his booze and paid a heavy fine and was glad to escape with his liberty. Now he doesn't think much of spare tires as a place in which to carry booze.

Mike Griffin had it all over Dennison as a thinker-up of schemes. "Too much trouble to put it in spare tires," opined Mike. "Officers too darn clever. One needle puncture and there you ain't. What you want is something so artfully concealed they'll never even think of looking for it. And I want transportation for containers. A quart brings eight bucks; a pint brings five, and a half-pint, three-fifty. Gimme it in half-pints and I grow rich, provided I buy 'em cheap enough."

Whereupon Mr. Griffin made *his* mistake (for all bootleggers make them, sooner or

PERSONAL GLIMPSES
Continued

later) and bought him a new, shiny, beautiful sedan car.

This he took to a shop where strange and curious things were done to it. To the eye, the bright and beautiful sedan was still but a sedan, beautiful and bright. But to Mike it was the road to wealth. And there was joy in the hearts of half-pint buyers, for the supply seemed inexhaustible. Mike would have 200 half-pints to-day, sell them, and reappear with a couple of hundred tomorrow.

But buyers exult too much. "Oh, t'ell with the Volstead act. I can buy all I want. Sure, good stuff. Get you some if you want." Some one says it to some one who says it to some one else who says it to some one who tells some one who is interested in prohibition. Mike Griffin was watched. And once he was seen to drive a beautiful and bright sedan out of the city in the morning and return the next morning the presumption was that the brightness and beauty of the sedan concealed something.

So they stopped and searched the car. Mr. Griffin here made his second mistake; he threatened the officers with all sorts of penalties for searching him without a warrant. One of the officers called his bluff, and insisted on taking him to the police station to make his complaint right there. Mr. Griffin went.

While he was complaining, the officer climbed into the sedan, slouched down in the seat, and stared at the upholstery above him. It was a trifle low, that upholstered ceiling, and "the officer poked gently at it." It appeared to be a good, hard ceiling, almost too good and hard, so—

He smote his club against it, smote vigorously, and was rewarded with the tinkle of glass and an odor which perhaps made him remember the "here's how" of the old days. The false ceiling, the concealed rack for half-pint bottles were a good scheme, but for the fact that a bright and beautiful sedan is not usually driven twice daily from city to city by a lone driver. Exit the half-pint-false-ceiling scheme and exit also Mr. Mike Griffin.

Bootleggers have tried every known part of a car as a storage space for booze. One Elias Grassmacher, whose name certainly is not a carefully chosen alias, was one of the many who thought gasoline tanks holding seventeen gallons, about thirteen gallons too big. He put a smaller tank inside the larger one, filled it with booze, and then filled around the smaller tank with gas. It's a grand scheme, if you don't run out of gas at the wrong place. Mr. Grassmacher chose a country garage beside the road to refill.

"Pretty near dry?" inquired the garage-man, pleasantly.

"Yep, can't go very far without gas. Fill 'er up," was Grassmacher's incautious reply.

The garage man filled her up—*and it took only three gallons to do it.* Two miles further on was a rope across the road, and a couple of local constables who told him they'd like to take his boat to pieces and see what made it go. Grassmacher threatened and pleaded and cussed and raved, but the local police were anxious to make a record, and a big gasoline tank filling was too inexplicable, especially with Mr. Grassmacher not having any too good a reputation in the nearby city to which a telephone inquiry had been sent. Now Mr. Grassmacher does sums in mental arithmetic which add the value of one car, to the value of one auxiliary tank, to the value of taking the gasoline tank apart and inserting the smaller tank and soldering it up and painting it again, to the value of one fine, to the value of thirteen gallons of perfectly good hootch, and, presumably is either inventing new schemes or going out of business.

But not all transportation of wet goods is such picayune stuff as this. There are those who won't deal with booze at all unless in large lots, where they make a whole lot of money at once. Such was the scheme of a super-dealer, who used tires in freight-car lots as concealers of his true merchandise.

Of course, by no means all schemes fail all the time. Mr. Al "Frisco" Johnson collects seven truck-loads of whisky. He gets seven purchasers in a city nearby. The load is worth a great many thousand dollars, too many to risk if a little money will serve to insure it. So "Frisco" buys himself a cheap, second-hand truck, and loads it with garden produce, under which he puts one case of whisky and several cases of near-whisky. The real whisky is nearest the end and has a top carefully broken open so an exploring hand can be easily inserted for investigation.

When the cavalcade is ready to start, "Frisco" calls up the police at the one place at which he fears interference. "Sh-shshshs," he whispers over the telephone. "This is Shifty Mike talking. I got it in for Dan O'Hara. Dan is starting a truck full o' booze for your burg to-night. He'll get there about twelve-thirty. By-by."

At twelve-thirty, sure enough, into the town and the arms of waiting policemen, drives Dan O'Hara (who has been hired to be arrested). The truck is captured. The open case is found, tasted, the load confiscated. The police disperse in triumph. An hour later the real whisky-laden truck drives unmolested through the town.

"Frisco" loses the truck. It is cheaper to let the prohibition forces have it than fight it.

Even to the lover of the forbidden liquids, and those who would not have wept had Mr. Volstead died when he was a baby, some mishaps of the bootleggers are funny. Among these anecdotes there is one which became a classic in a certain club, so much so that the "hero" of the tale resigned.

This gentleman had much money with which to gratify his whims, and decided his cellar was under-supplied. Inquiry developed the fact that a friend stood ready to remedy the condition with a brand-new, never-before-used tank truck labeled "Standard Oil." The tank truck was carefully cleaned, and filled with whisky; several hundred gallons, at about twenty-five dollars a gallon.

The "Standard Oil" truck safely got out of the city where it was loaded, safely negotiated the road and safely arrived in the city of its destination. The driver of the truck was uninstructed, and the garage chief of the wealthy man was equally innocent. The mislabeled truck drove to the rich man's garage and there ran the precious contents of the tank into the big gasoline tank in the garage, mixing the whisky with enough gasoline to make a mixture equally unfit for drinking or engine propulsion. And what, it may be asked, could the rich man do? Nothing. So he did it.

INVESTMENTS ▲ AND ▲ FINANCE

THE BANK RATE RETURNS TO NORMALCY

THE reduction of the New York Federal Reserve Bank rediscount rate to 5 per cent. seems to the New York *Sun* to be a definite indication of the return to normal levels for money in the financial center. It is noted that the "maximum rate of 7 per cent. was first reduced in May, another reduction followed in June and another in July," and that the latest reduction seems to have followed rather than anticipated general conditions in the financial markets. As *The Sun* comments editorially:

A "return to the normal of 1914" in the rediscount rate is an important step toward regaining stability and activity in commercial affairs; but it is by no means the only requirement. The gradual "thawing out" of credits has progressed sufficiently to justify the lower and now the normal rate on rediscounts, but so long as the various industrial and mercantile instituons lack orders, or buyers, or customers, the complete usefulness of the mechanism is not restored, and the wheels will not turn with requisite ease and the old rapidity. And would-be customers will not become actual and active buyers until they can buy at prices upon which they can figure a profit for themselves.

It remains to turn the valve and let the steam into the cylinders. For the motive power of brains and money cannot function so long as high prices prevent their free and unrestricted action.

In Boston, where the Federal Reserve Bank rate has also been reduced to 5 per cent., *The News Bureau* observes that the new rates themselves "give only a faint idea of the unparalleled financial deflation which has been going on for nearly two years." The Boston financial daily believes that "the figures of reserves, discounts, and circulation of the entire Federal Reserve system afford the true picture and emphasize the solid foundation upon which the new investment structure is based":

On March 12, 1920, the reserve ratio of the reserve system reached its record low figure of 40.5% (42.5% on the old basis of figuring and the commonly quoted low point). To-day it is 68.7%. A year ago it was less than 50%, actually 49.4%.

On November 5, 1920, bill holdings of the system reached their peak of $3,126,594,000. To-day they are actually $1,705,843,000 less, or in aggregate of but $1,420,751,000. Since last September they are off about $500,000,000.

Just before Christmas a year ago, December 23, 1920, circulation reached its greatest height, $3,404,931,000. In less than nine months it has contracted $930,255,000, until to-day it is $2,474,676,000.

The extraordinary phase of this deflation, amounting to nearly $1,000,000,000 in circulation and nearly $1,800,000,000 in discounts, has been the gain of over $800,000,000 in reserves at the same time. For total reserves September 21, 1921, aggregated $2,863,096,000 or $827,656,000 higher than the low level of $2,035,440,000, February, 1920.

This is explained by the anomaly of gold imports in the face of financial deflation and receding business. Some keen bankers do not anticipate a continuation of these cross currents and look for a tapering off of gold imports or a marked reduction in the speed of American deflation.

Following figures for the Federal Reserve system show what has been accomplished in the way of deflation since the winter of 1919 with its 7% discount rate and its repeated warnings from the Reserve Board:

RESERVE RATIO	
Sept. 21, 1921	68.7%
Nov. 12, 1920	40.5
BILL HOLDINGS	
Sept. 21, 1921	$1,420,751,000
Nov. 5, 1920	3,126,594,000
NOTE CIRCULATION	
Sept. 21, 1921	$2,474,676,000
Dec. 23, 1920	3,404,931,000
TOTAL RESERVES	
Sept. 21, 1921	$2,863,096,000
Feb. 20, 1920	2,035,440,000

THE WORLD FOOD PROSPECT FOR THE WINTER

WITH the food crops of the United States aggregating about 15 per cent. less than last year, and "with famine existing in Russia and reported in India, both former surplus producers, and drought threatening Argentina," the prospect is not exactly comfortable, *The Wall Street Journal* notes. Nevertheless, it adds, "a survey of the world's food situation shows that for another year there will be no need of any one going without sufficient food wherever it can be transported and paid for." For one thing, our large corn crop will make up for shortage in wheat. As *The Wall Street Journal* glances at the situation:

In the current season ending with July, 1922, Europe will need at least 550,000,000 bushels of foreign wheat, and other importing countries 50,000,000 more. Russia needs an immense amount, but it can not be transported, even if financed. Millions of Russians must pay their lives as a part of the Bolshevik destruction of the railroads. Probably 50,000,000 bushels will be a conservative estimate of the amount that can go to Russia. Europe also may economize, as it did last year when it bought according to its purse instead of its stomach. Six hundred million bushels is an irreducible minimum world demand.

Our September crop report forecasts 754,000,000 bushels of wheat, which is about 30,000,000 less than last year when we had also a large carry-over. Our present carry-over of wheat and flour is about 90,000,000 bushels, making the total supply 844,000,000. We consume 500,000,000 bushels a year, and allowing for seed and a minimum carry-over, our exportable surplus is 200,000,000 bushels. Canada will have about the same amount to ship. This leaves at least 200,000,000 bushels which the world must find elsewhere.

Manchuria should furnish 25,000,000

bushels. India is now importing wheat, but under ordinary weather conditions Argentina and Australia should be able to furnish the remainder of the world's probable demand. But those countries do not harvest until January. With three months to run before harvest and Argentina now needing rain, little can be said of the prospect. So that it seems that the world's wheat situation is just as acute as it was a year ago. Europe sees this, and at this time of the year, when its imports should be light, it is taking wheat from the United States at the rate of 30,000,000 bushels a month.

Our potato and rice crops, which supplement wheat, are about 20 per cent. smaller than last year, so domestic consumption of bread is not likely to be reduced. This makes certain that we, with the help of Canada, can not possibly supply more than two-thirds of the world's probable requirements of wheat. The supply for one-third the need must depend upon the southern continent. Fortunately we have a great corn crop as well as a big carry-over. Therefore, if the weather in the southern hemisphere should prove unpropitious, North America with its surplus of coarse grains can still feed the world until another harvest.

FRANCE RETIRING WARTIME PAPER CURRENCY

FRANCE is retiring and replacing with silver coins the "Chamber of Commerce paper" with which our soldiers who served in France became so familiar. This progress toward normalcy in France is reported by *Bradstreet's*, which gives the following history of the particular type of wartime currency now going out of existence:

Such "paper" was issued in 1 and 2 franc as well as 50-centime denominations, because the rise in silver at that time made the coining of the metal disadvantageous, and, furthermore, the silver coins were hoarded in France and seemed to disappear almost as soon as they were put into circulation. In view of those conditions, the country was divided into "Chamber of Commerce" zones, and paper currency was issued by the Chamber of Commerce of each zone, which usually included many towns and cities. The arrangement, however, did not work satisfactorily for a number of reasons, principally because the French people were unaccustomed to the new currency and tried to pass it along whenever possible, and to exchange it for silver coin or French bank notes. Then, too, the small change currency was printed on cheap paper and became worn out in a short time. Approximately 300,000,000 francs were issued in the small denominations indicated, and the French government, it is understood, is now retiring the issue gradually, by substituting therefor silver coins as rapidly as the mint can produce them. Possibly the entire amount will have been retired by the end of this year. The substitution will begin, it is stated, with the notes bearing the marking of the Paris Chamber of Commerce, whose bills are negotiable throughout France, and the process will be extended to the remotest provinces wherever the wartime paper is to be found. Coins to the value of 40,000,000 francs have already, according to report, been struck off for that purpose. The paper currency backed by the Bank of France will, of course, not be disturbed. It is expected

INVESTMENTS AND FINANCE
Continued

that not much more than one-half of the "Chamber of Commerce paper" issued for wartime convenience will be presented for exchange, since much of it has been lost, destroyed or otherwise made irredeemable.

LETTING EMPLOYEES FIX THEIR OWN SALARIES

THE most successful employer of to-morrow, declares the editor of *Forbes*, "will be the one who can tie up most closely with his employees so that each one will feel that he or she is a real partner and directly responsible for the results achieved." An interesting means towards this end has been adopted by one organization, the name of which is not given by the writer. The head of the concern thought up a plan for fixing salaries which is said to have worked ideally and to have taken all the worry in this connection off his shoulders. He simply lets the employees fix their own salaries. It is done like this, so the New York editor informs us:

The force is not large, so that they all know one another quite well. Once a year every employee makes out a list of the salaries he or she thinks the other employees are worth. Even the executives' salaries are fixed this way. The head of the organization takes all the lists submitted, figures out the average recommended for each employee, and that amount becomes the employee's pay for the following year. He told me the other day that he has never had any occasion to be dissatisfied with the working of this novel system. He declares that the employees can tell what one of their number is worth better than he could possibly judge.

"A curious incident happened this year," he remarked. "The salary recommended for a certain clerk was less than he had been receiving. Not one or two but practically every employee had marked down this one's pay. I sent for him, told him what had occurred, and asked what was the matter. He was quite confused for a little, but then blurted out that he probably deserved what had happened. He explained that he had been in love and had always been in a hurry to get away early. Also, his mind hadn't been as intent upon his work as it ought to have been. I asked him if he was really anxious to get married, and he said he was. I told him that if he cared to get married, I would raise his salary by a certain amount. He did get married and he is now back in his old form."

Model Youth.—A settlement worker was speaking of the relaxed moral standards that she found among the people in her district in New York—owing, she thought, to the upsetting conditions of the war period.

"One boy I knew," she said, "was recently sent to the reform school, and a neighbor was trying to console the lad's mother.

"'Yes,' said the mother, 'it is a shame. He was such a good boy, too. Everything he stole he used to bring right home to me.'"—*Youth's Companion.*

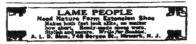

CURRENT EVENTS

FOREIGN

October 5.—A rear-end collision of two suburban trains in a Paris tunnel results in the death of thirty-three persons.

A strong attack by Turkish Nationalists near Afium-Karahissar has been checked by the Greeks, according to an official Greek statement.

Brazil, Belgium, China and Spain are reelected by the Assembly to the Council of the League of Nations. They are non-permanent members.

October 6.—The British Government assures representation for the Dominions at the Washington arms conference by allotting them half of the Empire's six delegates.

The Russian Soviet Government has dropt control of the schools and theaters and has turned them over to local governments, according to an announcement by M. Lunacharsky, former Minister of Education.

Dispatches from Milella, Morocco, state that the Moroccan rebels are fleeing before the Spanish troops, abandoning Xertes, Mizzian, and other places in which they had concentrated heavy reenforcements.

Professor Riccardo Zanella, leader of the Fiume People's Party, has been elected President of the new independent state of Fiume by the Constitutional Assembly, according to a dispatch from Fiume.

German and French Ministers sign an agreement whereby the German government is to deliver to France within three years, 7,000,000,000 gold marks' worth of building materials.

October 7.—The Council of the International Chamber of Commerce, meeting in Paris, adopts a resolution calling on the United States to join with the Allied Powers in plans to solve all the problems growing out of reparations and payment of the Allied debts.

Italian, British and French representatives agree to Italian mediation in the controversy between Austria and Hungary over Burgenland.

October 8.—The Russian Soviet Council of Commissars decides to create a state bank which will be authorized to make loans, afford credit facilities, develop industries, agriculture and trade, and control circulation and exchange. The bank will be capitalized at three trillion rubles.

The Irish peace delegates arrive in London.

October 9.—Eighteen people die when the Laird Line steamship *Rowan* collides with one ship and is sunk by another coming to her rescue.

Premier Briand announces in a public speech that France is ready to disarm provided she has Allied guarantees of security.

October 11.—Premier Lloyd George welcomes the Sinn Fein delegates to the London peace parley.

The British Government invites General Pershing to decorate the tomb of the British unknown warrior buried in

CURRENT EVENTS
Continued

Westminster Abbey with the Congressional Medal of Honor awarded by Congress.

DOMESTIC

October 5.—General Leonard Wood retires from the Army and is confirmed by the Senate in his nomination as Governor-General of the Philippines.

October 6.—The special committee appointed to inquire into the Canal Zone Government recommends to Secretary of War Weeks that open shop conditions be put into effect and that a substantial proportion of non-union men be employed in all departments at prevailing wages.

The Department of Labor reports that statistics on unemployment gathered from 1,428 firms having more than 500 employees each, and located in the 65 principal industrial centers, show that 18,050 more men were at work in September than in August. Thirty-eight cities reported increases in employment and 26 a decrease.

D. S. Swenson, of Minnesota, is nominated by President Harding to be Minister to Norway. Mr. Swenson has been Minister to Denmark and Switzerland.

October 7.—Representative Dowell, of Iowa, introduces a resolution which will compel a reduction of 25 per cent in freight rates on grain, grain products, hay, live stock, coal and cotton.

Representative Upshaw, of Georgia, introduces a resolution to investigate "each and every secret organization in the United States."

Edwin A. Shepherd, of New Jersey, is appointed Controller of the Shipping Board and Emergency Fleet Corporation at an annual salary of $7,500.

October 8.—Senator Kenyon introduces a bill providing penalties for profiteering in the coal industry and another for a comprehensive regulatory law empowering the President to take over the industry in emergency.

Chancellor V. J. Stricker, of Mississippi, holds that 84 insurance companies of that State are guilty of violating the Mississippi anti-trust laws, and fines them a total of $13,000,000. The companies will appeal.

October 9.—Students of more than 100 leading universities and colleges in the Eastern States are invited by the Senior Council of Princeton to send delegates there October 26 for a conference on means to solidify young men of the nation in a movement for international limitation of armaments.

October 10.—The Senate passes the Borah bill to grant free tolls through the Panama Canal for American coastwise ships by a vote of 47 to 37.

October 11.—The President's unemployment conference suggests as a program to aid the unemployed adjustment of rail rates, early settlement of taxes and tariff, and limitation of world armament.

Robert E. Tod, of New York, is nominated by President Harding to be Commissioner of Immigration at the Port of New York, in place of Commissioner Frederick A. Wallis, resigned.

CURRENT EVENTS
Continued

The United States Steel Corporation will spend $10,000,000 this year in construction work, it being understood that this step was approved by the Finance Committee to provide work for 100,000 idle men who normally are employed by the Corporation.

Personal Liberty.—A Hyde Park orator returning home flushed with his efforts, and also from certain spirituous causes, found a mild curate seated opposite in the tram-car. "It may interest you to know," he said truculently, "that I don't believe in the existence of a 'eaven." The curate merely nodded, and went on reading his newspaper. "You don't quite realize what I'm trying to make clear. I want you to understand that I don't believe for a single, solitary moment that such a place as 'eaven exists." "All right, all right," answered the curate pleasantly, "go to hell, only don't make quite so much fuss about it."—*Tattler*.

Confiscated Hootch Eats Lining Out of Sewers

SIERRAVILLE, CAL., Sept. 20.—Prohibition authorities will be asked to pay for repairs to the city sewers. The city claims that confiscated liquors, hootch and jackass brandy, poured into the sewer by the officers, removed the lining of the sewer for a distance of 304 feet.

The liquor was disposed of in this manner by Marshal Massey and Assistant Marshal Pierce on the orders of Federal Commissioner Arnold. City officials, who happened to be examining the spot, discovered the damage.—*Los Angeles Examiner*.

The Exacting Eel.—A profiteer bought a wonderful country home and set about making it even more wonderful. One of his proposals was a fish pond which should contain eels.

"But you can't keep eels in a pond," suggested his neighbor, to whom he had confided his idea. "They have to go down to the sea every year, you know."

"Well I wont have 'em," gasped the profiteer; "I always takes the missus and the kids every year, but I ain't going to take no eels."

Criminal Carelessness.—MRS. NEWLYWED—"Oh, Jack, you left the kitchen door open and the draught has shut my cookery book, so that now I haven't the faintest idea what it is I'm cooking!"—*Le Ruy Blas (Paris.)*

The Outstanding Case.—"Bitten by Insect 27 Years Ago, Suffers Great Pain Now," says a headline. That sounds almost like the first attack of the Presidential bee upon W. J. B.—*Philadelphia Record*.

Probing His Depths.—"When did you first become acquainted with your husband?"

"The first time I asked him for money after we were married."—*London Opinion*.

Brief, but Enough.—The sting of a bee is only a thirty-second of an inch in length.

Another example of a little going a long way.—*Life*.

THE SPICE OF LIFE

Men of Weight and Influence.—"Success brings poise," says a magazine writer. Especially avoirdupois.—*Cleveland News.*

To-day's Optimistic Thought.—Cheer up! When all the neighbors buy autos you can get a seat in a street car.—*St. Paul News.*

The Starting Crank.—Just because a crank can start something, he thinks he is the source of the horsepower.—*Baltimore Sun.*

Always in the Way.—It's easy to meet expenses these days. You run onto them every time you turn around.—*Jackson Citizen Patriot.*

Not So Simple.—"Jack, what causes those marks on your nose?"

"Glasses."

"Glasses of what?"—*London Mail.*

Below Expectations.—"Lenine says he is disappointed in the Russian people." Probably thought they could live without eating.—*Toledo Blade.*

Information Wanted.—MISTRESS (to new maid)—"Above all things, Jane, you must be reticent."

JANE—"Yes, mum—but what is there to be reticent about?"—*The Bystander.*

Undeserved.—JIMMY (tearfully) "Father, the d-donkey kicked me!"

FATHER—"Have you been annoying it?"

JIMMY—"No. I was only t-trying to c-carve my name on it!"—*The Passing Show, London.*

Surprizing Intelligence. — Those keen Eastern business men learn something every day. A candy store operator who has been making a 300 per cent. profit says he can cut prices in half and still make a profit.—*Seattle Times.*

Scientific Proof.—One day a teacher was having a first-grade class in physiology. She asked them if they knew that there was a burning fire in the body all of the time. One little girl spoke up and said:

"Yes'm; when it is a cold day, I can see the smoke."—*The Epworth Herald.*

Purely Inspirational.—The archbishop had preached a fine sermon on the beauties of married life. Two old Irish women coming out of church were heard commenting upon his address.

"'Tis a fine sermon his reverence would be after givin' us," said Bridget.

"It is indade," replied Maggie, "and I wish I knew as little about the matter as he does."—*Tid-Bits* (*London*).

Pot and Kettle.—"You have such strange names for your towns," an Englishman remarked to one of his new American friends. "Weehawken, Hoboken, Poughkeepsie, and ever so many others."

"I suppose they do sound queer to English ears," said the American, thoughtfully. "Do you live in London all the time?"

"Oh no," said the unsuspicious Briton, "I spend a part of my time at Chipping Norton, and then I've a place at Pokestogg-on-the-Hike."—*Harper's Magazine.*

The Real Totterers.—"Are Rents Tottering?" inquires the LITERARY DIGEST. No, but those who are paying them are.—*Greenville (S. C.) Piedmont.*

Too Much for Them.—"That's what I call killing two birds with one stone," said the jeweler as the couple dropt dead on hearing the price of the diamond ring.—*Sun Dial.*

Inexplicable.—Jud Tunkins says what makes him admire a mother's love and marvel at it is a photograph of himself taken at the age of eleven or twelve. —*Washington Star.*

"There's a Reason."—They laugh at the Music Box show when Florence Moore complains—"All the salesmen are so haughty this year. They're taking orders from no one."—*New York World.*

His Recipe for Luck.—FAIR ANGLER—"Mr. Rosenthall is so interesting when he is fishing."

ENTHUSIASTIC RODMAN—"Has he caught some big fish lately?"

FAIR ANGLER—"No. But he talks to the bait just like it was a pair of dice."—*The Catalina Islander.*

Still Missing.—JOHNNY—"Say, paw, I can't get these 'rithmetic examples. Teacher said somethin' 'bout findin' the great common divisor."

PAW (in disgust) — "Great Scott! Haven't they found that thing yet? Why, they were huntin' for it when I was a boy."—*The Christian Evangelist, St. Louis.*

Fashion Note.—CHLOE—"I sho' mighter knowed I gwine have bad luck if I do dat washin' on Friday."

DAPHNE—"What bad luck done come to yuh?"

CHLOE—"I sen' home dat pink silk petticoat wid de filly aidge what I was gwine keep out to wear to chu'ch on Sunday."—*Columbia (S. C.) State.*

Amenities of the Big Town.—Four immigrants at the Battery asked a taxi driver where they could get tickets to Iowa. He supplied them with subway tickets, charging them $6 each, and they did not learn they had been swindled until they were put off a train at 255th Street.

Three Japanese last week hired an open-face carriage and drove for two hours around Central Park. The driver charged them $12.50, and they paid it.

New York is certainly a wonderful city to visit—so courteous to strangers.—*New York World.*

Unforeseen Sequel.—Willie had been instructed by his father to clean up the yard, and he had promised to do so to the best of his ability.

That evening, however, when his father returned from the office and took a look at the yard, he became very angry.

"Willie," he called, "I thought I told you to clean up that yard!"

"Well, dad, I did," said Willie, virtuously. "I fired everything over the fence as soon as I could; but the kid next door threw everything back when I went downtown for mother."—*Harper's Magazine.*

THE LEXICOGRAPHER'S EASY CHAIR

In this column, to decide questions concerning the current use of words, the Funk & Wagnalls New Standard Dictionary is consulted as arbiter.

Readers will please bear in mind that no notice will be taken of anonymous communications.

"M. C. B.," Toronto, Ont., Can.—"Is this sentence correct English, 'He did it without *me* knowing it,' or should you say, 'without *my* knowing it'? Please give reason for your answer."

A participle used as a noun may be preceded by the possessive case of a noun or pronoun; as, "The *man's* leaving home was a surprize"; "*His* buying the property was a mistake"; "*My* going there was necessary." This is the regular construction, and any other would ordinarily be inaccurate. In the sentence you cite, *my* is correct, "He did it without *my* knowing it."

"B. R. F.," Troutville, Va.—"Please give the meaning and pronunciation of the phrase *sine die*."

The phrase *sine die* means, "Without day; finally; as, an adjournment *sine die* (that is, without setting a day for reassembling)." The phrase is pronounced *sai'ni dai'i—ai's* as in *aisle*, *i's* as in *police*.

"R. H. M., Jr.," New York, N. Y.—"Which is correct, 'Negotiations are *under way*,' or 'Negotiations are *under weigh*'?"

"Negotiations are *under way*" is correct.

"J. E. L.," Brunswick, Ga.—"Please tell me if the following sentence is grammatically correct, 'It is I, and not Crichton, who *am* paying you your salary.'"

The sentence you cite is grammatically correct. The antecedent of the relative "who" being "I," the proper verb to use is "am." A rearrangement of this sentence shows clearly what is the antecedent of the relative—"It is I who *am* paying you your salary, and not Crichton."

"F. S. Z.," Byron, Ill.—"Kindly inform me whether there is any such word in the English language as *worsened*. I found the word used as follows: 'Mankind has been *worsened* by the war.'"

Yes. *Worsen* is defined as a verb meaning, "To make worse; to get the advantage of; also, to become worse."

"F. C. H.," Danville, Va.—"Kindly tell me if there is such a word as *onto*, and if it is ever correct to say, for instance, 'It fell *onto* the floor.'"

Onto is a word meaning "upon the top of" that is avoided by purists as colloquial or vulgar. Condemned by Phelps as a vulgarism, it is now growing in popularity. Inasmuch as its form is analogous to *into*, *unto*, *upon*, all of which are sanctioned by best usage, Phelps's condemnation is perhaps a little premature. The word has been objected to by some critics as redundant or needless. "Considered as a new word (it is in reality a revival of an old form), it conforms to the two main neoteristic canons by which the admissibility of new words is to be decided. (See Hall, *Modern English*, pp. 171, 173.) It obeys the analogy of *in to*—*into*. It may also be held to supply an antecedent blank, as may be shown by examples. It never should be employed where *on* is sufficient; but simple *on* after verbs of motion may be wholly ambiguous, so that *on to*, meaning 'to or toward and *on*,' may become necessary to clear up the ambiguity. 'The boy fell *on* the roof' may mean that he fell while *on* the roof, or that he fell, as from the chimney-top or some overlooking window, *to* the roof so as to be *on* it; but if we say 'The boy fell *onto* the roof,' there is no doubt that the latter is the meaning. The canons for deciding the eligibility of new words appear, therefore, to claim for *on to* the right to struggle for continued existence and general acceptance."—*Standard Dictionary*.

"J. O.," Hong-Kong, China.—The name *Beatrice* is correctly pronounced *bi'a-tris*—first *i* as in *police*, *a* as in *final*, second *i* as in *hit*.

"A. H.," Arnold, Neb.—"Please give the correct pronunciations of the words *charmeuse* and *Eton*."

The word *charmeuse* is pronounced *shar''muz'*—*sh* as in *ship*, *a* as in *art*, *u* as in *burn*; Eton, *i'ton*—*i* as in *police*, *o* as in *atom*.

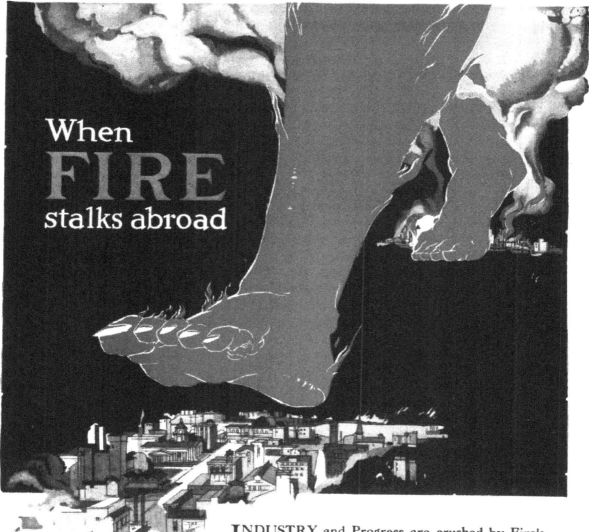

When FIRE stalks abroad

INDUSTRY and Progress are crushed by Fire's relentless feet. Its pathway is marked by smoldering ruins, halted production, and lost revenue. **Fire dangers always threaten but may be largely eliminated when proper precautions and care obtain.**

The Hartford Fire Insurance Company offers to make good the loss of property or of its use when caused by fire. Business quickly resumes its regular course when protected by a "Hartford" policy.

In addition the "Hartford" gives the service of trained fire prevention engineers to policy-holders who are willing to co-operate in eliminating fire dangers.

There is a "Hartford" agent near you. Ask him for information or write directly to the Company.

Hartford Fire Insurance Co.

Hartford Conn.

The Hartford Fire Insurance Co. and The Hartford Accident and Indemnity Co. write practically every form of insurance except life

Colored Map Showing Density of Population in U. S.

Per Square Mile, by Counties and States, According to New Census

MARSHAL FERDINAND FOCH

New York FUNK & WAGNALLS COMPANY *London*

PUBLIC OPINION *New York* combined with *The* LITERARY DIGEST

Kuppenheimer
GOOD CLOTHES

THIS SEASON Kuppenheimer Good Clothes give you everything—fine style, perfect fit, excellent fabrics at prices one-third less than last year. *A real investment in good appearance.*

The HOUSE *of* KUPPENHEIMER · *Chicago*

Just as the advertisement predicted

Depending on miracles

MOTHER leaves them with a sigh of relief. She takes it for granted the school is safe. She knows it has fire drills. She has seen its fire escapes.

She never thinks, any more than the school and city authorities, what a miracle it is when a fire drill in actual fire works as it does in practice!

But isn't it a miracle for children to keep a drill when unchecked flames are pouring up from the basement, cutting off the stairs, filling the building with stifling gases and smoke; flames bursting out windows and across fire escapes?

Isn't it a miracle under real fire conditions like these that children do not always break into a wild panic that crushes and maims them even before fire destroys?

The way to make a fire drill a certainty—not a miracle—is to put the fire out when it starts—automatically! This is what a sprinkler system does.

Read *"Fire Tragedies and Their Remedy"*

The Grinnell Sprinkler System insures the protection of your precious children's lives. It works automatically. When the fire starts, the water starts. In our booklet, "Fire Tragedies and Their Remedy," we have endeavored to show you just what penalty has been paid by the people who thought, "Tomorrow will be time enough," or who didn't think at all. Send us a postal card and the book is yours by return mail. It talks to you when you have time to listen. Address, Grinnell Company, Inc., 278 West Exchange Street, Providence, R.I.

GRINNELL COMPANY

Complete Engineering and Construction Service on Automatic Sprinklers, Industrial Piping, Heating and Power Equipments. Fittings, Pipe, Valves.

GRINNELL AUTOMATIC SPRINKLER SYSTEM—*When the fire starts, the water starts.*

Reproduction of an advertisement published last year in national magazines

ROCHESTER DEMOCRAT AND CHRONICLE

TWO CHILDREN LOSE LIVES WHEN LYONS UNION SCHOOL IS DESTROYED

Girls Who Were in Gymnasium Floor When Fire Broke Out While Others Had to Fl...

STEADY DOWNPOUR SAV... AS SPARKS FALL IN ...

ROCHESTER TIMES-UNION

Two Girls Die In Fire In Lyons High School; Building a Fire Trap

Fire Escapes Difficult of Access From Interior ...

ROCHESTER TIMES UNION: FRIDAY, DECEMBER 24, 1920.

BODIES OF LYONS GIRL FIRE VICTIMS FOUND TODAY IN RUINS OF SCHOOL

(SPECIAL TO THE TIMES-UNION.)

Lyons, Dec. 24.—(Noon)—Workmen engaged in searching the ruins of the Lyons Union School this noon came across the remains of the body of one or both of the two girls who lost their lives in the fire Wednesday evening. Searchers were not certain whether the little pile of bones and crisp flesh was of one or both of the two girls, Elizabeth Borne and Helen Belfert. A buckle found with the bones is believed to have been from the coat of one of the girls and will be used as a means of identification. The position of the remains of the bodies in the ruins clearly indicated that the girls had managed to make their way to the north wall of the ...

Photo by L. S. Lake, Lyons, N. Y.

How many Civics Clubs dance?

DOES your Civics Club depend on miracles—and *dance?*

Read this newspaper clipping of the Lyons, N. Y., school tragedy:

> "Owing to the tragedy, officers of the Lyons Civics Club *unanimously* voted to abandon the annual ball. . . . . This action was taken, club officials assert, as an expression of their feeling of *responsibility for not having protested* against existing conditions in Union School that made possible the gruesome tragedy."

The fire drill, the cool headedness of Lavinia Stoever, teacher, and the heroism of Janitor Eckerts could not save two little girls who ran back to the fire escape and perished while trying to open the window.

Civics Clubs can discharge their full responsibility by insisting on Automatic Sprinklers in every school and hospital. This is the one means that offsets all the dangers of old construction and of carelessness in management.

Fire escapes and structural changes do not discharge responsibility because they do not insure safety.

Read "*Fire Tragedies and Their Remedy.*"

"Fire Tragedies and Their Remedy" shows you just what penalty has been paid by the people who thought "Tomorrow will be time enough." Send for your free copy *today*. Address Grinnell Company, Inc., 274 West Exchange St., Providence, R.I.

GRINNELL

AUTOMATIC SPRINKLER SYSTEM

When the fire starts, the water starts

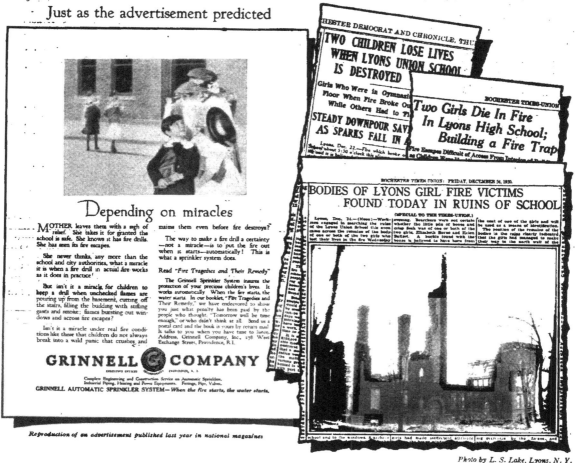

TABLE OF CONTENTS

TOPICS OF THE DAY: Page

- Are Rail Pay and Rates Blockading Good Times? . . . 7
- Density of Our Population. . . . 11
- Disarmament Not To Be Overdone . . . 12
- The Right to Criticise Chicago . . . 13
- On the Job to Make More Jobs . . . 14
- Silesian Riches Given to Poland . . . 16
- Topics in Brief . . . 17

FOREIGN COMMENT:

- Franco-German Team-Work Amid the Ruins . . . 18
- Famine Testing Lenine . . . 19
- The Greco-Turk Tug-of-War . . . 20
- Geography of China's Politics . . . 21

SCIENCE AND INVENTION:

- Is the Panama Canal Too Small? . . . 22
- To Treat Railway Cars More Gently . . . 23
- Dangers of Some Common Things . . . 23
- Getting Ready for Next Time at Pueblo . . . 24
- Seeing the Earth Move . . . 24
- Selling Land with Air Views . . . 25
- Coloring Oranges Orange . . . 25

LETTERS AND ART: Page

- America's Love for Dante To-Day and Yesterday . . . 26
- More Books and Less Bread for Devastated France . . . 27
- Half-Price for Half-Length Art . . . 28
- Our Resentment of Criticism . . . 29

RELIGION AND SOCIAL SERVICE:

- The Procession to the Vatican . . . 30
- The Church's Return to Drama . . . 31
- To Put the Bible in the Schools by Court Order . . . 32
- Claptrap in the Pulpit . . . 32

MISCELLANEOUS:

- Current Poetry . . . 34
- National American Speech Week . . . 36
- Personal Glimpses . . . 38-42
- Review of New Books . . . 43-49
- Investments and Finance . . . 50-51
- Current Events . . . 52-53
- The Spice of Life . . . 54-55

TERMS: $4.00 a year, in advance; six months, $2.25; three months, $1.50; single copy, 10 cents; postage to Canada, 85 cents a year; other foreign postage, $2.00 a year. BACK NUMBERS, not over three months old, 25 cents each; over three months old, $1.00 each. QUARTERLY INDEXES will be sent free to subscribers who apply for them. RECEIPT of payment is shown in about two weeks by date on address-label; date of expiration includes the month named on the label. CAUTION: If date is not properly extended after each payment, notify publishers promptly. Instructions for RENEWAL, DISCONTINUANCE, or CHANGE OF ADDRESS should be sent *two weeks* before the date they are to go into effect.

Both old and new addresses must always be given. PRESENTATION COPIES: Many persons subscribe for friends. Those who desire to renew such subscriptions must do so before expiration.

THE LITERARY DIGEST is published weekly by the Funk & Wagnalls Company, 354-360 Fourth Avenue, New York, and Salisbury Square, London, E. C.

Entered as second-class matter, March 24, 1890, at the Post-office at New York, N. Y., under the act of March 3, 1879.

Entered as second-class matter at the Post-office Department, Ottawa, Canada.

"It's the Chief Factor in Steady Growth of Our 1921 Sales"

L. H. Lewis Co. Dallas.

SOME firms are selling *more* this year than last! There's the L. H. Lewis Co. (Jobbers), Dallas. When business slowed up months ago they accepted our FREE trial offer. Now they write—

"We attribute the *steady growth* of our business since January 1st to the Addressograph."

Startling changes in selling methods are noticeable everywhere. The *increased use* of the Addressograph by small firms and large corporations for winning business is amazing. The following results prove that YOU, no matter what your business—can profit by trying the Addressograph FREE.

"Addressograph has so *increased* our business, do not see how we have done without it so long."—Kay-Dee Co. (Filing Devices), Lincoln, Nebr.

"Our *extraordinary growth* in 1921, due in great part to our Addressograph-ed direct mail advertising."—Van Den Berg Bros. (Furniture), Grand Rapids.

"Addressograph has *increased* our 1921 business over 1920."—Bert L. Daily Co., Dayton (Painter's Supplies).

Direct advertising is *easy!* You can get accurate, profitable lists of names at small cost or we will tell you how to compile your list with little effort.

FREE Trial Shows How You Can Sell More

SMALL cost of Addressograph for *increasing* your sales will *surprise* you. "Paying for it as you sell *more*" will *please* you! Free Trial will *convince* you! Mail the coupon *NOW* and *increase* your sales! No obligation—Just *good* business!

2 New Books to Help You Sell

—free with coupon

1—*"Mailing Lists—Their Preparation, Care and Uses."—By C. P. Ufford; Mailing List Expert, Goodrich Rubber Co.*

2—*"How Live Sales Promotion Puts the Sharp Edge on Dull Business." By A. J. Reiss, Sales Promotion Expert.*

Addressograph

TRADE MARK

PRINTS FROM TYPE

General Offices: 915 Van Buren St., Chicago Factories: Chicago, Brooklyn, London

Allentown, Albany, Atlanta, Birmingham, Baltimore, Boston, Buffalo, Butte, Chicago, Cincinnati, Cleveland, Dallas, Denver, Des Moines, Detroit, Duluth, El Paso, Grand Rapids, Houston, Indianapolis, Kansas City, Los Angeles, Minneapolis, Newark, New Orleans, New York, Omaha, Philadelphia, Pittsburgh, Portland, Salt Lake City, San Antonio, San Francisco, Seattle, Spokane, St. Louis, St. Paul, Syracuse, Toledo, Washington

Canada: 60 West Front Street, TORONTO—Vancouver—Montreal—Winnipeg—Calgary

FREE Trial Shows How You Can Sell More

MAIL WITH YOUR LETTERHEAD

To Addressograph Co., 915 Van Buren St., Chicago, Ill.

☐ SEND ON APPROVAL Hand Operated Ribbon Print Addressograph for 10 days free trial. If we don't buy, we will return it at your expense.

☐ HAVE SALESMAN DEMONSTRATE the Addressograph he carries with him.

☐ SEND SAMPLE 1c Blank Plate.

☐ SEND BOOK No. 1

☐ SEND BOOK No. 2

(10-29)

EAT AND BE WELL

A condensed set of health rules—many of which may be easily followed right in your own home, or while traveling. You will find in this little book a wealth of information about food elements and their relation to physical welfare; also effective weight control diets, acid and bland diets, laxative and blood-building diets, and diets used in the correction of various chronic maladies.

DIET BOOK SENT FREE

The book is for FREE circulation. Not a mail order advertisement. Name and address on card will bring it without cost or obligation.

Health Extension Bureau
64 Good Health Building
BATTLE CREEK MICH.

HIGHER EDUCATION

Courses in English, Spanish, Mathematics, Chemistry, Drawing, Education, Business and in 35 other subjects are given by correspondence. Begin any time.

The University of Chicago
30th Year Division 9, Chicago, Ill.

Learn to Dance

I CAN TEACH YOU, Fox-Trot, One-Step, Two-Step, Waltz and newest "up-to-the-minute" society dances in a few hours at home—in private by the wonderful

Peak System of Mail Instruction

REMARKABLE NEW METHOD. Easy—fascinating. RESULTS GUARANTEED. No music—no partner needed. Thousands taught successfully.

WRITE ME TODAY for my interesting FREE BOOK! Special low offer if you answer at once.

WILLIAM CHANDLER PEAK, M. B.
Studio 668 4737 Broadway Chicago, Ill.

CHICAGO, LOCK BOX 239 X
Lincoln-Jefferson University HOME STUDY
in Academy, College, Theological, Law, Music, Pharmacy, Business and Graduate schools leading to degrees.

AUTUMN ANNOUNCEMENT of THE LITERARY DIGEST SCHOOL and COLLEGE SERVICE

LITERARY DIGEST readers seeking educational advantages will find in our pages in 1922 a selection of military and non-military schools, girls' schools and colleges, co-educational schools (academic), vocational and professional schools, special schools, summer schools, and camps for boys and girls under expert direction in all athletic and outdoor sports.

From May 13th to September 9th, 1922, we shall publish a Classified Directory containing the names and addresses of many noted Educational Institutions. In the FIRST ISSUE of EACH MONTH—MAY to SEPTEMBER, inclusive—there will appear illustrated or descriptive copy of the schools. Our readers will be invited to correspond with the heads of these schools who are training the youth of our country.

The School Advisory Department continues to serve as it has for many years readers and schools without fee or obligation. All requests for educational information should be very explicit and must be written. We can give no advice by telephone.

The Literary Digest

WILL POWER AND WORK

by Jules Payot, Litt.D., Ph.D.

Authorized Translation from the French by Richard Duffy

(FIRST AMERICAN EDITION)

More than thirty editions of this author's previous work, "Education of the Will," have passed into the hands of forward-looking Americans, to their everlasting benefit. In this NEW volume, "Will Power and Work," M. Payot shows you how to increase your mental efficiency, how to intensify your power of accomplishment, how to link your will to your work. In a manner irresistibly helpful, you are given the theory and practise of self-culture.

You are shown how to read systematically and intelligently, how to build up a dependable memory, how to obtain control of that strangely uncertain instrument, the will, and how to supplement the lack or rightly assimilate the surplus of education that fate has decreed for you. As a clear, sympathetic, and authoritative guide to true wisdom, strength of character, and the development of that practical energy which makes for real success in life, this new book will be a boon to you.

Cloth, 12mo. 462 pages
At all booksellers, $1.75; by mail $1.87

FUNK & WAGNALLS COMPANY, 354-360 Fourth Ave., New York

A DICTIONARY OF NAPOLEON AND HIS TIMES

By Hubert N. B. Richardson, B. A.

A veritable treasure-house of information for the student of Napoleana and the general reader alike! In popular yet exact form, and with surprizing completeness, this incomparable work gives you a digest in dictionary style of all that has been written regarding Napoleon and the numerous satellites who circled around him.

Facts Revealed By Recent Research Included

Particulars of the personality of Napoleon and all that recent research has discovered regarding him is incorporated. The military, commercial, political, and artistic developments of his reign; biographical matter relating to his family from the earliest recorded member thereof down to its latest scion; his habits and idiosyncrasies; the great leaders who served or failed him; his more private life; the women he loved; and the contemporaries who set down their reminiscences of him—all are included in this work.

Gives a General Survey of the Napoleonic Period

This indispensable volume throws light on the social and political tendencies of his time, its art, literature, and industries. The military career of the emperor is fully treated. The various memoirs of Napoleon's life have been summarized and reviewed at length, many for the first time: a Chronological Table dealing with every important event in the Emperor's life and time has been added, as has also a select Classified Bibliography giving all the more useful, authoritative, and accessible books on Napoleon's career.

Crown 8vo; 496 pages; with maps, plans, and a chronological table. Price $7.00; postpaid $7.16

FUNK & WAGNALLS CO., 354-360 Fourth Ave., N. Y.

Highly Commended

"This book is alive with the essential spirit of romance—the allure of the unknown and untried, the subtle charm lent by the imagination, the experience of the joy of discovery, which is the experiencing of a beauty first felt in the mind and heart of the discoverer.

The veteran author's memories are recounted with beauty and vividness, but they are memories which hold alive and bright only the essentials of experience—the happiness, the fancy, the emotion of it." —*From The Sierra Club Bulletin.*

"Finally, 'Mountain Memories' may be pointed to as another instance which proves that devotion to the mountains and proficiency in alpinism stand for something more than eccentric enthusiasm and gymnastic prowess." —*From The Bulletin of the Geographical Society of Philadelphia.*

". . . The very reading of it will leave a permanent imprint—a fuller and richer life." —*From The Mountaineer.*

"A Pilgrimage of Romance"

The massed majesty of towering heights—the magnificence of mile after mile of jagged rocks boldly contrasted with glittering snow and ice, gigantic glaciers, majestic trees, velvety plains and roaring cataracts—the thrills of standing on the very heights of the world—all are vividly described for you by an eminent man who writes of his 30 years of mountaineering as a romance in a volume entitled

MOUNTAIN MEMORIES

By Sir Martin Conway, M.P., Litt.D., V.-Pres. S.A., V.-Pres. R.G.S., ex-Pres. Alpine Club, etc. Splendidly illustrated with 16 full-page half-tones of mountain scenery. 282 pages, 6¼" wide, 9½" high, 2" thick. Handsomely bound in maroon cloth. Title, etc., embossed in gold.

Not with the coldness and preciseness of a guide-book, but warmly, vividly, as an enthusiast reminiscent in the evening before a log fire—thus has the author given to you his clear impressions of not only the mountains, but the lakes, forests, the desert, the sea, the peoples and places which he has seen in his several decades of mountain climbing. He takes you to the Alps, the Himalayas, the Bolivian Andes, the peaks of Spitzenbergen and Fuegia—farthest north and farthest south to heights in lands where the explorer seldom adventures. And, through it all, he radiates a delightfully human philosophy which lends a mellowed atmosphere of exquisite charm to the entire book. *Price $5.00 postpaid.*

FUNK & WAGNALLS COMPANY, 354 Fourth Ave., New York

Lively Tales From La Grand Corniche

Most travelers write about places. Sir Frederick Treves, Bart., writes entertainingly about picturesque people—men and women who are famous (or startlingly infamous) for something; and who have lived and "flourished" and left their impress, good or bad, on the world.

NICE: A Street

Sir Frederick's new book, "The Riviera of the Corniche Road," is of stirring, gripping interest to everybody, especially to the thousands of American tourists who have been, or who expect to go, to Southern France for this memorable Corniche Road jaunt.

Like Sir Frederick's other books, "The Other Side of the Lantern," and "The Country of the Ring and the Book," the new work is *in no sense* a mere record of travel; it is *full of startling revelations of the past*—stories of romance, love, hate, jealousy, deceit, plunder or murder, in the old towns along the Grand Corniche Road.

REVELATIONS OF A EUROPEAN JAUNT.

For instance, you read private details in the sensational career of Jeanne, the beautiful and passionate queen of Naples, ending with her strangulation. You learn the touching romance of how Blanche d'Entrevannes, the beautiful nun of St. Pons, happened to elope and marry; how Madam Ugly Face saved Nice in the siege; how Gaspard de Caïs betrayed the impregnable town of Eze; how Claudine of Monaco, aged twelve, had to listen to marriage proposals; how a philanthropic princess gave her silver leg to the Laghet Convent; how an aboriginal woman at Mentone lived in a chilly cave seventy years without rheumatism. There are hundreds of droll incidents.

MENTONE: A Doorway

In whatever place you pause with Sir Frederick in "The Riviera of the Corniche Road" he shows you photographs of leading structures, while you listen to the tales he has to tell about remarkable people.

You will read this book with real relish, *over and over again.* Illustrated with ninety-two engravings from photographs by the author.

CROWN 8VO. 326 PP. $6, NET; POSTPAID, $6.16. BOOKSTORES, OR

Funk & Wagnalls Company, 354-360 Fourth Avenue, New York

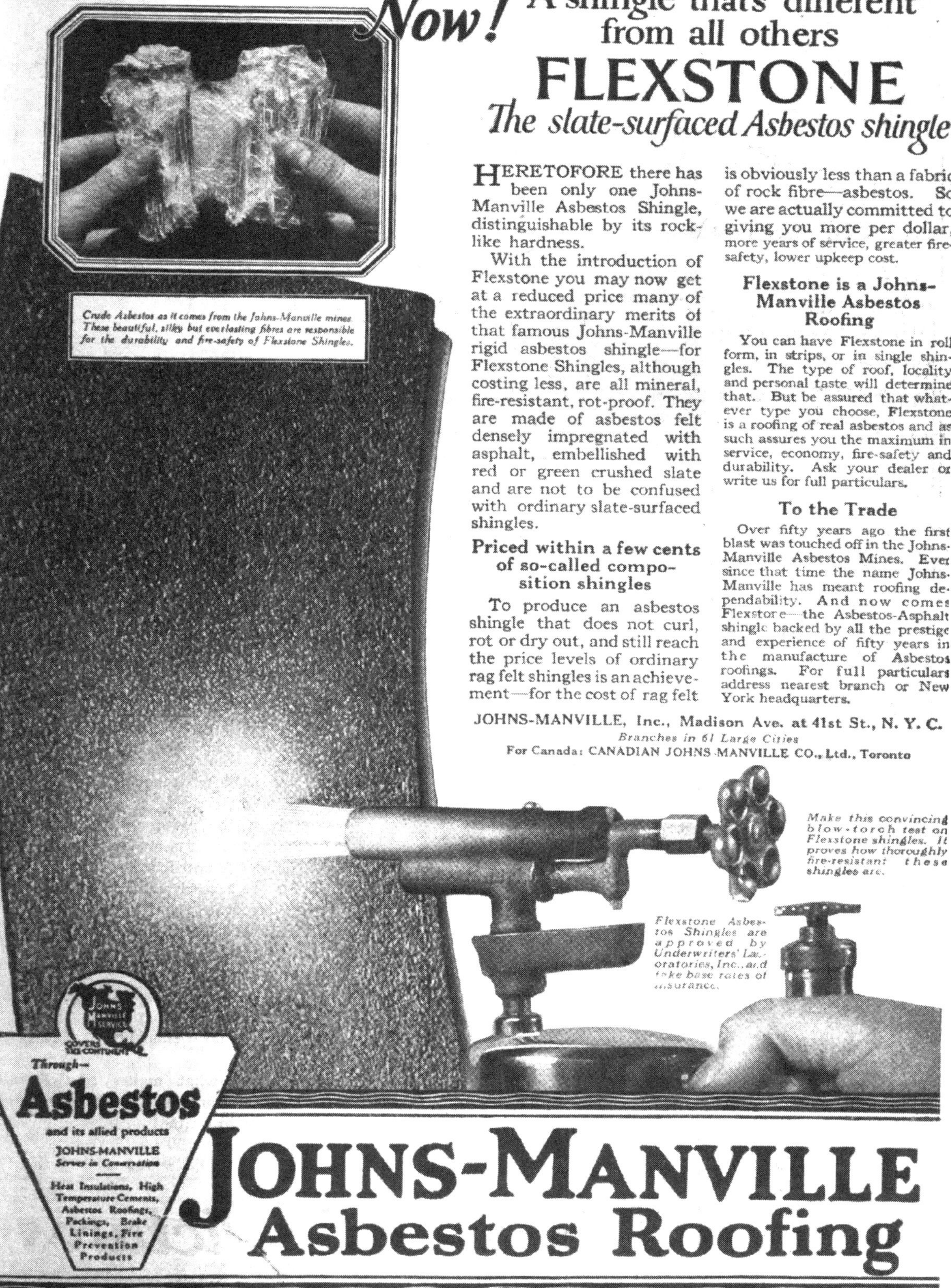

Now! A shingle that's different from all others
FLEXSTONE
The slate-surfaced Asbestos shingle
Crude Asbestos as it comes from the Johns-Manville mines. These beautiful, silky but everlasting fibres are responsible for the durability and fire-safety of Flexstone Shingles.
HERETOFORE there has been only one Johns-Manville Asbestos Shingle, distinguishable by its rock-like hardness.
With the introduction of Flexstone you may now get at a reduced price many of the extraordinary merits of that famous Johns-Manville rigid asbestos shingle—for Flexstone Shingles, although costing less, are all mineral, fire-resistant, rot-proof. They are made of asbestos felt densely impregnated with asphalt, embellished with red or green crushed slate and are not to be confused with ordinary slate-surfaced shingles.
Priced within a few cents of so-called composition shingles
To produce an asbestos shingle that does not curl, rot or dry out, and still reach the price levels of ordinary rag felt shingles is an achievement—for the cost of rag felt is obviously less than a fabric of rock fibre—asbestos. So we are actually committed to giving you more per dollar, more years of service, greater fire-safety, lower upkeep cost.
Flexstone is a Johns-Manville Asbestos Roofing
You can have Flexstone in roll form, in strips, or in single shingles. The type of roof, locality and personal taste will determine that. But be assured that whatever type you choose, Flexstone is a roofing of real asbestos and as such assures you the maximum in service, economy, fire-safety and durability. Ask your dealer or write us for full particulars.
To the Trade
Over fifty years ago the first blast was touched off in the Johns-Manville Asbestos Mines. Ever since that time the name Johns-Manville has meant roofing dependability. And now comes Flexstone—the Asbestos-Asphalt shingle backed by all the prestige and experience of fifty years in the manufacture of Asbestos roofings. For full particulars address nearest branch or New York headquarters.
JOHNS-MANVILLE, Inc., Madison Ave. at 41st St., N. Y. C.
Branches in 61 Large Cities
For Canada: CANADIAN JOHNS-MANVILLE CO., Ltd., Toronto
Make this convincing blow-torch test on Flexstone shingles. It proves how thoroughly fire-resistant these shingles are.
Flexstone Asbestos Shingles are approved by Underwriters' Laboratories, Inc., and take base rates of insurance.
JOHNS MANVILLE SERVICE
COVERS THE CONTINENT
Through—
Asbestos
and its allied products
JOHNS-MANVILLE
Serves in Conservation
Heat Insulations, High Temperature Cements, Asbestos Roofings, Packings, Brake Linings, Fire Prevention Products
JOHNS-MANVILLE
Asbestos Roofing

THE LITERARY DIGEST

PUBLIC OPINION (New York) combined with THE LITERARY DIGEST

Published by Funk & Wagnalls Company (Adam W. Wagnalls, Pres.; Wilfred J. Funk, Vice-Pres.; Robert J. Cuddihy, Treas.; William Neisel, Sec'y) 354-360 Fourth Ave., New York

Vol. LXXI, No 5 New York, October 29, 1921 Whole Number 1645

TOPICS - OF - THE - DAY

(Title registered in U S Patent Office for use in this publication and on moving picture films)

ARE RAIL PAY AND RATES BLOCKADING GOOD TIMES?

THE APPALLING THREAT of a nation-wide strike of railroad workers seems to have brought home to the public, if the newspapers are any index of public feeling, a conviction that high freight rates and high railway wages unite to form the most serious remaining obstacle in the path of returning prosperity. For, as the San Diego *Union* remarks, "at the present moment our best hope, perhaps our only hope, of readjustment to normal conditions is in the assurance of the utmost facility of distribution." When the Railroad Brotherhoods issued their call for a strike, to begin on October 30, it brought from the press of the country a virtually unanimous denunciation of a move which they regarded as, in effect, a "strike against prosperity" and a "declaration of war against the public." But many of them, in placing the blame for this crisis, accused the railroads as well as their men of considering self-interest before the public good.

Thus the Jersey City *Journal* is not alone in suggesting that the railroad executives proposed additional wage cuts with the deliberate purpose of provoking a strike, knowing that it could never come at a worse time for the strikers, and that one result would be to crush or cripple the powerful railroad unions. "There would be no danger of a strike if the railroad executives and the railroad labor organizations were obeying and intending to obey the law," remarks the Washington *Post*. "It is no longer a matter for dispute, but a plain fact, that railroad rates and railroad wages are both abnormally high," avers the Nashville *Banner*. Railroad wages, the same paper continues, "are abnormal with either pre-war wages or the present cost of living as a standard." "Freight rates must come down if the country is to go ahead, and wages must come down to permit rates to come down," declares the Tacoma *Ledger*, which argues that, since living costs have come down and workers in other important industries have accepted wage cuts, "the railroad workers are claiming what amounts to a preferred position, and any such claim is untenable."

BOTH: "HE'S TALKING TO YOU!"
— Knott in the Dallas *News*.

"Freight rates ought to come down at once," declares the Columbus *Ohio State Journal*, which thinks that "such a concession by the railroad managers would do much to stimulate general business and almost certainly would prove of direct financial advantage to the railroads themselves, as it surely would to the general public." But, it adds, "however stubborn and wrong-headed the railroad corporations might be on this point, popular sentiment would never support a strike of 2,000,000 men on their present grievances while two or three times that number are already unwillingly idle." "A reduction in freight rates would make a better feeling both with the men and with the people generally, and in the end the greater volume of business would mean greater profits to all the railroads," says the Cheyenne *Tribune Leader*. "Railroad freight rates have got to come down or we shall never reestablish American commerce," argues the Grand Rapids *Herald*, which however, adds this word of warning to the Brotherhoods: "To strike against this 12 per cent. reduction, at a time when millions of jobless workers are suffering a 100 per cent. reduction, would be to strike against immutable economic law." The public has not much sympathy with the railroads in this controversy, declares the Milwaukee *Journal*. Nor, it adds, is there any public sympathy "for any set of men who propose to make a terrible condition worse." "The agricultural bloc in Congress wants railway rates reduced, Secretary Hoover of the Department of Commerce wants them reduced, and the public wants them reduced," says the New York *Herald;* and the New York *Globe* adds the President's Conference on Unemployment to the list.

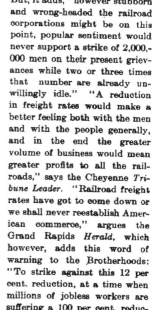

President Harding himself, according to Mark Sullivan's

Washington correspondence in the New York *Evening Post,* "is believed to hold that there should be both a reduction in freight rates and also a reduction in railroad wages." To quote further:

"The two constitute a cycle, and the only embarrassment the President has had was which of the two should come first. It would seem to be likely that he will take advantage of the present situation to bring about the two simultaneously."

This idea of simultaneous reduction in rates and wages is also advanced by two Texas papers. "The present rates of transportation are ruinous to productive industry and business; they must be substantially reduced, and a reduction of wages must come simultaneously," declares the Houston *Post;* and in the Dallas *Journal* we read:

SOMEBODY WILL BE THERE TO GRAB THE FRUIT.

—Knott in the Dallas *News.*

"Plainly the power to deal with both rates and wages ought to be lodged in a single body or else definitely coordinated. Railroad workers contend that lower rates should precede lower wages; railroad managers contend for a reversal of this program. There is no good reason why the reductions should not be simultaneous, nor is there any good reason why the removal of these humps in our economic structure should be postponed."

The charge that railroad labor asks to be treated as a privileged branch of the labor family seems to be sustained by the report of the Conference on Unemployment. According to a table of index figures prepared by the Conference "a general estimate of all union wage scales is about 89 points above the 1913 level," while "railway wages are 126 above." "The public," remarks the Hartford *Courant,* "does not look upon the railroad employee as poorly paid; there is no wide-spread feeling among the people that his face is being ground beneath the heel of a wealthy and unreasonable taskmaster." And the Utica *Press* cites the following figures:

"Before the Government took over the control of the roads the payroll was $1,468,576,394 while in 1920 it had grown to $3,698,216,351, hence it appears that as the result of the Adamson law the aggregate wages paid railroad employees increased $2,229,639,957. The cut of 12 per cent. ordered by the Labor Board to which the employees object and against which they propose to strike reduces the aggregate payroll less than half a billion dollars which is less than 25 per cent. of the increase in war times."

The railroads, on the other hand, complain that their expenses have for years been increasing faster than their revenues. The following long-range survey of the freight rate situation is presented by Julius Kruttschnitt, Chairman of the Executive Committee of the Southern Pacific Railroad:

"About 1905 wholesale prices of commodities and the rates of railway wages began climbing, until in May 1920, they reached a summit never before dreamed of. In the same year, 1905, railway freight rates began falling, and, continuing uninteruptedly, reached the lowest level in seventeen years in 1916 and 1917.

"The Federal Railroad Administration made a substantial rate increase in June, 1918, which, however, fell far short of establishing any proper relation between freight rates and costs of commodities.

"The Federal Labor Board, by a decision made effective in May, 1920, increased wages an average of 21 per cent., raising them to a level 240 per cent. above those of 1900; wholesale price were also 240 per cent. higher than in 1900, while freight rates were but 30 per cent. higher.

"The rate increase finally authorized by the Interstate Commerce Commission about the first of September, 1920, raised freight rates to a level only 59 per cent. higher than in 1900; wholesale prices then had fallen, but were still 203 per cent. higher than in 1900, while railway wages remained 240 per cent. higher. All industries except railroads (which under strict regulation were restrained from doing so) raised prices currently as costs went up, so that when at last the 1920 rate increase was granted, further increased expenses and the cost of disorganization under Federal control more than wiped out the increase. . . .

"A wide-spread propaganda is being carried on in favor of a general reduction of freight rates; whereas the fact is that ever since the rates have been advanced the cost of transporting a great many commodities which it is asserted cannot move at the increased rates is far less than the toll taken by commission merchants and retailers for buying and selling them. People are misled into believing that high rates have stopt the movement of a large amount of freight, and that the railways would make more money if they would reduce rates and thereby revive traffic.

"There is the strongest reason to believe that the great stagnation in business is due almost entirely to world-wide conditions which must inevitably have come if there had been no advance in freight rates.

"We have shown that the policy of the Government for many years was not to raise rates in normal or good times sufficiently to yield adequate revenues, and if rates are now to be lowered on account of bad times where will this leave the railroads?"

In an editorial in the *Railway Age* (New York) we read:

When the railways appealed to the Railroad Labor Board last spring for a reduction of wages they emphasized the fact that it was needed to save a large part of the companies from insolvency. Since the wage reduction on July 1 there has been a substantial increase in the net return earned. But the largest monthly net returns earned have not been equal in any month to the net return which it was expected the railways would earn every month under the present rates.

"It became evident, however, that the railways must heed the constantly increasing public demand for a general reduction of rates. Therefore, they decided upon the plan of asking for a further reduction of wages, and of giving a definite pledge that the benefit of any reduction of wages obtained would be given to the public in reductions of rates. . . .

"The whole argument for early reductions in railway rates is based on the proposition that it is needed to relieve industry of a heavy burden and help promote a revival of general business. The railways, however, are one of the most important industries in the country. A general reduction of rates without a corresponding reduction of wages would postpone indefinitely the time when they could begin to rehabilitate their properties and increase their purchases from other industries. If the reduction in rates were substantial it would financially ruin many railway companies. Would the indefinite postponement of an increase in purchases by the railways, and the financial ruin of many companies, promote a revival of business? On the contrary,

READY TO TAKE THEIR BREAD AND BUTTER AWAY FROM THEM.

—Walker in the New York *Call*

"AND NOW HERE YOU ARE AGAIN!"

—Alley in the Memphis *Commercial Appeal.*

OPPOSITE IDEAS OF WHO IS GRABBING.

nothing could be better adapted to protracting the business depression. . . .

"The railways are sure to be severely criticized in many quarters for refusing voluntarily to reduce their rates without a corresponding reduction of wages. Their position is, however, entirely defensible, not only from the standpoint of the rights of their owners, but also from the standpoint of the welfare of the public. There are intimations given that unless, regardless of whether there is a further reduction of wages, they soon make a voluntary reduction of rates, measures will be adopted to force them to reduce their rates. This means that the railways are invited to commit suicide, and told that if they do not do so they will be murdered. The presentation of such an alternative leaves the railways but one choice, and that is to refuse to commit suicide and find out whether, because of their refusal, they really will be murdered. If they must be ruined, it is not the function of their managers to ruin them. Their managers should let others do it, and then let those who do it assume the responsibility for the consequences."

A radiogram from Robert E. Thayer, London editor of *The Railway Age*, reports that to American business men in Europe "it seems inconceivable that American labor is so utterly ignorant of the world's economic conditions as to even think of fighting the present wage reduction." "Have our men at home grown to believe themselves so omnipotent that they still can demand cream which is but to fatten them for the slaughter?" asks Mr. Thayer; and he adds:

"Let them watch their step! They are no longer citizens of Pennsylvania, Illinois or California; they are citizens of the world. Their problems are no longer home problems, but world problems. They are not bucking the railways; they are bucking the world, the economic condition of which they seem to know but little about."

"No class, however powerful, can stem the economic forces which make for readjustment to normal conditions after the world upheaval of the war cataclysm," avers the Louisville *Courier-Journal*. "The persistency with which the Railway Brotherhoods fling this threat of a strike at the nation has become intensely irritating," remarks the Los Angeles *Express*, which suggests that—

"The fact might as well be determined now as at any time whether the whole body of the people are the rulers in America, or whether that small minority of the people embraced in the railway unions can assert a Hohenzollern sort of superiority over all the others and compel obedience to their will."

Turning to another group of critics, we find the New York *World* declaring that "the railroads have been whining around so long for public sympathy and government help as to have acquired the arrogance of the professional beggar along with his insistence"; and the Macon *Telegraph* avers that "the proposal of railway owners to further reduce the pay of employees was an error, unless it was for the purpose of forcing a strike." The Tulsa *World* also blames the railroads for "deliberately aggravating a situation which was by way of adjusting itself"; and the Raleigh *News and Observer* is convinced that the public "regards the further wage reduction by the railway executives as indefensible under the circumstances." In *Labor*, a Plumb Plan organ published in Washington, we find the position of the Brotherhoods defended and that of the railroads arraigned as follows:

"For more than a year and a half the railroad workers have been goaded and badgered by railroad executives, and if there is an interruption of transportation the responsibility will rest squarely with those officials who are charged with the responsibility of private operation of the railroads of the United States now seeking to establish a new and degrading industrial policy. Ten per cent. of the rate increase granted railroads was intended to cover the wage increase, but last July a large portion of the wage increase was taken from labor; but there was no corresponding rate decrease accompanying this cut in wages. It was estimated at that time that at least three hundred and sixty million dollars was saved to the railroads by that wage decrease. They now ask another decrease of three hundred million, with a promise to pass along to the public in lower rates the amount saved to the railways after recouping themselves for the losses inflicted by rate reductions already made. By the time they get through absorbing these reductions there seems to be very little left for the public. Isn't it time to deflate railway profits: to make investors in railroads bear the same risk and hazards that other private investors in other industries are required to bear? Is America ready to accept an industrial policy which protects the dollar at the expense of the man?"

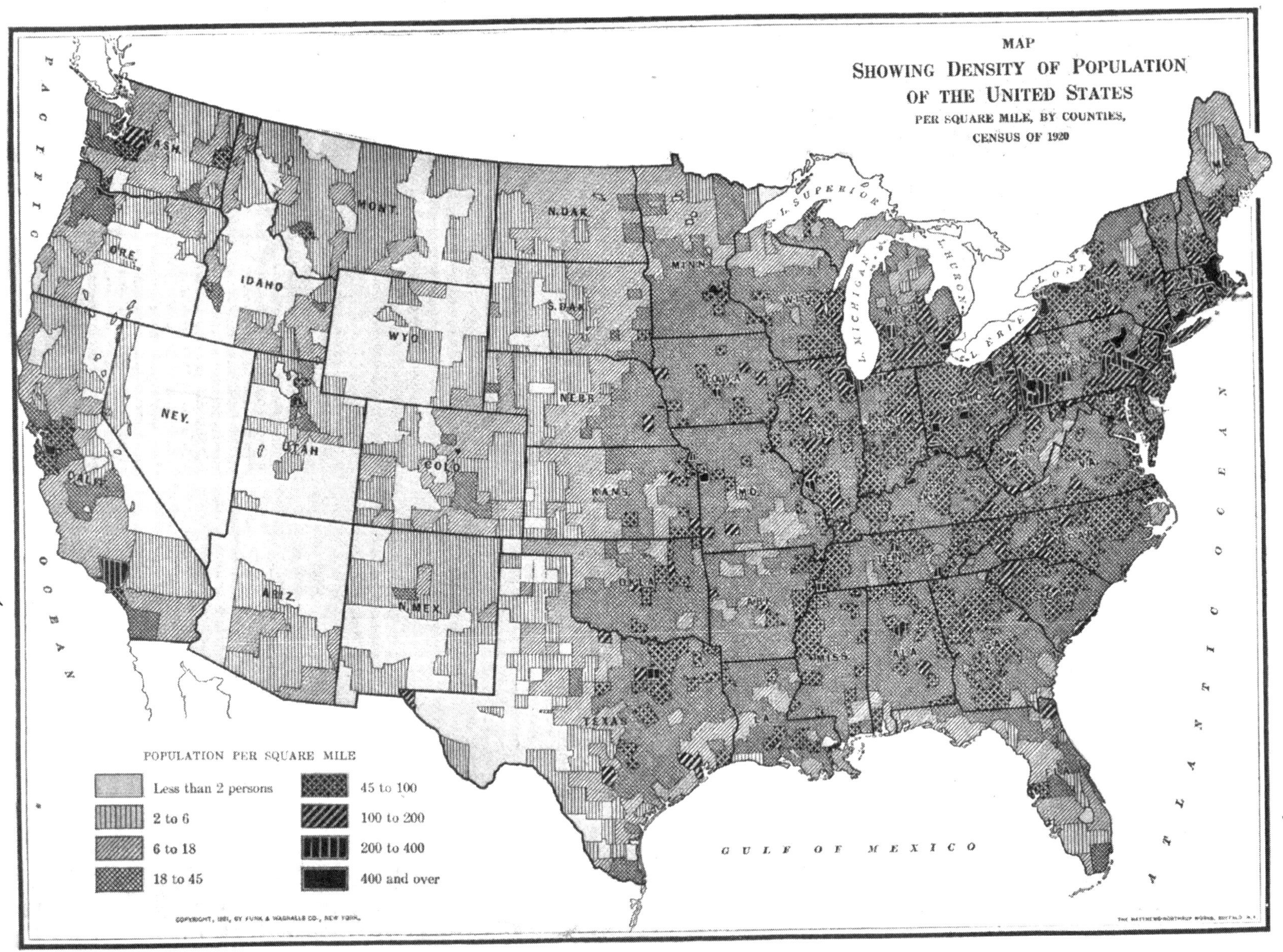
MAP
SHOWING DENSITY OF POPULATION
OF THE UNITED STATES
PER SQUARE MILE, BY COUNTIES,
CENSUS OF 1920
PACIFIC OCEAN
ATLANTIC OCEAN
GULF OF MEXICO
L. SUPERIOR
L. MICHIGAN
L. HURON
L. ERIE
L. ONT
WASH.
ORE.
CALIF.
IDAHO
NEV.
MONT.
WYO.
UTAH
ARIZ.
COLO.
N.MEX.
N.DAK.
S.DAK.
NEBR.
KANS.
OKLA.
TEXAS
MINN.
IOWA
MO.
ARK.
MICH.
OHIO
VA.
TENN.
MISS.
ALA.
GA.
FLA.
POPULATION PER SQUARE MILE
Less than 2 persons
2 to 6
6 to 18
18 to 45
45 to 100
100 to 200
200 to 400
400 and over

DENSITY OF OUR POPULATION

THOSE WHO THINK IT DESIRABLE that the American people should be more and more crowded may be pleased to learn from the census figures that we now have ten more persons per square mile than twenty years ago. In 1900 we had 25.6 persons per square mile; in 1920, 35.5. Another way of putting it is that in 1900 we had 25 acres per inhabitant, now we have 18 acres per inhabitant. Three of our States, Rhode Island, Massachusetts and New Jersey are approaching the crowded condition of England, Belgium and Holland. Those who deplore this increase will find their comfort in the fact that we still have one State, Nevada, with less than one person per square mile, a density less than any reported country in the world. Thus the Census meets all tastes. The accompanying maps and tables tell the whole story.

The small map shows the density of population per square mile, using the State as a unit, and the large full-page map, the density of population per square mile using the county as a unit. The latter, therefore, shows how the population is distributed inside of each State, and will tell each reader the density of his own county. We show 400 and over as the highest grade, in solid black. This takes in all counties in which there are large cities. Some of these counties have several thousand persons per square mile; for example, Philadelphia County, which is co-extensive with Philadelphia City, has 13,712 persons per square mile.

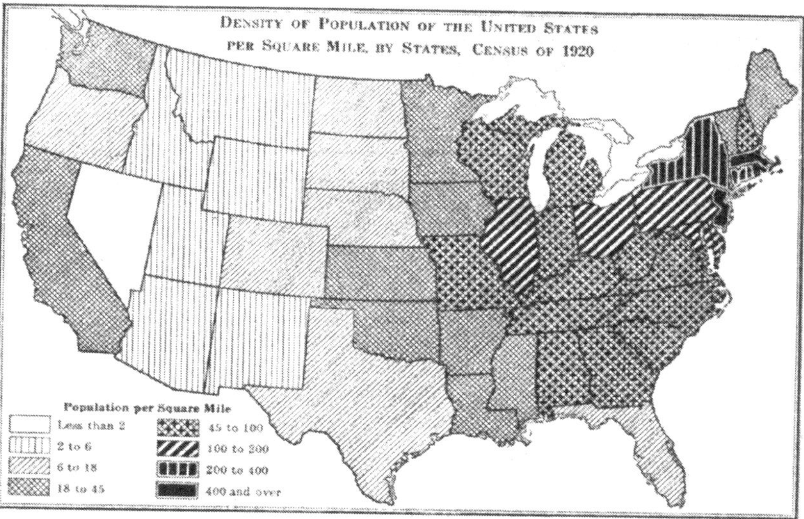

We give one table taken from the United States Census reports, giving the population, area and density per square mile, for divisions and States arranged geographically. Also, a table of the States arranged according to their density of population. For comparison we have placed the principal foreign countries, with their population per square mile, mostly taken from the 1921 edition of the Statesman's Year Book, alongside the States. Thus, Rhode Island, Massachusetts and New Jersey are nearly as thickly populated as England, Belgium and the Netherlands. Pennsylvania is more densely populated than France.

The Southern States are nearly all about the same density as Russia in Europe. The Mississippi Valley States east of the Mississippi have about the same average density of population as Czechoslovakia. The Mississippi Valley States west of the Mississippi compare with Sweden and Finland.

The Mountain States have an average of 3.9 persons per square mile. No country in Europe, and only Bolivia in South America, has as low a density.

The Pacific States have an average of 17.5 persons per square mile. This is less than Mexico with 19.2, and Norway with 19.1.

The average for the United States is 35.5, which is slightly higher than Sweden with 33.8 persons per square mile.

POPULATION PER SQUARE MILE

States	Pop. per sq. m.	Foreign Countries	Pop. per sq. m.
Rhode Island	566.4	England	669.2
Massachusetts	479.2	Belgium	652.7
New Jersey	420.0	Netherlands	542.9
Connecticut	286.4	Great Britain	481.9
New York	217.9	Japan	375.0
Pennsylvania	194.5	Germany	332.0
Maryland	145.8	Italy	326.5
Ohio	141.4	Japan Empire	300.1
Illinois	115.7	Switzerland	241.7
Delaware	113.5	Hungary	222.9
Indiana	81.3	Austria	196.8
Michigan	63.8	China	197.7
West Virginia	60.9	France	189.5
Kentucky	60.1	Denmark	188.7
Virginia	57.4	India	174.7
Tennessee	56.1	Poland	162.8
South Carolina	55.2	Scotland	156.5
North Carolina	52.5	Portugal	152.8
Missouri	49.5	Roumania	150.0
Georgia	49.3	Ireland	134.0
New Hampshire	49.1	Bulgaria	119.0
Wisconsin	47.6	Jugoslavia	118.5
Alabama	45.8	Spain	106.6
Iowa	43.2	Greece	105.0
Louisiana	39.6	Czechoslovakia	96.7
Mississippi	38.6	Albania	73.9
Vermont	38.6	Palestine	71.9
Arkansas	33.4	Russia in Europe	71.0
Minnesota	29.5	Cuba	65.3
Oklahoma	29.2	Turkey	54.4
Maine	25.7	Siam	45.2
California	22.0	Sweden	33.8
Kansas	21.6	Finland	26.0
Washington	20.3	Afghanistan	25.0
Texas	17.8	Iceland	21.0
Florida	17.7	Mexico	19.2
Nebraska	16.9	Uruguay	19.2
North Dakota	9.2	Norway	19.1
Colorado	9.1	Ecuador	17.2
South Dakota	8.3	Persia	15.1
Oregon	8.2	Chile	13.9
Utah	5.5	Paraguay	13.6
Idaho	5.2	Columbia	13.2
Montana	3.8	Brazil	9.3
Arizona	2.9	Venezuela	7.1
New Mexico	2.9	Argentine	6.8
Wyoming	2.0	Peru	6.6
Nevada	0.7	Bolivia	3.4
		Canada	2.0
U. S. Possessions		Siberia	2.0
Dist. of Col. (Wash.)	7,292.9	Australia	1.4
Porto Rico	378.4	Arabia	1.0
Virgin Islands	197.4		
Samoa	104.6		
Philippine Islands	90.0		
Panama Canal Zone	64.0		
Guam	63.2		
Hawaii	30.7		
Alaska	0.1		
United States	35.5		

POPULATON PER SQUARE MILE BY DIVISIONS AND STATES, 1920:

Division and State	Population	Area (sq. ms.)	Pop. per sq. mile
New England	7,400,909	61,976	119.4
Maine	768,014	29,895	25.7
New Hampshire	443,083	9,031	49.1
Vermont	352,428	9,124	38.6
Massachusetts	3,852,356	8,039	479.2
Rhode Island	604,397	1,067	566.4
Connecticut	1,380,631	4,820	286.4
Middle Atlantic	22,261,144	100,000	222.6
New York	10,385,227	47,654	217.9
New Jersey	3,155,900	7,514	420.0
Pennsylvania	8,720,017	44,832	194.5
East North Central	21,475,543	245,564	87.5
Ohio	5,759,394	40,740	141.4
Indiana	2,930,390	36,045	81.3
Illinois	6,485,280	56,043	115.7
Michigan	3,668,412	57,480	63.8
Wisconsin	2,632,067	55,256	47.6
West North Central	12,544,249	510,804	24.6
Minnesota	2,387,125	80,858	29.5
Iowa	2,404,021	55,586	43.2
Missouri	3,404,055	68,727	49.5
North Dakota	646,872	70,183	9.2
South Dakota	636,547	76,868	8.3
Nebraska	1,296,372	76,808	16.9
Kansas	1,769,257	81,774	21.6
South Atlantic	13,990,272	269,071	52.0
Delaware	223,003	1,965	113.5
Maryland	1,449,661	9,941	145.8
District of Columbia	437,571	60	7,292.9
Virginia	2,309,187	40,262	57.4
West Virginia	1,463,701	24,022	60.9
North Carolina	2,559,123	48,740	52.5
South Carolina	1,683,724	30,495	55.2
Georgia	2,895,832	58,725	49.3
Florida	968,470	54,861	17.7
East South Central	8,893,307	179,509	49.5
Kentucky	2,416,630	40,181	60.1
Tennessee	2,337,885	41,687	56.1
Alabama	2,348,174	51,279	45.8
Mississippi	1,790,618	46,362	38.6
West South Central	10,242,224	429,746	23.8
Arkansas	1,752,204	52,525	33.4
Louisiana	1,798,509	45,409	39.6
Oklahoma	2,028,283	69,414	29.2
Texas	4,663,228	262,398	17.8
Mountain	3,336,101	859,009	3.9
Montana	548,889	146,131	3.8
Idaho	431,866	83,354	5.2
Wyoming	194,402	97,548	2.0
Colorado	939,629	103,658	9.1
New Mexico	360,350	122,503	2.9
Arizona	334,162	113,810	2.9
Utah	449,396	82,184	5.5
Nevada	77,407	109,821	0.7
Pacific	5,566,871	318,095	17.5
Washington	1,356,621	66,836	20.3
Oregon	783,389	95,607	8.2
California	3,426,861	155,652	22.0

DISARMAMENT NOT TO BE OVERDONE

NUMEROUS GENTLE WARNINGS from Washington that the public should not expect too much from the coming Conference on the Limitation of Armament have not been received by everybody with that "sweet reasonableness" which many supporters of the Administration find in them. Indeed, these attempts to apply a mollifier to the peace-optimists and "idealists" of the country by an appeal for "practical measures" as against "undue hopes," have resulted, in certain quarters at least, in something more like a diapason of discords. Both Vice-President Coolidge and Secretary of State Hughes have issued warnings, but President Harding's reply to the letter of a member of the Citizens Disarmament Committee has brought the most wide-spread and immediate results. He argues for "a reasonable limitation," explaining—"By reasonable limitation I mean something practicable that there is a chance to accomplish, rather than an ideal that there would be no chance to realize. It is necessary to deal with actualities; to do the best possible."

"WE CAN'T MAKE IT IN ONE STEP!"

—Gale in the Los Angeles *Times*.

"Idealism is America's tradition and greatest hope," objects the Republican New York *Evening Mail*, whose editor finds in President Harding's latest reference to "practical policies" a misunderstanding of American psychology. And he adds: "We are not a practical people. The history of our nation runs counter to such a statement. Our traditions and our national life would lose all that is noblest and best in them if we were to turn aside from idealism because it is not practical. Had that been the line of reasoning followed from 1776 to 1781, there would have been no United States of America; had that been Lincoln's reasoning in dark and tragic periods throughout our war to achieve the ideal of human freedom, slavery would still exist on this continent." The Springfield *Republican* (Ind.) and the New York *Globe* (Ind.), also object to the "practical statesmanship" which emanates from Washington. "If we were to interpret the words 'reasonable limitation' in the light of experience and diplomatic tradition," observes *The Republican*, "the reduction of armaments brought about will not be noticed perhaps by the taxpayers." This editor, one of the milder critics of the President's warning, concludes:

"The price the President may have to pay for his insurance against popular disappointment is a paralysis of the popular will to disarm, and without that there can be no reduction in military expenditures and the economic burden of great armaments. It is our hope that the public in all the countries concerned, notwithstanding the danger of final disappointment, will still demand much and expect much of the Washington Conference, for governments must carry into effect, in the last resort, the will of the people who created them. Those who do not expect too much of politicians and diplomatists are apt to get too little."

The *Globe* thinks that, altho Mr. Harding became President at a time when "the market value of ideals was very low in the United States," that mood "apparently is passing. Every member of Congress brings back word to Washington of the eagerness of voters for practical limitation of arms. The enthusiasm for disarmament, which the Administration sees as a menace, is a native expression of the people." Democratic papers, naturally, use stronger language in dealing with the President's announcement that the country must not expect "too much" from the Conference. "Milk-and-water presentation of milk-and-water observations," cries the Dallas *Morning News*, "is not going to put battle-ships out of commission, or shut off the drain on our Treasury!" The Richmond *News-Leader* finds that "official Washington is far behind the country in its faith in the possibility of disarmament," and as for President Harding's warning—

"He writes more like a General Staff colonel than like a successor to Washington, to Grant or to Wilson. That which gives the greatest offense not only in Mr. Harding's references to international peace, but also in practically everything else that comes from Washington on the same subject, is the tacit suggestion that war and diplomacy are great mysteries that must be left by the people to the decision of the official clique in the national capitol. Why so? If taxes are to be imposed that will reduce a man's property, he is consulted, is he not, and is given a chance to be heard? If any 'interest' is involved in pending legislation, Congressmen and even some Cabinet officers show an exceeding tenderness and insist on long hearings. Are the destinies of boys to be jeopardized when property may not be?

"At this very minute the civilized world is spending its time and money and intelligence preparing the weapons that are to destroy us," exclaims the Pittsburgh *Leader* (Ind.). "Yet in the face of a world condition which is defying the best efforts of statesmen, of financiers, and captains of industry and commerce, when, to use the words of the man in the street, 'everything is shot to pieces' we are warned not to expect 'too much.'" The New York *World* (Dem.), one of the leading proponents of disarmament, complains that "the Administration's disarmament efforts at present seems to be directed mainly to warn the country against expecting too much from the Conference that Mr. Harding has called." The *World* scores the Administration for turning down the Borah resolution, which stipulated that the United States, Great Britain and Japan agree to suspend their naval building programs for five years. This objector concludes:

"Having dragged everything into the Conference that could be dragged in, including his mythical association of nations, the President is now astonished to find that people have been taking him seriously and are disposed to hold him to a strict responsibility."

"Wielding a wet blanket" the Brooklyn *Eagle*, also Democratic, calls the efforts of the Administration. "Nothing will be accomplished unless much is attempted," believes the Chattanooga

News, which opposes a "gospel of minimums," at this time and the Jersey City *Journal* observes that:

"The war was won, peace was established and the League of Nations set up because of high ideals. We are soon to see what is to be accomplished when something 'practicable' is the object to be attained and when high ideals are apparently to be out of place. The comparison will be most interesting. Many Americans, however, would be more certain of the success of the Disarmament Conference if they knew that America had a definite program to propose and that that program was inspired by idealism of a really high order."

Turning now to the other side of the argument, "common sense," "practical measures," and "wise moderation," are the watchwords of the editors who believe that the President, Secretary Hughes, and Vice-President Coolidge have been right in warning the country against over-optimism. We are approaching no "millennium," believes the Republican New York *Tribune*. "As Mr. Harding says, we have facts and not ideals to deal with," adds Mr. Hearst's New York *American*, and the New York *Times* speaks slightingly of "the amiable sentimentalists," who expect any considerable results from the Conference. "A reasonable and practical limitation of armaments ought to be possible of achievement," believes the Kansas City *Star*, adding, "idealism may be disappointed, but practical statesmanship will have won concrete results." "It is because the impossible is not to be undertaken that the President's confidence in the success of the Conference is justified," declares the Philadelphia *Inquirer*, which thus deals with a possible danger:

"It would be too much to hope, perhaps, that this plain statement will put a quietus upon all the organizations and individuals that are prepared to tell the distinguished delegates to the Conference precisely what they must do. The purpose of half-baked idealists of every stripe to bring to bear every possible influence in behalf of their fads and crotchets is obvious. Indeed, there seems to be a more or less deliberate attempt to create an atmosphere in Washington favorable to extreme action and unfavorable to such agreements as are feasible in existing conditions. It would be unfortunate from every point of view if the attempt so far succeeded that the practical work of the Conference should be obstructed in any way by a body of hostile opinion."

It is on this body of opinion, not necessarily "half-baked," but certainly and actively "hostile" in case the Conference does not live up to its promises, that most of those who have high hopes for a real disarmament conference depend. "The most conscientious of delegations could do no more at the Conference than the public saw fit to demand," says the New York *World*, and *Wallace's Farmer*, an agricultural weekly of Des Moines, Iowa, promises the American delegates that:

"So long as they strive honestly to cut down the tremendous price exacted from the people in money and men in maintaining the nation's place in the competitive armament race, they will have behind them a united popular support that will make failure almost impossible."

Courtesy of "Collier's." Reproduced by permission.

NO TIME FOR CEREMONIAL DEFERENCE.

A little crowding from those in the rear might help overcome some of this painful politeness.

—Darling in *Collier's*.

THE RIGHT TO CRITICIZE CHICAGO

BACK IN 1735 an old printer named John Peter Zenger so irritated the Colonial rulers of New York by attacks in his *Weekly Journal* that it was solemnly resolved in Council that certain of the Zenger writings should be publicly burnt by the common hangman and that the publisher himself should be charged with libel. The subsequent jury verdict of "not guilty" has been called "the morning star of that liberty which subsequently revolutionized America." No copies of the Chicago *Tribune* have been burnt in Grant Park, but *The Tribune* and *The Daily News* have been sued for libel by the city government on the ground that their criticisms of the municipal administration and their charges of "insolvency" were hurting the city's credit to the extent of $10,000,000. Judge Harry M. Fisher's decision that the city has no cause of action against *The Tribune* is greeted by the press with phrases recalling the historian's verdict in the case of old Zenger. "Free Government Upheld in Chicago," "The Freedom of the Press Vindicated," "No Crime to Criticize Officials," "A Victory for Free Speech," "Freedom of the Press," are sample headlines. The suit, according to the New York *Evening Post*, "was as impudent an attempt as has ever been made to silence criticism of public officials in this country." "Another insolent attack on the constitutional freedom of the press" has now been decisively repelled, says the Philadelphia *Bulletin*.

In Chicago, *The Evening Post* finds Judge Fisher's decision "a healthy thing for municipal government," upon which "the people of Chicago together with newspapers everywhere are to be congratulated." The Chicago *Tribune* itself, while remarking that any comment of its own might be discounted because of selfish interest, believes that Americans throughout the country "will realize that the decision is a noteworthy assertion of American constitutional right." If such a suit, it says, were to be sustained in law, "all criticism of public administration would rest under the paralyzing threat of exhausting or completely destructive attack by politicians in power," and "no more fatal assault upon the liberties of the individual could be devised." For the most part *The Tribune* contents itself with summarizing the Judge's decision, which goes deeply into the principles involved. Before the court hearings were held *The Tribune* announced to its readers that "to coerce or destroy *The Tribune* was the immediate purpose of this suit, the intimidation of all newspapers and prevention of free speech the second objective; and, as *The Tribune* has evidence to prove, the overturning of the republican form of government was its ultimate goal."

It appears from Judge Fisher's decision that the city government of Chicago took exception to a number of *Tribune* articles in the Small campaign, particularly to one referring to the city as "broke," "bankrupt" and "insolvent"; complaining that they gave the impression "that the management of the administrative and governmental affairs of plaintiff were conducted in a corrupt and incompetent manner," and finally that "said grievances" damaged the city in its "good name, reputation and financial credit" to the extent of $10,000,000. Judge Fisher holds that the right to free expression of opinion is only limited by restraints against blasphemy, immorality, sedition and defamation. But defamation or libel "is that class of prohibited publication which affects only private persons," and can not hold against municipalities. They "have no character or reputation to defend. They exist to conserve order and advance the public good." As regards the position of the press, the Judge said in part, as reported in the Chicago papers:

"It is not only a great privilege but, to my mind, a positive moral duty of those who have the facility to keep a watchful eye and to give generous expression on all public matters, the knowledge of which few citizens could obtain even when personally seeking it.

"Fortunately, while the good the press is capable of rendering, if unafraid, is without limit, the harm it can do has its own limitations. It cannot long indulge in falsehood without suffering the loss of that confidence from which alone comes its power, its prestige and its reward.

"On the other hand, the harm which certainly would result to the community from an officialdom unrestrained by fear of publicity is incalculable.

"The honest official seldom fears criticism."

"This action," said Judge Fisher, in summing up his reasons for giving judgment for the defendant, "is not in harmony with the genius, spirit and objects of our institutions. It does not belong to our day. It fits in rather with the genius of the rulers who conceived law not in the purity of love for justice, but in the lustful passion for undisturbed power."

It is not surprizing that a judicial decision which eulogizes the press while emphasizing its privileges should receive apparently unanimous editorial approval. A wire to Mayor Thompson failed to draw a word from him to help us state his side of the case. It is perhaps fair to assume that Corporation Counsel Ettelson spoke for the entire city administration when he told a Chicago *Tribune* reporter: "We have decided to make no comment except to say that we think Judge Fisher's decision is wrong."

"DO IT NOW!"

And put men to work, urges Col. Arthur Woods, as head of the National Unemployment Committee

ON THE JOB TO MAKE MORE JOBS

LESS THAN AN OUNCE of prevention of future unemployment may have come out of the Washington conference, but there is a general agreement in the press that the conferees made good at least to the extent of a pound of cure for the present crisis. President Harding says "the unemployment conference has borne rich rewards to the unemployed of this country." It has started, in the opinion of the Washington *Post*, "a movement which promises to alleviate and possibly cure the unemployment situation in the United States." While the less enthusiastic Newark *News* insists that "the conference did duck, evade, and side-step to keep from saying or doing anything at all embarrassing to the Administration, to organized labor intent on keeping up war wages, to employers pounding too hard for the open shop," it admits that much good has come in the shape of publicity and emergency relief. It will be remembered that the conference devoted its first attention to stimulating cooperation between city and state officials and business and labor organizations, urging each community to try to solve its own unemployment problen. So while the conference went on to discuss prevention measures at Washington, the cure was beginning to take effect, and in nearly every city and town in the United States, editors tell us, the fight against unemployment is under way, committees are busy compiling rosters of the unemployed, and individuals and organizations are devoting their energies to reduce idleness by methods suggested by the conference or thought of by themselves. To coordinate and assist these community efforts there is the clearing house established at Washington and headed by Colonel Arthur Woods. Colonel Woods is visiting the chief cities of the country to hear reports, give advice and stir up enthusiasm. "Do it now!" is his slogan, for both public and private enterprises. The only cure for lack of work is work, he insists, and "the way to get rid of unemployment is to provide employment." As he specified in his speech at Albany on the 19th:

"One way in which the conference has felt that it was sound to stimulate industry is by what we have called the 'spruce-up' campaign. Almost every one has about his home or his shop some repair upkeep work which he needs to have done.

"Another way that the conference figures industry can be stimulated in a sound way is through public works. There is a good deal of public work all over the country planned, approved, the money provided, which will be started in the ordinary course of events within the next few months or during the coming year. Much of it can be done during the winter.

"If such public works already approved and necessary for the community to have can be started now instead of later, here again work can be created which now does not exist. Men can be employed who are now unemployed.

"With the full realization of the great need of national economy now the conference recommended that Congress pass an additional appropriation for public roads and the conference further urged that all States try to match this appropriation at once and put the work immediately under contract so that the dirt may be made to fly right off, instead of a good many months later."

Signs are visible that powerful business leaders are falling into

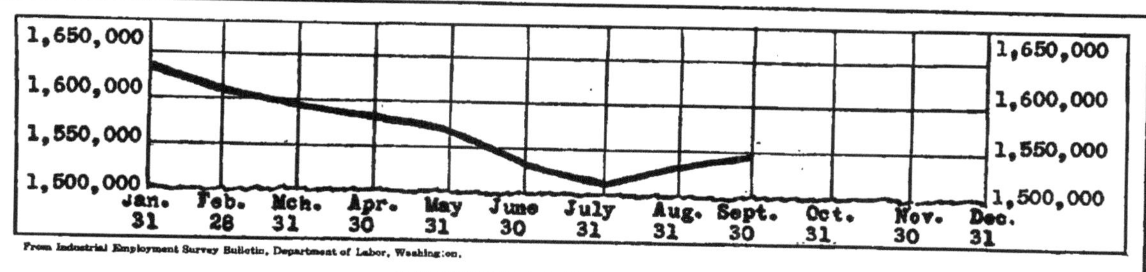

EMPLOYMENT RISING SINCE JULY.

This chart, based on the pay-roll records of 1,428 concerns in sixty-five industrial centers, shows the variation of employment in fourteen manufacturing industries during the past nine months of the year. The trough of unemployment was reached on July 31, when the number employed was 1,510,210. By September 30 it had risen to 1,544,529.

line with this advice, notes the New York *Globe*. "The action of the Steel Corporation, the Standard Oil Company and of the railroads in undertaking work now which might be postponed is entire gain." The decision of these groups to hire more men followed so closely the appeal of the unemployment conference that Mr. Hoover and his associates are fairly entitled, in *The Globe's* opinion, to recognition for the results. The Chamber of Commerce of the United States and the Department of Labor officials feel that the conference "mainly by suggestion and stimulation of interest in unemployment has already had its effect in improving conditions," so a New York *Evening Post* correspondent reports. President Samuel Gompers of the American Federation of Labor testifies that the conference recommendations to local authorities are already bringing results in relieving unemployment. The conference, declares the Rochester Post *Express*, must at least be given credit for waking up the country. What these papers mean by waking up the country is indicated by a number of facts collected by a New York *Herald* correspondent at Washington:

"That the manufacturing industry generally is beginning to respond to the call of the conference is seen in the announcement of the United States Steel Corporation that $10,000,000 worth of extension work is being undertaken to provide jobs for the idle during the coming months. Arrangements to carry a large number of men on its pay-roll are being made by the Standard Oil Company of New Jersey.

"Work for thousands of machinists will be afforded this winter by the railroads, which in the next three months are getting ready to spend more than $800,000,000 on repairs for equipment and rights-of-way, according to an estimate by Dr. Julius Parmelee, director of the Bureau of Railway Economics. The roads have in their employ at least 1,700,000 persons, Dr. Parmelee estimated, or within 300,000 of the total number at work during the war period.

"In the West the Federal and State Governments are cooperating in pushing reclamation work. With authority from Congress these jobs can be made to care for 40,000 unemployed, according to the findings of the conference. At the Capitol to-day several Senators and Representatives stood ready, they said, to introduce measures authorizing the Federal Government to undertake this work.

"Road-building totaling millions is being contracted for in many States, especially in the South, where such work can proceed all winter. Contractors from all sections of the country are sending bids to the Carolinas, two States leading in the work.

"In the building trades workers and employers of a dozen cities are negotiating new wage scales at lower rates, intended to stimulate building. New Orleans reports that building contracts are being let at a rate double that of a year ago.

"Reports to the Federal Reserve Board seem to indicate that a building boom is developing in many sections. Both the number of contracts and their value are on the increase in New York, Philadelphia, and other large cities."

Thus the patient would seem to be on the way to recovery partly at least as the result of the conference cure. But how about keeping him healthy in the future? Officials of the Department of Labor have assured a New York *Evening Post* correspondent that "enough momentum has been secured by the conference to warrant the idea that no other future emergency will find the nation quite so lamentably unprepared to cope intelligently with unemployment as it was a month ago." In its permanent program there is no "magic formula," but, observes the Omaha *Bee*, "some sane and worth-while methods for relieving the present situation are offered."

Some of this disappointment may be explained by the desire of the conference to be unanimous on its official recommendations. Suggestions involving contentious matters were offered as committee reports and made public without endorsement by the conference. While the emergency recommendations would seem to shift the responsibility for the unemployed from the nation to the states and cities, the official permanent program of the conference suggests specific tasks for Congress and the Federal Departments. Before adjourning the conference adopted eight recommendations declared essential to "constructive and immediate settlement if recovery in business and permanent employment are to be expeditiously accomplished." The New York *Herald* gives them in brief as follows:

Readjustment of railway rates to a fair business relation to the value of commodities.

Speedy tax revision with reductions.

Definite settlement of tariff legislation.

Quick financial settlement between the Government and railroads.

Limitation of world armament.

Stabilization of foreign exchange rates.

Elimination of waste in industry and seasonal operations.

Alignment of wholesale and retail prices.

While the unemployment conference has done "an enormously valuable thing" in trying "to improve business conditions in the hope of creating more opportunities for work" it has not, in the opinion of the New York *Globe*, really been giving its attention to unemployment:

"Neither the conference nor the country should imagine for an instant that unemployment as such has been considered adequately. It has not. Insecurity of the job is one of the most serious evils of a generation which lives by large scale industry. Insecurity means irregular employment and worry at almost all times and unemployment during a depression. Some time it must be considered in all its phases."

The conferees, writes Mr. William L. Chenery in *The Globe*, have simply been trying to stimulate business and they have served their nation to the extent to which they succeed. But, he concludes

"Unemployment will remain and its misery will not be permanently swept away until there arises a statesman willing to face unflinchingly the stark reality of industrial insecurity. In this country no such leader has appeared, and the spokesmen of labor are themselves dumb in the face of such an issue."

SILESIAN RICHES GIVEN TO POLAND

"THE TURNIPS FOR THE GERMANS, the mines for the Poles," is one bitter German's way of describing what the Council of the League of Nations has done in dividing Upper Silesia between Germany and Poland in such a way as to give the former most of the territory and the latter the best of the industrial area. Germany has been convulsed in a paroxysm of rage, say the correspondents. From editors and political leaders in the Fatherland come feverish protests against such "a dagger thrust in the back of German democracy," such "flagrant," "colossal," and "horrifying" injustice. The newspapers, we are told, do not dare print maps showing the new boundary line, and the very stability of the government is said to have been shaken. When Solomon was king, a mother found her wails against dividing an infant sufficient proof of her claim to it. But the Allies do not seem to be imprest enough by this judicial decision to make a like award of the Silesian industrial district. According to the correspondents, Poland, the Allied governments and public opinion in Europe alike accept with considerable satisfaction this settlement of a controversy which has been a trouble-breeder for many months. In this country the League's decision seems to receive the most wholehearted praise from pro-League journals which deem it a noteworthy feather in the League's cap, while several Republican anti-League dailies find it no settlement at all, but only a timorous makeshift.

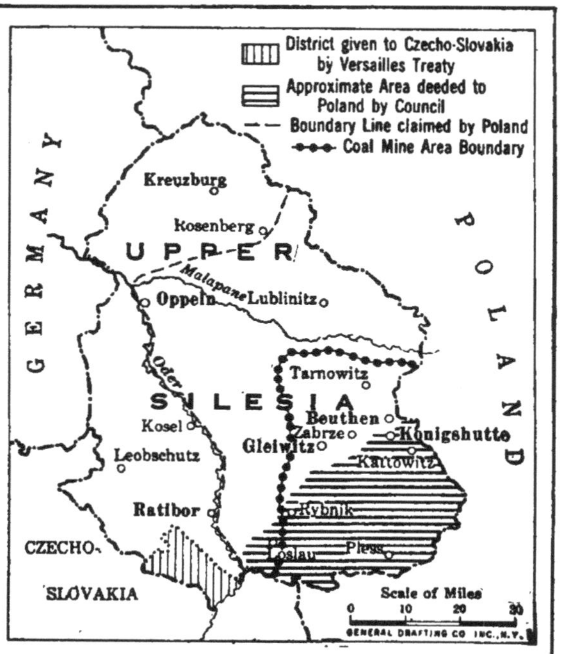

It will be remembered that altho the Peace Council first decided to take all of Upper Silesia from Germany and give it to Poland, the Versailles Treaty finally left the matter to a plebiscite. When the vote was taken last March 683 out of 1,280 communes in Upper Silesia voted for union with Germany while there was a total popular majority of about 200,000 out of a million votes in favor of Germany. But the Supreme Council, unable to agree on a division of the country in accordance with the plebiscite vote, turned the whole matter over to the Council of the League of Nations, which unanimously adopted the report of the special commission recommending a settlement according to the accompanying map. While "Le Chapeau," as the Silesian industrial district has been termed, in accordance with a fancied map resemblance to a cocked hat, is divided politically, provision is made for a certain amount of economic unity, under the supervision of an industrial commission.

Germany, as a Berlin correspondent of the New York *Times* understands it, loses 64 per cent. of the Upper Silesian anthracite production, that is, 67 anthracite coal mines which last year produced about 32,000,000 tons. She loses all her Upper Silesian zinc, or about 60 per cent. of her former total zinc production. It is believed that Germany loses about 63 per cent. of the Upper Silesian iron industries production, about 1,500,000 tons of iron and steel products. In coal deposits German experts declare they are losing 86 per cent. of Upper Silesian anthracite, or 42 per cent. of all the former German anthracite deposits.

WHAT POLAND AND GERMANY GET IN SILESIA

In England, a number of British economists have published a letter to the press asserting that the Upper Silesian decision is "perhaps the severest blow to the prospects of peace in Europe and its economic recovery." They feel that it brings the day of German default in reparation payments measurably nearer, since Germany's ability to pay is so greatly diminished by the loss of the large Silesian mineral deposits. Another line of British criticism is to the effect that the settlement is a mere temporary compromise, "a timid and time-serving decision," in the words of the London *Daily Chronicle*, in which no definite principle is adopted.

Here several American Republican papers agree. "A makeshift that settles nothing," is the Boston *Herald's* (Rep.) phrase; "a compromise which will not contribute to permanent peace," the Pittsburgh *Gazette Times* (Rep.) calls it. One thing seems clear enough to the Manchester *Union* (Rep.):

"There is no settlement of the Silesian dispute. There is no settlement of the question whether Germany is to be given a chance, or Poland is to be equipped for industrial growth as an auxiliary of France. The plebiscite is blithely set aside, the fringes of the industrial area are handed to Poland and Germany respectively, and the pestiferous little mining triangle is bisected and set up as an economic quasi-state under joint control, with partial free trade between its hostile parts, and a German money standard. Nothing is settled. The League could not bring itself to tell France she must accept an agricultural Polish ally, or Britain that she must accept a permanently impoverished German market, or Germany that she must get along without Silesia and let the Allies take their chances on reparation, or the whole lot of them, Poland included, that they must stand by the result of the plebiscite they had authorized or accepted. The League has simply patched up a complicated compromise which will probably be accepted tentatively because winter is at hand, but which has in it no solitary element of permanence."

But even in Republican circles some admit that the League has made a wise decision. It "puts economic considerations above political," observes the New York *Tribune* (Rep.), and will "probably contribute materially to peaceful reconstruction." It is the opinion of the pro-League New York *Evening Post* (Ind.), "that a League decision, arrived at after due judicial deliberation and after a solution by violence and diplomacy had failed, spells less trouble for the future than a decision that would have left Poland with the sense that it had been cheated. As against German discontent we must weigh the gain for the principle underlying the League of Nations and its authority." And it seems to the Boston *Post* (Dem.) that everywhere outside of Germany the Silesian decision will be regarded as based on "equity and an intelligent view of national claims"—

"To infer that the bitterly contentious question of Silesian boundaries has been put to sleep by the action of the League would be to rely too much upon the power of such a settlement to silence criticism. But that the bounds will stay as the League fixes them is pretty certain. There is a good deal of power, both actual and potential, in that big aggregation of all the great nations of the world—save one, or, perhaps, two."

TOPICS IN BRIEF

THE real Chinese puzzle is China.—*Little Rock Arkansas Gazette.*

SUCCESS is still operated on the self-service plan.—*Kingston Whig.*

THE Chicago cop who sold bootleg isn't a copper still.—*Albany Times 'nion.*

THE tailors are the only ones who are satisfied with an increase in rents.—*'ew York American.*

LODGE says the German treaty will help business. It will help Germany's usiness.—*Charleston Gazette.*

BETWEEN the demands of the unions and the Union, employers are up gainst it.—*Columbia Record.*

WE have come to a pretty pass if we can't advocate Americanism without earing a nightgown and a mask.—*Elmira Star Gazette.*

WE would never have believed, without having had it demonstrated, at George Harvey could remain quiet so long.—*Columbia Record.*

SPECIALISTS. Most of the holesale profiteering is done y the retailers.—*New York 'orld.*

"THE voice of the people" very much in need of megaphone. — *Columbia ecord.*

THE trip to normalcy seems involve a long stopover subnormalcy.—*Columbia ecord.*

IN the beginning the earth as made round, and it's ver been square since. — *olumbia Record.*

THE present situation af- rds considerable food for ought, if hash can be called od.—*San Diego Tribune.*

THE low estate of the Ger- an mark demonstrates that a scrap of paper" also mes home to roost.—*olumbia Record.*

THE politicians always anage to defeat the will of e people by sneaking in me sort of codicil.—*Colum- a Record.*

THE trouble about a skeleton in a closet is that it does not have enough nse to stay there.—*Charleston Gazette.*

APPARENTLY Japan's chief grievance is that Western nations will not let wrest peacefully.—*Norfolk Virginian-Pilot.*

SOMEBODY has invented a silencer for street cars. Too late. The motor s is doing the business already.—*Wichita Eagle.*

THE kind of elastic currency most people want is the kind that will retch from one payday to the next.—*New York American.*

WE shall probably understand the Irish question better when our own lipinos organize their Sinn Fein.—*Columbia Record.*

AN optimist is a man who thinks the grocers are going to reduce prices cause of their sympathy for the public.—*New York American.*

OUR Government seems to have finally decided that our foreign policy not an endowment policy.—*Columbian Missourian.*

ONE of the many fine things about baseball is that G. B. Shaw has not prest an opinion concerning it.—*Boston Shoe and Leather Reporter.*

DR. CRAFTS says he's going to put the Sun in Sunday. Now if the oc will put the pay in Payday and the mon in Monday.—*Brooklyn agle.*

THIS new yeast-eating fad saves a fellow a lot of embarrassment d self-consciousness when he buys a cake from the grocer.—*Columbia ecord.*

ANOTHER reason New York has a right to regard it as a real world series because it took forty-nine languages to interpret it to her populace.—*llas News.*

THE German mark is in a horrible way, but if the remainder of the world esn't get up and hustle the German trade-mark will get there first.—*lumbia Record.*

TAXES defy the law of gravitation.—*Greenville (S. C.) Piedmont.*

"BOLSHEVISM will live on," says Lenine. On what?—*Hutchinson Gazette.*

SUGGESTION to business: Money is a boomerang; turn it loose.—*Erie Times.*

THE laborer's hire is not always determined by the laborer's ire.—*Columbia Record.*

A CYNICAL writer asks what Bolshevism lives on. Certainly not on its reputation.—*Minnesota Star.*

WHATEVER it is that afflicts Congress, it would be fine if our speed maniacs could catch it.—*Harrisburg Patriot News.*

AN elephant lives four hundred years, but then baggage men don't handle his trunk.—*Jefferson City Capital News.*

WE didn't mind supporting the Government in extravagance during the war, but this post-bellum alimony gets our goat.—*Columbia Record.*

WONDERS OF AMERICA—THE BALANCING ROCK.

—Brown in the Chicago *Daily News.*

A PAPER scarcity would aid the rehabilitation of the finances of Germany.—*Boston Shoe and Leather Reporter.*

THE people should not permit any one to use the pipe of peace to create a smoke-screen. — *Columbia Record.*

WE believe that Mr. Harding's intentions are good, but the road to normalcy can't be paved that way.—*Columbia Record.*

WE surmise that John Barleycorn, tho uninvited, will also be a delegate to the conference for the limitation of armaments. — *Columbia Record.*

THAT the only cure for unemployment is employment may not sound like a very profound observation, but it falls much more gently on the ears of many than to say the only cure for unemployment is work.—*Kansas City Star.*

A SEVERE winter is predicted. This is the 1921st severe winter predicted during the Christian era.—*Wichita Eagle.*

THE industrial unrest doesn't impede our progress nearly so much as the industrial rest.—*Columbia Record.*

THE rate of exchange between Canada and the United States is now one quart for ten dollars.—*Cincinnati Times-Star.*

SOLDIERS are everywhere in the Balkans, ready for action. That section is normal, if not stable.—*Pittsburgh Gazette-Times.*

IT is estimated that there is enough coal in discovered fields to keep miners striking for 3,276 years.—*Fresno Republican.*

GERMAN liners are beginning to arrive in New York. But it will be a long time before the kaiser's ship comes in.—*Wichita Eagle.*

THE agent can demonstrate with it for six months, and it's new. But three days after you get it, it's a used car.—*Sherbrooke Record.*

ONE of the most important Pacific questions to be handled by the Administration is to keep California safely Republican.—*Washington Post.*

CLOSE observers say that Herb Hoover is an idealist, which is probably why we thought for a long time that he was a Democrat.—*Columbia Record.*

THE trouble about defeating Prohibition now is that we would have to beat the combined vote of the Prohibitionists and bootleggers.—*Columbia Record.*

THERE are people who invest in German marks just as there are men who believe that hair can be made to grow on bald heads.—*Boston Shoe and Leather Reporter.*

EVERYBODY is imploring Mr. Harding to "lead" Congress, but our notion is that it would be more effective for him to get in behind it and administer a swift kick.—*Columbia Record.*

FRANCO-GERMAN TEAM-WORK AMID THE RUINS

A REAL STEP toward the establishment of peaceful conditions in Europe is seen in the agreements signed October 7th and 8th at Wiesbaden by the representatives of the French and German Governments, by which Germany shall supply materials for the reconstruction of the devastated regions of France. We are reminded that France is the most pressing of Germany's creditors, and the one who would have to take serious steps to force collection, but "now she has entered into an agreement with her debtor which, so long as it is lived up to, removes the danger of further military action along the Rhine." Both Louis Loucheur, the French Minister of Liberated Regions, and Dr. Walter Rathenau, German Minister of Reconstruction, express their confidence in the good presage of the pact by a statement which reads:

A GERMAN JIBE AT FRANCE.

FRANCE: "What do you mean—reconstruction? We're going to make good money out of this as a show-place."
—*Wahre Jacob* (Stuttgart).

"The Wiesbaden agreement is a free-will agreement. The good-will of Germany joins with that of France for the purpose of peaceful reconstruction. It is a question on both sides of speeding up the reconstruction of the devastated regions of France. It means the beginning of international cooperation and is perhaps the symbol of universal reconstruction. To attain this end France needs an arrangement permitting her to push this work during a period of four years. Germany needs to pay in goods instead of gold.

"Germany takes upon herself a sacrifice, since her position is not that of a financial power. She accepts this sacrifice to prove that she wishes the restoration of Europe."

In Germany the Berlin *Vorwärts* points to the agreement as the best proof that the Germans are anxious to fulfil all their obligations. Meanwhile, the persistent hard feeling against the Treaty of Versailles is evidenced in the added remark that "the spirit of Wiesbaden is not the spirit of Versailles." *The Deutsche Allgemeine Zeitung*, one of the Stinnes newspaper organs, declares that in coming to terms France has been forced to recognize inexorable economic laws, and that the dangerous tension in the international money market which existed at the time of the first payment of 1,000,000,000 marks will not be repeated. The task which Germany has undertaken is immense, remarks the *Vossische Zeitung*, but the agreement must be accounted a notable success because it points virtually the only way to a restoration of peaceful conditions, and as "our labor is all we have to pay with, it is better to work to the utmost with head and hands, than to search fruitlessly in the world's markets for paper we cannot afford to buy."

In France the Paris *Temps* applauds the settlement as a showing of good faith by Germany as well as of France's wish to end squabbling and get down to the actual work of post-war clearance. Nevertheless, it adds:

"The Wiesbaden agreement most certainly marks progress in our relations with Germany, but it does not change our policy of exacting fulfilment of the Treaty of Versailles. It proves that, while France is perfectly able to safeguard her interests, she does not block the efforts of Germany to pay her debts, and that so far as she can France will make it easy for any loyal German Government to fulfil its obligations."

The Germans who oppose the Wiesbaden agreement, says the Paris *Journal des Debats*, are those "who wish to pay nothing at all," and those of our Allies who frown upon it, "give us the impression that they are not worrying about the restoration of our devastated regions." Paris correspondents point out that the Wiesbaden compact must be submitted to the French and German parliaments and to the Reparations Commission, where "it is reported it may meet some opposition from the British," and we read:

"This is because it provides for payment by Germany to France of materials worth 7,000,000,000 gold marks in the next five years, which is more than France would receive under the terms of the London reparation ultimatum. But French statesmen believe that they can offer arguments which will bring the British to withdraw their opposition."

The agreement runs until May 1, 1926, and provides for the establishment of a central office in France to which orders from the devastated regions will be directed, and in turn sent to a central office in Germany, which will distribute them to German industries. Germany will pay the manufacturer. To the extent of 1,000,000,000 gold marks yearly France will credit Germany on the part due her under the reparation payments, and we are further informed that what remains to be paid by Germany will be settled by a series of payments from 1926 to 1935. Altho the text of the agreement was made public only in part, the press publish an unofficial summary giving some of its important features, as for instance:

"A French buyer may negotiate directly with a German producer as to the amount of deliveries and the prices to be paid, provided he is able to come to terms with the Germans, but the agreement contemplates that transactions will be arranged between organizations created by the French and German Governments. If these respective organizations should be unable to reach an agreement respecting deliveries, prices, transportation and acceptance, decision as to disputed points will be left to a commission of three. This commission will be made up of

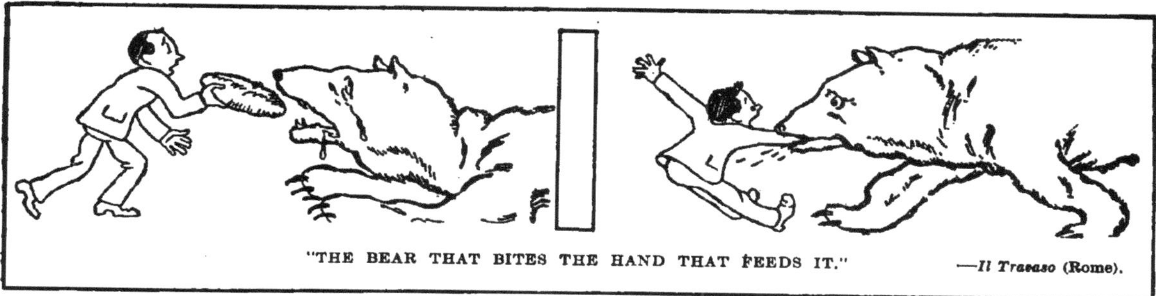

"THE BEAR THAT BITES THE HAND THAT FEEDS IT." —*Il Travaso* (Rome).

one Frenchman, one German, and a third person chosen by common consent, or appointed by the President of the Swiss Confederation. It will fix the price list every three months, and the list will correspond to normal prices in the interior of France, less customs duties and transportation charges.

"The semi-official summary does not deal with the question of exchange. Four supplementary agreements, dealing with deliveries of cattle, machinery, coal and rolling stock, drafted by experts to cover details and technical points, were signed by Mr. Loucheur and Dr. Rathenau."

This semi-official summary advises us that the credits to be made on the books of the Reparations Commission are subject to three limitations, as follows:

"1. Only 35 per cent. of the value of the merchandise (if the deliveries reach 1,000,000,000 gold marks), or 45 per cent. if the total amount of presentations do not reach 1,000,000,000 marks, will be credited.

"2. Germany will never be credited with more than 1,000,000,000 gold marks to May 1, 1926.

"3. Germany will never be credited with a sum superior to France's share in the yearly reparations."

An annex to the text of the agreement as reproduced in the press reads:

"Germany engages to deliver to France upon her demand all machinery and materials which would be compatible with the possibilities of production in Germany and subject to her limitations as to supplies of raw materials. Such deliveries will be in accord with the requirements necessary for Germany to maintain her social and economic life. This agreement shall date from October 1, 1921.

"In any case the present contract excludes the products it is specified Germany must turn over to the Allies in Annexes 3, 5 and 6, Part VIII of the Treaty of Versailles. The cumulative value of the payments in kind which Germany will supply France in execution of Annexes 3, 5 and 6, as well as deliveries Germany makes to France under the present contract, will not exceed 7,000,000,000 gold marks from October 1, 1921, to May 1, 1926.

"It is expressly stipulated that all deliveries shall be devoted to the reconstruction of devastated regions in France."

Paris dispatches inform us also that the Wiesbaden agreements are said to be precursors of further pacts because France is "beginning to realize that she can no longer depend on her European allies for protection against Germany, and that only an Entente with her late enemy can provide a firm basis for Europe's economic restoration."

FAMINE TESTING LENINE

THE HOUR OF DOOM has struck for Soviet rule, say the anti-Bolsheviks in Russia, while their opponents grimly retort that this government will stand the test of famine as it has passed safely through all former trials. The controversy rages, we are told, even as the terrible conditions of want blacken broad sections of the country, and one refugee, Professor A. Gorovtzeff, writes in the Prague *Volia Rossii* that "absolute collapse of the Soviet government is near," and because it can plainly be foreseen, there are grounds for believing that "in order to retard it, the Bolsheviks will stop at nothing." This writer further predicts that they will "employ the method employed so often by despotic bourgeois governments and try to divert the attention of the masses from the internal situation and inflame it with fears of international imperialistic policy." We read then:

"That is the more probable in this case, since such a move would achieve the happy combination of the idealistic task of world revolution with the purely material prospects of the seizure of grain supplies of the neighbors. To those who know that in Soviet policies there can be nothing unexpected, in the sense of their hypocrisy and dishonesty, it is not absurd to suppose that the very call for help is capable of having some peculiar provocational significance. The 'task' may be construed to mean that if it becomes clear that it is impossible through foreign relief to feed the 150 millions of the country's population, exhausted by the Soviet régime, the Kremlin dreamers might have legitimate grounds to address their call, not to Europe, but to the Soviet proletariat, exhorting them to go and take the grain which capitalistic Europe, you see, does not want to give them.

"At any rate the maintenance of a large army, which so sharply contradicts the Bolsheviks' loud protestations of their desire for peace, can not but cause most serious apprehensions in this respect. In particular, the concentration of the Soviet military forces on the Bessarabian frontier compels one to suppose that Bessarabia, perhaps sooner than any other neighboring territory, may be in danger of a Soviet invasion."

THE BOLSHY IN A DICKENS MAKE-UP.

URIAH HEEPSKI PLOTSKY: "Believe me, Mr. Bulovitch, I'm that 'umble, I could never deceive you."

JOHN: "I believe you. Turn out your pockets!"

—*The Guardian* (Manchester).

The *Vremya*, a democratic Russian daily published in Berlin, believes it is impossible to do effective relief in Russia while the Soviet government lasts, and says:

"The question naturally arises: Is it possible to render substantial assistance in the matter of reconstructing the national economy of Russia, the agriculture of the country in particular, if the economic policies adopted by the Soviet government are not abandoned? Are these policies, together with the political system of Soviet Russia and the social experiments and methods of government of the Communist rulers, not the primary cause of the calamity which has befallen the country and an obstacle in the work of the economic rehabilitation of our fatherland? In a word, the problem is whether international relief is expedient when there is no assurance that the Soviet government will choose other methods of administration to secure the country against a repetition of such calamities."

The comment of the Bolshevist journals tends to confirm the suspicion of their opponents. The Petrograd *Pravda*, for instance, remarks:

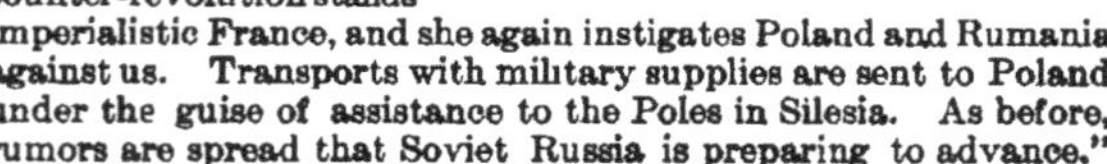

THE GRECO-TURKISH TUMBLERS.

Turkish War Report. Greek War Report.

—*The Passing Show* (London).

"The bourgeois press is in feverish excitement, for it imagines that the long-awaited moment of the downfall of the workmen's rule in Russia is arriving. Therefore it is probable that the capitalistic governments will endeavor to utilize this opportunity to organize a new intervention in Soviet Russia. From all parts of Europe there come reports of recruiting of whiteguards. As in the past, in the center of the counter-revolution stands imperialistic France, and she again instigates Poland and Rumania against us. Transports with military supplies are sent to Poland under the guise of assistance to the Poles in Silesia. As before, rumors are spread that Soviet Russia is preparing to advance."

This editorial further avers that ammunition is being sent to Rumania by way of Silesia and Jugo-Slavia and that Rumania is concentrating large military stores on the borders of Bessarabia. The Moscow *Izvestia* also dwells on the war preparations against the Soviet republic, and, discussing the union of the Baltic States, observes:

"One might think that the alliance of the Baltic States would be confined to the smaller border countries, as Latvia, Esthonia and Lithuania. Even the participation of Finland was doubtful for some time. If so composed, the Baltic Alliance would have had the character of self-defense in case of attack by a big neighbor—Soviet Russia or Poland. But what do we see in reality? It appears that the Baltic Alliance is planned without Lithuania, but with the active participation of Poland. And this at once changes its character; from a defensive it becomes an offensive alliance—and it is directed against Soviet Russia.

"To dissuade small countries from risky adventures, in which they can gain nothing and can only lose, would be a profitless undertaking. They are the tools of the big imperialistic powers, and are simply doing their will. The bourgeois governments know better than anybody else that Soviet Russia does not think of war, least of all of an offensive war. They know all that, and nevertheless continue in their old way, or, rather, follow Anglo-French instructions. That is their affair. We can only say what we have repeatedly said: Soviet Russia does not want war, but she will be able to defend her existence under all circumstances."

A Bolshevik communication, not designed for anti-Bolshevik consumption, is the appeal of the Central Executive Committee of the Third Internationale in Moscow to its Bureau in Western Europe, and the London *Daily Telegraph* describes it as "a confession of decaying influence," which reads in part:

"The proletariat of the west will be called upon in the next few days to undergo its first and very serious crucial test. This test will be the organized participation of the proletariat of the entire world in the struggle which at present the workers of Russia are waging to save 20,000,000 of their brothers from the clutches of famine. . . . The leaders of capital realize perfectly well that, with the help of provisions sent in time, with the help of a timely thrown piece of bread to the starving peasant, they will be able to undermine the confidence in the Soviet government which is at present being displayed by the working masses of Russia."

THE GRECO-TURK TUG-OF-WAR

WHEN GREEK MEETS TURK then comes not only the tug-of-war but also a fierce conflict of communiqués, we are told, and the outside world remains more or less in the dark. Yet editorial comments based on war reports, it is said, are calculated to let us read between the lines if we know how. Now the official Turkish Nationalist organ, the Angora *National Government*, has no editorial articles, but a plenteous array of detailed statements about the Nationalist and the Greek armies and their fighting. The following sentences, presented mostly in big type, give a fair impression of the tone of this newspaper:

"The Greek army is trying to escape from the *impasse* into which it has fallen by persistent expenditure of all its strength, but has been met by a wall of fire in every attempt. In the bayonet attack, with God's help, success always remained with us. The enemy is in retreat. The English papers tell of the sufferings of the Greek soldiers from heat and thirst. At Athens there is great anxiety on the part of King Constantine and the people regarding events in Anatolia. Evil news comes from Adrianople. A train loaded with soldiers and ammunition has been blown up. The Greeks fear Bulgaria exceedingly."

In Constantinople the *Peyam-Sabah* gives its leading article the cheerless title "The World Catastrophe" and traces its extent back to 1914. The writer, Ali Kemal, concludes his account of the evils that have befallen Turkey as follows:

"Our allies managed to secure a sort of peace, but we cannot lift our heads from war and calamity. The general war dragged on at disastrous length, shaking all the actors to the last degree. We were the weakest of them all; even if we had partially appreciated how weak we were, we might in some way have escaped the calamity that has overtaken us. How dark, how miserable that page of the record of the life of this nation which records that, as has been the case for centuries, those at the head of the government were a wholly incompetent set of men, ignorant of the steps necessary to be taken. If Sultan Abdul Hamid's reign had lasted five or six years longer, he would have found some way by hook or by crook to save this state from plunging into such an abyss. Well, the past is past. What we ought to have done the moment the armistice was signed was to seek for peace, to acknowledge the faults we had been guilty of for four or five years, to punish those responsible for what was done, and to consider immediately in all sincerity the restoration of relationship with the victors, and with very unaccustomed zeal and celerity to carry into effect wise plans to this end.

"When an opportunity like this was measurably within reach we put war in the place of peace. That seemed better when the decisions of Europe were against us! It did not enter the heads of the leaders to try to turn those decisions into peaceful relations. No, we are people used to war, used to hunger, want, distress, but still proud of our country, our state, our race. In words we are. But in acts, in fidelity to country, state and race, dare we face the record of these latest years?"

As to Greek affairs, Athens dispatches relate that, after having given an account of the military situation to the National Assembly, Premier Gounaris declared that "because of the international character of the Turkish problem a closer contact is necessary between Greece and the Entente in order to create a basis of solution." To this end he had sought an interview with Premier Lloyd George and Premier Briand, who accepted his proposal. According to Central News dispatches to London, the object of the Gounaris mission to that city, Paris, and other capitals, is to "raise a loan for prosecution of war against the Turks."

GEOGRAPHY OF CHINA'S POLITICS

THE LAY OF THE LAND is the superfactor in the puzzle picture of China's politics, we are told, and until railroads and waterways are adjusted properly, the puzzle will remain unsolved. Two thousand years ago when China had an excellent system of post-roads throughout the Empire, it had also political peace and prosperity. To regain this happy state means of transport and communication must be reorganized, according to *The North China Commerce* (Peking and Tientsin) which shows us China of to-day as split from east to west into three groups. The south, comprising the "progressive and somewhat radical Canton party," is led by Sun Yat Sen. The north is under the *de facto* government of the Chihli party. The Yangstze Valley is nominally under the northern rule, but practically indifferent to its mandates and representatives, altho the latter, with their armies, are said to enforce "a semblance of government." We read then:

"The big rivers of China run from west to east affording communication and commercial relations necessary to establish common understanding and friendly feelings among dwellers in the provinces through which the waterways run. Apart from the Grand Canal which connects Peking with the Yangstze Valley, and even then only along the eastern fringe of the continent, there are no natural communications running north and south.

"If we go back some two thousand years we will find an excellent system of post-roads, paved with big flat stones connecting the capital city with all parts of China, irrespective of geographical limitations, and coincident with this we find a politically undivided country, with its people living in harmony and enjoying a standard of culture and progressiveness hardly equaled by any contemporary civilization. Successive dynasties and the inroads of conquering Mongols and Manchus slowly but surely by the combined forces of misgovernment, corruption and individual indolence brought about a decay of the magnificent road communications, and incidentally a decline in the political state."

This commercial and political monthly believes a cursory study of their own history and geography ought to bring home to the Chinese the futility of struggling with faction against faction to establish a political unity that "can not exist without the indispensable basis of intercommunication." China "must first be united mechanically before it can be united politically." The political units, it is urged, either must agree to separate into self-governing states according to the will of their people, or else sink their respective individual aspirations and, for the sake of a united China, concentrate on the material factors through which alone their dream of political integrity can be realized. To this end—

"It must be made as easy to travel and trade between north and south as it is between east and west. In fact there must be even a greater inter-relationship between Peking and Canton to offset the separation of many centuries. It is not enough that steamer lines fringe the coast in their five-day journeys from north to south. The intervening regions, with their own opinions, shading off in ratio to their proximity to one or other of the principal units, must be linked up with a network of communications if not in proportion to population, at least equal to those of similar sized foreign countries.

"This vision of political unity probably was not lost sight of in the more material interests that caused the commencement of the Canton-Hankow Railway, not yet completed, but, were it emphasized to the contending factions, they would have sunk their disputes long ago and centered their energies on the completion of this first real step towards reunification. China needs not only a Canton-Hankow Railway but a Canton-Hangchow Railway, and Canton-Nanchang Railway, linking as they would with present northern lines to Shanghai, Kuikiang, Hankow and Peking. China urgently needs at least a half dozen through traffic lines from north to south, and a dozen more modern automobile roads and air routes."

This monthly expresses its good-will towards Sun Yat Sen and his Canton associates in their effort to achieve "what they believe to be the best form of government in China," and it tenders the like sentiment to the "efforts of a few northern administrators to establish in spite of militarist intervention a coordinate administration for the common welfare of China," but—

"The prime requisite in basing a state on solid economic foundations seems to have escaped their attention. And until such time as they come to reckon with this pressing need of intercommunication and inter-relationships to offset the geographical limitations we see no hope of a politically unified China."

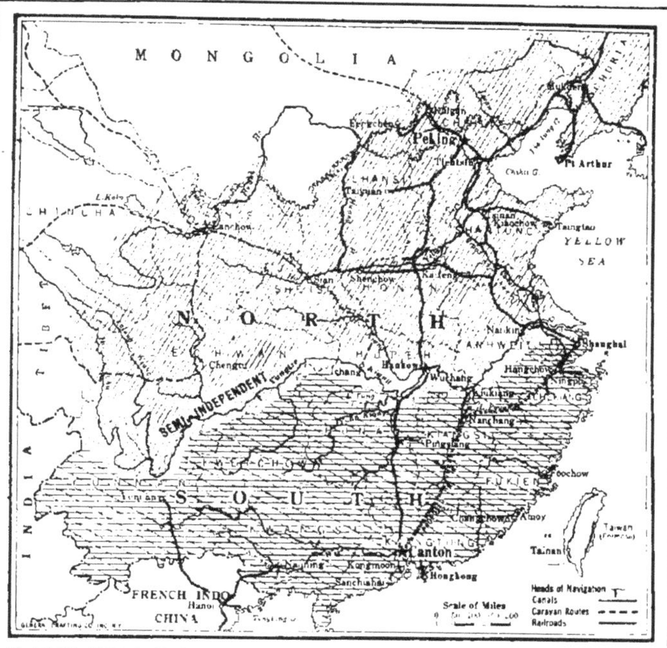

NORTH AND SOUTH CHINA AND THEIR LAND AND WATER ROUTES.
Two thousand years ago, when China had an excellent system of post-roads, it had also political peace, and her land routes and waterways "must be reorganized to regain this happy state."

Meanwhile Washington dispatches inform us that China has "plunged into a real civil war" on the eve of the Washington Conference, which has "decided in advance that a settlement of the Far Eastern problem is the necessary preliminary to any agreement upon a limitation of armament" and we read:

"Japanese influence is alleged to be involved in the new and significant development. Face to face with the determination of the Government of the United States to treat only with the Peking Government in dealing with China affairs, the South China Government, headed by Dr. Sun Yat Sen, together with Dr. Wu Ting-fang, Minister of Foreign Affairs, has decided to chance its fortunes upon an armed advance upon Peking.

"Three divisions of troops under personal direction of Dr. Sun, consisting of about 15,000 men each, representing the armed force of Kwangsi province, are marching upon Peking. Their hope of success is based on the theory that the northern provinces of China are not supporting the Peking Government.

"It is a desperate move which, if successful, will make Dr. Sun the leading Chinese figure at the arms conference. On the other hand, the standing of the South China Government at the conference will be entirely destroyed if it proves a failure."

Photo by Underwood & Underwood.

IS THERE WATER ENOUGH HERE TO SUPPLY THE PANAMA CANAL?

Overflow from Gatun Lake going over the Gatun Dam in 1912, before the canal was opened. This overflow is now used to operate the locks, and the question is whether it will always be sufficient.

IS THE PANAMA CANAL TOO SMALL?

IN TWENTY-FIVE YEARS or so the Panama Canal will be called upon to transport twice as great a traffic as it will now accommodate—three times as much, in fact, if we consider that its water supply is not sufficient to allow it to reach the mechanical maximum. This water supply is now important because the canal and its locks are largely filled with fresh water from Gatun Lake. If it were a sea-level cut, from ocean to ocean, like the Suez Canal, no such condition would interfere with its full operation. Such a cut we must have, in the not distant future, unless the canal is to become a back number. At least this is the conclusion of V. G. Iden, who contributes an article on this subject to *The Marine Review*. Says this writer:

"The canal has cost the country more than $360,000,000, which makes possible the passage of some forty vessels a day from one ocean to the other. It is a tremendous waterway, but will it be adequate to care for the heavy traffic of the future? The canal was opened to commercial shipping in the summer of August, 1914. During 1915 a total of 4,894,134 tons traversed it. During 1920 a total of 11,326,119 tons of shipping were locked through. It is estimated by engineers that the canal can accommodate only 50,000,000 tons of shipping a year. If the traffic increases at this same rate, the country will find, within the next twenty years, that its much proclaimed waterway at the isthmus is inadequate to care for the demands of commerce. The canal was designed after careful study of the isthmian meteorology, but records then covered a period of but fifteen years, and mistakes have since been found. For instance it was reckoned that the total yearly flow could not be less than 5730 cubic feet per second. From May to April, 1911-1912, it was 4626, that is to say, much below the minimum admitted by the engineers to insure the feeding of the canal.

"As an illustration, a ruling by the canal administration instructs every one in the zone to report leaky spigots. The water supply is too precious even during the wet season to permit a little thing like that to escape attention.

"In May, 1920, there was a scarcity of rain never before seen. This indicates a prospective calamity which no imaginable storage can counterbalance.

"From the estimates already made, it would appear that the Panama Canal is enclosed in a limited horizon of 30,000,000 tons of traffic per annum. On the other hand, there is every reason to expect a traffic of between 50,000,000 and 100,000,000 tons toward the middle of this century.

"The only sensible means of meeting this prospect is to enlarge the canal. It has been suggested that another channel be dug to parallel the present canal. But that is impossible, as the observations show that the present watershed will not yield an adequate supply of water. Then it would be necessary to cut through the isthmus at another point and tap a new watershed. That would be more expensive than the present canal.

"Ex-Secretary of War Baker suggested that the country might turn to the Nicaragua project and build that canal, but engineers have ruled against the scheme owing to the volcanic nature of the land in that neighborhood. And should a second canal be built through Nicaragua, what claims would Panama have against this country? The United States entered into a treaty with Panama to build the canal through her territory to connect the two oceans. That is an obligation which can not now be avoided. And if the Panama Canal is not enlarged the risk arises of having some other power step in and build a rival canal."

What is to be done? Mr. Iden pronounces unhesitatingly for a lock canal so constructed as to be gradually transformed into a wide and deep waterway. After the construction of the lock canal, the excavation would be entirely executed on water by dredges. The consulting board rejected this project because they did not know the progress made then in underwater rock excavation. Some expert engineers are now ready to reverse that decision, as they believe such excavation is entirely feasible. He goes on:

"The enlargement of the present canal would start with the dredging and the transportation by scows of the spoils in the lake created in the Chagres Valley above Gamboa. The work would begin by enlarging enormously the bed of the canal, especially in that short section at the divide where the slides have taken place. These slides themselves will be of no account if the width of the canal is increased to 1,000 or 2,000 feet at the actual level of the Gatun Lake. Much work could be carried out without interfering with the current operations of traffic through the waterway.

"America's dependence upon the canal is becoming more and more evident as the nation grows. When the United States undertook the task, it never dreamed of the possibility of becoming involved in a world-wide war. Now national security demands a quick and efficient channel giving access to either the Atlantic or Pacific coast.

"Culebra Cut is one of the most serious danger spots on the canal. A slight earthquake would open a fissure, in which case the canal would be destroyed the next day. A bomb dropt from the air might put the whole waterworks out of commission. A munitions ship was sunk in the Suez Canal during the late war, and in order to move her out of the way of traffic the British blew her up. There was no damage done, for the Suez is a sea-level canal. An obstruction in the Panama Canal could not be removed so easily.

"It is entirely possible to order the transformation of the canal under a law which would specify that the expenses must be kept within the limits of the funds to be borrowed by an emission of bonds bearing an interest not greater than the last yearly surplus of the revenues of the canal above current expenses. When the traffic reaches 20,000,000 registered tons, the canal will produce earnings more than covering all expenditures of maintenance as well as of interest on the capital of construction. Probably within half the time necessary for the transformation into a sea-level strait, the canal will have reached the financial equilibrium. Before the transformation is completed, the canal will earn also the surplus sum necessary to cover the interest on the transformation."

TO TREAT RAILWAY CARS MORE GENTLY

ARNOLD BENNETT says that American engineers always start and stop their trains with a jolt, while this is rarely the case in England. This may be due to our longer and heavier trains, or just to slap-dash, "don't-care" temperament. Treatment of this kind is annoying to the public, but what is perhaps more important to the railroads, it wears out the cars. Rough handling occurs even more in yards than on the open line, and it has been proved to be unnecessary. The roads are going to stop it, and they will be aided by a newly devised instrument named an "impact-recorder," which will tell them the extent, time, and exact location of cases of rough handling on each particular car. The facts noted above were ascertained with the aid of this instrument, as described in an article contributed to *The Railway Age* (New York). We are here told that service tests have been carried to a point which is said to have definitely established the practicability of the device. The writer goes on:

"Through a series of tests conducted with a view of creating actual cases of rough handling and observing the resulting vibration on the chart of the impact register the limit of rough handling was decided to be between two and three miles an hour speed at the time of impact.

"After the test had been completed, a number of machines were put into use in through merchandise cars operated on a regular loading schedule and handled at destination by the agent in charge. No traveling inspector accompanied the machines, but their records were removed by the receiving agents and mailed to the general office for investigation and tabulation. The movement of the machines was not advertised and train crews did not know at any time when they might be handling the register. Each case of rough handling which resulted was taken up with the superintendent on whose division it occurred and the crew responsible disciplined therefor.

"Studies of records indicate that 97 per cent. of the rough handling cases actually occur in yards. The question has been raised whether it is within the limits of reason to expect that cars may be handled under the conditions imposed on railway operation without a certain amount of rough handling. In answer to this it is noted from the record obtained in the tests that 27 out of 111 cars under observation moved from origin to destination over an aggregate distance of 10,000 car miles without a single case of rough handling. There are also repeated instances where cars moving over exactly the same route received widely varying treatment. It is, therefore, estimated that if 24 per cent. of the cars can be handled properly under present conditions of transportation with no rigid disciplinary measures in effect, the enforcing of proper discipline would enable the handling of at least 70 per cent. of the equipment in the same manner."

DANGERS OF SOME COMMON THINGS

ENVIRONMENT MAY ENDOW generally harmless articles with highly dangerous qualities. C. B. Scott, manager of the Chicago Bureau of Safety, tells in *The National Safety News* (Chicago) how in an electrical power plant, fishing-rods, derby hats, shoes or watch-chains may be fatal to the holder or wearer. Writes Mr. Scott:

"Once upon a time a man thoughtlessly walked into a generating station with a long steel fishing-rod over his shoulder, and the timely application of the prone pressure method of resuscitation saved his fast ebbing life.

"Ever after and even to this day men about the plant are telling how foolish the man was. It was indeed a foolish thing to do, but not more foolhardy than some of the everyday thoughtless things many experienced electrical workers do. A long steel fishing-rod is no better conductor of electric current than a wire in a derby hat, a concealed nail in a shoe. The long rod is only more conspicuously visible and easier to place in contact with the source of electrical energy. We have only heard of one fishing-rod incident, but we have also heard of fatal electrical accidents caused by the hat wire, the nails in the shoes, finger-rings and watch-chains.

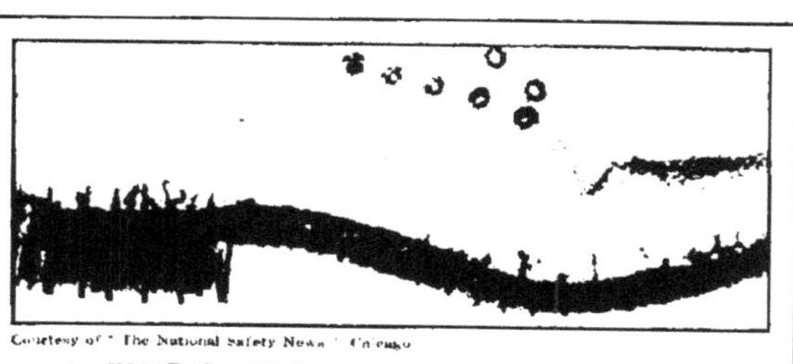

Courtesy of "The National Safety News," Chicago

A SUICIDAL SHOE FOR ELECTRICAL WORKERS.

The X-ray shows the nails that will conduct the fatal current.

"One reason why there are so many accidents due to electric current is because the current is not visible. Visible hazards are not so often disregarded as the ones which can not be seen. Unguarded moving machinery looks dangerous even to the inexperienced.

"Every person does not so readily distinguish the invisible current of electricity. Men employed in the business of electrical production and distribution often have to apply a test to ascertain if wires or equipment are electrically alive or dead. It logically follows that greater care is required in connection with electrical hazards than with visible sources of danger.

"Too little attention is given by electrical workers to the subject of unsafe clothing, and by unsafe clothing we mean clothing containing metal parts. No workman in a generating plant is safe while wearing shoes with metal nails, a hat with wire in the brim, metal finger-rings, watch-chain, clothing with metal buttons, glasses with metal or flammable frames.

"Men who persist in ignoring these things need urgent admonition just as much as did the unwise fisherman. In fact, they need it more, because any one could see and appreciate the folly of the man carrying the fishing-rod.

"Shoes worn by men subjected to electrical hazards should have wooden pegs instead of metal nails, derby hats and cap visors should be examined for metal parts, and if they contain these, should not be worn.

"Flammable visors or eye-shields should be prohibited. To sum it all up, particular precaution should be taken not to wear any clothing about electrically charged wires or apparatus which contains any metal or flammable part. No metal trinkets should be worn.

"The difference between visible and invisible hazards is clearly shown in the accompanying illustration of the anatomy of a pair of shoes which were worn by a deceased electrical worker at the moment of his decease. The picture is *prima facie* evidence of a danger almost as obvious as a picture of a man entering an electrical plant with a steel fishing-rod."

GETTING READY FOR NEXT TIME AT PUEBLO

IN TIME OF LOW-WATER prepare for floods, George Washington would probably have said, if asked his opinion on the subject. The man in Arkansas who didn't mend his leaky roof when the dry weather gave him opportunity, "because it didn't leak then," is not a safe guide for cities built on the flood plains of periodically overflowing streams. Hence the reason for the plans for making Pueblo immune to floods, described in *The Engineering News-Record* (New York). These include diversion of the river to the bluff side of the valley, the creation of an overflow channel, and the use of the railroad yards for extreme flow. If they are carried out, the next flood, when (not if) it comes, will be harmless, and property and lives will be saved. Other towns on floodable sites should take notice and act before disaster comes to teach them the way. We read:

"A noteworthy proposal for the control of the Arkansas River at Pueblo, Colo., to prevent recurrence of floods like that of the first week of June, has been put forward by Edward F. Rizer, civil engineer, of Pueblo. It depends upon provision of an overflow channel alongside the normal river channel, normally utilized as a park. This channel would make the capacity equal to the estimated flow of the 1921 flood. To provide for still higher floods, 50 per cent. greater than that of June, a wide belt of level ground, adjoining the overflow channel and in the plan assigned to railroad yard use, is made to serve as a secondary overflow channel, carrying water four and one-half feet deep in extreme floods. Levees provided with suitable spillways separate the river and the overflow channels from each other.

"In applying this flood control system to the Pueblo conditions, Mr. Rizer makes a relocation of the Arkansas River through the entire length of the city, shifting it from its present location (about the middle of the valley bottom) to the southerly edge, along the bluff. Complete revision of the railroad yards now occupying the south half of the valley bottom would be required, as well as elimination of a business and industrial district lying between the present river and the Union Depot, and a housing district.

"Pueblo's physical location will continue to invite flood disasters," says Mr. Rizer in explaining his proposal, "on account of the size, arrangement and steep slope of its drainage area, which make the river flashy. Three extreme floods have occurred within a thirty-year period, in each case doing large damage. By moving the river south against the bluff, one bank is secured; the bluff is of blue shale and will not require revetment. Taking the ordinary flood volume of 65,000 cubic feet, the proposed new channel is planned to be able to carry this flow. The 'flood channel park,' about 400 feet wide, along the north bank of the new river channel, would receive water over a spillway at a point near where the river enters the city. The area north of this channel, to the present river, would be devoted wholly to railroad yards, and would be kept available for peak flood flow, giving a total flow width of about 2,200 feet. The main part of the city to the north would be separated from the railroad yards by a retaining wall. Communication between this part of the city and the district lying on the south bluffs would be by viaducts like the one shown for Union Avenue.

"This plan was developed on the assumption that Pueblo alone would have to finance the flood-protection work, and correspondingly it gives protection to the city only. Should the Arkansas Valley as a whole be included in the project, a detention reservoir would have to be added to the local channel improvement. This would, roughly, double the cost, it is stated.

"Enlargement of the channel at its present location," Mr. Rizer says, "would destroy more property value than the diversion project. That part of the plan involving rearrangement of the railroad yards is also logical, as the present yards are poorly arranged and of inadequate capacity."

SEEING THE EARTH MOVE—With a bowl of water and some powdered resin one may observe the earth's motion, we are told by S. Leonard Bastin in *The Scientific American* (New York). It is commonly supposed, says Mr. Bastin, that it is not possible to demonstrate the movement of the earth without elaborate apparatus, which is far from being the case. He goes on:

"In the first place select a room that is fairly free from vibration. Then obtain a good-sized bowl or tub a foot or more in diameter and rather deep, and nearly fill it with water. Place this on the floor of the room in such a position that it need not be disturbed for some hours. Get some finely powdered resin and sprinkle a coating of this on the surface of the water. Any fine substance that would float and not be dissolved for some hours would do as well. Next secure a little coal dust and sprinkle some on the top of the resin in a straight line from the center to the circumference. Carry this line up over the rim of the bowl, and make it broad enough to be clearly seen—say about an inch in width. The bowl may now be left for several hours, at the end of which time it will be noticed that an interesting thing has happened. It will be seen that the line of the surface of the water has changed its position and that it no longer meets that which runs up over the rim of the bowl. As a matter of fact the black line on the surface of the water has swept around from east to west. What has happened is this: The water in the bowl has stood still throughout the time which it has been left, while the vessel itself has been carried around by the motion of the earth from west to east. Another way of putting it is that the earth has swung around through a considerable arc from west to east, leaving the water quite stationary."

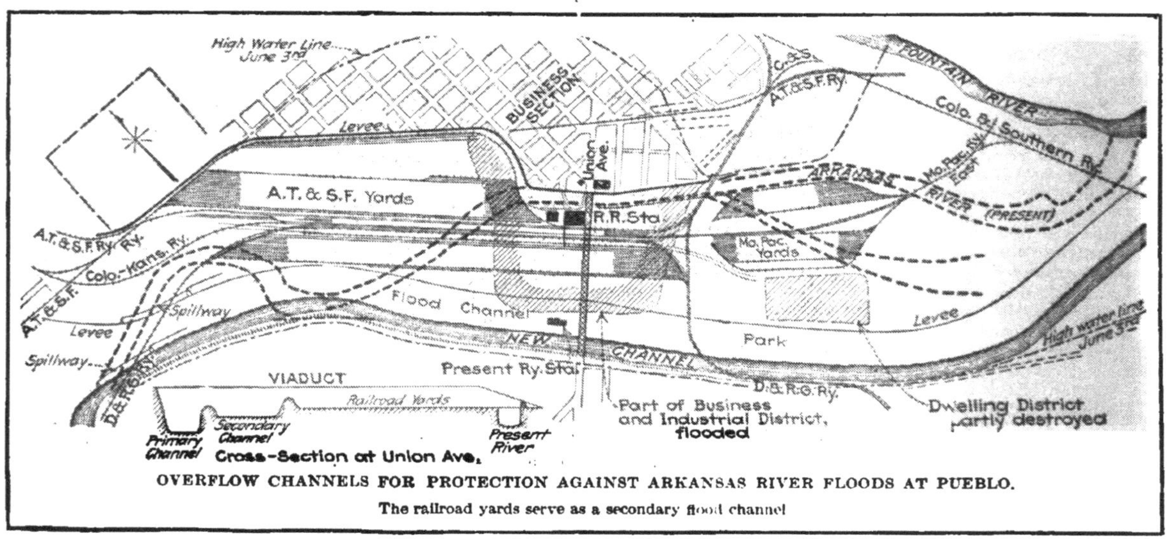

OVERFLOW CHANNELS FOR PROTECTION AGAINST ARKANSAS RIVER FLOODS AT PUEBLO.

The railroad yards serve as a secondary flood channel

Illustrations by courtesy of "The Popular Science Monthly," New York

AIR VIEWS AS USED BY TRADE ASSOCIATIONS TO ADVERTISE HOUSING AND TERMINAL FACILITIES.

SELLING LAND WITH AIR VIEWS

LESSONS LEARNED IN AERIAL PHOTOGRAPHY during the war are now applied to commercial use, says a contributor to *The Popular Science Monthly* (New York). There are firms, he goes on, that make a specialty of taking airplane views of factories or of communities. Manufacturers have discovered that an air photograph gives a more comprehensive idea of the plant, the location of the buildings, and the general layout than any number of ordinary views taken on the ground, or even on a tower. But the most interesting application of airplane photography is its growing use in the real estate business. We read:

"Real estate is a difficult thing to sell. An automobile, for instance, may be easily viewed as a whole. The prospective purchaser, if he chooses, may look on three sides of it at once or, by walking around it, obtain an impression of the entire car.

"But the real-estate man is up against it. When Mr. Smith walks into the office and announces that he is thinking of buying a 'home of his own,' the salesman starts at a disadvantage. He commences by describing roughly and usually inaccurately the various properties that might interest Mr. Smith. Sometimes he even goes so far as to show Smith some photographs of the houses.

"But Smith is a bit wary. He can not tell from the photographs whether the property is on a respectable street or whether it is hedged in by factories and small shops. So that, after all the salesman's talk, it is necessary to take Mr. Smith to every one of the properties. Too often, when he gets there, one glance is sufficient to tell him that it is not what he wants. His time and that of the salesman have been wasted. Now, had the real-estate office been a modern one, with an airplane as the salesman's assistant, Mr. Smith could have been greatly assisted in his search. In fact, it is probable that it would have been unnecessary for him to leave the office until his selection had been narrowed down to one or two available selections.

BETTER THAN A DOZEN GROUND VIEWS.

The air view gives the buyer a better idea of the estate.

"Harrington Emerson, one of the shrewdest industrial counselors and efficiency engineers in the world, has repeatedly stated that visualization is the greatest salesman in the world. Real-estate dealers are commencing to realize the truth of this statement, and in aerial photographs are finding the means to commercialize the fact.

"Nor does the use of air photographs end there. Real-estate dealers are finding it to their interest to have an annual photographic map made of their city, thus showing graphically its growth from year to year. Such a map would be of great value in bringing to the attention of prospective customers residing at a distance, the railroad, harbor, and docking facilities, and engineering projects under way or already in existence, such as large public buildings, canals, and traction lines. The cost of an annual map would be small compared to the returns."

COLORING ORANGES ORANGE—This would seem to be like "gilding refined gold, or painting the lily," but it is done only in cases where a really ripe orange looks green. We are so accustomed to orange-colored oranges that it is quite legitimate, thinks S. R. Winters, to gratify the public taste in this case. He says in *The Scientific American* (New York):

"The marketing of Satsuma oranges is being speeded up by an artificial process of discoloration developed by the Office of Horticultural and Pomological Investigations of the United States Department of Agriculture. Laboratory tests have determined the feasibility of applying an attractive coloring to oranges by exposing the fruit to an atmosphere of gases formed by an imperfect combustion of petroleum products. The Satsuma orange, strange to say, reaches its most inviting state for consumption several weeks prior to the attainment of a yellow color. If permitted to remain on the tree until it assumes the characteristic hue of a ripe orange, the fruit is robbed of its fine flavor. The time-honored habit of the buyers of oranges is to specify a fruit with a yellow color, long considered as the only sure earmark of a ripe orange. Obviously, the fruit salesman is at a disadvantage in marketing the green-colored specimens. Hence the efforts of the Bureau of Plant Industry to hasten the ripening process where nature left a gap."

AMERICA'S LOVE FOR DANTE TO-DAY AND YESTERDAY

TAKING A FALL OUT OF DANTE would seem in line with other literary criticism affected by our younger school. The "Divine Comedy" is found "to be largely piffle" by Mr. H. L. Mencken, if we may rely on a quoted opinion. Our authority is Mr. Ed Howe of the *Monthly*, who avows he is not unwilling to bolster up his confessed standing as "the worst literary critic in the United States" by quoting the man sometimes charged with being "the best" in the same line. And Mr. Howe admits he has also said Dante was "piffle." Despite these jarring notes, there is no denying this country's interest in such a great cultural subject, and the *New Republic* recalls the important part played by American literary scholars in the Dante revival at the six hundredth anniversary of his birth. The study of Dante, it points out, began with the romantic movement in culture. "George Ticknor must be accounted as the father of Dante scholarship, as of romance studies in general at Harvard." He was succeeded by Longfellow, Lowell and Norton, who held famous "Wednesday evenings" in Longfellow's study. We read:

THE PARIS CHURCH WHERE DANTE WORSHIPED.
Church of St. Séverin where the pillar seen at the right is dedicated to the Italian poet who, as Boccaccio asserts, once visited Paris.

"The account Norton gives of the cooperative effort of these scholars in colonial and provincial Cambridge, Massachusetts, so far away from the great currents of the world's thought, deserves to be quoted in the words which he spoke to the Dante Society on the occasion of Longfellow's death.

"'We paused over every doubtful passage, discust the various readings, considered the true meaning of obscure words and phrases, sought for the most exact equivalent of Dante's expression, objected, criticized, praised with a freedom that was made perfect by Mr. Longfellow's absolute sweetness and simplicity and modesty and by the entire confidence that existed between us. . . . They were delightful evenings; there could be no pleasanter occupation; the spirits of poetry, of learning, of friendship were with us.'

"Truly a discipleship not unworthy of the master, and an association that suggests the rare and tender charm with which Dante has recorded so many human relations.

"In 1865, the six-hundredth year of Dante's birth, Longfellow's translation of the 'Inferno' appeared, to be followed by the 'Purgatorio' and 'Paradiso,' and Norton's translation of the 'Vita Nuova.' In 1872 Lowell's essay on Dante appeared. Ten years later, on May 16th, 1882, the Dante Society was founded, with Longfellow as President, Lowell as Vice-President, and Norton as a member of the Council. In that year Longfellow died, to be succeeded by Lowell, and he in turn by Norton. The Dante Society has been a center of energy for interest in Dante in America and by its support most of the larger contributions to Dante scholarship have been made, especially the three concordances, that of E. A. Fay to the 'Commedia,' that of E. S. Sheldon to the minor Italian works, and that of E. K. Rand and E. H. Wilkins to the Latin works. The foundation of the Dante prize brought forward many young scholars, of whom the first prize winner, George R. Carpenter, showed by his essay on the Episode of the Donna Pietosa in the 'Vita Nuova' promise that was cut short by his absorption in other activities and by his untimely death. Latham's translation of Dante's eleven letters was another effort which owed its being to the society. It is indeed a remarkable testimony to its influence that under its inspiration so many men of note in other fields have made contributions to the study of Dante. Perhaps by reason of the eminence of its founders it has enjoyed a prestige which has enabled it to grant a sort of blue ribbon in American scholarship, and in the rising tide of academic interest in physical science, to maintain a proud distinction as a stronghold of literary study."

Why Dante makes such a special appeal as the history of American scholarship shows is a question suggested quite naturally. The writer here hazards the reply:

"The answer is perhaps to be found in a quality which the two most eminent American critics of Dante have noted in him. Lowell expresses that quality in declaring that 'Dante had discovered the incalculable worth of a single idea as compared with the largest heap of facts ever gathered.' The Puritans had a passion for unity, for a conception of the universe, as opposed to a pluriverse. This explains the predominance of monistic idealism in American philosophy, and the disappointment of Henry Adams when such a world view was denied him. The descendants of the Puritans, ranging from Unitarianism to Agnosticism, kept this desire, and if they could not find its satisfaction in philosophy they found it at least in literature, in the medieval Dante. One may ask why they did not turn rather to their own poet, to Milton. Obviously the reason is that Milton stood too near them. His world order is too closely an expression of the Christian mythology which they had renounced. Dante gave them the rich and perfect concept of a world unity, and that the faith which inspired it was alien from theirs made the appeal of his art so much the greater. And it is in this appreciation of the unity of Dante that Mr. Santayana with his Catholic heritage and classical attitude joins the neo-Puritan critics in saying:

"'His poetry covers the whole field from which poetry may be fetched, and to which poetry may be applied, from the innermost recesses of the heart to the outward bounds of nature and of destiny.'"

A MILITARY PAGEANT FOR THE ITALIAN POET.

Before the Palazzo Vecchio on September 17, Florence celebrated the return of her forces from the battle of Campaldino, where on July 11, 1289, Dante fought for the Guelphs against the Tuscan Ghibillines.

Two special Dante collections exist in this country, one is housed at Harvard and another at Cornell. The usefulness of these has been enhanced by careful bibliographical work. Universities, even as remote from Italy as Oxford, cherish the tradition that Dante once visited them. Little as scholars of the thirteenth century were travelers, it is undoubted that he once went to Paris.

MORE BOOKS AND LESS BREAD FOR DEVASTATED FRANCE

THE AMERICAN LIBRARY SYSTEM is making an entrance into France and showing some of the universal phases of pioneer work. Give us more books and less bread, was practically the request of the dwellers in the devasted areas, and the American Committee for the Devastated Region of France began at once after peace to replace its purely physical relief work by social and educational endeavors. The program includes public health, physical education, nursing, public libraries, manual training and playgrounds. Miss Jessie Carson, director of the committee's library activities, gave an account of the work illustrated by moving pictures before the Library Association of Manchester, England, and the report of her address in the London *Times* is the first information we have seen of these endeavors. The report does not give her words directly, but after the usual British newspaper manner:

"The territory covered by the operations of the committee extends over 103 communes and 128 villages in the neighborhood of Soissons. Fifty traveling libraries have been established by the library section in 50 different villages. There are five reading rooms with up-to-date furniture, made by French labor from pitch pine imported from America. Three American librarians are in charge of the work, with seven French assistants, one of whom is now on her way to the United States to receive professional training in librarianship.

"Miss Carson paid a warm tribute to the efficiency and intelligence of the women motor drivers, all British, who have been engaged in the necessary transport work for the village library. Popular library work for the people, she said, seemed to be unknown in France, yet the few books that survived the war were found by the people to be the greatest treasures imaginable. American workers were asked for books first. 'We will take less of the absolute necessaries of life if you will only give us some books,' was a common remark by the villagers. To-day 15,000 books were in use, specially selected as to subject matter, and these were distributed in five reading rooms and 50 permanent libraries. This was the achievement of 15 months. The cost had been only 200,000f. (about £3,770), including the purchase and binding of the books, all the initial expenses, the first subscriptions to magazines, and all salaries.

"Statistics, however, said Miss Carson, did not tell the whole story. The work had wonderful humanizing aspects. Altho the people of France loved good books they seemed to know nothing of the possibilities of library work, but by the means of these traveling village libraries in the devasted areas a real 'library atmosphere' had been created. Difficulty had at first been experienced in getting adolescent boys and girls into the libraries. Yet, without this, she would have considered the work a failure. Success had been achieved in getting these classes of frequenters into the libraries, as the film subsequently showed."

The London *Daily Telegraph* devotes a long editorial to this report and some of the problems that it brings forward:

"There could be no better proof of the keenness of these hungry souls than the postponement of their bodily hunger to the interests of their intellectual needs. In her experience Miss Carson has found a great lack of French translations of English works, especially of children's books and animal stories; and she wants to have Mrs. Ewing's tales and Mr. C. G. Roberts's admirable anecdotes made available for French boys and girls. Certain books have become popular. For instance, much of the work of R. L. Stevenson, to which might be added Fenimore Cooper's novels, 'Swiss Family Robinson'—despite its unscientific character—and the immortal 'Robinson Crusoe.' But the children have their dislikes as well as their favorites. Apparently they cannot make head or tail of 'Alice in Wonderland,' which can hardly surprize us, and, according to Miss Carson, Kipling is only popular for his 'Kim,' which is studied by Boy Scouts."

The Telegraph goes on to correct a possible impression that

Kipling is not "largely translated" into French or "tolerably well known in Paris":

"Some years ago there was a boom for Kipling in the French capital, and men like Robert d'Humieres and Savine and Louis Fabulet were busily engaged in rendering him into French. Above all, André Chevrillon devoted a good many pages to the poet of Imperialism in his 'Etudes Anglaises' in a discerning and critical spirit, which showed no little sympathy with a writer not perhaps very congenial to the French temperament. Of course it is by no means an easy task to make Kipling understood by the average French reader. Nor has the effort been always successful. For instance, Kipling wrote a curiously imaginative little story under the title 'They'—'they' meaning vague, phantom existences, especially the ghosts of little children which haunt the imagination of a spinster. To find in French the word 'Eux'—which is indeed a literal translation—seems somehow to strike an entirely different note. In an similar fashion we have the well-known anecdotes for children which Kipling called 'The Just-So Stories.' How is this title to be turned into French? 'Contes comme ça' does not seem particularly happy. Perhaps 'Contes qui s'expliquent' comes nearer to the sense of the original—stories which cannot help being what they are, stories which every child would accept in their entirety, as, for instance, the humorous account of the cat that walked by himself, to whom all places and times were alike, and who was cleverer than all the beasts of the field."

From this *The Telegraph* is easily led into an interesting consideration of the differences of the French and the English mind which the effort of translation so forcibly brings out:

"If a clever Frenchman wanted to understand Kipling, he would probably achieve his object through his familiar acquaintance with Pierre Loti, or, it might be, Guy de Maupassant. Loti would give him the interest, so strong in Kipling, of foreign regions and alien civilizations, 'exotisme,' as the French call it, the passion for the foreign. Maupassant would supply the realism, for both he and Kipling belong to the realistic school, and passionately desire to paint things as they are without romantic illusion. But when we come to individual pieces a strange divergence between the tastes and predilections of London and Paris is at once discernible. Take Kipling's novel, 'The Light that Failed.' What is the main theme? We should be inclined to say that the novelist's subject was the joys and sorrows, the temptations, the anguish, the despair of an artist. Naturally we are thinking of the hero, the unhappy *Dick*, who made such a tragic shipwreck of his life. But with Maupassant's 'Notre Cœur' in his hand, the Frenchman picks out for sympathy and praise the figure of *Maisie*, the heroine, a woman incapable of love. *Maisie*, with the limitations of her temperament, ruined *Dick*, and it is this side of the tragedy, engineered by the character of the heroine, which appeals to the French writer. Or let us take André Chevrillon's estimate of Kipling's great hymn, 'The Recessional.' He finds it '*haïssable*,' hateful. It is not easy for us, we will not say to accept such an estimate, but even to understand it. The 'Recessional' is described as an intensely egotistic poem, in which an Englishman thanks God in the spirit of the Pharisee that he is not like other men. He is accommodating himself to a passing mood of modesty which he does not in reality feel, he remains throughout the self-righteous egotist. It is a curious verdict; for the extra-ordinary thing about the 'Recessional,' when once we have got over our surprize that Kipling should have written it at all, is that it is so simple, so utterly devoid of self-consciousness. It might be the voice of some older Puritan in Cromwell's time telling us in grave and noble accents to beware of national pride. But however little appreciation is extended to the 'Recessional,' 'The Jungle Book' is given a very different reception. No book has won higher praise from French critics."

HALF-PRICE FOR HALF-LENGTH ART

ONE OF ENGLAND'S TITLED GENTLEMEN is apparently fond of being portrayed by famous artists, but he has his own opinions of the value of the results and the rights of ownership, and they may be said to vary considerably from the ideas Whistler used to hold of the rights of the artist on his own work. Whistler granted nothing more to the man who paid for the artist's work than the rights of reverent custodianship. If he were now living he might find in Lord Leverhulme material for an additional chapter to the "Gentle Art of Making Enemies." Lord Leverhulme sat a year or two ago to the famous painter, Augustus John, and when the canvas was sent home he trimmed off a generous margin because he found the picture an inconvenient size. Recently he has been painted by Sir William Orpen, and argues that the work is worth only half the original sum agreed upon because the painter persuaded him to be "done" sitting down instead of standing "full length," which he was in the beginning willing to agree would be worth £3000. The dispute furnishes an art topic for the British papers and convinces the London *Times* that the British public is often unjustly accused of indifference to art. At least—

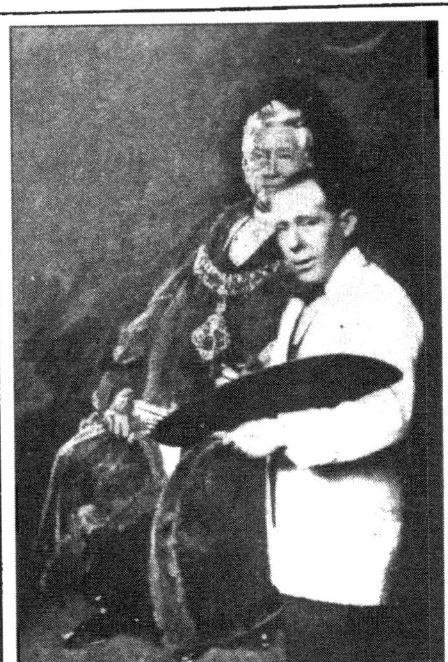

THE LORD AND THE PAINTER.
Sir William Orpen standing before the sitting "Lord Leverhulme" who thought such a portrait as done by Orpen worth only half a "full-length."

"It has a curious, irrelevant interest in art as a commodity, the price of which is incalculable. It is excited when some picture is sold for many thousands of pounds, because it can see no reason why that picture should fetch more than another; and often there is no intelligible reason. It is also excited when there is a dispute about the authorship of a picture, because, if it is by Romney, say, it is worth a great sum, while if it is by some one else it is not; and the public, naturally, cannot understand why this should be so. Finally, it is excited when there is a dispute between an artist and his customer about the price of a picture, again because this is a matter that does not appear to be determined by ordinary economic principles. At the present moment, for instance, there is a dispute between Lord Leverhulme and Sir William Orpen because Sir William, having agreed to paint a full-length portrait of Lord Leverhulme standing for £3,000, did in fact paint one of him sitting and demands the same price for it. This would seem to be a question not of art at all, but of business, and no more interesting than any other business dispute. Sir William contracted to supply a certain article for a certain price; and the only question is whether he has supplied such an article or one of less value. But no; to the public it is a question of art, because the price of works of art is incalculable and subject to laws of its own.

"We express no opinion on the dispute because we have no means of forming one, and because it is no more a matter of public interest than any other dispute about a contract. What is interesting is the prevailing confusion of thought on such questions. Art itself is, or should be, a matter of great moment; but not the price of works of art, except in so far as it is important that artists of merit, whether painters or writers or musicians or craftsmen, should be able to earn a decent living by their work. But on that point the public is not much interested; at least many artists of merit and even of genius are not able to earn a decent living. Van Gogh, whose pictures now sell for thousands, when he was alive—and he died only twenty years ago—could seldom get more than five pounds for a picture; the public interest in him grows in proportion as others profit by his work. But on this kind of interest art cannot thrive, because it is an interest not in art, but in prices. Sir William Orpen's portrait of Lord Leverhulme may be a masterpiece; but if it were the greatest masterpiece of modern times, and if the sum in dispute were not £3,000, but £30, we should hear nothing about it."

OUR RESENTMENT OF CRITICISM

ONE OF OUR OLDEST TRADITIONS, alongside that one which admits we are a young country, is that "we have no critics, no criticism." The reproach dates openly as far back as Poe, and appears to be in a peculiarly aggravated state at present. The radical journals who never let us forget our shortcomings are the ones now most exercised over this one. *The New Republic*, to be sure, is only half convinced of the truth, and quotes the charge from Mr. Conrad Aiken with the reminder that it has "an exquisite provincialism of its own." Poe "echoed the Colonial cry" that "we have no critics, no criticism," and Henry James came along to berate Poe's performance in that line as "provincial." *The New Republic* finds this in the nature of things:

SITTER FOR PORTRAIT CONTRIVES TO GET HIS KNEES IN AT HALF-LENGTH RATES.

—Dowd in *Punch* (London.)

"That James should have gone so wrong on Poe and Whitman is not, in the nature of things, extraordinary. It was the fashion of Colonials then, as it is now, to apologize for American literature abroad, to meet the charge of provincialism more than half way, to be a little masochistic. Not until France and England took a mandate for Poe and Whitman did they become reputable for the timid esthete in America."

The troubles of Mr. Aiken were brought about by disparaging criticism passed on Henry James by Mr. H. L. Mencken. The same gentleman precipitates another overhauling of our critical baggage in a contemporary member of *The Freeman*. The writer of the "Reviewer's Notebook" quotes a recent observation of Mr. William Allen White to the effect that "he would like to collect a number of the more or less youthful pessimists who are at present raking America with their criticism and duck them in the town pump." The "Reviewer" here admits that "of the critics in question few indeed are not open to the retort that they are themselves no more essentially civilized than the civilization they attack." But aside from "these same vipers" the "Reviewer" comes back to the old cry that "there is no criticism in America at all."

As a people we do not understand criticism, he declares, and the reason for our blighted condition is "because we have had none." Then to prove it:

"We have had, in all the course of our history, no such candid friend, no such 'national conscience' as every European country has had within the last two or three generations; and accordingly we can not seriously question Mr. Meredith Nicholson's belief that 'if there's any manifestation on earth of a divine ordering of things, it is here in America.' That is the sort of belief the Philistine majority in every population cherishes in its heart; but America is the only country in which for generations the Philistine majority has been able to utter that belief, retarding as it is, unchallenged. . . .

"There was Emerson who, deploring the imperfections of our life eloquently enough, was the very incarnation of a fatalistic optimism. There was Lowell, so conscious of a certain condescension in foreigners that he could not sufficiently draw the veil over the shortcomings of his countrymen. There was Howells with his rosy vision of the American scene, all the more deceptive because he profest an intransigent realism. There was Henry James, whom nothing could have induced to live in this country; did he not apologize in one of his prefaces for having referred disrespectfully to Northampton, Mass., adding just so much thereby to the ultimate obloquy that has befallen the traducers of the American small town? In the old days those who were unable to put up with life in the East went West, and those who were unable to put up with the country at all went to Europe; and the voices of the countless traveling foreigners who told the ugly truth about us in the early days of the Republic were all hushed after the Civil War. Every one waited, waited, by common consent, to see how the great democratic experiment was going to work out; we had sixty years of grace, while all the oracles were dumb. And at the end we found, naturally enough, that we had forgotten what an oracle is.

"In short, all sense of values had been submerged in the United States. We are obliged to take Mr. White and Mr. Nicholson at their word and assume that they do not know the difference between a banjo and a lute or between Kansas and the Kingdom of Heaven. We are obliged to assume again, in the absence of any evidence to the contrary, that the public which reads the best magazines has ceased to feel the distinction between Mr. Scott Fitzgerald and a real genius or between Mr. Edison and a real sage. Mr. Edison is permitted to occupy the pedestal of a national worthy while he offers a prize to any one who can express in five words the patent truth that the phonograph is 'more than a machine.' And as far as one is aware, none of the defenders of the American tradition has yet challenged Mr. Edward Bok for adopting the word 'Americanization' as a legitimate description of a career that has been consistently devoted to the vulgarization of American life. To the public in our day, in other words, the whole public virtually (save for the lunatic-fringe, the small protesting minority), one thing is absolutely as good as another. And therefore, being colorblind to the values in the name of which criticism speaks, it sees nothing but the animus in this criticism and regards it as merely insulting. This would be true if our criticism were ten times surer of its values than it is; we can be certain that Mr. White would just as readily duck an Ibsen as a Mencken."

Paying this tribute to our periodical literature, the writer says:

"The conservative reviews, in so far as they are critical at all, exist for the purpose of combating the radical reviews; they have themselves neither taste nor principle; otherwise they too would perceive that American life is far from amiable or beautiful or interesting or successful and would set about in their own way helping to make it so. As it is, they only give aid and comfort to the 'Americanism,' now dominant and all but unchallenged, the rise and spread of which through the world was the nightmare of those very European critics of the nineteenth century whose standards they themselves profess to uphold."

RELIGION-AND-SOCIAL-SERVICE

THE PROCESSION TO THE VATICAN

THE RUSH OF CIVIL GOVERNMENTS to the Vatican since the war is a remarkable phenomenon in the religio-political history of the day which is creating profound interest in all religious circles, especially since the present trend may bring a return of the Papacy to greater prestige in all the affairs of the world. Tho all these journeys back over a once well traveled path are said to be largely political in their inspiration, the movement, runs a National Catholic Welfare Council editorial published in Catholic papers, "goes deeper than that. The nations would not be much concerned about bettering their stand with the Vatican if they did not realize with impressive force that the Vatican has greatly bettered its position with mankind." Before the war the Vatican had diplomatic relations with a dozen states; now it has such relations, either by sending a representative or receiving one, or, in the large majority of cases, by both sending and receiving, with twenty-five. The recent return of France to her former ambassadorial relations "has raised the diplomatic edifice of Rome, the world-position of the Papacy, to such a height," writes L. J. S. Wood in the *Atlantic Monthly*, "that the world can not help noticing it. The Holy See—to change the metaphor—seems to be riding on a great wave resulting from the storm of world-war; and the world may wonder where, how far, and in what direction it may steer itself or may be carried." Quality of relations, too, as well as quantity, we are told, have bettered. Prior to the war the Vatican sent to foreign powers only five nuncios, including those of the second class, and two internuncios; it received only two ambassadors and twelve ministers from foreign states. Now it sends out nineteen nuncios and five internuncios, receiving eight ambassadors and seventeen ministers. Governments formerly without relationships have established them. Governments which had broken off relations have reestablished them. Governments which had secondary relations have raised them to first-class.

The British Empire is prominent in the first category. It sent a minister on special mission in 1914 to explain its aims, purposes and conduct in the war. Now the special mission has been converted into a permanent legation. Holland sent a representative to the Vatican in the spring of 1915, on the ground that it was to the country's special interest that peace should be brought about as soon as possible and that it should cooperate with the Vatican. Now that peace has come, Holland has made its relations permanent, receiving a separate internuncio instead of a subordinate share in the Nuncio at Brussels. In this category come Poland, Czecho-Slovakia, Jugo-Slavia and the other states which have risen from the war. In the second category France is the outstanding figure, having lived up to Cardinal Merry del Val's characterization of her that she was "too great a lady to come up the back stairs" and resumed full ambassadorial relations. The third is numerous: the German Embassy replacing the Prussian legation, and Belgium, Chile, Brazil, and Peru raising their legations to the full rank of embassies. All this has come about, we are told, without objective effort on the part of the Pope. The civil governments have approached the Pope, not the Pope the civil governments, tho a cordial welcome in every case has been extended. Notable as an exception in the general list is Italy, now practically the only great European nation without representation at the Vatican. The position between the Quirinal and the Papacy remains as it was in 1870, when the Pope was shorn of his temporal power and became a voluntary prisoner in the Vatican. But much water has flowed under Tiber bridges during the last fifty years, and various stepping stones have been cast along which a permanent pathway between the two may be built. Pope Benedict XV has relaxed the rule prohibiting the heads of Catholic states from visiting Rome, tho in his encyclical of reconciliation it is expressly stated that the concession "must not be interpreted as a renunciation of its sacrosanct rights by the Apostolic See"; and means of communication between the two authorities are kept open. Now, we are told, the next move must come from the Italian Government. If the question were put before the people, after the explicit example set by France, the writer assures us, "the proposal might go through—all other circumstances being favorable—on a wave of patriotic enthusiasm, in addition to religious satisfaction of the great mass of the people. The patriotic note would drown what little sectarian clamor might arise." But however the Italian situation may develop, the procession of other nations of the world toward the Vatican, declares the writer, "is certainly one of the great historical phenomena to be noted among the results of the great war."

"But to prophesy as to future historico-political possibilities arising from it would be premature, particularly in view of the very sudden way in which it has come about. There is a point, however, which rivets the attention. No one, in considering to-day's phenomenon, can help thinking of old times, when the Pope had relations and agreements with all the Powers of the world—the historico-political world that counted then—Europe. Such relations were between temporal sovereigns of states and the Pope—who also was temporal sovereign of a state, but at the same time supreme spiritual sovereign of the Catholic princes with whom he had relations."

Times have changed, as the Pope is reported to have said more than once lately; and "if we run down the list to-day we find His Most Catholic Majesty of Spain the only remaining sovereign of the class of the olden days." There are, of course, Catholic states represented at the Vatican, such as Poland, Belgium, Bavaria, even France, and others:

"But Rome's diplomatic relations with the world to-day are not with Catholic princes, but with 'democratic' states, represented by parliaments and prime ministers. It has been said in disparagement of limited companies that they have 'no souls to be saved or bodies to be kicked.' In the old days of Catholic princes and of the Temporal Power, both these conditions stood. Such entities to-day have the first half of the phrase only in the measure of righteousness of feeling exprest in the policy of the nation influencing the government; and the second half stands only in the lessened and entirely changed measure of adjustment of diplomatic differences. In truth, to-day Rome's aspect in its relations with the world flocking to it must be very different from that of olden days. How it will align itself will be matter for interesting study by future students of history.

"And it is for the future students of history, not for a passing note-maker of the time, to comment on another striking phenomenon. There is one great country to which the Pope's eyes turned specially in every crisis of the war; which, up to the very last minute, he believed never would come in; to which his eyes turned all the same after it had done so; to which the eyes of the Vatican are still turned, the more so in view of its evidently increased prestige and objective and subjective importance—and that is the one country which is not joining in the rush to Rome. The United States receives a purely religious representative of the Pope in the person of an Apostolic Delegate, but it has no diplomatic relations with the Holy See. That, too, is a policy as to which future students of history, at the Vatican and in America, will have opportunity for noting results and forming judgment."

THE CHURCH'S RETURN TO DRAMA

DRAMATIC PRESENTATION of stories and scenes from the Bible is having a vogue just now in several denominations, and is being found a valuable adjunct to the usual work of the pastors in intensifying the interest of the congregations in their churches and in instructing the young in the significant facts in Biblical history. Success in many instances in this revival of an ancient method of religious teaching has led to the formation of National Commissions on Religious Dramatics by a number of the Protestant churches, including the Methodist, the Baptist and the Episcopal. It has led also to the formation of a Dramatics Association of the Sunday schools of New York, and a similar one in New Jersey. Only recently a Council on Church Drama and Pageantry has been organized under the General Board of Religious Education. This council will, as speedily as possible, writes Martha Candler in *The Christian Herald* (New York), bring together all available material suitable for church production, and will act as a clearing house for information and assistance to the churches of the country. It is composed of representatives of the dramatics and pageantry departments, or educational departments, of all Protestant churches, and of dramatics experts of the Y. W. C. A., the Community Service, and other social organizations. As to the plans of this council, we are told that—

PAGEANT OF THE THREE MARYS.

Showing how drama may present significant Biblical facts.

"One of the greatest things it will attempt to do is to stimulate the celebration of the great church holy days by the production of suitable pageants. Ultimately it will aim to circulate especially arranged material for such production, and wherever wanted furnish directors to assist in the preliminary arrangements, and take charge of costuming, lighting and scenery.

"Meanwhile the church which has its musical and dramatic talent, or which has adequate leadership, may turn its attention to the dramatization of Biblical themes. 'We hope,' says Mrs. Donald Pratt, executive of the National Episcopal Commission on Biblical Dramatics and Pageantry, 'that the time will soon come when every church basement in the country will be a workshop where groups of children as well as adults are busy on costumes, on "properties," on all that goes toward the production of the visualized Sunday-school lesson. Nothing is so real to the child, to the youth—to any of us, in fact—as those things which we act out, and it seems safe to presume that the every-day application of the great moral lessons of the Old and the New Testaments will be immensely strengthened.'

"'Some who do not understand the almost sacramental purpose of our undertaking may be shocked,' said one minister whose church was about to present the dramatized ritual. But the significant thing there as elsewhere was that those who came half expecting to be shocked, went away profoundly moved."

Many churches have their own dramatics organizations which both study the principles underlying the best drama and produce plays as a part of the social center recreations. When the Union Methodist Church of New York City called upon the Community Service to establish a dramatic department in its social center, the work, it was stated, would have a two-fold purpose: To develop the latent ability for self-expression upon the part of the young people; and to make more vivid through the use of the drama the message of the church. To further the second end, a course in Biblical drama was launched for church workers. Specific themes studied and adapted, for presentation by Sunday schools or to form a part of Sunday evening services, varied in length from a fifteen minutes' presentation to an entire evening's performance. Plans went well, and, says the writer:

"The first performance to be given in the church was on Easter Sunday evening. The play, 'The Resurrection of Our Lord,' was a fragmentary medieval miracle play. A crowded house sat in hushed awe while, to the music of the immortal oratorios so closely associated in our minds with the scenes, Pilate brooded over having condemned Jesus Christ, the Marys lamented at the empty Tomb, and finally the Angel of the Lord appeared in a burst of radiance to the organ music of Handel's 'I Know That My Redeemer Liveth.'

"Recently, in Worcester, Mass., the Union Church presented a beautiful spectacle pageant, 'In the Days of the Judges,' arranged and produced by local church people. It is said that the people of that city learned more of the historical continuity of the Old Testament than they had ever known before. The deeply religious atmosphere of the play was sustained throughout by the accompanying soft music, and by the costumes and settings which were modeled after those in the world's most famous Biblical paintings, which had been studied by a special committee over a period of several months.

Illustrations by Courtesy of "The Christian Herald," New York.

A STRIKING TABLEAU OF THE NATIVITY.

A portrayal of the great event as presented in the Neighborhood House of a New York church.

"Several of the leading churches of Washington have for a number of years held Christmas Nativity plays which were enacted in the chancel. And these are but instances of local effort producing conspicuous results."

TO PUT THE BIBLE IN THE SCHOOLS BY COURT ORDER

THE RIGHT TO READ THE BIBLE in the public schools is to be tested in the United States Supreme Court by the Presbyterian Synod of Washington State, according to a report recently published in the New York *Tribune*, one of the chief arguments to be advanced in affirmation of the right being the charge that prohibition of Scriptural reading in the schools has resulted in filling up the jails and correctional institutions. The appeal, we are told, will be based on the Declaration of Independence, the Presbyterians claiming that the Declaration is a covenant between the American nation and God, and that the study of the Bible by American children is essential to an understanding of the covenant as well as to a full knowledge of God. "To exclude the Bible from the public schools," contend the Presbyterians in their presentment preparatory to an appeal, "is to violate one of the essential clauses of the opening paragraph of the Declaration of Independence. In the State of Washington the Attorney-General, and later the Supreme Court have rendered an opinion in which the Bible, in effect, is adjudged 'a sectarian book' and decreed to be unconstitutional to read or teach in the State schools." According to the published report,

"The Presbyterians declare this ruling erroneous and that the State constitutional provisions so construed are void as in conflict with and repugnant to the principles of the Declaration of Independence.

"'This ruling,' it is added, 'makes it impossible to obtain such knowledge in the school system of the State as all citizens are equally entitled to—instruction in the laws of nature and also of nature's God, which latter are spiritual and obtainable from the Bible.'

"Extensive arguments are presented to show that no State has a right to exclude from its system of education 'instruction in the science of religion as set forth in the Bible—the only book which sets forth the existence, laws and other attributes of the Divine Providence to which the Declaration of Independence is committed—without this exclusion being repugnant to the Declaration, and therefore void.'

"The presentment declares that within a few years after prohibiting the Bible from Washington schools it became necessary to create juvenile courts, jails and correctional institutions, and so great was the demand for their use that people of the town and city began to make efforts to supply Bible teaching and moral training of youth attending State schools and colleges and were knocking at the back doors of their schools to which the law required their children to be committed for education, seeking recognition of Bible instruction.

"It is declared that 'the course of the State toward religion and the Bible will overcome all others. It took less than twenty-two years during the reign of Ahab, by favoring the teaching of Baal over that of Jehovah, to reduce the well established Jehovah system to one prophet, while Baal's teaching had increased to over 450 prophets.'"

But "it is hard to imagine that a worse calamity could befall religion than to have it interpreted to the youth of the nation by our public schools as now conducted," declares *The Christian Century* (Undenominational). While the Church will never rest easy under a judicial decree which calls the Bible a sectarian book, the remedy is certainly not that being sought by the Washington Presbyterians, it says, and argues that tho it is alleged that since the Bible has been outlawed in the public schools juvenile delinquency has increased,

"There has not been enough Bible in the public schools anywhere in fifty years to make very much difference to the child. It would be more sensible tho not yet wholly fair to lay the increase of juvenile delinquency at the doors of the church. The church's slip-shod method of teaching religion a half hour a week instead of devoting much larger portions of the time to this task is as notorious as it is farcical. The lack of conscience among church people on religious education is a failure of church teaching. What the church does have a right to ask the state is that the time of a child shall not be so monopolized by secular studies that he can not pursue those fundamental studies which are the foundation of all ethical and spiritual attitudes. It requires in most states no new legislation to secure this fundamental right, since it is already conceded to Catholics, Lutherans and Jews and may be secured by evangelicals on demand."

CLAPTRAP IN THE PULPIT

"HOT STUFF" in the sermon is out of place, agree several critics who have been following the methods practised by sensationalists and noting the resultant congregational disturbances, tho, one paper points out, "there is certainly enough for a sincere reformer to talk about." "I have no patience with the claptrap of many modern pulpits," said Bishop Thomas Nicholson, of Chicago, before a recent Methodist camp meeting at Desplaines, as he is quoted in the press. "We need less of the frivolous, jocular and witty, and more of the spiritual." "The Bishop is right," says the Milwaukee *Sentinel*, "and his ideas of the methods to be employed in impressing the truths of religion are sound." It is true, we are told, that the Church must progress, "but the progress must not be along the lines of making the church service amusing or of providing in the pulpit a Sabbath substitute for the vaudeville show or even the moving picture theater." The majority of ministers in the United States are serious men, imprest with a sense of responsibility and the dignity of their calling, but, says the Milwaukee paper,

"Unfortunately, there are a good many men now occupying pulpits who imagine that if they amuse and entertain their congregations they have accomplished what they are placed in the pulpit for. Instead of attempting to inculcate the fundamentals of religion and morality, by which means alone they can fight effectively for reform, they spend their time in the much easier effort of sensational attacks on prevailing evils, humorous monologs concerning present day tendencies, and other performances which, while they bring wide publicity to the performer, react unfavorably on religion and the real work of the Church.

"It was these sensational publicity seeking preachers to whom the Chicago Bishop referred. A good thundering ecclesiastical denunciation of their works is a good thing—not that it will reform the erring brethren of the cloth, but that it will apprise the lay public that the churches have not yet come to regard religion as a humorous exercise."

"The proper place of a clergyman in his community is a disputed question nowadays," observes the New York *World*. "Standards are changing, and a reboiling of doctrine is no longer of much interest to anybody. But doctrine was always safe, whereas contemporary criticism, even the mildest and most sincere, is certain to arouse opposition." Ministers should not be engaged with particular examples of evil, says the Pittsburg *Gazette-Times*. "It is the great moral principles which should be dinned into the minds and consciences of the people." "Yet," believes the New Haven *Journal-Courier*, "one can allow quite a margin of error and some folly to a crusader who has the hard task of arousing a community, provided he is in earnest." Discretion is an essential in "setting a community on fire," and "the devoted incendiary may well pray for wisdom—he is pretty sure to make the judicious grieve." For

"The preacher qualified for this line of attack is rare. He may and should speak his mind in the presence of iniquity; his instructions are definite on this point. The peril of the pulpit to-day is not too much but too little frankness. But his presentation should accord with his gifts. He is not required by man or heaven to engage in tasks for which neither experience, training or qualities call him. He may denounce evil, but only here and there is one who is competent to impeach the police and the offenders and clinch allegation with street number and time of night. The man who can do this, whether preacher or layman, is on high levels of citizenship. He appears too rarely. But for one to engage in warring on wrong with little qualification save indignation is profitless as a rule. . . . Charity is needed for one that fights tigers, but there are limits."

Give your overworked telephone operator a chance

PRIVATE AUTOMATIC EXCHANGE

Combining

INTER-COMMUNICATION
CODE CALL SYSTEM
CONFERENCE WIRE
EMERGENCY ALARMS
WATCHMAN'S CALLS
and other related services.

The P. A. X. augments and completes but does not supplant local and long distance telephone service.

HAVE you ever sat by her desk for an hour during the busy part of the day? Counted the calls she handles—how many outside connections, how many inside? Listened in and noted the impatience of those compelled to wait? If you had made such an investigation you would realize what it would mean not merely to her but to your own organization if she could be relieved of more than half the load—the inside calls. You would not require further proof of your need for the P. A. X.

Better service for the outsiders calling in, better service for the insiders calling out. Instant communication between departments, code calls, conference wires—a means of making every member of your organization directly and quickly accessible to every other member. No operator necessary on the P. A. X.; no one can listen in.

The P. A. X. services are adjusted to meet individual wants. A request from you, and our field engineers will survey and recommend. Write or telephone our nearest office.

AUTOMATIC ELECTRIC COMPANY
Home Office and Factory
CHICAGO, ILL.

BOSTON OFFICE
445 Tremont Bldg.
PITTSBURGH OFFICE
608 Fulton Bldg.
DETROIT OFFICE
525 Ford Bldg.
NEW YORK OFFICE
21 East 40th St.
CLEVELAND OFFICE
415 Cuyahoga Bldg.

KANSAS CITY OFFICE
1001 New York Life Bldg.
ROCHESTER OFFICE
612 Mercantile Bldg.
PHILADELPHIA OFFICE
The Bourse Bldg.
COLUMBUS OFFICE
516 Ferris Bldg.
SAN FRANCISCO OFFICE
320 Market St.

CURRENT - POETRY

Unsolicited contributions to this department cannot be returned.

WITH nothing left, apparently, but his untamed spirit, in this world of defeated hopes, the Revolutionary stands and girds, knowing his day is not yet, unless he be some Russian with the satisfaction of destruction for its own sake. This is in *The English Review*, and Mr. Lawrence is one of the most defiant of England's literary artists:

THE REVOLUTIONARY

By D. H. Lawrence

Look at them standing there in authority,
The pale-faces
As if it could have any effect any more.

Pale-face authority,
Caryatids
Pillars of white bronze standing rigid, lest the skies fall.

What a job they've got to keep it up.
Their poor, idealist foreheads naked capitals
To the entablature of clouded heaven.

When the skies are going to fall, fall they will
In a great chute and rush of débâcle downwards.

Oh, and I wish the high and super Gothic heavens would come down now.
The heavens above, that we yearn to and aspire to.

I do not yearn, nor aspire, for I am a blind Samson.
And what is daylight to me that I should look skyward?

Only I grope among you, pale-faces, caryatids, as among a forest of pillars that hold up the dome of high ideal heaven
Which is my prison.
And all these human pillars of loftiness, going stiff, metallic-stunned with the weight of their responsibility.
I stumble against them.
Stumbling-blocks, painful ones.

To keep on holding up this ideal civilization
Must be excruciating: unless you stiffen into metal, when it is easier to stand stock rigid than to move.

This is why I tug at them, with my arm round their waist.
The human pillars.
They are not stronger than I am, blind Samson.
The house sways.

I shall be so glad when it comes down.
I am so tired of the limitations of their infinite.
I am so sick of the pretensions of the Spirit.
I am so weary of pale-face importance.

Am I not blind, at the round-turning mill?
Then why should I fear their pale faces?
Or love the effulgence of their holy light,
The sun of their righteousness?

To me, all faces are dark,
All lips are dusky and valved.

Save your lips, oh, pale-faces,
Which are slips of metal
Like slits in an automatic-machine, you columns of give and take.

To me, the earth rolls ponderously, superbly,
Coming my way without forethought or afterthought.
To me, men's footfalls fall with a dull, soft rumble, ominous and lovely,
Coming my way.

But not your foot-falls, pale-faces.
They are a-clicketing bits of disjointed metal
Working in motion.

To me, men are palpable, invisible nearnesses in the dark
Sending out magnetic vibrations of warning, pitch-dark throbs of invitation.

But you, pale-faces,
You are painful, harsh surfaced pillars that give off nothing except rigidity,
And I jut against you if I try to move, for you are everywhere, and I am blind,
Sightless among all your visuality,
You staring caryatids.

See if I don't bring you down, and all your high opinion
And all your ponderous roofed-in erection of right and wrong,
Your particular heavens,
With a smash.

See if your skies aren't falling!
And my head, at least, is thick enough to stand it, the smash.

See if I don't move under a dark and nude, vast heaven
When your world is in ruins under your fallen skies.
Caryatids, pale-faces
See if I am not lord of the dark and moving hosts
Before I die

WE might take it that Lawrence or his Revolutionary had sauntered arm in arm with Sitwell around the public garden of Florence and came upon the Marchesa as she is pictured here in *The Nation and the Athenaeum*. We can understand the rage of the Revolutionary if he doesn't happen to have the amused sense of drama that is evident in Sitwell:

GIARDINO PUBBLICO

By Osbert Sitwell

Petunias in mass formation
An angry rose, a hard carnation,
Hot yellow grass, a yellow palm
Rising, giraffe-like, into calm,
All these glare hotly in the sun,
Behind are woods, where shadows run
Like water through the dripping shade
That leaves and laughing winds have made
Here silence like a silver bird
Pecks at the droning heat. We heard,
Townward, the voices, stiff as starch,
Of tourists on belated march
From church to church, to praise by rule
The beauties of the Tuscan School,
Clanging of trams or trains, a flute,
Sharp as the taste of unripe fruit;
Street organs join with tolling bell
To threaten us with Heaven or Hell,
But through it all a nearing sound
As of stage-horses pawing ground.

Then, like a whale confined in cage
(In grandeur of a borrowed carriage),
The old Marchesa swam in sight
In tinkling jet that caught the light,
Making the sun hit out each tone
As if it played the xylophone,
Till she seemed like a rainbow, where
She swells, and, whale-like, spouts the air.

And as she drove, she imposed her will
Upon all things both live and still,
Lovers hid quickly—none withstood
That awful glance of widowhood.
Each child, each tree, the shrilling heat,
Became encased in glacial jet;
The very song-bird in the air
Became a scarecrow, dangling there,
And if you turned to stare, you knew
The punishment Lot's wife went through.

Her crystal cage moves on. Stagnation
Now thaws again to animation;
Gladly the world receives reprieve
Till six o'clock to morrow eve,
When, punctual as the sun, she'll drive
Life out of everything alive,
Then, in gigantic glory, fade
Sunward, through the western glade.

SYRIAN poetry has but one rhyme or rather verse ending. Once you choose, let us say *ana* for a suffix, it must remain *ana* for each. Some such experiment must have intrigued Robert Graves and we see in this from *The London Mercury* how badly the English language bends to such an artifice.

A LOVER SINCE CHILDHOOD

By Robert Graves

Tangled in thought am I,
Stumble in speech do I?
Do I blunder and blush for the reason why?
Wander aloof do I,
Lean over gates and sigh,
Making friends with the bee and the butterfly.

If thus and thus I do,
Dazed by the thought of you,
Walking my sorrowful way in the early dew,
My heart cut through and through
In this despair of you,
Starved for a word or a look will my hope renew.

Give then a thought for me
Walking so miserably,
Wanting relief in the friendship of flower or tree,
Do but remember, we
Once could in love agree,
Swallow your pride, let us be as we used to be.

A FABLE for subway travelers is furnished in the *Literary Review* of the New York *Evening Post*. But you must know your Canada and its Drummond:

DRUMMOND IN THE SUBWAY

By Hamilton Fish Armstrong

"Fourteenth!" My neighbor turned the page . . .
I caught the name of Lac St. Pierre. . . .
Into the Subway, stale with sweat,
Suddenly blew a vernal air

Clean with the scent of river fields
Where cornhills warm in August suns
(Altho the nights are chill and bright,
Telling how quick young Summer runs).

The patchy signs, the dizzy posts,
Whirring interminably by,
Give way to stalwart piny ranks
Against an open northern sky

Along the rutted river road
Rattles and sways my ancient chaise,
Leetle Bateese the charioteer
Of "Castor," steed of better days.

I smell again the sun-steamed flats,
Speckled with eel and pickerel grass,
And watch an errant seagull meet
His double in the looking-glass. . . .

The pulsing grind of steel on steel
Slows on the curve, and new lights flare.
No one has known the sights I've seen
In these black miles from Union Square.

Poor at twenty; Rich at forty;

Internationally famous at fifty

You are invited to have FREE a booklet that tells what few great books make a man think straight and talk well

POOR, friendless, with no education, Benjamin Franklin walked through the streets of Philadelphia alone. Yet at forty he was independent; at fifty his company was eagerly sought by the leaders of two continents.

What was the secret of such phenomenal success? Something mysterious? Not at all. His secret was nothing more than this: Every day of his life he added a part of some other man's brains to his own. He picked the few really great mind-building books and read them systematically a few minutes every day.

Are you bigger to-day than yesterday?

You have so few minutes in the day for reading; so few days in a busy life. Will you spend them all with the gossip of the newspapers, or the mere entertainment of fiction? Or will you, like Franklin, start now to make the great thinkers of the world your servants? Will you increase your own brain power by adding their brain power to it?

What are the few great books—biographies, histories, novels, dramas, poems, books of science and travel, philosophy and religion, that have in them the power to make of their readers men who can think clearly and talk interestingly—men who will not only be ambitious for success, but who will have acquired the broadness of vision necessary to achieve it?

All of these questions, so vital to you, are answered in the free booklet pictured below. You can have a copy of it for the asking. In it Dr. Charles W. Eliot, who was for forty years president of Harvard University, gives his own plan of reading. In it are described the contents, plan, and purpose of

Dr. Eliot's Five-Foot Shelf of Books

Every well-informed man and woman should know about this famous library. The free book tells about it—how Dr. Eliot has put into his Five-Foot Shelf "the essentials of a liberal education"; how he has so arranged it that even "fifteen minutes a day" are enough; how in pleasant moments of spare time, by using the reading courses Dr. Eliot has provided for you, you can get the knowledge of literature and life that every university strives to give.

Every reader of The Literary Digest is invited to have a copy of this handsome and entertaining free book. Merely clip the coupon and mail it to-day.

Send for This Free Booklet That Gives Dr. Eliot's Own Plan of Reading

FIFTEEN MINUTES A DAY

P. F. COLLIER & SON COMPANY
416 West Thirteenth Street, New York

Mail me the free book, "Fifteen Minutes a Day," telling about the Five-Foot Shelf of Books, and containing the valuable article by Dr. Eliot on what and how to read for a liberal education.

Name ....

Address ....

....

L.D. 10-29-21

NATIONAL AMERICAN SPEECH WEEK

November 6-12, 1921

Prepared Especially for School Use

"INVEST IN GOOD SPEECH—it pays daily dividends" is typical of the slogans that will be used during the "Better Speech Week" of November 6th to arouse the nation to the evils of slovenly speech—careless enunciation, ungrammatical constructions, mispronunciations, the use of slang, and poor choice of words.

A great army of disappointed men and women can testify that inability to talk clearly and forcefully has been to them a severe social and business handicap. Mr. H. Addington Bruce, the well-known author, observes that "there are men to-day in inferior positions who long ago would have commanded good salaries if they had only taken the trouble to overcome remediable speech defects. Strange how careful people are about dress—how sure that dignity and good taste in dress help to make one's success in getting on in the world—and at the same time how careless these same people are about speech, which is the dress of the mind."

Attention to speech is worthy of our respect not merely because it is an index of ability. It is a means of growth. Bishop Trench said: "Language is on the one side the limit and restraint of thought as on the other side that which feeds and unfolds thought." But pure, forceful American Speech is more than a personal matter; it is a patriotic duty. Dr. James C. Fernald says in "Expressive English": "Language is the expression of our national life brimming with the achievements of all its past and reaching on with shaping and molding power to the generations yet to be. Language molds the thought of those who speak it, exalting or degrading. *This molding power of our language is a mighty force in shaping the mingled people into one on American soil.*

The "Better Speech Week" of 1921 will be the third national observance of this movement. Directed by such powerful organizations as the National Council of Teachers of English and the General Federation of Women's Clubs, sponsored by the American Academy of Arts and Literature and the Society of Pure English, it is now unquestionably one of the most hopeful influences of our national life.

Our national leaders believe that "a clear, pleasant, forceful speech" is so essential to the high ideals of our American character that they are giving this splendid effort their active support. Governor Henry J. Allen in his proclamation for the observance of "Better Speech Week" of 1920 said: "Each man has tools peculiar to his vocation—the carpenter his plane, the miner his pick, the tradesman his price-list, the student his text-book; but every true citizen, whatever his occupation, should use his American language. 'Better Speech Week' calls attention to the importance of our language . . . I commend every effort made by the schools of the State to train our citizens in the cultivation of lucid, forceful, and uncorrupted diction."

As the direct outcome of the two previous drives, real speech improvement is evident in hundreds of towns and cities throughout the United States. The best results have been obtained where every possible agency in the community has given its cooperation. As a rule the several agencies have been encouraged and coordinated by some public-spirited club or society. The Chicago Women's Club has not only aided the "Better Speech" campaign in its own city but has fostered the movement throughout the entire country.

In many cities the various interests "joined hands" for this splendid purpose along the following plan: In one church the minister preached a sermon on "The Sanctity of Words," in another the church bulletin contained a carefully written announcement in regard to "The Value of Careful Speech." The Mayor issued an official statement calling on all citizens to aid in the patriotic effort to improve our national speech. The newspapers cooperated with news stories and editorials. Department stores used "Better Speech" slogans in their advertisements and displayed posters on counters and in the windows. One bookstore arranged an attractive grouping of books useful for speech improvement.

In Malden, Massachusetts, a specialist of one of the photoplay corporations gave his time in preparing two-minute films for presentation, these financed by the four cities in the north of Boston.

Valuable as "Better Speech Week" is as a general community influence, its greatest development has been, and will doubtless continue to be, in the school. Teachers report that as a result of the "Better Speech Week" celebrations their students have been stimulated as never before to work for a correct, distinct, and pleasant speech. Miss Claudia Crumpton, Chairman of the American Speech Committee of the National Council of Teachers of English, writes that the interest already shown would indicate that nearly every school in America will formally observe "Better Speech Week."

"The Guide to Better American Speech Week," from which the facts in this article have largely been taken, states: "Better Speech Week, as it is now observed, serves one of two purposes. It may be an intensive campaign for calling the attention of the community to the need of speech improvement, or it may have a definite place in a year's program for developing power in speaking." In any case it becomes a time for self-examination in speech and for pledges similar to the following, written by Grace Williamson Willet of the Chicago Women's Club:

"I love the United States of America, I love my country's flag, I love my country's language. I promise:

1. That I will not dishonor my country's speech by leaving off the last syllables of words;
2. That I will say a good American 'yes' and 'no' instead of an Indian grunt 'umhum' and 'nup um' or a foreign 'ya' or 'yeh' and 'nope';
3. That I will improve American speech by enunciating distinctly and by speaking pleasantly and sincerely;
4. That I will try to make my country's language beautiful for the many boys and girls of foreign nations who come here to live;
5. That I will learn to articulate correctly one word a day for one year."

"Better Speech Week" can accomplish permanent results only if it inspires its observers to all-year care in the matter of pure English; only if it causes every one to keep the powers of the mind invariably in tone and training by being ever vigilant against the enemies of American speech. And this means more than to talk grammatically and to enunciate clearly. It requires the more discriminating use of overworked words such as "nice," "splendid," "awful," "elegant," "fierce," etc.; the elimination of worn-out expressions like "bold as a lion," "the acid test," "the staff of life," "the arms of Morpheus." "Slang saves the trouble—and the glory—of thinking."

Since Armistice Day comes on Friday of this year's "Better American Speech Week," it is fitting that homage be paid by word and deed to the ideals for which the nation has fought, that America rededicate herself to preserving her language, as an emblem of national unity, in "its native freshness and vigor," a language "inherited by us from our grandfathers and by us to be handed down to our grandchildren unimpaired in vigor and variety, in freshness and nobility."

Friction—
the unseen enemy of production
in your plant

Getting the Upper Hand

of Friction's Drag on Production

YOU AND YOUR COMPETITOR both pay for power.

If you can get more production, than he, out of your dollar's worth of power, you have an advantage in lower production cost.

Incorrect lubrication of any piece of machinery invites preventable friction—and "friction, the destroyer" is never slow to accept the invitation.

As you go through your plant, you may not see the unnecessary power loss that occurs wherever two moving metal parts meet.

What will guard you against this loss?

Correct lubrication. Nothing else.

If you seek lower production costs—more work out of each dollar's worth of power—we suggest you get in touch with our nearest branch.

We can put before you correct lubricating recommendations for your plant which are based on—

1. The experience and knowledge gained in the manufacture and application of high-grade lubricants for over 50 years.
2. Constant field contact with industry the world over.
3. Close engineering study of the operation of all types of machinery.
4. Standardized and specific recommendations through a central Board of Engineers whose standing you can readily ascertain.

These recommendations will make for

§ *Less wear on your machinery.* § *Less upkeep cost.* § *Less power waste.* § *More* USEABLE *power.* § *Better production.* § *Better profit.*

Stocks of Gargoyle Lubricating Oils are carried in principal cities throughout the country.

GARGOYLE

Lubricating Oils

A grade for each type of service

For Lower Production Costs

Steam Cylinders

Gargoyle Steam Cylinder Oils minimize power losses and undue wear in steam cylinders the world over. No other steam cylinder oils are so widely endorsed by engine builders.

The well-known Gargoyle Cylinder Oil 600-W and several other Gargoyle Lubricating Oils are specially manufactured for cylinder and valve lubrication to meet conditions in all types of Steam Engines, Steam Pumps, Steam-driven Compressors, Locomotives, etc.

Turbines

A worry of every turbine operator is sludge. Gargoyle D. T. E. Oils are manufactured and especially treated to meet the exacting requirements of turbine lubrication. These oils separate readily from moisture and impurities and thus provide remarkable freedom from sludge.

Internal Combustion Engines

The severe lubricating requirements of gas engines, Diesel engines and oil engines are scientifically met by Gargoyle D. T. E. Oils.

Compressors and Vacuum Pumps

Correct lubrication is of unusual importance in compressor work. Carbon in the air cylinder has sometimes caused explosion. Gargoyle D. T. E. Oil Heavy Medium is made especially to minimize carbonization. It is correct for air or gas compressors and vacuum pumps.

Bearings

A wide range of Gargoyle Bearing Oils is provided to meet all specific operating conditions of engines and machines involving size, speed, pressure, temperature and lubricating methods.

* * *

THROUGH our nearest branch or distributor, we shall be glad to assist you in selecting the correct Gargoyle Lubricating Oils for use throughout your entire plant.

Stocks are carried in principal cities throughout the country.

Domestic Branches:

New York (*Main Office*)
Boston
Philadelphia
Pittsburgh
Buffalo
Rochester
Albany
Chicago
Detroit
Indianapolis
Minneapolis
Des Moines
Kansas City, Kan.
Dallas

VACUUM OIL COMPANY

PERSONAL ▾ GLIMPSES

DEMOCRATIC RUMBLINGS IN JAPAN

CROWN PRINCE HIROHITO OF JAPAN, who lately broke all the precedents of his country by going visiting in Europe, is said to have democratic tendencies—"probably because he is shrewd enough to recognize the increasing power of Japanese labor, and the slowly growing Japanese tendency away from imperialism," comments the writer of a syndicated editorial for the Newspaper Enterprise Association. With the death of the present Mikado, predicted for the near future by recent press dispatches, Hirohito "seems likely to swing Japan, the last stronghold of absolute monarchy, from autocracy to democracy," predicts a news dispatch from Tokyo. Even tho students of the Japanese form of government report that the island Kingdom is now ruled rather by a sort of close corporation of big business and military men than by the invalid Emperor, Hirohito's power is sure to be considerable, and the forces which are inclining him to take a more democratic view of things, testify half a dozen recent journalistic investigators, are likely to become stronger rather than weaker. Among current commentators, Nathaniel Peffer in *The American Legion Weekly*, Frazier Hunt in *Hearst's Magazine*, and Emma Sarepta Yule in *Scribner's*, find signs of the times in the protests of "the common people," of the "new women," and of the radical labor unionists.

There is said to be a new spirit, also, in the universities. Mr. Peffer, writing in the Legion's weekly under the heading of "Democracy's Growth in Japan," testifies that—

Photo from Adachi

AN ARGUMENT FOR MORE FOOD AND LESS WAR.

Mrs. Haku Kihuchi, a worker in a muslin factory, appealed to the first great mass meeting of Japanese women workers to change the conditions under which the workers are crushed by taxes levied to keep Japan prepared for war. In the spread of democracy among the "common people" many American investigators find the surest basis for peace in the Pacific.

Not from the bitterest anti-Japanese among Chinese have I heard such blighting denunciations of Japanese militarism as from groups of Japanese students with whom I have sat around little charcoal *hibachi* in wood-and-paper houses near a college campus in Tokyo.

In every progressive movement, whether it be suffrage, equal rights for women, labor unions, freedom of speech or equal distribution of wealth, the students are represented. They get out a large number of vivid little papers translating news of liberal movements all over the world and crying to the Japanese people to awaken and assert themselves. They send delegations to China and Korea to get together with Chinese and Korean students to undo the evil done by Japanese militarists and soften the bitterness against Japan that now fills the people of other Far Eastern countries, especially China. They denounce universal military service. They are watched by the police, and sometimes arrested. It is something like the old Russia.

The same is true of university professors. Just as the professors are the loudest prophets of militarism and the loudest singers of Japan *uber alles*, so also are professors in the forefront of protest. They have established contacts with the leading thinkers of the West and the modern literature of the West, they do a great amount of translating of such literature and serve as the inspirers of the demand for greater freedom. I have met Japanese professors who as pioneers of freedom in a wilderness of subjection take their place with the great spirits of western countries.

If you go among the ordinary merchant and professional classes in Japanese cities now you will hear these same rumbles of discontent. It is unorganized and hardly analyzed, but it exists nevertheless. These are the people who read newspapers, and they read in their newspapers discomfiting things. Jingoistic as is the overwhelming majority of the Japanese press, there does nevertheless creep in, even if involuntarily, some echo of protest. Certainly there is reflected therein the world-wide suspicion of Japan and its motives. Reading this, the Japanese people naturally ask themselves why. They cannot help making the connection of ideas between this suspicion and the burden they bear of taxation for armies and navies. They see also their helplessness. They do not know what is wrong—they only know something is wrong. They see their country grow stronger and stronger, and themselves worse and worse off in their own intimate and daily lives. The economic pressure is their strongest evidence. In Japan also men think deepest from the pocketbook.

It is very easy to exaggerate the meaning of all this, admits Mr. Peffer, and he calls to mind the fact that "about 40 per cent. of German voters were out-and-out Socialists before the war, and men said Germany could not make aggressive war because the Socialists would not support it." Japan is far from being as liberal as was pre-war Germany, he believes, but the leaven is working. Frazier Hunt, telling the story of one of Japan's most consistent radicals, Kagawa of Kobe, is much more optimistic about the situation. Much of his account reads like a Socialist report of labor troubles in America. He first heard Kagawa, the anti-militarist, "at a thrilling labor meeting in Tokyo," writes Mr. Hunt. He goes on:

A cordon of policemen stretched from the street to the entrance, and once inside the assembly hall they lined the walls and strung down the aisles.

GENASCO LINE

- Trinidad Lake Asphalt (For streets and roofs)
- Standard Trinidad Built-Up Roofing
- Bermudez Road Asphalt (For road building)
- Genasco Roll Roofing
- Genasco Sealbac Shingles
- Genasco Latite Shingles
- Genasco Vulcanite Mastic Flooring
- Genasco Acid-Proof Paint
- Genasco Industrial Paint
- Genasco Boiler Paint
- Genasco Asphalt Putty
- Genasco Asphalt Pipe Coating
- Genasco Asphalt Fibre Coating
- Genasco Tile Cement
- Genasco Waterproofing Asphalts
- Genasco Waterproofing Felts and Fabrics
- Genasco Battery Seal Compound
- Genasco Mineral Rubber
- Genasco Mineral Spirits
- Genasco Base Oils
- Genasco Flotation Oils
- Genasco Motor Oils
- Genasco Soluble Oils
- Genasco Saturated Asphalt Felt
- Genasco Deadening Felt
- Genasco Insulated Paper
- Genasco Red Sheathing Paper
- Genasco Stringed Felt
- Genasco Wall Lining
- Iroquois Road-building Machinery

When Winter's ice-sharpened claws tear at your roof—

when bitter winds and driving snow sweep down from the North—is your home warm and cozy or is it filled with cold, comfort-destroying draughts?

Look to your roof. The comfort, health and happiness of yourself and family depend on its staunchness—whether it is snow-proof, cold-proof and storm-tight.

Genasco Sealbac Asphalt Shingles shut out cold and dampness and keep in warmth and comfort. They defy the icy blasts and destructive thaws of the North as well as the blazing sun and torrential rains of the tropics.

Genasco Shingles are ideal for all buildings demanding beauty, harmony and distinction in a roof. Their colors—rich warm red and cool grayish green—are of crushed slate—therefore natural and non-fading.

Genasco Roll Roofing is recommended for buildings where less ornamental roofs than shingles are desired. It is the only roofing furnished with the celebrated Kant-Leak Kleets—the most efficient roof-fastening made.

Genasco Shingles and Roll Roofing are made of densely-compressed, long-fibre felt, coated on both sides with Trinidad Lake Asphalt Cement. They cost little more than ordinary roofing—are extremely fire-resisting and last a lifetime.

Other Products of the Genasco Line are listed in the panel. If your dealer does not yet handle the Genasco products, ask any architect or builder where to obtain them, or write to us.

Let us send you booklets describing the various types of Genasco Ready Roofing.

New York
Chicago
Pittsburgh

THE BARBER ASPHALT PAVING COMPANY
PHILADELPHIA

St. Louis
Kansas City
San Francisco
Atlanta

Genasco
Asphaltic Roofing, Flooring, Paints and Allied Protective Products

PERSONAL GLIMPSES
Continued

Probably five hundred men were at this labor meeting, and certainly no less than seventy-five policemen, who divided their time between open-mouthed attention to the speakers' magic words of liberty and and more rice and their job of preserving the majesty of worn-out laws.

A liberal sprinkling of blue-capped students gave a tone to the crowd. For the most part the men were skilled workmen and petty clerks, with groups of students, but here and there you caught the lettered jacket of some coolie—a coolie who only yesterday was a serf and to-day was fettered to a submerged class.

A young boy in the uniform of a Tokyo mail-carrier was the first to open the mouths of these undersized cops: "I work long hours and yet I must live in a cold, unlighted room and I am hungry, and ninety per cent. of the men who work with me want what I do—a real democracy and real freedom and real living wages." And the police, thinking of their own half-filled rice-bowls—the average wage of the Japanese policeman is something like ten dollars a month—forgot their majestic pose and became striving hungry humans, with mouths to fill and children to dream of.

But a minute later when a square-jawed coal-miner from the striking districts began telling how gendarmes and soldiers were beating up the miners in their camps, a police captain loaded down with a half-ton of gold braid blew a whistle and the fight was on. It was a neat battle for a few moments and then, while the crowd jeered, the officers carried out two men feet first. These Tokyo cops, like their American models, swing a wicked baton.

So it went for an hour. Once there was a fairly general fight. That time I stood on my chair and almost cheered. It was good for your soul just to look on. The miracle had happened—the Japanese worm was actually turning.

Kagawa, called "the saint of new Japan," graduated from Princeton a few years ago, and has since secretly formed the Federation of Labor of Western Japan. "A young David who is out to slay the Goliath of a militant Japan," he is called. Mr. Hunt tells of him in his surroundings, among the "bewildered laborers" and outcasts of Kobe:

> I wish you could see these slums of his—tiny crooked alleys, less than four feet wide, banked on both sides with narrow, wooden dog-kennels, six by eight feet, and probably five feet high. Here 20,000 outcasts live like homeless dogs; each human kennel crowded with squalling, quarreling creatures of filth and vermin, rotting with crime and tuberculosis and disease. Outcasts of all kinds—White, Black, Eurasian, Chinese—dregs of an old, old East. God, what a sore on the earth!
>
> Crowding the doorways and filling the winding alley paths are hundreds of poor, outcast children in filthy rags, whose eyes light up with happiness when they see Kagawa, this teacher of kindness, approach. For him it is always a triumphal march; shrill little voices herald his coming, while thin, hungry, half-clad little bodies scramble to hold his hand or even to touch his kimono. No Pied Piper ever had a more willing, a more joyful train.
>
> You follow him with real tears in your

eyes—this teacher of Shinkawa—wan and undersized, smiling with warm, brown eyes, preaching God; a young Christ, walking among outcasts, murderers, and broken lives of the lower depths, preaching a living, breathing Christianity.

That first night I met him, we wandered about these forbidden streets for an hour, and then he led the way to the blackened two-story mission house where he holds his little school, gives out his free medicines, and brings God to these God-forgotten people. I took off my shoes at the door, and in my stockinged feet walked up the stairs and into the matted and immaculate study. For hours we talked of "Dangerous Thoughts," and Kagawa told me the thrilling story of Young Japan opening her eyes, and seeing visions, and daring real Democracy.

"Dangerous thoughts," the government here calls them. America would call them "Inspiring Thoughts," "Glorious Thoughts," "Winning Thoughts," because they are all about the hope of a people struggling up to the light. And that's the greatest gripping romance in the world—the struggle and fight and dreams, not of individuals, but of millions opening their eyes for the first time, stretching themselves and realizing their strength.

Other signs of the forces at work in the remaking of Japan are pointed out in an article called "Japan's New Woman," by Emma Sarepta Yule, in *Scribner's Magazine*. The writer has lived in Japan for a number of years. "Japan's new woman waves no red flag," she writes, and yet, to quote:

Some embattled fisherwomen in 1919 made the first strictly feminine militant move in the history of Japan, when they started a near-riot in protest against the high cost of rice. A shuddering gasp went through the Land of the Gods. The thing was so unwomanlike, so unheard-of, and for Japanese women to act so like foreign barbarians, it was shocking! These sturdy fighters for their right to sustenance without supporting food profiteers were not, by any means, *atarashi onna*. They were just village women who were asserting, in the only way they knew, their right to life, with no mention of the pursuit of happiness. A strike in a girls' school tells that assertion is not restricted to illiterate fisherwomen. Strikes in boys' schools are too common for comment, but for young girls!—well may heads wag in woful interrogation as to the future.

Also, according to the author, the women of Japan are beginning to take an interest in public affairs, an interest that may serve as a foundation for Japanese democracy. She writes:

There seems to be not a little interest in public affairs among Japan's thinking women, perhaps more than it is reasonable to expect when their restrictions in most things and their simplified education are considered. In elections they are concerned more with the candidate as an individual than with party affiliations.

It amazes somewhat, that, with all the centuries of teaching in meekness back of her, the new woman in her public utterances is quite fearless, does no begging, nor does she hesitate to criticize. In an article a few months ago on the universal suffrage movement and excitement, that in Tokyo was often near-rioting, Mrs. Akiko Yosano

PERSONAL GLIMPSES
Continued

so phlegmatic. She averred that the universal suffrage should have been granted twenty years ago, and would have been had the men of the country any mettle in their make-up. She further said that, as a whole, Japanese men took little interest in what affected the whole country. They at times get excited and worked up over some matter, but are incapable of sustained interest and long-continued struggle for an end.

All these signs of liberalism are of the utmost importance, says Mr. Peffer in the conclusion of his article in *The American Legion Weekly*, because—

There is little likelihood, in my opinion, gained from a long residence in the Far East and a long observation of the working out of Japanese policies, that there will be any voluntary revision on the part of the Japanese military and imperial classes. The men who make up the government of Japan are too wedded to their present ambitions to change voluntarily.

I take it that no American likes to contemplate the possibility of war. War has been proved a wasteful, criminal, and futile method of settling international problems. The change, I believe, can not be forced from without; even if it could, I believe the price would be too big. I think it must come from within. The only thing that can bring it from within is the power of the Japanese people. That can come only from their own change of heart, from the growth of public opinion among them, and their determination to compel it. And that must be by evolution of democracy in Japan.

It is for that reason that Japanese liberalism is of such importance. On it depends the future course of the Japanese Empire and the future peace of the Pacific.

Fine Points in English.—The man had just informed the Pullman agent that he wanted a Pullman berth.

"Upper or lower?" asked the agent.

"What's the difference?" asked the man.

"A difference of fifty cents in this case," replied the agent. "The lower is higher than the upper. The higher price is for the lower. If you want it lower you'll have to go higher. We sell the upper lower than the lower. In other words, the higher the lower. Most people don't like the upper, altho it is lower on account of it being higher. When you occupy an upper you have to get up to go to bed and get down when you get up. You can have the lower if you pay higher. The upper is lower than the lower because it is higher. If you are willing to go higher, it will be lower."

But the poor man had fainted!—*The Epworth Herald.*

Circumstantial Evidence.—The Bingville board of selectmen had held many sessions and finally formulated a set of auto laws that was the pride of the county. So the constable felt no worriment when he stopped a motorist.

"Ye're pinched for violatin' the auto laws," he pronounced.

"Which one?" inquired the traveler.

"Durned if I know, but ye certainly hain't come all the way down Main Street without bustin' one of them."—*The Ameri-*

REVIEW OF NEW BOOKS

THE BREAK-UP OF ENGLAND

INTERESTING as Mr. Galsworthy's novels are, it is perhaps as well that with "To Let" (Scribner's, $2.00) he has brought to an end the story of the Forsyte family, which began with "The Man of Property" and has continued through five volumes. By this time the descendants of the original Forsyte are as the sands of the sea as regards numbers, and it has become increasingly difficult to link them all up properly, attaching to each couple its own form of marital unhappiness, for unfaithfulness, drink and gambling have been rife among the members of the tribe, afflictions endured by their victims with various forms of stoicism.

The story concerns itself with the love-affair of two young Forsytes, between whose families there is a feud, owing to a dark past that can never be surmounted. Fleur is the daughter of Soames Forsyte, young, beautiful and hard, a girl whom her own cousin had described as "having" and who said of herself, "when one wants a thing fearfully, one does not think of other people." Quite different is young Jon Forsyte, a boy of her own age, ardent, sweet-natured and devoted to his mother. The two young people meet almost by chance and are dimly aware that some kind of feud has kept the two branches of the family apart, but it is not until their love-affair is well advanced that they learn the true state of the case. Briefly, young Jon's mother was Soames Forsyte's divorced wife before her marriage to Jolyon Forsyte, Jon's father, and judging her by the law of the land and the ten commandments, she has a questionable past behind her. But the author has many excuses to make for Irene, and she certainly shines in contrast to one or two other women in the story who have never openly transgrest.

When this love-affair comes to the knowledge of the young people's parents, it is felt at once on both sides that it must be stopt. To do this Jon's father, seriously ill of heart disease, forces himself to write a letter to his son, telling him the whole story, an experience which proves so agitating to him that it kills him. It almost kills his son, too, for he feels it impossible to go on with the affair, and when Soames Forsyte, urged thereto by his great love for his daughter, brings himself to appeal to young Jon personally, the lad answers: "Tell Fleur that it is no good, please; I must do as my father wished before he died."

This refusal comes as a great blow to Fleur; she has been rejected, and her pride suffers so much that within three months she marries young Michael Mont, a youth who has been infatuated with her for some time, and the reader feels that only the most strenuous self-denial on the part of the author will prevent his starting upon a fresh record of matrimonial unhappiness with Mr. and Mrs. Michael Mont as the chief performers.

As a story of incident the book need not be considered. It is a record of first love, ardent, unforeseeing, content with the present. At least such is its nature in Jon's case, for Fleur is a type of the modern girl—hard, self-seeking and with little affection even for the father who is wrapt up in her. She has the strong instinct (inherited from that father) of possession, and the author is continually contrasting, perhaps unconsciously, this unlovely trait

How Old Man Burns

"Advertising? I never saw much in it," said Old Man Burns.

"Nor I," agreed Jackson, the lawyer whose shrewd rebuilding of a certain nationally-known corporation is bringing new interests his way with requests that he duplicate the job for them.

"Now hold on a minute," continued the Old Man, "you haven't heard me out. I was going on to say that I never saw much in advertising—until after the war."

Jackson leaned back with his cigar cocked at the show-me angle.

"During the war," said the Old Man, "our problem was filling orders. Logical markets, prospective markets were neglected and ignored—you know they had to be—the situation with nine out of ten manufacturers, I suppose. After the Armistice orders, orders, orders, and then—the slump. We hitched up our trousers, worked out new discounts, had efficiency men tell us how and where to save, put on still more men, introduced some novelties, but the slump went right on slumping. One morning I found on my desk a circular from an advertising agency headed, 'Why don't you advertise?' I wrote back 'Why should I?' Next day a man from the ——— advertising agency came in—a real businessman. And it was he who gave me the franchise idea."

Lawyer Jackson sat up. "Franchise" was a word out of his dictionary. The Old Man noted this sudden display of interest with an amused snort.

"Yes, franchise—the sort of thing you lawyers know all about. Right at the start that advertising man convinced me that I had always had the wrong slant on advertising. Up to that time I had thought of advertising as a tuneful second fiddle to the excess profits tax."

Jackson grinned.

"I did hear something to that effect. The rumor reached me that quite a bit of money was spent that way."

The Old Man waved his hand at the interruption.

"Let me get to the franchise," he continued. "My agency man showed me how to build advertising into my business and in turn make it build my business. As I worked along with him and his agency, I learned that modern advertising has back of it the same principles of patient research and scientific accuracy as the latest engineering exploits. The men in charge of our advertising agencies today are practical men of affairs who do not depend on trick writ-

(Continued on opposite page)

Got His Franchise

ing and fancy speeches to pull them through. Just think of the work those advertising men put in before they gave me their copy and layouts and schedules. Why they learned my plant by heart and, between you and me, Jackson, they showed me one or two things I had never thought of. They suggested a new quota system for sales that has worked out beautifully; they sat in with us on a change in routing; they tackled our jobbing problems in a helpful manner. Their suggestion that we cut out some of our dead lines and keep to the sellers sounds like a simple one to make, but I'd hate to admit how much it has saved us. I know," he said quickly at signs of an interruption on Jackson's part, "you are going to pooh-pooh the idea that an outside organization can step in and perfect something we've been laboring over for fifty years. But here's the answer. Get an agency that sticks closely to its specialty—the making of more and better sales—and you're bound to profit. So that's how I got my franchise—"

"Hold on," said Jackson, "where does the franchise come in?"

"Well, this franchise of mine isn't on paper exactly, though it starts with paper, after all. It's the most valuable of our assets—the franchise of good-will that comes from new and old consumers of our product all across the country. There are men and women who read and believe our selling-story because it is honestly and interestingly told by those who believe in it. To-day advertising is as much a part of my business as the machines in the factory—and I hope it always will be."

"There's a lot in what you've said," mused lawyer Jackson, "I'll think it over. It's shaken my ideas up a bit. Seems to me that advertising of the sort you've described might very well fit into some of my clients' plans for 1922."

The Literary Digest

354 FOURTH AVENUE, NEW YORK 122 SO. MICHIGAN AVE. CHICAGO

Bankers, heads of industrial enterprises, lawyers whose clients discuss advertising with them are invited to send for a DIGEST *representative. We are frequently able to give good advice leading toward a proper solution of the application of advertising to business enterprises.*

REVIEWS OF NEW BOOKS
Continued

characteristic of the man whose life has been outwardly respectable, with the unselfish affection displayed by the two who have, at least once, overstept the bounds of morality. Another contrast drawn by the author is that between the old and the new order of things which is beginning to be so marked in England. The description of the funeral of old Timothy Forsyte, "the one pure individualist left, the only man who hadn't heard of the Great War," is a striking picture, and his extraordinary will represents a last stand in favor of entailed property. Soames Forsyte represents the spirit of owning, and only occasionally, and as it were by chance, does a glimpse of the truth come to him, "that the body of Beauty has a spiritual essence, uncapturable save by a devotion that thinks not of itself" and the book closes with a picture of him, seated in Highgate Cemetery, dreaming over his career. " 'To Let,' the Forsyte age and way of life, when a man owned his soul, his investments, and his woman, without check or question. And now the State had, or would have his investments, his woman had herself, and God knew who had his soul. 'To Let,' that sane and simple creed!

MATRIMONIAL MISFITS

"A BOND dissoluble at will in the divorce court is not a foundation upon which civilized society can endure. . . . There should be a positive law forbidding remarriage under any circumstances. . . . In the home lies the strength of the nation. Disrupt that, and it crumbles. . . . We ought to make it clear that loyalty to the marriage tie and to the home is required not only by the law of God, but by love for country, and that whoever, by his example, weakens the foundation of the home, sins against the very life of the state."

So runs a brief summing-up of the conclusions reached by Mr. Charles G. Norris in his new novel, "Brass" (Dutton, $2.00). But it must be admitted that to the disinterested reader its teaching might be condensed into the one word which was the advice of "Punch" to those about to marry, "Don't!" For it is a sad and forbidding picture of various kinds of matrimonial misery which Mr. Norris draws. Out of all the couples he presents, one, and only one, make a real success of their venture—principally, it would seem, because they lived in the country, and the woman was a notable housewife, with the strength and endurance of a horse. The rest are wretched in various ways, but when they try to get rid of the "ring about your neck" which has proved to be "brass, not gold," they soon find that they have but exchanged one brass ring for another of the same metal.

Philip Baldwin was only about twenty-two when he married pretty Marjorie Jones. Philip was stupid, clumsy and somewhat stubborn; Marjorie was selfish, spoiled and moody. To make matters more difficult, they began by living with Marjorie's mother and elder sister, who had petted and given in to her all her life. Trouble began almost immediately. A quarrel over the opening or shutting of their bedroom window brought about a separation. But they still loved each other, and an accidental meeting led to their reunion. For a while they were happy in a love, the happiness nor the reunion lasted very long. A child was born to them, and Marjorie found it a thorough-going nuisance, while the little flat which had amused her at first soon began to bore her. "She intensely disliked 'duties,' preferring to do things impulsively, or when it suited her. . . . She rebelled at the slightest criticism. . . . She was discontented, forever quoting her friend, Virginia, enviously commenting on that lady's freedom, her easy and luxurious life." Virginia had a rich husband, and no children. She was fond of Marjorie, made her handsome presents, and brought her into her own racketty, set, of which Roy North and his wife were members.

Philip's life with Marjorie became "a mockery of marriage." The little home was exchanged for two rooms in "a small family hotel," and their relations went from bad to worse. At last came an actual fight, during which Marjorie "sunk her small teeth deep into the flesh of his hand below the thumb." The subsequent divorce was a relief to both of them; they hated each other. And presently he heard that Marjorie had married Roy North, who was also divorced.

Philip's business prospered, owing to his clever partner, Wilbur Lansing, the husband of his sister Lucy. He was quite well-to-do when he met Mary Rowland, and fell in love with her. She was beautiful, and highly educated, yet she, too, fell in love with him, and promised to marry him. Not until then did he tell her that he was divorced, and had a son. Mary was a devout Catholic; she could not and would not marry a man who had a wife living. She wrote Philip a note of farewell, and sailed for England, leaving him, as he thought, heartbroken.

It was some little time after this that Leila Vale became an important factor in Philip's life. Leila had a good social position but no money. Philip was now a rich man, and his sister had ambitions for him. He was not really very much in love with Leila, but he drifted into marriage. Leila, like Mary, was a Catholic, but in her case, "an obliging priest had found a way out of the difficulty" of Philip's previous marriage. Marjorie had never been baptized, and "The Church refused to recognize a marriage with an unbaptized person." But Philip's second marriage was no more successful than his first. He lost his money; and poverty changed the elegant Leila into a vulgar shrew. But their little daughter held them together, even after Leila's inheritance of a fortune had turned Philip into a nonentity in his own house. It was just at this time that he again met Marjorie, who had become a successful motion-picture actress, and realized, as she did, that had divorce not been easy for them, they might have stayed together and been happy after all. As it was, the only time Philip was contented was when he was living with Mrs. Grotenburg, who literally slaved for him, considering all his desires and never permitting herself to have any of her own. Whenever she saw him coming she flew into her kitchen: "The waiting sirloin must be clapped over the hot embers; the yellow batter poured into the sizzling frying pan. . . . Mrs. Grotenburg always ironed his trousers for him, and kept his clothes brushed and on hangers." Considering what a first-class valet and general houseworker she was, it is a little difficult to see how Philip could look upon her as "a form of charity." But he did.

There are some half-dozen mismated couples in the book. Philip's parents

REVIEWS OF NEW BOOKS
Continued

among them. His mother is held up to the reader's admiration because she condoned her husband's numerous infidelities; but when one remembers that two out of her three children were divorced, and the third on the highroad to ruin when he was rescued by his model wife, the results of Mrs. Baldwin's endurance do not seem to have amounted to much. Tho the novel is badly in need of cutting, there is much in it that is very good, the best being the description of Philip's first marriage. From the moment when he and Marjorie are married in the cheap little flat to the time of their final separation, the portrayal is thoroughly natural, absolutely realistic and convincing, enough in and by itself to make "Brass" a notable novel.

HALL CAINE'S MORALIZING AND MELODRAMA

OLD-FASHIONED melodrama, with a moral not suggested, but shrieked aloud in strident tones, over and over again —of such is Hall Caine's latest production. Long-winded and slow-moving, it sets forth the machine-made and highly improbable history of Victor Stowell, who while still under thirty became Deemster of the Isle of Man, and by virtue of this very important office, "The Master of Man." (Lippincott, $1.75).

So far as any one could see, Victor Stowell's lines were cast in extraordinarily pleasant places. He had power and position, money enough, and love as well. He was engaged to beautiful Fenella Stanley, the only daughter of the Governor of Man, and, so we are told, a model of all the virtues. But alas, and likewise alack, there was a dark secret in Victor Stowell's apparently blameless life. Under circumstances of peculiarly strong temptation he had an affair with a young country woman, Bessie Collister. After a great deal of mental perturbation he had decided to marry Bessie, first having her educated. But during the process, Bessie fell in love with another man, Alick Gell, Stowell's best friend, and he with her. So Victor Stowell thought he was going to escape unpleasant consequences, not knowing that the author had decided to pile them on his unlucky head. Preparations were being made for his marriage to Fenella, and he was having a perfectly lovely time, when Bessie's child was born. Bessie killed it. She did not mean to do it any harm, the death was purely accidental. But dead it was. She tried to hide the body; some curious neighbors saw her, and dug it up. She was arrested and tried for murder.

This was only the beginning of Stowell's difficulties. Tho he tried his very best to wriggle out of it, he found himself obliged to sit as judge at Bessie's trial for the murder of her child, and his. For a while it seemed as tho she might be acquitted, but Alick Gell, who was defending her and firmly believed in her innocence, wanted to make assurance doubly sure, and in the endeavor, ruined everything. Bessie was convicted. But she had told all her story to Fenella, and Fenella repeated it to the jury. They declared Bessie guilty, but followed their verdict with a recommendation to mercy. Under ordinary circumstances she might have escaped; not with Hall Caine determined to make "The Story of a Sin"—so the book is sub-titled—as lurid as possible. For no logical reason save that it suits the author's purpose, the Governor took a hand, and reported against the recommendation to the authorities in London, thereby practically making certain Bessie's death on the gallows, while his daughter upbraided Victor with much emphasis, breaking her engagement.

So after undergoing a lot more mental anguish, Stowell decided that somehow Bessie must be helped to escape from her prison. Of course, his oath as Deemster was against his breaking the law, but he made up his mind that as Bessie's fellow-criminal his first duty was to her. She must escape; and some one must go with her. He resolved that Alick Gell should be that some one; "He must unite those two injured ones. And perhaps some day, when they were gone from the island and safe in some foreign country, the Almighty would accept his act as a kind of reparation and cover up all his wretched wrong-doing in the merciful veil which is God's memory."

The next question was that of managing Alick, who had almost become insane with grief and rage. At least, he must try. He went to Alick, and Alick "struck him in the face and laid open his cheek-bone . . . But Stowell remained standing, and then said, with a break in his voice: 'I have well deserved it.' That was too much for Gell."

The friends were reconciled, and all necessary arrangements made A fog helped them, and Bessie and Alick escaped in a fishing-boat. But the Governor was highly indignant. And of course the disappearance of Alick Gell at the same time that Bessie vanished convinced everybody that it was he who was the guilty man. The Governor demanded that Stowell, as Deemster, sign the warrant for Gell's arrest. Stowell decided to tell the Governor the truth, and confess that it was he who had helped Bessie to escape from her cell in Castle Rushen. Then came the news that there was rioting in Douglas over the failure to arrest Gell, and that the Governor had telegraphed for troops. If they came there would be still more trouble: "The guilty man in this case must give himself up . . . to save the island from ruin."

After hearing voices and seeing a vision of his dead father, who assured him that: "No man can run away from the consequences of his sins. If he flies from them in this life he must meet them in the life hereafter, and then it will be a hundredfold more terrible to be swept from the face of living God"—whatever that may mean —Stowell went to the Governor and denounced himself. But that obdurate person refused to accept his denunciation, and still insisted that he sign the warrant for Gell's arrest. Whereupon Stowell, after pausing by the way to rescue a small child, went before the High Bailiff, who was holding court that day in Douglas, and asked to be arrested and sent to jail. The obliging bailiff consigned him to Castle Rushen. Fenella followed him there, got a position as female warder, and after he had been condemned to two years' imprisonment, married him. "Well she knew that the victory had been won, that the resurrection of his soul had already begun, that he would rise again on that same soil on which he had so sadly fallen, that shining like a star before his brightening eyes was the vision of a far greater and nobler life than the one that lay in ruins behind him, and that she, she herself, would be always by his side—to 'ring the morning bell for him.'" Altogether, she seems to have known a very great deal!

INVESTMENTS ▲ AND ▲ FINANCE

GERMAN MARKS AND AMERICAN "GAMBLERS"

"GAMBLERS and nothing else," is one newspaper's description of Americans who have invested in German marks hoping to reap a rich harvest upon the return of German money to the normal exchange level. Speculation in foreign currency bonds, foreign currencies, bills of exchange and deposits of money in foreign banks, declares Mr. Thomas B. Pratt in *The Annalist*, has reached proportions "far beyond that of any similar craze for oil stocks, gold mining or railroad shares, in the palmiest days of gambling in such ventures." It has reached every class in the population of the United States, "the corporation executive, the clerk, the farmer, the laborer, professional men and women of all classes have succumbed to the arguments and propaganda of the distributors of foreign currency 'investments.'" And the speculation, we read, "has been all the more insidious because of the plausible arguments that have been advanced about the profits that might be realized when these currencies return to normal or par." Of course there has been no actual fraud in connection with this business. The currency that is sold has a price that is quoted daily, and is as good as the credit of the government issuing it. But investments in it are speculative and unsound, says this writer, who here agrees with many financial authorities, because the buyers do not understand foreign exchange and "because in the case of many currencies, there is little or no reason to believe that they will ever return to normal, and, in fact, there are plenty of reasons why they should go still lower and stay there." Not that this applies to all foreign currencies at present depreciated. But there has not been a great deal of speculation in the currencies of such countries as Great Britain, the European neutrals, and the principal South nations. The bonds of these countries, it is mentioned in passing, are a perfectly legitimate investment. But a warning, we are told, "should be issued against speculation in the currencies of some countries that are decidedly shaky."

Speculation in German marks has been greater than in any other foreign currency, and the recent spectacular drop of the mark is the occasion for a history of this particular speculation by a writer in the New York *Times*. He notes one banker's guess that a hundred million dollars' worth of marks have been sold in the United States since the armistice at a price averaging around 2½ cents. On the basis, and at the present quotation of less than a cent, "approximately 60 cents of every American dollar put into marks has been lost." Another banker, it should be added, is said to place the investment in marks at nearer fifty billions. The story of the buying and selling of marks proceeds as follows:

> It was not until midsummer, after the armistice was signed, that quotations in the German mark were resumed. They started at 7¾ to 8 cents per mark. In the meanwhile, many bales of the German currency appeared in the United States, and were sold surreptitiously to those of known German sympathy. This traffic did not come into the open until the resumption of foreign exchange dealings in the midsummer of 1919. In the intervening two years the United States—and every other country, for that matter—has been fairly flooded with the paper marks of Germany as fast as the printing-press could turn them out.
>
> New York appeared to be the center of this distribution. Small stores sprang up on prominent corners, where the paper currency of Germany was sold to the extent of thousands of marks. This traffic, too, burrowed into the bank accounts of small investors with but $100, $500 or $1,000 to risk, and which gave him in return for his dollars a few prettily colored pieces of paper, turned out within the month by the overworked printing-presses, running unrestricted. "Foreign exchange" stores began dotting the country as well as the cities. At one time no less than six were running day and night on Broadway. The exchanges of other countries could be purchased at these stores too, but chiefly they were ostensibly and openly concerned with the conversion of German marks into dollars.
>
> Peddlers also hawked the paper marks about the streets, selling from 1 mark up. One enterprising distributer last Fall sent a large crew of canvassers over the city, to call from door to door. Even the part-payment system was adopted, in some cases, and many persons to-day are paying out of their earnings, week by week, agreed sums which eventually will give them ownership of stipulated numbers of German marks.
>
> This traffic evidently was carefully planned to attract those unfamiliar with the purchase of foreign exchange, in the regular manner, and through a bank. Compared to the transactions handled through banks it was but a small part of the total, but it put thousands of good American dollars into Germany's till, and no doubt aided the country in amassing the first reparations payment of 1,000,000,000 marks gold, recently discharged.
>
> The appeal of the traffic in German currency was directed at those familiar with Germany and her industrial and financial efficiency in pre-war days. With the mark selling at 5, 4, 3, or 2 cents, the point was made that the German Government would soon be on its feet, and that her financiers would quickly bring the mark back to 23.8 cents, its pre-war worth. The bait was attractive. The investment of a few thousand dollars promised a small fortune to the lucky holder of marks, when the currency regained its equilibrium, it was pointed out.
>
> The bulk of the business in marks, of course, was done through the foreign exchange market. The transaction was simple, after the reopening of the exchange market to Germany by the Allies. An investor or speculator, merely went to his

banker and procured mark exchange either securing the bank's voucher for so many marks, to be delivered at a future date, or ordered the transfer of so many marks to his account in a German banking institution. Thousands of new American accounts were opened in German banks during 1919 and 1920, representing drafts sold by American bankers on their Berlin correspondents.

Some bankers who have dealt heavily in German marks—both the actual currency and in the exchange, for speculation—assert that those who put their money into marks did not do so for a "quick turn," that they have faith in the future of Germany and her industrial and banking recovery and that the mark, ultimately, will return to a price at which they may reap a profit. Between the present quotation for the paper mark—less than one cent—and its 23.8 cent nominal value, however, stand the German printing-presses, grinding away ceaselessly. Some figures on this tremendous increase in the circulation are timely.

Germany's payment of her September 1 instalment on reparations was coincident with a renewed outpouring of paper marks which raised the circulation of the Reichsbank between August 20 and September 3, 1921, from 68,423,000,000 marks to 71,960,-000,000 marks, an increase of 3,500,000,000 marks in two weeks. In the same period the Reichsbank gold reserve was reduced from 1,091,543,000 to 1,023,708,000 marks. The gold reserve is microscopic.

But what can the investor in German marks do about it now, how can he make the best of what at present seems to be a bad bargain? In answer to this obvious question, *The Times* quotes an authority on mark exchange as suggesting that the remedy is for the investor to use his marks or marks credit to purchase German municipal bonds:

> The German marks will fall; the municipal bonds, with their real estate backing them, will rise and the increment will be greater than the shrinkage of the foreign exchange value of the German currency.

THE WORLD'S SHIPPING IN 1920

WITH the principal countries of the world in the throes of business depression, and the world possessing something like a third more ships now than it did before the war, it is no wonder that we see idle tonnage tied up in every harbor and the United States Shipping Board trying frantically to dispose of its ships. Figures compiled by Lloyd's and reprinted in *Bradstreet's* show an increase of 36 per cent. in the steam tonnage of the world between 1914 and 1920. Germany, it may be noted, is the only nation to show a decrease in shipping. The figures are given in millions of gross tons as follows:

Country	1914 *Gross tons*	1920 *Gross tons*	*Increase or decrease* *Gross tons*	*P.ct.*
United King...	18,900	19,300	+ 400	+ 2
United States*.	2,000	13,500	+ 11,500	+575
Japan.......	1,700	3.400	+ 1,700	+100
France.....	1.900	3.300	+ 1.400	+ 73
Norway......	2,000	2.400	+ 400	+ 20
Italy.........	1,400	2.500	+ 1,100	+ 79
Holland	1.500	2,200	+ 700	+ 47
Germany....	5.100	700	— 4.400	— 86
Other countries	8,900	11,600	+ 2.700	+ 30
Total .	43,400	58.900	+15.500	+ 36

CURRENT EVENTS

FOREIGN

October 12.—The trial of Bulgarians accused of war crimes opens in Sofia before peasant judges elected by the people.

Anti-tax riots break out in Pueblo, Mexico, and many factories are reported closed.

October 13.—German volunteers in Upper and Lower Silesia have obtained large supplies of arms and ammunition and are reported ready to seize that part of Upper Silesia allotted to Poland by the League of Nations.

Twenty thousand unemployed parade London streets on a "hunger march."

The Australian Minister of the Navy announces that the Commonwealth's seagoing fleet has been reduced to two light cruisers, one training cruiser, two sloops, four destroyers, three submarines and a few auxiliary ships. The estimate for the coming year is $12,720,000.

October 14.—Two thousand tons of food have been used in Petrograd to alleviate the famine, it is reported, and food sufficient to feed 1,000,000 for five months is on its way to Russia.

The new Russian state bank opens in Moscow, and five branches are to be established in as many cities.

October 15.—A state of siege is declared in the Bethuen District, Upper Silesia, and the inter-Allied Commission warns both Polish and German factions that force will be used promptly to suppress disorder.

General Leonard Wood is sworn in as Governor-General of the Philippines at Manila.

October 17.—General Pershing lays the Congressional Medal of Honor on the tomb of the unknown British warrior in Westminster Abbey. In return King George expresses the desire that the tomb of America's unknown warrior be decorated on Armistice Day with the Victoria Cross, the highest honor within the gift of the British Empire.

Protest meetings are held in all parts of Germany against the reported decision of the League of Nations in awarding the greater part of Upper Silesia to Poland.

October 18.—The Ulster volunteers begin remobilizing as the result of reported concentrations of Sinn Fein troops in Ulster.

Premier Lloyd George announces himself, Arthur J. Balfour, Lord President of the Privy Council, and Lord Lee of Fareham, First Lord of the Admiralty, as the English members of the Washington Arms Conference.

DOMESTIC

October 12.—Senator Philander C. Knox of Pennsylvania dies suddenly in his home in Washington in his 69th year.

The American delegates to the Arms Conference effect a permanent organization to decide on questions of policy in the negotiations.

The House passes a bill prohibiting transmission through the mails of newspapers publishing betting odds on horse-races, prize-fights, and similar contests.

The Senate adopts the compromise plan for repeal of all the transportation taxes on January 1.

October 13.—President Walter C. Teagle, of the Standard Oil Company, announces that approximately $2,000,000 will be spent on repairs and reconstruction work in the New Jersey refineries in order to increase employment.

Alexander M. Howat, President of the Kansas Mine Workers' Union, and his administration, are suspended from office by John L. Lewis, President of the International Union, because of the former's refusal to order certain striking miners back to work.

October 14.—President T. De Witt Cuyler, of the Association of Railway Executives, announces that the executives will request the United States Railway Labor Board to authorize a ten per cent. cut in the wages of train service employees, pledging themselves to make corresponding cuts in rates when the wage decreases are approved.

The House blocks a proposed increase in membership by recommitting to the census committee, by a vote of 146 to 142, the Siegel bill to increase its size from 435 to 460 members.

Secretary of the Treasury Mellon announces that Federal expenditures for the current fiscal year will be kept within the agreed limit of $4,034,000,000, and denies reports that additional deficiency appropriations of $370,000,000 will be asked.

Between 4,000 and 5,000 Kansas coalminers adopt resolutions upholding the administration of President Alexander M. Howat, suspended by the International President John L. Lewis.

October 15.—The five big Brotherhoods of railroad employees, involving nearly 750,000 men, are ordered to begin a strike on October 30. President Harding summons the public group members of the Railroad Labor Board and members of the Interstate Commerce Commission to a joint meeting to attempt a settlement of the issues involved.

October 16.—Immediate translation of the reduction authorized last July in the wages of railroad employees into reduced freight rates is suggested by the public group of the Railroad Labor Board to settle the railroad controversy.

Retail cost of food in September was 1.1 per cent. less than the average cost in August, announces the Bureau of Labor Statistics. Wholesale figures did not change materially.

October 17.—Postmaster-General Hays announces that the threatened railroad strike will not be permitted to interfere with the movement of the mails.

State Senator William E. Crow is appointed United States Senator by Governor Sproul to fill the unexpired term of the late Philander C. Knox of Pennsylvania.

October 18.—The Senate ratifies the Treaties of Peace with Germany, Austria and Hungary by a vote of 66 to 20.

At the request of President Harding a meeting of the United States Railroad Labor Board and the heads of the five unions which have authorized their men to strike is called for to-morrow, to attempt a settlement of the railroad dispute. A canvass is ordered of all military commands in the Eighth Army Corps area, comprising five states, for soldiers experienced in operating rail-

THE SPICE OF LIFE

Ready to Oblige.—John, can you let me have a little money?"

"Certainly, darling. About how little?" —*London Mail.*

Sing a Song of Rent Bills.—The rose is red, the violet's blue, and so is a man when his rent falls due.—*Western Christian Advocate.*

Not Going Up.—STAGE MANAGER—"All ready, run up the curtain."

STAGE HAND—"Say, what do you think I am, a squirrel?"—*Froth.*

Just So.—CARRY—"Why did kings tap men on their heads when they knighted them?"

TARRY—"Perhaps the stars made the knights more realistic."—*The Widow.*

Inhuman Treatment.—HEROINE (in the melodrama)—"What are those shrieks?"

VILLAIN (relentlessly)—"They have tied an American to a chair and are showing him a bottle of Scotch."—*London Passing Show.*

Judging by His Habits.—VISITOR—"Does Mr. Crawford, a student, live here?"

LANDLADY—"Well, Mr. Crawford lives here, but I thought he was a night watchman."—*The Goblin.*

Relieving Her Anxiety.—OLD LADY—"Oh, conductor, please stop the train. I dropt my wig out the window."

CONDUCTOR—"Never mind, madam, there is a switch just this side of the next station."—*Octopus.*

No Chances.—"Judge," cried the prisoner in the dock, "have I got to be tried by a woman jury?"

"Be quiet," whispered his counsel.

"I won't be quiet! Judge, I can't even fool my own wife, let alone twelve strange women. I'm guilty."—*Houston Post.*

He Could Prove It.—"Well," said the waiter to the student, who had just had his coffee cup refilled for the seventh time, "you must be very fond of coffee."

"Yes, indeed," answered the student, "or I wouldn't be drinking so much water to get a little."—*Lehigh Burr.*

Poor Fodder.—"Did you read in the paper about the squirrels storing away golf balls?"

"Yes, and old-timers say it presages a hard winter."

"It certainly does for those squirrels."—*Boston Transcript.*

Easily Explained.—The fancy shop proprietor had ransacked his shop in an endeavor to please the rather exacting woman who wanted to purchase a present.

"Now, are you sure this is genuine crocodile skin," she inquired, critically examining a neat little satchel.

"Quite, madam," was the reply. "You see, I shot the crocodile myself."

"It looks rather dirty," remarked the customer, hoping to get a reduction in terms.

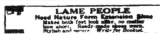

"Yes, madam," replied the shopkeeper, "that is where the animal struck the ground after it fell off the tree."—*London*

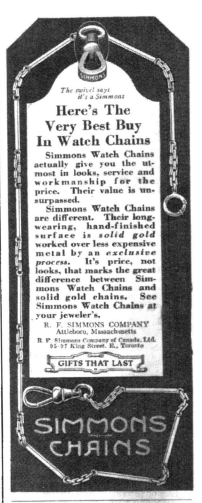

Snuff.—"Sneagle."
"Snotneagle, snowl."
"Sneither, snostrich."—*Lehigh Burr.*

Death Rattles.—They say jazz is dead. We thought it was dying from the weird noise it made.—*Boston Transcript.*

No Mixed Tricks.—"Would you marry a widower, Maude?"
"No. I prefer to tame my husband myself."—*Judge.*

What Gave Them Value.—"Why does the boss always keep his desk locked?"
"Important papers."
"He never locked up his papers before prohibition came in."—*Detroit Free Press.*

Accent on the "Skeet."—We liked Doug Fairbanks in "The Three Musketeers," but the young lady in the next seat, who called it "Three Muskeeters" evidently thought she had been stung.—*Arkansas Gazette.*

Just Before the Explosion.—VOICE AT THE OTHER END—"Is that you, darling?"
GOUTY PATER—"Er—yes."
VOICE—"Oh, good! How's the old boy's gout, my pet? I mean to say, if he still has it, I'll come round to-night, but if he hasn't, we'll go out to some show!"—*The Passing Show, (London).*

Crowned with Lightning.—A white streak searing the withered grass tops, a hurtling human mass, then a stab of lightning followed in a trice by a bolt which dealt final destruction—and the Giants were crowned kings of the baseball universe!—*Opening paragraph of the report of the last world-series game in the New York Herald.*

The Next Best Thing.—"Willie, where did you get that black eye?"
"Johnny Smith hit me."
"I hope you remember what your Sunday-school teacher said about heaping coals on the head of your enemies."
"Well, ma, I didn't have any coal, so I just stuck his head in the ash-barrel."—*Boston Transcript.*

Making Him Careful.—LAWYER—"And what was the defendant doing meanwhile?"
WITNESS—"He was telling me a funny story."
LAWYER—"Remember, sir, that you are under oath."
WITNESS—"Well, anyway, he was telling me a story."—*Pearson's Weekly.*

All Wrong.—ACCUSED OFFICER—"I admit dat I wuz drunk and insulting people; but I was off duty and in citizen's clothes, sir!"
POLICE COMMISSIONER—"That is just the point, sir. When you are off duty and in citizen's clothes you have no more right getting drunk and insulting people than anybody else, sir."—*New York Globe.*

Experienced.—Mrs. Jones was entertaining some of her son's little friends. "Willie," she said, addressing a six-year-old, who was enjoying a plate of cold beef, "are you sure you can cut your own meat?"
The child who was making desperate efforts with his knife and fork replied,
"Yes, thanks. I've often had it as tough as this at home."—*The Christian-Evangel-*

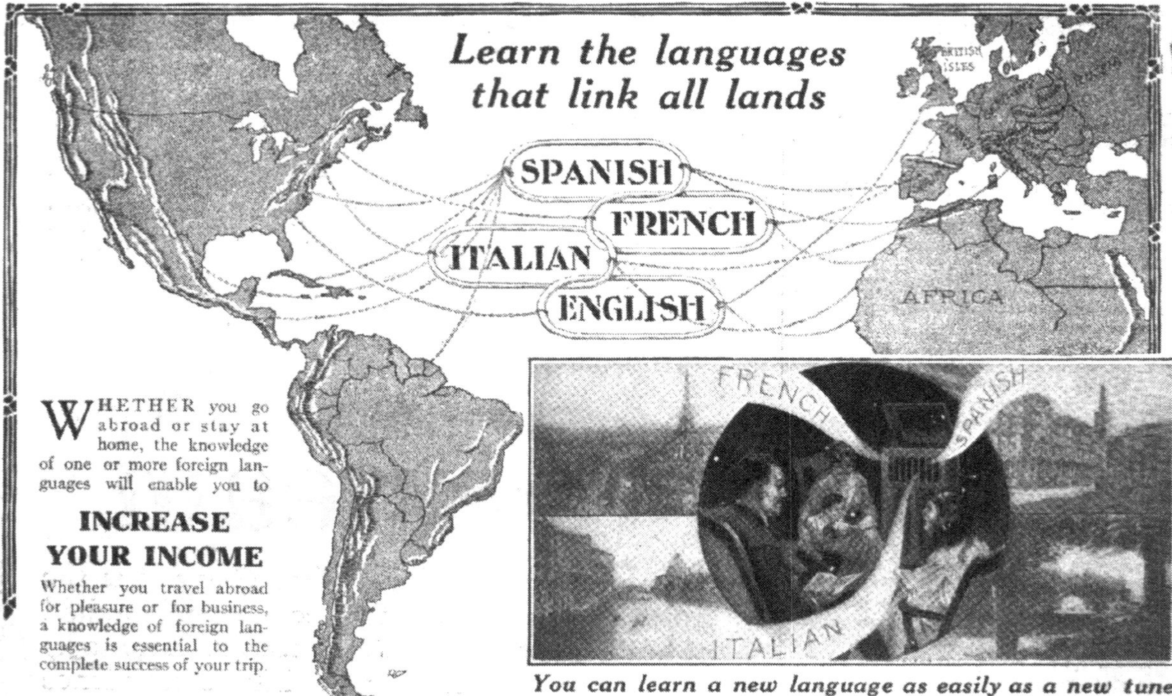

You can learn a new language as easily as a new tune

THERE are thousands of opportunities for "two-language" men and women. Whether you are an employer or an employee, a clerk or an executive, a professional man or woman in any branch of law, medicine, art, literature, music, science, divinity, pedagogy—another language will help you increase your income, enlarge your social and business prestige, multiply the pleasures of travel and reading. Men and women familiar with one or more foreign tongues are in demand. They are needed for responsible office-positions and on the road, in our own country, as well as to travel abroad. To-day, linguistic ability commands high pay.

LANGUAGE PHONE METHOD

(Title Reg. U. S. Pat. Office)

WITH ROSENTHAL'S PRACTICAL LINGUISTRY

Anyone can learn to speak, read, and write a foreign tongue, easily and quickly—by the Rosenthal Language Phone Method.

A Few Minutes of Spare Time

You study in the comfort and privacy of your own home. You choose your own time—whenever you are in the mood. You can use your own phonograph (any make) or we will furnish one.

From the very first lesson, you begin to speak the language you take up. You say and understand phrases that will be of constant practical use.

No Rules to Learn

You do not have to learn any rules of grammar or syntax or conjugations. Yet perfect pronunciation and correct diction are assured.

Progress is surprizingly rapid. It is also intensely interesting—as hundreds of students have written us.

Francis W lson, the famous actor, has lear ed several languages by means of the Rosenthal Method. He says: "It beats a teacher all hollow, for it is the teacher itself plus something else—that is, the power of patience and repetitive energy which no teacher could possibly possess."

Better Than Living Abroad

It is even better than learning by living in a foreign country, for there you pick up the language in a haphazard, hit-or-m'ss way. You learn as circumstances necessitate—slowly and incompletely. You hear much bad grammar, and crude pronunciation, and so inevitably form many bad habits of speech.

By the Rosenthal Method, you learn quickly, correctly, methodically.

One-third of Our Population Speaks a Foreign Tongue

Exporting and importing are but two of the many fields in which a knowledge of languages is of great value.

Over thirty-two million people in the United States—nearly one-third of the population—speak a foreign language You can interest a man more thoroughly and convince him more quickly by talking or writing to him in his mother-tongue.

When you visit foreign countries—for pleasure or business—familiarity with the native languages is indispensable.

Used in Famous Universities

The Rosenthal Method has been praised, endorsed, and used by teachers of languages in scores of famous colleges and universities, including Columbia, Yale, Harvard, Princeton, Cornell, Johns Hopkins, New York, Boston, Stevens Institute of Technology, College of St. Francis Xavier, St. Joseph's Seminary.

A Social Recreation

It is not a selfish and isolating pastime, but one that can be shared by any number—the whole family and groups of friends.

FREE—A 64-PAGE BOOK THAT TELLS YOU

How to Increase Your Income, through a knowledge of a foreign language, whether you are an employer or an employee, young or old, a professional man or woman, a practitioner of any of the arts or sciences—*whoever, whatever, and wherever you are.* How to Acquire Conversational Fluency in a Foreign Tongue Quickly—and devote only ten minutes, three times a day, to study. How familiarity with even one foreign language Increases Your Prestige—in the drawing-room, the club, the office; Widens Your Circle of Acquaintances—social and commercial; Multiplies the Pleasures of Travel and Reading; Broadens Your Intellectual Horizon.

FUNK & WAGNALLS COMPANY, 533 [illegible], New York, N. Y.

Please send me by mail (without obligation of any kind) the free book about Language Study, together with details of your offer of a fr e trial, in my own home, of The Language Phone Method for Spanish, French or Italian.

Name ....

Address ....

City .... *State* ....

An OLD-WORLD TOWER *in* NEW YORK

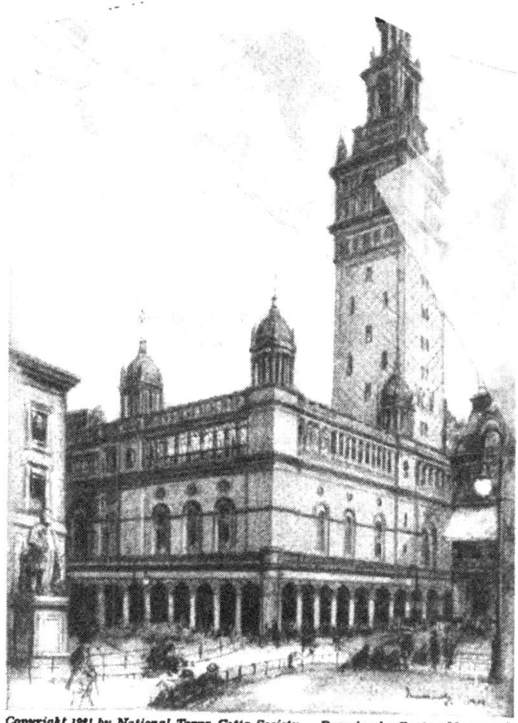

Copyright 1921 by National Terra Cotta Society. Drawing by Carton Moorepark

MADISON SQUARE GARDEN
NEW YORK CITY

Trim and Ornament, Buff Unglazed Terra Cotta — McKim, Mead & White, Architects

To become familiar with Architecture, follow this Series of Details. No. 15 will appear in The Literary Digest of Dec. 3, 1921.

HOW TO RECOGNIZE ARCHITECTURAL DETAILS

TERRA COTTA SERIES No. 14

Palladian Arch from sub-cupola on tower of Madison Square Garden.

Palladian Motive

This treatment of the arch, named after Palladio, the great Italian Renaissance architect, consists of springing an arch from two pieces of architrave each shorter than the the span of the arch. The ends of the two pieces of architrave rest on columns, and the two narrow openings on either side of the arched opening emphasize the arch. The Palladian motive is used for windows, doors and loggias, as well as in such applications as illustrated.

Corinthian Column, Italian Renaissance

This column illustrates the characteristic Italian Renaissance manner of embellishing the Classic Orders. The garlands hanging from the neck of the column, and the beads in the two lower sections of the flutes, give the column a finer scale and a greater richness of effect.

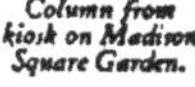

Column from kiosk on Madison Square Garden.

(All the material described is Terra Cotta)

WHEN Madison Square was the center of all that was brilliant in New York, the tower that rose at its northeast corner, with Diana glinting in the sun, was the tallest and most beautiful of up-town buildings. It is still the most beautiful.

Inspired by the Hispano-Moorish tower of La Giralda, in old Seville, the master architect Stanford White skillfully translated the detail into that of Renaissance Italy. And wishing to create in New York a building with that mellow richness of antiquity which is the architectural charm of the Old World, he thought and designed in Terra Cotta.

For he realized the ready response of the clay to the hand of the modeler, the ease of repetition of intricate forms, the mellow antiquity of texture and color immediately obtainable with this material. He used Terra Cotta exactly in the manner of the great architects of Renaissance Italy—and achieved a masterpiece.

Madison Square Garden was built in 1890. Although three decades have passed since then, the detail modeling is as clean-cut as on the day the Terra Cotta came from the kiln. Even the lightest marks of the modeler's tools are easily discerned; there is not the slightest trace of erosion.

Unquestionably the beauty of Madison Square Garden will endure as long as man permits the building to stand; for its beauty is cast in Terra Cotta—and Terra Cotta knows neither youth nor age. It is as enduring as Time itself.

If you are interested in buildings of any kind, write to the National Terra Cotta Society. We are a bureau of service and information. And we will be glad to send you a brochure or other information illustrating Terra Cotta's value and achievements in the class of buildings you are interested in. Address National Terra Cotta Society, 1 Madison Ave., New York, N. Y.

TERRA COTTA

Permanent *Beautiful* *Profitable*

Actual photo of one of our rebuilt Underwood Typewriters

GUARANTEED REBUILT
Shipman-Ward
CHICAGO
UNDERWOODS

$3 DOWN And It's Yours

Standard Underwood

Rebuilt like new. Every typewriter is factory rebuilt by typewriter experts. New enamel — new nickeling — new lettering – new platen – new key rings — new parts wherever needed – making it impossible for you to tell it from a brand new Underwood. An up-to-date machine with two-color ribbon, back spacer, stencil device, automatic ribbon reverse, tabulator, etc. In addition, we furnish FREE waterproof cover and a special Touch Typewriter Instruction Book. You can learn to operate the Underwood in one day.

From factory to you

Yes, only $3 brings you this genuine Rebuilt Standard Visible Underwood direct from our factory, and then only small monthly payments while you are using it makes it yours; or if convenient pay cash. Either way, there is a big, very much worthwhile saving, too. Genuine new Underwood parts wherever the wear comes — genuine standard four row, single-shift keyboard — thoroughly tested — guaranteed for five years.

$3 Puts It in Your Home

You don't even have to scrimp and save to pay cash. Instead, you pay only a little each month in amounts so conveniently small that you will hardly notice them, while all the time you are paying, you will be enjoying the use of and the profits from the machine.

10 Days' Free Trial

Remember, you don't even have to buy the machine until you get it and have used it on 10 days' free trial so that you can see for yourself how new it is and how well it writes. You must be satisfied or else the entire transaction will not cost you a single penny.

FREE TRIAL COUPON

TYPEWRITER EMPORIUM
SHIPMAN-WARD MFG. CO.
2558 Shipman Bldg., Montrose and Ravenswood Aves., Chicago

Send by return mail Bargain Offer No. 2558 of a Standard Visible Writing Underwood. This is not an order and does not obligate me to buy.

Name ....

Street or R. F. D. No. ....

.... *State* ....

Use Coupon

Now is the time when every dollar saved counts. Let us save you many dollars. Don't delay. Get this wonderful easy payment bargain offer now, so you can send for and be sure of getting your Underwood at a big saving — and our easy terms or for cash.

Act Now–

Send Coupon Today!

Typewriter Emporium
Shipman-Ward Mfg. Co.
2558 Shipman Bldg., Montrose and Ravenswood Aves., Chica

All shipments made direct to you from our modern factory (shown above) – the largest typewriter rebuilding plant in the world.

November 5, 1

The Literary Digest

(Title Reg. U.S. Pat. Off.)

PAYING OUT THE TRAWL

New York FUNK & WAGNALLS COMPANY London

PUBLIC OPINION New York combined with The LITERARY DIGEST

Vol. 71, No. 6 Whole No. 1646 November 5, 1921 Price 10

Pass the Buck to Fairbanks

—the Best Purchasing Agents Do It

EIGHT-HOUR days have arrived for purchasing agents. The old bulging record of supply sources is no more. The bids from a dozen or more firms for every purchase have gone unmourned. And with all this wasted energy, lost motion and worry, have gone the complaints about that last batch of so-and-so's not being as good as the first ones.

Fairbanks O. K. Service has changed the buying habits of thousands of purchasing agents and other buyers of mill, mine and railway supplies.

The engineers of the Fairbanks Company place their O. K. on supplies, equipment and tools that merit the Fairbanks guarantee of quality and service. It may be a machine tool, a wheel barrow, a valve or a union—everything from Adzes to Zig-zag Rules that Fairbanks makes or sells, is sold with the Fairbanks O. K. tag attached—the Fairbanks O. K. of unvarying quality at a Fairbanks O. K. price.

Don't take your purchasing troubles home. Take them to Fairbanks. Let Fairbanks O. K. Service work for you as it is working for wise P. A's in the biggest industries and public service companies.

THE FAIRBANKS COMPANY

Administrative Offices: New York

Albany, Baltimore, Birmingham, Boston, Buffalo, Chicago, Detroit, Hartford, Newark, New Orleans, New York, Paterson, Philadelphia, Pittsburgh, Providence, Scranton, St. Louis, Syracuse, Tulsa, Washington

Rochester

Havana · Kingston · London · Paris

Birmingham · Glasgow

HARTMANN

WARDROBE TRUNK WEEK

SEE OUR NEW LINE AT YOUR DEALER'S

November Fifth to Twelfth

ALL over America Hartmann Wardrobe Trunk dealers will unite in an exhibit of the complete improved line of Hartmann Wardrobe Trunks. Those careful buyers who are looking for real service and values in the trunks they buy will find much to guide their choice in this demonstration.

The exhibit will feature Castle-Grande, the only steel frame trunk ever built—the only trunk without a nail in its construction. It is not only remarkable for its strength, but gives to travelers a clothes care and protection never before possible. It is absolutely the last word in Wardrobe Trunk creation, as it combines in complete harmony the utmost of beauty, durability and practical convenience.

Here, too, will be shown the world-renowned line of Hartmann Gibraltarized Panama Wardrobe Trunks. These are the only round edge trunks actually built with a patented solid interlocking re-inforcement. This round edge construction is imitated by others, but in outward appearance only. And the display of popular priced Hartmann Rite-Hites proves conclusively that no practical, serviceable Wardrobe Trunk can sell for less money. Hartmann Wardrobe Trunks range in price from $30 to $200.

To merely speak of Hartmann exclusive features in this announcement would not mean much, but to see them actually demonstrated will be enlightening. For instance, by actually seeing the operation of the patented cushion-top, an exclusive Hartmann feature, one can understand why the Hartmann Wardrobe Trunk so perfectly prevents clothes from shifting or wrinkling under all conditions of travel.

Be sure to visit your dealer's exhibit. Then you will know the truth; that even though Hartmann is highest praised, it is the most economically priced wardrobe trunk

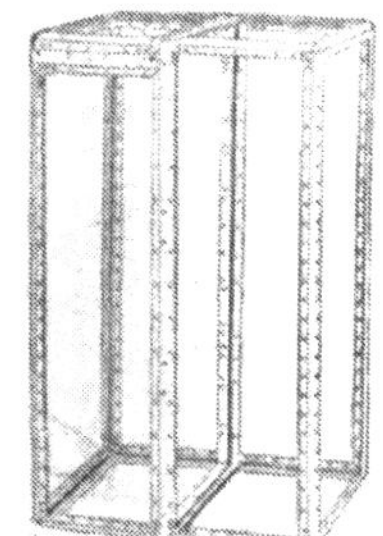

Steel frame of CASTLE-GRANDE *the only trunk without a nail in it*

HARTMANN TRUNK COMPANY, *Racine, Wisconsin*

BE SURE THE HARTMANN RED ✕ IS ON THE TRUNK YOU BUY

Volume 71 No. 6

TABLE · OF · CONTENTS

November 5, 1921

TOPICS OF THE DAY: Page

Mr. Harding's British-American "Doctrine." 5
The Forlorn Hapsburg Hope 7
Railway Wage Facts 8
The Anarchists and the Ambassador 9
A Close-Up of Unemployment 10
Topics in Brief 12

FOREIGN COMMENT:

Must Uncle Sam Forgive His Debtors? 13
Chinese Labor Organizing 14
Peril of "Empty Australia" 15
"Unearned" Wealth to Relieve the Jobless 16
Japan's "Official" Propaganda 16

SCIENCE AND INVENTION:

A Plan to Give Each Man a Job to Fit His Brains . . . 17
Improbability of Life on the Planets 18
Tracking Criminals by Their Pores 19
Woman's Friend, the Corset 20
Hunting Seals from the Air 20
Must the World Die of Thirst? 21

SCIENCE AND INVENTION *(Continued)*: Page

How Nature Swats the Fly 21

(*Continued on page 54*)

LETTERS AND ART:

The "Blue Boy" and the "Tragic Muse" for America . . 22
The Music Assembler 23
Actors Bilking Shakespeare 23
Dull Teaching of History 24
Forgetting How to Read 25

RELIGION AND SOCIAL SERVICE:

The Dispute over the Holy Land 26
Protestant Growth in France 27
Religion Rising above Genesis 28
A Drive to Recruit Catholic Youth 28

MISCELLANEOUS:

Current Poetry 30
Personal Glimpses 32-41
New Books for Young Folks 42-58
Investments and Finance 58
Current Events 60-61
The Spice of Life 62-63

TERMS: $4.00 a year, in advance; six months, $2.50; three months, $1.50; a single copy, 10 cents; postage to Canada, 85 cents a year; other foreign postage, $2.00 a year. BACK NUMBERS, not over three months old, 25 cents each; over three months old, $1.00 each. QUARTERLY INDEXES will be sent free to subscribers who apply for them. RECEIPT of payment is shown in about two weeks by date on address-label; date of expiration includes the month named on the label. CAUTION: If date is not properly extended after each payment, notify publishers promptly. Instructions for RENEWAL, DISCONTINUANCE, or CHANGE OF ADDRESS should be sent *two weeks* before the date they are to go into effect.

Both old and new addresses must always be given. PRESENTATION COPIES: Many persons subscribe for friends. Those who desire to renew such subscriptions must do so before expiration.

THE LITERARY DIGEST is published weekly by the Funk & Wagnalls Company, 354-360 Fourth Avenue, New York, and Salisbury Square, London, E. C.

Entered as second-class matter, March 24, 1890, at the Post-office at New York, N. Y., under the act of March 3, 1879.

Entered as second-class matter at the Post-office Department, Ottawa, Canada.

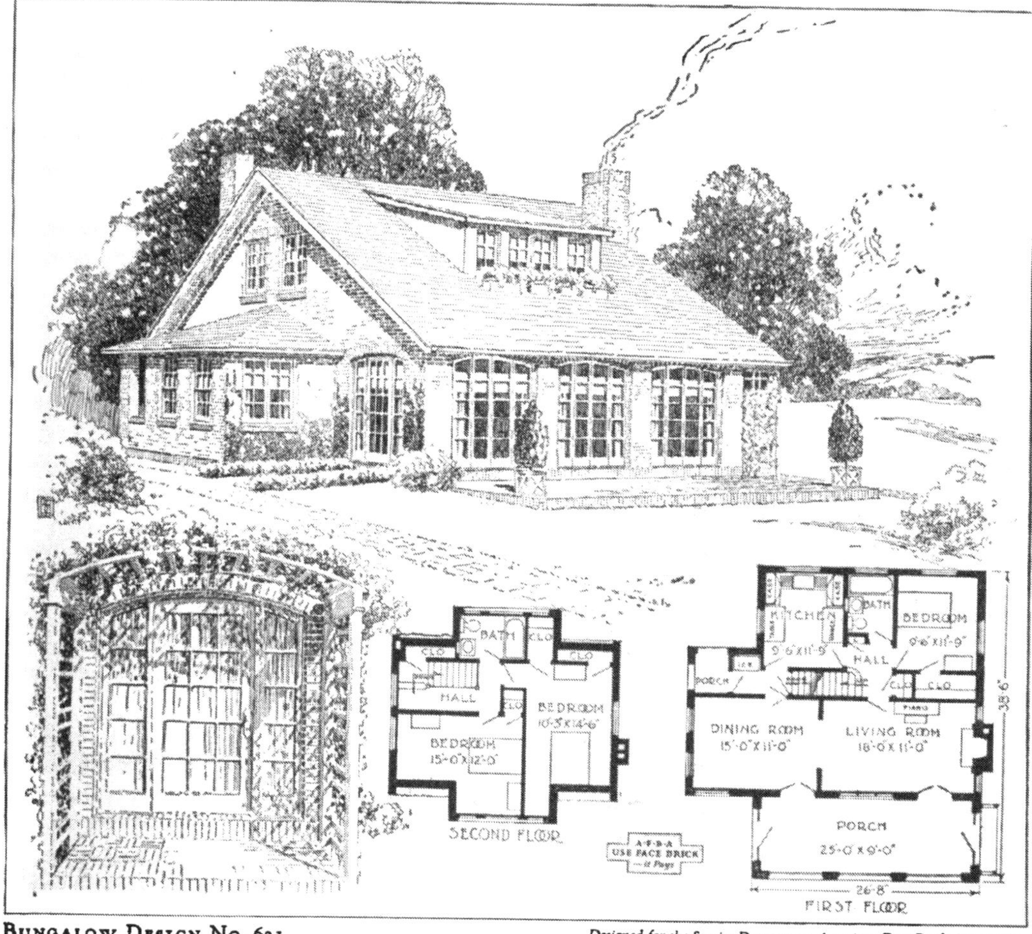

BUNGALOW DESIGN NO. 621

Designed for the Service Department, American Face Brick Association

This airy, sunny cottage is one of the designs in our "Face Brick Bungalow and Small House Plans." The large porch, ample living and sleeping quarters, and the generous windows, assuring plenty of light and ventilation, combine to make this an exceptionally livable house.

Beautiful, Economical Face Brick Homes

THE joy and satisfaction of your new Face Brick house is only enhanced by the years. Time mellows its beauty, weather cannot mar it, and age does not undermine its strength. It will serve you a lifetime and be a heritage to your children.

Costing but a little more than less beautiful and less enduring materials, it becomes in a few years the most economical house you can build; for the Face Brick house depreciates almost imperceptibly, requires no repairs and little painting around doors and windows, and saves money in fuel costs and insurance rates.

"The Story of Brick," an artistic booklet with numerous illustrations, discusses these matters in detail. It has much helpful information for all who intend to build. Sent free.

"Face Brick Bungalow and Small House Plans" are issued in four booklets, showing 3 to 4-room houses, 5-room houses, 6-room houses, and 7 to 8-room houses, in all sixty-four, each reversible with a different exterior design. These designs are unusual and distinctive, combined with convenient interiors and economical construction. The entire set for one dollar. Any one of the booklets, 25 cents, preferably in stamps.

We have the complete working drawings, specifications and masonry quantity estimates at nominal prices. Select from the booklets the designs you like best and order the plans, even if you are not going to build now, for their study will be not only interesting and instructive, but helpful in formulating your future plans for a home.

You may want "The Home of Beauty," fifty designs, mostly two stories, representing a wide variety of architectural styles and floor plans. Sent for 50 cents in stamps. We also distribute complete working drawings, specifications and quantity estimates for these houses at nominal prices.

Address, American Face Brick Association, 1134 Westminster Building, Chicago, Illinois.

THE LITERARY DIGEST

PUBLIC OPINION (New York) combined with THE LITERARY DIGEST

Published by Funk & Wagnalls Company (Adam W. Wagnalls, Pres.; Wilfred J. Funk, Vice-Pres.; Robert J. Cuddihy, Treas.; William Neisel, Sec'y) 354-360 Fourth Ave., New York

Vol. LXXI, No 6 New York, November 5, 1921 Whole Number 1646

TOPICS - OF - THE - DAY

(Title registered in U S Patent Office for use in this publication and on moving picture films)

MR. HARDING'S BRITISH-AMERICAN "DOCTRINE"

WHEN GROVER CLEVELAND TWISTED the British lion's tail, in a dispute over a Venezuelan boundary, so vigorously that war seemed imminent, little attention was paid to Arthur Balfour's prophecy of a new British-American doctrine that would some day be formulated. Said Mr. Balfour, speaking in the British Parliament in that crucial hour that is now twenty-five years behind us: "The time will come, the time must come, when some one, some statesman more fortunate even than President Monroe, will lay down the doctrine that between English-speaking peoples war is impossible." Is Mr. Balfour one of those rare prophets who live to see their prophecy fulfilled? President Harding, speaking at Yorktown on October 19, at the spot where the British General, Lord Cornwallis, surrendered his forces to General Washington one hundred and forty years ago, declared that to-day a breach of the peace between this country and Great Britain is "unthinkable."

In this declaration he finds himself in head-on collision with the published convictions of George Bernard Shaw, Horatio Bottomley, William Randolph Hearst, and a considerable part of the Irish-American journals. Nevertheless, his words seem to find a wide and cordial welcome in the American press. "The President reflected practically the unanimous sentiment of the American people," says the Richmond *Times-Dispatch;* "did no more than give voice to the sentiment of all sensible persons of both countries who have given thought to the subject," remarks the Columbia *Record.* "We like to think that this is the American attitude," says the Charleston *Gazette,* "and we repeat, coming at this time, it is a very wise policy." Similar expressions are found in papers from Norfolk, Detroit, Toledo, Philadelphia, Brooklyn and New York. In Canada the Montreal *Herald* welcomes this evidence that "Mr. Harding sees the light," and the London, Ontario, *Advertiser* exclaims enthusiastically: "More power to the speaker, be he President of the United States or the humblest layman in the constituency, who has vision enough to reiterate to the point of monotony that another break in the friendly relations between United States and Great Britain is unthinkable."

"By emphasizing the supreme necessity of close union between the United States and Great Britain the President strikes at the heart of the peace problem," declares the New York *Tribune.* But, urging that we show respect for a great cause by candor, it goes on to say:

HOW NOT TO ENCOURAGE REDUCTION OF ARMAMENTS.
—Knott in the Dallas *News.*

"It is said war between the two peoples is unthinkable. Would it were so. But, alas! too many not only think it but talk of it. More than one generation of petty American politicians have devoted themselves to twisting the British lion's tail.

"Sometimes it has been to hoodwink those whose emotional center is Ireland, and recently it has been to cater to those whose major interest is Germany. In every conceivable way there have been attempts to keep alive feelings born of the misdeeds of George III, of the War of 1812, and of the unhandsome behavior of many British leaders when disunion threatened the life of the Republic. Public men might be friends to Great Britain in their closets, but not on the stump.

"Men and women who have recognized that a statute of limitations runs against memory of old wrongs and have seen that it was peculiarly desirable to have concords between peoples which in many things are strikingly alike have been browbeaten—attacked as Anglomaniacs, as contemptible imitators of alien ways. To dwell on the good qualities of other peoples was permissible, but Great Britain was always bad. Thomas Jefferson, ignoring the outrages he had catalogued, wrote before his death that he would rather have good relations with Great Britain than with any other Power, and exprest a hope, if war ever came to us, that we would fight on the same side with our former foe.

"But Jefferson was about the last American statesman to express such opinions. It has been a convention of our politics that robust verbal antagonism to Great Britain was safe. Indeed, one vainly racks memory to recall another American President who has spoken as President Harding did at Yorktown. . . .

"Great Britain seems to have permanently shaken off her old anti-American psychology. All her parties and elements join in wooing America. In return we must, if we would have peace, conquer the remains of any Anglophobia that still grip us—must subdue the prejudices such as Hearst foments."

Turning for a moment to those sections of our press that are dubious concerning the President's Yorktown doctrine, we find the New York *Irish World* exclaiming ironically: "What a consolation it will be to the people of the United States, when the blow falls, that their President had found it unthinkable!" Another Irish-American journal, the New York *Gaelic American*, characterizes the President's picture of the relation between the United States and Great Britain as "wholly fanciful," and argues

THE TREACHEROUS DOPER.

Look out for this chap, Samuel! He masquerades as a patriot.

—Racey in the Montreal *Star*.

that the marine rivalry between these two great Powers "must ultimately lead to war." It goes on to say:

"Nobody wants war, but peace can only be ensured, for a time, by the United States ceasing to contest English Commercial Supremacy and her Mastery of the Sea. If President Harding does not know this, he has misread history and wofully misunderstands the present world situation."

In the same frame of mind the New York *Sinn Feiner* remarks that "whenever international statesmen are found throwing bouquets at each other, it is a sure sign that there is something wrong; they are trying to stave off something which they believe should not occur at the moment." And it goes on to warn its readers that "the prime purpose of the approaching Washington Conference is not disarmament." As *The Sinn Feiner* sees it:

"International 'experts' are moving heaven and earth to get the United States into an alliance with the British Empire. To bring about this the British Empire is willing to throw over Japan, or, at any rate, to scrap the Anglo-Japanese alliance.

"We say to the gentlemen in Washington that such a scheme can not be consummated. We say to them that the American people are resentful at the monstrous expenditure of their money occasioned by the bringing together of this confab.

"Secret intrigue will never assure world peace. On the contrary secret intrigue is an unfailing breeder of war."

"We have no desire to interfere with or obstruct Anglo-American friendship," says the Philadelphia *Irish Press*, "but it must be friendship of the right kind, not an imperialistic screen." The German-American *New Yorker Herold* characterizes the President's utterance as "a pious wish," and adds: "As a matter of fact the peoples push hard against each other in space, and their separate interests bring about conflicts without concerning themselves with pious wishes." "Unthinkable things have repeatedly happened in history," the Baltimore *Sun* reminds us; and the Chicago *Daily News* says of war between this country and Great Britain: "It is the imperative duty of both countries to make it unthinkable and impossible by removing its potential and probable causes."

A few days after President Harding's Yorktown speech Lord Northcliffe, speaking in Manila, declared that "despite slight surface difficulties, the English-speaking peoples of the world are insensibly drawing near to each other." And he added significantly: "The process will be greatly accelerated by any sign of hostile action from the peoples of the Far East."

In his address at Yorktown the President said that American participation in world affairs was "inevitable," and exprest a hope that general cooperation "to the common good" would usher in a new day of international relationship. At the same time he sounded a warning against the impairment of national sovereignty in the name of international unity. Of our past and future relations with Great Britain he said, speaking on the spot where the Revolutionary War was won:

"We must not claim for the New World, certainly not for our Colonies alone, all the liberal thought of a century and a half ago. There were liberal views and attending sympathy in England and a passionate devotion to more liberal tendencies in France. The triumph of freedom in the American Colonies greatly strengthened liberal views in the Old World. Inevitably this liberal public opinion, deliberate and grown dominant, brought Great Britain and America to a policy of accommodation and pacific adjustment for all our differences. There has been honorable and unbroken peace for more than a century, we came to common sacrifice and ensanguined association in the World War, and a further breach of our peaceful and friendly relations is unthinkable. In the trusteeship of preserving civilization we were naturally arrayed together, and the convictions of a civilization worthy of that costly preservation will exalt peace and warn against conflict for all time to come.

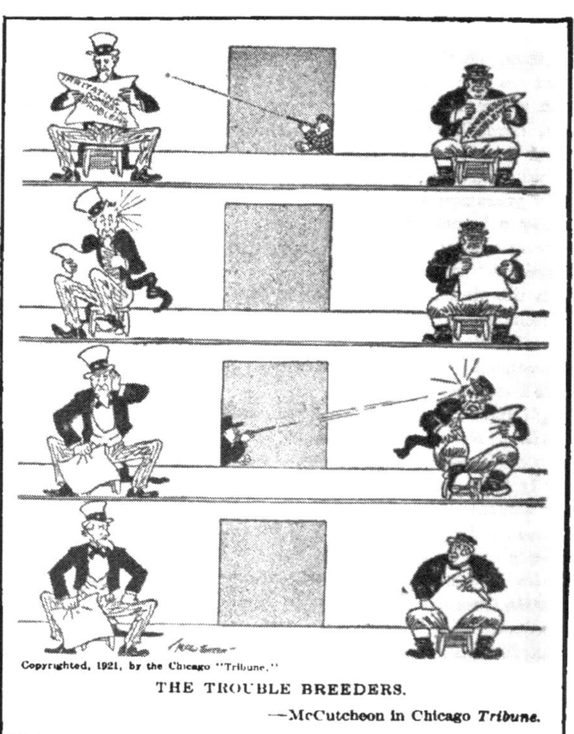

THE TROUBLE BREEDERS.

—McCutcheon in Chicago *Tribune*.

"Our thoughts have lately been concerned with those events which made history on the scale of a world, rather than of a continent. Yet the lesson is the same. It is the lesson of real interdependence among the nations which lead civilization."

Wide World Photo.

PEOPLE OF BUDAPEST STREWING FLOWERS IN THE PATH OF ADMIRAL HORTHY, REGENT OF HUNGARY.

Horthy's defeat and capture of Charles rather damps the early rumors that he was merely keeping the throne warm for his return.

THE FORLORN HAPSBURG HOPE

"IMPERIAL SPRING FEVER" was the excuse brought forward by the New York *Tribune* last March when former Emperor Charles failed to regain the Hungarian throne. That attempt, cables the Vienna correspondent of the New York *Times*, "was a burlesque; his October coup has resulted in a tragedy, for Charles now stands at the end of all his hopes. He has not only lost his crown, but the claims of his dynasty to the throne will be forfeited." Furthermore, declares the president of Switzerland, "the door of this country are definitely closed to him." Having for the second time broken his formal promise to refrain from political activity and not to abuse the asylum Switzerland accorded him, the former emperor is now a man without either a country or a home. Few seem surprized at his attempt, but at least his method of transportation was a novel one—for kings. "He came as 'the man on horseback' should come in this day and generation," thinks the Syracuse *Post-Standard*.

About noon of October 20th the former emperor, his wife, and two others seated themselves in a large airplane near Zurich and were carried over the Swiss Alps and down the Danube past Vienna to Odenburg, the chief city of Burgenland, a distance of several hundred miles. Here Charles was hailed as Hungary's king by approximately 15,000 insurgent Hungarian troops. The events which quickly followed were a disastrous clash with troops of Admiral Horthy's Hungarian Government, and the capture and internment of Charles and his wife. As the New York *Evening World* puts it, "Charles was a Hapsburg, doomed to go down, like the rest of the Hapsburgs, in a vain struggle with a Europe that has outgrown them."

"What made the present moment favorable was the agitation in Hungary over the award to Austria of the border territory of Burgenland," notes the Springfield *Republican*. "With much to gain, and apparently little to lose, he might have been expected to make another venture," remarks the Brooklyn *Eagle*. Then, too, suggest foreign editors, Charles probably believed that neither France nor Italy would actually send troops into Hungary to prevent his return. Austria has denied Charles and his descendants all right to the throne of Austria, but he was still the titular King of Hungary. Yet, points out the Philadelphia *Record*, he must have known that his return would be opposed by Roumania, Jugo-Slavia and Czecho-Slovakia, "all of which acquired large blocks of Hungarian territory in its partial dismemberment, and which now constitute the Little Entente." With Austria they entirely surround Hungary, which could make no effective resistance to their concerted action. Moreover, adds the Providence *Journal:*

> "Great Britain and France are intimately concerned because the restoration of Charles would give the friends of William Hohenzollern a good excuse for trying to set him up again at Berlin. The Bulgarian Royalists might also seek to recall Ferdinand, and the whole structure of peace with victory would then be in danger of collapse.
>
> "It is probable that within the borders of Hungary the opposition to Charles is stronger than his support. Admiral Horthy, who became Regent with the understanding that he would remain in office only as long as the Allies were against the King's return, has not been idle during the last two years. He has built up his own political machine and won over most of the Hungarian Army. He is ambitious; indeed, there is good reason to believe that he has designs upon the throne. Naturally, therefore, under pretense of acceding to the wishes of the Allies, he is opposed to a Royalist return."

"The case of Charles is not like that of Constantine," explains the New York *Globe*. "Charles, it will be remembered, is the leader of the house which precipitated the World War, and while he is not a forceful personality, his traditions and ideas are dangerous to the peace of Central Europe. Charles is not a Napoleon, but a fool can light a fire as well as a genius."

Nevertheless, points out the Pittsburgh *Dispatch*, "the suspicion that the restoration of Charles to the throne is only a question of time, in view of European diplomatic dickering and military strategy, will not down." As we read in the Troy *Record:*

> "The life figuratively went out of Austria and Hungary with the fall of the proud and historic House of Hapsburg. Charles is the legitimate representative of that House, and there unquestionably is very intense and wide-spread sentiment in his favor in both Hungary and Austria. Such sentiment only awaits the opportunity for expressing itself. That is why such a sudden move as that made by Charles is always apt to meet with success. History repeats itself, and we may expect monarchies to be overthrown and monarchies to be restored. Democracies are not made in a day; they are the result of long training. Europe, in spite of the war and in spite of the idealism the United States carried to Europe, remains monarchical in thought and precedent."

RAILWAY WAGE FACTS

RAILWAY WAGES, the Conference on Unemployment found, "are 126 points above the 1913 level, while union wages in general are about 89 points above." In fact, avers the Newark *News*, "the average railroad employee to-day gets more than twice what he got six years ago, while the rank and file of American workers are enjoying no such increase. And the brotherhoods are bent upon making permanent the highest wages ever paid, wages that were increased because of the advanced cost of living." Yet, points out the New York *Journal of Commerce*, "since the middle of last year the cost of living has fallen more than 18 per cent., so these workers are receiving higher real wages than they were when the business depression set in." Instead of resisting a cut, therefore, "railroad labor should get in line with conditions just the same as all other classes of labor and general business," thinks the New York *Commercial*.

AVERAGE DAILY RAIL PAY IN 1917 AND NOW.

(New York Herald)

CHICAGO, Oct. 23.—Statistics compiled by the United States Railroad Labor Board show that the average daily rate of pay for all grades of railroad employees now is $4.54, compared with $2.87 in 1917. The present rate includes the wage cut of about 12½ per cent., authorized July 1 by the Board.

The following table is taken from Labor Board figures:

	Percentage of cut in July	Percentage still above Dec., 1917, wages.	Average daily rate of pay now.	Average daily rate of pay in 1917.
Supervisory forces	6.3	63.4	$8.01	$5.34
Clerical and station	12.2	64.6	4.18	2.54
Maintenance of way and unskilled	17.4	55.7	3.35	2.15
Shop employees	10.5	54.0	5.47	3.55
Telegraphers, &c	8.9	82.8	4.84	2.65
Engine service employees	9.4	59.9	5.81	3.83
Train service	10.7	64.5	5.35	3.32
Stationary engineers and firemen	12.7	92.3	4.19	2.18
Signal department	10.0	66.6	5.50	3.30
Marine department	9.8	33.3	6.69	5.02

But the actual wages earned by railway men are far below those quoted, declares W. Jett Lauck, labor economist, in the New York *Globe*, because the following items are not taken into consideration in working up figures on average railroad labor wages:

1. Overtime, which inflates the average wage figures.
2. Salaries of highly paid officials, which do the same.
3. Irregular employment, which reduces the workers' income.

The president of the Brotherhood of Railroad Trainmen gave as additional reasons for the decision to strike in October, "the 12 per cent. wage reduction of July 1; proposed further reductions, and proposed elimination of rules which would mean still further reductions.' It is his contention that—

"Railroad transportation employees, even when peak wages were paid, did not receive advanced wages in keeping with the increased living costs. The daily rate paid transportation men was fixed for all classes in the United States in 1913, and regardless of the increased costs of living, there were no increased wages for these employees until January 1, 1918.

"The rate of a freight brakeman between Chicago and New York was $2.67 a day. It does not take long to determine how much could be earned in a month of thirty days at a rate of $2.67 per day. Until January 1, 1918, $80.10 was the princely wage some 50,000-odd railroad men received in what is known as the Eastern Territory. Other wages were in proportion to the wages of the freight brakeman.

"With the reduction in wages of July 1, 1921, the present wage of this employee is $134.40 for 30 days in the month, and he is fortunate, indeed, if he is able to work every day in the month.

"Let it be understood that no transportation wages are paid unless the time is made. It is true that the railway companies show wages earned in much higher amounts than those quoted, but they do not tell that the higher monthly amounts represent full time and overtime."

It was the Railroad Labor Board which gave railway workers a wage increase of approximately 25 per cent. in 1920. As we are told by the Newark *News:*

"The average annual wage of all classes of railroad workers, including unskilled labor, in 1915, was $830. In 1920 it had risen by frequent graduations to $1,908, an increase of 130 per cent. That marked the highest peak of wages in the history of American railroading.

"All classes did not share alike, of course, in the increases, but a few examples will help to make the thing clearer. The average passenger engineer got $2,141 a year six years ago. His present average pay is $3,016. The average freight engineer got $1,864 back in 1915, and now he gets $3,136. Freight and passenger firemen got, respectively, $1,136 and $1,287 then, and now get $2,253 and $2,288. Unskilled labor that got $560 a year in 1915 now receives an average of $1,206."

To understand the present situation, thinks the Springfield *Union*, it is necessary to have in mind the chronological order of recent changes in relation to railroad operation in this country, which began in 1916. In *The Union's* resumé we learn that—

"The condition of the roads was such that for a few years before the war their credit was impaired and their service deteriorated. Such was the situation when the so-called Adamson Law was passed under a threat of the brotherhoods of a general tie-up. Congress, under the influence of the Administration, threw up its hands and passed the bill, which became effective January 1, 1917, or about three months before we entered the war. From a railroad point of view the effect of the law was a blanket increase of about 25 per cent. in wages.

"After the Government took over the railroads on January 1, 1918, labor began to bring pressure on the Railroad Administration, and the first move was General Order No. 27 in May, making both a blanket and a percentage increase in wages, retroactive to January 1. According to Director of Railroads McAdoo at the time, this order increased the total labor cost about $360,000,000 a year. A month later freight rates were increased 30 per cent., which, however, did not offset increased labor costs that so far had amounted to 55 per cent. Another readjustment led to a further large increase in costs of operation through an entire change in labor classification and a minute designation as to the kind of work that could be performed by special classes. Director McAdoo himself admitted that this change added over $200,000,000 a year to costs without any increase in the amount of work done. Railroad executives claim that it was much greater.

"The increasing deficits of railroad operation were made up out of the public treasury, and the next year, September, 1919, came the change that, with the Adamson Law and the reclassification, took the railroads largely out of the hands of managers and foremen, and added still more largely to the costs of operation. This change was the acceptance by the Government of the so-called national agreements. A marked result of these agreements was to secure to the men full or overtime pay for much time in which no work was done.

"On March 1, 1920, Federal control ceased, but regulations were continued to September 1 by the provisions of the Transportation Act, which also established the Labor Board to deal with disputes. Since September the rules and regulations have virtually been continued by the Labor Board, but meantime, July 20, 1920, the Board again increased the wages of railroad employees 21 per cent., retroactive to May 1, 1920, the increase adding $600,000,000 to cost of operation. This was at the height of war inflation and prices. In September the Interstate Commerce Commission granted another increase in rates amounting to about 35 per cent. Last spring the Board declared the termination of the national agreements and directed the railroads and employees to make their own agreements. But as such agreements could not be made, the national agreements are practically in force, for the Board declared the old agreements to be in force until others could be made.

"In May this year the Board authorized a reduction averaging about 12 per cent. in wages, effective July 1. However, the increased cost of labor in operation is not due entirely to increase in wages, but very largely to rules and regulations in the national agreements forced on the Railroad Administration."

THE ANARCHISTS AND THE AMBASSADOR

THE INSANE MALCONTENT who believes that he can reform the world by bomb-throwing has not altogether disappeared, notes the New York *Evening Mail*, as it comments upon the recent attempt in Paris to "avenge 'comrades' or to terrorize the American courts by killing Ambassador Herrick." The anarchist "comrades" to whom *The Mail* refers are Nicolo Sacco and Bartolomeo Vanzetti, who were pronounced guilty in the first degree of murdering the paymaster and guard of a Massachusetts shoe factory and escaping with the company's payroll. Both, we are told, are Italians, radicals and draft evaders, and these facts, charges *The World Tomorrow*, were used by the prosecutor to arouse the passions and fears of the jury. The trial, avers *The New Republic* (New York) "was held in an atmosphere of armed guards and solemn precautions that could not but have had its effect in impressing the jury with the dangerous character of the defendants." This is denied by the New York *Tribune*, which notes that the trial judge in concluding his charge to the jury said:

"In the administration of our laws there is and should be no distinction between parties. I therefore beseech you not to allow the fact that the defendants are Italians to influence you or prejudice you in the least degree. They are entitled to the same consideration as tho their ancestors came over in the Mayflower."

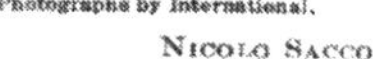

Photographs by International.

NICOLO SACCO — BARTOLOMEO VANZETTI

THE MEN WHOSE FATE ENRAGES THE COMMUNISTS.

Altho admitting that the two men "are anarchists in their social beliefs," the Socialist Milwaukee *Leader* declares that "there is nothing to indicate that they would indulge in an ordinary robbery and murder." "Unprejudiced observers," continues this paper, "unite in the belief that they are innocent —or, at least, that there is a great lack of sufficient proof that they are guilty." Nevertheless, points out the Boston *Post*, "the two defendants were heavily armed when arrested, and the bullets which killed the paymaster and guard came from exactly the same type and caliber of revolver as carried by one of the defendants."

The bomb set off in the home of Ambassador Herrick, asserts the Baltimore *Evening Sun*, "was exploded in the name of Sacco and Vanzetti." It followed Communistic demonstrations against the conviction of the two men in front of the American Embassies at Brussels and Rome, and the receipt by the Ambassador of more than two hundred threatening letters, according to the Paris correspondent of the New York *Herald*. Milan, Rio Janeiro, Bordeaux, Brest, St. Nazaire, Lyons, and Marseilles were scenes of other Communistic gatherings of protest, while in Paris some twenty persons were injured at the close of a similar meeting by the explosion of a hand-grenade. All these happenings, notes a Boston correspondent of the New York *Herald*, "appear to have accomplished the aim of the Communists; the eyes of the radical forces of the world are centered on the cells of the two prisoners, the murder has taken on an international importance, the radicals are assured of a world audience—and the money is coming to help the condemned men. If it is a campaign, it must be credited with being successful, for there is apparent on all sides to-day a disposition to give the condemned men every advantage."

"It is not," declares the New York *Telegram*, "that the European Red cares a whoop what happens to Sacco and Vanzetti, but their conviction provides the Reds with an opportunity to attack the system which they oppose." "It is anarchy seeking to thrust its hands into the administration of justice in the United States," adds the Buffalo *Times*. As the Cleveland *Plain Dealer* sees it:

"Here is a shining exemplification of anarchist logic. The anarchist must have a weak brain to be an anarchist at all, but it seems that any one who would try to kill an ambassador in Paris to prevent the electrocution of two obscure murderers in America must be wholly lacking in cerebral substance. For scaring the nations into accepting anarchism such tactics are as ineffective as was the German *schrecklichkeit* for scaring them into accepting Prussianism."

While the evidence against the two men is said to have been largely circumstantial, in the opinion of the Washington *Star*—

"The criticism of the prosecution in this case is wholly unwarranted. The men had a perfectly fair trial and there remained practically no doubt of their guilt. The crime was a brutal one for gain, and the perpetrators deserve the extreme punishment, tho they have not yet been sentenced. No amount of demonstration either here or abroad will cause any slackening of the procedure.

"A peculiar aspect of the affair appears in the fact that the Sacco-Vanzetti case was tried before a State court and that the United States has no jurisdiction over it. The President of the United States could not, if he would, pardon these men, nor could the Federal courts order a new trial. Thus the demonstration against the American Ambassador, who represents the Federal Government, is merely a gesture which betrays the agitation as having no sincere relation to the Sacco-Vanzetti conviction. The conclusion is inevitable that the European radicals have simply seized upon this matter as an excuse for a parade of their objections to organized government."

The New York *World* is at a loss to explain the wide-spread interest among Communists in the Sacco-Vanzetti case. Says this paper:

"It is an extraordinary fact, most difficult to understand on this side of the Atlantic, that the Communists of Europe have passed over the hysterical drive on the radicals which came to a climax in the United States after the war, the continued incarceration of Debs, the ousting of the Socialists at Albany and the passage of the Lusk laws in New York, without much comment, only to fall foul of a verdict in a Massachusetts murder case which had no political significance whatever. If the verdict rendered in the case of Sacco and Vanzetti was unjust, as appears possible, the Massachusetts courts can still correct the error.

"Radicalism has sometimes had one saving grace—intelligence. But in the madness over Sacco and Vanzetti there is no intelligence whatever."

"In any case, Sacco and Vanzetti belong to a school of thought which makes them potential, if not actual, assassins, and a sort of moral partnership has been established between the Communists who have caused the recent disturbances and the prisoners," maintains the Baltimore *Sun*. But, *The Sun* goes on.

"All the explosives in France, Italy and Russia will not be permitted to swerve or affect the course of justice in the humblest court in the United States. We will concede everything to reason, but nothing to force."

A CLOSE-UP OF UNEMPLOYMENT

THE LETTERS FROM THE TRENCHES used to bring home to us the realities of war more strongly than pages of official reports. In the same way, the whole truth about unemployment can not be learned from columns of Labor Department statistics, reports of the Unemployment Conference, or even from the formal statements of such well-informed men as Herbert Hoover and Samuel Gompers. The editor of a trade union paper in Bridgeport, or South Omaha, may not be able to make an elaborate analysis of nation-wide unemployment, but he has something to tell us about the proportion of jobs to workers in his own city. And this editor is also likely to have a very definite idea of what ought to be done about it. To bring together for LITERARY DIGEST readers these various close-up views, and thus to give a more vivid realization of what those nearest the workers think about the lack of work, we have asked several hundred labor editors to tell us whether they find things growing better or worse, and what remedies they would recommend. As a whole, the answers—which come from thirty States and forty important industrial cities—bring cheer, for they seem to show that the Unemployment Conference's program for immediate relief is succeeding, and that the situation is improving.

"NOT CHARITY, BUT A JOB."

—Grant in *Better Times* (New York).

Half of the answers received report a lessening of unemployment, while fewer than a score of labor editors believe conditions are becoming worse. In a very general way conditions seem to be worse in the East than in the West and South. The most pessimistic reports come from New England, New Jersey, and Pennsylvania, and from such important cities as New York, Chicago, Pittsburgh, Omaha, Cincinnati, Duluth, Des Moines, St. Paul, and Washington, D. C. Mechanics in Pennsylvania, quarry workers in Vermont, bakers in Chicago, and butchers in Omaha report a dreary outlook, as do also cigar-makers and wood-carvers. Hotel and restaurant employees are joining the ranks of the unemployed in growing numbers, says their organ, *The Mixer and Server* (Cincinnati), owing to "the steady increase of the self-serve or cafeteria style of 'eat-shop.'"

On the other hand, we hear of improved conditions in up-State New York, Ohio, West Virginia, Illinois, Indiana, Michigan, Tennessee, Georgia, Alabama, Florida, Texas, Oklahoma, Missouri, Iowa, Colorado, Utah and California. Certain editors in Kansas and North Carolina report that the unemployment situation has not been critical in their respective States. A large number of replies tell of increased activity and consequent reemployment in printing and allied trades, and there are also assertions of more work in the various building trades, in the textile mills, in the iron and steel plants, and in the mines.

The "Do-It-Now" campaign, launched by the Unemployment Conference and supervised by the committee headed by Colonel Arthur Woods, seems to have been stirring up a number of committees to immediate activity in the construction of public works, by which thousands of men have been given jobs. And it is significant that this particular campaign is the only remedy suggested by any large number of the labor editors who have replied to our questions. Nearly half of them insist upon this method of immediate relief. Undoubtedly, writes an Ohio editor, "much could be accomplished if effort were made to advance building programs, encourage work of a public nature, such as street repairs, grading, sewering, extension of waterways, improvement of park lands, county and State road work." And much, they tell us, is being accomplished. Two labor weeklies of Rochester, New York, speak of the large public building program which has been launched by their city government. The Lone Star State is especially active, Texas labor papers report. The State has a definite program that was delayed on account of the war but has now been urged into being again in order to employ farm workers during winter, and keep them from crowding into the cities. San Antonio is starting the construction of long-delayed public buildings and street improvements. Fort Worth is now building fire-stations and swimming-pools to provide for future demands, and is eliminating all its railroad grade crossings. Private citizens have agreed to do their building and repair work at once instead of waiting, and a building loan company will encourage would-be home-owners. The county authorities will spend $100,000 a month for some time to come on road-building and repairs. Dispatches in the daily papers tell of similar activities in Portland, Me., Springfield, Mass., Worcester, Mass., Buffalo, Dayton, Savannah, and Tulsa.

The taxpayer, of course, pays the wages of the men employed on public works. But labor editors would not leave the entire burden there. Let employers provide work, say several, irrespective of profits. Employers will be able to provide more work for wage-earners, it is suggested, if they spend less money on high-salaried executives, expensive advertising and so-called "efficiency systems." Or, if the employers can not provide more work, let them, in the words of *The Pennsylvania Labor Herald*, "reduce the hours and employ all men part time." A shorter week and shorter hours are suggested. Establish a universal eight-hour day, advises a Kansas editor, then "if all are not employed, make a six-hour day till there is enough work for the eight-hour day." Then, it is suggested, if employers can not or will not furnish work to all, let them step down and allow the Government or the workers to take over the idle plants.

Among the large number of miscellaneous suggestions appear a few admissions that wages might be lowered. The Erie (Pa.) *Labor Journal* feels that "workers should realize that the war-time wage is a thing of the past," just as retail business men should be willing to take their losses and be satisfied with the profits they made during the war. And a labor editor in Indiana remarks that "workers are too choicy about their jobs as a rule; plenty of farm work needing men, but not at seven or eight hours a day, or double time for overtime; plenty of work for those who will work in the old-fashioned way, and help to do things." These suggestions contrast with a larger number of protests against wage reductions. "Give the workers wages that will allow them to buy the commodities which must be sold," says one. "Cheap wages never made a good town," observes another, and a North Carolina paper states the argument for high wages as follows:

"The wage-earner must function in a dual capacity: as a producer and as a consumer. With modern power-driven machinery and the factory method, as a producer, he is highly successful; he produces all the necessities and luxuries of life in superabundance. But as a consumer he cannot buy according to his desires or needs, he can buy only to the limit of his wages, and his wages are sufficient to buy off the market only a small part of the goods his labor has put on the market.

"Obviously then, the higher wages are, the more the wage-earner can buy, and the more he can buy, the greater the number that can be employed in producing."

Sharp demands are made for lower retail prices and lower prices on building materials. Many of these spokesmen for labor can find something more for the Government to do than to start building new bridges and post-offices. A prompt revision of taxes is essential to the return of prosperity, we are told. Speedy tariff revision is demanded by several editors, some of whom want it "down," and others "up." There are protests against the waste of government funds in war construction. The Federal Government is also requested to set up an employment service, to reestablish price regulation, to repeal prohibition, to nationalize the mines, to build a system of Federal highways, to launch new water-power and reclamation projects, to deport alien laborers, to give ex-service men their bonus, to assume control of finance, and to investigate Wall Street.

The financial side of unemployment is taken up by a number of editors who believe that the banks ought to extend credit more freely, that they are making it too difficult for builders and business men to carry on and employ. "Stop the bankers' strike," cries the Cincinnati *Labor Advocate*. And the Sacramento *Tribune* denounces the bankers as the "slackers" of to-day, saying:

"The banks must loosen up their hoards of money, factories must run, farmers must have money, merchants must have money, and as the bankers have it all tied up, solving the unemployed problem is up to them."

ON THE ROAD TO NORMALCY.

—McCutcheon in the Chicago *Tribune*.

Better relations between capital and labor are essential to any permanent cure of unemployment, say several labor editors. Until the employers' organizations have definitely called off the "so-called union shop fight," "employers in many lines will be timid and ultra-conservative in their operations," declares *The Labor Herald* of Newport, Kentucky. The Duluth *Labor World* feels that some of these anti-unionist employers are really responsible for unemployment. "The men who control the industrial destiny of America," it says, "are not yet ready for the return of good times. They have not succeeded in beating wages down as low as they want them to be. They have not completed the job they started at the close of the war." Other writers are less bitter, simply asking employers to try harder to cooperate with the workers.

Several interesting suggestions are made regarding the railroads. The call for lower freight rates is frequent. No building or industrial boom, says *The National Labor Tribune* (Pittsburgh), can be started until freight rates drop. There is a call for government ownership and operation. It is suggested that all the other railroads copy the methods used by Henry Ford on his Detroit, Toledo and Ironton. An organ of railroad workers does not understand "just why thousands of good cars and locomotives slightly out of repair on the 'rip tracks' of railroads throughout the country should be kept out of service when needed to accommodate the business of the country." If the railroads would repair these instead of waiting for the construction of new rolling stock, "it would be the means of placing at work many men out of employment and preventing an actual waste in timber and metal." The most sensational suggestion comes from a Buffalo labor editor who would rebuild the entire railroad system of the country. Railroad tonnage, so to speak, has not increased in comparison with lake and ocean tonnage. Increase the railroad's carrying capacity, he urges, by widening the existing standard gage by two feet and rebuilding all rolling stock accordingly. "You can readily see," he continues, "that there would be plenty of work for everybody. This improvement must be done by all roads sooner or later to meet the demands of the commerce of the country. Why not do this work now when we need work the worst?"

There ought to be lower rents and more building, agree several labor editors, and as a means to that end it is suggested that municipalities provide for tax exemption on new buildings. The readjustment of so-called "seasonal" occupations would help, thinks one writer, while another asks for the elimination of the middleman. The "buy-now" movement has its friends, while such mottoes as "do-it-now," "have faith" and "just hustle" find occasional utterance. When asked to suggest a means for reducing unemployment, an optimistic Iowa editor replies: "Nothing except to hustle for business; do one's full share in purchasing things needed in business and home life; eliminate fear and pessimistic thoughts; accept TO-DAY as *near-normal* and forget to make comparisons with 1914 or previous periods." A no less hopeful Georgian writes: "The only thing we know is that those who want work can get it if they look for same."

In sharp contrast with these replies is that of the Fort Wayne *Worker*, which can see no permanent improvement while our cities are filled with people who have lost jobs and will not be wanted in them again for years. The real unemployment problem, it says, is "how to get great numbers of our people out of the towns and onto the agricultural lands." And this labor editor is inclined to agree with the Eastern banker whom he quotes as saying: "We must starve hundreds of thousands of families out of our towns and cities, out on to the rural lands; STARVE them out, because there is probably no other way to get them out." Likewise *The Baker's Journal* of Chicago finds conditions growing worse and none of the suggested remedies of any real value. It says:

"All attempts to solve the unemployment problem, together with other economic questions connected with it, are nothing but wasted effort under our present social system. The employing class insists on its profits, and these profits can be made only at the expense of the working class. Temporary relief and so-called reforms are nothing but patchwork, and do not advance us one pace toward the solution of this important economic question. Only by substituting a better and more humane social system for the one we now have can permanent relief and a solution to the question at issue be found."

TOPICS IN BRIEF

The future of the shimmy is declared to be shaky.—*Dallas News*.

The Empire may be Invisible, but we begin to see its finish.—*Dallas News*.

If it keeps on, the German mark will soon be completely erased.—*Indianapolis Star*.

Prosperity seems to be skidding just a bit coming around that corner.—*Columbia Record*.

Evidently railroad labor realizes that a strike would not be a hit.—*Norfolk Virginian-Pilot*.

We imagine that in the "Invisible Empire" time is told by Ku-Ku Klocks.—*Brooklyn Eagle*.

And now comes the season when the wise hunter disguises himself as a deer.—*Detroit Free Press*.

It is revealed that there are some volunteers in the army of the unemployed.—*Pittsburgh Gazette Times*.

The late summer recess is about the only thing that the present Congress has really completed.—*Norfolk Virginian-Pilot*

Germs are frequently caught on the fly.—*Greenville Piedmont*.

Divorce suits are always prest with the seamy side out.—*Lincoln Star*.

All-night movies might solve the housing shortage problem.—*Greenville Piedmont*.

A menace: Any part of the world in which you do not happen to dwell—*Hartford Times*.

What salary reduction have the Brotherhood leaders received?—*Wall Street Journal*.

An optimist is a person who eats candy off an uncovered street stand.—*New York Evening Mail*.

About the only kind of strike now popular in this country is an averted one.—*Chicago Daily News*.

"No beer, no work" wasn't very successful as a protest, but it was an excellent prophecy.—*Boston Post*.

As business sees it, highways of prosperity can be reached only through buy-ways.—*Norfolk Virginian-Pilot*.

Russia, having failed to produce a superman, should acknowledge Mr. Hoover as the supper man.—*Brooklyn Eagle*.

If a hitch does come in the British-Irish negotiations, it's a safe wager it will not be the Irish who are hitched.—*Manila Bulletin*.

We may be getting back to normalcy, but we seem to be a darned long time in passing a given point.—*New York American*.

The difference between Socialism and football is that in football the kicking is done after the gains are made.—*Sioux City Journal*.

How can Obregon expect us to recognize Mexico? It doesn't look like the same old place since he's been president of it.—*New York World*.

Secretary Davis says 1,000 Christian Asiatics are fleeing to the United States. Probably they are coming as missionaries.—*Columbia Record*.

Another reason Irish negotiations are slow is because the Sinn Fein want to be sure of their parachutes before they come down off their high horse.—*Dallas News*.

The old system of following the leadership of party whips has been abandoned in Congress. Operations there are now directed by bloc heads.—*St. Louis Post Dispatch*.

TO GET RID OF THEIR SHADOWS.

—Thomas in the Detroit *News*.

This foreign paper money would be worth more if they printed a comic strip on one side.—*Greenville Piedmont*.

If all our pro-Germans invested in German marks we can bear the blow with Christian fortitude.—*Wall Street Journal*.

The only collar that galls the free American is the one the laundry has tried to convert into a saw.—*Springfield State-Register*.

If there is any corrective value in suggestion, it might be well to place perpendicular steel bars on the windshields.—*Chicago Journal*.

American manufacturers want foreign buyers so they can pay the American wage scale to their foreign employees.—*Manila Bulletin*.

We are slowly getting to the point where we can eat a piece of steak without feeling that we are taking it away from starving Europe.—*New York Evening Mail*.

One nice thing about the Disarmament Conference is that it will be held far enough from Europe to escape the noise of several wars now in progress.—*Detroit Journal*.

The former Kaiser has taken personal charge of his own garden. That's all right: there isn't the slightest danger that he will be able to raise his favorite crop on it.—*Cincinnati Enquirer*.

FOREIGN - COMMENT

MUST UNCLE SAM FORGIVE HIS DEBTORS?

WORLD TRADE CAN NOT REVIVE until the international debts that weigh down all countries are crossed off and wiped out, is the cry of some English newspapers, which declare that "only then can the exchanges be quieted down." The foundation upon which "the pyramid of paper" rests is the German indemnity, says the London *Outlook*, and once it is recognized that Germany can not pay the Allies, "we in this country will be ready to agree that France and Italy can not pay us what they owe, and America will realize (but when?) that she can not collect the ten milliards of dollars owed her by Europe." America occupies a unique position in the discussion of war debts, for, "on her lonely pinnacle she holds demand notes aggregating more than two and a half milliards of pounds and owes nobody anything." At the same time this weekly notes that America is "now in the throes of the worst business collapse since 1893, and is trying to find enough crusts to keep six million unemployed alive." Meanwhile, it adds:

"Our argument has been that unless the outstanding international debts be wiped out, enemy and friendly debts, we can not stabilize the exchanges, and we can not hope to recover our trade and our prosperity. This implies that not only must we forgive our debtors, but we must be forgiven by our only creditor—America. Self-respect, we agree, forbids us to ask America to cancel the debt. The offer must come from across the Atlantic. But candor compels us to admit that there comes no sign over the cables that such a proposal will be made; on the contrary, Anglophobe politicians already commence to foam at the mouth because we have not paid principal or interest, and the Washington Administration significantly refuses to permit the world trade question to be raised at the November Conference. We would then seem to be deadlocked; honor will not permit us to appear as suppliants; it follows that honor requires us to starve while our trade dwindles to zero."

UNEMPLOYED.
—*The Bystander* (London)

But *The Outlook* has a formula to suggest which it thinks may help Britain out, and that formula implies "talking frankly and honestly" to America somewhat in this fashion:

"We do not ask you, gentlemen, to cancel that milliard odd we owe you out of generosity, idealism, recognition that we did more fighting than you did, or because we lent most of the money involved to other nations who can't pay it back to us. In fact, we do not ask you to cancel the debt at all. We merely state our opinion that you *will* cancel it, not out of generosity or out of idealism, but out of sheer self-interest. The only question is when you will do so. You must cancel it, for until you do, your industries will be crippled, your trade at a standstill, your people out of work. We make no suggestion, beyond expressing the opinion that the sooner you look into the situation and do what you will have to do before long in any event, the better it will be for you and for us. If you do not now agree, or rather if you will not trouble to examine the world trade position, since if you do you must agree, ask for your money—we will mortgage our credit, we will send you our gold, until such time as you discover how that metal feels when poured in a molten state down one's throat."

The formula "does not err on the side of humility," it is admitted, for the British Lion "must not fawn for sugar at the feet of Uncle Sam." But the Lion loses no dignity when he suggests to Uncle Sam that they are "both in a sinking boat" and that Uncle Sam "being blest with arms instead of paws, had better start bailing rather quickly or Lion and Uncle will founder simultaneously." We read then:

"We are far from claiming that the cancellation of world debts will altogether cure the economic ills of the world; we do devoutly believe that until this step is taken, no serious progress can be made towards exchange stabilization and a resumption of trade. The opposition to cancellation will come from America. Let American publicists, and her politicians, tell us how the world and America herself can recover without cancellation! None of them, so far as we are aware, have yet attempted the task. Do they intend to wait until an export trade which has sunk from thirteen to ten, has gone down from ten to two, before they come to grips with reality?"

With a glance at the Washington Conference, the London *Pall Mall and Globe* says that "a matter like the outstanding war debts of the Allied countries must come up for review" there and this the more particularly because "the principal creditor of Europe is the Power which has summoned the Conference and has taken the lead in proclaiming a gospel of mutual consideration." This daily continues:

"The other great civilized Powers have incurred sacrifices of blood from which America has been exempt, and have spent their wealth also in defense of the common liberty. American appeals to philanthropy can scarcely sound convincing if they are to be taken as coming from a nation that insists upon its full financial rights over an exhausted and impoverished world. Englishmen can raise this question of debt without any shamefacedness, because what they owe to America is less than half of what stands in their ledger to the account of Europeans nations. The public on the other side of the Atlantic are beginning to realize that while such obligations are in some cases a very dubious kind of asset, they are most effectually blocking the channels of trade, and particularly the creditor's powers of export."

A financial authority, the London *Statist*, points out that the United States Government is confronted with the problem of its own internal short-dated debt as well as with the problem of the credits it has extended to foreign countries, and relates:

"The total gross debt of the American Government on May 31 last amounted to 23,953 million dollars, of which 7,884 million dollars was short-dated debt. In the first eleven months of the fiscal year 1920–21 there has been a reduction of approximately 350 million dollars, the retirement being confined almost exclusively to short-term liabilities. Further reductions since May have brought the figure of early-maturing obligations down to 7,500 million dollars approximately. By far the most important item in that sum is the Victory Loan, which is due for repayment on May 20, 1923. The amount of the loan as originally issued was 4,495 million dollars, and on May 31 last the total outstanding was 4,022 million dollars. The United States Treasury hopes by the issue of notes and by periodical retirements of debt out of current surpluses to spread the 7,500 million dollars of short-

UNCLE SAM REVIEWS THE WEALTH OF NATIONS.

—*Kladderadatsch* (Berlin).

dated debt, which is now concentrated in relatively few maturities, into a progressively smaller aggregate amount of maturities extending over the years 1923 to 1928."

Under the Liberty Bonds Act, we are reminded, cash advances made to foreign governments up to June 23d last were:

"Great Britain	$4,277,000,000
France	2,997,477,800
Italy	1,648,034,050
Belgium	349,214,468
Russia	187,729,750
Czecho-Slovakia	61,256,207
Serbia	26,780,466
Roumania	25,000,000
Greece	15,000,000
Cuba	10,000,000
Liberia	26,000
	$9,597,518,741

"Payments received in respect of this debt up to the same date comprised:—Great Britain, $110,681,642; France, $46,714,862; Roumania, $1,794,180; Belgium, $1,522,902; Cuba, $974,500; and Serbia, $605,326, making a total of $162,293,412."

The American Government, as *The Statist* notes, holds in respect of these loans demand obligations of the various foreign governments bearing interest at the rate of 5 per cent. per annum. More than 451 million dollars have been paid in interest up to the present, we are told, as follows:

Great Britain	$245,557,186
France	129,570,376
Italy	57,598,853
Belgium	10,907,282
Russia	4,832,354
Cuba	1,282,370
Greece	784,153
Serbia	636,059
Czecho-Slovakia	304,178
Roumania	263,314
Liberia	861
	$451,736,986

Meanwhile Washington dispatches tell us Congress has provided for a commission of five, one of whom is to be the Secretary of the Treasury, which is empowered to determine when and how the debts should be paid and at what rate of interest. Representative Mondell, the Republican leader, said in the House that the commission would have minority representation and pleaded with the Democrats to trust the President, who in the last analysis will "make this settlement," for "whatever is done by the commission is done with the approval of the President."

CHINESE LABOR ORGANIZING

ORGANIZED LABOR IN JAPAN has been making itself increasingly felt of late years, but only recently have we record of the fact that Chinese workingmen also are banding together in defense of their interests. In some quarters, in fact, it is charged that they are a little too strenuous as far as their own interests are concerned, so that they overlook considerations affecting their employers. In *The Trans-Pacific* (Tokio) a writer expresses the fear that the labor movement in the big cities of China is "destined to become one of the greatest problems of the Far East, where hitherto labor has been counted as a chief commodity." This informant tells us further that the Chinese workers of Hongkong and Canton have "embarked on a scheme of organization almost parallel to that known in European and other foreign countries" and he adds:

"A report has just been issued by the Hongkong Government which states that one of the most interesting and important recent developments has been the rapid increase in the number of workingmen's societies, avowedly run on Western trade union lines, copying trade union methods and using trade union phraseology. This increase, the report continues, is only partly due to the greater liberty given such societies by the new ordinance, for the chief encouragement came from the great fitters' and engineers' strike of April, 1920. This was conducted by the Chinese Engineers' Institute, and the men were successful in gaining an increase of 32½ per cent. on their former wages. Concurrently with this trade union development, there has been a series of trade disputes, often developing into small strikes. Fortunately, most of these have been settled by agreement and all have resulted in leveling up the men's wages and, in some cases, decreasing the hours of labor. In one case, where the masters ended the strike by importing fresh men from up country, the dissatisfied men took the novel step of opening a shop and working on their own account.

"So well organized are the workers of Hongkong becoming that they have succeeded in large measure in gaining control of all labor."

WANTED—A GOLD CURE.

UNCLE SAM MIDAS: "Whatever I touch becomes gold! If this confounded witchery doesn't soon cease, I shall starve!"

—*Die Muskete* (Vienna).

PERIL OF "EMPTY AUSTRALIA"

AN EMPTY AUSTRALIA is a standing temptation to a painfully packed Asia, and this thought, underlying a speech made by Lord Northcliffe in Australia, raises echoes of perturbation as far away as Canada. Not only Australians, but Canadians and Americans also, should think of this matter, exclaims the Montreal *Daily Star*, which considers it "the most highly explosive question that lies embosomed in the twentieth century." The island is an "outpost of the white race," we are warned, and "if Asia ever awakes, it presents itself as the logical, almost inevitable first point of attack upon white expansion." This newspaper believes that "an aroused and armed China might seize Australia for her overflow before even the people of India had concluded to get along without British tutelage and protection," and the question is asked:

"Can the English-speaking peoples protect Australia as a white man's country? They can to-day. But at a time when the energetic and capable Americans are very dubious whether they could even to-day protect the Philippines against a Japanese attack, it is not without pertinence to point out that any defense of Australia must be accomplished very far from the home bases of both Great Britain and the United States—and that an armed China would have enormous man-power at its disposal.

"None of us could afford to let Australia perish without a fight. None of us could afford to lose that fight. An Asia which had won it over the united power of the English-speaking races would be quite as 'cocky' as the Japanese were after defeating great Russia. Such an Asia, with its uncounted millions, would be a dangerous neighbor just across the Pacific. Yet such a fight at the antipodes would be very hard to win. Thus it will be just as well to utilize the coming Washington Conference to lull Asia comfortably to sleep and not to pin-prick it into maddened activity as some superficial 'statesmen' seem so ready to do."

THE GREAT AUSTRALIAN GAMBLE.

COLORED RACES: "Here, let us into this game—you're putting all your money on one end of the board."

—*The Bulletin* (Sydney.)

Any people who imagine that this condition of an "empty Australia" can go on indefinitely, says *The Star*, have neither "read history, studied human psychology, nor taken into account the ordinary humane motives which are supposed to govern the actions of Christian nations," and it adds:

"The Australians must fill Australia with the sort of people they want for neighbors; or the over-spill of Asia will fill it for them, whether they like it or not. No outside Power can forever keep Asia penned up in her murderous congestion. Our American neighbors are often nervous lest Japan become the champion of the less well-equipped Asiatic peoples who can not even rid their own countries of European interference, let alone find territories abroad to which they can emigrate. So far there seems to be little reason for this nervousness, because the Chinese are so jealous and fearful of the Japs that they would never dream of accepting rescue at their hands. They think that their active and ambitious little neighbor only wants to expel the European to come in himself.

"But what if Japan frankly withdrew from China and then offered to force an entry for her festering millions into empty Australia? Might not that appeal to the Chinese soul?"

An Australian view of the matter appears in the Melbourne *Argus*, where a contributor quotes Australia's Prime Minister Hughes as having said at the American Luncheon Club in London that "the Pacific question largely arises from the rapidly expanding population of Japan," for that country is "unable to find room for her natural increase within her present territories, yet must find room for them somewhere." There is no room for Japan in the already overcrowded countries of the East, says the contributor to the *Argus*, nor is there room for them in North America—

"if the people of the United States pursue their present declared policy of building the largest navy in the world, and if their 110 millions can prevent any attempt to seek room in that continent. Equally obviously Premier Hughes fears, and fears rightly, that Japanese eyes are turned towards Australia. His speech breathes that fear throughout. But he pins his faith to the British Navy, to the Anglo-Japanese Alliance, and to an understanding with America. He appeals to America. 'If she can not agree with Japan, how is she to help Australia?' But does America really want to help Australia in the event of Japan's insistence on freedom of entry? It has long been obvious to the thinkers of the great Republic that Japan must soon 'find room somewhere for her rapidly expanding population.' And she is taking the necessary steps to preserve the purity of her own white race. But it does not follow that she is equally anxious about the purity of the Australian section of the European race. It is actually in the mind of many Americans that Australia, being the only empty area of any magnitude in the world, and more closely connected with Asia than any other land, is the natural sphere of Japanese extension. 'Why,' they ask amongst themselves, 'should America pour out blood and treasure in an attempt to defeat the natural aspirations of the most important and only civilized Eastern race?' Were Australia thrown open to Japanese immigration the danger to America would be postponed for at least a hundred years, if not forever, they think, and with much reason."

Premier Hughes also said "our continent is able to support 100,000,000, yet we have only 5,000,000," but the writer in *The Argus* retorts:

"This brings one to our real danger: the over-estimating of our capabilities to the world at large. Japanese public opinion will eagerly note the emptiness (it constantly bears it in mind) and envy the limitless possibilities for a successful invader, so advertised by our leading citizen. But while the first condition is undoubted, the second is by no means established. Australia, because it is the same size as United States of America, is often compared therewith. But size is their only similarity. Because the United States of America has increased from 5,000,000 to over 100,000,000 people in a century, it does not follow that Australia can possibly equal that increase. Of the total area of the United States 60 per cent. is estimated to be tillable, and of that portion nearly one-third was planted in 1918. Will any one who actually knows this continent dream that a sixth of its total area can ever be brought under cultivation? If not, how is an equivalent population to be fed? A third of the Commonwealth has under ten inches of annual rainfall. With the exception of the Murray system, the rivers from which irrigation water may be drawn are negligible."

Even as a pastoral country, Australia is not rich compared with New Zealand, according to this informant, who tells us that while it is nearly thirty times greater in extent, it carries only four times the number of cattle, and less than four times the number of sheep. In the eight years ending 1918 Australia's number of live stock showed but little increase. Horses increased by only 400,000 and cattle by 1,000,000, but sheep decreased by 5,000,000, and pigs by 100,000. The writer adds:

"In other words, the live stock, as a whole, did little more than hold their own. Occasionally the census shows a very large decrease. There were nearly 11,000,000 fewer sheep in 1918 than in 1890. Of course, the reason for the great fluctuation is the recurring droughts. This was especially manifest in 1914–15. The 'Year Book' (p. 318) states 'the falling off in the number of sheep in 1915 was 9,343,145; of cattle, 1,120,157; of horses, 144,252; and of pigs, 108,754; being 11.91, 10.14, 5.72, and 12.61 per cent. respectively.' Is it reasonable to expect that a country subject to such vicissitudes will ever carry a population approaching the optimistic estimates of the Prime Minister, at all events, with any degree of safety and comfort?"

ALL HANDS ON DECK!

CAPTAIN LLOYD GEORGE: "Now, me lads! Shake a leg, shake a leg!"
—*The Mail* (Birmingham).

"UNEARNED" WEALTH TO RELIEVE THE JOBLESS—Relief for England's unemployed is so imperative that every resource of the country is being probed, and the London *Nation and Athenaeum* comes forward with the proposal that money should be exacted from "the rich districts" and those districts containing "appreciating property," for—

"There exists in all parts of the country, especially in the great cities, a large fund of unearned wealth, chiefly the product of war-conditions, upon which an emergency levy should be made. We allude to the immense accretion of value to land and real estate. In London, especially, landlords have been reaping, and for some time will continue to reap, enormous gains out of the miserable shortage of housing, by profitable sales, high rents, fines and fees on renewals, etc. These gains, like those taken in the later war-years by agricultural landlords who had the wisdom to sell in time to prosperous farmers, have never paid their tribute to the Exchequer or the local treasury. Why not? Not merely are they unearned by their possessors. They are the direct product and measure of the needs of that very population whose evil case we are considering. The urgent pressure of a large and growing industrial population upon the restricted house accommodation has forced up these land and house values. Here is a fund specially fitted to finance our emergency, a large unearned increment, the levy upon which not merely disturbs no incentive to industry, but actually provides a stimulus for putting all land to its most productive uses. It is not, however, enough to group the constituent sections of a city together for the purpose of this unemployed finance. As the main causes of our unemployment lie within the sphere of national policy, so must the financial provision be planned upon a national scale. Not only are poor London boroughs, but poor industrial cities, quite unable out of their separate local resources to meet the dimensions of such a disaster as confronts us."

JAPAN'S "OFFICIAL" PROPAGANDA

IF JAPAN IS MISUNDERSTOOD, as Japanese authorities so often say, is it because she has not enough "official propaganda" in foreign countries, or because she has too much? The question is suggested by a Japanese correspondent of the *Journal de Pekin*, who believes that Japan's propagandist efforts have "rather served to put in high relief Japanese imperialism, and the menace it offers to universal peace." On the other hand, some newspapers remind us that since Germany "gave propaganda a bad name" almost any publicity work is suspected. What is more, they say that the "inaccessibility of the Japanese language" to the world in general justifies the Japanese in their belief that "it pays to advertise." The correspondent of the *Journal de Pekin*, however, views the matter rather grimly, and tells us that "not even the Germans before the war attached so much importance to political propaganda as do the Japanese." We read then:

"The central office which distributes good news about the Empire of the Rising Sun is under direct control of the government, while the secondary offices in foreign countries are under surveillance of Japanese embassies, legations, consulates, vice-consulates, and consular agencies. In their efforts to win foreign opinion the descendants of the Samurai only follow customs much in honor in western and American countries. However, official propaganda has not so far been very successful in the field of politics, yet it is pleasant to admit that travel propaganda has had great success, especially in the United States. The uninterrupted flow of visitors to the Nipponese islands is the most striking proof of this fact."

The consequence is that "the prevailing opinion among the subjects of the Mikado is that their country is not known or is not sufficiently known." This surely can not be for lack of organization and this writer continues:

"At London and at Washington, to mention only these two great centers, we find two Japanese associations operating directly under the control of the Japanese Embassies in these two cities. These associations have their periodicals and their newspapers, they have their speechmakers who hold forth at meetings and dinners to which they are invited, or to which they secure invitations, to give light on the policy of Japan and the intentions of the Mikado's government. This light, of course, being exclusively official, is always favorable. Englishmen and Americans take part in these meetings, and in the similar organizations known as Anglo-Japanese or American-Japanese. Their pro-Japanese activity is as great as their zeal. Naturally, their attitude has given rise to criticism."

A Japanese naval officer, who is to "play an important rôle" at the Washington Conference, shows his belief in high publicity by declaring that "if I had my own way about the thing, there would be wide-open sessions all over the place." He is quoted by Adachi Kinnosuke, American correspondent of the Tokyo *Jiji*, in a Washington dispatch to the New York *World* as saying further: "Our blunders and our sins are bound to find us out in the end. The one question for practical statesmanship is just this: whether our enemies will bring them to light, or we do it ourselves. And we are apt to be more just to ourselves than our enemies."

A PLAN TO GIVE EACH MAN A JOB TO FIT HIS BRAINS

THIRTEEN YEARS is the average intellectual age of Americans fit for military service. So the psychologists said after examining 1,700,000 army recruits. Of our hundred million population, it is reckoned that less than one-third are above this average, and only 4½ per cent. are of superior intelligence. Is democracy possible with a low intellectual majority? Yes, thinks Dr. Henry Herbert Goddard, director of the Ohio Bureau of Juvenile Research. There can be no democracy without leadership, and democracy has always shown itself willing to accept the leadership of the intelligent. So long as there are in our country nearly five millions of persons of superior intelligence, we need not despair, but we should see to it that each man is placed in a job requiring just the degree of mental acumen that he possesses. These conclusions are put forth in Dr. Goddard's Princeton lectures recently gathered in book form. Our quotations are from a review by Paul Popenoe in *The Journal of Heredity* (Washington). Writes Mr. Popenoe:

"In Dr. Goddard's opinion, with the army experience it is no longer possible for any one to deny the validity of mental tests, even in case of group testing; and when it comes to an individual examination by a trained psychologist, it cannot be doubted that the mental level of the individual is determined with marvelous exactness.

"Such considerations throw real light, the author thinks, on the search for national efficiency. For the first time society has an instrument with which to work. If the mental level of every individual in the nation should be determined, it would be possible to apportion the available jobs intelligently, preventing good men from wasting their time on inferior jobs, and protecting the public from having mentally inferior persons in positions of responsibility, where they now often are.

"In the light of this doctrine, it is easy to see why human society is relatively inefficient. Knowing nothing of mental levels beyond a crude appreciation of the fact that some men are certainly more intelligent than others, we have made no serious attempt to fit the man to the job.

"When one contemplates the enormous proportions of misfits that must exist in the industrial world and that such misfits mean discontent and unhappiness for the employee, one can but wonder how much of the present unrest in such circles is due to this fact.

"Looking at the larger problem, what about democracy itself? Can we hope to have a successful democracy where the average mentality is 13?

"There are, as was pointed out, thirty million above the average, and 4,500,000 of very superior intelligence. Obviously there are enough people of high intelligence to guide the Ship of State, if they are put in command.

"The disturbing fear is that the masses—the 70,000,000 or the 86,000,000—will take matters in their own hands. The fact is, matters are already in their hands and have been since the adoption of the Constitution. But it is equally true that the 86,000,000 are in the hands of the 14,000,000 or the 4,000,000. Provided always that the 4,000,000 apply their very superior intelligence to the practical problem of social welfare and efficiency."

When children enter school Dr. Goddard believes their mental level should be determined. Several groups will be found. At the top are those who are exceptionally intelligent, well endowed, who test considerably above their age. This group subdivides into two: first, those who are truly gifted children, and second, those whose brilliancy is coupled with nervousness. The superior mentality of the truly gifted will mark them throughout life. They should have the broadest and best education that it is possible to give.

"The nervously brilliant group is a very important one. These children are in a stage of instability which, while it happens to make them keen, acute, and quick, is exceedingly dangerous, since experience has taught that a little pushing or overwork may very easily throw them over definitely on the insane side. These children should be treated with the very greatest care.

"A second group comprises the moderately bright children, a little above average and yet not enough to be considered especially precocious. They should, however, have their condition taken into account and they should not be compelled to drudge along with the average child.

"Then comes the *average child* for whom our school systems are at present made, and the only group whom they adequately serve. The question whether the training in the public schools is the best that can be devised is not for us to discuss here.

"Our next group is the backward. This group should be carefully watched from the start. Some of them may catch up with the average child. Some of them will go through their whole educational career with the same slowness, nevertheless they will get through.

"Finally there is the group of definitely feeble-minded. This group will ultimately divide into the morons and the imbeciles, and each of these should receive special training and treatment.

"The lower grade imbeciles will probably not get into the school, but will be recognized at home as defective and kept there until they can be placed in an institution for the feeble-minded."

Children who are doing regular school work should be given mental tests whenever it is proposed to promote them to an advanced grade, Dr. Goddard thinks. Whenever it is shown that they have not the capacity, they should be transferred to special work, and their development carefully watched. There is a prevalent idea that every child who has the means and gets through high school should go to college. The teachers in college have long known that many who enter should never attempt to do college work. We read further:

"The same principle might be applied, Dr. Goddard thinks, to the various professions and occupations. 'Why should we not ascertain the grade of intelligence necessary in every essential occupation and then entrust that work only to those people who have the necessary intelligence? This would not be at all difficult to do. It would in some cases require considerable labor, but that is all. For example, how much intelligence does it require to be a motorman on a street car? To ascertain this, it is only necessary to give mental tests to all the motormen, and then ascertain from employers which ones are highly successful, which ones moderately successful, and which prove to be failures. It would then be discovered that men of a certain mental level fail, men of another mental level are fairly successful, men of still a third mental level are highly successful and efficient.'

"Why should we not ascertain the mental level of people in various activities and when we find any inefficient, clearly on account of their lack of intelligence or other qualities, why should not society have the right to transfer that individual to some other line of work where he would be more efficient? This may be too advanced a step to be taken at once, but it will surely come to that eventually. Many a person is inefficient because of an uncongenial environment which a better intelligence would prompt him to change.

"In stating clearly—even baldly—the doctrine of mental levels and pushing its application to a logical conclusion, Dr. Goddard has done a real service to biology. One need not agree with all the author's statements, to agree with him that the recognition of the innate and inalterable differences among human beings is fundamental to social progress. This will eventually make it possible 'for the intelligent to understand the mental levels of the unintelligent, or those of low intelligence, and to so organize the work of the world that every man is doing such work and bearing such responsibility as his mental level warrants.'"

IMPROBABILITY OF LIFE ON THE PLANETS

THE EVIDENCE for the existence of life in the universe, elsewhere than on this earth, is reviewed and discust in *Science* (New York) by W. D. Matthew, of the American Museum of Natural History, who concludes that altho the chances favor the existence of life of some sort somewhere on other worlds, it is extremely unlikely that such life is intelligent, and practically impossible that it has developed anything like what we call civilization. He scoffs at Martian "canals" and planetary "signals." Mr. Matthew calls attention to the fact, which he considers worthy of note, that astronomers take the affirmative and biologists the negative side of the argument. There may, he thinks, be two reasons for this, and he proceeds to give them as follows:

"1. Astronomers, physicists, mathematicians, are accustomed to hold a more receptive attitude, an open mind, toward hypotheses that can not be definitely disproved. This frame of mind is natural and adapted to their work. They are accustomed to deal with problems which can be solved by mathematical and deductive methods. A limited number of solutions appear, all of them to be receptively considered until they can be definitely disproved.

"The biologist, on the other hand, deals with a different sort of problem. His evidence is almost always inductive, experimental. His subjects are far too complex, too little understood, to admit of mathematical analysis, save in their simpler aspects. And always he is compelled to adopt toward the illimitable numbers of possible explanations, a decidedly exclusive attitude, and to leave out of consideration all factors that have not something in the way of positive evidence for their existence. If he fails to do so, he soon finds himself struggling hopelessly in a bog of unprofitable speculations. A critical rather than a receptive frame of mind is the fundamental condition of progress in his work.

"2. The second reason is that the astronomer or cosmologist has in mind when he thinks of this problem the physical and chemical conditions that would render life possible. If these be duplicated elsewhere he sees life as possible, and by the incidence of the laws of chance probable or almost certain, if they be duplicated often enough. Viewing the innumerable multitude of stars, each of them a solar system with possible or probable planets analogous to our own, he sees such multitudinous duplications of the physical conditions that have made life possible on our earth, that it appears to him incredible that all stand empty and lifeless.

"The biologist, on the other hand, has at the forefront of his mind the history and evolution of life on the earth. He knows that altho these conditions favoring the creation of living matter have existed on earth for many millions or hundreds of millions of years, yet life has not come into existence on earth save once, or at most half a dozen times, during that time. The living beings on earth are reducible at most to a few, and probably to one primary stock, all their present variety being the result of the evolutionary processes of differentiation and adaptation. It must appear therefore to him that the real conditions for the creation of life on earth have involved, not merely the favoring physical conditions, but some immensely complex concatenation of circumstances so rare that even on earth it has occurred probably but once during the eons of geologic time. If the conditions necessary to creation and evolution have not been duplicated on earth during the whole of the recorded history of life from the Cambrian down to the present day, it appears to him infinitely less probable that they have been duplicated elsewhere than on the earth."

That the "man in the street" should be sympathetic with the astronomer's rather than the biologist's conclusion is natural enough, Mr. Matthew thinks. The physical probabilities are obvious; the complexity of life he does not realize; nor does he sense the minute relative proportion of time during which intelligent life has existed upon earth. Moreover, to admit the probability of extra-mundane life opens the way for all sorts of fascinating speculation. He continues:

"Such life, if it exists, would surely be evolved *ab initio* on independent lines of adaptation, and the probabilities would be overwhelming that the results of the eons of its evolution, if by some rare chance it developed intelligent life simultaneously with its appearance on the earth, would be a physical and intellectual type so different fundamentally from our own as to be altogether incomprehensible to us, even if we recognized it as being intelligence or life at all. Who that has studied the ant or the bee has failed to be imprest with the unplumbed mysteries in its sensations, its psychology, its inner life! We are far from any full understanding of the intelligence, if I may use the word, of the social insects, relatives, albeit distant relatives, of our own, brought up under the identical environment of terrestrial conditions. How much farther would he be from any comprehension of the intellectual processes of a race of beings whose ultimate origin was wholly different from ours, whose evolution was shaped under conditions that, however closely parallel, could not have been identical with those of the earth. Indeed, if we are to take a receptive attitude in this matter, why limit ourselves to protoplasm as the basis of life? Other substances, solid, liquid, or even gaseous, may have similar capacities. We know of nothing of the sort. But would we know of it if it existed, even if it existed upon earth? Would there be any conceivable method of communication, any common ideas, interests, or activities, between such beings and ourselves? It does not appear probable. How much less the probability of communication across the void of interplanetary space.

"To suppose that parallel evolution could go so far as to produce similar methods of exploiting the earth to those used by civilized man—irrigation canals, cities, or other such phenomena of the immediate present—in life evolved independently in different planets—and to produce them at an identical moment in geologic time—would seem to be the result of those limitations of constructive or creative thought which are characteristic of myth and fairy-tale, of the anthropomorphic god, or the animal that thinks and talks like a man. Civilized men can not form any real concept of intelligent life on Mars save in terms of civilized life on earth. Yet, so far as we may judge from earth conditions, if life exists at all on Mars, it is a thousand to one that it is not intelligent life, for intelligent life on earth is a phenomenon that has existed for about a thousandth part of the geologic record of life. And it is a hundred thousand to one that it is not civilized life, for civilized life has existed at the utmost for a hundredth part of the time that man as such has been on the earth."

In sum, it appears to Mr. Matthew as a paleontologist that the case may be stated as follows:

"1. The complex concatenation of circumstances necessary to bring about the initiation of life has occurred upon earth half a dozen times at most, probably but once, in an environment that has apparently been favorable for a thousand million years. The probability of its occurring in a substantially similar environment upon another planet is so slight as to be practically reducible to a mathematical zero in any particular instance.

"2. The number of solar systems being almost infinite, we might regard the number of such possible favorable environments as amounting practically to infinity.

"3. The resultant of these two considerations is that there is a finite and reasonable chance that life has existed or will exist somewhere else in the universe than on this earth alone.

"4. The probability that intelligent life exists is vastly less, and that anything in the least analogous to our civilization exists at the present time is so slight as to be negligible.

"5. If any life involving the development of self-consciousness, of abstract thought and introspection analogous to the higher intelligence of mankind, or the control of environment and utilization of natural resources that we call civilization, should develop independently upon some other planet out of the preexisting simpler phases of life, it probably—almost surely—would be so remote in its fundamental character and its external manifestations from our own, that we could not interpret or comprehend the external indications of its existence, nor even probably observe or recognize them.

"6. In any specific instance, such as other planets of our own system, the probabilities of the existence of any kind of life amount to practically zero. The probabilities of an intelligent life upon Mars or Venus or elsewhere in our system so similar to our own in its character and manifestations as to be indicated by irrigation canals, cities, or other manifestations of human civilization, appear to be zero of the second degree. The most that one can allow as a reasonable possibility is that there may be some form of life existing somewhere else in the universe than upon our planet. That we have or shall ever get evidence of its existence appears to me practically impossible in the light of present knowledge and limitations."

TRACKING CRIMINALS BY THEIR PORES

IDENTIFICATION by arrangement of the pores of the skin—a method christened "poroscopy"—is described and illustrated in *Discovery* (London, October) by G. F. Frederick Lees. This method is effective when the finger-print is so imperfect that the whorls and ridges, by which identification is usually effected, are not numerous enough for this purpose. And even if they are, it is a fortifying adjunct to the usual method, and is, we are told, likely to be more convincing to a jury. The finger-print, Mr. Lees reminds us, has long been held to constitute irrefutable evidence. For the intricate pattern of curved lines we bear on our hands is never identical in two persons. Moreover, from birth to death, finger-prints never change. It is not possible for any one to hide his or her identity by the use of chemicals, by burning, or by rubbing—all practises which are resorted to by the criminal classes. He continues:

"Stated thus, theoretically, the problem of criminal investigation and identification looks very simple, but in practise all kinds of difficulties are encountered, introducing an element of doubt which has had such weight with some juries that they have rightly refused to convict. The principle generally admitted among judical authorities is that identity between two finger or palmary prints is incontestable when at least a dozen guiding marks, consisting of the beginnings of lines, bifurcations and islets, are in every respect the same. To be able, however, to come to this clear conclusion, it is necessary to have a fairly large portion of a print under the microscope, and unfortunately the traces which are so carefully collected by the experts of police laboratories on the scene of a murder, burglary, or other offence, are often very fragmentary. Sometimes too, they are partly obliterated by the prints of persons who have arrived there before the police. Or, again, the criminal may have taken the precaution to cover his hands with gloves or cloth, in which case he may leave but a very small number of utilizable guiding marks behind him.

"Supposing that only a very fragmentary finger or palmary print is under examination, showing no more, say, than three or four points of comparison with the print from the hand of a suspected person, is there any other means of arriving at a proof of guilt? Writing in *La Province Medicale* as long ago as 1912, Dr. Edmond Locard, the Director of the Police Laboratory of Lyons, was the first scientist to answer this question in the affirmative. 'I believe it is possible, in many cases,' he wrote in the course of a detailed statement of this new method of identification, 'to make up for the insufficiency of the print considered from the sole point of view of its guiding marks by studying in the trace under examination the arrangement of the pores.' Here we have a method—brought to perfection since 1912, and only recently set forth by this distinguished investigator in a work which ought to be translated into every language—which is infinitely more fruitful in results than the one known by the name of dactyloscopy. Like the patterns on the fingers, the pores between those patterns are unchangeable. Moreover, in shape and in size they are extremely variable, and when the trace of these sudoriferous glands has been enlarged by microphotography, we are provided with an infallible means of identification. The smallest portion of a finger-print may thus be utilized, for there are from nine to eighteen of these glands per millimeter. Between one person and another there is also infinite variety in the distances between the pores. 'In brief,' says Dr. Locard, 'the pores, because of their immutability, permanency, and variety, constitute a sign of identity of the first order. Poroscopy (as this science is called), the only method of identification in the case of very small fragments of prints, is, in all cases of dactyloscopic analysis, an important complementary proof. A jury, unimprest by thirty or forty homologous characteristic points, will be struck by the concordance of shape, position, and number of some hundreds of pores found to be identical in two compared prints. Poroscopic research, which is difficult and hard to carry out on the original traces, even by the use of a lens enlarging five times, is practised by means of large photographic enlargements. With an enlargement of sixteen the work is already easy. For demonstration before a jury one can usefully enlarge up to forty-five times. In practise, poroscopy has very often enabled fragments of prints measuring but a few square millimeters to be used, or half-effaced prints in which only a few points were visible. Above all, it enables one in numerous cases to be clearly affirmative, and strengthens the evidence due to dactyloscopy in a most efficacious manner.'

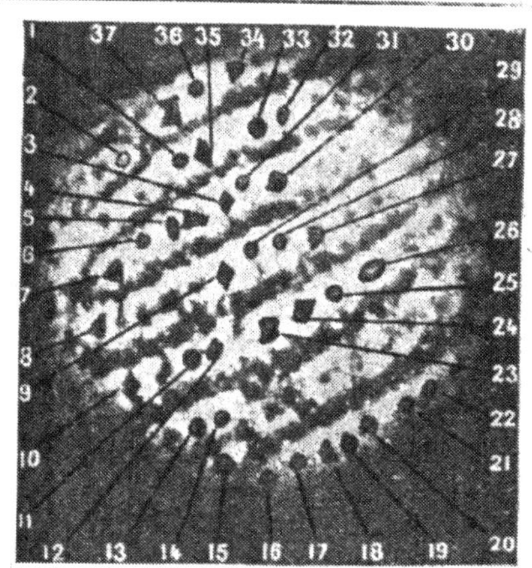

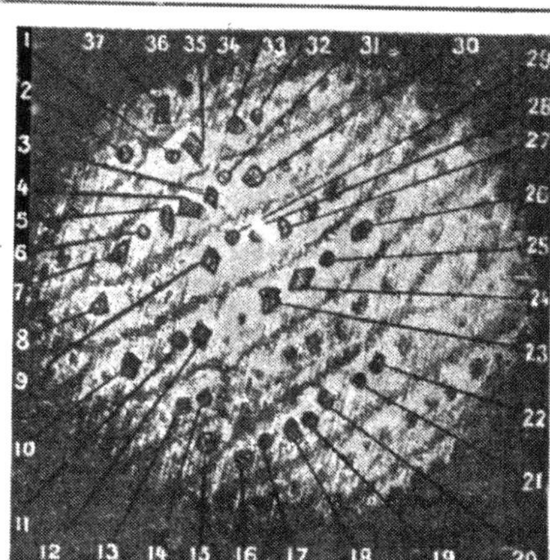

EVEN THE SMALLEST TRACES OF FINGER-PRINTS

Can be photographed up to show the pores. Here the identity of the two impressions is unmistakable.

"Dr. Locard cites a large number of cases in which this fresh advance in criminology has been successful. As a good example we may take the Boudet Simonin case, in which two men with these names were arrested on a charge of burgling a flat in Lyons, on June 10, 1912, and stealing a quantity of jewelry and 400 francs. There were no witnesses of the robbery, and nobody could furnish the slightest piece of information regarding the burglars. But a rosewood cabinet, from which the jewels and money had been taken, was literally covered with finger-prints. These were revealed by the aid of carbonate of lead, and photographed. Search was then made in the finger-print archives of the Lyons Police Laboratory, with the result that certain prints were found to be indentical with those of a man, Boudet, who had been several times convicted of theft. The man's record at the Sûreté showed that he often worked in collaboration with a man named Simonin. Both were arrested. And it was then found that the finger-prints which were not Boudet's were Simonin's. Thirteen prints from the former's hand presented 78 characteristic points; two prints made by the latter, including that of the palm of his left hand, showed 94 points of comparison. In the case of the middle finger of Boudet's left hand 901 pores were identified, while in that of Simonin's palm more than 2,000 homologous pores were pointed out to the jury. On this sole piece of evidence the men were sentenced to five years' hard labor, the jury refusing to grant them the benefit of extenuating circumstances. 'I am convinced,' comments Dr. Locard, 'that the demonstration of the homology of the pores played, in the minds of the jurymen, the principal rôle.'

"Stockis, another well-known criminologist, proved experimentally that the wearing of leather or india-rubber gloves need not prevent the formation of finger-prints, and in February, 1912, in the S—— case, Dr. Locard put theory into practise by identifying a gloved burglar without any other proof than his finger-prints. The print was naturally less clear than that of a bare hand, but nevertheless a fairly large number of guiding marks could be distinguished."

WOMAN'S FRIEND, THE CORSET

NOT ALWAYS, but under certain conditions, says Dr. D. M. Dunn, head of the women's department of the Life Extension Institute, writing in *The Forecast* (Philadelphia). Apparently "whatever is" is wrong, in the judgment of the hygienists. Our mothers, who wore trailing skirts and tight corsets, were urged to reform, on the ground that the former were dirty and the latter deforming. Now that our women wear short skirts and low corsets, or none at all, they are equally targets for condemnation. One of the remarkable features in the career of the corset, says Dr. Dunn, is the attraction it has always had for the public eye. Not only the health crank, the dress reformer, the physician, the physical culturist, but city editors, ministers and college professors have always taken it upon themselves to condemn, condone or advocate, but always to mention, this intimate article. He goes on:

"These winds of contention have swept every one into three groups: Those who stand for the total abandonment of the corset; those who accept it unthinkingly as a mere adjunct to dress; those who, believing it can be reconciled with laws of health, take it seriously enough to select it with the greatest care.

"More than a year ago the International Conference of Women Physicians assumed the first position, adopting the principle of No Corsets for Women. Strangely enough, this theory of certain learned reformers is practised as a matter of convenience by the two most influential groups of young women in the country—college girls and débutantes. 'Let joy be unconfined' they cry, much to the chagrin of their instructors, mothers and chaperons. Naturally these groups of elders are in a panic—'Are corsets doomed?'

"To the older generation this question has almost a moral significance. They themselves were brought up in corsets almost from babyhood and never questioned either their place in the toilet or their effect upon the health. Midway between these two extremes are they who do not condemn the corset wholesale nor accept it on fashion's terms, but believe it useful if conforming to health in make and fit.

"There are some authorities in hygiene to whom they can turn for a program of moderation. Such a body is The American Posture League, whose purpose is to promote standards of correct posture and to approve commercial products which attain them. They have stated that 'Corset support is unnecessary only when skirts and underwear are not made with bands; when the weight of clothing is borne at the shoulders well in toward the neck (not from the tip) and from the hip joints; when the weight of the stockings should be distributed evenly and borne by the hip joints (round garters should not be used).'

"This organization will even furnish an approved list of corsets, since they believe that women have a right to ask the expert to direct their buying.

"The wrong corset is a subtle enemy, which emphasizes all the bad features of posture and encourages the slump which is injurious to health. 'But, doctor, what shall I do?' In exceptional cases it might be safe to say: 'Give up your corset and strengthen your abdominal muscles, depend upon them to keep you erect and well poised.' But the command would go unheeded by all the 'smart' well-groomed women to whom the proper hang of a skirt is a social obligation. On the other hand, it wouldn't be safe to advise the sudden abandonment of corsets for the overweight woman, for the woman recently under surgical treatment, nor for the underweight woman whose muscles are flabby and thinned-out.

"The nervous strain of modern city life to which women are not yet adjusted, together with lack of exercise, has resulted in a wide-spread condition known as visceroptosis—or sagging of the abdominal organs. Constipation, debility, headaches, backaches, sallow complexion, appendicitis, general weakness, are some of the ailments associated with this condition. A corset is useful in proportion to its success in alleviating this weakness by supporting the cavity and reinforcing the muscles. Such a corset must be a firm, low support, so made that its lines pull upward and back. The boning must be flexible enough to allow the body to bend easily, sideways, as well as backward and forward.

"It ought to be individually fitted even more carefully than are shoes. Ideally, the corset should be made to order by a good corsetière, that its lines may be perfectly planned for the figure. The garments on the market which most nearly provide for such individual variation are the best ones to select. At least careful measurements are necessary for proper fitting. The difference in cost between the made-to-order garment and others is at present marked, but from the standpoint of health it is worth every extra penny.

"Suppose now you succeed in obtaining a corset satisfactory to you in its texture and to your doctor in its line and its effect upon your posture. Are you absolutely safe, warranted to improve in health without sacrificing style? 'No,' says the hygienic advisor. 'There is yet much for you yourself to do.' The depressing effect of these words will probably deepen when, after you have mustered up enough courage to ask in a weak voice: 'What?' the answer comes—'Exercise.'

"Without exercise a woman is bound to depend on her corset exactly as a vine does on a trellis. The best corset that was ever made could not relieve its wearer of all danger of weakening muscles. The only way to keep muscles firm is by *working* them. To allow your muscles to become thinned out, and flabby, is almost as bad an offense against health as to fail to keep your teeth clean.

"But here is balm for your rising protest. A few minutes of hard work night and morning will turn the trick. One hour of brisk walking a day is also, without any other form of outdoor sport, enough to keep your muscles in good condition.

"A low corset, which lifts the figure, individually fitted, worn by a woman who keeps her muscles taut by daily exercise, is a boon to health. Until in some glad hygienic day women assume the perfect posture as a matter of course, to wear such a garment is much better for the average woman than to try to do without it."

HUNTING SEALS FROM THE AIR

HOW AIRMEN recently have been assisting the hunters along the Grand Banks of Newfoundland in tracking down seals, is told by Edgar C. Middleton in *The Illustrated London News*. Our quotations are from excerpts in *The Aerial Age Weekly* (New York). Says Mr. Middleton:

"It happened in this way. A Newfoundland sealing captain who had returned to his calling from the war had watched the airmen hunting down U-boats among the gray wastes of the North Sea. He became aware of a certain similarity to his own business of sealing. There is something of the seal in a submarine, more than the fact that their habits are similar. The sealing captain put two and two together. An aerial observer who could spot the elongated form of a submarine from a distance of forty miles at 5,000 feet should add many hundreds to the catch when it came to seal-hunting.

"His idea materialized, and in March of this year there arrived at the Bay of Exploits, northward from which lie the great sealing grounds, a small party of British airmen. Led by Mr. F. S. Cotton, a young Australian, this party included another and a spare pilot, a couple of mechanics, and two machines, and forthwith they got to work erecting their hangar on the shores of the bay.

"Within a few weeks they were flying out hundreds of miles over the ice, cooperating with the ships in the sealing. In all, they covered 2,000 miles of the ice-fields, or something like 20,000 square miles, in the first expedition, one flight taking them very far from their base. This aerial cooperation assisted in a catch of 110,000 seals.

"Belle Isle is the center of the great seal fisheries. There the seals pass the winter. There the flipperlings—young seals—are born, and from there, as the ice begins to break up with the spring, they and their parents come floating southwards on huge blocks of ice. Every year, regular as clockwork, towards the end of February, the ice-floes start floating south. Every year, between March 21 and March 25, the entire seal nursery arrives off Fogo, where the sealing fleet waits their arrival.

"The actual bagging of the seals is a comparatively simple matter. Immediately they are sighted, the entire ship's company take to the boats, and, clambering on the ice, club the seals over the head, skin them, and haul their skins and fat back to the ships, at the rate of thousands a day.

"Like the old proverb, tho, you must first catch your seal 'before you sell his skin.' In these vast seas it is no easy matter to track down even an army of 100,000 seals. From the time that the ice-floes arrive until the seals take to deep water again, far beyond the hunter's reach, is only a matter of a few weeks at most. In that brief spell either the sealers have made their catch, or they return to harbor empty-handed for another twelve months."

MUST THE WORLD DIE OF THIRST?

CHEERFUL SCIENTIFIC PROPHETS at various times have assured us that the human race will burn up, freeze, starve, or murder each other in war. Now a French scientist suggests that the earth is drying up. This happy thought is based on the belief that fresh-water streams are gradually finding their way into underground courses, where we can not get at them. If this interesting possibility beats the others to our fate, then we may imagine the last survivors of the race huddled in our deepest mines drilling in day and night shifts for the elusive fluid. In a book published in Paris by E. A. Martel, a French geologist, a chapter is devoted to this subject, and an abstract, translated from *La Nature* (Paris) appears in *The Scientific American Monthly* (New York). The retreat of surface waters to sub-surface courses appears to have been going on, the writer thinks, since remote geological epochs. Whether it is proceeding appreciably still, is open to question, but as early as 1861 this was maintained by a French geologist. Many explorers have held the opinion that the dried-up ravines of the Sahara carried great volumes of water in the Quaternary era. De Lapparent thought that during that same era the bottom of the Grand Cañon was filled with a much more powerful current than that of our time. The lowering of the level in the ancient lakes of Lahontan and Bonneville (Great Salt Lake), the ancient river borders and terraces, the plateaus of Provence, the desiccation of certain regions in Africa, Central Asia, etc., have long been pointed to as signs of an increasing spread of dryness. Says the reviewer:

"But most of all it is the recent researches in the interior of the ground itself which have 'transformed from a hypothesis to a certainty the idea that the waters are gradually making their escape into the sub-soil and that there is a substitution of a modern subterranean circulation for an ancient surface circulation.' Martel enumerates and describes a great many very curious examples of the disappearance of springs, the deepening of subterranean rivers, the going dry of wells, etc., which make the future desiccation of our globe seem inevitable. He says 'humanity must prepare for a fight with thirst.'

"One of the most convincing of the arguments offered to this effect is the perforation of the bottom of the upper galleries in caverns where subterranean rivers have dried up in the course of ages through an actual drawing off of their waters into profounder depths. This has been noted particularly in many of the caves among the Pyrenees. In the Mammoth Cave of Kentucky, the largest cavern in the world, the upper galleries are perforated repeatedly in this manner by great orifices through which their ancient waters have escaped.

Illustrations used by courtesy of "The Scientific American."

WHERE ONE RIVER WENT.

Subterranean river entrance in the Rocky Mountains.

"Even under our very eyes we may see the capture of waters by the depths below. The valley of the Nesque now loses on the top of Monieux its stream of water, which is taken captive by the famous fountain of Vaucluse, and it requires very violent storms to cause even a temporary flood to run in the bed of this superb dry ravine.

"There is a lively dispute as to whether this process has been actually manifested during historic times. . . . While a number of authorities agree that there is evidence of the 'tangible visibility and rapidity of the phenomenon' in modern times, others hold that there has been no perceptible diminution of the waters upon the earth's surface during the period of historical record."

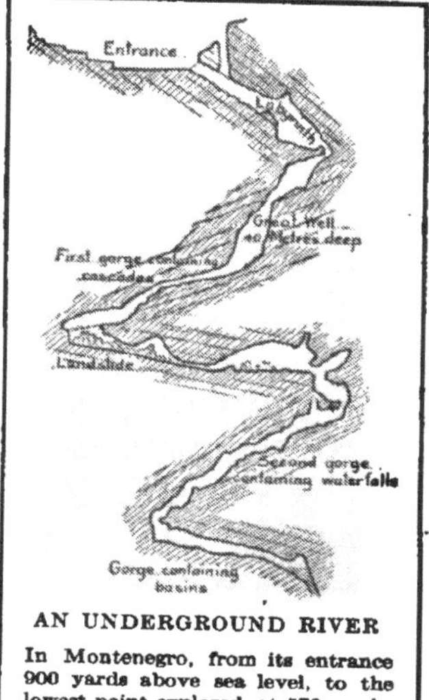

AN UNDERGROUND RIVER

In Montenegro, from its entrance 900 yards above sea level, to the lowest point explored, at 570 yards.

Still another controversy rages as to causes. Some geologists, including Martel and his school, ascribe it to the enlargement of fissures in the subsoil, together with a decrease in the amount of rain. Still another school makes this last cause entirely responsible. Some writers think that all the observed facts proceed only from regional changes in the distribution of rainfall, and thus remain purely local; others still hold that there is a progressive desiccation of the earth's surface, but declare that it is due to deforestation. Still another group believe that the phenomenon is due to the intensive cultivation of the soil.

HOW NATURE SWATS THE FLY.—Nature's method for getting rid of the house-fly is thus described editorially in the Bridgeport (Conn.) *Telegram*, by I. Foster Moore:

"About this time of year, as the cool days of Autumn begin to make us think that the morning ablutions are getting to be more or less of a nuisance, you will notice, now and again, house-flies on the window-panes, walls, or any convenient place which they have chosen for their demise. Your probable conclusion on such an occasion would be that the poor thing had been overcome by the autumn chill, but such is not the case, for *Musca domestica* died of *Empusa musae* (sounds bad enough to kill anything). If you should examine *domestica*, beg pardon, the fly, closely, you would notice that the body was slightly enlarged, having somewhat the color of yeast and something of its consistency; also the filaments of this yeast-like substance have glued the fly to its resting-place. *Empusa musae* is a fungus which attacks flies from early in the fall until winter finishes the job. This section is very favorable to the fungus disease of the house-fly, as moisture in the air causes rapid development of the hyphal bodies, as the fungus fragments that fill the body of the fly are called. The fly is attacked by floating spores, which attach themselves to it and throw out a thread which enters the body and, by budding and division, as in the lower protozoa, eventually fill the victim with the growth, feeding on the softer parts until death ensues. The local government board on public health and medical subjects of the City of London started a campaign under the direction of Dr. Julius Bernstein for a detailed study of this fungus and an attempt to cultivate the spores by artificial means, hoping to use it in the destruction of the house-fly on a large scale. It is probable that all insects have some fungus growth which attacks and kills them, and the entomologists have already studied and named many of them which attack many different species. So the next time you find an embalmed fly you will know what ails him. Meanwhile the fungus goes on performing a duty which commands our gratitude."

THE "BLUE BOY" AND THE "TRAGIC MUSE" FOR AMERICA

TWO BRITISH INSTITUTIONS have finally been sacrificed to Hard Times. Gainsborough's "Blue Boy" and Reynolds's "Tragic Muse" are reported sold by the Duke of Westminster to a firm of art dealers, and their ultimate destination is regarded as likely to be found in this country. To call these two pictures national institutions is not to exaggerate their importance in the realm of English culture. To bring the "Blue Boy" here would be like bringing the "Mona Lisa" from France, observes the New York *Times*. This painting was the repudiation of a claim that blue could not be used as the predominant color of a picture. Gainsborough and Sir Joshua Reynolds took opposite sides in this contention and the former painted the picture in proof. In mere money value nothing in the way of painted canvas has ever reached its selling price, which is reported to be £170,000 (nearly $680,000). Its coming to America may revive a lively dispute of the last centuries when New York auction rooms sold to the late George A. Hearn a "Blue Boy" that Mr. Hearn always maintained was Gainsborough's "original" and the Duke of Westminster's but a "replica." Of the two pictures the New York *Herald* writes:

GAINSBOROUGH'S "BLUE BOY."

A national institution supposedly as immune as the "Mona Lisa," but sacrificed to the stress of Hard Times.

"This portrait of Mrs. Siddons was painted by Sir Joshua Reynolds in 1783 when the actress was at the zenith of her career and apparently a year or two earlier than the almost equally well-known portrait of her in walking-dress by Gainsborough. The gallant Sir Joshua was so delighted with the work that when he had finished it he said, 'I cannot lose this opportunity of sending my name to posterity on the hem of your garment.' And he wrote his name—he seldom signed his paintings—in large characters upon the gold embroidered border of the dress. In 1822 the painting came into the possession of the Grosvenor family and remained one of the chief pieces of their famous private gallery.

"The 'Blue Boy' hung in the same gallery until at the beginning of the World War it was removed for safekeeping to the National Gallery. This painting, which is very generally considered the best of Gainsborough's works, is believed to be the portrait of a youthful scion of the house of Bottall, wealthy iron founders of London. Its name is said to have come from the fact that it was painted by Gainsborough after a dispute with Sir Joshua Reynolds as to the value of making blue the predominant color in a portrait. From the family of the iron founder the portrait passed into the possession of Prince George of Wales, who sold it to a famous beau of the period, John Nesbitt. It was acquired by Earl Grosvenor and added to his collection early in the last century."

The sale has "created endless gossip both in artistic and social circles in London," says a cable dispatch to the *Herald*. The Duke of Westminster, with more than a square mile of London property covered by the fashionable districts of Belgravia and Mayfair, is "understood to be the one peer who is not in serious financial difficulties." When great art changes hands to-day the money element is the chief feature of discussion, and the *Herald* continues:

"The price paid for the two paintings is said to be £200,000, or at normal rates $1,000,000, the 'Blue Boy,' according to report, bringing £170,000, and the portrait of Mrs. Siddons £30,000. One of the highest prices previously recorded for a portrait by an English artist was the 52,000 guineas paid early in 1919 for George Romney's picture of the Beckford children, in the Duke of Hamilton's collection. Over this sale began the lively controversy, which has continued ever since in Great Britain, regarding the dispersion of the private art treasures of England. It was really the first time that the country found itself confronted with the problem of preserving its richest art possessions.

"One of the reasons for this was that the wealthy collector had confined himself largely to the Continent. But the best of the private collections there had been well culled over and what remained came to be rigorously protected, especially in Italy,

France and the Netherlands, against removal from the country by stringent laws and high export taxes. There remained thus but one source in Europe for the obtaining of these treasures, and that was Great Britain. After-war conditions compelled the breaking up of many of the great estates and also forced upon the market some of the most jealously guarded and most prized paintings of the country. Strong appeals were made to British patriotism for the retention of these works in England. A plan of purchase through public subscription of the Romney portrait failed; in fact, the whole effort to preserve to England her famous paintings, either by the imposition of heavy export tax or the formation of special purchasing funds, failed because the matter was complicated through the demands for copyrights and concessions to modern painters and their families.

"That the two famous paintings from the Duke of Westminster's gallery will come to America for a short time at least, is a matter of much satisfaction. This country is rapidly becoming the home of the great masterpieces of the world. A London comment on the sale is to the effect that after all there may be relief in the fact 'that it is the generous wont of American millionaires to leave their spoils of European art treasures to public galleries.' This has been markedly true in the past. Mr. Morgan presented to the Metropolitan Museum of Art some of the most distinguished of his art treasures; the collection of Mr. Altman, left to the same institution, is perhaps the richest collection of paintings of the Dutch and Netherland artists outside of Holland. The splendid collection of old masters' works left by Mr. Frick will also no doubt eventually be open to the public. There is every reason to believe that our great collectors of the future will not depart from the generous policy of their predecessors."

THE MUSIC ASSEMBLER—A film which is merely accompanied by more or less "suitable" airs of the rumty-tumty order is a thing of the past. Musical accompaniment has become one of the exacting features of a successful picture, and its creation is not left to the orchestra leader, but to the member of a "new profession" which the London *Daily Mail* thus describes:

"A rough-and-ready formula grew up: slow waltz for sentiment, funeral march for death scene, ragtime for humor, drum for motor-car. But no real subtlety in the provision of musical atmosphere could be achieved unless picture and accompaniment were wedded by a *musician*.

"Hence the arrival of the film music assembler—who must be endowed not only with an encyclopedic memory of musical literature and a highly sensitive dramatic instinct, but also be himself a gifted composer and have the elaborate possibilities of orchestral technique at his fingers' ends.

"Sitting in the darkness of the private theater, he is shown the film repeatedly, and as it passes before his eyes he makes lightning memoranda of the various motives involved. All the chief characters, treated by the modern method, must have their own musical motives; the subject as a whole must have its main musical theme; every incident or series of incidents must be either musically illustrated, harmonized with, or commented upon—sometimes seriously, sometimes ironically, but always with the object of providing that essential factor, an 'atmosphere'—and providing it at exactly the right instant. . . .

"In the fulness of time a young musician may become as celebrated for having composed the incidental music to a film as, say, the incidental music to such a play as 'Monsieur Beaucaire.' And meanwhile the assembling of musically atmospheric passages, their dramatic interruption by what Handel called 'valuable silences,' the harmonious linking up of separate tunes, is itself arriving at the dignity of an art. . . .

"Way Down East" and "The Bigamist" were immediately hailed as masterly blendings of picture and music. The former's music embellishment is the work of an American; the latter's was that of an Englishman, David Brooks."

ACTORS BILKING SHAKESPEARE

NO OTHER PROFESSION would take so complacently the charge Mr. Sothern has made against actors. With ranks overcrowded, the kind of players needed for a Shakespearean performance are barely to be found among the denizens of our stage. Should he lose the faithful group he has long gathered about himself and Miss Marlowe, their substitutes could not be produced, and Shakespeare would have to be shelved for lack of fit interpreters. Worse than this, when these veteran Shakespearean players proposed founding a school to teach deportment, diction and fencing—the accomplishments needed in the poetic drama—they found no pupils willing to attend. Our younger actors or would-be actors were satisfied with themselves as they are. "This particular instance," says Mr. J. Rankin Towse in the New York *Evening Post*, "has its significance because it illustrates what there is only too much reason to believe is a widely prevalent attitude." This:

MRS. SIDDONS AS THE "TRAGIC MUSE."

Sold by England, sought by France, but destined for America, one of the most famous of Sir Joshua Reynolds's paintings.

"As Mr. Sothern justly remarks, proficiency in such accomplishments, with all that it implies in the important matters of deportment, diction, and gesture, is just as much a necessary equipment in all the better forms of modern drama as it is in the romantic or classic. The almost universal neglect of it fully accounts for that lack of finish, distinction, and real vitality so characteristic of many contemporary performances. Too many players, he hints, have an aversion to anything like systematic study or hard work. They are content to rely upon the promptings of what they are pleased to consider their own intuitive genius. Everybody knows what that means. That is why there are so few first and so many second-rate actors.

"Old and uncontradicted as these arguments are, it is as well that they should be borne in mind. They lead to an unescapable conclusion. The theater, of course, will continue to exist and, after a fashion, grow. The question is not one of survival, but of character and influence. Few will dispute the contention of Mr. Sothern that it is only by great plays that great acting can be developed. It is a truism which has its corollary. Without great plays there can be no great actors. Doubtless many players have reaped fame and fortune by the display of some extraordinary faculty in pieces of no inherent worth. Liston as *Paul Pry*, Robson in 'The Porter's Knot,' Jefferson as *Rip*, Owens as *Solon Shingle*, E. H. Sothern as *Dundreary* are examples that instantly come to mind, and many others might be quoted. But none of these cases, taken individually, would justify the inclusion of the performer in the exclusive category of the 'great,' because there was nothing in the subject matter either of rare conception or loftiness of ideal that called for or permitted the highest type of powerful, noble, or imaginative interpretation. It might even be asserted that the artistic dimensions of the acting are precisely limited by the intellectual and imaginative proportions of the play.

"This, after all, is only a roundabout way of saying that the play is the thing. Upon it, ultimately, every estimate of the theater must rest. Clever acting occasionally may confer a temporary fictitious value upon inferior kinds of drama, but cannot give it worth or durability. Moreover, as has been proved to the hilt during recent decades, a general decline in the standards of drama must inevitably be accompanied by a corresponding decay in the general efficiency of acting. It is this consideration that makes an intelligent direction of the theater so vital to its future not only from the artistic but from the commercial point of view."

In this failure of the stage the public is absolved from blame. They demand Shakespeare. The Sothern-Marlowe Company has been appearing at the Boston Opera House and will move to the Century Theater in New York—the largest houses these cities afford for the speaking drama. Mr. Mantell, Mr. Hampden, Mr. Lieber and Mr. John Barrymore are also employers of candidates for Shakespearean acting. But apparently the economic law of supply and demand parts here. The Indianapolis *Star* comments:

"People who attended the theater years ago and still visit it occasionally will agree that finished acting was far more common then than now, nor was it confined wholly to the 'stars.' A good many English actors came to America in those days and one of their noticeable characteristics was their speech, with its clear enunciation and pronunciation and the ease with which the voice was managed. English speech as we often hear it from casual visitors and occasional lecturers is not always clear or free from faults by any means, so that the vocal powers were evidently helped by special training. But our own leading actors were equally satisfying in this respect. It was a pleasure to listen to them.

"A change came about, however. Vocal training began to be neglected. Even the otherwise great Mansfield had an indistinctness of speech. As fine an actress as Mrs. Fiske has marred her career by her failure to enunciate clearly. Once the stage served as a model of what correct speech should be. Now it is far from that. Actors and actresses too often clip their words or run them together or fail to throw their voices properly. There are happy exceptions, and the natural conclusion must be that such men and women have really studied their art. But it does not often happen that any one on the stage suggests Shakespearean possibilities."

The rewards that are given actors of the rank of Mr. Sothern would seem to be a sufficient bait, but is the same thing true of the support? Herein might lie the answer. The New York *Herald* almost touches the point:

"There are constant reports that the profession of acting is overcrowded. There are said to be seven applicants, on the average, for every available post. Yet there is so little interest in one kind of acting that Mr. Sothern and other distinguished actors of Shakespeare are able only with great difficulty to find recruits for their companies. One branch of the profession certainly does not appear to be overcrowded."

DULL TEACHING OF HISTORY

HISTORY AND CONTEMPORARY THOUGHT have a poor show in the teaching of our schools and colleges. It is not charged that teachers do not know enough, but they fail to impart what they know so as to get under the skull of the pupil. The reason is that the student body have intellectually grown out of hand. "The material on which we operate," says President M. Carey Thomas of Bryn Mawr, "the boys and girls in the schools and the students in our colleges, has been transformed under our hands into something entirely new and strange." The apparatus of teaching, lectures, recitations and text-books, belongs to the scrap-heap, "especially our text-books." She thinks that not alone text-books, but teachers, college executives and what not "are no longer vital in the eyes of our students." Speaking at the Founders' Day celebration of Mount Holyoke College, Miss Thomas gave the younger generation a place hardly granted them by the most advanced modern English fiction. "The profound interests to which they vibrate, their currents of passionate thought, sweep by us in secret channels unknown to us." And to choose an illustration she takes Wells's "Outline of History" as the kind of book this "passionate" generation ought to be set to study. Reported in the New York *Times* her words are:

"It is history of a wholly new kind and makes a world-wide appeal to the younger generation. Its inaccuracies, if there are any that are avoidable in so vast an undertaking, do not matter at all in comparison to its gripping qualities. Yet how few historians are making use of it. One courageous professor told me that he was using it, and he added that to his astonishment his habitually indifferent men students turned into famished kittens and lapped it up like new milk. All our text-books must be rewritten from this new point of view.

"But this new and almost universal appreciation of the power of education has brought upon us what I regard as the most terrible menace to American schools and colleges and to free and liberal thought that has come in my lifetime. The Federal and State Governments, Boards of Education, Americanization societies, American Legions and organizations of every kind are demanding that children and college students should be taught patriotism, concrete citizenship and 100 per cent. Americanism. This means that school teachers and college professors, as yet only in public schools and State universities, but unless the movement is determinedly opposed sooner or later everywhere, are being required to teach not how to make things as they should be, but that things as they are right; that the United States Constitution, as written 134 years ago, is perfect; that our highly unsatisfactory Government must not be criticized; that the United States flag, which, as we all know, flies over many cruel injustices which we hope to set right, must be reverenced as a sacred symbol of unchanging social order, of political death in life.

"The Lusk law passed in New York State is a hideous example of what may happen any day in any and every State. It is impossible to teach in our schools definite political or religious doctrine without arousing conflicting parties, one faction of which will surely rise up and rend the other. All the conservative forces now in control of the world are seizing upon this propagandist teaching in order to capture the younger generation and so save their ancient privileges. What this perversion of education did for Germany it may easily do for the United States. We need now progressive leadership of the most liberal kind to save the world from revolution. It can come only from the younger generation now in school and college. In our generation there is no such light or leading. One hundred per cent. Americanism such as this will strangle free thought in its cradle. Cut-and-dried opinions on practical matters are almost sure to be wrong. Agreement on contemporary questions is impossible.

"If our young people are to be instructed what to think on controversial subjects of contemporary politics, teachers and professors must teach the majority opinion held by Boards of Trustees and Boards of Education and the communities in which they teach. There is no other way out. Otherwise their official heads will inevitably roll into the basket. Our professors and teachers will then become timorous souls with no light and leading. Now is the time above all others to affirm as never before the freedom of teaching and freedom of opinion, to refuse utterly to teach cut-and-dried opinions, to claim as our highest right liberty to train our students to think for themselves and to work out for themselves after they leave school and college their own practical applications. Unless the youth of the world now in school and college can develop leadership there will be none in the next generation. Without vision our civilization will surely perish."

Refusing to be carried away by the sweeping eloquence of the speaker, described by *The Independent* as "but one of a host of up-to-the-minute educational reformers," this paper analyzes the particular book she "wishes to substitute for the outworn methods of the past." And in doing this it calls to its aid the long review of Wells's book by Dr. J. S. Schapiro appearing in *The Nation*. The reviewer is called "a professor whose radicalism does not submerge his learning or his regard for truth." We quote:

"For Mr. Wells's 'unusual powers of imagination,' for his capacity to write 'superlatively well,' for his power of holding the attention of the reader, for his extraordinary feat in presenting the story of prehistoric man, and of man's forerunners, in a way at once scientific and thrilling, the reviewer has unqualified admiration. Far different is it with Mr. Wells's treatment of the history of the past two thousand years. Is this—as Miss Thomas nonchalantly assumes—because of his occasional inaccuracies? Not at all. 'Altho he makes comparatively few downright errors,' says the reviewer, 'his story of the Roman Empire, the Middle Ages, and Modern Times is tragically disappointing in view of the hopes he has raised in the earlier sections.' Let us look at a few of the specifications:

"'The various periods and countries are badly integrated, and the reader loses sight completely of the great path that humanity has traveled since its appearance on the earth.

"'Book V is the history of the Roman Empire. As may be expected, the children of Mars fare badly at the hands of the anti-militarist Mr. Wells. . . . The Roman Empire was "a colossally ignorant and unimaginative empire." It foresaw nothing. It had no conception of statecraft. . . . Even tho one may dislike the Romans, the fact nevertheless remains that, during a period of six centuries, they did unify the Western world and did create a world polity—that thing so much desired by Mr. Wells; they did create the system of private law upon which modern jurisprudence is largely based; they did create an administrative system which functions to this day in Latin Europe.

"'He gives us no evidence of being aware of the vast social changes that were taking place during the fourth and fifth centuries, the silent economic massacre of the lower middle classes, the sinking of the free laborers to a condition of serfdom, the race suicide—phenomena that surely offer some explanation for the decay of the Roman world.

BRYN MAWR'S PRESIDENT.

Miss M. Carey Thomas, who thinks teachers of to-day fail to get under the skulls of their pupils.

"'So deeply hostile is Mr. Wells to Christianity that when he does say something nice about it he says something which is erroneous.'"

A footnote to the review appended by one of *The Nation's* editors speaks of the history as "one of the great English pamphlets"; and *The Independent* echoes:

"A great 'pamphlet' it certainly is; and the word may well serve to define the issue between our colleges on the one hand and the up-to-the-minute reformers on the other. Is the latest thrilling pamphlet—however brilliant in nature and however expanded in size—to furnish the ground work of the education of our young men and women? Is it to be the chief concern of the colleges to feed the minds of our 'new and strange' young people with stuff which they will 'turn to like famished kittens' and 'lap up like new milk,' as Miss Thomas tells us has happened with Well's 'Outline'? Is their desire for a delightful thrill to be gratified at the cost of the sense of intellectual responsibility, to say nothing of the habit of sober study and painstaking thought? The notion that either in history or in any other subject, a propagandist pamphlet that brushes aside all difficulties—that presents everything from the simplified standpoint of a facile writer exploiting a pet theory—can give to students that intellectual equipment which is the prime purpose of the colleges is worthy rather of some happy-thought journalist than of a representative of learning or culture."

FORGETTING HOW TO READ—Once a person has been taught how to read it has seemed that he ought to remain literate. But war-time statistics have shown that this has not been the case. A primary education has not insured that a pupil would go through life with ability to read, nor is that education necessarily to blame, argues the Springfield *Republican*, "tho when anything goes wrong it is customary in this country to blame the schools." The cause might equally lie outside, and demands an investigation.

"Society is not wrong in looking to education for a cure of many of the ills that afflict it. But it is mistaken about the dose. Primary schooling cannot be counted upon as a kind of vaccination which will last through life. If men lead illiterate lives early instruction will not save a considerable part of them from lapsing into illiteracy. And even if by intensive methods everybody could be carried onward and upward to the point of reading newspapers, consider how many other things which the schools are painfully trying to teach must be forgotten because of neglect. It is not fair to put all the blame on the schools; part of it is scattered among individuals too dull, shiftless, and indolent to use what education they have, but a good deal of it can be traced straight back to society as a whole which has been steadily dumping its problems upon the schools without granting enough time and money for their solution. The schools have been exhaustively investigated; now let us have a little investigation of why millions of adults have forgotten how to read."

RELIGION-AND-SOCIAL-SERVICE

THE DISPUTE OVER THE HOLY LAND

RESCUE PALESTINE from the "Jewish danger," runs a recent appeal said to have been sent to President Harding by an Arab delegation journeying to this country on the same ship with a Zionist delegation coming to spur on the cause of Zionism. The Arab Mohammedans and native Christians have already appealed to the British Government not to put into effect the Balfour Declaration, because, they say, the Zionists wish "to evict and dispossess the Arab population of Palestine," where now Jewish colonists are engaged in the industrial and agricultural rehabilitation of the home of their ancestors. The Balfour Declaration, issued in November, 1917, approves, it will be recalled, "the establishment in Palestine of a national home for the Jewish people," and states that the British Government will use their best endeavors to facilitate this object, while at the same time reserving to all non-Jewish communities their full civil and religious rights. So, reasons *The Day*, a New York Jewish paper, "the whole world knows that the Zionists are coming to Palestine not to destroy, but to build. The Zionist ideal has always been to live in harmony with the Arab population, which has everything to gain from a populous and prosperous Palestine." The Arabs, however, appear to have visions of their country, their holy places, and their lands taken from them and given to strangers, and of being gradually forced out by a massed immigration of Jews. The native Christians, allied with the Mohammedans in this cause, have said in various utterances that they will never agree to live under a Jewish government. The Vatican, too, has definitely arrayed itself among the Zionists' enemies, declares the Chicago *Israelite*, an anti-Zionist paper, "and the Pope has appealed to the Christian Powers to counteract Zionist activities in the Holy Land."

Copyrighted by Underwood and Underwood

MODERN METHODS IN ANCIENT SOIL.

Jewish farmers find American plows handier than the sharp sticks their fathers used.

But the Zionists assure the native peoples that their fears are groundless. "Our policy in regard to the Arabs, as in regard to all our problems, is clear and straightforward," said Dr. Chaim Weizmann, president, in his address to the Twelfth Zionist Congress, recently held at Carlsbad. He declares, furthermore, we read in press dispatches:

"We intend to abate no jot of the rights guaranteed to us by the Balfour Declaration, and recognition of that fact by the Arabs is an essential preliminary to the establishment of satisfactory relations between Jew and Arab. Their temporary refusal to recognize that fact compels us to give thought to the means by which we can best safeguard our Yishub against aggression. Self-protection is an elemental duty. But we proclaim most solemnly and unequivocally that we have in our own hearts no thought of aggression, no intention of trespassing on the legitimate rights of our neighbors. We look forward to a future in which Jew and Arab will live side by side in Palestine, and work conjointly for the prosperity of the country. Nothing will stand in the way of such a future, when once our neighbors realize that our rights are as serious a matter to us as their rights are to them."

In trying to assuage the animosities and suspicions of both sides, Sir Herbert Samuel, the British High Commissioner under the mandate, and himself a distinguished Jew, occupies a difficult position. He has been accused of being too lenient with Arab outbreaks on the one hand, and of being not sufficiently Zionistic on the other. However, in his recent report to Parliament he declares that the policy of the British Government "contemplates the satisfaction of the legitimate aspirations of the Jewish race throughout the world in relation to Palestine, combined with a full protection of the rights of the existing population." He is convinced that the means can be found to effect this combination, and says: "The Zionism that is practicable is the Zionism that fulfils this essential condition." It is the clear duty of the Mandatory Power, insists the Commissioner further, to promote the well-being of the Arab population, for "if the growth of Jewish influence were accompanied by Arab degradation, or even by a neglect to promote Arab advancement, it would fail in one of its essential purposes. The grievance of the Arab would be a discredit to the Jew, and in the result the moral influence of Zionism would be gravely impaired." Then too—

"Simultaneously, there must be satisfaction of that sentiment regarding Palestine—a worthy and ennobling sentiment—which, in increasing degree, animates the Jewries of the world. The aspirations of these fourteen millions of people also have a right to be considered. They ask for the opportunity to establish a 'home' in the land which was the political, and has always been the religious, center of their race. They ask that this home should possess national characteristics—in language and custom, in intellectual interests, in religious and political institutions.

"This is not to say that Jewish immigration is to involve Arab emigration, that the greater prosperity of the country, through the development of Jewish enterprises, is to be at the expense, and not to the benefit of the Arabs, that the use of Hebrew is to imply the disappearance of Arabic, that the establishment of elected Councils in the Jewish Community for the control of its affairs is to be followed by the subjection of the Arabs to the rule of those Councils. In a word, the degree to which Jewish national aspirations can be fulfilled in Palestine is conditioned by the rights of the present inhabitants."

But the fear that Palestine will eventually become a Jewish political state persists, whether or not it is the result of agitation, and, says *The Christian Science Monitor*, "it is just this threatened process of absorption which the Arab is determined to resist." Syrians, Mohammedans, Christians, and even Jews, loudly protest against the consummation of the plan, declares *The Christian Observer* (Presbyterian). "All parties alike are antagonistic to the Zionist movement, which aims at the settlement of Palestine with a class of Jews, either extremely poor or extremely devout," in neither case "desirable material from which to build up a new commonwealth. . . . Thus 'the mills of the gods grind slowly,' and we can only stand by and study with absorbed interest the slow unfolding of the roll of destiny as regards the Holy Land and the promises of the Book concerning it."

PROTESTANT GROWTH IN FRANCE

SURVIVING THE AGE-LONG RELIGIOUS WARS, Protestantism in France is to-day declared to be in a flourishing condition, according to the first complete report to reach this country since the armistice, and there are said to be factors in its growth which indicate that its roots have withstood all efforts to weed them out and are at last firmly established in the soil. Protestantism had its beginning in France in the early part of the sixteenth century under the Huguenots, and, in spite of continued and violent conflict, received so many converts that in 1561 there were 2,150 Reformed churches. But, at length, the sanguinary outbreaks against the new faith culminated in the tragic "Massacre of St. Bartholomew's Day," which is branded with other persecutions as "odious" by The Catholic Encyclopedia. These had their effect, and in the early part of the seventeenth century the Huguenots, who had once formed a tenth of the population, were reduced to a few hundred thousands. In 1802, according to The Encyclopedia Britannica, there were left only 121 pastors and 171 churches; in Paris there was only a single church with a single pastor. The Church had no faculty or theology, no schools, no Bible societies, no asylums, no orphanages, no religious literature. Now, according to the Statesman's Year Book, there are about 1,000,000 Protestants in France, and a comparative study of the report contained in the *Agenda-Annuaire Protestant* for 1921 with the report of 1918, writes Reginald L. McAll in *The Intelligencer* (Reformed Church), reveals some additional interesting facts. Excluding Alsace-Lorraine, there are, according to Mr. McAll's summary, 840 ordained ministers, as compared with 872 on the list of 1918, a decrease explained by the fact that more than one-half of the ministers were mobilized, many of them never to return to their work. In this figure are represented seven denominations, of which the two branches of the Reformed Church number together 644 clergy. The Lutherans have 73, Eglise Libre (Free Church), 42; Evangelical Methodists, 28; Baptists, 28, and various independent churches, 15. In addition, there are ten French pastors working under the American Methodist Episcopal Church. In their home missionary work these churches maintain, or assist in supporting, more than 550 preaching stations, annexes or Sunday schools, which possess their own buildings. Many of these are under the control of the Société Centrale Evangelique and the Mission Populaire, while the Geneva Evangelical Society and the British and Foreign Bible Society furnish many lay helpers and colporteurs for evangelistic work. The return of Alsace-Lorraine restores to France a large number of Protestants, chiefly Lutherans. Among them are 209 ministers, who serve 265 churches. The vitality of all these churches is exprest, we are informed:

"Firstly, in the variety and extent of their Christian philanthropy and social service. They support 53 hospitals and general asylums, including the well-known Asiles John-Bost at Laforce, established in 1848. Local charities and mutual aid societies exist all over the country. Thirty orphanages care for girls and nineteen for boys. Some of the twenty-four institutional plants for special work are noteworthy. One hundred Patronages serve as social centers and homes for children and young men and women.

Several agencies have developed for sending young people and children to the country in the summer, and permanent country homes are being purchased by the Mission Populaire. . . . There are about sixty Protestant schools, and the number is increasing. The two most important theological faculties of Paris and Montpelier report a shortage of students. Many French pastors, however, come from the five Protestant seminaries in Switzerland.

"The foreign missionary activity of French Protestants gives further evidence of their vitality. In the French West Africa colonies, for which they are entirely responsible, there are 179 French missionaries, both men and women. In 1918 the number was 185. This is in the proportion of one missionary for every five pastors at home. The corresponding ratio for the year 1918 in the United States was one to sixteen.

"The record is the more remarkable when it is remembered that most of the French churches are small, and weak financially.

"Yet we find that in 1918 the French churches gave for foreign missions 16.5 per cent. of all the money they raised. At that time American Protestants gave about 8.3 per cent. for their foreign work, or about one-half the proportion raised in France. While the financial data for 1920 is not at hand, we certainly have far to go to equal the sacrifices being made to-day by French Protestants to spread the Gospel in their own mission fields. . . .

"But most important of all, the *Agenda* indicates that the vigor of French Protestantism is due to the spiritual fidelity and intellectual integrity of its leaders. While using institutional methods with great skill, they allow nothing to obscure their first aim, that of saving souls. They have fire, they preach the faith once delivered to the saints, and they are reaching the unchurched masses of the French people."

ZIONIST COLONISTS AT WORK IN PALESTINE.

An advance guard of the "massed immigration" feared by the native Arabs.

RELIGION RISING ABOVE GENESIS

UNFETTERED THINKING in theology will not do violence to our religion, asserts that liberal thinker, Dean W. R. Inge, of St. Paul's Cathedral, London, whose own theology apparently has in nowise been shaken by rejection of the accounts in Genesis and acceptance of the theory of evolution. To ascribe only legendary origins to these accounts, he declares in effect, does not impair, but rather strengthens, his belief in God. "The Gloomy Dean," as he is familiarly known in England, is regarded as their arch enemy by evangelists of the old school and by the modern literalists, and he has frequently been challenged in press and pulpit for his open rejection of certain cardinal teachings common to both the Protestant and Catholic branches of the Christian Church. To him this means that there are many persons who think that whatever advances may be made in human knowledge, the teaching of the Church must remain congealed and petrified, forbidden to change in any particular. Yet, he declares, this sort of religion, which is kept in a watertight compartment, which never has interchange of play on secular experience, which leaves its problems of faith and practise to the priest to work out, has proved impotent for the regeneration of society. "The failure of Christainty" has become a commonplace, and he argues in *The Evening Standard* (London) that "it was unable to prevent the World War; it did nothing to prevent the war from being waged with unexampled barbarity; it has had no success in mitigating the bitter antagonism of class against class." Therefore, "something is clearly wrong. We have a great and costly machinery for bringing the Gospel of Christ to bear on the world, and its influence seems to be very small indeed." Now, however, that "materialism and secularism have landed Europe in a terrible disaster," he thinks there is a chance that men will be willing to listen to the religion of Christ —if put before them as a form of practical idealism—as a way of living based on the standard of values found in the New Testament. As things are,

"The enemy of Christianity is secularism—that false standard of values which takes life in the world, the world of the senses, the world of claims and counter-claims, as the ultimate reality. This creed of 'practical men' has proved impracticable; it has brought our civilization to the brink of ruin. We Christians believe that we know the way out; and we wish to see what we believe to be the truth put fairly and simply before our generation.

"We believe that Christianity, as a moral and spiritual revelation, is final; we none of us wish to alter it in any way. But we find that one of the obstacles which prevent it from being accepted is that it is brought before the people mixed up with a great deal of obsolete science. A few centuries ago it was thought that we must choose between Christ and Galileo. Fifty years ago it was thought that we must choose between Christ and Darwin."

But every educated man, says the Dean, knows that the main facts of organic evolution are firmly established, and that they are very different from the legends borrowed by the ancient Hebrews from the Babylonians. These stories, he asserts, "are no part of the Christian religion; they are not part of religion at all." Nor have the discoveries of science "diminished the awe and reverence which we owe to the Creator of the universe." Similarly "our faith can hold its own without difficulty in the field of philosophy. It is practical, not theoretical, materialism which is the danger, and those who are affected by it are not scientists, critics, or philosophers, but people of a very different stamp." And here Dr. Inge asserts his belief that in the field of Christian mysticism "is the region in which immediate certainty of the reality of the spiritual world is attainable." Some "have had moments at least in which they have passed beyond the veil." So,

"The cause of religion must be won on its own field—that of the devout life Religion can be neither proved nor disproved by anything outside itself. It is real to those who live in it; it justifies itself progressively to those who will make the necessary sacrifices in order to find the pearl of great price. All the best modern thought is converging in this direction. In a sense, it makes the attainment of truth more difficult, because 'it takes all there is of us' to win it; but it also makes it much simpler.

"We are not required to do violence to our reason by rejecting the assured results of modern research. It will be a happy day when we feel ourselves free, as indeed we are. Every branch of truth is sacred; every new discovery of the methods of nature is a new revelation of the law of God's world. Truth, Beauty and Goodness are the three attributes under which the Creator is known to us; or, if we prefer it, we may use St. John's words and say that God is Light, Life and Love. In Him is no darkness—no obscurantism—at all.

"Traditional Christianity must be simplified and spiritualized. It is at present encumbered by bad science and caricatured by bad economics, both of them the result of latent materialism. Real Christianity is 'an other-worldly religion,' inasmuch as it 'looks not at the things that are seen, but at the things that are not seen.' But the things that are not seen are the strongest things in the world. We have tried in vain to transform society by trying experiments with the machinery of a secularist civilization. We might as well try to lift ourselves by our boot-laces, as an American said.

"It is other-worldliness which alone can transform the world. This is, in Matthew Arnold's words, the secret and the method of Christ; and the more convinced we are of this, the less disposed we shall be to stake the existence of our faith on superstitions which are the religion of the irreligious and the science of the unscientific."

A DRIVE TO RECRUIT CATHOLIC YOUTH

A VIGOROUS CATHOLIC MOVEMENT is on throughout the world to recruit membership in Catholic Youth societies, which correspond in general aim to the Y. M. C. A., organized under Protestant auspices. Considerably more than a million members were represented, we are told, at the international congress recently held in Rome, where Pope Benedict said that "they are the hope of the Church of the future." Europe, Asia, Africa and North and South America were represented. Even China had a spokesman at the congress. According to the National Catholic Welfare Council News service, which supplies the Catholic papers,

"Reports submitted by the delegates showed that the organization of Catholic young men in Europe had been growing very successfully notwithstanding the social and economic upheavals caused by the World War. In Austria there are 600 young men's organizations with 300,000 members. Belgium has 300 clubs and 10,000 members. There are 86,000 members in the young men's association of Czecho-Slovakia, and 3,162 clubs with 340,000 members in Germany. The French Catholic Juvenile Association had 150,000 members before the war, but this total has been materially reduced.

"Thus far China has no separate organization of young men, but Catholic youth of the Republic are numerous and zealous. Their activities are really part of the general Catholic movement. Spain has a national confederation of Catholic students. Its membership is about 15,000. In Holland both young men and young women are organized. The parochial sections number 25,000 young men and the syndicates of Catholic juvenile workers represent a considerable strength.

"The Brazilian Catholic Union has 3,000 members, but notwithstanding its relative weakness in numbers it has a secretariat, wages campaigns against immoralities of all kinds, conducts spiritual retreats and operates a library. In Switzerland the Catholic youth have a national organization which concerns itself with religious and social questions.

"The Catholic Copts of Egypt are but a small minority, yet an association for young men has been formed and is doing good work. Its membership is recruited from among the youth of the various nationalities belonging to the several oriental rites represented in the Catholic household of Egypt. The Catholic young men of Jugo-Slavia have been gathered into a strong organization and are showing initiative and energy in defending their Christian patrimony from their enemies."

MADE BY THE MAKERS OF CAMPBELL'S SOUPS

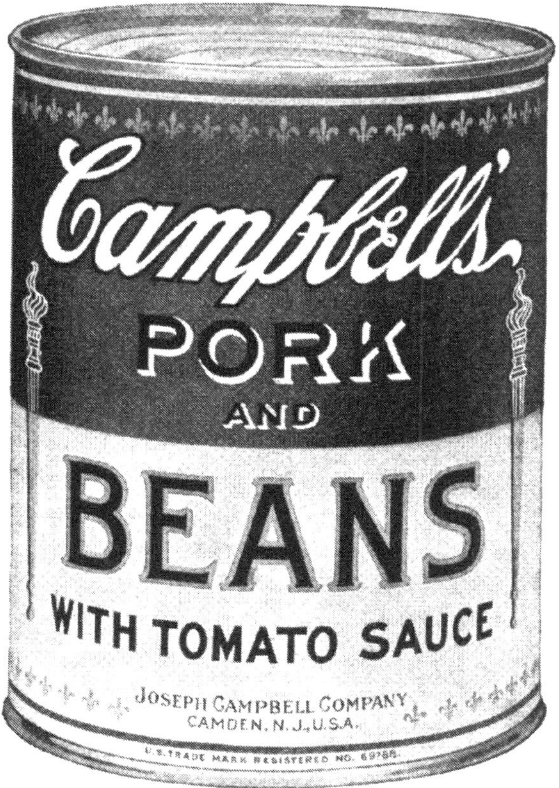

Why are they slow-cooked?

Because this makes them wholesome and easy to digest. The real enjoyment you get from eating them is all the greater because you know that they will agree with you. Campbell's Beans are so thoroughly cooked that they are spendidly beneficial food for every member of the family, from the kiddies up. And how good they taste!

12 cents a can

Except in Rocky Mountain States and in Canada

Campbell's BEANS

LOOK FOR THE RED-AND-WHITE LABEL

CURRENT - POETRY

Unsolicited contributions to this department cannot be returned.

POEMS that express an emotion or a thought are frequent, but we do not often find one that defines a philosophy of living. Such a rarity appears in the London *Westminster Gazette*, and it possesses the added charm of suggesting the affection between France and England that persists despite all political bickerings. As to its philosophy of living, what could be more reasonable and attractive than "to have a temperance of goods and gold," "to love a woman," and "to live with justice, vision, and no hate."

LE PETIT MANOIR

By Viola Garvin

"Avoir une maison . . ."

To have a house, clean, comfortable and sweet,
Where France's shoulder—if it so might be—
Naked and snowy woos the Channel sea,
Fringed with sea pinks where chalk and clover meet—
To have a house, clean, comfortable and sweet,

To cultivate our garden, with a prayer,
To say, when autumn mellows the red wall,
"This is September; this is best of all."
Spring brought a fever, summer many a tear—
To cultivate our garden, with a prayer.

To have good wine, ripe fruit, a table spread—
To hook the shutter back at noon and say,
"I can see England—I smell rain to-day,"
And coffee freshly ground, and baking bread—
To have good wine, ripe fruit, a table spread.

To have a temperance of goods and gold,
To pass the window, and look in and see
The other waiting where one used to be
Alone; and asking if the tale were told—
To have a temperance of goods and gold.

To love a woman. Tranquil and serene,
To take her hand, and to forget a span
The old, long loneliness that shadows man;
With no waste word of what might once have been—
To love a woman. Tranquil and serene.

To live with justice, vision, and no hate,
See without looking; See—but not without
Giving slow judgment clemency's last doubt,
Knowing too well the tyranny of fate—
To live with justice, vision, and no hate.

To wait for death with patience and content,
To sleep eternally; nor yet to shirk
A reawakening once again to work
If for such hidden purpose we are meant—
To wait for death with patience and content.

THE *Far East* (Tokyo) gives us a view of the lotus flower somewhat different from its common Western attribute as a drug. The writer here says—"The prettiest memory I have of the summer was seeing my little sisters and their cousins dancing in a ring, and singing the 'Lotus Song' in their clear, soft voices."

LOTUS SONG

By B. L. S.

The children gather in a ring;
They swing and sway, and softly sing
About the lovely lotus white
That blooms by day, and dreams by night.

They spread their little arms out wide,
Then meet, with hands held high inside;
And this is what the children sing
When dancing in the lotus ring:

"Opened, opened! What flower has opened?
The lotus flower has opened
Scarce has it bloomed, when, lo! it is closed again.
Closed, closed! What flower has closed?
The lotus flower has closed.
Scarce has it slept, when, lo! it awakens."

WHILE on the subject of Japanese feeling we find in the *Freeman* this little group of lyrics that give us further glimpses into the different feeling of the East and the West.

JAPANESE LYRICS

The Shogun Sanetomo

(Twelfth century.)

(Translated from the Japanese by Madame Yukio Ozaki)

THE UNDERGROUND RIVER

The subterranean river takes its rise,
And flows unseen beneath the hills;
Like this my love; and I indeed am sad
Because I may not tell my love.

HOPING AGAINST HOPE

Sore vexed for being made to wait so long
I would no longer wait for her;
But, even then, that night the Moon alone
Came o'er the summit of the hill.

AUTUMN SADNESS

In autumn evenings, on the plain,
Even the leaves of trees and flowers,
That neither think nor love, are wet with dew.

My eyes are all bedimmed awaiting her,
So that I can not clearly see the moon;
E'en thus my heart o'ershadowed is with gloom
Which can not be dispelled before she comes.

THE EVENING HOUR

The Regent Gokyoku

(Kamakura epoch)

(Translated from the Japanese tanka of thirty-one syllables.)

Thinking of you,
Watching the evening sky where you must be,
If people turn their heads and question me,
What shall my answer be?

SIGHS

Manyoshu

(Written by a lady a thousand years ago when her husband departed to Korea on an Imperial Mission.)

My lord, when tarrying beyond the seas,
You watch the mists arise,
Know that in them I sadly send to thee
My breath of sighs.

FROM a Rugby schoolboy comes this through the columns of the *Morning Post* (London). The classics become humanized by English schoolboys in a way rather outside our experience:

HERO AND LEANDER

By J. T. G. Macleod

All the long night a-weary of thought she kept
Her storm-swung vigil, lingering there alone
With open eyes that watched, but had not wept
These many hours, for doubt of the unknown;
Filled with faint fears that could not speak, and tears
That would not fall, and with soft hope that soon
Leander's lips would kiss away her fears,
She stood, a moonbeam paler than the moon.

Beneath her window, in a bed of scent
From the bruised cyclamen, Leander lay,
While gentle ripples, rocking penitent
For cruel strife that tossed his soul away
Lulled him to his long sleep. Above, moonbeams
Strewed love upon pale Hero as she slept
Calm now, no dread to purple all her dreams;
And thus his tryst her tired Leander kept.

THE note of the exile, whether merely expatriate or absentee doesn't matter, is poignantly sounded in these lines from the New York *Times*. Ireland's woes divorced from politics can touch all.

IN THE TENDER IRISH WEATHER

By Lillian Middleton

Oh! the calm, brown mountain and the endless miles of heather,
And the rugged, grave horizon where the white clouds roll;
And my cheek against the soft cheek of the tender Irish weather,
And in all the space around me not a soul—not a soul!

There the skylark and the blackbird and the linnet sing together,
With ne'er a one to still them nor human voice to speak—
Oh! 'tis long since I have lulled me in the tender Irish weather,
And my heart is hot within me for the touch of her cheek!

But they say that on the mountain where I've lain among the heather,
With the plover's note a-mourning thro' the haze of blue,
That the cold and dead are lying in the soft cheeked Irish weather,
And oh! my heart is breaking for the mountain that I knew!

THIS poem in the New York *Times* is a little homily for to-day, but the lesson is implied not exprest. It shows the outside and the inside of one's consciousness dealing with the question of work and no work, and many, alas, will respond to it:

UNEMPLOYED!

By Florence Van Cleve

Only last week he viewed the Hopeless Ones
With pity in his heart for such as they—
Pity and scorn—for surely (so he mused)
There must be, at the bottom, reason for it;
Surely no able man need want for work:
The World cries out for hands to do her tasks—
For brains to solve the problems facing her;
The War's grim wreckage must be cleared away;
The starving nations look to us for food;
Two blades of wheat must grow in place of one:
So much—so much to do!
And yet today
He looks around him with bewildered eyes,
For he is one of these! They recognize
His kinship by his furtive, frightened air;
Self-confidence is gone—he fears the worst!

How empty seem the streets he used to know
Alive with workers on their daily march!
Last week he stepped out boldly with the rest,
Ready to meet his fellows with a smile;
But now he shuns them—goes his doubting way
Down unfrequented streets, afraid lest one
Should ask him "what he does there at that hour."
Last week the Universe was on his side;
But now each human face looks sinister;
Cosmos is Chaos; he is Unemployed!

How the Right Shoes Increased Her Sales

A true story with a lesson for all men and women

"MISS GREEN, you and eight other girls out of seven hundred have shown increased sales during the last three months. All the others show losses. Why have you been able to increase your sales?"

"Who are the eight girls?" asked the young woman.

The president of the store read the names. The girl seemed happy to answer:

"Shoes—Cantilever Shoes. I got them first. Later I took each of those girls, in turn, to the Cantilever Shop. In Cantilevers, you see, our minds are off our feet. The business gets all our attention. We don't feel cross, cranky or tired. I suppose that's why our sales are good."

That afternoon the president of the big store walked into the Cantilever Shop and asked a salesman to explain the features of Cantilever Shoes.

The Cantilever salesman took a shoe and bent the sole at the shank, showing how the shoe conforms to the human foot, even to having a flexible arch like the foot. He said, "the arch of the foot should flex with every step, according to nature, yet ordinary shoes are made rigid by a concealed metal shank-piece that forbids free movement of the muscles. There is no rigid shank in Cantilevers. The 'waist' is designed to hug the instep, the shoe fits and supports the arch restfully. The flexibility allows the arch muscles free play and this, together with the natural lines of the shoe, permits perfect circulation.

"It is important to allow the foot muscles to exercise, to keep well and strong. The forepart of a Cantilever Shoe is shaped to look well, while allowing the toes to lie in their normal position. Cantilever heels are moderately high—high enough to be smart, without throwing the posture of the body out of balance as exaggerated heels do, causing unnatural pressure and strain on the nerves and the internal organs. By wearing Cantilever Shoes a woman avoids headaches and backaches, irritability and nervousness. She is brighter and happier."

"The subject is of great importance to the business woman who is required to stand during the greater part of the working period. The tired feeling often complained of at the end of the day's work may be attributed to ill-fitting shoes.
—Dr. Wilmer Krusen, head of the Department of Public Health of Philadelphia.

"Pain is a great foe to good looks. Comfort works just the other way. If you are comfortable, you are apt to be pleasant, and pleasantness and prettiness are often synonymous terms. Eliminate as many of your worries as you conveniently can—and your tight shoes."
—Grace Margaret Gould on "Good Looks" in *Woman's Home Companion*.

"Working women are the worst offenders. It is the girls who are on their feet most who persists in wearing the highest heels. Sensible women have learned that they can increase their efficiency and even earn bigger salaries by wearing shoes built for solid comfort and health."
—Dr. Evangeline W. Young of Boston.

If no dealer listed at the right is near you, the Manufacturers, MORSE & BURT CO., No. 1 Carlton Avenue, Brooklyn, N. Y., will mail you the Cantilever Shoe Booklet and the address of a nearby dealer.

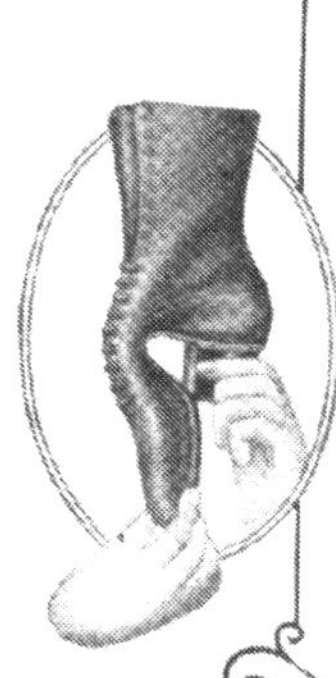

Cantilever Stores

Akron—11 Orpheum Arcade
Altoona—Beudheim's, 1302—11th Ave.
Asbury Park—Best Shoe Co.
Asheville—Anthony Bros.
Atlanta—Carlton Shoe & Clo. Co.
Austin—Carl H. Mueller
Baltimore—325 No. Charles St.
Battle Creek—Bahlman's Bootery
Bay City—D. Bendall Co.
Birmingham—219 North 19th St.
Boston—Jordan Marsh Co.
Bridgeport—W. K. Mollan
Brooklyn—414 Fulton St.
Buffalo—639 Main St.
Butte—Hubert Shoe Co.
Charleston—J. F. Condon & Sons
Chicago—30 E. Randolph St., Room 502
Cincinnati—The McAlpin Co.
Cleveland—Graner-Powers, 1274 Euclid Av.
Colorado Springs—M. B. Rich Shoe Co.
Columbia, S. C.—Watson Shoe Co.
Columbus, Miss.—Simon Loeb's
Columbus, O.—The Union
Dallas—Leon Kahn Shoe Co.
Davenport—R. M. Neustadt & Sons
Dayton—The Rike-Kumler Co.
Denver—A. T. Lewis & Son
Des Moines—W. L. White Shoe Co.
Detroit—T. J. Jackson, 41 E. Adams Ave.
Easton—H. Mayer, 427 Northampton St.
Elizabeth—Gigl's, 1053 Elizabeth Ave.
Elmira—C. W. O'Shea
El Paso—Popular Dry Goods Co.
Erie—Weschler Co., 910 State St.
Evanston—North Shore Bootery
Fitchburg—Wm. C. Goodwin
Fort Dodge—Schill & Habenicht
Galveston—Fellman's
Grand Rapids—Herpolsheimer Co.
Greenville, S. C.—Pollocks'
Harrisburg—Orner's, 24 No. 3d St.
Hartford—86 Pratt St.
Houston—Clayton's, 803 Main St.
Huntington, W. Va.—McMahon-Diehl Co.
Indianapolis—L. S. Ayres & Co.
Jackson, Mich.—Palmer Co.
Jacksonville—Golden's Bootery
Jersey City—Bennett's, 411 Central Ave.
Johnstown, Pa.—Zang's
Kansas City, Kan.—Nelson Shoe Co.
Kansas City, Mo.—Jones Store Co.
Knoxville—Spence Shoe Co.
Lancaster—Frey's, 3 E. King St.
Lansing—F. N. Arbaugh Co.
Lawrence, Mass.—G. H. Woodman
Lincoln—Mayer Bros. Co.
Little Rock—Poe Shoe Co., 302 Main St.
Los Angeles—505 New Pantages Bldg.
Louisville—Boston Shoe Co.
Lowell—The Bon Marche
Macon—The Dannenberg Co.
McKeesport—Wm. F. Sullivan
Meridian—Winner, Klein & Co.
Milwaukee—Brouwer Shoe Co.
Minneapolis—21 Eighth St., South
Missoula—Missoula Merc. Co.
Mobile—Level Best Shoe Store
Montgomery—Campbell Shoe Co.
Morristown—G. W. Melick
Muncie—Miller's, 311 So. Walnut St.
Nashville—J. A. Meadors & Sons
Newark—897 Broad St. (Opp. City Hall)
New Britain—Sloan Bros.
New Haven—153 Court St. (2d floor)
New Rochelle—Ware's
New York—22 West 39th St.
Norfolk—Ames & Brownley
Oklahoma City—The Boot Shop
Omaha—1708 Howard St.
Pasadena—Morse-Heckman Co.
Passaic—Kroll's, 37 Lexington Ave.
Pawtucket—Evans & Young
Philadelphia—1300 Walnut St.
Pittsburgh—The Rosenbaum Co.
Pittsfield—Fahey's, 234 North St.
Plainfield—M. C. Van Arsdale
Portland, Me.—Palmer Shoe Co.
Portland, Ore.—353 Alder St.
Poughkeepsie—Louis Schonberger
Providence—The Boston Store
Raleigh—Walk-Over Boot Shop
Reading—S. S. Schweriner
Richmond, Va.—S. Sycle, 11 W. Broad
Rochester—148 East Ave.
Rockford—D. J. Stewart & Co.
Rock Island—Boston Shoe Co.
Saginaw—Goeschel-Brater Co.
St. Louis—516 Arcade Bldg., (Opp. P. O.)
Salt Lake City—Walker Bros. Co.
San Antonio—Guarantee Shoe Co.
San Diego—The Marston Co.
San Francisco—Phelan Bldg. (Arcade)
San Jose—Hoff & Kayser
Santa Barbara—Smith's Bootery
Savannah—Globe Shoe Co.
Schenectady—Patton & Hall
Seattle—Baxter & Baxter
Shreveport—Phelps Shoe Co.
Sioux City—The Pelletier Co.
Sioux Falls—The Bee Hive
South Bend—Ellsworth Store
Spokane—The Crescent
Springfield, Ill.—A. W. Klaholt
Springfield, Mass.—Forbes & Wallace
Stamford—L. Spelke & Son
Syracuse—136 S. Salina St.
Tacoma—Fidelity Building (8th floor)
Tampa—Glenn's, 507 Franklin St.
Terre Haute—Otto C. Hornung
Toledo—LaSalle & Koch Co.
Trenton—H. M. Voorhees & Bro.
Troy—W. H. Frear & Co.
Tulsa—Lyons' Shoe Store
Vancouver—Hudson's Bay Co.
Waco—Davis-Smith Booterie
Walla Walla—Gardner & Co.
Washington—1319 F. Street
Waterbury—Reid & Hughes Co.
Wheeling—Geo. R. Taylor Co.
Wichita—Rorabaugh's
Wilkes-Barre—M. F. Murray
Winston-Salem—Clark-Westbrook Co.
Worcester—J. C. MacInnes Co.
Yakima—Kohls Shoe Co.
Yonkers—Louis Klein, 22 Main St.
York—The Bon Ton
Youngstown—B. McManus Co.

NEW SIDE LIGHTS ON T. R.

"POSTERITY WILL KNOW ROOSEVELT more completely than it will know any of his predecessors," predicts President Harding in a letter to the Roosevelt Memorial Association, quoted in one of the numerous articles inspired by the ex-President's birthday, on October 27. Lately the newspapers have taken up the campaign, and "the Colonel has been back on the front page again," observes Hermann Hagedorn, writing in *Leslie's Weekly*, "thus revealing even in death the characteristic resiliency." Two new Roosevelt volumes reenforce the magazine and newspaper comment. One of them, "My Brother, Theodore Roosevelt," by Corinne Roosevelt Robinson (Scribners), has been running in *Scribner's Magazine*. "Almost confidential personal recollections," Mrs. Robinson calls her book. The other, "Roosevelt the Happy Warrior," by Bradley Gilman (Little Brown) is described as "a biography, written *con amore* by a Harvard classmate, that is full of illuminating anecdotes and memories of this great American." Mr. Gilman, by consultation with a number of men who were acquainted with the young Roosevelt during his college course, has collected much new material, dealing with the beginning of the future President's career. In those college days of '76-'80, Roosevelt, says his latest biographer, "had all the mental and physical energy and less sophistication than he acquired, inevitably, afterward." The writer goes on to present some of the little illustrative incidents that are liberally scattered through his narrative:

Photo from "Roosevelt, the Happy Warrior," (Little Brown).

IN HIS SIDE-WHISKERED PERIOD.

Members of a Harvard Dining Club which Roosevelt, the only youth shown with whiskers, enlivened during his "salad days." He lacked sophistication, says his latest biographer, but he had "pep" to spare.

In our classroom, in our lecture hours, it was not often that any student broke in upon the smoothly flowing current of the professorial address. But Roosevelt did this again and again, naively, with the evident aim of getting at the more detailed truth of the subject. One of my classmates, who was in his section of Political Economy (Pol. Econ., for short) writes me that he recalls Roosevelt's pushing questions at the instructor, and even debating points with him. This novel action made Roosevelt a subject of wonder and comment. Free Trade was the undergraduate fetich, at Harvard, at that epoch, and probably was the topic most debated.

Another letter from another classmate goes more in detail. I quote from the letter, literally: "I recall an incident in one of the classes when the instructor, Professor D——, a much beloved man, was discussing the differences between curly-haired races and those with straight hair. The opinion was presented by him that straight-haired races greatly excelled. Whereupon Roosevelt—you remember he had brown curly hair—arose and declared very forcibly, that he did not agree with the instructor. At once the whole section 'Wooded up', with much laughter. And Professor D—— joined in it. Roosevelt was by no means dismayed, but, now with his smile, stuck to his point. 'I'm right in my view, just the same.' Then he sat down."

From a classmate's letter I quote: "I was with Roosevelt in Rhetoric section. Just who the instructor was I can not say. But I remember that it was always difficult to get any definite statement out of him, on any subject. One day Roosevelt tried. I remember distinctly his vain efforts to get 'Yes' or 'No' in reply to his question. Perhaps so brief a reply could not have been given. At any rate, Roosevelt did not get it. And I recall distinctly his characteristic and unconcealed gesture of impatience and disgust as he settled back in his seat."

From another source I have an illustration of the same unquenchable spirit. Roosevelt engaged in a public debate at the Harvard Union, then situated on Main Street, near Central Square. What the topic of debate was I do not know. But Roosevelt's side lost, as adjudged by the referee committee. He acquiesced cheerfully in their decision, and at the close of the meeting, going up to the two opponents and shaking hands cordially, he congratulated them on their good work. Then he added firmly, "But we had the right of the question, for all that."

Roosevelt was always, it appears, what might be called "a hearty eater." "Two helpings," we are told, were usually called for and consumed. The writer goes on, with increasing intimacy:

When he received his portion, he was accustomed to retain his spectacles and prepare it carefully on his plate. When prepared, he took off his glasses and devoted himself pretty exclusively to eating. He seemed to be keeping up a line of absorbed thought as he ate. As one of this group told me, "He did not seem to enjoy eating very much, but ate as we might stoke a furnace—because it must be done. He did not live to eat, but he ate to live." He seemed to have a deliberate purpose in this matter of eating, as he did in nearly all his acts. Many years afterward, when he was starting upon what looked like an exhausting political campaign, he said—in sketching his plans to a former college classmate—"And I'm going to eat. If a man doesn't eat, he can't work."

At times, in the intimate little dining club, he put on his glasses and joined in some discussion, not frequently, but always with vigor. Apropos of his office as peacemaker, I recall the account given of another attempt of his to quiet a noisy group. One evening he and several friends went to a theater in Boston. After the performance they drifted into "Ober's"—a somewhat promiscuous restaurant just back of Washington Street, near Winter Street. Here "all sorts and conditions" of men—and women—and drink—were to be found. Roosevelt's group became somewhat heated and enthusiastic and demonstrative. There was no saying what the climax might have been. Suddenly Roosevelt leaped upon a table and, gesturing vigorously, cried out above the din, "I say, fellows, let's not go too far! We mustn't carry this thing too far. We've about reached the limit, fellows. Let's get out!"

Somebody bigger and stronger than himself promptly pulled him off the table, amid a roar of good-natured laughter. And he and his noisy companions soon started for the sequestered academic groves of Cambridge.

There was never any danger to his reputation as a vigorous, virile fellow in his doing a thing of that sort. His game qualities in sparring and wrestling and in debate were too well known for that. As one man who had sparred and wrestled with him frequently said to me recently, "He was such a fair-minded fellow. Open, square, generous, an awfully fierce fighter, but always a good sport."

Altogether Roosevelt, in his college days, took his place as a

His story, in his own words, is printed in the free book offered below, "Increasing Your Output and Income."

Corona helped him to success

Send for the free booklet that tells how Corona can increase your output and income

HIS name is Harry Botsford; he is editor of The Dodge Idea, and publicity advisor to five corporations besides.

He came back from the war to find his business position gone and so he journeyed out to the oil fields.

"I had always been a reader of magazines," he writes, "and one day while I was hard at work, the BIG IDEA came—why not rent a typewriter and see if I could write some articles and sell them?

"I managed to rent an old-fashioned typewriter and carried it three miles on my back. By the time I got to the house, I will swear that machine weighed a ton! Then and there, I quietly registered a vow that I would buy one of those 6½ pound Corona typewriters I had heard so much about.

More income in the evening than he earned during the day

"Every night, tired and weary physically, I put in two hours before that typewriter, trying to write salable articles. Fortune indeed smiled, for my first attempt was accepted by a small trade paper.

"At the end of the first two months, I checked up on my income and found to my joy that the two hours I had put in each night had netted me more money than had the eight and a half hours at heart-breaking labor.

Finish his story in this free book

The rest of the story—just how he moved forward in income, step by step, how he has travelled all over the country with faithful little Corona, is told in a free booklet entitled "Increasing Your Output and Income."

The book tells also the stories of many other men and women, in all sorts of businesses, who have found Corona a faithful little private secretary and are doing more and better work with its help.

There is a copy of the book *free* for every reader of this magazine. It will be sent by mail without obligation; merely fill in the coupon and mail.

"Fold it up—take it with you—typewrite anywhere"

The Personal Writing Machine

TRADE MARK

Built by CORONA TYPEWRITER COMPANY, Inc., Groton, N.Y.

There are more than 1000 Corona Dealers and Service Stations in the United States

You need not put off owning your own Corona—for its total cost (including the case) is only $50—and you can buy it on easy payments.

CORONA TYPEWRITER COMPANY, Inc.,
105 Main St., Groton, New York

Without obligation to me, please send by mail your free booklet No. 5, entitled "Increasing Your Output and Income."

Name ....

Address ....

....

PERSONAL GLIMPSES
Continued

somewhat unique personality. The normal conventional kind of man could not make him out, but respected and wondered at him. Whether he would turn out a crank or a leader of some new order stood a puzzling question. William Roscoe Thayer, Harvard '81, speaks of sitting with Roosevelt on the window-seat of a room in Holworthy, and chatting about what they intended to do after their college course. "I'm going to try to help the cause of better government in New York City," declared Roosevelt, "altho I don't know exactly how." And Thayer comments, "I looked at him inquiringly and wondered whether he was the real thing or only a bundle of eccentricities." Results have shown that he was indeed "the real thing."

Again and again his classmates have been asked, "Did you see signs in him, in those days, of the greatness which he afterward showed?" I do not find anybody except Charles G. Washburn, of our class, who quite asserts that he saw greatness in Roosevelt in college. Washburn was one of the original eight members of a dining club which included Roosevelt, and had opportunities to know him well. A few years ago he wrote an excellent and discriminating book about his classmate whom he profoundly admired. In it he says, "It became evident very early that Roosevelt was a person *sui generis*, and not to be judged by ordinary standards. Very early in our college life I came to believe in his star of destiny."

I have implied, perhaps, in my recital of his outspokenness in the classroom, that he was not unduly sensitive and shy. The whole truth of the matter is that he was really shy, but he persistently struggled, in this field as in so many others, to overcome a natural defect which he saw tended to hamper him in whatever work he might engage in. There are several pieces of evidence pointing to this conclusion. To any person who saw and heard him frequently, in his later public life, as he made speeches and gave addresses, countless in number, it might have seemed as if he had never known shyness or stage fright.

One incident which reveals his undergraduate shyness and sensitiveness has been given me by one of the participants in the scene. It appears that a committee of three students presented themselves before President Eliot, to state some grievance. Roosevelt was to be the spokesman. The president entered the room. No American citizen whom I have ever known, and no European royalty whom I have ever seen, equaled him in dignity and majesty of mein. And when Roosevelt confronted that dignity and majesty, his "tongue clave to the roof of his mouth"—for the moment only. Then he burst out, "Mr. Eliot, I am President Roosevelt—" which confused him still more, and for several moments he could say nothing.

All this timidity he triumphed over, in due time. Doctor Edward Everett Hale, a past master in public speaking, was once asked by an eager but shy young man how he could overcome his extreme shyness in public. "Speak every time anybody asks you to," replied the honored author of "The Man Without a Country." And the advice was sound. Roosevelt's experience in New York politics took away all his shyness.

In private, he never had any real shyness about talking, altho as a child he had always spoken rapidly, and sometimes, in his eagerness, incoherently. But his difficulty was one of the tongue and larynx, not of the mind and will He could talk, and at times he could refrain from talking. One of my classmates, a most genial, likeable man, has given me an illustration of this from his own experience. Speaking of hunting and other outdoor sports, my friend said: "That was one of the points I held in common with Roosevelt, at college. I liked shooting. And he went, again and again, up into Maine with 'Bill' Sewall, to camp and hunt. Several times Roosevelt asked me to come to his room to talk about some trip I had taken in the woods or along the shore, in search of game. He would ask the most minute questions about the cries and habits of the birds and animals which I had hunted. He cared far more for that side of the subject than I did. But when I had told him all I knew, I recall that he suddenly ceased his questions, took up a book or magazine, and began to read."

During the period when he lived on a ranch, says his biographer, Roosevelt bore his share of the tasks and hardships so willingly and with such persistent endurance that he soon made friends everywhere among the cowboys, even among those who had looked with distrust and contempt at this bespectacled "dude" from the East. This did not prevent several adventures, however, which followed the best tradition of Wild West fiction. The author proceeds to give some instances:

Roosevelt had very little lasting difficulty with the better class of cowboys. They held their elemental moral virtues, as did he, and the two types soon recognized and approved each other. But there were many "bad men" scattered over the new country, and with one or another of these he came into collision. One evening the young Easterner entered a "hotel," fatigued after a hard day's riding. The barroom was the living-room of the resort, and it was well filled with cowboys and cattlemen. He took a seat in a corner, out of the way. But a local bully, the worse for drink, caught sight of his unusual face and figure and made advances. Roosevelt's account of the scene is vivid and very readable. "As soon as he saw me he hailed me as 'Four Eyes,' and said I was going to treat. I joined in the laughter, but made no response. He came over near me and with a gun in each hand used foul language."

Here comes to the rescue—as several times in Roosevelt's life—his experience in boxing. "He was foolish to stand so near and foolish to stand with his heels together, in a very unstable position. He ordered me to get up and treat.

"I rose slowly, remarking, 'Well, if I've got to, I've got to.' Then, looking past him casually, I suddenly struck, quick and hard, with my right on his jaw, then with my left, and again my right. Down he went, his head hit the corner of the bar, and he lay senseless. Whereupon the crowd approved heartily of my action, disarmed him, hustled him out, and put him in a shed."

Only a trained boxer would have noted the "heels too close together." And the "first the right, then the left, and again the right" was the ripe fruit of those athletic days in "the Gym" at Cambridge.

Thus he lived through the robust experiences of his ranch life. He was an

PERSONAL GLIMPSES
Continued

exotic in this land of elemental force, yet there was such a wide reach in his nature that he took the vigorous, rigorous experiences as if born to them. And throughout them all, underneath the outer, exactint routine of the day, he carried on an interior life of which his hardy companions knew little. He wrote and read much, somewhat to their perplexity. If he had done nothing but hold a book and a pen he would have stood condemned in their eyes. But he shared the zest and strain of the hunt and the round-up with them so joyously and efficiently that he commanded their respect. And his frank, warm nature won their affection.

Take that incident—in two parts—which his friend Bill Sewall recounts with artless brevity. It reads like a tale from Plutarch. "While Roosevelt was away on this hunting trip, we heard that a bad man on a nearby ranch had said he would shoot Roosevelt at sight. I told Theodore about it, when he came back. He said, 'Is that so?' Then he rode straight over to the shack where the man lived and told him he had heard that a man intended to shoot him. 'And,' said Theodore, 'I want to know why.' The man was flabbergasted and denied that he had ever said anything of the sort. He said he had been misquoted. The affair passed off pleasantly, and he and Roosevelt were good friends after that."

That is the first half of the story. Here is the second. That same "bad man" lived on the ranch of a Marquis de Mores. And the Marquis, irritated by some fancied slight, sent Roosevelt a letter which hinted at a challenge to a duel. "The challenge did not actually come," explains Sewall, "but Roosevelt expected it. And he said that altho he did not believe in dueling, he would accept it if it came; he would not be bullied. As the person challenged, he said, he had the right to choose the weapons. And he would choose Winchester rifles, at a distance of twelve paces. 'I'm not a very good shot,' he said, 'and I want to be near enough to hit.' The two principals were to 'shoot and keep on advancing—until one or the other was satisfied.'"

It would seem that with Winchesters, at twelve paces, "satisfaction" would soon be reached.

Always Roosevelt had believed in "the square deal," long before he had so formulated the idea, even back in the days of his Sunday-school class when he had rewarded the small boy who had resented the stealing of his marbles. And now, at Medora, when three lawless tramps stole his boat on the river, promptly and tirelessly he set about retribution and recovery. Altho his fellow ranchmen advised him not to undertake a well-nigh hopeless chase, he persisted. With two other men he went down the river a hundred and fifty miles, dangerous in places; and after three days of swift pursuit he overtook the thieves, recovered his property, and brought back the men to serve a term in jail.

These early western experiences helped to identify him with the big and untamed spaces of the West. "It is fitting," writes Le Roy Jeffers, President of the Explorers' Club, in *Leslie's Weekly*, "that the greatest National Memorial to Theodore Roosevelt should be the creation of a National

Park." To quote briefly from his description:

From east to west the proposed Roosevelt-Sequoia Park is seamed with the tremendous canyons of the Kings River and its branches. The unequaled scenery of the park culminates on the crest of the High Sierra, which for seventy miles will form its eastern boundary. Here is Mount Whitney, 14,502 feet, highest of all the peaks in the United States proper; and there are scores of summits all along the range that are but little lower. It is intended that the Roosevelt-Sequoia Park shall comprise about 1,365 square miles.

AFTER KLONDIKE GOLD, WITH JACK LONDON

WITH the "optimism bred of a stomach which could digest scrap iron and a body which flourished on hardships," Jack London was among the first adventurers who led the great gold rush over Chilkoot Pass and into the Klondike field. He was twenty-one and full of the passion for adventure, as Charmian London, his wife, describes him in her remarkable new biography, "The Book of Jack London" (The Century Company). He managed to get together a "grub stake" by a partnership arrangement with his brother-in-law, an elderly man not very well fitted for the hardships of pioneering. He bought "fur-lined coats, fur caps, heavy high boots, thick mittens, and red flannel shirts and underdrawers of the warmest quality—so warm that Jack had to shed his outer garments when packing over Chilkoot Pass, and blossom against the snow a scarlet admiration to Indians and squaws." The brother-in-law turned back, but young London kept on, at the risk of his neck, and made true his father's prophecy that "Jack is going to make a success out of the Klondike—whether he digs it out of the grass roots or not." The young adventurer dug little gold out of the grass roots, but there he found the great dog "Buck," together with the characters and surroundings that appeared in "The Call of the Wild," the solid foundation of his later fame and fortune.

Mrs. London thus tells the story of the latter part of Jack's journey to the land of gold:

Forty-two miles northwest of Juneau they reached the end of their crowded voyage and stretched themselves on the beach at the Indian village of Dyea, a mere cluster of huts above the reach of high tide on the Chilkoot Inlet of Lynn Canal. The party—now swelled to five, for Jack and Captain Shepard (his brother-in-law) had formed a partnership with Fred Thompson, "Jim" Goodman, and one Merritt Sloper—found the beach a shouting bedlam of gold-rushers amid an apparently inextricable dump of ten thousand tons of luggage. Many of the arrivals were like lunatics fully as responsible as newly headless fowl in this scramble into an unpitying frozen land. (It was in this same Lynn Canal, in 1918, that the steamer *Princess Sophia* foundered, with the loss of all

PERSONAL ▾ GLIMPSES

"MARTIAL LAW" AGAINST RAILWAY BANDITS

HIGHWAY ROBBERY, common in the good old days when outlaws rode the roads of Merrie England, has cropped up, in an improved and far more lucrative form, in these contemporary United States. Brigands with guns hold up the mails, and nothing heretofore has seemed to stop them. They operate with equal facility in the heart of what we used to consider the Wild West, or in the wilds of the most populous districts of New York and Chicago. Last year the highwaymen took over $6,000,000, usually without getting themselves into any particular trouble, and lately, 1,000 Marines, "expected to act as a little army to keep the mails from being stolen at will," have been supplied by the War Department, with instructions to "shoot to kill." "The orders given by Secretary Denby to the Marines entrusted with guarding the mails read like a passage from a thriller," observes the Louisville *Times*, quoting a part of the Secretary's order, which reads: "When our men go on guard over the mail, that mail must be delivered or there must be a Marine dead at the post of duty." The editor observes:

BY CRIMINY, THESE MAIL ROBBERIES HAVE GOT TO STOP!
U.S. MAIL

MAIL ROBBERS, BEWARE!

—Knott in the Dallas *News*.

Getting the drop is the crucial thing in stories of banditry on the plains and in the cities. But getting the drop is not the deciding point when the Marines are on guard. For the guards are instructed not to recognize the drop. They are to proceed to shoot, as soon as the robber shows his intentions. They are not to put up their hands in any case. Their duty is to fire, regardless.

Positive knowledge that the Marines will do exactly this should go a long way toward discouraging the nerviest of the bandits. Where two Marines are on guard, death for one or more of the robbers is a foregone conclusion. It will be suicidal for bandits to continue to operate.

Possibly a few will be so desperate as to invite certain death. But in the main the bandit is not looking for translation. He is seeking easy money, not a bullet through the heart. Banditry should soon cease to be a popular sport in all cases where the rifle of the Marine is to be brought into play.

Several Mexican editors, taking the cue from our own newspapers, coyly remind us of the time when America was considerably disturbed by banditry to the south of the border. None of the exploits of the Mexican bad men, they hint, measure up to the bold robberies lately carried off by American highway men in our two largest cities. The calling out of the Marines amounted practically to a declaration of martial law, the Cleveland *News* reminds us, and "when martial law is proclaimed in a city, and Federal troops are ordered into the State to restore order, the taking of such military measures is universally accepted as proof that conditions of extraordinary disorder and danger required resort to the extreme remedy. The country is now given to understand, in the same unequivocal manner, that pillaging of the United States mails throughout the country has grown to an extent constituting a dangerous emergency, and demanding extreme measures." As the Cleveland editor observes:

Mail robberies in recent months have been bold, successful and frequent beyond all precedent. Toledo, Chicago, Milwaukee, Bayonne, N. J., and Detroit furnished astounding instances. In Illinois a few nights ago a gang of mail robbers staged a shocking attack on a train, getting little loot but showing complete contempt for law by dynamiting and burning a mail-car and fighting off attack for nearly an hour. On lower Broadway, in the heart of New York city, mail bandits recently helped themselves to registered packages containing more than a million dollars, and got away scot-free—as the mail robbers usually do. Three postal superintendents have now been suspended in consequence of that startling crime—as to which Postmaster-General Hays confesses himself uncertain "whether it was an inside or outside job."

"When robbers haven't anything else to do they amuse themselves by robbing the mails," observes the Milwaukee *Leader*. The same page of one New York newspaper (November 9), contains an account of the reorganization of the New York Post-Office Department, following the million-dollar robbery in the city, followed by the story of the looting of a New York Central train near Paxton, Illinois. Immediately following this story a dispatch from Minneapolis illustrates the versatility of the modern highwayman. "Three robbers," it reads, "entered the Republic State Bank, drove officials and patrons into the vault, and escaped with $15,000 in cash. They fled in an automobile, kept in readiness by a fourth bandit. A few days later, on November 16, to quote the New York *Tribune*:

Roy Gardner, one of the most notorious and daring mail-train robbers in the country, who in the last nineteen months has committed at least four mail robberies, escaped from guards on trains three times, and from the Federal penitentiary at McNeil Island, Tacoma, Wash., last September, was captured here last night, in another robbery attempt, by a mail clerk who took the pistol away from the robber when ordered to throw up his hands.

Herman Inderlied, of Phoenix, who is six feet two inches tall and weighs 215 pounds, is the clerk who captured the desperado. Inderlied was alone in the mail car, which was attached to an Atchison, Topeka & Santa Fe train in the station due to depart for Los Angeles. Ten minutes before the time of departure Gardner, masked and carrying a pistol, entered the car unobserved by Interlied. The bandit placed his pistol against the clerk's body and ordered him to throw up his hands.

Interlied struck his assailant, took his gun away from him, knocked him down and sat down on him, shouting for help. Marine guards in a nearby mail-car rushed to his aid.

When Gardner was taken to the county jail he gave his name as R. P. Nelson, of Chicago, and warned the Sheriff that he intended to escape.

He admitted his identity to-day when confronted with descriptions sent out at the time of his last escape. He will be sent

GULBRANSEN Player-Piano

(Pronounced Gul-BRAN-sen)

Grandfather—"You sing so much better, Mary, now that we have the Gulbransen for accompaniments."
Mary—"Yes, Dad, you see I don't have to think about playing; Bob does it now."

Many a Woman Has Found Her Voice—thru the Gulbransen

The sweet song of a woman's voice in your home—what joy it would bring! Imagine it growing ever sweeter, with a repertoire that an opera star might envy. It can be, if you wish it.

In thousands of homes the Gulbransen has freed busy women from the drudgery of hand-practicing their accompaniments. It is no trick at all to play one's own accompaniment on the Gulbransen. So every spare moment for music can be devoted to actually singing.

And in the evening, you'll find the head of the house coming home with a new roll or two—keenly enjoying his wife's improving voice. Yes, eager to show improvement in his own playing of the Gulbransen. This famous instrument comes to you with instruction rolls that teach you how to play well.

Nationally Priced

Gulbransen Player-Pianos, three models all playable by hand or by roll, are sold at the same prices to everybody, everywhere in the United States, freight and war tax paid. Price, branded in the back of each instrument at the factory, includes set of Gulbransen instruction rolls and our authoritative book on home entertaining and music study with the Gulbransen.

White House Model $700 - Country Seat Model $600 - Suburban Model $495

GULBRANSEN-DICKINSON CO., CHICAGO

Canadian Distributors: Musical Merchandise Sales Co., 79 Wellington St., West, Toronto

Gulbransen Trade-Mark

Get Our New Book of Player Music—Free

The only book ever published showing the complete range of player-piano music of all kinds. This book is so classified and arranged that it is a guide to musical education for any player-piano owner. Sent free, if you mail us the coupon at the right.

Did you know the wonderful Gulbransen Player action can be installed in any piano (or old player-piano)? Yes, grand or upright. Check coupon for details.

To Gulbransen Owners: Keep your Gulbransen in tune—at least two tunings a year. You'll enjoy it more.

Try the Gulbransen Only Ten Minutes

At our dealer's store you can prove to yourself in ten minutes that the Gulbransen is easy for you to play well—a marvelous instrument—positively fascinating. The coupon below brings you dealer's address and full information.

Check here if you do not own any piano or player-piano. ☐

Check here if you want information about having a new Gulbransen player action installed in your present piano (or player-piano). ☐

Write your name and address in the margin below and mail this to Gulbransen-Dickinson Co., 3230 W. Chicago Ave., Chicago.

to Leavenworth, Kan., to finish serving sentences hanging over him when he escaped.

At the prison to-day Gardner held his hand out to Inderlied and said:

"You haven't got any hard feelings, have you?"

"I've got a wife and child at home," Inderlied replied.

"So have I," responded the prisoner, "and if you had had a gun last night your wife would have been a widow to-day. I never hurt an unarmed man. But next time a gun is stuck against you, you put up your hands—it might not be Roy Gardner behind the gun."

It was announced that Interlied would receive a reward of $7,000 for Gardner's capture. Of this $5,000 is the standing reward offered for the capture of any person attempting to rob the mails, and $2,000 is a special reward offered for Gardner's capture.

Copyrighted by the International Film Service.

CONVICTED OF MAIL ROBBERY.

"Big Tim" Murphy, a Chicago labor leader, has lately been found guilty of complicity in the $100,000 mail robbery which took place at Pullman, Illinois, last summer.

The Philadelphia *Record*, looking at the revival of banditry in a pessimistic frame of mind, observes:

Here we are on the eve of the millennium. We have put away the flowing bowl, out of which it was represented that serpents wriggled. We have closed the saloons, where we were told nine-tenths of the crime originated. And what kind of a time are we having? Murder is at least as rife as ever, and probably more common. The burglary insurance companies have had to raise their rates two or three times on account of the increase in the amount of robberies. And after the Postmaster-General had armed all the men who handle the mails, and encouraged them to shoot, the number of mail robberies has increased until it is necessary to put marines on all mail-cars. What is the matter? Possibly we have taken the wrong road to the millennium.

A less sweeping explanation is given by the Indianapolis *Indiana Daily Times*, which thus follows the history of mail-robbing in this country:

Throughout a long period of years the nation succeeded in protecting its mails from marauders through the prestige of the Government which had been built up in the early days when mails were carried through dangerous territory by pioneers who were as speedy with their weapons and as determined as any of the lawless.

As civilization extended its borders the carrying of the mails became less hazardous and the mail service invited into itself men whose training was less hardy. Concurrently, preparations for the defense for the mails grew less thorough and safety was measured in a way by the reputation the Government had for swiftly punishing those persons who interfered with the post-office functions.

Gradually the post-office authorities and the Federal courts were submerged in the handling of law violations of lesser importance than mail robberies and the popular estimate of their efficiency was weakened.

Ten years ago a criminal hesitated to violate a Federal statute, while he had little compunction about trespassing on State laws. He believed, and had good grounds to believe, that he could not with impunity risk offending the Government. To-day, he knows that there is less likelihood of swift punishment for violation of Federal laws, and in his desperation he is willing to "take a chance" against the Federal authorities as well as those of the States.

The result is a large number of mail robberies which have reached such serious proportions as to justify consideration by the Cabinet of the United States.

United States mails must be protected at all costs.

No longer does it appear that they are exempt from raids merely because they are United States mails.

The situation calls for drastic steps, not only to guard the mails, but also to make it apparent to those who are lawlessly inclined that the United States will never falter in its efforts to bring swift and summary punishment on those who do not respect its insignias.

A writer in the New York *Times*, taking a more general view, observes:

Now we have with us days to match those of the robber barons and of the Dick Turpins and the beady-eyed Bedouins, who lay in wait for the rich caravans from Sarmacand. The recent order of Postmaster-General Hays, which last week placed armed marines in charge of the trucks carrying registered mail, brings back vividly the days of pirates and buccaneers and knights of the road. It is one of the anomalies of this present-day civilization that despite the millions of dollars spent in the policing of a city like New York, a wagon should be held up within the traditional stone's-throw of a police station and more than $1,000,000 worth of securities taken from the care of the drivers by bandits. The mail-wagon robbery of the night of October 24 in the streets of the Metropolis, which has resulted in an offer of $20,000 for the arrest of the four criminals and the issuing of a four-page circular describing the valuable securities taken, was the largest which has been reported in recent years.

Copyrighted by the Keystone View Company

CAPTURED AS HE TRIED TO ROB.

Roy Gardner, who is charged with committing at least four mail robberies in the last nineteen months, succumbed to the bare fists of Herman Inderlied, a mail clerk.

Crime waves of this kind have come and gone, and this one has risen higher, no doubt, because of the general slackness of morals which seems always to come in the wake of war. The same conditions obtain practically in even the more well-ordered parts of Europe, while the situation in some of our Manhattan streets is not unlike that which has overspread darkest Russia. Despite the presence of the uniformed police force, and of detectives innumerable in our large cities, and of nattily upholstered and holstered mounted police in the country, both the Federal Government and private owners are obliged to depend upon their own efforts to keep their trucks from being looted by the modern brigands which infest metropolitan streets and country crossroads.

At a conference last Thursday (November 10), attended by Postmaster Morgan and Chief Inspector W. E. Cochran, the arrangements were made for the safe conduct of mail through the streets of New York in these piping times of peace.

Sixty-five marines from the Brooklyn Navy Yard are now on duty with the mail trucks, and before long at least two hundred will be in this warlike duty. Orders have been given for many steel-clad trucks, which will be heavily armored, enough, at least, to deflect ordinary revolver bullets. These vehicles will supplant the present open-work trucks of loose wire, which resemble circus cages. The new type of truck is to be provided with suitable loopholes, or apertures much like those which were put in the walls of the tanks which used to crawl over the enemy trenches and spread terror and machine-gun bullets on every hand. Within each truck will be a marine armed with rifle, and also with revolver, and as partner he will have a clerk equipped with a sawed-off pump shotgun, which is just about as good at short range as a machine-gun, as far as execution is concerned. On the front seat of the present trucks, as there will be in the armored ones, supposed to be ready next week, will be another armed marine, sitting beside a chauffeur who can also reach for a revolver if he needs it. It is planned to have a steel shield on either side of the seat, which can be brought into use in double-quick time if it is needed.

By this arrangement, remarks the writer, the United States mail will have fairly good protection from the local gunmen and thugs as they go through the streets of the largest stronghold of

STEINWAY

THE INSTRUMENT OF THE IMMORTALS

ON the 26th of March, 1827, died Ludwig van Beethoven, of whom it has been said that he was the greatest of all musicians. A generation later was born the Steinway Piano, which is acknowledged to be the greatest of all pianofortes. What a pity it is that the greatest master could not himself have played upon the greatest instrument—that these two could not have been born together! De Pachmann once said: "If Beethoven could hear his compositions played upon a Steinway, he would not know such beauty for his own. Tears of joy would flow from his eyes and run down his cheeks." Though the Steinway was denied Beethoven, it was here in time for Liszt, for Wagner, for Rubinstein. And today, a still greater Steinway than these great men knew, responds to the touch of Paderewski, Rachmaninoff, Hofmann, and their brilliant contemporaries. Such, in fact, are the fortunes of time, that today this Instrument of the Immortals, this piano more perfect than any Beethoven ever dreamed of, can be possessed and played and cherished not only by the few who are the masters of music, but by the many who are its lovers.

Steinway & Sons and their dealers have made it conveniently possible for music lovers to own a Steinway. Prices: $875 and up, plus freight at points distant from New York.

PERSONAL GLIMPSES
Continued

civilization in the world. The truck will be locked fore and aft, and those within can make a strong defense, at least until the police reserves are attracted by the sound of the firing, or the garrison at Governors Island called on for relief. Other antibandit plans are afoot:

Wall Street is taking heed how it sends its stock certificates, its silver and gold about the city. There are revolvers handy for the employees who escort the securities to the safety deposit vaults. Not long ago when the New York Trust Company transferred its assets to a new office, it used heavy trucks with convoys of armed guards and an escort of police. It is said that sharpshooters were stationed near at hand, to pick off any bandits who might suddenly appear upon the scene. This was not in the war zone, but in the heart of a city declared by the present Administration to be the best governed in the world. Leading banks also have arrangements for releasing tear gas, turning loose machine-guns, or deluging maurauders with hot steam, if the emergency comes. The Subtreasury is under the vigilant watch of armed men, and when its riches are sent out into the world they are attended by expert revolver marksmen mounted on motorcycles.

The companies and firms which belong to the Silk Association of the United States are not taking any chances. They put their bales in heavy trucks, which are provided with steel wire doors at both front and back. Some of these trucks also have steps which can be drawn up and hidden when they are in transit. The drivers and their helpers are armed. They have special permits from the authorities for the carrying of revolvers. As the trucks are driven through city streets, and for the most part along highways which lie through thickly populated regions, they seem to belong to the age of licensed violence rather than to this one of high-pressure civilization. Italy in the time of the Renaissance, when dukes and petty princes were attended by bands of well-groomed murderers, might have produced creaking wains of silken bales which had to be so guarded, but there are police in New Jersey and other States through which such processions pass in these days.

There is a New York and Philadelphia motor-truck express company which has carried the convoy system of transporting valuable goods to a high state of efficiency. Sometimes the large manufacturers, who want to keep their goods safe, send two or even three motor trucks in company. Several manufacturers may even combine to make up a caravan which is in charge of armed guards. The express company in question goes further than that, for it makes up a caravan or train of six or seven heavily laden motor trucks and starts them out to Philadelphia in a procession. It would be a foolhardy bunch of bandits who would essay to capture such an argosy of the land as this, for each driver is well armed. The trucks are of about the same power, and, therefore, can be kept at approximately the same speed. Playing around them, sometimes at the side of the road, and more often bringing up the rear, is a swift runabout in which are several guards armed with plenty of revolvers and a short-barreled shotgun or so for good measure. This caravan, proceeding on its way, either by day or in the watches of the night, has all the appearance of a great baggage train attached to an army.

HOW LIEUTENANT MACREADY KEPT FIT—EIGHT MILES UP.

AT AN altitude of eight miles, which was that attained by Lieutenant Macready in his record-breaking aeroplane flight in September, there is very little oxygen—only about one-fourth the amount at the earth's surface, and the cold is intense. Mere existence in this thin, icy air is a feat, without counting the ascent as a trial of skill. The power of adjustment to these greatly altered conditions, which a record-breaker must have, and which all aviators do not possess, interests medical men especially, we are told in an editorial by *The Journal of the American Medical Association* (Chicago). Without the establishment of "a physiologically endurable environment," which is the fruit of various successful inventions, the most daring and skilful bird-man could not hope to reach altitudes that have now been surmounted, and will ultimately, no doubt, be far surpassed, writes the editor:

To the medically trained who bears in mind the limitations of the human machine at high altitudes, these aeroplane records awaken appreciation of scientific acumen and technical ingenuity in overcoming the handicaps which unaided nature has placed upon man as a flying animal. High altitudes or low barometric pressure are well known to interfere with physiologic functions. What is true of mountain sickness is equally applicable to the other more modern forms of altitude sickness which the balloon and subsequently the aeroplane brought into scientific prominence.

The experts of the Medical Research Laboratory of the War Department's Air Service have pointed out that men differ greatly in their power of adjustment to changes of environment. Hence, it is found that mountain sickness befalls some individuals at a lower, others at a higher altitude; but it is also certain that no one who proceeds beyond a certain elevation—the critical line for him—escapes the malady. An elevation of 10,000 feet, or even less, might provoke it in some; others may escape the symptoms up to 14,000 feet, while only a very few, possest of unusual resisting power, can without much distress venture upward to 19,000 feet. At a height of six miles the content of oxygen in the air has been reduced from approximately 21 per cent. found at sea level to 6 per cent.; at a height of eight miles, reached by Macready, it must be less than 5 per cent. The breathing of an atmosphere containing only 10 per cent. of oxygen, equivalent to an altitude of 19,400 feet, is a venture which only a few possest of unusual resisting power can undertake with any hope of success.

These facts attest the physiologic significance of the devices which have been perfected to supply oxygen successfully in the flights at great altitudes. In addition to the respiratory problems are the perhaps less formidable, but nevertheless immediate needs of conserving body temperature in the cold environment of the higher atmosphere. In this respect, too, the difficulties have been overcome.

REVIEWS - OF - NEW - BOOKS

THE AMORIST IN SPITE OF HIMSELF

WITH its scenes laid partly in the "Black Country"—the English mining district—and partly in the farm lands which lie along the once turbulent Welsh border, Mr. Francis Brett Young's new novel "The Black Diamond" (Dutton, $2.00) portrays several phases of the life of an English laborer. Born on the edge of a colliery, there where: "The pit-mound stands up black, and over beyond the Stour valley a desert of blackness stretches westward, with smokestacks thronging thick as masts of shipping in a harbor," Abner Fellows, the son of a miner, looked forward to becoming a miner himself as a matter of course. Yet he disliked the underground work, and when his football successes brought him the favor of the chief clerk at the nearby iron-works, he was glad enough to leave the mine. But when he refused an offer of ten pounds, a bribe to let the other side win in the next contest, he lost the easy job which had been his and went back to the mine.

He had to go back, for the money he earned was urgently needed. His own mother had died when he was very little, and his father, John Fellows, had married again. The second wife, Alice, was a girl but little older than Abner himself. An accident at the mine sent his father to the hospital, and he was obliged to support Alice and his little half-brother. Trouble soon began. Youth turns toward youth, and Alice found Abner far more companionable than the middle-aged, drunken husband of whom she was more than a little afraid. But their relations were innocent enough, and if Abner had not won a brooch at a shooting match and given it to Alice, everything would have been all right. But John Fellows came home drunk one night, saw the brooch, and put the worst possible interpretation on the affair. In his drunken fury he would have killed Alice if Abner had not knocked him senseless. Then there was nothing for Abner to do but leave his home. He had long been restless; he had fairly ached for liberty, but now: "He did not know which way to turn; he was dazed by the suddenness with which the freedom so long and so patiently awaited had come to him. In the bewilderment of the moment he could scarcely even realize that it was sweet." And he was destined to keep it but a very little while.

After various adventures on the road, Abner got a job at Mainstone, on the Welsh border, where they were putting in water-works. There he met and took an immediate liking to young George Malpas, who offered him a lodging at Wolfpits, the house where he lived with his pretty young wife Mary and their two small children. For a while, Abner was contented. Then he began to spend his evenings with George at the Pound House, a nearby tavern where there was a pretty barmaid, Susie Hind. He also took to poaching, partly for love of excitement, and this and his affair with Susie earned him the enmity of Badger, the gamekeeper. One night, when they were all more or less intoxicated, a drunken Irishman's insults started a fight which ended when George Malpas and the policeman, Bastard, fell to the floor together, Malpas on top. Bastard did not get up again. He had struck his head violently on the stone floor. He was dead.

Malpas was arrested, charged with manslaughter, convicted, and sent to prison. Abner offered to remain at Wolfpits, to care for the young wife Malpas had deceived and neglected, and for the two children. Malpas declared: "By God, you're the only pal I've got that I can trust!"

So for the second time in his life Abner Fellows found himself responsible for another man's family. He did odd jobs about the house, played with the children, and gave Mary all but a few shillings of his wages. And before many weeks had gone by tongues began to wag. George's mother, old Mrs. Malpas, hated Mary, and blamed her for all his shortcomings. She began the gossip, and others quickly took it up, including the vicar and the vicar's wife, who were angry with Mary because she refused to take a position they offered her, and send her children to the workhouse. Things went from bad to worse. Abner lost his job, and when he found another, the daughter of his employer, a farmer, fell in love with him. He cared nothing for her, but one evening she cried, and he kissed her. Those kisses cost him his place. The story regarding himself and George Malpas's wife was common property now, and he was boycotted.

It reached their ears at last, and they realized that there was this much truth in it; they were in love with each other. They planned to run away together, and then, on the very evening they made their plan, word came that George had been released, and would soon be home. It was, Abner thought, "Like a warning!" And so it presently happened that for the second time in his life he stood looking at a man who lay senseless on the floor, and heard a woman sobbing. And for the second time in his life the bonds that had held him to one place were broken, and he went out into the night, alone. "He was conscious of a strange physical lightness, as though a material load had slipped from his shoulders." And again, his freedom did not last long. When we leave him, he is on the verge of being subjected to a new and very different form of discipline. He had wanted to be free; again and again he had felt: "The restlessness with which his spirit was so familiar; the desire that had come over him in fierce gusts ever since the days of his childhood, the will to be free, to cut all coils and launch out into the life to which he had a right. * * * Breaking free from Mawne and reaching out over these hills, he had merely passed from one prison to another." And always, in one way or another," a woman had been at the bottom of his slavery." He was attractive to women; and that attractiveness was his undoing.

The book has in it little of the mystical element one finds in so much of this author's work. It is a little too long, but it is interesting, and its people are real, if not especially likable. Liquor flows freely through its pages, and is the cause of much of the trouble, both in the Black Country where: "Even tho the fires of the furnaces and factories had been banked down for the holidays they could still smell the heat which had scorched and blackened this volcanic country on every side," or out on those Welsh borders where: "With a sudden fervor unknown in more temperate climes, spring came. The sloes were sprayed with light; the hue of hawthorn twigs paled; in the space of a single week the whole earth broke in a green flame."

PURSUED BY ONE'S PAST

IT is hard, when one has made a position for oneself in the business and social world, accumulated a good deal of money and occupies a public position, to have a man turn up who is cognizant of certain actions in one's past that would best be forgotten. Yet that is the situation in which Mr. Cotherstone of Highmarket finds himself when his new tenant, one Kitely, drops in to the office of Mallalieu and Cotherstone, Builders and Contractors, to pay his rent.

For twenty-five years the firm had been doing business in Highmarket and had won the respect of the inhabitants, so much so that Mallalieu is Mayor of the town and Cotherstone is the Borough Treasurer. Their past seemed safely hidden and in no danger of being revealed that afternoon when Mr. Kitely stopped in. Kitely is a retired detective; on first seeing Cotherstone, the face of the contractor had seemed familiar, but it was not until a day or two later that he remembered having seen his landlord thirty years before when he was being tried at the assizes in Wilchester with his present partner for embezzling the funds of a building society of which they were treasurer and secretary. The opportunity for blackmail is too good to be lost; the firm is prosperous, and Cotherstone's only child is engaged to a promising young man; naturally a father would pay heavily to insure his daughter's happiness, and so Kitely suggests to Cotherstone that he and his partner should confer together and make him an offer for his silence. He will come to the office the next day and hear what they have to say. That night, about ten o'clock, Kitely is found dead in the woods near Cotherstone's house, strangled by a piece of cord drawn tightly about his neck.

There is a young barrister staying in the town named Brereton, who becomes interested in the case and devotes himself to the discovery of the murderer. No one knows of the hold Kitely had over Messrs. Mallalieu and Cotherstone, but certain facts that come to light cause Brereton to wonder where those two gentlemen were at the time Kitely was killed. Then the cord is traced to the house of a mysterious character in the neighborhood, named Harborough who, tho he denies any knowledge of the murder, declines to say where he was at that time and is arrested and held for examination. Further suspicion is attached to him by the fact that he was known to have been in the bank when Kitely was drawing out money on the morning of the fatal day, and more than twenty pounds is found upon him after his arrest. Kitely had a queer old housekeeper, Miss Pett, who is examined, and Brereton, who has undertaken to defend Harborough, begins to think there are suspicious circumstances connected with her.

Break down that wall between you and your boy!

That baby whose first smile was directly into your eyes, that toddler who took his first steps with his little hand gripped round your fingers, is he growing away from you?

It is natural that he should outgrow his first complete reliance on your care and love. You and his teachers are constantly urging him to think for himself. More and more he is weighing, judging, making his own conclusions. Each careless rebuff to his natural and spontaneous spirit of investigation cautions him to build a wall of reserve against ridicule. Each misunderstanding of his dreams, his schemes and his enthusiasms builds the wall higher and thicker.

Between the ages of 10 and 20 what boys most need is association with fellows and men of strong character, who understand them and whom they understand. They need to work with them and play with them, seeing the real world as it is, meeting experiences and boy-adventures with them, learning the right way to think and the right way to act.

This is the companionship that more than a half million boys are finding and being developed by in

THE AMERICAN BOY

"The Biggest, Brightest, Best Magazine for Boys in All the World"

It is edited by men who have never lost their understanding of the boy heart. Its stories teach a boy to know himself and trust himself, to understand motives, principles, temptations, to know courage and to use it, to distinguish between the clean and ignoble and to choose the clean, to understand the virtue of unselfishness and to practice it.

Each and every story is written to let boys face a real boy-problem and it teaches them how a regular fellow will meet and solve it. There is nothing preachy about THE AMERICAN BOY. (How boys do hate preaching!) There is nothing namby-pamby or wishy-washy about it. Its articles are instructive, boy-building, man-building, and have an instant power to suggest all that is best and healthiest to a boy.

Each issue is full of sports, as champions play at them; mechanics, that a boy can practice; the great outdoors, which is boyhood's natural element.

Your boy's feet are already on the road leading to somewhere. THE AMERICAN BOY will easily persuade him to walk with you, while he gains the poise and stature of a man.

Right now you are facing the Christmas season. What an opportunity to break down the wall that separates you and your boy. Make him a present of a year's subscription to THE AMERICAN BOY. You'll never make an investment that will pay such large dividends in increased understanding between him and you, nor one that will bring him more hours of genuine enjoyment.

Perhaps there is also some other boy in whom you are interested. Make this a great Christmas for him. Send him THE AMERICAN BOY.

Price Reduced! THE AMERICAN BOY is again $2.00 a year by mail! 20 cents a copy at newsstands. Subscribe for a year, or leave a standing order at your news-dealer's.

THE SPRAGUE PUBLISHING COMPANY
No. 272 American Building, Detroit, Mich.

Enclosed find $2.00, for which send THE AMERICAN BOY for one year, beginning with the Christmas, 1921, number, to

Name..

Address..

REVIEWS OF NEW BOOKS
Continued

It is a case of too many clues, and the barrister realizes that the only way to a solution is to find a motive for the crime. A large reward is offered for the detection of the murderer and, stimulated by this, a clerk of the contractors, who thinks he has got hold of something important, starts upon a tour of inquiry which ultimately discloses to him his employers' secret, but before he has time to take any action he meets with a violent death. Finally Brereton's astuteness reveals the past record of Messrs. Mallalieu and Cotherstone, and they are arrested.

One might think the solution in sight, but the author is above such obvious methods, and there is plenty of incident yet to come. Mallalieu, upon whom suspicion rests most heavily, escapes and his further adventures form the most thrilling part of the book, the climax of which will prove a surprize to many.

"The Borough Treasurer," by J. S. Fletcher (Macmillan $2.00) is a thoroughly enjoyable story and will uphold the author's reputation as one of the best of the present writers of mystery fiction.

IS WAR A BIOLOGICAL NECESSITY?

By virtue of long service as well as on account of his official position during the Great War, Colonel Frederick Palmer is recognized as the dean of American war correspondents. Twenty-four years have elapsed since he had his baptism of fire in accompanying the Greeks during their disastrous war against the Turks in 1897. In the years between that petty war and the outbreak of the Great War he saw thirteen different nations in battle. His "The Last Shot," a work of fiction, depicting with a startlingly prophetic vision the events that so quickly and unexpectedly followed, was published in the spring of 1914. Frederick Palmer did not approve of war then; still less does he like it now. To his mind it is summed up in the title which he gives his new book, the one real book that every human being has in him out of the experiences of life, the "Folly of Nations." (Dodd, Mead & Co. $2.00).

Specious argument may momentarily obscure, but it never can totally hide the great and simple truths. As old as the eternal hills, the folly and absurdity of war are as plain as fires on the hills. War began when Cain killed Abel. Cain probably had preparedness and Abel had not. Or if Cain had not preparedness he struck his brother a foul blow without any preliminary declaration of war. Modern casuistry would call that "outraged national emotion." That affair of Genesis was settled because Abel was killed outright. If Abel had been merely wounded he would have crawled away to some cave and there would have begun his preparations for revenge by the secret invention of a new form of battle-ax. In due course there would have been a new cause for strife and this time, Abel, having achieved preparedness, would have killed Cain. Thereupon Cain's sons would have seen that their father's mistake had been in giving quarter in the first place. In revenge they would have sought to kill Abel's sons, who in turn would have sought to kill Cain's sons, and so on. There you have Colonel Palmer's four hundred odd pages of illuminating argument reduced to a primer. Its strength lies in its simplicity.

It was as a youth in his early twenties that Frederick Palmer first began to see war in its true aspect. He had been the lucky one to whom his editor had said: "Go to Greece for the war," and with visions of the glory of witnessing and describing battle in the fabled land where Leonidas fought and Homer sang, he found himself sitting at a café table in Larissa, the little capital of Thessaly. The beginning of the truth was a tall, gaunt, scarred man, who sat silent and observant amid all the boast and clamor. "I knew," writes Palmer, "that he had been at Plevna, in the Soudan, at Majuba Hill, and in the Chilean and Chino-Japanese wars." A platitudinous Greek deputy was extolling war, promising that even defeat would be a benefit, uniting Greece and rousing the national spirit. Then the Soldier of Fortune spoke, thoughtfully, a trifle didactically, not to any one present, but to the distance, possibly to old Olympus. "There are no good wars. All wars are bad wars." Palmer doubted then. But in the days that followed, with the resourceful old soldier of fortune by his side, and in the agony of the Thessalian plain he learned to doubt no more.

Martially, Colonel Palmer sums up the latter part of the nineteenth century as "McAndrew's Epoch." It was the epoch of little wars, of Kitchener and Cecil Rhodes; of Chamberlain and the Jameson Raid; of the jingo Americans who "spread-eagled" about our destiny to overrun the American continent at least as far as Brazil. Kipling was its singer. His "White Man's Burden" encouraged us to our task in the Philippines. In the Filipino rebellion Palmer was one day writing a dispatch in the shade of a mango tree and contemplating the columns of smoke that marked the advance of the American column. Dismally poking about the smoking ashes of his home was a bent, elderly man. To console him the war correspondent sought to convey to him the national purpose of this sweep of soldiery across the land. Its real name was "benevolent assimilation." "We are here to help you—to bring order and progress," explained Palmer. The old man pointed to the ruins of his home. "Do you call that helping us? Is that progress?" It was the idea of progress of the McAndrew Epoch. Kipling, a genius child, who played about the bazaars in the land where two hundred million natives were ruled by a handful of outlanders, "he pictured in the imagery of the East the 'Arabian Nights' wonder of the white man's increasing mastery of material forces, which spread his dominion over the world. 'Soldiers Three' were our regulars who did our fighting for us. 'McAndrew's Hymn' sang the song of our mechanical power, and the 'Soldiers Three' were the policemen serving ruler McAndrew."

The unthinking man in the street contents himself with the reflection that war "always was and always would be." That saves him the trouble of analysis. The cynical man of learning expresses it differently. He concludes that war is a biological necessity. But Colonel Palmer continually returns to the "Why? of the old Greek shepherd whom he found herding his sheep in the midst of the carnage of Thessaly. Rulers have since the dawn of time been using the creeds of the man in the street and the cynical man of learning to further their ends and ambitions. And to what purpose? The effort to attain national power is praiseworthy. "But," says the

REVIEWS OF NEW BOOKS
Continued

militarist, "we would conserve this power through complete military preparedness." William II. of Germany and Napoleon I. both tried this and they failed. Full preparedness has to deal with one element of human nature that does not change: that which makes common cause of all nations against the nation falling victim to the illusion. Full preparedness may win one war and give a good start in another, but until one nation is strong enough to conquer all other nations it will inevitably lead to eventual defeat.

Above all that is so in these days when bravery is a common attribute supported by the common intelligence of all democracies. In former wars even the best drilled and stoutest infantry unit was expected to break when it had suffered a loss of thirty per cent. In the Great War units stood losses of forty, fifty, and sixty per cent. In all armies the reserve officers from offices and shops were as gallant as the professional officers.

The Folly of Nations was based on the old ideas which the events of the last seven years should have exploded. Once it marched to the cry of a false patriotism. The true patriotism, Colonel Palmer holds, means a willingness to fight, if necessary, for relief from wrongs, and with steel if you must, but preferably to fight with every-day actions in peace. The patriotism which holds that, because you are born of a given nationality, you can lick three men of another nationality should have been given its quietus in the World War. It is ridiculous and cheap boasting, and those who indulge in it most freely do not excel in their fortitude under the fire of modern arms. If you think in this old-fashioned way, keep your thoughts to yourself so as not to encourage your potential enemy to disprove your contention; for if he tries, you may be sure that, as you face your first artillery bombardment, your generals will be calling for the superior numbers which to them still remain the prime essential of victory.

THE PATHETIC EGOIST

BEING an egoist is no easy job. There is a great deal of the sad side of life mixed with the natural pleasure, and the price of egoism, like that of liberty, is eternal vigilance.

In Miss Sinclair's latest novel we meet an egoist and come to know his joys and sorrows with a terrifying intimacy. Merciless she is in her exposure, yet there is the kindness of comprehension in the portrait she draws of "Mr. Waddington of Wyck" (Macmillan, $2.50), and again the truth of the French adage that to know all is to pardon all becomes manifest. To be sure, we laugh at Mr. Waddington, as his wife and his friends laugh at him, but we pity him too, as they also pity.

Mr. Waddington has one passion; to be at all times the center of interest, the most charming, intelligent, powerful personality in his world, forever young, forever to be desired, in a word, IT. Most of the time he is satisfied that he is all this, but at times, horrible times, he doubts. As Miss Sinclair explains, he hated to have you catch him in any gesture that was less than noble. Yet there are moments when no one can be noble, even a Waddington of Wyck. And then. . . .

We sense Mr. Waddington before we

meet him. Miss Sinclair is past master at creating an atmosphere, and in a few swift strokes she sets us in the heart of the Waddington home. An old Tudor house, he refers to it as his "seat" rather than by any other term. His is an old family and the most important in Wyck, all of which is a solemn matter. The things that are not solemn are his wife and his wife's cousin, Ralph, and Barbara—only he does not realize this about Barbara till near the end.

Ralph *was* Mr. Waddington's secretary. Barbara *is* his secretary. Ralph was given to jokes and Mr. Waddington couldn't stand that. Moreover, Ralph tried to write Horatio's book for him. After you get to know Horatio—the whole name is Horatio Bysshe Waddington—you understand about that book.

Barbara has only just come to Lower Wyck Manor, and has not yet met the lord thereof. Mrs. Waddington was an old friend of her mother, but the girl had not met her till she arrived, after the mother's death, to be secretary to Horatio, and companion to Fanny—with the ultimate idea in Fanny's head of adopting the young thing. In the drawing-room, and Fanny, who is herself adorable, had made the room so too, with its tulips in Lowestoft vases, its faded Persian carpet, its air of being lived in, in this room hung Horatio's portrait, revealing him as a large and florid person, handsome, nobly posed, extraordinarily solid, and seemingly absorbed in solemn thought. Barbara stood staring at this portrait, wondering what her host-employer was like, and Fanny finds her staring.

"'Well, what do you think of him?'"

"'I think he's jolly good-looking. . . .' and later, gazing again at the picture, she adds: 'I wonder what he's thinking about?'

"'I used to wonder.'

"'And now you know?'

"'Now I know. . . .'"

Yes, she knew. And Ralph, her cousin, knew. And presently Barbara knows too. It was himself. Always himself; solemnly and wonderfully himself.

In the frame of his family—there is a young son, too—we see Mr. Waddington pursuing the pathway of his life. This inner circle regards him with a kind of rapture. "*What* will he do next?" they ask each other, as he emerges from one great scene or another, unabashed at what to a lesser man would have been humiliating failure or the acme of the ridiculous. For he can shield himself behind that colossal self-satisfaction, can always escape from the world as it were into himself. There was, for instance, The League of Liberty. There is a precious scene where Mr. Waddington, for a few awful moments, fears that Sir John Corbett is going to accept the offered chairmanship of the Committee—offered by himself, to be sure, but only in the sure hope of a refusal, for Sir John is a lazy man. In the end Waddington manages to make Sir John see that a tremendous amount of work is involved in being president of the League, and Sir John utterly refuses, suggesting that Waddington himself—yes, it came out perfectly, and Sir John never even guessed.

To be sure, Sir John was telling Lady Corbett as Waddington disappeared up the drive that "any one could see the fellow wanted it for himself. I put him in an awful funk, pretending I was going to take it," but then, Waddington never saw the reverse side of himself, to express it that way.

The League soon comes to smash, but it

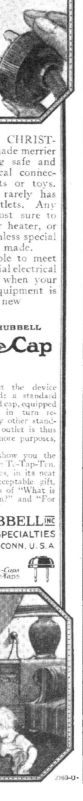

REVIEWS OF NEW BOOKS
Continued

was entirely over the heads of the people, or, as Horatio explained it, "It's a bit too big for 'em. They can't grasp it. Sleepy minds. You can't rouse 'em if they won't be roused."

"He emerged from his defeat with an unbroken sense of intellectual superiority."

There follows the remarkable experience with Mrs. Levitt, ending with her slapping him and calling him an old imbecile. That was hard to turn to his advantage, it was difficult there to come away with the noble gesture intact, but he manages it. As Barbara and Ralph have said all along, he is magnificent.

It is hard to choose between the time when he is taken ill. and lies in bliss while the whole household gyrates about him, and even Sir John calls to inquire every day, and the time when he is photographed for his book. Which is the more gloriously Waddingtonian? They are perhaps merely different, but equal. The illness is a sequence to the photographing, since it seizes upon him after severe exposure in being taken out playing in the snow, a sign of his superb, unshaken youth and vigor, but it is complete in itself. And even as the illness came on through the photographs he had taken of himself, so did his last and finest gesture develop because of the illness. For it is during that that he decides that dear little Barbara is in love with him.

And then indeed things are a bit stiff for Mr. Waddington. He has poured out a great man's devotion at the feet of his "little April girl" and she laughs at him:

"Not Mrs. Levitt's laughter, gross with experience. He had borne that without much pain. Girl's laughter it was, young and innocent and pure, and ten times more cruel.

"'You don't know,' she said, 'you don't know how funny you are,' and left him."

Left him to go to the young Ralph, whom she did love, left him to Fanny, who had seen, who understood—and who felt immensely sorry. As she says afterwards to Barbara:

"'I was *glad*. I thought: If only he could have one real feeling. If only he could care for something or somebody that wasn't himself. . . . I think he cared for you, Barbara. It wasn't just himself. And I loved him for it."

He wanted to be young, handsome, admired. And he was only laughed at. It was that which made Fanny unhappy, even tho she too laughed at him. For one couldn't help it. And tho he carries things off somehow, and saves himself after a fashion, yet deep down he suffers. It is hard work, bitter work to be an egoist in a world full of people who simply will not take anything seriously.

We leave him on his way to his mother. To her he remains young, and has always been perfect. There he will be healed, and come out again, noble in his forgiveness, great once more in the true Waddington manner.

A LONG WINTER

IF A. S. M. Hutchinson's recent novel, "If Winter Comes" (Little, Brown & Co., $2.00) were not so well written, had it depended upon incident instead of character for its interest, it might be cataloged as a hard-luck story. As it is, the history of Mark Sabre is one of the most poignant in recent fiction, only endurable to the keenly sympathetic reader because of the promise held out in the title. "If Winter comes, can Spring be far behind?" They are the concluding words of Shelley's Ode "To the West Wind," and they serve to sustain the hope that the hero of Mr. Hutchinson's story will win through to happiness.

Mark Sabre's mind is of that rare type that always sees the other man's point of view so clearly and sympathetically that his own convictions sometimes suffer for it. Thoughtful, sensitive and inarticulate, he meditates much upon the inconsistencies and futilities of life, always seeking a solution for its many problems. He is married to a woman the unthinking would pronounce an excellent wife. She is a good housekeeper, she is pretty and well dresst, and her conduct is always irreproachable, but she is, nevertheless, a most detestable person, narrow-minded, unintelligent and censorious. Mark's ability to put himself in another's place stands him in good stead in his married life and the allowances he is constantly making for Mabel are astonishing.

Before his marriage there had been another woman in his life, but Nona Holiday had decided in favor of Lord Tybar, handsome, brilliant and engaging, only to discover when too late that those qualities hid a gracelessness (there is no other word for it) that renders her life wretched.

The story of Mark Sabre is one of vicissitudes. He is badly treated by his business firm: his relations with Nona ultimately reach a point where little is needed to precipitate matters, and only the outbreak of the war prevents action on his part. He enlists when the need for men causes the physical test to be less exacting, for he has a weak heart, and he comes back from the front, crippled. The charitable stand he takes concerning a girl and her illegitimate child causes his ostracism, and gives Mabel an opportunity to leave him and sue for a divorce, while later the suicide of the unfortunate girl drags the matter before the public and Mark's name in the dust. A cerebral hemorrhage ensues and a long illness follows, but fate now seems to have done her worst and things begin to brighten. Mabel secures her decree, Lord Tybar is killed, and we leave Mark and Nona with every prospect of happiness before them, tho Mark has destroyed the letter by which his name might have been publicly cleared.

The character-drawing in the book is something remarkable, so clear and so varied. Mark's personality pervades every page and the virtuous but obnoxious Mabel rouses hatred in the most gentle breast, but perhaps Lord Tybar will be longest remembered. Nona describes him thus: "Utterly graceless. Without heart, Marko, without conscience, without morals. . . . He hasn't got any feelings at all. . . . and it simply amuses him to arouse feeling in anybody else. There have been women all the time we've been married and he simply amuses himself with them until he's tired of them and the next one takes his fancy, and he does it quite openly before me, in my house, and tells me what I can't see before my own eyes, just for the love of the suffering he sees it gives me." And this is the man whose gallantry wins him the Victoria Cross, who is mortally wounded leading his men at Arras, and who dies with a message for another woman than his wife on his lips.

The minor characters are no less well done. There is Freddie Perch and his irascible old mother to whom he is devoted and who is devoted to him. Mr. Fargus,

New Series Coupe

A Revelation of Goodness and Beauty

The fine Coupe reveals at a glance so much beauty and goodness that its price seems almost unbelievable. Inviting as the details may sound, they are as nothing compared with the surprise that awaits you in an examination and demonstration of the car itself.

The Outstanding Value of the Good Maxwell Coupe, New Series

Larger, handsome radiator and hood.

Drum type head lamps and cowl lamps, nickel trimmed.

Cord tires, non-skid, front and rear; 31x4 inch, straight side.

Disc steel wheels, demountable at rim and hub; or wood artillery wheels, without extra cost.

Unusually long springs promote comfort, tire economy, roadability.

Four-passenger capacity. Fourth seat, unfolding from under cowl, faces forward.

Broadcloth upholstery; Turkish cushions.

Back-cushion springs of new and special design, extremely comfortable. Adult-size seats, deep and wide and roomy.

New type windshield, hinged at top of upper part and bottom of lower part. No windshield inside drip in driving rain. Windshield wiper; windshield visor. Rear vision mirror.

Crank regulator for door windows. Non-rattle device for side windows.

Special inside locking device on left door. Yale lock on right door.

Body lower and larger. Car is lower, without sacrificing headroom. Floor level with chassis frame. Wool carpet on floor.

Parcel compartment behind driver's seat; luggage under rear deck.

Mechanism more simple and more accessible. Alemite chassis lubrication.

New steering comfort—wheel so placed that driver's hands reach it naturally, comfortably and without stretching.

Clutch and brake action, steering and gear-shifting, made remarkably easy.

Handsome and accessible instrument board. Best switches. Improved dash gas adjustment.

Maxwell Motor Corporation, Detroit, Michigan
Maxwell Motor Company of Canada, Limited, Windsor, Ontario

Touring Cars *Roadsters* *The Good* *Sedans* *Coupes*

MAXWELL

REVIEWS OF NEW BOOKS
Continued

with his large wife and six domineering daughters, whose theory of life is "that everybody was placed in life to fulfil a divine purpose and invested with the power to fulfill it." The Reverend Boom Bagshaw, tho he appears but for a moment or two, is such a clear-cut figure as to cause us to regret that, as far as fiction is concerned, we have no Established Church.

It is impossible to help comparing "If Winter Comes" with the many sordid and dismal novels that have for some time defaced American literature. The most successful of these, "Main Street" sinks to its true level when compared with the vicissitudes of Mark Sabre's career. The one is a record of happenings in a dull little town where a shallow and conceited woman finds herself as bored as is usual with those who have no mental resources, and whose character at the end of some years has neither developed nor improved. The other is the story of a high-minded man whose nature, tried in the fire of adversity, emerges triumphant. The book is one of the very best that has recently appeared.

A RIVAL OF THOMAS HARDY

DARTMOOR is Mr. Phillpotts's favorite background for his stories, and in "Orphan Dinah" (Macmillan, $2.00) it is the scene of a tale which shows that the city does not monopolize all the movement of life, but that among the slower-witted rustic population dramatic events often play a part.

Dinah Waycott is the step-daughter of a well-to-do farmer, Ben Bamsey by name, and between the two is a great love that is somewhat trying to his second wife and their daughter Jane, for Dinah is the daughter of Bamsey's first wife by her first husband, and so no kin whatever to the Bamseys. It is the knowledge that such an engagement would please her foster-father that has led Dinah to be "tokened" to Bamsey's son John, but a reluctance to name a date for the marriage has begun to show her that her affection for John is only that of a sister, and that she has made a mistake which fortunately it is not too late to rectify.

Near Buckland village lies Falcon Farm where dwells Joseph Stockman and his daughter Soosie, and the opening of the story finds Stockman expecting two new hands, a horseman and a cowman for, according to himself, he has hitherto lived a most laborious life and must now have relief. Altho in perfect health, he pleads his advanced years as an excuse for not working, and has succeeded in imposing this view of himself upon most of his neighbors. His two men arrive, Thomas Palk, the horseman, and Lawrence Maynard, whose domain is the cow-yard. The latter is the cleverer of the two, and yet it is the slower-witted Palk who first sees a discrepancy between Stockman's benign conversation and his ability to work his men to the utmost. Palk is helped in his clear-sightedness by a growing admiration for Soosie and pity for the thraldom in which she is kept by her father, none the less exacting because lovingly endured.

Little is known concerning Lawrence Maynard in the village of Buckland; Dinah does not get to know him well until after she has broken her engagement with John Bamsey, and it is still later when she and Maynard find themselves deeply in love with one another. But there is an obstacle in the way of their marriage. Maynard, it seems, has a wife whom he has not seen for years and, contrary to the usual procedure in story-telling, it is he who realizes the formidableness of this barrier and Dinah who insists that it exists only in his imagination. Where is the man who could resist such arguments? Dinah's reasoning prevails and they lay their plans for a departure for Australia, separately from Buckland, together from a nearby seaport, and marriage as soon as the vessel reaches her destination. But their flight is not so easily accomplished. Altho their plans have been laid with a due regard for secrecy, they have been obliged to communicate by letter, and their correspondence has fallen into the hands of Jane Bamsey. Jealousy and spite do their work, and when Lawrence arrives at Shepherd's Cross, the place of rendezvous in the forest, he is set upon by half a dozen of his neighbors, most of whom are actuated by a desire to save Dinah from disaster. It is something of a surprize to them when she appears and, denouncing them for their stupidity and narrow-mindedness, shows that not only does she know Maynard's history but is convinced of the rightness of her own position towards him. Even the rustic mind perceives that here is no cause for action, and reluctantly Lawrence and Dinah are allowed to depart upon their way to Australia and happiness, a happiness which proves to be perfectly legal, tho they are not aware of it.

The book is full of good characters. The reader rejoices when Soosie and Palk decide to marry and are pleased at old Stockman's dismay at the emancipation of his patient slave. The old bed-ridden huntsman, Enoch Withycombe, is a wonderful personality, full of the wisdom gained by reflection and experience, and the description of his funeral is most striking, with the dead sportsman's master, the huntsman and the whipper-in, and two brace of hounds following the chief mourners. Chaffe the carpenter is another pleasant character, his goodness and piety shining forth mixed with his shrewd observations on life. The author is able to depict these rustic sages without making them appear unnatural in a way, that to my mind, surpasses Hardy. It is a small thing, but yet noticeable that the author puts into the mouths of two Dartmoor men two distinct Americanisms, "pure cussedness" and "up against it." "Orphan Dinah" is a delightful book.

EDUCATION FOR THE NEXT GENERATION

OWEN JOHNSON has taken a step forward in this new book, "The Wasted Generation" (Little, Brown & Co., $2.00). He is not satisfied merely to tell a good story, to build a seller. He has thought over this novel, and felt over it, and he makes the reader go with him in thought and feeling. He is not afraid to write of the war, he approaches various American problems with considerable freedom, he looks at dangers with an open eye.

It is a story of a man of the privileged classes, brought up in the usual way, with the usual school and college training, and turned out with plenty of money and time to do what he likes. He comes from stout New England stock. This is how he puts the matter:

"I have received the deplorable education of the day. Everything that possibly

REVIEWS OF NEW BOOKS
Continued

could be done was done to make me hate the pursuit of knowledge. I am, indeed, an excellent example of the failure of American education—the failure to provide for the utilization of a developed type. My father and my grandfather and his father before him were brought up to public service as the result of a system of society and education which demanded service of them. What, all at once, has happened to our generation? We have everything to make us leaders . . . yet the only result . . . of our education has been either to divert our unquestioned energy towards a heaping up of material comforts or to make us triflers and dilettanti. . . . It may have been our fault, but I think it was deeper—the fault of national thinking. . . . We are a generation wasted."

These reflections are the outcome of service in France in the Foreign Legion, during a time of recuperation. For this spoiled rich boy, who had been a couple of years in Paris enjoying himself, had been caught in the tremendous enthusiasm of the mobilization and had volunteered. He had weathered two years of warfare, years that had done something to him inwardly as well as outwardly. For the first time in his life he began to think.

Thus thinking it occurred to him to set down, faithfully and truly, all he knew about himself and what his reactions were to the events of his life. He reaches back into the past first to portray himself as he was, and incidentally those who are of his time and place in society, next to give you what he is, and from then he carries you on with him in what develops.

He has been, or has thought himself, in love several times. There was an early episode, a young country miss eager to capture the scion of a rich house—a girl no better than she should be, but whom he idealized and adored with all the fair generosity of youth. That affair was ended by Ben, his older brother, who proved to him that his lady love was not averse from being made love to by himself. David was enraged and hurt, but it had a lasting effect upon him. "From that time forth vulgarity had no part in my life. Milestone number 1."

His next episode was with a young girl, the friend of his sister and the only child of a man of wealth and importance, a fine man. The two had been the best of chums when suddenly friendship changed, with the lad, to love. That ended the happy chumming, for the girl was not ready for love. Their intimacy received a check, their frankness with one another was over. It ends with David's departure for France. And next comes an evil infatuation.

Letty, Madame de Tinquerville, is one of those who do harm for the love of it. She lived an outwardly conventional life, under the mask of a madonna. She had married, as a young girl, a worn-out roué, who had died early in the game. Since then she had fed her love of excitement and power, her furious vanity, at the expense of any one who interested her.

David interested her, and she set out to capture him, a thing laughably easy. Then she proceeded to dominate him.

"She was, I am certain, thoroughly conscientious in everything she did. The corruption she exerted over me was both mental and moral. I had come back to Paris filled with enthusiasm and ambition. My self-discipline disappeared. I threw myself into a life of pleasure and dissipation. . . . I obeyed only the craving for excitement, movement and rapidly succeeding sensations. My old philosophy, simple and proud, yielded to the worldly wisdom of the facile luxury which surrounded me. . . . What had been an orderly, measured mode of life, contemplative, tolerant and good-humored, now became a tumultuous succession of days and nights when every nerve was raw to the exposure. . . . I found myself quick at offense and wincing under the new tortures which she invented each day for the perverse delight of proving to herself how completely she held me in subjection."

The affair drags on, altho David, disillusioned and disgusted, tries to free himself. But always Letty draws him back to her. It is a lie that breaks the thing at last, a lie and jealousy discovering that it had grounds. The scene is well done, but too long to give. A few days later war breaks out and David joins the Legion.

The French background is wonderfully conveyed. Mr. Johnson knows and loves France and he can make us at home with the French and their lovely country. The war is sufficiently suggested. And then, suddenly, David finds himself on the way back to America on a two months' permission, which has been procured for him through the efforts of Mr. Brinsmade, father of the young girl friend whom David had fallen in love with. That early flame has died, however, in the man. In the girl it appears to be coming into being. Brinsmade is eager for the match. He likes David, and he wants a real man for his daughter, a man who can handle the great responsibilities of wealth. As he says:

"I said I want you as my son-in-law, David. It's more than that; I want to invest what I've made in a man that counts. I want you with me. I want to feel that when it comes time for me to step out, that I'm passing on the power to count for big things to some leadership I've inspired. . . commerce, science, public affairs. You like a man's job. That's where it lies, and it's our kind that must lead. . ."

David ponders these statements, and feels their effect. But he knows one thing above all, that he must return first and help finish up the job in France; with the French until America comes in, and both already see that America must come in, with his own people after that event.

But there is something waiting for David on the ship. A new experience, a new development. Real love, at last!

Among those who are boarding the ship he perceives a young French woman to whom an old peasant is saying good-by. Both are terribly moved. The old woman cannot summon strength to tear herself away from her mistress, and David, stepping forward, offers his assistance in conveying the poor old mourner back to the dock. The service is accepted. From that moment he cannot free his mind of this young woman, cannot keep his eyes from her. It is love at first sight, tho he does not realize this immediately.

Mr. Johnson has spent himself in painting this passion, which rapidly becomes dominating. There is a mystery about the woman. She is evidently of the aristocracy, yet she travels without attendants, and her name is plebeian. She tries to avoid all intercourse with David, but circumstances gradually work on his side, and in the end it comes to a declaration. He finds that Bernoline (whose first name he has discovered by accident) loves him. But he learns from her that the love is utterly hopeless, and she demands from

REVIEWS OF NEW BOOKS
Continued

him a promise that he will not see her nor try to communicate with her again, after reaching shore. He gives this at last, broken-hearted but unable to refuse her evident terror and despair, as well as the high nobility of her character, which has made him realize that what she does must always be done from the finest motives only, must be the one right thing that is to be done. They separate, he to return to his home in Connecticut, she to go to a convent in the city.

Mr. Johnson uses the time on the ship for other purposes than this love episode, however. He groups together Brinsmade, a socialist named Magnus, David and the French woman, each with their ideas of country, duty, patriotism or humanity, contrasts them with a crowd of careless young Americans returning from one or another sort of service in France, and discusses through these media the future of America; contrasting the devoted love of country so evident in France with the careless attitude of our own countrymen. David, who knows the French love for their country, wishes he could love his own with that same burning passion, to which the girl replies:

"My country has been centuries in the making. In every family some one has died that France might remain France. We are an old race. We have lived together, been proud together, suffered together, a long while. That does not come in a day. . . . Our young men are brought up to think of France as something outside themselves, that must go on, that must live—an ideal that is not selfish. That is what we all feel, from top to bottom. What difference what happens to us, if France remains."

It is toward such a cohesion, such an ideal, that America must march, David feels, and it is toward this that her leaders should strive. Her leaders that must be found, if not in this, the wasted generation, then in the young and coming one. On the other side is the picture of America falling into the hands of our swarming aliens, becoming something featureless, international, confused. For this surging under-force is powerful, and it is a challenge that must be met with something real, something devoted, not with an artificial power. The mere fact that Americans have been leaders will not keep them leaders.

The rest of the book is devoted to the love affair between Bernoline and David, which ends tragically. The mystery that kept them apart is expounded. She has been ravished by a German, and has borne a war child. She is afterwards married to this German, a prisoner, by her brother, and the man is killed. There is no good reason for the departure of Bernoline with her child; it is unlike her character to yield a spiritual victory to the German brute simply because she lacked the physical strength to protect her body from him. However that may be; and it seems unnecessarily melodramatic; David, the war over, returns to his own home and marries Anne, the girl love, Brinsmade's daughter, or is on his way to this when the story closes. The two of them are dedicated to the true service of their country, are linked by real affection and respect, and are suited by an equal inheritance of custom and training to make a success of life.

The SOUND of SAFETY

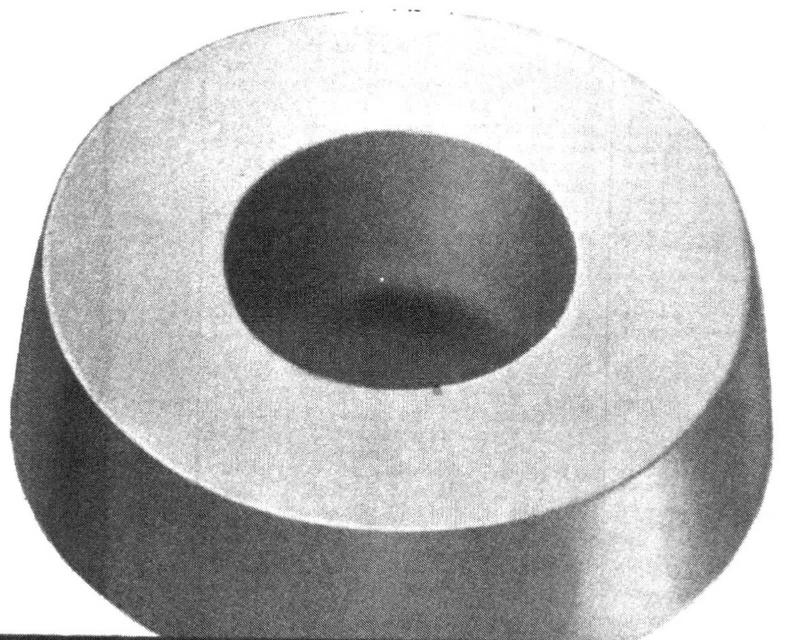

Pennsylvania VACUUM CUP CORD TIRES

More Than a Thousand Vacuum Cups

exert the *grip—hold—letgo* principle of *suction* on wet, slippery pavements, when your car is fully Pennsylvania equipped.

More and more every day you hear the deep purr-like rhythm—*the Sound of Safety*—of these massive Cups, as Vacuum Cup Tires carry the cars of prudent drivers straight and true, without loss of speed or power, over pavements made treacherous by oil and water.

Skid-freedom is the mission of Vacuum Cup Tires, plus sustained *highest quality* at prices always on a parity with those of *ordinary* makes.

Hence the *guaranteed* effectiveness of the Vacuum Cup Tread on wet, slippery pavements and the *guaranteed* mileage of Vacuum Cup Cord Tires—per warranty tag—of

9,000 Miles

PENNSYLVANIA RUBBER CO. *of* AMERICA, Inc.
JEANNETTE, PA.
Direct Factory Branches and Service Agencies Throughout the World.

TO EDUCATE THE NEXT GENERATION AGAINST WAR

(*Continued from page 13*)

and especially coming men and women, as represented by our school children, should carefully study its every document and loyally in every way assist in striving for a satisfactory solution of those problems which mean everything for civilization and world prosperity and happiness. Frankness, honesty and integrity of purpose mean more than all the diplomacy of the ages. May America take this lead and establish a new beacon light for the guidance and welfare of the world.

J. B. A. Robertson, Governor of Oklahoma—The Limitation of Armament Conference in Washington will accomplish through its deliberations the most thorough, illuminating, and practical survey of the past development and future progress of our civilization that can ever be achieved. This study of the history and discussion of the future of the nations and the peoples of the world is of such vital importance that the proceedings of the Conference should be read and reviewed as a part of the daily course in all our schools, colleges and universities in order that the rising generation may be fully educated upon the cost and folly of war.

Pat M. Neff, Governor of Texas—The history that is now being made by the Disarmament Conference at Washington will be frequently referred to by writers, speakers and thinkers for generations to come. It constitutes an epoch-making milepost that ineffacably marks the march of man. The students of to-day who are to be the men and women of to-morrow should have as a part of their daily curriculum the detailed proceedings of this worldwide Conference now assembled in our country, as it seeks to turn the tide of civilization away from the war-wrecked shores of the past.

MOUNTAIN STATES

Jos. M. Dixon, Governor of Montana—The Disarmament Conference marks a mile-stone in world history. Upon its success or failure largely depends the permanency or failure of the present social order. The last number of The Literary Digest was a veritable treasure-house of information regarding the scope and possibilities of this historic international Conference. The public schools and colleges of the country can perform no greater service to the nation than that of giving courses, during the sitting of the Washington Conference, to their students regarding the great questions involved. If we can fully impress upon the minds of these young people the tremendous danger involved and the impelling necessity for world disarmament, the possibility of future war will be greatly reduced.

D. W. Davis, Governor of Idaho—It will be my pleasure and privilege to request our Department of Education to follow out the forward-looking and statesmanlike suggestion of the Governor of Massachusetts. We need more thoughtful and constructive educational suggestions such as this to truly build the intellects of our future citizens. There is an astonishing lack of sound information among our citizens of the political and economic history of the world. Should the true situation be spread before the boys and girls to-day there would dawn a better to-morrow, because the dominating characteristic of the average citizen is his desire for betterment.

Robert D. Carey, Governor of Wyoming—The history of the Disarmament Conference should be imprest upon the minds of the school children of America. The United States leads in a movement that promises more for the peace of the world than any gathering of statesmen since the dawn of history. Through our Educational Department I have requested that the schools of Wyoming shall study every phase of the Conference, from its inception to final adjournment. With the minds of the studénts of the nation focused upon the proceedings of the Conference, the chief actors will feel a keener incentive to make their conclusions conform to the dominant will of the peoples of the earth. Wyoming is for disarmament and the peace of the world.

Oliver H. Shoup, Governor of Colorado—We can conceive no better way to train the citizens of to-morrow for the discharge of their most important duties than by encouraging their study of the proceedings in Washington at the great Conference. While thè program laid down was to many a complete surprize and is far-reaching in its effect, yet we believe if consistently carried out it will be the foundation of a permanent peace that will be world-wide for all time to come.

Merritt C. Mechem, Governor of New Mexico—I think it vitally important to instruct the youth of the country relative to the great historical event now transpiring at the Washington Disarmament Conference. America contributed her mighty strength and influence to make the world safe for humanity. America is now taking the lead in the demand for reduction of war machinery, and our children should be helped to understand thoroughly what is being done to prevent a recurrence of the horrible world tragedy we are now emerging from.

Thomas E. Campbell, Governor of Arizona—Regardless of its outcome, the Armament Conference is of such tremendous importance to the future welfare of the young people of America that they should take advantage of every possible opportunity to follow the proceedings in detail. What the ultimate outcome is to be depends largely on their intelligent understanding of the problems now being discust and their appreciation of the tremendous issues involved. Upon their shoulders will fall the responsibility of carrying out to its logical conclusion any agreement that may be reached, or the terrible burdens which a continuation of the present race for sea power will necessitate if unchecked.

Charles R. Mabey, Governor of Utah—The Disarmament Conference now in session constitutes a landmark in human progress, the significance of which cannot yet be conceived. By all means let us study earnestly its deliberations that understanding among all peoples may be the result. Not only should the course of the Conference be closely observed by those of mature age, but it is essential to posterity that the youth of the nation comprehend the full meaning and purposes of the gathering. With such a basis of familiarity they will best be prepared to perpetuate and bring to complete materialization the aims and ideas now being proposed.

Emmet D. Boyle, Governor of Nevada—I heartily approve your suggestion that the

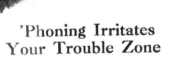

TO EDUCATE THE NEXT GENERATION AGAINST WAR

(Continued)

school children study contemporary history in the making of the Arms Conference. The movement is an educative one and should extend to the children upon whose intelligence and sense of justice the future of the nation rests. As Roger Williams said, it is a pity they did not save some before they killed so many.

PACIFIC STATES

LOUIS F. HART, GOVERNOR OF WASHINGTON—It is preposterous to think that disarmament, if possible at all, can be accomplished in a day, for reckoning in terms of centuries, the present Conference is but an atom of time. Strife has continued incessantly between individuals since Cain killed Abel, and between nations almost since the birth of government, and each succeeding war has been more terrible and devastating than the one before. Some new life-destroying instrument has been produced in each new struggle. There is much truth in the argument that human nature will have to undergo a change before war can be eliminated. It does not follow, however, that human beings can not agree among themselves to restrain their passions to the utmost. The "gun-toter" of to-day is a criminal, but in the earlier days of the nation even the most protected citizen carried arms. Human nature has changed in this respect, and largely through education of the fact that "It does not pay." A beginning has been made, a bold, fearless step, such as an unselfish nation like the United States might be expected to take, but after all its greatest value is educational—the problem remains for future generations. By all means let the children of the land study closely the Disarmament Conference.

BEN W. OLCOTT, GOVERNOR OF OREGON.—In an epoch-making document, Mr. Hughes has turned over the leaf to a new era. If success is achieved at the Disarmament Conference, as it now appears it shall be, history will hold no record of achievement for world good comparable to it. Consequently history may hold nothing more vital for the study of our youths and all citizens than the progressive steps of this gathering. May the eyes of our future home-makers and nation-makers be opened to the great trust to-morrow will repose in them. It may be ours to will that there shall be no more wars. It will be theirs to keep forever sacred and inviolate that pledge of their ancestors.

WILLIAM D. STEPHENS, GOVERNOR OF CALIFORNIA—Never before in the history of the world has a limited group of men been given an opportunity to relieve a war-weary world of the awful burdens of destructive warfare. Never before has it been possible to relieve the mothers, the children and the toilers of the world of the heartaches, the heart-breaks, the want and misery and slighted education, the almost unbearable taxes, and other economic sacrifices brought on by war. May we not pray that God will guide aright all those who participate in the proceedings of the great Disarmament Congress now in session in Washington? In my judgment it will be good for the future of the Republic if all school children give earnest study to the proceedings.

SCIENCE AND INVENTION
Continued

WHEN LUMINOUS DIALS DON'T SHINE

FOR some years luminous watch-dials have been on the market, the luminosity being not produced by any salt of radium, as is commonly supposed, but usually by a salt of a more common metal. It has hitherto been supposed that all that was needed to cause the figures on these dials to become luminous was absolute darkness. However, this is contradicted by a curious observation made by a traveler in Europe. Having just bought a new watch with a luminous dial, he took it out in the first tunnel he came to. To his astonishment the dial remained entirely dark, and this was the case in all the other tunnels through which he passed. He determined to send it back as defective, as soon as he reached his journey's end. However, when night fell, while the train was still above ground and the porter turned off the lights in the car, he was astonished to see the figures on the dial blaze brilliantly forth. This observation led to experiments with other watches having luminous dials, and it was found that at a distance of twenty feet under the surface of the earth all lost their radiance. Experiment has demonstrated that the humidity of the air in the tunnel is not responsible.

These facts appeared in *Kosmos* (Stuttgart) and roused great interest throughout Germany, many letters commenting upon it being received by the editors. In the June number they acknowledge these and explain the probable reason, substantially, as follows:

There is, as a matter of fact, no need of making an effort to explain the matter by forcibly twisting the laws of physics. Those of physiology offer a more logical explanation. When one goes from outdoors, that is from full daylight, into a perfectly dark room, from five to twenty minutes, according to the degree of the light-fatigue of the eye, must elapse before the eye becomes capable of perceiving faint impressions of light such as come, for example, from small cracks in the door or from "phosphorescent" luminous substances. As we commonly say, the eye must become accustomed to the dark. If, however, one remains for a while in a room illuminated with ordinary artificial light before going into the room which is entirely dark, the sensitiveness of the eye to feeble impressions of light appears at once, or after a very short time. This is due to the immense difference of intensity between daylight and our sources of artificial light, and also to the fact that daylight contains very intense light of all wave lengths from violet to red. On this account the receiving eye is fatigued with respect to red and yellow after being in an artificially lighted room for some time, but only slightly to green and blue, which are the chief rays emitted by phosphorescent substances. Thus we see why the watch-dial failed to shine during the brief ride through the tunnel but was on the job at night.

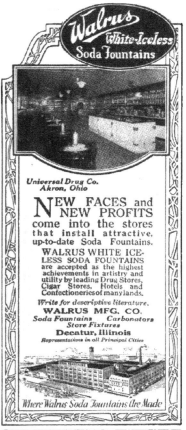

INVESTMENTS • AND • FINANCE

PRICES, WAGES, INTEREST AND RENT

THAT one of the great hindrances to a return to normal levels of business activity is the mal-adjustment between prices of different commodities, was noted in these columns last week. The New York Trust Company, in its current *Index*, adds that the inequalities between the four basic economic factors, production, labor, capital and returns of real estate form an extremely important factor in the situation. Prices, wages, interest and rents must, we are told, come into a closer relation before there will exist a substantial and permanent basis for business activity. It is apparent from the New York Trust Company's chart here reproduced, that while wholesale commodity prices "reached the highest peak of inflation, they have also, relatively to their rise, gone through the greatest degree of deflation." It is a matter of common knowledge that retail prices have not come down to anything like the extent that wholesale prices have, a point strongly emphasized in a recent speech by that great employer of labor, Judge Gary. Wages, on the other hand, it will be noted, have suffered the least deflation of all. Interest did not advance to the heights which were attained by commodities and wages and the after-war readjustment has brought it the nearest of any of these four factors to the pre-war level. The chart at the bottom of this page is further explained by *The Index* as follows:

> The index of commodities [wholesale prices] is that of the United States Bureau of Labor.
>
> The wage index is that compiled by the New York State Industrial Commission on returns from factories employing approximately 500,000 men and women.
>
> The interest index has been compiled by taking the monthly average of the weekly high and low rates on 60- to 90-day commercial paper. The base represents the average for the years 1911 to 1915. It happens, however, that the July, 1914, rate is approximately the same as this average. The trend here plotted seems to afford an accurate picture of fluctuation in price of capital.
>
> The rent index covers only house rents, as no returns on commercial, industrial or farm rents were available. It is the housing item compiled in the cost of living index by the National Industrial Conference Board, and the base used is July, 1914. In fact, the base used for all four indices is approximately the same, namely, June or July, 1914, which puts them on a comparable basis.

A GOVERNMENT WARNING TO INVESTORS—American investors have been warned by the watchful Department of Commerce to be very careful in purchasing foreign bonds payable in depreciated currencies. Certain concerns in this country are said to be offering national, municipal, and industrial issues exprest in such currencies, calling attention to the possibility of the investor realizing enormous profits. Most of these issues, it seems, are payable in the currencies of Germany, Austria, Poland, Czecho-Slovakia, Roumania, Jugo-Slavia and Hungary. As the warning is further summarized in a New York *Journal of Commerce* dispatch from Washington:

> In some cases the prices at which these securities are offered are unduly high in view of the actual exchange rate of the given currency. There have been instances where there has been great disparity between the sale price of the advertised securities in terms of dollar and the price at which they could be purchased with American money in the foreign country.

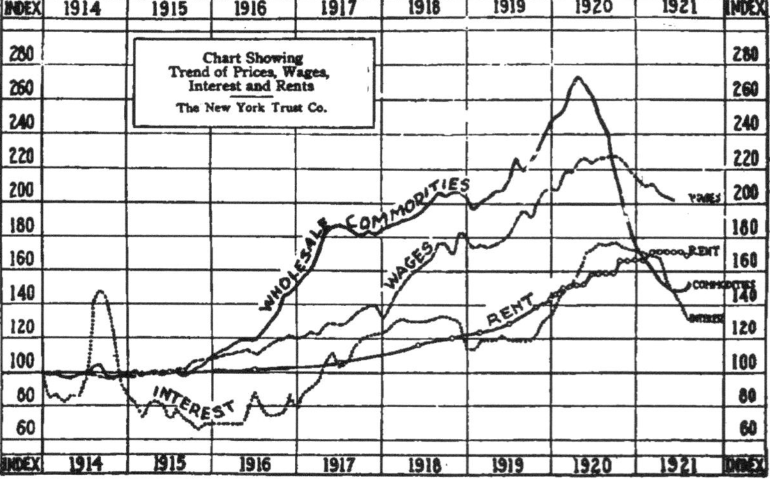

Twenty-five little baby bodies in a garbage cart

National Committee

Rt. Rev. C. P. Anderson, D. D.
Dr. Frank Billings
Harriot Stanton Blatch
Cornelius N. Bliss, Jr.
Alfred J. Boulton
Arthur Brisbane
John Graham Brooks
Mrs. Cora Haviland Carver
C. P. Coleman
Edward Cornell
Fred M. Corse
Charles R. Crane
John W. Davis
Jerome T. DeHunt
Charles W. Eliot
John Lovejoy Elliott
Harry M. Fennimore
Irving Fisher
Hon. Joseph I. France
Hon. David R. Francis
Col. Michael Friedsam
John A. Gade
E. F. Gay
Samuel Gompers
Rev. Percy Stickney Grant, D. D.
Norman Hapgood
Robert Herrick
Rabbi Emil G. Hirsch
William M. Johnston
Alexander Kahn
Dr. Gertrude Kelly
William Kent
E. F. Ladd
Col. Herbert Lehman
James G. McDonald
John A. McSparran
Rabbi Judah Leon Magnes
Capt. Wm. A. Maher
Anne Martin
Hon. Ogden L. Mills
William Fellowes Morgan
Walter M. Nelson
Morgan J. O'Brien
Fremont Older
Herbert Parsons
Francis G. Peabody
Mrs. Gifford Pinchot
Glenn E. Plumb
Ernest Poole
James H. Post
Mrs. John T. Pratt
William C. Redfield
Very Rev. Howard C. Robbins, D.D.
Raymond Robbins
Dr. Frank F. Rosenblatt
Julius Rosenwald
Rev. John A. Ryan
Mrs. Vladimir G. Simkhovitch
Alfred E. Smith
Mrs. Willard D. Straight
Henry W. Taft
Thomas D. Thacher
Norman Thomas
Mrs. Charles L. Tiffany
Oswald Garrison Villard
B. C. Vladeck
Lillian D. Wald
J. H. Walker
George P. West
George W. Wickersham

THE cart creaks and stops in front of the hospital. The twenty-five baby bodies are loaded in.

Tomorrow, while you sit at dinner, the cart will stop again and twenty-five more baby bodies will be loaded in—

The next day there will be twenty-five more. And so on . . . twenty-five . . . twenty-five . . . until Spring comes in Russia and there are no more babies in that town . . .

"You Could Hear the Children Crying Two Blocks Away"

says Anna Haines who, for more than a year has represented the Quakers over there. "A steady wail that kept up like a moan, all the time growing louder as we got nearer. The nurses could do nothing except to go around every morning and separate the ones that were going to die from the others; and they went around at different times and felt them to see if they were cold, and took them out . . ."

And once a day the garbage cart called, creaking, and stopped for its ghastly load.

Fifteen Million Are Starving to Death in Russia

In hundreds of cities and towns scenes like the one described above are enacted every day. Men, women, and children—*millions dying.*

They are asking for $5,000,000—every cent of it to be spent in this country for the most necessary articles of food.

How Many Will You Feed?

Ten dollars will save ten lives for a month.

A hundred dollars will save a hundred lives for a month.

A thousand dollars will save a thousand lives for a month.

The cart creaks and stops; you can hear it creak. Between the rich courses at your dinner table you can hear it creak. And the little bodies are carried out.

In God's name let us do what we can

Russian Famine Fund

Distributing through the

American Friends (Quakers)

Charles H. Sabin, ***Treasurer***
RUSSIAN FAMINE FUND
15 Park Row, New York

I enclose $....... as my contribution toward the relief of the suffering in Russia. Please send acknowledgment to

Name..

Street..

City..

State..

THE SPICE OF LIFE

Juvenile Edition Wanted.—"Mamma," said little Fred, "this catechism is awfully hard. Can't you get me a kittychism?"—*Baptist Boys and Girls.*

Worth Believing In.—"Do you really believe in heredity?"

"Most certainly I do. That is how I came into all my money!"—*London Mail.*

Where They Show It.—"We women bear pain better than men."

"Who told you that? Your doctor?"

"No, my shoemaker." — *Karikaturen* (*Christiania*).

Up-to-Date.—MOTHER (reading fairy-story)—"And when they had walked a great distance they came upon a woodchopper."

HAROLD—"I know! It's the Kaiser!" —*The Passing Show* (*London*).

The Young Genius.—MOTHER—"Willie, how is it that no matter how quiet and peaceful things are, as soon as you appear on the scene trouble begins?"

WILLIE—"I guess it's just a gift, mother."—*Life.*

Everybody In.—"Auto for Every 5½ Persons in Los Angeles."—Headline, the *New York Sun.*

The ½ persons are pedestrians who have been run over at least once.—*Detroit Motor News.*

An Arizona Ultimatum.—Judge Perry yesterday assessed a Phoenix speeder ten dollars. Those birds must learn that it don't pay to come over here and burn the coating off our new pavements.—*Tempe* (*Ariz.*) *News.*

Forearmed.—THE SECRETARY — "This speech may get you into trouble."

THE HONORABLE—"Then you had better prepare a statement saying that I was misquoted by the newspapers."—*The Christian Register*, (*Boston*).

Long - Distance Shooting. — The new night-watchman at the observatory was watching some one using the big telescope. Just then a star fell. "Begorra," he said to himself, "that felly sure is a crack shot." —*Toronto Goblin.*

His Great Regret.—NEW OFFICE BOY— "A man called here to thrash you a few minutes ago."

EDITOR—"What did you say to him?"

NEW OFFICE BOY—"I told him I was sorry you weren't in."—*Chicago Herald and Examiner.*

Making Them Useful.—TRAVELER— "It's a nuisance—these trains are always late."

RESOURCEFUL CONDUCTOR—"But, my dear sir, what would be the use of the waiting-rooms if they were on time?"— *Numero* (*Turin*).

Our Versatile President. — "President Harding has taken the bull by the horns with admirable skill, and simultaneously he may be able to forge this rainbow of peace into a real shearing knife, and then use the knife to cut down the naval appropriations and the taxes."—*Moody's Weekly Review of Financial Conditions* (*New York*).

CURRENT EVENTS

FOREIGN

November 16.—Nearly 700 Moplah rebels are killed, and one British officer and three men are killed and 34 are wounded, in an attack by the rebels on the Pandikkag Post in India.

Belfast Unionists in three meetings emphatically protest against the British Cabinet's treatment of Ulster.

November 17.—By an overwhelming vote the Unionist Party, in session at Liverpool, endorses the British Government's policy in its effort to bring about peace in Ireland.

Four policemen are killed and 30 seriously injured in an uprising by the followers of Mahatma Gandhi, the Hindu non-cooperationist leader, when the Prince of Wales arrives in Bombay to begin his tour of India. The rest of the population accords the Prince a tumultuous welcome.

Jugo-Slavia denies before the Council of the League of Nations that Jugo-Slav troops have invaded Albanian territory contrary to the terms of the Covenant of the League of Nations.

November 18.—The British Government issues orders suspending all construction work on the four new super-Hood battle cruisers, as the first step towards naval armament reduction.

Thirteen Mexican revolutionists are killed in battle and four more executed after summary court-martial near Algagones, in Lower California.

A new state bank is opened in Moscow by the Soviet government. It is announced that 3 per cent. interest will be paid on current accounts, and 5 per cent. on time deposits.

November 19.—The British Labor Party issues a manifesto promising support of any steps necessary to make the American proposals for naval armament reduction effective, and calls for the extension of the proposals to all forms of armament. The manifesto also asks for the non-renewal of the alliance between Great Britain and Japan.

November 20.—Renewal of the outbreaks in Bombay by the non-cooperationists is reported in advices to London, and Mahatma Gandhi, their leader, is said to be trying to quell the rioters.

November 21.—A hunger riot breaks out in Berlin, large crowds of men and women raiding provision shops and demanding relief from the high cost of living.

November 22.—Twenty-one persons are killed and scores wounded in an outburst of rioting in Belfast coincident with the assumption by the North Ireland Parliament of control of Ulster's local affairs in accordance with the Home Rule Act under the recently signed order-in-council.

The bethrothal of Princess Mary of England, only daughter of King George and Queen Mary, to Viscount Lascelles is announced by the King.

The German Government officially denies the charges of Premier Briand, of France, in his address before the Washington Conference that the German police forces and the Reichswehr constitute a nucleus for a future German army.

DOMESTIC

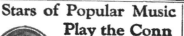

November 16.—Dr. Alfred Sze presents to the Armament Conference China's demands for recognition of her territorial integrity throughout her geo-

The Gift to Make to Your Friends

Naturally you wish to give something substantial. But the conventions of society hold one within quite narrow lines. It is hard anyhow to foretell just what will please. There is no accounting for tastes, you know.

Good Reading Matter Popular

But—

Everybody appreciates good reading, as is shown in the fact that more than a million and a quarter copies of The Literary Digest are printed and sold every week.

And so we suggest —

By far the simplest and easiest solution of the holiday gift-giving problem is described in detail on this page. Please read it carefully.

You will see how The Literary Digest has arranged to supply you with handsomely engraved Subscription Presentation Cards to be filled in with your name as subscription donor and forwarded to the persons to whom you wish The Digest to be sent for the ensuing year.

A Worth-While Present

In this way you not only give presents that are worth while, that will be highly appreciated and heartily enjoyed week after week, but your thoughtfulness and good judgment will be brought directly to the reader's attention every time a copy of The Digest arrives—52 times within the course of the year.

Those Who Will Appreciate The Digest

For your son, daughter, niece, nephew or cousin at college; the relative in some distant city; the stenographer and bookkeeper at the office; the clerk, salesman, saleswoman or heads of departments at the store; the special customers or clients that should be remembered, or the old friend or relative who by reason of advanced age or infirmity is no longer in active life, but who still wishes to know what's going on, there is scarcely anything that you could send as a holiday gift that is more sensible and that would represent so much genuine and long-continued satisfaction to the recipient as a year's subscription to The Literary Digest.

Others Remembered

Some of our subscribers send The Digest to their clergymen, their doctors and dentists, the trained nurse that has served in the family. Maybe there is some friend you haven't heard from in years whom you would like to remind of your existence and who would feel complimented to be remembered after so long an interval of silence.

There is no one thing you could select that would be more appealing or more appropriate as a gift to any man or woman of intelligence than The Literary Digest, the national news magazine that offers a complete, well-balanced and broad-minded presentation of the world's events and the opinions of the world's press. To tell you the merits of The Digest is superfluous.

> I Wish You a Merry Christmas
> That my good wishes and your enjoyment of
> them may last throughout the year
> I have ordered
> **The Literary Digest**
> sent to you as a message from me every week for a year
> With the Compliments of the Season
>
> ____________________________

Our Holiday Offer

While The Literary Digest has one fixed yearly price—four dollars, in order to co-operate with our patrons in their generous purpose during the holidays we are now filling Digest gift subscription orders on the following basis:

2 Subscriptions . . . . $3.90 each
3 to 9 Subscriptions . . . . 3.75 each
10 or more Subscriptions . . . 3.60 each

(One of the subscriptions may be your own.)

For postage on Canadian subscriptions, an extra charge of 85c is required; on foreign subscriptions, $2 extra.

A facsimile of the engraved Presentation Card we supply is shown on this page in slightly reduced size.

We will send the cards either to you and you can fill in your name and mail them and thus advise the recipients of your courtesy, or, we will sign your name to the cards as the donor and mail them to the parties direct—Indicate in order form which method you prefer.

Thousands Subscribe for Others

The Literary Digest has been making this holiday offer for several years. Thousands of its subscribers take advantage of the opportunity afforded to quickly dispose of part of their holiday gift problems and send in their Digest subscription renewals at the same time. Merely make out the list of names and addresses and send them in to The Digest with one check or money order to cover all and the deed is done without shopping around in crowded stores — without jostling in hurrying crowds. There can be no question as to whether the gift suits; The Literary Digest appeals to all classes who read English.

Promptness Important

Send in your order NOW while there is still time to get out the Presentation Cards before Christmas. Indicate in the order form whether you desire the Presentation Cards sent to you for mailing or direct to the recipient.

Use This Subscription Form

Publishers of The Literary Digest
354-360 Fourth Ave., New York

Gentlemen: My name and address is. . . . .

. . . .

and I enclose $. . . . ., for which please send The Literary Digest for one year to the names and addresses below. Send the Presentation Cards direct to me ☐ or to the parties listed, each bearing my name ☐. (Indicate your preference.)

Name . . . .
Local Address . . . .
Postoffice . . . . State . . . .

Name . . . .
Local Address . . . .
Postoffice . . . . State . . . .

Name . . . .
Local Address . . . .
Postoffice . . . . State . . . .

Name . . . .
Local Address . . . .
Postoffice . . . . State . . . .

Name . . . .
Local Address . . . .
Postoffice . . . . State . . . .

CURRENT EVENTS
Continued

graphical domain, for the principle of the open door with equal opportunity to all nations, and for the expulsion of all foreign powers as soon as possible.

Reductions in carload freight rates on farm products, which will bring the aggregate reductions since September 1, 1920, up to 10 per cent., are approved by executives of nearly every railroad in the country. The cuts apply to every section of the United States except New England.

Ellis Loring Dresel, of Boston, and now American Commissioner to Germany, is nominated by President Harding to be Chargé d'Affaires to Germany.

November 17.—The other nations represented at the Armament Conference accept in principle China's proposals that she be admitted to the family of sovereign nations.

Ordinary expenditures of the Government are increased by more than $37,600,000 during October as compared with September, while disbursements on the public debt fall off by $627,000,000, according to the monthly statement issued by the Treasury.

November 18.—President Harding receives from the heads of 12 nations and from Pope Benedict XV messages assuring their cooperation and wishing complete success to the Arms Limitation Conference.

The anti-beer bill prohibiting the use of beer and malt liquors as medicine is passed by the Senate by a vote of 56 to 22, and goes to President Harding for signature.

The employees of Armour & Company, Swift & Company, and Wilson & Company, Chicago meat packers, agree to a wage cut, to be fixed later.

President Harding issues a proclamation declaring peace between the United States and Austria.

November 19.—The American Federation of Labor, through its executive council, endorses the American plan for the reduction and limitation of armament.

November 20.—A natural gas field covering an area of 212 square miles is discovered in Northern Louisiana, according to a report made public by engineers of the United States Bureau of Mines.

November 21.—Premier Briand promises the Armament Conference that France will soon cut her military service from three years to one year and a half, and on his request that France be not left to defend liberty alone, assurances of moral support are given by the delegates of those nations which fought with her in the war.

Eight powers sign a resolution presented by Elihu Root to respect the sovereignty of China and provide her with the fullest opportunity to develop for herself effective and stable government.

November 22.—The six unions comprising the Federated Shop Crafts notify the general managers of the railroads of their intention to proceed for an increase of 13 cents an hour over the present rate of 77 cents an hour.

Señor Felix Cordova-Davila, Resident Commissioner of Porto Rico, is asked by a majority of the members of the Porto Rican Assembly to request President Harding immediately to remove Governor E. Mont Reily.

BY THEIR SHADOWS YOU SHALL KNOW THEM

Every man casts two shadows: one, the shadow of the outward man, which you may see upon the sidewalk as he passes in the sun; the other, the shadow of the inner man, the reflection of his accomplishments and his ideals. Something more than a hundred years ago you could have seen the shadow of Benjamin Franklin, reflected by the dim street lamps of Philadelphia, as he passed along the street. Tonight, you can see the shadow of his genius, reflected by the miracle of electricity, upon the lighted skyline of every city in the land.

Across oceans and across time, the shadow of Abraham Lincoln hovers over the councils of nations, uplifting their ideals and influencing the destinies of the world.

Just as there is the shadow of a man, so is there the shadow of a business and of its products—a shadow that reflects the ideals of the one and the quality of the other.

The man in New England is asked to buy a product made in Illinois by a manufacturer he never heard of, and whose ability and integrity he must take on faith. He has no opportunity to visit the factory that he may view its efficiency, nor to inspect the raw materials that he may be convinced of their quality. And so he must judge the product by its shadow—by the image of its worth, by the reflection of its desirability, which has been made upon his mind.

Yesterday, in thousands of stores in hundreds of cities and towns, something like this took place:—a salesman showed a woman two similar products made by two different manufacturers. The name of one product was unfamiliar to her ears; the name of the other was familiar. To her it was like hearing the name of a friend in a strange company. Had it been, instead of a product, a person, she might have said: "I feel as if I know you, because I've heard so much about you."

The shadow of that product had reached into her mind, and lingered in her memory. And the shadow of the product was its advertising.

N. W. AYER & SON *ADVERTISING HEADQUARTERS*

NEW YORK PHILADELPHIA BOSTON CLEVELAND CHICAGO

Drawing by Hugh Ferriss

ASCHER'S ROOSEVELT THEATRE
CHICAGO, ILL.

Black spotted cream enameled
Terra Cotta with polychrome ornament

C. Howard Crane, Architect

To become familiar with Architecture, follow this Series of details. No. 16 will appear in The Literary Digest of January 21, 1922.

om *the* OPEN-AIR HILLSIDE
the MOTION PICTURE THEATRE

the early days of the Greek Theatre, actors delivered their lines from behind rude nasks. There were leering ones for comedy and sneering, glowering ones for tragedy. h the passing of the centuries such primitive limitations disappeared. But it has re- ed for the last several decades to bring forth the stupendous versatility and grandeur roduction we find in our theatre today.

And the theatre building itself has traversed a cycle of development fully as great—from ncient Greek open-air hillside to our magnificently equipped modern structure.

Ascher's Roosevelt Theatre, Chicago, sums up the progress of the centuries. In its chaste k design is seen the heritage of its fine old Classic origin. And in its structural and utili- n features it reaches the peak of modern development. It is a building worthy of housing brilliant offspring of 20th Century Science and Ancient Art — the Modern Motion ire.

This theatre's facade, dramatically flood-lighted by night, strikingly impressive by day, esses the architect's vision in that most versatile and plastic of all facing materials— a Cotta. Note the delicately modelled bas-relief in the pediment—cream figures against ue background—all of Terra Cotta. See how the panels between the pilasters, also -relief treatment, relieve the massive expanse of plain Terra Cotta! Examine the strong ntricate detail, the coping, the eagles flanking the pediment—all so expressive of Terra a's plasticity, its marvellous adaptability to form.

Architects design in Terra Cotta because of its expressiveness, and its economy in the zation of ambitious designs.

If you are interested in buildings of any kind, write to the National Terra Cotta Society. are a bureau of service and information. And we will be glad to send you a brochure or r information illustrating Terra Cotta's value and achievements in the class of buildings are interested in. Address National Terra Cotta Society, 1 Madison Ave., New York.

HOW TO RECOGNIZE ARCHITECTURAL DETAILS
TERRA COTTA SERIES No. 15

Motive running between pilasters of main facade, Ascher's Roosevelt Theatre

Greek Wave Motif
(Evolute Spiral)

One of the most characteristic running ornaments in Greek art is the "wave motif." This design, possibly the earliest form of ornament known, was adapted from the earlier Egyptians. Its origin, often erroneously ascribed to a wave, was purely geometrical.

Ionic Pilaster Capital

Capital surmounting pilaster on main facade, Ascher's Roosevelt Theatre

This fine example of the capital of the Ionic Order, as used for a pilaster, is elaborated with a single anthemion (Greek conventionalized honeysuckle) centered between the spiral volutes. Others are found on the neck below.

Panel between pilasters on main facade, Ascher's Roosevelt Theatre

Bas-Relief

Bas-relief, meaning low relief, is the term used to designate slightly raised ornamental figures against a flat background. It is often seen in friezes, panels, and medallions.
Bas-relief is to be distinguished from ornament and figures that stand three-quarters free and from statuary.

(All the material illustrated is Terra Cotta)

TERRA COTTA

Permanent *Beautiful* *Profitable*

Look under the lid!

The picture "His Master's Voice" is a registered trademark of the Victor Talking Machine Company and identifies all Victor products.

The word "Victrola" is also a registered trademark and applies to the products of the Victor Talking Machine Company only.

To be certain the instrument you buy is a Victrola, be sure to see the Victor dog and the word "Victrola." Look under the lid!

Victrola instruments $25 to $1500.

Victor Talking Machine Co.
Camden, New Jersey

Victrola

REG. U.S. PAT. OFF.

December 10, 1921

The Literary Digest

(Title Reg. U.S. Pat. Off.)

RESTFUL WOODS—By Charles S. Chapman, A.N.A.

New York FUNK & WAGNALLS COMPANY London

PUBLIC OPINION New York combined with The LITERARY DIGEST

Vol. 71, No. 11. Whole No. 1651 December 10, 1921 Price 10 Cents

Which of these two men has learned the secret of 15 mi

The secret is contained in the free book o idea how much 15 minutes a day can mea

HERE are two men, equally good looking equally well dressed. You see such me at every social gathering. One of them can tal of nothing beyond the mere day's news. The oth brings to every subject a wealth of side light an illustration that makes him listened to eagerly.

He talks like a man who had traveled wide though his only travels are a business man's tri He knows something of history and biograp of the work of great scientists, and the writi of philosophers, poets and dramatists.

Yet he is busy, as all men are, in the affair every day. How has he found time to acquire so rich a mental background? When there is such a multitude of books to read, how can any man be well-read?

The answer to this man's success—and to the success of thousands of men and women like him—is contained in a free book that you may have for the asking. In it is told the story of Dr. Eliot's great discovery, which, as one man expressed it, "does for reading what the invention of the telegraph did for communication." From his lifetime of reading, study, and teaching, forty years of it as President of Harvard University, Dr. Eliot tells just what

Send for this FREE bo that gives Dr. Eliot's o plan of reading

P. F. COLLIER & SON COMPANY

Publishers of Good Books Since 1875

Which of these two men has learned the secret of 15 minutes a day?

The secret is contained in the free book offered below. Until you have read it you have no idea how much 15 minutes a day can mean in growth and success. Send for your copy now

HERE are two men, equally good looking, equally well dressed. You see such men at every social gathering. One of them can talk of nothing beyond the mere day's news. The other brings to every subject a wealth of side light and illustration that makes him listened to eagerly.

He talks like a man who had traveled widely, though his only travels are a business man's trips. He knows something of history and biography, of the work of great scientists, and the writings of philosophers, poets and dramatists.

Yet he is busy, as all men are, in the affairs of every day. How has he found time to acquire so rich a mental background? When there is such a multitude of books to read, how can any man be well-read?

The answer to this man's success—and to the success of thousands of men and women like him—is contained in a free book that you may have for the asking. In it is told the story of Dr. Eliot's great discovery, which, as one man expressed it, "does for reading what the invention of the telegraph did for communication." From his lifetime of reading, study, and teaching, forty years of it as President of Harvard University, Dr. Eliot tells just what few books he chose for the most famous library in the world; why he chose them and how he has arranged them with notes and reading courses so that any man can get from them the essentials of a liberal education in even fifteen minutes a day.

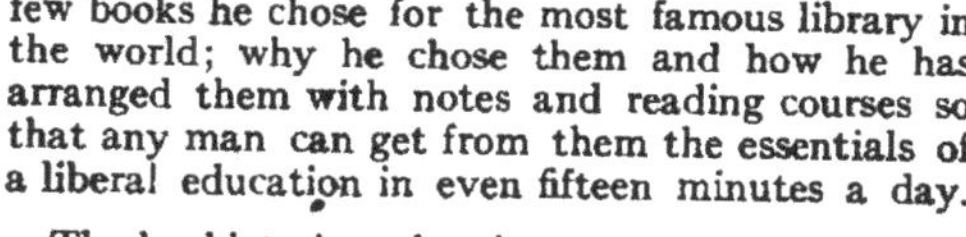

The booklet gives the plan, scope, and purpose of

Dr. Eliot's Five-Foot Shelf of Books—

The Fascinating Path to a Liberal Education

Every well-informed man and woman should at least know something about this famous library.

The free book tells about it—how Dr. Eliot has put into his Five-Foot Shelf "the essentials of a liberal education," how he has so arranged it that even "fifteen minutes a day" are enough, how in pleasant moments of spare time, by using the reading courses Dr. Eliot has provided for you, you can get the knowledge of literature and life, the culture, the broad viewpoint that every university strives to give.

"For me," wrote one man who had sent in the coupon, "your little free book meant a big step forward, and it showed me besides the way to a vast new world of pleasure."

Every reader of *The Literary Digest* is invited to have a copy of this handsome and entertaining little book. It is free, will be sent by mail, and involves no obligation of any sort. Merely clip the coupon and mail it to-day.

Send for this FREE booklet that gives Dr. Eliot's own plan of reading

P. F. COLLIER & SON COMPANY

Publishers of Good Books Since 1875

P. F. COLLIER & SON COMPANY L. D. 12-10-21
416 West Thirteenth Street, New York

By mail, absolutely free and without obligation, send me the little guidebook to the most famous books in the world, describing Dr. Eliot's Five-Foot Shelf of Books, and containing the plan of reading recommended by Dr. Eliot of Harvard.

Name ....

Address ....

....

Do You Kn
How t

No, this is not a joke. So many people do not kno
how to behave, do not know the right thing to do a
the right time, the right thing to say at the righ
time. They are always embarrassed and ill at ea

AT THE DANCE, at the theatre, as a guest or in public—wherever we chance to be, people judge us by what we do and say. They read in our actions the story of our personality. They see in our manners the truth of our breeding. To them we are either well-bred or ill-bred. They credit us with as much refinement and cultivation as our manners display — no more.

Do you know the correct and cultured way to make introductions?

Very often, because they are not entirely sure, because they do not know exactly what is correct and what is incorrect, people commit impulsive blunders. They become embarrassed, humiliated. They know that the people around them are misjudging them, underestimating them. And it is then that they realize most keenly the value of etiquette.

Etiquette means correct behavior. It means knowing just what to do at the right time, just what to say at the right time. It consists of certain important little laws of good conduct that have been adopted by the best circles in Europe and America, and that serve as a barrier to keep the uncultured and ill-bred out of the circles where they would be uncomfortable and embarrassed.

What Etiquette Does

To the man who is self-conscious and shy, etiquette gives poise, self-confidence. To the woman who is timid and awkward, etiquette gives a well-poised charm. To all who know and follow its little secrets of good conduct, etiquette gives a calm dignity that is recognized and respected in the highest circles of business and society.

In the ballroom, for instance, the man who knows the important little rules of etiquette knows how to ask a lady to dance, how many times it is permissible to dance with the same partner, how to take leave of a lady when the music ceases and he wishes to seek a new partner, how to thank the hostess when he is ready to depart. The lady knows how to accept and refuse a dance, how to assume correct dancing positions, how to avoid being a wallflower, how to create conversation, how to

What would you do or say in this embarrassing situation?

What W

If you were
ball and w
wallflower?

If you made
at a formal
suddenly co

If you receive
gift from so
invited to th

If you were
celebrity a
him or her

conduct herself
that commands

What It

Perhaps you
to do in a cert
what to say at a
Etiquette will h
blunders. It w
out a particle
and what is inc
at once all the
that others acc
cial contact wit
people.

Do you kn
weddings, fun

Do you know th
havior at publi

you to do,
is absolute
exactly wh
expected
you for th
alone with
what cloth
what to w
the eveni
respect a
whom yo

The Fa

The B
one of th
authoriti
This sple
of home
enabled
social w
ileges.
immune
to know

Do You Know How to Behave?

No, this is not a joke. So many people do not know how to behave, do not know the right thing to do at the right time, the right thing to say at the right time. They are always embarrassed and ill at ease in the company of others. They make mistakes that cause strangers to misjudge them. Pretty clothes and haughty manner cannot hide the fact that they do not know *how to behave.*

AT THE DANCE, at the theatre, as a guest or in public—wherever we chance to be, people judge us by what we do and say. They read in our actions the story of our personality. They see in our manners the truth of our breeding. To them we are either well-bred or ill-bred. They credit us with as much refinement and cultivation as our manners display — no more.

Do you know the correct and cultured way to make introductions?

Very often, because they are not entirely sure, because they do not know exactly what is correct and what is incorrect, people commit impulsive blunders. They become embarrassed, humiliated. They know that the people around them are misjudging them, underestimating them. And it is then that they realize most keenly the value of etiquette.

Etiquette means correct behavior. It means knowing just what to do at the right time, just what to say at the right time. It consists of certain important little laws of good conduct that have been adopted by the best circles in Europe and America, and that serve as a barrier to keep the uncultured and ill-bred out of the circles where they would be uncomfortable and embarrassed.

What Etiquette Does

To the man who is self-conscious and shy, etiquette gives poise, self-confidence. To the woman who is timid and awkward, etiquette gives a well-poised charm. To all who know and follow its little secrets of good conduct, etiquette gives a calm dignity that is recognized and respected in the highest circles of business and society.

In the ballroom, for instance, the man who knows the important little rules of etiquette knows how to ask a lady to dance, how many times it is permissible to dance with the same partner, how to take leave of a lady when the music ceases and he wishes to seek a new partner, how to thank the hostess when he is ready to depart. The lady knows how to accept and refuse a dance, how to assume correct dancing positions, how to avoid being a wallflower, how to create conversation, how to conduct herself with the cultured grace that commands admiration.

What would you do or say in his embarrassing situation?

What Would YOU Do—

If you were not asked to dance at a ball and wished to avoid being a wallflower?

If you made an embarrassing blunder at a formal affair and found yourself suddenly conspicuous?

If you received a wedding or birthday gift from some one who had not been invited to the entertainment?

If you were introduced to a noted celebrity and were left alone with him or her?

What It Will Do for You

Perhaps you have often wondered what to do in a certain embarrassing situation, what to say at a certain embarrassing time. Etiquette will banish all doubt, correct all blunders. It will tell you definitely, without a particle of a doubt, what is correct and what is incorrect. It will reveal to you at once all the important rules of conduct that others acquire only after years of social contact with the most highly cultivated people.

Do you know the correct etiquette of weddings, funerals, balls, entertainments? Do you know the correct manner of making introductions? Do you know the correct table etiquette? Do you know how to plan engagement and wedding receptions, dances and theatre parties; how to word cards, invitations and correspondence?

Do you know the correct behavior at public places?

The existence of fixed rules of conduct makes it easy for you to do, say, wear and write only what is absolutely correct. Etiquette tells you exactly what to do when you receive unexpected invitations, when people visit you for the first time, when you are left alone with a noted celebrity. It tells you what clothes to take on a week end party, what to wear to the afternoon dance and the evening dance, how to command the respect and admiration of all people with whom you come in contact.

The Famous Book of Etiquette

The Book of Etiquette is recognized as one of the most dependable and reliable authorities on the conduct of good society. This splendid work has entered thousands of homes, solved thousands of problems, enabled thousands of people to enter the social world and enjoy its peculiar privileges. To have it in the home is to be immune from all embarrassing blunders, to know exactly what is correct and what is incorrect, to be calm in the assurance that one can mingle with people of the highest society and be entirely well-poised and at ease.

In the Book of Etiquette, now published in two large volumes, you will find chapters on dance etiquette, dinner etiquette, reception etiquette and the etiquette of calls and correspondence. There are interesting and valuable chapters on correct dress, on how to introduce people to each other, on the lifting of the hat, the usual every-day courtesies. You may often have wondered what the correct thing was to do on a certain occasion, under certain puzzling circumstances. The Book of Etiquette solves all problems—from the proper way to eat corn on the cob, to the correct amount to tip the porter in a hotel.

What should the gentleman say when the music ceases and he must leave one partner to seek another?

Send Coupon for Free Examination

Let us send you the Book of Etiquette. It is published in two handsome blue cloth library volumes, richly illustrated. Our free examination offer makes it possible for you to examine these books without expense in the comfort of your own home. Just send the coupon—no money. We want you to see them for yourself, to examine them, to read a chapter or two. You may keep them at our expense for 5 days, and after that time you have the privilege of returning them without obligation or sending us $3.50 in payment.

Don't delay—mail the coupon NOW. This may be your last opportunity to examine the Book of Etiquette free. Clip the coupon and get it into the mail-box at once, this very minute!

How should the young man who calls for the first time be entertained?

Nelson Doubleday, Inc.
Dept. 3912, Oyster Bay, N. Y.

Nelson Doubleday, Inc.
Dept. 3912, Oyster Bay, New York

Without money in advance, or obligation on my part, send me the Two Volume set of the Book of Etiquette. Within 5 days I will either return the books or send you $3.50 in full payment. It is understood that I am not obliged to keep the books if I am not delighted with them.

Name ....
(Please write plainly)

Address ....

☐ Check this square if you want these books with the beautiful full leather binding at five dollars with 5 days' examination privilege.

THE LITER

PUBLIC OPINION (New York)

Published by Funk & Wagnalls Company (Adam W. Wagnalls, Pres.; Wilfred J. Fu

Vol. LXXI, No. 11 New York,

TOPICS - O

(Title registered in U S Patent Office

WHAT THE HARDING P

A DEATH-BLOW would be dealt the League of Nat certain prophets have maintained, if President Hard "Association of Nations" ever came into exist These international organizations for the perpetuation of p they saw as two deadly rivals. But now that the Ha plan has taken its first definite step toward materialization with the proposal that the present Washington Conference be ultimately enlarged to include all nations and be made a recurring event, we find many ardent friends and champions of the League of Nations in the forefront of those who applaud the advent of its supposed rival. "Senators who are for the League of Nations welcome the Harding plan either as a step in the direction of a league or as a practical carrying out of the league movement," reports a Washington correspondent of the New York *Tribune*; and a *Times* correspondent quotes other pro-Wilson Senators as predicting that the new plan would lead us at last into the League that is already organized and functioning without us. And from the League's enemies in the Senate come the most vigorous upon this plan that was to put the League out of Thus we find Senator Borah of Idaho, a leader ar Republican "irreconcilables," leading the fight ag proposed "Association," while Senators Watson of Ge Shields of Tennessee, anti-League Democrats, ral support.

ONLY A SM
APPEA

Before President Harding gave his proposal to Washington correspondents hint, the foreign dele sounded on the subject, and were found sympath as the pro-League Louisville *Courier-Journal* remind

"With the exception of the American delegates, participants in the Armament Conference are me officials of the League of Nations. There is no m League man than Balfour. Viviani always takes a l in League meetings. Schanzer is one of the most useful of the Leaguers. Koo is president of th Council. Dr. Wang is one of the judges of the L manent Court of International Justice. Karnebeek of the League's Assembly. And there are about a

THE LITERARY DIGEST

PUBLIC OPINION (New York) combined with THE LITERARY DIGEST

Published by Funk & Wagnalls Company (Adam W. Wagnalls, Pres.; Wilfred J. Funk, Vice-Pres.; Robert J. Cuddihy, Treas.; William Neisel, Sec'y) 354-360 Fourth Ave., New York

Vol. LXXI, No. 11 New York, December 10, 1921 Whole Number 1651

TOPICS - OF - THE - DAY

WHAT THE HARDING PLAN MEANS TO THE LEAGUE

A DEATH-BLOW would be dealt the League of Nations, certain prophets have maintained, if President Harding's "Association of Nations" ever came into existence. These international organizations for the perpetuation of peace they saw as two deadly rivals. But now that the Harding plan has taken its first definite step toward materialization with the proposal that the present Washington Conference be ultimately enlarged to include all nations and be made a recurring event, we find many ardent friends and champions of the League of Nations in the forefront of those who applaud the advent of its supposed rival. "Senators who are for the League of Nations welcome the Harding plan either as a step in the direction of a league or as a practical carrying out of the league movement," reports a Washington correspondent of the New York *Tribune*; and a *Times* correspondent quotes other pro-Wilson Senators as predicting that the new plan would lead us at last into the League that is already organized and functioning without us. And from the League's enemies in the Senate come the most vigorous attacks upon this plan that was to put the League out of business. Thus we find Senator Borah of Idaho, a leader among the Republican "irreconcilables," leading the fight against the proposed "Association," while Senators Watson of Georgia and Shields of Tennessee, anti-League Democrats, rally to his support.

ONLY A SMALL PART OF AN ICEBERG APPEARS ABOVE THE SURFACE.

—Thomas in the Detroit *News*.

Before President Harding gave his proposal to the press, Washington correspondents hint, the foreign delegates were sounded on the subject, and were found sympathetic. Yet, as the pro-League Louisville *Courier-Journal* reminds us—

"With the exception of the American delegates, the leading participants in the Armament Conference are members and officials of the League of Nations. There is no more ardent League man than Balfour. Viviani always takes a leading part in League meetings. Schanzer is one of the most active and useful of the Leaguers. Koo is president of the League's Council. Dr. Wang is one of the judges of the League's Permanent Court of International Justice. Karnebeek is president of the League's Assembly. And there are about a dozen other participants in the Armament Conference who are connected with the League."

These men, the *Courier-Journal* argues, must believe that the suggested new association would be "not an extirpator, but a handmaiden of the League." Declaring this to be its own view, the Louisville paper goes on to say:

"There would never have been an Armament Conference but for the League of Nations. The spirit that impelled the calling and directs the work of the Conference was aroused by the League of Nations and animates the League of Nations. It is the spirit which was never given concrete expression until so exprest in the League of Nations. The prospective association's object of world peace is the object of the League, and in so far as the association might succeed in promoting it the association would be a helpmeet of the League.

"The United States has not been permitted to join the League. If it is to be permitted to participate in a new tho feebler association, with the same ends in view, then godspeed to the new association. It would at least get us into the habit of international conference, which would be a good thing in itself. If it succeeded in accomplishing anything in the promotion of its purposes, that would be so much to the good for which the League of Nations exists."

After remarking ironically, for the benefit of the anti-League Senators and others who are haunted by a fear of foreign entanglements, that the Harding plan would be "no more entangling than a rainbow," the pro-League New York *Evening World* predicts that any new "Association of Nations" will be as sure to merge finally with the League "as the scattered efforts of a community to keep order are sure to converge ultimately in a common council and a police force." Otherwise, says the New York *World*, the Harding plan "would remain a side issue to the League, a second-best, a limited partnership." "If it is seriously considered by its author as a rival of the League of Nations," adds this strongly pro-League paper, "then is the shadow rivaling the substance that it mocks." "So far as it is revealed, this association is at best a shadowy structure, so vague in outline that little foundation is given for either approval or adverse criticism," complains the pro-League St. Louis

Globe-Democrat; but it adds: "In so far as it may tend to accustom the people to the fact that we have, and always must have, international relationships, that we have international obligations, and that our own welfare is dependent upon the recognition and fulfilment of these obligations, the President's idea, vaguely as it is presented, is so much to the good." Mr. Harding's proposal, remarks the pro-League Newark *News*, has these points of identity with the League:

IF HE'S HEADED THAT WAY, WHY NOT HIT THE MAIN TRAIL?

—De Mar in the Philadelphia *Record*.

"It aims to get the nations together in periodical conference to discuss international problems, and that is the predominating essential for peace.

"It recognizes that isolation is an impossible policy for the United States, which can not keep out of the world's affairs, try as hard as it may.

"It moves toward the inclusion of all the nations, Germany not excepted, just as the League of Nations stipulated, and by so doing abandons the idea that we should not become involved in European questions.

"It is built around the International Court of Justice established by the League of Nations largely through the influence and help of Mr. Root."

The same paper in another issue hails the President's proposal as "the biggest thing that has come out of the Disarmament Conference." The plan, as it is understood and interpreted by the Washington correspondents, differs fundamentally from the League of Nations in that it contemplates no political organization. "It would be even more an 'association with the nations' than the much-talked-of 'association of nations,'" writes Robert Barry in the Philadelphia *Public Ledger*. Another correspondent explains that it would be "an association of nations for conference." And he goes on to say:

"Such an association of nations, it is known to be President Harding's belief, would not be a rival or an undermining agency to the League of Nations. The President usually refers to the League of Nations as the 'European League,' and such a designation has been construed to imply that the League is capable of undertaking to settle European difficulties, in which the United States is not involved in a military way."

Still another correspondent, claiming the White House as the source of his information, assures us that "whatever association of nations may grow out of the Conference for the Limitation of Armament will not be aimed at the League of Nations." In another dispatch the plan is described as "an annual meeting of nations around a conference table for the purpose of discussing international problems, including econon ics, finance and commerce, and for the dissemination of international good-will." Moreover, the agreements reached at these conferences "would be based on 'understandings,' not on covenants or treaties." We also read that "an international court will be a necessary feature of the plan," and that "nothing has been said to indicate that the court established by the League of Nations would not be satisfactory for this purpose." Wickham Steed, editor of the London *Times*, who is now in Washington, predicts that—

"When the President's views are more definitely expounded, it will be found that he has in mind a series of gatherings for precise objects. Such gatherings may, indeed, become a peripatetic association of the principal nations that will neither resemble the existing League of Nations nor invade the legitimate functions of the League.

"The tendency of American thought is rather toward the association of the United States with other nations for the treatment of immediate and definite problems, than toward the creation of any hard-and-fast international organization."

The Republican platform on which President Harding was elected, we are reminded by more than one editor, indorses the idea of an international association such as "shall secure instant and general conference whenever peace shall be threatened by political action, so that the nations pledged to do and insist upon what is just and fair may exercise their influence for the prevention of war." Moreover, in his inaugural address the President announced his international policy in the following words:

Copyrighted 1921, by the New York "Tribune", Inc.

LOOK WHAT'S GROWING OUT OF THE JUNK PILE!

—Darling in the New York *Tribune*.

"We are ready to associate ourselves with the nations of the world, great and small, for conference, for counsel, to seek the ‹prest views of world opinion, to recommend a way to ap-roximate disarmament and relieve the crushing burdens of ilitary and naval establishments. We elect to participate in ggesting plans for mediation, conciliation and arbitration, and ould gladly join in the exprest conscience of progress which eks to clarify and write the laws of international relationship id establish a world court for the disposition of such justiciable uestions as nations are agreed to submit thereto."

Recalling that the President "has confidently declared that e League is dead," and that he "has interpreted the result the 1920 election as a mandate that he shall have nothing do with it even under reservations protecting this country om enforced participation in foreign affairs," e Brooklyn *Eagle* goes on to say:

"What Mr. Harding did in calling the Washington onference was to make the United States a leader the adjustment of foreign complications, irre-ective of the League. What he proposes to do the future is to continue that work indefinitely."

Turning to the uncompromising opponents of the resident's plan, we are assured by Philip rancis, a Washington correspondent of the New ork *American*, that "Mr. Hughes' Association of ations is on its way to join Mr. Wilson's League of ations," and that "the American people do not ant anything to do with either of them or with any reign alliance or entanglement of any kind." And another Washington dispatch to the same paper e read that, on the tentative announcement of e plan, "sharp opposition to the proposed as-ciation immediately developed among sections of e Senate, the irreconcilables leading in expressions antagonism to what they regard as an attempt foist on the country a modified form of the eague of Nations." "There can not be any ssociation of nations' subterfuge without the resident's consent," declares Arthur Brisbane, and he will neither betray the people that voted r him in his 'no League of Nations' campaign nor lay the undation of an overwhelming Republican defeat at the next ection." Senator Borah, an anti-League bitter-ender, sees the President's plan "a new league" which he regards as ven worse, in some respects, than the League of Nations. a statement issued to the press he says in part:

"The proposed association of nations has not yet been reduced form nor yet defined. But from what one can gather here id there, it is the old League of Nations under another name. will be engaged in precisely the same kind of work and doing e same kind of things that were proposed by the League. . . . .

"It is claimed by the advocates of the League that the present eague has been of much service to Europe. If so, there is no ason for asking Europe to scrap the old League and try a new ie. If we are going into Europe, we ought to go in. If we are ot, we ought not to be handing her a new league every ninety ays.

"The United States operates under a written constitution. reat Britain has no written constitution. One of the argu-ents being put forth now in favor of the Association of Nations that Mr. Wilson made a mistake in giving his plan a written onstitution, that we should adopt the British idea and under-ke to conduct the League or an association of nations without ny written constitution or written covenant whatever; in ther words, that the new association will consist of representa-ves of different Governments coming together with no limita-on upon their jurisdiction or power or authority other than eir own discretion.

"A conclave of diplomats, sitting behind closed doors with othing to direct or limit their powers save their own will and iscretion, would be a rather interesting proposition. I am clined to think that if the American people choose a league, ey will choose one which has its powers defined, or at least an ttempt to define them, rather than trust their destiny to the nbridled discretion of a few men."

PHILIPPINE INDEPENDENCE PUT OFF

"HE CAME; HE SAW; HE ACCEPTED." In such brief fashion does the Manila *Bulletin* paraphrase the history of General Leonard Wood's six-months investigation of the Philippines, and his resignation from the United States Army to become Governor-General of the Islands. The University of Pennsylvania, which had held out to him, as an inducement to head that seat of learning, a yearly salary of $25,000 and the use of a house, rent free, will have to wait. For the new Governor-General finds, contrary to his predecessor's opinion, that the Filipinos are not yet ready for independence.

GENERAL WOOD FACING THE PHILIPPINE PROBLEM.

Which, according to one American editor, "is more acute than at any time since McKinley appointed Taft Governor-General." The present Governor-General is here seen meeting a native Provincial Governor.

He has made, in fact, a lengthy report to the President, but, as the Springfield *Republican* remarks, "the complete report is not likely to see the light while the Washington Conference remains in session." Excerpts from the report, however, tell us that, in General Wood's opinion independence for the Philippines should be indefinitely deferred. In this opinion he is joined by W. Cameron Forbes, a former Governor-General, who assisted in the investigation. Also, it might be said, the Wood-Forbes opinion is concurred in by the majority of editors throughout the United States, and by the editors of *The Times* and *The Bulletin*, American papers of Manila.

"Independence at this time for the Philippines would be ruinous," thinks the Kansas City *Star*, while the New York *Times* notes more specifically that "autonomous government, with Filipinos occupying the important offices of trust and responsibility, has not been notably successful." "We have lifted a people from the jungle, and delivered them from despotism and graft; we need them, and they need us. When they are ready for self-government, it will be granted to them, just as it was granted to Cuba," declares the Cincinnati *Enquirer*. In the meantime, says the Wood-Forbes report in part:

"We are convinced that it would be a betrayal of the Philippine people, a misfortune to the American people, a distinct step backward in the path of progress, and a discreditable neglect to our national duty were we to withdraw from the Islands and terminate our relationship there without giving the Filipinos the best chance possible to have an orderly and permanently stable government.

"We feel that, with all of their many excellent qualities, the experience of the last eight years, during which they have had practical autonomy, has not been such as to justify the people of the United States in relinquishing supervision of the Government of the Philippine Islands, withdrawing their Army and Navy and leaving the Islands a prey to any powerful nation coveting their rich soil and potential commercial advantages.

"We recommend that under no circumstances should the American Government permit to be established in the Philippine Islands a situation which would leave the United States in a position of responsibility without authority."

"The native politicians want a comfortably insured independence—with American guaranties against outside aggression," believes the New York *Tribune*. "But," explains this paper, "in such a case the United States would have responsibility — involving war, perhaps—without either sovereignty or authority." "It is, therefore, our duty to keep our flag on the Islands, where it means protection and prosperity, at least until world conditions become more settled," concludes the Providence *Journal*. As the Manchester *Union* sums up present conditions there:

Copyrighted 1921, by the Chicago "Tribune."

HE'S BETTER OFF ON BOARD.

—McCutcheon in the Chicago *Tribune*.

"Admittedly, affairs have not gone well in the Philippines. The administration of justice is criticized widely. Public improvements have not been carried on with conspicuous wisdom. Something has been done in the way of sanitation, but not enough. Racial problems have grown acute. There is unnecessary friction between Americans and Filipinos, and the old feud between Mohammedans and Christians in the southern islands has been embittered. There is widespread unrest. There is the uncertainty as to the general political status of the Islands.

"Quite as pressing is the difficulty due to the sad tangle into which finances have come. Altogether, the situation is sufficiently grave. It means that administration, to be successful, must pass into hands that are firm, trained and capable."

Because Uncle Sam is the guardian of the Philippines, "the decision as to when the time for independence has come must rest with the United States, even tho the people of the Islands grow restless in the meantime," maintains the Washington *Post;* "the question of independence must be settled in Washington, not in Manila."

Nevertheless, "We want independence!" was the slogan of the thousands of natives who greeted the Wood-Forbes mission when it landed at Manila. "If independence is not given now, it will be necessary for the United States to set a date when we may expect it," argues Manuel Quezon, Nationalist leader of the Philippine Government. This suggestion the New York *Evening Post* finds "wholly reasonable."

"In finance the natives have made a sorry showing," quotes the New York *World* from its contemporary, *The Times*, but, it asks, "is it any worse showing than New York City has made in its local affairs?" "Clearly," says a California paper, "we are hanging on to the Philippines for our own benefit, and not for the welfare of the inhabitants."

"We have had hard times in the Philippines, but so has the United States and every other country. Mistakes we have made, but who has not made them?" asks the director of the Philippine Press Bureau of Washington. In spite of these things, he contends, "conditions in the Islands to-day are better than conditions in any of the independent countries of the world."

A "MAKESHIFT" TAX LAW

DAMNED WITH FAINT PRAISE by its very sponsors, received with uncivil leers and jeers by the Democrats, the new Republican revenue law came as a most unwelcome guest on the eve of the national day of feasting and thanksgiving, newspaper writers very generally agree. The joy bells are seldom rung to herald the coming of a tax-gatherer, and many find it difficult to smile with Pollyanna while making out income-tax blanks. But now we are asked to pay Federal taxes in accordance with a law which, as the New York *Globe* (Rep.) notes, is "not satisfactory even to the men who voted for it." The Indianapolis *News* (Ind.) reminds us that Republican Senators and Representatives, "almost without exception, are at least cool toward it." Senator Smoot (Rep., Utah), who voted for the law, says it will be "condemned by the American people." Senator Calder (Rep., N. Y.) calls it "a disappointment." President Harding is said to be "frankly disappointed" with certain important features of the bill, and Senator Penrose (Rep., Pa.), responsible for the measure in the upper house, calls it "a temporary makeshift" which "does not place the tax system on a stable or scientific basis." When the baby looks like this in the eyes of the parents and family, the remarks of the neighbors may well be left to the imagination. It will suffice to note the Democratic New York *World's* characterization of the tax revision as "the most bungling piece of financial legislation that was ever sent to a President for his signature," and the assertion of a well-known New York accountant that it ought to go down in history as "the crime of 1921."

But even some of the sharpest critics of the new law find some good in it, or at least some improvement over the existing law. "Bad and wrong as the law is," admits the Democratic New York *Times*, "it does have the virtue of repealing the excess profits taxes." The change which, in the opinion of the Washington *Herald*, is likely to "promise the most immediate relief and benefit to business, is the repeal of the railroad traffic taxes; these have been paid directly by the shippers and have been a burden especially on the farmers, in many instances making the difference between profit and loss." The three per cent. tax on freight rates and the eight per cent. tax on passenger fares are repealed to take effect January 1. It is estimated that because of this the American public will pay $80,000,000 less to travel on the country's railroads in 1922 than they paid this year.

Any one who charges that the tax revision is relieving only the rich and not the poor is thinking about the reduction of the maximum income tax surtax from 65 per cent. to 50 per cent., but, says the Washington *Post*, he is failing to take into account "the increase from $2,000 to $2,500 in the exemption allowed to heads of families or the increase from $200 to $400 exemption allowed for each dependent." Since this concerns such a large number of our readers, we quote *The Post*, at some length:

"The head of a family earning up to $2,500 will, under the new law, pay no income tax whatever. Assuming that he has no dependents, if he earns $3,000 a year he will pay a total tax of $20, as against $40 under the old law. Since $3,000 represents approximately the average earnings of probably the largest class of citizens under existing conditions, it will be seen that millions will receive a reduction of 50 per cent. in their income tax. These as a rule are people to whom $20 is a very considerable item, much greater, in fact, than several times that amount would be to those of larger incomes. On $4,000 earnings the tax will be $60 instead of $80 under the former law and on $5,000 it will be $100 as against $120. The levy increases at this ratio up to incomes of $20,000, which will now pay $1,720 in tax instead of $1,990.

"Increasing the exemption for heads of families from $2,000 to $2,500 applies only to those with total incomes of $5,000 or less, but the actuaries of the Treasury Department estimate that more than 2,000,000 taxpayers in the country will benefit by this provision. Doubling the exemption for dependents—from $200 to $400 each—it is estimated will affect about 2,750,000 taxpayers."

This Washington daily, close to official sources of information, also explains that the increase in income-tax exemptions takes effect at once, that is, they apply to the taxes to be paid in 1922 on the income of the calendar year 1921. The reduction of the surtax, however, does not take effect until a year later, that is, the old rates will be paid next year on the income of 1921, but the new reduced rates will be paid in 1923 on the income of 1922.

In the same way excess profits taxes will be paid at existing rates next year on the profits of 1921, but there will be no tax to pay in 1923 on the profits of 1922. The increase in the corporation tax also takes effect in 1923 on the business of 1922.

"WE CALLED FOR *RELIEF!*"
—Harding in the Brooklyn *Eagle*.

According to Senator Penrose more than eight hundred modifications were made by the Senate in the old revenue law, but the comparatively small total change is indicated by the following summary of the outstanding features of the new law, made by a Washington correspondent of the New York *Times:*

"A reduction in taxes of $70,000,000 for this year and a reduction of $835,000,000 forecasted for 1922; the repeal of the excess profits tax as of January 1, 1922; reduction of maximum surtax on individual incomes from 65 per cent. to 50 per cent.; increase of the corporation income tax from 10 to 12½ per cent.; repeal of the transportation taxes as of January 1, 1922; increase of the personal exemption for married persons with incomes of less than $5,000 from $2,000 to $2,500, and for each dependent from $200 to $400, and the repeal of most of the so-called nuisance taxes."

"AW, IT MIGHT BE WORSE!"
—Sykes in the Philadelphia *Evening Public Ledger*.

According to Congressman Fordney, the bill will yield a revenue for the current fiscal year of $3,216,000,000, about $46,000,000 less than the Treasury has considered necessary. But Mr. Fordney believes the difference can be bridged by means of further economies on the part of various departments.

Since so much has been said of the wide-spread criticism of the bill, the chief objections should be noted, as set down by one of the less violent and less politically biased critics. The new law, says the New York *Journal of Commerce*, adds to and increases the general weight of taxation in these two ways:

"(1) By enlarging certain classes of taxes, such as those on corporation income.

"(2) By adding immensely to the severity of the administrative features, severe as these already were."

It seems to *The Journal of Commerce* that the "nuisance taxes" will be about as oppressive as ever. Certain administrative provisions dealing with stock issues, transfer, capital gains and losses and the like are possibly of some aid to "big business" but are of "no direct assistance to the ordinary business man." Even though it has been slightly reduced, the income surtax rate is still "so high as to drive what remains of the surplus income of the community into tax-free investment, so that we are not only holding back investment as a general process but are also directing what is left of it into unproductive channels as represented by Government, State, municipal and land bank bonds." Concludes this organ of business:

"The pity of the whole situation is that instead of giving relief to the average man, as it was expected no doubt by politicians that the new plan would do, the bill as now drafted will hurt him. Already it has wrought a bad effect upon credit, and especially upon the railroad prospect, and this influence may be expected to go much further. It will intensify the evils of the credit system which were already so obvious, largely as a result of tax exemption, and almost as strongly as ever discourage investment in productive enterprise.

"Altogether it will be a sorry day for the employed man who depends upon his labor when this bill takes effect. His soi-disant friends in Congress have stabbed him in a vital spot while pretending, and perhaps really thinking, that they were able to help him."

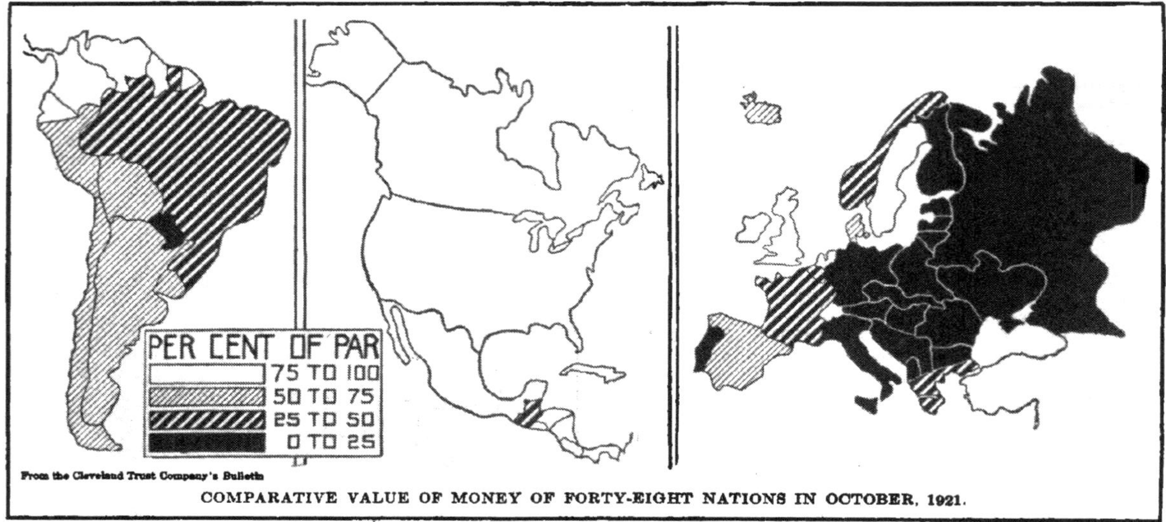

COMPARATIVE VALUE OF MONEY OF FORTY-EIGHT NATIONS IN OCTOBER, 1921.

HOW TO KEEP EUROPE GOING

THE PICTURE OF CIVILIZED EUROPE falling back into a state of "citylessness, illiteracy and the peasant life," such as Mr. Wells describes, is not a pleasant one, especially when we are reminded by bankers and business men that our own prosperity and the end of unemployment here depend on Europe's ability to buy from us. We have surplus goods to sell, but we also have more money than we need, while Europe is penniless and already heavily in debt to us. While the suggestion to cancel the Allied debts keeps cropping up, it does not seem to have won any wide support, and financial authorities are cudgeling their brains to devise some scheme for stabilizing exchange and getting American capital busy in Europe. Two interesting suggestions made by Frank A. Vanderlip, and the popularity of the ter Meulen scheme abroad make timely a brief outline of some of the plans for helping Europe which are taken most seriously by the press. It might be said here that several important financial papers declare that no purely financial scheme will be of any avail until the European Governments begin to set their houses in order, slow up the presses for turning out paper money, try to make revenues and expenses balance, and reform the political conditions which make investors afraid to put their funds into countries where property rights are insecure, tax methods confiscatory, and police protection uncertain. "Cure Europe's political ills," says *The Wall Street Journal*, for instance, and industry and finance will be in a fair way to take care of themselves.

It is evident to many that the present low value of the franc as compared with the dollar is of less importance than the fact that nobody knows what it is going to be worth from one day to another. So a good many of the plans for helping Europe center around what is called the stabilization of exchange. According to the press correspondents, a conference of bankers will soon be called in Europe to consider the effect of the German reparations payments on exchange, and the United States is likely to be represented, at least unofficially. Because America holds so much of the world's gold—40 per cent., roughly speaking—America alone, declares the London *Times*, can "stabilize credit by devising some scheme for financing the nations now hovering on the brink of insolvency." Reflecting the opinion of a number of financial authorities, both here and abroad, the New York *Tribune* remarks:

"Since it would seem impossible to raise to gold par the vast volume of paper currencies, it follows that there must be a refunding in some fashion—in some nations perhaps a repudiation of the paper, allowing it to go to sleep in the pockets of the last holder, even as did our first Continental currency and as did the assignats of Revolutionary France. . . .

"An international congress is required to bring pressure to compel each country to revalue its currency, and thus bring it into some sort of relation to fact. The mark, the franc, the lira, the pound, must have some definite value—if not in gold, then a value based on a composite of the current prices for the principal world commodities."

It has been suggested that exchange could be "pegged" effectively by an international bank which might also issue an international currency based on gold. While several plans for the formation of such a bank have been put forward, that outlined in some detail by Frank A. Vanderlip has received most attention. Mr. Vanderlip's "Gold Reserve Bank of the United States of Europe," with a paid-in capital of $1,000,000,000, would be controlled for the present in America and would use the dollar as a unit. It would establish branch gold reserve national banks in those European countries desiring to join the undertaking. These banks, says Mr. Vanderlip, could issue $5,000,000 gold-backed notes "in which the whole world would have confidence and which would be uniform in character throughout

AS YE SOW, SO SHALL YE REAP.

—Thomas in the Detroit *News*.

the territory adopting the scheme." This proposition from so eminent an American financial authority is said by Polish representatives here to be "the best news to Poland since the defeat of the Bolshevik armies." In this country it seems "ingenious and fairly simple" to the Philadelphia *Inquirer;* the Columbus *Dispatch* thinks the plan deserves the careful attention of the world's financiers. "Right in theory and workable if a way can be found to raise the capital and to overcome national jealousies," is the way the New York *Journal of Commerce* sums up Wall Street banking opinion. Editorially, *The Journal of Commerce* is skeptical, observing that "there is no cheap and easy way" to correct Europe's political, social and economic troubles "by the establishment of some gilded bank which will do all sorts of impossible things." This paper, *The Wall Street Journal*, and the Chicago *Journal of Commerce* agree that there is much more hope of relief in the more limited ter Meulen and Edge Law bank projects.

Mr. Vanderlip also has a plan for handling the Allied indebtedness to the United States, which totals well over $10,000,000,000. Mr. Vanderlip would insist on the payment of the debt, but he would have it understood that a considerable part of the money received would be "used as a revolving credit fund to be loaned to nations to help them accomplish specific purposes, purposes which we had carefully analyzed and believed to be economically sound and for the general good, purposes which would accomplish substantial and permanent economic and social results. The funds so loaned could in time be repaid." Under such a plan, it seems to Mr. Vanderlip that "the sting of our insistence would be taken away even from the minds of those who to-day see with the least clearness their moral obligation," and "if we convert the debt due to us into a debt to humanity, the whole world will want to see it paid."

While Mr. Vanderlip's debt plan has been regarded favorably in New York banking circles, several dailies point out that he misses the real difficulty, namely, that the European debtors have not the money to pay us, whatever we might intend to do with it. And the New York *Journal of Commerce* adds that if the European nations were in condition to make payments on their debts, American capitalists would be rushing in to invest in their industrial enterprises. In fact, "Europe can have our capital just as soon as she shows a disposition to restore order, balance her national budgets, and meet her obligations." And, we read elsewhere, the Arms Conference is helping Europe to do this by relieving some of the Powers of heavy military expenses.

The ter Meulen bond plan simply provides the machinery whereby under international supervision governments can issue bonds backed by national assets, which their importers can use as collateral in buying essential commodities. The plan is sponsored by the League of Nations and is approved by many bankers and government officials here and abroad.

A BLOW AT THE BUILDING COMBINE

A NEW ROAD TO PRISON has been discovered by Federal Judge William C. Van Fleet, of California, who is temporarily sitting in New York City. By sentencing to prison four business men who pleaded guilty to violating the anti-trust section of the Sherman Act, "he rendered a vastly greater service than merely by fining them," thinks the Newark *News*. In addition he created a precedent, for in the thirty-one years that the Sherman Act has been on the statute books, remarks the New York *Times*, "no business man has ever seen the inside of a jail for violating it." The four who received jail sentences were singled out, we are told, because of their activities in preventing competition in the tile and marble industry; "building-trust profiteering," the Boston *Herald* calls it. Judge Van Fleet's action, in the opinion of the New York *Globe*, "will have an immediate and salutary effect upon the tendency to reform shattered price combines. Fines were merely a tax on the bulging pockets of illegitimate business; prison terms are a knife-thrust at its very heart."

JUDGE VAN FLEET IN A LESS SEVERE MOMENT.

He is here shown swearing in Miss Annette Adams, the first woman to be appointed an assistant to the Attorney-General of the United States. The Judge's recent decision sentencing four building material dealers to jail for violating the Anti-Trust Law is hailed as an "emancipation proclamation for the home-builders of the country."

Two of the men sentenced by the Federal Judge were presidents of tile and mantel associations, and each of the two others played an active part in his particular association, it is said. "The conviction and sentence of the 'tile-trust' officials," notes the Springfield *Republican*, "is a direct outcome of the Lockwood legislative committee's investigation of the building situation in New York. Under the State law, labor leaders who were found guilty went to Sing Sing, but the guilty contractors and dealers were liable only to fines. There are more teeth in the Federal law." As Judge Van Fleet declared from the bench:

> "Ample facts have been adduced showing that the abnormal prices of building materials, as well as the lack of new building construction and the resultant lack of proper housing for the multitudes of human beings in large cities throughout the country, are traceable directly to an interlocking series of criminal conspiracies and combinations in the building trades, of which this case is typical.
>
> "With these practises prevailing in this particular association and with like combinations holding a grip throughout the country upon the various building trades, it is not a matter for surprize that the building industry throughout the great cities of the country has been for several years virtually at a standstill."

The total fines imposed by the Judge upon the four who received jail sentences, and forty-eight other individuals and corporations, amount to about $125,000, notes the Boston *Herald*, "but no fines would count for much as a penalty or as a deterrent by comparison with these terms in prison." As the New York *Evening World* put it:

> "By a system of mutual protection and collusive bidding, these tile manufacturers maintained abnormal prices at a time when the high cost of building materials was one of the chief

obstacles in the way of relieving the housing shortage. They were merciless toward the public. They deserve no mercy from the law. Fines are all in the day's work to men who combine to dictate prices, but there is still a strong prejudice against spending even four months in jail. If that prejudice weakens, lengthen the jail term."

"Public sentiment, when it is reflected how the people have been at the mercy of rent profiteers through the housing shortage, will eagerly back the Court in imprisoning all such offenders," believes the Pittsburgh *Post*. In years gone by, notes The Philadelphia *Public Ledger:*

"The public has seen trusts 'dissolved' by the courts under the Sherman Act without being able to observe that the business practises of these trusts were in any appreciable way altered. It has seen fines imposed upon violators of the law, and its conclusion as to that was that men who would violate the law would not at all be above assessing the amount of the fine upon the next transaction they undertook. In other words, the public became convinced there were no 'teeth' in the Sherman Law, and it lost interest in the law except as to whether or not the missing 'teeth' could be put in. Judge Van Fleet has done that for us."

Editors throughout the country opine that the so-called building trust has received, in the words of one of them, a "smashing blow," and that a new era in anti-trust law enforcement is now upon us. As we read in the Baltimore *News:*

"Thirty years ago it would probably have been a sheer impossibility to send a man to prison for organizing business combinations. It was difficult enough to establish at all the authority of the law in such cases, even tho the necessity for some defense of the public interest had become obvious. A law is not merely an inscription upon the statute book; it is also a state of mind, an attitude on the part of public opinion. The statute can be inscribed easily enough; the process of building up the opinion which is necessary to make it really effective is a long and difficult one, and we are just now seeing it brought to completion in the matter of anti-trust legislation.

"The Sherman Act is thus vindicated; but the Sherman Act was only a beginning. A vast deal has been done in other directions, and much must still be done before we shall have adjusted our laws and jurisprudence to the conditions of modern industrial life. The present case is interesting as an illustration of how that adjustment must proceed—not by a sudden introduction of sweeping and unenforceable laws, but by a slow development and growth in the living body of law."

Despite the precedent that Judge Van Fleet appears to have created, the Pittsburgh *Dispatch* asserts that "only a moral victory" has been gained. The Sherman Law has been vindicated, avers this paper, but nothing has been done to relieve the building trades, and through them the public. Continues *The Dispatch:*

"The victory can not be graded higher than a moral conquest. From the practical view-point the victory is hollow, involving nothing more deterring than a severe prison sentence for one man, nominal prison terms for a few others, and the payment of fines from a gigantic profit through illegal practises thoroughly proved in all the trials. Aside from these effects everything remains as before the inquiry. Prices have refused to drop as an admission of wrong-doing and to round out the victory for law; and conditions surrounding the use of building materials are unchanged in practical sense. The housing shortage is as remorseless as before. Exposure of the methods of manipulation and monopolistic guardianship has brought no relief. Buyers are still forced to pay extortionate prices and to give compulsory consent to imposed conditions for the use of materials. Exposure of methods, convictions, pleas of guilty, fines, and even imprisonment, have failed to break up the practises which brought these penalties."

THE ROW IN PORTO RICO

THE "TEMPEST IN A TEAPOT," as one writer refers to the agitation which has raged in Porto Rico for some months, has now reached the stage where delegations from the island are arriving in the United States to ask President Harding to remove the Governor. He has undoubtedly been guilty of "gross tactlessness," declares the independent New York *Evening Post*, altho it reminds us that in reading the complaints from Porto Rico we must remember that they are the complaints of a party—the Unionist party. This party, says its leader, "demands a régime of self-government." "Out of nineteen Senators all but four, and out of thirty-nine Representatives all but twelve, are Unionists," we are told. In a cablegram to their Washington representative the Unionists make these specific charges against Governor Reily:

Copyrighted by Harris & Ewing

GOVERNOR REILY.

"That he removed judicial officers without stating the cause and threatened removal of others.

"That he annulled the 'moral power' of judges by announcing that they would be removed if a decision was rendered 'considered by the Governor unjust.'

"That he pardoned criminals 'to please Socialist leaders,' and that these criminals immediately committed new crimes.

"That he 'directed or permitted' the police to break up a reception organized to greet Antonio Barcelo, President of the Senate and leader of the Unionist Party, 'later promoting the police officer who broke up the demonstration.'

"That he encouraged and rewarded all who offended the majority party.

"That he appointed three departmental heads 'opposed to the spirit of the organic act and to the laws of Porto Rico,' on the recommendation of 'corporations whose Directors reside outside Porto Rico.' "

"A steady stream of complaint has followed his inauguration," notes the New York *World* (Ind. Dem.). Even the staunchly Republican Washington *Post* is of the opinion that "if the usefulness of Governor Reily has been ended by unfortunate occurrences, a change should be made forthwith."

"Governor Reily is a tyrant whose methods of misgoverning Porto Rico can only lead to enmity toward the United States," avers Antonio Barcelo, President of the Porto Rican Senate, who is said to be at the head of the opposition to Governor Reily. As the Governor's secretary writes to the New York *Journal of Commerce:*

"This new offensive against Governor Reily, through a channel involving financial interests, one that is more far-reaching than whims of sentiment or diplomacy, has its origin in the operation of Antonio R. Barcelo, leader of the secessionist movement and president of the Unionist party, a relative of whom is at the head of a delegation now in the States on the mission against Governor Reily."

The New York *Herald* (Ind. Rep.), quotes this letter written to Barcelo by the Governor:

"I am sorry, my dear Barcelo, that you still fail to comprehend my business here. You seem not to understand that the old order has changed. I want you to fully understand that I shall never appoint any one to any office who is not an advocate of independence. . . . All my appointments will be made strictly by me, as I do not intend to be hampered or held up."

The Herald congratulates Porto Rico on having "a man who knows why he is in the palace at San Juan, and what he is about."

TOPICS IN BRIEF

The pen is mightier than the battle-ship.—*Columbia Record.*

What little of business is left ought to be sound.—*Charleston Gazette.*

Hughes to the line, let the ships fall where they may!—*Columbia Record.*

Only disarmament can sink the world's floating debt.—*Farmville (Va.) Herald.*

The world craves that peace which passeth all misunderstanding.—*Norfolk Virginian-Pilot.*

The world has now learned that the dogs of war are not a howling success.—*Asheville Times.*

The reason business conditions are unsettled is because so many accounts are.—*Elizabeth Journal.*

We can not take our interest out of Europe without taking some interest in Europe.—*Asheville Times.*

Political junkers have kept war alive; naval junkers will try to end it. —*Nashville Southern Lumberman.*

When soldiers are entirely unknown then the unknown soldier will be sufficiently honored.—*Charleston Gazette.*

There is poetic justice in the reduction of German currency to what she once said treaties were.—*Dallas News.*

There will be about as much giving as usual this year, unless the ten-cent stores run short of stock.—*Detroit Free Press.*

As we understand the tangled Far Eastern question, American business wishes to bring orders out of chaos.—*Tremont Tribune.*

You can say one thing for beer as a medicine. You don't find any half-empty bottles standing about on shelves. —*Minneapolis Star.*

Just now we are hearing what the nations want, but a little later will learn what they will get. —*Boston Shoe and Leather Reporter.*

Open door in China is the front door, and it may be important to settle who carries the key of the back door.—*Wall Street Journal.*

There is something strangely suggestive about Judge Landis's contention that Babe Ruth shouldn't make money on the side.—*Fort Wayne News.*

And now when a doctor speaks of a case, you don't know whether he is talking about the patient or the prescription.—*Pueblo Star Journal.*

The newspapers tell of the death of New York's champion bootblack. Death, it seems, still loves a shining mark.—*Nashville Southern Lumberman.*

The Soviet has issued paper money to the extent of five trillion, seven hundred and fifty billion rubles. That is a dollar and seventeen cents in American money.—*Seattle Argus.*

The *West Virginia*, America's mightiest battle-ship, has been launched with the prospect of being scrapped in a few months. Best prospect any battle-ship ever had.—*Omaha World-Herald.*

Mr. de Valera says: "There is no clause in the English proposal which gives us what we want." The only clause which could give him all he wants is Santa Claus.—*Nashville Southern Lumberman.*

Objection is made that public demonstrations at the arms conference are against diplomatic precedent. Perhaps the sort of diplomacy we have been treated to heretofore didn't deserve applause.—*Seattle Times.*

Britannia, briefly, will golden-rule the waves.—*New York Tribune.*

The big tax issue is settled—all but getting the wherewithal to pay.—*Washington Star.*

Isn't it funny that the mail robbers never interfere with your monthly bills?—*Asheville Times.*

Germany is at least free from the crooks who used to make counterfeit marks.—*New York World.*

The nations should make peace first and then they should make it last.—*Norfolk Virginian-Pilot.*

Karl tried two coups and failed; but the Hungarian Government is hoping that his present coop will prove successful.—*Nashville Southern Lumberman.*

THE RILING REILY DID.

—Fitzpatrick in the St. Louis *Post-Dispatch.*

Nations could safely lose their arms if statesmen wouldn't lose their heads. —*Lansing Capital News.*

Next thing somebody will be prosecuted for passing Russian rubles for cigar coupons.—*Seattle Argus.*

Scrapping navies is the surest way to put a stop to navies' scrapping.—*Nashville Southern Lumberman.*

Crowded mourners' benches emphasize the need of speeding up that business revival. —*Norfolk Virginian-Pilot.*

You see, by reducing navies we can save money enough to build far-cruising and heavily armored aircraft.—*Lincoln Star.*

Marshal Foch has gained ten pounds but was probably weighed with his new medals on.—*Boston Shoe and Leather Reporter.*

All will yet be well if the open door in China can only be attained without making it a jar.—*Philadelphia Evening Public Ledger.*

Don't be too optimistic. Congress will find some way to spend the money we save by disarming.—*Boston Post.*

There is one consoling thing about a war with Japan. It would be a naval war, and the desk men couldn't wear spurs.—*Waterbury Democrat.*

While agreement at the Washington Conference is not to be expected before snow flies, it is to be hoped for before fur flies.—*Norfolk Virginian-Pilot.*

The rice-growers are putting on a campaign to increase the use of rice. Why don't they start a matrimonial bureau?—*Nashville Southern Lumberman.*

The French say lasting peace hinges on security. Every one who is reasonable must admit that lasting security hinges on peace.—*Louisville Courier-Journal.*

Over in the Pacific are two contiguous islands named respectively New Britain and New Ireland. And still we talk of peace in that region.—*Columbia Record.*

It must be very discouraging to Mr. Hearst, after all the work he has done, to see Japan displaying such an amicable attitude towards us.—*Nashville Southern Lumberman.*

After watching the Army-Navy football game the foreign delegates to the Arms Conference are likely to figure that we don't need any weapons but those we were born with.—*New York World.*

The Literary Digest speaks of a "plan for giving every man work to fit his brains." But just think how many people that would throw out of work permanently.—*Nashville Southern Lumberman.*

FOREIGN - COMMENT

LORD CURZON'S "PLAIN WORDS" TO FRANCE

A SHARP WARNING to France, by Lord Curzon, Britain's Minister for Foreign Affairs, that if she attempts to pursue "an isolated or individual policy" she will fail in the long run both to injure Germany and to protect herself, throws a brilliant new light on Anglo-French relations. Until Premier Briand made his speech before the Washington Conference, Americans had not particularly noticed the jarring European policies of England and France. Rumors of occasional disputes between the two nations were heard faintly from afar, but when Mr. Briand "spoke right out in meeting" at Washington, we are told, and Lord Curzon "answered back" at a public luncheon in London, then America became a close spectator of Anglo-French differences. Even some English observers concede that France is justified in looking out for herself by her strong right arm, because except for the occupation of the Rhine, her safeguards against German aggression are "nebulous." First there is the League of Nations, which, it is pointed out by British opponents of that organization, was unable even to save Armenia, and in which America has no share and little sympathy. Then, there was the proposed triple compact between Great Britain, France and the United States, which never matured because of the abstention of the United States. Some adverse critics of England say, moreover, that England is much too friendly in spirit to Germany not to cause disquiet if not suspicion in France; and there is the familiar Polish argument that England "would like to see a strong France in Europe, but not too strong; and similarly a strong Germany in Europe, but not too strong." This aspiration of England, in the view of some, is at the root of all the wordy squabbles between France and England arising from their cross-purposes since the armistice, and the verbal climax is reached, we are told, in the speech of Lord Curzon, from which we quote the following:

DAVID FEELS SAFE.

LLOYD GEORGE (to France): "There's nothing to be alarmed about! What can a million Bavarians do without a single battle-ship?"
—*La Democratie Nouvelle* (Paris)

"In what lies the real strength and protection of our great ally across the Channel? It does not consist in the valor of her soldiers, great as that is. It does not consist in the strength of her armies, potent as they are. It does not consist in the inexhaustible spirit of her people. It does not consist even in the justice of her cause.

"It exists in the fact that the conscience of the world and the combined physical force of the world—and in that I include America—will not tolerate the reappearance in the heart of Europe of a great and dangerous Power which has always rattled the sword in the scabbard and which is a perpetual menace to the peace of the world. We shall convert Germany into a peaceful member of the International Court of Europe only if the great Powers combine not merely to enforce the Treaty but to make it clear that no policy of retaliation or revenge would be tolerated by them, and that they will assist Germany to play her part, provided she shows sincerity and good-will. So long as Great Britain, France and Italy hold together I am hopeful of this result.

"The sole question of the recovery of the peace of the world is not the old idea of splendid isolation by any individual power. There is not much splendor in isolation, after all. It is harmonious cooperation of Powers as a whole."

This part of Lord Curzon's speech refers obviously, it is said, to Premier Briand's address at the Washington Conference, but the British Foreign Minister took advantage of his opportunity to speak also of the situation in the Near East, where France has made a separate treaty with the Turkish Nationalist Government while the Greeks and Turks are still actively at war. In this connection, Lord Curzon said:

"Much more important than the victory of either party is that there should be no victory, but that there should be peace. This will never be achieved if any one Power tries to steal a march on another and conclude arrangements on its own account. This takes us to a blind alley, a cul-de-sac out of which we shall never get unless the Powers work together with perfect loyalty."

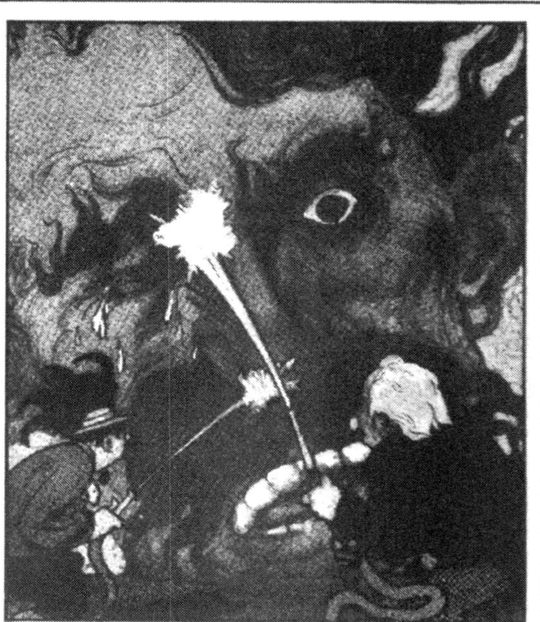

"THE FIRE BRIAND"

LLOYD GEORGE (to Italy): "This wild man from France threatens to reduce Europe to ashes."
—*Kladderadatsch* (Berlin)

The British Premier's London newspaper, *The Daily Chronicle*, discusses Lord Curzon's speech at length and warns France against the mistake made by Germany of "trusting only to the size of her biceps. Germany did this, and she fell. So would France if she did the same." Reverting to the Paris Conference, this newspaper informs us that:

"Few know, but every one ought to know, that Lloyd George, if he could have had his way, would have persuaded the Allies to disarm after Germany had disarmed. Had his proposals been accepted they would have marked the definite dethronement of force in our political ideas and the conversion of the world to new ways of thought, and the recent history of the world would have been different. The door is still open, but if France bangs it, frankly we do not know what is to become of old Europe."

A COMMUNIST JIBE AT FRANCE.

THE FRENCH MOTHER'S LAMENT: "The home in France means a disabled father, a son serving under the colors in the Near East, and the youngest getting ready for next year's class of recruits."

—*L'Humanité* (Paris).

Lord Curzon's speech is "a very grave public utterance" and seems "entirely true" according to the Liberal London *Daily News*, which adds:

"The question for Frenchmen is simply whether they are more likely to attain the security which they desire by a policy which haughtily disregards the wishes and even the urgent necessities of their neighbors, or by working in concert with them even at the cost of sacrificing some of the immediate steps which may seem to French eyes necessary to the protection of France.

"The answer admits of no doubt. France alone assuredly cannot keep Germany permanently weak. It is probable that the whole of Europe cannot do that, and it is not desirable, if it could be done."

On the other hand, the extreme Unionist London *Morning Post*, which would be supposedly one of Lord Curzon's supporters, describes his luncheon speech as "unfortunate" and observes:

"The safeguards given to France against German aggression apart from the occupation of the Rhine, were the League of Nations and the triple compact. As the League of Nations could not save Armenia, we do not suppose that the short and rickety arm of Geneva could do much to save France. The triple compact has been dissolved owing to the abstention of the United States. Was that any reason why Great Britain should withdraw?

"The responsible British authorities ought to have assured themselves at the time that President Wilson had behind him the support of the American people and their elected representatives. They blundered on that point, and then on realizing the blunder backed out of the solemn obligation without giving the British and the French peoples any valid excuse for such precipitate action. If France then is acting alone, she is doing so because her friend has deserted her."

The Morning Post declares furthermore that France is not afraid of Germany, and is merely asserting her right to take necessary precautions against a renewal of the horrors of 1914. Another critic of Lord Curzon is the London *Times*, which calls his speech "a defense and an apology rather than a clear statement of constructive policy," and proceeds:

"If we rightly interpret Lord Curzon's veiled allusions, he desired to explain the manifest inadequacy of the foreign policy of the British as being due to the fact that, as the result of the war, the British Government are no longer able to act independently, but form part of a system whose imperfect working is responsible for the irregularities that still trouble the world at large and ourselves in particular."

This famous English daily points out further that on several occasions since the war Great Britain has not acted consistently, and reminds us that to France, not to England, is due the credit of repelling the Red army from the gates of Warsaw.

Altho the first impressions among the Paris press were that Lord Curzon's speech might do harm to Franco-British relations, there was a unanimous second thought as exprest by the Paris *Intransigeant* that "there has been a great deal of violent talk over very little." Nearly all the Paris newspapers endorse Mr. Briand's attitude at Washington, altho the *Journal des Débats*, which is not at all pro-British, criticizes the French Premier for failing to reach an understanding with England about the Angora agreement before he went to Washington. The Paris *Liberté* points out that the recent hostile demonstrations towards France in Italy, however ill-founded, should serve as a warning that Great Britian and France should learn to understand each other better.

It is the view of the semi-official Paris *Temps* that the unity of of policy which Lord Curzon demands has not been preserved by England since the Armistice, and the British Foreign Secretary is reminded that England has repeatedly adopted policies with regard to Russia, Poland, Turkey, and even Germany, in which France could not and did not join, so this important daily wonders whether by unity of policy Lord Curzon means acquiescence by France in all the plans which his Government proposes.

A DAY DREAM FROM HOLLAND.

EUROPE: "Ah, if there were only some one like you, Napoleon, to bring order into my turbulent household!"

—*De Amsterdammer* (Amsterdam).

Wide World Photo.

"LONG LIVE THE GERMAN REPUBLIC!"

Following the murder of Matthias Erzberger by the "Monarchist Murder Gang," thousands of German Republican loyalists took occasion to express their fealty to the German Reich and their opposition to Monarchist reaction by endless parades in the larger cities and by massing in public squares to hail speeches asserting and pledging the imperishability of democratic government in Germany. As monarchist and militarist are said to be interchangeable terms in Germany, these public demonstrations have "special significance for the foreign observer."

GERMAN MILITARISM IN BRITISH EYES

WILD AND EXAGGERATED as were the threats and fears of a genuine civil war when Erzberger was murdered by the German Monarchists, and peaceful as is the compromise that has followed this tragic event, it would be erroneous, say some British observers, to pooh-pooh the whole episode as a mere tempest in a teapot, "artificially created by a handful of extremists on either side." The murder, it is recalled, followed bickerings between Bavaria and the Central Government over the latter's determination to fulfil the Peace Treaty. It was described as a political murder hatched by the "murder gang" which had found a safe asylum in Bavaria, and the enemies of Berlin declared that the Republic was in instant danger of overthrow by the Monarchist reactionaries. To sweep away the mass of reaction in Bavaria, Dr. Wirth and President Ebert issued the famous decree of August 29 based on Article 48 of the Weimar Constitution, which states explicitly in its second paragraph that "when public order and security are materially disturbed or endangered in the German Reich, the President of the Reich is empowered to take the necessary measures to restore public order and security, and in case of necessity to have recourse to armed force." As far as the legal aspect of the quarrel between Bavaria and the Berlin Government is considered, Berlin seems to have the right on its side, we are informed by a contributor to the London *Fortnightly Review* (November), who concedes meanwhile that the main interest in the conflict for outsiders is "not so much in the legal and administrative niceties involved, as in the forces operating with more or less of concealment in the background." Europe as a whole is said to have been curious to know whether Bavaria was seriously considering the idea of separating from the Reich, whether there was any immediate likelihood of a Monarchist *coup d'état* and whether the plans for maintaining Germany's military organization were really as formidable as they were often represented. The notion that Bavaria might be detached from the Reich has "long been coquetted with in certain French circles," according to this writer, who tells us that while the Bavarian "may be as cantankerous as he will towards his compatriots over domestic affairs . . . in questions with foreign Powers he is and will remain as good a German as any." The questions of a monarchical restoration and of secretly keeping up a German army, it is said, "grow together in many respects, since it is mainly the same body of men who are striving after these objects." Nevertheless, there are comparatively few German Monarchists who think "an attempt immediately to restore the Empire would be successful" for—

"To be successful the monarchy must either be backed by a sufficient military force or repose upon the willing adhesion of a people which shall have regained the confidence of Europe, and can be trusted to ensure that the restored monarchy, if restored, would be incapable of reverting to its former militarism.

"Whether a Hohenzollern would ever consent to remount the throne hedged round by such restrictions, or whether, if he did, he would do so with any real intention of abiding loyally by the conditions imposed upon him, may well be open to doubt. . . . Since an immediate restoration is both an impolitic and impossible object to pursue, the intention of the reactionaries is to prepare the way by the establishment of a temporary dictatorship, military or otherwise. There are many people who think that this is the ambition of General Ludendorff, and it is certainly significant that this hero of the military party, recently honored by Königsberg University in terms of extravagant chauvinism, should have been taking an increasingly active part in public functions. Nor are members of the Entente likely to be gulled by his recent statements to a correspondent of the *Matin*, in which he ridiculed the feasibility of Germany waging a war of revenge on France, and declared that the real danger is Bolshevism, against which Great Britain, France and Germany should combine."

Important elements in Germany are "consistently and obstinately trying to avoid the fulfilment of their obligations under the Treaty of Versailles," says this British informant, who adds that the exposure of the Erzberger murderers has proved again, if such proof were required, that "many officers of the old army are banded together in associations spread not only over the whole of Germany, but reaching also into adjacent countries."

SOCIALISTS AND LABORITES IN ITALY

IT IS NOT EASY to say in a word how the Socialists and the Laborites of Italy are differentiated from each other, we are told, nor must it be thought that the Socialist party operates in direct opposition to the Labor party, and that therefore the strength of the Labor party is a safeguard against Socialism. The latter notion lulls some foolish minds in Italy, writes a distinguished authority, Luigi Einaudi, in the Milan *Corriere della Sera*, who says that "hats" predominate in the Socialist party and "caps" in the Labor party. The remark on head-gear means that there are "more organizers in the Labor party and fewer lawyers, professors and philosophers than in the Socialist party." The lawyers and their ilk are said to be "mostly prattlers and people who have chosen the Socialist party as a more expeditious way to a career." On the other hand the Labor party is "composed mostly of secretaries of leagues, of the chamber of labor and of organizers who come from factories and the fields." We read on:

"Some time ago there was a reaction in the Labor party against the traitorous intellectual element which was not sufficiently repressed. After a brief interval, during which the intelligentsia were disbanded, a violent and extreme section reasserted itself and took up with the Socialist movement. The Socialist party is dominated by prepossessions of those directing it who have not properly felt the problem of the workers. The Labor party may easily be blamed for sinning in the opposite direction, by concerning itself only with the concrete problems of the worker. The laborer in town and country may also acquire a certain culture by reading and thus learn by heart the evil teachings of the Socialist creed and become truly impassioned with the idea of immediate and rapid reform in wages, work and moral and intellectual conditions. . . .

"Very numerous among the Socialist party leaders are rich people and those who live on incomes or earnings in the liberal professions. Such as these invent sophisms to demonstrate that there is no contradiction between taxation and taking property without indemnification; also that it is perfectly logical to speak of the Army, of the royal guards and of the nobility as if speaking of another race, while they themselves are all the time living in luxurious apartments with many servants.

"In the Labor party organizers predominate and the leaders here usually derive their incomes from the stipends and proceeds of their offices. Some amass conspicuous sums . . . and it has been reported that one leader got between 50,000 and 100,000 lira in one year. Yet all the time the recipients of such revenue speak, live, and dress as workingmen and are not out of harmony with their environment."

Theoretical tendencies abound in the Socialist party, we are told, because the leaders of it are bred on some few books and periodicals such as they have access to in the universities and in the law courts. They are not prepared to understand the concrete economic problems of the worker. Their desire is to leap suddenly into power, which they fear to do lest they should be expelled from the party or perhaps "because they know instinctively that they would commit many errors." On the other hand the Laborites, it is said, are indifferent to all theoretical matters and confine their interests to lockouts, organization, cooperative societies, etc.

The result is, according to this informant, that in Italy, the leaders of the Socialist party are chiefly concerned with their own political advancement, while the leaders of the Labor party busy themselves most in "seeking millions for cooperative societies, urging public work and drafting law projects in behalf of the working man." He adds that insofar as the Labor party leaders succeed in their enterprises, Italy shows practical Socialism in being. Over these reforms of the Laborites, he tells us, Socialist leaders exult and claim all the credit for having brought them about. Incidentally, it is recalled that about a year ago all the bourgeois and intellectuals among the Italian Socialists aspired to be Lenines and Trotskys, but as events have developed in Russia, such dictatorial ambitions have fast dwindled to the vanishing point.

NORWAY'S FOURTEEN PER CENT. PROHIBITION

WINES AND LIQUORS containing not more than 14 per cent. of alcohol do not free Norway from the prohibition bone of contention, it seems, and many familiar arguments for and against prohibition were heard in the recent Parliamentary elections very similar to those we hear in America. But an argument new to American disputants is the effect prohibition has on export and import trade in Europe, for such wine-producing countries as France, Spain and Portugal are important markets for Norwegian exports, notably fish; and the anti-prohibition cry is that if alcoholic beverages from France, Spain, and Portugal are barred, naturally these countries retaliate by barring out Norwegian fish. The Norwegian press recall that the late government concluded an agreement with France by which Norway undertook to import certain quantities of brandy and strong wines in return for being treated as a most favored country by the French customs authorities. Negotiations with Spain and Portugal are in progress; but meanwhile the Norwegian "wets" find ammunition in the fact that both Spain and Norway have abrogated their most favored nation clauses. The consequence is that Norwegian klipfish sent to Spain and Spanish wines and fruits shipped to Norway are subject to maximum tariffs, which "in the long run will probably be intolerable to both countries." Similar retributive action was lately taken by Portugal, in a quintuple increase of the customs duties on Norwegian products and a considerable rise in the harbor dues on Norwegian ships.

Altho the Conservative elements triumphed in the Parliamentary elections held toward the end of October, and the Rights and the Agriculturists have a clear majority in the new Storthing, various Norwegian editors agree that "the effect of this majority on prohibition in Norway cannot as yet be foretold with any certainty." Nevertheless there are journals which predict that the "drys" will still have a majority in the Storthing because of prohibition advocates among the Agriculturists. Norway's first taste of prohibition was a temporary war measure and the new law which puts a permanent ban on all wines and liquors containing more than 14 per cent. of alcohol is characterized by the Christiania *Morgenbladet* as "a sacrifice designed to secure the prohibitionist vote." On the other hand the chief organ of the Socialists, the Christiania *Social-Demokraten*, declares that prohibition was not an issue in the election. The fact is that the law had been made and it must be supposed that "all parties that joined in bringing about the referendum are agreed that no changes can be made in the prohibition laws without a new referendum." Then "everybody can take his stand on the prohibition question, without regard to other questions." As an indication of the divergence of view on the effects of prohibition, we cite first the conservative Christiania *Aftenposten*, which blames prohibition for spoiling the young, and says:

"A few years ago the young people of Norway were very temperate. Even in the space of time covered by one man's memory an immense advance had been made in the progress of temperance among the young people. This progress has ceased and all because of the prohibition policy."

In sharp contrast to the above, the Government press maintain that just the opposite is the case and that the good results of prohibition will become even more obvious after the first difficult transition period has passed. Says the Stavenger *Aftenblad:*

"We know that prohibition has decreased misdemeanors caused by drunkenness by fifty per cent., despite the fact that no product in any country has received so much advertising lately as liquor in Norway. The result does honor to the power of resistance of the Norwegian people."

SCIENCE - AND - INVENTION

TO MAKE MANHATTAN ISLAND SIX MILES LONGER

SHALL a great part of New York Bay be filled in so that Manhattan Island may be made larger? To do this would merely be to carry out on a greater scale what has already been done with Governors Island, in the bay, whose size has now been greatly multiplied by filling in the shallows just to the south. That enlargement would be engulfed in the proposed new filling, and Governors Island would cease to be a separate entity. The extension would make Manhattan about six miles longer, and the North and East Rivers would join at a new "Battery" not far from the entrance of the Narrows. The plan is detailed in the following description which we quote from *The Illustrated World* (Chicago):

"New York, now credited with being the most populous city in the world, must find more territory. The congestion in certain areas is tremendous. Manhattan Island. Staten Island and Long Island—the last ninety miles in length—would seem to offer sufficient land for even so great a metropolis, but the commercial interests must have certain favored sections for proper operation, and also the problems of getting to and from work are becoming more and more serious. The most up-to-date methods of transportation cannot overcome these obvious drawbacks, and more land is necessary.

"But where is this additional territory to be found? If man has used up all the available resources nature had placed at his disposal, apparently there is nothing to do but get along as best he can. However, it has suddenly occurred to the New Yorker that the land he has been seeking lies at his very door. The map shows that Manhattan Island is a narrow strip of land, about thirteen miles in length and in no place wider than two, lying between the Hudson on the one side and the East River on the other. At the north it terminates at a narrow stream, known as the Harlem River, and on the south at the Battery, overlooking the Upper Bay. Now it is proposed to extend Manhattan out into the bay so as to include about six more square miles and come within close range of Staten Island. Congress, by its passage of the Edge-Ansorg bill, signed by President Harding, has given free rein to New York City to make their great improvement. Plans are already being drawn up to put this permission definitely into effect.

"As an engineering feat the filling-up of this part of the bay will not be a gigantic one. The water is shallow and no exceptional features are involved, at least none that have not already been met and solved by engineering science. The building of a series of great coffer-dams, the pumping out of the stagnant and—it must be confessed—rather dirty waters, the pouring of endless loads of earth and stone upon the erstwhile sea bottom—these are the steps that will constitute the procedure to be taken.

"The 3,840 acres of terra firma thus added to the great city's area will be worth considerably over a million dollars more than enough to pay off the present total indebtedness of the municipality.

"It is proposed to construct a model city on the most scientific pattern compatible with the peculiar needs of the business section on this new land. Every building—if this part of the admirable plan goes through—will be a block square. There will be three, perhaps four, levels. There will be streets in as many tiers or decks. The lowest level will be used for subway and trains; the next higher for heavy auto and truck traffic; the last for light vehicular and pedestrian traffic."

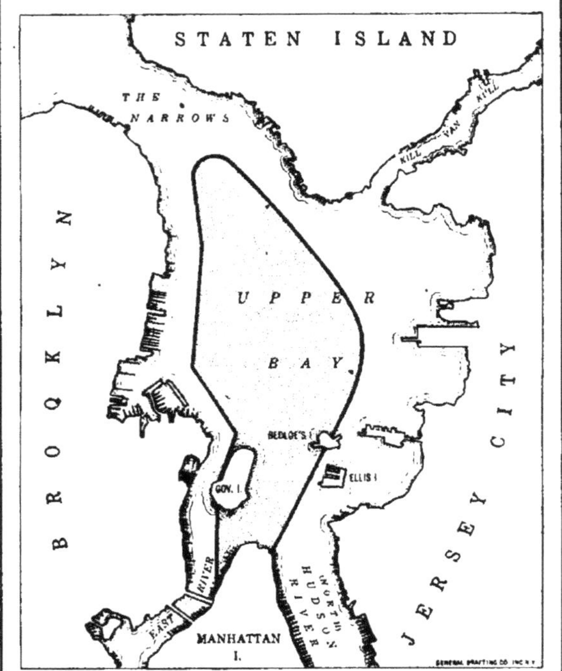

MAP OF THE PROPOSED NEW ADDITION.

Extending six miles down the bay and adding 3,840 acres to Manhattan Island. The value of the land would not only pay for the expense of making it, it is claimed, but would pay off the municipal debt and leave a million dollars for the city treasury. This map faces south, to correspond with the view on the opposite page.

Tunnels will run under this new made land, connecting Brooklyn with Staten Island and the Jersey shore. The water-ways at present separating the three main sections of New York City would be practically bridged by the great fill-in. Accessibility would be assured for any one section with the others. It would take thirty minutes to go from Staten Island to Manhattan by the ferries, and in winter and in foggy weather it sometimes takes hours to make the passage. Further:

"The rail route to Philadelphia would be cut down by ten miles and that from Philadelphia to Boston by twenty. Also, freight is tied up for days on the Jersey side of the Hudson at the present time. It is estimated that the facilities brought about by the improvement would reduce this delay by an average of ten days. As freight terminal charges for this period mount up to two dollars and fifty cents a ton, the saving on many thousand tons of freight is obvious, and naturally the cost of living in New York City—particularly on Manhattan or Staten Island—would be correspondingly reduced.

"An engineering authority says of the fill-in: 'It will give terminals on Manhattan Island for all railroads, thus increasing the radius of centralization. It will give twelve miles of much needed new protected docks; it will open up the vast territory of Staten Island and South Brooklyn for the coming millions, and it will keep the Wall Street zone the permanent logical center of Greater New York forever.'

"Still another advantage to the scheme will be the clearing out of these stagnant waters, for the sewage not only of New York but of the cities all the way up the Hudson finds an outlet here. With the waters narrowed to the width of a mile on either hand, the stream would be deeper and swifter, thus carrying these fever-breeding pollutions rapidly out to sea.

"The Federal authorities are keenly interested in this great project."

Photo by Brown Brothers

LOOKING DOWN NEW YORK BAY: THE NEW LAND WOULD TAKE IN MOST OF THE WATER IN SIGHT.
Including Governors Island, at the left, and Bedloe's Island, with the Statue of Liberty.

THE MONOTONY OF PERFECT TUNING

"DON'T TUNE THE PIANO; it sounds better out of tune," a modern composer is said to have remarked. That lack of perfect concord may furnish needed variety to music is also the opinion of Professor C. K. Wead of Michigan University, who expresses himself to that effect in *Science* (New York). Prof. Wead quotes a musical trade paper to the effect that a phonograph dealer in Chicago had two similar pianos tuned alike, except that in one of them one string belonging to each set of three that belong to each note was tuned a trifle out with the other two. Then the public was asked which tuning it preferred; a large majority chose the one that was slightly out of tune. "What is the use," the editor went on to say, "of trying to keep a piano in tune when a mistuned one is really liked better?" Professor Wead comments as follows:

"This does not seem to me to involve the question of being out of tune in the ordinary meaning of the term; if a chord is struck two thirds of the strings will sound together in the usual way, tho the accuracy of tuning will be somewhat blurred or masked by the beats due to the other strings.

"But a similar even more marked effect has long been obtained in other ways and has often been proposed by inventors. It is akin to the tremolo which is familiar as a means of expression on many instruments and which in vocal music may be a sign of emotion or even weakness. On the violin a tremolo may come from the rolling of the player's finger along the string, and on mechanical violins from intermittent pressure on the tail piece. Even more closely analogous to the effect in the piano experiment and long known are the results of the 'Celeste' stop on the reed organ that brings into use two sets of reeds which beat slightly with one another; and in the pipe organ of the 'Vox Celeste' or 'Unda Maris' stop that brings on two sets of pipes which beat producing a very few waves per second.

"So the Chicago experiments seem to me to indicate, not that hearers object to having the notes of the piano in tune, but that they welcome a new way of introducing variety, vitality, into piano tone. After the key is struck there comes the loud thud characteristic of the piano sound and then the gradual dying away of the sound; the musician can do nothing with the tone but let it die away till he is ready to drop the damper. The player of most other instruments has considerable control over the loudness of a continued sound and occasionally to some extent over its pitch and quality; this is obviously true of most orchestral instruments, and of the organ with its swell and the harmonium with its 'expression' due to pumping.

"This double control, of loudness and pitch, was realized in the old clavichord and was sought for in the 'Steinertone' patented and built by the late Morris Steinert fifteen or twenty years ago. I have recently learned from the makers that in the reproductions built some years ago by Chickering & Sons under direction of Mr. Dolmetsch 'the clavichord was tuned with one string of each note two or three waves sharper than the others, and on the harpsichord the second unison was slightly sharper than the first.' So the Chicago experimenters and listeners are in good company."

RAIN AND RAINMAKERS

THE ACTIVITIES of so-called "rainmakers" in western Canada and elsewhere have received wide publicity. In an article in *The Times* (London), an account is given of the achievements of one of these; and in *Nature* (London) Dr. Harold Jeffreys comments on what he reads therein. Dr. Jeffreys notes that the method used is not described in detail. A tank filled with unspecified "chemicals" was exposed 25 feet above the ground, and it is claimed that this had the effect of producing eight inches of rain in three months at Medicine Hat, 22 miles away. The theory is that the apparatus draws clouds from other parts to the Medicine Hat district and causes them to precipitate their moisture there. Dr. Jeffreys goes on:

"No direct observations of the motions of clouds are mentioned in confirmation of this theory, tho they should not have been difficult to obtain.

"The official rain-gage at Medicine Hat during May, June and July, the period of the contract, recorded 4.8 inches, which was 1.3 inches below the normal for the station for those months. Further comment on the success of the experiments is unnecessary.

"The financial side of the rainmaker's contract with the Agricultural Association of Medicine Hat is interesting, for the association was apparently prepared to pay him as if 8 inches of rain had fallen.

"Still more interesting is the fact that he was promised $4,000 for 4 inches, and $6,000 for 6 inches. Since the normal rainfall is 6.1 inches, the rainmaker would have been much more likely than not to make a substantial profit even if he had done nothing at all.

"It may be mentioned that at Calgary, Alberta, the rainfall was 3.0 inches below normal; at Edmonton it was 3.1 inches above; and at Qu'Appelle (Sask.), 300 miles to the east, it was 3.85 inches above normal.

"It is also stated that at Los Angeles, in the first four months of 1905, he guaranteed 18 inches of rain, and that his own rain-gage showed 29.49 inches. If this is correct the rainfall must have been extremely local, for the official rain-gage at Los Angeles in those months showed only 14.98 inches. Still, this was 4.4 inches above normal.

"At San Diego, however, which is 200 miles away, the excess was 4.6 inches, and it appears likely that the abnormality at both stations was due to more wide-spread causes than the rainmaker's chemicals.

"Attempts have on many previous occasions been made to produce rain by artificial means, but the results have been uniformly unsuccessful. The reason is not difficult to see. To make the water vapor in the air condense it is necessary to cool the air in some way to a temperature below the dew point. This may be done in two ways. One may cool the air directly, for instance by the evaporation of liquid carbon dioxide or liquid air. This certainly would produce a little condensation; the fatal objection to it is that it would be thousands of times cheaper to distil sea water. The other method is to raise the air.

The pressure decreases with height, and to reduce the pressure on a particular mass of air is known to cool it. The difficulty is to raise it enough. To produce an inch of rain over an area of 100 square miles requires the condensation of six million tons of vapor, and to achieve this some hundreds of millions of tons of air must be lifted up.

"The distance it must be raised depends on how nearly saturated it was originally, but it could not be less than a kilometer in ordinary fine weather conditions. We have no source of energy at our command great enough to achieve this.

"It is often suggested that rain may be produced by exploding shells or otherwise agitating the air. The action is compared with that of a trigger, a large amount of energy being released by a small effort.

"An essential feature is, however, overlooked. For a trigger to work, there must be a large supply of potential energy only awaiting release. Precipitation from partially saturated air would require an actual supply of new energy. Therefore a trigger action can not produce precipitation."

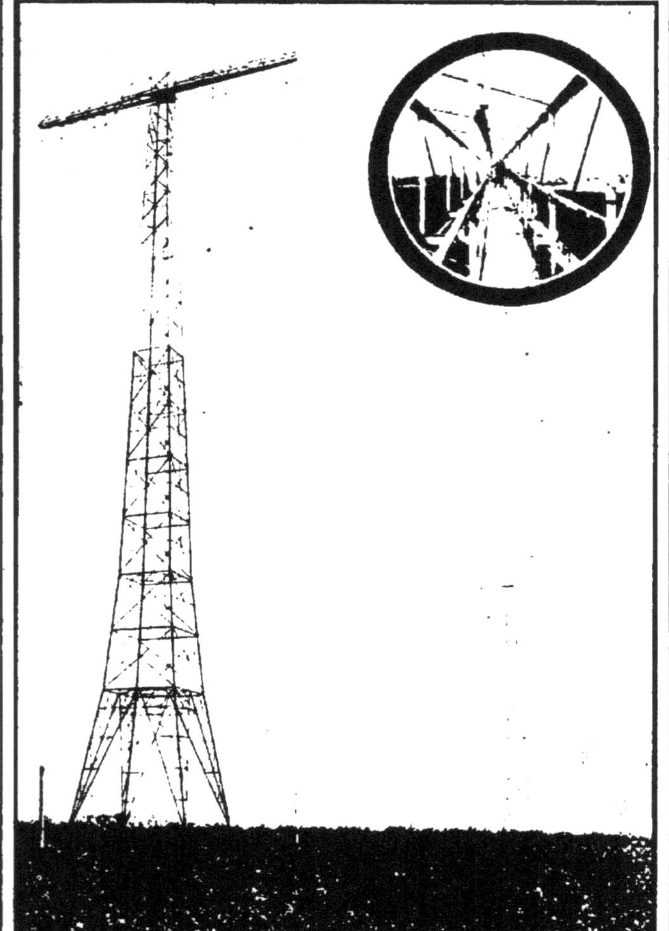

Courtesy of "The Electrical World," New York.

ONE OF THE TOWERS. INSET: HALF OF ONE CROSS-ARM.

THE WORLD'S LARGEST AND MOST POWERFUL RADIO STATION.

Its sending range is virtually world-wide. Altho only two rows of six towers each are installed at present the ultimate development will involve twelve antennas radiating from a single point like the spokes of a wheel. Three spokes will be for transpacific communication or radio-telephone purposes to Europe. Another group of three will be for South America, and each of the remaining spokes for England, France, Germany, Sweden, Denmark and Poland respectively. The towers are 410 ft. high and 1250 ft. apart. The cross-arms are 150 ft. long and support sixteen parallel conductors. It is on Long Island, about 70 miles from New York.

THE WORLD'S BIGGEST RADIO STATION

PRESIDENT HARDING opened on November 5th the central station of the Radio Corporation of America, asserted by the company's engineers to be the most powerful so far constructed. Seated at his desk in Washington, the President prest a key and an automatic sending device began to send out an official message to receiving stations in twenty-nine countries. Within a few minutes replies were received from England, France, Norway and Italy. The station, we are told by *The Electrical World* (New York), is near Port Jefferson, Long Island, about seventy miles from New York. The site covers ten square miles, and when completed the station will resemble a huge wheel with twelve spokes, the power house and sending station forming the hub, while each set of antennas, mounted upon six towers, will form a spoke. At present only two sets of towers have been erected, each 410 feet high, while the cross-arms are 150 feet long. We read on:

"A sending speed of 100 words a minute is possible with each unit, so that when the entire installation is completed twelve different messages may be sent simultaneously, each at the rate of 100 words a minute. The transmitting range of the station is virtually world-wide, preliminary tests having been heard in all parts of Europe and in Australia, South America and Japan. The station is to be operated by remote control from the New York office of the corporation, over wire lines built by the forces of the New York Telephone Company.

"The receiving station is at Riverhead, L. I., sixteen miles away. No operators are stationed there either, the signals being automatically transferred to wire lines and received at the New York office. The action is simultaneous from the time the signals are transmitted abroad, picked up by the aerial, to the moment of actual transcribing by the receiving operators in New York at the central traffic office, 64 Broad Street.

"The formal opening of the station took place before about 400 visitors who had been brought from New York by the Radio Corporation on a special train. There were present a large number of men prominent in electrical and governmental circles.

"In the absence in Europe of Edward J. Nally, president of the corporation, the guests were addrest by Owen D. Young, chairman of the board of directors. Mr. Young said at the opening exercises 'that America now stood in the van of the world in radio communication, but that only courage, skill and the use of financial resources would continue to keep her there.

"'England has taken advantage, and properly, of her geographical position to control European cable lines, and America should follow the same method.' said Mr. Young. 'With the construction of this station America becomes the center of radio communication. Poland has contracted with us for a station there, and we have just come from Europe, where an agreement was made with French, British and German representatives that the station to be built in Chile shall be jointly owned and operated. Another station is proposed for Brazil, and still more will be built in South America as the need arises. Of all these, Radio Central will be the center.'

"Mr. Young gave great credit to the engineers and executives of the General Electric Company, the Westinghouse Electric & Manufacturing Company, the Western Electric Company and the United Fruit Company for their aid in working out commercial, financial and technical problems. He announced that these companies all had agreed to turn over to the Radio Corporation all inventions dealing with radio for a period of twenty years so that the progress of American-controlled radio would not be hindered by any patent litigation whatever."

MUCH SKILL IS REQUIRED TO GET HENS TO ARRANGE THEMSELVES SO REGULARLY IN ALL PARTS OF THE DESIGN.

WHY HIGHWAYS "BLOW UP"

UPHEAVALS IN CONCRETE ROADS, sometimes causing serious accidents, may occur where no expansion joints or equivalent devices are provided, says a writer in *Concrete* (Detroit). Many road-builders, he tells us, have come to disregard expansion and consider contraction only as a source of breakage, necessitating jcints. Expansion, it appears, is not to be disregarded, however. He goes on:

"On a concrete road near Wichita having no expansion joints, a serious buckle occurred at the top of a long vertical curve. The part which raised was seven feet on one side, and eight feet on the other, and raised twenty-two inches shortly after the break occurred. A touring car driven at a high rate of speed, in turning out and attempting to miss this obstruction, turned over and a woman and child were very seriously injured.

"The instance suggests the value of placing steel dowels across the construction joints. These are now being used in several States, and usually consist of five three-quarter inch round plain bars about five feet long, embedded for half their length in the end of the slab at the close of the day's run. The next morning the projecting ends are soaped or oiled, or sometimes wrapped in tar paper, to prevent bonding of the concrete in the second slab to the rods. Thus, the rods are solidly embedded in the end of one slab, but are free to move slightly with longitudinal expansion in the adjoining slab.

"This design is used in Indiana and in Los Angeles County, California, where the range of temperature is quite extreme. None of the Los Angeles pavement so built has expansion joints.

"The present practise of the Pennsylvania State Highway department is to provide a joint filled with premolded, compressible material at intervals of not over 100 feet. Joints are also especially located at the beginning and end of all curves, both horizontal and vertical. As the topography of Pennsylvania compels frequent curves in the highways, this means that the expansion joints are frequently at much closer intervals than 100 feet. The fact that Pennsylvania highways are uniformly reinforced may have some bearing on the fact that they have had no serious upheavals due to expansion. It is reported from Pennsylvania expansion does occur in the warm weather and that it is not uncommon to find the slab on one side of a joint heaving perhaps as much as one inch above the adjacent slab. This is not a serious matter, as it occasions no danger to traffic.

"Similar reports are received from other States, such as Colorado, Washington, etc., where it is the practise to provide true expansion joints at intervals from 30 to 50 feet."

Upheavals are rare, even in concrete roads built without expansion joints, when steel dowels have been used across construction jcints. When expansion occurs, the concrete is under compression, which may be rather high in extreme cases. If there is a jcint or a crack where this compression may be localized and the crevice is not exactly at right angles to the surface there is a tendency for the slabs to buckle at such a point. If the concrete is good it should not shatter under compression, nor crush above the steel dowels. The joints cost something extra, but——

"It is pointed out, however, with the increasing amount of concrete pavement being built, if provision is not made for expansion, a proportionate number of upheavals due to expansion may be expected. Some of these may occur at points distant from a town or any point of quick communication. Such an upheaval as that at Wichita, Kansas, might cause a serious accident before the authorities could warn traffic."

HENS IN GRAPHIC FORMATIONS—Letters and designs formed by massed men in camps, or by pupils in schools, are familiar, but similar figures composed of poultry are something of a novelty. *The Poultry Item* (Sellersville, Pa.) presents the accompanying picture of the initials P. P. F. formed by single-comb white Leghorns, and taken at the Pennsylvania Poultry Farm, Lancaster, Pa. We quote the following comments from *The Guide to Nature* (Sound Beach, Conn.):

"Designs made with human beings were a comparatively easy task, as the actors were under orders and would 'stay put.' But this poultry farm excels us, if the owners can make a white Leghorn hen stay for half a minute where she is put. Another thing that interests us in this unique photograph is the fact that the hens are so evenly distributed over the letters. We suppose the design was marked out with food attractive to these restless birds, but that does not solve the problem. According to our experience with white Leghorns, in such conditions they would pile themselves together two or three deep in one spot, eat that place clean and proceed to clear up another without the slightest hesitation. We therefore offer our appreciation of the photographer's technique, and feel sure that even the professional artist will recognize the difficulties that have been so perfectly overcome. In regard to the docility of the hens, we are speechless."

HOW LONG CHILDREN SHOULD SLEEP — Children who have become tiresome are probably only tired, suggests a writer in *The California State Journal of Medicine* (San Francisco). No child nutrition worker, says this paper, citing the U. S. Public Health Service, can hope to get satisfactory results without insisting on enough sleep for her charges. Besides damaging the nervous system, late hours cause "sleep hunger" and make children fidgety. The Service commends the following precepts just issued by the London County Council:

"School children aged four years need twelve hours' sleep a day; aged five to seven, eleven to twelve hours; eight to eleven, ten to eleven hours; and twelve to fourteen, nine to ten hours. Children grow mainly while sleeping or resting; do you want yours to grow up stunted? Tired children learn badly and often drift to the bottom of the class; do you want yours to grow up stupid? When children go to bed late, their sleep is often disturbed by dreams and they do not get complete rest; do you want yours to sleep badly and become nervous? Sufficient sleep draws a child onward and upward in school and in home life; insufficient sleep drags it backward and downward. Which way do you want your child to go? Tiresome children are often only tired children; test the truth of this. That a neighbor's child is sent to bed late is not a good reason for sending your child to bed late; two wrongs do not make a right. Going to bed late is a bad habit which may be difficult to cure; persevere till you succeed in curing it."

CHRISTINE NILSSON

ONE NAME, so long as the Metropolitan Opera endures, will stand out beyond all the others who have filled its walls with song—Christine Nilsson. It was she who sang *Marguerite* on the opening night, October 22, 1883, and anniversaries must always name her. To hear that she has just died at Copenhagen brings that early date back for many devotees of opera, tho other stars hold her throne at present. Nilsson may not have been the equal of Patti, but she was her most formidable rival in the seventies and eighties. She came to this country first in 1870, when Patti, who was remembered as a child wonder, had disappeared into foreign lands, which were much more remote than now. Nilsson was here often in the following decade while Patti was winning European laurels, and she had acquired a firm hold on her public when Patti returned in the early eighties to challenge her position. She also held the strategic position at the new Metropolitan while Patti continued at the old Academy of Music. Nilsson was another "Swedish Nightingale," but her vogue fell somewhat short of Jenny Lind's, perhaps because America had grown more sophisticated in music. Four New York papers pay their tribute to the dead prima donna on the editorial page, the New York *Evening Post* pointing to the fact that the lands of song are not always of the South:

THE RIVAL OF PATTI.

Nilsson was aided in her triumphal career by the fact that she was a violinist as well as a singer.

"We are apt to associate a good voice with the sunny climate of Italy, but it is a singular fact that three of the most famous American singers—Annie Louise Cary, Lillian Nordica and Emma Eames—came from Maine, our only State where sugar-cane cannot be grown, while Geraldine Farrar's ancestors also came from that State. In Europe we find, at the opposite extreme from Italy, a cold country which gave the world two world-famed singers, Jenny Lind and Christine Nilsson. Each was called 'the Swedish Nightingale' by her admirers. Lind was twenty-three years old when Nilsson was born. Both were of humble parentage, both worked hard and long to attain their eminence—a hint to the thousands of our girls who seem to think that a popular coach can prepare a young singer in three months for operatic triumphs. The career of the two Swedish Nightingales emphasizes the fact that great singers are usually made as well as born—altho Patti and Melba apparently contradict this statement.

"Like Sembrich, Nilsson was greatly aided in her triumphal career by the fact that she was a musician as well as a singer. As a little girl she earned her living by playing the violin at dances, and at one time she played a violin concerto by Berwald in a Paris concert. Indeed, for some time she hesitated whether she should give her life to the violin or to singing.

"Her operatic triumphs are still fresh in the memory of music lovers. She came to America in 1870 and again in '73, '74 and '84. She was admired equally in Italian, French and German operas; perhaps her best operas were 'Traviata,' 'Lucia,' 'Lohengrin,' 'Don Giovanni,' 'Faust,' and 'Hamlet,' in which she created the part of *Ophelia* at the request of Ambroise Thomas himself. Colorature and passionate dramatic expression were not her strongest points, but her voice was singularly pure, rich and sweet. Concerning her *Violetta* in 'La Traviata' Sutherland Edwards wrote: 'She seemed to die, not of phthisis, aided and developed by dissipation, but of a broken heart, like *Clarissa Harlowe*, or like that Shakespearean lady who never told her love. Mlle. Piccolomini's *Violetta* was a foolish virgin; Mlle. Nilsson's a fallen angel."

The World gives us a hint of the changed time and changed manners. A prima donna walks our street to-day unnoticed by the crowd, but does a popular pugilist? The following strikes the note of wonder:

"With the death of Christine Nilsson there passes a great European operatic soprano of the last generation who was in a peculiar sense a public favorite in this country. Do New Yorkers nowadays pelt prima donnas with flowers as they drive through the streets? Perhaps it is a less emotional age, possibly famous sopranos are relatively more numerous. But certainly the two visits to the United States of this second and last of the 'Swedish Nightingales' in 1873 and again in 1882 were popular triumphs, the memory of which is still vivid.

"Christine Nilsson followed the traditionally romantic path to fame—the gifted child of poor peasants, singing at village fairs and rising to be the world's queen of song. Was her voice unmatched not only in her time but in ours? The phonograph will dispose of such questions for future generations, but for us there is only the enthusiastic testimony of our opera-going forbears. Whether Mario was greater than Caruso, whether Grisi and Jenny Lind and Nilsson outshone Metropolitan stars of the later period, remains in the domain of conjecture.

"But at least the death of Nilsson will convey a sense of personal loss to an older race of New Yorkers in spite of the length of years since she had left the stage."

Those interested in musical history will read with pleasure this evocation in the New York *Herald:*

"At the opening of the Metropolitan Opera House, on the night of October 22, 1883, one of the great events in the operatic history of this city, Mme. Nilsson had already a high place in the regard of not only the fashionable attendants in the opera boxes but of the crowds who struggled for seats in the upper galleries whenever it was announced she was to sing. An interesting phase of this devotion to a great singer, and one which seems to indicate New York's loyalty to a favorite, was that at this memorable opening performace she was no longer in her prime, she was in fact forty years of age, and her voice and her artistry had both begun to show that they had not withstood the wear of time.

"'Faust,' in which she could appear to the best advantage, was chosen as the opening opera. She had recreated the character of *Marguerite* when the opera was remodelled for its Paris production, and her voice and skill had contributed not a little to the popularity of this masterpiece of Gounod. The critics report that the performance aroused little enthusiasm until Mme. Nilsson sang the scintillating waltz song in the garden scene. This was received with a storm of applause. Flowers were rained upon the singer from the boxes, and in the midst of the rich offerings of bouquets was a velvet casket enclosing a wreath of gold bay-leaves and berries. The name of the donor was not given, the gift bearing only the inscription 'In commemoration of the opening of the Metropolitan Opera House.' This was perhaps the greatest triumph of her artistic career."

ART IN THE HINTERLAND

WHEN THE GERMANS ENTERED ST. QUENTIN and carried away the collection of pastel portraits by Quentin de Latour, people outside France wondered why the work of so precious a master should not be kept at the French capital. One reason was that St. Quentin was the native place of the artist, and so entitled to be the custodian of his work, and another was that it is the policy of France to cultivate its provincial museums. France, being a bureaucratic government, looks after many things that in our land are left to the benevolence of individuals. Mr. Huntington's recent purchase of Gainsborough's "Blue Boy" is a case in point, for this great work along with Mr. Huntington's other priceless books and art works are destined for the permanent enjoyment of the people of California. England might have cause for grief, thinks the New York *Evening Post*, if she had merely "lost her $728,000 treasure to New York City, already rich in art." As it is:

"To lose it to California, which is trying hard to build up the Crocker Gallery in Sacramento and the galleries left by the San Francisco and San Diego expositions, should seem less of a hardship. California has an active native school of painters and sculptors and the exposition showed that their work is popularly appreciated.

"In one recent year, 1916, seven art museums were established in this country. Whereas thirty years ago a report to the French Government upon American art listed no galleries beyond the Mississippi and but four beyond the Alleghanies; now they are springing up in every section. Even the South, as the recent opening of the Brooks Museum in Memphis reminded us, is being invaded. It is possible that some museums are an artificial growth. In the spirit in which Cleveland and Detroit, Seattle and Tacoma, Birmingham and Atlanta compete for population and manufactures, one city may decide that its neighbor's erection of a fine marble gallery to wait for art windfalls challenges it to build one twenty feet longer. But the spirit is usually one of genuine esthetic enthusiasm.

"If the community appears to have little taste for fine art, the founders of its museum can employ Haydon's answer to those who decried English taste. Give the people a chance to view fine works, he said, open galleries and classes in design, as on the Continent, and see. Nor need regional museums wait for such exceptional riches as bequests from millionaires. Just as poor men of taste and discernment can build up collections of valuable first editions, museums can use slender incomes to obtain the work of men more promising than prominent and to acquire objects which time multiplies in value."

PAINTING WITH LIGHT

"TRANSFORMATION SCENES" were the *pièces de resistence* of the old pantomime and burlesque. The unfolding rose would reveal the coryphée. People might like to believe they were deceived, but it is hard to think one couldn't, even on the gas-illuminated stage, "see the wheels go round," if one looked sharp. Science has finally brought it about that the quickness of the electric switch deceives the eye. What first appears to be a rocky grotto merges in an instant

Photograph by Edward F. Townsend.

NICHOLAS DE LIPSKY.

Who has put into operation a new principle of light, color and design in the theater.

into a sylvan lake, and no wheels go round. This is the miracle revealed in Madame Pavlowa's recent season in a new ballet called "Dionysus" with the effect described produced by the invention of a young Russian refugee, Nicholas de Lipsky. Interviewed by P. J. Nolan for *Musical America*, Mr. de Lipsky reveals how simple are the causes which produce so remarkable a result:

"'It is merely an arrangement of lights and colors,' he explained, when asked about it; and, taking the visitor into his studio, he showed him a small sketch done in pale red and blue colors which overlapped each other and ran riot in broken lines. It resembled a crudely designed combination of the 'Dionysus' scenes, a jumble of rocks and trees.

"'Look at it through this!' he enjoined, holding out a sheet of red gelatine.

"Behold! the trees had vanished, the crudities had disappeared, the sketch was admirable in its order and design. Under the red transparency only the precipitous rocks and canyons of the first 'Dionysus' scene were revealed.

"'Now see it through this!' and he held up a blue transparency.

"There, on the same sketch, was revealed the placid lake scene with the overhanging trees, and not a trace of the rugged mountain country.

"'That's the whole thing!' he exclaimed. 'That's all that happens in the theater.'

"The two sketches are painted on the one canvas and are then separated by the use of lights which obliterate the tones in one or the other. Very simple it all seems; and yet, Mr. de Lipsky says, it is exceedingly complex in the study required for the proper choice of colors for these sketches. 'The whole principle is to secure true harmony between light, color and design,' is his explanation. He began the investigation of this subject in Russia some years ago, he says. He was then an art student in the Imperial Arts Academy of Petrograd; and one of his earliest recollections is of observing the effect which changing hues produced upon a scarlet sash, and seeing that beneath a red light its tones vanished, and that beneath a blue light it became black. In order to study the scientific principles of the operation of light, he entered the Polytechnic in Petrograd. Then came the war, and the revolution, and he was obliged to leave the country. He went to England, and there began to design scenery, and in October, 1920, he came to America."

Courtesy of the Bohemians, Inc.

UNDER THE RED RAYS.

A scene in the Greenwich Village Follies presents this warm interior. The effect devised by Mr. de Lipsky is a partnership between paints on canvas and light from the wings.

The same thing seems to have been done even more elaborately in London by another Russian named Samoiloff, who not only changed his mise-en-scène, but the costumes worn by his actors. In the London correspondence of the New York *Times* we read:

"The wonders accomplished in transforming scenes, costumes and actual figures from one period of history to another by a mere change of light on the stage of the Hippodrome has set all London talking. In a revue now playing there is a scene representing a very modern damsel sighing for her lover in a frowning mountain pass. She sings, the echo answers and the audience is beguiled by the sweet sentimentality of the situation.

"Then behind the scenes somebody does something and everything is altered in a flash. The grim mountains become a Hindu temple, the frowning rocks melt into sands and palms, and the tall, slender young woman turns into a stout Indian maiden. It has all been brought about by a change in light, by the manipulation of more than one hundred different switches at the same moment, and the audience is carried back three thousand years and from one continent to another. Every detail is transmogrified, and the girl, who was clad conventionally in a yellow artificial silk blouse with blue facings, and a rust-red golf skirt, appears now with her bust draped in white, embroidered in black and brown, with her waist unclothed and her trousers-skirt pale cream with a graceful figured pattern.

"An Oriental scene follows, with the customary dances. Men and women in all the finery of the East enter and weave in and out in the mazes of the ballet. The lover comes on, to all appearance robed in the loose white garments and the trousers of certain castes of Hindus. The action grows fast and furious; the heroine is threatened by a rival; she runs to the hero for protection, and as he clasps her to his arms some one throws those switches again.

"Back goes everything to the mountain gorge, and a very modern young man in a brown lounge suit of unexceptionable cut is seen embracing the young woman in the crowd of equally modernly dressed people."

Here the changes of costume seem to create the greatest curiosity and these effects have been thus accounted for by Mr. Samoiloff:

"'It's merely amatter of establishing and utilizing a harmony between light, line and color. Is it new? Well, all the elements of it have been known for years; I have merely brought them together and worked them out scientifically and systematically. Do you remember, for instance, the postcards we had as children, which showed one inscription in one light and another in another? Well, that's part of it. Then during the war we heard a lot about "dazzle" and camouflage, and how a few apparently random lines of paint would alter to the distant observer the shape of the outline of a vessel. That's part of it, too. I have merely worked along these and similar lines until I got the results I wanted'

"'But the girl's skirt and blouse in the mountain scene seemed to be of solid color and heavy material while in the Hindu scene they were quite flimsy and covered with embroidery. How about that?'

"'That's quite simple,' replied M. Samoiloff. 'To the colors I use in the mountain scene I applied two methods of analysis. First, I took their spectra; then I analyzed the paints used chemically. From the spectra I found into what colors the first would split up by the application of the proper kind of strong light, and by chemical analysis I discovered that a great variety of substances had been used in the original paints and colors to produce the original hues. Take, for example, several pieces of red material; they will seem to match exactly, but chemical analysis will show that one contains radium bromide, another phospherine or zinc, and a third no special chemical at all. In ordinary daylight they look exactly alike, but when I begin to throw my specially prepared lights upon them they change in different ways according to the chemicals they contain. When you have worked this out very carefully, as I did, it will be quite simple for you to make a plain blouse look like a mass of embroidery.

"'Perhaps you noticed in the Oriental scene three of the dancers who seemed to be clothed in quite different ways; one looked as if she were wearing merely a skirt, another was draped to her shoulders, and so on. Yet when the light was changed all three were found to be clad in modern gowns, the only difference between them being the colors of their costumes. It's really merely an application of the knowledge of how light affects colors.'"

Mr. de Lipsky exhibited his art also in the Greenwich Village Follies, whose two scenes we are able to reproduce here. Those acquainted with photography will realize the difficulties attending any reproduction of these scenes. A few personal words on the inventor are given in *Musical America*:

"Mr. de Lipsky, who was born in Petrograd, was an officer in the court of the Czar when the revolution broke out in Russia, and was assigned, with other members of the corps, to the defense of the British Embassy. For his services on that occasion he received the British Distinguished Service Order. He was later arrested and told that he would be shot; but he escaped during the night and made his way to Odessa, and thence to Constantinople."

BOLSHEVISM FATAL TO SCIENCE

"IF TOLSTOY HAD LIVED, he would have been one of us!" so Trotzky is reported to have remarked to the sage's daughter, Countess Tatiana. But the Countess had her doubts, and so Trotzky let her sister remain in prison and took no steps to help repair the damage to the Tolstoy home, Yasnaya Polyana, now falling into ruin through depredations of the Commissars. This shrine, which even the Bolsheviki pretended to venerate, seems to be a symbol of the disregard shown by the now dominant power in Russia to the whole intellectual fabric of that nation. Russian scientists, refugees from Soviet Russia, recently held a conference in Prague, and passed a resolution protesting against the mistreatment of their colleagues who are still remaining in their native land. No one has described their tragic case more graphically and sympathetically than M. Restortziff, himself a former professor and a member of the Russian Academy of Sciences. In an article published in the *Sovremenniya Zapiski* (Paris) he writes:

"I get from time to time letters from refugees from the Bolshevik paradise, where the arts and sciences are flourishing, from my teachers, colleagues and pupils. And each letter contains first of all a list of those who have perished, with uniform notations: 'died of hunger', 'shot,' 'committed suicide'—dozens of names, one greater than the other, dozens of images of self-sacrificing workers in the field of science and education, professors—idealists, who bore their cross of apostles of knowledge. Their life was not easy, and their death was supremely tragic. They were pariahs under the old régime, and they remained pariahs in the Bolshevik paradise. Their ideals of liberty and their seeking after truth were not compatible with the sad reality of Russian reaction—the Black under the Czar and, even to a greater degree, the Red at present. But one must give the old régime its due: it was no friend to the professors, and it made things very hard for many of them, but it never reached that Herculean extent of oppression and lawlessness which characterizes the rule of the Bolshevik commissars. The unanimous opinion of all my colleagues who have escaped from Russia is: Messrs. Kasse, Shwartz, Delianoff (Ministers of Education under the Czar) are mere children in comparison with any commissar of Bolshevik education. Never did it come into the heads of the Ministers of the old régime that it is possible to execute without trial a scientist of note, just because somebody denounced him to the authorities, as was done by the Bolsheviki in the case of the well-known Slavist, Professor Florinsky of the Kieff University, and with that mild, truly Christian man, in the best sense of this term, the historian of the Church, Prof. I. D. Andreyeff of Petrograd University, who was shot in Eletz. Never before did they disorganize the system of education so ignorantly, so impudently, so barbarously, as during the encumbency of the 'enlightened' dictatorship of Lunacharsky (Commissar of Education). . . .

"It is not to be wondered at that in that atmosphere the men of science are dying one after another, not so much of hunger as of complete nervous exhaustion; are committing suicide, as was the case of the noted Moscow jurist, V. Khvestoff, the Moscow philosopher, Victoroff, and the celebrated mathematician Liapunoff, my colleague in the Academy of Sciences. It is not surprizing that all who can do so flee at the first opportunity, knowing beforehand that they will encounter there, whither they flee, poverty, disdain, or at best cold indifference. There are among them men of venerable age, celebrated scientists, as N. P. Kondakoff, men in the prime of life, as D. D. Grimm, and young men with their enthusiasm and thirst for knowledge, who are in despair over the state of their native culture and education. Never has the world witnessed such a terrible spectacle. And the Bolsheviki send triumphant radio messages after that: 'Never before did science flourish so richly in Russia, as now, never before have scientists had such an easy life, and since the time of the Medici the world has not seen a government which was so solicitous of the progress of science and art as the Soviet government is.' . . . Why are the universities empty in that paradise of education? Why are thirty of the sixty chairs in Petrograd University vacant? Why is it that at the Medical Academy, so necessary to the Bolsheviki, who are struggling so hard against spotted typhus, forty-five chairs are vacant and not a single physician will be graduated next year? Why? Probably because it is impossible to live in that heavenly environment.

THE BLUE RAYS WORK THIS MIRACLE.
The change from the scene opposite is effected by merely switching the lights from red to blue.

"Those who have succeeded in escaping from Russia may yet some day return thither, or perhaps may be able to labor for science and education in their exile. Not all hopes are lost yet. Western Europe may at last understand that it is criminal to dissipate the vital forces of a great people and that the cultural solidarity imperatively demands that they be supported and safeguarded, and an opportunity to work be given to these fragments of Russian culture. But those will not come back who have gone to, let us hope, a better world, have gone with outraged souls and in dark despair."

The Soviet government, on the other hand, insists that it is doing all it can for the men of science. The Commissar of Education, Lunacharsky, in an interview with press representatives, denied that the status of scientists was worse than that of other citizens. He said:

"The condition of our scientists is not an easy one, but our entire population is in a much worse state. The scientists enjoy privileges. Only after overcoming the unparalleled crisis, for which the support of the richer countries is necessary, will Russia be able to make the life of the scientists secure. Instead of hypocritical protests, the emigré ought to protest against the blockade, against procrastination in the matter of relief to the famine sufferers.

"Unfortunately, among the scientists of Russia a great many are engaged in counter-revolutionary activity. Such scientists can not claim immunity, no matter how great their scientific labors. He to whom Russian science is dear must contribute to the successes of Soviet Russia. Let European public opinion be easy on account of the fate of our scientists, whose lot the Soviet government will improve as soon as bourgeois Europe will give Russia a chance to take up her internal problems. Fight for credits to Soviet Russia, then the sufferings of the scientists will cease. Then the hard times will pass for millions of less learned, but nevertheless not less deserving of happiness, citizens of a country which is being ruined by the intrigues of international reaction."

STRIPPING THE DEAD TO CLOTHE THE LIVING

TAKING FROM THE HUNGRY to feed the starving, the Russian Soviet Government is resorting to heroic measures to avert the annihilation of millions from famine and disease, and, contrary to common report, the Soviet heads are said by American workers not only to be thoroughly honest in cooperation with them, but to be sincere in their own efforts to plan an effective program of relief. The Russian Commission of the Near East Relief found the Soviet officials to be "uniformly earnest, hard-working, to all appearance sincere men, as well equipped for their work as the average officials of any country, and certainly, so far as the members of this Commission could judge, profiting in no way personally by whatever power their position placed in their hands." More than this, the Soviet Government is said to be not a beggar at the hand of charity, but to be willing to guarantee the country's natural resources in payment for foreign aid.

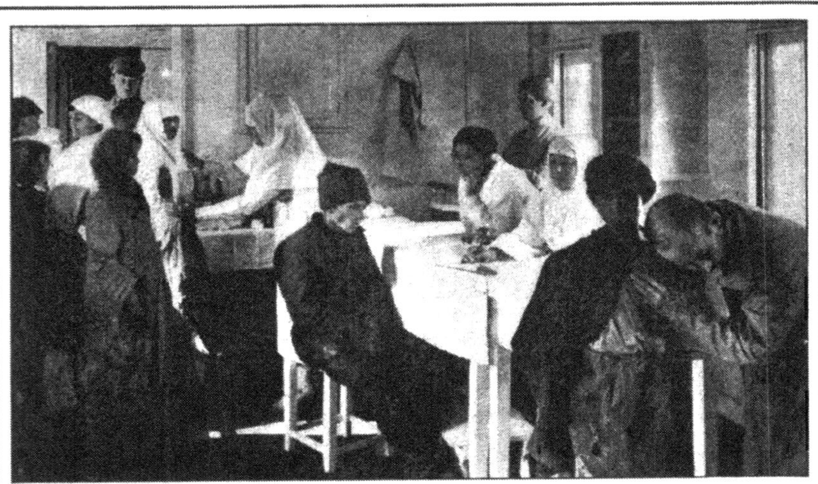

Copyrighted by International

EXAMINING RUSSIAN FAMINE VICTIMS.

Half-starved children find help on the hospital train of the American Relief Administration.

At present the situation is described as the worst within the knowledge of American investigators long experienced in Europe's troubles. Children die by the wayside, and are buried naked in order to clothe the living; others more fortunate are clad in made-over flour-bags that have been emptied of their contents; mothers starve themselves in order to save their little ones. Through this picture of horror and despair shine rays of heroic self-sacrifice. Tho in some provinces the peasants are fleeing from impending doom, in others they are living on acorn flour and other substitutes while sowing for their children a harvest they may not themselves live to reap. But, in spite of these measures of relief, and of the help being afforded by American relief commissions and a British fund, the problem is said by visitors recently returned from the field to be not for Russia alone, but for the whole world to tackle.

"Practically all Russia is to-day short of food supplies," said Secretary Hoover to the House Committee on Military Affairs when this body recently took up the question of giving surplus army supplies to the Russian destitute. "Of the twenty-five governments that formerly produced a surplus for export," Mr. Hoover is quoted in the Committee's official report, "not more than two or three are capable of affording any surplus at the present moment." In the Volga area, ordinarily Europe's greatest granary, are from six to seven million children to whom the American relief societies are giving, but the adult population, we are told, must be left to shift for themselves or to depend upon some other means of help. From its present resources the American Relief Association has undertaken the direct support of 1,200,000 until September 1, 1922, when it is hoped the next harvest will be sufficient to meet the need. The organization is now reported to be feeding 400,000 children and daily increasing the number. They hope to reach the million mark in January. Other societies contributing are the American Red Cross, which has given $ 3,000,000; the Friends' Service Committee (the Quakers), the Jewish Joint Distribution Committee, the Y. M. C. A. and the Y. W. C. A., the Federated Churches, the Catholic Welfare Society, the Knights of Columbus, the Lutheran Society, and some others. How tremendous is the task they confront may be judged from Dr. Vernon Kellogg's statement to the committee, that "it is an extraordinary thing that in this day and age 100,000,000 people should have practically but one thought and interest, a veritable obsession, and that is, 'How are we to get food for to-day and to-morrow?'" Dr. Kellogg has been associated with Secretary Hoover in all the latter's relief undertakings since May, 1915, and has traveled extensively in Russia. He informed the committee that there are in Samara some fifteen detention homes, filled with children picked up on the streets of villages and on the roadways from the villages to the capital, and added:

"I visited five of them. In one of the homes there were 150 children, and they were gathered together for their noon meal. This meal consisted of a little horse meat and a little coarse kind of porridge, called kasha, made of broken coarse grains and chaff. The children were all emaciated, and some showed the worst sign of hunger and famine, the so-called 'hunger belly,' filled out with bark and clay bread that does not digest; these children soon pass away. As I say, there were 150 of them, and they were sitting in one large room on the floor leaning against each other.

"There were three cots in the room; there were five children on one, three on another, and four on another. They were the only ones lying down, except those lying down on the floor. They were given the food, and I asked where they would go after eating it and was told they would stay there. There were two haggard looking women with them, with their hair cut short—all the children have their heads shaved in order to avoid typhus lice—and I asked where they slept. The women said: 'They sleep here.' I asked whether they had any mattresses and they said, 'We have none.' I asked whether they had any blankets and they said, 'We have none.' The children eat there and sleep there, leaning against each other on the floor. That is the situation which is represented in those fifteen children's homes, and there are another fifteen like them in Kazan. In all my experience with hunger situations I have never seen anything to compare with it. I simply say bluntly that in six years' experience of seeing distressing conditions in many places this is so far beyond anything I am acquainted with that it is almost incredible to me, even after seeing it."

The consequences of the situation "may be far-reaching and entirely unforeseen," according to the report of the Russian Commission of the Near East Relief, summarized in *The Nation* (New York). Because of almost continuous warfare for the past seven years and the consequent loss of man power and draft animals, not to speak of the poor methods of farming resulting from the old system of landlordism, agriculture broke down, and then came the droughts of 1920 and last April to cap the climax. Under these trying conditions the peasants themselves are exercising the utmost fortitude and patience. Says the report:

"It is the observation of this Commission that there is no tendency whatever on the part of the peasant farmers of Russia voluntarily to reduce their production to a minimum, for any reason whatever. They are to-day, and they have been throughout, eager to cultivate the maximum land at their disposition and for the cultivation of which they still have equipment. This Commission is well aware that this finding may upset a preconceived idea of the situation in Russia to-day which is current abroad. It is, however, true that this Commission has seen the land being plowed and sown in the heart of the famine area, in anticipation of a crop next year, when those who were plowing and sowing the land in question were actually living on bread made of flour of acorns, 'soosak,' sunflower seeds, and millet and when they were consciously facing a failure of even this inadequate form of nourishment by January 1, 1922."

GIVE YOURSELF A CHRISTMAS PRESENT OF SAVED LIVES

OUR readers no doubt noticed the heart-touching statement of the Russian famine situation on page 59 of our issue of last week, as presented by the Russian Famine Fund Committee, of which Mr. Allen Wardwell is Chairman and Mr. Charles H. Sabin is Treasurer. The situation baffles description. It is appalling. This committee is trying to save as many as possible of the 15,000,000 of all ages who are now starving to death. So grave is the crisis that every gift saves lives. Our own check for $2000 is already on its way, and we hope many of our readers will join their gifts in this splendid work. The fund is administered through the American Friends (Quakers), whose noble record in and since the war has commanded the confidence and admiration of America and Europe. Everyone who reads this statement should send a check to-day to Charles H. Sabin, Treasurer, Russian Famine Fund Committee, 15 Park Row, New York City. Ten dollars will save ten lives for a month. One hundred dollars will save a hundred lives for a month. A thousand dollars will save a thousand lives for a month.

WHEN PREACHERS WORK AND WORKERS PREACH

A TEN-YEAR STRIKE HOLIDAY could be won if militarism were ousted from industry and the Golden Rule substituted by employers and employees in its stead, agree Boston preachers and labor leaders who recently gathered on a common forum to discuss terms of peace to end the present economic war. "The solution of all our problems in industrial and international life," exclaimed Arthur Nash in historic Faneuil Hall, "is the philosophy of Jesus Christ," and this statement seems to sum up the general opinion exprest in Boston on "Golden Rule" Sunday. Mr. Nash is a Cincinnati clothing manufacturer who is credited with having successfully established the Golden Rule policy in his factory.

THE SOVIET COMMITTEES COOPERATE WHOLE-HEARTEDLY.

The Soviet officials are said by American relief workers to be "as well equipped for their work as the average officials of any country," and "profiting in no way personally by whatever power their position placed in their hands."

The movement for this mutual discussion of the industrial problem by Church and Labor was started by the Greater Boston Federation of Churches and other religious organizations, with the cooperation of the Boston Central Labor Union and a group of employers, and Jews, Catholics and Protestants participated. Besides the one in Faneuil Hall, meetings addrest by pastors and labor leaders were held in the Old South Forum and in thirty Protestant churches, and Cardinal O'Connell issued for the occasion a special pastoral in which he declared that the right to strike was inherent, tho, like war, to be considered as a last resort. Preliminary to the meeting and in order to gain a sympathetic insight into the problems and difficulties of the workingman, several Protestant pastors donned overalls and for a day accepted jobs at anything which critical foremen thought they could do. Unaccustomed hands grasped pick, hod and shovel. One pastor carried a hod weighing 73 pounds up three stories during his shift, after which, we are told, he probably slept well, even if he did not learn much about the particular problem which the hod-carrier has to meet. Some doubt is exprest as to the practical value of one day spent with a pick or wheelbarrow. The introduction of union workers into Boston pulpits may have served to spread a better understanding of labor's difficulties, observes the Philadelphia *Record*, "but why certain pastors should ostentatiously take off their coats and take laborers' jobs for a day or two, just to complete the picture, isn't so clear. It smacks of patronizing condescension or a too eager desire to seem sympathetic to the working men." Still, this paper admits, "anything, even a faulty plan, that will serve to bring the Church and the worker closer together is to be commended."

Not always is the counsel of the Church welcomed in labor disputes, but Miss Maude Foley, of the Garment Makers' Union, said from a Methodist pulpit that she believes the Church is the best agency for bringing capital and labor together. "If the Golden Rule were to be applied in business and to the relations between the employer and the labor unions," said Martin J. Casey, of the Electrotypers' Union, from another pulpit, "I think that it would iron out most of the difficulties that exist to-day." "The evils and abuses of the present industrial system can not be too strongly deplored," declares Cardinal O'Connell in his pastoral, and he counsels both employer and employee to follow the ideals of Christ and to be "just and charitable," the one to pay a living wage and the other to give a full day's work. "The hostility to employers, the tendency to drift toward radicalism or into harmful political activity, the fostering of useless strikes, the limiting of output, the demand for wages independently of merit and skill, are evils incidental to unionism, but not necessary," and the Cardinal believes that the more intelligent and better disposed trade unionists greatly deplore these abuses and earnestly seek to remedy them. On the other hand this observer argues:

"Strikes are called more frequently on account of failure to pay a just wage than for any other reason. If employers would recognize man's right to a just wage, another great milestone of progress toward industrial peace would be passed. 'Remuneration ought to be sufficient to support a frugal and well-behaved wage-earner.' There should be enough for the worker and his family to live in decent comfort. There is plenty to go around in this rich country of ours and where the just wage, which often ought to be more than a living wage, is not granted by obdurate employers, the moral law of natural justice should be enforced."

"It is gratifying that after 1,900 years there is a rapprochement between the church and the workers," says the Milwaukee *Sentinel*, but the Indianapolis *Star* makes light of the swapping of jobs by pastor and laborer, and thinks that, "prompted by their aching backs," the pastors "certainly will be in favor of lighter bricks and more smoothly running wheelbarrows. In order to improve the spiritual life of the workers they may be able to induce the employers to permit daily vesper services. . . . At any rate, the conclusions of the clerical band will be awaited with the greatest curiosity, not to say impatience, by the directors of the United States Chamber of Commerce."

Wide World Photo

A NEW USE FOR FLOUR SACKS.

Jewish orphans at Brest-Litovsk cut the cost of clothing and still keep themselves warm after disposing of the bags' contents.

SAVING CHILDREN BY SLAVERY

SLAVERY IN A MILD FORM still exists in China, where it is generally regarded as a necessary institution, since "a few live slaves are better than a whole dead family." The main cause of the traffic in human beings in that part of the world lies in the extreme poverty of the people, so often increased by drought or flood, and the only effective cure, we are told, would be some means of supplying all with work at wages sufficient for the support of the family, in which case "the little ones would be cherished just as tenderly as the children are in any other country." It will be recalled that a great increase in the traffic in girls was reported during the famine which last year wiped out whole communities in the northern provinces; but we are assured that in the great majority of cases these girls were destined only for household service and that the evils of slavery in China are much lighter than those which are associated with the institution in other lands. There are no slave markets in the country, says the Hankow *Central-China Post*; but there are go-betweens who are equally ready to hunt up a bride or a yatou (maid-servant) for any family needing them. The bride must be of the same standing as the bridegroom, but the yatou will come from some poor family which parts with her for the monetary consideration they had in view at the outset, and but for the prospect of which they might never have reared the child at all. These maid-servants are as a rule well treated, and should some mistress become cruel the neighbors or authorities will intervene. When the maid-servant comes of marriageable age it is the custom to find a husband for her, and the period of her servitude comes to an end. Boys are also bought and sold, and bring much better prices than the girls. But, says the *Post*.

"The parents will not dispose of a boy save as the last resort. The sons are relied upon to become the stay and support of their parents in old age, and blest is the family which has a quiverful for, to the credit of the Chinese, it must be said that the young men seldom seek to repudiate their responsibility. Hence the boys have to be kidnapped, and hence also the kidnapper when caught will be dealt with most drastically. If he falls into the hands of the people they will put him to death without mercy.

"Sometimes a boy will be bought by a childless couple with a view to adoption, and if all goes well he will become to them as a son. But the bulk of them pass into the hands of slave-drivers who want them because of the work which may be got out of them. They are employed in shops where small crafts are carried on. They are compelled to work any length of hours the master pleases; they may be poorly fed and wretchedly clad, but there is no escape till they have grown up to man's estate and become able to shift for themselves.

"A time of famine offers a grand opportunity for pushing the slave-dealer's trade. The destitute victims are no longer able to support their children. To sell them ensures that they will be fed and the money received assists to keep themselves alive."

What Men Should Know

About film on teeth, and modern ways to end it

These are vital discoveries made by able men, at the cost of years of research. They have brought to millions, the world over, whiter, cleaner, safer teeth.

No man can afford to ignore them. The benefits are most important—often life-long in extent. They apply to the entire family.

Every man should send this coupon, make this test, then watch results and judge them for himself.

The film problem

Film is the teeth's chief enemy—that viscous film you feel. It clings to teeth, gets between the teeth and stays.

If not removed—and frequently—it may do serious damage. Most tooth troubles are now traced to film.

Film absorbs stains, making the teeth look dingy. Film is the basis of tartar. Smokers in particular suffer these discolorations.

Film holds food substance which ferments and forms acid. It holds the acid in contact with the teeth to cause decay. It breeds millions of germs. Many serious troubles, local and internal, are now traced to them.

One great problem in mouth hygiene has been to find ways to daily fight that film.

Two ways discovered

Dental science has now found two effective film combatants. Able authorities have subjected them to many careful tests. The results are beyond dispute. So leading dentists everywhere are urging their daily use.

A new-type tooth paste has been created to comply with all modern requirements. The name is Pepsodent. In that tooth paste are embodied these two film combatants.

Other problems solved

Another problem has been starch deposits on the teeth. They also cling and stay, and often ferment and form acid. Nature puts a starch digestant in the saliva to digest those starch deposits. But with modern diet that agent is usually too weak.

So modern authority has decided that the tooth paste should stimulate that agent. Every use of Pepsodent multiplies that starch digestant.

Mouth acids formed another problem. Nature puts alkalis in the saliva to neutralize those acids which attack the teeth. But they also, with modern diet, are generally too weak.

So a factor is used in Pepsodent to multiply those alkalis. Thus every use increases vastly those acid neutralizers.

Now used by millions

Pepsodent is rather new, yet the use has already spread nearly all the world over. Careful people of some 40 races now employ it daily, largely by dental advice. To millions of people it is bringing a new era in teeth cleaning.

The results are quickly seen and felt. No one can doubt the benefits they bring. Someone in every home should make this test and show the effects to the family.

Pepsodent REG. U. S. PAT. OFF.

The New-Day Dentifrice

A scientific tooth paste, made to comply with all modern requirements. Endorsed by authorities and advised by leading dentists almost the world over.

All druggists supply the large tubes.

10-Day Tube Free 768

THE PEPSODENT COMPANY,
Dept. 534, 1104 S. Wabash Ave., Chicago, Ill.

Mail 10-Day Tube of Pepsodent to

....

....

....

Unsolicited

LUCIEN BOYER, the author of "Madelon," which became the French song of the soldiers in the World War, is a guest of this country, his mission being to create a greater interest in America in the songs of France. The following, from the New York *Tribune*, is a translation of the French verses read at the dinner at which Marshal Foch was the guest of honor of the Alsace-Lorraine Society of America and Allied Franco-American organizations of New York.

THE CONQUEROR

By Lucien Boyer

So New York was awaiting the Marshal of France
And wishing also to see the Conqueror's arrival.
Many humble buildings felt the pain
Not to tower as the skyscrapers.

City Hall said to Woolworth: "Well, big brother,
Don't you see him coming, Monsieur le Maréchal?"
Answered the giant: "I am looking and I hope"—
And stiffened up his paradoxical head into the sky.

Of a sudden Woolworth says: "I see a point which
gleams:
A new star has burst into the night!
Tho I see no flag nor ship,
Yet, and I don't know why, I am sure it is *he*."

At last the *Paris* glided into the light. . . .
Down, before her, burst with fervor,
And suddenly thrilled upon her granite pedestal,
"*Bonjour!*" Liberty greets her savior.

Oh! not for long, all moves so quickly in old U. S.:
Even for a conqueror, great moments are brief
They know how to prepare for him a triumph
. . . electric . . .
Pfft! a Pullman. . . . Pfft! a banquet. . . .
Pfft! an address.

True! But here hearts are never forgetful,
Sacred names are ever tinkling like sleigh bells.
What they love in Foch is also Lafayette,
And he was in their minds in the Bois de Belleau

Upon the gorgeous cities which will be born
Near Lake Michigan or near Missouri,
Already we divine the names which will be written:
Foch, Verdun, Saint Mihiel, Belleau, Chateau
Thierry.

But we ourselves have seen one thing! . . a
thing
Which Americans of the future will not believe.
We saw Wall Street, for that apotheosis,
Tear up its files and scatter them broadcast!

Yes, all these financiers, these bankers, these
brokers,
Were scrapping into confetti their accounts,
And, thanks to these eccentrics one could only see
A little man in blue beneath white butterflies.

And, indeed, proud of his hegemony,
Flatiron cried cheerfully:
"Now I know what is a Marshal of France:
It is a ray of azure which glides along Broadway."

And then, raising his voice with emphasis
So as to be heard by the swarming crowd,
Woolworth shouted: "I was only gothic,
But Marshal Foch has made me flamboyant!"

THE little problem posited here may be debated endlessly. London's *New Witness* prints it:

LA DANSEUSE

By Elsie Paterson Cranmer

Beneath the swaying poplar's shade,
There stands a little dancing maid,
With lips half parted, eyes a-glo...
Feet tiptoeing on th...

CURRENT - POETRY

Unsolicited contributions to this department cannot be returned

LUCIEN BOYER, the author of "Madelon," which became the French song of the soldiers in the World War, is a guest of this country, his mission being to create a greater interest in America in the songs of France. The following, from the New York *Tribune*, is a translation of the French verses read at the dinner at which Marshal Foch was the guest of honor of the Alsace-Lorraine Society of America and Allied Franco-American organizations of New York.

THE CONQUEROR

By Lucien Boyer

So New York was awaiting the Marshal of France
And wishing also to see the Conqueror's arrival.
Many humble buildings felt the pain
Not to tower as the skyscrapers.

City Hall said to Woolworth: "Well, big brother,
Don't you see him coming, Monsieur le Maréchal?"
Answered the giant: "I am looking and I hope"—
And stiffened up his paradoxical head into the sky.

Of a sudden Woolworth says: "I see a point which gleams:
A new star has burst into the night!
Tho I see no flag nor ship,
Yet, and I don't know why, I am sure it is *he*."

At last the *Paris* glided into the light. . . .
Down, before her, burst with fervor,
And suddenly thrilled upon her granite pedestal,
"Bonjour!" Liberty greets her savior.

Oh! not for long, all moves so quickly in old U. S.:
Even for a conqueror, great moments are brief
They know how to prepare for him a triumph . . . electric . . .
Pfft! a Pullman. . . . Pfft! a banquet. . . Pfft! an address.

True! But here hearts are never forgetful,
Sacred names are ever tinkling like sleigh bells.
What they love in Foch is also Lafayette,
And he was in their minds in the Bois de Belleau.

Upon the gorgeous cities which will be born
Near Lake Michigan or near Missouri,
Already we divine the names which will be written:
Foch, Verdun, Saint Mihiel, Belleau, Chateau Thierry.

But we ourselves have seen one thing! . . . a thing
Which Americans of the future will not believe.
We saw Wall Street, for that apotheosis,
Tear up its files and scatter them broadcast!

Yes, all these financiers, these bankers, these brokers,
Were scrapping into confetti their accounts,
And, thanks to these eccentrics one could only see
A little man in blue beneath white butterflies.

And, indeed, proud of his hegemony,
Flatiron cried cheerfully:
"Now I know what is a Marshal of France:
It is a ray of azure which glides along Broadway."

And then, raising his voice with emphasis
So as to be heard by the swarming crowd,
Woolworth shouted: "I was only gothic,
But Marshal Foch has made me flamboyant!"

THE little problem posited here may be debated endlessly. London's *New Witness* prints it:

LA DANSEUSE

By Elsie Paterson Cranmer

Beneath the swaying poplar's shade,
There stands a little dancing maid,
Frail and translucent as a pearl
Glimmers the little dancing girl.
Slowly she comes to earth again,
For dreaming only ends in pain.
Warm as a fairy flower that glows
Flushes the wildling human rose.
Her lips are open for a kiss,
Men think the end of dance is this
Yet somehow it seems wrong to me,
To smirch the mind's virginity,
For dancing lifts the soul on wings,
Away from human, earthly things.
Some good folk think it isn't so,
But no one minds such folk, I know.
Surely a God Who creates dance,
Would never leave a soul to chance;
And little dancing girls have mind,
The same as other human kind.
Oh, lithe-limbed body all a-glancing,
Setting the lyric heart a-dancing,
Sweet little feet that gleam and dart,
Thanks for the music in this heart!

AMONG the verses inspired by the Unknown Soldier this in the Hollywood *News*, is among the few where the Unknown speaks in his own behalf:

VOICE OF THE UNKNOWN DEAD

By Herbert Stotesbury

Oh, my people! Do ye wonder
Whom the spades are digging under,
To the gun's saluting thunder
And the bugle's final call!
Was I one of starved affection?
Was I bowed with imperfection?
Oh, until the resurrection
It shall matter not at all!

What I was hath passed behind me
With the dust that God assigned me;
And the grave that once confined me
Hath been opened for a space
That my voice may speak in thunder,
While the spades shall dig me under,
Of the wrath that tears asunder,
Or opposes race to race.

And my words shall prove a treasure
If ye think, in toil and pleasure,
That as ye shall justly measure,
God shall mete to you; nor cease
Till His world be wrapt in wonder,
Where the guns no more shall thunder
And the spades that dig me under
Be the symbols of His peace.

A FASCINATING fad is the rebuilding in miniature the ships of bygone ages, and some of these reproduced to the minutest detail vie in auction values with the most precious articles of *vertu*. The sentiment they may inspire is happily exprest in this from the Springfield *Republican:*

THE "GOLDEN STEP"

By Anne Johnson Robinson

I can hear the stalwart sailors singing chanties;
As they weigh the dripping anchors at your bow.
The tropic sun's a-glare upon your mainsail,
And the spray is flashing up before the prow.

There's a pungent smell of tar upon your rigging.
And the salt of seven seas—if all were told—
While the air is heavy sweet above the hatches
With the perfume of the spices in the hold.

'Tis thus I see you sailing out of Malta
With your black hull eager for the spray.

ONE of war's strange ironies is touched by Mr. LeGallienne in his lines to be found in the "Silk-Hat Soldier," (John Lane Company). It makes us revise all our thoughts about war even to its battle songs, and this will take us far back in humanity's history.

THE ILLUSIONS OF WAR

By Richard Le Gallienne

War
I abhor;
And yet how sweet
The sound along the marching street
Of drum or fife, and I forget
Broken old mothers, and the whole
Dark butchering without a soul.

Without a soul—save this bright treat
Of heady music, sweet as hell;
And even my peace-abiding feet
Go marching with the marching street,
For yonder goes the fife,
And what care I for human Life;
The tears filled my astonished eyes,
And my full heart is like to break,
And yet it is embannered lies,
A dream those drummers make.

Oh, it is wickedness to clothe
Yon hideous, grinning thing that stalks
Hidden in music like a queen
That in a garden of glory walks,
Till good men love the things they loathe;
Art, thou hast many infamies,
But not an infamy like this.
O, snap the fife and still the drum,
And show the monster as she is.

OUR November days have given us a fellow feeling with these languid verses in the London *Outlook*. It is a feeling akin to the pulse of the year just before lying down to winter's sleep:

IN A WARM OCTOBER

By Archibald Y. Campbell

Only a memory is the lilac now;
The nightingale not even a memory.
Two months, three months back, did the cuckoo fly;
One month before that took his Trappist vow.
Gone are the swallows even, when? whither? how?
Yet one great rich rose blazes garishly;
And once more crawls the meditative plough;
And still the suns soar cloudless, hot, and high.

Glad tho not thrilled I walk, even as the year;
See little, think little, blink, feel the sun.
Birds there may be yet, none I care to hear;
Hopes I may nurse, but would not mention one.
What still is with me, I reflect how dear;
If I have lost some things, their thought I shun.

POETRY has this fearful warning for any who are light in love:

THE JILT

By Agnes Lee

Why should I curl my hair for him?
He said the trouble couldn't be mended,
He said it must be good-by and go;
And he took up his hat, and all was ended.
So all was over. And I'm not dead!
And I've shed all the tears I'm going to shed!

And now he's wanting to come again?
Perhaps he's sorry, perhaps he misses
The hill-top girl. Well, let him come!
But no more love and no more kisses—

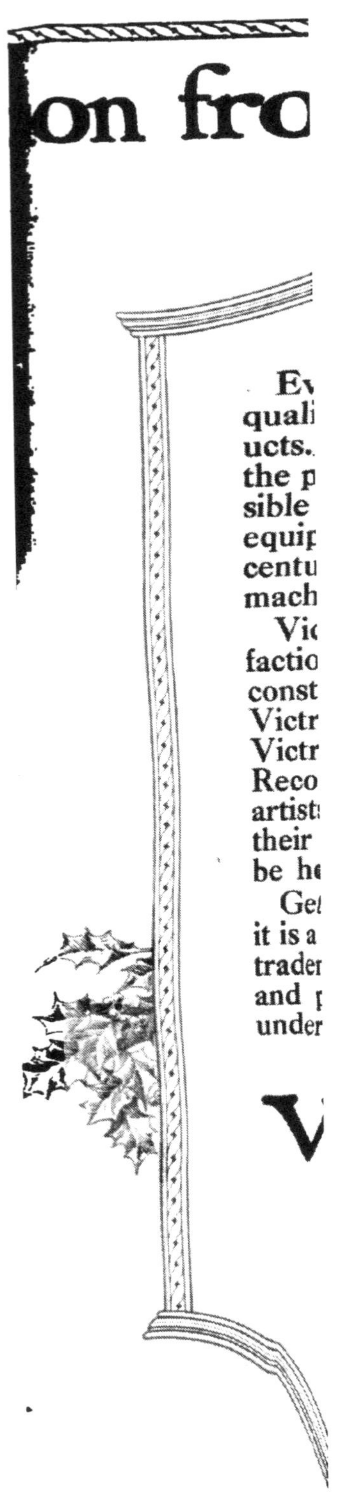

on fro
Ev
quali
ucts.
the p
sible
equip
centu
mach
Vic
factio
const
Victr
Victr
Reco
artists
their
be he
Get
it is a
trader
and p
under
V

pany, Car

PERSONAL ▾ GLIMPSES

OUR COMMUNIST "MARTYRS" DISTURBING THE WORLD

"SAVE SACCO AND VANZETTI!"

Most of the countries of Europe and South America, even Mexico, it is said, are better acquainted with this slogan than is America, where it originated. Within a few weeks a Massachusetts court will decide whether the two Italians convicted of murder shall have a new trial, and in the meantime bomb outrages, boycotts of American goods, and general strikes throughout the world will emphasize the International Communist conviction that the men are being railroaded to death, not because of what they did, but because of what they thought. Thus far, bombs have been sent to the American Ambassador in Paris and to the American Consul General in Lisbon. American representatives in Havana, Peru, Buenos Aires, and Juarez, Mexico, have been warned that their own deaths will follow the execution of the two Italian Communists. American goods are boycotted in several places in South America; demonstrations have been held in front of the American Embassy in Brussels; 5,000 Parisian police were mobilized in Paris following the receipt of a bomb and some fifty threatening letters by Ambassador Herrick; many men and women who had gathered in Rome to protest against the "American judicial murder" were injured, and more than 100 arrested, in a conflict with the police. Judge Webster Thayer, who is reviewing the evidence to determine whether a new trial shall be granted, has received threats and letters enough to constitute, in his own words, "the boldest attempt to influence the court in the history of Massachusetts." The radical *Minnesota Daily Star* (Minneapolis) reminds him of the disbarment of Daniel H. Coakley and two other Boston lawyers in connection with the "$100,000-shake-down" following a dinner party to a well-known movie star at the Copley-Plaza Hotel in 1917.

MADE HEROES BY WORLD-WIDE PROPAGANDA

"An infamous, haughty capitalist-judiciary threatens to drag to the electric chair these two most impeccable Italian citizens.' So runs a literal translation of the beginning of a widely circulated Italian poster, headed by the photographs and the dramatic drawing shown above.

concludes the Minnesota paper, "Mr. Coakley would have slipt over to Dedham and talked to Judge Thayer." A good many other editors, radical and otherwise, are wondering whether the two Italians had as fair a chance for their lives as American justice customarily allows.

What is the basis of this international protest, which started with "three men in a dim-lit, scantily furnished office in Boston"? Samuel Spewack, a staff correspondent of the New York *World*, takes us back to the day of the murder for which Vanzetti and Sacco now await execution in the electric chair. The *World* investigator presents:

> Pearl Street in grimy South Braintree in the mid-afternoon of April 15, 1920. The three o'clock train from Boston screeches into the New Haven Railroad Station nearby.
>
> Two men, the paymaster and his guard, of the Slater Morrell shoe factory, leisurely make their way to the street, bearing in two boxes the weekly payroll.
>
> Revolver shots sound over the grinding in the factories. The paymaster and the guard stagger to the ground. Two men, revolvers in hand, seize the boxes and leap into an automobile containing three other men.
>
> Windows are thrown open in the factory. Frightened employees peer out into the street. The automobile speeds over the railroad tracks. Passers-by and workmen rush to the two fallen men—Alexander Berardelli and Frank Parmenter. They are dead.
>
> This is the crime a jury in Dedham fastened upon Nicolo Sacco and Bartolome Vanzetti.
>
> Three weeks after the murder these two Italian laborers were arrested in Brockton, nearby. Vanzetti was linked with still another crime, and both men with the Pearl Street tragedy.
>
> Evidence against the two men was largely circumstantial. Judge Webster Thayer, who presided, told the jury that "there is a most strenuous contest or dispute as to the identity of the murderers. The real issue that you must determine (the identity) is a very narrow one."
>
> Both men had alibis supported by reputable witnesses. Sacco had been in the Italian Consul's office in Boston upon the day of the crime, a clerk in the office testified. Vanzetti, so other witnesses swore, had spent that day selling fish in Plymouth, thirty-five miles away from South Braintree.
>
> Before their arrest neither of the men had been convicted of a crime. Sacco was a shoe worker and a watchman, and one employer testified to his honesty. Vanzetti had done menial work. Of late he had been peddling fish in the Italian colonies near Boston.

Both men were radicals. Shortly before their arrest they had arranged a mass meeting of protest against the death of Salsedo, the radical who committed suicide by leaping from the Department of Justice Building on Park Row, New York, after, it is charged, he was rendered half-insane by "third degree" methods. Salsedo's companion was deported, and the incident was never explained. Both Sacco and Vanzetti were active in strikes, altho their friends assert they never were paid leaders. As for their connection with the South Braintree murder, the

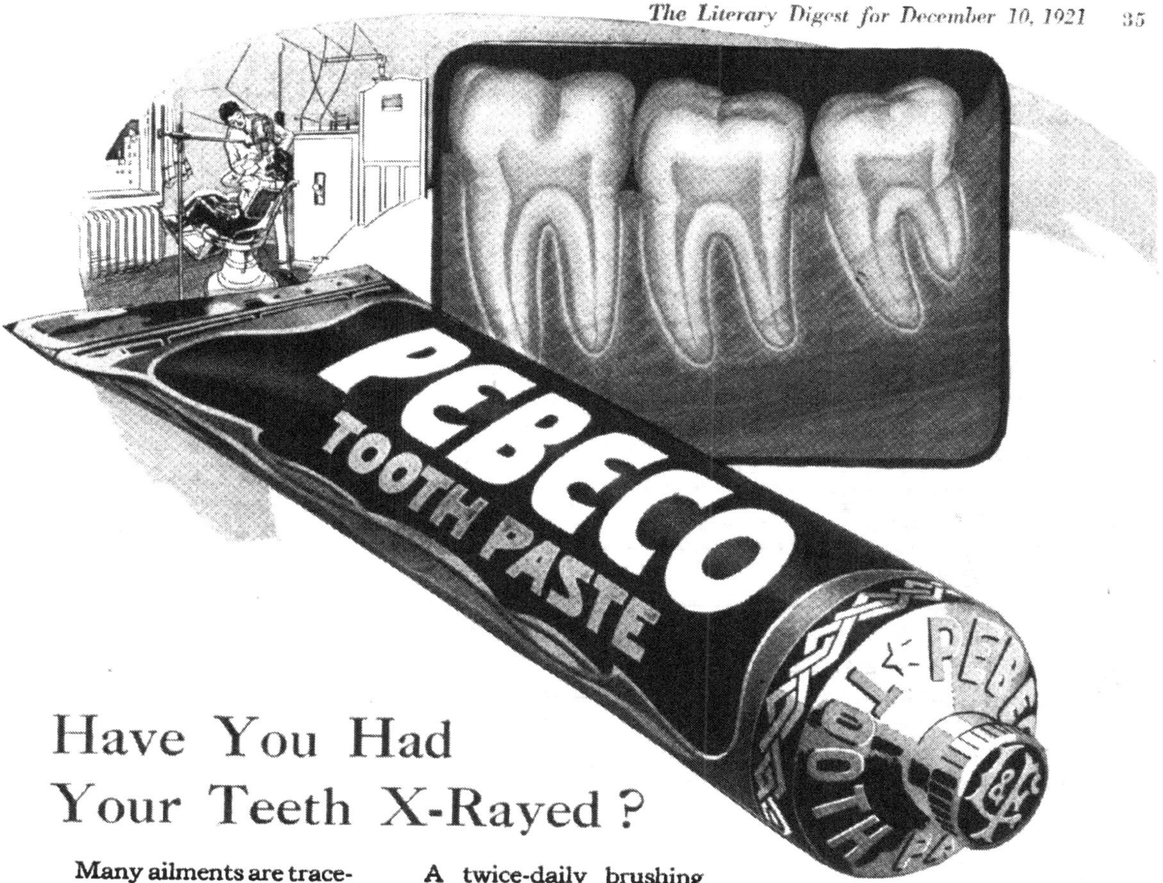

PEBECO TOOTH PASTE

Have You Had Your Teeth X-Rayed?

Many ailments are traceable to conditions of the teeth that an ordinary examination cannot disclose. Trouble in a tooth socket is not always locally painful. The fact that such trouble can be diagnosed from an X-ray plate by a competent specialist is another one of the blessings of modern science.

When professional treatment of the teeth has extended itself to take in X-ray photography, it seems strange that there are still people who neglect the ordinary daily care which may prevent real trouble later on.

A twice-daily brushing of the teeth and gums with Pebeco Tooth Paste will, first of all, make the teeth clean and white.

In addition to making the teeth pleasing to the sight, Pebeco leaves a fresh invigorating sensation in the mouth—a feeling of fine cleanliness.

Finally, Pebeco used night and morning tends to counteract the condition known as "Acid-Mouth," a condition responsible for most tooth decay. A simple test will show whether or not your mouth is in an acid condition.

LEHN & FINK, Inc.,

635 Greenwich Street, New York

Harold F. Ritchie & Co., Selling Agents for the United States and Canada
171 Madison Avenue, New York City — 10 McCaul Street, Toronto

Also Makers of Lysol Disinfectant, Lysol Shaving Cream and Lysol Toilet Soap

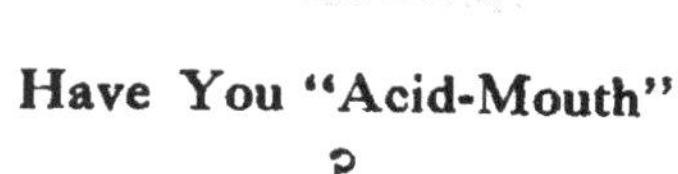

Have You "Acid-Mouth"?

It Is Thought To Be the Chief Cause of Tooth Decay

These Test Papers Will Tell You—Sent Free With Ten-Day Trial Tube of Pebeco

There are probably many causes that contribute to decay of the teeth, but dental authorities seem to agree that in the vast majority of cases decay results from over-acidity of the mouth. You can easily tell if you have "Acid-Mouth," and also see how Pebeco tends to counteract this tooth-destroying condition, by the simple and interesting experiment with the test papers, which we will gladly send to you upon request.

Moisten a blue Litmus Test Paper on your tongue. If it turns pink, you have "Acid-Mouth." Brush your teeth with Pebeco and make another test. The paper will not change color, thus demonstrating how Pebeco helps to counteract "Acid-Mouth." Just send a post-card for Free Test Papers and 10-Day Trial Tube of Pebeco.

First prejudicial evidence against the men centered upon the fact that they carried revolvers. In answer, the defense maintains that all members of the Italian colony own weapons—no license is needed in this State to have a weapon at home—and that many carry revolvers without knowledge of the law. Further, Sacco had frequently carried a revolver as a watchman.

Briefly, the points made by the prosecution were these:

1. A group of witnesses identified Sacco and Vanzetti either as the hold-up men or "suspicious" men seen loitering in South Braintree.

2. A police captain, who claimed to be a revolver expert, linked the bullet found in Berardelli's body with Sacco's revolver.

3. "Consciousness of guilt" was manifested by the two men upon the night they were arrested—that they made evasive statements and lied about their movements.

Replying the defense argued that:

1. Three of the prosecution's star witnesses had changed their testimony from the preliminary hearing a year ago. Then they were not positive. At the trial they insisted upon the identification.

2. Witnesses against the men were at some distance from the hold-up men, and yet several men who stood close by the assailants could not identify either Sacco or Vanzetti.

3. Experts called from revolver factories contradicted the prosecution's expert.

4. "Consciousness of guilt" was betrayed because the men knew of the Red raids; they had heard of Salsedo and did not, therefore, wish to be enmeshed with the Department of Justice.

treat briefly of two other contested points not linked directly with the crime:

1. Police said the men acted as if they were about to draw revolvers when they were arrested. This, the defense says, is a conclusion from the nervous manner of the two men.

2. Vanzetti's conviction upon a hold-up charge is declared a "frame-up" by the defense. When the two men were arrested Vanzetti was brought to trial for quite another hold-up in Bridgewater. Then, after conviction and sentence to fifteen years' imprisonment, he was brought to trial with Sacco for the South Braintree murder. The story of this is not treated in detail here, as the world-wide protest dealt only with the South Braintree crime.

Nevertheless, the defense contends introduction of the previous conviction stamped Vanzetti a criminal. The defense, summarizing the case, emphasizes that radicals do not commit crimes; that nothing in the Communist theory sustained a petty hold-up and shooting of employees. For that matter, the Communists insist they do not contemplate violence, and certainly Communists seen by this writer in Boston are as mild mannered as schoolmasters.

Here is the prejudicial testimony against the two men:

Mary E. Splaine and Frances J. Devlin, office workers for the Slater Morrell concern, saw the hold-up men from the second floor of the building, a distance of eighty feet, the defense say.

Miss Devlin gave a minute description of the hold-up man, nevertheless—color of hair, build, and so on. She positively identified Sacco as that man.

Yet a year ago she had said at the preliminary hearing: "I do not think my opportunity afforded me the right to say he is the man." She admitted that after a visit to Police Headquarters she could not, after studying Sacco minutely, identify him.

Miss Splaine was equally certain. She too at the preliminary hearing said she was not positive of her identification. At the trial she made an unqualified identification.

Louis L. Wade was in the street when the shooting occurred. "three telegraph poles away." He identified Sacco, but he too had indicated his doubt at the preliminary hearing.

Louis Pelzer, a shoe worker, swore he saw the shooting from a first-story window. He identified Sacco, but three men who worked with him testified Pelzer was frightened and did not gaze out into the street long enough to obtain more than a fleeting glance at the hold-up men. Further, shortly after the crime was committed, Pelzer told a detective he had not seen the tragedy. He explained this by his desire to avoid being a witness.

Thirteen witnesses, some of them within a few feet of the fugitive murder car, could not identify the two men.

There is the testimony of numerous individuals who saw two "foreigners"—Sacco and Vanzetti, they were convinced—in various parts of the town several hours before the crime was committed. In answer the defense states that this was absurd; that men planning a crime would not loiter in the neighborhood, particularly as Sacco, as a shoe worker, was well known.

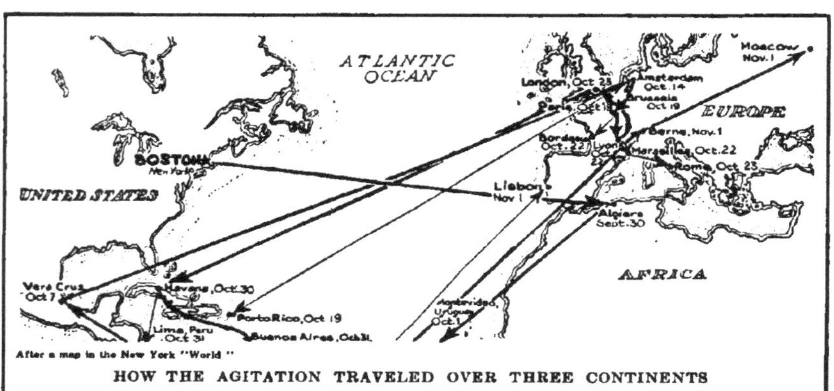

HOW THE AGITATION TRAVELED OVER THREE CONTINENTS

Beginning in Boston, the course of the propaganda in favor of Sacco and Vanzetti followed the lines shown on the map, with places and dates of protest. The American agitation is said to be just getting under way.

One of the circumstantial phases at issue involved a Buick car found abandoned near Bridgewater. Witnesses testified it was this type of car that the hold-up men had used.

Sacco, Vanzetti, Michael Boda and Orciani—the two latter agitators and friends of the convicted men—went to a garage upon the night of the arrest to take out Boda's car. Boda owned an Overland.

The proprietor had been told by the police to notify them if Boda appeared. He was to be questioned in connection with Communist activities. The police were notified. Meanwhile the four, sensing danger, disappeared. A half hour later Sacco and Vanzetti were arrested upon a street car.

The prosecution introduced witnesses to show Boda had used a Buick. Boda and Orciani disappeared.

Significant in the analysis of the case is the atmosphere surrounding the trial. The defense maintains—and impartial investigators with it—that the political beliefs of the two men struck fear into many of the provincial in Dedham. Five hundred residents were examined before a jury could be chosen; a court officer was compelled to go into the street to gather talesmen, and during this process, the defense says, the officer chose nine men from a Masonic meeting.

Much has been written of the Judge's charge, particularly abroad. Radicals have claimed that Judge Thayer practically told the jury to convict the two men because they were Communists. That is not true.

Judge Thayer did tell the jury to deliberate with the courage "such as is typified by the American soldier boy as he fought and gave up his life upon the battlefields of France." But he urged at the same time that no distinction of race or political belief should influence the verdict.

Sympathizers of the two men who attack Judge Thayer maintain that altho legally fair his statements of "courage"

Michael Levangie and Harry Dolbeare linked Vanzetti with the crime by testifying they had seen him in the fleeing automobile. Levangie is the gate tender at the station. He said a man in the automobile pointed a revolver at him. He identified the man as Vanzetti. Levangie's testimony was contradicted by witnesses for the defense who were near the station at the time. Dolbeare saw the profile of one of the occupants of the automobile. His testimony, he conceded, was vague, but he identified Vanzetti as the man.

The prosecution endeavored to prove that Vanzetti's revolver was taken from Berardelli. The guard's revolver had been recently repaired for a broken spring. There was no evidence that Vanzetti's revolver had acquired a new spring, altho witnesses did testify to a new hammer.

For the defense more than a hundred witnesses were called. Twenty of them supplied alibis for the two men. Witnesses for Sacco included the Vice-President of the Haymarket National Bank in Boston, a grocer, a photographer, the clerk in the consulate office where Sacco said he had been that day

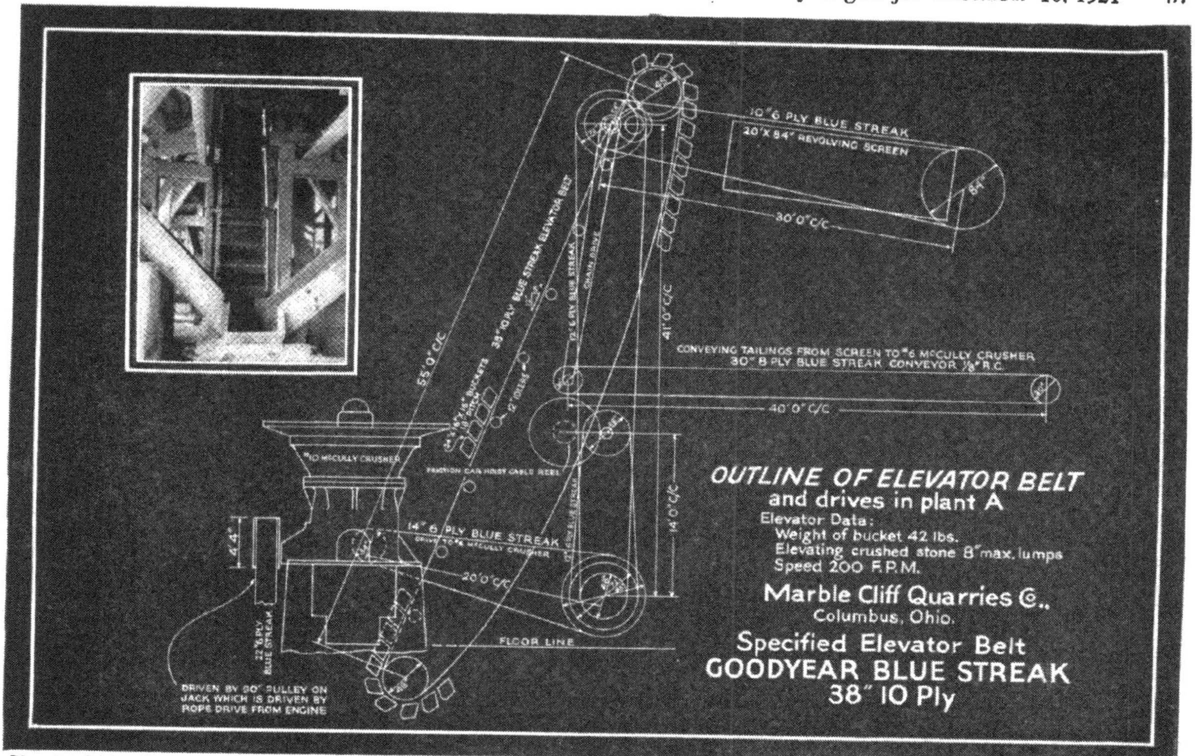

OUTLINE OF ELEVATOR BELT
and drives in plant A
Elevator Data:
Weight of bucket 42 lbs.
Elevating crushed stone 8" max. lumps
Speed 200 F.P.M.

Marble Cliff Quarries Co.,
Columbus, Ohio.

Specified Elevator Belt
GOODYEAR BLUE STREAK
38" 10 Ply

Blueprint sketch and insert photograph of Goodyear Blue Streak Belted Bucket Elevator in the service of The Marble Cliff Quarries Company, Columbus, Ohio

Five Years of Lifting—and the G.T.M.

"The best record ever made on elevator service in our plants," says H. J. Kaufman, Assistant General Manager of The Marble Cliff Quarries Company, Columbus, Ohio, "was made by a Goodyear Blue Streak Belt, specified to the job by a G.T.M.—Goodyear Technical Man."

Every quarryman knows the punishment a belt gets in bucket elevator service. It is exposed to changing weather. It is showered constantly with grittily abrasive stone dust. It is subjected continually to sudden and severe strains as the buckets take up their loads of rock. It has to stand up to the steady pull of the loaded buckets as they rise.

No wonder that ordinary belts, coming to such a job without any special construction in their favor, swiftly developed the troubles the Marble Cliff's superintendent experienced with them for years. They averaged only a few months in life; the very best of them lasted two years, and was regarded as a marvel.

Then the G.T.M. came along, and his proposal, to analyze the elevator requirements and specify a belt exactly to those requirements, impressed the Company's officials. His study included every mechanical detail of the problem—the weight and number and spacing of the buckets, the average load, the belt speed. The plant superintendent co-operated, supplying full data on the working conditions.

A Goodyear Blue Streak Belt, 38-inch, 10-ply, was the G. T. M.'s recommendation. It was installed in 1914—the first year of the World War. It was removed from the pulleys on May 1, 1919, five months after the end of the war, with the trouble-free service record of having carried between 1,500,000 and 2,000,000 tons. After withstanding every hardship in the day's work for five whole years, it was retired in favor of the new Goodyear Blue Streak Belt that is already in its third year of lifting.

The Goodyear Analysis Plan, the expert services of the G.T.M., and the inbuilt worth of Goodyear Belt construction may be put to work profitably in your plant. Whether your problem is one of Conveyor or Transmission Belts, whether it involves a single drive or an entire factory, the G.T.M. will gladly undertake the study of it for you. For further information about the G.T.M. and Goodyear Belts, write to The Goodyear Tire & Rubber Company, Akron, Ohio, or Los Angeles, California.

PERSONAL GLIMPSES
Continued

Vanzetti produced eleven witnesses to testify to his presence in Plymouth that day. Joseph Rosena, peddler, who sold Vanzetti some suiting, placed the day by a receipt for payment of taxes. Various women testified they had bought fish from him. A boat builder remembered meeting him that day.

No effort was made to trace the $15,000 contents of the two boxes seized by the hold-up men. Various explanations were offered, but none substantiated.

The case was presented to the jury on July 14 after a trial of two weeks. The jury deliberated five hours and brought in a verdict of first degree murder.

The Springfield (Mass.) *Republican*, in its consideration of the nearby case, has brought out an argument, introduced by Professor Hurley of the Suffolk Law School, to the effect that the Italians "were convicted by atmosphere, not evidence." The radical papers of the country, of course, take this attitude, exprest in a far less restrained manner. "Truth crusht to earth in North America, arises in Paris, in Spain, in Italy, in the Argentine Republic!" cries the Butte *Bulletin*. "The Sacco-Vanzetti demonstrations have shown the kept-press editors that the time has passed when the guiltless can be quietly strangled for their views of the social order. They can be strangled, perhaps, but not quietly!" The New York *World*, which has been investigating the case, notes that the "Propagandists have played a safe game. If Sacco and Vanzetti are set free it will be hailed as a victory over the forces of injustice; if they are executed, they will be looked upon as martyrs. In either case great numbers of people in foreign lands will think the worst of American courts." Nevertheless, declares *The* World, "if there was a mistrial, the United States will be as much interested as Europe to find it out and to redress the wrong."

In the course of its investigation, *The World* editor says:

Among the first findings are an obscure office in Boston from which publicity has been issued and three very much astonished young enthusiasts who set out to discredit the evidence in a murder trial and ended by creating what looks like an international issue. Their cry of "Save Sacco and Vanzetti!" has been taken up by so many voices that they are swept away in the confusion.

Taking up "the mushroom growth of this new *cause célèbre*, hatched in a Boston office and transplanted into Italy, South America, Switzerland, Belgium, Mexico, Portugal—leaving its imprint in violence and bloodshed," *The World's* investigator writes:

Actual violence commenced upon October 21—more than a week preceding the day upon which sentence was to have been pronounced upon the two labor

Everywhere the hoarse shouting of the "Internationale"—the clarion call of revolution—was blended with the appeal of the Boston office: "Save Sacco and Vanzetti!"

Then—

PARIS, Oct. 19.—A hand-grenade exploded in the home of Ambassador Herrick. It was deposited upon a table in the embassy, carefully wrapt in a box labeled "Perfume." Ambassador Herrick's valet was wounded.

BRUSSELS, Oct. 19.—Belgian Communists attended various meetings in protest of the Sacco-Vanzetti conviction. Demonstrations were held in front of the American Embassy. The police attacked the crowd and dispersed it.

PARIS, Oct. 21—Hundreds of mass meetings preceded a street demonstration and a march upon the American Embassy. This was planned by the Anarchist Alliance and the radical newspapers. Two squadrons of cavalry, helmeted troopers, armed police, charged mobs near the embassy. A bomb was thrown by a fanatic in the midst of violent encounters. Twenty were killed. Six policemen were wounded.

PARIS, Oct. 22.—Ten thousand troops guarded the city while as large a number of radicals paraded the streets. Minor conflicts with the authorities were reported in various parts of the city.

BORDEAUX-MARSEILLES-LYONS, Oct. 22.—Clamorous crowds gathered in front of the offices of the American Consuls General in these cities and demanded the immediate release of Sacco and Vanzetti.

Not only in the big cities of France did such things as these take place. The Sacco-Vanzetti case filtered into the provinces. Parisian papers carry accounts of visits of agitators to the villages, where, to quote *Libertaire*, "the peasants listened, interested, with their mouths a little opened. What could they do, these isolated ones, except to pour out their pennies that others might carry on the struggle?"

The course of the movement in France included the demand for a boycott of American goods; incessant appeals for demonstrations in front of the American Embassy. "Stop at nothing," rang the slogan—and French Anarchists heeded.

PARIS, Oct. 23.—Fifty threatening letters were received by Ambassador Herrick. Five thousand of the Parisian police were mobilized. The members of the Republican Guard, battalions of infantry and cavalry were drafted. The city wore "the aspect of a state of siege."

ROME, Oct. 23.—Thousands gathered in the streets in demonstration for Sacco and Vanzetti. This followed mass meetings, verbal and printed propaganda. In a conflict with the police more than one hundred men and women were arrested.

Meetings were held in Galliate, Sulmona, Orvisto, Luino. Orders of the day were voted to boycott American goods. Each meeting, so the newspaper reported, roused listeners "to the boiling point." In the Chamber of Deputies the Radical members demanded intercession by the Italian Government. This was promised if Sacco and Vanzetti were condemned finally.

LONDON, Oct. 23.—Sylvia Pankhurst planned a demonstration of Anarchists to Ambassador Harvey's home, but few responded.

STOCKHOLM, Oct. 26.—Resolutions were passed at a meeting of labor unions demanding the release of Sacco and Vanzetti. These were forwarded to Ira Nelson Morris, the American Minister.

PERSONAL GLIMPSES
Continued

General Hollis's office. Mr. Hollis kicked it with his foot but was not injured. He had received many threatening letters from Sacco-Vanzetti sympathizers.

HAVANA, Oct. 30. — Major-General Crowder and the members of the United States Legation were menaced by radicals distributing Sacco-Vanzetti literature through the streets. Seven of the radicals were arrested. The literature called conviction the "dagger of vengeance of the bourgeoisie."

BUENOS AYRES, Oct. 31.—William H. Robertson, the American Consul General, received letters warning him that unless Sacco and Vanzetti were saved a "stick of dynamite would be prepared."

LIMA, Peru, Oct. 31.—The American Embassy received a letter stating: "If these two innocent beings are put to death you will pay with your lives."

PORTO RICO, Oct. 19.—Radical newspapers and organizations call for release of Sacco and Vanzetti.

AMSTERDAM, Oct. 14.—French newspapers reported an "incessant agitation in Holland from one end of the country to the other." Here too American representatives were flooded with appeals for Sacco and Vanzetti.

VERA CRUZ, Oct. 7—"Crime of North American imperialism" is discust in Anarchist papers. Literature distributed at Communist meetings.

ALGIERS, Sept. 30.—Robert Oliver appealed to the French and Italian colonies. Various meetings were held. Oliver's appeal is: "The Algerian proletariat must join its protest to that of the proletariats of of other countries so that these two latest victims of imperialism shall not be assassinated. Algerian comrades, get together, and let us act before it is too late.

MONTEVIDEO, Uruguay, Oct. 1.—Metal workers and chauffeurs proclaim boycott of American products and general strike. Big posters bearing the photographs of the two men were placarded over the city. For two days the city was paralyzed. American representatives bombarded with protests.

BERNE, Nov. 1.—"Space is lacking to give a complete report of the agitation made in Switzerland for Sacco and Vanzetti," reports *Il Rieveglio*. Protests were sent to the American Legation by 600 members of the Workingmen's Union at the first congress here.

MOSCOW, Nov. 1.—Swiss newspapers reported street demonstrations in Moscow for Sacco and Vanzetti. Agitators distributed literature upon the streets. The Third Internationale in Moscow is now behind the world-wide demonstrations through its organizations in various countries.

This is the list of cities thus far available. Minor protests in other parts of the globe are not included. In each city mentioned the Sacco and Vanzetti case was not merely an incident—it was a vital issue. In each city mentioned American representatives were harassed, America denounced.

A postscript to the list given above is contained in a dispatch from Washington dated November 26, which runs:

> John W. Dye, American consul at Juarez, has been threatened with death if the United States Government permits the to a cablegram received at the State Department to-day.
>
> A letter warning him was forwarded by Dye to the Department. It was signed "Committee for the Syndicate of Truckmen, Port of Vera Cruz."

Even such liberal, if not radical, American weeklies as *The Nation* and *The New Republic*, deplore the "direct action" of the Communists. "Bomb throwing in Paris is likely only to bring Sacco and Vanzetti nearer to the electric chair," says *The Nation*, which believes that "in a larger sense it is not so much Sacco and Vanzetti as American justice which is on trial. One hundred and thirty years ago French mobs hailed America as the seat of liberty; to-day they call us the center of capitalism's worst tyranny." *The New Republic* observes that "The men were convicted of a private crime on what seems to have been insufficient evidence. The chance of saving them from execution depends largely on arousing public opinion on their behalf." Nevertheless, concludes the editor,

> The American public is jealous of foreign interference and sensitive on the subject of social crime. Once convinced that these men are dangerous to society, and that they are for that reason the object of intervention by foreign radical forces, public opinion is too likely to react strongly against them, to hold that whether guilty or not they should be handled as enemies of the social order and that it is a matter of national prestige to hang them. The lesson of the Chicago anarchists' case is obvious.

A rather more general, and more conservative, view is taken by the Philadelphia *Inquirer*. Under the headline of "Fictitious Martyrs to a Futile Cause," it observes:

> It will not be surprizing if the disorderly demonstrations in Europe in behalf of the two Italian Communists found guilty of murder by a Massachusetts jury are repeated in American cities. Such is said to be the program of American Radicals. They have a perfect right, of course, to protest against what they believe to be injustice. The wisdom of doing so is more open to question. The likehood that violent language will be used, leading, perhaps, to violent acts, is giving the police of Boston, which appears to be the headquarters of the agitation, some concern. They fear lest bombs may form a part of the argument.
>
> The case of Sacco and Vanzetti, of comparatively little importance in itself, has become, as it were by chance, a rallying point for the forces of revolution. The issue which they have thus raised is a false one. The two men were fairly tried. Whether they were fairly convicted may be doubtful. There is a conflict of evidence as to their identity with two men who undeniably committed highway robbery and murder. It is said that both have complete alibis. The jury that convicted them were obviously not convinced of this, tho possibly they should have been.
>
> Objection is also taken to the judge's charge, which is described as prejudiced and partial. For this accusation there appears to be no sufficient ground.
>
> If Sacco and Vanzetti are indeed innocent, they have nothing to fear, nor is all

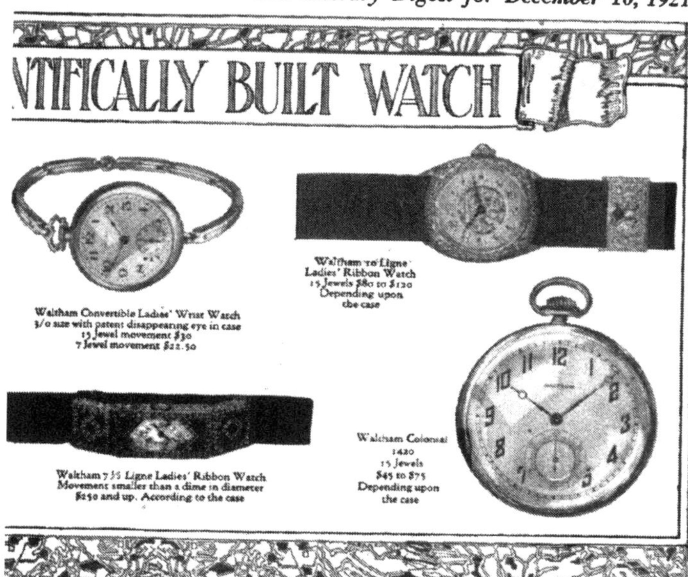

For Sixty-Seven Years he Christmas Gift of Gifts

'OR sixty-seven years the Waltham Watch been the American of gifts.

ır after year it has ved its lasting merit. "works" contain the hest watch-making ievements in the world. re is no watch movet like it. It has demonted its unchallenged lership in international petition.

Waltham Watch is the ily watch of our bed country. It has transd its service from par- to children's children. housands of instances the most prized perıl possession.

Waltham accuracy is world famed.

Every Waltham Watch is backed by Waltham integrity. It is the world's standard of watch values.

What more worthy gift for Christmas! What gift more lasting! There is a Waltham Watch for every pocket-book. Make one of these dependable, beautiful Waltham time-keepers *your* Christmas Gift of Gifts.

Your jeweler can supply the Waltham Watch that you desire. If it is not in stock, write us, and we will see that he obtains it immediately.

for a valuable booklet that is a liberal "Watch" education. Sent upon request. The Waltham Watch Company, Waltham, Mass.

VALTHAM

THE WORLD'S WATCH OVER TIME

Where you see this sign they sell Waltham Watches

PERSONAL GLIMPSES
Continued

courts essential to their protection. An appeal for a new trial is pending, and if that is denied the case will probably go to the Supreme Court of the Commonwealth. Furthermore, a large sum of money has been raised for their defense and able counsel have been provided.

"EDUCATIONAL" PRISON LIFE UNDER THE SOVIETS

IRONY of the bitterest sort is found, by a recent well-equipped investigator from Czecho-Slovakia, in the Bolshevik boast that they were going to turn their prisons into "educational institutions," from which the prisoners would emerge "not criminals as from bourgeois prisons, but well-educated citizens." Prison life in Russia, this investigator found, had become immensely more common, if not more popular, but the "educational features" were not so apparent. Anything or nothing, he testified, may result in prison terms. The investigator is I. Ochakovsky, a member of the staff of *Volia Rossii*, a Russian daily published in Prague. He went to Soviet Russia to inquire into conditions at first hand, enjoying an advantage over most investigators in his knowledge of Russia and the Russians. He traveled extensively, for the most part on foot, worked in factories, and also had occasion to spend some time in prisons. A translation of his description of this last investigation runs:

At the present time, even in small towns, the "educational institutions" occupy several private houses. The old prisons are not destroyed, but simply overcrowded. The new "homes" usually are on the main street of the city or town, probably to impress everybody with the fact that the people's commissars are doing much for education, the need for which is so great in Russia. In the city of Proskuroff the prison is in an immense building. Inside the big and badly neglected court, where heaps of refuse and garbage are seen, there are two houses with iron bars surrounded with barbed wire, in front of which Red Army guards stand with rifles in their hands.

When one enters the dirty damp structure, one finds himself in a large room, which could accommodate at most thirty people, and an extraordinary sight greets the eye. About eighty people, women and men are sitting on the floor closely pressed together. Their faces are gaunt, pale and dirty. Nearly all of them are dressed in rags. The men are naked to the waist. All are earnestly engaged in doing something. This occupation is called "reconnaissance" by the inmates.

When the guard opens the door to admit a new prisoner, the odor almost knocks him off his feet. As soon as he steps over the threshold, all inmates raise their heads and greet him with a wretched smile on their yellow faces: "Come in, comrade, make yourself at home. If you have not got 'them' yet, they are sure to come."

The guard slightly pushes in the puzzled newcomer and bangs the door shut after him. I do not know how that affected others, but I shiver even now, recalling that moment in the detention house. I stood, looked around myself, unable to make up my mind to join the prisoners. In a corner I noticed a priest with long hair, without a shirt, who was busily engaged in destroying a certain species of insect. Not far from him sat a lady of cultured appearance engaged in the same task. She was a public school teacher, an intelligent and well-educated woman. When some time earlier she came to the Cheka to change her Ukrainian passport, issued by Petlura's agents, for a Soviet document, she was detained for "a couple of minutes" (all are detained for "a couple of minutes"), and several days later she was told that she was charged with counter-revolution, espionage and banditry.

Further in the corner sat a peasant woman from Volhynia and near her a lad of about eighteen, her son. Following the example of the men, the old woman took off her shirt, and also engaged in the destruction of the vermin. On the other window sill sat a man of imposing appearance, with an extremely kindly face, and next to him a tall and broad-shouldered old man, clean shaven but with gray hair on his head. The former was the principal of the Polish high school in Proskuroff and the latter a former Polish landowner who had a model estate near Proskuroff, which now was completely destroyed.

In the middle of the room stood Yankel Yankelevich, a former military tailor. . . . He had just been locked up, and he could not make up his mind to settle anywhere, being afraid to let the vermin into his half-torn fur coat. Suddenly he noticed the principal of the high school, for whom he used to make uniforms. He made a step in the direction of the principal and exclaimed: "Thank God, you are here. . . . Now I feel a little better, because I see there are decent people here. I thought I was put in the same cell with bandits."

The principal smiled and shook the hand of his old acquaintance. "Why were you imprisoned?" he asked.

"Why was I imprisoned? Just so, just for nothing. All these months I have been embroidering stars for Red Army commanders. The chairman of the Special Section comes to me and says: 'Yankel, make me a star for to-morrow without fail.' 'I can not,' I say to him, 'I have much work for to-morrow.' He got awful mad and began to shout: 'If you don't make it, I'll arrest you, I'll have you shot, that's sabotage.' And, my God, what a scandal he made! But I didn't get frightened and didn't make the star, because I couldn't. And I had no material. And what do you think? On the next day I got an order to go to Zhmerinka: to get material there. I got a pass, which was entered in about a hundred books, and went to the station. Suddenly I was arrested there by order . . . whose order, do you think? By order of the chairman of the Special Section, and I am charged with attempt to travel on a false pass. How do you like that? And, I had with me about two hundred small stones for self-igniters which I wanted to exchange for something in Zhmerinka, so I am charged with profiteering. Then when searching my house they found two pairs of old officer's shoulder straps, which I cut up in order to make new stars, so I am charged with being a Monarchist, and they threaten to shoot me. And I have, you know, six children, and the seventh one will soon come. There is no money at home, upon my honest word, not a copeck. And what will my poor wife do without me?"

BIRDS - BEASTS - AND - TREES

JOHN DANIEL, CIVILIZED GORILLA

LIFE in a jungle in the French Gaboon country may differ slightly from the ways of an English household, but that did not especially trouble "Johnny Gorilla," as his intimate friends called him. He did not find eating at table disconcerting on the contrary, his table manners were really very good. And as for sleeping in a bed, he soon found it was rather a lark to stand on the top rail of the bed and jump on the springs, head over heels, like a mischievous boy. Of course he did not arrive at this advanced stage of sophistication all in a moment. He had to be "brought up," like any other child. His civilized life began when he was captured, very young, and brought to Havre by a French ship captain. The friends who adopted him saw him first entertaining the crowds in the zoo of an English department store, toward the end of 1918. Major Rupert Penny, who was interested in primates, bought the gorilla, with the idea of seeing how much mentality could be developed in this member of the highest ape family. So John came to live with his owner's family in London, and the story of his domestic life and his quaint habits is told by a member of the household, Alyse Cunningham, in the *Zoological Society Bulletin* (New York):

Courtesy of the Bulletin of the New York Zoological Society.

HE WAS FOND OF CHILDREN.

This three-year-old girl was a frequent visitor and beloved playmate.

We converted a small room into a cage for him, separated from another room by bars, so that he could see and be near to people all day. The cage was heated by an electric radiator. One of the windows of the cage we had taken out, and the space was covered with several thicknesses of muslin, to allow fresh air to be filtered through.

We soon found it was impossible to leave him alone at night, because he shrieked every night, and nearly all night, from loneliness and fear! This we found he had done in the store before coming to us. He always began to cry directly he saw the assistants putting things away for the night. We found that this loneliness at night was trying on his health and appetite, besides which, we were afraid the people in the neighborhood would complain. As soon as possible my nephew had his bed made up every night in the room adjoining the cage, with the result that John was quite happy, and at once began to grow and put on weight.

By this time I was getting to like John, and to take a great interest in him. I fed him, washed his hands, face and feet twice a day, and brushed and combed his hair—which he would try and do himself whenever he got hold of the brush or comb. He soon got to like all this. My next idea was to teach him to be strictly clean in his habits. This training occupied quite six weeks.

John's appetite seemed to tire of foods very quickly. The only thing he stuck to was milk, which he always liked best when warmed. We began by giving him a quart a day, raising to three and a half quarts a day. I found that he preferred to choose his own food, so I used to place for him several kinds, such as bananas, oranges, apples, grapes, raisins, currants, dates and any small fruit in season, such as raspberries or strawberries, all of which he especially liked to have warmed. These displays I placed on a high shelf in the kitchen, where he could get them with difficulty. I think that he thought himself very clever when he stole anything. He never would eat anything stale. He was extremely fond of jelly, especially fresh lemon jelly, which was often made for him, but he never would touch it after the second day.

Courtesy of the Bulletin of the New York Zoological Society

A BIT COY, PERHAPS, BUT HAPPY.

When he was taken from Miss Cunningham to live among strangers, the gorilla died.

Oranges or apples, or any fruit that had been cut he would never eat after a few hours. He loved roses, *to eat*, more than anything! The more beautiful they were the more he liked them, but he never would eat faded roses. As a consequence I hardly

catalog
ooks, let us send
36-page catalog
ys and girls. It
of the more than
s published by
—all arranged for
ht book for the
L D. 12.
ROBERT RIGGS

The Open Door to the Fairyland of Dreams—

Memories of boyhood and girlhood days are rose-tinted with recollections of precious hours "when Daddy read," and later of that joyful day when the magic story unfolded itself before our own enlightened eyes.

Mother Goose and Cinderella, and Jack and the Beanstalk, and King Arthur and His Knights, and Ivanhoe and Robinson Crusoe—these were not make-believe characters in the Fairyland of Dreams. They lived!

And today they still live in picture and in story in RAND McNALLY Books for little tots and older boys and girls. RAND McNALLY is not only the world's largest maker of maps, atlases, and map systems but it is also the largest publisher of the best juvenile books.

More than 500,000 copies of just one RAND McNALLY book—*The Real Mother Goose*—have already been sold. Practically every one of the many other RAND McNALLY juvenile books has run into three, four, or five editions.

In addition to the best content and finest workmanship there are three other reasons for the ever-increasing popularity of RAND McNALLY books: (1) clear, readable type; (2) illustrations by such famous artists as Milo Winter, Hope Dunlap, Ruth Hallock, Maginel Wright Enright, Blanche Fisher Wright, Margaret Evans Price; (3) clean, wholesome text that educates and inspires the youthful mind.

RAND McNALLY BOOKS *are for sale in all shops where books are sold.*

RAND McNALLY & COMPANY—*Headquarters for Juvenile Books*
536 S. CLARK STREET, CHICAGO

RAND McNALLY *Editio*

BIRDS, BEASTS AND TREES

Continued

ever was able to have roses in the vases. He also liked nibbling twigs, and to eat the green buds of trees.

When he first came to us, I found that nuts gave him dreadful spells of indigestion, for after eating them he would lie down on the floor and groan. As he grew older he became very fond of peanuts baked in the oven, and they seemed to agree with him very well. He never cared very much for nuts of any other kind, except walnuts. With coconuts he was very funny. He knew that they had to be broken, and he would try and break them on the floor. When he found he couldn't manage that, he would bring the big nut to one of us and try to make us understand what he wished. If we gave him a hammer he would try to use it on the nut, and on not being able to manage that, he always gave back to us both the hammer and the coconut. He knew what hammers and chisels were for, but for obvious reasons we never encouraged him in anything to do in the line of carpentry.

John loved to have people come to see him in his home, says Miss Cunningham, and when they came he would show off like a child. He would take them by the hand and lead them round and round the room. If he saw that his visitors were at all nervous about him, he would run past them and give them a smack on the leg, and, she says, you could see him grin as he did so. His mischievousness took various diverting forms, she continues:

A game he was very fond of was to pretend that he was blind, shutting his eyes very tightly and running about the room knocking against tables and chairs. He loved to take everything out of a waste paper basket and strew the contents all over the room, after which he would always pick up everything and put it all back when told to, but looking very bored all the while. If the basket was very full he would push it all down very carefully to make room for more. He would always put things back when told to do so, such as books from a book-shelf, or things from a table.

His table manners were really very good. He always sat at the table, and whenever a meal was ready, would pull his own chair up to his place. He did not care to eat a great quantity, but he especially liked to drink water out of a tumbler. I always gave him some butter with his breakfast, but he seldom liked bread. Sometimes he would take a whole crust or round of toast when you least expected him to and eat it all. He always took afternoon tea—of which he was very fond—and a thin piece of bread with plenty of jam; and he always liked coffee after dinner. He was the least greedy of all the animals I ever have seen. He never would snatch anything, and always ate very slowly. He always drank a lot of water, which he would get himself whenever he wanted it, by turning on a tap. Strange to say he always turned off the water when he had finished drinking. He seemed to thrive on water, and this never prevented his taking his milk as well.

John seemed to think that every one was delighted to see him, and he used to throw up the window whenever he was permitted. If he found the sash locked he would unfasten it, and when a big crowd collected

BIRDS, BEASTS AND TREES
Continued

of a burden, and his friends felt they must part with him. Miss Cunningham outlines the tragedy that followed:

Understanding he was to be placed in a private park in Florida, and believing that these would be ideal conditions for him, we signed the contract to sell him, only to find out too late what the real conditions were to be. Unfortunately also the man sent to take him across to America had not the slightest notion how to treat him, because, altho we stipulated he would stay with John for six weeks, he was with John only a very few hours. Thus was poor John Gorilla taken away from us by a complete stranger to him, with the result that from totally changed conditions and homesickness he soon became ill, and my presence was called for by cable entirely too late for me to find him alive. He died in Madison Square Garden Tower in the last week of April, 1921.

UNDERWATER DUEL OF THE OTTER AND THE PIKE

A WILD chase is going on in the depths of the biggest bog-hole. The rushes bow their sheaves and the flags their fans. Black mud is stirred up in whirlpools, seething bubbles come to the surface and burst. The otter has invaded the water-hole of Grim, the pike. The fisher had just caught a fish and started on its way to a little island, intending to have its meal peacefully under a willow, when it was suddenly attacked and robbed of its prey. It caught a glimpse of the indistinct outline of a great fish, who was Grim herself, and exasperated at such audacity, it turned hotly to chase the robber. Now it tries to get beneath Grim, in order to seize her round the gills or by the belly, but at the decisive moment Grim turns aside, so that the otter has to set his teeth where he can, a little behind Grim's neck, and, we read in "Grim, the Story of a Pike," translated from the Danish of Svend Fleuron (Knopf, New York):

The instant it has taken hold Grim darts into deep water with her assailant. The otter backs, extends his fore and hind legs far out from his body, and spreads his web, so as to offer as much resistance as possible. Just as the weasel lets itself be carried away by the hare in whose neck it has fixt itself, so now the otter allows himself to be dragged through the bog by the lynx of the waters.

Grim soon sees that this pace is wearing out her strength, and pauses for a moment.

As she does so, she feels as if an eel were winding its pliant body round her chest. She rolls round, unable to use her fins. She quickly regains her balance, however, frees her body from the pressure, and sets off, with sudden twists, and leaps from the bottom to the surface, turning so suddenly that the fish-snatcher's body swings out and hangs down in the water.

But the otter only keeps a firmer hold. He is used to these desperate rallies, which always become fiercer and more violent as the quarry is on the point of giving in. He takes care, however, in turning, not to let any of his legs hang in front of the pike's mouth; he is too well acquainted with the teeth of the fresh-water shark!

Up and down, the two well-matched opponents dive incessantly.

Whenever Grim goes to the surface, a puffing and growling is heard. The otter hastily gasps for breath, and tightens his hold with his fore-claws; but when they are on their way down to the depths, and air-bubbles, like silver beads, roll through the water behind him, he has only to hold on and let himself go.

Once Grim is lucky. An old snag sticks up in the water, and, in turning, the otter's body is dashed against it. It sends a shock through the animal, but as Grim for the moment has exhausted her energy and succumbed to one of the well-known fits of weakness common to her species, the otter once more apparently gets the upper hand.

Thus with varying fortunes the battle rages for some time.

They lie fighting on the surface—a golden-streaked, slimy, scaly fish twisted into a knot with a dark, hairy, furred body!

Once more there is a pause in the fighting.

Unobserved by Grim, who has just fallen into one of her apathetic fits, the otter endeavors carefully to float the pike up under one of the large mounds, in order to drag her up with an effort of strength on to dry land; but the attempt fails utterly: he is simply unable to manage so great a load.

Now Grim's strength returns once more. With a powerful stroke of her tail, she disappears with lightning rapidity from the surface, and goes to the bottom with her rider, whose merry-go-round jaunt makes his head swim. She is trying to get hold of his leg or body, and therefore twists round with him so that he flaps like a loose piece of strap on an axle; but she is not sufficiently supple to reach him. Her back aches, her flexor muscles hurt. At last she has met with an opponent who puts her judgment, her ingenuity, and her endurance to the extreme test.

Down on the bottom, sticking out from the bank, are the roots of the willow-bushes on the edge. In her mad rush down, Grim has come near these, and instinctively seeks shelter beneath them. At full speed she runs her long body into the network and sticks fast, rapidly twisting her tail-screw both ahead and astern.

The otter treads water now on the right, now on the left side of her, and tries, by utilizing the roots as steps, to lift her up with him. But in vain, he cannot even stir the huge fish!

His teeth are still far from having forced their way through; it seems as if, short and rounded as they are, they cannot reach the bottom. But he makes tremendous exertions, whipping his tail in under the peat-bank, while with his hind paws he seeks for support in clefts and cracks. Suddenly he feels one of his feet seized. The grasp tightens, so that his whole leg aches; he tries to draw in his foot, but it is held immovable.

What has happened? A new character has entered the watery drama. A monster crayfish, that has become so stiff with age that it can scarcely manage to strike a proper blow with its tail, has made for itself, in fear of Grim, a reliable place of refuge in the hole. For a long time it has patiently followed the battle through its feelers, and hoped that some morsel would fall to its hungry stomach; now, with

BIRDS, BEASTS AND TREES
Continued

gratitude to Providence, it closes its great claw upon the warm-blooded fisher. But alas! it returns its thanks too soon. When the crayfish seizes upon the animal, we read:

A growing uneasiness steals over the otter. With the grasp on his leg, his lungs begin to warn him, his throat contracts, and his eyes seem on the point of bursting. Up! Up! With or without his prey!

He has let go of Grim, and now makes his escape from the hole with so sudden a jerk that the old crayfish accompanies him; he slips out from among the roots, and is already rising; and as he approaches the surface and finds the blessed light beating more and more strongly upon the mud about his eyes, he hastens his flight, until, with an eager sniff, he reaches the surface.

Grim is close behind him, and as the otter lands, there is a loud splash. It would have been all over with the brown beast if the old crayfish, on its way down from the surface, where it had at last let go its hold, had not dropt like a stone straight into Grim's mouth. Grim has now to content herself with sending her opponent a cold, dull, fishy glance, and let the Nipper continue its journey down into her draw-bag.

THE MISSIONARY BIRD THAT CONVERTED OLD CAESAR

OLD Cæsar would go fishing on Sunday. Otherwise he was a well-behaved old slave. It was in the Puritanical days of the pioneers of Dorchester backwoods, and he was notorious for this bad habit. His orthodox master berated him and often warned him who and what would get him if he did not mend his ways, but Cæsar was obdurate. Winthrop Packard, secretary of the Massachusetts Audubon Society tells in *Our Dumb Animals* (Boston) the legend which gave the brown thrasher the name of "the missionary bird" among those colonists:

One pleasant May morning, after a special lecture on Satan and Sabbath-breakers, Cæsar, nevertheless, slipt away down behind the barn to the little lake, rowed out from shore in his boat a little way, and began to fish. And as he fished there came a brown thrasher to the near-by birch-top and sang; and these were the words which Old Cæsar, with his guilty conscience stirred, thought he heard him sing:

"Cæsar, Cæsar,
Go to church, go to church,
Fishy fisher, fishy fisher,
Devil catch you!"

Cæsar stop this fishing, aghast. Nothing like this had ever happened to him. He listened, and the brown thrasher sang it over and over again. Whereupon he caught up his oars, rowed ashore, rushed up to the house, got into his good clothes and hurried to church, a little bit late, but safe. Therefore, they called the brown thrasher the missionary bird because he converted Old Cæsar, who was never known to go fishing on Sunday again.

Whether this be true or not, or whether it is one of those farm-hand folk tales which

This is the Year to see China

CHINA is the place to go this year. Thousands of Americans are going. Swift new American ships have made China more accessible—and have made the journey across the Pacific as comfortable and as luxurious as days in the finest American Hotels.

There is more to see in China now. Side by side you may see the China of yesterday and the China of tomorrow. On one street corner you may see the China of Confucius. On the next you may see the undeniable handiwork of China—the modern Republic.

The Sunshine Belt

The Pacific Mail Steamship Company is operating these new U. S. Government owned ships. For 73 years this Company has been known in every port on the Pacific for the excellence of its service.

Now, under its direction these new ships have broken the speed record over "the Sunshine Belt to the Orient." They sail from San Francisco to Hawaii, Yokohama, Kobe, Shanghai, Hong Kong and Manila, on the Southern route. Stop-overs in any Eastern country may be arranged. A day's stop is made at Honolulu so that the traveler has plenty of time to see the picturesque life, to visit the beach at Waikiki, and view the nearby scenic wonders.

New Comforts

Every stateroom is on the outside. American beds have taken the place of old fashioned berths. Running water, electric fans, electric radiators, and bed reading lamps equip each room. Most of the rooms have private baths.

For information in regard to sailings and accommodations, address

Pacific Mail S. S. Co.

508 California St. - - - - San Francisco, Cal.
10 Hanover Square - - - - New York, N.Y.
Managing Operators U. S. Shipping Board

Send for Booklet

Your Government wishes the name of every prospective traveler so he may be sent literature and official information. If you are a prospective traveler, send the coupon now—no matter when you intend to go. You will want to know about this new trans-Pacific service—and what your ships are doing in other parts of the world. Sending the coupon puts you under no obligation but it brings you valuable information. Send it now.

P.M. INFORMATION BLANK
To U. S. Shipping Board
Information Division 2419
Washington, D. C.

Please send me without obligation the U. S. Government Booklet and descriptive literature about the places I may visit.

I am considering a trip to The Orient ☐ South America ☐ Europe ☐.

If I go date will be about________

*My Name*________

*My Street No. or R. F. D.*________

*Town*________ *State*________

BIRDS, BEASTS AND TREES
Continued

CAN A SNAKE CHARM A BIRD?

"THEY say that snakes can charm birds by their gaze and draw them into their open mouth by first overcoming them with their poisonous breath. Helpless, the bird plunges headlong into the creature's horrible gullet," said Louis, one of the children in "Animal Life in Field and Garden" (The Century Company, New York). In this book Jean Henri Fabre, the great French naturalist, masquerading under the name of *Uncle Paul*, tells many stories of the little neighbors about which the children ask him. As for snakes, says *Uncle Paul:*

There is a grain of truth in what you say, but far more untruth, the result of popular superstition which deliberately credits the serpent with sorcery. In the first place, the breath of a serpent, or of any reptile whatever, has nothing poisonous about it, nothing magically attractive, nothing supernatural. You all have too much common sense to make it necessary for me to dwell on these ridiculous tales. There remains only the belief that the bird is charmed by the reptile's hard, fixed gaze. The marvel of this amounts in reality to very little.

Some of our snakes are very fond of birds' eggs. They climb trees, search out the nests, and eat the eggs when the mothers are not there to protect them. More than one human nest-robber who thought he was seizing a jay's or a blackbird's brood has put his hand instead on the cold, coiled body of a reptile in the bottom of the nest. I have even known instances in which the plunderers, seized with horror at this unexpected encounter, fell backward from the tree-top and did not come out of the adventure without broken bones. A warning to others. The larger snakes do not content themselves with eggs, but devour the young birds as well, even those that are outside the nest when they can catch them, which fortunately is not easy. Imagine an innocent little bird surprized by a snake in the underbrush. The poor little thing suddenly sees before it a mouth horribly wide open and glittering eyes regarding it steadily. Scared almost to death, the bird loses its head and is powerless to take flight. In vain it beats its wings, cries plaintively, and finally falls from the branch, paralyzed and dying. The monster lying in wait catches the poor thing in its mouth.

The power to charm that serpents are supposed to have is therefore in reality only the power so to terrify a bird that it can not fly. We ourselves, on being suddenly confronted by an appalling danger—do we always retain the presence of mind necessary to face it? Are there not plenty of persons that get bewildered, lose their wits completely, and make matters worse by acting foolishly? The charm exerted by serpents all comes down simply to that. I am inclined to believe that a bird, on being surprized by a snake, usually is able to overcome the first feeling of terror and to take flight as soon as it sees the reptile's horrible gullet yawning to receive the expected prey; and so the serpent's attempt to paralyze its victim has a chance to succeed only with very young and inexperienced birds. What paralyzes with fright an ignorant young nestling hardly affects a bird that is master of itself.

The motorist who has driven a Buick longest is the one who appreciates Buick most

W. C. Jessup, President and General Manager of the E. H. Hotchkiss Company, Norwalk, Conn., is a staunch admirer of Buick. He tells why:

"My Model 29 Buick, purchased in 1911, has now run 150,000 miles.

"Winter and summer, it has traveled over every kind and condition of road. It has gone through miles of mud at a stretch. It has traveled for hours over Florida sands. It has plowed through snow drifts. Yet in all these years I have never had to get out of my car except for tire trouble. It always keeps going.

"The same clutch, cylinders, transmission, differential, etc., that were in the car when it was delivered are still in perfect working order."

Mr. Jessup's account of his Buick's performance is characteristic of the service given by Buicks everywhere, and accounts for the overwhelming sentiment—You can always depend on Buick.

BUICK MOTOR COMPANY, FLINT, MICHIGAN

Division of General Motors Corporation

Pioneer Builders of Valve-in-Head Motor Cars

Branches in all Principal Cities—Dealers Everywhere

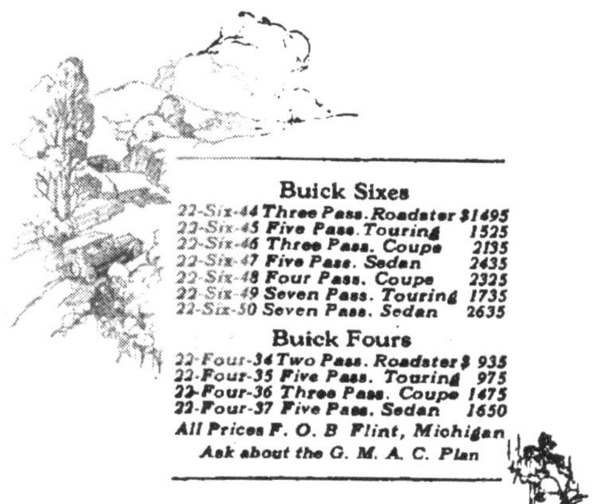

Buick Sixes

22-Six-44	Three Pass. Roadster	$1495
22-Six-45	Five Pass. Touring	1525
22-Six-46	Three Pass. Coupe	2135
22-Six-47	Five Pass. Sedan	2435
22-Six-48	Four Pass. Coupe	2325
22-Six-49	Seven Pass. Touring	1735
22-Six-50	Seven Pass. Sedan	2635

Buick Fours

22-Four-34	Two Pass. Roadster	$ 935
22-Four-35	Five Pass. Touring	975
22-Four-36	Three Pass. Coupe	1475
22-Four-37	Five Pass. Sedan	1650

All Prices F. O. B Flint, Michigan

Ask about the G. M. A. C. Plan

WHEN BETTER AUTOMOBILES ARE BUILT, BUICK WILL BUILD THEM

SCIENCE AND INVENTION
Continued

FRUIT PRODUCTS, TRUE AND FALSE

THE chemical "Fruit Product" is to some extent a sequel of the crop-failure, we are told by M. S. Noyes, director of research of the Welch Grape Juice Co., writing in *The Chemical Age* (New York). The public, educated to the distinctive characteristics of a product, is unable to get it on an off year, and the synthetic manufacturer, who is not bothered with frosts or droughts, cleverly steps in with his "something just as good." He thus gets a foothold, and finally becomes an active competitor of the pure fruit manufacturer. Mr. Noyes recommends the methods of chemical research to control this situation. Variations of climate and soil, the chemistry and physiology of nutrition, improvements in factory methods—all, he says, will bear additional study in order that an abundance of high-quality fruit may be grown and that it may reach the consumer in attractively edible form.

Pure food laws are hard to enforce beyond a certain point, Mr. Noyes says; for we have so many varieties that no exact analysis or formula can be given as the standard to which product must conform. Each year's crop is the result of seasonal conditions and in some years the same crop, grown on the same land, is different from that of the year previous. He continues:

"Pure food products are different to-day from what they were twenty years ago. Methods of handling and processing are different. Sterilization, the use of improved machinery, larger units and better transportation facilities make it easier to produce a higher-class product from a given material than was the case a few years ago.

"Food preserving is an art; in fact, in its inception it was a household art, and it is fair to say that some people are condemning fruit products that are purer and of higher quality than those they are accustomed to, simply because they do not look like those made by cruder methods a few years ago.

"The pure food manufacturer finds that prejudice for a product that looks like what the same-named product did twenty years ago is a temptation to him to go backwards rather than forwards.

"It is a disappointment to the manufacturer with good intentions, who has spent effort and money in developing sanitary methods and vacuum cooking, to have his product unfavorably received because it does not have the charred color and cooked taste that he has worked hard to overcome. It also is a great disappointment to have a product unfavorably received by the public because it is not highly-spiced to cover up the pomace and oxidation products present in previous products of its kind.

"The sugar industry was among the first food enterprises to put its processes under the direction of the chemical laboratory. The problem of putting out uniform food products of high quality is complicated. Agricultural experiment stations have been testing different varieties

Can A Printer be happy working for you?

THERE is a type of printer who is very snappy. He sits down at your desk to take an order and says, "Yes, yes, yes. I got you, I got you, I see," and so forth. And the chances are he hasn't "got you" at all, and doesn't understand what you are trying to tell him.

There is another kind of printer who studies over what you show him and who is likely to break out and say, "Wait a minute; I am not sure I quite understand how you want this done. You had better explain that a little more."

And then you start in to explain and realize that your own understanding was just a little hazy. So you clear things up together and when this printer goes away he knows how to use his judgment to please you.

The basis of nearly all friction between a printer and his customer is a lack of mutual understanding of exactly what is wanted.

better paper better printing

Where the work is not organized at the time it is started—where the most important decisions about the job are made as questions come up, the buyer of printing is pretty certain to invoke his divine right to be irritable.

If you want your printer to go about your job happy and confident that he is going to please you, just be sure that his conception of the work agrees with yours.

IN the interests of Better Printing, S. D. Warren Company has prepared a series of books of dummy-making material. These books contain all sorts of specimens of type, borders, page arrangements, illustrations, decorations, etc. Each book is printed on one of Warren's Standard Printing Papers. The book issued last month is on Warren's Silkote, a non-lustrous dullo-enamel paper which will print simple or difficult subjects with equal charm. This month's book is on Warren's Cumberland Machine Book.

These books are in the hands of paper merchants in different cities who sell Warren's Standard Printing Papers. They are given to printers, buyers of printing, advertising managers, artists, and book designers. If you do not know the paper merchant to whom you should apply for a copy, write us for his name.

S. D. WARREN COMPANY, BOSTON, MASS.

WARREN'S
STANDARD PRINTING PAPERS

connection with variations in the fruit produced from them. Different soils and crops of the same section are being investigated in the same way. At the present time 43 acres of grapes are under special fertilizer tests. The larger portion of this acreage is under tests where each fertilizer element is added both separately and in combination. This gives a basis for observing plant characteristics developed under the same climatic conditions, but with different nutrition balances.

"During the last few years much work has been done to ascertain the constituents of food which are most beneficial to the human system. This department is giving attention at the present time to variations in the ash constituents which are in fruits and pure fruit products. Variations in soil and plant composition in relation to variations in fruit analyses have advanced to the point where a new fruit section has been started for the production of one fruit used in large quantities.

"The research work on fruit beverages and preserved products involves the collection of information regarding the chemistry of the jell-making constituents in their naturally-occurring variations. Methods of preserving natural color, natural taste and appearance have caused the inauguration of about forty lines of experimentation, including theoretical, bacteriological and chemical problems.

"The research department keeps constantly in touch with factory methods and materials. In this way the entire line of products is constantly and gradually being improved."

OIL FROM GRAPE-SEED—The seeds of the grapes used in the manufacture of grape-juice may be employed profitably as a source of an oil which can be utilized as a food and as a dressing for salads. This announcement is made by Frank Rabak, of the U. S. Bureau of Plant Industry in an article in *The Journal of Industrial and Engineering Chemistry*. Our quotations are from an abstract in *The Chemical Round Table* (Washington). Says Mr. Rabak:

In the grape-juice industry of the United States, there results annually as a by-product approximately 1100 tons of grape-seeds. These seeds are at the present time wasted, probably because of lack of knowledge of the proper method of converting them into products of value. The utilization of these seeds largely for the oil they contained has long been under consideration in foreign countries where the seeds result as by-products of the wine industry. The principal variety of grapes grown for the manufacture in the United States is the commonly known Concord. The seeds from these grapes have been found to contain varying quantities of oil, the variation being probably related conditions of ripeness. The average yield of oil from the clean, dry seeds is about 13 per cent. The expert says that the oil obtained from the seeds by pressure, after being bleached and refined, is of a pale straw color and a bland, sweetish, nutlike taste and practically odorless. On account of the ease of refining grape-seed oil the chemist thinks that it should find most important commercial use for the table, just as the oil of the olive is employed. He therefore recommends it as an edible oil and suggests that the waste seeds from the grape-juice industry in the United States can thus be made of economic value.

connection with variations in the fruit produced from them. Different soils and crops of the same section are being investigated in the same way. At the present time 43 acres of grapes are under special fertilizer tests. The larger portion of this acreage is under tests where each fertilizer element is added both separately and in combination. This gives a basis for observing plant characteristics developed under the same climatic conditions, but with different nutrition balances.

"During the last few years much work has been done to ascertain the constituents of food which are most beneficial to the human system. This department is giving attention at the present time to variations in the ash constituents which are in fruits and pure fruit products. Variations in soil and plant composition in relation to variations in fruit analyses have advanced to the point where a new fruit section has been started for the production of one fruit used in large quantities.

"The research work on fruit beverages and preserved products involves the collection of information regarding the chemistry of the jell-making constituents in their naturally-occurring variations. Methods of preserving natural color, natural taste and appearance have caused the inauguration of about forty lines of experimentation, including theoretical, bacteriological and chemical problems.

"The research department keeps constantly in touch with factory methods and materials. In this way the entire line of products is constantly and gradually being improved."

OIL FROM GRAPE-SEED—The seeds of the grapes used in the manufacture of grape-juice may be employed profitably as a source of an oil which can be utilized as a food and as a dressing for salads. This announcement is made by Frank Rabak, of the U. S. Bureau of Plant Industry in an article in *The Journal of Industrial and Engineering Chemistry*. Our quotations are from an abstract in *The Chemical Round Table* (Washington). Says Mr. Rabak:

In the grape-juice industry of the United States, there results annually as a by-product approximately 1100 tons of grape-seeds. These seeds are at the present time wasted, probably because of lack of knowledge of the proper method of converting them into products of value. The utilization of these seeds largely for the oil they contained has long been under consideration in foreign countries where the seeds result as by-products of the wine industry. The principal variety of grapes grown for the manufacture in the United States is the commonly known Concord. The seeds from these grapes have been found to contain varying quantities of oil, the variation being probably related conditions of ripeness. The average yield of oil from the clean, dry seeds is about 13 per cent. The expert says that the oil obtained from the seeds by pressure, after being bleached and refined, is of a pale straw color and a bland, sweetish, nutlike taste and practically odorless. On account of the ease of refining grape-seed oil the chemist thinks that it should find most important commercial use for the table, just as the oil of the olive is employed. He therefore recommends it as an edible oil and suggests that the waste seeds from the grape-juice industry in the United States can thus be made of economic value.

INVESTMENTS ▲ AND ▲ FINANCE

A HIGHER STANDARD OF LIVING FOR WAGE-EARNERS

IT is rather difficult to investigate anything so vague as the standard of living, but the National Industrial Conference Board has been carrying on an inquiry which the New York *Commercial* finds impressive. The Board concludes that there has been a decided improvement in the American workers' standard of living since 1901. That is, in 1918 the wage-earners of the United States were spending a larger proportion of their income for clothing and sundries and a small proportion for food and shelter than was the case in 1910. The proportion spent for fuel and light did not appreciably change. *The Commercial* regards these facts as very strong evidence of the advance of the standard of living. As it proceeds to argue:

It is hardly to be presumed that families deliberately chose to be less well fed and less well housed in 1918 than in 1901, or deliberately chose to spend more for sundries, which include all kinds of luxuries, at the same time going hungry and poorly housed. The presumption on the other hand is very strong that if they spent relatively more on clothing and on sundries, including luxuries, in 1918 than in 1901, it is because they had more money left over to spend for such things after satisfying their needs for food and shelter.

Allowance has to be made for the advance in the cost of living, but where the increased expenditure for separate items more than keeps pace with their increases in cost and, at the same time, a larger proportion is expended on less necessary items, a higher standard is indicated. It is further shown that the increase of expenditures for living in 1918 was greater than the increase made necessary by the higher cost of living, that is to say, wage-earners spent more not merely because they were forced to by the higher cost of living, but because they had more to spend, and were living better in 1918 than they were in 1901.

And *The Commercial* knows of other evidences of the higher standard of living which are not included in the Industrial Conference Board's report:

No mention is made, for example, of the tremendous influx of students in recent years to high schools and colleges. It is also not quite clear as to just where the report differentiates between necessities and luxuries. There was, for instance, a tremendous amount of buying of furniture, pictures and home furnishings generally, and while what we are pleased to call a period of hectic prosperity was in existence, there was a heavy demand for the better grades of clothing for both men and women.

All of these manifestations could not be classed as extravagances, but, on the contrary, as reflecting a natural desire on the part of these people to realize some of their ambitions. It is a great asset to the community to have its members striving for better things, such as higher education, more comfortable homes and suitable dress to accompany these things.

GERMANY'S NEW DEMOCRATIC POSTAGE STAMPS

THE substitution of figures of workingmen for crowned heads on the new postage stamps being issued by the German Government have considerable political significance, in the opinion of the Boston *News Bureau*. They "speak emphatically for the radical change in public opinion," and "argue rather convincingly of a continued strengthening of democratic sentiment." As the Boston daily explains:

The stamps are in three series of six designs, one having the figure of a smith, the other of a miner, and the third of a farmer. The first series, with a value of 60 pfennig (dark violet) and 80 pfennig (red), show smiths of different ages at the anvil; the next in value 100 pfennig (green) and 120 pfennig (ultra-marine), show miners with pick, chisel or hand-car; the last in value 150 pfennig (orange) and 160 pfennig (blue-green), carry farmers mowing grain and binding sheaves.

The 120 pfennig stamp will be the unit for foreign postage. The 60 and 120 pfennig stamps have now been issued. The other stamps will not be issued immediately as the government has a supply of old stamps to be exhausted.

It is interesting that the government takes official cognizance of the depreciated mark, since the 120 pfennig stamp equals 30 cents gold, pre-war parity. That a larger depreciation is not recognized is undoubtedly due to the greater value of the mark in Germany than outside.

In any case the stamps are noteworthy as indicating the passing of the crowned head as a symbol of Germany.

TIRE PRICES NOW BELOW PRE-WAR LEVELS

THE cost of new tires is so large an item in the upkeep of a motor-car that the announcements of downward price revisions by several of the leading manufacturers ought to cheer the motorist's heart. Leaving cord tires out of the comparison, and noting that "consumption of 30x3½ fabric tires is equal to about 50 per cent. of the consumption of all tires, and the 34x4 casing is a popular size for medium-weight cars," *The Wall Street Journal* presents in its news columns the following tabulation of price quotations by two representative companies:

	—"A" Company—		—"B" Company—	
	30x3½	34x4	30x3½	34x4
At present	$10.95	$27.35	$12.55	$27.35
October, 1921	13.95	30.40	13.95	30.40
November, 1920	17.85	33.50	17.85	34.65
March, 1920	23.50	40.10	23.50	40.10
May, 1919	20.00	34.10	20.00	34.10
April, 1918	21.35	36.45	23.00	40.00
April, 1917	17.95	30.15	18.15	31.35
January, 1916	15.60	26.20	14.70	24.55
February, 1915	14.20	23.80	13.35	22.30
August, 1914	18.40	28.50	22.95	33.85
December, 1913	20.95	34.30	19.95	30.50
April, 1912	24.00	37.90	25.00	37.60

The Utility of a Closed Car

JUST a little while ago people thought of a closed car as a rich man's other car.

Now a lot of people who intend to keep only one car are buying closed models instead of open models.

The closed automobile is entirely practical for all-year-round utility, and utility is at the bottom of most of today's automobile investments.

When the Standard Steel Car Company began to build the Standard Eight, automobiles were looked upon as luxuries. This company looked ahead and planned ahead to a day when usefulness and long service even in fine cars would be the things the buyer wanted to know most about.

An outstanding feature of the Standard Eight is its power. Especially in the carefully built closed models this power shows to advantage. It affords freedom of movement under almost any conditions and an easy, effortless motion at all speeds. These cars are well made.

Vestibule Sedan, $5000 *Sedan, $4800* *Sedanette, $4500* *Coupé, $4500*
Touring Car, $3400 *Sport, $3400* *Roadster, $3400* *Chassis, $3150*

Above prices f. o. b. Butler, Pa.

STANDARD EIGHT

A POWERFUL CAR

STANDARD STEEL CAR COMPANY

Automotive Dept. *Pittsburgh, Pa.*

THE SPICE OF LIFE

A Drop too Much.—"I think I'll drop in on the boys," said the miner as he fell down the shaft.—*Froth.*

Adding Machine Needed.—HE—"How long have you been engaged?"

SHE—"This time or all together?"—*Lord Jeff.*

Wasted Breath—"A lot of eloquence," said Uncle Eben, "ain' no more practical use dan hollerin' 'Come seven!' in a craps game."—*Washington Star.*

The Belligerent *Blade.*—The Toledo *Blade* proposes a Tell the Truth Week. What do they want to do—start another war?—*Cleveland Plain Dealer.*

Luck That Turns.—Wolves think it a fine thing when sheep are introduced in their neighborhood, but it is the coming of the sheep that leads to the extermination of the wolves. Moral, etc.—*St. Louis Globe-Democrat.*

Helpmeats.—A very beautiful home wedding took place at the residence of Sol T. Ham and wife Sunday evening at 6 o'clock, when King Bone and Miss Mattie Ham were married.—*Sharp County Ark. Record.*

The Retort Crushing.—TRAFFIC COP—"Say you! Didn't you see me wave at you?"

MIRANDY—"Yes, you fresh thing, and if Henry were here he'd paste you one for it."—*Sun Dodger.*

No Allowance for Lateness.—Jonas has been to visit his son in America and, on his return remarks: "They say that the sun rises six hours later in America than in Sweden, but I had to get up at the same time, anyhow."—*Strix, Stockholm.*

Dad's Awful Fix.—A tiny maid, held up to hear her father's voice on the telephone, burst into tears. "What are you crying for?" asked her mother.

"Oh, mamma," sobbed the child, "however can we get dadda out of that little hole?"—*Morning Post.*

The Lesser Evil.—Following a recent earthquake in a region that shall be nameless, five-year-old Jimmy was sent by his fond parents to a distant uncle's home. Three days later they received this wire: "Am returning your boy. Send me the earthquake."

One Thing Saved.—"The thief took my watch, my purse, my pocketbook—in short, everything."

"But I thought you carried a loaded revolver?"

"I do—but he didn't find that."—*Copenhagen Klods Hans.*

Changing the Basis.—"Mr. Smith," a man asked his tailor, "how is it you have not called on me for my account?"

"Oh, I never ask a gentleman for money."

"Indeed! How, then, do you get on if he doesn't pay?"

"Why," replied the tailor, hesitating, "after a certain time I conclude he is not a gentleman, and then I ask him."—*Harper's Magazine.*

THE KIMBALL

—an ideal gift for those who wish to give wisely and well.

GIFT-GIVING at Christmastide is a custom that will endure so long as the heart of the world throbs with sentiment. And in no way can one more happily express the season's sentiment than by the gift of a KIMBALL musical instrument — world-famed for its sweetness of tone, visible beauty and sturdiness of construction.

KIMBALL products, now serving a Nation of Music Lovers, include—

GRAND Pianos, Upright Pianos, Player Pianos, Reproducing Pianos—the artist's identical rendition; Phrasonome Pianos—a revelation in Phrasing control; Pipe Organs, Phonographs and Music Rolls.

Descriptive catalog of KIMBALL products, also nearest dealer's address, sent to you on request.

W. W. KIMBALL CO.
(Established 1857)
Factory and Executive Offices
CHICAGO, U. S. A.

To the WEST INDIES

Panama, South America and Windward Islands

THE CANADIAN PACIFIC

offers two remarkable Cruises de Luxe by the splendid

"EMPRESS OF BRITAIN"

22,200 tons displacement

THE LARGEST STEAMER TO THE TROPICS

Oil-burning; no coal dust—cinders—soot

Leaving New York

Jan. 21st and Feb. 21st

Each Cruise 27 Days **Fares from $300.00**

Havana (*Cuba*), Kingston (*Jamaica*), Colon (*Panama*), La Guayra (*Venezuela*), Port of Spain and La Brea (*Trinidad*), Bridgetown (*Barbados*), Fort de France and St. Pierre (*Martinique*), Charlotte Amalia (*St. Thomas*), San Juan (*Porto Rico*), Nassau (*Bahamas*), Hamilton (*Bermuda*).

All the Comforts of the Best Hotels

Luxurious Suites, Cabins with Bath, Cabins with Toilet, Electric fans in every room. Wide promenade spaces, swimming pool. Special orchestra carried.

NO PASSPORTS REQUIRED

For rates and full information apply to local agents or

CANADIAN PACIFIC RAILWAY
Traffic Agents

CURRENT EVENTS

FOREIGN

November 23.—Great Britain and Afghanistan sign a treaty of friendship, recognizing the complete independence of Afghanistan.

November 24.—The Ukrainian movement against the Russian Soviet government is abandoned by General Petlura, according to a report from Warsaw.

Angered by alleged cheating during a vote, women Communist members of the Prussian Landtag throw sneeze powder bombs in the Chamber.

Two persons are killed and eight wounded by a bomb explosion in a Belfast streetcar carrying a load of shipyard workers.

November 25.—The Crown Prince Hirohito is designated Regent of Japan, owing to the illness of Emperor Yoshihito.

November 26.—Official figures place the number of persons killed during the last few days in disorders in Belfast at 27 and the number of wounded at 92. Of the killed 13 were Protestants and 14 Catholics, and of the wounded 61 are Protestants and 31 Catholics.

Anti-French demonstrations break out in Naples, Italy, after the publication of erroneous dispatches reporting a clash between Premier Briand, of France, and Senator Schanzer, of Italy, at the Washington Conference.

November 27.—The anti-French rioting spreads in Italy, and several demonstrations are attempted against the French Embassy in Rome.

November 29.—After Premier James Craig's announcement to the Ulster Parliament that the British Government's recent proposals could not be considered, Premier Lloyd George offers the Sinn Fein a new basis for settlement of the Irish problem in which the question of an immediate all-Ireland Parliament is ruled out, but provision made for a new boundary between the North and South.

France, Italy and Spain are reported to be considering intervention in Portugal as a result of the serious internal situation in that country.

DOMESTIC

November 23.—The tax bill is passed by the Senate by a vote of 39 to 29, and is signed by President Harding. The bill is expected to raise $3,216,000,000 for the current fiscal year.

The Interstate Commerce Commission orders a general investigation to determine if any further reduction of railroad rates can be required.

The anti-medical-beer bill is signed by President Harding.

The extraordinary session of Congress adjourns until December 5, when the regular session begins.

November 25.—A White House statement suggests that the Armament Limitation Conference be the first step towards the calling of annual meetings of all the nations to consider international affairs.

The Chinese delegation at the Washington Conference asks that the system of extra-territoriality under which certain areas are governed by foreign powers be abolished, and that China be permitted complete control of her customs.

November 26.—The Armament Conference agrees to the abolition of foreign postal systems in China "as soon as conditions warrant."

Fifteen American warships are to be sold at auction, announced Secretary of the Navy Denby.

The final order expelling Alexander Howat and all his followers from the Kansas miners' union for refusal to obey the orders of the international organization is issued by the latter body.

A block and a half of the business district of Augusta, Georgia, is destroyed by fire, resulting in a loss of about $2,000,000.

November 27.—Five people are killed and several hundred injured in a fire which destroys a motion-picture theater in New Haven, Connecticut.

Tax receipts of the Government in the current fiscal year decreased approximately $1,000,000,000, as compared with the previous year, while the cost of collection increased 32 cents for each $100, according to the annual report of the Bureau of Internal Revenue.

November 28.—Japan abandons her fight for an increase in proportion of battleship tonnage as compared with Great Britain and the United States.

Secretary Hughes formally denies published reports that Premier Briand, of France, had used harsh words to Senator Schanzer, head of the Italian delegation to the Washington Conference.

November 29.—The Conference on Armament Limitation agrees to appoint an international commission to investigate China's demand for abolition of extraterritorial rights and to report within the year whether these rights may be abandoned "progressively or otherwise."

Six men are killed and twenty-six injured in the collapse of a theater building in process of erection in Brooklyn, New York.

The Philippine Islands should remain under control of the United States until the people have had time to master the power already in their hands, Governor General Leonard Wood, and W. Cameron Forbes, Former Governor General, advise in their report to President Harding.

The Long and Short of It.—GROCER—"What was that woman complaining about?"

CLERK—"The long wait, sir."

GROCER—"Well, some people you never can please, anyhow. Yesterday she complained of the short weight."—*Western Christian Advocate (Cincinnati).*

Remarkable from the First.—The teacher had told her pupils to write a short essay about Lincoln, and one boy handed in the following:

"Abraham Lincoln was born on a bright summer day, the twelfth of February, 1809. He was born in a log cabin he had helped his father to build."—*Republic Item.*

Simple Remedy.—"The bluff, cheery optimism of the late Senator Frye," said a Lewiston divine, "could not brook a whiner. Once at a dinner here in Lewiston, a whiner seated opposite Senator Frye said dolefully, 'I have only one friend on earth—my dog.' 'Why don't you get another dog?' said Senator Frye."—*Boston Herald.*

Low operating cost

DODGE BROTHERS
SEDAN

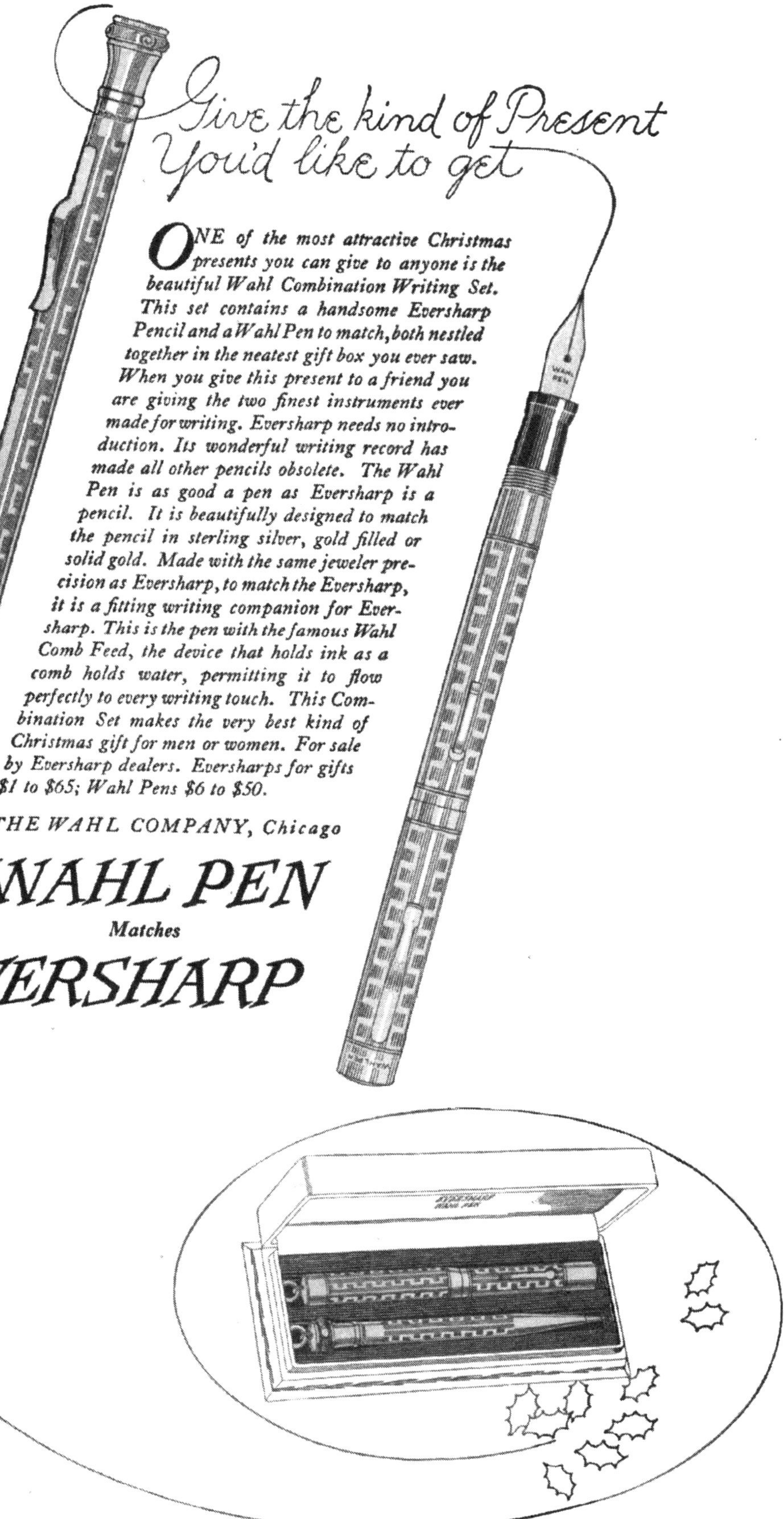

Give the kind of Present
You'd like to get
ONE of the most attractive Christmas presents you can give to anyone is the beautiful Wahl Combination Writing Set. This set contains a handsome Eversharp Pencil and a Wahl Pen to match, both nestled together in the neatest gift box you ever saw. When you give this present to a friend you are giving the two finest instruments ever made for writing. Eversharp needs no introduction. Its wonderful writing record has made all other pencils obsolete. The Wahl Pen is as good a pen as Eversharp is a pencil. It is beautifully designed to match the pencil in sterling silver, gold filled or solid gold. Made with the same jeweler precision as Eversharp, to match the Eversharp, it is a fitting writing companion for Eversharp. This is the pen with the famous Wahl Comb Feed, the device that holds ink as a comb holds water, permitting it to flow perfectly to every writing touch. This Combination Set makes the very best kind of Christmas gift for men or women. For sale by Eversharp dealers. Eversharps for gifts $1 to $65; Wahl Pens $6 to $50.
THE WAHL COMPANY, Chicago
WAHL PEN
Matches
EVERSHARP

THERE is a Corona dealer near you who will gladly deliver Corona for you at Christmas time, gaily wrapped in this attractive holiday box over its own smart traveling case. If you don't know his address, the coupon below will bring it to you.

Give a Corona this Christmas

Corona is "Private Secretary" to thousands of busy men

So little and so light—it is at home on milady's dainty desk

A student without a Corona is handicapped at the start

To Mother—it will make letter-writing a joy.

To Father—no more evening work at the office.

To the Invalid—to make the long hours fly.

To any Ambitious Friend—as a certain help toward success.

To the College Boy or Girl—for better work; higher marks.

To your Business Associate—a traveling private secretary.

To your Pastor—for his letters and sermons.

To your Literary Friend—for more acceptable manuscripts.

Of all people in the world, an invalid will appreciate Corona

What shall we give the boss? Corona is the happy solution

The younger a child learns coronatyping the better

NOTE: The cash price of Corona, including the smart traveling case, is only $50. If you do not wish to pay the entire amount just at Christmas time, you can arrange to buy on easy terms.

Look in the telephone directory for the nearest Corona dealer; or clip the coupon and we will send you his name and address. The coupon will bring you, also, an interesting book about Corona.

The Personal Writing Machine

TRADE MARK

Built by CORONA TYPEWRITER COMPANY, Inc.
105 MAIN STREET GROTON, N. Y.

There are more than 1000 Corona Dealers and Service Stations in the United States

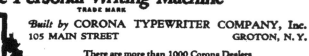

CORONA CHRISTMAS COUPON

(Please mark an X before items wanted)

☐ Without obligation, please reserve for me a Corona in a holiday gift box.

☐ Please send me the latest Corona Booklet No. 5.

☐ Please tell me the address of the nearest Corona store.

Name..

Address..

....

cember 17

erary Digest

(Title Reg. U.S. Pat. Off.)

ON TRAIL—By Frank Tenney Johnson

NAGNALLS COMPANY London

New York combined with The LITERARY DIGEST

December 17, 1921 Price 10 C

Spiced Walnuts

2 cups Diamond Walnut meats; 1 cup sugar; ⅛ cup water; ¾ teaspoon cinnamon or ginger.

Mix sugar and water and boil until it hardens when dropped in cold water. Take from fire, stir in cinnamon, and add Walnuts. Stir until the nuts are thoroughly coated with syrup. Spread on platter to cool.

Delicious Walnuts are

The Food of Foods

—don't use them only as holiday delights

THE crisp, delicious flavor of Walnuts and the part they play in making other foods more attractive is by no means their whole service to you.

Buy them for the holiday, of course, but *use them* also *the year 'round* for their incomparable value as a food!

Some foods lack one essential and supply others in excess. Walnuts supply *all* of the *vital* food elements in ideal proportions. They are over 96% pure nutrition.

Use Walnuts in dressing for fowls, in meat substitutes, in desserts, in cakes, and in salads. Of course, you'll want the best Walnuts, especially since they cost no more than ordinary kinds. Ask for Diamond Walnuts. They are hand-sorted, crack-tested, and selected with infinite care.

Thin shells permit the kernels to be extracted whole. The plump, sweet, tender nut-meats are exquisite in flavor.

Your Dealer has a sack marked with the Diamond Trade Mark like that shown at the bottom of this page. Ask him to take yours from this sack.

Walnut Fruit Salad

1 slice pineapple; 12 dates; 1 orange; ½ cup Diamond Walnut meats, 1 sliced banana; Golden salad dressing.

Cut in cubes, pineapple, dates, and orange which has been peeled. Add to these Diamond Walnut meats broken in pieces, and sliced banana. Mix thoroughly, adding enough Golden Salad Dressing to moisten. Serve individually in lettuce cups, or in salad bowl, masking with dressing. Garnish with Maraschino cherries.

DIAMOND California WALNUTS

More Meats Per Pound

DIAMOND Shelled Walnuts are packed in a high vacuum to preserve indefinitely the fresh, sweet flavor characteristic of the newly matured California Walnut. The can contain Halves for topping and facing, as well as Pieces for filler and salads. The glass contains only carefully selected Halves for table use and fancy dishes.

MANY recipes just as tempting as these, are contained in the revised edition of "100 Delicious Walnut Recipes," which includes the favorite dishes of the Wives of the Walnut Growers, as well as those of a leading culinary expert. Send the price per pound you have been paying for Walnuts and a free copy will be mailed you. Address Dept. 62,

California Walnut Growers Association.
A purely co-operative, non-profit organization of over 4,000 growers.
Our yearly production more than Forty Million pounds.
DEPT. 62, LOS ANGELES, CALIF.

California Walnut Growers Assn.,
Dept. 62, Los Angeles, Calif.

Please send me, without charge, your book of tested and proved recipes for Walnut dishes. I have been paying for Walnuts this season..........c per pound.

Name..........

Address..........

....

....

The MASTER FORMULA

During the Civil War a certain material used in making one of the Squibb products became very scarce and its price extremely high. A young chemist suggested to Dr. Edward R. Squibb that another ingredient be substituted—one which cost less and was easier to obtain, but was not so satisfactory. "By changing your formula in this way," the young man argued, "you will save money and most people will never know the difference."

"Young man," was the reply, "I am always willing to change a formula when I can improve it. But please remember that the Master Formula of every worthy business is honor, integrity and trustworthiness. That is one formula I cannot change."

We all know that there are men and women who devote a lifetime to some science, art or profession with no thought of wealth or profit beyond that which naturally follows worthy achievement. Not only are there such men and women, but there are such business institutions as well.

Such institutions are interested primarily in making something as fine as it can be made, and only secondarily are they interested in the profit.

Of all manufacturers, this honor, integrity and trustworthiness should guide the maker of pharmaceutical and chemical products. Of all things used by mankind there are none where purity and reliability are more important.

For sixty-three years, the House of Squibb has adhered to "the master formula" in a way which has won worldwide recognition for the supremacy of Squibb products. For sixty-three years, the House of Squibb has shared with the world its scientific discoveries. It has used no secret formulas and has made but one claim: That its products are as pure as nature and science can make them, *and that there is never an exception to this.*

For sixty-three years the name Squibb has been recognized as full guaranty of skill, knowledge and honor in the manufacture of chemical and pharmaceutical products made exclusively for the medical profession, and used only by the physician and the surgeon.

The name Squibb on HOUSEHOLD PRODUCTS is equally valued as positive assurance of true purity and reliability.

Squibb's Bicarbonate of Soda—exceedingly pure, therefore without bitter taste.

Squibb's Epsom Salt—free from impurities. Preferred also for taste.

Squibb's Sodium Phosphate—a specially purified product, free from arsenic, therefore safe.

Squibb's Cod Liver Oil—selected finest Norwegian; cold pressed; pure in taste. Rich in vitamine.

Squibb's Olive Oil—selected oil from Southern France. Absolutely pure. (Sold only through druggists.)

Squibb's Sugar of Milk—specially refined for preparing infants' food. Quickly soluble. In sealed tins.

Squibb's Boric Acid—pure and perfectly soluble. Soft powder for dusting; granular form for solutions.

Squibb's Castor Oil—specially refined, bland in taste; dependable.

Squibb's Stearate of Zinc—a soft and protective powder of highest purity.

Squibb's Magnesia Dental Cream—made from Squibb's Milk of Magnesia. Contains no soap or other detrimental substance. Corrects mouth acidity.

Squibb's Talcum Powder—a delightfully soft and soothing powder. Boudoir, Carnation, Violet, and Unscented.

Squibb's Cold Cream—an exquisite preparation of correct composition for the care of the skin.

Squibb's Pure Spices—specially selected by laboratory tests for their full strength and flavor. (Sold only through druggists.)

Sold by reliable druggists everywhere, in original **sealed packages**.
The "Priceless Ingredient" of every product is the honor and integrity of its maker.

SQUIBB

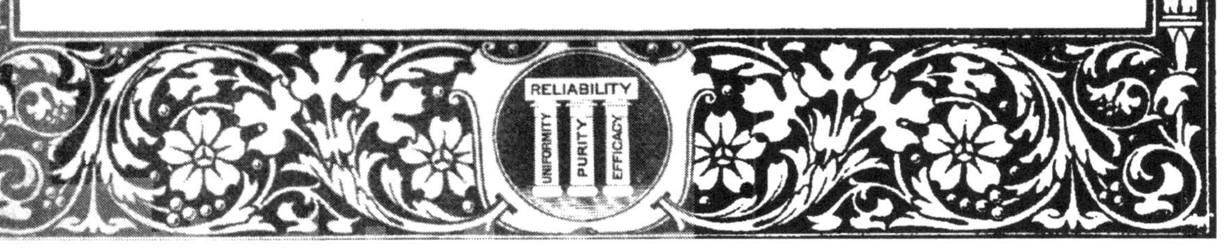

Hello Boys!

A.C. Gilbert's Own Column

THIS week I am going to ask your indulgence while I take all the space in my column to tell you something of my own story.

My reason for this is that I want my boy friends (and I think I may count more of these in the world than any other single individual) to know what I have been through myself and why I feel that every boy should be trained for skill, adeptness, knowledge, popularity and leadership.

I am not very far past boyhood myself. It seems only yesterday that I landed at the little university in Oregon from my boyhood home in northern Idaho.

I was interested in three outside things: athletics, sleight of hand and scientific experiments.

In the Northwest I went in for wrestling, got beaten the first year and the second year won the Pacific Coast championship.

I also went in for pole vaulting and broke the Northwest record, beside winning the track championship of that section.

Then I went to Yale, won the "Y" in three different branches, took the wrestling championship of the United States, took first honors as all-round gymnast, and twice broke the world's pole vaulting record.

But all the time I devoted every possible spare moment to my scientific experiments. This work of making science understandable, fascinating and useful to boys helped me earn my way through college and led me into my life work of making mechanical toys.

This is a lot for a man to talk about himself you will admit.

But I want you to know these things to see therein where I got the inspiration to build the Master Hand Library for Boys which my publishers are now offering.

The real
story of a real boy

Keeping

In which Jim Craig

WE HAVE a new game at o
brothers and I. We call it '
Father." We just hit on the name
last Christmas day while we were ,
pictures and titles of ten corking
had smuggled in on the quiet and p
ents. It sounds funny, but we co
other presents for a while.

But you want to know about th
we named it.

Well, father is a very busy man
tremendous lot of interesting thin
and engineering, and chemistry, an
veying, and electricity. He has a
about magic and tricks of all kinds.
like these things too.

Then he discovered that set of b
right into a lot of wonderful secrets.

Here are some of the things we
to do the strange rope tricks of
Brothers, who, as you know—th
before—made everybody think they
tic powers until their secrets were e

How to do some of the most amazi
coin and card tricks that made su
Herrmann and Kellar famous.

How to build all kinds of things
few tools and a carpenter's bench.

How *to be able to talk about big*
explain *them to others.*

How to understand the wonders o
and the wireless, and how to experim
in many simple ways.

The set contains books on Ch
Weather Bureau, Light Experiments,
and Facts, Coin Tricks, Handkerchie
and Splices, Carpentry, Civil Enginee
Engineering.

I think I have told you enough abo
to make you wish that you had a se
to give you any real idea of all the spl
tion there is in these books is beyond
of having a quick answer to such que

1. How can you bear yourself t
2. What makes the compass p
3. How is invisible signaling do
4. Why can you see in the dark
5. How tall do you look to a fi
6. What is a cross-cut saw?
7. How does the weather man going to rain?
8. What is a cantilever bridge?
9. Who were the greatest mast and coin tricks?

I only hope for your sake that some
this great set of books this Christmas
you right now that if your father ge
he will have just about as much fun
do. I know my father has.

But here! I haven't told you the na
or who wrote it.

It is called The Master Hand Libr
in all), and it was got up by Mr.

·Iello Boys!

·.C. Gilbert's ·)wn Column

·HIS week I am going to ask your indulgence ·ile I take all the space my column to tell you ·mething of my own story.

My reason for this is that ·vant my boy friends (and ·think I may count more these in the world than ·y other single individual) know what I have been ·rough myself and why I ·l that every boy should trained for skill, adept- ·ss, knowledge, popularity ·d leadership.

I am not very far past ·yhood myself. It seems ·ly yesterday that I land- at the little university in ·egon from my boyhood ·me in northern Idaho.

I was interested in three ·tside things: athletics, ·ight of hand and scientific ·periments.

In the Northwest I went for wrestling, got beaten ·e first year and the second ·ar won the Pacific Coast ·ampionship.

I also went in for pole ·ulting and broke the ·rthwest record, beside ·nning the track cham- ·nship of that section.

Then I went to Yale, won ·e "Y" in three different ·anches, took the wrestling ·ampionship of the United ·ates, took first honors as ·round gymnast, and ·ice broke the world's pole ·ulting record.

But all the time I de- ·ted every possible spare ·oment to my scientific ·periments. This work of ·king science understand- ·le, fascinating and useful boys helped me earn my ·y through college and led · into my life work of ·king mechanical toys.

This is a lot for a man to ·k about himself you will ·mit.

But I want you to know ·ese things to see therein ·ere I got the inspiration build the Master Hand ·brary for Boys which my ·blishers are now offering.

The real story of a real boy

A story for wide-awake fathers

Keeping Up With Father

In which Jim Craig tells how he got new power of leadership

WE HAVE a new game at our house, my two brothers and I. We call it "Keeping up with Father." We just hit on the name all of a sudden on last Christmas day while we were going through the pictures and titles of ten corking books that father had smuggled in on the quiet and put with my presents. It sounds funny, but we couldn't "see" our other presents for a while.

But you want to know about that game and why we named it.

Well, father is a very busy man but he knows a tremendous lot of interesting things about science, and engineering, and chemistry, and magic, and surveying, and electricity. He has always been keen about magic and tricks of all kinds. So he got us to like these things too.

Then he discovered that set of books that let us right into a lot of wonderful secrets.

Here are some of the things we learned. How to do the strange rope tricks of the Davenport Brothers, who, as you know—though we didn't before—made everybody think they had spiritualistic powers until their secrets were exposed.

How to do some of the most amazing handkerchief, coin and card tricks that made such magicians as Herrmann and Kellar famous.

How to build all kinds of things at home with a few tools and a carpenter's bench.

How to be able to talk about big inventions and explain them to others.

How to understand the wonders of the telephone and the wireless, and how to experiment with sound in many simple ways.

The set contains books on Chemical Magic, Weather Bureau, Light Experiments, Magnetic Fun and Facts, Coin Tricks, Handkerchief Tricks, Knots and Splices, Carpentry, Civil Engineering and Signal Engineering.

I think I have told you enough about these books to make you wish that you had a set yourself, but to give you any real idea of all the splendid information there is in these books is beyond me. Just think of having a quick answer to such questions as these:

1. **How can you hear yourself think?**
2. **What makes the compass point north?**
3. **How is invisible signaling done?**
4. **Why can you see in the dark?**
5. **How tall do you look to a fish?**
6. **What is a cross-cut saw?**
7. **How does the weather man know it is going to rain?**
8. **What is a cantilever bridge?**
9. **Who were the greatest masters of card and coin tricks?**

I only hope for your sake that someone gives you this great set of books this Christmas. And I'll bet you right now that if your father gets one for you, he will have just about as much fun with it as you do. I know my father has.

But here! I haven't told you the name of this set, or who wrote it.

It is called The Master Hand Library (ten books in all), and it was got up by Mr. A. C. Gilbert. You know, the man who invented the building sets and all those other sensible toys we get at Christmas—I mean the mechanical ones that teach us engineering and carpenter work, and wireless, and magic and chemistry.

Believe me, he knows how to write for boys! He ought to, for he was "some boy" himself.

That game I told you about—"Keeping up with Father"—is more fun than anything we ever played. That's pretty strong when you think of foot-ball, hockey and all that.

But this is another kind of fun. It is planning and building and doing experiments in chemistry and everything else that men do.

It beats school learning all to pieces, and you haven't any idea what a lot of interesting things that you never dreamed of before, you can get from Mr. Gilbert's books in almost no time.

JIM CRAIG

Don't Send a Penny

Fathers, mothers, sisters, brothers, aunts. You have read Jim's own story. He knows what he is talking about because he has read the books. He didn't tell you, but they have wrought a wonderful change in Jim. His father tells us he has gone ahead with leaps and bounds—so far as popularity is concerned—since he began reading and using The Master Hand Library. Jim wasn't naturally a leader, but somehow he seems to be chosen now for that job whenever the boys get together.

How about the Boy you have in mind? Don't you think these books would make a great Christmas for him?

Just send the coupon by next post without any money and we will send you the entire set of ten cloth-bound books for five days' examination. You see, it costs nothing to look them over.

Then, if you decide (as we believe you will) that Mr. Gilbert's Master Hand Library is "just the thing" for Bob, or Bill or Jack or all of them, send one dollar and the set is yours to give him, or them, for Christmas. It is ready for immediate shipment.

Then, you send us one dollar a month for the next nine months to complete your payment.

Upon receipt of your coupon we will send you with Mr. Gilbert's compliments, a copy of his 100-page book, Boy Engineering in which you will find many interesting and fascinating things. This book is yours free of all charge whether you buy the Library or not.

SEND THIS COUPON

The Master Hand Publishing Company
New Haven, Conn.

Please send me A. C. Gilbert's Master Hand Library for boys. I agree either to return the books to you after five days inspection or to send you $1. and to pay $1. per month for nine months, when the books will be fully paid for.

Name ....

Address ....

.... L. D. Dec. 17

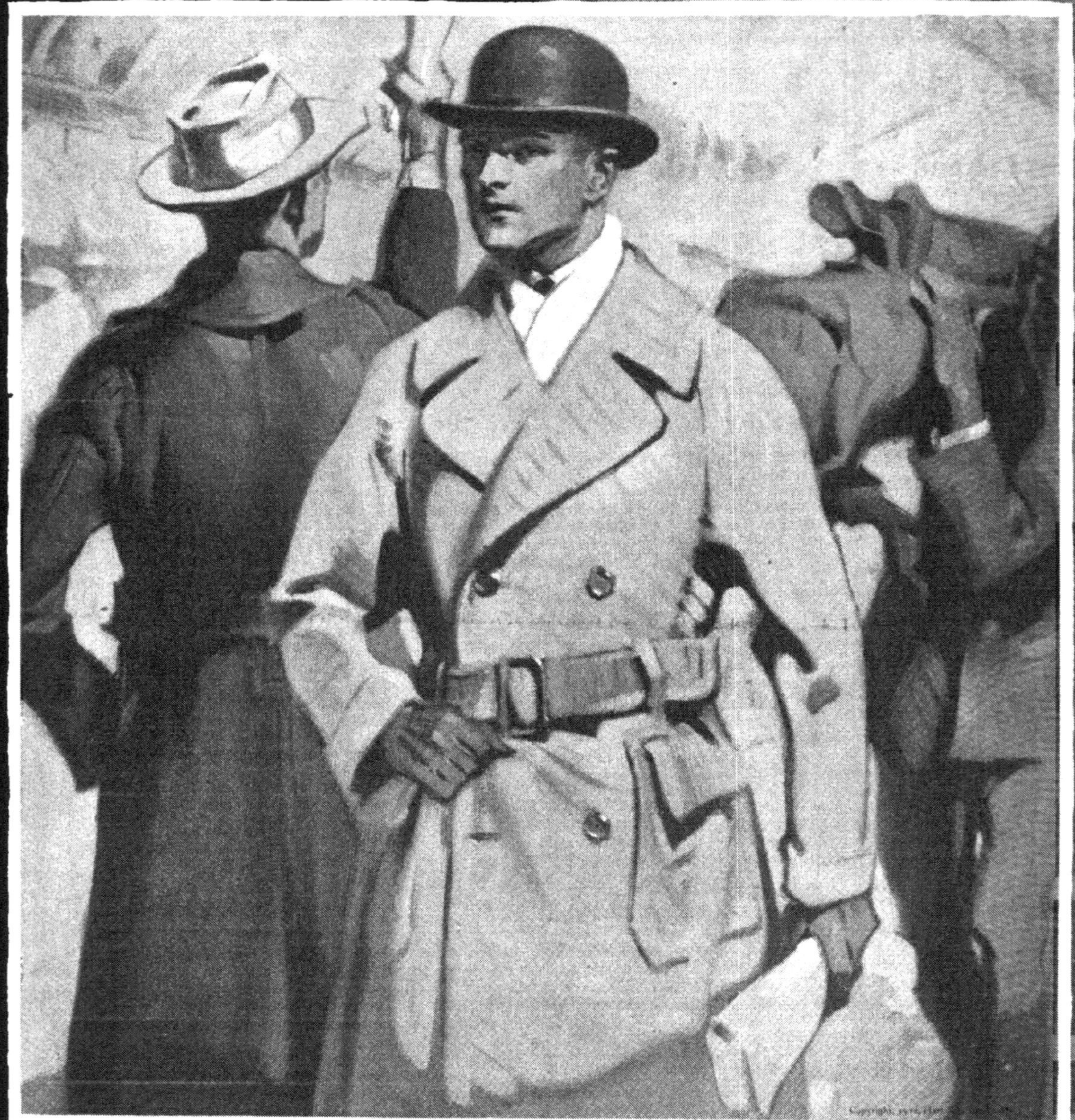

You'll find the best style in Hart Schaffner & Marx clothes

The designing is right to start with; beautiful all-wool fabrics add a note of good taste; the expert tailoring gives the smart drape Get it all

THE LITERARY DIGEST

PUBLIC OPINION (New York) combined with THE LITERARY DIGEST

ished by Funk & Wagnalls Company (Adam W. Wagnalls, Pres.; Wilfred J. Funk, Vice-Pres.; Robert J. Cuddihy, Treas.; William Neisel, Sec'y) 354-360 Fourth Ave., New York

l. LXXI, No. 12 New York, December 17, 1921 Whole Number 1652

TOPICS - OF - THE - DAY

(Title registered in U S Patent Office for use in this publication and on moving picture films)

THE IRISH FREE STATE

"WE WILL SIGN. IT IS PEACE." These six words, addrest to Lloyd George, Prime Minister of Great Britain, by Arthur Griffith, head of the Sinn Fein egation, marked the climax of Ireland's seven-hundred-year iggle for freedom. Nor was the drama of the moment lessened the fact that they were spoken in that same room at No. 10 wning Street in which was signed nearly 140 years ago the aty sealing the freedom of the United States. It is widely erted, moreover, that this later treaty, signed by the tish and Sinn Fein delegates in the early morning hours of cember 6 will do much to ninate a feeling of hostility vard England that has per-ed with some sections of population since the War Independence. "For Amer-ns," avers the New York *be*, "the salient aspect of settlement continues to be promise which it holds of a closer friendship be-en England and America." many ways we have been arena here in America erein Sinn Fein and the own have contended," notes Philadelphia *Public Ledger*. t has been said that the sh question is as much an erican as a British affair," remarks the Portland *Oregonian*, nce the United States has 14,000,000 people of Irish blood, ile only 4,500,000 Irish are in Ireland." "The removal of tion between Ireland and England will remove sources political friction in this country," believes the St. Louis *be-Democrat*, which goes on to say:

'The Irish question will cease to be a disturbing element in domestic and foreign relations. 'Twisting the lion's tail' will longer appeal to the Irish vote. On the contrary, the interests Ireland as a sovereign state within the British Empire will npel it to resent unjustifiable attacks upon the integrity of the ipire, and the Irish in America will have no sympathy for h attacks. With that great obstacle to friendship removed, way is opened for a continuous Anglo-American accord, and cooperation for the maintenance of peace and justice that uld be of inestimable benefit to the world."

The Irish agreement as signed by the delegates is in the form "a treaty between Great Britain and Ireland," consisting of hteen articles. It gives Ireland the title of the Irish Free ate, with virtually the same constitutional status as Canada, stralia, New Zealand and South Africa. The treaty does not quire Ulster's assent to make it effective, but Ulster is given the option of withdrawing within one month of the passing of the act that will confirm the treaty. The Sinn Fein delegates made concessions in the question of an Irish Republic, and a compromise was reached regarding allegiance to the Crown. The oath which the members of the Irish Parliament would take under the agreement reads:

"I do solemnly swear true faith and allegiance to the Constitution of the Irish Free State as by law established, and that I will be faithful to his Majesty King George V. and his heirs and successors by law, in virtue of the common citizenship of Ireland with Great Britain and her adherence to and membership of the group of nations forming the British commonwealth of nations."

News that the delegates had reached this agreement was received with expressions of enthusiasm by friends of Ireland generally, altho here and there a doubting or critical voice was raised. King George declared himself "overjoyed at the splendid news," and celebrated it by releasing all political prisoners interned in Ireland. Pope Benedict sent messages of congratulation to both King George and Eamon de Valera. Cardinal Logue, Primate of Ireland, characterized the agreement as "a fair enough settlement," and the British delegates to the Washington Disarmament Conference are all quoted as rejoicing over the outcome. As a Washington correspondent of the New York *Herald* reports: "Every member of the British delegation seems convinced that the Irish agreement is an extremely important step in the general direction of universal peace and bound to have a beneficial effect on the developments of the Washington Conference." "It is a lesson in peace-making for all the world, and its happy termination comes auspiciously during our own Disarmament Conference and in this season of good-will," adds the Rev. John J. Wynn, editor of the "Catholic Encyclopedia."

On the other hand, Justice Daniel F. Cohalan, of the Friends of Irish Freedom, thinks that Ireland will not be satisfied with the agreement; and Diarmuid Lynch, of the same organization, regards what is offered as "an insult to the dead who died fighting for an independent Irish Republic." Judge Cohalan is quoted by the New York *World* as saying:

"Lloyd George has won the greatest diplomatic triumph of his career. He has braced up the tottering British Empire for

PRESIDENT HARDING'S APPEAL FOR STARVING RUSSIANS

While we are thinking of promoting the fortunes of our own people, I am sure there is room in the sympathetic thought of America for fellow human beings who are suffering and dying of starvation in Russia. A severe drought in the Valley of the Volga has plunged 15,000,000 people into grievous famine. Our voluntary agencies are exerting themselves to the utmost to save the lives of children in this area, but it is now evident that unless relief is afforded the loss of life will extend into many millions. America can not be deaf to such a call as that. —See page 59.

the moment by attaching to it an apparently satisfied Ireland. He hopes, largely as a consequence, as the London papers and their echoes here show, to proceed now to attach America similarly. He seeks through these actions to get for his country the breathing space she must have in order to survive.

"But his triumph is dexterous rather than solid. He has, it is true, kept the substance of power and given his inexperienced opponents only the shadow, but he has been compelled to recognize the essential right of the people of Ireland to determine their own form of government."

Copyrighted by the Keystone View Co.

WHERE AMERICA AND IRELAND BOTH FOUND FREEDOM.

In this council room at No. 10 Downing Street, nearly a hundred and forty years ago, we signed the treaty that confirmed the independence of the United States. Here also, at 2:30 A. M. on December 6, 1921, the Irish settlement was signed.

From Paris also comes the unfavorable comment of Sean O'Ceallaigh, President of the Irish Republican Parliament. As quoted by a Paris correspondent of the New York *Herald*, he says the agreement still holds Ireland a vassal to the British, because laws must be submitted to the Governor-General for ratification, as in the case of Canada. "Altho in Canada's case this is a pure formality, as the laws are invariably ratified by the mother Government," he said, "there is a principle of vassaldom created which cannot coincide with our desire for absolute independence." In London, virtually the only paper that does not welcome the settlement is the *Morning Post*, which explains the terms on the theory that "a tired government is trying to administer the affairs of a tired people, which would sacrifice nearly everything for peace and quiet." This same Tory paper quotes Lord Carson, former Ulster leader, as saying: "I never thought I should live to see a day of such abject humiliation for Great Britain."

Turning again to American journals, we find the Sinn Fein *Irish Press* of Philadelphia, hailing the agreement as the "triumph of the Irish Republic." We read:

"Many people will say the name Republic has been dropt. No such thing has happened. Ireland is to be a Gaelic not an English nation, and at the first sittings of Dail Eireann the Gaelic name for the recreated nation was adopted. That name is 'Saor-stat'—pronounced *seer-stath*. If England prefers the correct English translation of the Gaelic term, which is Free State, instead of the Latin word Republic, Ireland should be quite happy that England has made such a choice. . . .

"Putting aside all meaningless phrases, if the treaty made is approved and carried into effect, Ireland again becomes an independent sovereign nation among the nations. The English army of invasion and occupation betakes itself forever from the shores of Ireland, and may God be as merciful to its sponsors as Ireland will be forgiving for the centuries of wrong she has suffered at England's hands once she is again master in her own house.

"The army of Ireland will take possession of the strongholds held by the British for centuries. The Irish flag will soon be seen on every sea, a menace to no nation or people, seeking only the right of fair trading with the world and bringing peace and good-will wherever it appears. May its folds never be stained in the pursuit of empire. Let every Irish heart be lifted up to his Maker in gratitude for this approaching blessing which apparently He has willed to bestow. May no treachery of Ireland's ancient enemy or lack of caution by Ireland's friends longer prevent the realization of Ireland's absolute freedom."

The Kansas City *Star* hails the Irish settlement as "something for the whole English-speaking world to rejoice over." On all sides tribute is paid to the political and diplomatic genius of Lloyd George, and to the breadth and ability of the Irish negotiators. Credit must also be given, points out the Baltimore *Sun*, "to the zealous and intelligent efforts of liberal and labor forces in Great Britain." The outcome was due to the fact that concessions were made on both sides, notes the Columbus *Ohio State Journal;* and the Boston *Transcript* remarks that "when all is said and done the agreement is seen to represent mutual sacrifice, mutual tolerance, and a mutual abhorrence of strife and bloodshed."

Now that the Irish have their Free State, what will they do with their state of freedom? What will the results be in politics, in economic and cultural development? The first task that confronts Free Ireland, says the New York *Evening Post*, answering some of the questions which Americans, Englishmen and Irishmen are asking, "is to make herself a united Ireland." The most convincing proof Irishmen can give of their ability to govern themselves "is to win Ulster's acquiescence in a government of Ireland by Irishmen." "Ireland's immediate concern

AT LAST!
—Kirby in the New York *World*.

is the wooing of Ulster." In case Ulster is willing to begin negotiations with Dublin, we are reminded, "the terms of the settlement provide for a broad charter of guaranties for Ulster, guaranties with regard to patronage, finance, trade policy, local militia, minority rights, and above all the free exercise of religion and all its implications. In the face of such safeguards, in the face of pressure from overwhelming British public opinion, in

HOPING TO GET THEM TO LIE DOWN TOGETHER.
—Reid in the New York *Evening Mail.*

the face of economic forces that work for unity in Ireland, the Ulster temper must be rockribbed indeed if it clings to a policy of isolation." True, with all the racial, religious, economic, and cultural points of difference the problem of joining the North and the South not again to be put asunder is far from a simple one, yet *The Evening Post* is confident that it will be solved.

Here an Ulster man, a manufacturer from Belfast, who writes in one of a series of articles by Irishmen in a recent special number of *The Survey* (N. Y.), agrees that "it is only by winning the confidence of the northern government that ultimate fusion can be achieved." He continues:

"It would seem evident that if Dail Eireann can rule its own part of Ireland economically and well, if it can foster trade and agriculture, and administer the law fairly between man and man, if it can show that it has no bitterness against those of alien blood and different faith, then it can, by the mere spectacle of its success, force Ulster to ask for the privilege of sharing the benefits of such rule. But until these benefits are proved and seen, Ulstermen will not give up what they possess; they will not embrace a change which may risk the whole fabric of their commercial achievements. The northerners are weary of the age-long conflict, but their desire for peace will not make them betray their native caution.

"A few years' waiting is but a little thing in the long and troubled history of Ireland. The northeast corner must be won by conviction. It must have proved to it the capacity of Celtic Ireland to govern itself wisely and unselfishly. The suspicion which clouds the relations of the two peoples—suspicion which is the natural legacy of so many centuries of racial strife—can be removed only by the spectacle of the task of legislation and administration carried on successfully for a certain number of years. Could this suspicion be so removed, the miracle would be performed. Ulster would be reconciled and Ireland would be one."

That the leaders of the new Irish Dominion have in mind the necessity of winning over Ulster by such a policy as is here described, would seem to be evident from statements made by Arthur Griffith, head of the Irish delegation to the London conference. He says, as quoted in the press dispatches, that the Sinn Fein leaders would consult with Southern Unionists about giving the latter a full share of representation in both Chambers of the Irish Parliament. "We desire," he added, "the willing cooperation of the Unionists, in common with all other sections of the Irish nation in raising the structure and shaping the destiny of the Irish Free State."

Ireland, as several writers remark, will be more than a mere new political state. Mr. Dudley Field Malone, a well-known American of Irish ancestry, predicts that "in ten years Ireland will have the most modern and useful economic program in Europe, and Dublin will be recognized as one of the greatest cultural centers." In the issue of *The Survey*, already quoted, George W. Russell, the Irish publicist and writer, better known as "A. E.," tries to answer the question, "what will the Irish do with Ireland?" He thinks that an Irish government will foster a knowledge of the Gaelic language and literature. On the economic side he reminds us that Sir Horace Plunkett and his colleagues of the Irish Agricultural Organization Society have "cast a new economic generalization into the minds of the Irish people." About 130,000 Irish farmers, "and these the best," are now united in over a thousand cooperative associations.

IT'S ONLY TAKEN ABOUT 750 YEARS, BUT IT SEEMS LONGER.
—Darling in the New York *Tribune.*

"These were originally started for some one particular purpose, such as butter-making, the purchase of requirements, or the sale of produce, but very soon these societies for special purposes began to change their character, to enlarge their objects, until they became what I might call general purpose societies." If this tendency goes on, and Mr. Russell expects it to, "we shall find rural Ireland in the next generation with endless rural communities, each covering an area of about four or five miles around the center of business, all buying together, manufacturing together, and marketing together, using their organization for social and educational as well as for business purposes. These again would be linked up by national federations, or groups of them would conspire together for enterprises too great for parish associations to undertake."

Also writing for *The Survey*, Mr. Erskine Childers predicts and declares that the new Irish Parliament will continue on the lines of the Dail Eireann with wide suffrage including women, proportional representation, two chambers of parliament and an executive directly dependent upon parliament. "The all-powerful weapon of finance, for the first time in Irish hands, will undoubtedly be used," thinks this Sinn Fein leader, "on the one hand to secure economy in the wasteful, administrative chaos that now exists, and on the other to plan with deliberate forethought the building up of the economic and cultural life of the country hitherto under the overpowering influence of England, on healthy independent lines." Finance, he continues, "will probably be used also to foster an Irish merchant marine now hardly existing, to further scientific industrial education, temperance, and the cooperative movement, and to raise the standard of living for labor. Education will be endowed with far greater funds, reformed, and made Irish as well as rationally efficient." Mr. Lionel Smith-Gordon, who is secretary of the Sinn Fein bank, believes that "an increase in tillage is one of the first conditions of prosperity in Ireland, and its promotion will be one of the first cares of the national government. Agriculture in itself is insufficient to maintain a self-contained country, but in such a country as Ireland the industry should grow out of agriculture." Chief among other possibilities of the economic future of Ireland which require expert handling are:

"The development of the water-power resources of the country and the utilization in a scientific manner of our vast reserves of peat. We have also various other natural resources which have so far been very little exploited, if at all. The seaweeds of the western coast are rich in potash, which is in constant demand for farming operations, as well as iodine and other by-products. The coal-fields which exist in various parts of the country are no doubt capable of development, altho difference of opinion exists as to their ultimate value. The same may be said of the mineral deposits, of which the most striking are probably those of the Avoca valley. Turning then to the manufactures which already exist, we find that while Belfast is the well-known center of the ship-building and linen industries, Dublin can hold its own in such lines as biscuits, matches, jams, sweets, cocoa and coffee, soaps, and a number of smaller products, while the whole world is familiar with the names of the celebrated brewers and distillers whose products bulk so largely in our export trade."

On the cultural side, James Stephens, the Irish author is inclined to predict that "Ireland will turn more and more completely from England and will cultivate the human relations she requires in quite other directions." In summing up the responses made by its Irish contributors to its questions as to what the Irish will do with Ireland, *The Survey* observes editorially that they all agree on one point:

"Build up a new Irish civilization. And the new civilization which Ireland is about to contribute to the world is a rural civilization. This is one of the most encouraging signs of the times—development of rural communities on a cooperative basis; each community to have so far as possible its own general store for supplies of common need; each community to manufacture what it can do advantageously with a common mill, creamery, bacon factory, electric plant, buying the commodities that can not be supplied at home, and selling its products; each community to establish schools, recreation halls and libraries, organize community pageants and games; each community to have its town council where common problems and new plans may be discust.

"Such community life will recreate anew the Gaelic genius. The stormy times have left the leaders little leisure to think out the details of an administrative scheme against the day when an Irish government will take hold of the destinies of the nation. Leisure is necessary for such thinking, and Ireland has been busy fighting and thinking in terms of war. But the constructive program has been forming in the minds of Ireland's leaders. Their common vision is to build up a nation by making each community rediscover its own soul."

The relations between the new Irish state and the British Crown shall be modeled on the existing relations between Canada and the Crown. The "Treaty Between Great Britain and Ireland" which brings peace to Ireland, adds one to the Dominions of the British Empire, and takes one unit out of the United Kingdom, contains eighteen articles which outline the relations between the two governments. The Irish Free State, it is specified, shall have the same status as the older Dominions, "with a parliament having powers to make laws for peace and order and good government in Ireland, and an executive responsible to that parliament." The Irish Free State assumes liability for its proportionate share of the British public debt. Until an arrangement is made for Ireland to share in her own defense the Imperial Forces are to defend the coasts of Ireland, but the Irish Government is responsible for the maintenance of vessels to protect revenues and fisheries. The British Government is to have certain specified harbor and other facilities in time of peace, and in time of war such facilities as are needed for purposes of defense. If the Irish Free State sets up a military defense force it "shall not exceed in size such proportion of the military establishments maintained in Great Britain as that which the population of Ireland bears to the population of Great Britain."

If Ulster does not decide to join, a commission is to be appointed to decide the boundaries between northern Ireland and the Irish Free State. Northern Ireland is to retain its powers under the Home Rule act of 1920, but the Parliament of the Irish Free State shall have jurisdiction over all of Ireland, including Ulster, in respect to those powers given by the new Treaty but not given by the Act of 1920. For the present, the Council of Ireland set up by the 1920 act will have its Southern members chosen by Parliament of the Irish Free State. If Ulster does not join, it is further provided that its representatives shall join with the provisional government of southern Ireland to discuss "(A) safeguards with regard to patronage in northern Ireland, (B) safeguards with regard to the collection of revenue in northern Ireland, (C) safeguards with regard to import and export duties affecting the trade and industry of northern Ireland, (D) safeguards for the minorities in northern Ireland, (E) settlement of financial relations between northern Ireland and the Irish Free State, and (F) establishment and powers of a local militia in northern Ireland and the relation of the defense forces of the Irish Free State and of northern Ireland respectively," the decisions of this conference to be binding. The whole of Article XVI, which deals with religious freedom, is worth quoting:

"Neither the Parliament of the Irish Free State nor the Parliament of northern Ireland shall make any law so as to either directly or indirectly endow any religion or prohibit or restrict the free exercise thereof or give any preference or impose any disability on the account of religious belief or religious status or affect prejudicially the right of any child to attend school receiving public money, without attending the religious instruction of the school, or make any discrimination as respects State aid between schools under the management of the different religious denominations, or divert from any religious denomination or any educational institution any of its property except for public utility purposes and on the payment of compensation."

Proper powers will be extended to members of a provisional government in Ireland "as soon as each member thereof shall have signified in writing his or her acceptance of this instrument." The treaty is to be ratified by the British and the southern Ireland parliaments. An annex to the treaty provides for regulation of air and cable communication, and air defense.

TWO BILLIONS SAVED THE TAXPAYERS

A CASE "WHERE FIGURES ARE NOT DULL," as one editor puts it, appears in the new budget presented to Congress last week, which promises savings to the taxpayers that are regarded as little short of stupendous. In two years a load of more than $2,000,000,000 will be thrown off the Treasury. This most welcome relief in taxation may even be increased as a result of the Limitation of Armament Conference, for approximately two hundred millions is allowed in the budget for new naval tonnage that may not be required. At any rate, there will be a saving of half a billion dollars over the 1922 estimates, and of two billions over the 1921 expenditures. The New York *Tribune* thus summarizes the figures:

"The new Federal budget estimates receipts for 1922-'23 at $3,338,000,000 and expenditures (including reduction in the principal of the public debt) at $3,505,000,000 These figures exclude postal revenues and expenditures, which practically balance each other

"The sweeping reductions in taxation and expenditure which have been under way since the Harding Administration came in are shown by comparisons with the receipts and disbursements of 1921-'22 and 1920-'21 In the year 1920-'21, ended June 30 last, receipts were $5 624,000,000 and outlay was $5,538,000,000. For 1921-'22 receipts are expected to reach $3,943,000,000 and expenditures $3,967,000,000. In the year 1922-'23, for which approximations are to be made at this session, the Director of the Budget Bureau anticipates receipts of $3,338,000,000 and expenditures of $3,505,000,000. The deficiency of $167,000,000 for 1922-'23 is to be met, however, not by taxation, but by a bookkeeping reform, which will make $100,000,000, now unnecessarily tied up in the naval supply account, available, and by additional economies in government operation.

"From 1921 to 1922 government expenditure has fallen $1,570,000,000. From 1921 to 1923 it will have fallen $2,032,000,000."

As the budget stands, the five larger items are for wars, past or future. Correspondingly, as the New York *Globe* observes, the reduction in the new budget is due to the tendency toward disarmament, the general lessening of war expenses, and the beginning of a period of falling prices. For instance, roughly, six hundred millions less will be spent by the War Department in 1922 than was expended in 1921, and the amount will be even smaller by twenty millions in 1923. Two hundred millions less will be spent by the Navy Department in 1922, whose 1923 expenditures will be even less by forty-seven millions. Similarly, savings are brought about in Shipping Board and Fleet Corporation expenditures, which are reduced fifty-seven millions in 1922 and eighty millions in 1923 over 1921 figures. Roughly, $393,000,000 less will be spent by the Railroad Administration than was expended in 1921.

"That Director Daws should have done so much in so short a time is truly amazing," thinks the Philadelphia *Inquirer*, yet, as the Brooklyn *Eagle* observes, "it is obvious that he played few, if any, favorites—he has hewed to the line, let the chips fall where they might, and he is entitled to a corresponding credit." The day of "log-rolling" for appropriations, whether in departments or in Congress, is over, several editors agree; department heads will be required to live within their incomes. There are to be no more haphazard appropriations; no more deficiency appropriations. As the New York *Evening Mail* speaks of the new era:

"This country will in future estimate what it needs to spend in any given year, raise enough money to spend just that amount, and see that the spending is accomplished with as much care as a great industrial corporation exercises. There will no longer be the independent spending of moneys by departments without reference to the general state of Uncle Sam's firm. A careful watch will be kept over the firm as a unit."

Likening the Federal Government to a business corporation, General Dawes points out the following faults, which, it is estimated, have wasted billions in taxes:

"The President of the corporation (the President of the United States) gave practically no attention to its ordinary routine business.

"The administrative Vice-Presidents (members of the Cabinet) were allowed to run their several departments as if each separate department was an independent authority in all matters of routine business.

"Because of a lack of any outlined business plan, no system existed for making purchases or in selling material along business lines under a unified policy.

"No balance sheet of the corporation as a whole was ever prepared.

"The Treasurer kept no accurate account of the contingent obligations of the various Federal departments, thus resulting in money being drawn from him continually in excess of the estimated annual running expenses.

"The corporation, in effect, seldom reconsidered an unwise project entered into by any department.

"The administrative heads of the departments were selected as a rule with little reference to their business qualifications, and were compelled to rely largely upon the advice of subordinates wedded to the theory of the right of independent operation of the department."

The financial Boston *News Bureau* goes more into detail:

"Imagine a corporation where the president ignored routine business; where the vice-presidents had no contact; where departments had no coordination in operating, in buying or selling; where there was no effort at profit, and an assured levy on stockholders (taxes) to rely on; where balance sheets and inventories were lacking; where departments were told they could draw so much credit as they liked, but the treasurer never had more than the roughest estimate of what they would take; where they came to feel they must spend such totals, needed or

HIGH LIGHTS IN THE PRESIDENT'S MESSAGE

PRESIDENT HARDING first asks Congress in his message of December 6 to pass the pending bill giving the Executive power to fund and settle the "vast foreign loans growing out of our grant of war credits."

He explains that the harm which it would do to world trade justifies him in failing to give notice, as the Jones Act requires, "of the termination of all existing commercial treaties in order to admit of reduced duties on imports carried in American bottoms." But he limits the need of Congressional "tolerance of noncompliance" to "a very few weeks until a plan may be presented which contemplates no greater draft on the public Treasury and which, though yet too crude to offer it to-day, gives such promise of expanding our merchant marine that it will argue its own approval."

The President urges the early enactment of the pending "permanent" tariff bill. He also wishes a more flexible tariff policy and suggests that the President be given authority to modify customs duties "to meet conditions which the Congress may designate," acting, of course, upon the advice of the Tariff Commission. Mr. Harding realizes that there are differences of opinion over the "American valuation" plan, and suggests a provision in the tariff law, "authorizing proclaimed American valuation, under prescribed conditions, on any given list of articles imported."

"Something more than tariff protection is required by American agriculture," and in particular "every proper encouragement should be given to the cooperative marketing programs." Congress is asked to give earnest attention to the development of "a general policy of transportation, of distributed industry and of highway construction to encourage the spread of our population between city and country."

Labor's right to organize should be recognized, but certain "well defined principles of regulation and supervision" should be applied. To provide against strikes and lockouts a code of practise should be developed for dealing with industrial controversies and "it should be possible to set up judicial or quasi-judicial tribunals for the consideration and determination of all disputes which menace the public welfare."

Partly in order to provide homes for ex-soldiers, the President recommends government aid in reclaiming 20,000,000 acres of irrigable land and 79,000,000 acres of swamp and cut-over lands.

Finally, the President suggests a possible amendment to the Federal Constitution. He thinks "our tax problems, the tendency of wealth to seek non-taxable investment, and the menacing increase of public debt, federal, state and municipal, all justify a proposal to change the Constitution so as to end the issue of non-taxable bonds."

not; where they resented executive control and made plans involving policy which belonged only to the executive.

"Only a rich Government could stand all that. And even that rich Government stops the folly none too soon for the stockholders' comfort."

"Before the Dawes plan can have its full effect, however," thinks the Boston *Globe*, "a financial revolution will be necessary in Washington, for Congress has always looked upon itself as the keeper of the public purse." "The great saving shown in the budget estimates are due to two separate but related forces," we are reminded by the Springfield *Republican*,—"to the President's constant pressure upon the various departments and miscellaneous bureaus to keep their expenses down to a diminishing minimum, and to the activities of the Bureau of the budget in expertly advising such reductions." General Dawes thus outlines the three principles on which the budget-making is based—

Copyrighted 1921, by the Chicago "Tribune"

A BAD CONDITION.

—McCutcheon in the Chicago *Tribune*.

"First—That the business organization of Government hereafter assumes that the minimum amount of money to be expended in any fiscal year is not of necessity the sum appropriated in advance by Congress, but the smallest amount upon which the business of the Government can be efficiently administered under the program outlined by Congress.

"Second—That there should not be in the minds of the business administrators of Government a too easy reliance upon the custom of deficiency appropriations.

"Third—That where Congress has directed the expenditure of certain sums for specific purposes, an Executive pressure will now be exerted for more efficient and economical administration in order to produce greater results from the given expenditure, and also, wherever possible, to complete the given project for a less amount than the total appropriated for the purpose."

"The budget," believes the New York *Globe*, "is bound to call the attention of the people in an effective way to the financial condition of the country, and make public opinion a factor of growing importance in agreements between the legislative and executive, and in the shaping of the national policy in general." Regarding the principles enumerated above, and in agreement with *The Globe*, the New York *Journal of Commerce* says:

"The merits of these principles are so evident as to command immediate assent, and it need only be said that both the President and the Director of the Budget will have the hearty support of the financial community in their effort to carry them into effect. The work that has been done on the budget would in ordinary times stand out as an achievement. It has been obscured by more immediate and more sensational factors. These should not prevent so important a piece of constructive work from receiving its due at the hands of the sober element of our citizenship."

The estimated cost of maintaining the Navy Department, the War Department, the United States Veterans' Bureau, and of paying pensions and meeting the interest on the public debt is given in the following table by the New York *Times:*

	1922	1923
War Department	$389,091,406	$369,902,107
Navy Department	478,850,000	431,754,000
Pensions	258,400,000	252,350,000
United States Veterans' Bureau	438,122,400	455,232,700
Interest on the public debt	976,000,000	975,000,000
Total	$2,540,463,806	$2,484,238,807

"With the addition of smaller expenditures, the true war total for 1923 is estimated at about $2,900,000,000—83 per cent. of the budget total—while Government costs other than military will be only $600,000,000," points out the New York *World*. Legislative expenses for 1923 are expected to be two millions less than they were in 1921; the State Department requires approximately two millions more; Treasury expenditures in 1921 were $476,352,192.21, whereas they are expected to be only $168,997,160 in 1923. And so on. All of which leads the New York *Evening Post* to inquire:

"How is it possible to cut half a billion dollars out of a budget which had already been cut to the bone? Economy accounts for it only in part. A larger part of the reduction is due to the deferring of expenditures. This is not a mere bookkeeping juggle; it represents a change in fiscal policy. Hitherto appropriations for a given year have borne no close relation to expenditures for that year. The appropriations have been intended to cover the obligations incurred, whether those obligations had to be met during the year or were spread over a series of years. In addition, there have been permanent and indefinite appropriations which required no annual action by Congress. The new policy is that Congress shall appropriate only money which is to be expended during the fiscal year.

"This policy is expected to reduce the sum finally spent, partly by putting an end to the practise by the departments of making expenditures in excess of the year's estimates, but chiefly by compelling an annual resurvey of projects which are under way. Instead of voting a continuing appropriation and then forgetting about it, Congress will annually reexamine the work authorized, preliminary to voting more money for it."

"The casual reader who stops when he learns that there is to be a reduction in expenditures of more than two billions will be imprest with the obvious economies of the Bureau of the Budget," notes the Cleveland *Plain-Dealer*—

"But any one who stops to analyze the comparative expenditures of the three years in question will observe that the saving is to be effected much less by the elimination of unnecessary employees and mistaken fiscal practises than by the termination of heavy expenses attributable directly to the war.

"If, for example, allowance is made in the estimates for the next fiscal year for reduced expenses of the War and Navy Departments, the Shipping Board and Emergency Fleet Corporation, and the termination of the Railroad Administration, there is very little left to show for the economies of the present method of budget-making over the old. But a careful reading of Director Dawes' report on the operation of the Budget Bureau for the first five months of its existence will convince the most skeptical that through the Bureau the Government is working in the right direction, and that through it a degree of business enterprise is going to be introduced into the activities of the Government that has not before been known.

"Incidentally, Dawes tells us that his term is of limited duration. It is to be hoped that before retiring he will have achieved a degree of success as the nation's first Budget Director no less than that which has marked his other undertakings."

TO HELP GERMANY PAY UP

IF SHYLOCK HAD NEEDED THE MONEY, he might have been quite willing to take the ducats instead of the pound of flesh from Antonio's body. So to-day the Allied ɔvernments seem to be coming to the conclusion that a literal ısistence on their treaty rights is less important than to keep ermany working steadily for their benefit. And the cor-espondents agree that the French and British Governments ·ill soon join in accepting a "pay-as-you-can-without-bank-uptcy" program for future German reparations payments. n so far as this involves what might be called a "mor-torium," or debt holiday, it does not meet with the ntire approval of our press. "There will not be and should ot be, any moratorium" declares the Boston *News Bureau*, "that would let the Germans go scot free for a while longer, and ·ee also meanwhile to tangle things up fiscally for themselves nd for everybody else." Other American editors are far from eing convinced that Germany is really on the verge of bank-uptcy. The Columbus *Dispatch* believes that Germany could apidly repair her own credit "by taking up the work of repara-ions payments with the same grip with which France met the demnity assessed upon her in 1871." The Providence *Bulletin* omes back to the well-known fact that the war "left the eco-omic resources of Germany virtually untouched." What ermany is facing, the New York *Times* explains, "is really not n economic bankruptcy, but simply a currency bankruptcy." 'he New York *Tribune* believes that if Germany is now given a breathing space," she will turn up with a new set of excuses t the expiration of the period. The truth is, declares *The 'ribune*, "that Germany has refused to levy taxes to meet the eparations payments. There has been no substantial sub-raction from German wealth and conversion of the revenue into quid forms of capital." On the other hand, *The American 'anker*, taking up the moratorium in its broadest sense, to "in-lude suspension of German indemnity payments and those ue this country from the Allied nations," quotes with apparent pproval the forcible statement of a New York brokerage ouse that "a five-year moratorium accompanied by the slogan, five years more to work like h—— and clean up our past ébris and debts' should be effective." Indeed, "it might be period of universal commercial activity and social betterment nore pronounced than anything we have seen in many years."

Opinions in high financial and governmental circles differ ·idely about the justice and practicability of the reparations ayment plan of May, 1921. Before quoting certain repre-entative statements from these sources, it might be well to note he developments of recent weeks which have led to the press ispatches asserting that the Allies have agreed to help Germany o pay up, and to note precisely where Germany stands in this natter of payment. A clear outline of the reparations situation ppears in a recent *Federal Reserve Bulletin*. Germany, it is oted, agreed last May to pay annually to the Allies 2,000,000,-00 gold marks (a gold mark is worth nearly 25 cents), plus a um equivalent to 26 per cent. of the value of German exports. t was agreed that these sums were to be paid in two series of uarterly instalments, i. e., five hundred million gold marks on ach of the four dates, January 15, April 15, July 15 and October 5; and the export payments on February 15, May 15, August 15 nd November 15. The reparations agreement does not state or how many years these payments must be made, since this epends upon the size of export trade. These payments are to edeem bonds to be delivered by Germany to the Allies to the otal amount of 132,000,000,000 gold marks. Some of these bonds ave been delivered to the Allies, and others are to be delivered ater. None of them as yet have been issued to the public, but ·hen issued Germany will be responsible for the interest on them. Counting the payment of a billion marks last May, and earlier payments, more than five and a half billion gold marks have now been paid on reparations which must be subtracted from the total sum due the Allies. The sum due on November 15 has been met by payments in goods. The coming payments will be partly met by coal deliveries and by the Wiesbaden agreement, signed October 6, under which Germany pays France in goods for the reconstruction of the devastated regions. It might be stated here that the Reparations Commission has insisted on the payment of the January and February sums, and that the German Government has agreed to pay, altho it is asserted that three-fourths of the money will have to be borrowed abroad.

All through the autumn press correspondents have reported that Germany has been enjoying great prosperity, based partly

THEY ARE ALL ON THE SAME ROPE.
—Morris for the George Matthew Adams Service.

on industrial activity, partly on the fall of the mark, which leads every one to try to get rid of his paper money for goods and securities. This boom has been punctuated by Bourse panics and bank failures, and several observers predict a complete col-lapse by spring. According to Federal Reserve Board figures, German paper note circulation has grown from 2,600,000,000 marks in 1913, to 84,000,000,000 during last summer. In the meanwhile the gold reserve to back this currency has actually decreased, so that the ratio of gold to paper has dropped from 55.8 per cent. to 1.3 per cent. Financial authorities estimate that by the end of the year German note circulation will have reached the one hundred billion mark, and in the meantime the mark has dropped to an exchange value of about half a cent.

In November, the Reparations Commission told the German Government that the January and February payments would be expected on time, and that Germany must be more business-like, lay heavier taxes, and make its revenues equal expenses. A new tax program has been laid before the Reichstag involving heavy levies on corporate incomes, profits and property. But it is explained that these taxes will not produce their maximum before 1923 or 1934, and that while the Reichstag has been talking about them the fall of the mark with the consequent rise in prices has rendered the budget quite out of date. While

German officials protest that they can not pay, German business men like Hugo Stinnes and Walter Rathenau have been making mysterious visits to London. Correspondents hear remarkable stories of plans for paying reparations by handing over the German Government railroads to private control and by developing Russia, Mesopotamia and other backward regions by German workers under international supervision. Talk of a moratorium or an international loan to Germany has been appearing almost daily in the dispatches for several weeks. The plan is naturally popular in Germany and has considerable favor in Great Britain. France, say the correspondents, would prefer to let Germany go bankrupt and then arrange for an Allied receivership. Last week's dispatches told that the French Government was willing to consider a method of helping Germany out which would be based on currency deflation and larger taxation in Germany. A plan worked out by the Reparations Commission and reported in press dispatches of December 6 calls for the abandonment of the hard-and-fast-payment schedule for perhaps five years. During this time the Allies are to guarantee a series of long-term German loans, the greater part of the proceeds to be applied on the reparations account. The Allies under this plan would supervise the German budget and try to prevent Germans from investing heavily in other countries than their own, and thus avoiding taxation.

HIDDEN TREASURE.

LLOYD GEORGE AND BRIAND: "Of course, it may be all you've got, Fritz, but we mean to go a little deeper into the matter."
—*Reynolds's Newspaper* (London)

The Germans, of course, try to emphasize the financial straits of their country. Herr Stresseman, a political leader, says: "Unless America coerces the Entente Powers to recognize a moratorium which will give Germany a chance to breathe, I see a terrific crash." We read similarly in *Vorwaerts:* "If the German mark reaches the level of the Austrian crown, then it will wreck the economic system of Germany and that of the rest of the world with the force of a terrible explosion." The banker, Von Gwinner, asks for "a breathing space." Then, he says, "let the best heads of all countries sit round a table and see what can be done."

The central difficulty, as *The Wall Street Journal* points out, is that "if Germany is not required to pay, she is not making reparations justly due, while insistence upon payment," at least so the Germans say, "may result in bankruptcy to Germany and disruption to the trade of other countries." That trade is already being "disrupted" by the German reparations situation is shown by a recent statement from Professor Blondel, the French economist. Because of the new German competition French warehouses are to-day "overstocked with manufactured goods, tools, textiles and machinery, for which there is no market and which had been turned out for English consumption which the Germans are now supplying."

The fall of the mark is variously accounted for. Mr. Kiddy, the British financial expert, in one of his letters to the New York *Evening Post* says it is due partly to the reparations payments, partly to "watering of currency," and partly to speculation. Our own Federal Reserve Board thinks the drop in the mark has been to a large extent "the outcome of the inflation policy of the German Government and the inflation policy in turn is due in part at least to the terms of the reparations agreement." Germany's diplomatic representative at Washington declares the depreciation is due to the enforced payment of reparations in gold francs. Many Allied economists, however, the New York *Journal of Commerce* notes, "maintain that the depreciation of the mark has been artifically brought about by the machination and trickery of German financiers. They point out that Germany is much more prosperous in comparison with other European countries and that, while there is a great contrast between the extreme of wealth and poverty in Germany, speculators are making millions and nearly every one is at work, even if at low wages."

In a careful estimate of Germany's ability to pay, Mr. Charles H. Grasty writes to the New York *Times* from Paris that Germany has a distinct advantage because "first she has all her splendid pre-war plants untouched by devastation or depreciation; second, and more important still, all the labor, whether manual or mental, in the country, has been disciplined and obedient." The latter "was one of the good things that Kaiserism left behind." There is now evident, however, a slow but sure decline in efficiency, due to new ideas of individual rights, the increased power of the unions, and the comparative weakness of the government. Touching on the hints of bankruptcy and a "smash," Mr. Grasty observes in conclusion that "with all the difficulties now facing Germany, that country will still compare favorably in potential solvency with any other in Europe, and men with a real stake in such a handsome estate—and it happens that this class of which Hugo Stinnes is the chief, has a considerable influence at present—are not likely to yield immediately to counsels of desperation."

Several American financial writers point out that much hinges on the German people's "will to pay," and the monthly letter of the Alexander Hamilton Institute calls attention to the fact that to-day "the German business interests lack the patriotic support for their Government which the French displayed in 1871."

It seems to Mr. De Sanchez of the French Commission in the United States that public sentiment in Germany is alining itself to aid reparations payments, that Germany is "beginning to realize, dimly at least, that she can only regain the good-will of the world by making good in a measure of her utmost capacity the damage she did." Another French expert on economics emphasizes rather the ability of the Allies to force German payments by compelling fiscal and financial reforms and the repatriation of German capitalists' foreign holdings.

To conclude with a quotation from an English authority, we may note Mr. J. A. Hobson's remarks in *The Nation* (New York), about the tariff and other barriers that the Allies have put up against German goods, which would almost persuade one to think "that the Allied governments wished to receive from Germany the least possible amount of reparation." This English economist would cancel all the injurious economic clauses of the Versailles Treaty, would remove all restrictions on German trade, would give Germany positive assistance in putting its industry and finance upon a sound basis, and calls for the appointment of a neutral commission to fix a new reparations figure which Germany can afford to pay within a generation and which "the Allies can afford to receive without injurious reaction upon their economic system."

WHAT CHINA WANTS

LIKE THE SUICIDE OF PROTEST, still in vogue in China, the Secretary of the Chinese Delegation at the Arms Conference resigns in protest against "conditions that have arisen in the Conference," and declares flatly that "governments and vested interests oppose the liberation and regeneration of China, and her rehabilitation as a sovereign nation." Immediately after the secretary's action came the resignation of China's chief military adviser, her chief financial adviser, and her chief naval adviser and assistant director of customs. In fact, the Chinese question now holds the center of the stage at the Washington Conference. Once the most enlightened and prosperous country in the world, China, in the words of the Cincinnati *Enquirer*, "is now the world's bone of contention." The United States, Great Britain, France, Japan, and four other nations recently subscribed to the principles outlined in the Root resolution, thus declaring their intention to respect the sovereignty, independence and integrity of China; to provide it with an opportunity to develop a stable Government; to maintain equal trade opportunities for all countries, and to refrain from seeking special privileges which would abridge the rights of citizens of friendly States. "But China has heard all this before," notes the Newark *News*. True, "if the eight Powers actually respect the sovereignty of China, and so forth, the Conference will have removed once and for all the greatest obstacle to lasting peace that remains," declares the Brooklyn *Eagle*, and "interpreted in a liberal spirit, the Root resolution would go far to solve the Chinese problem," agrees the Springfield *Republican*. Many editors, in fact, hail the adoption of the Root resolution as a "Magna Carta for China," but, we are reminded by the Boston *Herald*, "these principles are merely 'general principles' upon which to proceed in the adjustment of details." Furthermore, asserts Charles Merz in the New York *World*, "only the Pollyanna section of the press believes that China has gained a victory." "Much of this talk of great gains for China is for consumption in China," observes the New Haven *Journal-Courier*. "Before the ink was dry on the Root proposals," points out the Norfolk *Virginian-Pilot*, "some of the parties subscribing to them in principle were in sharp disagreement as to their import in practise."

THAT CHINA EGG.

—Brown in the Chicago *Daily News*.

"What China wants," notes the Sacramento *Bee*, "is nothing more than the right of self-determination, a right which can not be denied a country with 400,000,000 people." As the Washington *Post* puts it: "China has two cardinal needs—First, a guaranty against further encroachments by an agreement among the Powers assembled at Washington; and second, an opportunity to recover the ground lost by previous encroachments on the part of the Powers."

"The sort of sovereignty which China now has is a mockery," maintains the New York *Evening Mail*. Perhaps the Republic's chief complaint is that it is not allowed to fix its own tariffs, and that while these are set at 5 per cent., they have in reality, according to the Chinese delegates, dwindled to 3½ per cent.—a totally inadequate amount for carrying on the Government. What China wants is to have the privilege, or, as the *Evening Mail* remarks, "to exercise the inalienable right of setting up such a tariff as will help to build up her own industries." At present this impost duty yields about $40,000,000 yearly; China would like to double it. And, as the New York *World* remarks:

"The arguments of Mr. Wellington Koo for the restoration to China of the power to fix her own tariff can not be ignored by the Committee on Pacific and Far Eastern Questions, or by the Conference itself, unless the talk about Chinese integrity and the Chinese nation is simple hypocrisy. There can be no such thing as Chinese sovereignty while the tariffs of China are regulated for her by other Powers; there can be no such thing as a solid and responsible Chinese Government until there is a Government in China that controls its own income."

"China's revenues are so completely shackled by foreign treaties and agreements as to prevent that country going forward upon any financial domestic program," avers the Washington correspondent of the New York *Times*. "Her loss from restrictions of various kinds amount to about $300,000,000 yearly," we are told, "yet the revenues could be increased with the greatest ease if the Powers would consent to the abrogation of the treaties." Customs receipts and railroad revenues, under the present agreements, are deposited in foreign banks, so that China banks gain little or nothing from this source of revenue. Then, too, says the *Times* correspondent, "all revenue from the salt mines, aggregating perhaps $45,000,000 gold annually, is placed in foreign banks."

China also wants extraterritorial rights in that country abolished. Extraterritoriality, we are told, means the immunity of the foreigner from Chinese law, and his right to trial by a foreign court and under foreign law. This, says a Chinese delegate, "infringes on China's sovereign rights, and produces confusion in the courts." The Chinese delegation, therefore, asks that the Powers now represented in the Conference relinquish their extraterritorial rights in China at the end of a definite period.

Another infringement on China's territorial and administrative integrity, avers a delegate to the Conference, is the "evil of the foreign postal system." The Chinese charge that through these post-offices, particularly those controlled by Japanese, opium is smuggled into China and the "cream of the postal business skimmed." In Manchuria alone, say the Chinese, approximately 5,000 chests of opium are distributed through Japanese post-offices, China having no authority to inspect Japanese mail-sacks. The Japanese Government, they aver, reaps $20,000,000 a year in revenue from this source.

The exclusion of Shantung from the agenda of the Conference is a disappointment to the Chinese delegates; they would prefer to discuss the return of this Province to China in the open. At this writing Japan has agreed to waive all preferential rights with regard to foreign assistance, thus opening Shantung to the trade and investments of all nations. Japan has further restored the port of Tsingtao to the Chinese maritime customs, the New York *Tribune* informs us, but the railroad from the Shantung peninsula, which the New York *Times* considers the "core of the Shantung problem," remains under Japanese control. And control of the railroad, say the Chinese delegates, carries with it political control of the whole Province.

The maintenance of foreign troops in China is another sore

LOOKS LIKE A DIFFICULT CASE. —Brown in the Chicago *Daily News*.

point. As Frederick Palmer writes in the New York *Evening Post*, "Japan would have the open door of China guarded by a Japanese sentry." There are, moreover, said to be twenty-seven Japanese police agencies in China, which, the Chinese delegates contend, should be withdrawn.

China's railways, it is said, are the principal source of revenue, and it was because the consortium could be interpreted to give international control to China's railways, according to her ex-Minister of Finance, that China refused to accept it. United States officials, however, are hopeful that the consortium will be accepted by China, as one of the steps in the financial rehabilitation program, after some objections have been eliminated. The chief technical adviser of the Belgian delegation, who spent twenty years in China, and is one of the pioneer railroad builders in that country, has this to say regarding China's financial needs:

"No matter what is done for China by the Conference, she will remain under the tutelage of Japan unless she can obtain financial assistance of unprecedented magnitude from abroad to enable her to repay or make some new arrangements with regard to the loans she received from financial groups in Japan during the years of the World War."

Altho there is much sympathy in the American press for China's desire to control her own destinies, many editors declare that China's own impotence in dealing with internal questions almost places the Republic beyond hope for the time being. "The failure of the Canton and Peking governments to agree upon a delegation is the best proof of China's impotence," remarks the Brooklyn *Eagle*. "The country is torn by civil war, it has repudiated its obligations, its finances are utterly disrupted, and the Peking government, which the Washington delegation represents, has but a precarious hold." The French delegation, indeed, has asked the Chinese delegation with what authority they presume to speak for all China in disregard of the protests of the South China government at Canton, of which former Minister Wu Ting Fang is a leading member. It is this government, notes the Philadelphia *Record*, "which arraigns the Peking authorities for subservience to Japan."

"To treat China as wholly free to run her business her own way would doubtless evoke praise as a great act of international morality," remarks the Baltimore *News*, but, thinks the Norfolk *Virginian-Pilot*, "if China wishes to avoid foreign interference, she must first bring order into her own divided household." As for immunity to foreigners, "extraterritoriality obtains in China because of necessity," avers the Manchester *Union*.

The Baltimore *News* says of China's financial problems:

"The question of Chinese finance, which the Conference is now taking up, is infinitely complicated. Putting China on her feet will involve something more than raising the customs tariff.

"A strong financial administration will have to be secured in some way; if not by the Chinese, then with the aid and supervision of the other Powers. But if such an administration can be set up, the chances for future peace in the Pacific will have been vastly improved."

Then there are the existing rights which China has guaranteed to friendly Powers. Of these Powers and their concessions the St. Louis *Globe-Democrat* says:

"Superficially the right thing to do would be for all of them to get out of China and leave her to manage her own affairs. But that is not easy. It may not be entirely possible. Many millions of dollars have been invested in China by public or semipublic agencies in railroads and other developmental enterprises, and the disposition of these calls for consideration. Assuming the most sincere desire on the part of every government to give China the fullest control of her own affairs and her own resources, there are difficulties in the way of accomplishing this that may be immediately insurmountable."

Lastly, observes the New York *Journal of Commerce:*

"What are the facts of the case? As reported by disinterested observers on the spot, a month ago, it was, briefly, as follows: Chinese bankers had declared that they were drained dry by the requirements of Peking and that unless the Government could secure money to repay them, at least in part, there would be a grand financial collapse.

"Peking officialdom had seen the situation coming for many months, but with characteristic obstinacy refused to admit it, and tried to hide the Government's real distress and utter helplessness by playing politics with an assumption of power and assurance. And now Peking is penniless and resourceless; a number of payments on foreign loans are falling due, the Chinese banks are tottering, and the life of the Government itself is in imminent jeopardy.

"If the Powers were weak enough to allow Peking to collect the customs revenue and the proceeds of the salt tax, there would be immediate default on foreign loans and confessed national bankruptcy. Of the sources of national revenue which remain in Chinese hands, like the land tax, 80 per cent. is consumed in the cost of collection and in the personal pickings and stealings of the collectors, while Peking gets a steadily diminishing share of the remainder.

"It is an old story, and the only difference between the Republic and the Empire is that official graft is to-day more open, more impudent and less restrained than it was under the Manchus. Until a capable, honest and generally respected and acknowledged government can take hold of the finances of China, it is a mere waste of time to discuss questions of tariff 'autonomy.'"

TOPICS IN BRIEF

SOMEONE forgot to put "vision" in tax revision.—*Wall Street Journal.*

IT was a great mistake to locate Ulster in Ireland.—*Columbia Record.*

"GERMANY Seeking Credit," says a headline. Credit for what? —*Dayton News.*

MARSHAL FOCH is for peace, but then he is a soldier, not a politician.—*Pittsburgh Dispatch.*

GERMANY, we read, denies Briand's charges. It looks as if they must be true.—*Hartford Courant.*

GERMANY gets almost cheerful over bankruptcy as reparation time draws near again.—*Dallas News.*

A CHRONIC victim of seasickness expresses the wish that berth-control were possible.—*Brooklyn Eagle.*

SOMEHOW the proposal to preserve the integrity of Russia is embarrassed by the common belief that she hasn't any.—*Dallas News.*

YELLOW perils and red perils and orange and green contests need not disturb a world that is determined to act white.—*Minneapolis Star.*

A HISTORIAN says that women ruled the world 2,500 years before the birth of Christ. They also have ruled it 1,921 years since.—*Charleston Gazette.*

HAVING pledged themselves to respect China's integrity, the powers should now pledge themselves to respect their own integrity.—*Norfolk Virginian-Pilot.*

"THE Story of Mankind" is the title of a new book. If it runs true to name and the censors do not stop its circulation, they will stand for anything.—*New York Morning Telegraph.*

THE Treasury department regularly sends out voluminous propaganda regarding the advantages of thrift and economy, but apparently Congress is not on their mailing list.—*Nashville Southern Lumberman.*

CHINA has a number of friends with taking ways.—*Greenville Piedmont.*

APPARENTLY one good Conference deserves another.—*Philadelphia Evening Public Ledger.*

IT will also be necessary to scrap a few ambitions along with the fleets.—*Lansing Capital News.*

SLOWLY the German mark is approaching the value of Grover Cleveland Bergdoll.—*Detroit Journal.*

WHEN the bride promises to obey, she waives her rights; but it isn't a permanent waive.—*Lincoln Star.*

MOST of the football teams have now been put away for the winter in plaster casts.—*New York World.*

THAT loud noise you don't hear is Aristide Briand and Germany cheering each other.—*Nashville Tennessean.*

THE end of the stunt flyer is near, states a headline. The end of the stunt flyer always is near.—*Kansas City Star.*

WE often wondered whether the squad of fat reducers in New York ever tried eating in restaurants.—*Charleston Gazette.*

FRENCH statesmen insist that their army is necessary in order to preserve the mind of Germany from temptation.—*Washington Star.*

THAT Kansas hospital janitor who threw $5,000 worth of radium into the furnace probably thought it was cheaper than coal. —*Washington Post.*

HENRY'S great interest in the Muscle Shoals property may be due to the natural affinity between a shoal and a ford.—*Nashville Southern Lumberman.*

A FORMER cabinet minister says Germany is in entire sympathy with the Association of Nations idea. In other respects it seems to be a good plan.—*New York Morning Telegraph.*

THE finding of a headless body has caused the arrest of an American dentist. Our experience with dentists is that the head doesn't really come off; it just feels that way.—*Manila Bulletin.*

ANOTHER unequal tax is having to pay the same amount of salary to all kinds of Congressmen.—*Washington Post.*

SOME nations show a willingness to disarm if somebody will guarantee to lick their neighbors in case of trouble.—*Brooklyn Eagle.*

THE conviction of the rich that the poor are happy is no more foolish than the conviction of the poor that the rich are.—*Boston Post.*

LOCAL government progress reminds one of the sudden evolution of heating systems at home. First it was hot air and now it's hot water.—*Manila Bulletin.*

THEY have discovered an illicit distillery in one of the cells at Sing Sing. I always have been of the opinion those Sing Sing boys would bear watching.—*New York Morning Telegraph.*

A PHILADELPHIA economist says that "The consumer is king." And everybody knows in what portion of the anatomy the kings have been getting it during recent years. —*Nashville Southern Lumberman.*

Copyrighted by George Matthew Adams

SANTA CLAUS: "Say, Uncle Sam, why don't you leave some for me?"

—Morris for the George Matthew Adams Service.

ADVICE to nations about to open the door in the Far East: look for the catch.—*Norfolk Virginian-Pilot.*

"KING CONSTANTINE'S Hold Slipping," says a headline. That's what he gets for trying to stick to Greece.—*Charleston Gazette.*

"SCRAPPING battle-ships is all right," concedes W. P. H., "but why not destroy aeroplanes and thus reduce the overhead?"—*New York Tribune.*

THE Russian Soviet government has condemned a man to death for stealing a ton of leather. Lenine simply won't tolerate petty thievery.—*Seattle Times.*

MR. HUGHES suggested a naval ratio of 5–5–3. The Japanese statesmen didn't like it, and are scrapping for 10–10–7. A ratio that would suit us first-rate would be 0–0–0.—*New York Call.*

REDUCING the battle-ships and permitting the use of submarines is like making a law prohibiting citizens from carrying flintlock muskets while permitting the use of pocket pistols.—*Nashville Southern Lumberman.*

FOREIGN - COMMENT

SCRAPPING THE ANGLO-JAPANESE TREATY

ONE SURE RESULT of the Washington Conference, it is predicted in some quarters, is the scrapping of the Anglo-Japanese Alliance, and not as a theatrical stroke, but rather as a routine matter of business, because of its supersession by the projected agreement of America, Great Britain, Japan, and possibly France, to guarantee the integrity of China, and at the same time observe certain limitations of armament along the main lines proposed by Secretary Hughes. London dispatches advise us that England is giving "heart-felt but guarded acclaim" to these reports emanating from Washington correspondence, but while a Pacific understanding is warmly welcomed, the London *Evening Standard* points to the danger of excessive optimism before the projected treaty is ratified by the United States Senate and the Japan Government. Nevertheless it states in its news columns that consent of the British Government is assured, and it speaks editorially in these words:

"On the whole, we are inclined to believe that the courage and statesmanship of President Harding will have their reward despite the stubborn American prejudice against any form of entanglement, and especially against entanglement with more than one Power. The British people can have only one feeling in regard to the enlargement of the treaty so as to include other interested Powers and get rid of the really frightful possibilities of danger and expense involved in their antagonism."

THE RAINBOW.

—*The Daily Express* (London).

On the other hand, press dispatches from Washington indicate that the agreement will take the form of "anything but a treaty" and one American correspondent says: "It might be a collective resolution. It might be a protocol, signed by the interested nations, but not technically a treaty that would go before parliaments for ratification. It might be an exchange of notes. It might be several other things."

Yet, although London dispatches concede that President Harding and his Secretary of State have not entered into any hard and fast undertaking, in the form of a treaty, which would have to be submitted to the Senate for ratification, it is held that this is the "logical eventuality." Lloyd George's newspaper, the London *Daily Chronicle*, observes:

"It is said, on what appears to be good authority, that President Harding has made up his mind to submit to the Senate a treaty of alliance for the defense of certain declared objects of policy in the Far East. The members of this alliance are to be Great Britain, the United States, Japan, and possibly, also, France, and it is said they are to guarantee each other's island possessions in the Far East against attack, besides guaranteeing the integrity of China as defined.

"That would be a way of scrapping the Japanese treaty very much to our liking, for it would substitute for it something bigger and better. No reasonable Englishman has ever regarded the Japanese treaty as an end in itself or as a perfect instrument, but only as better than no treaty at all or than a mere series of declarations with no sanction behind them.

"But a larger treaty with improved sanctions is a very different proposition, and if it be true that the President has brought himself to support it, one great cause of anxiety would be removed."

The Japan Foreign Office is reported in Tokio dispatches as disclaiming "official advices" on the subject of the new pact, but is quoted as inclined to "believe the plan is a possible one, and that such a solution would be welcomed throughout the world." Some Tokio newspapers regard the suggested entente as likely to prove the philosopher's stone for the happy solution of many difficult problems confronting the Conference. By the inclusion of France with Great Britain, Japan and the United States, it is argued, America would find less difficulty in entering the proposed association, while France thereby would be rescued from possible isolation. Great Britain and Japan, it is pointed out, would have nothing to complain of, since the fundamental object of the Anglo-Japanese Alliance would be attained, and given even greater authority through French participation. On the subject of the alliance the Tokio *Yomiuri* remarks:

"We have stated from time to time in the past that the object of the Anglo-Japanese Alliance has already been achieved and its treaty is nothing but a dead letter. Especially at this time, when it has been made clear that the alliance will not be applied to the United States in any and all cases, and when Russia and Germany, which were once constituted its objectives, have collapsed entirely, the alliance is of no use except as the reminder of its past usefulness and efficiency, as well as a chain linking the peoples of Britain and Japan in amity and friendship. From this view-point, we have adhered to the opinion that the existing pact of alliance between the two countries should be maintained so long as it does no harm in Japan's relations with other countries. However, now that we hear adverse opinions and views from the lips of so eminent a journalist as Lord Northcliffe, and also in view of a very delicate relation of Japan with the United States, we strongly and emphatically insist upon the abrogation of the treaty of alliance with Britain without delay."

The Tokio *Nichi Nichi* also alludes to Lord Northcliffe's utterances and proceeds:

"Needless to say, the opinion of the United States, which has a vital relation to the Pacific question, should be taken into consideration when the treaty of the alliance is to be renewed, but we consider that, as long as the Anglo-Japanese Alliance purposes the maintenance of peace in the Orient and has no sinister designs against the United States, it should be continued as heretofore. We are not aware how much Lord Northcliffe is conversant with the actual state of things in Japan and China, but we are solicitous that he will at least bear in mind that Japan has no territorial ambition toward China, and her actions in that country have been and are strictly in keeping with the principle of equal opportunity and the Open Door agreed upon with other Powers. We also wish to say that the opinions of our militarists are not the representative opinion of our people, especially toward China."

Some editorial observers recall the first suggestion of the new agreement as embodied in a speech of Premier Lloyd George on August 18 last in the House of Commons, in which he said in part:

"The alliance with Japan could emerge into a greater understanding with Japan and the United States on all problems of the Pacific; that would be a great event which would be a guaranty for the peace of the world. The United States, Japan, the British Empire and China—these four great countries are primarily concerned in having a complete understanding with regard to the Pacific. The surest way of making a success of the Disarmament Conference is first to have such an understanding."

The speech was made in a résumé of the work of the British Imperial Conference, and the Premier's further utterances about the United States were as follows:

"We were all agreed in the Imperial Conference in the desire to have complete friendship with the United States of America and to make arrangements which would remove every conceivable prospective obstacle to such friendship. Nothing would please the British Dominions, as well as the mother country, more than a settlement which would make them feel that the British Empire and the United States could work side by side in common partnership for the preservation of peace and for guaranteeing the peace of the world.

AND THE SENTENCE IS—
10 Years! (Without the option.)
—*The Daily Express* (London).

"I do not know any guaranties that would be equal to that—the United States of America and the British Empire in common agreement on the principle on which a world policy ought to be based. I am still hopeful that such an understanding as would make us feel that this partnership could be established will ensue as a result of the coming Conference in Washington."

RUIN OF RUSSIAN COOPERATIVES

ONE WOULD HAVE THOUGHT that where the Bolshevik leaders found something like a communal organization in working trim, they would have allowed it to function, or at most attempted to improve it, say various observers who note the self-satisfied declaration of Soviet officials that the Russian Cooperative organizations, whose membership numbered about 20,000,000, and whose yearly turnover amounted to hundreds of millions of dollars, have

THE BUDDHA OF MOSCOW, TO WHOM ALL BOW DOWN.
—*La Democratie Nouvelle* (Paris).

been completely and deliberately destroyed by the Bolsheviks. This information is given by Z. Lensky in the *Sovremenniya Zapiski*, a Russian paper published in Paris, who quotes as proof the statement of Chairman Lezhava of the New Sovietized Central Union of Cooperatives, as follows: "We can say with satisfaction that after a struggle of three years with the old Cooperatives nothing is left of them." Meanwhile we learn that the few remaining members of the old Cooperative Board of Directors were sentenced to fifteen years in concentration camps, having been found guilty of giving support to Kolchak and Denikin, "whose activity was directed against the economic policy of the Soviet Government." This was the last act in a series of measures initiated by the Bolsheviks against the Cooperative organizations, of which Mr. Lensky speaks in detail to this effect:

"The building of the Soviet cooperative organization began soon after the Bolshevik coup. In the beginning of 1918 Commissar Shlikhter worked out a project of 'consumers' communes,' which were to embrace the entire population and serve as the sole organization for the distribution of products among the people, in accordance with the plans elaborated by the Commissariat of Food. The consumers' communes, in his scheme, would fulfil not only distributive functions, but also carry on the exchange of products. This project, which aimed at the destruction of the existing cooperative consumers' organizations, met then with the unanimous and decisive opposition on the part of the general as well as workmen's cooperative organizations. In view of that opposition, the Soviet Government made a compromise, which took the form of a decree on April 12th, 1918. Lenin characterized the measure as 'a compromise with the bourgeois cooperative organization and with that element of workmen's cooperatives which has not yet discarded the bourgeois viewpoint.'

"The decree of April 12th, 1918, on consumers' cooperatives, permitted the existence in each locality of not more than two consumers' societies (one general and one workmen's), excluded definite groups of the population from the management of the cooperatives, and placed the organizations under the control of special government bodies, 'cooperative bureaus' of the Councils of National Economy.

"This decree was regarded by Soviet leaders . . . as the first step 'in the consolidation of the cooperative organizations in the system of economic establishments of the Soviet republic,' as the beginning of the transformation of cooperatives from a private organization into one which dovetails with the economic organs of the Soviet Government. At the congress of the Councils of National Economy in May, 1918, it was emphasized that the process must not at all be confined to consumers' cooperatives; it must include all other forms of cooperative organization, as credit, agricultural, butter-producing, etc."

At first the Bolsheviks centered their attention on the workmen's cooperative organizations, which, being in the cities, were easier to get hold of. The writer continues:

"Taking advantage of the decree of April 12th, 1918, which permitted only one general and one workmen's cooperative organization in each locality, the Communists began to found in many places 'central workmen's cooperatives,' for the most part fictitious organizations, with which, however, all other workmen's cooperatives existing in the city, with all their membership, capital and enterprises, had to consolidate."

In the period between that decree and December, 1918, the Bolsheviks passed several measures still further restricting the activities of the independent cooperative organizations. The Moscow People's Bank, the largest cooperative financial institution in the country, was made a branch of the State Bank; the decree on the organization of the supply of products, by abolishing private trading, turned the central and regional consumers' societies into mere agents of the Commissariat of Food, and appointed representatives of the Soviet government on their Boards of Directors.

In December, 1918, a congress of workmen's cooperative organizations was assembled and the Bolsheviks, by political trickery, we are told, succeeded in showing an apparent majority of votes. But later, in January, 1919, when the Bolsheviks failed to gain a majority on the Board of Directors of the Central Union of Cooperatives, "they had recourse to direct action," and by a decree of March 20th, of that year, enabled themselves to put any number of appointees on the Board. This decree completely changed the foundation and structure of the all-Russian Central Organization of Consumers' Cooperatives, we are told, and the same policy was pursued in Siberia after its re-capture from Kolchak. By the end of August, 1920, Mr. Lensky adds, the Soviet Government had completely destroyed all independent cooperative organizations, and it is the exprest opinion of Soviet officials, he says, that there is no need of cooperative organizations in Soviet Russia, and the sooner they are absorbed by government departments the better.

But the Soviet officials frankly admit present conditions in Russia "do not permit a purely communistic state," we learn from a Moscow United Press correspondent, and justify their "dictatorship" policies, because the present illiteracy of the people—about ninety per cent. can neither read nor write—"demands a more or less paternalist, disciplinary form of government."

"BRIGHT AS A DOLLAR."

THE DOLLAR: "Say, you guys look worried; what's the matter?"
THE SOVEREIGN AND THE FRANC: "Just that little scrap in France, son. Don't you remember?"

—*The Bystander* (London).

WALL STREET AND AUSTRALIA

LONDON'S FINANCIAL SUPREMACY begins to wane before the rising prestige of New York, say some Australian journals, in taking note of the fact that the Queensland State Government floated its latest loan in Wall Street. But such an inference is unwarranted, in the view of the Melbourne (Victoria) *Argus*, which declares that there is plenty of money for loaning purposes among British investors, as is proved by the fact that in the early part of October British investors readily lent large sums to India and South Africa, have underwritten a loan of £3,000,000 to New South Wales, and have promised Victoria a loan. All these loans are made "on better terms" than have been obtained by Queensland from Wall Street, we are told, but this does not "indicate lack of resource or any attempt to starve the Dominions financially." The terms on which the British Government arranged to fund the war-debts of the Commonwealth were generous when the state of the money market at the time is considered, and *The Argus* has no doubt that if the Commonwealth should desire to fund the £5,000,000 of treasury bills floated by the Australian Federal Government recently in London, it would have no difficulty in carrying through the transaction. Any objection to Queensland going to New York, therefore, can be based only on sentimental grounds, according to *The Argus*, which proceeds:

"London so long ruled as the mistress of finance that thoughtless persons may hold it to be a sign of decadence that Empire borrowers have to apply to outside countries for funds. . . . The interest rate is the highest yet paid by State or Commonwealth. In addition, the unsettled state of exchange has created speculative factors which should be considered in attempting to ascertain what price must ultimately be paid for the loan."

Nevertheless this Melbourne daily goes on to confess that "it would be foolish to disregard the present-day position of the United States in the money market" for—

"It stands as the great creditor nation, and therefore is a force that British financiers have to reckon with. Still, America rests uneasily in the position in which she finds herself. The state of international exchange is affecting her trade. The situation has become more complicated by the pressure for an almost prohibitive tariff. Hence every device is being adopted by bankers, manufacturers, and traders to extend commerce. The Jones Law, which will restrict the transport of United States goods to her mercantile marine, is one instrument. The Edge Law, to allow of the granting of extended credit to outside importers, is another; and the greater willingness on the part of her bankers to lend to necessitous countries is a third. Great Britain cannot complain of the last two devices, and it is unlikely that she will protest against the Jones Law. Still, it is most probable that the presence of Queensland in Wall Street will quicken the desire of British statesmen to place home finance on such a footing as to checkmate any transfer of business from London to New York."

Meanwhile we read in the *Australian Trade Commissioner's* correspondence to the United States *Commerce Reports* that "financial conditions in Australia continue to improve so that on the whole the situation is much better than it was a few months ago."

POLAND'S NEW ALLY

POLAND HAS A GOOD FRIEND on the western boundary of Germany in her ally France, and now she makes another on Germany's eastern border by the "accord" with Czecho-Slovakia, say those writers who welcome the new arrangement as an important act in the solidification of Central Europe. Incidentally, Czecho-Slovakia is also bound up with Roumania and Jugo-Slavia in the Little Entente, which showed its "big stick" on the occasion of the recent air journey of Karl of Hungary. In Czecho-Slovakia the news comes welcomely, says the *Gazette de Prague*, because of the serious events in Hungary, the first of which was the opposition to treaty conditions affecting Burgenland, and the second the abortive monarchist attempt of Karl of Hungary and his adherents. The signing of the agreement at Prague on November 6th is taken as one more manifestation of the new spirit in European and in world politics which "tends to make sure the peaceful existence of national democracies and the peaceful development of free nations on the basis of reciprocal respect for rights determined by mutual understanding." The agreement was concluded by Constantine Skirmunt, Poland's Foreign Minister, and Dr. Eduard Benes, Foreign Minister of Czecho-Slovakia, and the Polish Bureau of Information (New York) summarizes the main points as follows:

"1. To guarantee to each other their territorial possessions based on the treaties from which results the independence and organization of the two countries.

"2. If one of the contracting parties is attacked by neighbors, the other one is bound to maintain friendly neutrality and allow free transit of war material.

"3. Czecho-Slovakia declares herself uninterested in the question of Eastern Galicia and Poland declares herself uninterested in the question of Slovakia. Consequently, each party undertakes to dissolve any military formations or organizations on its territories as well as to suppress all active propaganda intended to tear away any territory belonging to the other party. Neither state will tolerate on its territory any political or military organization directed against the integrity and safety of the other party.

"4. A commercial agreement has been arrived at.

"5. Both parties have agreed to submit any difficulties to arbitration, either by specially selected umpires or by the Arbitration Tribunal at The Hague.

"6. Neither state may enter an agreement contrary to this agreement.

"7. The agreement is arranged for five years. Either government may terminate it after two years by giving six months' notice. Special arrangements have been made to set up a Common Commission to settle all disputes between national majorities and minorities in those border districts which have a mixed Polish and Czecho-Slovakian population. This special commission which has been set up may intervene in all affairs relating to national conditions, as regards schools, economic conditions, etc. The only remaining boundary dispute (a small one) between the two countries is to be settled by arbitration within six months."

The Polish official view of the new accord is presented by the Polish Foreign Minister Skirmunt in a statement to the Prague *Narodni Politika*, in which he says:

"Poland and Czecho-Slovakia owe their new life to the same event and the same treaties of peace. Thus they have each the same task, which is to consolidate the new European situation and to maintain peace. This common aim, despite the difficulties of the first years, has enabled our reciprocal good-will to conclude this political accord, which gives us reason to hope for the solidifying and strengthening of our two countries in Central Europe."

A new era begins, remarks the Prague *Ceskoslovenska Republika*, and it is full of promise, "despite the skepticism that will inevitably declare itself here and there and despite the attempts that will be made from this side or that to damage it." This daily adds:

"We believe that the work begun by the visit of Polish Minister Skirmunt will have lasting value. It is not the product of transient emotions, but of profound understanding of the needs of the two nations. This accord not only justifies joyous confidence in the future, but has a real importance in the present hour. In effect it is a clear refutation of all theories about the Balkanization of Central Europe."

The *Prager Presse* avers that public opinion not only in Poland and in Czecho-Slovakia, but wherever there is interest in the development of Central Europe, does not need the publication of the accord in order to appreciate its high importance and meaning, and adds:

"The officials representing Poland and Czecho-Slovakia solemnly avow their purpose to devote themselves by common effort to the work of peace, and to the systematic reinforcement of the friendly bonds uniting the two countries. Everybody who understands the importance of the issues of the New Central Europe, which has been born of the Peace Treaties, will welcome this event with enthusiasm."

CENTRAL EUROPE'S NEW BALANCE IN PROCESS.

A clear refutation of all theories about the Balkanization of Central Europe is said to be found in the accord between Poland and Czecho-Slovakia, by which the influence of the Little Entente is extended. Dotted sections above show Czecho-Slovakia's colleagues of the Little Entente, Roumania and Jugo-Slavia, cheek by jowl with Hungary and Austria; and also France, Poland's first ally and Germany's neighbor at the west. Striped sections show Czecho-Slovakia and Poland, Germany's neighbors at the east.

GENERAL SMUTS'S CRITICISM OF THE CONFERENCE

— Compare what happened at the Peace Conference with what is now happening in connection with the Washington Conference, says General Smuts, as quoted in a Pretoria press dispatch to London, and you find that at Paris the Dominions had all the advantages of "recognized individual status," and of consultation and mutual support. In the British Empire delegation at Paris, he adds, "our individual standing was unquestioned, while our team-work made us a really effective force." This is "a great precedent which has settled our international status, and which I feel should be followed in future," but the South African Premier points out that—

"Now, at the first great international conference called after Paris, the Dominions, despite the Pacific position of three of them, have been simply ignored. At Washington there will only be the British Delegation, in which the Dominions as such will not be found."

General Smuts denies the charges that he seems to be wishing to play "a lone hand," and declares: "I want the Paris precedent to be followed at Washington and at every subsequent conference. I want the British Empire represented through its constituent and equal States; there is no other way of giving it representation." He says further that he has no intention of striking a jarring note, but wishes merely to stand up for that Dominion status "which to me and, I feel sure, to the nations of the Dominions, is the reality and the basic constitutional reality of our free Imperial Commonwealth."

SCIENCE - AND - INVENTION

SOURCE OF HUNDREDS OF FOODS, MEDICINES, OILS, SIRUPS AND STARCHES.

"The golden kernels have locked up in their mysterious cells untold possibilities of wealth, health and comfort-giving. It may yet prove that the most important fact in connection with the discovery of America was the discovery of corn."

MYRIAD NEW USES FOR CORN

GREEN CORN AND JOHNNY-CAKE are by no means the only products of the corn-field. The list of modern corn products embraces hundreds of foods for man and beast, medicinal preparations, oils for the chemist, manufacturer and cook, sirups and sugars for the table and the confectioner, and starch in its myriad forms and still more varied uses. E. W. Hellwig, who has devoted the past twelve years to intensive work upon food products, describes some of these uses of corn in *The American Food Journal.*

Corn, Mr. Hellwig reminds us, is distinctly a New World product. From the point of view of America, it is the most valuable and most important of all our cereal crops. We are now growing more than three billion bushels—the money value alone is almost as great as that of all the wheat, potato, rye and cotton crops put together. He continues:

"The kernel of corn is composed of three parts—the germ, the endosperm, and the hull. The hull is the hard and horny outer covering; the endosperm, a white body, mostly made up of starch, but with a certain percentage of gluten; the germ a small, oily nitrogenous point.

"Each of these is capable of being worked up into various products—some of which differ radically from the substance from which they were originally derived, as will be seen later.

"To the general reader the uses of corn are more important than is its chemistry—altho upon its chemistry depend its uses. These uses are many and varied, some thirty different products being developed from the cereal.

"Chief among these is a refined oil, derived from the germ, and marketed as a salad and cooking oil.

"Each bushel of corn yields approximately a pound of refined oil.

"The residue from the refining of the oil is treated with an excess of alkali. The resulting soap stock is then separated out, cooled, and allowed to harden. This substance is used in the making of soap powder, soap and soap chips.

"From the corn germ is also extracted a gum, known as 'paragol,' used as a substitute for rubber in many ways. One of the most familiar of these is the 'red rubber' bath sponge, now quite generally supplanting the old sponges, becoming more and more scarce because of their prohibitive price.

"Many millions of eraser tips for lead pencils are also annually made of this substitute; while it is said also to contribute some 20 per cent. to the synthetic soles of shoes.

"The residue of the germ also enters into the composition of oil cake and oil meal—largely used as a milk producer or milk increaser for cattle.

"One of the best-known of all corn products is cornflakes, familiar to every family in the land as a breakfast cereal and appetizing luncheon dish."

The starch grains of the corn—which constitutes 55 per cent. of the kernel—are converted into a great number of products, invaluable for dietetic and industrial uses. This starch is used in the manufacture of corn sirup, dextrine, sugar, edible starch and laundry starch. The edible starch is exceptionally pure and clean, for it is especially washed and milled to remove all traces of gluten, etc., and reeled until all small lumps and gritty substances are removed. We read further:

"In making corn sirup unmixed and sugar, the starch is treated under pressure in closed bronze converters, with the addition of steam and a small amount of hydrochloric acid.

"The addition of the hydrochloric acid is necessary to convert the starch into dextrine. This is the same action as that which develops in the stomach when starchy food is eaten, the hydrochloric acid in the stomach converting the starch into glucose, so that it can be assimilated by the digestive organs.

"After the starch has been converted, it is neutralized with sodium carbonate to change any excess of acid into wholesome sodium chloride—common table salt. The neutralized liquor is then filter-prest, to remove small particles of gluten, or any unconverted substance which may have been carried along by the starch.

"The clarified liquor used in the manufacture of sugar is converted to a higher per cent. dextrose than that used in sirup-making. When the sugar liquor is run on tables and allowed to cool, it crystallizes or solidifies in large cakes. The cakes or slabs are chipped in fine pieces and sold to brewers, canners and vinegar makers.

"The slab sugar is also prest to remove the uncrystallized liquor called hydrol, and then ground and dried. This product is of a very high purity, and is the cerelose or bread sugar used by bakers, and in the manufacture of numerous food products.

"There are many other substances derived from the manufacture of starch. For instance, the dry, milled starch is packed in barrels and bags to supply pearl and powdered starch for cloth sizing, paper, etc.

"A portion of the starch from the mills is partly cooked with steam, to increase solubility, then prest into cylinders. This produces laundry starch, or lump starch.

"One of the principal by-products in the manufacture of corn products is gluten feed, which is partly derived from the steep-water, concentrated in vacuum pans. This steepwater is rich in proteins, which, with the hull or skins of the corn and the gluten separated in the various processes, is valuable as a tissue nd muscle-building food for stock, as well as a milk-producing gent.

"The germ which was separated in the first part of the process dried, passed through rolls and then the crude oil is prest out. he residue is ground very fine, is used as oil-cake meal and og-meal.

"Within the past year hundreds of clinical experiments have een made with a new corn product—anhydrous glucose, or extrose, 99.6 per cent. pure.

"This pure dextrose can be given in very large amounts ithout disturbing the digestion, or without developing any vidence of sugar intolerance.

"So perfect is the absorption and utilization of anhydrous lucose that there is a strong likelihood that may completely change the present ethods of treating many organic disorders, sulting from disturbances in metabolism.

"For one thing, experiments conducted y careful observers seem to show that dex-ose can be given to diabetic patients, for hom all other forms of sugar are forbidden.

"Dextrose has also been used as a feeding igar for dehydrated, toxic babies—doomed die of malnutrition. In numbers of cases has saved life, and turned puny little celetons, listless and almost devoid of the nergy that enabled them to continue to reathe, into rosy, active babies.

"What is destined to prove one of the ost valuable of all corn derivatives was iscovered in 1900 by Dr. Posternak, in Paris.

"In supplying the phosphorus required y the nerves and tissues it is absolutely ssential to have an organic phosphoric acid its salt—as found in plants and cereals.

"Because of this fact Professor Gilbert is oroughly justified in proclaiming the dis-overy of phytin, 'the solution of the prob-m of phosphorus therapy,' and in adding at it has become possible, for the first me, to supply the organism with sufficient hosphorus in an assimilable form, and erefore to obtain therapeutic effects never et obtained with any other phosphorus reparation.'

"Phytin, as found in corn, contains about 2 per cent. of pure organic phosphorus. s introduction and ultimate production n a commercial scale may revolutionize e present treatment of nervous diseases, nemia, and disorders of nutrition.

"The golden kernels have locked up in their mysterious ells untold possibilities of wealth, health and comfort-giving. may yet prove that the most important fact in connection ith the discovery of America was the discovery of corn."

USES OF THE CORN-COB—Science, according to *The Chemical ound Table* (New York), has also found a way of utilizing all the orn-cobs, short or long, in the manufacture of various chemicals. says:

"Formerly the only use for the lowly cob was to feed the rnace or to provide fuel for the cook stove. Only a part of the utput could be used in this way, however, and the chemists ave found that with the millions of bushels of corn which must e shelled in this country there are many tons of cob which can be ade to serve commerce and industry. As the corn-cob consists ostly of cellulose, which is valuable for the making of many roducts, such as celluloid and paper, it is considered desirable save the substance of the cob. The furfural, therefore, is ken from the extract which is obtained by boiling the cob in ater, and the cellulose can thus be kept for other purposes. urfural is employed for many purposes in industrial chemistry, nd can be so treated that it will yield a bright green dye, which much liked by women of fashion. If it is desired merely to repare furfural and not to save the cellulose, the process could e made continuous from the start. It should be emphasized, owever, that the cellulose may have as great a value as the rfural in technical operations, and it is of great importance to reserve it from injury by overheating. From corn-cobs, aluable glues and adhesives may also be prepared."

WHO INVENTED THE AEROPLANE?

SOLE INVENTORS are rare birds; possibly they are non-existent. Most great inventions are growths; the man who gets the name of being the originator rather completes than originates; it is he who puts on the finishing touch and makes the device practical. The writer of a leading editorial in *Nature* (London) compares this work of completion to the setting of a keystone in an arch. The inspiration of this editorial is a recent paper read by Griffith Brewer before the Royal Aeronautical Society in London on "The Langley Machine and the Hammondsport Trials," dealing with what Mr. Brewer terms an "attempt to rob the Wright brothers of the credit of inventing the aeroplane." Says the London paper:

HE GAVE "A HELPING HAND,"

Said the Wright Brothers of Professor Langley, while Langley himself admitted that others must complete his work.

"The argument turns on a usual interpretation of the word 'inventing,' and it is not suggested that the credit of establishing the principles of aeroplane design is in doubt. The dispute as to the relative importance of the pioneers S. P. Langley and the Wright brothers arose in the course of certain legal actions as to the validity of patents taken out by the latter. In connection with the defense of the Curtiss Aeroplane Co. against a charge of infringement, arrangements were made with the Smithsonian Institution for the loan of the original man-carrying aeroplane designed and constructed by Langley. The design was modified in certain ways before it was taken into the air at Hammondsport, and the contention of Mr. Brewer in putting the case for the Wright brothers is that the modifications were such as to invalidate the claim that the original Langley aeroplane had been flown.

"The trials of the modified aeroplane were made late in the development of the subject, the loan by the Smithsonian Institution being dated April, 1914. The public European flights of the Wright brothers had taken place some six years prior to this, whilst the date of the first successful flight of about one minute's duration is stated to be December, 1903. It is perhaps worth while to clear up the historical facts of the trials, but the paper tends to give an erroneous impression of the importance of the part played by the Wright brothers in spite of Mr. Brewer's note to the effect that Langley himself did not make the claims to which exception is taken, nor would he have been likely to do so had he been alive to hear of the controversy.

"The difficulty appears to arise from a not uncommon type of mental blindness which is readily produced by the contact of financial interests with development. It is rather like making the assumption that, because an arch can not be used as an engineering structure until the keystone is in place, the keystone is therefore the most important element in it; the rest of the structure appears to be unseen. Applied to Mr. Brewer's paper, the simile suggests that the keystone was provided by the Wright brothers, and that the much more laborious work of preparing for its reception is to be found in the scientific experiments of Langley.

"Readers of *Nature* will find in its volumes references which indicate, in a calmer atmosphere, the part played by Langley in the development of aviation. So far back as July 23, 1891, a paper on his experimental researches is to be found in *Nature* showing that the flight of a man-carrying aeroplane was possible, and enunciating the fundamental principles for obtaining a design. Matters were so much advanced in 1896 that on May 28 of that year *Nature* was able to give a description of the flight of the Langley model aeroplane under its own power.

"This was a remarkable achievement, since it required a solution of the problem of inherent stability, a quality almost certainly not possest by the Wright aeroplanes of 1908. The great addition to aeronautical knowledge and practise made by the Wright brothers was the introduction of the system of wing warping which gave adequate lateral control even to an unstable aeroplane."

Langley's researches, the writer goes on to say, have been described on many occasions, and their relation to the problem of flight is shown in Sir Richard Gregory's book, "Discovery," from which the following extracts are given: On p. 288 Langley is quoted as saying, in relation to his experiments before 1897:—

"I have brought to a close the portion of the work which seemed specially mine—the demonstration of the practicability of mechanical flight—and for the next stage, which is the commercial and practical development of the idea, it is probable that the world may look to others. The world, indeed, would be supine if it does not realise that a new possibility has come to it, and that the great universal highway overhead is now soon to be opened."

The Wright brothers are equally clear in their acknowledgment of Langley's work:—

"The knowledge that the head of the most prominent scientific institution of America believed in the possibility of human flight was one of the influences which led us to undertake the preliminary investigations that preceded our active work. He recommended to us the books which enabled us to form sane ideas at the outset. It was a helping hand at a critical time, and we shall always be grateful."

The editorial writer sums up as follows:

"One feels that in relation to such remarks by the two great American pioneers of aviation the matter under discussion is unimportant. The transactions appear to have been rather sordid and to reflect discredit on those commercial systems of the world which exalt 'patentability' at the expense of solid service which is not patentable."

SOAPS THAT FADE DYES—Some soaps not only remove the dirt from textiles, but a generous share of the color also. Dr. Martin H. Fischer, speaking on "Soaps" before the Cleveland Section of the American Chemical Society, said on this phase of the subject, as quoted in *Drug and Chemical Markets* (New York):

"'The commercial soaps employed at the present time are blunderbuss mixtures containing larger or smaller fractions of different soaps. This makes it possible to use common toilet and laundry soap in a wide variety of circumstances, tho, of course, not with economy.' Some of the yellow laundry soaps are faulty, in the opinion of Dr. Fischer, because when used with very hot water they set free rosin and alkali. The rosin settles in the clothes and tends to make the fiber of woolen 'mat,' while the alkali eats the clothes. Woolens washed in this way are likely to become hard and stiff. Blankets and woolen garments, therefore, should be washed with soaps which do not suffer such decomposition and are soluble in water which is not too hot. When the garments are rinsed, therefore, soap of this kind readily leaves them. Dr. Fischer said a course in laundry chemistry has been established at the Washington Irving High School, New York City. The main object of the course is to teach the proper use of materials employed in the cleansing of clothes and to avoid damage to the goods. Dr. Fischer said the fading of dyes, which has been falsely attributed to errors in manufacture, may be traced to excessive use of improperly prepared washing materials. The laundry industry in this course is giving its employees thorough instruction in the nature of dyes and colors, and gives special attention to the proper handling of fabrics which have been colored with direct dyes, mordant dyes, vat dyes, sulfur dyes, and anilines. There is also a lesson in bluing."

THE WORLD'S TINIEST RAILROAD

THE ESKDALE RAILWAY, in Cumberland, England, seven miles long, with a fifteen-inch gage, has features of great novelty and interest. At first sight, says a writer in *Conquest* (London, November), it is difficult to regard it seriously, and some of our illustrations will inevitably provoke a smile. Nevertheless, it is not a toy or model, but is of real commercial utility, and as an engineering feat on a small scale is unique. It is the result of a remarkable development of the model locomotive beloved of most boys, and, indeed, by many more adults than one might suppose. We read:

"Constructed in 1876, the line was originally of 2 feet 9 inches gage, and was used to convey iron ore from mines in the neighborhood of Boot, a little village in Eskdale, to Ravenglass, on the coast of Cumberland, where it joined the Furness Railway. After serving a useful purpose, both as regards mineral and passenger traffic, for many years, the mines at Boot were closed down, and, after valiant efforts to maintain it, the railway itself fell into disuse in 1913. In 1915, however, a company known as Narrow Gage Railways, Ltd., obtained a lease of the line, which they converted to 15 inches gage, the original rails, weighing 40 pounds a yard, being relaid. The line was then equipped with the biggest model locomotives and rolling stock in existence.

IRTON ROAD, ONE OF THE PRINCIPAL STATIONS.

"The line is just seven miles long and passes through charming scenery. There is an excellent service of trains each way.

"There is a hoary old joke against one of our big railways to the effect that passengers are requested not to alight and pluck flowers while the train is in motion. We do not know whether the management of the Eskdale Railway offer facilities in this respect to passengers, but at any rate, persons desiring to join a train may do so at intermediate points between stations by means of hand-operated signals.

"A maximum speed of thirty-five miles an hour is attained by the locomotives, which are also capable of drawing a load of 17 tons on the level at a speed of fourteen miles an hour—quite a respectable performance. The journey occupies about thirty minutes, and about seventy-six passengers constitute a full load for a passenger train.

"Each open coach accommodates eight persons (two abreast), the weight of an empty coach being about 800 pounds. Wind screens and awnings are provided for protection in wet or in hot weather. For winter traffic closed bogie coaches are run that weigh 2400 pounds empty, and seat twelve persons inside and four on end platforms. An ordinary summer train comprises nine open coaches.

"Without question the most fascinating features of the Eskdale Railway are its one-quarter scale model locomotives. The most up-to-date models are of the 'Pacific' type. Their weight is 3 tons each in working order, their over-all length 18 feet 2 inches, and height from rail level to top of chimney 3 feet 8 inches. The boiler working pressure is 140 pounds per square inch, the cylinders are 4⅜ inches diameter by 6¾ inches stroke, and—to complete the refinement of design—the engines are fitted with superheaters, and the rolling stock is provided throughout with vacuum brakes! There are, in all, five locomotives, twenty-three goods cars, and twenty-seven passenger coaches.

"It is an interesting fact that, whereas the development of narrow gage railways generally has been a matter of accommodating practise on broad and standard gage lines to smaller gages, in the case of the Eskdale Railway it has been a case of development in the opposite direction, namely, of improving upon the design of scale models and constructing model locomotives capable of doing really useful work.

"Scarcely a Yuletide passes without some artist depicting a scene in which the children of a Christmas party are deprived by their elders of their mechanical toys, and we have already hinted that the equipment and running of model railways is not confined children. The writer knows more than one ·ious business man who devotes much of his spare ne to this form of amusement, ostensibly for the tertainment of his children, but in reality because possesses a fascination that leads him to spend any an hour with his trains—surreptitiously and in ar of being discovered. The reason for such diffi-nce is not hard to guess, especially when it entails awling about the floor on hands and knees; yet ere is at least as much exercise of intellect in such occupation as in the majority of pastimes in ich we indulge. Personally, the writer is ready confess that, altho indoor clockwork trains do not ssess much attraction for him, one of his minor bitions is to construct an outdoor model electric lway on realistic lines, not necessarily on the scale the Eskdale Railway, but one capable of with-nding the weather."

ONE OF THE SMALL BUT POWERFUL "PACIFIC" LOCOMOTIVES.

Used on the Eskdale Railway. Thirty-five miles an hour can be attained when "running light," and the engines can easily haul a full train of 76 passengers.

"MILK" FROM RICE

RICE CAN BE LIQUEFIED into the form of milk, we are told by W. M. Queen, writing in *The Rice Journal* (Beaumont, Texas). is discovery marks a new chapter, he asserts, in e history of dietetics, and opens up an enlarged field consumption for the grain. Throughout the ages, Mr. Queen es on to say, the transformation of natural elements into a lk has been carried on through the water roots of the rice ant, "upon the same principle," he assures us, "as that by ich the milk is drawn from Mother Nature through the veins the cow into the udder." He proceeds:

"In the rice plant the sun's heat performs the work directly d in a most perfect manner, requiring more time than the cow complete the process of making its milk. The result is the e kernel, which is nothing more than a concentrated, crys-llized milk—which in turn, may by a natural process be rned into the flowing liquid form.

"S. Christensen, one of California's leading rice growers, who s in the dairy and butter business in Denmark years ago, rted in his early youth to study and experiment with rice. He served that the cereal is both a grain, in the ordinary sense of e word, and a water plant. Unless submerged it may grow to a thing of beauty, but, of course, is valueless.

"It is known that rice at first grows like any ordinary grain, t later puts forth its milk veins, which have been called water ots, above the surface of the ground. These draw a milk m the elements in the water.

"This is no longer a matter of speculation. Providentially, it uld seem, the two men who could together coax the milk from e rice, by reason of their long and patient experiments, have et. A milk containing 7 per cent. fat has been produced. It 100 per cent. rice.

"The writer has tasted this milk, fifty-five hours after its production, when it had become a buttermilk, and can vouch for the fact that it is refreshing, invigorating and stimulating.

"J. H. Sasseen, who with Mr. Christensen, is producing the new product from the rice, was born in Richland, Iowa. He attended the Iowa State Dairy School and left that institution in 1902, engaging in practical work with private interests until 1915, when he commenced his duties with the Iowa State Dairy and Food Commission, with which he continued for four years. After spending a portion of the War period in Columbus, Ohio, he went to Texas, where he brought the experiments with rice as a base for ice-cream he had started in Iowa, to a more perfect stage of their development. His products were already being made experimentally in the form of an emulsion and also in a frozen state as a substitute for ice-cream and sherbet.

"At this point Mr. Sasseen brought his discovery to California, drawn there by the famous rice belt and the proximity of a wide variety of fruits for use in his new food products. There he met Mr. Christensen, the rice grower, whose researches covering a long period of years were so supplemented by Mr. Sasseen's invention that between them they have opened a new field for the development of rice with possibilities hitherto undreamed.

"In the near future a factory will be started in San Francisco or Oakland, which serving as a base for operations on the Pacific Coast, will be the nucleus of a world-wide industry of colossal magnitude.

"What this move will mean to the rice interests can be imagined when it is taken into consideration that the new rice milk can be used with greater economy, and with remarkable benefit to health, in any case where cow's milk has been employed. It must not be overlooked that it is richer than ordinary milk, being in fact a cream superior to that which comes from the cow.

LOADED TRAIN DRAWN BY ENGINE "COLOSSUS."

"Rice will be made the base of a host of delectable and nutritious foods. It will appear in a jelled form for use at soda fountains, in sundaes of all flavors. It will be adopted in candy factories as a filling for French creams, etc.

"In the frozen state it will be served in the same manner as ice-cream and sherbet, but, as will be seen, it can be eaten more freely and by persons who have hitherto had to abstain from frozen dainties.

"Only lately, after incessant educational advertising and publicity, have people come to know the importance of the vital element, vitamines, which is lacking in many of our daily foods. Ordinary meat and fish do not contain it at all. Milk is not as rich in it as was once thought. Too many everyday foods have been robbed of their vitamines in the process of manufacture. Care has been taken to avoid this fault in the preparation of rice milk.

"The use of rice as a milk, which will make it an important ingredient of the products of the bakery, candy factory, soda fountain and a host of other industries, as well as increasing its consumption in the home, marks a beginning of a new chapter in the history of dietetics."

LETTERS - AND - ART

LITERATURE DRAMA MUSIC FINE-ARTS EDUCATION CULTURE

RISE OF A NEW OPERATIC STAR

"THE KING IS DEAD, LONG LIVE THE QUEEN," might have been said at the Metropolitan Opera on the night of December 1. For if it does not happen that the throne left vacant by Caruso is taken by a woman, then the signs will fail. Marie Jeritza, the Jugo-Slav soprano whom Mr. Gatti has brought here from Vienna, has already given two exhibitions of her power as a singing actress, and her triumph came in the less expected place. *Tosca*, the somewhat threadbare heroine of melodramatic opera, and not *Marietta*, the newest candidate for melodramatic vogue in an opera of the latest school, was her vehicle to fame. The critics say that the Metropolitan was shocked out of its composure at the power she showed as the Sardou-Puccini heroine. Opening her career here in the young Korngold's opera, "Die Tote Stadt," written for her, there was expectation of a sensation such as did not exactly realize itself. It was felt that the merciless young composer had set her vocal tasks that were beyond the powers of almost any human voice. To judge her thus as a singer seemed unfair. So the audience came together for her representation of *Tosca* with somewhat of the "show me" air. What the singer achieved in the testing second act was a revelation that came "like an avalanche which swept thousands into a frenzied demonstration of enthusiasm." No one is better qualified to speak such words than Mr. Krehbiel, of the New York *Tribune*, who has doubtless been present on every great occasion in the history of the house. "We can not recall a similar scene in all the history of the opera house, which has witnessed many a great artistic triumph. It was not applause; it was an emotional tumult; a tempest." Mr. Krehbiel goes on:

A NEW *TOSCA*,

Who gave the well-worn Puccini rôle such life that the sophisticated New York Opera House rose to her.

"We have had a number of fine representatives of the *Tosca* of Puccini and his librettists, and memory deals kindly with them all—with Ternina, Eames, Fremstad, Farrar. Mme. Jeritza's impersonation differed from them all. It was more than an embodiment of the operatic heroine, dramatically and musically; it was an incarnation of a woman far greater than the one conceived by the creators of the opera. It was Illica, Giacosa and Puccini, plus the soul of Sardou. It was Sardou sublimated by the subtle and powerful alchemy of music. Pose and gesture of infinite variety and grace, vocal utterance of irresistible eloquence gave meanings to phrases of which perhaps neither dramatists nor composer had dreamed. The line of demarcation between speech and song seemed to have been eliminated, and the clogs which music places upon action seemed non-existent. The entire gamut of vocal color was played upon to intensify the musical declamation, yet there was no hint at studied effect. The emotional stimuli seemed spontaneous, unvolitional; they came from within.

"Yet it was a manifestation of art, of a lofty conception of the province of art, and a marvelous capacity to embody that conception. The climax of the second act did not come with the vulgar killing of a libertine; it was reached when *Tosca*, perplexed in the extreme, poured out her agony in a heartbroken wail, which rose to passionate supplication and ended in the broken accents of despair.

"'Vissi d'Arte' has generally been a concert intermezzo, embarrassing to the progress of the tragedy. It has been sung so that the prima donna's admirers might applaud it, might even demand a repetition. Last night it was the despairing exhalation of a crusht heart, and on it the drama soared to its psychological height. It was sung as Mme. Bernhardt might have spoken it, yet it was song. It was dramatic song, like every word of dialogue which Mme. Jeritza uttered, the song of an actress who was a trained and gifted singer, of a singer impelled by the spirit of a great tragedienne.

"It was small wonder that Signor Scotti felt the inspiration of such a companion and revivified his always superb impersonation of *Baron Scarpia*. Gracefully, gallantly, almost reverentially, he made his homage to Mme. Jeritza every time the torrential applause summoned the pair before the curtain."

That Mme. Jeritza's triumph did not come on the occasion of her first appearance was due perhaps to a combination of causes. True, there was a loud welcome then and much applause, but to some it bore an air of speciousness, to which "Mephisto" furnishes the key in *Musical America:*

"She got a great reception and others during the opera and at the end, all of which she deserved, tho there were very many Germans in the audience that afternoon. They had come to welcome and support a compatriot and a person who had won distinction not only as an artist but as a renowned beauty.

"On her singing I would not like to render an opinion. The voice seemed a little hard in the upper register. When it comes to some of the high notes which have to be sustained, it sounds as if she were scooping them up from some musical reservoir. It were better to reserve full opinion with regard to her as a singer till she has had an opportunity in some other rôles, for it would not be fair to judge her by a first appearance, and especially in such an opera as Korngold has written."

Korngold, it may be interesting to recall, was a youthful prodigy in 1914, and THE LITERARY DIGEST of March 14 of that year contained an article on his "Sinfonietta," performed in Berlin by the Philharmonic orchestra under Arthur Nikisch. Richard Strauss then spoke of him as "one of the most remarkable musical geniuses that this age has seen." At the age of eight he began composing, and even in 1914 he had a considerable achievement to his credit, tho he was but sixteen. The war years made him drop out of sight to Entente nations, but now at twenty-three he reappears with an opera, "Die Tote Stadt," whose leading part was sung by Jeritza, for whom, in fact, it was written. Of this opera Deems Taylor writes in the New York *World:*

"In general, the faults of the score are those that would be expected of youth—lack of individuality, overemphasis, bad taste and emotional immaturity. Of Korngold's talent for composition there can be no question. 'Die Tote Stadt' is an amazing performance for a boy of twenty-two. He has rhythmic vigor, a sense of color and apt harmonization, and an unerring sense of what will get across in the theater. All that is incomplete is Korngold himself. He is not yet an individual. His score is crammed with reminiscences not only of other men's themes but of other men's minds and reactions. He not only sounds like Puccini and Mendelssohn and Wagner and Bizet and Liza Lehmann; he *is* each of these in turn. Once in a while one hears a new note, a voice as yet halting and almost inarticulate, that offers a promise of eloquence when the speaker shall have grown up. Unimportant as much of this music is, it always has vitality, always demands a hearing. Only, Korngold's voice is changing, spiritually speaking."

KORNGOLD AT 16. KORNGOLD OF TO-DAY.

The composer of "Die Tote Stadt," who began to lisp in original numbers.

A rather complicated plot is this very modern opera, but Mr. Max Smith has given it in brief form in the New York *American:*

"In the ancient city of Bruges the morbid *Paul*, obsessed with a ghastly mania for *Marie*, long since among the departed, turns the cult of her memory into a sort of religious observance. Having discovered in *Marietta*, member of a traveling opera troupe, an extraordinary likeness to his former wife, he transfers his affections to her, callous to the entreaties of his friends.

"Falling into an ecstatic sleep, the true character of the worthless dancer is brought home to *Paul* in a series of visions that extend from the first act to the close of the third and last, when the poor dreamer, awakened no doubt by the fancied effort of strangling his mocking paramour with a treasured strand of *Marie's* golden hair, decides that the time has come to quit Bruges and to abandon his perverted cult of the dead."

Of Jeritza's performance in this opera, one paragraph from Deems Taylor in the *World* summarizes her difficulties and her achievement:

"If Marie Jeritza were not of heroic build and proportions the part of *Marietta* would be utterly impossible for her. As it is, she 'swooped' badly—that is, slid up to her high notes—in the last act of 'Die Tote Stadt.' If a woman of less strength, or a coloratura soprano (coloraturas are not expected to combine much volume of tone with their high notes) tried the part she would be voiceless before the middle of the second act. No wonder neither Mme. Jeritza nor Mr. Harrold was able to give a perfect performance, vocally speaking. The wonder is that they could give any performance at all. 'Modern opera does not produce great singing artists,' said Mr. Gatti-Casazza during his first interview with the newspaper men this fall."

BRITISH DEFENSE OF ARTEMUS WARD

THE JOYS OF LIFE may be spread thicker here than in foreign lands, so that those same lands have no idea of permitting us to scrap any of our armament of humor. When some of our college professors are for scrapping Artemus Ward as outworn and outlived, the London *Punch* comes to his rescue. The battalion against Ward must be formidable since North and South join in the attack. Prof. George Frisbie Whicher of Amherst thinks that his humor merely "marked the initial stage in the inevitable progress from pioneer jocularity to urbane irony." Prof. Nathaniel Wright Stephenson of the College of Charleston, S. C., as the Boston *Transcript* interprets him, "seems to suppose that he condemns Ward in linking his humor up with that of Abraham Lincoln, who, as a type, he says, 'illustrates the American contentment with the externals of humor, with bad grammar and ironic impudence.'" Lincoln, says Professor Stephenson, "shared the illusions of his day about Artemus Ward; when he tried to write humorously he did the same thing himself." *The Transcript* in mediating this difference of view between *Punch* and our professors observes as an axiom that "humor is an imponderable and an unmeasurable thing"; that—

"No professor was ever able to map it or chart it. The only thing certain about it is that all gravity is its legitimate prey—grave criticism along with the rest. The humorist may not be always funny, but the critic who seeks to weigh and measure humor never is anything else."

The Transcript recalls that *Punch* "made very good use of Ward while in England he was singing his swan song of fun and prodigiously amusing the whole British nation." Therefore there is good reason for their coming stoutly to Artemus's defense:

"Not only does it recall the whole world's spontaneous delight in him while he lived, but cites sayings of his that stand the test still. *Punch* challenges any normal person to read Ward's essay on 'Cats' to-day without a broad smile; if you can do it, quoth *Punch*, you 'must either be a prig or a professor—or both.' And *Punch* is right. The taste in humor changes, and the fine perfume of a man's wit fades away with the disappearance of the man himself from the scene. Yet the sayings of Artemus abide. We echo him unconsciously every day. His humorous discoveries have become commonplace. His noble sacrifice of his wife's relations on the altar of his country survives; we still praise G. Washington for never slopping over; we seek the reason of 'this thusness'; we are 'saddest when we sing,' and so are those who hear us; we quote the showman, and Betsey Jane; we have long since made a proverb of Artemus. His humor, whether or not it belonged to the order of buffoonery, was native, spontaneous, surprising and delightful. He could even bring satire to bear, as when he wrote of 'Traters'; 'Traters I will here remark are a onfortnit class of peple. If they wasn't they wouldn't be traters. They conspire to bust up the country—they fail and they're traters. They bust her and they become statesmen and heroes.' His personal sketches are broadly irreverent. If irreverence and the suggestion of incongruity are at war with true humor, then indeed our professor friends may be quite right in their judgment. . . .

"Even the greatest humorists, after they are dead, need to be judged in the light of their personal quality, their look, their touch, while living. Artemus Ward has been gone so long that it may be difficult to do that. Yet we may all be glad that he lives again in the pages of such a biography of him as that of Don C. Seitz, a book now some three or four years old, in which a man who knew the conditions of life and the native flavor out of which Charles Farrar Browne sprang, and who himself possesses abundant humor, has enabled us to see Ward as he was, and to get into the spirit and genial current of his soul. We feel his influence, and we sorrow with him, for Ward was the victim of his humor. Entertaining the world, he was himself entertained to death. In the 60's the penalty of good-fellowship was terrible; in Ward's case it was tragical. The condition is illustrated—and the surprizing quality of Ward's humor is also exprest—in one of the stories Mr. Seitz tells. On his lecture tours, after finishing his public appearance, the humorist was expected to put in most of the rest of the night with the 'reception committee.' At one town in the West this committee was headed by the local magnate, who was also a distiller. He manufactured a brand of whisky of which the slogan was, 'Not a headache in a hogshead of it.' The distiller's product was plentifully set out, and the ceremonies took until about three in the morning. At about eleven the next day Ward came in to the local newspaper office looking very much the worse for wear. 'Oh, dear,' he said, 'I wish I'd taken a hogshead of it, because he said there wasn't a headache in a hogshead!'"

OUR DISAPPOINTING YOUNGSTERS

THE SHIVERS DOWN THE SPINE of the older generation that Ibsen taught us to expect from the knockings at the door at the hands of masterful youth seem not to function at present. Or, rather, the younger generation itself has ceased to function, if we take to heart the words of a writer in the New York *Evening Post*. With a disconcerting gesture he sends the younger generation "back to its muttons" with the admonition to "attend to its most pressing business, which is to create." Literature must go a-begging if they do not soon look up. It seems not enough to "dislike Tennyson," "believe in realism," "read De Gourmont," and disclaim responsibility for the war, which this writer sees as the hall-marks of the younger generation. The warning that is offered our youngsters must sound like a sort of knell: "The younger generation must pay its debt to time before it grows much older or go down among expectations unrealized." They have no small burden to bear in the face of the "uncounted hoards of the youthful in appearance who support the movies, are stolidly conservative in the colleges, never heard of De Gourmont, and have forgotten the war." So from this diagnosis, we must infer that the younger generation are far from a unity. To prove that their high peaks are not conspicuous the writer sets before them the older generation—"what actually it is, and who in reality they are":

"The general impression seems to be that they are the Victorians, they are Howells and his contemporaries, they are the men and women who created the family magazine, invented morality, revived Puritanism, and tried to impose evolution on a society that preferred devolution by international combat. But these men are all dead, or have ceased writing. They are not *our* older generation. It is true that they are famous and so convenient for reference, but it is not accurate nor fair to drag them from their graves for purposes of argument.

"The true older generation, of which one seldom hears in current criticism except in terms of abuse, remains to be discovered, and we herewith announce its personnel, so that the next time the youthful writer excoriates it in the abstract all may know just whom he means. Among the older generation in American literature are H. L. Mencken and Mrs. Edith Wharton, Booth Tarkington and Stuart P. Sherman, Miss Amy Lowell and Mr. Frank Moore Colby, Robert Frost and Edwin Arlington Robinson, Vachel Lindsay and Carl Sandburg, Mrs. Gerould and Professor William Lyon Phelps, Edgar Lee Masters and the editors of *The Literary Review*, Joseph Hergesheimer and most of the more radical editors of New York. Here is this group of desiccated Victorians, upholders of the ethics of *Mr. Pickwick*, and the artistic theories of Bulwer-Lytton. Here are the bogies of outworn conservatism, numbered like a football team. Mark their names, and know from now on that most of the books that you have supposed were solid in artistry and mature in thought, tho perhaps novel in tone or in method, were written by the older generation.

"Perhaps when the younger generation pretend to confuse their immediate predecessors with Ruskin and Carlyle, with Browning, Emerson, Hawthorne, Longfellow, and Matthew Arnold, they are merely strategic. For it is still dangerous to assault the citadels of the great Victorians with no greater books than the youthful volumes of 1918–1921, no matter how many breaches the war has left in the walls of their philosophy. It is far easier to assume that they are still alive in pallid survival, and to attack a hypothetic older generation, which, representing nothing real, can therefore not strike back."

It must be a sad blow to the youngsters, burdened with their responsibilities, to hear its generation summed up thus:

"It is vigorous, prolific, and, to our judgment, full of promise, but so far has done little or nothing not summarized in these words. It must pay its debt to time before it grows much older, or go down among expectations unrealized. It has few hours to waste upon attacking an older generation which, as it is described, does not exist except in youthful imagination, a generation actually of the middle-aged which in the meantime is bearing the burden of invention, creation, revolution in art while the youngsters are talking."

THE ILLS OF WELLS

WHETHER MR. WELLS WILL EMERGE as the Playboy of the Conference the further development of his case will decide. He came as a reporter and he remained as a censor, particularly of France, with opinions so "indecorously" exprest that the London *Daily Mail* relinquished his services. "Tell Wells that the anti-French bias of his recent articles is destroying their value in this country and in France, and they are thereby falling very far below the magnificent promise of his first articles, which I think was one of the best newspaper articles ever published." So ran the message from the editor of *The Daily Mail* to its special correspondent in Washington. Wells replied that he couldn't change his opinions; and the answer was: "Tell Wells I am not asking him to change his opinions but to express them more decorously with regard to France." The exchange did not seem to mend matters and Mr. Wells's articles ceased appearing in *The Daily Mail*. Newspaperdom both here and in England were amazed. "It is the most extraordinary chapter in the history of editors and contributors I can recall," says a writer in the London *Evening Standard:*

"What interest can the public conceivably have in the correspondence of editor and contributor? It is the very essence of such correspondence that it should be regarded as confidential. The whole value of Mr. Wells's opinions consisted in fact that they were Mr. Wells's. Some people agree with Mr. Wells, others are violently at variance with him, but the great number of people who care very little for what *The Daily Mail* thinks on any subject care a great deal for what Mr. Wells thinks on every subject, and it would be quite fatal from Mr. Wells's standpoint if the idea gained currency that his views were colored by editorial suggestions at any time."

The New York *World*, which engaged Mr. Wells, told him to "write what he regarded as truth" and reminded *The Mail* that they were but sub-contractors, saying in a telegram, as their columns inform us:

"In what circumstances did *The Mail* assume to attempt to give instructions to Wells, who is writing for the *World*, not *The Mail*? *The Mail* has been guilty of grave discourtesy and one that the *World*, and no doubt Mr. Wells, resents. Any communications with Mr. Wells are to be made through this paper. We must insist that you refrain from further communication except through us.

"Mr. Wells is under the same instructions every member of the *World* staff is, which are that there are no instructions beyond the obligation to write the truth as he sees, with no leaning one way or the other because of any implied position of the paper's editorial policy. The *World's* news columns have no policy except the publication of the truth.

"With regard,

"THE NEW YORK WORLD."

When the matter reached this stage, the London *Star* comments:

"It now appears when the editor of *The Daily Mail* took upon himself to 'tell Wells to moderate his tone in regard to France' he was guilty of a great piece of presumption, inasmuch as he merely held a kind of right to second publication of Mr. Wells's Washington articles, which were written for the New York *World*. Incidentally, the *World* lays down a very sound conception of journalistic ethics."

The Manchester *Guardian* thought France could hardly take offense, however frankly Mr. Wells exprest his views, since "French publicists have never hesitated to express themselves with all point and sting about the British Government and Premier when they disagreed with our actions." But Mr. Ferdinand Tuohy cables from Paris to the *World* another view, quoting Jacques Bainville, the foremost writer on international policies, to this effect:

"It must always be remembered that Wells is a Socialist. Who are France's greatest enemies all over the world if not the Socialists and Liberals generally? Our greatest friends in all countries are the reactionaries. In England the newspaper most friendly to us is the *Morning Post*, the journal of the British reactionaries.

"Mr. Wells gets his views of France from *Humanité* and other of our Socialist papers. His ideas are not new, but at least forty years old.

"I have the greatest admiration for him as a novelist, but his ideas on politics are only worthy of being consigned to the waste basket. He is out of his right place in Washington. It is just as if France had sent Jules Verne to do political journalism when he was at the height of his fame.

"The great part of hostility to France in the Anglo-Saxon world is traceable to Mr. Wells's non-conformist upbringing. The case of Premier Lloyd George is exactly similar to that of the writer. To people who preach in chapels it always seems peculiarly easy to find grievances against France."

In accord with this, too, is Auguste Gauvain, editor of the *Journal des Débats*, who regards Wells as "no reporter at all," but "a romancer who is full of ideas, but gets carried away with them." The *Petit Parisian* bought the French rights to the Wells articles, but also ceased publication, as Senator Paul Dupuy, its owner, explains,

"on account of the flagrant bias against France that they showed. The incident raises a most important question. The very growing responsibility of the press on international politics renders ill-considered, exaggerated pushing of ideas extremely dangerous."

To point this quarrel we quote a paragraph from Mr. Wells's article in the New York *World* on the day following Premier Briand's address:

"The plain fact of the case is that France is maintaining a vast Army in the face of a disarmed world and she is preparing energetically for fresh warlike operations in Europe and for war under sea against Great Britain. To excuse this line of action M. Briand unfolded a fabulous account of the German preparation for a renewal of hostilities; every soldier in the small force of troops allowed to Germany is an officer or non-commissioned officer, so that practically the German Army can expand at any moment to millions, and Germany is not morally disarmed because Ludendorff—M. Briand quoted him at some length—is still writing and talking militant nonsense.

"Even M. Briand has to admit that the present German Government is honest and well-meaning, but it is a weak Government. It is not the real thing. The real Germany is the Germany necessary for M. Briand's argument. And behind Germany is Russia. He conjured up a great phantom of Soviet Russia which would have conquered all Europe but for the French Armies and Poland. That iniquitous attack of Poland upon Russia last May was, he assured his six quiet-eyed auditors and the rest of us, a violent invasion of Western civilization by Russia.

"'There were those in Germany,' he said, in a voice to make our flesh creep, 'who beckoned them on.' The French had saved us from that. The French Army, with its gallant Senegalese, was the peacemaker and guardian of all Europe.

"One listened incredulous. One waited still incredulous to hear it over again from the interpreter. Yes, we were confirmed; he really had said that. Poor, exhausted Russia, who saved Paris, desiring nothing but to be left alone; bled white, starving, invaded by a score of subsidized adventurers; invaded from Esthonia, from Poland, from Japan, in Murmansk, in the Crimea, in the Ukraine, on the Volga, incessantly invaded, it is this Russia which has put France on the offensive-defensive!"

THE JOURNALISTIC WELLS,

Whose reports from the Conference have set the newspaper caldron boiling.

Apparently Mr. Wells's behavior need have surprized nobody, for before he ever began to speak everybody must have known what was to be expected of him. This seems to be the assumption of one of Mr. Mark Sullivan's letters to the New York *Evening Post:*

"Of course, Mr. Wells is not really going to 'report' the Conference. It would be a most uneconomical use of genius for him to do so. Mr. Wells has a set of ideas about the future relations of the nations with one another which he believes in with exalted ardor. He has also a body of readers which composes a following probably larger than is possest by any other English or American writer. Obviously, what Mr. Wells is going to do is to use the pulpit from which to preach these ideas. In this rôle the presence of H. G. Wells outside the Conference door is fully as important an event as the presence of any one statesman who is going to be inside. Mr. Wells is a very great man. To say that he is the greatest of living writers of English is, perhaps, a loose and indolent way of describing him; but it is a description with which those who agree far out-number those who disagree. To say that Mr. Wells is in Washington to report what is going to be said and done by, let us say, Arthur Balfour, would reflect a conspicuous defeat in the sense of relative values. A more accurate picture of the true proportion of things would be to have Mr. Balfour acting as stenographer to Mr. Wells."

PROHIBITION UNDER THE FIRE OF RIDICULE

"THE UNITED STATES is falling off the water wagon," declares an investigator who has quested through the country for information, hobnobbed with bootleggers, talked with enforcement agents, and followed some of the well-traveled rum routes which to-day lace the country in a thoroughly organized traffic. Blame for this state of affairs is laid largely to the fact that prohibition has become the nation's chief butt of ridicule. It is in danger of being laughed out of court. The indications are that "we have come to the last test of prohibition in the United States," writes William G. Shepherd in the *Cosmopolitan Magazine*. Mr. Shepherd was especially employed by this magazine to gather information on the extensiveness of bootlegging, and he reports that "studying the stages through which we have passed, any investigator who follows the liquor trail through the United States to-day as I have, who feels public opinion, and then dips into the bootlegger's world to converse with its hardy, daredevil, but richly repaid members, must realize that unless there is shortly a change of sentiment in the United States, prohibition is done for."

Photos by courtesy of the "Cosmopolitan," New York.

WHISKY CARRIERS ANCHORED BY ENFORCEMENT AGENTS.

Small craft like these run the gantlet daily to smuggle whisky into the United States.

Rum-running and bootlegging, we are told, have become an industry which makes millionaires almost overnight. It is said to be possible to get whisky anywhere in the United States. Near the Atlantic seaboard the law is so easily evaded that whisky costs only three times its pre-prohibition price. Leaks which revenue officers and enforcement agents are unable to plug extend all along the Canadian and Mexican borders, and along the Gulf Stream runs daily a cargo of intoxicants which dribbles all through the country. Open and flagrant mockery of the law helps make all this possible, and if this joking stage is the last and final stage through which the law is to pass, says this investigator, "then prohibition has been laughed out of court, in the old American fashion, and the United States is going to be wet, tho saloonless. The fourth stage, if there be one—and there is every reason for an observer who has scoured the country as I have to believe that there will be a fourth stage—will have few laughs in it." Ten years hence somebody will be drinking alcohol in the United States. "Whether it will be all of us or only a few of us depends, at this very moment, on how the every-day man in the United States—the man who wanted his home dry and was willing to go dry himself—regards the prohibition law and its enforcement. Judges may interpret its horns off, but he can laugh it to pieces."

We must admit that the situation is very grave, observes *The Christian Statesman*, organ of the National Reform Association, declaring that "the American people are on trial as certainly as is the Eighteenth Amendment," and that "America will sink decidedly in the moral scale in the eyes of the world, if prohibition is nullified." Little discernment is required to discover that recently "the American people have become the victims of a country-wide system of propaganda in favor of the liquor traffic," asserts *Zion's Herald* (Methodist). This attempt to mold public opinion, it says, proceeds by subtle suggestion and indirection. "News items chronicling the failures of prohibition in various localities, reports of a tremendous increase in the use of narcotic drugs as a result of the dry movement, assertions as to the 'breakdown' of the courts because of the multitudes of violators, stories and interviews showing that 'there is more liquor drunk now than before we had prohibition,' and other similar pieces of newspaper intelligence help to poison the thinking of the American public." Criticizing the spirit of jocularity being excited against the law, *The Herald* declares:

"The situation indicates a plain duty for every Christian. Instead of calmly enduring these floods of misstatement, abuse, and ridicule of the temperance reform, which stands for the highest welfare of the race, earnest, thinking men and women should protest against the propaganda in the name of respectability and righteousness. Editors of newspapers ought to be challenged to reveal the source of their information when manifestly misleading statements appear in their journals. Cartoons slandering preachers and temperance reformers should bring letters of rebuke from decent people, with the warning that the guilty journal must not repeat such presentations. A little robust reaction from the readers of publications that have become channels for the distribution of propaganda created by the liquor forces will speedily open the eyes of easy-going editors and publishers to the folly of lending themselves to the nefarious business of espousing the cause of intemperance.

"Ridiculing prohibition, however, has wider implications than those involved in the attempt to nullify temperance legislation. Let newspaper writers, cartoonists, vaudeville players, and moving picture actors, in league with the actual breakers of the Volstead Law, continue their attempts to make a joke out of prohibition and they will succeed in undermining respect for all law. Already, in these United States, there is too little regard for moral and civic authority, accompanied by a growing tendency to consider an act in violation of law legitimate, provided the perpetrator is not caught. There may be too much autocracy in Europe, and too much servility on the part of the common people, but even to-day on the Continent, war-torn as it is, men and women have a more wholesome respect for law than do the vast majority of Americans. The miners and sappers of the liquor traffic are at work here on the very foundations of our liberty. By the use of money and by their blatant disregard for the will of the majority, they are promoting a state of open anarchy.

"It is the duty of church people and all lovers of decency to educate, if possible, these enemies of freedom in the manners of respectable society, which requires that the desires of the individual be surrendered if necessary for the sake of the well-being of the majority in the group. If, however, these lovers of liquor cannot be trained into worthy citizenship, then they must be restrained and kept from doing harm. This coercion is also the business of a virile Christianity."

Whether Prohibition can be made to work "depends largely upon the support of public sentiment," says Bishop William Lawrence, of Massachusetts, in a symposium published in *The Churchman* (Episcopal). "Persistent education of the people in the facts and improved conditions wrought by prohibition will help much." In the same symposium Clinton S. Quin, bishop coadjutor of Texas, declares that the attitude of the clergy on "the prevalent evasion of the Prohibition Amendment should, without a shadow of a doubt, be one of clear-cut, emphatic, strong and fearless support, without a suspicion of weakness or equivocation."

MOONSHINERS FIND NEW USE FOR THE ATTIC.

Wily "hooch" makers keep Prohibition agents running from cellar to roof to ferret out their stills.

THE NEED FOR PERSONAL DISARMAMENT—Murder decreased in the United States last year, "but not enough to brag about," and the need for individual disarmament goes without saying. While peaceful collectively, this nation, says the New York *Herald*, "is over-much militant individually in some regions." Dr. Frederick L. Hoffman, statistician of the Prudential Insurance Company, estimates, we are told, that there were 9,000 murders in the United States in 1920, or slightly fewer than in 1919. A glance over the homicide record of the last twenty years is discouraging, admits the *Herald* in thus summarizing Dr. Hoffman's report:

"In the thirty-one cities of which Dr. Hoffman keeps track, the average homicide rate for each 100,000 of population has risen from 5 to 8.5. Memphis retains the lead it has held for years, altho it fell from 70 homicidal deaths in 100,000 of population—its record just before the war—to 63.4. Memphis is followed on the list by other Southern cities where negro populations are large; Savannah, 44; Atlanta, 40; Charleston, 36. Baltimore, with 7, is the most peaceful of Southern cities.

"The safest of the thirty-one cities is Rochester, with a rate of 1.3, but Reading is close behind with 1.8. New York has 5.9 homicides in each 100,000 of her people. Philadelphia's rate is about the same. Milwaukee, with 3; Newark, with 3.4; Buffalo, with 4.1, are in the moderate class.

"There are wide contrasts in the homicide rates of the States. Maine is the most law-abiding, with only 1.5 homicides yearly in 100,000 people. New Hampshire and Vermont are next. The darkest record is that of Mississippi, where the rate is 19. Of all the Northern States Montana is reddest, her rate being 13.

"Some American cities, like Memphis and Savannah, should confer among themselves on the limitation of individual armament."

HOMES BETTER THAN ORPHAN ASYLUMS

NORMAL FAMILY LIFE for dependent children is far better than institutional upbringing, according to a recent experiment carried out in Ohio, and the change, in addition, represented a financial saving to the community. When the children's home in Hancock County, Ohio, became too ramshackle for further use, the State Division of Charities suggested, as it had often suggested before, we are told, that the boarding-out system be tried. An ordinary dwelling in Findlay, the county seat, was rented as a receiving home, and boarding homes were secured for the little inmates through the efforts of a visitor, after a thorough, personal examination as to their fitness. The success of the experiment, writes Mary Irene Atkinson, of the Ohio Department of Public Welfare, in *The Survey* (New York), was at once proved in the better health of the children, and was hailed by former doubters as a great step forward in the rearing of these wards of the State. The writer quotes from a commendatory letter from the president of the county board of trustees, who had been possest of the "institutional habit," written to the Department of Public Welfare, from which we give this extract:

"You should hear our doctor. He told me only two days ago that he hoped a new orphans' home would never be built. We told him it would not be, if our board had anything to say about it. He said, 'When you first started this scheme last January, I thought it was the darndest plan I ever heard of, and I was about ready to quit looking after the children. I thought I could not possibly do it if they were scattered all over. But I am simply delighted with the results. The children are so different. They act just like other boys and girls now. They come to my office and I can do much better by them. Now that we have finished our routine of reexaminations and corrections for the year, I can see the greatest difference in the physical condition of the children, as well as their more normal social reactions. I hope to live to see the day that the big institution which houses normal children will be a dead proposition.'"

The school work of all the children also showed a marked improvement, says the writer. Instead of going to the same school building, the "orphans" were scattered through the various school systems of the city, and the new contact and the breaking up of the institutional group was found to be a tremendous advantage. "The stranger who came into the school-room could not possibly distinguish the dependent children from the others." As for the health of the children the writer says that—

By courtesy of "The Continent," Chicago.

THE YOUNG SHAREHOLDERS OF NEW YORK COMMUNITY CLUB ENJOYING THEIR OWN BACKYARD.

"In August, 1920, when the nurse from the Institution Inspection Bureau assisted the local physician in making physical examinations of the children it was found that 48 per cent. were of normal weight. In July following, 72 per cent. were of normal weight. While there were changes in population, the type of children being cared for was practically the same. The food under the old régime was wholesome and the change in nutrition is due not so much to food as to better living conditions and individual care and attention.

"The boarding-out plan has not interfered with finding free homes. The visitor is continually investigating applications of prospective foster families. Some of the boarding homes have developed into free homes."

A GIRLS' INVESTMENT IN THEMSELVES

THE MOTHERHOOD OF THE NATION to-morrow depends on the girls of to-day, and that is the idea behind the Girls' Community Club in New York City—a club in which every girl is a shareholder and a director. The girls—three hundred of them—govern themselves, their home, their business and their social life, and have all sorts of privileges which they could not enjoy singly or unaided. Knowing that cumbersome government is slow-moving and unsatisfactory, and that in these days of intellectual freedom there is much casting of yokes, writes Ada Patterson in *The Continent* (Presbyterian), this club made its constitution a brief one and its by-laws are nearly wordless. "It tolerates no 'lights out' laws, no 'Home at 10' tyranny," so that the girls may stay to the last act when they go to a movie. Operated something like a Christian republic, says Miss Patterson:

"It is an upright, eye-to-eye, shoulder-straight government. Its declaration of independence is: 'We believe in respect for ourselves, for each other, in winning it from the world.' No institution, no patronized 'home,' no 'beneficiary of my bounty,' is the club, but a paying proposition yielding, according to the season and conditions, from 4 to 10 per cent. on the investment, a fact which would cause any business man to assume the square-shouldered, frank-eyed attitude of the republic of girls."

The organization was founded about two years ago by Miss Cornelia Marshall, with the aid of several wealthy women of New York interested in the problem presented by the city girl whose pleasures and privileges are limited by the lightness of her purse. Then "girls who had fought the fight for health and sustenance at—let us say, inadequate—boarding-houses, or in hopeless rooming-houses and 'eating out,' filled the sunny, airy rooms, strolled the rear balconies, overflowed upon the large gardens at the back, breakfasted, lunched and dined in the appetizing cafeteria, slept upon clean, fresh beds that wooed sleep." The joy of possession was followed by a sense of responsibility:

"It was their home, but they must manage it. They must make it pay. Accordingly, they formed a council and divided into committees. The entertainment committee arranged evening entertainments, including dances at the club. There were parlors in which they might receive their men friends. No more street strolling nor park lingerings in pursuit of those confidential chats that make for understanding. Dignity was to be added to their romances. No longer dread of the casual passer-by who, catching their mutual gaze, says with cruel distinctness: 'Another pair of spoons!' The parlors had pleasant corners and alcoves in which privacy was assured.

"The library committee learned the tastes of the club members, arranged a list of suitable books and placed them on the waiting shelves. It sternly guarded its new books, threatening a fine for loss or defacements. The garden committee cut the grass, planted, weeded and watered the flower plots. The club council presided seriously over all. It met, heard reports of the committees, recommended ways and means. Last winter it was determined to increase its own board rates.

"The club developed the spirit of a large and harmonious family. There are clerical workers, private secretaries and stenographers, librarians, students, milliners, textile designers, saleswomen, social workers, waist models, dress models, kindergarten teachers, illustrators, a dressmaker, a messenger and a dramatic coach—all enjoying the benefit for from $9 to $12.50 a week."

The girls' club is supplemented by a club for landladies known as The Association to Promote Proper Housing for Girls, which is kept interested and up-to-date by frequent lectures on sanitation and decorations, furnishings and diet. Two model rooming-houses next to the bureau are always open for interested inspection. Standards are kept always to the front—cleanliness, suitable furnishings, ample heat, telephone in the house or near by. Boarding-houses and rooming-houses are thus classified by the association:

"A. Provides accommodations which can be recommended to the person of critical taste. It must be in charge of a woman of ability and excellently kept. It must have a parlor for the use of its guests.

"B. A comfortable place for an average person; must also be in charge of a responsible person. It may or may not have a parlor, but only adults will be sent if there is none.

"C. A comfortable place for the business girl or woman. The requirements for a responsible person in charge and for a parlor are emphasized, and if there is no parlor only adult women are sent."

MADE BY THE MAKERS OF CAMPBELL'S SOUPS

How good they taste!

Added to the rich, full bean flavor you like so much, is the spicy tang from juicy tomatoes! When you eat Campbell's Beans you completely satisfy your hunger and enjoy a deliciously tasty dish. Beans of best quality are slow-cooked until thoroughly digestible and wholesome. And then made doubly appetizing by their famous tomato sauce.

12 cents a can

Except in Rocky Mountain States and in Canada

Campbell's BEANS

LOOK FOR THE RED-AND-WHITE LABEL

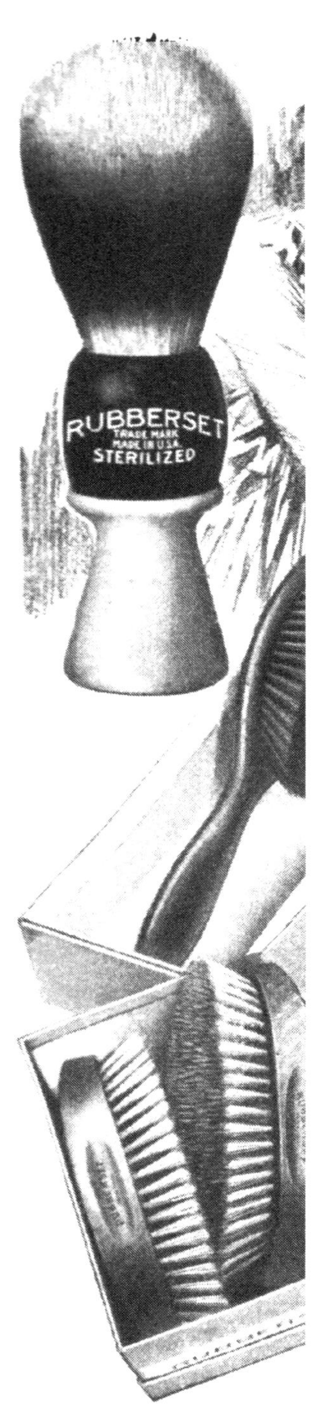
RUBBERSET
TRADE MARK
MADE IN U.S.A.
STERILIZED

RU
Every bristle gri

RUBBERSET
TRADE MARK
MADE IN U.S.A.
STERILIZED
Rubberset Brushes—
as welcome as the day itself,
as lasting as its memories.
Here is the wide assortment at your disposal:
World's Standard Shaving Brushes
A complete range in Badger Hair and French Bristle, from $1.00 to $15.00 each, to suit your fancy and your pocketbook. Each one in handsome gift box.
Sanitary
Hair Brushes
Black Walnut and Myrtle Backs. Regular models, $2.00 to $6.00 each. Military models, $2.50 to $10.00 per pair.
Everlasting
Nail Brushes
Black Walnut Backs, $1.00, $1.25, and $1.50 each, or White Alberite Backs, $1.75, $2.25, and $2.50 each.
Safety
Tooth Brushes
Imported French Bristle, White Alberite Handles. All sizes, stiffnesses and styles. 35 cents to 60 cents each.
at YOUR store
or postpaid direct on receipt of remittance if your dealer lacks the ones you wish.
RUBBERSET COMPANY
(R. & C. P. Co., Props.)
NEWARK, N.J., U.S.A.
RUBBERSET COMPANY
LIMITED
TORONTO, CANADA
TOOTH BRUSH
NEWARK N.J.

RUBBERSET

Every bristle gripped *everlastingly* in hard vulcanized rubber!!

KATO AS "THE SOUL-MAP OF JAPAN"

A SMALL MAN, "suffering from an embarrassment of riches in the form of bones," sat beside Secretary Hughes in the first of the official carriages that met the Japanese delegation when it arrived at Union Station in Washington. "I watched the scene from amidst the curious mob that packed either side of the driveway," writes Adachi Kinnosuki, the Japanese author and publicist, who is reporting the Arms Conference for the New York *World*. "I watched it with mingled emotion, marveling at the hugeness of responsibility of our envoys, and at the slenderness of the shoulders upon which such stupendous responsibility was resting." One of the correspondent's neighbors remarked, pointing at Admiral Kato: "He doesn't look like he ever had a square meal in his life; looks a bit like the map of Japan." This casual remark of a stranger, says Mr. Adachi, "portrays the ranking member of the Japanese delegation to the Arms Conference much truer than the official biography of Admiral Baron Tomosaburo Kato, Minister of the Navy of Japan, ever thought of doing." This is especially true, we are told, "if the author of the careless remark meant what he did not mean, namely, that in that slender collection of skin and bones we know under the name of Admiral Kato there rests a dauntless spirit that looks like the soul-map of Japan." The writer goes back to Kato's great moment in the Russo-Japanese War:

Photo from Adachi

JAPAN'S ADMIRAL-DELEGATE, WITH HIS SMALL SON.

The head of the Japanese group at the Arms Conference, Admiral Tomosaburo Kato, was Togo's chief of staff in that great battle which destroyed the Russian Baltic fleet. He is said to be taciturn and unemotional, but determined.

It was on the 27th of May and the year was 1905—perhaps the most fateful year in the life of the New Nippon. The *Mikasa* was leading the combined fleet of Japan out of a Korean base athwart the Korean Strait to intercept the Baltic Squadron of Russia. Early in the afternoon of the day the leading ships of the Russian fleet blurred the horizon to the port of the Japanese ships. Upon the bridge of the *Mikasa* were two silent figures. One of them was Admiral Togo, the Commander-in-Chief of the Combined Fleet, and the other was his Chief of Staff, the then Rear-Admiral Tomosaburo Kato.

At the sight of the Russians, signals began to fly thick and fast. All the commanding officers of various Japanese ships called for instructions; all of them were impatient for orders, and some of them demanded to know the reason for the delay. Not only did the commanding officers of individual ships of the fleet show their impatience at the delay of the order for immediate course of action, but there were aboard the flagship itself a number of young tacticians among the members of Togo's staff boiling with a hundred suggestions on the plan of battle.

In all this turmoil Admiral Togo stood there on the bridge, as calm, as silent, for all his outward appearances told, as the silhouette of Tsushima, looking on the fateful drama, and not far from the Commander-in-Chief stood his Chief of Staff pale, lean, frail and as silent as his chief. About the only difference between them was that Kato had his arms folded across his breast.

Was Kato to order the Japanese fleet to steer the opposite course to that of the Russians and rake the enemy ships with the port broadsides as they steamed past? Or was he to order our ships to steam in a parallel course and fight the Russians as they made their northward way? Those were the two main lines of action in the minds of almost all the commanding officers with the Japanese fleet. And there stood Kato, with the key of life and death of the entire fleet in his hand—silent and still. And the Russians came on.

Suddenly the folded arms of the Chief of Staff uncoiled themselves; the signal flew and the plan of battle whose daring passed all the understandings of swivel-chair tacticians, passed into history.

And the same silent figure, Mr. Adachi continues, is now in Washington. This time, of course, he is not on the bridge of Togo's famous flagship, "but his country is calling to him once more to decide the course the ship of state is to take in the fateful hour. And the eyes of practically the whole world are upon the silent sailor and his fellow envoys to the Arms Conference."

"What manner of man is this silent sailor?" asks the writer, and thus continues his appreciation:

In the historic town of Hiroshima, on the world-famed Inland Sea of Japan, there is a street called Ohtemachi. And in it is a humble house, incredibly frail for having seen something like three-quarters of a century come and go. It was there in that old house that the child destined for one of the title rôles at the Arms Conference at Washington saw the light of the world. Admiral Kato's sister, in her eighty-second year, still lives there. And this is what she told a reporter the other day about a certain bad boy who happened to be her youngest brother:

"Tomo deskai?" began the old lady. "He lost his father when he was very young. He was reared almost entirely at the hand of his mother. But his mother, too, went soon after. So of us all he deserves the most sympathy. His elder brother, Tanenosuke, was more than seventeen years his senior, and took a fatherly interest in the boy. After the death of the parents, you might say, he was reared almost entirely by his elder brother.

"Naturally enough, he showed the effect of this even while he was a small boy. His brother was noted for his ruggedness of character, a soldier in spirit and by profession. Most likely that was the reason why the child was surprizingly high-spirited and full of mischief and fond of fights, which one would never have suspected from the looks of him.

"I recall the time also when his small fingers would steal along the shelf where tempting morsels of sushi used to be kept and his cheeks would acquire a sudden fullness which did not come from clear conscience and robust health. I shall say this about him, however: He never sulked. He never worried or bored people to extinction with tales of woe or by his obstinacy. Oh, yes, he had temper sometimes, a good deal more than his blood relations would find altogether entertaining. He used to fly into a fit of temper when he came home and found his room in disorder. A curious child in that respect. He always wished to see his own

"That rug simply makes the room—and just think what we've saved!

"I could have paid much more for woven rugs—and they wouldn't have been one bit prettier than my Gold-Seal Art-Rugs!"

Not alone by their colorful patterns have Congoleum *Gold-Seal* Art-Rugs won the favor of the modern housewife.

For these inexpensive floor-coverings are as durable as they are beautiful. They lie perfectly flat without fastening. Being thoroughly waterproof and sanitary, a damp mop cleans them in a quarter the time, with a quarter the effort required by woven rugs.

Popular Sizes—Popular Prices

$1\frac{1}{2}$ x 3 feet	$ .60	3 x $4\frac{1}{2}$ feet	$1.80
3 x 3 feet	1.20	3 x 6 feet	2.40

The rugs illustrated are made only in the sizes below. However, the small rugs can be had in colors to harmonize with them.

6 x 9 feet	$ 9.75	9 x $10\frac{1}{2}$ feet	$16.60
$7\frac{1}{2}$ x 9 feet	11.85	9 x 12 feet	19.00

Prices in the far West average 15% higher than those quoted: in Canada prices average 25% higher. All prices subject to change without notice.

Look for the Gold Seal

The Gold Seal pasted on the face pledges absolute satisfaction, and protects you against inferior imitations. Don't be misled into buying a substitute. Be sure to look for the Gold Seal.

CONGOLEUM COMPANY
INCORPORATED

Philadelphia New York Chicago San Francisco
Dallas Boston Minneapolis Kansas City
Pittsburgh Atlanta Montreal

Keep thes
and we'll All

4 million like him need work now

YOU owe it to the man without a job to find one for him, if you have work that needs to be done.

You owe it to the man without a job, to buy—and buy now—materials that his labor can supply, if you or your business have good use for these materials.

Every extra day's work you cause to be done *now* takes men off the streets.

Every dollar you use *now* for worthwhile purposes puts money into circulation.

Every dollar you put into circulation employs men—checks business depression — hastens business prosperity.

Relieve Unemployment by Maintaining Your Property

Mr. Herbert Hoover, Secretary of Commerce and Chairman of the President's Conference on Unemployment, has rendered a report giving the recommendations of the conference. Please read the sixth clause of that report:

Private houses, hotels, offices, etc., can contribute to the situation by making repairs and alterations and doing cleaning during the winter instead of waiting until spring, when employment will be more plentiful.

The eleventh clause, which deals with the construction industry, contains this:

Considering all branches of the construction industry, more than 2,000,000 people could be employed if construction were resumed.

The findings of the conference showed clearly that acute unemployment can be promptly relieved, *if the public will act.*

Property maintenance presents a large field where *action* will benefit equally both the owners and the unemployed.

You have an interest in or own some kind of property—your home, an automobile, a factory or store—perhaps a railroad.

Neglect of your property means direct loss to you and economic loss to the whole country.

A firmly established principle that applies to the maintenance of practically every kind of property is *surface protection* by means of paint or varnish.

Paint and Varnish NOW!

Winter is as good a time as any for all kinds of interior painting and varnishing. Don't wait 'till spring to have it done. Painting and varnishing done now will relieve unemployment, when relief is most needed, and will save the surface of valuable property.

The paint brush is our greatest weapon against property deterioration and its by-products—dirt, disease, ugliness, depression.

The painter's brush spreads more than paint and varnish. With every stroke it spreads economic maintenance, cleanliness, health, beauty, cheer—the ingredients of prosperity. Put the paint brush to work *now*—this winter—and you will share in a public service to meet the national emergency of unemployment.

* * *

TODAY it costs less to paint than it did. The cost of materials has led in the downward economic trend of manufactured products. But no matter what it costs, the fact remains that it always costs more not to paint than to paint. Rust and rot go on till you check them. The logical time to paint and varnish is NOW.

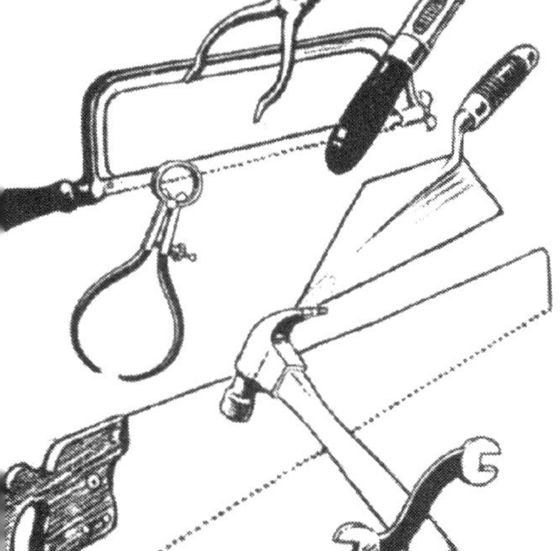

Keep these Busy and we'll All Prosper

SAVE THE SURFACE CAMPAIGN, 507 The Bourse, Philadelphia.
A co-operative movement by Paint, Varnish and Allied Interests whose products and services conserve, protect and beautify practically every kind of property.

"Save the surface and you save all"—Paint & Varnish

PERSONAL GLIMPSES
Continued

write a daily postcard in simple words to one of his grandchildren, or into his cabin for work, an aide summoned by an almost imperceptible glance.

Once a bold spirit requested the Admiral to desert the "go" games and have his photograph taken. He assented with the slightest of nods, stepped out on deck, sat in the chair until all the cameras had clicked, bowed acknowledgment to the fiends' thanks and faded quietly out of the picture.

Each year the Minister states the Navy's needs to each house of the Diet. He is one Minister who has never been entangled in his own statements by the members' rapid fire of questions. The Navy consumes one-fourth of the nation's annual income, but no unnecessary words or wavering in policy by its Minister has ever afforded a loophole for attacks by press or opposition.

The eight-eight program, a Navy of 200 ships, is to be the crowning achievement of a career of half a century, entering the Navy in 1873, when he was a lad of twelve years. The appropriations for all of it have been voted. Next March it will be completed to eight-four, in 1924 to eight-six and in 1928 to eight-eight. If other nations agree, he is willing to give up his life's dream on the eve of its realization. The quiet man's horizon is broad.

HOW HUGHES MEASURES UP WITH THE "VETERAN DIPLOMATS"

IS SECRETARY of State Hughes endeavoring to conceal the fact that he is a great idealist? Men in Washington speak of his "exaltation of spirit" these days, reports a Washington correspondent, who has gathered impressions leading to the conclusion that Mr. Hughes, like President Harding, is being revealed as more of an exponent of high ideals every day. A French newspaper man of long experience commented that President Harding's recent addresses sounded very much like Woodrow Wilson. Harold Phelps Stokes, Washington representative of the New York *Evening Post*, reports that Mr. Hughes, also, is coming to have a suggestion of ex-President Wilson about him. Hughes may be a realist, and insist on putting his policy on the familiar bases of self-interest, economic necessity, and other very realistic matters. Nevertheless, we are told, his ends are much the same as those sought by the repudiated War-President. There is this difference between them, says Mr. Stokes: "Wilson hitched his wagon to a star. Hughes has chosen rather to hitch his star to a wagon." As for the reality of the "exaltation of spirit" shown by the Secretary, Mr. Stokes reports:

I believe it, tho perhaps the Secretary of State himself would not care to have the report credited. He has chosen rather to clothe his purposes in the cloak of realism. But there is such a thing as exaltation of spirit which can refresh the idealism of a leader's purposes without impairing in one whit that realism of its methods, and it is that exaltation which I believe fills Mr. Hughes to-day.

Mr. Hughes has a fancy for the homely metaphors of the card-table. He knows games where the players put all their cards on the table, and he knows games where you hold them close to your chin. He likes to talk of these two kinds and of their comparative merits, and you would think from his talk that he was an expert at them. I once heard him, in a most informal way—apropos of reparations or mandates or some other controversy in which the United States was involved at the time—characterize the general purpose of the United States as "a fair deal all around, with Uncle Sam sitting in for what he's entitled to."

That is not the way Woodrow Wilson would have exprest it. Perhaps it could not safely be left to history as a formal expression of the country's purposes. It would, for instance, give the impression of a group of men dividing up the spoils—an impression which was far from Mr. Hughes's mind, I am sure. Then, too, while reflecting his lawyer's sense of a client's rights, the quotation falls short of a full expression of Mr. Hughes's own exalted purposes, which he has chosen—consciously, I believe—to keep always in the background. But it will do well enough as a rough-and-ready slogan of the Administration's attitude, and one perhaps peculiarly responsive to what seems to be the country's mood.

But the star is there, I firmly believe. I believe while Mr. Hughes has chosen deliberately to talk about oil, and cables, and armaments, he has been thinking of international law, and international tribunals, and international cooperation, and international good-will—yes, even of international association. Let those who will smile at so ingenuous a faith in the ulterior idealistic purposes of an avowed realist like Hughes. Only let the doubters remember what Lord Northcliffe, who is no ingenu, wrote of Hughes when he was here:

"The failures of others may have taught him that the surest way to attain a lofty end is not always to proclaim its loftiness in advance. He may have learned that the presence of a spice of self-interest, national or individual, is often helpful in persuading men of worth and of ethical principles. Hence, perchance, his insistence upon 'interests' of the United States as the main concern of Mr. Harding's Administration. When the full catalog of those 'interests' comes to be made up, there may be found among them such matters as the promotion of good-will among nations, the assurance of peace on the Pacific and the elimination of armaments among the Powers chiefly 'interested.'"

No man who sees Mr. Hughes from day to day, as the Washington correspondents do, can come away from those conferences without marveling at the vigor of the man. I wonder what it is in him that enables him to radiate such energy and assurance. Is it golf? Is it prayer? Is it a consciousness of the rectitude of his own purposes and the conviction of their assured success? I do not know. Perhaps it is all four—with just a dash of calculated policy thrown in. For confidence is contagious.

Remember what he said in his address to the beginners in the consular service: "The man who succeeds in this work in any position where there are a great many burdens and demands is the man who can keep quiet and placid when there is very severe pressure, who can keep his head and intelligence, *at the same time* giving the

Works of the Western Electric Company; the manufacturing department of the Bell System

Economical Equipment

Forty years ago the management of the Bell Telephone System organized for a supply of the apparatus which it foresaw would be required in the development of its new industry—telephone service.

The telephone in some countries is the luxury of the rich, but in America it is used by practically all the people. This universal service is due in large measure to foresight in engineering and manufacture.

Switchboards with millions of parts, other apparatus of highest efficiency, and all necessarily of complex and intricate design, cables and wires and a multitude of technical devices enable our country to lead the world in telephone service.

All this telephone equipment is made in a factory which is recognized throughout the world as having the largest production and the highest standards of workmanship and efficiency.

This factory, controlled through stock ownership by the American Telephone and Telegraph Company, has been for forty years the manufacturing department of the Bell System; with the result that the associated companies secure equipment of the highest development, made of the best materials, produced in accordance with the requirements of the public, and with the certainty of moderate costs.

Economy in the Bell System begins with the manufacture of equipment.

"BELL SYSTEM"

AMERICAN TELEPHONE AND TELEGRAPH COMPANY
AND ASSOCIATED COMPANIES

One Policy, One System, Universal Service, and all directed toward Better Service

PERSONAL GLIMPSES
Continued

too much bald logic about it, and too little understanding. Other instances could be cited.

This may be a weakness, but it is not necessarily a vital one. It can be balanced by Mr. Hughes's strength of character, his extraordinary power of analysis, his broad tolerance of the other fellow's point of view, and his political talents, which, apart from this single angle, are of no mean order. With consummate skill he has steered the foreign policy of the United States in such a course that while the strongest partizans of the League of Nations, on the one hand, and the irreconcilables, on the other, may be alike dissatisfied, in the main he has the whole country behind him and the nations of the world ready to cooperate with him.

CRIMINALS AND FAKERS BETRAYED BY THEIR SKINS

THE human skin, under the stress of emotion, alters its ability to conduct an electric current. Thus, with an appropriate detector, we may tell real emotion from false, test a suspected criminal by his inner reactions, and study the responses of different individuals and different races to injury, pain or even threats. This, at any rate, is what we are told by Ronald Campbell Macfie, who writes in *The Chronicle* (London). This variation in the electrical resistance of the skin under the influence of emotion was first noticed, Mr. Macfie tells us, by the French physiologist, Féré, in 1888, and has since been studied by other scientists, offering a fascinating field for research. He goes on:

> The variation, sometimes termed the "galvanic reflex," is of value as a criterion of emotional manifestations, not only in neurasthenic subjects, but in all kinds of people, under all kinds of conditions. Emotions are notoriously deceptive. The histrionic can simulate emotions suitable to any situation, and can deceive not only onlookers, but also themselves. The hysterical can make "much ado about nothing" with a great deal of plausibility. The stoical can suppress all outward manifestations of feeling.
>
> But histrionics, hysteria, humbug, hypocrisy are all betrayed by the skin. Louis XVI, surrounded by a fierce mob, challenged: "Am I afraid? Feel my pulse?" But tho his pulse might have been steady, his skin would probably have told another story.
>
> The pseudo-poet may roll his eye in a fine frenzy, but the little galvanometer-needle will prick him like a gasbag. The romantic lover may sigh like a furnace, but the still finger will point scorn at him. The tub-thumper may thump his tub, but unless he be sincere the needle will not budge.
>
> It seems, indeed, quite certain that every genuine emotion, whether due to physical or psychical causes, produces an alteration in the electrical conductivity of the skin which can be registered by a galvanometer.
>
> By no possible effort can a man suffering from genuine emotion inhibit the reflex and steady the needle. On the other hand, no simulated or imaginary emotion, however violent in its outward manifestations, makes the needle even wobble, for fictitious emotions are not even skin-deep.

Dr. Golla, of St. George's Hospital, who has made a special study of the skin reflex, states in a recent lecture:

> The reflex can not be inhibited by any voluntary effort on the part of the subject. I have sought for evidence of inhibition, either of the response to physical or verbal stimuli in over a hundred subjects, but have never met with evidence of any direct voluntary power either to inhibit or modify the reflex.
>
> On the other hand it is impossible to evoke it by simulation of affective states, such as fictitious rage, nor can the mere recitation of emotional poetry, no matter with what emphasis it be declaimed, produce a reaction, unless by some chance a phrase acts as a stimulus to evoke some association with a personal experience of affective import.

As illustration of these statements, Dr. Golla quotes a case:

> One young soldier, suffering from hysterical contracture of the foot, broke down during an examination; tears rolled down his cheeks, he addrest his dead brother in language savoring of a South London melodrama: he asked why he himself had not been killed in his brother's place so that the favorite son might have been left to comfort his poor old father, and all the time whilst he wailed and wept, the spot of light from the galvanometer mirror remained steady.

The writer in *The Chronicle* goes on:

> We have accordingly in the galvanic reflex an unfailing means of discriminating between fictitious and genuine emotion; and it is possible for a man to test even his own emotions by testing the galvanic response of his own skin, and to measure them by the swing of the galvanometer needle.
>
> It must be noted, however, that tho there can never be genuine emotion without an equivalent galvanic reflex, and tho the galvanic reflex is always lacking when emotion is fictitious, yet there can be galvanic reflex in the absence of genuine emotion, since it is found that a stimulus which has once produced emotion and the reflex, may, on repetition, reproduce the reflex without reproducing the emotion. But this qualification detracts little from the value of the criterion.
>
> It is probable that many interesting objective measurements of character and mentality might be made by the galvanometer. For instance, the comparative response in different races and different individuals to physical injury, to insult, to actual pain, and to threat of pain. There is reason, indeed, to believe that it might be possible even to measure imagination and intelligence by this reflex, for Miss Waller tested the skin responses of 70 students to a series of standardized stimuli, and found that the students whose responses were most active made most marks at a subsequent examination. But more investigations in these directions are required.
>
> Whatever the practical uses of the physiological phenomenon may be, it is at least a most interesting illustration of the intimate relationship between mind and body.

HOW TO KEEP YOUNG IN WINTER

WE grow old in winter rather than in summer, says the medical correspondent of the London *Times*. Winter exercise is therefore especially important for the middle-aged. Many an hour of ill-health, he assures us, may be spared us by such exercise, properly taken. "Spurts" should be avoided, as likely to be injurious. Swimming, games, home exercise—all are good, when taken in moderation. The difficulty is, says the writer, that at the very period when exercise is most necessary it becomes most difficult to obtain. The business man must leave home at an hour which makes early morning exercise practically impossible. When he returns home again it is already growing dark or quite dark. Thus his opportunities for outdoor recreation are practically withdrawn altogether, except at the week-ends. Our further quotations are from an abstract in the New York *Times:*

Young people are better off. The majority of them dance once or twice a week, and manage to get in some vigorous exercise on Saturday and Sunday. Sometimes middle-age follows this lead; more often not. In spite of our elderly enthusiasts, dancing is youth's pastime. Adventures into the world are not, generally speaking, to be recommended to the senior members of the community.

Nor is the vigorous Saturday or Sunday a solution that can be called satisfactory. There is too much of the "spurt" element in such exercise. Youth can sustain and benefit from spurts; middle-age had better avoid them. The sudden strain is as likely to do harm as to do good.

Middle-age, indeed, demands above all steadiness and continuity in its recreation. There is so much waste to be got rid of every day. If this is allowed to accumulate to the week-end, the tissues of the body become clogged, symptoms of poisoning show themselves, and it is increasingly difficult to get rid of them. Like a piece of machinery that has been allowed to lie unattended, the mechanism of the body deteriorates.

You can not safely set a piece of machinery going at its top speed and then neglect it for a week and repeat the process.

What then is the middle-aged man to do in the coming months? The answer depends to some extent on his temperament. But more important than temperament is determination.

Some men solve the difficulty by playing a game of squash three or four times a week. They simply "take" the necessary time, and they are fortunate in belonging to clubs which have the necessary accommodation. Other men adopt swimming, and make a point of going to their baths nearly every afternoon for half an hour.

This latter method has a great deal to recommend it. There is little or no danger of catching cold if ordinary care is exercised, and the swimmer obtains really thorough exercise of all his muscles. He obtains this, too, without strain, for the water supports the weight of his body.

The chief difficulty is time. It is often difficult to get away, and often, in cold weather, the tendency is to shirk the exercise. This is a matter which must be left to the individual. It can be said, however, that an hour spent in this way is never an hour wasted; on the contrary, it may save many an hour of ill-health.

MIDWINTER BATHING ON THE BEACH AT WAIKIKI, HAWAII'S FAMOUS SEASIDE RESORT.

THIS SEASON'S WINTER TRAVEL will be attended by several important developments in water and land transportation. Among these are increased steamship accommodations for regular routes, and the return of that pre-war favorite with many travelers, the special "cruise." On both land and water lines there will be a saving in the cost due to the removal of the government tax.

Unusual varieties of cruises to the tropics are now available, and for European tourists Mediterranean cruises have been restored. Steamship service to South American ports also is improved. More ample accommodations for meeting the heavy winter traffic to Hawaii are offered. Coastwise sailings are restored practically to pre-war days.

One effect of the new Revenue Bill is the repeal of the tax on transportation, which means a reduction of eight per cent. on the purchase of tickets after January 1st. It is estimated that this reduction will result in a saving on the American public's travel bill for 1922 of approximately eighty million dollars. For instance, a ticket from New York to San Francisco with lower berth will cost $11.54 less after the removal of this tax. Another lowering of travel expenses is due to the marked trend toward reduced dining-car prices.

On this and following pages we present a brief survey of trips and vacation lands mainly within warm winter latitudes. While the north country with its frosty tang, its snowshoe, ski, skate and toboggan appeals to many who visit the carnivals at such headquarters of the Frost King, as Saranac and Lake Placid in the Adirondacks, Quebec and Montreal in Canada, or Mt. Rainier National Park, open to the public this winter for the first time with dog-sleds, reindeer sledges and Alpine sports for the public, the majority of winter tourists migrate to warmer climates.

A digest of only the more important of these winter playgrounds with brief glimpses of their attractions and directories of routes can be given here. If these suggestions arouse interest in any particular place or trip, detailed information should be obtained either directly from transportation or resort managements, or through the leading well-equipped tourist agencies. Cares and annoyances in travel often may be avoided by obtaining complete bookings through these experienced agencies, or by joining their especially arranged tours under escort.

Another convenience for the tourist traveling in our country or foreign lands, are the travelers' checks, issued for our own and foreign currency, and obtainable from express offices and some of the larger banks. These checks obviate trouble over exchange rates, and are acceptable in every part of the world.

WINTER PLAYGROUNDS IN THE SOUTHLAND

From the Virginia capes to the Gulf lagoons of Texas extend winter playgrounds in infinite variety. Every range of climate is available from temperate to sub-tropical and tropical. Every location is provided from seashore to mountain, lake or river.

To these regions there is a great migration from colder parts of our country each winter of those seeking comfort, recreation and health. So ample are the facilities for realizing these ends that many families are building winter homes in the Southern and Southwestern States.

The migration from Eastern cities to the South flows through three great rail arteries and connecting lines—the Southern Railway, Seaboard Air Line, and Atlantic Coast Line. Through trains are operated by each of these roads from New York to Washington over the Pennsylvania system.

From the Middle West the important routes to Southern resorts are the Illinois Central, Chicago and Eastern Illinois, Louisville and Nashville, Southern Railway, Queen and Crescent, and its connections, the Big Four and Pennsylvania Lines.

Excellent coastwise steamship service, described elsewhere, is available to or from the Southland.

It is a territory so vast, with resorts so numerous, that only the briefest survey can be presented here. Traveling southward, we meet a series of distinctive resort groups, including the high altitude regions in the southern Alleghanies, the Long Leaf Pine districts, the seaboard cities, and the Gulf coast. Florida is considered separately in another part of these articles.

A stop-over at Washington en route will reward the southbound tourist. The nation's Capital is fairly crowded with points of interest to every American, and there are equally impressive scenes nearby, such as Arlington National Cemetery and Mount Vernon, Washington's home on the Potomac. From the moment the visitor emerges from the magnificent Union Station the city, with its stately Government buildings and their interior executive machinery, claims his attention. The rail routes from the North are the Pennsylvania and Baltimore and Ohio systems.

In the midst of the Alleghanies is the mineral spring region of the Virginias, notable among numerous resorts being Virginia Hot Springs with its famous thermal baths and hydro-therapeutic facilities, and the White Sulphur Springs of West Virginia. "Old White," as the latter was affectionately known by a past generation, was popular in the days when railways had not penetrated these green valleys. Washington, Jefferson and Van Buren were among distinguished visitors. In our own day these resorts are among our most fashionable playgrounds. Fox trots have replaced the hops of crinoline days; the motor has supplanted the carriage; golf provides a modern recreation; stately hotels stand near the sites occupied by taverns a century ago, and the outside world is closely linked by Pullmans over the Chesapeake and Ohio system.

Continuing southward we come to another famous mountain playground designated "The Land of the Sky," of which select Asheville, North Carolina, is the center. With its high altitude, averaging 3,000 feet, the winter climate here is distinguished by bracing and tonic qualities, which delight those who go in for the favorite pastimes—golfing, mountain-climbing and horseback riding. "The Land of the Sky" is reached by the Southern Railway system, as are also Aiken and Augusta, among the South's more fashionable resorts.

Nearer the coast in the Carolinas is the Long Leaf Pine region, made famous by that Mecca of the winter golfer, Pinehurst, and its neighbor, Southern Pines. All winter the disciples of Colonel Bogey flock thither. Indeed, Pinehurst proudly boasts four championship courses, while Southern Pines is supplied with excellent links. The Seaboard Air Line is the direct route to these golf headquarters.

Along the coastline of the middle South are cities which have much charm for the winter tourist, of which Charleston, South Carolina, with its colonial atmosphere, its historical points of interest, including Fort Sumter, its ancient churches, its Isle

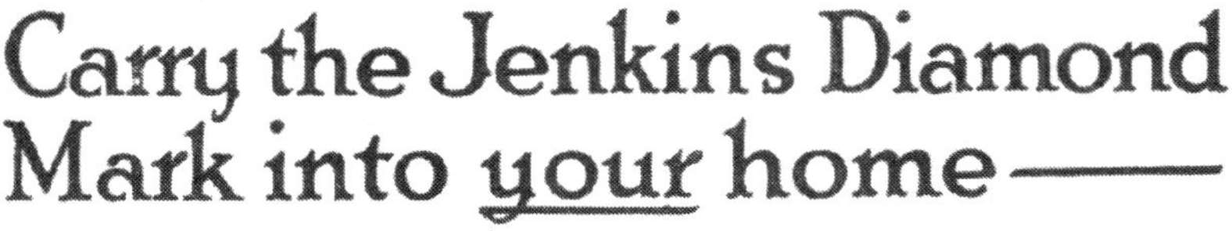

EQUIP your radiators with identified valves that bear the symbol of assured satisfaction—Jenkins "Diamond Mark" Valves. Provide for yourself in your own home the same dependable and lasting service that Jenkins Valves give in thousands of places—power plants, factories, office buildings, hotels, residences, in fact, everywhere that safety, convenience, and economy are planned and secured.

A heating system, no matter how good, can be no better than its valves—trouble is frequently traceable to cheap, light-weight valves. So supply your steam or hot water system with Jenkins heavy, strong, substantial valves. Valves that open easily, close tightly, do not leak, and thus facilitate proper heat control. Enjoy the comforts they assure: the luxury of dressing in a warm room on winter mornings; and coziness throughout the house at all times.

Good, heavy valves are of equal importance to the proper functioning of your plumbing. Throughout your home permit your architect to specify and your contractor to install genuine Jenkins "Diamond Mark" Valves—a recognized standard for over 57 years.

Jenkins Valves are made for all domestic and industrial purposes—guaranteed for the maximum service, not merely the average. At supply houses everywhere.

For engineers, architects, plumbers, steamfitters, executives, and others, data on Jenkins Valves for any purpose. For home owners, interesting plumbing and heating booklets.

JENKINS BROS.

80 White Street . . . . . New York
524 Atlantic Avenue . . . . . Boston
133 No. Seventh Street . . . . . Philadelphia
646 Washington Boulevard . . . . . Chicago

JENKINS BROS., LIMITED
Montreal, Canada. London, England

FACTORIES:
Bridgeport, Conn. Montreal, Canada Elizabeth, N. J.

WINTER TRAVEL
Continued

of Palms, with broad beaches and magnolia gardens, and its country club and Belvidere Links, is one of the most attractive. Savannah, Georgia, with its superb parks, shaded streets, excellent motoring roads, eighteen-hole golf course, modern hotels and places of unusual historic interest, is another. Both cities are on the rail lines of the Atlantic Coast Line, Seaboard Air Line and Southern Railway. Each city also has direct steamer connections with New York. Clyde Line steamships operating between New York and Jacksonville, Florida, call at Charleston en route. This winter the Savannah Line resumes full pre-war service between New York and Savannah and Boston and Savannah. Among Southern ports reached by various divisions of the Merchants and Miners Transportation Company's vessels are Norfolk, Baltimore, Savannah and Jacksonville.

The Gulf Coast of Florida, Alabama, Mississippi, Louisiana and Texas is a winter resort region gaining rapidly in favor and destined soon to become the great American Riviera. The Mississippi River is a natural division between two Gulf Coast regions; the first extending between Tampa, Pensacola, Mobile and New Orleans; the second between New Orleans and the long chain of Texas water-front places.

From Pensacola to New Orleans the coast is paralleled with a series of islands, the shore continuously indented with deep bays and innumerable estuaries. There are many miles of smooth shell roads, shaded by huge magnolias and live oaks, draped with Spanish moss. Back from the sandy beaches stand forests of pine, combining with the salt air to contribute health-giving qualities to the warm, genial climate. The Gulf abounds in gamey fish, including the tarpon, and here are waters most tempting to yachtsmen. In this back country there is excellent hunting. Tampa, Pensacola and Mobile, situated on broad bays, are delightful cities for a winter visit. West of Mobile stretch a long series of resorts including Pascagoula, Ocean Springs, Biloxi (settled by the French two centuries ago), Mississippi City, Gulfport, Long Beach, Pass Christian and Bay St. Louis, near New Orleans. Tampa is on the Seaboard Air Line and Atlantic Coast Line; Mobile on the Southern Railway and the Louisville and Nashville; while the resorts between Mobile and New Orleans are on the Louisville and Nashville System.

Few cities on the continent have a greater variety of fascinations than New Orleans. Here within one municipality the visitor finds two distinct cities—the "old town," "Vieux Carre" of the Creole, a continental city with French-Spanish architecture and buildings exceeding the two-century mark, and just across the canal the "new city" of skyscrapers, distinctively American to the core. About the French Quarter cluster tradition and romance, dating back to the days when France or Spain ruled the city. Here the sightseer may still enter the Cabildo, which in 1795 was the headquarters of the French Colony of Louisiana, the ancient Cathedral of St. Louis, built in 1737, and the "Haunted House" on Royal Street, once the residence of Lafayette, Marshal Ney and Louis Phillippe. Here one may wander down to the levee where great ocean steamships and Mississippi "stern wheelers" are strangely commingled, and see in action the open-air French market. And of course no one ever visits the old town without dining at one or more of the quaint cafés where Creole dishes, superlatively prepared, are served. In the "new city" there is much to see, too—the brilliant shops, miles of handsome residential streets, parks, and imposing public buildings.

Direct steamship service from New York to New Orleans is provided by weekly sailings of the Southern Pacific Atlantic Steamship Lines, connecting at New Orleans with the "Sunset Route" of the Southern Pacific rail lines for California. New Orleans is one of the important northern ports of the United Fruit Company's fleet. It is the eastern terminus of the Southern Pacific's "Sunset Route," heretofore mentioned, while among the other rail lines entering the city are the Louisville and Nashville Southern Railway, Texas and Pacific, Illinois Central and Gulf Coast Lines.

The western Gulf Coast has the unusual characteristic of facing for hundreds of miles a series of lagoons and it, too, is indented with numerous rivers and bays. On the largest of these bays stands Galveston, the shipping metropolis of Texas and one of the most important deep-water ports of the country. The city faces an imposing harbor and is protected from its waters by an immense sea-wall. Extensive shipping interests include lines to domestic and foreign ports. Galveston is an attractive city for the winter tourist, its climate being delightful and its hotels famous. It is the terminus of the Mallory Line ships with semi-weekly sailings to and from New York. Five rail lines enter the city, including a division of the Southern Pacific; Gulf Colorado and Santa Fe; International and Great Northern; Missouri, Kansas and Texas; Galveston, Houston and Henderson.

Famous among the resorts in this region are Corpus Christi and neighboring waterside playgrounds, including Rockport, Ingleside, Port Aransas, Portland, Flour Bluff and Boerne. Rail access is by the San Antonio and Aransas Pass System from Houston, Waco, and San Antonio.

AMERICAN RE-DISCOVERY OF FLORIDA

Altho the Spaniards discovered Florida hundreds of years ago and it has been held at various times by Spain, Great Britain, and France, between 1559 and 1861, its rediscovery as the Land of the Fountain of Youth goes back to comparatively recent years. Further, more Americans and visitors from foreign lands keep on discovering its salubrious charm month after month, for Florida has come to possess a strong appeal as a summer as well as a winter resort. But it is during the fall and winter months especially that the great trend of travel turns to the peninsula. Here Americans are learning the secret of long life and comfort, as they have previously mastered the problem of hard work and success. Each autumn the seasonal visitors "pour over the borders of the State like an invading army" we read in the *Florida Tourist* (Tallahassee), a quarterly issued by the Florida Department of Agriculture, which proceeds:

"Florida has all types of hotels, from the most palatial, elaborately furnished, with giant domes looming against the cloud-decked blue in barbaric splendor, to the simplest hostelry. There are winter homes, from magnificent villas to humble bungalows. Lack of accommodations to meet the influx of visitors has led many to own or rent winter homes. Many tourist's parks have been provided for those who prefer outdoor life to hotel accommodations. The State is penetrated by the

Voyages Modernes

PARIS—*nom glorieux*—synonymous with beauty, charm and *l'élégance*—the city of a thousand wonders is truly typified by the giant French liner, the S. S. "Paris." Its *salons magnifiques*, its commodious cabins, broad stairways and tasteful decorations combine to make it a Parisian palace afloat. The traveler will particularly enjoy its *cuisine renommée*, as well as the manifold forms of entertainment including the celebrated orchestra, and the *guignol*—the unique Punch and Judy show.

Write for our interesting booklet D also descriptive literature regarding fascinating French Line auto tours in Morocco and Algeria

French Line

COMPAGNIE GÉNÉRALE TRANSATLANTIQUE

19 STATE ST. NEW YORK

WINTER TRAVEL
Continued

The principal rail gateways to Florida are Jacksonville on the northeast, Tallahassee on the north, Pensacola on the northwest. All the great rail arteries or their connections from northern and western States, including the Atlantic Coast Line; Seaboard Air Line; Southern Railway; Pennsylvania System; the Big Four; Michigan Central; Chicago & Eastern Illinois Railroad; Illinois Central; St. Louis and San Francisco, etc., contribute to the Florida traffic through the Jacksonville gateway. Jacksonville is also the Southern terminus for the Clyde Line and a division of the Merchants and Miners Transportation Company. The rail system serving East Coast resorts from Jacksonville southward, including St. Augustine, Ormond, Palm Beach and Miami is the Florida East Coast to the southern tip of the State, thence crossing the ocean and Coral Keys to Key West, where connections are made with steamer for Havana. The central, western and northern resorts are served by the Atlantic Coast Line, Seaboard Air Line, Southern Railway, Louisville and Nashville Railways and their connections.

BERMUDA, ISLES OF SUNSHINE AND FLOWERS

A conversation recently overheard on a returning ship from Bermuda is eloquent of the charm of the place. One woman passenger exprest her regret at leaving—she had been there only ten days. "Oh," replied the other, "it would be just as bad later on. I've been there a month and it breaks my heart to come away."

As the steamer nears the islands on the morning of the third day out from New York, the picture that greets the eye more resembles an exquisite marine painting, whose source is imagination rather than reality. The sea takes on every shade of turquoise blue imaginable, varying with the depth of the coral reefs below the surface. Every day these colors seem more and more beautiful, changing with the position of the sun and the condition of sky. Resting in these colorful waters are the low hills of pure white limestone, dotted with green cedars, against which nestle houses of pink and white.

Ashore one enters a land of sunshine and flowers, with a winter temperature averaging 70°.

The quaint town of St. George's is to some the most interesting and picturesque spot in Bermuda. This is the oldest English settlement now existing in the Western Hemisphere.

About sixteen miles from St. George's is the city of Hamilton, the largest town in Bermuda. This is now the capital, and here are the government buildings, some of the largest hotels on the island, and fine residences.

Among some of the other points of interest in Bermuda which tourists should not miss are the Crystal Cave, with its thousands of crystal stalactites; the Sea Gardens near Hamilton, fairy submarine forests with trees, plants, coral roses, branch coral, and brainstones.

The chief ocean gateways are St. George's and Hamilton. The St. George's passengers land by tender, the ship continuing along the north shore of Bermuda, thence through the McDundonald and the Two-Rock Channel into Hamilton Harbor.

Steamship service between New York and Bermuda this winter will be the best offered in many years. The Royal Mail Steam Packet Company will inaugurate in January weekly sailings by its twin-screw 17,500-ton cruising steamship *Araguaya*.

The Furness Bermuda Line, operating their new steamer *Fort St. George*, also steamer *Fort Hamilton*, will also provide sailings at seven-day intervals throughout the winter.

VOYAGING OVER THE SPANISH MAIN

To sail over tropical seas and to visit lands over which hover legends of explorers, buccaneers, and marooners, are pleasures of cruises to the West Indies and beyond. Here groped their way over unknown seas Columbus, Balboa, Ponce de Leon. Here lurked under their "Jolly Rogers" Captain Kidd, Sir Henry Morgan, Edward Leach, "Blackbeard." The galleons have sailed away forever, but they have left in and about the Caribbean treasures of romance and tradition. For the tourist of to-day, the West Indies provide delightfully mild winter voyages, combined with visits to unusual scenes ashore.

AT NASSAU IN THE BAHAMAS

Lying off the Atlantic Coast in about the same latitude as southern Florida, the Bahamas, since 1629 a British possession, include a labyrinth of some three thousand islands, islets, coral keys and reefs. The capital and chief seaport of the group is Nassau, on the island of New Providence. This city is also the tourist headquarters. Its popularity with American and European winter travelers has been long established. With an average winter temperature of 72° and fanned almost continually by the trade winds, the climate is delightful. At Nassau you may play golf on a nine-hole course within sound of the surf, and containing within its limits forts centuries old. There are numerous tennis courts, shaded by palms, still-water and surf bathing, yachting, fishing, and interesting drives.

Steamship service between New York and Nassau is provided by frequent sailings of Ward Line steamships, and weekly by the Munson Line. Nassau and Miami, Florida, are connected by the Peninsular and Occidental Steamship Line.

VISITING THE CUBAN CAPITAL, AND BEYOND

When the steamship passes the grim walls of Morro Castle and glides into the busy waters of Havana Harbor, the winter tourist enters upon scenes characteristically foreign. To the American visitor Havana has a charm of both ancient and modern origin. Here one may view remains of the Spanish dynasty with their tragic memories, and here enjoy the brilliant life of the present-day Republic's capital city.

But Cuba's attractions are not confined to Havana or its immediate environs. There are many attractive trips, both short and long, into a region which imprest Columbus as "the most beautiful land eyes have ever beheld."

The chief railway systems of the Republic are the United Railways of Havana, the Western Railway of Havana, and the Cuba Railroad. Steamship service between Havana and New York is performed by Ward Line, United Fruit Line, and various special cruise steamers. Daily sailings between Key West, Fla., and Havana are made by the Peninsular and Occidental Line in connection with its Port Tampa-Key West division. Direct service between New York and Eastern Cuban ports is afforded by the Munson Steamship Line.

SIGHTSEEING IN JAMAICA

On the West Indian cruise Kingston, Jamaica, is a favorite port of call with winter travelers. This island, a British possession, mountain-crowned, bordered by sapphire harbors, intersected with superb motor roads, and providing every form of outdoor recreation, is a tropical fairyland. Visits to ancient "Spanish Town," the old-time capital; to the world-famous botanical gardens; the river and mountain scenic attractions; to Blue Hole, a pirate rendezvous of past centuries, provide interest. Kingston, Jamaica, is a port of call on West Indies cruises described elsewhere.

WHAT TO SEE IN PORTO RICO

Porto Rico has been famed for its attractions since Juan Ponce de Leon, so imprest with its beauty, founded the present city of Ponce in 1508. In few other places may we see the old and the new in such vivid contrast as in San Juan, the principal port, in Ponce, and other towns of the island.

Among the points of interest are these scenic drives—Coamo Mineral Springs, sugar plantations, historic fortresses, and other buildings, etc. All forms of outdoor sports are available.

Between New York and Porto Rican ports steam the vessels of the New York and Porto Rico Steamship Company, offering attractive sixteen-day tours.

UNDER THE STARS AND STRIPES AT CHARLOTTE AMALIE

Of increasing interest to Americans, now that the archipelago is a United States possession, are the Virgin Islands—St. Thomas, St. John, St. Croix. Charlotte Amalie, St. Thomas, is the chief port in picturesque mountain and harbor setting. Legends of the buccaneers of old who brought their gold to these islands abound. Beyond, on the course of ships bound to and from South America, are the Barbados, "Little England," with many points of interest to the tourist. Charlotte Amalie, St. Thomas, and Bridgetown, Barbados, are ports of call on West Indian cruises described elsewhere.

EXPLORING THE CARIBBEAN COAST COUNTRIES

Sailing southward from the West Indies, steamship lines extend across the Caribbean Sea to lands rich in interest. In Central America there are Honduras, Guatemala and Salvador, which were consolidated last October into a new republic—the Central American Federation. Visitors to Honduras and Guatemala should see the Maya ruins, among the most extensive remains of a prehistoric race in existence. Temples, monoliths, columns, with inscriptions in an unknown language, offer a fascinating spectacle. Costa Rica is noted for its impressive scenery, and tourists should visit San José, the capital, reached from Port Limon after a rail climb of 3,816 feet over the wildest scenery. On the northern coast of Colombia are Cartagena, Spain's treasure city, until captured by Sir Francis Drake; Puerto Colombia, seaport for the interesting city of Barranquilla, twenty miles inland on the Magdalena River, and Santa Marta, founded in 1525.

PANAMA, WORLD'S ENGINEERING MARVEL

Panama, marine junction of Atlantic and Pacific shipping, is the goal of an ever-increasing tide of winter tourists. The government-owned and operated Hotel Washington at Cristobal, the Caribbean entrance, affords all the attractions of a first-class resort hostelry. From this point the great engineering features of the Canal may be visited and side trips made to other points of interest. These and other near-by ports are included in the itineraries of various West Indies cruises.

Cruises to the West Indies by the United Fruit Company's fleet include the following sailings from American ports:

23-day cruise from New York to Havana, Cuba;

The same company has also chartered the S. S. *Ebro* of the Pacific Line, sailing to Valparaiso on the west coast of South America by way of Havana and the Panama Canal. Members of the party on this cruise may cross the continent to Buenos Aires, returning to New York by the Munson Line S. S. *American Legion*. Another cruise under the same auspices is that sailing from Baltimore January 7 on the *Buckeye State* of the Matson Line to Hawaii.

Raymond & Whitcomb Company have chartered the S. S. *George Washington* for a cruise leaving New York February 14 and visiting the Azores, Madeira, Spain, Gibraltar, Algiers, Sicily, Italy, Athens, Constantinople, Syria, the Holy Land, Egypt, Corfu, Jugo-Slavia, Corsica and the Riviera, thence via Cherbourg to New York.

This same company has also chartered the S. S. *Hawkeye State* of the Matson Navigation Company for a cruise to the Hawaiian Islands.

Thomas Cook and Son have chartered the *Caronia* of the Cunard Line for a tour leaving New York January 28th to Madeira, Cadiz, Gibraltar, Algiers, Monaco, Naples, Alexandria, Haifa, Constantinople, Athens; and on the return, Naples and Gibraltar.

GETTING ACQUAINTED WITH OUR SISTER CONTINENT

For those who would embark upon a travel experience unlike any other on land or sea the call of South America is irresistible. An ocean voyage crossing the Equator, scenery of surpassing grandeur, picturesque living races, awe-inspiring monuments of extinct races, superb cities, mighty commercial enterprises, fill the cup of travel adventure to overflowing. If you have a taste for archeology, ethnology, or the wonderful in nature; if you simply go for the fun of seeing the unusual or to learn at first hand some of the rudiments of Latin-American trade in the world's commercial reconstruction, you will be satisfied.

If the traveler's time permits of no further exploration, the journey from New York to Buenos Aires, with calls at Pernambuco, Bahia, Rio de Janeiro, Santos and Montevideo on the east coast will provide a trip of extraordinary interest. But with three or, better four, months, at his disposal the tourist who would obtain a more comprehensive insight into South American wonders will take the great circle trip through the Panama Canal, down the west coast, with visits ashore at Ecuadorian, Peruvian, Bolivian and Chilean points of interest, crossing the Andes by the Trans-Andean Railway to Buenos Aires, and returning home via the east coast ports heretofore mentioned.

On the journey down the west coast the first stop for most visitors is Callao, port for Lima, City of the Kings, founded by Francisco Pizarro in 1535. The magnificent cathedral completed in 1625, with priceless historical treasures; the museums with their rare collections; the ancient residence of the viceroys of past generations, now the Government Palace; the oldest university in the Americas; the shops with their unusual wares; the colorful costumes of the people, all hold the visitor's interest.

On the second morning after leaving Callao the steamer reaches Mollendo. Here the tourist may disembark for the remarkable rail trip to Arequipa, Cuzco, and La Paz, visiting Titicaca, the sacred lake of the Incas, highest navigable water on the earth's surface.

Leaving Mollendo, the train crosses the Desert of Islay and then plunges i[illegible]

The same company has also chartered the S. S. *Ebro* of the Pacific Line, sailing to Valparaiso on the west coast of South America by way of Havana and the Panama Canal. Members of the party on this cruise may cross the continent to Buenos Aires, returning to New York by the Munson Line S. S. *American Legion.* Another cruise under the same auspices is that sailing from Baltimore January 7 on the *Buckeye State* of the Matson Line to Hawaii.

Raymond & Whitcomb Company have chartered the S. S. *George Washington* for a cruise leaving New York February 14 and visiting the Azores, Madeira, Spain, Gibraltar, Algiers, Sicily, Italy, Athens, Constantinople, Syria, the Holy Land, Egypt, Corfu, Jugo-Slavia, Corsica and the Riviera, thence via Cherbourg to New York.

This same company has also chartered the S. S. *Hawkeye State* of the Matson Navigation Company for a cruise to the Hawaiian Islands.

Thomas Cook and Son have chartered the *Caronia* of the Cunard Line for a tour leaving New York January 28th to Madeira, Cadiz, Gibraltar, Algiers, Monaco, Naples, Alexandria, Haifa, Constantinople, Athens; and on the return, Naples and Gibraltar.

GETTING ACQUAINTED WITH OUR SISTER CONTINENT

For those who would embark upon a travel experience unlike any other on land or sea the call of South America is irresistible. An ocean voyage crossing the Equator, scenery of surpassing grandeur, picturesque living races, awe-inspiring monuments of extinct races, superb cities, mighty commercial enterprises, fill the cup of travel adventure to overflowing. If you have a taste for archeology, ethnology, or the wonderful in nature; if you simply go for the fun of seeing the unusual or to learn at first hand some of the rudiments of Latin-American trade in the world's commercial reconstruction, you will be satisfied.

If the traveler's time permits of no further exploration, the journey from New York to Buenos Aires, with calls at Pernambuco, Bahia, Rio de Janeiro, Santos and Montevideo on the east coast will provide a trip of extraordinary interest. But with three or, better four, months, at his disposal the tourist who would obtain a more comprehensive insight into South American wonders will take the great circle trip through the Panama Canal, down the west coast, with visits ashore at Ecuadorian, Peruvian, Bolivian and Chilean points of interest, crossing the Andes by the Trans-Andean Railway to Buenos Aires, and returning home via the east coast ports heretofore mentioned.

On the journey down the west coast the first stop for most visitors is Callao, port for Lima, City of the Kings, founded by Francisco Pizarro in 1535. The magnificent cathedral completed in 1625, with priceless historical treasures; the museums with their rare collections; the ancient residence of the viceroys of past generations, now the Government Palace; the oldest university in the Americas; the shops with their unusual wares; the colorful costumes of the people, all hold the visitor's interest.

On the second morning after leaving Callao the steamer reaches Mollendo. Here the tourist may disembark for the remarkable rail trip to Arequipa, Cuzco, and La Paz, visiting Titicaca, the sacred lake of the Incas, highest navigable water on the earth's surface.

Leaving Mollendo, the train crosses the Desert of Islay and then plunges into the

WINTER TRAVEL
Continued

Andes, climbing up to Arequipa at an altitude of 7,500 feet.

From Arequipa the railway climbs to the divide at an elevation of 14,666 feet, thence descending to Juliaca. From here one stem continues to Cuzco, the other to Puno, port of departure for the Lake Titicaca trip.

Cuzco, ancient capital of the Incas, is one of the most impressive of all South American cities. Its imposing plaza, great cathedral, Monastery of Santo Domingo, standing on the foundation of the Incas Temple of the Sun, its picturesque market and the neighboring Inca Fortress, one of the first among the world's archeological wonders, contribute to make it a city of intense interest.

Returning from Cuzco to Juliaca, thence to Puno, the train is abandoned for a sail over South America's lake of the sky.

Lake Titicaca is twelve thousand five hundred feet, or more than two miles, above the sea, 135 miles in length and 66 miles broad.

From Guaqui to La Paz is a rail ride of about sixty miles, and on the way another collection of pre-Inca ruins should be visited.

La Paz is a colorful city, nestling in a canyon on either side of the Chuquiapu River, teeming with Indians and herds of llamas, presenting a novel picture to the tourist.

From La Paz two railway lines extend through the wildest of mountain scenery to Pacific ports, one terminating at Arica, the other at Antofagasta. From each the west coast tour may be continued by steamer to Valparaiso.

At Valparaiso the majority of tourists cross the continent to Buenos Aires. Others who have the time and desire to view the island fairyland of the southern Chilean coast and the stern majesty of Magellan Straits embark on the continent-encircling voyage.

Valparaiso is a busy, cosmopolitan city, its harbor crowded with shipping.

Leaving Valparaiso for the transcontinental journey, a train is boarded for Santiago, 2,000 feet above the sea.

This capital city of the Chilean Republic stands at the base of the Cordillera of the Andes, a superb city in all respects.

The trans-Andean trip begins here. Of all mountain railway rides this is most inspiring. It is beside rushing torrents, up narrow canyons, over dizzy bridges, in and out of tunnel mouths.

Buenos Aires, capital of the Argentine Republic and metropolis of South America, is often styled also the Paris of South America. Visitors will find the comparison appropriate. The Avenida de Mayo is in many respects a replica of the famous Paris boulevards. Palermo suggests the "Bois de Boulogne," while the great theaters, stately government buildings, brilliant shops, imposing statues, fashionably drest men and women, all carry out the atmosphere of the French capital. Buenos Aires is not all splendor, however.

Voyaging northward along the east coast the next important port is Montevideo, capital of Uruguay.

Then comes Santos, the most important coffee exporting center of Brazil. It is the port for São Paulo, a bustling modern city, two hours by rail inland.

Continuing the coastwise journey, the steamship enters the great mountain gateway of Rio de Janeiro Harbor, and there comes into view a city with setting probably unequaled elsewhere on this or any other continent. Among the points of interest are the National Library, Fine Arts Museum, Cathedral, Botanical Gardens, etc.

At the easternmost part of the continent are the ports of Bahia and Pernambuco, each of high commercial importance, and beyond them Para, at the mouth of the mighty Amazon, the world's first port in the export of raw rubber.

A brief directory of the more important South American steamship service follows:

From New York to west coast ports via Panama Canal are regular sailings by express steamships of the Pacific Steam Navigation Company, calling en route at important west coast ports as far south as Valparaiso, connecting there with the steamship route to Puntas Arenas.

At Cristobal west coast steamers make connection with United Fruit and Panama Railroad steamships.

A special cruise-tour of South America will be made this winter from New York by S. S. *Ebro* of the Pacific Line, southbound to west coast ports, returning up east coast by Munson Line S. S. *American Legion*. There will also be a special cruise-tour by the new S. S. *Vandyck* of the Lamport & Holt Line south bound to Rio de Janeiro, Montevideo, and Buenos Aires, returning up the West Coast from Valparaiso by the S. S. *Ebro* of the Pacific Line.

Between New York, Rio de Janeiro, Montevideo, and Buenos Aires, calling at Santos northbound, are operated steamers of the United States Shipping Board under control of the Munson Steamship Line.

The Lamport and Holt Line's fleet plys between New York, Rio de Janeiro, Montevideo, and Buenos Aires, calling at Barbados northbound.

The Norton Line American Mail S. S. *Crofton Hall* provides sailings between New York, Montevideo and Buenos Aires.

ROUTES TO THE PACIFIC COAST

Which route is a perplexing question with many travelers. Each has its individual attractions, and it is customary with most tourists to go by one route and return by another. As an aid in making the itinerary we give a brief outline of the main rail highways with the routing over them of important transcontinental trains. The Central and Southern routes are favored by the majority of winter tourists, yet many enjoy the bracing air and winter scenery of the northern mountains.

OVER THE CANADIAN NATIONAL-GRAND TRUNK ROUTE

The coast-to-coast route of the Canadian National Railways, extending from Halifax, Sydney and St. John on the east to Prince Rupert and Vancouver on the Pacific Coast, with steamer connection for Victoria and Seattle, traverses scenery of great variety and charm. It includes the forests of New Brunswick, the shores of the St. Lawrence, the cities of Quebec (over the great St. Lawrence Bridge) and Montreal, the Lake Region of Ontario, the vast Canadian prairies, the Canadian Rockies, and the valleys of the Thompson and Fraser rivers.

Between the maritime Provinces and Montreal are operated the "Maritime Express" and the "Ocean Limited," connecting at Montreal with the "Continental Limited" through to the Pacific Coast. Tourists from Toronto connect with this train by taking "The National" express to Winnipeg.

THE CANADIAN-PACIFIC ROUTE

From the Atlantic to the Pacific stretches the steel highway of the Canadian-Pacific, with many ramifications. The main stem after leaving Montreal continues to Ottawa, follows the north shore of Lake Superior to Fort William, thence to Winnipeg, Regina,

When Evangeline came to Louisiana

"THE Eden of Louisiana" is what the Acadians called the beautiful Bayou Teche country near New Orleans. With its live oaks, hanging moss and picturesque plantations it is as fragrant and charming today as when Longfellow's beautiful heroine sighed for her lover under the moss-draped oak that bears her name.

Stop over in New Orleans on your Sunset Way to California and revel in the ways and byways of this fascinating Southern City. You can visit the old French quarter—see relics of the Spanish regime—explore busy markets—dine at quaint restaurants—visit the Haunted House and Duelling Oak and enjoy a hundred delightful experiences.

SUNSET LIMITED

New Orleans **Los Angeles**
San Antonio **San Francisco**

Operated over a mild, sunny route all the way, free from ice and snow. Observation Car, Through Dining Car and other modern travel comforts. Daily Through Tourist Sleeping Car Service between Washington, D. C. and San Francisco. Tri-weekly Sleeping Car Service to Globe, Arizona, for the side trip to ROOSEVELT DAM on the APACHE TRAIL.

Take the
Sunset Route
to California
Every mile a scene worth while
SOUTHERN PACIFIC

For Information and Literature address

SOUTHERN PACIFIC LINES

New York
165 Broadway

New Orleans
Pan American Bank Building

Houston
Southern Pacific Building

Tucson, Arizona
Score Building

San Francisco
Southern Pacific Building

WINTER TRAVEL
Continued

daily train from St. Paul to Seattle and Portland via Helena, Montana.

THE SHASTA ROUTE

This route of the Southern Pacific provides the only main artery of travel from North Pacific coast points to California. Superb views of Mount Shasta are had as the train passes over the summit of the Siskiyous and into the canyon of the Sacramento River, thence into the Sacramento itself and across the valley to Oakland and San Francisco. All trains over this route stop at Shasta Springs to permit passengers to sample these famous waters. "The Shasta" and "The Oregonian" between Seattle, Tacoma, Portland and San Francisco are important trains.

THE OVERLAND ROUTE AND CONNECTIONS

With its main feeder from Chicago to Omaha, the Chicago and Northwestern System, the Union Pacific System, between Omaha and Ogden, follows the old Overland Trail of pioneer days along the Platte River. Near Cheyenne the great wall of the Rocky Mountains comes into view, the Continental Divide being passed at Creston, this route descending through Echo and Weber Canyons to the great Salt Lake Basin. Before Salt Lake has been reached, however, the northern arm of the Union Pacific has diverged at Granger, stretching northwestward to the Columbia River, thence along its shores to Portland. From Ogden junction is made with the Southern Pacific's Ogden Route, continuing westward on its great Lucin Cut-Off, built for many miles over the Great Salt Lake, thence following the trail of the "Forty-Niners" to Truckee, and down the Western slope of the Sierras, following the rim of the American River Canyon to the Sacramento Valley and San Francisco. At Salt Lake City the Union Pacific's southwestern arm continues to California, through Utah and Nevada, following the Old Mormon Trail and terminating at Los Angeles.

Among famous trains to the Pacific Coast by the Overland Route and its connections are the "Overland Limited" from Chicago to Omaha via Chicago and Northwestern System; Omaha to Ogden via Union Pacific; Ogden to San Francisco via Southern Pacific.

"The Pacific Limited," via Chicago, Milwaukee and St. Paul to Omaha, provides a morning departure from Chicago and unusually fast time from San Francisco to New York, Eastbound.

"The Los Angeles Limited," Chicago to Omaha via Northwestern System, thence over the Union Pacific System to Los Angeles via Salt Lake City. Over the same route is operated "The Continental Limited."

THE RIO GRANDE-FEATHER RIVER CANYON ROUTE

From Denver or Colorado Springs to Salt Lake City by the Denver and Rio Grande Western and from Salt Lake City to San Francisco by the Western Pacific railways this route includes the Pikes Peak region (Colorado Springs, Manitou, Pikes Peak, etc.), the Royal Gorge, through which the railroad passes, Collegiate Peaks, Tennessee Pass, Continental Divide, Canyons of the Eagle and Colorado rivers, Ruby Canyon, Price River Canyon, Castle Gate, Soldier Summit (summit of the Wasatch Range), the Great Salt Lake, Feather River Canyon and the "Sierras."

From Chicago and Omaha (direct connections from St. Louis and Kansas City) by way of Denver en route to California, the Burlington, in connection with the foregoing railways, operates through service over this central scenic highway. Through cars are also operated in conjunction with the Missouri Pacific system from St. Louis to Denver, and connections are made at Denver with Rock Island and Union Pacific trains. A feature of this service is the fact that the schedule has been so arranged that all of the major scenic attractions are passed during the daylight hours.

Leading trains to California include the "Scenic Limited" and "Salt Lake and San Francisco Express," with connections at Ogden via Southern Pacific.

THE SANTA FE TRAIL

The Santa Fé route from Chicago to California, closely paralleling between the Missouri River and the Rockies the old Santa Fé Trail of pioneer days, provides many points of interest for winter tourists. Among the foremost are the ancient city of Santa Fé and its environs and the Grand Canyon of the Colorado River in Arizona.

THE CITY OF SANTA FE

antedating both Jamestown and Plymouth, was founded in 1605 by the Spaniards. Seventy-six Mexican and Spanish and nineteen American rulers have successively occupied the governor's palace on the plaza.

The real Santa Fé of the traveler's anticipation—the Mexican quarter—consists of low adobe huts, divided by narrow winding lanes, where burros loaded with firewood pass to and fro. The American section has substantial buildings, and the new museum and art gallery is a Mecca for artists of national reputation.

Santa Fé is the center of archeological research in America. Work is being carried on among the prehistoric cliff dwellings at Pajarito Park, Puyé and Rito de los Frijoles.

Within a few hours' ride are several Pueblo Indian and Mexican villages. Ascend Pecos River to the rangers' camp at Panchuela, past Valley Ranch, and the scenic beauty of the surrounding mountains is evident. Few tourists will wish to miss that unique hostlery near the city, the Bishop's Lodge formerly an old mission. Farther on this route, at Adamana, tourists stop over for a visit to the Petrified Forest and Painted Desert, and continuing westward and merging at Williams there is that most stupendous of all natural wonders,

THE GRAND CANYON

The Grand Canyon National Park is open throughout the year.

Charles F. Lummis has written of it. "Ten thousand pens have 'described at' this Indescribable, in vain. It is alone in the world. The only Mountain Range in Captivity—a hundred miles of unearthly peaks, taller from their gnawing river than Mt. Washington above the distant sea; all countersunk in a prodigious serpentine gulf of living rock; a Cosmic Intaglio, carved in the bosom of the great Arizona Plateau. Nowhere else can you look up hundreds of 7,000-foot cliffs whose tops are but three miles from a plummet to your feet. And from their Rim, look down upon such leagues of inverted and captive skies—of rainbows in solution, and snow and thunder tempests far below you; and brimming fogs that flow with the moon, and with dawn ebb and ebb—till one by one the white, voiceless tide reveals the glorified

'Islands' of its countless archipelago of glowing peaks.

"To all it is a Poem; History; an imperishable Inspiration. Words cannot overtell it—nor half tell. See it, and you will know why!"

The Santa Fé System enters California near Needles on the Colorado River, the Southern Division for Los Angeles and San Diego diverging at Berstow, and crossing the mountains through Cajon Pass; the northern lines continuing through the central valleys to San Francisco.

Over the Santa Fe Route four daily trains are operated to the Pacific Coast: "The California Limited," for Los Angeles and San Diego (with through Pullman via Grand Canyon); "The Navajo," Chicago and Kansas City to Los Angeles, San Diego and San Francisco; "The Scout," Chicago and Kansas City to Los Angeles, San Diego and San Francisco; "The Missionary," Chicago and Kansas City to Los Angeles, San Diego and San Francisco (Pullman via Grand Canyon). The first three trains are operated via La Junta and Albuquerque; the fourth, via Amarillo and Belen.

THE ROCK ISLAND-GOLDEN STATE ROUTE

The Rock Island Route in conjunction with the El Paso and Southwestern and Southern Pacific Systems to California affords an attractive low altitude trip to the Coast from Chicago, St. Louis, St. Paul, Minneapolis, Kansas City or Memphis.

From Chicago the route is through the Illinois River Valley, crossing the Mississippi at Rock Island, thence to Kansas City, where connection is made from the Twin Cities on the east and St. Louis on the south. From Kansas City the tourist passes through Kansas, Oklahoma and Texas. At Tucumcari, just across the New Mexico border, the division from Memphis joins the main line.

El Paso with the Mexican city of Juarez on the opposite shore of the Rio Grande; Tucson and San Xavier Mission; a side trip to the Roosevelt Dam from Bowie or Maricopa are among points of interest, this route entering California through the picturesque Carriso Gorge, a scenic wonderland described under "The Sunset Route."

The Rock Island's premier train to the Coast is the "Golden State Limited" from Chicago to Los Angeles, San Diego and Santa Barbara; also "The Californian" from St. Louis and Kansas City to the Coast. At Kansas City cars from Minneapolis and St. Paul join the train and at Tucumcari from Memphis.

Tourists desiring to go to California via Denver and Colorado Springs are provided direct service from Chicago or St. Louis to these two cities over the Rock Island Lines.

THE SUNSET ROUTE

The Sunset Route of the Southern Pacific Lines from New Orleans across Spanish America to California is rich in attractions for the transcontinental tourist. This route may be combined with a delightful voyage from New York to New Orleans by the Southern Pacific's well-appointed steamships plying between these ports. Rail connections to New Orleans from Eastern and Middle Western States are provided by the Southern Railway, Louisville and Nashville, Illinois Central, Gulf Coast Lines, Missouri Pacific, and their various connecting systems.

After leaving the fascinating "Crescent City" the route is through tropical scenery, including forests of cypress, sugar plantations, stretches of rice fields and pine forests to Houston, an interesting city, with an attractive side trip to Galveston, the "Atlantic City of the Southwest."

WINTER TRAVEL

Continued

The line now gradually ascends the Texas plateau to

ANCIENT SAN ANTONIO

Here, adjacent to skyscrapers, one may see the old time adobes, and that shrine of American valor, the ancient Alamo. Near-by are ruins of missions dating back centuries. The San Antonio of to-day, with its sulphur springs, golf-links, fine motoring, and modern hotels, is one of the most popular winter resorts in the Southwest. San Antonio may be also reached from St. Louis by the Missouri Pacific and Missouri, Kansas and Texas systems.

From San Antonio to El Paso the "Sunset Route" passes over its highest altitude, which is only 5,082 feet, making this the lowest altitude route to the Coast. At El Paso the Chicago, Rock Island and Pacific-El Paso and Southwestern-Southern Pacific, known as "The Golden State Route," described in detail elsewhere, joins "The Sunset Route." Thence the way leads on to Bowie, Arizona, where a side trip diverges to Globe for a tour of

THE MARVELOUS APACHE TRAIL

This, says a recent writer, "was the historic route followed by the Apache hordes in their descents upon the far-flung settlements of the encroaching whites. To-day. . . . instead of the muffled hoof-beats of flitting ponies, the grim canyon now re-echoes to the throb of pulsing pistons."

Seven-passenger automobiles afford attractive one-day trips over the Trail to the Roosevelt Dam providing, in addition to the wonderful natural scenery, a visit to the Cliff Dwellings of a pre-historic race. To see the entire Apache Trail the trip may be continued from Roosevelt Dam to Phoenix, thence to the Pacific Coast via Maricopa and Yuma. However, through Pullmans are operated over the Southern Pacific to Bowie and Globe, where tourists can have a one-day automobile trip over the Apache Trail to Roosevelt Dam and return to Globe, continuing that night in same car to the coast, or vice versa. Farther westward the Sunset Route passes Tucson and on to the California line.

The Sunset Route of the Southern Pacific System now has two entrances, each emanating from Yuma on the Colorado River. The newest and most southerly of these is the recently completed line which four times crosses the Mexican Border and leads directly to San Diego. Through tunnels, over lofty bridges, and along precipitous mountain-sides it penetrates California's southernmost natural wonder, the multi-tinted mountain chaos of the Carriso Gorge. The other entrance from Yuma follows the southern slope of the Chocolate Mountains, skirts the Salton Sea, crosses the divide by San Gorgonio Pass, thence descending into the San Gabriel Valley to Los Angeles. Certain trains of the Rock Island and Southern Pacific Systems are operated to the coast via El Paso and the Carriso Gorge. From Los Angeles to San Francisco extend the coast and valley lines of the Southern Pacific northward, the Sunset Route providing a ride close to the surf, and the "Big Trees" to San Francisco, connecting there with the Shasta and Ogden Routes.

Two trains are operated over the Sunset Route from New Orleans to San Francisco the first being the "Sunset Limited" and the second, the "Sunset Express." Between Chicago, El Paso, San Diego, Los Angeles and Santa Barbara is operated the Chicago, Rock Island and Pacific-El Paso and Southwestern-Southern Pacific's "Golden State Limited" and between Kansas City, El Paso and Los Angeles the same system's "Californian."

CALIFORNIA IN WINTER

One of the greatest thrills the winter tourist ever experiences is that of dropping down over night from the ice and snow of the Rocky Mountain Peaks into the orange groves in the heart of Southern California.

The contrast is so tremendous and the new surroundings are so delightful that it is almost impossible to believe you are still in our same little world.

Every month in the year is vacation time for tourists in California, but it is those who arrive in January who constitute the greatest advertising force of California's charms, because the warm days and nights, the sunshine, myriads of flowers and ripening fruits form such a contrast with what they have just left behind.

For many of those who still have in store their first trip to California, it is difficult to realize that the state extends along the Pacific Coastline from a point opposite Boston on the Atlantic Coast to the Mexican line parallel to Atlanta, Georgia.

With this large latitude and a variation of altitude of fourteen thousand feet between sea level and the highest peaks, it is not surprizing that California can serve to her tourist friends, almost any kind of climate at any time of year.

The Mecca for the traveler desiring to escape the rigors of winter at home, is the bay region of San Francisco, south.

If you enter California through the new Carriso Gorge route, one of the most scenic and expensive bits of railroad engineering in the world, you will begin to see California at its far southern extremity, as did the Spanish explorer, Cabrillo, 350 years ago from the harbor of San Diego.

San Diego is a clean appearing American city of probably 100,000. It has no smoke, and little dust, and provides somewhere to go and something to do sufficient to fill every hour. It is but five minutes' walk from your hotel to the harbor to visit the latest type of dreadnought floating peacefully at anchor, or three-score torpedo boats and other naval craft, or to watch the big naval flying boats skimming the water or circling overhead in battle formation, with occasionally a blimp or group of army planes.

With many visitors the first question asked is how to get to Tijuana, a little town across the Mexican Border. There is not a thing worth while to be seen there unless it might be a bullfight or a horse race, but tourists go for the novelty of setting foot on Mexican soil, buying a Mexican souvenir and startling their friends at home with postcards bearing Mexican stamps.

Most of the old San Diego Exposition buildings of 1915–16 still stand amid flowers and foliage more beautiful than in Exposition days, with a few of the most interesting exhibits still retained, and every day at three o'clock the world's largest out-of-door pipe-organ peals forth its melodies free to all.

The auto trip through Old Town, stopping at the adobe home of Ramona's Marriage Place, to the end of Point Loma, the southwest corner of the United States, are pleasures never to be forgotten. Few views in the old world or the new surpass in grandeur the panorama from the end of Point Loma.

Beautiful Coronado is only thirty minutes' ride, partly by ferry across the bay.

and La Jolla forty-five minutes by automobile. Old Mission, mountain and valley trips by automobile over splendid boulevards, superb golf-links, games in the stadium, and various other forms of pleasure will keep one entertained as long as he cares to stay.

So much in California is different. There is always something new and unexpected. The magnificent Magnolia Drive of Riverside has been famous for the past quarter of a century, but did you ever hear of the Mission Inn? A quaint hotel of most charming design with a chapel that is an old mission itself, and from the cloisters and archives in the basement to the belfry, it is furnished with the most exquisite appointments of the Spanish padres and filled with ornaments, trinkets, and various art works of the days of Junipero Serra. Nowhere else in the world is there a hotel just like it, where the peace and quiet take one back involuntarily a hundred and fifty years.

From Smiley Heights at Redlands, half an hour's ride from Mission Inn, itself a bower of foliage and glory, one looks out over the orange and lemon groves for fifty miles to the west, while to the right are the mountain peaks of Old Baldy and Gray Back topped with snow, forming a picture never to be forgotten.

The old arrowhead on San Bernardino Mountain stands out as plainly as tho hewn there by human hands. At its foot are hot sulphur springs and another resort.

In two hours from here by motor over paved roads, by train or electric trolley, the tourist reaches Los Angeles. A book might be filled with description of points of interest to be seen here. Probably the best idea can be formed by the realization that in the past twenty years more than 500,000 tourist visitors have returned to Los Angeles to live, and they are returning to-day in larger numbers than ever before. Many who have come to California to retire, develop new energy, and as an outlet, enter some business or industry. More than four thousand factories, it is claimed, now call Los Angeles their home, and the total output of manufactured goods last year exceeded nine hundred million dollars.

In two hours from Seventh and Broadway, you may have ascended the incline railway to the Lick Observatory at Mt. Lowe, five thousand feet elevation. In thirty minutes over the famous Pacific Electric Railway system you can find yourself at any of a dozen beach resorts, Long Beach, Ocean Park, Venice, Redondo, Huntington Beach, and many more, with all the fun, frolic and frivolities of life, or you may motor for days over paved roads through the most magnificent resident districts, with green lawns and flowers on every side, geraniums to the eaves of the bungalows, and every style of residence construction known.

Ten miles to the north and just on the edge of the foothills is Pasadena, the city of roses, and to the west about the same distance is Hollywood, the home of the motion picture industry, where, at certain hours every day, visitors are taken behind the scenes to see the pictures being made.

One should visit the museum where have been assembled actual skeletons of the first residents of Southern California, saber-toothed tigers, the giant sloth and mastadon, mammoth elephants, and more than a thousand other beasts who basked in the sunshine there two thousand years ago, then wandered into an asphaltum mire and so were preserved through all these ages.

A most profitable day is the trip to Catalina Island, twenty miles from the main-

WINTER TRAVEL
Continued

parent waters, glass-bottom boats, and submarine gardens, etc.

In Los Angeles as in San Diego, hotels and apartments are everywhere, all prices and all classes.

In three hours by train from Los Angeles, or four by automobile, you will arrive in Santa Barbara, the winter home of many millionaires. It is a charming little community of probably 25,000 happy, contented folks, living there just because they like to do it.

Santa Barbara nestles right in the mountains, with a series of roads and boulevards winding here and there among the oaks and overlooking the ocean and beach below. Here also is the Santa Barbara Mission, one of the best preserved relics of its kind.

Over night by train or in eight or ten hours by motor from Santa Barbara north is beautiful Monterey Bay, Del Monte Hotel, in its gorgeous setting of parks and golf-links, Carmel-by-the-Sea, the famous artists' and authors' retreat three miles away, the seventeen-mile drive among the pines and rugged ocean crags, and many other interesting features to make you want to prolong your visit here.

And then San Francisco! Even the fire of 1906 could not change the character and romance of San Francisco. Daring buccaneers do not walk in and out of swinging saloon doors and shoot up the town as in the days of '49. Jack London would miss many haunts of the characters he created, and the Barbary Coast is presumably abolished, but it is still San Francisco and San Franciscans live to enjoy themselves.

It is big and busy, and some parts are "smelly," but somehow tourists feel at home and rather like the bustle and noise.

San Francisco handles the bulk of the trade from the immense Sacramento and San Joaquin Valleys, some three hundred miles in length, so it is in nowise a tourist town, but there is enough of sights not to be found elsewhere to consume every moment left of your vacation.

There are many interesting trips to be taken from San Francisco, but the temptation is to loaf about town and live over again the stories one has read about this fascinating city.

Yosemite National Park in all its glory is now a year-round resort, and if you are here to "do California," a side trip of three days to a week may be profitably spent in a visit there. The important rail gateways to California are described under "Trips to the Coast."

A WINTER VACATION IN HAWAII

The Hawaiian Islands form the goal of a delightful six-day ocean voyage, which after two days out from the Pacific Coast continues through soft trade winds and tranquil waters, terminating at palm-embowered Honolulu. Leaving the United States through the Golden Gate, the tourist reenters United States territory as the ship passes under the brow of Diamond Head and into Honolulu harbor.

With a maximum temperature of 85° in summer and a minimum of 55° in winter, and bathing-beaches where waters average 78°, Hawaii is a year-around resort.

Honolulu, island of Oahu, is the tourist headquarters, with countless points of interest within its limits and island environs.

Among the scenic wonders and attractions of the islands are: Hawaii National Park, including the continuously active volcano, Kilauea, the intermittently active summit crater of Mauna Loa, the inactive crater of Haleakala; Waimea Canyon; the Pali, a 1,200-foot precipice; Waikiki beach; Diamond Head; Mount Tantalus and Punchbowl Crater; sugar plantations; pineapple fields and canneries.

The difficulties of obtaining steamer accommodations to the Hawaiian Islands in the height of the winter season will be largely alleviated by a material increase throughout 1922 of sailings between the Pacific coast and Honolulu, including:

Canadian-Australasian Royal Mail Line—From Vancouver and Victoria, B. C., to the Antipodes via Honolulu; an outbound steamer approximately once a month.

Alaska Steamship Co.—From Seattle to Honolulu only; new route recently opened.

Matson Navigation Co.—From Seattle to Honolulu only; new route recently opened.

Matson Navigation Co.—From San Francisco; regular weekly sailings to Honolulu and other points in the Hawaiian Islands.

Oceanic Steamship Co.—From San Francisco to the Antipodes via Honolulu.

Pacific Mail Steamship Co.—From San Francisco to Oriental ports; with increased first-class passenger accommodations on six new shipping-board vessels.

Matson Navigation Co.—From Baltimore to Honolulu and Hilo, via Havana, the Panama Canal, Los Angeles and San Francisco.

THE CALL OF JAPAN

Now more than ever Americans are interested in the Far East, because they have come to learn so much about Japan and China from the discussions at the Washington Conference. Mr. John D. Rockefeller, Jr., on returning from his Far East tour, is quoted in the press as saying: "I have come home with a tremendously deepened interest in the problems of the Orient, with the warmest feelings of friendship for both the Chinese and the Japanese people, and desirous of doing everything possible to forward international peace, good-will, and cooperation between these great nations and the peoples of the west." Mr. Rockefeller's message of peace and good-will epitomizes the impressions of many visitors to the Far East. The fascination and instruction to be enjoyed in Oriental travel were never so appealing as to-day, when you can visit these fairy-like regions through the most modern rail and waterways, while your stop-overs are spent in the best appointed hotels. In Japan, for instance, railway travel is only fifty years old, and the government railways of Japan, we learn from their bulletins of information, date back only to 1869, a few years after the doors of the Hermit Nation, that had been jealously kept closed for more than two thousand years, were thrown wide open to admit the flow of foreign civilization. In 1872 rail traffic was opened by a line of some twenty miles running between Tokio and Yokohama, and to-day there are government lines of more than 6,500 miles, and private lines of some 2,000 miles.

The Japanese Empire with its population of 70,000,000 extends along the Eastern shores of Asia, and consists of five large islands and countless smaller ones. Japan itself is the Eastern center of world traffic. On the coast bordering the Pacific Ocean and the East China Sea, Yokohama, Kobe, and Nagasaki are the main ports of call for ocean liners to and from America, Australia and Europe; while the port of Tsuruga on the Japan Sea is connected with Vladivostok. Connections between Japan proper and Chosen (Korea) are maintained by steamers of the government railways between Shimonoseki and Fusan. At the latter port begins the Chosen line of

Railway Company, which forms an international thoroughfare in conjunction with the company's Manchurian line for China.

As the dominions of Japan extend almost to the frigid zone in the north, and to the tropical zone in the south, the climate varies according to the locality, altho there are sections, much frequented by travelers, where the temperature is not subject to extreme changes. Generally speaking, from the middle of March to May in the spring, and from the middle of September to November in the autumn, are the pleasantest months for traveling. But Japanese writers point out that each and every season of the year has its characteristic charms.

ROUTES TO THE ORIENT

Excellent steamship service between the United States, Japan and other Oriental countries is provided in two main routes, the first beginning at Seattle and the second at San Francisco. Following is a brief directory of transpacific lines operated from these ports.

Over the short "Great Circle" steamship lane between Puget Sound and Yokohama are being operated, under the American flag, fast new American-built passenger steamships of the Admiral Line (Pacific Steamship Company). The passage from Seattle to Yokohama is made in eleven steaming days. After leaving Yokohama the ships continue to Kobe, Shanghai, Hong Kong and Manila.

Also over the North Pacific Route steam the "Empress" fleet of the Canadian Pacific Steamships Limited from Vancouver to Yokohama, thence to Kobe, Nagasaki, Shanghai, Manila and Hong Kong.

A third Northern route is from Seattle to Yokohama and other important Oriental ports, provided by the Nippon Yusen Kaisha (Japan Mail Steamship Company).

Over the central route, sailing from San Francisco via Honolulu thence to Yokohama, Kobe, Nagasaki, Shanghai and Hong Kong steam under the American flag vessels of the China Mail Steamship Company, Ltd. and the Pacific Mail Steamship Co., via Honolulu, Yokohama, Kobe, Shanghai and Manila to Hong Kong.

From San Francisco to Hong Kong are also operated steamships of the Toyo Kisen Kaisha (Oriental Steamship Company), via Honolulu, Yokohama, Kobe, Nagasaki, Shanghai, Dairen and Manila.

TRANSATLANTIC SAILINGS

There is a noticeable rise in the tide of European winter travel. The winter of 1921 was the first tourist season for Egypt and the Mediterranean since the beginning of the war. The winter of 1922 promises to exceed it in volume of travel. Numerous winter cruises are planned to include Spain, Gibraltar, Algiers, The Holy Land, Athens, Italy and the Riviera. Below is a brief directory of the leading transatlantic lines, with sailings from New York.

International Mercantile Marine (White Star Line, American Line, Red Star Line) New York to Cherbourg, Southampton and Mediterranean ports.

Compagnie Generale Trans-Atlantique (French Line) New York for Bordeaux and Havre.

Cunard-Anchor Line for Cherbourg, Southampton, Liverpool, Londonderry and Glasgow; also Mediterranean ports.

United States Mail Steamship Company, New York for Bremen, Danzig and Queenstown.

Holland-American Line, New York for Plymouth, Boulogne-sur-Mer, Rotterdam.

Royal Mail Steam Packet, New York to Cherbourg, Southampton and Hamburg.

Norwegian-American Line, New York to Christiania.

Scandinavian-American Line, New York to Christiania and Copenhagen.

Swedish-American Line, New York to Gothenburg.

Navigazione Generale Italiana, New York to Naples and Genoa.

INVESTMENTS ▲ AND ▲ FINANCE

WHY BUILDING BOOMS WHILE BUSINESS LAGS

THERE is a long cherished tradition to the effect that building is one of the last of the industries to recover from an economic slump. But this, says *Bradstreet's*, has now "been exploded and relegated to the place where so many other economic theories, which passed current before the Great War, have gone." The returns from 157 cities show the total value for building permits for October to be $167,386,660, as against $149,506,906 in September and only $92,175,533 in October a year ago. Thus there is a gain of 11.9 per cent. over the previous month and of 81.6 per cent. over October a year ago. The October figures, we are told, exceed those for August, 1921, and August, 1919, and are second only to the aggregate of April, 1920, "when the building boom reached its crest." And, if the lower values of material and wages as compared with April, 1920, are taken into account, "the October volume of building will be found to have exceeded even that hitherto peak month and the curious situation is presented of a great boom in building construction at a time when nearly all other lines of industry are either deprest or painfully recovering from the depths of past depression." *Bradstreet's* explains this condition of affairs by the fact that "much absolutely necessary building was postponed owing to preoccupation in the war or to high prices and high wages following that struggle, and this is apparently now being pushed to completion, to the confounding of the theories and the theorists." Other authorities report a continuance of the building boom, and the *Federal Reserve Bulletin* says "the activity of building has been particularly noteworthy because of its continuance beyond the time when a seasonal reaction would ordinarily occur."

FRANCE'S NEW FINANCIAL POLICY

FRANCE'S position as a debtor to her allies and to the United States, and as a preferred creditor of Germany, make her financial policy a matter of world-wide interest. The Briand Government's new program, which has just been endorsed by the Chamber of Deputies, includes, according to a recent Associated press dispatch from Paris:

> Strict execution of her engagements by Germany and conservation by France in her dealings with the Allies of all guaranties of payment. No new taxes to be levied till the maximum revenue has been obtained from those in existence. Avoidance of any increase in fiduciary issue. Limitation of public expenditure to strict necessity and organic reforms with a view to economy. Progressive reduction of the number of functionaries to that of 1914. Encouragement of the economic development of France and the colonies in a free spirit and transformation of State monopolies as rapidly as possible where to the general interest.

TREMENDOUS BUSINESS DONE BY GREAT DEPARTMENT STORES

WITHIN the last fifty years the great department stores of New York, Chicago, Philadelphia, London and Paris have come into existence and have built up businesses comparing favorably with those done by important manufacturing and transportation companies. The largest retail store in the world is that of Marshall Field of Chicago, which does a business of from $65,000,000 to $73,000,000 annually in normal times. Other equally famous department stores do a business only slightly less.

The Wall Street Journal, which has been collecting these figures, notes that there are aggregations of stores or chain stores under a single management that do a bigger business than the department stores, "notably Woolworth with 1,111 stores and $140,000,000 of gross business; the United Cigars, 1,400 stores with aggregate business of $75,000,000; and Kresge with 194 stores and a gross business of between $50,000,000 and $60,000,000."

Probably the biggest retail business in dollars and cents that has ever been done, we are told, is "that of the mail order house of Sears Roebuck & Company, which for the first three months of 1920 did a business of $90,000,000 gross or over $1,000,000 a day."

The astonishing thing about the department store business is said to be not size but the large expense in service:

> Formerly department stores did business with expense of 10% and 12% for rent, salaries, delivery, management and all overhead. To-day the public is served by the big department stores at an expense exceeding 30% of the gross sales.

The 1920 figures for the business done by the department stores of the world do not set a record, being estimated as a whole at something like 5 per cent. below the normal pre-war or 1913 basis. *The Wall Street Journal* goes on to present the 1920 figures for business done by the leading establishments, as gathered from reliable trade sources:

Selfridge & Co.	London	$30,000,000
Bon Marche	Paris	40,000,000
Marshall Field	Chicago	65,000,000
Carson, Pirie & Scott	"	50,000,000
R. H. Macy & Co.	New York	25,000,000
Franklin Simon Co.	"	21,000,000
Lord & Taylor	"	20,000,000
Gimbel Bros.	"	20,000,000
Altman & Co.	"	18,000,000
John Wanamaker	"	28,000,000
John Wanamaker	Philadelphia	27,000,000
N. Snellenburg & Co.	"	40,000,000
Lit Bros.	"	33,000,000

While Death Plays Santa Claus

GAY colored lights—glittering tinsel—the laughter of children—the Tree—Home—*and off there in the Volga country people are starving to death.*

Holly and mistletoe—bulging stockings by the fire in the living-room—red and white candy canes—little packages tied with red and green ribbons—Mother—*and off there in the Volga country the nurses are separating the babies who are going to die today from the ones who won't die until tomorrow.*

Dad carving the turkey and spilling gravy on the tablecloth—the family laughing at Baby as she sucks the drumstick bone—teasing Mother because she didn't put enough sugar in the cranberry sauce—*and off there in the Volga country they're eating bread made of dried grass and ground-up horses' hoofs.*

While our lights are gay and our homes are filled with Christmas cheer—

Death plays Santa Claus.

Off there in the Volga country fifteen million people are dying of hunger while we say "Merry Christmas" and celebrate the birthday of Jesus Christ.

$10 will save 10 lives for a month
$100 will save 100 lives for a month
$1000 will save 1000 lives for a month

Every dollar spent in America—Every dollar spent for relief

RUSSIAN FAMINE FUND

Distributing through The Society of Friends (The Quakers)

National Headquarters 15 PARK ROW, NEW YORK

With committees in

BOSTON, PITTSBURGH, PHILADELPHIA, NEW YORK, CHICAGO, MINNEAPOLIS

and other American cities

Executive Committee

Allen Wardwell, Chairman
Jane Addams
Mrs. August Belmont
Charles C. Burlingham
William M. Chadbourne
Paul D. Cravath
Lewis S. Gannett
Robert Morss Lovett
Walter W. Pettit
Frank L. Polk
Charles H. Sabin, Treasurer
Graham Romeyn Taylor
Helen Todd
Felix M. Warburg
L. Hollingsworth Wood
Harry Powers Story, Secretary

National Committee

Rt. Rev. C. P. Anderson, D.D.
Dr. Frank Billings
Harriot Stanton Blatch
Cornelius N. Bliss, Jr.
Alfred J. Boulton
Arthur Brisbane
John Graham Brooks
Mrs. Cora Haviland Carver
Bayard M. Christy
C. P. Coleman
Edward Cornell
Fred M. Corse
Charles R. Crane
John W. Davis
Jerome T. DeHunt
William C. Edgar
Charles W. Eliot
John Lovejoy Elliott
Harry M. Fennimore
Irving Fisher
Hon. Joseph I. France
Hon. David R. Francis
Col. Michael Friedsam
John A. Gade
E. F. Gay
Samuel Gompers
Rev. Percy Stickney Grant, D.D.
Norman Hapgood
Robert Herrick
Rabbi Emil G. Hirsch
William M. Johnston
Alexander Kahn
Dr. Gertrude Kelly
William Kent
E. F. Ladd
Col. Herbert Lehman
Cyrus H. McCormick
James G. McDonald
John A. McSparran
Rabbi Judah Leon Magnes
Capt. Wm. A. Maher
Anne Martin
Hon. Ogden L. Mills
William Fellowes Morgan
Walter M. Nelson
Morgan J. O'Brien
Fremont Older
Herbert Parsons
Francis G. Peabody
Dr. Raymond V. Phelan
Mrs. Gifford Pinchot
Glenn E. Plumb
Ernest Poole
James H. Post
Mrs. John T. Pratt
William C. Redfield
Very Rev. Howard C. Robbins, D.D
Raymond Robins
Dr. Frank F. Rosenblatt
Julius Rosenwald
Rev. John A. Ryan
Mrs. Vladimir G. Simkhovitch
Alfred E. Smith
Mrs. Willard D. Straight
Henry W. Taft
Thomas D. Thacher
Norman Thomas
Mrs. Charles L. Tiffany
Oswald Garrison Villard
B. C. Vladeck
Lillian D. Wald
J. H. Walker
Robert Wardrop
Robert W. Webb
George P. West
George W. Wickersham

CHARLES H. SABIN, Treasurer
Russian Famine Fund,
Room 1836 15 Park Row, New York

Dear Sir:

I enclose $................ as my contribution toward the relief of the suffering in Russia. Please send acknowledgment to

Name ....

No. .... Street ....

City ....

No Propaganda—No Politics—FOOD!!

The number of the nation's unemployed has decreased by more than a million during recent weeks, according to an estimate of the National Conference on Unemployment.

The Philippine legislature requests of President Harding that the Filipinos be consulted on any questions coming up in the Washington Conference which involve their interest.

The Emergency Fleet Corporation plans to sell everything it owns "as fast as it can and at what prices it can get," announces President Joseph W. Powell.

December 3.—Great Britain, France and Japan agree at the Washington Conference to surrender important leaseholds in Chinese territory, tho Japan insists that she has no present intention to relinquish her rights in Manchuria.

December 4.—Great Britain and Japan, it is announced, will insist that the naval armament limitation agreement be put in the form of a treaty and ratified by the Senate.

A special deputation from the Far Eastern Republic of Chita arrives in Washington to lay before the Conference the plea of that government for withdrawal of Japanese troops from Siberia and to secure recognition of the Chita administration.

Textile union officials meeting in New York announce that they are preparing the organization of a united textile labor union in opposition to the American Federation of Labor.

December 5.—Nineteen persons are killed and more than a score are injured in a head-on collision between passenger trains near Woodmont, Pennsylvania. Some of the passengers are burned to death when the wooden coaches catch fire.

The first budget of government expenditures, transmitted to Congress by President Harding at the opening of the regular session, calls for estimated expenses in the fiscal year ending June 30, 1923, of $3,505,754,727, half a billion less than for 1922, and more than $2,000,000,000 less than the actual cost of government for 1921.

Japan agrees at the Washington Conference to return to China administrative control of Shantung, but demands that the railway from Tsing Tao to Tsinan be placed under a joint Japanese-Chinese administration.

December 6.—In his message to Congress, President Harding advocates legislation for judicial settlement of troubles between capital and labor, renewed tax revision, repeal of the provisions of the Jones Shipping Act that would abrogate commercial treaties, alteration of the Fordney tariff bill to give the executive power to fix duties to meet problems as they arise, and an amendment to the Constitution releasing non-taxable bonds for taxation without disadvantages resulting to the States.

Three advisers to the Chinese delegation at the Washington Conference resign because of their belief that China will "get nothing" from the Conference.

Calming His Fears.—One of the fifth division (speeding homeward on the "Limited")—"What if this bridge should break and the train be dashed into the river?"

Conductor—"Don't worry lad, the railroad company has a lot more trains."—*The Arklight.*

The number of the nation's unemployed has decreased by more than a million during recent weeks, according to an estimate of the National Conference on Unemployment.

The Philippine legislature requests of President Harding that the Filipinos be consulted on any questions coming up in the Washington Conference which involve their interest.

The Emergency Fleet Corporation plans to sell everything it owns "as fast as it can and at what prices it can get," announces President Joseph W. Powell.

December 3.—Great Britain, France and Japan agree at the Washington Conference to surrender important leaseholds in Chinese territory, tho Japan insists that she has no present intention to relinquish her rights in Manchuria.

December 4.—Great Britain and Japan, it is announced, will insist that the naval armament limitation agreement be put in the form of a treaty and ratified by the Senate.

A special deputation from the Far Eastern Republic of Chita arrives in Washington to lay before the Conference the plea of that government for withdrawal of Japanese troops from Siberia and to secure recognition of the Chita administration.

Textile union officials meeting in New York announce that they are preparing the organization of a united textile labor union in opposition to the American Federation of Labor.

December 5.—Nineteen persons are killed and more than a score are injured in a head-on collision between passenger trains near Woodmont, Pennsylvania. Some of the passengers are burned to death when the wooden coaches catch fire.

The first budget of government expenditures, transmitted to Congress by President Harding at the opening of the regular session, calls for estimated expenses in the fiscal year ending June 30, 1923, of $3,505,754,727, half a billion less than for 1922, and more than $2,000,000,000 less than the actual cost of government for 1921.

Japan agrees at the Washington Conference to return to China administrative control of Shantung, but demands that the railway from Tsing Tao to Tsinan be placed under a joint Japanese-Chinese administration.

December 6.—In his message to Congress, President Harding advocates legislation for judicial settlement of troubles between capital and labor, renewed tax revision, repeal of the provisions of the Jones Shipping Act that would abrogate commercial treaties, alteration of the Fordney tariff bill to give the executive power to fix duties to meet problems as they arise, and an amendment to the Constitution releasing non-taxable bonds for taxation without disadvantages resulting to the States.

Three advisers to the Chinese delegation at the Washington Conference resign because of their belief that China will "get nothing" from the Conference.

Calming His Fears.—One of the fifth division (speeding homeward on the "Limited")—"What if this bridge should break and the train be dashed into the river?"

Conductor—"Don't worry lad, the railroad company has a lot more trains."—*The Arklight.*

THE ▲ SPICE ▲ OF ▲ LIFE

Sad Example.—Crookedness never pays in the long run. Look at the corkscrew.—*Burlington News.*

Old Friends.—A Chinese play 600 years old was recently performed in English. Several score present-day music-hall gags were recognized.—*New York Star.*

When They Laugh.—Frenchmen have a strong sense of what is funny. We English-speaking peoples find it out when we try to talk to them in French.—*St. Louis Globe-Democrat.*

Fair Warning.—If your leg is loose get it tightened before the table tips and breaks your dishes. All work guaranteed.—*Furniture Repairer's ad. in the Bremerton Evening Searchlight.*

How to Save Your Family.—Fire destroyed another beautiful Salina home. Happened while husband was away caused from soot in the chimney. Why take the chance, think of your wife and babies at home. Have them inspected, repaired and cleaned.—*From an ad. in the Salina Union.*

Heredity Again.—"Late for reveille again, I see, O'Malley," snorted the irate captain. "How do you account for this persistent tardiness?"

"'Tis inherited, sir," answered Pvt. O'Malley. "Me father was the late Michael O'Malley."—*The American Legion Weekly.*

It Looked Bad.—"Why you call my boy a poor nut?" queried an indignant mother, who confronted the dietitian of a New Jersey charities association the other morning at her office door. And the latter has not yet found a way of convincing Mrs. Caruso that "poor nut" on the face of Angelo's card stands for poor nutrition.—*Survey.*

The Easier Job.—"What are you going to be when you grow up, Jennie?"

"I'm going to be an old maid."

"An old maid, dear. Why?"

"'Cause I don't think I'd like to kiss a man a hundred times and tell him he's handsome every time I do shopping. I'd rather earn money and buy things for myself."—*Baptist Boys and Girls.*

Husbanding Her Resources.—He was cycling through a quaint, old-fashioned village, when he was thrilled by the sound of a woman's cry for help, followed by the muffled tones of a man's voice. He quickened his pace, to find a woman holding on to the handle of a cottage door, while from within it was evident that somebody was endeavoring to force it open.

"Give me a hand, mister," she cried. "I daren't let him come out!"

The cyclist dismounted, and by adding his strength to that of the woman the door was kept closed.

"Your husband I suppose?" he said.

"Yes," was the breathless reply. "He's got one of his crazy fits on to-day."

"Well, I should think you would be pleased to let him out."

"Not till this policeman's passed," panted the woman. "You see, Bill's very nasty with policemen when he's like this, and this one's too valuable to lose. I do his washing."—*Tit-Bits (London.)*

The Only Explanation.—"One never hears a breath of scandal about her."

"Why? Hasn't she any friends?"—*London Mail.*

Our Text-Book Age.—"If I only knew what to do with baby!"

"Didn't you get a book of instructions with it, mother?"—*Kasper (Stockholm).*

Health Resorts.—He—"I spent a lot of money at Kelley pool this winter."

She—"Did you like it as well as Hot Springs?"—*Purple Cow* (Williams).

Where Ignorance Is Safety.—A Virginia man never saw an automobile until last Friday, his 98th birthday. That's one reason he's 98!—*Schenectady Gazette.*

His Grasping Disposition.—"Why did they put Bob out of the game?"

"For holding."

"Oh, isn't that just like Bob!"—*Virginia Reel.*

First Things To-day.—The first thing some people want when they get a little money is a car; then the first thing they want when they get a car is a little money.—*American Lumberman.*

Poultry First.—As I need more room for the Poultry Business I have moved my barber shop to the rear room, but am still doing business in the barber line.—*From an ad. in the Jamestown, N. Dak., Alert.*

Postponing the Day.—The convert who recently got up at a prayer meeting and thanked the Lord that he had three wives in heaven was (so it is rumored) subsequently observed paying sixpence at a bookstall for a copy of "How to Prolong Life."—*Eve.*

His Prize Lamp.—Father (reading a letter from his son at college to mother)—"Myopia says he's got a beautiful lamp from boxing."

Mother—"I just knew he'd win something in his athletics."—*Orange Owl* (Oregon Agri).

Restaurant American.

"Scrambled eggs," ordered a customer in a city market restaurant. "Milk toast," murmured his companion, who was not feeling well.

"Scramble two and a grave yard stew," sang out the waitress with the Titian hair.

"Here," corrected the second man, "I want milk toast."

"You'll get it Buddy," replied the girl. "That's what they call milk toast down in Pittsburgh, where I worked."

The two customers held a conference and decided to "put one over" on the "fresh young thing" from Pittsburgh. The first one wanted a glass of milk and the second a cup of black coffee.

When the girl appeared to put a "set up" of the restaurant artillery in front of the men the second man gave the following order:

"A bottle of lacteal fluid for my friend and a scuttle of Java with no sea foam for me."

"Chalk one an' a dipper of ink," shouted the girl. She didn't even grin.—*The Arklight.*

THE LEXICOGRAPHER'S EASY CHAIR

In this column, to decide questions concerning the current use of words, the Funk & Wagnalls New Standard Dictionary is consulted as arbiter.

Readers will please bear in mind that no notice will be taken of anonymous communications.

"D. K.," Bournemouth, Dorset, England.—The name of the county of *Hampshire*, England, is derived from the Anglo-Saxon *Hamtun-scir*, from *Hamtun*. In the Anglo-Saxon Chronicle for A. D. 837 *Southampton* is the name given to *Hampshire*. *Hampton* is from Old English *ham* home, and *tun*, estate or farmstead on rich, riparian pasture land; by extention, town.

"H. H.," Colorado Springs, Colo.—"Will you please express your opinion in regard to the use of the words *begin* and *commence?* Modern writers seem fond of using the long and cumbersome French *commence* in preference to the short and virile Anglo-Saxon *begin*. Writers also seem to prefer the noun *commencement* instead of the verb form.

Commence is frequently substituted for *begin* when used with "work" where the change should not be made. *Begin* is applied to order of time: *commence* relates to the work on hand with reference to its subsequent completion. The man who strikes the first blow *begins* a fight, but both parties to a law suit *commence* litigation at the moment when they severally undertake the first step.—Vizetelly, "Desk-Book of Errors in English."

The Latin *commencement* is more formal than the Saxon *beginning*, as the verb *commence*, is more formal than *begin*. *Commencement* is for the most part restricted to some form of action, while *beginning* has no restriction, but may be applied to action, state, material, extent, enumeration, or to whatever else may be conceived of as having first a part, point, degree, etc. The letter A is at the *beginning* (not the *commencement*) of every alphabet. If we were to speak of the *commencement* of the Pacific Railroad, we should be understood to refer to the enterprise and its initiatory act; if we were to refer to the roadway we should say "Here is the *beginning* of the Pacific Railroad." In the great majority of cases *begin* and *beginning* are preferable to *commence* and *commencement* as the simple, idiomatic English words are always accurate and expressive. "In the *beginning* was the word," John i, 1.—James C. Fernald, *English Synonyms, Antonyms and Prepositions.*

"F. A. A.," New Hampton, N. H.—The word *peripety* is a variant form of *peripetia*, which means: "That part of a drama in which the plot is brought to a conclusion; the dénouement: applied, by extension, to life."

"K. W. Mack," St. Paul, Minn.—"What is the correct pronounciation of the word *erudite?*"

There are two pronunciations, the first is *er'u-dait*—*e* as in *get*, *u* as in *full*, *ai* as in *aisle*; or *er'yu-dait*—*e* as in *get*, *yu* pronounced like *you*, *ai* as in *aisle*.

"E. T.," Danville, Ky.—"How is a check payable to a woman customarily written, as, 'Susan N. Smith' or 'Mrs. John Smith'; 'Kate Brown' or 'Miss Kate Brown?'"

In drawing a check to the order of a married woman, it may be drawn either to "(Mrs.) John Smith" or to "Susan N. Smith"; the latter is the better form unless it is desired to show that she is the wife of "John Smith." In the case of an unmarried woman, the usual form is to make the check payable to "Kate Brown." The essential thing to do is, however, to indorse the check *exactly* as it is drawn on the face.

"O. B.," Ann Arbor, Mich.—"Do you consider that the Anglicized pronunciation of foreign names is ever allowable? I often hear such names as *Ascencion* and *Chile* so pronounced, and have considered it as a mark of uncultivated speech. To one who speaks Spanish, the twisting of South American names out of their own beautiful sound is distressing to listen to."

It is the duty of a lexicographer to place only the best usage on record. The rule generally followed is to give the pronunciation of educated persons. The names of many foreign countries and cities have become so thoroughly Anglicized that to give them in the pronunciations used by their citizens might lay one open to a charge of affectation. Who, for instance, in America, would use *Paree* for *Paris*, or *Me'hi-ko* for *Meks'i-ko?*

DRIVING intricate automatic machinery in factories, furnishing motive energy to unnumbered types of household and office appliances, Robbins & Myers Motors for nearly a quarter of a century have won admiration for the reliable character of their service. Through every step of their manufacture, from the winding of armatures to the final assembly, R&M products are subjected to critical scrutiny by expert inspectors. To measure to the standard inferred by the Robbins & Myers name plate is a test calling for all that a product has of honest merit, and one that is applied without exception to every R&M Motor built.

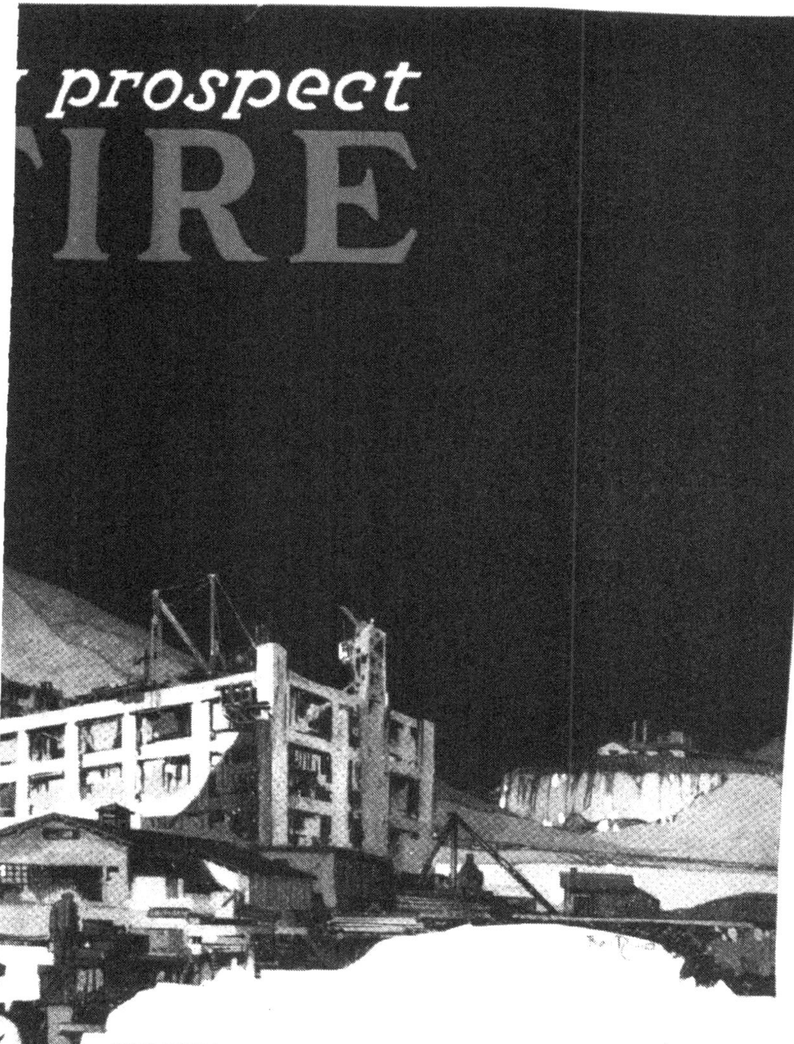

EVERY new building is a prospect for fire—a source of possible loss to its owners.

The Hartford Fire Insurance Company offers sound insurance against loss if fire comes. In addition the Hartford's Fire Prevention Engineers will plan with you to prevent a fire and this cooperation should begin when plans are made. There is no fee or charge for consultation.

For over a century the Hartford has made good the losses of its policy-holders. It will sell you sound insurance.

If you own property it should be insured in the Hartford. There is a Hartford agent near you. If you do not know him write to the Company.

Fire Insurance Co.

Hartford Conn.

urance Co. and The Hartford Accident and Indemnity Co.
ractically every form of insurance except life

The Woman whose sleep is habitually disturbed—

May make a failure of her children

There is nothing in the world more likely to create a nervous, irritable disposition than the constant loss of sleep

If YOUR nerves are irritated so that sleep only comes after hours and hours of tossing around restlessly, and then is broken and fitful and unrefreshing, your nerves cannot be in proper condition.

As a matter of fact, your nerves are not properly nourished. They may be actually starved, because it is during sleep that the reconstructive processes in your body are busiest.

Therefore, the woman whose nerves are irritated and kept on edge, can never do herself justice. She cannot possibly show the forebearance and consideration for her children that she would if her nerves were calm and rested.

If you are accustomed to drinking tea or coffee, you are taking into your system elements which, sooner or later, may bring about nerve-bankruptcy. For tea and coffee contain thein and caffeine—well-known drugs.

If you want to know the joys of sound, restful sleep and strong virile nerves, stop drinking tea and coffee, and drink Postum in tead. You will like its delicious, savory flavor.

Postum is the nationally-known, pure cereal beverage. It helps to build up the nervous system, by permitting you to get sound, refreshing sleep.

Go to your grocer today and get a tin of Instant Postum—made instantly in the cup. Drink it for 10 days instead of tea or coffee, and see how much more vigorous and enduring you will feel. Then you can make up your mind to quit tea and coffee forever.

Instant Postum *for* Health

"There's a Reason"

December 24, 1921

The Literary Digest

(Title Reg. U.S. Pat. Off.)

©

THE STORY OF CHRISTMAS—by Norman Rockwell

New York FUNK & WAGNALLS COMPANY London

PUBLIC OPINION New York combined with The LITERARY DIGEST

Vol. 71, No. 13. Whole No. 1653 December 24, 1921 Price 10 Cents

The Nash Four
The New Nash Six

The Nash Four—a quality car at a popular car price.

The Nash Four was designed and built as a light weight high-quality car and even at its original price of $1395 created a new standard of value.

Now at its new reduced price, the Nash Four will find wide acceptance as the most remarkable motor car value in America.

Ranking with the finest of four-cylinder automobiles in every attribute of appearance, comfort, and performance—in its wonderful acceleration, speed, dependability and power, such value is made possible only through volume production and the narrowest margin of profit. Let the Nash dealer go over this car with you—then drive it.

New model, series 691, the greater Nash Six with new straight-line body, Delco Equipment, perfected valve-in-head motor and wonderful new springs.

Observe the beauty of its new straight-line body with lowered top and windshield. Then drive this car over some rough road. Feel the quick response, great power and flexibility of its Nash Perfected Valve-in-Head Motor—but most of all the wonderful riding quality of its new type springs.

This new series in both open and closed cars brings a new standard of riding comfort, a vast development in performance capability and a striking distinction in body designs, now ready at your dealer's.

NASH FOUR MODELS

5-passenger touring — *3-passenger coupe*
2-passenger roadster — *5-passenger sedan*

All Nash passenger cars have cord tires as standard equipment

NASH SIX MODELS

5-passenger touring — *4-passenger sport model* — *7-passenger touring*
2-passenger roadster — *4-passenger coupe* — *7-passenger sedan*

See these Nash Values at the Automobile shows

THE NASH MOTORS COMPANY, KENOSHA, WISCONSIN

The "Ayes" have it!

"All in favor of this motion appropriating $7,000 for automobiles for the Safety Department and Building Department signify by saying 'Aye'."

"The Ayes have it. It is so voted."

"We come now to a consideration of the proposed Sprinkler System for the Elm Street Grammar School. The cost I believe is $5,500. Conditions I understand are very "

"I move the matter be laid on the table."

"Second."

"All in favor say 'aye'."

"The ayes have it. It is so voted."

And six months later the local paper in writing up the fire in the Elm Street Grammar School where two children were killed and a fireman fatally burned in rescue work, complimented the city officials on their speed in arriving at the blaze to take charge.

Speed is the whole thing when fire breaks out. The paper might better have noted that if $5,500 had been put into a sprinkler system, the water would have beaten the officials to the fire by half an hour and no lives would have been lost.

We have prepared a book which shows the danger of school fires. It is "Fire Tragedies and Their Remedy." If you are a wide-awake citizen you will want it. It will answer convincingly every question you ask about Automatic Sprinklers. It will wake you up to the penalty paid by those who have neglected to provide adequate fire protection. Write us today for your free copy. Address Grinnell Company, Inc., 274 West Exchange Street, Providence, R. I.

GRINNELL

AUTOMATIC SPRINKLER SYSTEM

When the fire starts, the water starts

Volume 71 No. 13

TABLE ▾ OF ▾ CONTENTS

December 24, 1921

TOPICS OF THE DAY: Page
- Workability of the Four-Power Peace Pact 5
- "Viper" Weapons 8
- The Farm Bloc—a Peril or a Hope? 10
- The Railroads' Christmas Carol 11
- The Battle of Packingtown 13
- Topics in Brief 15

FOREIGN COMMENT:
- America's New Triumph 16
- Mexico's Era of Reconstruction 17
- A French Vision of Greek Gloom 18
- Russia's New Bourgeoisie 19

SCIENCE AND INVENTION:
- A Warning Against Eye-Glasses 20
- Plant Indications of Oil 21
- An Eat-as-You-Go Lunch Room 21
- Changing Our Medical Superstitions 22
- Accidents Due to Fatigue 22
- Why and When Watch-Springs Break 23

LETTERS AND ART: Page
- Shakespeare Recreated by a Woman 24
- Chicago's Unlettered State 25
- France's Greatest Living Composer 25
- Kitchener's Death in the Movies 27

RELIGION AND SOCIAL SERVICE:
- Christmas as a Day of Prayer for Disarmament 28
- Changing Women Into Human Beings 29
- Crime Decreasing in England 30
- The Glitter of Bahaism 30

MISCELLANEOUS:
- Current Poetry 31
- Personal Glimpses 32-34
- Notable Books of the Season 36-41
- Current Events 42-43
- Investments and Finance 44
- The Spice of Life 46-47

TERMS: $4.00 a year, in advance; six months, $2.25; three months, $1.50; a single copy, 10 cents; postage to Canada, 85 cents a year; other foreign postage, $2.00 a year. BACK NUMBERS, not over three months old, 25 cents each; over three months old, $1.00 each. QUARTERLY INDEXES will be sent free to subscribers who apply for them. RECEIPT of payment is shown in about two weeks by date on address-label; date of expiration includes the month named on the label. CAUTION: If date is not properly extended after each payment, notify publishers promptly. Instructions for RENEWAL, DISCONTINUANCE, or CHANGE OF ADDRESS should be sent *two weeks* before the date they are to go into effect. *Both old and new addresses* must always be given. PRESENTATION COPIES: Many persons subscribe for friends. Those who desire to renew such subscriptions must do so before expiration.

THE LITERARY DIGEST is published weekly by the Funk & Wagnalls Company, 354-360 Fourth Avenue, New York, and Salisbury Square, London, E. C.

Entered as second-class matter, March 24, 1890, at the Post-office at New York, N. Y., under the act of March 3, 1879.

Entered as second-class matter at the Post-office Department, Ottawa, Canada.

Unlock the Treasure-Vaults Of Your Mind

—Here Are the Keys!

There are certain qualities that every man must exercise if he would win promotion, more pay, more influence and power. You possess these qualities to a greater or lesser extent. Develop them—use them—profit by them! In the majority of men these qualifications are dormant—they are locked up in their minds. These ten books are the keys that will unlock them! They create the characteristics that win power, position, and happiness for all who will master them. Nearly two hundred thousand men and women own these unusual volumes, and it is safe to say that to **them they have brought new hope, rekindled the fires of ambition, and lifted them joyously to higher and more influential places in the world.**

"The volume on 'Practicality' alone is worth many times the price paid for the ten books." *Joseph I. Cantarow, Ph. G.*, Hartford, Conn.

"They are really indispensable. A real student is bound to take his place in the first rank of constructive, efficient, and consequently successful business men." *Elmer H. Dearth*, Pres. Manufacturers and Traders Casualty Co., Detroit, Mich.

"You have not done them full justice in your advertisements. They not only treat the subjects more copiously than I had anticipated but the logical and thoro development of each topic renders them valuable to all." *David D. Stiles*, Chicago, Ill.

POISE: *How To Attain It*

Here the immense value of poise is explained, with instructions for acquiring the ability to be thoroughly at ease and self-controlled in all situations, even under the most trying circumstances. A clear explanation is given of how one man can dominate a situation without appearing to do so; how to rid yourself of uncertainty; how to hold an individual or an audience; how to create the favorable first impression that counts for so much in business and social life, etc., etc.

TIMIDITY: *How To Overcome It*

This volume shows you how to get rid of doubt of yourself which is the cause of all timidity. It describes the way to attain thorough self-confidence; how to develop moral courage, courage of your convictions; how to develop physical courage; how to gain the power that will give you mastery of yourself and mastery of others. It explains the handicap in business and society that timidity places on you, and how to overcome it.

PERSEVERANCE: *How To Develop It*

Of all the modern "keys to fortune" none more easily turns the tumblers of the lock than Perseverance. This volume analyzes this quality, points out all the factors which contribute to great perseverance, and then shows you how you may develop it in yourself. How to exercise self-control; how to throw off worry and fatigue; how to keep fresh, keen, and enthusiastic for your job; how to train your mind to concentrate, create, apply itself to any task you will—these and many other phases of the subject are explained for you.

OPPORTUNITIES: *How To Make the Most of Them*

This is an inspiring and suggestive branch of mental efficiency which shows how fortune and good luck are nothing more than seizing opportunities that present themselves, or going ahead and making the opportunities yourself. How to know a good opportunity and take the fullest advantage of it; how to acquire resourcefulness; how to handle every situation so that you may make of it an opportunity to gain some advantage; how to develop the winning combination of audacity and good judgment, etc.

PERSONALITY: *How To Build It*

The important part that personality plays in all the activities of life is described. You are shown the characteristics that make up the man or woman of personal magnetism and power, and how you may develop them in yourself. Habits to cultivate, mistakes to avoid, qualities needed and how to acquire them—every phase of personality building and exercising is explained. Remarkable suggestions as to how to "arrive" in society or business are offered.

INFLUENCE: *How To Exert It*

It is your personal influence on your associates that determines your place in life, and to be successful you must exert it intelligently. This volume explains how to concentrate all the laws of mental efficiency in the building and exercising of your personal influence; how to assume and hold authority; how to develop personal magnetism and self-confidence; how to command your associates, sway an audience, persuade those you meet to your way of thinking; how to exercise your influence wisely and to your greatest advantage in every situation.

COMMON SENSE: *How To Exercise It*

This volume shows why simple common sense is such a rare quality—and such a valuable one. And it gives thorough instructions for developing it. How to see all sides of everything and then take the wisest course; how to weigh advice and judge its value; how to dispel illusions and overcome unwise impulses; how to analyze evidence and make intelligent deductions; how to train yourself to be governed in all your actions by common sense—these and many other phases of the subject are explained fully.

PRACTICALITY: *How To Acquire It*

This volume explains how you may control all your thoughts and actions so that they may be of practical advantage to you. How to acquire the knack of easy application to any task. How to break up bad habits without difficulty; how to get the substance of a book from one reading; how to use your full strength and overcome your weaknesses; how to know false practicality, and avoid errors in foresight; the stock in trade of the practical man and how he uses it, etc.

SPEECH: *How To Use It Effectively*

The expression of many of the powers of the mind depends largely upon your ability to use speech effectively. This volume shows you how to talk to win in every phase of life—whether in a dinner-speech, in a social conversation, on a platform, in a business interview, or anywhere else. It gives you the secrets of appealing to the fundamental instincts of human nature; it shows how to present your facts and opinions to the best advantage; it explains how and when to arouse the different emotions, etc.

CHARACTER: *How To Develop It*

Only by intelligent development can the full force of your character be put into play. This volume explains the best methods of development. How to make the most of your strong points and strengthen your weak ones; how to conquer fear and foolish sentiments; how to see things clearly and make wise decisions; how to concentrate; how to develop the reasoning powers, the analytical powers, the creative powers, and coordinate them all to work to your greatest advantage.

These Books Show You How To

Win by force of character	Banish fear and worry
Create opportunities and make the most of them	Overcome foolish sentiment
Analyze and solve the problems of your daily life	Avoid all kinds of excesses
Organize all your faculties and use them to your greatest advantage	Banish indecision
Speak with greater power	Overcome nervousness and lack of balance
Be always self-confident and at ease	Judge and use advice
Impress and influence those you associate with	Arouse enthusiasm in yourself and others
Develop executive ability	"Size up" an audience and determine upon the right appeal
Understand and overcome your weak points	Develop business instinct
Appreciate, develop, and use your strong points	Weigh the practicality of any plan
	And hundreds of other equally important subjects

10 Books Sent for Only $1 FOR EXAMINATION

You need not write a letter to order these books. Just sign and mail the coupon below with $1.00 stamps, cash, money order or check. If the volumes do not please you, you can send them back at our expense, we will refund the $1.00 and you will owe us nothing. If you keep them, you pay only $2.00 per month for seven months—$15.00 in all. Don't delay—because of the constantly rising costs the next edition of these books may be priced higher. They are big value at the present figure. **Bound in Beautiful Dark Brown "LUXART"—Semi-Flexible and Richly Embossed in high-relief.**

FUNK & WAGNALLS COMPANY
354-360 Fourth Ave., New York

Enclosed find $1.00. Send me, carriage prepaid, the new ten-volume MENTAL EFFICIENCY LIBRARY bound in semi-flexible "Luxart," richly embossed. If the books are unsatisfactory, I will send them back to you, at your expense, within ten days after receipt; you will refund my money and I shall owe you nothing. If I keep them, I will send $2.00 a month for seven months.
L. D. 12-24-21

Name ....

Street Address ....

City .... State ....

WHO PAYS FOR THE SPECIAL DISCOUNT?

Maybe your dealer has offered you a "special discount" on this or that make of tire.

Think his proposition over.

Ask yourself who pays for this sales inducement.

Is the dealer generously sacrificing his profit—the manufacturer his?

Or is the equivalent of the discount being taken out of the tire?

Think it over.

The immense popularity of Goodyear Tires has been built up without the aid of fictitious sales inducements of any kind.

The extra profit we might have allowed the dealer for the purpose of "special discounts," we are putting into the tire in extra value.

Wouldn't you rather have it there, than in a "special discount"?

Wouldn't you rather buy mileage, than a "bargain"?

We are building Goodyear Tires better today than ever before.

We are making them larger, heavier, stronger, more durable.

Are *you* using them?

More people ride on Goodyear Tires than on any other kind.

THE GOODYEAR TIRE & RUBBER COMPANY
Offices Throughout the World

Goodyear Heavy Tourist Tubes are especially thick, sturdy and long-lived. They come packed in a heavy, waterproof bag. More people ride on Goodyear Tubes than on any other kind

GOODYEAR

THE LITERARY DIGEST

PUBLIC OPINION (New York) combined with THE LITERARY DIGEST

Published by Funk & Wagnalls Company (Adam W. Wagnalls, Pres.; Wilfred J. Funk, Vice-Pres.; Robert J. Cuddihy, Treas.; William Neisel, Sec'y) 354-360 Fourth Ave., New York

Vol. LXXI, No. 13 New York, December 24, 1921 Whole Number 1653

TOPICS - OF - THE - DAY

(Title registered in U S Patent Office for use in this publication and on moving picture films)

WORKABILITY OF THE FOUR-POWER PEACE PACT

THE SAME GROUP of "irreconcilables" who led the fight against our participation in the League of Nations have now rushed to arms to rescue the nation from the Four-Power Pacific Treaty. The result of their former fight is well known. The Hearst papers were credited with much of the influence that defeated the League. Now we find Mr. Hearst's New York *American* warning us that the agreement for peace in the Pacific is really a "war breeder, not a peace-maker," and that its ratification by the Senate would mean the "surrender of our old safeguards" and the acceptance of partnership with "the only three imperialisms and militarisms left in the world—England, France and Japan." "To go into partnership with these international highwaymen is to become an insurer of their stolen goods—to pledge our military, naval and financial help to the thieves whenever the rightful owners of the goods try to regain their property." In another issue of the same paper Mr. Arthur Brisbane pictures England, France, Japan and the United States as four "gentlemen highwaymen trying to agree not to cut each other's throats over the spoils." Another of Mr. Hearst's Washington correspondents declares that the treaty represents for Great Britain "one of the greatest diplomatic triumphs of her history"; and still another denounces it as an attempt to "supersede the Monroe Doctrine" and to "force us to recognize the League of Nations." On the latter point we read:

"Article 18 of the Covenant of the League of Nations provides that: 'Every treaty or international engagement entered into hereafter by any member of the League shall be forthwith registered with the Secretariat and shall as soon as possible be published by it. *No such treaty or international engagement shall be binding until so registered.*'

"This makes it mandatory to Great Britain, France and Japan, who signed the covenant, to register this new proposed agreement with the Secretariat of the League of Nations, and the United States recognizes the League of Nations *ipso facto* when it enters into an agreement which, it knows, must be approved by the League of Nations before it becomes binding."

THE FOUR-POWER AURORA BOREALIS OF THE PACIFIC AND FAR EAST.

—Bushnell for the Central Press Association.

"The proposed Anglo-American-Franco-Japanese alliance in the Pacific has been acclaimed by the same blare of newspaper headlines that prophesied a speedy ratification for the League of Nations in 1919," writes another Washington correspondent of the New York *American*, who goes on to say:

"But treaties are not ratified by newspaper headlines, nor by editorials. The Constitution has entrusted that power to the United States Senate.

"The newspaper acclaim which greeted the birth of Woodrow Wilson's League of Nations was powerless to prevent its ignominous death at the hands of the Senate a year later. There are many promises that the tragedy will be repeated.

"In the case of the League of Nations, months were required before the skeptics could make themselves heard. More months passed before the apologists for the League began to work on reservations intended to make it palatable to Americans."

"Treacherous, treasonable and damnable," seems this new treaty to Senator Reed (Dem.) of Missouri, whose views on international matters are very often in agreement with those of Mr. Hearst. It is, he says, "nothing more nor less than a proposition to refer our rights to a tribunal of four, in which we have but one voice." Senator La Follette of Wisconsin promises to do all in his power to prevent the ratification of the treaty, on the ground that it has "all of the iniquities of the League of Nations, with none of the virtues claimed for that document." In a statement to the press he goes on to say:

"The league purported to embrace all the nations in the world, and to preserve and protect the boundaries of each of them. The proposed alliance is, on the face, a coalition of four powers, who, at this time, are best able to dominate by force the rest of the world.

"This alliance is a challenge to Germany, Russia, and other

great nations, now prostrate, and will ultimately drive them into a similar alliance, greatly exceeding in potential man-power the coalition to which the United States is invited to bind its destiny."

Besides the agreement of the four Powers to cooperate peacefully in the Pacific for ten years, the new treaty provides for the termination of the existing Anglo-Japanese alliance. So the Socialist New York *Call* concludes that "what the agreement

FOLLOWING THE LEADER: OR THE FOUR GREAT POWERS TREATY.

—Walker in the New York *Call*.

accomplishes in reality is to bind Asiatic imperialism into a partnership with three western imperialistic Powers instead of one." This may possibly be the point of view also of Mr. Ma Soo, a spokesman for the South China government of Canton, who is quoted as saying that "if the Pacific Treaty is recognized by the Senate, American prestige in the Orient will be entirely destroyed." And the Norfolk *Virginian-Pilot* similarly finds very little to wax enthusiastic over in this result of the deliberations of the Arms Conference:

"What is of importance just now is to grasp the central fact that the entente is not what Senator Lodge wants us to believe it is. It does not bring within the purview of the 'higher impulses of mankind' any disputes that may be expected to endanger the peace of the world. Altho the entente includes Great Britain and France, its machinery of conciliation can not be invoked to adjust the growing dissension of these two Powers with respect to reparations and the Near East. Altho it includes Japan and the United States, its good offices can not be invoked to settle disquieting differences between these two Powers over immigration and mandates. Altho the entente includes the four Powers most likely to develop sharp conflicts over the complicated problem of China, its arbitral functions are, in respect to an adjustment of this most ominous of all conflicts, inoperative."

But on the other hand Senator Lodge, who led the fight against the League of Nations, is the sponsor and official champion of the Pacific Treaty. This treaty, signed on December 13 by representatives of the United States, Japan, France and Great Britain and read to the Conference by the Massachusetts Senator, is worded as follows:

Article 1.

The high contracting parties agree as between themselves to respect their rights in relation to their insular possessions and insular dominions in the regions of the Pacific Ocean.

If there should develop between any of the high contracting parties a controversy arising out of any Pacific question and involving their said rights which is not satisfactorily settled by diplomacy and is likely to affect the harmonious accord now happily subsisting between them they shall invite the high contracting parties to a joint conference to which the whole subject will be referred for consideration and adjustment.

Article 2.

If the said rights are threatened by the aggressive action of any other power, the high contracting parties shall communicate with one another fully and frankly in order to arrive at an understanding as to the most efficient measures to be taken, jointly and separately, to meet the exigencies of the particular situation.

Article 3.

This agreement shall remain in force for ten years from the time it shall take effect, and after the expiration of said period it shall continue to be in force subject to the right of any of the high contracting parties to terminate it upon twelve months' notice.

Article 4.

This agreement shall be ratified as soon as possible in accordance with the constitutional methods of the high contracting parties and shall take effect on the deposit of ratifications, which shall take place at Washington, and thereupon the agreement between Great Britain and Japan which was concluded at London on July 13, 1911, shall terminate.

The American representatives signed with the following reservations:

1—That the treaty shall apply to the mandated islands in the Pacific Ocean; provided, however, that the making of the treaty shall not be deemed to be an assent on the part of the United States of America to the mandates and shall not preclude agreements between the United States of America and the mandatory Powers, respectively, in relation to the mandated islands.

2—That the controversies to which the second paragraph of Article 1 refers shall not be taken to embrace questions which,

THE WAY TO PUT HIM OUT OF BUSINESS.

—Hanny in the St. Joseph *News-Press*.

according to principles of international law, lie exclusively within the domestic jurisdiction of the respective Powers.

"I firmly believe that when the agreement takes effect we shall have gone further in the direction of securing an enduring peace than by anything that has yet been done," said Secretary Hughes after the reading of the treaty. "If we enter upon this agreement, which rests only upon the will and honor of those who sign it, we at least make the great experiment and appeal to the n and women of the nation to help us sustain it in spirit and truth," said Senator Lodge in his address to the delegates. . Viviani pledged France's "full adhesion to the pact that has t been read," and Prince Tokugawa declared that "all Japan approve" and "will rejoice in this pledge of peace upon the ific Ocean." Mr. Balfour, after paying a warm tribute to an as a loyal and faithful ally of England for twenty years ler the Anglo-Japanese Treaty, went on to say:

THAT'LL HOLD HIM!

—Sykes in the Philadelphia *Evening Public Ledger*.

'Great Britain found itself between the possibilities of two understandings—a misunderstanding if they retained the aty, a misunderstanding if they denounced the treaty—and have long come to the conclusion that the only possible way of this impasse . . . was that we should annul, merge, troy, as it were, this ancient and outward and unnecessary eement, and to replace it by something new, something ective, which should embrace all the Powers concerned in the t area of the Pacific."

Turning to the American press, we find the friends of the new aty overwhelmingly in the majority. If Balboa could come k, one editor remarks, he would find a new and more inspiring son for naming as he did the ocean he discovered four hundred rs ago stretching before him in dazzling tranquillity as he ed upon it from "a peak in Darien." For, avers the Troy *nes*, with the signing of the four-Power pact "the Pacific omes the text for pacific settlement of international conversies." This agreement paves the way for still more comhensive agreements of the same kind, and for the limitation naval armaments, notes the Houston *Chronicle*, which adds: 'hus the Pacific is to be made the home of a new policy—a icy of reduced fleets, of fewer fortifications, of less aggressives, of reliance on peaceful adjustments."

This treaty "may be a small thing in itself," says the New rk *Journal of Commerce*, "but it is the expression of a great nciple—that of international association for the preservation peace." "Concerts of this sort need not be limited to the cific, but can be extended to other parts of the world where bilization is sought and where American cooperation is irable," remarks the New York *Tribune*. And it notes ther that by ending the Anglo-Japanese alliance the new treaty "pleases not only this country but Canada, Australia, New Zealand and South Africa." "To have terminated this dual compact without offense to either Japan or Great Britain is a diplomatic achievement of great importance," *The Tribune* adds. The Pacific agreement is "a long step in the direction of the preservation of world peace," says the Los Angeles *Times;* and the Denver *Rocky Mountain News* remarks that it also "brings very much closer the English-speaking peoples."

The agreement "can not be sanely attacked as an entangling alliance," argues the Cleveland *Plain-Dealer*, because, while it safeguards the Pacific interests of each of the four Powers, "it does not bind the signatories to coercive action or to warlike cooperation." Opposition to its ratification, predicts this Cleveland paper, will ultimately simmer down to a few "irreconcilable isolationists." And once the treaty is in force, it adds, "it is inconceivable that Japan and the United States could even approach the brink of war."

The workability of the pact is insured by the extreme simplicity of its terms, many papers aver. "Embodying a new departure in world relationships and establishing far-reaching changes, it is phrased in terms so utterly simple that they exclude misunderstanding and require no interpretation," says the Philadelphia *North American*, which adds: "The great fact

BURYING IT IN THE MIDDLE OF THE PACIFIC.

—Darling in the New York *Tribune*.

is that statesmanship has found a formula for the establishment of peace which is an expression of the advanced thought of an awakened civilization—not a complex scheme attempting to reorganize the whole world under a supergovernment backed by force, but a simple arrangement of understanding and cooperation based upon candid conference and good faith."

Among the virtues of the Pacific Treaty proclaimed by the Boston *News Bureau* and many other papers is the fact that "it has no Article X," which was the section of the League most generally attacked in this country. In Article X members of the League of Nations "undertake to respect and preserve as against external aggression the territorial integrity and existing political independence of all members of the League of Nations." As the New York *Times* sees it, however, Article II of the Pacific pact is only "a clumsy paraphrase" of Article X of the League Covenant, with the implied guaranty cloaked in vague phrases. This view seems to be shared by the Washington *Herald*, in which we read:

"Article II provides that 'if the said rights are threatened by the aggressive action of any other power, the high contracting parties shall communicate with one another fully and frankly in order to arrive at an understanding as to the most efficient measures to be taken jointly or separately, to meet the exigencies of the particular occasion.'

"It has been said this is more like The Hague than Paris. It is just about as much like The Hague as hootch is like skim milk. It means that if Russia, Germany, or both, or any other combination, threatens aggressive action, the four are morally bound to stand together. It is diplomatic language for a defensive alliance, no more, no less. And why not? The United States has as much to gain as any of the rest. It means peace, good-will, good trade, security with the only Power that is a possible menace. It means changing the only source of trouble to a source of friendship, good-will and understanding. If this article is a defensive alliance, no other combination of Powers will fool around the Pacific. If it is only a wobble, a pretense, a sort of sneak-trick, then some day some other combination may try it out.

"There are just the four whose territorial possessions are contiguous, as it were. They agree to respect each other's possessions and keep away any marauders. These possessions are all away off by themselves in the world's greatest ocean. Article X of the covenant carries exactly the same agreement as to all continental countries and their possessions everywhere. The one may be child's play as compared to a man's job, but they are 'sisters under their skin.'"

The New York *World*, which led the newspaper fight for the League of Nations, urges all friends of the League to support the new treaty. Says this journal:

"To the irreconcilables of the Senate the four-Power treaty must inevitably be as bad as the covenant of the League of Nations, assuming that these Senators believed what they said during the debate on the Treaty of Versailles. Anybody who professes to think that a strict construction of Washington's Farewell Address is the last word in the foreign policy of the United States must inevitably be against a treaty that associates the United States, Great Britain, Japan and France in a common agreement to maintain the status quo in the Pacific for ten years.

"The answer to that argument is that the 'isolation' of this country is fiction. It has nothing to do with fact. It was a transparent fraud when it was used against the covenant of the League of Nations, and it is no less a transparent fraud when it is used against the four-Power treaty.

"Senator La Follette, who is one of the irreconcilables, insists that 'the proposed treaty has all the iniquities of the League of Nations, with none of the virtues claimed for that document by its advocates.' Senator Lodge would probably retort that it has all the virtues of the League with none of its iniquities. Neither statement is the whole truth nor a wholly acceptable half-truth.

"The four-Power treaty unquestionably draws its inspiration from the covenant of the League of Nations. Except for the covenant it would never have been framed; it would have no existence. Moreover, under Article XVIII and Article XX of the covenant the treaty must be registered with the Secretariat of the League and must conform to the covenant.

"In the opinion of *The World*, Democratic Senators who vote against the treaty will have no higher motive than the Republican Senators who voted against the League because it was Mr. Wilson's League.

"The Battalion of Death Senators will inevitably revive all the myths that were invented during the debate on Article X, but it is surely no proper function of Senate Democrats to assist in making these myths permanent in respect of the foreign affairs of the United States.

"Every consideration of policy, party expediency and public service is a summons to the League of Nations Democrats in the Senate to support the four-Power treaty."

"VIPER" WEAPONS

THAT POISON GAS WARFARE is "humane" in character may come as a surprize to the thousands of "doughboys" who have not yet recovered from the effects of gas during the World War, believes the Seattle *Times*. Yet that is the contention of Brigadier-General Fries, Chief of the Chemical Warfare Service of the United States Army. His opinion, moreover, is upheld by a resolution by the American Institute of Chemical Engineers, and by American Army officers in general, according to the New York *World*. General Pershing, on the other hand, recommends that poison gas be abandoned in warfare. "Here is practical military knowledge against civilian chemical theory," remarks the Philadelphia *Evening Bulletin*, which reminds us that the civilian non-combatant population near the front in any war are the chief sufferers, since the death-dealing clouds of gas cannot be controlled, and may be carried by the wind for miles. "It is the business of the Chemical Warfare Service chief to develop the use of poison gas, and nothing is more natural than that he should be partial to its use, but his view is narrowed by his occupation," thinks the Louisville *Courier-Journal*; "as a man lives, so does he think." His theory, however, "will not appeal to the majority of laymen," declares the Pittsburgh *Chronicle-Telegraph*. "And the stand of such a distinguished professional soldier as Pershing should have a tremendous effect upon public opinion everywhere," points out the New York *Evening Mail*.

Among other proponents of chemical warfare is Professor Zanetti, of Columbia University, who was a Lieutenant-Colonel in the Chemical Warfare Service during the war. In a letter to the New York *Times* he sets forth views similar to those of his former chief:

"No right-minded person can seriously entertain the idea that any weapon of war, let alone chemical warfare, should not, if possible, be set aside. To dwell on the horror of chemical warfare and characterize it as a 'viper weapon' is a platitude. . . .

"The manufacture of a new gas, discovered in some obscure laboratory, could go on in some remote chemical factory for years; enormous stocks could be accumulated and stored and, if necessary, harmlessly labeled, until the moment came to use it. Who can guard against such a contingency? Would we dare in the light of past experience to expose our men to a slaughter similar to that suffered by the French and British at Ypres and run the risk of its consequence? . . .

"The knowledge that both sides are fully equipped and ready at a moment's notice to retaliate in kind would make more toward preventing a chemical war than—as experience has shown—any treaty, no matter how clear and definite."

"It is no secret," writes Frederic J. Haskin, in the Little Rock *Arkansas Gazette*, "to say that the chemical experts of all countries are hard at work devising new poison gases." Advocates of this new weapon contend that its use is justified on the ground that it will shorten hostilities. As we read in *Chemical Warfare*, the official organ of the Chemical Warfare Service, of which General Fries is the head:

"Chemical warfare with its unlimited choice of weapons and its unlimited methods of making war intolerable, will make warfare universal, and better than any other means, will bring war home to its makers. Jingoes, great and small, will hesitate long before they start war in the future, knowing that they themselves, as well as their armies and navies, may be subject to its terrors. Their strongholds can now be easily reached by chemical agents delivered from aircraft. Knowing that the war of the future will be brought home to every individual, the effort will be made to avoid it at all costs."

By the use of airplanes, bombs, and poison gases of various sorts, "a great city could be destroyed in five minutes," maintains Thomas A. Edison in a New York *American* interview; "and in half an hour every living creature in the vicinity—men, women and children—could be burned to death or suffocated by these deadly gases." Yet, asserts Dr. Raymond F.

Bacon, director of the Mellon Industrial Research Institute at Pittsburgh, "chemists know that the use of poison gases during war has come to stay." W. Lee Lewis also has this to say in the *Chemical Bulletin:*

"Poison gas is the most economical and humane weapon yet devised by the mind of man. Its efficiency is shown in the wide-spread casualties of the recent World War produced by this agent: Thirty per cent. of the American casualties; a fourteen hundred per cent. increase in British casualties after the introduction of mustard gas; its capacity to harass and handicap an army through the mere enforced wearing of the gas-mask."

"All of which goes to show that it is a pretty tough villain who is so bad that nobody can be found to make out a case for him," remarks the Duluth *Herald*. "The theory that by making war more and more horrible you diminish the chance of a war is an amazingly faulty theory," asserts the Baltimore *American*, and as the Louisville *Courier-Journal* puts it:

"There never will be a method of warfare so terrible that men will refuse to engage in it. Flirting with death is inherent in human nature. The invention of firearms was, perhaps, just as radical an improvement in the art of killing as was the introduction of poison gas. Firearms might have been called 'intolerable.' But they did not put a dampener on war, any more than did the use of the war chariot or the long-bow or the metal sword. Compared with the trireme, the modern battle-ship is a horrible engine, but its appearance did not spell the cessation of naval warfare.

"General Fries overlooks the fact that as soon as an 'intolerable' instrument of death appears, the immediate sequel is the invention of protection against it. Armor counteracted swords and the battle-ax, just as the gas-mask was almost coevil with gas.

"There is a way, however, to prevent nations from using chemical poisons in warfare—the creation of a militant public opinion against the practise, and the agreement of nations to refrain from their use. If dum-dum bullets were eschewed by both sides in the last war, why is it not possible to ban gases?"

CRUSH THEM NOW!

—Pease in the Newark *News*.

Many editors hail the report of the American Advisory Committee of the Washington Conference, advocating the abolition of poison gas, liquid fire, and other chemical agents in warfare. The Committee, it should be said, keeps in touch with public sentiment on certain matters that come before the Conference, and advises the American delegates accordingly.

"America's influence at the Conference," declares the St. Louis *Star*, "should be thrown against the weapons that are directed against non-combatants—the submarine and poison gas."

THE MODERN GOD OF WAR.

—Morris for the George Matthew Adams Service.

"Since a gas attack is uncontrollable, chemical warfare falls into the well-poisoning class," agrees the Norfolk *Virginian-Pilot*, while the New Orleans *Times-Picayune* maintains that "as to the barbarity of chemical warfare . . . there is no argument." "For the present Conference to adjourn without a vigorous condemnation of such uncivilized weapons would be an evasion of its plain duty," avers the Pittsburgh *Chronicle-Telegraph*. "What is this 'humane' method of warfare of which the chemists speak?" asks the New York *Evening Mail*—

"Is it the spreading of gas that will torture and poison honorable and gallant men not only through their lungs but through their skins, that will reach far behind the fighting lines and send women and children to horrible death, that will kill all vegetation and secure the starvation of peoples for years after war ceases? If this be a chemist's idea of humane warfare, God deliver the world from its chemists! Evidently it is not a soldier's idea of warfare, or General Pershing would have indorsed it. And, be it remembered, the soldier fights on the field, not in the laboratory."

When all is said and done, however, agree the Louisville *Courier-Journal*, the Des Moines *Register*, the Baltimore *Sun* and a dozen other newspapers, "it is useless to forbid inventions; the only way to prevent the use of aerial bombs, submarines, and poison gas in war is to prevent war." Adds the New York *Globe:*

"Some gases do not kill, some kill without pain, some torture as well as kill, but these statements are also true of rifle and artillery fire. There is no more to be said in favor of tearing men to pieces with shells or bombs, macerating their flesh with high-power rifle bullets, or stabbing them in the face or intestines with bayonets than there is for suffocating or burning them with gas.

"War is slaughter, and can never be anything else, and victory will always go to the contestant who is best at killing."

THE FARM BLOC—A PERIL OR A HOPE?

THE "KEN-CAP-CLAN" that "cares not three corn-belt or cow-country whoops for the Republican program or the old seats of Republican strength" is "in the saddle in Congress," or, to shift to another editor's figure, it "has taken the bit in its teeth and run away." Be it horse or rider, the New York *Times* professes to take the agricultural bloc in Congress very lightly, and prophesies that "it will pass with the depression from which it sprang, like the Wheel, the Brothers of Freedom, the Society of Equity, the Farmers' Alliance, the Greenbackers, and other shadows." But to a goodly number of other newspapers, it is far from a joke that, as the Seattle *Times* puts it, "after political upheavals in the country which were inspired by the presence of spokesmen for business minorities in the Houses," the agriculturist clan led by Senators Kenyon and Capper should "calmly proceed to build up a machine in Congress infinitely more powerful than any that business ever possest." The farm bloc, observes this paper's Washington correspondent, "is aggressive and cohesive and knows precisely what it wants and how to get it." Various correspondents remind us that this group succeeded in having its way with much of the tax revision, including the retention of a high surtax on large incomes, and that it was able to force through at the last session of Congress the passage of the billion dollar Farm Export Credit Act, the Capper-Tincher Bill regulating grain exchanges, legislation for government control of meat packing, the Emergency Tariff Act, and two measures increasing the effectiveness of the Farm Loan System. In the coming session, they tell us, these "embattled farmers" intend to fight for the enactment of a cooperative marketing bill, reduction in freight rates, and more financial aid to farmers. Recent dispatches report that the bloc will defeat any sales tax in connection with a Soldiers' Bonus Bill. "The farmers' program is far from completed, and the farmers are far from satisfied," is the way a New York *World* correspondent puts it, and he predicts that "the agricultural bloc will make itself felt again when the tariff is considered no less than when a new tax revision measure is brought forward."

RATHER DIFFICULT DRIVING.

—Pease in the Newark *News*.

This new political development, this prodigious activity—is it a menace or a promise? The answer would seem to be to a considerable extent a matter of occupation and geography. At least, Senator Capper, who was born in Kansas and owns a chain of farm papers, believes that the efforts of the farm bloc are helping to bring national prosperity, while Secretary Weeks, who was born in New Hampshire and is a banker and broker by profession, sees in the new bloc system a real menace to our institutions. Eastern newspapers and business organs generally are inclined to agree with the Secretary of War. In the opinion of Mr. Weeks, who has served in both Houses of Congress, the activity of such a powerful bi-partizan group "has had a tendency to weaken effective government, has resulted in irresponsible legislation, prevented both parties from carrying out the pledges made in their platforms, and in time will divide the legislative branch of the Government into groups, each group championing a special cause, and we will see one group combining with another to bring about a control of legislative action in the interests of a particular faction." "Carried to its logical conclusion," the bloc system, we are told, might divide the country "into hostile factions or groups, one class plundered by another, and the country powerless to defend or maintain its interests, national or international." Here the Boston *Herald* concurs with the Secretary. "This is political brigandage pure and simple," avers the New York *Herald*, likewise agreeing. The antipathy to blocs seems to the Philadelphia *Bulletin* to be "due to sound political instinct," for "in so far as the system succeeds, it deprives the people of any real control of parties, or any real method to make the will of the actual majority effective in legislation." Farther south the Richmond *News Leader* joins the chorus of alarm, and the Lexington (Ky.) *Leader* says that "the blocs which are being formed in Congress tend in the wrong direction and cloud the future."

When we turn to the business press we find the Chicago *Journal of Commerce* protesting against the "group selfishness" of the agricultural and other blocs in Congress: "born of honest, patriotic, and worthy impulses, they have in too many cases sunk into vicious, vindictive, and sordid practises." Their program is shortsighted, too, according to *The American Banker*, for—

"Just as the agricultural bloc with its tariff tinkering spoiled part of the farmer's market, it has wrought the same effect by causing the defeat of the bill exempting from taxation American capital invested in foreign business enterprises."

But to these and all the other critics of the farm bloc, Senator Capper, one of its most influential members, says in a recent letter to his *Capper's Weekly* (Topeka), after explaining that the farmer is really the backbone of the nation:

"Wall Street and Big Business should be aiding instead of fighting its best friend; should be aiding instead of opposing the efforts of farm blocs in Congress.

"I believe that for the next quarter century the outstanding policy of this nation should be the carrying out of a great constructive program for the encouragement and upbuilding of its farm industry. The much maligned Farm Bloc has such a program well started in Congress. If all its measures are enacted, they will lay a broad foundation on which may be erected the world's best and most enduring system of agriculture. That also would mean the upbuilding of what would be the world's most enduring and most wide-spread and genuine national prosperity."

And the Secretary of War's grave condemnation of the farm bloc is thus picked to pieces by the New York *Globe:*

"The history of representative government in this country and wherever liberty has advanced among men, has been the record of group action. The barons who wrested the Magna Carta from King John at Runnymede were a bloc, and an agricultural bloc at that. As new bodies of citizens came to power they have always demanded a share in the fruits of govern-

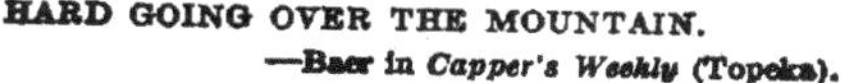

HARD GOING OVER THE MOUNTAIN.
—Baer in *Capper's Weekly* (Topeka).

THE SHORN LAMB.
—Baer in *Labor* (Washington).

A FARM AND A LABOR VIEW OF RAILROAD ILLS.

ment. In this country the agricultural bloc is the oldest, and formerly it was the richest and most respectable of all in power at Washington. The industrial and financial interests for which the Republican party has been spokesman during recent decades was counted an upstart bloc, an intruder, during the first half of the nineteenth century. . . .

"The underlying objection to the agricultural bloc is thus not to the bloc as such. Secretary Weeks has never evinced any alarm over the business bloc, which is active. His dismay arises from the fact that a new political power threatens the sway of his own group. That is not an evil. Representative government looks to the enfranchisement of all classes and groups. Laws in a democratic country are, in effect, collective bargains. The interests of Secretary Weeks's financial bloc clash with those of Senator Kenyon's agricultural bloc, and the result is a compromise between them and others. It would be bad for the country for either the agriculturists or the financiers or the manufacturers or the merchants or the organized unionists or for any other single group to dictate the national policy. But it is gain and not loss to have the farmers and all others who exercise political power coming frankly into the open and asking for what they want. The objection is not that they have ceased to pretend, but that they are so powerful. During this time of transition they possess the balance of power, and they are feared. But what they are doing is of the essence of democracy."

This, of course, is not all that the newspapers are saying about the bloc. One offers comparisons between it and political developments in European legislatures. Another predicts the end of our traditional two-party system. More than one Democratic paper suggests that the Republican party leaders in 1920 are entirely to blame for these bloc developments in Congress. Correspondents enlighten us about the personnel of the agricultural bloc. They agree that there is an inside group of twenty or less in the Senate, but that as many as thirty-five can generally be counted on to vote with the "hard and fast regulars," led by Senator Kenyon. In the Senate group there are about two Republicans to one Democrat. There is also a less highly organized non-partizan body of Representatives who vote together to further agricultural interests. There are other groups composed of Senators or Congressmen acting together, but the only ones that have actually organized, besides the farm group, are these, according to the New York *Herald:*

"Pacific Coast bloc, irrigation bloc, ex-service men's bloc, and the new or 'baby' Congressmen's bloc."

THE RAILROADS' CHRISTMAS CAROL

"YES, VIRGINIA, there is a Santa Claus," one hears our editors saying in effect to the railroads as they look at that little $50,000,000 gift in annual savings, which the roads have just received through the Railroad Labor Board's recent revision of working conditions. The rôle of Santa Claus in this particular Christmas party would seem to be thrust upon the railroad employees, for besides what they give up under the new working rules, 1,650,000 of them are being asked by the executives to accept a wage cut of from ten to twenty per cent. in order to strengthen the carriers' financial position. The public, which in years gone by used to be a rank outsider when the railroads gave their parties, has been carefully invited this time, and is informed that it may find a few sugar plums on the Christmas-tree. Both the farmer as producer and the city man as consumer of food are favored guests. The reduction of approximately 16 per cent. on Western freight rates on hay and grain, taking effect on the 27th, is expected to profit the shippers by about $32,000,000. Then there is the nationwide ten per cent. reduction in rates on farm products offered by the roads and being considered by the Interstate Commerce Commission, which would mean a saving of about $55,000,000 to the shipping public.

Everything considered, says Mr. Ben W. Hooper of the Railroad Labor Board, in a cheerful pre-Christmas statement, "the railroad situation is more conducive to optimism than it has been for many months. The absence of any serious general labor disturbance, combined with the disposition of the carriers to make voluntary reductions in freight rates, will contribute to the restoration of sound business conditions." There is ample testimony, agrees the Troy *Times*, "to show that there is both on the part of the public and the railroads a better temper than existed during the period of most severe stress. This encourages belief that problems remaining to be adjusted will be solved in a spirit of conciliation and fair play." And the Troy paper also finds good reason for Christmas cheer in renewed railroad activity:

"Among the most encouraging indications of improvement in transportation and industrial conditions are the resumption of work in railroad shops which have been closed for long periods, and the orders placed by some of the large companies for new or additional equipment. A writer who has given special attention to this phase of the situation mentions several of the leading locomotive-building companies and supply concerns as having received such orders, adding that the plants affected 'are in for a fairly busy winter and spring.' It is mentioned that the orders given include 'stock, box, gondola, refrigerator, convertible, ballast, coal and various other kinds of cars.' That is, the companies are acquiring an outfit of rolling stock adapted to meet every phase of railroad operation. One company's big order is for fifty-five locomotives, 127 steel passenger cars and 7,300 freight cars.

"The meaning of all this is unmistakable. Some of the leading railroads of the country are anticipating a great increase of business and are preparing to meet the expected demand on their facilities. The developments are all the more significant because they follow a period of exceptional stagnation in industry and of grave difficulties faced by railroads."

Mr. Scrooge appears at this Christmas feast in the shape of the Providence *Journal*, which gloomily remarks that altho the war was ended three years ago, a "beginning has hardly been made" in the work of railroad readjustment. There is evidence, it says, that notwithstanding the 12½ per cent. wage reduction ordered by the Labor Board some time ago, "the schedules are still excessive in comparison with that of workers in other lines of industry." "Besides," *The Journal* adds, "the effect of the long postponed modification of rules upon operating expenses can not be determined. The railroad situation, accordingly, is not satisfactory.

During the holidays, a discussion of railroad rates and wages and working conditions may not seem particularly appropriate, but it is this current readjustment of rates and rules that dozens of newspapers agree to look upon as indications of progress toward normal conditions of railroading. Normal conditions of railroading will go far to bring about normal conditions in all business and industry, and there is no Christmas present which the country would welcome more gleefully than a definite promise of a revival of business in the early months of the New Year.

Turning first to the new railroad rules we note that they are a revision by the Railroad Labor Board of the nation-wide regulations which were established during government ownership, which will affect 400,000 railroad shopworkers, perhaps 450,000 when normal conditions return. It will mean a saving of $50,-000,000 to the roads, a sum equal to that lopped off the payrolls by the similar revision of six months ago. The decision was followed a few days later by a reduction of overtime pay for certain kinds of railroad labor. The revision of the rules has been called an "open shop" decision in the headlines because it affords provision for a representation of non-unionized minorities in the shops. But, says a statement issued by members of the Board, "the existing unions are recognized by the Board and by the Transportation Act as representative of the majority." What has been done, as Associated Press writers point out, is to lend elasticity to working arrangements. "Under previous agreements with the shop crafts, including the national agreement, it has been the custom to define and detail the various types of work belonging to each craft." The railroad managers have objected to some of these classifications. "For example, work not requiring a mechanic's skill was assigned to a skilled mechanic, thus making efficient and economical operation impossible, according to the railroads." The new rules broaden the scope of each worker's activities. For instance, "the machinist working on running repairs may connect or disconnect any wiring, coupling or pipe connections necessary to repair machinery or equipment. This work was previously assigned to electricians and sheet metal workers only."

Copyrighted 1921, by the New York "Tribune" Inc.

ISN'T IT RATHER DANGEROUS NOT TO HAVE THE TWO HITCHED TOGETHER IN SOME WAY?

—Darling in the New York *Tribune*.

Railroad executives and labor leaders have not been saying much about this for publication. Both seem to doubt, remarks a New York *Times* writer, whether the roads will really save anything like the $50,000,000 estimated by the Labor Board statisticians. Mr. B. M. Jewell, who heads the Railway Employees Department of the American Federation of Labor, points out in somewhat cryptic language that the railroads have now received about all they ought to have in the way of direct and indirect wage revisions. President Samuel E. Felton of the Chicago Great Western admits that the new rules "should tend to remedy to some extent the waste and inefficiency" caused by the old ones. But, he continues, "the decision does not give relief from the bad effects produced by the application of most of the working rules throughout the country regardless of widely varying local conditions."

This is not very hearty thanks, but the editors are more enthusiastic over the railroad's Christmas gift from the Labor Board. The Brooklyn *Eagle* finds the relegation of "the McAdoo mechanic" to his proper place an "impressively revolutionary development." "A boon for the railroads," is the Boston *News Bureau's* phrase. "By every count the award is welcome," declares the Richmond *News-Leader*. The new order, says the Rochester *Post-Express*, "will conduce to both the profit and efficiency of the roads." Similar observations come from papers in New York, Chicago, Indianapolis, St. Louis, Washington, D. C., Baltimore, Philadelphia, Seattle, Cleveland, Dallas, and Newark, N. J. Several papers insist that while the railroads gain the workers do not lose. The New York *World* and *Herald* point out that the change is a good thing for the skilled workman, who is entitled to a higher rating than his unskilled brother. It seems to the Indianapolis *Star* that "the railway shopmen will profit more from efficiency and the prosperity of the transportation companies than they could hope to gain by maintaining useless jobs and restrictions that increase living costs to everybody and are a drag on the normal development of business activities." But to a radical spokesman for labor like the Butte *Bulletin* the Labor Board

DRAGGING HIM INTO IT. —Brown in the Chicago *Daily News*.

decision seems a great triumph for reaction and for the "capitalists":

"Low wages, long hours, petty tyranny and discharge without appeal will from now on be the order of the day. The railway worker will be at the mercy of as conscienceless a gang of bandits as ever operated in a country which is a Mecca for this species."

The railroad wage cuts will be rather late for Christmas, if they come at all, for they are still to be submitted to the Labor Board. Formal notices have already been posted by Eastern and Western railroads calling for conferences on wage reductions, and Southern lines are expected to make similar announcements. Reductions varying from ten to twenty per cent., according to the class of labor involved, will affect more than 1,650,000 men. It will be remembered that the Railroad Labor Board gave an increase of 22½ per cent. in pay May 1, 1920. Last July the Board cut the pay by about 12½ per cent. Now the railroads, as the newspaper writers explain, would like to lop off the remaining ten per cent. to bring wages back to the early 1920 level. But "this means a finish fight," says one labor leader, and certain groups of railroad workers have gone on record as demanding wage increases of from five to seventeen per cent., so that the Railroad Labor Board will have a far from simple problem on its hands. Some editors expect a decision as soon as February.

Finally, the freight rate situation needs a few words of explanation. There have been a number of reductions in various sections and for various commodities from the level established by the Interstate Commerce Commission in August, 1920. Last October the Commission suggested a decrease approximating 16 per cent. in rates on hay and grain west of the Mississippi. Late in November the decision was made mandatory, to take effect on or before December 27. In the meantime, the railroad executives have agreed on a ten per cent. cut in carload freight rates on farm products. This reduction, which it is thought might cost the roads $55,000,000 a year, is to be generally applicable throughout the United States except on traffic moving wholly within New England. The reduction, it is explained, would include the sixteen per cent. reductions and would not be added to them. Hearings on this suggestion have been begun by the Interstate Commerce Commission. Typical of much editorial comment is the following from the Indianapolis *News:*

"The belief generally prevails among men versed in commercial and industrial affairs that a return to better conditions has been largely checked by high transportation costs, and that as these costs decline conditions will improve.

"That the rate cut will do much to help conditions among the farmers can hardly be doubted, nor can it be doubted that the farming business needs stimulation."

THE BATTLE OF PACKINGTOWN

RED PEPPER, TEAR-GAS, AND BULLETS were freely used in the recent Chicago riots, when mobs numbering a hundred thousand persons surged about the stockyards. Packing-house strikers and their sympathizers gave battle to strike-breakers and the police, with the result that two men were killed and scores injured, we are informed by the Chicago *Daily News*. True, we were told in November that employees of the "Big Five" packing-houses had themselves agreed to an average wage reduction of eight per cent., after an examination of the company books, but at the time, points out the Baltimore *American*, "there were indications that perhaps things were not as simple as they seemed." Certainly, if the report were true, other editors remarked, the fixing of wages in a national industry by a "plant congress" of workers and executives was an unprecedented move. It seems, however, according to a Department of Labor statement, that "both union and non-union workers were alike aroused by the proposed reduction," and a strike affecting some 45,000 packing-house workers in fifteen cities was the result. Serious rioting, however, occurred only in Chicago, it is said, altho National Guardsmen were called to St. Paul. Legal proceedings instituted by the packers to restrain the strikers from interfering with the operation of packing plants in various Middle Western cities seemed to be of little avail, but finally the advent of two Federal and two State mediators had a quieting effect in the midwest metropolis.

"The Chicago controversy has been the most serious in the packing industry in a dozen years," remarks the Springfield *Republican*, which does not believe that the "company union," or "plant congress" "as a substitute for the abandoned system of collective bargaining, with impartial arbitration, has established itself as an insurance against strikes." The present strike "has long been foreseen, and never should have occurred," avers the New York *Evening Post*, "and for its occurrence the packers are chiefly to blame." "They may be perfectly correct in their contention that their economic situation makes a cut in wages imperative," *The Evening Post* goes on, "but if this position is unassailable, they could have submitted it to arbitration." As this paper explains:

"During the war the industry was upon a wage-and-hour basis fixed by Federal Judge Samuel Alschuler, acting for the Department of Labor. The strike threatened last March was forestalled by a supplementary agreement under the same arbitrator, embodying marked wage cuts and good until September 15. Union leaders have been willing to continue on an arbitration basis as regards wages, but the packers have instead tried to establish 'plant assemblies' or 'company unions' and to induce them to accept the 10 to 15 per cent. cut in pay and the ten-hour day. Armour's obtained this acceptance, and the Swift, Morris, Cudahy and Wilson companies have demanded the same basis. But the workers declare that the 'company unions' are unrepresentative, being mere creatures of the packers. A strike vote of 35,354 to 3,490 gives force to this contention."

AT THE END OF THE BAYONET.

—Callaghan in the Minneapolis *Minnesota Daily Star* (Labor).

Judge Alschuler acted as arbitrator in the packing business from 1917 to last autumn, notes the New York *Globe*. Then—

"Judge Alschuler ceased to serve because the packers no longer desired his intervention. Having eliminated the kind of supervision which President Harding is now proposing for all industry, the packers organized shop councils and immediately lowered wages. The wage reduction may have been just or it may not. The essential fact is that neither the public nor the workers are now in a position to judge. The packers would to-day be better off, the workers would be undisturbed, and the nation would have been spared the shame of a pitched battle between police and women and little children had the system of arbitration been continued.

"It is a tragedy that governmental aid was refused months ago. The mistake should not be continued. President Harding should call for an investigation in which Secretaries Hoover and Davis participate."

"The public would rather see a frank refusal to treat with the workers at all than an attempt to cover up such a refusal under sham forms," believes the Baltimore *American*. For, as the Chicago *Evening Post* remarks, "the public is always the chief victim when either capitalism or unionism get the upper hand over the other." "The shop representation plan," in the opinion of this Chicago paper, is still an experiment, "but it is a step of cooperation directed with apparent sincerity toward the ending of industrial warfare." In this the New York *Times* agrees, but adds:

"It has often failed; when successful it has not always been permanent. On the part of both employers and employed it calls for a high degree of intelligence, self-control and vigilant liberality of mind. Capital perforce must abandon the idea that it can do what it will with its own; labor has to learn that it can earn more and receive more only by increased efficiency, to which trained and capable management is necessary."

Then there is the other side of the question, as set forth by the Memphis *Commercial-Appeal*. "The reduction in wages, which caused the strike," it reminds us, "was suggested by the plant conference boards of the packing-houses, which are made up of representatives both of the packers and the workers themselves."

"For this very reason, then, the strike will set back the cause of employee representation in the conduct of great industrial institutions in so far as this conduct has to do with the employees themselves, their wages and their working conditions. It will revive the discredited and increasingly costly plan of conducting industrial affairs upon the basis of conflict rather than cooperation. The packing-house industry at least will be back again upon the wholly indefensible position that employers and employees are enemies rather than friends.

"But a more imminent danger to the success of the strike lies in the great number of unemployed men in the nation. Many of the packing-house employees are of the unskilled class and others are of the not highly skilled character, so that it will be no difficult matter to fill their places. The packing-house managers have announced that the men will lose their jobs for good, and that their places will be filled by others who will be taught the trade. And the prospects offered by such a determination are not any too bright for those who may have decided to quit their jobs.

"The railroad employees, whose places would have been hard to fill, were prevented from striking largely by the force of public opinion, and it would be well if the packing employees would give earnest consideration to the motives that actuated their brother workers. The chances for harm growing out of the strike to both employers and employees, as well as to future industrial relationships, are almost limitless; the chances for good are nil."

REMEMBER MRS. O'LEARY'S COW.

—James in the St. Louis *Star*.

"It is difficult to see what the riotous element among the packing industry's employees expect to gain by their defiance of law and order," agrees the San Diego *Union*; "even if their cause is just, they are not going about it in the right way to compel recognition of its justice."

TOPICS IN BRIEF

Gene Debs is for the open door.—*Dallas News.*

Where moonshine comes from is a secret still.—*New York American.*

Doesn't freedom in Ireland make you feel wistful?—*Wall Street Journal.*

The Mad Mullah seems to have taken his last death quite seriously.—*Punch (London).*

"Microscope reveals 22 teeth in a mosquito." We believe it.—*Asheville Times.*

Never was it more necessary to handle China with care.—*Wall Street Journal.*

The Chinese should be good at ironing out differences in the Far East.—*Asheville Times.*

How easy it would be for nations to reform if there was nothing left to grab.—*Binghamton Sun.*

China will now follow Japan into our wonderful alliance of English-speaking peoples.—*Indianapolis Star.*

The English-speaking people agree in most things except the English they speak.—*Greenville Piedmont.*

Canada and the United States found the right armament ratio a hundred years ago: 0-0.—*New York Evening Post.*

The Chinese question would be difficult enough if the Chinese themselves could agree upon what it is.—*Indianapolis Star.*

GETTING THE KNOTS UNTIED.

—Pease in the *Newark News.*

Presents also make the heart grow fonder.—*Asheville Times.*

The dove of peace isn't kept in a diplomatic coup.—*Passaic News.*

Joshua couldn't make the modern son stand still.—*St. Joseph Gazette.*

It isn't what a man stands for, as much as what he falls for.—*Cape Girardeau Southeast Missourian.*

A fare fight is not always a fair fight.—*Greenville Piedmont.*

If prosperity will only return, we will ask no questions.—*Asheville Times.*

The present dream of Middle Europe is a square meal.—*Albany Times-Union.*

Edison has found the road to success paved with good inventions.—*Asheville Times.*

There are two kinds of marks—and one kind buys the other kind.—*New York World.*

Really, it begins to look as if Senator Tom Watson's silence is the most golden there is.—*Dallas News.*

During the shortage of nurses "Roll Your Own" is the motto in baby-carriage circles.—*New York American.*

They talk much now of professional women. Personally, we have never met an amateur.—*New York American.*

A man never becomes so lost to decency and righteousness that he can't see the other fellow's duty.—*New York Telegram.*

Chang-Tso-Lin, China's great general, has five wives and was once a brigand. That's why he can afford five.—*Washington Post.*

It will take a generation of dime novels to make the Far East as dear to the heart of America as the Far West.—*Canton Repository.*

It looks as tho the professional Irish-American politicians would have to hustle around and get a new issue.—*Kansas City Times.*

Some people are so busy worrying about the general depression that they haven't time to go after new business.—*Rochester Times-Union.*

If it is true that there are no cuss words in the Japanese language, how do the Japs start a Lizzie on a cold morning?—*Newark Ledger.*

The difference between a pedagog and a demagog is that one works against ignorance and the other gets a profit out of it. —*Elizabeth Journal.*

You see, each Power must have islands in the Pacific so it can establish a naval base for the protection of its Pacific islands. —*Elmira Star-Gazette.*

"Europe will never concede that we are cultured until some of our celebrities begin to make farewell tours over there." *Evening Telegram.* Well, what about Bergdoll?—*New York Morning Telegraph.*

German bands are said to be looting and raiding in Upper Silesia. We should think they could make enough trouble by merely playing.—*New York World.*

And if Ulster decides not to accept, will there be two Orange Free States on the map of the world?—*Kansas City Star.*

In return for independence China ought to be willing to surrender the laundry privilege in the United States.—*Portsmouth Times.*

If you are superstitious just add up 5-5-3 and maybe you can account for Japan's objection to it.—*New York Morning Telegraph.*

If Duffy in the Gaelic language becomes Dhubhthaigh, what would Lake Muchelookmeguntic look like in Gaelic?—*New York Evening Post.*

A writer says nine-tenths of the people know how to drive a car. Evidently he hasn't studied the police court records.—*Mansfield News.*

Senator Watson might make another hit by demanding a Senatorial investigation of some of the lynchings in Georgia.—*Columbia Record.*

Those who claim credit for inaugurating the disarmament movement are a little late. The movement was begun 1921 years ago.—*Fremont Tribune.*

The four-Power agreement talked of at the Washington Conference is not to be an alliance but a concert. The Powers will transact their business by an exchange of notes then.—*Kansas City Times.*

FOREIGN - COMMENT

AMERICA'S NEW TRIUMPH

THE CERTAINTY OF A NAVAL HOLIDAY was one triumph for America, and in less than a month she achieves a second, by the conclusion of the quadruple pact in the Pacific, is the happy exclamation of various French editors who say American prestige has never been higher since she entered the war in 1917. No less enthusiastic is the acclaim of their English colleagues, who are unreserved in their eulogies of President Harding and Secretary Hughes for their "invigorating essay of idealism in action," which the London *Observer* describes as "sweeping aside the stale, stagnant pessimism about the future of peace and war, and showing the world that international problems of the most stubborn order will yield to negotiators who have peace as their purpose, and the world as it is before their eyes." The details of the terms and extent of the agreement as well as the opinions of the leading delegates of the signatory Powers, will be found in the leading article of this issue. Meanwhile, in recording the verdicts of the overseas press, we find the London *Daily Chronicle*, called Lloyd George's newspaper, expressing the belief that "it is possible now to regard the Conference as having put an end for the present to the evil prospect of a Pacific armaments race and the fateful friction and jealousies in China, and also as placing Pacific affairs on a most satisfactory footing of mutual consultation, recognition and guaranty." To this newspaper occur four specific comments, as follows:

THE PIPE OF PEACE.

—*Sunday Chronicle* (Manchester).

"First—The British Empire has the most varied and vulnerable interests in the Pacific and will proportionately be an immense gainer by the elimination of militarism and rivalry from that vast region.

"Secondly—The Power outside the new concert—Holland—won't lose, but will gain by its establishment.

"Thirdly—We entirely indorse what Mr. Balfour said about our excellent relations with Japan, and are most gratified that the bond between us has not been severed, but only enlarged so as to bring in other friends.

"Fourthly—That prospect thus opened of close, definite cooperation with the United States corresponds to the dominant political instinct of all British democracies—both in Britain and those in the Dominions."

The London *Daily Telegraph* avers that by this achievement alone President Harding's Administration has "justified to the full the bold magnanimous stroke of statesmanship which amazed the world six months ago." *The Westminster Gazette* declares it has "earned the good-will of the world by the success of its initiative" in leading the world out of "a nightmare of misunderstanding about secret motives," and adds:

"With the Anglo-Japanese Alliance out of the way England will occupy a stronger position as an honest broker in any dispute between America and Japan, and Anglo-American relations should be immeasurably happier and Anglo-Japanese relations no worse."

The London *Daily News* recalls that long ago it "suggested that the Japanese alliance might be obviated simply by extending it so as to include other Powers." But it believes a pact of the Four Powers is much more than an extension of that kind, and that "a formal agreement between America, Great Britain, France and Japan about anything on earth is a factor of the first moment in the consolidation of the world's stability." The London *Daily Mail* thinks world friendship will be greatly strengthened by the pact and "by the disappearance of our own treaty with Japan which has increasingly obstructed a complete understanding with the United States." Says the London *Times:*

"Never has a document of greater promise to mankind been adopted by the representatives of four such mighty States; never has an agreement upon a subject of such unprecedented importance been so easily, so gladly sanctioned by the spokesmen of nations whose most vital interests it concerns. In lands where peace is cherished as the chiefest of blessings it will be welcomed with profound satisfaction."

The London *Morning Post* describes the pact as "the greatest achievement of our time in constructive statesmanship" and points out that altho it "concerns the Pacific, its existence necessarily involves cordial cooperation on all other matters between America and Great Britain, the two nations which above all are resolved to maintain peace." It believes that Article II of the new agreement which meets any "aggressive action of any other Power" is a much surer guaranty against a breach of world peace than all the "machinery of Geneva," and adds:

"In a word, the proceedings at Washington show that after the turmoil of war and the distorted imaginings which its horrors awoke in the minds of well-intentioned but hysterical men, the world is at last returning to common sense, and the way of common sense is the way of peace. We are sure that his country, remembering the many services of his great career, is convinced that at Washington Mr. Balfour has reached the highest pitch of unselfish patriotism and supreme statesmanship."

This London newspaper thinks the inclusion of France is of the happiest import, being "in substance the accomplishment of that tri-partite agreement which, had it not been unfortunately prevented, would have served so powerfully to settle distracted Europe." Moreover, the inclusion of France has done much to bridge the gap between Paris and London, we are told by the French press, and the semi-official Paris *Temps* sees everyone's interests enhanced by the quadruple pact, including the states not signatory to it, such as the South American republics and the Netherlands. As to the part of the Japanese in the new combination, *Le Temps* observes:

"In dissolving the Anglo-Japanese alliance for the Treaty of Four, Japan is sacrificing nothing essential. The Anglo-Japanese alliance gave Japan her entry among the great nations of the world, and now the Washington treaty confirms her place there. England would never have held to the treaty against America in case of war, but now the Japanese position as an Asiatic power with a rôle in Asia, is more confirmed than ever.

"For ten years Japan can send to Asia her formidable excess population, and the thinly peopled districts along the Pacific Coast will have nothing to fear. Later we shall see what will happen. Each generation has its peculiar problem."

THE YANKEE MAGICIAN.

His disappearing ship trick.

—*Asahi* (Tokyo).

Turning to Japan herself, Tokyo dispatches state that the international standing of Japan is now raised much higher, and eminent Japanese officials assert that what she lost through the abrogation of her alliance with Great Britain she will regain through the new agreement. Men in public life are quoted in the press as expressing genuine enthusiasm over the arrangement, we read, not as a new scheme, but as a continuance of the present valuable alliance. Moreover, they give out the impression that in their belief there is a possibility of realizing President Harding's "association of nations" in which Japan would remain one of the great Powers, which means much to Japanese self-respect.

In Italy the Rome *Tribuna* remarks:

"America's signal success in the agreement represents the guaranty that no nation will be able to attempt any warlike action without the previous consent of all four big nations. It is a guaranty of peace, soundly constituted, just where the danger of another war was greatest. The United States has won a noteworthy advantage in obtaining from the world's major Powers a guaranty of its own security."

A JAPANESE HINT.

"Why object to Japan's little knife, when you yourself carry such a big sword?"

—*Asahi* (Tokyo).

While the press of The Netherlands welcomes the announcement of the pact, it expresses some wonder as to how far the American Senate is willing to collaborate in the matter. Also it is interesting to note the avowal of The Hague *Nieuwe Courant* that Holland's delicate position in the Pacific prevents her from joining the entente, for if Holland did so, she would thus declare the same policy as other powers—namely, that there are possibilities of her coming into collision with other nations. Holland's real work at Washington, according to this newspaper, must be to "maintain the ideals of former President Wilson," and it says that this work should be the logical continuation of The Hague and Geneva.

Australian newspapers welcome the pact, and Premier Hughes, in a public statement, says it is "especially significant for Australia," which has its own very important Pacific problem, and that "it insures our security."

MEXICO'S ERA OF RECONSTRUCTION

A VAST CHANGE has recently come over the people of Mexico and, what is more to the point, over those who shape its destinies· but to determine in advance the final outcome of this change, especially in view of the "system of obstruction with which it has to cope abroad," is a task for a prophet. This is the frank declaration of a famous expert foreign observer, Dr. E. J. Dillon, who says the best a conscientious chronicler can undertake in Mexico is to describe and characterize the principal signs and tokens of its reconstruction, and he finds them eminently favorable. His opportunities of observation were exceptionally good, he tells us in the London *Contemporary Review*, for he traveled with General Obregon, Mexico's President, over thousands of miles of the republic. Under the Carranzist régime he had become familiar with many parts of Mexico, and he reminds us that in those days soldiers had to escort the trains, and there was always fear that brigands might derail or blow up the trains in order to kill, rob, or hold the passengers for ransom. This was about May, 1920, since which time we are told that—

"A complete transformation has been undergone by the country, and it is interesting to note the people's mental reactions with the purer and exhilarating moral atmosphere created by the new régime. I have observed the beneficent change everywhere, among all classes and in all walks of life. I accompanied General Obregon on his various journeys. Our trains were not escorted by soldiers; we generally traveled in second-class carriages, mingled with the people, listened to what they had to say, observed their demeanor towards the new authorities, and learned their grievances and aspirations. . . .

"Already the Government is assiduously repairing the damage caused by its predecessors and their enemies. The railways are being returned or about to be returned to their owners. Rebellions have ceased. Even Villa, who for years was the ineradicable plague of the country, has repented and found salvation, and he and his partizans have become ardent tillers of the soil. The Government is dealing magnanimously with all its enemies. Gambling hells have been closed peremptorily, and without a day's grace, wherever the writ of the Federal Government runs. The liquor laws are being rigorously enforced. The autonomy of the individual States—despite the undesirable results which it occasionally produces—is being respected by the Central Government. The army has been materially reduced. The law everywhere is being left to take its course. Traveling is once more perfectly safe; and it looks as tho in truth a new era had already begun. In a word, this is the first of Mexico's recent revolutions after which, to use one of Obregon's winged words, it is not necessary to liberate the nation from its liberators."

This distinguished informant goes on to say that General Obregon is confronted with perplexing problems drawn from every conceivable sphere, from the domains of foreign policy as well as from internal legislation, constitutional law, national economy, railways and waterways, labor, finance, and the army. Some of these problems are "uncommonly delicate," but we are told that—

"The new President is gifted with an unusual stock of common, or, rather, uncommon sense, with the rare quality of leadership, and, altho still young, has vast stores of experience to draw upon. This is another striking instance of his personal luck. For 'experience,' as the Turkish proverb puts it, 'is usually a comb presented to us by destiny when our hair is all gone.' But while genius in a statesman can achieve much, it can not achieve everything. The greatest kneader of human wills when charged with reconstructive work depends for results very largely upon those to whose lot it falls to translate his ideas into acts. Even an autocrat is to that extent restricted in the exercise of his power, just as a skilled artizan finds his natural limitations in the materials and the implements of which he disposes. And whether General Obregon will find enough coadjutors and subordinates of the right kind for a task of this magnitude remains to be seen."

QUEER COLLATERAL.

TINO: "I say, sir, couldn't you just advance me something on account of that little thing of mine you have sticking in your back?"
—*Evening News* (London).

Of all the tasks confronting General Obregon, we are told, that which will most severely strain his ingenuity and resourcefulness is the transformation of the revolutionary republic into a pacific and well-ordered community. Mexico "must become an elective law-abiding commonwealth on pain of extinction as a sovereign state," says Dr. Dillon, who holds that the alternatives are as certain "as if fate had embodied them in a formal decree." If Obregon were suddenly to pass away to-day, Dr. Dillon proceeds, his work and the best fruits of the revolution would vanish with him, but "as long as Obregon continues to direct the affairs of his country, peace and order may be deemed secure." But this is not enough, for—

"The test of a great ruler is so to govern the State and educate its members as ultimately to enable it to dispense with his services. . . . I have often talked with him on this topic, and his conception seemed to me on the whole perfectly sound. Altho neither a historian nor a politician, his views of contemporary history and politics are those of a man who has deeply meditated on the course of human affairs and their larger aspects, and who firmly grasps the main factors in the politico-social currents of his time. He realizes—much more fully than most European statesmen—the interdependence of peoples and their unconscious but continuous approximation toward an informal community of the whole human race based on the highest interests of each. His own ideal is a universal civil society cemented by justice, and his belief in its ultimate establishment is unshaken by recent events. His active undersense and feeling of the whole, joined to a keen understanding of the integral parts, constantly impels him so to adjust the interests of his country to those of humanity that the two can be closely associated. This is the quality which distinguishes him from the best of his predecessors in the Presidency, entitles him to a foremost place among the best statesmen of modern times, and warrants the high hopes entertained of his work by those who know his views and appreciate his intentions."

A FRENCH VISION OF GREEK GLOOM

NOW THAT DISSIMULATION about the complete failure of the Greek campaign in Asia Minor is no longer possible, and that the Greek evacuation of Anatolia becomes obligatory, the Athenian public is beginning to ask itself just what good has come to it out of the restoration of Constantine to the throne. Thus writes the Athens correspondent of the semi-official Paris *Temps*, who reminds us that as it is just one year ago the elections were held which resulted in the downfall of Mr. Venizelos and his party, it seems timely for the people to cast up their accounts and find their losses and gains of the past twelvemonth, especially as the present Premier Gounaris is at last forced to avow the failure of his policies. This Athens correspondent passes over the ministries of Premier Rhallys and Premier Călogeropoulos, because "everybody knows that even in those ministries Mr. Gournaris was the soul of the Government," and that the two men who preceded him were not at the head of the Cabinet because of the strength of their party, but "simply because it was necessary to delude the Entente by presenting names less compromised than that of the present Premier." We read then:

THE KING AND THE ANGORA.

TINO: "I could have captured that goat, but I never wanted to."
—*The Daily Express* (London).

"It may be said in so many words that Mr. Gournaris, in close contact with King Constantine, has been governing Greece for the past year; and it is of interest therefore to see with what effect. Outside of the question of the restoration of the King, the program of the anti-Venizelist coalition contains the following features: Immediate demobilization, lowering of the cost of living, and constitutional reform. Now none of these projects has been realized, and in the matter of demobilization and the cost of living conditions to-day are much worse than they were a year ago. The number of mobilized classes is doubled, and the cost of living has risen enormously in proportion to the equally enormous decline of the drachma. Moreover, after a year of Parliamentary gabble, constitutional reform has not advanced a single step. In this matter the unproductiveness of the régime is so striking that people are beginning to ascribe it not to chance or to the incapacity of those in power, but rather to their deliberate calculation. Nor must it be forgotten that the Assembly, which dabbles with the constitutional question, is a Constituent Assembly, and that even the royal power itself can not dissolve it without a *coup d'état.* Herein lies a precious advantage which the deputies both use and abuse. Some of them, in a moment of expansion, have said: 'As long as our Assembly is indissoluble, as long as it remains constituent, we shall take care to make the discussion of constitutional reform last more than three years if necessary.''

The *Temps* Athens correspondent goes on to say that many divers questions are raised, such as for example the creation of a Second Chamber, and they are so energetically forwarded by their sponsors that it will take long months to reach an agreement on them. A more singular discovery, he writes, is that Parliament has done nothing but make promises, even in the obvious matter of indemnity legislation promised to the former opposition parties, which are now in the saddle. Surely, this has not been for lack of good-will on the part of Parliament, but if all demands of all parties were to be satisfied, "it would have been necessary to sacrifice more than a milliard of drachmas." Now the State Exchequer is empty, he tells us, and no one seems to know how to replenish it, so that possibly, the government was lavish and easy with its promises "because there was no possibility of fulfilling them." Whoever suffered under the Venizelos régime, or pretends to have suffered through the agency of the Greek Government, or of the other Powers which were then acting in concord with the Greek Government, has the right to an indemnity, and this informant explains:

"The text of the bill on this point is conceived in such fashion that the individuals who carried on spy work in Macedonia for Germany, and against the Allied army of Saloniki, and who on this count should have been imprisoned or deported, are considered as victims of the Venizelist régime. Now the government of Mr. Gournaris recognized the right of these good servants of Germany to be indemnified for the violent treatment to which they had been subjected by the French military authorities of Saloniki. Unfortunately, it is necessary that they wait for their indemnity. But why? Simply because France or England's consent to a loan is indispensable. In any event, the French public and the English public have the right to know whether the money they lend to Greece is for rewarding services to Germany.

"So it is that Mr. Gournaris has not been able to realize any features of his program up to the present. But, it may be asked, has he kept intact the handsome inheritance received from Mr. Venizelos? Alas, disorganization is rife in the interior. Ionia, the dream of so many Hellenic generations, Ionia for which thousands of Greek soldiers have died in these latter months, Ionia itself is lost. This is perhaps an avowal not only of military weakness, but even more an avowal of diplomatic weakness."

Despite this situation, only a few weeks ago Mr. Gournaris, abusing the credulity of the Greek people, declared to them calmly that he enjoyed a confidence among the Powers of the Entente that Mr. Venizelos had never been able to acquire. He affirmed that as soon as he landed in Paris or in London he would be able to secure everything he asked, and the writer continues:

"Now he did go on his journey, and he did ask for what he wanted, but he found himself faced with a hostility and distrust, or a disdain so definitely marked, that even he himself was obliged to recognize it. The Greek people who saw him set out with so many illusions, either sincere or feigned, only now begin to understand that there is no alternative for the Greece of Constantine and Gournaris, except to abandon Asia. Venizelist Greece meant the reconstitution of the great Greek Empire of the East; Gournarist Greece means a little Greece once more, humbled, and condemned through her own fault, to perpetual vassalage towards one or the other of the great Powers."

RUSSIA'S NEW BOURGEOISIE

BOLSHEVIK CHESTS have always swelled, it is recalled, with prideful boast that Bolshevism wiped out the Russian bourgeoisie, that well-drest, well-fed, moderate, if conventional-minded class, whose very content was anathema to the discontented Bolshevik. But now comes a Bolshevik writer, A. Borissoff, who tells with disgust and indignation of the appearance of a new bourgeoisie in Russia, which is "cunning, impudent, ignorant, stops at nothing, lacks all moral restraint, and has no cultural traditions." In a Russian newspaper issued at Berlin, the *Novy Mir*, this informant goes on to say:

"The new bourgeoisie is seldom a member of the old bourgeois class. Usually it is a former small shopkeeper, a usurer, a saloonkeeper, a traveling salesman, perhaps a professional gambler, or one who deals in stolen goods. As I have already said, he has no cultural traditions, he has not even that little resemblance of external culture which the old bourgeoisie had acquired. . . .

"Without contributing to life in Soviet Russia either material values or cultural, or possessing even elementary 'virtues' of

A WISER AND A SADDER JOHN.

TINO: "Come over here."
JOHN BULL: "Never again!"

—*The Daily Express* (London).

ordinary decency, the new bourgeoisie represents a purely negative force in the economic and cultural sense.

"Crude, impudent, tasteless, primitively greedy, it is a source of moral decomposition and cultural savagery.

"Notwithstanding the primitiveness of these vulgar newcomers, they are already becoming a great force in Soviet Russia. They subordinate to themselves separate parts of the Soviet apparatus, they make the Soviet officials serve them—not the nation—that is, betray the country. The Soviet apparatus under the pressure of the bourgeoisie suffers such changes in its functions as to become substantially anti-Soviet."

One of the most shuddering indictments brought by this Bolshevik writer against the new bourgeoisie is that it "fights the Soviet government by means of bribery" and "buys the materially insecure and morally unstable portion of the Soviet bureaucracy." This is sad enough, in the view of some, but what is to be thought of a Bolshevik who laments the annihilation of the old bourgeoisie, and remorsefully wishes they had never vanished from Russia, for the writer argues:

"The entire economic policy, in so far as it affects industry and trade, depends upon the legalization of the bourgeoisie, which performs definite normal functions in the economy of the Soviet Republic. Of such a bourgeoisie there is only the smallest representation. There is need for this representation to expand and increase, and it probably will thus grow in the atmosphere created by the new policy of the government."

A WARNING AGAINST EYE-GLASSES

A WARNING against all eye-glasses is given by Dr. George M. Gould, an eminent authority on eye-strain, in *American Medicine* (New York). By "eye-glasses" he means any lenses that are not steadied by bows. In other words, spectacles should always be preferred to nose-glasses. And even when spectacles are worn, the lenses should be properly cared for—something that Dr. Gould says few persons know how to do. He begins by reminding us that the objects of eye-glasses and spectacles are to increase or sharpen vision, to lessen, prevent, or cure eye-strain, and to avoid the diseases caused by it. And yet he believes that nearly all of the eye-glasses and many spectacles in actual use are often injuring the eyes and general health of the wearers. He continues:

HOW NOT TO DO IT.

"In view of the fact that many of such glasses have been ordered by oculists and opticians, this may at first seem to be a decided exaggeration. But not so! Because all of us know that, warn, urge, advise, and repeat, however frequently and earnestly we may, to keep the lenses in proper position and perfectly polished, however illustrated with handkerchief or lens-cloth—it will usually go for naught. However frequently and emphatically the urging, they may return to report 'glasses of no use,' 'can't wear them,' etc. If one asks for an illustration of how they do it, such patients may use the bare fingers, or a dirty or dusty handkerchief. Few can understand that the lenses are smudged by the slightest touch against the lashes or lids in putting them on. The big, round lenses now in stupidity-fashion, moreover, strike the cheeks, nose and eyebrows, and are at once smeared with sweat and vapor. There is no limit to the rage for the wrong ways and tools to treat eye-strain. Still another bad way is to rub the lenses so hard that they are made semi-opaque by a thousand scratches which destroy transparency. If we fail to get at least one way successively practised, we fail in duty to the patient's vision and health. And foggy, moisture-laden atmosphere, in factories, homes, and sometimes out-of-doors, will at times make the job still more difficult.

"One rule should, therefore, be unexceptional: Abolish eye-glasses and order only spectacles. All useful lenses have optical centers, and it is only by means of the temple-pieces of spectacles, curved behind the ears, that accurate and constant adjustments are possible. If we lose our patient, let him (or her) go with goodly warnings, repetitive and explanatory, begging at least that eye-glasses shall be used only for distance, company, party, and going-to-meeting occasions. Vanity and migraine are old friends, and vanity decreases—sometimes—with age, and surely with years and suffering long and well combined."

The extent of the morbid, popular mania for ill-fitting eye-glasses may be judged, Dr. Gould says, by the examination of photographs reproduced in the Sunday supplements. It would seem evident, he goes on, even to a blacksmith, that something is decidedly wrong, and that the glasses must be harmful, not helpful tools to the wearers. He proceeds:

"To oculists who know about astigmatisms, and their rôle of ill if the axes are misplaced, there is no doubt about the matter. The worst of the fashions is that of the sillies, who dangle a long black ribbon from one side of their eye-glasses, which displaces the axes of the astigmatism of the lenses from 20 to 30 degrees, according to several quickly changing conditions, the movements of the head, the weight of ribbon, the slipping of the springs, etc.—an optical farce!

"The nasal triangle upon which the eye-glasses are clamped causes a change of the lenticular axes according to the weight of the eye-glasses, the moisture of the skin, the motions of the head, the shape of the nasal bridge, the drag of the cord, and other conditions, so that the displaced axes of the lenses are constantly changed.

"The whole affair thus becomes a tragical farce, so far as physiologic optics and the relief of eye-strain are concerned. The patient pays for the wretched tools which often increase his suffering and inefficiency. It is neither good business, good medicine, nor good morals. The prescription or sale of such tools should be adjudged as malpractise and subject to heavy penalty.

"Some patients pinch a roll of skin above the bone, causing a wobbling of the lenses with every movement of the head or eyes, and there ensues a jerking and dancing of the image, imperfect images, and amblyopia, according to the manifold tasks demanded, the conditions of illumination, the size and placing of the object, etc. The demand of the eyes and brain is, therefore, for spectacles, only and always, where eye-strain exists. At least in the great majority of cases we should tell patients that if they will not wear spectacles for the constant daily work, we can not in future continue to prescribe. There are plenty of others who will gladly receive them as patients.

"It is usually less harmful to wear no glasses than to wear those that do not correct the ametropia. An astigmatic axis misplaced is worse than no correction whatever of the astigmatism. As worn, eye-glasses almost always decidedly change the axes as determined by the conscientious oculist and his scientific trial-frame."

SHALL WE TEACH ELECTRICAL ARITHMETIC?—There is no good reason, thinks *The Electrical World* (New York), why the elementary facts on which the calculation of electric service bills is based should not be taught in the public schools along with the other weights and measures taught in simple arithmetic. It says:

"In school textbooks the pupil is taught to deal with common weights and measures and the methods of computing the cost of the various articles that he must buy or sell in everyday life. Excepting the avoirdupois units of weight and those of linear measure, it is questionable whether any of these units enter into the daily life of the American family so fully as the units of electrical measure do. The engineer who allows his mind to dwell on the intricate foundation on which the system of electrical measurements is built may be inclined to declare that teaching the subject is impossible. But no one will deny that great good would result from a better popular understanding of such units as the watt and kilowatt, the watt-hour and kilowatt-hour and the horsepower. The calculation of the large majority of service bills is based on the use of these units in combination with simple arithmetic.

"The introduction of tables and examples showing how the kilowatt and kilowatt-hour are developed by the use of appliances and how these quantities enter into the service bill would be a powerful factor in placing the electrical measurements in which the public is most vitally interested in the same familiar light that from long habit has come to surround other units of measure."

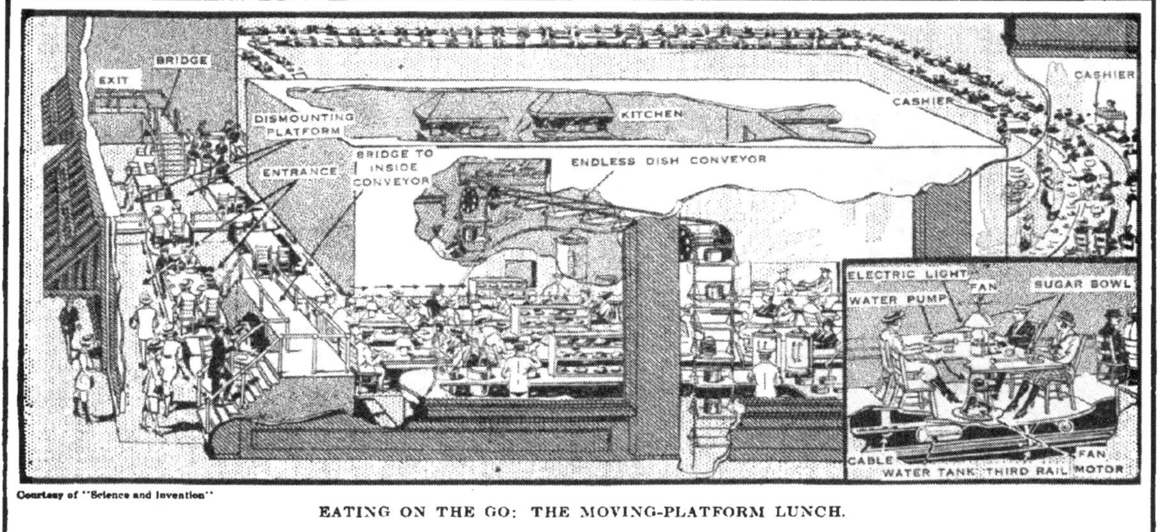

Courtesy of "Science and Invention"

EATING ON THE GO: THE MOVING-PLATFORM LUNCH.

PLANT INDICATIONS OF OIL

THE IDEA THAT SUPERFICIAL INDICATIONS can be relied on to some extent in prospecting for petroleum, and in particular that the character of forest growth may be relied upon for this purpose, as stated recently in *The Engineering and Mining Journal*, is not favored in a press bulletin of the U. S. Geological Survey (No. 475), entitled "Hints on Oil Prospecting." Where surface conditions are reliable, they are geological, we are told; and in most cases the oil itself is visible, either as a film on water, or in the pores of strata. Under the subhead "False Signs," the bulletin gives us this information:

"It is often said that a country 'looks like oil'—that is, the surface gives the speaker the impression that it must be underlain by oil. This remark means only that the country looks like some other oil-producing region which the speaker has visited. The surface appearance of a region, however, means absolutely nothing as indicating the presence of oil, for oil may occur under a surface of any kind, from the orange groves of California to the alkali plains of Wyoming; from the ice-encircled hills of Alaska to the sun-blistered table-lands of Utah. And, similarly, in many regions where the surface is of exactly the same type as that in certain oil-fields there is not a drop of oil. Some men declare that a guide to oil may be found in the vegetation—the trees, bushes, grasses and flowers. But oil is found as abundantly in the treeless plains of Kansas or the Gulf coast as in the pine-covered ridges of Pennsylvania and West Virginia or the 'black-jack' and hickory covered hills of Oklahoma."

In a letter to THE DIGEST, Paul S. Reed, of Tulsa, Okla., has this to say of the pine tree as an indication of the non-existence of an oil-field:

"In January of this year the El Dorado, Arkansas, field was brought in. The Busey well threw a stream of oil, over twice the height of the derrick, which painted evergreen trees black on all sides.

"The field which has been developed at El Dorado during this year has been a big one, extending over ten miles and producing a great volume of oil. The latest estimates which I have seen place this production at close to 50,000 barrels a day.

"The Mexia, Texas, field, brought in during the spring of this year, is located in a forested region of the same kind as that at El Dorado. This is a field with a production estimated at close to 50,000 barrels a day.

"It has often been said that you can not find oil where there are pine trees. This delusion may have affected wild-catters more than is realized, and as a result it is likely that evergreen regions have not been tested as much as others. It does not appear that the pine is a tree that tells where oil is not."

AN EAT-AS-YOU-GO LUNCH ROOM

THE CAFETERIA in its latest form obviates the necessity of walking past a counter to select your food and be "checked up" by the cashier. You may do all this now while sitting comfortably at your table, which is carried slowly along on a moving platform. This happy device is the invention of Lazarus Muntean of Highland Park, Mich., and it is described and illustrated in *Plant-Restaurant Management* (New York), which gives credit to *Science and Invention* (New York). Besides providing the novelty of traveling along as you dine, Mr. Muntean's scheme is one for serving a large number of people in a minimum of time. We read:

"In the first place, Mr. Muntean's scheme calls for one or more loops of a moving platform, to be driven by electric motors or otherwise, and which platforms encompass the kitchen department, as the accompanying illustration shows. In the kitchen we find the necessary ice-boxes, steam-tables and ranges, etc. The victuals are supplied to the serving-counters in front of which the diners move at their tables, by means of moving conveyors, as shown in the illustration. The patrons sit down at the first empty table that comes along, and either consult a menu to be found on each table, or have already consulted a menu at the entrance of the restaurant. The inventor has provided means whereby special dishes can be ordered when the patron first enters the restaurant, so that they will be ready when he arrives before the proper department service counter—meats, vegetables, pies, ice-cream, etc. A small personnel is required only to dispense coffee and tea and keep the shelves of the serving-counter filled with food."

The moving platform arrangements can be built in different ways to suit the requirements of different-sized restaurants and different numbers of people to be served during the rush hour. The table and chair platforms may be hooked up in trains, or they may also be joined to form a continuous platform or chain of tables. The writer goes on:

"Of course the speed at which the tables move is slow so that the patrons can easily pick up the dishes they desire. After passing the last serving-counter, the diners pass before the cashier's desk, where they pay for the amount of food they have selected. The diners may sit at their table and travel around the circuit until they have finished their meal; then if they desire any more food, they select it and pay for the same when they make the second trip past the serving-counters and cashier. Soiled dishes are transferred to endless belts which carry them to electric dishwashing machines in the kitchen.

"The individual dining-tables which move along on the plat-

Courtesy of "The Iron Trade Review," Cleveland.

TWO VIEWS OF THE SAME SHOP, BEFORE AND AFTER THE WALLS AND MACHINES HAD BEEN PAINTED WHITE.

The white paint is said to prevent accidents. Note that the work on the table and in the machines appears in sharp contrast against the white surfaces. It is said that pure white surfaces are not objectionable from the standpoint of glare, unless an unusually strong direct natural light is present.

form are most ingeniously designed. Each table is fitted with an electric lighting fixture and shade, as well as electric motor operating a fan.

"In the center of the table the inventor provides a fountain from which ice-cold drinking water may be drawn from the spigot, the ice and water being contained in a compartment under the platform. The drinking-water system is operated by an electric motor-driven pump. Thus, if the diner wants a breeze, he has but simply to push a button and the fan starts up, or if he wishes more light he clicks on the lamps in the electrolier.

"Necessary electric current is supplied to the motors and lamps on each table through a third rail and contact shoe arrangement, as the drawing clearly shows."

CHANGING OUR MEDICAL SUPERSTITIONS—Drug superstitions are dying out and are being replaced with others, such as psychoanalysis. This statement is quoted from *The Prescriber*, apparently with approval, by *The Medical Record* (New York), which is, however, inclined to think that, "superstition" aside, drugs are more valuable and more efficient than ever, altho their value has somewhat depreciated in the minds of the medical profession. What is needed, in the view of this journal, is to reorganize the whole system. As it sees the situation:

"For considerable time there have been those who have denied to all but a very few drugs any real therapeutic virtues, while there are cynics as to the merits of drugs, and there are even yet drug nihilists.

"Moreover, there have sprung up within recent years various other methods of treating disease and conditions of ill-health, such as vaccine therapy, radiotherapy, and lastly those much overrated methods of diagnosing and treating certain affections, psychoanalysis and psychotherapy. All this at a first glance would seem to imply that belief in the efficacy of drugs in the treatment of disease has diminished. Perhaps, however, when the matter is looked into more closely it will be realized that it is not the use but the abuse of drugs that is on the wane. Drugs are not out of date, but, on the whole, are more efficient than ever. What is required to place drug therapy on a sound basis is to reorganize the entire system, to weed out those that are useless and sometimes even dangerous, to improve and perfect those which have proved themselves of true value. Drugs also to exert their best effects must be prescribed with more or less exact knowledge of their action, and especially must be furnished with discretion. It is sometimes the fault of the physician that drug therapy fails."

ACCIDENTS DUE TO FATIGUE

ACCIDENTS MAY HAPPEN TO WORKERS simply because they are overtired. Elimination of fatigue is therefore one of the most vital of safety measures, we are told by Frank B. and Lillian M. Gilbreth in a paper read before the National Safety Council in Boston and printed in *The Iron Trade Review* (Cleveland, O.). Shop welfare study of all kinds, including that of the elimination of eye-strain by proper coloring, and that of ascertaining the easiest and fewest motions necessary to accomplish a given item of work, tends directly toward the reduction of fatigue and is hence an important measure of accident-prevention. Dr. and Mrs. Gilbreth lay great stress on the efficacy of white paint, which they greatly prefer to the "battleship gray" or other neutral tones now generally used by manufacturers for machine tools or metal-working equipment. These were chosen to reduce glare, but after some years of study the authors are convinced that white is the better color for such purposes. We read:

"Fatigue study is the first step in safety work. It lowers the number of accidents, decreases the wastefulness of operating methods and therefore lessens the number of problems that must be considered.

"The problems of fatigue and of safety bear a peculiar relation to one another. Fatigue causes accidents, while fear of accidents causes fatigue.

"Rest periods, chairs for work and rest, and other means of improving the conditions of work have an aspect of accident prevention as well as of fatigue prevention.

"The importance of proper lighting often is underestimated. Too much emphasis cannot be laid on the old-fashioned idea of 'light from the left side for right-handed workers.' 'White paint and white walls everywhere' should be not only a slogan but a law. The belief in 'neutral tones' of interior paint is founded on a fatigue amateur's guess and not on the results of research.

"The method of finding the one best way to do work, which is a fundamental part of the science of management, has been thoroughly worked out and is identical to the methods of minimizing fatigue and reducing the number of accidents. Habit, so long considered a cruel master, now is realized to be the most useful of helpers; automatically or firmly established habit may become dexterity and, finally, skill.

"As far as possible, useless, inefficient and ill-directed motions are discarded, and the sequence of necessary motions is determined, so that the body can perform these with least effort and fatigue and the largest resulting wages."

WHY AND WHEN WATCH-SPRINGS BREAK

WATCHMAKERS BELIEVE that thunder-showers cause watch-springs to break. Investigation by S. R. Williams, of Oberlin College, Ohio, reveals the interesting fact that more springs do break in summer, the season of electric storms, than in winter, when few or none occur. He believes, however, that electricity has nothing to do with the breakage, which is caused by rust, due to moisture, and promoted by high temperature. This belief is confirmed by laboratory experiments, which also show that oiling is effective in lowering that amount of breakage. "Oil your watch-springs," ought therefore to be good advice, provided there is any way of doing this without clogging the delicate mechanism. Mr. Williams reports his results in *School Science and Mathematics*, beginning his article with a mention of some other odd trade ideas that seem to have foundation, altho, as held, they are erroneous. He writes:

"Blacksmiths have an idea that if the red-hot end of an iron bar is suddenly plunged into water, while the other end is held in the hand, that the smith can notice a very rapid and perceptible increase in temperature of the portion held in his hand. In other words, they believe that the water very suddenly drives the heat from the hot end to the cooler one. Curiously enough, careful investigation of this idea was made by two departments of physics of leading universities of this country and quite independently they could not find, by sensitive instruments, the changes which the blacksmiths seem to pretty generally recognize.

"Again, there is a belief among many barbers that a thundershower dulls their razors and that special attention must be paid to sharpening them after the thunder and lightning.

"It is well to remind ourselves that a blacksmith named Arstall once conceived the idea that an iron rod would change its length, if magnetized. He spoke to Joule, a prominent physicist of England, about it, who became sufficiently interested in the suggestion to test it and found, indeed, that such was the case.

"While the explanations offered by the trades for their ideas are not always supported by scientific reasons, there are fundamental principles back of them which show why they persist in the minds of those who believe in them. For instance, in the case of the iron rod whose heated end is very suddenly plunged into cold water, in all probability the steam arises from the water where the heated rod enters it and this steam ascending envelops the hand grasping the other end and gives the sensation of a sudden increase of temperature. At any rate the ideas are frequently worthy of further investigation as the following may well illustrate.

Courtesy S. R. Williams, Oberlin College.

TESTING THE WATCH-SPRINGS.

"Inquiry among a number of those engaged in the business of watch repairing reveals a persistent notion that the electricity present during a thunder shower is accountable for a large number of mainsprings snapping during and immediately following a thunder-shower.

"To ascribe this breakage to electricity may be ruled out at once, for the mainsprings are coiled in a metal barrel, which in turn is inside of a metal case, and the combination makes absolute protection against any electrical disturbances. Magnetic effects were looked for, but none could be discovered.

"Through the courtesy of Messrs. Herrick and Shreffler of Oberlin, Ohio, and Mr. Chas. H. Savage of Elyria, Ohio, they allowed a search of their records to be made and the number of mainsprings replaced each month was recorded over a continuous period of five years, 1915, '16, '17, '18 and '19. In curve A is shown the composite for the five years as taken from the records of Messrs. Herrick and Shreffler, while curve B shows the average number of thunder-showers per month over the same five years. Curve C shows a similar study from the records of Mr. Savage of Elyria, Ohio. There seems to be a real connection between these curves. If electricity and magnetism are not the causes, what is? Moisture is the obvious answer, and so the next study was an experimental one, in which the breakage of pieces of watch-springs under tension was observed when they were in a moist atmosphere and when they were in a dry one. The results seem very conclusive.

"A watch-spring was cut into pieces, each alternate piece being thrown in one pile and the others in another pile. These were put in a state of strain by bending them in a small loop and holding the ends together by a clamping device. One set of springs was then placed in a jar in which a vessel of water was located and the other set of springs was placed in a similar jar but with a vessel of calcium chloride present to keep the air inside the jar dry. Both jars were sealed air-tight. They were observed for a period of time, and the number which broke in each jar was recorded. The results of a number of different tests are given in the following table:

Exp. No.	*Sample in each jar*	*Days under observation*	*No. broken in dry air*	*No. broken in moist air*
1	22	7	0	11
2	28	52	0	17
3	30	41	0	10

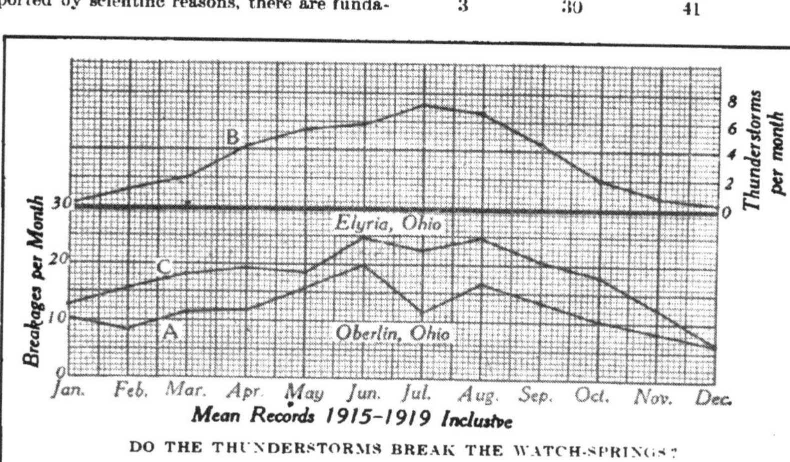

DO THE THUNDERSTORMS BREAK THE WATCH-SPRINGS?

"The moisture therefore seems to be the main cause of the seasonal breakage. Investigation of the springs under a compound microscope showed minute rust spots at the points where the springs had broken, indicating that moisture had promoted rusting there which had broken the skin effect of the spring. Once a crack starts the rust then works in, causing still greater weakness, and it breaks."

SHAKESPEARE RECREATED BY A WOMAN

A WOMAN RUSHES IN where men have feared to tread. Will Shakespeare has proven too much of a theatrical nut for his own sex to crack, but he is shown up in a four-act drama by one of England's young ladies of the pen. And she seems to have emerged with something of a triumph for her intrepidity. Shaw has attempted *Shakespeare* in a "one-act squib," as a Manchester *Guardian* reviewer puts it. "Many write Shakespeare plays for the study, in the safe knowledge that they will never be acted." Miss Clemence Dane is the woman of courage who "must have written with a fair confidence that her Shakespeare would take form upon the stage, and be judged in the flesh by men and women who have built up lovingly in their minds some picture of their country's greatest poet, a figure all the more bewitching, because he is one of history's secrets." What she did was this:

From "The Sphere," London.

SHAKESPEARE AND MARY FITTON

The "Dark Lady of the Sonnets" has come to the dressing-room after playing *Juliet*, and is captivated by Shakespeare's genius. In the inset is *Punch's* picture of the Bard of Avon after being told by Queen Elizabeth to get on with his work.

"'Will Shakespeare: An Invention' was produced at the Shaftesbury Theater. That it could satisfy everybody could never be hoped, but it will satisfy very many. Miss Dane attempted the impossible with high courage, and she has written a play that will live.

"The program begins with an author's note: 'This play does not claim to be true to history. It is no more than an attempt to suggest the nature of the experiences which went to the development of Shakespeare's genius.' Miss Dane has indeed snapped her fingers at history with a flourish.

"*Shakespeare* has sent a play from Stratford to London, and *Henslow* comes down to claim him for the Court. He goes, breaking *Anne Hathaway's* heart. At the Court, he meets and loves *Mary Fitton*, the dark lady, and she plays *Juliet* when a boy fails. But *Mary Fitton* has an affair with *Marlowe*, and Shakespeare pursues her to her meeting with *Marlowe* at Deptford, and it is in a fight between the two poets that *Marlowe* is stabbed by his own hand. The *Queen* hears of the scandal, banishes *Mary* from Court, and *Mary* goes out; there are other men, and she has heard of *Shakespeare's* wife. Then *Shakespeare* is left with his remorse, his burned-out embers of passion, his wolfish, devouring pessimism. The *Queen* prescribes a remedy. Let him work.

The play is thus seen to be "pure fantasy, and one must honorably accept the convention and not boggle about dates and facts." But—

"She who takes this high hand must justify her daring and face a more searching test of poetic truth than the humbler pedestrian folk who abide by the chronicle. This *Shakespeare* had stature of spirit. Mr. Philip Merivale, who played the part, made him big, but not a giant. And there was so much left out. He had no humor. True, that at the close he played to receive that gift. But *Shakespeare* did not need to supplicate half-way through his career for the boon of laughter. That surely must have been his from birth.

"Nor was this *Shakespeare* sensual, driven to frenzy alike by the fascination and the horror of physical love. He struck one as good, possest of a moral logic, wholly modern and quite un-pagan. He was weak and given to wrestlings with conscience, like a Puritan. Was the real *Shakespeare* really so haunted as this one by the presence of his deserted life?

"Miss Dane has not accepted the idea that Shakespeare's passionate love of love and passionate loathing of love sprang both from his esthetic emotions and not from an ethical instinct. Her *Shakespeare* was concerned more with the rights and wrongs of his love than with its beauty and its ugliness. Yet Miss Dane had only two hours and a quarter (exclusive of pauses) to reveal the most many-sided man that ever lived. She could not do all. What she did, she did well. Would that the players had done as as well for her as she for them!

"The play is in verse, often inspired, always dignified. And it was gabbled for the most part, not spoken."

"Honorably accepting" this lady's convention does not come

so easily for *Punch*, who, personated by "O. S."—Sir Owen Seaman?—finds some things against his gorge:

"One may be permitted to sympathize a little with Miss Clemence Dane's *Shakespeare* (as distinguished from the real one) in his resolve to escape to London from his exigent *Anne* (Miss Dane's again). But he needn't have done it—and in fact the real Shakespeare didn't do it—before she had had time to bear him a child. And he needn't have behaved to her like an insufferable boor, flinging her age in her face and reminding her that the advances had been on her side. ('Did you not look at me as tho I were God?' says this offensive prig.)

"One never got over that ugly picture. And one's opinion of the fellow was not improved by his obvious insincerity when, ten years later, he was informed of the mortal illness of the son that he had never set eyes on. Ah! (he tells us) had he but known that the child was a boy, how he would have cherished him! And yet he had never had the curiosity to inquire about the sex of this infant whose advent, and the probable date of it, had been very frankly discust before he deserted his wife.

"Actually, as everybody knows, Shakespeare did not leave Stratford to make a career in London till after the birth of his first child (a girl) and subsequent twins (including the boy Hamnet). So that his hasty and total desertion of his wife is a pure figment of Miss Dane's lively imagination. I hope I am not pedant enough to resent the perversion of history for stage purposes; but, if you must pervert it, it is just as well that you should not make it appear that your object is to bring your hero into contempt.

"There may be some excuse for presenting on the stage the private life of lyrical or first-personal poets whose work betrays no delicacy in regard to self-revelation. But the dramatist, by the nature of his art, can not very well expose himself directly, and, if he knows his job, he will avoid the temptation to do it indirectly by projecting his own personality into his characters. And of all dramatists Shakespeare is the least communicative about his own affairs and emotions. Practically nowhere do we get at the man himself, except in the Sonnets, and then only conjecturally. For if 'with this key Shakespeare unlocked his heart,' as Wordsworth asserts ('Did Shakespeare? If so, the less Shakespeare he!' retorts Robert Browning), he still contrives to leave one guessing. One is tempted to question Miss Dane's sense of proportion when she relies for the romantic interest of her play upon the vague evidence supplied by the Sonnets, which, after all, were only the by-play of a working dramatist."

CHICAGO'S UNLETTERED STATE—The young and eager spirits of Chicago may thank the town for at least one small vehicle of expression," says Mr. Henry B. Fuller, in the New York *Evening Post*. He refers to *Poetry, a Magazine of Verse*, that serves a wider field than Chicago. Its loneliness has never been so brought home to us before:

"Chicago, for a community of three millions, is astonishingly lacking in organs of opinion, whether general or specifically literary. Where are the weeklies, monthlies, quarterlies proper to a metropolis? Trade journals are indeed multitudinous, but even newspapers are few; and some of these latter prefer to treat literature (and the arts in general) with a business-like bluntness as news, and others as gossip, with an excess of smart chatter. In some fields Chicago still does little for the support and refreshment of the human spirit. Meanwhile the town, in all its welling variety, is bursting the bounds set by editorials, 'features,' and news stories. There are finally other things to say, and young minds to say them. Certain small theatrical enterprises, certain small coteries of radicals, certain small advances on the part of 'society'—all these have helped make the local mind more pliant and more self-confident. Space is not the first of youth's demands; place, rather. Our poetical practitioners are learning how to express, within set limits, a wide variety of things: their city, with its beauties and blemishes, its ideals and its lapses; the wide Middle West, conscious of its growing—indeed, its preponderant—importance in the developing life of the nation; America itself (even if but sporadically), with some reference to man and his destiny, as an individual or in the mass; their own young selves, with their various egoisms and generosities; finally, and importantly, a pure estheticism, with man and man's practicalities minimized by an idealizing youth that is not yet ready to hake itself down to the common level of life's prose. That always arrives soon enough."

FRANCE'S GREATEST LIVING COMPOSER

ALONG WITH MARSHAL FOCH, France's greatest soldier, we "have with us" Vincent d'Indy, France's greatest composer. It is suggested that the coincidence is not accidental nor its propagandist value unforeseen. These purposes are given a sharper test by the presence of Richard

FRANCE'S MUSICAL WIZARD.

Who respects tradition, but is also so advanced in musical expression that French audiences have hissed him—Vincent d'Indy.

Strauss, Germany's greatest composer, and it can not be denied that there is more limelight for the latter. Another fact is pointed out by Mr. Krehbiel, the New York *Tribune's* music critic, and that is that we hear barely nothing from Dr. Strauss besides his own compositions, whereas Mr. d'Indy draws his programs impartially from the world of music, including Mozart of his late enemy country. Mr. Vincent d'Indy is one of the founders and present head of the Schola Cantorum of Paris, an educational institution, as Mr. Krehbiel describes it, which "began as the conservator of ancient tradition in respect of the performance of the Gregorian Chant, but has come to be looked upon as the exponent of advanced thought in French music. . . . also the significance of the Schola Cantorum at the present time lies quite as much in what it has done to preserve the old as to make propaganda for the new in music generally as well as in specifically French music." Mr. Krehbiel reviews Mr. d'Indy's position here among us:

"This circumstance may have determined the character of the program which M. d'Indy presented at the two concerts, which had an archaic character at the beginning and after disclosing works by two of his pupils ended with the latest symphonic creation of M. d'Indy himself. If propagandism entered into its purpose (a thought which is at least invited by the presence of the composer in America at this juncture) it was at least propagandism of a more liberal spirit than that represented in the concerts thus far given under the direction of Dr. Richard Strauss, for thus far the latter has brought forward only music of his own composition, except at the concert of last Tuesday, which was given for the purpose of exploiting a singer new to the United States; and these exceptions were two arias by German composers. M. d'Indy's list, on the contrary, contained a composition by Claudio Monteverde, an Italian; Mozart, a German; Michel de Lalande, a Frenchman who was in the service of Louis XIV and died nearly two hundred years ago; and three contemporary Frenchman, himself included."

Much was said during the war about our slavish dependence upon German music and lack of curiosity about the tonal expressions of other nations. Now that we are at peace again it is easy to see who are most active in trying to guide our complacent footsteps. Dr. Strauss's "program" music seems to offer no trying problems for our present comprehension. It is the established mode everywnere, among the French and Italians, too, as we are led to see:

"The compositions by M. d'Indy's pupils and associates were an orchestral dirge, 'To the Dead,' by Paul Le Flem, and a movement from a suite with the general title 'Evocations,' called 'The Gods in the Shadows of the Caves,' by Albert Roussel. Much, overmuch, elaboration, harmonically and instrumentally, of themes not worthy of so much labor, might be said in description of the two works; or, more sententiously, 'Much ado about nothing.' However, considering them in relation to something that has come to us recently from Italy, Germany and England, it is possible to see in them one element deserving of commendation. The Frenchmen (let us now include M. d'Indy as disclosed in his new work) still believe in logical and symmetrical structure—M. d'Indy needed not to be hesitant about calling his 'On the Shores of the Seas,' a symphony, for a free symphonic form, exprest in the arrangement of themes, their development and a succession of moods, obviously hovered over him during the work of composition. In all the pieces, we found the obsession that the scenes, or imaginings from which the composers proceeded, were accepted by them as the contents of their music. To them they may have been so, but they needed not to be to a single one who listened to them. M. Le Flem's piece, being a lamentation, may have been an evocation of grief greater than individual dolor, but M. Roussel's could be called an evocation of vanished gods, seen as shadows in a vast cave only by a listener willing to surrender his ear and fancy into the hands of a literary guide. M. Roussel may have felt while composing his work as if he were a Dante who had placed his hand in that of Virgil, but to us he was neither the great Florentine nor the greater Mantuan.

"In one respect the music of pupils and master stirred the demon of curiosity within us. Why do so many latter-day pieces begin in the depths? Why do their themes emerge from grumbling tubas and muttering double basses, like primal organism wriggling out of primeval, primordial protoplasmic slime? Great heaven! Are we never again to have a composer make a proclamation as Brahms does in his third symphony? 'All at once and nothing first, just as bubbles do when they burst.' When a contrasting second subject is necessary, why does it present itself in the form of a frivolous dance, and why must this dance be made silly or macabre by the tones of a xylophone? Wood alcohol has done mischief enough of late. Must there be an infusion of it in every piece of music, even in tonal visions of the limitless sea, with its mourning eternal and its smiles innumerous? In the glory of every sunrise? If the classic formularies are monotonous, what shall be said of the ceaseless reiteration of such cheap and vulgar devices?

"There are pages of splendid music in M. d'Indy's 'On the Shores of the Seas'; music which sprang from noble emotions and is calculated to evoke noble emotions and uplifting fancies in the listener. But has he sounded 'The Tranquillity of Light' or 'The Joy of the Deep Blue' or 'Green Horizons?' Are there blue and green pigments in music? Dalliance with smiles in musical analysis is as old as the hills—so is the notion that sound and color are correlated. Has such correlation ever been made intelligible? Does the tone of the oboe resemble any color in the solar spectrum? Or the bassoon or trombone? Colors, odors, tastes, sounds, arouse emotions, sometimes definite emotions, in some persons, but the emotions are individual, not shared by all.

"When all men are made over the same psychological last, perhaps a musical composer will paint the red-headed woman whom Strauss said to Mottl he had pictured in 'Don Juan.' Until then we must perforce remain blind, or deaf, or auricularly sightless to the blues and greens of M. d'Indy's 'poem.'"

THE LINK BETWEEN ENGLAND AND BERLIN.

According to the film, it was the monk Rasputin who passed on the word that brought about Kitchener's end.

To give another report of the Frenchman, we quote from the editorial comments of the *Musical Courier* (New York). After speaking of Strauss, and declaring "that the strange genius of the man reaches every one with whom he comes in contact; his cerebral vibrations are irresistible," the writer turns to the other:

"Last Thursday and Friday a French gentleman, *compositeur de musique*, stood up at Carnegie Hall and conducted the New York Symphony Orchestra. He was Vincent d'Indy, and in several respects he made one auditor think of Richard Strauss. Like the latter, d'Indy is a stage figure, slim, dignified, self-contained, imperturbable. Again, like Strauss, he goes at the business in hand without visible display of emotional disturbance, but gets splendid results from the band under his command. To complete the analogy between the two men, d'Indy was an artistic 'revolutionary' early in his career, was attacked as an 'enemy' of art, and in the end prevailed as a master spirit and to-day is considered eminently safe and respectable, musically speaking. Walter Damrosch led the orchestra in a fanfare as d'Indy stepped on the stage. In Paris he frequently was greeted in former years with catcalls and hisses. *Tempus fugit*, and so does the idea that compositions not written in the method or spirit of those already existing and accepted must necessarily be insincere art creations and bad music. D'Indy led his own new symphonic poem, 'On the Shores of the Sea.' All is serene, lovely, poetical, sunshiny, translucent. Soothing and brightly colored music it is, but also highly imaginative and orchestrated with a delicate and sure hand. The listeners liked d'Indy, liked the work, and liked the way it was played. Their applause made all that clear. The rest of the program, indicative of the visitor's scholastic tastes was typically French, typically refined, typically stimulative."

The reviewer for *Musical America* had some of Mr. Krehbiel's difficulties with color significances of sound, saying: "The essential element of this new work is its obvious effort to correlate color and tone. Whether, if it bore another title—say, 'From the Summit of the Years'—it still would suggest depths of green, is debatable. Even with the program notes before the eyes, the 'deep blue' of the second movement and the 'all-enveloping green' of the third, seemed to the writer much the same. However, you either believe in a definite relationship between colors and musical effects, or you don't."

KITCHENER'S DEATH IN THE MOVIES

ONE OF THE MYTHS of the Great War seems to have been thoroughly exploded, and the instrument of its destruction has gone up in the general conflagration. It is a movie film in England that set out to show just "How Lord Kitchener Was Betrayed." The whole story is branded a myth and the film has been barred by the War Office, for all that one of the actors for the camera was a one-time secretary of Lord Kitchener and latterly his biographer. The film had but one showing and that before a large audience supposed to comprise none but members of the two houses of Parliament and their friends, for whom a private exhibition had been arranged. Many objections followed the representation, one from Lord Kitchener's sister. In the London *Daily Telegraph* is an account of this singular happening, and a summary of the film story. Thus:

THE FILM KITCHENER.

Portrayed by Mr. Fred Paul, but not to go beyond the archives of the War Office.

"It had been rumored beforehand that the Government was opposed to the film being exhibited in public, and the ostensible object of yesterday's exhibition was to obtain the opinion of members of Parliament as to what justification there was for such alleged hostility. Much stress was laid on the absolute authenticity of the story told by the film in its main details, and it was noted that Sir George Arthur, Lord Kitchener's confidential friend, played personally in the film, and that extracts from his life of the great soldier were thrown on the screen to explain much of the action. For these and other reasons the audience yesterday was in a very critical mood, and followed all the incidents depicted on the screen with sustained attention.

"The film opens with the departure of Lord Kitchener for Egypt, 1914. We see him embark on the Channel steamer at Dover. Then, just before the vessel casts off from the quay, a special messenger from the Prime Minister dashes up, and Lord Kitchener returns to London to take up the reins at the War Office. Thereafter various scenes display the awakening of Britain's manhood and the magic growth of the great armies that were to save civilization. Up to this point, in spite of the fact that not sufficient care has been displayed in many details, such as uniforms and so on, there is not much that a layman can object to, if one excepts a few of the subtitles, which may not be considered in the best of taste by some persons. In one the definite claim is made that the whole idea of 'the greatest invention of the war,' the tank, was conceived by Lord Kitchener on September 5, 1914, and carried out by Captain Bede Bentley, who makes a momentary appearance on the screen in person.

"The 'great betrayal' is shown as the work of a German woman, the widow of an English officer, killed in the early days of the war. She apparently discards mourning almost immediately, and is seen at a fashionable modiste's buying clothes she cannot afford. The tempter steps in, in the guise of a suave German agent, who offers to pay her well if she will act as a spy. She consents without much reluctance, and eventually worms out of a young English officer who is to accompany Lord Kitchener to Russia all the details of the journey. The German agent who employs her thereupon exclaims, before he despatches the news abroad, 'The war has been won, and won by a woman.' Rasputin is shown in the wireless room at Tsarskoe-Selo apparently communicating the information to Berlin. Orders are immediately sent out for the torpedoing of the *Hampshire*, and the young officer whose indiscretion is supposed to have led to the tragedy is drowned, as well as Lord Kitchener.

"On the completion of the exhibition, which lasted nearly two hours, those present were invited to express their opinion about the film. It was immediately obvious that the general impression was by no means favorable. Admiral Sueter protested against the claim put forward in connection with the invention of the tanks. Several members of Parliament strongly objected to the claim made that the story told was authentic, and none liked the idea of mixing up a sensational story of such a kind with the name of one of the Empire's greatest soldiers. One speaker even went the length of saying that the exhibition in public of such a film was a scandal that should not be tolerated. A lady, understood to be the sister of the late Field-Marshal, exprest her abhorrence of a film which showed a British officer betraying his trust. General Von Donop, who said he had worked in close association with Lord Kitchener during the war, was indignant at what he described as a travesty of the true facts, as well as at the whole tone of the film. He said he had often discust the tragedy of the sinking of the *Hampshire* with Lord Jellicoe. Altogether, it may be said that the general impression left on the audience was that the film is objectionable from several points of view and not very interesting or well constructed. The French Government, it was stated, had asked to be supplied with a copy for the State archives."

Following the published account of the film exhibition is a letter in the London *Daily Mail* from an apparently authentic source giving what must be the officially accepted facts of the great warrior's death:

"To the Editor of *The Daily Mail*.

"Sir—May I confirm your statement that the story of espionage in connection with the loss of the *Hampshire* and Lord Kitchener is a piece of silly fiction?

"It is practically certain, however, that the mines which the *Hampshire* struck were those of U-75 (a large German submarine minelayer carrying 36 mines), and not of the Whiten mine-field laid by the *Mœwe* farther to the westward.

"U-75 laid her mines on May 29 as a preliminary part of the Jutland operations, which were based on the idea of the German Fleet showing itself in the North Sea and enticing out the British Fleet, which was then to be attacked by submarines lying off the Orkneys, Moray, Firth and Forth for the purpose.

"The plan miscarried, so far as the submarines were concerned, and they returned to Germany on June 1.

"Lord Kitchener arrived at Scapa on June 5. In ordinary circumstances he would have sailed by the east side of the Orkneys. But a strong northeasterly gale was blowing. . . .

"On account of the gale Lord Jellicoe decided to send him up the western coast—an eleventh-hour choice which in itself rules out the possibility of espionage, for the mines were laid on May 29 and the choice was made a week later.

"The *Hampshire* struck a mine and was lost.

"The rest of the mines were discovered as soon as the weather moderated. They were laid deep in a strong tideway and in a normal sea the *Hampshire* would have passed over them.

ALFRED C. DEWAR (Capt. R. N., retired).
Caledonian U. S. Club, Edinburgh."

The War Office, according to the New York *Herald*, has disposed of the claim of the woman, Elbie Boecker, who "boasted to any willing listener that she received 10,000 marks for the information of Kitchener's impending departure for Russia. . . . Elbie Boecker was sentenced four weeks before the *Hampshire* sailed, and before arrangements for the trip had been made, to two months' imprisonment and expulsion for violating rules regulating alien enemies. The fact that she was never at large after May 8, 1916—the *Hampshire* sank June 5—effectively disposes of her claim that she was arrested on suspicion after the sinking of the vessel and deported on account of her suspected share in the disaster."

CHRISTMAS AS A DAY OF PRAYER FOR DISARMAMENT

CELEBRATE CHRISTMAS DAY by "rooting" for the Arms Conference, suggests **Edward S. Martin**, editor, in *Harper's Magazine*, declaring that the thing to do, if possible, is to mix the two proceedings, for until the Conference, or some succeeding one, makes a satisfactory performance, Christmas is apt to be a waning festival, and unless there is an infusion of the season's spirit into its work, "the results are not likely to meet the situation." Prayers for the success of the Conference, which has as its aim "Peace on earth and good-will to men," were offered up in every church in the land the week before the deliberations began, and recently every post of the far-flung Salvation Army joined at a certain hour in a similar petition to God. Following the example set by the evangelical churches of Rome, Ga., the Federal Council of the Churches of Christ in America has suggested that congregations everywhere observe Christmas Day by holding a second concert of prayer and by sending to their respective Senators and Representatives in Congress an urgent appeal to use their influence for the reduction of armament. Further evidence of world support for the Conference is not lacking. No less than in America, the churches in Great Britain and Japan, we are told, have sent up, and are sending up, petitions in its behalf. Pope Benedict, as an ardent advocate of peace, has warmly commended the present movement, and is praying for its success. It seems then, as Mr. Martin says, that "we all know that we need peace on earth, and we all know and are constantly reminded—particularly on the quarter day, when some of us have to pay a tax—how much we need it. We all know, or begin to realize, that we won't get it except at the price of good-will to men." No less a spirit of earnestness is required now, when we want peace, than was needed when we went to war, and the world is looking to the Conference and to us for salvation. So—

Copyrighted by the Philadelphia "Inquirer."

LOVE AND HATE.

—Morgan in the Philadelphia *Inquirer*.

"It is constantly put up to us that we are an indispensable part of the machinery of the modern world, and that unless we recognize our importance and our duties, and function as we ought to, there is no assurance that civilization can recover from its recent setback. Not that it will die; it can hardly perish; but it can be put back a long time, and if civilization is so put back, make sure that we shall be put back with it. We shall not forge ahead on our own account after failing in our duty to the rest of mankind. National progress does not come out of duty slighted, but out of duty met and fulfilled. We can not skulk, we can not shirk, and hope to get anywhere. Skulking and shirking are not even good for business. . . .

"We can do a great deal from the outside. The atmosphere the Conference works in is very important. If we can create an atmosphere that will sustain its hope and encourage its best thoughts and best efforts, that will be a great service. It has a better chance than the Congress at Versailles because the war is far away and the consequences of it are better understood and the immediate future can be much better calculated."

All forward-looking people, then, we are urged, should work together for the success of the Conference, and especially the religious people. "Everybody should get over the idea that religion is something apart from knowledge and not practical. Religion is not a thing apart. All knowledge belongs to it, and it belongs to knowledge, and is a supremely important branch of it." All the more valuable, then, are the facts which make for confidence in religion, and in its power to rescue the world from its present plight. Mr. Martin assures us:

"The very pith and essence of religion is the belief in an invisible world to which our visible and material world is related by the closest ties, and out of which it is possible to get help in the solution of our earthly problems. That is the sort of help we need for the Washington Conference, and the call for universal prayer at the opening of it was an instinctive recognition that that help is needed. We want spiritual assistance. So much anybody of intelligence will admit. Anybody who thinks will concede that materialism has made a mess of the job of managing this world and that we need an infusion of what might be called spiritualism into the management, if we are to salvage what is left. But where do they expect to get their spiritualism—their spirituality? Is it a product of the material and visible world that they are so concerned about? No; it isn't! It is a product of the spiritual and invisible world, about which so many good and valuable people have only vague and timorous ideas, and no belief positive enough to accomplish what they would. They want spirituality —something to temper the selfishness of men, but the price of it is belief—an urgent, practical belief in a spiritual and invisible source of the spirituality that they want, and they can not pay that price. They have not got it."

However, some have this spirituality, and "they are, as usual, the hope of the world, and should be the best helpers of the Conference. It is they, perhaps, who can furnish its inspiration." And on whether the Conference secures this help and inspiration depends whether it will be successful—a serious task for the Church and religious workers to realize, for after all, believes the writer:

"Our best hopes for the Conference and for any radical improvement in the methods of conducting human life on this planet are, frankly, religious hopes, based on the birth we celebrate at Christmas, and the ministry and the teachings that followed. If there is not enough in Christianity to save our present edifice of civilization—enough wisdom, enough illumination, enough

) REFORMERS AT THE WOMAN'S CHRISTIAN COLLEGE OF JAPAN AT TOKYO.
which are helping downtrodden Eastern women to achieve an economic and social status.

., for other means have here are only ruins to ave.

an imperfect record of se those earlier civiliza- ey crumbled. In that r fathers, and there is of history, we have viv- r surpassing in destruc- proceeding out of very those that destroyed in We know more clearly before what lies ahead and the ways of human our grasp if civilization n it. We see destruction hat growing knowledge our case is and some of Washington Conference actically operative. It we can do to make that r civilization from what e, and all the rest."

from every part of the Federal Council, come ropose to abate in any of Christian methods in eetings are still pushing ng success to the issue told, "a new spirit in e must be, first of all, much of our own rights own duties and others' ir nation, not as an end of nations under a com- pen to the incoming of can bring lasting peace a has spread around the led as a remarkable public churches. After stressing post-war conditions of the in the outcome of the lat- society, these churches say:

the Limitation of Arma- final purpose of complete e Kingdom of God upon Divine Lord, the Prince of e an opportunity to unfold

tal necessity for the Chris- e their efforts in rendering the Conference successful."

CHANGING WOMEN INTO HUMAN BEINGS

FOR THOUSANDS OF YEARS WOMAN in the laggard countries of the Far East has been little more than a beast of burden, a creature without a soul; but, under Western influence, this condition is now reported to be changing, and already in China and Japan the women are trying to keep pace with their Western sisters in obtaining an economic and political status. In China the women are successfully rebelling against the ancient custom of foot-binding, and in India the wailing against child marriage and the degradation of women in the lower ranks of society no longer goes unheeded. To Christian colleges established by foreign missionary societies a large part of the credit for this leavening in the great mass of ignorance seems to be due, for, as we are told, they are affording valuable assistance in the great reformation which the Orient is now undergoing. Before the war, writes Mrs. Henry W. Peabody in the *Missionary Review of the World*, there were three or four experiments in higher education for women, all under denominational direction. It was found extremely difficult, however, for any one denomination to provide proper buildings and sufficient equipment, and the women's boards of foreign missions decided to cooperate, with the result that it is becoming possible to provide adequate, standardized, well-equipped institutions. Yenching College, at Peking, which is affiliated with the Imperial University, is one of the leavening institutions which is said to have a particularly striking history. According to a booklet prepared by Mrs. Frame, formerly acting president, and quoted by Mrs. Peabody, the women graduates are active "in administration, in education, medicine, literature, as religious workers, social workers, lecturers, in social reform, as home missionary pioneers in distant, lonely fields, as Y. W. C. A. secretaries." Moreover—

"In a hundred ways their patient endeavor is helping their sisters to meet the new social complexities and changes with dignity and intelligence. But none the less constructive is their work as home-makers and mothers. Comrades of their husbands, everywhere they work together, quietly weaving a strong fabric of community life out of the patriarchal family life of the past and the democracy of the present. To leaven the new social order is surely the greatest work of Christian education. All the direct or indirect training Yenching can give her students, whether by courses in Education, Sociology or Home Economics, in society or in class organizations, by debates and plays and pageants, by athletics and music and social service, to develop a spirit of initiative, poise and considerate cooperation, counts in this.

"Leaders in constructive patriotism, in Christian social service, in education, literature, journalism, in molding the new social order—these, then, are the answer that Yenching tries to give to the clamoring needs of China, the part she tries to play in preparing the alert young womanhood of North China to do its share with vision and distinction."

Ginling College, at Nanking, which opened its doors in the old home of Li Hung Chang in 1915, and is, therefore, looked upon as "one of our war babies," has "already made a good record," and "many preparatory schools in East and Central China are sending up their girls, who will go back with their college degrees and their thorough training to build up the missions from which they came. They will also take important positions as educators, writers, doctors, reformers, teachers, in the new educational system of China." Other colleges listed by the writer are one at Tokyo; one at Lucknow, affiliated with Allahabad University; another at Madras; and the Vellore Medical Missionary School, about four hours south of Madras. The college at Madras, opened in 1915, is, we are told, an international experiment in which Great Britain, the United States and Canada are bound together, and for whose maintenance twelve boards are united—six in Great Britain, five in the United States, and one in Canada. A plan of campaign to build up and maintain all these institutions is now being promulgated by all the cooperating boards, in which are included Baptist, Christian, Congregationalist, Canadian Methodist, Canadian Presbyterian, Lutheran, Methodist, Presbyterian, Reformed Church, and Methodist Episcopal, South. They are begun on a great venture, for, as the writer says, in India—

"There are many millions of women and there are so few doctors—not one to a million. With child marriage and child motherhood we can easily imagine the frightful conditions. This effort to train Indian Christian women in medical work, sending them out as doctors to their own women, is one of the most important events of this century. There is no lack of students. One hundred and fifty were turned away last year, as there was no building in which they could live, no class-rooms adequate."

CRIME DECREASING IN ENGLAND

THE ENGLISH CRIME RECORD for 1920-1921 is greatly less than that for the year preceding the war, this fortunate change being due, we are told, to the advance in education and to the generally improved condition of the people. It is true that the number of prisoners is greater by 10,000 than in 1919–1920; but this may be regarded, it is said, as a passing phase, for which wide-spread unemployment and industrial unrest may be held responsible. Sentences to imprisonment increased in these two years from 34,000 to 42,000, and the number of persons imprisoned as debtors or on civil process rose from 2,800 to 5,200. Male prisoners increased by 8 per cent., while female prisoners fell off by 2 per cent. As between 1920–1921 and the year before the war, however, the following table shows what is considered to be a remarkable improvement:

OFFENSES	1913–14	1920–21
INDICTABLE:		
Murder, manslaughter, wounding, etc.	474	389
Burglary, housebreaking, etc.	1,960	1,548
Larceny, embezzlement, receiving and false pretenses	19,126	12,995
NON-INDICTABLE:		
Assaults	8,666	3,312
Drunkenness, etc.	51,851	8,752
Police regulations, offenses against	8,661	1,948
Poor law, offenses against	4,275	1,222
Prostitution	7,952	2,938
Begging and sleeping out	15,019	2,539

This is an extraordinary decrease, says the New York *Times*, informing us that

"The Commissioners attribute it to various causes—better education, better working conditions, higher wages, larger savings, temperance, war pensions, juvenile courts, the disappearance of the extreme destitution of the days before the war. The Governor of Durham Prison, speaking of first offenders, whose number was 18,000, compared with 45,000 in 1913–14, says:

"'A new stamp of offenders has sprung into existence. Men and women of respectable antecedents and parentage, in regular employment and in no respects associated with the criminal class, are taking to serious crime (embezzlement, fraud, false pretenses, housebreaking and robbery) with astounding facility.' He disputes the theory that lawlessness learned in the war is responsible for these crimes. The proportion of women among these offenders contradicts that theory. It is more probable that many who have been used to 'big money' and can no longer get it, steal to provide themselves with luxuries and amusements to which they have grown accustomed. On the other hand, some men who learned motor-mechanics in the war are given to breaking into garages and stealing motors. There is a sort of adventure about this crime; and the men who practise it are 'usually intelligent and of fairly good education.'"

THE GLITTER OF BAHAISM

ABDUL BAHA, "SERVANT OF GOD," and head of the Bahaistic doctrine of universal fellowship, is dead, but, as the Charleston *Gazette* observes, "there will be no falling off in attendance at the churches devoted to worship of the great moralist who was born in Nazareth and whose birthday the world is preparing to observe." All religions are said to come from the East. Bahaism sprang up in Shiraz, Persia, where the son of a wool merchant, a young man of genius called the Bab, in 1844 broke away from Islam to preach an "all-embracing gospel of universal brotherhood." After six years of teaching, the head of the new cult suffered martyrdom, and his disciples were persecuted. But another man came forth to lead the movement in the person of Mirza Hosein Ali of Nour, who, we are told, assumed an inspired leadership and proclaimed the doctrine of a peaceful reunion of faiths and aspirations. He became known as Baha'o'llah, which means the Glory of God. He also is said to have been of the fiber of which martyrs are made, and he suffered forty years of exile and imprisonment. He was succeeded by his son, Abdul Baha Abbas, who has just died. In the meantime, says the Boston *Transcript*, Baha'o'llah's "benevolent, but vague and indefinite, doctrine or holy hope of a universal religion which shall replace or reconcile all the warring creeds has spread abroad through the earth, until its acknowledged followers are found in all Christian countries at least." Its devotees, we are told further, do not find their acceptance of the Bahaist doctrine to be inconsistent with their membership in existing churches. Concerning the ideals of the "quietist" cult, the *Transcript* says:

"It is a mélange of Christianity and idealistic Mohammedanism, suffused and inspired by a very glowing hope. It contains nothing new; it is, in the words of Baha'o'llah, 'an ocean of generosity manifested and rolling before your faces.' It is a gorgeous glitter of intense benevolence, which derives whatever it has of proselyting power from its dramatization in a saintly personality. It is the old story of the attempted incarnation of an idea—the idea itself being so vaguely generous and noble that no one could possibly object to it. Long before the present movement for an international organization of peace, Baha'o'llah had proclaimed the following as one of its cardinal 'doctrines'—that is, aspirations:

"'We desire but the good of the world and the happiness of the nations. That all nations should become one in faith and all men as brothers; that the bonds of affection and unity between the sons of men should be strengthened; that diversity of religion should cease, and differences of race be annulled—what harm is there in this? Yet so it shall be; these fruitless strifes, these ruinous wars shall pass away, and the "Most Great Peace" shall come. Do not you in Europe need this also? Is not this that which Christ foretold? Yet do we see your kings and rulers lavishing their treasures more freely on means for the destruction of the human race than on that which would conduce to the happiness of mankind. These strifes and this bloodshed and discord must cease, and all men be as one kindred and one family. Let not a man glory in this, that he loves his country; let him rather glory in this, that he loves his kind.'"

CURRENT - POETRY

Unsolicited contributions to this department cannot be returned

TWO poems in the Christmas number of London *Sphere* sound the season's emotion. The second one which speaks the harmony of the dumb beasts with the faith of the world is a fine appeal for universal sympathy.

NOËL

BY M. M. JOHNSON

"Noël, noël,"
Earthward fell
Voice of Gabriel,
Like a golden bell.
"Noël, noël!"
Good tidings to tell
To shepherds with sheep
Upon hills asleep.
"Noël, noël!"
Hollow and dell,
Sweet with the spell
Of that best knell.

I have no sheep
On hills to keep,
And yet, I wist,
I too may list
Good Gabriel
His tidings tell,
And I as well
May sing, "Noël,
Noël, noel!"

THE HOLY STALL

BY M. M. JOHNSON

There's a warm hollow in the hay
Where the Baby Jesus lately lay,
For Mary has taken her Child away,
And the cattle speak with their eyes and say,
"Where is our Shepherd Babe to-day?"

Mournfully thro' the dusk they gaze
(Around no holy Starlight plays):
Till for grief their rugged heads they raise
And snort and bellow in deep amaze
That Joseph and Mary have gone their ways.

In stable and shed and dark city,
Great Shepherd, on beasts have sweet pity,
For rarely go they merrily;
And once, o'er Thy humility,
With fragrant breath they worshiped Thee.

Once o'er Thy state most pitiful
Wept at Thy side the fearsome bull,
And gave Thee shaggy locks to pull:
Thrust thou Thy fingers in white wool
Of sheep, that frisked thy cries to lull.

HERE is an old legend restated in the New York *Herald* with considerable felicity:

THE ARTIST'S SIGNATURE

BY EDITH M. THOMAS

Grieve not, to offer to some reigning power
Though 'tis but of the hour,
Deeming this must we do, to make our way
Until some Reckoning Day!
For so it happens much the same to us
As once to Sostratus.
His story? Here it is in brief annexed
Reduced from Lucian's text:

He builds a lighthouse on a sharp fang'd reef
Where many came to grief
When they would enter Alexandria's Bay—
He builds, and builds to stay! . . .
Outside, the Pharos bore a monarch's name
(Long lost of mocking Fame!),
But mason work the marble's face o'erlaid,
And in some years betrayed!
Then, gradually, but sure, there came to light,
Cut in the marble white,
Another charactery, unread before,
From wave or from the shore:
"I, Sostratus, this Pharos did erect
To them who do protect
The Mariner . . ." These words outstanding wrought
Magic in all men's thought,
But most the artist's—that the maker's craft
The last of all had laughed!

Build to the Gods (if build we can). Care not
How long your name's forgot!
Make of Obscurity a wily friend—
Far in her shadow bend:
Expediency—she, too, you hate so much
Has her own salving touch . . .
The work's your own, your signature inheres—
O trust it to the Years!

MANHATTAN has had many invocations, but when has she been called kind as well as beautiful? In the New York *Times* is one that gives us a fresh insight into the heart of a great city:

MOTHER MANHATTAN

BY MARY SIEGRIST

They say that you are cruel—those who glance
Carelessly on your haughty roofs and towers;
They claim that you are cold and pitiless,
That you devour the driven ones who fly
To you for sanctuary—that you draw
Blind youth to you, then Circe-like, destroy.
But we, who know your every passing mood,
We, who have sought you out of all the earth,
Sensing your large awareness, we have found
Within your moving throngs a shadowed peace—
That your deep maze holds many a holy shrine
We know that you are swiftly answering,
We know that you are beautiful and kind.

Many are phantom-led and slip, dust-blind,
Hourly from out your marts, the goal unwon:
Yet each has found you not unbeautiful.
In all the world what towers are like to yours;
So calm, uneager, self-sufficing, still?
They say that you are cruel—those who look
Unseeing on your unmoved, wind-swept spires,
These have not heard your large, wide silences:
They have not guessed your wise indifference;
Nor have they shared your silent sorrowing
Beneath your lilting laughter, for your tears
You hid from them beneath a mask of smiles.
But we, who know you, Mother, find you great,
And we, who know you, Mother, know you kind.

FAIRY lore hasn't taken deep root in our folk consciousness, so while we may not feel the force of the picture we can still respond to the lesson. In the London *Spectator*, Philpott's poem is preceded by this note: "A pleasant maxim of old time directed the gardener to leave one corner as Nature planned it, for the little people. Thus welcomed, they might be trusted to show their human hosts good will, friendship, and service."

THE PIXIES' PLOT

BY EDEN PHILLPOTTS

You have it, or you have it not:
The cantle of the Pixies' plot,
Where never spade nor hoe shall ply
To break that treasured sanctity.
Touch no bloom there; uproot no weed;
Let what will blow,
Suffer the thistle, briar, and thorn to grow,
The dandelion to seed.

Though full the garden of your mind,
Well planted on a soil that's kind:
Your hedges gay, your borders clean,
Your seasons fair, your clime serene,
Yet trammel not the Pixies' mite,
For welcoming
Chance little, wandering, weary, fairy thing
Lost in the dim owl-light.
Still virgin, free and set apart,
Ordain one dingle of your heart,
Where visions home, and wing to you
The golden dreams that might come true.
Herein a gentler dawn than day
Shall often break
For foot-sore spirits, tired of reason's ache,
And children come to play.

THE broad highways are for everyday and for the multitude, but trails and half-hidden paths and old woodroads are for the exploring soul, as this from the *Independent* shows so well:

TRAILS

BY CHARLES WHARTON STORK

A trail's a careless human sort of thing,
Much like a casual turn of speech. Altho
You can't tell who began it or just why
It wanders here or there, still if you're set
To go somewhere, you'll mostly find a trail.
You think it's like
An unsophisticated country girl,
Confiding; who, taking your hand in hers,
With lifted eyes and berry-pouting lips,
Will lead you guilelessly. All it wants,
You think, is to reveal perchance a glade
Eager with fireweed; and soft nets of fern;
A lichened log; a shallow rivulet,
Brown over mud, but crystal over beds
Of pebbles, where its tiny wavelets crisp
To silver in the laughter-dimpling lights.
So you drift heedlessly, until you strike
A slope. You clamber up the jagged steps
Of a pink cliff of granite, quickly cross
A smooth stretch under boughs of stunted pines,
But then meet other crags to scale, with tufts
Of blueberries or of bristling juniper,
When with a great lift of the lungs and soul
You leap out on a summit, breast to breast
With the great clouds that melt in softest blue,
While far below the dim earth lies a-dream
In veils of violet haze, and off to the east
The titan ocean spreads his purple cloak
Broidered with runic islands.

You know the trail deceived you with its air
Of shy rusticity; you're in love, in love—
You that went out but for an idle walk—
Madly in love with the informing soul
Of what you gaze on!
That was where the trail
Led you. Do you forgive it?

A MEMBER of the Junior Class in Hamilton College contributes this to the *Hamilton Literary Magazine*, and our contributor thinks that spreading it broadcast "as a sample of what the American undergraduate can do" will encourage others:

TO SHELLEY

BY CHARLES GRANT LOOMIS

He silently took the fleece of a dream
And washed it clean with the dust of a star;
He wove in the fleece a lyrical theme,
And a mystical vision caught from afar;
It was never a cloud that sailed the sky,
But a naiad's soul all draped in a shroud;
It was never a luster that shone in an eye,
But a mirrored mind with beauty endowed.
Be it summer breeze or a moonbeam lone,
New music recaught from an echo fled,
Be it rainbow spray from a fountain blown,
That dies in the dusk when the sun has sped,
O'er these with the fire of impetuous Truth
Thou reignèd, sovereign guide, through an ageless youth.

OUR DOUGHBOYS' "OLD BOSS" ON A VISIT

MARSHAL FOCH, recently the guest of the American Legion on a tour of the United States, is "above all, a plain man, a simple man, an unaffected and unspoiled man," reports one of his hosts, who had an opportunity to know him at close range on his private train from Boston to New Orleans. The man who planned the defense of France "smoked a Missouri corn-cob pipe and enjoyed it." The soldier who wrote the Armistice terms shaved himself, using a steady hand and an old-fashioned straight-edged razor. Stories galore about the French Commander came out through the small army of newspaper correspondents who accompanied him about the country, altho the Marshal, unlike many notables who visit our shores, had no press agent. This little incident, related by the correspondent of the New York *Herald*, shows how the Allied Commander linked our Middle West with his France, in a bond of his own humanity:

Copyrighted by Paul Thompson

"A SAGACIOUS, KEEN-WITTED OLD EAGLE."

The Allies' Commander-in-Chief, Marshal Ferdinand Foch, lately the guest of the American Legion, has given hundreds of thousands of Americans a glimpse of the real genius of republican France. He is shown in the new photograph, reproduced above, as he stood at salute before Jeanne d'Arc's statue in Riverside Drive, New York.

A woman at the station platform in a little town in Indiana had managed to get away up front, near the observation end of Foch's special train. The train paused less than a minute. But she rushed past the policemen and the secret service men to thrust into the French soldier's hands a potted geranium.

"My boy died near Soissons," she told the Marshal. "Will you plant this flower when you get back home? He was a gardener and raised beautiful geraniums."

That night some one moved the geranium into the baggage-car. Foch missed it in the morning, and made inquiries.

"Fetch it back," he ordered, when informed that it had been taken out of his way. "I shall attend to it myself, because I intend keeping it alive and planting it in my own garden for that woman's boy."

He didn't say this to reporters. None of his staff came running back to the correspondent's car to tell them how thoughtful this Marshal was. The incident was overheard inadvertently. The professional press agent would have sown the story in every State in the Union.

Something of a point was made by American newspapers of arrangements by which Foch and his party might be guaranteed table wine, after the French custom, during their tour. As a matter of fact, Foch drank no wine during his visit, and James E. Darst, in *The American Legion Weekly*, relates this significant story, told by members of the Marshal's staff:

At a certain formal dinner in Paris, shortly after the Armistice, a foreign dignitary became equally overwhelmed by Foch's greatness and sparkling Burgundy. He persisted in leaving his place at table and running up to the Marshal to wring his hand. He kept exclaiming:

"Marshal, you are great. Tell us how you did it."

Foch, smiling and imperturbable, finally answered the query. He lifted his glass of water and bowed to his bibulous admirer.

"By drinking this, my friend," he said.

"That is Foch, alert, serene—ready, but kindly and tolerant." Mr. Darst goes on:

This gray man of France millions of Americans saw to be a sinewy figure, five feet and seven inches tall and weighing probably 150 pounds, his face rugged and furrowed with lines, his voice ringing and clear, his movements quick and energetic.

Those who were privileged to be with him on his country-wide triumphal trip found that Foch was always the same; that he was not a man to show one face to a throng in an auditorium and another to his companions at dinner. And his mood was always interested and genial. No one ever saw the Marshal in a bad humor. His perfect control over his mind—a control that sent him to sleep promptly at night, no matter what had been the excitements of the day—would not permit him to be abstracted or gloomy or disturbed.

The Marshal always left what is known in hotel parlance as a 7:30 call. He rose, shaved and drest himself. *Petit dejeuner* was served after he had donned a bathrobe, dark and somber in hue. He invariably ate a roll or a piece of toast, and drank tea instead of coffee.

Emerging from his compartment, clad in his horizon blue field uniform, Foch would greet everyone with a cheery "*Bon jour, Monsieur.*" Always the greetings—and the conversation —were in French. The Marshal refused to dally with English.

If the party remained on the train, Foch turned to his famous black pipe. It is a slightly curved affair, with apparently tremendous possibilities, particularly when loaded with the deadly French tobacco that the Marshal clings to. The pipe had the air of being a companion rather than a solace; a sort of grizzled crony of many high adventures, silent, scarred and devoted. A "Missouri meerschaum" supplanted the briar for a time, but became too vigorous and was discarded.

Newspapers made much of the Marshal's purported statement that he would abstain from wine in deference to the law of our land. He did so abstain, but his aides declared that as a matter of fact the Marshal seldom touches anything, even in France.

On his tour, the usual day's routine found Foch the honor

guest at a luncheon. There were occasions, however, when the party remained on the special train, whereupon Foch dined with his official party in his private dining-room. The Marshal made an exception to this rule when the train was going from New Haven to Providence. He suggested that a family gathering be held in the main dining-car and asked everyone to eat with him. During the dinner he bubbled with good humor.

Captain Réné l'Hôpital, his personal aide, went to the baggage-car and dragged out Theodora, the wild-cat kitten (or wild kitten, whichever it is) that Montana Legionnaires gave the Marshal at Kansas City. Except for a few desultory spits, the kitten was complacent and Captain l'Hôpital brought her to the table of the Marshal of France. You know the adage about the cat and the king. It held for the cat and the most famous living soldier. The cat squirmed, after she had had her look, and the Marshal poked a gingerly finger at her and admired the markings of her fur. Her purrs filled the car.

HIS OLD BOSS.

—Thomas in the Detroit *News*.

Incidentally, the cat will be interned as a dangerous alien in the Paris Zoo, with a tablet telling the world that the Legion presented it to the Marshal.

This particular meal, like all the others, found Foch sparing of appetite. He favored American soups and plain roasts. The familiar legend "All kinds of pies," failed to intrigue his interest. He took to ice-cream like a farm-boy. American food seemed to make a hit with him. He had been offered the privilege of bringing his own chef, but he refused to do so. The meals were Broadway Limited standard, and the Marshal and the rest of the French party demonstrated their approval.

The Pennsylvania Railroad made up the special train that carried the party, and Pennsylvania officials arranged the routings and made the way easy and comfortable. On the road's famous Horseshoe Curve in western Pennsylvania an amusing incident occurred. Foch noticed a large number "57" on a signboard, advertising a brand of pickles. He asked Pershing its significance. Pershing got as far in his explanation as the word "pickle" and was stumped. A Frenchman in the party advanced the theory that the word should be "peekle." Foch got it. He was delighted with this sample of American advertising enterprise.

Foch is credited with revising "our national opinion of him" during his eight weeks' stay. Americans, says Mr. Darst, had heretofore thought of him as a stern and implacable warrior—curt, cold, efficient. But—

His stay among us showed him to be pre-eminently human—not a thinking machine, but a man of family and friends and warm sympathies and ideas.

Crowds saw him alert and quick, reminding them of a sagacious and keen-witted old eagle. The movements of his head were quick and birdlike. At functions he studied the persons about him, and evidently based his speeches on the mood of the listeners. Foch spoke extemporaneously, except on a few occasions. His poise was always superb; he had himself well in hand. When he alighted from trains, amid bustle and confusion, he noted carefully the moves of those with him and quickly fell in with their directions.

The humanity of Foch was shown by his interest in children; not the politician's kiss on the cheek, but the kindly old man's affection for the latest generation to step into this old world of ours. The same real affection was exhibited whenever a poilu in his baggy blue uniform greeted the Marshal. When he landed at Battery Park, New York, he spied two uniformed French veterans in the outskirts of the crowd. Foch left the frock-coated ring about him and went to the side of his own men. He grasped their hands, and tears ran down their cheeks as their old C. O. wished them well.

The great leader is intensely religious. All have heard the stories of his refuge in prayer when days were darkest. A devout Roman Catholic, Foch always attended mass, usually choosing the simplest service. At the same time, his liberality impelled him to the utmost regard for the religious convictions of others, and his demeanor was intensely respectful no matter what the form of ceremony at which he was present.

Foch traveled light. Two locker trunks and a pair of suitcases were all he required. His uniforms were the horizon blue field attire and the dress uniform of a field marshal.

The Marshal was seventy years old on October 2d, but he looks not more than sixty. His health on the trip was excellent. In the early stages he did not even have a cold, altho he was subjected to all the rigors of our changeable November weather in all parts of the country. His personal physician, Dr. André, who was by the Marshal's side throughout the war, accompanied him.

LIBERTY'S DEFENDER GREETS OUR LIBERTY BELL.

Marshal Foch visited most American shrines and places of historic interest during his tour of the country, and is credited with standing the strain very well, in spite of his seventy years.

What chiefly interested Foch? Every distinguished visitor to our shores has this question fired at him as he comes up New York harbor. The conventional answer is 'tall buildings and the American girl.' Now, the Marshal has a mathematician's interest in great buildings and the average man's eye for a pretty girl. But his tastes are broad and varied.

The great steel works at Homstead, Pa., were immensely

interesting to him. Colonel Frank Parker, who accompanied him on the trip, said that Foch asked more questions there than at any other spot—what was the daily output, how were the men treated, what were their hours and wages, how did they live, how long did they last?

Always was the Marshal interested in people. He was a student of the characters of those about him on the trip. In a surprizingly short time he knew the faces of everyone and bowed pleasantly when he ran into them, either on the train or away from it. He commented frequently on the youthful appearance of Americans and their genius for large enterprises.

"I can understand the greatness of the American doughboy after seeing his parents and his wife," he burst forth enthusiastically one day.

WHEN THE IRISH GOVERNMENT WAS RUN "ON THE RUN"

THERE is a story, mostly untold, of what the people of Ireland did, without firing a single shot, to set aside the rule of England. There were plenty of shots fired by Irishmen, of course, in the period that preceded the Anglo-Irish agreement, and a great deal has been written about these fighters. Behind the Irish "army" however, there was a "hide-and-seek" sort of Irish government. Its attempt to run the country while the British Government was still very much "on the job," constitutes "a comedy without bloodshed, an extravaganza without violence," in the words of Samuel McCoy, who calls it "the strangest story I ever heard, and found to be true." The actual attempt of the Irish to govern Ireland goes back, says Mr. McCoy, to September, 1919. It was then that "the job of conducting a brand-new nation began, in a land where there was already a government in full swing, and possest of all the machinery of government." Writing in *Leslie's Weekly*, Mr. McCoy goes on to give a brief history of this anomalous enterprise, now recognized as the legitimate Irish Government:

Three million Irish people had made up their minds that they would have none of that other Government. They had elected a Congress of their own (they call it *Dail Eirann*) in December, 1918, and from this Congress their governmental cabinet was formed in the following spring. The delay was due to the fact that thirty or more members of the congress had been kept in English prisons until then.

The first thing the cabinet did was to appoint a "commission of inquiry into the resources and industries of Ireland."

You might ask why this was done. Surely, you say, the English Government has had plenty of time in which to examine and report on the resources and industries of Ireland. Yes, it has. It has appointed commission after commission, has issued report after report. It has cataloged everything.

But—and this was a very large "but"—

The people of Ireland weren't satisfied with these reports. They wanted their *own* experts. They maintain that they can develop their own coal-fields, peat-bogs, water-power and agriculture far more satisfactorily than they have been developed under English rule. They knew that to make a new survey of their own of all these things would require years, but, they said, we should worry about time. We are here to stay!

So the commission got to work at once. Its first job has been to make an exhaustive survey of the coal resources of Ireland. The job took two years. The report has just been published.

The total coal resources of Ireland, anthracite and bituminous, are estimated at *two billion* tons. Previous estimates placed them at half a billion tons!

The people of Ireland use very little coal for domestic purposes. They depend upon peat fuel, which grows at their doorsteps. If you want a fire, you simply step outside your own door and carve a chunk of fuel out of the ground. Therefore, at the present rate of Ireland's consumption of coal—about 5,000,000 tons yearly—the coal deposits of Ireland, if the Irish survey is accurate, will supply the nation for 400 years to come.

Until this report, the Irish had always believed what English and Welsh coal operators had told them—that they must depend upon imported coal. It may be true the Irish coal is not of as high quality as that of coal-exporting nations, but, at the worst, they figure, it will be cheaper to mine and use it in Ireland than to import coal. All that is needed is capital to mine it.

There was not much of the dramatic about this work of the commission—altho one might mention that when it went to hold its sessions in Cork in the city hall, a detail of British soldiers at once swooped down upon the building and drove them out at the rifle's point; and that when the members of the commission then withdrew to another building, they were chased out of that place also; and that since then it has collected all its statistics by dint of evading the vigilance of "the Military."

Imagine "that dignified body, the Interstate Commerce Commission of the United States, skipping about by back alleyways," suggests Mr. McCoy, "in order to conduct hearings without interruption from a body of scrapping Marines!" However—

The Irish commissioners proved that it could be done. With dry humor, their official bulletin remarks: "For some time this obstruction continued, but the commission found little difficulty in circumventing the attempts to render its efforts abortive."

The gleeful game of hide-and-seek was well on its way. I used frequently to meet young Darrell Figgis, the secretary of the commission, on the streets of Dublin. Figgis, who collated the reports of the coal experts for publication, had been arrested so many times by the British for his political opinions that they had grown tired of arresting him. And it was easy to "spot" him, too—he being adorned with a flaming red beard which he refused to sacrifice under any circumstances. Figgis is the originator of The Figgisian Theory, which is that empires must tremble before a bold front.

Elusive and triumphant as a mosquito, the Commission collected data and reported on the Irish dairy industry, the breeding of dairy cattle, the manufacture of industrial alcohol, and on the sea fisheries of Ireland, in addition to its report on the coal-fields; the British giant all the while making tremendous wallops at the pesky mosquito and striking heavily on thin air.

This was all well enough, but it didn't satisfy the 3,000,000 Irish who wanted their own government to get going, and get going quick.

So they instituted their own law courts.

If there was any one thing which rubbed the Irishman against the grain, it was that he could never enjoy a legal fight with another Irishman without taking it into a court which was not of Ireland's creating. "The British law courts, more than any other British institution, brought home to Irishmen the fact of British rule."

"We'll soon change *that!*" said Mr. Austin Stack, with a confident grin.

The mere fact that Austin Stack was behind the bars of a British prison when he made this cheerful prediction discouraged neither himself nor any of his constituents.

Austin Stack is the husky chap who captained the famous Kerry football team years ago when it licked every football team in all Ireland—and there seem to be more football teams in Ireland than in all America.

When he was arrested for his political opinions he was Minister for Home Affairs in the Irish Republican Government. The proposed establishment of Irish courts, in rivalry with the British courts in Ireland, fell within the province of his department. These courts were decreed by *Dail Eirann* in June, 1919, but not until May, 1920, after the veteran football star had made a sensational dash out of prison, were the details of the scheme worked out.

Try now to visualize the conditions under which this apparently mad project was to be carried out.

There were, on an average, 3,000 British soldiers and constables, the latter operating as troops, in each county in Ireland. They held the stone barracks in a hundred different centers; they swept along every country road in armored cars and armored motor trucks. There was not a public building in all Ireland in which a "rebel" meeting could be openly held.

Were the Irish overawed for a moment?

Well, in May, 1920, Austin Stack announced that national arbitration courts were to be set up immediately by the Irish themselves; and, at the end of the following month, a land settlement commission (to decide all disputes about land) and a system of civil courts with jurisdiction in criminal cases were simultaneously established. Every Irishman might choose between them and the British courts. By the end of August, 1920, the new system was in full operation all over Ireland.

The British Government, of course, did their best to break up these rank infringements on their legal prerogatives. But even tho they were "underground," the people patronized the Irish courts to such an extent that the British courts convened in empty halls.

Ho, for the merry Christmas-tide
The bells and the glistening tree!
The thrill of the gifts and a dashing ride
And the dinner with Campbell's for me!

A Merry Christmas to all!

And a feast as happy as the day, with the laughter of children for its music, sunny faces on every side and a table smiling with all good things! Campbell's Soup, of course, to give the dinner its first spark—spoonfuls of hot and savory deliciousness, inviting your most genial mood.

Campbell's Pea Soup

brings the glow of early springtime to your winter's day—the delicate, enticing flavor of dainty, fresh, young peas, the sweetest on the vines. Rich country milk, smooth creamery butter, spices added with the nicest care delight the palate and satisfy the appetite. A soup that gives the touch of luxury to introduce your dinner.

21 kinds **12 cents a can**

Campbell's SOUPS

LOOK FOR THE RED AND WHITE LABEL

NOTABLE BOOKS OF THE SEASON

LUCAS, E. V. LIFE AND WORK OF EDWIN AUSTIN ABBEY, R. A. With two hundred illustrations. 2 vols. New York: Charles Scribner's Sons. $35.00.

No adequate impression, in small space, can possibly be given of the richness of these two volumes—both in color of personality, and in wealth of pictorial value. As a biographer, Mr. Lucas has accomplished an agreeable if difficult task; he has traced the whole history of art in America and England during the time Abbey flourished, and he has had access to correspondence which is graphic and distinctive in style. Mr. J. S. Sargent has lent a hand in the choice of pictures which have been reproduced in *de luxe* fashion, thus making of this book an art treasure as well as a literary asset. Elsewhere, at some future time, we will more lengthily detail the record of Abbey's life; but except to emphasize again the beauty of the illustrations, including Abbey's Boston work, his Harper drawings, and his coronation canvas, it will be impossible to do more now. Lovers of beautifully made books should seek these rare volumes which will enthrall them for hours.

ROBERTSON, SIR WILLIAM. From Private to Field-Marshal. Boston: Houghton, Mifflin Co. $5.00.

Here is a fascinating narrative of personal rise and adventure, which might well be a fit companion volume to Admiral Fiske's reminiscences, "From Midshipman to Rear-Admiral." The book not only gives a graphic panorama of military conditions in the British Empire confronting an ambitious young soldier, but it records, as well, the development of the military machine, under the influence of modern invention. It carries the reader through many punitive expeditions, through the South African War, and, in valuable comment, through the Great War, when Sir William became Chief of the General Staff and Chief of the Imperial General Staff. The pen portraits of such men as Kitchener and Foch illustrate the writer's quick perception of character, and his frank comments on the short-sightedness of England's war policy, together with his fearless emphasis of the lessons to be learned from the conflict, make of the second half of this book an invaluable commentary on military history during the war. The volume is well printed, and carries a series of entertaining photographs.

STONE, MELVILLE E., FIFTY YEARS A JOURNALIST. Garden City: Doubleday, Page and Company. $5.00.

No better book could be adopted for study in our schools of journalism than this autobiography by the former General Manager of the Associated Press. There is no flourish in the writing; it is in itself an excellent piece of journalism, showing the editorial type of mind. Mr. Stone has recorded the incidents in his rise as a newspaper man; but more than that, he has traced the growth of modern journalistic ideas, as they came to him in the middle west, when he worked with Victor Ivanson. You get, in these pages, a first-hand analysis of the press, a frank analysis of the value of news, and of how best to gather it; you also are given a near view of the way in which papers are established, and the features which constitute their making or undoing. From news gathering to news service, out of which came the Associated Press—Mr. Stone holds the interest of his reader, not by his style, but by the value of his material. He was a wide traveler, and a canny interviewer of people from the Pope to the Czar; in that way he assured his foreign services. He likewise had a fascinating coterie of friends at home, like Eugene Field, Bill Nye, George Ade, and others. So that "Fifty Years a Journalist" is not merely a record of journalistic methods, but a record of friendships as well.

TUMULTY, JOSEPH P. WOODROW WILSON AS I KNOW HIM. Garden City: Doubleday, Page and Company. $5.00.

To the followers of Mr. Wilson, this intimate statement of inside happenings will come as a vindication of a misunderstood man; to the enemies of Mr. Wilson, there will be nothing in the pages but a grotesque imitation of a lesser Boswell. But on whatever side of the fence you are, you will be compelled to learn much of the character of Mr. Wilson which will dispel the many myths as to his strongheaded unwillingness to accept advice or to consult authority. Private correspondence quoted for the first time, presidential soliloquies as to national events, secrets of preparation for war, the whys and wherefores of his trip to Paris and subsequent tour for the League—all these matters are seen through Mr. Tumulty's eyes in a manner interesting to read and logical to study. Even tho Wilson's enemies may discount the secretary's statements as to reported conversations, it is scarcely conceivable—in spite of Tumulty's declaration that Mr. Wilson was not consulted in the making of the book—that his distinguished Chief was totally ignorant of the statements published so broadcast in the New York *Times* and elsewhere. And even if he was, there is small doubt that Wilson has read the articles before they were later embedded in book form. So far there has been no denial from the former President that the manner in which Tumulty "Knew Him" was not the correct way. So, this story of Woodrow Wilson may be taken as authentic stuff of inside White-House problems during a trying administration.

YOUNG, FILSON. WITH BEATTY IN THE NORTH SEA. Boston: Little, Brown & Co. $5.00.

It is always a relief to read a book, half technical in its scope, written by a man who has a feeling for words, insight into character, and enthusiasm for a life into which events have suddenly precipitated him. Through influence, Mr. Young became a close associate and observer of his chief, Admiral Beatty, on board the flagship *Lion*, during those momentous days when Scarborough was being raided, and off Dogger Bank, when the German fleet challenged the efficient use of super-dreadnaughts as fighting units in the North Sea. Those who recall the acid tone of Lord Fisher's "Memories and Records" will relish Mr. Young's description of him: "I remember the grim and yellow aspect of the old man as he sat at the blue cloth-covered table." "With Beatty in the North Sea" abounds in such lines; no writer on the naval aspects of the war has written with such pure delight in service, such zest for excitement, such unafraid, disinterested criticism of the gap between Admiralty and Navy, as Mr. Young. With the sharp eye of the born writer, he sketches the ingredients of a modern naval battle, and with an imagination colored with acute observation, he writes a chapter, "Foundations of the Future," which is valuable criticism.

WILSTACH, PAUL. POTOMAC LANDINGS Photographs by Roger B. Whitman and others Garden City: Doubleday, Page and Company. $5.00.

It is well to love a river; its features are like a face worthy to be remembered; its life in the past like memories to be stored away. It flows through history, as a thread that determinines a design works through tapestry. Mr. Wilstach, with his accustomed sensitiveness to material with which, from time to time, he has been called to work, has made a bewitching book out of "Potomac Landings." He has unearthed history, in every bend; he has landed hither and thither, where mansions have held infinite social graces, and where furniture and graceful stairways and hospitable doors measure the artistry of our ancestors. Season in and season out, he has revived for his readers the temperamental atmosphere of a river whose share in the nation's life has been ample and worthy. And the publishers have made of this narrative a handsome book, well printed, and copiously embellished with excellent photographs. Lovers of travel should relish it, and take it with them the next time they venture up and down the Potomac.

EVARTS, HAL G. THE PASSING OF THE OLD WEST. Boston: Little, Brown and Company (Illustrations by Charles Livingston Bull.) $2.50.

Usually, books preaching the gospel of conservation, are full of comparative statistics, proving our national wantonness, our extravagance, and drawing therefrom conclusions as to our future regretfulness. The beaver disappears, the buffalo no longer becomes the familiar feature of plain landscapes, the forests are denuded of their most valuable timber, and the elk takes his last stand—all in the name of Progress of Sport. Even our national parks are not protected from such depredations as mark the passing of the old West. Mr. Evarts preaches conservation in a new fashion; he writes a story full of human interest, and points his moral in no dry, matter-of-fact manner; he gives a setting full of characters, and upon them dawn the enormity of our national indifference to our national unresponsiveness to the wealth with which nature has endowed us in the past. With what result? That, in the end, "Oldmart had seen the symbol of the Mad God—Overdevelopment." Such a book as this is bound to win for conservation friends whose indifference is largely due to ignorance of the enormous problems involved.

GIBBS, SIR PHILIP. MORE THAT MUST BE TOLD. New York: Harper and Brothers. $2.50.

This new book by one of the most graphic of recent war correspondents, is a gratifying advance over its companion volume, "Now It Can Be Told." It is a pleasure to measure the growth of a constructive observer who combines the efficiency of a newspaper reporter with a certain steadying sense of the historian. It would be well if every young man who went across seas could study Mr. Gibbs' series of illuminating essays. They are full of sharply painted portraits of leaders with whom he came in contact; they team with vivid flashes of analytical comment; they palpitate with conviction that unless a new spirit is drawn from these disastrous times, just as a moral is drawn from a fable, the white people of the world will be swallowed up forever. Mr. Gibbs, in his ten chapters, presents a horde of economic and social evidence to show that the old régime, however much it tried to rehabilitate itself at the Peace Conference, is an antequated régime, and needs must go. He does not hedge, either in his comment on England or America, in his judgment on Ireland, or in his suggestions regarding Germany. The book is a gripping bit of reportorial history—profound, interesting, and in every respect human.

GILMAN, BRADLEY. ROOSEVELT: THE HAPPY WARRIOR. Boston: Little, Brown and Company. $3.50.

A most pleasingly made book, this, from the manufacturing standpoint—clear type, broad margins, interesting illustrations. We only wish the text had kept pace. The title should have been "Roosevelt: My Classmate"—for author and subject were at Harvard together. What a pity it is that, in books of this character, adulation should inundate and spoil memory of events. One can imagine what Dr. Gilman might have done in re-creating the Harvard days; instead of which he has cataloged Roosevelt's virtues, with none too illuminating remarks thereon, and quoted from other books to prove his points, as well as gathered, through correspondence, anecdotes short and trivial. Many books, written *con amore*, are measures of their author's devotion, but they are nearly always disappointing.

HUNEKER, JAMES. VARIATIONS. New York: Charles Scribner's Sons. $2.50.

To write on a variety of themes was always James Huneker's privilege and pleasure; and he always wrote with authority. This posthumous volume is prefaced by the publishers who say of the present collection of essays: "It presents . . . a wide-reaching diversity of esthetic material for the consideration, the illumination, and—preeminently—the entertainment of the cultivated." The subjects treated show the bohemian in Huneker tempered by a fine perspective which somehow always balanced this critic of the Seven Arts. He writes of George Moore, Baudelaire, Flaubert, Brandes, Cezanne, Chopin, Verdi, Liszt, Caruso—and always one can detect in him the brilliant continentalist, rather than an American. His discriminating eye was never labored: he was always sure of his judgments, hence his authority. His mind was tenacious; he was an omniverous reader, a fact which took away from the force of his originality; for often we get echoes of others in Huneker's writings. We noted this particularly in "Iconoclasts." But "Variations" is mature. A delightful collection of essays, reminiscent in parts, always laden with information and with a fresh point of view.

McISAAC, F. J. THE TONY SARG MARIONETTE BOOK. Illustrated by Tony Sarg. With two plays for home-made Marionettes, by Anne Stoddard. New York: B. W. Huebsch.

In small compass, here is a book to please young and old alike. For the technical side of amateur marionette production must be studied out carefully by wiser

NOTABLE BOOKS OF THE SEASON
Continued

heads before younger ones can hope to manipulate the strings. Mr. Sarg has not written the book; he has detailed to another the mysterious manner in which he has humanized cardboard and other flimsy materials; he has given away lavishly the tricks of his cunning trade, knowing full well that an amateur needs must develop technique to create illusion with such mannikins as he suggests building. You can build a marionette stage, under Mr. Sarg's supervision, if you have this book; you can work the strings as easily as a prestidigitator can remove a hen's egg from a gentleman's hat, if you develop dexterity, and follow carefully the intricate lines connecting joints with fingers. Then, when you are skilled, two plays are given by Mr. Sarg for your experiment and pleasure. Evenings of pure delight are here suggested.

NORMAN, HENDERSON DAINGERFIELD (Translator.) PLAYS OF EDMOND ROSTAND. 2 vols. New York: The Macmillan Co. $10.50.

All that is necessary for the translator of Rostand is to catch the glare of his romanticism: the very force of the drama's action will carry the rest of the way. It is true that "Chanticleer" is full of play on words, difficult to transmute from French to English. But one tests Mr. Norman's "Cyrano" with that of Gertrude Hall, which Mansfield used, and his "The Eaglet" with Louis N. Parker's "L'Aiglon," which Maude Adams used, and the patriotic fervor of the French Theater is in both. We are glad to see published such a satisfying edition of Rostand's plays—a beautiful example of press work, agreeably bound. The dedication is to Woodrow Wilson.

ROBINSON, CORINNE ROOSEVELT. MY BROTHER THEODORE ROOSEVELT. An intimate account of his childhood, boyhood, youth, and manhood. New York: Charles Scribner's Sons. $3.00.

Thick and fast come the books about Theodore Roosevelt. From every angle they are written to show the variety of this many-sided man. Mrs. Robinson has produced an invaluable record—naturally intimate in its approach, and exceptionally rare in the new material dealing with the "Colonel's" life. Such a human figure as that of Roosevelt must be viewed outside its political setting. No more refreshing book has come to us in years than the sheaf of Letters written to his children while in the White House. So, here, we get a host of memories which Mrs. Robinson generously shares with the public—recollections of the nursery, of college, of the Elkhorn ranch, of rough-riding, and of the White House. Biography rarely has the opportunity of telling a story so full of personal association as this. It is full of entertaining reading.

ROBINSON, EDWIN ARLINGTON. COLLECTED POEMS. New York: The Macmillan Co. $4.50.

Robinson, as a poet, has never made concessions, either in subject matter or in form; he is in tradition, yet out of it; he is fanciful yet profound; he is realistic, yet a mystic. He has fervor, yet philosophic stability. We are glad, in this collected series, to be able to judge Robinson under one roof, so to speak. All lovers of poetry will be pleased to own all his poetry, so conveniently bound.

ROBINSON, JAMES HARVEY. THE MIND IN THE MAKING: The Relation of Intelligence to Social Reform. New York: Harper and Brothers. $2.50.

Since the day of the Armistice it has generally been conceded that what the world was most in need of was a change in mind. Various philosophers have been preaching what that change should be. But now comes a seasoned historian, with philosophic insight, who tells us that were it possible for us to be freed of our intellectual bondage, which can be traced in the broad aspects of history, then that "race between education and catastrophe"—which H. G. Wells has spoken about—would have a hopeful end. Is it possible to "open our minds" so that we may reach an "unprecedented attitude" to cope with "unprecedented conditions," calling for the use of "unprecedented knowledge?" We speak of reconstruction times, as applying merely to social relationships and economic laws. But the individual mind needs reconstruction. Professor Robinson's book is an acute analysis of the mind's history, from its animal emergence; and the author graphically describes its medieval subjection, its scientific shaping, and its various forms of modern repression. With the scholar's grasp of the past, and with an idealist's love of the future, Professor Robinson shows how closely he is in touch with the imminent needs of the present. A book for the thoughtful who are wondering what will be the outcome of the world's chaos.

HAGEDORN, HERMANN. ROOSEVELT IN THE BAD LANDS. Boston: Houghton, Mifflin Co. $5.00.

This is the first of the publications of the Roosevelt Memorial Association. In the same spirit with which Albert Bigelow Paine visited Missouri, to re-create the early life of Mark Twain, has Mr. Hagedorn traveled far and wide to fix graphically, poetically, appreciatively, the life of Theodore Roosevelt in the Bad Lands, from 1883 to 1887. Western frontier life is described with the zest of the romancer. The writer has been a careful collector of first-hand material; he has drawn from Roosevelt's rough associates anecdote and comment of the struggles of bad men, red devils, and picturesque cow-punchers. "It was Mr. Roosevelt himself," writes Mr. Hagedorn, "who gave me the impulse to write this book"—a "gay and romantic experience." This is not merely a record; it is also a large canvas of a phase of American life now of the past, which shows Roosevelt—as the hero of it—against a background which only the more represents to us what a typical American he was. The Memorial Association is to be congratulated on the successful outcome of their first offering to Rooseveltiana.

FORBES, W. CAMERON. THE ROMANCE OF BUSINESS. Boston: Houghton, Mifflin Co. $1.65.

Knoblock, the dramatist, wrote a play called "My Lady's Dress," which detailed in a number of attractive acts, the human stories connected with those who were involved in the making of those elements out of which the dress was fashioned. Mr. Forbes here attempts to take from business its strictly utilitarian character, to read Romance into the market places of the world, to make us feel that at the breakfast table, under our arc-light, in all the inventions which have transformed the world of distance into nearness, the most interesting stories are involved in the very conveniences of daily life. Modern commerce is full of romance, and young readers who are about to enter the commercial field should approach it with a high conviction, not only of its usefulness, but of its adventurous, exciting character. Read Masefield's short-poem, "Cargoes," and you will see the golden dreams suggested even in the hogsheads of trade!

ROOSEVELT, KERMIT. QUENTIN ROOSEVELT: A Sketch, with Letters. New York: Charles Scribner's Sons. $2.50.

It is a pleasure to record praise for such a straightforward insight into the character of an eager boy—one whose two bents lay in the realm of mechanics and literature. The larger part of this book, compiled by Kermit, deals with "The Young Eagle's" part in the Great War—his cheer, his perseverance, his comments on men and things, his eagerness to do his share. The greater proportion of the book also consists of open and direct correspondence with Quentin's family. The boy wrote well, had literary taste and feeling; what is more, he possest sensitiveness and imagination, two qualities easily detected in the selection given from his youthful writings. Three chapters in the book constitute an anthology of praise for the boy who so gallantly gave up his life.

VINCE, CHARLES. THE STREET OF FACES: Glimpses of Town, Drawings by J. D. M. Harvey. New York: E. P. Dutton & Company.

There is no more charmingly printed book for the holidays than this, and no quainter sheaf of essays. Would that some writer would attempt for other cities what Mr. Vince has done for London—made vivid vignettes of the minor notes of city life, in a vein reminiscent of Lamb, and of Lamb's biographer, E. V. Lucas. It is a charming song Mr. Vince sings in these light essays—about motor-bus conductors, ash-bins, street-signs, peddlers, and the like. To him, with his charm of imagination, the open-air salesman, the spinning of tops, lighted windows—all have their charm, and are in turn charmingly treated. To lovers of London this should be a welcome gift; to believers in the city, it should prove what all lovers of city life claim, that the casual thing in crowded streets has its own particular poetry. The drawings are effective.

FABRE, HENRI. BOOK OF INSECTS. Retold from Alexander Teixeira de Mattos' translation of Fabre's "Souvenirs Entamologiques." By Mrs. Rodolph Stawell. Illustrated by E. J. Detmold. New York: Dodd, Mead and Co. $5.00.

A rare Christmas issue is this, blue and gold in cover design, colorful in illustrations, and generously typed and margined. Young readers will delight in knowing what Fabre has observed about the beetle, cicada, mantis, glow-worm, mason-wasp, grasshopper, cricket, locust, and other winged mysteries. This "insect's Homer," as Maeterlinck once called Fabre, has the touch of Queen Mab to his pen; he vivifies insect life until it spells romance. A good gift for the young naturalist.

DE BOOKE, LORD WILLOUGHBY. THE SPORT OF OUR ANCESTORS. Being a Collection of Prose and Verse setting forth The Sport of Fox-Hunting as They Knew It. Illustrated by G. D. Armour. New York: E. P. Dutton & Co. $10.00.

Very jealous is this compiler to use the word "sport," not as a term applied to golf, football, lawn-tennis, hockey, and the like, but as applied strictly to field sports. In 1750, foxhounds used to be bred for speed; from that time till the mid-Victorian period, real sport existed, in the eyes of the compiler, for the English country gentleman. It entered literature, and the writer who was a lover of sport sang of foxes as Homer sang of the gods. Here you are given selections from the true recorders of sports—Egerton Warburton, Major Whyte Melville, Bromley-Davenport, Beckford, "Nimrod" (Mr. Apperley),

Five Big Little Wonder Books At a Bargain Price

Better Say

Gives the correct pronunciation of frequently mispronounced words and corrects errors in using words and phrases. Packed with important and highly interesting facts, dealing specifically with such problems as the use of "lay" and "lie"; "can" and "may"; "shall" and "will"; "who" and "whom"; "went" and "gone"; "you" and "I"; "their" and "they"; "stop" and "stay"; "raise" and "rise"; "of" and "off"; "love" and "like"; "bad" and "badly," and a host of others.

Who? When? Where? What?

20,000 facts on makers of History, Art, Literature, Science and Religion. Gives you dates of birth and death (wherever authentic information is available) of Ancient, Medieval, and Modern Celebrities, together with the nationality, dignity, calling, profession or occupation, and the principal achievement of each person; dates of Battles; names from Mythology; names of Characters in Famous Writings. Provides you with the correct spelling, pronunciation, and syllabication of names and other bits of valuable information.

Mend Your Speech

1,000 hints on the correct usage of many words and idioms most commonly misused. Brimful of helpful facts.

Each Book is 3¼ inches wide and 6¼ inches long

Faulty Diction

Clearly explains puzzling word usages, and gives concisely, so you can easily apply them, the reasons for their correct use. Corrects faulty pronunciation of words, gives their accurate syllabication, and provides a generous quantity of illustrations in sentences of correct and incorrect forms. Invaluable information on the use of correct English.

Foreign Phrases In Daily Use

A reliable guide to popular and classic terms in French, Italian, Latin, Spanish, Greek, and German, with explanations of their meanings in English. Defines the puzzling foreign phrases you find in current books and periodicals, as well as the mottoes of various countries, famous people, and states. Indispensable!

These books give you the right and wrong usages of words and phrases in common use. No need to struggle through pages of grammatical rules. These five big little books give you the facts briefly, concisely, and to the point, with all the authority of FUNK & WAGNALLS NEW STANDARD DICTIONARY behind them. They are gold-mines of information!

You Save Nearly 25%

These five big little wonder books, strongly bound in cloth, and printed in clear type on durable paper, are yours for a limited time for only $1.39 instead of $1.83 postpaid, the regular price—a saving of nearly 25%.

People Say:

"Worth $10 to me—if I couldn't get another set."

"They'll help me get a raise in pay!"

"Send me four sets. I want them for the use of my office assistants."

"Just what my high-school children need!"

"The handiest little books I have found for the use of busy men who take an honest pride in making their written words command attention and response."

Send No Money In Advance

Just fill in and return the Money-Saving Order Coupon. We will send the books to you by mail, you pay the postman only $1.39 and the books are yours. No extras—no collection fees. You pay $1.39 and that is all! If they don't satisfy, return them at our expense, and we will refund your money instantly.

MONEY-SAVING ORDER COUPON

FUNK & WAGNALLS COMPANY Dig. 12-24-21.
354-360 Fourth Ave., New York, N. Y.

Send me the five little wonder books—regular price $1.83. I will pay the postman $1.39 when he delivers the books to me, which is to be payment in full. If I am dissatisfied I will send them back to you within ten days, and you are to refund all the money I have paid.

Name ....

Street Address ....

City .... State ....

Watch Your English

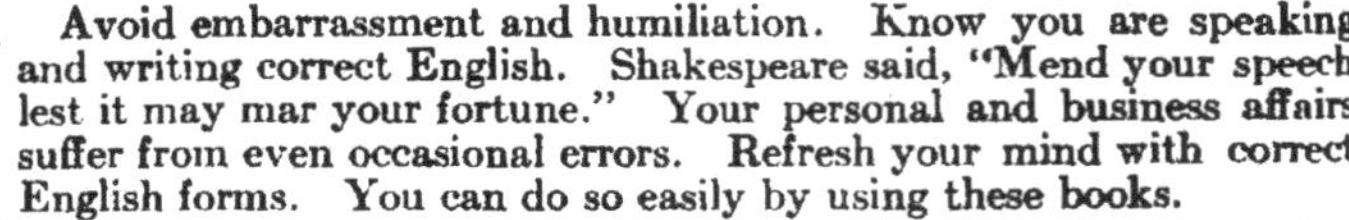

Avoid embarrassment and humiliation. Know you are speaking and writing correct English. Shakespeare said, "Mend your speech lest it may mar your fortune." Your personal and business affairs suffer from even occasional errors. Refresh your mind with correct English forms. You can do so easily by using these books.

In the home, the office, the study—for all who write or speak—they are of highest permanent value.

FUNK & WAGNALLS COMPANY, 354-360 Fourth Ave., New York

NOTABLE BOOKS OF THE SEASON
Continued

and Anthony Trollope. And what makes the book doubly attractive is the real spirit of the chase, riding to hounds, and traveling in the coach, depicted in line and color by G. D. Armour. Rarely has a sporting book such a wealth of hunting action about it. I wonder what the compiler thinks of Masefield's "Reynard the Fox"—one of the biggest narratives of the chase I know! Here is a book for the center table, for all sorts of readers.

GAY, JOHN. THE BEGGAR'S OPERA. Garden City: Doubleday, Page & Company. $4.00, $10.00.

This is a beautiful edition of a piece made famous in 1728, and made doubly famous to modern audiences by its distinctive revival in London and New York. The book is very handsomely printed and bound in yellow boards, backed by black cloth. Green and maroon stickers carry the title on the side and back. The color plates are the costume designs, in flat tones, for the different characters, done by Claud Lovat Fraser, whose memory is beautifully appreciated by John Drinkwater in a prefatory note, where is written, "alike in his theater design and his tender landscape, beauty of spirit flowed in everything he did into beauty of execution." Mr. Fraser himself prepared an explanatory word for this edition, detailing the difficulties besetting the path of a scenic artist desirous of reproducing, before a modern, sophisticated audience the atmosphere of an early eighteenth century play. As to the costuming of such a piece, let us use our imaginations over these words from a designer, to whom much of the charm of "The Beggar's Opera" revival was due. "I have kept faithfully to the outlines of the age, the close-fitting bodice, the flat hoops, the square-toed shoes, but I have taken considerable liberties in the manner in which I have shorn them of ribbons and laces and—for the sake of dramatic simplicity, be it remembered—I have eliminated yards of trimming." A good book for all lovers of the drama and the theater.

HALLOWAY, EMORY (Edited by). **THE UNCOLLECTED POETRY AND PROSE OF WALT WHITMAN.** 2 vols. Garden City: Doubleday, Page and Company. $7.50.

Whitman students will bless the devoted labors of Mr. Halloway, who has collected, from many sources—newspaper files and note-books—a variegated collection of hitherto unused material from the pen of Walt Whitman. You get here a jumble of book reviews, of matter of local interest pertaining to Brooklyn and New York, of music and the theater—all forming the subject of essays. The life of Whitman's time is all the better understood by the perusal of these isolated bits, some of them signed with the unfamiliar superscription, "Walter Whitman." What has been the purpose of the editor? "To collect all of Whitman's magazine publications not found in his 'Complete Prose' and to select from his countless newspaper stories, book reviews, editorials, criticisms of art, music, drama, etc., such as have particular biographical or literary value, with such others as may be needed fairly to indicate his thought and style of composition in each stage of his pre-poetic career." This statement in itself sufficiently describes the enormous source-character of the two volumes here offered in an attractive library edition.

COLVIN, SIDNEY. MEMORIES AND NOTES OF PERSONS AND PLACES. 1852-1912. New York: Charles Scribner's Sons. $3.50.

The dedicatory letter, which prefaces this volume, shows that the biographer of Keats has set himself the task of writing his impressions of persons and places that have filled his life. But the fund of reminiscences with which such a rich life as Colvin's must be filled is here partly put in the background by his critical bent, which is given to estimating the worth of such men as Ruskin, Burne-Jones, Rosetti, Browning, Stevenson, Meredith, and others whose paths crossed his. This tendency on his part makes it sometimes difficult to disentangle what Professor Colvin has seen for himself, from what he has gleaned of his reading from others. None the less, this volume is fascinating—not light in treatment, but solid in matter for the serious reader.

THE PHYSICALLY UNFIT

"IN THE army I was made responsible for the proper nourishment of troops," writes a reserve officer. "I was harassed by the thought that, if I could have started with those boys in their infancy, I might have made well-nourished soldiers of them. Their bad teeth, deficient feet and subnormal brains might have been prevented. I began twenty-five years too late to do them any good. Some say we will not have another war. But, I say, in order to raise another army, Uncle Sam should begin twenty-five years before war is declared," comments *The American Journal of Chemical Medicine* (Chicago):

This excerpt relates to what has been a sore point with all medical men having to do with the examinations of men for the selective draft service. An undue number of young men, in the proper age periods to serve their country in war time, was found deficient physically. The fact that similar and even worse conditions existed in European countries does not entitle us to lay the flattering unction to our souls that, after all, we are a superior nation. If the people of the United States of America proudly feel, even tho they do not always express it in so many words, that they are the most intelligent, the most progressive, the most advanced nation on earth, the physical findings in recent years were sufficient to dampen our nationalistic feeling of self-complacency in this respect. Newspaper writers and novelists delight in describing the "typical American young manhood," and select as their subjects imaginary young men as they are drawn by Gibson and others, but as they are found in actual life so infrequently as to be almost typical. And yet, with a sensible, deliberate utilization and husbanding of our national resources, with a proper application of the lessons learned in recent years, it would be easy to correct existing evils and to bring it about that the youth of the American nation actually would become the flower of the young people all over the world. This can not be done by talking. It requires years of persistent effort. It must be kept in mind, further, that the problem is not merely one of physical training and proper feeding, but it is exceedingly complex, social and economic conditions of all classes being intimately concerned in it."

CURRENT EVENTS

FOREIGN

December 7.—King George signs a proclamation summoning the British Parliament to meet December 14 in special session to ratify the Irish settlement.

Messages of congratulation have been sent by Pope Benedict to King George and Eamon De Valera for the part they played in the Anglo-Irish agreement, according to a dispatch from Rome.

The administration of President Carlos Herrera, of Guatemala, was overthrown at midnight Monday, the President surrendering his powers to a provisional government headed by General José Maria Lima, according to a dispatch from Guatemala City.

December 8.—Eamon De Valera issues a statement saying that he can not recommend the Anglo-Irish settlement to the Dail Eirann or to the country, on the grounds that the agreement is in conflict with the wishes of the majority of the nation as exprest at elections during the last three years.

December 9.—Three released Sinn Fein prisoners are injured by the explosion of a bomb thrown into a train leaving Ballykinlar camp at Thurles.

Premier Lloyd George invites Premier Briand to a consultation over a proposed revision of the German war debt.

December 10.—Germany has failed to pay 190,000,000 gold marks, due during the first two weeks of December under the schedule of payments calling for 26 per cent. of her exports and certain portions of her customs duties, it is announced. The German government informs the Reparations Commission that the decrease in the value of the mark makes it impossible for conversion into gold marks of the fund of paper marks accumulated to meet these payments.

December 11.—According to a dispatch from Berlin, the Russian State bank has announced the following rates of exchange: the pound sterling, 450,000 rubles; the dollar 110,000 rubles; the German mark, 500 rubles.

December 12.—Sir James Craig, Premier of Ulster, urges Ulster to stay out of the Irish Free State on the ground that the province was not invited to sign the Anglo-Irish treaty, and that it has pledged itself to remain a part of Great Britain.

The natives of Allahabad, British India, boycott the Prince of Wales by deserting the streets on the occasion of his visit to that city.

December 13.—The Cuban Congress passes a resolution requesting the United States to withdraw American troops stationed in Cuba.

DOMESTIC

December 7.—Nine persons are shot and a score are otherwise injured in rioting in the Chicago Union Stockyards.

Neutrality for China in the event of war is guaranteed in an agreement reached by eight powers represented in the Committee on Pacific and Far Eastern questions.

Representative Julius Kahn, of California, introduces a resolution requesting the American delegates to the Arms Conference to initiate an international conference for the suppression of the opium traffic.

December 8.—The Chinese delegates to the Arms Conference warn the Japanese delegates that if the direct negotiations over the Shantung controversy are not expedited with a view to the immediate and unconditional surrender of the province they will withdraw and place the responsibility for settlement on the full Conference.

Attorney-General Daugherty announces in his first annual report that the movement launched by the Third Internationale at Moscow to gain control of the trade and industrial unions throughout the world is meeting with marked success insofar as it relates to syndicalist unions in the United States.

December 9.—Representatives of more than fifty railroads east of the Mississippi River and north of the Ohio River announce a wage reduction of from ten to thirty per cent. or more to become effective by Christmas. More than 750,000 employees will be affected.

December 10.—The Senate Finance Committee approves the bill funding the $11,000,000,000 debt owed to the United States by foreign governments into obligations maturing not later than June 15, 1947.

The House passes a bill to increase the number of Federal judges by twenty-two.

A delegation from Porto Rico headed by President Barcelo, of the Porto Rican Senate, and Judge Felix Cordova-Davila, resident Commissioner, urges President Harding to remove Governor E. Mont Reily from the Governorship of Porto Rico.

December 11.—The General Committee on the Limitation of Armament—a citizens' body headed by Samuel Gompers and Oscar S. Straus—suggests to the Arms Conference an international economic conference to be held at the invitation of the United States.

In his annual report to the President Secretary of Agriculture Wallace says that the worst of the economic slump is over and that gradual improvement may now reasonably be expected.

The American birth rate advanced 1.4 per cent. in 1920 as compared with 1919, announces the Census Bureau. The birth rate was 23.7 per 1000 population last year and 22.3 in 1919.

December 12.—Employees of the local plants of the "Big Five" meat packers in New York walk out in connection with the Western meat-workers' strike.

Ten persons are killed and a number of others injured, and heavy property damage is done as a result of railroad accidents and landslides caused by floods in western Washington.

Japan grants the United States cable and radio rights on the Island of Yap, and agrees not to fortify the Marshall or Caroline Islands, nor to establish any military or naval bases on those islands.

On the recommendation of Secretaries Weeks, Denby, and Hoover, Chairman Winslow, of the House Commerce Committee, introduces a bill authorizing the purchase of the Cape Cod Canal for $11,500,000.

December 13.—A treaty pledging them to respect each other's insular possessions and dominions in the Pacific Ocean, to have recourse to mediation in case of disputes concerning those possessions, and to take concerted action in the event of aggression against their rights in the Pacific by any other power is signed by the delegates of the United States, Great Britain, Japan and France.

It is announced in the Navy Department that orders have been issued to reduce the personnel of the Navy by about 5,000 men because of shortage in appropriation for the pay of enlisted men.

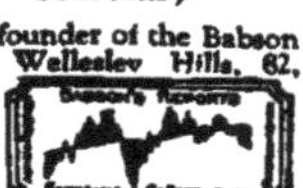

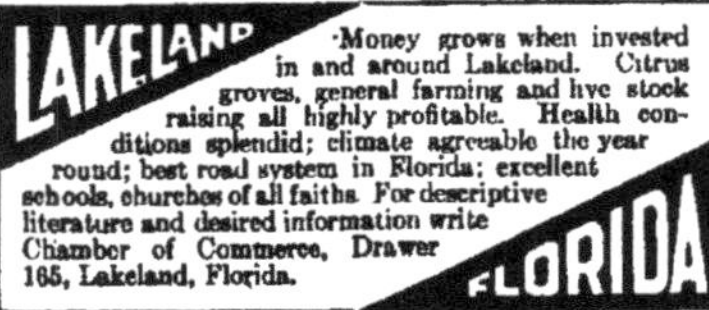

INVESTMENTS AND FINANCE

"UNBALANCED" BUDGETS AMONG THE ALLIES

In all the current discussion of Allied war debts and remedies for foreign exchange conditions we hear constant references to the necessity for better balanced national budgets in Europe. During the last two or three weeks there has been a decided upward move in foreign exchange. One New York banker quoted in the New York *Times* attributes it chiefly to a "covering" movement on the part of European speculators who have bought exchange "short." Another, however, thinks the movement too broad to be accounted for by any speculative operations, and says: "It is a discounting of the improved financial conditions in all parts of the world that we are seeking in the foreign exchange market to-day." Some light on the extent to which financial conditions abroad are improving is furnished by the Boston *News Bureau* in outlining from official figures the present state of the budgets of the chief Allied powers.

Great Britain expects to make her books balance this year, altho there are some British authorities who fear that the trade depression has cut so heavily into revenues as to wreck once rosy budget prospects. The British fiscal year, we are reminded, runs from April 1 to March 31. "The 1921-22 budget carries estimated receipts of £1,216,650,000, and expenditures of £1,039,728,000, with an apparent surplus of £176,922,000. However, owing to liabilities that could not be definitely calculated, officials estimated final surplus at not over £80,000,000." At the present rate of exchange the British pound is worth a little better than $4.00. Great Britain's improving financial position—which is reflected in the rise of sterling—can be shown by the fact that whereas her actual deficit in 1919 was £1,690,000,000 and was £326,000,000 in 1920, there was a surplus of £230,000,000 for the year that ended last April, and a substantial surplus is again expected.

But in France, according to a recent report of the French Chamber of Deputies, there will be a heavy shortage for both this year and next. The French fiscal year, by the way, corresponds with the calendar year. It is feared that the estimated receipts for the present year will fall short of official estimates by a billion francs. The franc is now worth a little over eight cents. French after-war financing is briefly outlined by the Boston *News Bureau* as follows:

Calendar year:	*Expenses millions of francs*	*Receipts millions of francs*	*Deficit covered by loans*
*1922	32,000	22,000	10,000
*1921	42,321	23,000	19,321
1920	47,932	19,287	28,645
1919	49,029	11,098	37,931
1918	54,537	6,987	47,550

*Estimated.

In the above figures subsequent to 1919 expenditures recoverable on reparations from Germany are included as follows:

"Recoverable" expenditures in—	
1922 (estimated)	7,158,000,000 francs
1921	15,913,000,000 "
1920	20,751,000,000 "

Tho France is still borrowing heavily to meet the emergencies of the post-war period, a writer on the financial page of the New York *Evening Post* calls attention to the growing confidence in French finances, shown by the recent rise of the franc in the world's money market, a rise from 7.31 cents on Dec. 1, to 8.16 cents on Dec. 14. And, he reminds us,

> This is the France which has already corrected its trade balance, which has reduced its note circulation by three billion francs during the past year, whose Government has repaid to the Bank 1.7 billion francs of the extraordinary war advances, and whose income from taxation is improving.
>
> It is a France, furthermore, which has seen the worst of the world depression and whose people are noted for their thrift and recuperative power.

For Italy, whose fiscal year ends June 30, official statistics are said by the Boston *News Bureau* to be encouraging, as summer months show a decided increase of revenue over the same months of 1920. The actual deficit for 1920-21 was nearly four billions of lire less than had been expected. The improvement, says the Boston *News Bureau*, "is due to increasing returns from taxation." It was expected last fall that the deficit for 1921-22 would be ten billion lire, but it is at present figured at only half that. The betterment is said to be "the result of better methods of financing grain supply and the fall in the prices of imported wheat." "Owing to the peculiar method of framing Italian budgets it is not possible to do other than estimate expenditures and receipts," we read. It should be remembered that the lira, with a par value of 19.3 cents, was worth 4.66 cents in New York last week. Budget figures for four years are set down as follows:

Year Ending June 30:	*Rev. in millions of lire*	*Expend. in millions of lire*	*Def. in millions of lire*
1921–22	17,000	22,000	5,000
1920–21	16,132	26,432	10,300
1919–20	14,100	28,134	14,034
1918–19	21,947	33,337	11,390

The Boston editor explains that one of the reasons why the Italian lira is worth less than five cents, or 60 per cent. of the French franc, is the size of Italy's foreign debt. As he puts it:

> France's foreign debt is relatively nominal. The French Government pays interest mainly to her own people, but Italy is under obligation to make heavy payments to people in foreign lands.

How Many Words Do YOU Know?

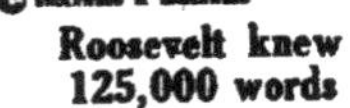

Roosevelt knew 125,000 words

Lloyd George knows 100,000 words

Shakespeare knew 24,000 words

THE EDITOR of the New Standard Dictionary states that "the average well-educated American knows from 60,000 to 70,000 words. Every well-read person of fair ability and education will be able to understand, as used, 50,000 words."

Compare the estimated vocabularies of Roosevelt and Lloyd George with Shakespeare's, which was the largest of the 16th century. Milton's, the next largest, numbered 13,000 words. It is apparent how amazingly the English language has grown.

To-day in order to keep abreast of the times—to be among *"the well-read people of fair ability"*—a man must know twice as many words as did the Bard of Avon. To forge ahead—to be a "well-educated American"—he should treble the master dramatist's vocabulary.

Learn More Words and Earn More Money

CAN you put into graphic words the ideas and plans that your mind conceives? Words so clear and convincing that others can readily understand your thought and are willing to cooperate in carrying it out? Words so vivid and eloquent that you are enabled to put through big business deals, make large and numerous sales, close important contracts? Words so forceful that you carry your hearers or readers enthusiastically with you—so interesting that you hold their attention and gain your object?

Do your business letters fully accomplish their purpose? Do your advertisements carry conviction—produce adequate results—sell your goods or bring inquiries, in sufficient quantities?

Those stories that are so vivid in your mind—can you write them so that editors will accept them? Those sermons, the thought of which uplifts your own heart—can you compose them so that they will move, inspire, comfort, and guide your congregation?

We think in words and images. The larger our vocabulary, the more varied and interesting our thoughts. Men climb to eminence in public life and in business on ladders of words. The man whose speech is limited and crude is limited and crude in his ideas—his aspirations. His life is drab and uninteresting. He makes no progress. He arrives nowhere.

FREE

"How to Become a Master of English"

This free booklet will show you how the **Kleiser Personal Mail Course in Practical English and Mental Efficiency** will enable you to add thousands of expressive words to your vocabulary—Use the right word in the right place—Write convincing and resultful letters, advertisements, stories, articles, sermons, etc.—Win promotion and higher pay—Become an interesting talker—Make yourself welcome in good society—Become influential in your community.

A Few Spare Minutes

Fifteen minutes a day—at home or in office—will result in surprizing progress.

This course is the busy man's short-cut to a full expressive vocabulary and correct grammar. It does away with the time-consuming study of abstract rules. It teaches correct speaking and writing quickly and practically.

All lines of business, all trades, all professions, arts and sciences are represented among the thousands of Mr. Kleiser's students. There are officers, directors and department heads of great industrial organizations as well as their subordinates. There are men and women, boys and girls.

Previous education or lack of it makes no difference.

Enthusiastic endorsements of this remarkable Course have been written by such masters of English as John Burroughs, Mary Roberts Rinehart, Booth Tarkington, Irvin S. Cobb, Rupert Hughes, Ellis Parker Butler.

FUNK & WAGNALLS COMPANY,
354-360 Fourth Avenue, New York, N. Y.

Gentlemen:—Send me by mail, free of charge or obligation, the booklet, "How to Become a Master of English," together with full particulars of the Grenville Kleiser Course in Practical English and Mental Efficiency. L. D., 12-24-21

Name . . . .

Local Address . . . .
Street and No. or R.F.D.

Post Office . . . . .

Date . . . . *State* . . . .

THE SPICE OF LIFE

A Case for Prayer.—We are the posterity our forefathers prayed for—can you blame them?—*Evansville Courier.*

A Line to Get 'Em.—Who'll be the first dealer to advertise: "Get an automobile or an automobile will get you?"—*Greenville (S. C.) Piedmont.*

Enchanting Distance.—Posterity will call these "the good old days" because posterity won't know all that we know.—*St. Louis Globe-Democrat.*

Powerful Remedy. — Professor Coué thinks that many illnesses can be cured by suggestion. The mere suggestion of the doctor's fee often has the desired effect.—*Punch (London).*

The Thrifty Scot.—BIX—I wonder why a Scotchman always says 'hae' for 'have'?"

DIX—"Possibly it's on account of his thrift—he saves a 'v' every time he does it."—*Boston Transcript.*

Expert Advice.—"The lungs are best expanded by deep breathing," says one of our most brilliant medical men. This is much better than using a glove-stretcher for the purpose.—*Punch (London).*

He Knows.—Elihu Mink of Long Island learned to make it from an advertised recipe and will not have any trouble making it any more. The funeral was held from the house.—*New York Evening Mail.*

Save and Have.—Suggestions are being made that Germany should be allowed three years before making further reparation payments. By that time of course they may be able to buy another war.—*Punch (London).*

Perfect Politeness.—On the arrival of a train in Nairobi Station the other day three lions entered a carriage. It speaks well for the courtesy of the passengers that to a man they gave up their seats.—*Punch (London).*

Force of Habit.—"Why was Dr. Kutter so severely reprimanded by the club librarian?"

"They caught him absent-mindedly removing the appendix from the book he was reading." — *The American Legion Weekly.*

Fickle Favor.—"Weren't you encouraged by the manner in which your audience applauded?"

"Not much," admitted Senator Sorghum. "A lot of those folks will go downtown to-night and cheer just as hard at a vaudeville show."—*Washington Star.*

There to Stay.—The pile of flints still to be broken was a very large one, thought the stone-breaker, as he gazed at it disconsolately between his bites at a large sandwich of bread and cheese. A minister came along and gave him a cheery "Good-morning," remarking afterward that he had a deal of work to get through yet.

"Aye," said the eater, "them stones are like the Ten Commandments."

"Why so?" inquired the genial parson.

"You can go on breaking 'em," came the reply, "but you can't never get rid of em."—*The Christian-Evangelist (St. Louis).*

Mild but Firm.—A telephone pole never hits an automobile except in self-defense.—*Toledo Blade.*

A Socialist Peril.—Furthermore, when all the capitalistic countries become socialistic, who will feed the famine victims?—*Dallas News.*

Safe and Sane.—It is reported that on humanitarian grounds America has decided to give up playing football and get back to the old-fashioned lynchings.—*Punch (London).*

Reincarnated Immortals. — Headline — "Dante Lectures at Amherst." And as a bookstore window card announces, "Dickens Works Here Today for $5."—*Boston Transcript.*

Swamped by Degrees.—We can conceive of no more pathetic figure than Marshal Foch trying to explain to the folks at home the meaning of those various college degrees that have been thrust upon him.—*Buffalo Express.*

The Lengthy Kind.—"I wonder if my little boy knows how many seconds there are in a minute?"

"Do you mean a real minute, mother, or one of those great big wait-a minutes?"—*Boston Transcript.*

A Family Affair.—"Did you give the penny to the monkey, dear?"

"Yes, mamma."

"And what did the monkey do with it?"

"He gave it to his father, who played the organ."—*Boston Transcript.*

The Horrors of Disarmament.—First Sailor (searching vainly for his ship after a few hours' leave)—"But she was 'ere when we went ashore, wasn't she?"

Second Sailor—"It's them blokes at Washington. They've started scrappin' the Fleet, an' begun on us."—*Punch (London).*

Improved Specifications.—Manager (to applicant for office boy vacancy)—"Aren't you the boy who applied for this position a fortnight ago?"

Boy—"Yes, sir."

Manager—"And didn't I say I wanted an older boy?"

"Yes, sir. That's why I'm here now!"—*London Evening News.*

The Seeing Eye.—How do you visualize your job? The story of the three stonecutters leaves nothing of wisdom to be said. They were working on a stone. A stranger asked the first what he was doing. "I'm working for $7.50 a day," he replied. "And you?" the stranger asked the second. "I'm cutting this stone," growled the laborer. When the question was put to the third stone-cutter, he answered, "I'm building a cathedral."—*The Christian Register (Boston).*

Precept and Example.—Early in October, while the business manager was away on sick-leave, our long-trusted bookkeeper and advertising manager, E. F. M——, author of "The Socialization of Money"—departed with four thousand dollars. We have made every effort to apprehend him, short of instituting proceedings which would result in his being put in jail, and that we do not want to do.—From a page appeal for immediate financial assistance in the current *Liberator (New York).*

High resale value

DODGE BROTHERS, DETROIT

Locked Out!
—on Christmas Eve
With roaring, window-rattling blasts—with driving snow or pounding rain—WINTER keeps battering at your home, seeking a way in.
GENASCO Latite Shingles lock your home against the WINTER weather. Rain, dampness and chilling draughts are locked out—every comfort-and-health-destroying breath of WINTER is barred.
GENASCO Latite Shingles lay tight and stay tight even when used over old worn-out wooden shingles. A patented key device holds them together in an unbreakable, vice-like grip.
These wonderful asphalt shingles defy time and the weather. The wind can't budge them, the sun can't make them curl or frost pry them apart. They are beautiful, durable and fire-resisting.
Whether your home is a mansion or a cottage, a GENASCO Latite Shingle Roof will give it added dignity, beauty and charm. And they actually cost less than ordinary asphalt or asbestos shingles.
Go to your dealer and "See that Key" that locks them on. If he does not yet handle Genasco Latite Shingles, ask any architect or builder where to get them. Write to us for a copy of "New Roofs for Old."
New York
Chicago
Pittsburgh
THE BARBER ASPHALT PAVING COMPANY
PHILADELPHIA
St. Louis
Kansas City
San Francisco
Atlanta
"See that key"
LATITE
Genasco
Asphaltic Roofing, Flooring, Paints and Allied Protective Products

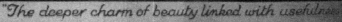

"The deeper charm of beauty linked with usefulness"

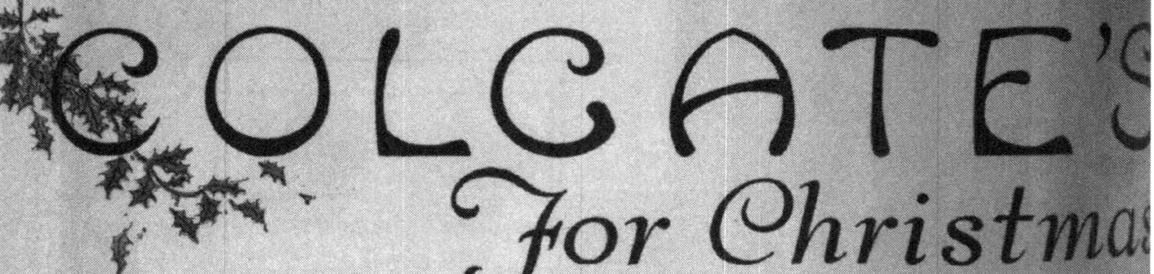

All at your favorite store:

Cashmere Bouquet Soap
Large size, three cakes in a box—70c.
Medium (10c) size, six cakes in a box—55c.
Florient Perfume, $1.00 to $10.00.
Colgate's Toilet Waters, 50c to $3.25.
Cha Ming Talc, Florient Talc, 25c.
Compact Face Powder, 35c.
Charmis Cold Cream, 25c., 40c. and 65c.
"Handy Grip" Shaving Stick, 35c.
Refill for "Handy Grip", 25c.
Colgate's Ribbon Dental Cream—large size, 25c.
Special Florient Gift Boxes, $4.80 to $12.00.

YOU can almost fill your Christmas shopping list from this group Colgate articles. Each article is favorably known and widely used your circle of relatives and friends. The fragrant Cashmere Bouquet —Florient Perfume—the soft, perfumed Talc in decorative boxes— water, face powder, Charmis Cold Cream—the familiar "Handy and old faithful Ribbon Dental Cream—all are accepted as standard

In fact the name "Colgate" on toilet articles corresponds to "Sterling" on silver.

A dozen cakes of Cashmere Bouquet Soap (four boxes), or a year supply of Ribbon Dental Cream—wouldn't you yourself rather receive *such* a gift than some more costly trifle that isn't what you would have selected for yourself?

It is always safe to select Colgate articles for Christmas gifts.

COLGATE & CO. *Est. 1806* NEW YORK

December 31, 1921

The Literary Digest

(Title Reg. U.S. Pat. Off.)

New York FUNK & WAGNALLS COMPANY London
PUBLIC OPINION New York combined with The LITERARY DIGEST
Vol. 71, No. 14. Whole No. 1654 ★ December 31, 1921 Price 10 Cents

Painted by M. D. Bakke for Cream of Wheat Co. *Copyright by Cream of Wheat Co.*

"A BUSINESS MAN'S BREAKFAST"

How Little Social Errors Ruined Their Biggest Chance

VIOLET CREIGHTON was proud of her husband. And she had reason to be. Six years ago he was at the very bottom of the ladder. Now he was almost near the top. One more decisive step—and they would be ready to step across the boundary, into the world of wealth, power and influence.

No wonder Ted was elated when he brought the good news home. "Well, Vi, it has come at last!" he beamed. "Crothers has left and I'm to have his place. I'm actually going to be one of the vice-presidents of the company."

Violet was duly surprised—and delighted. "The wife of an officer of the company," she laughed. "Sounds good, doesn't it?" and together they planned for the wonderful days to come, of the big things he would accomplish and the charming functions of which she would be hostess. Yet beneath their happy planning was a subtle, unexpressed fear which both realized—yet which both ignored.

An Invitation Is Received

The next evening, Ted brought even bigger news. They were to dine at the Brandon home—actually to be the guests of William Brandon! Violet knew how happy Ted must be, how he had dreamed of and longed for this very opportunity. Yet, when he told her of the dinner invitation, there was a sudden tug of pain at her heart.

Oh, she was happy enough, and proud that Ted had reached his goal. But were they ready for it—would they enter their new social sphere gracefully and with a cultured charm, or would they make a blundering mess of it? She was afraid. She knew that failure now would hurt more than ever. And with a woman's instinct, she knew that there was something Ted and she lacked.

"But do you think you should have accepted, Ted?" she queried. "You know how elaborately the Brandons entertain, and how—well, formal they are. Why, I don't even know whether it is correct for me to wear an evening gown!"

Ted was silent for a moment. "I couldn't possibly refuse," he said slowly. "We'll simply have to see it through. Mr. Brandon wants to have a long chat with me before the final arrangements are made. But I'll admit I'm kind of worried myself. Now, do you suppose I may wear a dinner jacket or must I wear full dress?"

For the first time, the Creightons realized that there was something more than business status if they were ever to be real successes—they realized that personality, culture and social charm played an important part. And they felt keenly their lack of social knowledge, their ignorance as to what was correct and what was incorrect.

"I hope we don't make any bad breaks," Ted whispered, as they drew up before the Brandon mansion. And way down deep inside, Violet made a secret vow that she would try to be at her best tonight, to be polished and well-poised and impressive—for Ted's sake.

Bad Mistakes Are Made

They reached the Brandon home immediately before the arrival of Mr. Roberts and his wife. There was a certain tacit understanding that if anything prevented Ted from stepping into the vacancy, Mr. Roberts would take his place. He was a severely dignified gentleman, and his wife had a certain distinction that immediately commanded respect and admiration. Violet was embarrassed when introductions were made and mumbled a mechanical, "Pleased to meet you" several times. She wished she had prepared something brilliant to say.

Violet sat between Mr. Brandon and Mr. Roberts at the table. From the very first she felt uncomfortably ill at ease. Ted, sitting opposite her, was uncomfortable and embarrassed, too. He felt out of place, confused. Mr. Brandon immediately launched into a long discourse on the influence of women in politics, and under cover of his conversation the first two courses of the dinner passed rather pleasantly.

But then, something happened. Violet noticed that Mrs. Roberts had glanced at her husband and frowned ever so slightly. She wondered what was wrong. Perhaps it was incorrect to cut lettuce with a knife. Perhaps Ted should not have used his fork that way. In her embarrassment she dropped her knife and bent down to pick it up at the same time that the butler did. Oh, it was humiliating, unbearable! They should never have come. They didn't know what to do, how to act.

He knew that the others were watching them reading in their embarrassment their lack of social knowledge.

Mr. Brandon was speaking again. Ted was apparently listening with rapt attention, but inwardly he was burning with fierce resentment. It was unfair to expect him to be a polished gentleman when he had had no training! It wasn't right to judge a man by his table manners! But—why did Violet seem so clumsy with her knife and fork? Why couldn't she be as graceful and charming as Mrs. Roberts? He was embarrassed, horribly uncomfortable. If he could only concentrate on what Mr. Brandon was saying, instead of trying to avoid mistakes!

The Creightons Suffer Keen Humiliation

Violet, sitting opposite, listened quietly to the conversation. She wished that Mrs. Roberts would not watch her, that she would not make any more mistakes, that the ordeal would soon be over. The butler stopped at her side with a dish of olives.

"I say, Creighton, are you listening to me or not?" With a start, Ted turned toward his host. He had *not* been listening. He had *not* been paying attention. How could he, when directly opposite him, before all the guests, his wife was taking olives with a fork! Violet glanced up and saw the look of horror in his eyes. She crimsoned, became embarrassed. But though Mr. Brandon seemed mildly surprised and Mrs. Roberts seemed very near the verge of smiling, the incident was smoothed over and conversation began once again.

For Ted, the evening was irretrievably spoiled. He knew that the others were watching Violet and him, reading in their embarrassment their lack of social knowledge, condemning them as ill-bred and uncultured. But when the ladies rose from the table to retire to the drawing-room, and he rose to follow, he knew by the amused glances of the others that they had hopelessly failed, that they had socially disgraced themselves.

He wasn't surprised, then, when Mr. Brandon remarked, after the other guests had left and Violet had stepped into the next room for her wraps, "I'm sorry, Creighton, but I've decided to consider Roberts for the vacancy. I need a man whose social position is assured, who can meet men of any position on their own footing. The executives in our company must be able to make a good impression wherever they go, and they must be the type of men one instinctively trusts and respects."

An Opportunity Is Lost, But a New One Is Found

At home that night, Violet refused to be comforted. "It was all my fault—I have spoiled your best chance," she cried. But Ted knew that he was as much to blame as she.

"Another chance is bound to come," he said, "and we'll be ready for it. I'm going to buy a reliable, authoritative book of etiquette at once."

It was only when the famous Book of Etiquette was in her hands, and she saw how easy it was to acquire the social knowledge, the social poise and dignity they needed, that Violet was happy again. They would never make embarrassing blunders again. They would never be humiliated again. Here was the very information they needed—clear definite, interesting information that told them just what to do, say, write and wear on all occasions, under all conditions!

Ted and Violet read parts of the Book of Etiquette together every evening. It revealed to them all the mistakes they had made at the Brandon home and told them exactly what they should have done. It was positively a revelation! By the time they had finished that splendid book they knew that they would ever after be well poised and at ease even in the company of the most brilliant celebrities!

The Importance of the Book of Etiquette to YOU

The Book of Etiquette is recognized as one of the most dependable and up-to-date authorities on the conduct of good society. It has shown thousands of men and women how to meet embarrassing moments with calm dignity, how to be always at ease, how to do, say, write and wear always what is absolutely correct. It has made it possible for people everywhere to master quickly the secrets of social charm, enabling them to mingle with the most highly cultured people and feel entirely at ease.

In the Book of Etiquette, now published in two large library volumes, you will find valuable and interesting information on every question of social import. The entire subject of etiquette is covered completely, exhaustively. Nothing is omitted, nothing forgotten. You learn everything—from the correct amount to tip the porter in a foreign country to the proper way to eat corn on the cob. Wherever old traditions are attached to present conventions, they are revealed—why the bride wears a veil, why calling cards are used, why ostrich plumes are worn at Court. Every phase of etiquette has been brought up to date, and no detail, no matter how slight, has been omitted.

Five-day FREE Examination

We would like to send you the famous Book of Etiquette free for 5 days, so that you can examine it at leisure in your own home. There is no obligation, no cost to you. Simply fill in the coupon and mail it to us at once. The complete, two-volume set of the Book of Etiquette will be promptly sent to you, and you have the privilege of examining and reading it at our expense for 5 days.

The Book of Etiquette is published in two handsome library volumes, bound in cloth and richly decorated in gold. Each volume contains interesting and valuable information that will be of permanent use to you—whenever you come into contact with men and women. Don't overlook this opportunity to examine this remarkable set without cost—mail the coupon NOW.

Within the 5-day examination period, decide whether or not you want to keep the Book of Etiquette. You have the privilege of returning the set to us within the 5 days, or keeping it and sending us only $3.50 in full payment. But remember, that this places you under no obligation—you may return the Book of Etiquette to us without hesitancy if for any reason you are not delighted with it. Clip the coupon and send it off *today!* Address Nelson Doubleday, Inc., Dept. 3012A, Oyster Bay, L. I., N. Y.

Nelson Doubleday, Inc.
Dept. 3912A, Oyster Bay, L. I., N. Y.

Without money in advance, or obligation on my part send me the two-volume set of the Book of Etiquette. Within 5 days I will either return the books or send you only $3.50 in full payment. It is understood that I am not obligated to keep the books if I am not delighted with them.

Name ....

Adress ....

☐ Check this square if you want these books with **beautiful full leather binding** at five dollars with 5 days' examination privilege.

Volume 71
No. 14

TABLE · OF · CONTENTS

December 31, 1921

TOPICS OF THE DAY:	Page
What We Will Do if France Is Attacked Again	5
What the 5-5-3 Victory Means	9
A Federal Bill to Halt Lynching	11
$20,000,000 to Send Food to Russia	13
The Kansas Industrial Snag	14
Topics in Brief	15
FOREIGN COMMENT:	
Canada's Liberal Landslide	16
The Tragic Paradox of Russia	17
Italian Parties Finding Themselves	18
Third Year of the German Republic	19
SCIENCE AND INVENTION:	
Houses Made of Straw	20
What Is the Matter with the Moon?	21
Cost of Private Transportation	21
Assassination with Germs	21
Alaska's Glacier Highway	22
Hypodermic Preservation of Wood	22
Mystery of the Sun's Heat	23

LETTERS AND ART:	Page
Chaliapin—Another Thrill	24
Heifetz Playing for Helen Keller	25
To-day's Spirit in Novel and Play	25
Are Our School Histories Now too [illegible]ish?	26
Macbeth Again in a Single Scene	27
RELIGION AND SOCIAL SERV[ICE]:	
A Dwindling Crop of Bad Boys	28
Disarming Religious "Jingoes"	29
Catholic Revival in France	29
Saving Sailors from Moral Shipw[re]ck	30
MISCELLANEOUS:	
Current Poetry	31
Personal Glimpses	32-38
Investments and Finance	42-43
Current Events	44-45
The Spice of Life	47
The Lexicographer's Easy Chair	47

TERMS: $4.00 a year, in advance; six months, $2.25; three months, $1.50; a single copy, 10 cents; postage to Canada, 85 cents a year; other foreign postage, $2.00 a year. **BACK NUMBERS**, not over three months old, 25 cents each; over three months old, $1.00 each. **QUARTERLY INDEXES** will be sent free to subscribers who apply for them. **RECEIPT** of payment is shown in about two weeks by date on address-label; date of expiration includes the month named on the label. **CAUTION:** If date is not properly extended after each payment, notify publishers promptly. Instructions for **RENEWAL, DISCONTINUANCE,** or **CHANGE OF ADDRESS** should be sent *two weeks* before the date they are to go into effect.

Both old and new addresses must always be given. **PRESENTATION COPIES:** Many persons subscribe for friends. Those who desire to renew such subscriptions must do so before expiration.

THE LITERARY DIGEST is published weekly by the Funk & Wagnalls Company, 354-360 Fourth Avenue, New York, and Salisbury Square, London, E. C.

Entered as second-class matter, March 24, 1890, at the Post-office at New York, N. Y., under the act of March 3, 1879.

Entered as second-class matter at the Post-office Department, Ottawa, Canada.

© HARRIS & EWING Pershing · Haig · Sims · Wilson · © INTERNATIONAL Mercier · Foch · Hindenburg

Old World Intrigue Laid Bare!

HOW the murder of a prince and his wife in a little Serbian town in 1914 gave a pretext for declaring war—almost overnight. And then—how "diplomacy" was like a joke in Europe. Treaties between sovereign states became "scraps of paper." Constitutional rights of countries were violated. Nation after nation was drawn into the vortex—England, France, Russia—thirty in all. The greatest—and the worst—war of modern times was fought.

Now that correspondence of the intrigues and secret diplomacy that brought on this war has been revealed, it has been carefully collated and printed for your information in the opening pages of

The Literary Digest

History of the World War

THIS GREAT WORK, in TEN big volumes, is the result of four years' labor. It tells the WHOLE STORY as never told before, of that terrible struggle, which, despite twentieth century civilization, lasted five years, killed or injured nearly thirty million human beings, destroyed six thousand ships, brought about "meatless" days and suffering throughout the United States, laid waste vast parts of Belgium, Poland, and Serbia, completely changed the face of Europe, and imposed a tax on every one of us that we are still paying to-day. You ask how such a conflict would rage so long among nations professing to be religious and most of them worshiping the same God? For answer read this remarkable History. It will give you a clearer insight into the causes underlying the war—'way back of that royal couple's murder in Serbia—than you can possibly get from any other source.

Generals as Historians

The Literary Digest History of the World War is not a mere one-man history. It is a careful compilation by Francis Whiting Halsey of official reports and thrilling personal experiences supplied by distinguished officers and enlisted men in the fight; by war correspondents, strategists, statesmen and other authorities.

You will read what was said by General Pershing, Marshal Foch, Admiral Hugh Rodman, Field Marshal Haig, Major-General von Bernhardi, Field Marshal von Hindenburg, Major-General Maurice, and other noted officers on both sides.

You will find elaborate reports, official and otherwise, of blood-stirring happenings, deeds of daring, suffering, sacrifice, cruelty, torture, massacre. One tells you of works of kindness and charity. Another tells of acts of wholesale murder and destruction.

Full Accounts of Battles

You will read thrilling reports of battles in France, Belgium, Italy, Russia, Japan, China, Egypt, the Holy Land, everywhere—on land, on and under the water, in the air. You will read—perhaps for the first time—carefully guarded information about the transportation of two million American soldiers to Europe, notwithstanding German submarine activity.

You will discover the remarkably quick turn in the tide of the war when the "Yanks" finally landed on the firing line.

You will devour the memorable campaigns of "Our Boys"—maybe of YOUR boy—thru every glorious engagement, including the memorable moment at Chateau Thierry, where the French had been fighting almost hopelessly for days, when the American officers hurried up, saluted and spoke eight words to the French: "Vous êtes fatigués. Vous allez partir. Notre job." ("You are tired. You get away. Our job.")

From that point you will follow the triumphant course of our armies thru the Marne salient, in the Argonne, at the St. Quentin Tunnel and on to the overwhelming victory under General Pershing at the St. Mihiel salient.

Was Your Boy There?

These battles, with the names of troops taking part, have gone down into history and taken their rightful places with the battles of Bunker Hill in 1775, New Orleans in 1815, Gettysburg in 1863, Manila Bay in 1898. The Literary Digest History of the World War in your home tells of these glorious deeds and will lead your children and generations to come to revere the memories of their ancestors as we now do homage to the valorous achievements of Washington, Lafayette, Andrew Jackson, Grant, Lee, Dewey, and others who gave us our heritage of freedom and made possible the United States as it is to-day.

EVERY American home should have this History—for study and reference. Especially should it be in homes from which a father or son or husband or brother went into the war. Perhaps you never have heard the whole story of what HE did! And so you should have this History. You should have a complete, authentic record of HIS achievements as shown in accounts of when and where HIS company or regiment or division went "over the top," and how HE helped to strangle German imperial autocracy. This History links HIS life and HIS heroism with the greatest military victory of civilization.

More Than a War History

The Literary Digest History of the World War does not end with the signing of the armistice in 1918. It vividly describes all the events of reconstruction days, including the surrender of Germany's ships. It tells of the abdication of Wilhelm, the German Kaiser; his flight into Holland; his life at Amerongen. It gives long-suppressed facts about the abdication, imprisonment and cold-blooded murder of Nicholas II, Czar of Russia.

You have all the facts about President Wilson's activities in the war, from his proclamation of neutrality in 1914 to and including trips to the Paris Peace Conference, and his veto of the Knox Peace resolution in 1920. The story has never been published before in such readable form.

Nothing But Praise

General Pershing said he was "very pleased to have this valuable History in his library."

Ex-Secretary of the Navy *Josephus Daniels* said: "It is remarkable how full and clear and informing this narrative is. It will be of lasting value and its pages will be drawn upon by future historians to emphasize this or that phase of the great struggle."

Major-General Leonard Wood said: "Your work will give the general public a very satisfactory and interesting story of the war and furnish information which the reading public is anxious to obtain and will enable it to follow the progress of the war from the beginning to end. It will also furnish a useful reference for the military student."

Send $2—You Get the Books

On receipt of $2 and a copy of the coupon below we will forward to your address, ALL CARRIAGE CHARGES PREPAID, the ten volumes of The Literary Digest History of the World War. The remaining $23 of the purchase price you can send in instalments of $2 a month.

Remember we DELIVER the books without expense to you. Our guarantee of satisfaction is backed by nearly HALF A CENTURY of great publishing achievements. Copy this coupon on a post-card or letter—NOW.

10 Beautiful Volumes—4000 Pages

Bound in Dark Blue Ribbed Cloth.

Titles in Gold

Printed on High Class Paper From Large Clear Type.

1000 Illustrations and Maps in Black and White and in Colors.

COUPON Dig 12-31-21

FUNK & WAGNALLS COMPANY Dept. 545
354-360 Fourth Avenue, New York, N. Y.

I enclose $2 for which send me, carriage charges PREPAID for ten days examination, THE LITERARY DIGEST HISTORY OF THE WORLD WAR. If satisfactory I am to send you monthly payments of $2 each to pay $25 in all. If the History is not satisfactory, I will return the books to you within 10 days at YOUR expense, you are to refund the $2 I have paid, and I shall owe you nothing.

Name ....

Street ....

City .... State ....

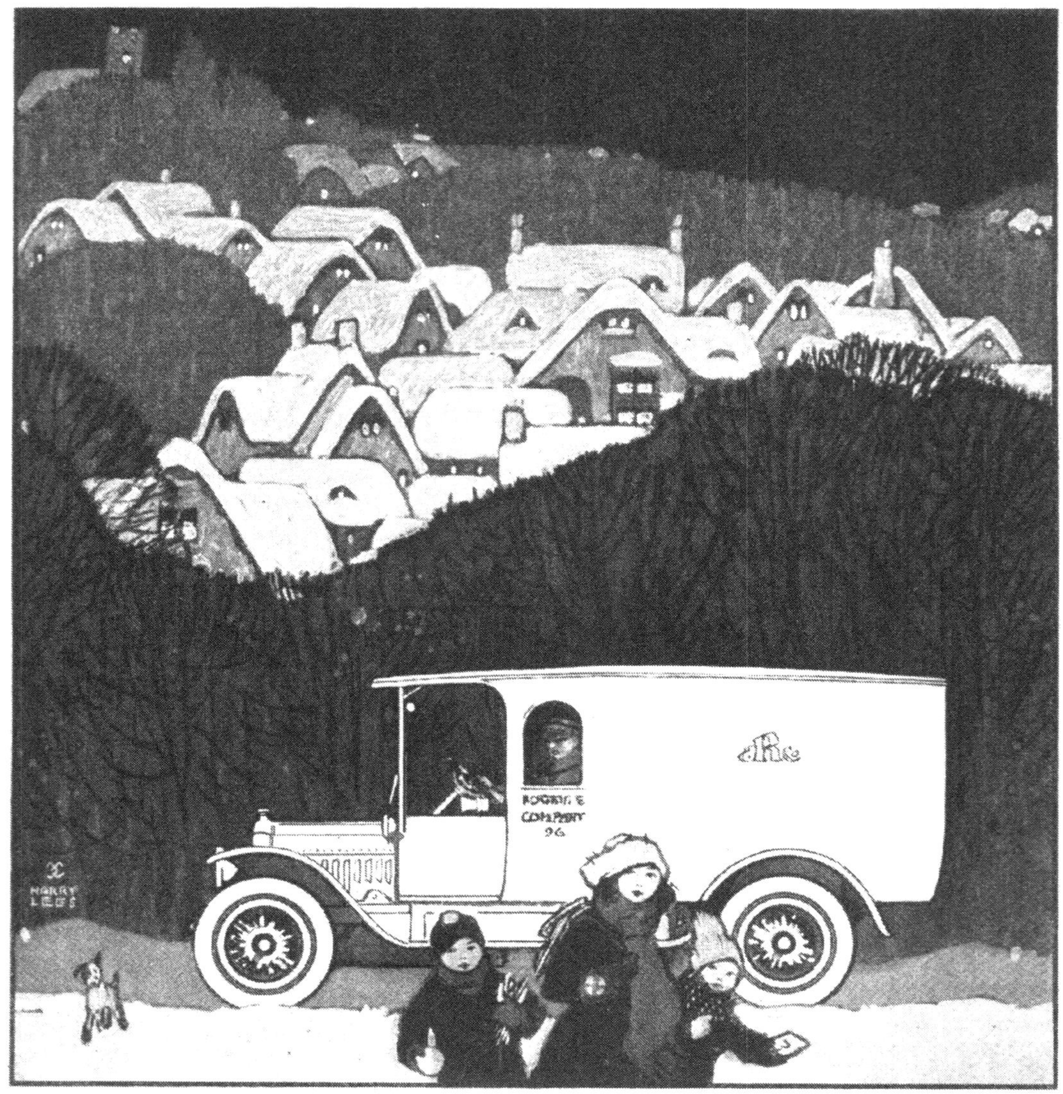

THE advantage of a White Truck to its owner is not merely in a very low cost of delivery. It is a strong competitive weapon—a rolling advertisement of superior service.

THE WHITE COMPANY, ***Cleveland***

White Trucks

THE LITERARY DIGEST

PUBLIC OPINION (New York) combined with THE LITERARY DIGEST

Published by Funk & Wagnalls Company (Adam W. Wagnalls, Pres.; Wilfred J. Funk, Vice-Pres., Robert J. Cuddihy, Treas.; William Neisel, Sec'y) 354-360 Fourth Ave., New York

Vol. LXXI, No. 14 New York, December 31, 1921 Whole Number 1654

TOPICS - OF - THE - DAY

(Title registered in U S Patent Office for use in this publication and on moving picture films)

WHAT WE WILL DO IF FRANCE IS ATTACKED AGAIN

REPORTS FROM FRANCE AND GERMANY, brought by cable, by returning travelers, and by European newspapers, tell of deep bitterness between these two ancient enemies which leads Germans of the militarist type to look forward to a day of revenge on France, and leads the French, in turn, to keep up their Army, to form alliances with Poland and the "Little Entente," and to ask what America will do if the Germans come pouring across the Rhine again a few years hence. This question was presented squarely to America by Premier Briand at the Arms Conference when he pictured the danger of German aggression and raised the question whether "France is to remain alone," or whether "the other nations were to offer to share France's peril." When Mr. Briand sat down, Mr. Balfour rose and assured him of the active sympathy of Great Britain in a cause where she has already lost a million men. Mr. Balfour was followed by Senator Schanzer and Baron Kato, and Secretary Hughes eloquently declared that "No words ever spoken by France have fallen upon deaf ears in the United States," and "what has been said will be read throughout this broad land by a people that desires to understand."

The speeches raise sharply the question of our attitude toward France in the situation portrayed by the French Premier. What is the wish of the American people? What would they say in reply to his suggestion in the words quoted above? To sound American sentiment on this critical question, which may become a burning reality some day if French fears are correct, we sent a letter to every daily newspaper in the United States, on the idea that the editors know the public feeling in the territory for which they speak, and taking the replies of the newspapers of the country, we can obtain the verdict of America pretty accurately. We asked the editors these two questions:

1. What do you believe to be the feeling or wish of the American people toward France in case of unprovoked outside aggression?
2. Do you believe our attitude should be exprest in the form of a treaty, and, if so, what should the treaty provide?

These questions went to newspapers, small and large, in every section of the United States, in the belief that from the small city and town, from the rural State, the "country editor" has as much right to speak American opinion as his brother in the huge city. The replies have come in hundreds, as the accompanying table shows, and give an index of the country's views that is most impressive. With few exceptions these editors declare that the sentiment of America to-day would be the same as has existed between the United States and France for the past hundred and fifty years. Whether America should interfere and go to the aid of France with men, money, and munitions, however, is another matter. A dozen editors, for instance, hold that France is "saber-jingling a little herself, and the fact that the aggression was unprovoked would have to stand out pretty clearly," in the words of the Duluth *Herald*. Other editors are just as certain that "the American people would do again exactly what they did in 1917," as one editor puts it. Many, however, who are in favor of extending every aid to France are nevertheless decidedly against an explicit treaty of any kind. There are, in fact, 123 out of the total who are in favor of aiding France, but who are not in favor of a treaty. "Public sentiment is a stronger force than a treaty," declares the Buffalo *Express*, "and might be weakened by a treaty tending to involve us generally in European problems."

WHAT AMERICAN NEWSPAPER EDITORS THINK	
Number of replies received to THE LITERARY DIGEST'S questionnaire	273
For military and financial aid to France in case of unprovoked outside aggression	228
For expression of our attitude toward France in the form of a treaty	66
For aid, but against a formal treaty with France	123
For membership in the League of Nations as a solution of the problem	48
Belief that France is in no danger, and that there is no need for aid	45
Belief that neither aid for, nor a treaty with, France is desirable	36

Of the two hundred and seventy-three editors, sixty-six not only "would not sit idly by if France was made the object of unprovoked attack," but would, moreover, make a treaty agreement so that all the world should know, on the theory that this would itself make France safe from attack. By saying to France, " 'we will be at your side if Germany or any other nation crosses your frontier without cause,' world-wide peace could be guaranteed," thinks the editor of the Atlanta *Constitution*. Not a few editors are of the opinion that this treaty should be a covenant, like the one in the League of Nations. "Nothing else will suffice," believes the editor of the Jackson (Miss.) *News*, and in this he is supported by some forty-eight other editors in various States.

While we find that 123 editors of representative daily newspapers would aid France, but would not enter into a treaty to do so, we find thirty-six who would not aid her in any way, nor, of course, would they enter into any sort of treaty. "Hands off *all* European problems unless they directly affect the honor of the United States," writes the editor of the Washington *Times*. "The American people love France, but sentiment is an expensive luxury," notes the editor of the Jacksonville *Metropolis*; "we proved our loyalty to France, and now it is France's turn to prove her loyalty to the world by cooperating in the business of the limitation of armament." Furthermore, asserts the editor of this paper, "there can be no universal peace as long as nations engage in treaties for offense and defense." As the Nashville *Banner* sees it:

"Secretary Hughes assured M. Briand of the strong sympathy and friendship this country feels for France, in all of which he spoke the truth, but there is small assurance that this country will ever send another army across the ocean, and, like Great Britain, it has no army to meet emergencies like that which came so suddenly in August, 1914."

WHY IS AN ARMADILLO?

PRUSSIAN VULTURE: "Excuse me, mein herr, but couldn't you persuade him to leave his shell off? It is so provocative!"

—From the London *Evening News*.

While the great majority of editors are for aid to France, yet more than half this number are against expressing our sentiments in a treaty. In fact only 66, or one-quarter of the whole, would make a definite pledge in treaty form. Some believe we should not aid France in particular, but should join the League of Nations; and others would neither aid France nor enter into a treaty with her. Since the majority would go to France's assistance, but would not enter into a treaty, let us consider their arguments first. "France need fear aggression from but one source—Germany," avers the editor of the Philadelphia *Public Ledger*. "Should it come next year or within fifty years we would get 'over there' in about a third the time it took us to get 'over there' the last time."

"The feeling of the United States always will be one of active sympathy for the French so long as they are in the right," explains the Muncie (Ind.) *Press*. "In case of unprovoked aggression, the sympathy of the people of the United States would unquestionably be with France, and would probably seek expression in moral and financial support in generous measure," believes the editor of the Milwaukee *Sentinel*. "But she would do this as an ideal of what is due every people, not as an act of special friendship," thinks the Houston *Chronicle*. "There is not, and never can be, moral isolation for any nation that actually stands as a defender of truth, justice, and actual right," declares the editor of the Oshkosh *Northwestern*. "France had American sympathy from the first as a country attacked by Germany without provocation and in defiance of efforts for peace," we are reminded by the editor of the Springfield (Mass.) *Union*, "and France would have it again in like circumstances." In this the Oakland (Cal.) *Enquirer* fully agrees:

"California public opinion would unquestionably sustain the national Government in whatever measures might be necessary to assist France in case of any unprovoked attack upon her, and especially in case of attack by Germany. The service of France to the cause of human liberty everywhere is fully appreciated on the Pacific Coast."

In the opinion of the editor of the Boston *Herald*, "it is inconceivable that the United States would remain a passive spectator of an unprovoked and wanton assault upon the French Republic by a great military power. "Americans have not forgotten 1776; they will not forget 1914." This sentiment is shared by the Portland (Ore.) *Journal*, Detroit *Free Press*, the Everett (Wash.) *Herald*, the Buffalo *Express*, the Buffalo *Commercial*, the New York *Evening Mail*, the Baltimore *American*, the Baltimore *News*, the Kansas City *Star*, and nearly two hundred other editors. A typical opinion is found in the Watertown *Times:*

"We were slow in going to her assistance in the last war, but there is nothing to indicate that we would be slow again, for, if an attack of this character were made upon France it would be another attack upon world democracy and humanity."

This peril is pointed out by the Tampa *Tribune:*

"France sees in Germany the same old enemy. France knows, as we at this distance believe, that Germany is doing all possible to bring back the day when it shall again strike terror into the heart of France.

"So long as Germany remains unconquered, and, as we believe, unhurt in its military, its industrial and its financial vitals, so long must France be prepared for attack; and when, if ever, that attack comes, not all the alliances of associated nations, or the gentlemen's agreements that can be made to the contrary will prevent the American people from going to the aid of France against our common enemy."

"The German is a strutting goose-stepper when he is having his own way. He is a whiner when he is licked. But at no time is he, in the collective national sense, to be trusted," thinks the Tulsa (Okla.) *Tribune*; "France, we must remember, is the nation that must be the first to face any outbreak from the people that have trained themselves in the art of treachery.

Moreover, adds the Schenectady *Union-Star:*

"If France is apprehensive of militaristic tendencies manifesting themselves across the thin border-line between France and Germany, it is only because France has had reason in disastrous experience to suspect militaristic tendencies. A country which has been overrun two or three times in a century by the same neighbor has the right to be apprehensive.

"Germany ought to rid itself of the idea that anybody anywhere is seeking its destruction. That is the last thing the world wants. The disruption of Russia has been costly enough to make the world shun more of that sort of thing."

But there is still another danger, points out the editor of the Erie *Herald*—the danger of a German-Bolshevik combination. The German menace, however, it is generally agreed, is much greater. Besides, as the Philadelphia *North American* reminds us, Germany has yet to fulfil her various pledges—

"France, bleeding from a thousand wounds inflicted by a wanton aggressor, found herself assailed at the Paris Peace Conference as greedy, vindictive and imperialistic. Her supreme requirements were reparation for the injuries she had suffered and security against future attack, but she obtained neither. Induced to relinquish strategical guaranties she had [illegible] o exact, in return for written assurances of reinfor[illegible] danger, she was to see those pledges discarded, and to [illegible] task of compelling by her own strength fulfilment of term[illegible]

Copyrighted by Underwood & Underwood.

"LAFAYETTE, WE ARE HERE!"

General Pershing at the tomb of Lafayette, July 4, 1917.

Germany was determined to evade and which France's allies were eager to abate.

"For two years she had to carry on this heavy undertaking, withstanding at once the venomous hostility of Germany and the criticism incited in countries that should have been her friends. In the face of these difficulties France held her position by sheer determination and endurance. Tho staggering under tremendous financial and economic burdens, her people supported the Government in maintaining armed forces large enough to compel Germany's reluctant obedience to the vital terms of the treaty. And it is an incontrovertible fact that France's military strength has been the one agency that has prevented the collapse of the whole settlement—the one agency, moreover, that has preserved Europe from an irruption of anarchism out of Russia. She remains 'at the frontier of freedom' alone; moral approbation is stimulating and precious, but it does not diminish her need for vigilance or the heavy burden of sustaining it. Yet the mission of her foremost statesman has justified itself by a great achievement; for he takes back to France assured knowledge that the enlightened governments and peoples of the world, if they will not stand guard with her, at least will not obstruct her efforts to vindicate her rights and preserve the liberties of mankind."

To stand by and see France's house afire, and not help to put out the flames is unthinkable, maintains the editor of the Atlanta *Constitution*, which goes on to recall:

"Twice within the last fifty years Germany has unceremoniously swept down upon France, seeking her destruction. And to-day the same Germany—more populous and more powerful in resources—still her enemy, stung by defeat and craving revenge, would not hesitate a moment under favorable conditions, to even up the score of war.

"France, Briand has repeatedly stated, would gladly scrap her armies and thereby relieve her people of the tremendous burden of maintaining her defenses: but for her to do that under conditions now existing would be akin to suicide."

Thus these editors of representative newspapers would show that France can not disarm unless she is sure the United States would come to her aid in a crisis. "We want no entangling alliances, but this is a unique situation and menace," writes the editor of the Providence *Journal*, for, he says—

"Germany can not be excluded from account as a future disturbing factor in international affairs. Her rising generation is still being taught that war is a natural and proper state of society. The old Prussian ideals are still inculcated. The Junker influence continues to be exerted, quietly but earnestly. Does any one suppose that if she saw a chance to tear Alsace-Lorraine from France she would hesitate, or that her irreconcilables have forsworn their old ambition to dominate the world?

"France stands to-day, and will continue to stand, as the first bulwark of civilization. She is the first line of defense against a repetition of Germany's mad onslaught. And she is entitled to know, positively and formally, that in the event of an unprovoked Teutonic attack in the future she can rely on our assistance to beat the invader back."

These statements are concurred in by such papers as the Indianapolis *News*, the Philadelphia *Inquirer*, the Tampa *Times*, the Council Bluffs *Nonpareil*, the New Haven *Journal-Courier*, its contemporary, the *Times-Leader*, the Springfield (Ill.) *State Journal*, the Scranton *Times*, the Altoona *Tribune*, the York (Pa.) *Dispatch*, the Pottsville *Republican*, the Columbus (Ohio) *State Journal*, the Springfield (Ohio) *Sun*, the Lowell *Courier-Citizen*, the Wheeling *Intelligencer*, and the Montgomery *Advertiser*—all of whom are in favor of aid for France in case of unprovoked aggression, and also in favor of expressing this country's attitude toward France by a treaty. From the Fairfield (Iowa) *Ledger-Journal* we get the interesting viewpoint of the doughboy who went overseas from the central West:

"Out here in the great agricultural West there hardly can be but one answer. We hear a lot of criticism of the French and the British by the doughboys who served with them, but sifted to the bottom it is just the result of the irritation and annoyance that naturally would come from mixing nationalities with the hundreds of years of differing traditions. But ever since the boys began to come back from France, we have been interested in their attitude toward France in the event of another war. We have asked many of them if they would fight again. The answer usually has had a preamble of criticism of the other peoples, the slackers and the profiteers, but hardly an instance can we remember where the returned soldier did not finally say determinedly that he would fight again for France and freedom as readily as he did before.

"And what the soldier thinks is about what the rest of us think. Liberty, democracy, and the ideals of America are just as dear and just as bright to us now, even in the throes of the financial depression and the injustices of readjustment, as they ever have been."

Among the scores of editors of representative newspapers who believe that the United States should stand by France, but who are not in favor of a formal alliance—who in other words believe that the long standing "alliance of sentiment" is sufficient—are the Memphis *Commercial-Appeal*, the San Francisco *Chronicle*, the Spokane *Spokesman-Review*, the Savannah *Press*, the Houston *Chronicle*, the Syracuse *Post-Standard*, the Lansing (Mich.) *State Journal*, the Waterbury *Republican*, the Bridgeport *Star*, the Des Moines *Capital*, the Burlington (Iowa) *Hawk-Eye*, the Duluth *Herald*, the Fort Wayne *Sentinel*, the Phœnix (Ariz.) *Republican*, the South Bend *Tribune*, the Davenport (Iowa) *Times*, the Allentown (Pa.) *Leader*, the Scranton *Republican*, the Bayonne (N. J.) *News-Review*, the Troy *Record*, the Sioux Falls (S. D.) *Press*, the Boise (Idaho) *Capital News*, the Parkersburg (W. Va.) *Sentinel*, the Staunton (Va.) *Leader*, the Burlington (Vt.) *News*, and the New York *Evening Mail*. The editor of the last-named paper tells why America's attitude should not be exprest by a treaty—

"This Government should never enter into 'offensive and defensive' alliances with other governments; they are war-breeders. History proves their futility; to try them again would be merely to repeat failures of the past and to perpetuate feuds and militarism.

"Let nations try another way. Germany is now effectively disarmed on land and sea; the Versailles Treaty insures this condition for approximately forty years. The Allies should, at the proper time, bring Germany into the world-wide disarmament program now in its initial stage at Washington; this should be done, not for Germany's sake, but to convince France that there is to be no army entrenched on the east bank of the Rhine ready and eager to grapple with her should she not have an army permanently entrenched on the west bank. An army in either country will inevitably mean (and justify) an army in both countries. A Germany on a basis of permanent disarmament is a better assurance to France against aggression than would be alliances or the maintenance of a French army, for both have failed miserably in the past; the Allies, led by America, are now in position to compel such a Germany. That is the service that America can and should undertake, not alone for France, but for humanity."

"Special and restricted alliances have proved the curse of the Christian world," agrees the Houston *Chronicle*—

"The basic idea of such an alliance is force, pressure, physical strength, intimidation, and even tho brought forward in the name of self-defense, it has never yet failed to develop an imperialistic, aggressive policy:

"Fundamentally, they are designed and intended to array force against force, to shape the evolution of events by means of artificial pressure, to handicap some peoples, while helping others, by a mobilization of physical power along arbitrary lines.

"The theory of dominating international affairs by grouped interests and power balances, is far more tyrannical in its operation, far more irritating in effect, far more disturbing in suggestion, than an independent militaristic policy on the part of single governments.

"The United States stands, and has always stood, for justice to all nations. This forbids her to recognize the logic or practicability of special alliances. The American view is that a special alliance of two, three, or four nations can be productive of nothing more quickly, or more inevitably, than the birth of a counter-alliance."

Still another argument against a treaty at this time is furnished by the San Francisco *Chronicle:*"

"This is not an opportune time to pledge the nation to engage in a future war, even in a just cause. It suggests that we have no confidence in what we are doing at the Washington Conference."

A treaty, agrees the Buffalo *Commercial*, is not necessary. "The strongest of international guaranties," it observes, "are not embodied in scraps of paper, but in mutual understanding." "Our entry into the recent war demonstrated that," agrees the Boise (Idaho) *Capital News*. Continues *The Commercial*—

"It is against public policy for the United States to enter into any treaty of alliance for offensive or defensive purposes. Therefore, it is useless to expect this country to guarantee protection to France against invasion. But there can be an understanding given at this Conference and made so emphatic as to have the sanction of a treaty, that the countries represented in this Conference will regard any attack upon France from any quarter as an act of aggression against the peace of the world. In her position with respect to Germany France is at least entitled to the moral support of the nations."

"There are always difficulties in interpreting treaties," we are reminded by the Kansas City *Star*, and the St. Louis *Star* is afraid that if we sign a treaty backing France it would give that country "too free a hand in Europe, just as the recently abrogated Anglo-Japanese treaty gave Japan too free a hand in China." Moreover, intimates the Boston *Herald*, "a treaty with France alone would have hard sledding in the United States." "If we should sign such a treaty," adds the editor of the Detroit *Free Press*, "we would become a party to all the petty squabbles in which France might indulge in the future." As we read in the Milwaukee *Sentinel:*

"The sentiment of the United States is, as it is easy to perceive, strongly against alliances in arms, such as would be the only possible result of such a treaty. The matter should be left for the nation to decide when, if ever, the necessity for such decision arises, resting on the basis as exprest by Secretary Hughes, that 'No words spoken by France have fallen on deaf ears in the United States."

"Of course, the opinion exprest in reply to the first question is predicted on the continuance of existing conditions. It is easy to conceive how in the course of years the complexion of affairs might be so altered as to bring about entirely different sentiments on the part of the American people. And in this fact lies one of the strongest objections to any treaty which would seek to bind the United States to a course of future action which might be found so repugnant to the sentiments of its people as to render it impossible of performance."

"There should be no treaty," maintains the editor of t[illegible] Hibbing (Minn.) *Tribune;* "France, if her cause is just, nee[illegible] no bond from the United States." "The good faith of nations is better than treaties," agrees the editor of the St. Cloud (Minn.) *Journal-Press*. A more effective way to protect France from aggression, thinks the Brazil (Ind.) *Times*, would be to let the world know "just what our attitude toward France is—a sort of understanding, like our Monroe Doctrine." "We should not bind ourselves," believes the editor of the Columbus (Ind.) *Ledger*. In the opinion of the Staunton (Va.) *Leader*, "America should always be in a position to act independently in every crisis." In circumstances similar to those of 1914, declares the editor of the Canton (Ohio) *News*, "America would not be neutral; she dare not." As the Des Moines *Capital* puts it:

"An agreement or pledge made openly and before the entire world would be as effective as a formal treaty and would avoid many difficulties such as ratification by the Senate. Any pledge made openly i[illegible] an assembly such as the Washington Conference would have a[illegible] [illegible]al force of a treaty."

"The [illegible] al European nations proves the inadequacy of trea[illegible] s of crisis," declares the editor of the Bayonne *New*[illegible] they serve their part during ordinary [illegible] w[illegible] opinion becomes unsympathetic they m[illegible] [illegible] is far better for the friendship of the two [illegible] [illegible]d upon mutual understanding and sympathy.

into words and subject it to constant discussion and ation," in the opinion of the Troy *Record*. "A treaty," he Elmira *Star-Gazette*, "is a promissory note, payable d, and Uncle Sam does not want to sign one." As va (N. Y.) *Times* puts it—

ices are not pleasant things. They come up to plague t times and put them in false or uncomfortable posi- Vashington's well-known advice about entangling alli- emembered and has had its influence down through the Vhile the world is closer together than it was in his day ation can now be aloof, still America should keep free gations made in advance that may be harmful or em- g to it in the future. France will have to rely upon will of America, and if her cause is just she never need that America will come to her aid, as was done in the ar."

other hand, those who maintain that we should sign a ith France set forth a number of reasons in support of tention. It is their belief that a guaranty of French would prevent any German aggression against France. s brave defense of civilization, her war-drained and d condition to-day, and her future surely justify a ledge," writes the editor of the Lorain (O.) *Times-Herald*. g but a treaty could be permanently binding," believes r of the Long Branch (N. J.) *Record*; "a change in the ration at Washington might vitiate a 'gentlemen's agree- er night," he observes. "Why not put it down in black e?" asks the editor of the Fairfield (Ia.) *Ledger-Journal*. ean to aid France, why not write it down so the world ?" "Any agreement looking to the maintenance of ust be guaranteed by treaty," asserts the Erie (Pa.) 'no mere 'gentlemen's agreement' could be equally bind- esides, we are reminded by the Council Bluffs (Ia.) *Non-* if we furnish France the guaranty which she rightfully France can disarm. With such a guaranty in force it e utterly futile for the German Junkers to attempt to heir war machine." "Nothing but a formal assurance e's safety will set at rest the French apprehensions which ing back the recovery of Europe," declares the editor of eling *Intelligencer*. "Germany should be informed that loes not stand alone," believes the Philadelphia *North n*, while its neighbor, *The Inquirer*, has this to say:

easy in a conference such as we have at Washington to t pleasing phrases and profess friendship. But France something more than that. Secretary Hughes went so was justified in going, when he declared that 'no words ken by France have fallen on deaf ears in the United The Secretary no doubt intended to imply that if vere again assailed without cause she could depend upon ntry.

why not say so outright? Why not put it into official The problem of France's great army would be solved in ing were the United States and England to enter into an nt to support France in case her liberty and that of tions were menaced. With such a moral understanding, night reduce her army in confidence."

editors vote against a treaty with France because they the editor of the Akron *Times* expresses it, that "our n with the League of Nations would cover the whole and reduce the possibility of attack to the minimum." is entitled to some guaranty, such as would be provided League if the United States were a member," declares the kee *Journal*. "Now that the League is functioning, our ould be suffici ... the guaranty she seeks," e editor of th ... the United S ... nents, and ... by Presi ... Wa ... innovat ... Ne ... nation can ... general idea of the League ... of the most

(Continued on page 39)

WHAT THE 5-5-3 VICTORY MEANS

"ON THURSDAY, December 15, 1921, the Race for Armaments came to an end." With those uncompromisingly optimistic words the Philadelphia *Public Ledger* celebrates the signing by Hughes, Balfour and Kato of the Three-Power Naval Agreement, establishing a naval ratio of 5-5-3 for the United States, Great Britain and Japan, and fixing the status of present and future fortifications in the Pacific. The retention of the *Mutsu* by Japan and the consequent re-adjustments in the British and American programs, together with the difficulties temporarily raised by France and Italy, are regarded by many of our papers as detracting little or noth-

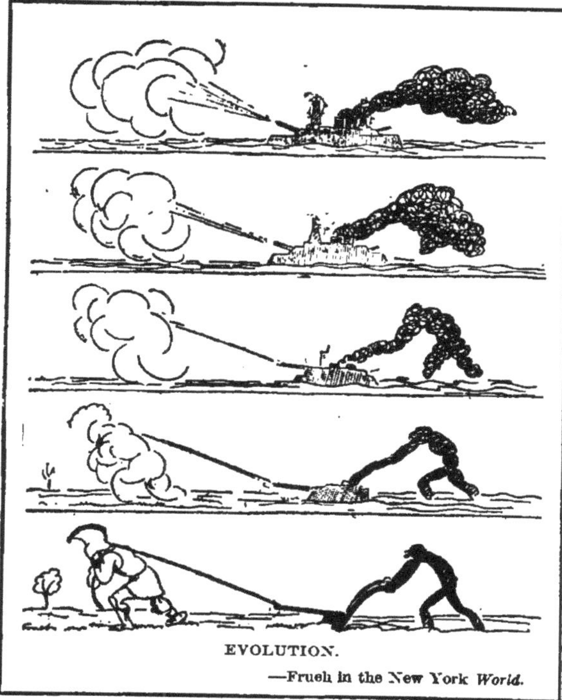

EVOLUTION.

—Frueh in the New York *World*.

ing from the significance of an event which they hail as an unprecedented triumph of American diplomacy and a great victory for peace and disarmament. In fact, the Philadelphia paper quoted above declares that "this is the world's greatest achievement for peace in all its long and crowded history." "Welcome, '5-5-3!' Tho your total is thirteen you have made it a lucky number!" exclaimes the Troy *Times*, which continues in whimsical vein: "This expression of a naval ratio is probably the most important of all numerical restrictions since that imposed in Eden, Noah's Ark, and modern marriage, and which may be colloquially exprest by the phrases 'the best two out of three' and 'two's a company, three's a crowd.'" This agreement, it adds, closes a hole in the pocket of industry.

"The miracle of naval disarmament has been wrought," says the Cleveland *Plain Dealer*, which characterizes the agreement as "the most vital achievement of the Washington Conference." And in the Philadelphia *Public Ledger* we read:

"There have been shiftings, compromises and concessions; ... have been within the iron limitations of the great ... name of America by Secretary Hughes ... set forth on that day, the 5-5-3 ratio ... world's three great naval Powers keep ... naval forces will not be increased above ... set down in the Three-Power Agreement.

"It is more far reaching than that. Japan and England and

the United States will stop pouring millions into the fortified islands and naval bases of the Pacific. Japan will not fortify Formosa against an attack from the Philippines. We will go no further with frowning Corregidor or at Cavite. England will halt where she is with her Hongkong and Kowloon areas of defense.

"The bold outlines of the Hughes plan emerge intact from the grind and hammering of the conferences. The 5-5-3 ratio is

GETTING CLOSER TO THE BASKET AT EVERY TRY.

—Ireland in the Columbus *Dispatch*.

unshaken, altho Japan saves her sentiment-financed *Mutsu* built from the yen and the sen scraped from the pockets of her poor. We keep the *North Dakota* and the *Delaware;* and England to keep the three-Power balance true, may build two super-*Hoods* of a definitely limited tonnage.

"The only place where the Hughes plan was dented and bent is in the proviso that for as many as three, and possibly for six, years England's navy yards may work upon the two new *Hoods*. Our own yards may work for some months yet upon the 90 per cent. completed *North Dakota* and *Delaware*. Then the hammers will be stilled. As for Japan, it would appear that she has built the last capital ship she may build other than for agreed replacements."

Comparing this agreement with the naval disarmament program as originally formulated by Secretary Hughes, the St. Louis *Globe-Democrat* says:

"The number of Japanese ships will be the same as was proposed in Secretary Hughes's plan, the number of American ships the same, and the number of British ships two less. The capital ships of the American and the Japanese navies will be of slightly larger tonnage and power, and those of the British Navy of a little less tonnage and a little more power. . . . The original proposal, as explained by Mr. Hughes, called for the scrapping of 66 ships with a tonnage of 1,878,343 tons. Under the agreement 68 ships with a tonnage of 1,861,643 tons will be scrapped. The original proposal allowed Great Britain to retain 22 capital ships with a total tonnage of 604,450, to be reduced later to the same tonnage as America's 18 ships with a tonnage of 500.650 tons. The agreement gives to Great Britain 20 capital ships with a tonnage of 582,050, and to the United States 18 with a tonnage of 525,850 tons. Japan by the proposal would have had 10 ships of a tonnage of 299,700. By the agreement it has 10 ships with a tonnage of 313,000. The naval holiday of ten years is agreed to, except for permission to Great Britain to build the two ships referred to, which are not to exceed 37,000 tons each. It is also agreed that no more fortifications shall be constructed in the Pacific island possessions of the three Powers, excepting the islands of Japan proper, Australia, New Zealand and Hawaii."

Turning to the difficulties that still lie in the path of naval disarmament the same paper goes on to say:

"While all this has been definitely decided upon, there yet remain some questions at issue which must be harmonized and settled before a naval armament treaty can be arranged. The capital ships, ratio and tonnage of France and Italy will have to be agreed upon, and the matter of submarine tonnage decided. Great Britain strongly desires total abolition of the submarine as an instrument of civilized warfare. It is not likely to insist upon that, for it stands alone in that position. But it is understood that it is pressing for a considerable reduction of the submarine tonnage proposed in the American plan, and perhaps for the outlawing of large sea-going submarines capable of offensive warfare upon merchant ships. Their experts contend that the experience of the late war has shown that the submarine is not an effective weapon of defense or offense as against battle-ships. The German submarines, they say, did little damage to British or other warships, except in the early days of the war. Its only success was in the destruction of the ships of commerce, in which it horrified the world. This paper has often exprest its antagonism to the submarine as an instrument of war. The submarine and poison gas are both weapons that ought to be discouraged instead of encouraged, and it should not be difficult for the governments to come to an understanding that would at least provide for their close limitation, if elimination is not yet practicable. What a strange conclusion it would be if this whole agreement were defeated by this thing, this submarine, which was the direct cause of all our losses and all our woes!"

According to the New York *Tribune's* Washington Bureau the naval agreement will mean "$100,000,000 a year saved to the United States or $3 for each taxpayer." These figures, however, are multiplied by five in an estimate published by the New York *Herald*, in which we read: "The actual cost of the upkeep of our Navy under the Hughes plan will be between $500,000,000 and $550,000,000 each year. The actual upkeep of the whole Navy, if not limited by the Hughes plan, with all the proposed ships

IN THE WAITING-ROOM.

—Ket in the Oakland *Tribune*.

completed, would be well over $1,000,000,000 a year, including necessary replacement construction."

Discussing the bearing on American interests of some of the alterations in the original Hughes plan the Springfield *Republican* says:

"The agreement provides for something ... sympathy, ... in the original Hughes proposal, to wit, the maintenance of the status quo as to fortifications on the Pacific islands in open waters and exclusive of Hawaii and the islands off the Japanese, Australian and New Zealand coasts. That means definitely that the fortifications of the United States island of Guam can not be carried to their completion and that, consequently, the United States gives up the only fortified naval base that could have made possible a naval campaign for the defense of the Philippine islands or for the military restraint of Japanese aggression on the continent of Asia or in Asiatic waters.

"It can doubtless be truly said that Japan's consent to the 5-5-3 naval ratio has been bought by our Government's agreement not to utilize Guam as an advanced naval outpost, yet the price paid is explained by certain facts which should not be lost sight of. Even with a fully fortified Guam, our Navy reduced to a purely defensive basis under the Hughes plan could not hope to command the far eastern seas. Further costly expenditure on the fortifications would be a waste of money—at least during the 10-year holiday—and could be justified only on the ground that the 10-year period would be followed by naval rivalry and possibly war. Guam should have been completely fortified before this Conference was called, if the United States Government was to escape making such a concession as has now been wrung from it.

"It is to be hoped that no more modifications of the ten-year holiday as originally planned will assume serious form. There is talk of permitting the construction of capital ships during the decade under certain restrictions so as to anticipate the end of the holiday and incidentally to help maintain the technical integrity of naval shipyards during the lean period, but such concessions need not be a grave impairment of the grand project. Another hope may be exprest—that the raising of the maximum tonnage limit of capital ships built for replacement purposes from 35,000 to 37,000 tons will not force the United States to increase the width of the Panama Canal at large cost to the American taxpayer. A battle-ship of 35,000 tons could barely crawl through the present canal without scraping its sides."

One of the curious effects of the naval agreement, notes the Newark *News*, is that it leaves the United States without a single battle-cruiser:

"The rather extensive tests made prior to our entrance to the war off this coast were then taken as showing that the American dependence on torpedo destroyers as scouts was not worth much, and the addition of scout cruisers alone made the condition but little better. It was decided that there was needed a high-speed, big-gun ship to protect these 'eyes and ears' of the fleet. The result was that our naval program as then laid down included six battle-cruisers carrying six sixteen-inch guns and being capable of thirty-five-knot speed.

"The first of these is not over a quarter completed, and will be scrapped. Great Britain now has ten of this type of which she will keep four, and Japan has four of which she will keep all. It may be that the British losses at Jutland rather discredited this type of ship, altho the one major vessel the British have built since that time is the battle-cruiser *Hood*. Perhaps in a similar way the doubt of the dreadnought herself as against air attack has helped along the general proposal that no more of these forty-million-dollar ships be built for ten years."

But "it is in the fact of the agreement itself, and not in the details of the armament limitation plan, that the world will read the victory for peace that has been achieved by the Washington Conference," remarks the Richmond *Times-Despatch*. As the New York *Tribune* discusses certain implications of the agreement:

"It is recognized that one nation may legitimately take notice of what another is doing. The domain of the common concern is thus immensely enlarged. Heretofore each nation has assumed that what it did in the way of arming itself was exclusively its own affair; that no questions could be asked; that it was justified in resenting anything that even hinted at restraint of its liberty of action.

"The doctrine is scrapped. In its place is established the one that the naval program of one country is the proper business of all. Here is a wholesome novelty in international law, and the seed planted at Washington will multiply.

"Another innovation is of almost equal importance—namely, that one nation can trust the word of another with respect to matters of the most delicate nature."

A FEDERAL BILL TO HALT LYNCHING

LYNCHING WILL BE LESS FASHIONABLE if the Federal anti-lynching bill sponsored by Representative Dyer (Rep., Mo.) becomes a law. Also, notes a Southern paper, the Columbia *Record*, "chicken-livered and rabbit-hearted officers of the law, with backbones no stiffer than empty flour-sacks," will be dealt with rather severely if they continue to surrender prisoners and jail keys as in the past, for heavy penalties to both the officer and the county he represents will result if every precaution is not taken to prevent the lynching of a prisoner, white or black. "The Dyer Bill is drastic, but a drastic remedy is needed for the loathsome lynching disease," declares the New York *Tribune*, which reminds us that "since January 1, 1921, there have been sixty known lynchings—a record of shame for a civilized nation." Moreover, another editor recalls, "the records of the past thirty years show that more than one-fifth of the 3,224 victims of lynchings in that time were white men." Southerners, therefore, should not feel that the Dyer Bill is aimed wholly at them, points out the Manchester (N. H.) *Union*, for, as the New York *Globe* remarks, "both Northerners and Southerners have offended, and both whites and blacks have been lynched."

In the opinion of Attorney-General Daugherty, the passage of legislation by Congress penalizing failure by a State to give equal protection of the laws to any person within its jurisdiction would be constitutional. Southern Congressmen, on the other hand, attack the constitutionality of the Dyer Bill. Besides encroaching upon a State's rights, they add, the bill, if it becomes a law, will increase crimes which cause lynchings. The bill provides, according to a summary of the Chicago *Daily News*, that—

"Any State or municipal officer charged with the duty of protecting the life of any person who may be put to death by a mob and who fails to make all reasonable efforts to prevent the killing, or any such officer, who, being charged with the duty of apprehending or prosecuting any person participating in a mob murder, fails to make all reasonable efforts to pursue the matter to final judgment, shall be punished by imprisonment for not exceeding five years or by a fine of $5,000 or less, or by both fine and imprisonment. Any person who participates in a mob murder is declared to be guilty of a felony and subject to imprisonment for life or for a term of not less than five years.

"It is provided further that 'any county in which a person is put to death by a mob or riotous assemblage shall forfeit $10,000, which sum may be recovered by an action therefor in the name of the United States against such county, for the use of the family, if any, of the person so put to death; if he had no family, then to his dependent parents, if any; otherwise for the use of the United States.' Payment may be enforced by the United States District Court in which the judgment is obtained. If the person put to death shall have been transported by the mob from one county to another and there put to death, each county through which he was transported is made jointly liable with the others for the $10,000 forfeit."

Some States, it is said, such as Minnesota and Illinois, already have enacted drastic laws against lynching, and have provided severe penalties for officers and communities that fail to protect the life of the accused. Should the Dyer Bill pass, however, the Federal Court, rather than a local tribunal, will institute proceedings should a sheriff or deputy be charged with neglect of duty. That it is practically impossible in most cases for State officers to deal with mobs bent upon lynching, is the contention of the San Antonio *Express:*

"Since April 11 last 38 lynchings, including two burnings at the stake and four burnings of bodies after lynching, have been perpetrated in the United States, as follows: Georgia 10, Mississippi 7, South Carolina 5, Louisiana 4, Arkansas 3, and Texas 3. Meanwhile, the 1920 record stands as the basis of indictment and comparison—and Texas heads that record. Last year its mobs out-lynched Georgia's.

"However sincere and courageous the Southern Governors'

Photograph from American Relief Administration.

WHEN THE TRAIN COMES IN WITH FOOD FROM AMERICA.

Scene at Samara station with a thousand children waiting for tickets admitting them to the American Relief Administration's train.

efforts to stamp out lynching, they come to naught. In the lynching States, spoken and written appeals to the spirit of civilization and Americanism, to lawful government and order, have encountered but eyes closed against them, mind fast shut against them, ears deaf to them.

"Congress, however, has both the right and the power to legislate for the genuine, effective operation of every mandate of the Constitution; it should pass the Dyer Anti-Lynching Bill."

"If, under the Dyer Bill, communities are made to pay for tolerating lynchings, lynchings will stop," asserts the New York *Tribune;* "if officials can be imprisoned for not doing their best to discourage mob violence, local sentiment will turn against such outbreaks." Meanwhile, adds this paper:

"No State can well complain if Congress takes a hand in ending the lynching evil. Our foreign relations have been troubled many times by the lawless hanging of other nationals. The Federal Government is bound under treaties to give equal protection to citizens and aliens. Yet it has no hold on the States through whose negligence aliens are lynched, and punishment for such crime is not exacted. It is likewise an affront to the Constitution that citizens of the United States are not protected by the States in their personal rights."

"As long as mob law maintains its hold in America the life of no individual is safe, be he rich or poor, high or low," points out the Houston *Informer.* Therefore, contends the New York *Globe:*

"No argument should be necessary in defense of this bill, which is a clear and direct application of the constitutional provision that no State shall deprive any person of life, liberty, or property without due process of law. Lynching can not ordinarily take place without the connivance of the local authorities. If they will not act, the Federal Government should. To call this assertion of the constitutional rights of every citizen a violation of State sovereignty is to deny sixty years of history."

"To reenforce State statutes by such Federal provisions as are contained in the Dyer Bill will impose no injustice upon any one, but will maintain equal rights for all," believes the Boston *Herald*, and the Detroit *News* remarks that "by this time it ought to be realized that the lynching spirit leads to more trouble than it can possibly correct."

Several Southern editors and Congressmen, however, take the opposite view. The debate in the House of Representatives, say Washington correspondents, "is fanning political and sectional flames as nothing else has done in many months." Southern Democrats who consider the Dyer Bill aimed at the South aver that Northern Republicans are trying to make political capital out of a bill which they know will accomplish nothing. Representative Sumners of Texas, in fact, declares that "there is not a lawyer on earth who can defend the bill on constitutional grounds." "It is an encroachment on States' rights, because it gives the Government the right to dictate to States how they shall exercise police powers," avers the Congressman from Texas. Representative Byrnes of South Carolina argues that even if the Dyer Bill should become a law, and should be held constitutional, "it would not prevent lynching, for similar laws in Ohio, Illinois and South Carolina have failed to do so." "The bill will increase the number of crimes and the number of lynchings," predicts Representative Aswell of Louisiana, while Representative Pou of North Carolina asks that Southern people "be left alone to work out their own problems."

"It is extremely doubtful if it would be wise to delegate to the Federal authorities the power which this bill would give them," thinks the Savannah *News*, while the Nashville *Banner* marshals the following reasons why the States should be allowed to "hoe their own rows"—

"Lynchings are essentially local. They violate State laws. The victim is usually taken from a county jail or from the custody of county officers. The offense is within the State, against the peace and dignity of the State, and should be punished by the State alone.

"Federal interference with the enforcement of the criminal laws would not be effective because it would be in the face of public sentiment, and State efforts would be correspondingly relaxed.

"Every possible exertion everywhere should be used to put down lynchings, but to give their suppression into the hands of the Federal Government would be subversive of State authority and a dangerous innovation. . . . It would also have a bad effect on the South, where it would be construed as were the reconstruction measures plainly intended to "put black heels on white necks." The Constitution was both overridden and amended by the Republican fanatics in power at the time, in the effort to create negro supremacy in political affairs, and it served to create race animosity more intense than would otherwise have existed, while the white man continued to hold the supremacy more jealously than he would otherwise have done. . . .

"Lynchings are not confined to the South. A mob in Massachusetts recently attempted to lynch three negro prisoners held for 'the usual offense' that is likely to excite mob fury wherever it occurs; but this anti-lynching bill is aimed at the South and is in line with the usual Republican endeavor to bring the South, in all matters where the negro is concerned, under strict Federal control. It has been a mischievous policy that has done much to engender race animosity and sectional ill-feeling that would not otherwise have existed.

"The best element of Southern citizenship is using all possible endeavor to suppress lynchings and to create a sentiment that will not tolerate the evil. This endeavor will in time prevail, but it would be hampered and hindered by attempted Federal interference."

$20,000,000 TO SEND FOOD TO RUSSIA

"DEADLY, DAMNABLE INDIFFERENCE to the fate of millions," is Philip Gibbs's description of the attitude of the rest of the world towards starving Russia, as the snows of winter come to cut off the escape of fugitives from the famine lands, and to add enormously to the difficulty of transporting food. A famine "too big for private charity" calls upon the governments of the world to act. The New York *Herald* agrees that except for Russia itself and what is left of Austria, there is scarcely a nation in Europe "that could not contribute something." The Washington *Post*, however, feels that it is to America alone that Russia must look for relief: "European countries have their own problems which prevent them from bestowing charity, however generous their impulses may be. The United States alone has the food in plenty, the money and the means for undertaking this work of relief." It is to supplement the work of private organizations that the Congress has acted on President Harding's recommendation and Secretary Hoover's appeal and appropriated, with a unanimous vote in the Senate, $20,000,000 to buy corn, seed grain, and certain staple food products in the United States to be sent to Russia.

Photograph from American Relief Administration.

RUSSIAN CHILDREN EATING AMERICAN FOOD

In a restaurant car of an American Relief Administration train.

No such stinging phrase as "deadly, damnable indifference" was used by Secretary Hoover, but the thought is evident in what he said to the House Foreign Affairs Committee:

"It is necessary to come to the American Government to get the money. Public charity will respond when it can, but it has been shown that this is not an auspicious time to depend upon public charity. I don't think the total collections of diligent organizations working for this cause have been $500,000 since August.

"It has been questioned whether our own economic condition warrants this expenditure. Briefly, can we afford it? Well, the American public spends a billion dollars annually on tobacco, cosmetics, and the like, and I do not think $20,000,000 too much. The supplies are already here, and we are now feeding milk to hogs and burning corn under boilers.

"There will be no economic loss to the United States in exporting these grains. It is true we transfer the burden from the farmer to the taxpayer, but there will be no net economic loss. If we get into the market now and buy we will afford some relief to the American farmer, also."

These remarks, the New York *Globe* comments, "seem to describe some other America than that emotional nation which gave generously enough to Belgian relief." *The Globe* itself says editorially of our indifference to Russia:

"The fact is that we are still open-handed, as individuals, in the matter of giving tips to people who have done nothing to earn them and in other forms of ostentatious display. We keep ourselves well supplied with chewing-gum, face powder, tobacco, fur coats, gasoline, and other luxuries that we can pay for or get credit for. But since August we haven't been willing to cut down on our gum or gasoline by even the imperceptible amount necessary to give food to starving Russian children. Mr. Hoover even thinks it necessary to prove that the proposed governmental aid won't really cost anything. Our defect may be lack of imagination, but the picture isn't flattering even with that emendation."

In this same New York paper Mr. Bruce Bliven reminds us that there are about 3,000,000 children—perhaps as many as there are in New York State—in the famine zone, that the American Relief Administration, which feeds children only, will be feeding 1,200,000 when it reaches the peak of its endeavors in January. What is to become of the others? Nothing, but "to die a lingering, cruel and peculiarly horrible death." Of the corn and seed wheat the Relief Administration looks for as a result of the Senate action, Mr. Bliven says, writing from Washington to *The Globe:*

"Twenty million bushels of corn would 'break' the famine and save nearly all the lives now threatened, except of those too far gone for aid. Three million bushels of seed wheat would permit a spring planting pretty close to normal, so Russia could feed herself after the harvest of next August. If the wheat isn't planted, the famine just goes on another year.

"Selling ten or twenty million bushels of corn would be a welcome relief to American farmers whose corn-cribs are glutted with it. They're burning it in the Middle-West as fuel—burning it while children starve in Russia and one thousand of the Shipping Board's big steel ships lie rusting at their anchors for lack of work!"

No better way could be found to start the New Year right in each of the million and a half homes to which this magazine comes than to send a gift of food to starving Russia. It is literally a gift of life. Read again the statement on page 59 of our issue of December 17 and send your check to the Russian Famine Fund, 15 Park Row, New York. Every $10 will save ten lives for a month. Every $100 will save one hundred lives for a month.

But with all the practical and emotional pleas for the Russian appropriation the newspapers note that it did not pass the House of Representatives unanimously or without objection. One Congressman alluded to the "dangerous precedent" involved; another to the necessity for charity at home; another to the necessity for economizing, and still another to the assertion "that the Russian Soviets are themselves mostly to blame for their suffering."

THE KANSAS INDUSTRIAL SNAG

GOVERNOR ALLEN'S LEGAL LIGHTNING-ROD, as the New York *World* terms the Kansas Industrial Court, while designed to avert strikes and lockouts, apparently "does not prevent Kansas getting hit quite as often as any other State." Instead of industrial peace, we see conditions which the Newark *News* considers "almost, if not entirely, without parallel in American labor history in the Kansas coal region, where mounted National Guardsmen have taken the field to quell rioting by women directed at union miners." For an unusual aspect of the situation is that "outlaw" workers are striking against the union. The women demonstrators, it is said, are relatives of the "outlaw" followers of Alexander Howat, deposed United Mine Worker president of that particular district.

Alexander M. Howat, for twenty years a figure in labor controversies in the Kansas coal-fields, and his aid are now serving sentences of six months each for violating the State Industrial Court Law by calling strikes in an industry which is "essential to the public welfare"—coal-mining, and several thousand of their followers are striking in protest against the incarceration. Meanwhile the United Mine Workers have taken over the administration of their former district president, now expelled from the organization, but the supporters of Howat have a rival organization and are making matters rather uncomfortable for Governor Allen. "They are hiding behind the skirts of their women," as the Chicago strikers did, charges the Buffalo *Commercial*, altho the Topeka *Capital* reports that the meetings at which the women planned their campaign were attended only by women. Arrests are being made among the leaders of these women, Governor Allen informs the editor of the New York *Herald*, "and also among the male agitators who are responsible for the movement." Continues the Kansas Governor:

"A peculiar feature of the case is that the miners who are working are regular members of the international union. The miners who are striking have been outlawed by their international organization. It is said to be the first instance in history where non-members of the union have led a strike against the union."

The point involved in the controversy, thinks the New York *Evening Mail*, "is of extreme importance because it involves the great question of whether the people can establish a real government of industrial relations for both employer and employee in an essential production like that of coal." We find a nearby view of the situation in the Kansas City *Times:*

"The issue in the Howat controversy is that of the honor of organized labor. It is the issue of whether or not collective bargaining shall stand the test when its representatives show bad faith.

"The question at stake is whether the national organization of coal miners has the power to compel its own men to carry out the contracts which the organization has made. In other words, it is the question of whether organized labor shall exist. For once organized labor breaks faith with the public through bad faith in the keeping of its contracts, then organized labor will lose its one great asset of public sympathy and approval.

"If President Lewis fails in his effort to establish the honor and good faith of the union in the Kansas coal-fields, and leaves the field again in the hands of Howat and his radicals, the State is as sure to take action as the sun is to rise to-morrow. It is one thing for the politicians of the labor movement to defy the laws of their own order, and quite another for them to defy the laws of the State of Kansas."

THE JAILED LABOR CHIEF

Alexander M. Howat, who has been called "the Czar of the Kansas coal fields," is serving a prison sentence for his defiance of Governor Allen's Industrial Court. So his followers have struck work.

The Supreme Court of Kansas already has declared the Industrial Court constitutional. The opposition of the trade union movement, we are told, arises primarily from the fear that the Court will act as a check upon unionism. As the Rochester *Democrat and Chronicle* reviews the work of the Kansas Court:

"Since this new Court began to function in the life of Kansas, there have been no serious strikes or walkouts in the mines, the welfare of the public has not been jeopardized, and the miners themselves have shown a disposition to leave their grievances for the court to settle. Both labor and capital have a hearing before this tribunal, but the decisions are left to competent and qualified judges. The case of the public is always considered in its awards."

"More than thirty cases already have been brought before the Court for adjudication, the majority of them by labor union leaders," avers the New York *Herald* editorially. Furthermore—

"Twenty-eight of the cases have been decided, and out of these twenty-eight decisions, all of them affecting wages, working conditions and contracts, twenty-seven have been accepted as entirely satisfactory, both to employees and employers."

Mr. Howat, however, declares from behind prison bars that the Court "is for the purpose of destroying organized labor; if it succeeds in Kansas, every State will copy it."

The Kansas miners have the sympathy of the Illinois District United Mine Workers of America, altho the president of the International organization expelled Howat, who was then president of the Kansas District. As the president of the Illinois District writes in an open letter to the miners of Illinois:

"The Kansas miners are waging a heroic fight against great odds, against the power of State and Federal governments, against organized capital and against the misused power of their own Union. Their desire and hope is to free themselves of the Industrial Court Act."

"It seems incredible that the Kansas Supreme Court would say this Industrial Court Law was sustained by public opinion," remarks the weekly news-letter of the American Federation of Labor. "This Court takes no notice of hostility of many Kansas legislators, and the growing conviction of thinking Kansas citizens that the act was inspired by 'big business,' and that the increased rates charged by numerous public utility corporations sustain their suspicions." Referring to what several editors term "civil war" in Kansas, the New York *World* says:

"Since the Court's decision could not be attacked in any other fashion, they have appealed to violence. The State has appealed in turn to the militia, and with the militia at a loss, it begins to look as if something else would have to be appealed to unless the issue is to be fought out to a finish. In the end the Kansas authorities will have to be reasonable and hit upon an agreement by conciliation, as they might have saved time and trouble by doing in the first place.

"For the principle of the Industrial Court is wrong. Industrial disputes can not be settled by governmental fiat. Courts make errors; Governments, as the workers know, are not infallible; the question of how much a man shall get for a day's work is not a legal question but a problem in human adjustment. Kansas has that lesson still to learn—and is learning."

TOPICS IN BRIEF

DOGS of war feed on bones of contention.—*Greenville Piedmont.*

LENINE and Trotzky are Russia's Gold Brick Twins.—*Asheville Times.*

THE difference between hog and pork is about thirty cents a pound.—*Marion Star.*

THE concert of nations will be improved by addition of the Irish harp.—*Greenville Piedmont.*

PUTTING Europe back on her feet will get her off our hands.—*Wilkes-Barre Times-Recorder.*

IF they can have peace in Ireland, there is no reason why the whole world can't have it.—*Toledo Blade.*

No wonder a hen gets discouraged. She can never find things where she lays them.—*New York American.*

CHINA might feel more kindly toward the open door if she doesn't have to serve as the mat.—*Toledo Blade.*

THERE are true friends of Irish freedom and then also there are friends of a free fight.—*New York Morning Telegraph.*

CHINA wants to run her own post-offices, and that ought to make her forget some of her other troubles.—*Columbia Record.*

THE silk stocking was invented in the sixteenth century, but not all of it was discovered until recently.—*New York American.*

IF there are any saloons left in New York, you can't describe them as "the poor man's club."—*New York Morning Telegraph.*

WHAT did Mr. Tumulty see "in the White House looking-glass"? Only one guess is allowed each person.—*New York Evening Mail.*

BRITAIN wants to abolish submarines, but the Hughes plan provides for converting a big proportion of the exciting fleets into under-water craft.—*Nashville Southern Lumberman.*

WELL, we guess the idea of a quadruple alliance has been pretty well received by everybody as all even Senator Reed of Missouri says against it is that it is treacherous, treasonable, damnable.—*Ohio State Journal.*

WHAT we have read of the climbing of Everest convinces us that its name should be Neverrest.—*Philadelphia Evening Public Ledger.*

THE reason nations can't decide concerning their duty to Russia is because she is too rich to neglect and too big to spank.—*Mansfield News.*

WELL, we'll scrap the ships. But we still cling to the conviction that we could have licked any other navy in the world.—*Akron Beacon-Journal.*

THE LITERARY DIGEST tells of the invention of talking pictures. But any of the old masters could paint a speaking likeness.—*Nashville Southern Lumberman.*

WE surmise that the most profitable employment of the German paper marks would be to use them in feeding goats for the market.—*Columbia Record.*

IF a four-Power agreement will keep the peace of the Pacific, why will not the fifty-one-Power agreement of the League of Nations keep the peace of the world?—*Philadelphia Record.*

I will respect the customs of your country and drink no liquor
BLUSH
Thassa good one
FOREIGN DELEGATE

KIDDING US?

—Thomas in the Detroit *News.*

IF we should win another war soon we'd be ruined.—*Columbia Record.*

THE cost of living is still about the same—all a fellow has.—*Toledo Blade.*

IT is a striking coincidence that "American" ends in "I can."—*Greenville Piedmont.*

CONGRESS would accomplish more with fewer "blocs" and more tackle.—*Columbia Record.*

AGRICULTURAL sections are slowly recovering from the bump of bumper crops.—*Steubenville Herald-Star.*

WHILE business is on the up-grade, a lot of sand is needed to keep the wheels from slipping.—*Columbia Record.*

THE Irish Free State already has two emblems of sovereignty: a flag and some outstanding bonds.—*Kansas City Star.*

ANOTHER grandson has been born to the ex-kaiser of Germany. We congratulate the little fellow on his pluck.—*Punch (London).*

IT was probably force of habit that made Mr. Harding insist on reservations to his own four-Power treaty.—*New York World.*

OUT West, in the corn belt, the farmers have found a way to beat the coal men. They grow their own fuel.—*Detroit Free Press.*

NOW let us have a series of one-Power treaties, each Power agreeing with itself to behave as it thinks the rest ought to behave.—*New York Evening Post.*

IF they must have an American as king of Albania, why not choose a baseball umpire? He ought to be able to stand anything.—*New York Evening Mail.*

THE straw that disvertebrates the camel's back 's
The last instalment of the income tax.
—*New York Evening Post.*

UNDER our new agreement slavery is prohibited in the Island of Yap. That is to say, no inhabitant of Yap will be permitted to enslave the other inhabitant.—*New York Morning Telegraph.*

IF the United States agrees to disarm, provisions should be made for the retention of enough marines to guard our mail trains.—*Nashville Southern Lumberman.*

WE shall eventually have to loan the Germans the money they were going to take from us if they won the war.—*Columbia Record.*

THERE was one good thing about old Dobbin. You didn't have to haul corn to town to swap for something to run him with.—*Buffalo Evening News.*

SOMEBODY ought to frame up a separate peace between the Friends of Irish Freedom and friends of the Irish Free State.—*New York Morning Telegraph.*

MISS LIZETTE WOODWORTH REESE says that free verse poets lack humor. She might go further and say that too many of them lack poetry.—*New York Evening Post.*

THE coal miners want more money. The operators want more money. The dealers want more money. What will the consumers who want coal have to have? Correct.—*Detroit News.*

FOREIGN - COMMENT

CANADA'S LIBERAL LANDSLIDE

SUCH A TREMENDOUS Liberal sweep as marked the Canadian elections on December 6th was entirely unlooked-for, according to the Conservative press, which concede, however, that the defeat of the Meighen Conservative government was "not altogether unexpected." The Windsor *Border Cities Star* (Ind.) calls it "one of the most notable landslides in the history of Canadian politics," which could not have happened in the judgment of the Toronto *Mail and Empire* (Cons.) if public opinion had been "in a more normal state." For instance, the Toronto daily tells us that Quebec went to the polls "in a frame of mind far from judicial, but not farther than at any other time since the beginning of the war," for its people were "determined to punish the men in office who had placed on the statute book and enforced the Military Service Act for the purpose of reinforcing our defenders at the front." As to the Canadian West, *The Mail and Empire* says it suffered from "aberration" resulting from "a class propaganda that had been successfully carried on, and public opinion there hinged largely on occupational instead of national interests."

In consequence of the verdict at the polls, the Conservative party drops to third place, below the rank of the Farmers' or Progressive party, and the Canadian press informs us that the standing in Parliament now is: Liberals, 117; Progressives, 65; Conservatives, 51; Labor, 2. The standing when Parliament was dissolved last October was: Conservatives, 120; Liberals, 84; Progressives, 14. According to some Montreal correspondents, the victory of the Liberal leader and new Premier, W. L. Mackenzie King, was won on the tariff issue, and is considered a "strong utterance by the country in favor of reciprocity with the United States."

International Photo.

CANADA'S NEW PREMIER.

Elected in a Liberal landslide that is considered chiefly a reaction against the wartime and after administration, Honorable William Lyon Mackenzie King takes office at the head of a government that "has no majority" in the House of Commons and will "no doubt have its own troubles."

Premier Meighen, we are told, had warned the voters in his campaign against the "economic absorption of Canada by the United States," while Mr. King advocated large reductions in the tariff in order to reduce the cost of living. Nevertheless the inclusion of such ardent Protectionists as Sir Lomer Gouin, the former Prime Minister of Quebec, and the Honorable Walter Mitchell, formerly Provincial Treasurer, among the victors, as well as the fact that the solid phalanx of successful candidates from Quebec, tho Liberal, are convinced Protectionists, is said to "dispose effectually of the cry raised by the Conservatives that the Liberals will tinker with the tariff until they bring about Free Trade."

Montreal dispatches further relate that business men feel that their industries are safe, and attention is called to a stock market rally following election, as a reflection of "satisfaction with the defeat of a government which had been greatly criticized by industrial interests." Conservatives themselves are said to admit that the policy of railway nationalization "had much to do with the downfall of the government," and "the big interests represented by the Canadian-Pacific Railway and the Bank of Montreal are understood to have favored the Liberals."

Among the Conservative press, the Montreal *Gazette* considers the victory "decisive," for not only has the government fallen, but the Prime Minister has "suffered defeat in his own constituency, while a number of his colleagues are also among the casualties." But one good result of the general elections is the return of party power, according to this daily, which believes that the sooner the restoration of the old two-party system, represented by the Conservative and Liberal divisions, is brought about, the better for Canada, and it points out that—

"The Liberal party, during the makeshift arrangements of recent years, retained its identity and something of its organization, and it has come back. The Conservative party, in a moment of national crisis, and for the achievement of a high purpose, gave its support to the Union Government. What the Union Government forgot was that the Conservative party was its sheet-anchor and its strength. It undertook, after the union or coalition had served its purpose, to retain the support of Liberal Unionists by the ingenuous method of adopting a new name. It abandoned the substance of Conservative loyalty for the shadow of Liberal support, and even that shadow flitted. The Borden Government's neglect of party organization and indifference to party support was made manifest very soon after 1911, and became notorious. The mistake then made culminated in the adoption of the name 'National Liberal and Conservative Party,' a cumbrous absurdity, in 1920. Little or no organization remained and, with the lack of a party spirit, there was nothing upon which to build. An attempt was made to erect a new structure without a foundation and the fabric, not unnaturally, fell to pieces."

Among the Independent press the Montreal *Daily Star* charges that the new leaders of the Conservative party "pursued a policy for the last few years that has driven from their side most of the powerful influences which range themselves under the Conservative banner," and in consequence of such "non-Conservative" procedure, it advises us that:

"This time, the railway interests distrusted and feared them. This time, British sentiment was not enlisted in their favor. This time, there was no reason why industry should dread a Liberal victory with Sir Lomer Gouin and his stalwart Protectionists at headquarters. The new National and Liberal-Conservatives had neither the flag to wave nor menaced industry to marshal nor imperilled railway systems to come to their support. The wonder is that they saved so much from the wreck. The cure is to get back to Conservative principles."

The Independent Liberal Vancouver *Sun* says that there has been "no real prosperity in Canada under Conservative rule," and assures its readers that Canada has now gained "a government of the people, by the people, and for the people; absolutely freed from the control of special and privileged classes; from unequal levies and intentional discrimination." Again the dependent-Liberal Kingston *British Whig* avers that "Toryism the Borden-Meighen type has received its death-blow," and the Saskatoon *Daily Star* (Ind.) admits that the Ministry nt down to "disastrous defeat" and the election is "curiously finite in its expression of disapproval of the course of adminis-tion in Canada for the past few years," nevertheless it remarks at it is "singularly indefinite in the expression of the wish of people as regards future policy." Thus it may be said at the whole country "exprest disapproval of high pro-tion as a fiscal policy, but only the West may be regarded as ving declared strongly for vigorous tariff reform." The ronto *Globe* (Ind.) says:

'On the tariff question we may hope for a return to common-ise from the frenzy of the campaign, with its predictions of free de, wreck and ruin. It is not necessary to rush to the other reme, and regard the present tariff as almost perfect and uiring only minor changes. There must be a compre-isive review of the whole situ-on, followed by a thorough ision. The revision should re regard to the general in-ests of the country, and all activities in town and field. put aside free trade as a sibility is not to treat lightly benefits of greater freedom, effect not only easing the rdens of the housekeeper and consumer, but stimulating ustry."

The Winnipeg *Manitoba e Press* (Ind.) remarks at for the first time in ny years Western opinion on the large questions of olic policy will be set forth Parliament "without being sored or suppress in the erests of a party which given hostages to special stern interests, and the re-tant good to the West and to Canada at large should be at." As to the Progressive rôle in Parliament, this newspaper lains its importance as follows:

'The Progressives will not have in the next Parliament the vy responsibility, wholly or in part, of conducting the affairs the Dominion; but they will have the very considerable re-nsibility of adhering to their program in Parliament and ampioning the principles it embodies. The Progressives, we e it, will not regard themselves as a political party out of ce and, therefore, bound to bring about, if possible, the wnfall of the Government of the day. Rather, they will ard themselves as holding a watching brief for the public, to that the promises of better government and wiser policies de in the campaign are fulfilled. If the Liberal government ves worthy of its name and lives up to the engagements made on behalf of his party by Mr. Mackenzie King, the Progres-es will pursue, we have no doubt, a course of sympathetic l useful cooperation with the new administration. There , it is very clear, strong reactionary elements in the Liberal ty as returned to power. The presence in the House of ty odd Progressives may be very useful to Mr. King in making possible for him to hold them in check.

'In any case, it is a bright omen in our politics that an inde-dent, non-office-seeking group, some sixty strong, will have ts in the new Parliament. The services they can render the ntry are not easily calculable. The future of the Progressive ty will take care of itself. If the Liberal party devotes itself progressive policies and shows itself in office devoted to the blic interests, there may be little need in the future for a gressive party. But if the great and powerful influences, whom all governments look alike, succeed in making a Liberal ernment the instrument of their policy, as they will most tainly attempt to do, the public will have in Parliament in Progressives effective champions of their interests."

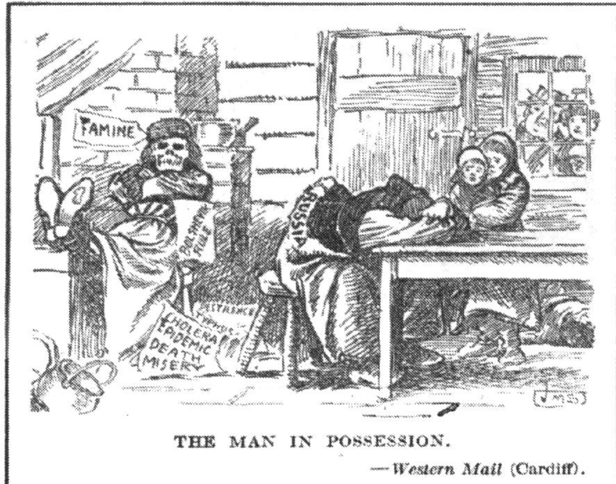

THE MAN IN POSSESSION.

—*Western Mail* (Cardiff).

THE TRAGIC PARADOX OF RUSSIA

HOW CAN IT BE POSSIBLE in this modern civilized world for ten million people to be starving on one side of it, when on the other side there is a surplus of grain rotting because there is no buyer? This question is put by no less authority than the Right Hon. J. R. Clynes, M. P., who is amazed at the paradoxical fact that the obstacle in the way of a rapid and energetic attack upon Russian famine conditions is the political view of those "who think they see in a starving Russia a defeated Bolshevism." The problem is above politics, in his judgment, and is sheerly human and international, for on the immediate solution of it depend the lives of millions of Russian men, women and children. In the Manchester *Guardian* he writes further:

"Is it our duty to look upon these people as traditional Bolshevists, craving the use of the weapons of propaganda and cruelty in order to overturn the rest of the world, or must we remember that in the great afflicted areas of Russia the peasants —poor women and little children, uneducated and helpless in the face of calamity—are just simple, suffering human beings? There can be no denying the fact that it is an international problem, for the failure of the Russian harvest has made it almost impossible for the peasants to help themselves. Under the pressure of hunger seed corn has been eaten, and the prospect for the future is even darker than is the terrible present.

"There exists an international organization for dealing with such problems—the League of Nations. Dr. Nansen, the Norwegian delegate, recently made an impassioned appeal to the assembled Governments of the world, reminding them that even five million pounds, half the cost price of a battle-ship, would assure the safety of the dwellers in the threatened areas until Christmas. Dr. Nansen had formulated an efficient scheme of distribution. Transport was available. Only money was lacking. The British Government effectively cut short the argument by instructing Mr. Fisher that it could vote no funds. The other Governments followed suit. The pitiable result was that the League gave its blessing to Dr. Nansen's scheme, said that his intentions were very laudable, and that if he could raise the money through charity the machinery was there for administrative purposes. But the Governments themselves could find no money."

Mr. Clynes goes on to say that those who have suggested that the unemployment problems of England might be alleviated by setting men to make machinery, boots, cloth, and other goods so urgently needed throughout Russia, have been met by Sir Robert Horne's question: "Where is the gain to us in sending goods to Russia?" Sir Robert Horne holds that the English would then be "giving" merchandise to Russia, and that "every one knows we are in no position to make presents to anybody." Thus, Mr. Clynes declares:

"The voice of Business raises itself above the voice of Humanity, booming out: 'Russia owes us money! Russia refuses to pay! Let Russia starve!'

"Before we could even decide whether relief was necessary a commission of inquiry had to be held, and it was decided that the form and extent of relief must depend on guaranties to repay all 'repudiated' debts. This matter of debts, now fortunately moving to a settlement, was raised by the British representatives at the Brussels Conference. Does it not savor of the broker's man? Is it consistent with traditions of British fair play and straightforwardness to carry through such discussions as have taken place between Russia and this country without mentioning

Tsarist debts, and at the moment of crisis suddenly to bring out such a highwayman's argument as a reason for delaying the provision of relief? Dr. Nansen has stated that his own representative at Moscow, who, together with one Soviet representative, would have charge of the international relief operations, will be a British subject. Does not such a promise dispose of the argument that the schemes are without guaranty?"

As to defeating Bolshevism by starving Russia, Mr. Clynes points out that a starving Russia will be "an unclean, diseased Russia," and a center of pestilence, and misery, "radiating death throughout Europe." Therefore—

"If the question is to be settled on a basis of sheer selfishness it might very well be questioned whether those who 'want their money back from Russia' are taking the most advantageous course by holding up relief. Might they not stand a better chance of getting their money back, and might we not as a nation stand a better chance of avoiding wide-spread dangers of disease and discontent, by offering help to Russia than by withholding it?

"Now that the chief obstacle to political relations with Russia is on the way to complete removal, human considerations should have the fullest freedom to rise to the level of famine requirements. The Russian Government has offered to recognize the debts of the Tsarist Government, and as long as these debts were not acknowledged diplomatic and political relations with Russia were deemed to be impossible. But now the prospect of repayment hereafter of money due to France and to Britain should enable us to apply immediately the measures of relief for which starving people can no longer wait."

THE PROTEST OF PEACE.

PEACE: "Has Italy got rid of the World War, only to be scourged with warring factions at home?"

—*Il 420* (Florence).

ITALIAN PARTIES FINDING THEMSELVES

IN THE TROUBLOUS POLITICAL WEATHER of Italy's after-war years, new parties launched their ships and old ones changed their rigging, and the consequence has been, according to some informants, that not much headway has seemed to be gained. But now these various craft are beginning to find themselves, and the best evidence of the fact is said to be presented in three important political conventions recently held. The Socialists met first, the Popolari (Catholic) party came next, and the Fascisti (anti-Socialist) last, their convention ending about the middle of November. The Socialist convention at Milan, we learn from a Rome correspondent of the Manchester *Guardian*, was primarily convoked to decide on the much debated question of Socialist cooperation with the Government. Cooperation elements were represented by the famous Socialist leaders Treves and Turati, and we are told that:

"They maintained that even the so-called Maximalists have practically accepted this principle, as they are no longer loath to climb the stairs of the various Government offices to solicit favors for their adherents, and accept financial support from the State Treasury so as to save the Socialist cooperative societies from bankruptcy. The Maximalists in Italy have nothing left now but their name, as they have practically given up their Communist notions. Neither do they think any more, as they did a year ago, of starting a revolution. They have simply returned to their much milder pre-war method and program."

The Popolari or Catholic party met at Venice, and the *Guardian's* correspondent reminds us that this organization, which sprang into being after the war, has had a remarkably rapid growth. It is represented in the Lower House by 108 members, and some of the most important of the Government Departments have been assigned to them—namely, the Department of Justice, which "according to an uninterrupted tradition, had always been assigned to men of the purest and safest liberal color." He continues:

"At the Convention of Venice this party was to solve a problem of internal equilibrium between opposite tendencies: those of the right wing, more orthodox and well under Church control, and those of the left wing, of which Miglioli is the exponent, which would drag the Catholics down to the ground of class strife and turn the party into an instrument for the spoliation of the *bourgeoisie*, in competition with the Socialists. This party is non-sectarian—*i. e.*, it is not necessary to be a Roman Catholic to be a member of it. Practically, however, its electoral influence is largely due to the clergy and the clerical organization. It must be remembered that the Pope, so as to help in checking the revolutionary tide, repealed the *non expedit* and permitted the clergy to go to the polls. The Convention has therefore deemed it expedient, for electoral purposes, to examine the condition of the clergy, which certainly is not prosperous. The general trend of the discussions has revealed the Radical spirit to be rather predominant in the party, whose policy, however, will continue along the present lines of cooperation with and participation in the Government."

Of the Fascist convention at Rome, this correspondent tells us that there was an imposing muster of nearly 40,000 Fascists, "with their flags, their military decorations, organized in a military way, many of them being armed," and he proceeds:

"Add to this their resolute bearing, which, to many, appeared to be rather provocative, and also their way of compelling people to salute their flags, and you will easily understand the Socialist reaction which culminated in a general strike which for four days deprived the whole region of its street-car service, newspapers, and other public services, and generally upset Rome, a city remarkable for its peacefulness. The Roman tumults caused more noise than damage, tho half a dozen people were killed and about a hundred wounded, a total which included those who were merely scratched.

"It was far from the Fascists' intention to become the cause of such a disturbance. Mussolini, the supreme leader of Fascism, in his address to the Convention, first of all urged the Fascists to abstain from every act of violence and provocation, and then went on to define the aims of the Fascist movement, which is now ripe for its final transformation into a real and solid political party, capable of exercising a permanent influence. In its political bearings his speech may be termed a Liberal speech, even tho it came from the mouth of a Conservative."

There is no doubt, says the *Guardian's* correspondent, that after its transformation, the Fascist movement will prove useful, for through its patriotism, courage, and youthful enthusiasm it will stir the sluggish Liberals whose parliamentary action has become "altogether too accommodating and weak." It will quicken Parliament with its own peculiar spirit, which, despite many drawbacks, proved beneficial to Italy at a time when it seemed on the verge of falling a prey to a Communist minority. At the same time, the writer points out that "the new Fascist party will certainly have to rid itself of many questionable characters who are the exponents of that spirit of adventure and of military arrogance which are a legacy of the war."

THIRD YEAR OF THE GERMAN REPUBLIC

THE "GREATEST CRIME IN HISTORY" was commemorated on November 9th, the third anniversary of the founding of the German Republic, say the German Conservative and monarchist press, and the Berlin *Deutsche Allgemeine Zeitung*, a Stinnes organ, declares there is no greater illusion than to see in November 9th "anything but a national catastrophe." The day should not be celebrated jubilantly, according to this newspaper, and it even advises the Social Democrats, who are "united on this solitary issue," to spend the day in sackcloth and ashes as one of "universal mourning." A very different tone is that of purely democratic journals, and we find the *Frankfurter Zeitung* flatly describing November 9th as "a terrible and deserved day of judgment for a political structure that was rotten within, and stood on sham foundations," and the *Vossische Zeitung* observes:

"Because they could find no way of escape from destruction, the political leaders resigned at that time, and now they jibe at the incapacity of their successors. The press of the organizations of the Right abound in scorn and abuse for November 9th and its consequences. They have no occasion to jubilate over themselves. Instead of scolding against the errors and frailties of others, in such puffed-up righteousness, they should meditate on the acts of those who are responsible for the day."

Much more satisfied and intrepid is the attitude of Social-Democratic organs, among which the *Vorwärts* points out that Germany would have sunk into chaos when the old order passed away, if the workmen had not assumed leadership and built up the German Republic, and it proceeds:

"This is a glorious fact in the history of the German Labor movement despite its later errors in internecine conflict and division. It is right to have pride in the workmen who remain faithful to the Social Democratic party in all its trials, as they most intelligently realized the needs of the hour. As the result of their political training, they saw that, in the moment of her defeat, Germany had become ripe for no other status than that of a democratic republic. They understood that this goal must be attained and held obstinately in order to make way for further progress. If the masses of workers had not been so politically mature, if they had been seduced by the chimera of Soviet Russia, how terrible a disaster would they not have incurred for themselves and the entire German people.

"In a state whose movements are dictated by the might of the victors in the World War, we Social Democrats are still in a minority. Therefore, let us not be deceived, and let us recognize that our power is limited both at home and abroad. . . . We must try untiringly to obtain more freedom of effort for our state abroad and for our party more power at home. These two aims are intimately joined. The struggle against Entente nationalism can not be fought by German nationalism, but only by German and international Socialism. The nationalism of our country and of other countries sets might up against might. With such weapons we shall be defeated. Brute force must be opposed with the might of ideas by German and by international Socialism. Only thus can we hope for victory."

WHAT GERMAN CHILDREN CRY FOR.

"Every German child born into the world owes 40,000 marks."
THE CHILD: "Good Heavens! When did this happen?"

—*Lustige Blaetter* (Berlin).

GERMANY'S NEW CÆSAR.

"Augustus Stinnes Triumphator."

—*Lustige Blaetter* (Berlin).

In sharp contrast to the satisfaction above exprest is the feeling of the Independent Socialists that, as the *Freiheit* says, in staving off Bolshevism and the Monarchy the Majority Socialists have "made an idol of the bourgeois republic, which, instead of leading to Socialization, has led to Stinnesation." Says the Communist *Rothe Fahne:*

"Altho the peasants and workers of Russia are ragged, hungry, and frozen, they face the lords of the earth strong and free. . . . The German people, under its industrial and banking potentates, its broken-down generals, without arms, without credit, without honor, rattling their tongues instead of their swords, is crawling in serfdom or sweated toil. This Germany of Stinnes, Wirth, Ludendorff, and Ebert, belongs neither to the forces of revolution nor of counter-revolution, and is rotting in an iridescent swamp."

To this playful remark is added the prophecy of "absolute certainty that the November days of 1922 will witness liberation from the illusions of November 9, 1918," that is, as the Communists believe, "they will dawn under the standards of the advancing proletarian Socialist revolution, and of victorious Communism."

SCIENCE - AND - INVENTION

HOUSES MADE OF STRAW

SOME OF US can remember when the only protection against cold feet afforded by our street cars was a thick layer of straw. Fresh and clean and comfortable at first, it soon became a dirty mass, intermingled with snow and mud. Our modern electrically heated cars are a vast improvement.

FILLING THE FRAMEWORK WITH STRAW BRICKS.

At the same time it is true that straw affords a good deal of warmth, as many a hobo can testify who has found a cosy bed in a barn or a haystack. It is a common practise, too, in the country, to bed down horses on straw, and Suzette, the famous trained chimpanzee at the New York Zoo, makes herself comfortable for the night in the same sort of a bed. The reason for the warmth afforded by this light and flimsy material resides in the fact that it enmeshes large quantities of air, thus acting as a non-conductor of heat. This quality has been taken advantage of in the straw mattresses common in some parts of the country. A Frenchman named Feuillette makes use of it in the construction of houses. He compresses straw into solid blocks, which he uses as fillers within a light framework of wood. Writing in a recent number of *La Science et La Vie* (Paris), Gustave Lamache observes in regard to this invention:

READY FOR THE CEMENT COATING.

"The restoration of the houses and holdings of the peasants, in the regions devastated by the enemy, may be accelerated by the utilization of materials which are both cheap and abundant and solve the problem of providing houses for workmen.

"This last point of view was not least of the motives which inspired M. Feuillette in his attempts to find a method of building a house which should be comfortable, hygienic, of considerable permanence, and agreeable to live in, while, at the same time, capable of being erected at a cost compatible with the small income received by clerks, laborers and others of modest resources."

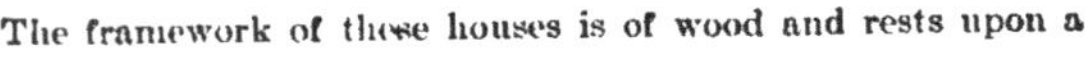

The framework of these houses is of wood and rests upon a foundation adapted to the nature of the ground; in all cases, however, it is comparatively inexpensive because of the lightness of the structure which surmounts it. The foundation is covered with sheets of tar paper to prevent dampness. The blocks of compress straw, which fill the hollow space in the wooden framework, are shaped like bricks, their width corresponds with the desired thickness of the walls, and their length with the distance between the uprights. After the hollow walls have been filled in by these bricks of straw, both sides of the wall are covered with fine-meshed wire netting. This in turn has a suitable coating on each side, as of cement outside and of plaster inside. The internal partitions consist of panels formed of uprights and laths covered with plaster. The floors are of joists supporting ordinary flooring; the ceilings, of sheets of reinforced plaster suspended upon the joists. There is a system of pipes through which disinfectants, such as formaldehyde or carbon bisulphide, can be sent to destroy rats, mice, and other vermin. We read further:

"The possibility of producing the units in standardized form insures a very low price and rapid construction by workmen not possest of great skill. In spite of the thickness of the walls, about 15½ inches on the average, they form a light and elastic ensemble, which can be erected upon comparatively shallow foundations, or even upon a base made of wood, concrete or brick. The variations of outside temperature are scarcely felt within these houses, so that M. Feuillette is quite justified in calling them *isothermic houses.*"

These houses are especially recommended for stables, garages, storehouses for perishable foods, and other places where uniform temperature is desirable. Numbers of them have been erected already in the Aisne and other parts of France, and have been very successful. They are recommended, too, for countries subject to earthquake shocks.

THE STRAW HOUSE COMPLETED.

WHAT IS THE MATTER WITH THE MOON?

AS A MEMBER of the solar system the moon is rather insignificant. All of the planets are larger, as well as some of the satellites of the outer planets. Yet like the small boy of the family, it causes a lot of mischief. Ask the astronomer what member of the sun's family causes him the most trouble, and he will reply undoubtedly "the moon." The greatest mathematical geniuses of the past and present have wrestled with the problem of the moon's motion, and have acknowledged defeat. Says Isabel M. Lewis, of the U. S. Naval Observatory, writing in *The Science News Bulletin* (Washington, D. C.):

"The moon simply will not travel according to schedule. Tables have been constructed from time to time according to the Newtonian theory, and predicted positions of the moon given to the highest degree of refinement. The latest and most valuable of these tables now in use by Almanac offices are compiled by Prof. E. W. Brown. By including terms and corrections, as in the past, whose source is unknown, the moon is fairly well harnessed for the time being, but Professor Brown has exprest the opinion that the moon's motion is not in accord with theory, and some unknown cause for its erratic behavior must be found.

"An excellent test of the accuracy of the predicted places of the moon is obtained from total solar eclipses. The astronomer predicts from his lunar tables the time for the beginning and ending of the eclipse to tenths of a second of time, but the moon delights in being six or eight or eighteen seconds ahead of time—or late, possibly—an unpardonable error in the eyes of the astronomer. An error of several seconds of arc in the moon's position throws the path of totality on the earth several miles from its true position, and because the astronomer does not trust the moon he locates his eclipse expeditions as nearly in the center of the predicted path as possible that he may not find himself bathed in sunlight at a time when he was anticipating total eclipse.

"Theorists delight in advancing reasons for the erratic behavior of our satellite. Frankly, the cause is unknown. Some unknown law may be involved, but the problem still awaits solution.

"When two bodies in the solar system are at a considerable distance from one another, or when one of the bodies is attended by satellites that are comparatively very small, it is a fairly simple matter to predict accurately their relative positions for any time. This is what astronomers call the problem of the motions of two bodies When a third body is introduced, however, comparatively large and near to one of the bodies, as in the case of the earth and moon, the two form with the sun the complicated problem of the motion of three bodies, and to follow the motion of three mutually disturbing bodies is a work for mathematical geniuses only. Such a problem is furnished by the moon, and after solving it in a highly satisfactory manner, as has been done by Professor Brown, the astronomers find that there is still something that does not conform to theory.

"We might go through the entire list of speculations—perturbations by an unknown satellite, action of electromagnetic forces, resisting mediums, variable gravitational attraction, etc. None has solved the problem, and we are faced with the simple fact that the erratic behavior of fair Luna has not been accounted for up to the present time."

COST OF PRIVATE TRANSPORTATION—One of the most common comments to-day, says an editorial writer in *The Electric Railway Journal* (New York), is that the private automobile is the greatest competitor the railway has. Why not tell these auto users how much it is costing them, and do it in a national way? He continues:

"A case comes to mind of a railway engineer who, in a social evening, asked two of his neighbors to make estimates of the cost of going to and from work in their private automobiles. One answered $1.70 and the other $1.45. His own figures indicated $1.30 (they all had cars of the same make). It took no more than the comparison of these estimates with the known 15 cents on the street car to make street-car riders of these neighbors. There are millions—surely many, many thousands—of such cases, scattered nation-wide. A nation-wide educational campaign should be started to deal with it."

ASSASSINATION WITH GERMS

POISONING A VICTIM with disease germs, altho we read of it in detective stories, and occasionally in the papers, is extremely rare, we are told by a contributor to *The Lancet* (London). In fact, there are only two authenticated cases, and these are not strictly in point, for one of them was unsuccessful and the other was not done by means of bacteria but of a toxin—a bacterial product. An article that will dampen the spirits of those contemplating anything of this sort, written by a German authority, Lempp, in the *Archiv für Kriminologie*, furnishes the facts cited in the paper from which we quote:

"Glancing at ancient literature, for instance, Thucydides's account of the Athenian plague, and medieval history, he pronounces, naturally enough, that these reports of pestilence spread through the action of enemies are in the great majority of cases merely fanciful. Just as baseless are the tales of aviators dropping bon-bons containing pathogenic cultures, or of laboratory workers contaminating water-supplies, which were recently given currency by, and perhaps often originated in, the sensational press. He states that on the German side such reports received for the most part immediate official investigation and discountenance. Probably the only authenticated instance of the use of pathogenic bacteria in warfare is, curiously enough, the practise of the warriors of the New Hebrides, of dipping the points of their weapons in marsh mud, which contains many tetanus spores. Equally scanty is indubitable evidence of murder by the means under notice; for probably there are but two properly recorded cases; and the second of these, that of the druggist and artist Hopf, did not go beyond an attempt. In 1914 Hopf was convicted of poisoning his first wife with arsenic, and of attempting to murder his third one by means of typhoid and of cholera germs. The latter infection was quite abortive, and examination of the culture in his possession showed it to have lost all virulence.

"The typhoid bacilli, on the contrary, were extremely pathogenic, having particularly high agglutination, a quality evident also in a strain isolated from the blood of an attendant, who also sickened. It was suspected that Hopf infected some of the entourage in order to give the impression of an ordinary small epidemic. Five days after poisoning his wife's food he began to take her temperature regularly; it duly rose two days later, but she recovered. He had caused her to make a will directing that her body should be cremated. The cultures—to the number of 30 within nine months—he had obtained from a private laboratory, asking particularly for the most virulent strains.

"Accounts have appeared in American newspapers of murders, or attempted murders, in the United States by means of bacteria, the only specified kind being again typhoid bacilli; the statement even being made that it had been proposed to erect in Chicago—a city with one of the worst records for murder in the world—an institute expressly for combating this particular crime. However, the only documented example of a fellow to Hopf is that of a Dr. Pantschenko, who, bribed by a relative of the victim, murdered a rich young Russian by injecting, not bacteria, but a bacterial product—namely, diphtheria toxin. The injection was pretended to be of spermin, for therapeutic purposes, and the defense was an admission that the syringe might have been not properly clean, thus causing fatal septicæmia. Septicæmia was, indeed, the diagnosis first arrived at, by an independent medical man, while a second one took the condition for septic gangrene.

"The site of injection became bluish-black, the temperature rose to 40° C., and death followed in a week. There were two autopsies, the second only revealing the truth, by means of the discovery of a detachable gray membrane in the pharynx, of cardiac dilation, and of peculiar thinning of the skin at the site of injection, appearances closely paralleled in experiments on animals—namely, guinea-pigs—which also died on the seventh day. It was proved that Pantschenko had obtained diphtheria toxin from a laboratory, and also, on a previous occasion, cholera endotoxin and cholera bacilli, a poison suggested by the instigator aforesaid. Pantschenko was sentenced to fifteen years' forced labor.

"The paper concludes with a review of current legal precautions against such crime, which seem in many countries to be altogether lacking, a state of things which its apparent great rarity does not wholly excuse."

MENDENHALL GLACIER—A GOOD VIEW OF THE AGE-OLD ICE-MASS

Which is destined some day to offer intensely interesting study to the scientist, when the highway entices tourist travel to the region.

ALASKA'S GLACIER HIGHWAY

AN ALASKAN GLACIER BY AUTOMOBILE! Few persons realize that such a trip is possible; and yet one can hire a car in Juneau at any garage, and by a drive of only eleven miles, over a good road, visit Mendenhall Glacier. This drive, says John D. Guthrie of the U. S. Forest Service, writing in *American Forestry* (Washington), is over a part of what is to be known as the Glacier Highway, which, when completed, will extend from Juneau, the capital of the territory, some sixty miles north to Berner's Bay. It will be entirely within the Tongass National Forest, except the small portion within the city limits of Juneau. This highway is being constructed under arrangement by the Forest Service, the Bureau of Public Roads, the Alaska Road Commission (composed of Army Engineers), and the Territorial Road Commission. When completed it will be one of the show places of all Alaska. Mr. Guthrie continues:

"The road starts at Juneau, follows north along Gastineau Channel, past canneries and sawmills, then by farms and dairy ranches, with several silos in sight, for a distance of some eleven miles, where a branch road turns off to Mendenhall Glacier. Autos may approach within a few hundred yards of the glacier, and visitors, by a short walk past the power plant, may go out on the glacier. There is a camping site nearby which is used by Juneau people who drive out, bringing tents and camping outfits, and spend a night under the shadow of this interesting age-old ice-mass.

"On the steep, rock slopes of the surrounding mountains may be seen the carvings of this slow-moving ice-river as it has relentlessly moved downward for centuries. A roaring stream issues from beneath the mass, tearing at the edges of the immense ridges of rock and gravel ever being shoved ahead by the enormous bulk of ice behind. The forest, through centuries, has been struggling to cover the smooth rock sides of the valley, and has begun to creep up on the terminal moraines, aspen first, flaunting its quivering banners—now green, now yellow—with spruces following slowly behind. Here a country in the making can be seen.

"Leaving Mendenhall Glacier the highway swings along the west side of Auke Lake where there are fish, boats and bathing. From the highway here magnificent views are to be had on one side, of Mendenhall and Herbert Glaciers, with high above them rugged, snow-capped peaks, and on the other, glimpses of Favorite Channel and Lynn Canal through the heavy stands of spruce timber. Auke Inlet, with points of timber running out almost encircling it, offers charming vistas which will some day delight the tourist. Along the shores of Auke Inlet are a summer home or two, and several canneries, almost hidden from the highway by the fringe of forest between. Altho only some fifteen miles of the proposed sixty have been built to date the Bureau of Public Roads is now at work on the construction of the portion along Auke Inlet, and will extend the preliminary survey work to Eagle River. In the vicinity of Eagle River there are extensive agricultural lands, some of which are even now being made productive by the eight or ten homesteaders who have settled there.

"One rancher is said to have cleared $200 from one-half acre of strawberries in 1919. Fine strawberries and raspberries, and such vegetables as cabbage, cauliflower, rhubarb, potatoes, carrots, turnips and celery are now grown, as well as a bewildering array of flowers. The extensive meadow lands produce a fine quality of native hay, and here are seen sleek cattle and horses in pasture and chickens around the door-yards.

"The Glacier Highway will open up the markets of Juneau, Treadwell and Thane for the produce of these farming lands. Even now one rancher is planning on buying a Henry, ahead of the completion of the road to his ranch.

"The Glacier Highway will be a wonder-way for the tourist a few years hence. It will afford alternate views of glaciers, ice-capped peaks, sea meadows, rivers, rugged mountains, forested islands and inlets, farms, and canneries, and will be practically at sea level for the 60 miles of its length. Four large and wonderful glaciers, each covering thousands of acres, are visible from it—Mendenhall, Herbert, Lemon and Eagle—where these intensely interesting ice-masses may be visited by the tourist and pleasure-seeker or more leisurely studied by the scientist.

"When completed undoubtedly the steamship companies will arrange their boat schedules to enable tourists to leave the boats at Juneau, take the trip over the Glacier Highway through this wonderland of the Tongass National Forest to Berner's Bay, and catch the steamer again on its route to Skagway."

HYPODERMIC PRESERVATION OF WOOD—A new process has been recently employed in Germany, according to the *Deutschen Wald*, quoted in *Die Umschau* (Frankfort) for impregnating wood with a protective antiseptic by means of injection. This method is known as the "Cobra Process." We read:

"By means of a hollow hypodermic needle, having an oval section, the protective fluid is injected into the freshly felled tree-trunk while it is still in the forest. Since the trunk is still full of sap, this fluid, which is used in highly concentrated form, quickly spreads through the tissues of the trunk by diffusion. Through a mechanical device the needle is withdrawn and pushed forward at regular intervals, so as to produce a spiral line of holes about the trunk; these are from one and one-half to three inches deep and from two to three inches distant from each other. While various liquids may be used for the purpose the experiment has proved that one of the best consists of a mixture of five parts of pulverized copper sulphate with fifteen parts of potassium chromate and eighty parts of a saturated solution of calcium chloride. This process can also be employed to prevent rot in wooden piles, posts, telegraph poles, etc., etc., which are already in position."

Illustrations by courtesy of John D. Guthrie, U. S. Forest Service.

DISTINGUISHED VISITORS AT THE GLACIER.

Chief Forester Greeley and District Forester Cecil.

MYSTERY OF THE SUN'S HEAT

THE SOURCE OF THE SUN'S ENERGY remains unknown in spite of years of speculation by astronomers and physicists. But Dr. H. D. Curtis, of Allegheny Observatory, believes that this energy may result from the breaking up of atoms rather than from ordinary chemical and physical processes. The disintegration of radium releases at least 10,000,000 times more energy than is produced by any chemical action known. In the sun there certainly is lead and helium, both of which are radioactive products. The existence of radium has been suspected in the sun. But radium alone is not sufficient as a source of the solar energy, we are told in *The Science News Bulletin* (Washington). Were the sun composed entirely of uranium and its radioactive products, the heat involved would be only about one-fourth of the actual amount. The writer continues:

"Astronomers are driven thus to a confession of ignorance; they do not know precisely how the sun's heat is maintained. The most probable assumption, and it is largely an assumption as yet, is that there may well be some dissociation in the atoms of other sorts of matter, similar to that observed in uranium and radium, and that from such stores of subatomic energy comes the greater part of the sun's truly prodigal outflow of energy.

"Thirty years ago, the general belief was that the heat of the sun was produced by the resistance that matter encountered as it moved gradually inward as the sun contracted through gravitation.

"This contraction theory rests solidly on known physical laws and because the amount of the contraction needed to produce the required heat is extremely small, only some 200 feet a year, it would take 10,000 years to produce a measurable change, so the theory could not be proved or disproved by observation.

"But geologists objected when Kelvin found that by the contraction theory the sun could not have existed for more than some 18,000,000 years in the past, nor last more than 10,000,000 or so years longer. They considered 10,000,000 years merely as a day in the making of this earth, and they refused to be satisfied with so picayune an allowance of time for geological development.

"This great heat engine has been operating for certainly a billion, and more probably a hundred billion years and is, so far as we can see, giving out constantly almost the same amount of heat.

"The temperature of the sun is between 5,000 degrees and 8,000 degrees Centigrade, every square yard of the surface emitting energy to the amount of about 75,000 horse-power. There are few terrestrial power-plants which produce as many horse-powers as does a space three feet square on the surface of the sun. To produce it would require the burning of a layer of coal twenty feet thick every hour. The sun is continually emitting about half a trillion trillion horse-power; or to use a less familiar unit, about half a sextillion horse-power. Most of this seems to be wasted in space; our earth intercepts about one two-billionth of it, amounting to about one horse-power per square yard, if we could use it. Could we utilize all the solar energy falling on an average-sized roof, it would go far toward lighting a modern city. When the day comes of the discovery of some method to extract the greater part of this solar energy, we shall move out of the age of steel and the age of electricity into an age of energy.

"This tremendous heat energy can not be caused by mere combustion. Were the sun made of solid coal, burning in oxygen, it would be black in less than 5,000 years. Emden, with true Teutonic preciseness, puts it at 2,630 years; months, days and hours omitted."

A VIEW OF THE GLACIER FROM THE HIGHWAY.

Automobiles may approach within a few hundred yards of the glacier and there is a fine camping site nearby for the benefit of those who wish to spend more time in the neighborhood.

CHALIAPIN—ANOTHER THRILL

THE SENSATIONS are all at the Opera this season. After Jeritza comes Chaliapin, and the staid old Metropolitan forgets its dignity and goes off its head with enthusiasm. What has happened that "the greatest singing artist of the world," as many proclaim the Russian, should create furors in 1921 while the same artist in the plenitude of his powers, with unimpaired vocal quality should be rejected in 1908? More of his countrymen are here to hear him now, and what they acclaimed in his impersonation of "Boris Godunoff" were the agonies of a ghost-haunted and dying Czar, for whom their natural sympathies are supposed to have cooled. So we are to assume that it was Chaliapin's art that won them. Mr. Krehbiel maintains that "there was nothing to indicate possession of such artistic puissance in the man when he was a member of the Metropolitan Opera Company in the season of 1907–08." The objection then was one of taste. "There was a vulgarity in his *Don Basilio* (in Rossini's 'Barber') which was repelling if not repulsive, and much also in his acting which prevented him from being a dominant figure in any of the four operas in which he appeared." Mr. Aldrich of the *Times* practically agrees, saying that in that other day Mr. Chaliapin was "by no means accepted as a great artist without cavil." Then he goes on to say that "Russian opera has conquered a great place for itself since then in the Occidental opera houses. It is understood, appreciated, admired, and in the operas of the school of his native land, Mr. Chaliapin has made his greatest name." All of which may make one question whether the artist or the audience failed. When Chaliapin left us he said he'd never return, but wars and Bolshevism were not dreamed of then. He can find small fault with such a tribute as Mr. Krehbiel's:

Copyrighted by the Keystone View Co.

RETURNING TO TRIUMPHS.

Chaliapin, the Russian basso, with Mme. Lucrezia Bori, landing from the *Adriatic*. When he left us in 1908, he vowed never to return.

"Centenarians with memories stored with recollections of Kean, Macready and Forrest, as well as Salvini (if there are any such alive), might have attended the performance of 'Boris Godunoff' at the Metropolitan Opera House last night and felt such swellings of the heart as they experienced when tragedy was in its prime in New York. Echoes of only the American and Italian worthies live in our comparatively youthful mind, but they were powerfully stirred when Mr. Chaliapin addrest the grisly horrors which his crime-haunted brain conjured up in the second act of Moussorgsky's lyric tragedy. We heard again the roar of Forrest's marvelous voice, tho attuned to more measured music; felt a thrill like that inspired by his postures, facial expression and gestures as Macbeth, and for the first time realized the greatness of the Russian as a dramatic singer, or a singing actor. . . .

"Last night nobility of action was paired with a beautiful nobility of voice and vocal style, and his *Boris* stood out of the dramatic picture like one of the old-time heroes of tragedy. He tugged at the heart-strings of the audience till it seemed as if he would tear them in pieces.

"There were storms of excited applause after the second act and again at the close. He sang in Russian; and tho it was possible even for those unfamiliar with the language to feel some of that intimacy which must exist between the original text and the music, the effect upon the Russians in the audience was akin to a frenzy. All that we have heard of the supreme greatness of his impersonation of the character of *Boris* was made plain. It was heartbreaking in its pathos, terrible in its vehemence and agony.

"Such things are so new and strange in opera that comparisons and precedents fail us. Only one picture looms up in our memory as comparable in moving power with the vision-haunted and dying Czar; it is that of Niemann's delirious *Tristan* at the first representation of Wagner's drama in New York. Then we saw an admired actress with blanched face and limbs relaxed, her eyes staring with horror, lean against her escort for support. Niemann was warned and never after tore the bandages from his wounded side as he did that night."

Chaliapin comes to us from Russia where his art helped to mitigate the hardships of the people, and his reward from the Soviet Government is said to have been extra rations of food. He stopt in England on his way here and gave concerts. Mr. Ernest Newman, writing from London to the Manchester *Guardian*, declared it "a pitiable reflection on the present state of operatic music in London that the greatest operatic artist in the world can come to the leading capital of the world and not find either opera or an opera house to sing in." London had him "like a fashionable *prima donna* with many of the *prima donna* stunts." Critics like Mr. Newman take a different view from ours of his past and present:

"Time and Messrs. Lenin and Trotsky between them have taken a good deal of the old power and beauty from his voice, but what remains is enough to leave him still without an equal among singers.

"English audiences will be able to test him fairly as a pure singer, for in no other way can he make an appeal to listeners who are ignorant of Russian. Even those of us who have a slight knowledge of the language were very glad to forget it and give ourselves up to the sheer joy of Chaliapin's singing. In the old days what made him so remarkable was not only the glory of his voice but the extraordinary command he had of it. We have had other basses with voices as huge as his, but none with such power of shading. Last night this art of his was as wonderful as ever; it really seemed as if we had heard no real singing since he left us in 1914."

Mr. Newman then proceeds to analyze:

"His art, like that of all the greatest artists, seems so simple because it is so complex. Many threads have gone to the weaving of that wonderful texture. Every phrase, every part of every phrase, is modeled upon the words. The mystery is how, with this close fidelity to verbal literalism, he contrives to make his voice sing with the freedom of line and the infinite variety of shading of a great instrumental player. How careful he is over his verbal points can be seen by any one ignorant of Russian who listens to him in German songs or songs derived from the German. He translates not only the poems but the music into Russian. Truth to tell, there were many things in his interpretation of 'The Two Grenadiers' and Grieg's 'Es war ein alter König' that were musical solecisms, but for this the peculiarities of the Russian language are responsible. There is no European language that shapes alien music more imperiously, more cruelly, to its own image. But if Chaliapin's Grieg and Schumann were musically as well as verbally only translations, what marvelous translations they were!

"The nine or ten Russian songs were almost all of the melancholy order—all to our advantage, for they gave him every possible chance to show the infinite modulations of which his voice is capable.

"He plays upon it like an instrumentalist; in its noble pathos it suggests a 'cello. His greatest triumphs, indeed, were precisely those of the great string player who draws such beauty from his instrument by mere tone and phrasing that we forget the banality of the music.

"One of Chaliapin's Russian songs was in itself as wretched a piece of music as any English drawing-room ballad, but it was upon this song that, as if by way of challenge to us, he lavished his subtlest art. It made us believe in the stories we read of Garrick drawing the soul out of his hearers by his recitation of the Lord's Prayer."

HEIFETZ PLAYING FOR HELEN KELLER—Closing the doors of the senses is not the same as conquering the will. This has been proved by Helen Keller in a hundred ways, but a new proof is revealed by the Denver *Post* when Jascha Heifetz, the great violinist, played for the blind and deaf woman at the Brown Hotel in Denver. Thus:

"For once when Heifetz was playing the audience was more interesting than the player. All eyes were on the blind woman as she placed the tips of her wondrously sensitized fingers under the belly of Heifetz's Stradivarius. The bow swept the strings, and the woman quivered as a thoroughbred race horse under the whip. The melody swept through her being. Her body responded to every note.

"She seemed to feel everything that the Cremona was trying to say to her. Heifetz was playing 'The Hymn to the Sun' from the opera 'Le Coq d'Or.' As the magic tones mounted the scales, the woman seemed to rise with it; her whole being quivered with an ecstasy that made those who looked on wonder if it was all delight.

"But it was not only the tempo to which she responded—the vibrations of the strings, fast or slow. She seemed to divine the real message of the music.

"'So tender, so tender,' she murmured once.

"Then Heifetz played 'La Chasse,' an old French hunting song—a gay, rollicking tune. The blind and deaf woman laughed with delight. There remained no doubt. She was hearing it all. It was as tho her whole being vibrated with the violin itself.

"The master of the violin was playing on a greater instrument than any ever turned out from the workshop of Antonio Stradivari. He was playing on what is probably the most highly attuned organism in the world—Miss Helen Keller."

TO-DAY'S SPIRIT IN NOVEL AND PLAY

DEBATES, LIKE COMPARISONS, are odious because they never settle anything. But people seem always to be debating, perhaps because thus they get a chance at each other. Whether "the modern drama more accurately reflects the spirit of the age than does the modern novel" was the

CHALIAPIN AS *BORIS.*

Four thousand people were inside The Metropolitan at the second representation of the opera, and as many outside failed to get in.

question of a recent debate between John Drinkwater and Hugh Walpole, two Englishmen of wide-spread reputation in America. The scene of their contention was the Cambridge Union Society at the home of that venerable British University. The London *Morning Post* calls it "a great and cheering debate" which it seems literally to have been, since both men received an ovation from an audience that filled every available space. A sort of preliminary skirmish over the field of the debate in England seems to be taken by two officials not known to us. They are the "proposer" and the "opposer." A brief abstract of their remarks serves to show how near they may come to stealing the thunder of the principal contestants:

"The proposer was Mr. R. L. Slater (Emmanuel). He admitted that he was merely the introduction to the two great protagonists who were to follow. Then with quaint humor and in quaint Midland accent he proceeded to make an excellent debating speech in which Shaw and the cinema seemed to meet with similar scorn. As a result of the war he found that there was a new spirit of idealism abroad. This idealism had spread into the world of drama, but, according to Mr. Slater, it had left the novelist cold. From this stricture he would not even except Mr. Walpole, and with this final fling at the Opposition he concluded his speech.

"The opposer was Mr. E. L. Davison (St. John's), a poet, the editor of the *Cambridge Review*, and a serious man. He pointed out that the motion was essentially a discussion of the comparative merits of the present-day drama and the present-day novel. Then, by some art known only to the practised Union orator, he managed to drag in a little discussion of post-war unrest and a good deal of Labor Party atmosphere. At length he came to the Drama, and, of course, Mr. G. B. Shaw. He appealed to the House not to take 'Back to Methuselah' as modern drama, and as for 'Heartbreak House' all the original thought was in accordance with Shaw tradition in the preface, and these prefaces were not modern drama. Coming to historical drama and Mr. John Drinkwater's 'Abraham Lincoln' in particular, the speaker said that such plays idealized a character and a period which was past but had little relation with the present. Turning to the novel, Mr. Davison, to the embarrassment of Mr. Walpole, quoted a passage from 'The Young Enchanted,' to show that here was true reflection of the feeling of young men and women in post-war days. The novel was the abstract and brief epitome of the times."

When the debate began in earnest, Mr. Drinkwater led off after telling a "semi-tragic story of a multiple christening," not further reported. It was in lieu of the joke which he declared he could never think of "save sometimes when by himself in a country lane." His words reported by the *Morning Post* are turned into "direct discourse" for easier conformity with American newspaper style:

"I announce with great pleasure that I read no modern novels, but as for plays, I have read them all, published and unpublished, produced or unproduced; in fact, I know modern drama to excess. During the past century the first-rate writers were thrown out of the theaters, and the actors more and more became dominant for the purpose of exploiting their own personalities. A breed of tame playwrights arose to feed these actors. With the advent of Ibsen there came the beginning of a change, and such men as Shaw and St. John Hankin came along. From some people, such as Miss Horniman, of Manchester, and the Abbey Players, we have found help to revive the true dramatist. The novel never has had such difficulties to face, and has had one long unbroken history. It is tradition in art which matters most of all in art, and it is here that the novelist has the advantage. Dramatists are a small and struggling body. Look at the list. Oscar Wilde's one achievement was the 'Importance of being Earnest.' St. John Hankin wrote some plays of charm. The really first body of plays written in modern times came from G. B. Shaw. Others are Granville Barker, John Masefield, John Galsworthy, and Arnold Bennett.

"The dramatists of to-day can but make a very small show against the huge array of modern novelists. There are only St. John Ervine, Lennox Robinson, Clemence Dane, and Eugene O'Neill in the little van of notable playwrights. In the motion there is reference to 'the spirit of the age,' yet in my view the spirit of one age is very similar to the spirit of another, and each generation discovers life and adventure seemingly for the first time. I regard the novel as a happy means of passing the ordinary, but not the great, moments of a man's life. The drama, tho, is meant for greater and more passionate moments, which only art can appeal to. Take Miss Clemence Dane's work. It stands for the heroic values in life, and there are others of the little band of dramatists who know of this ideal and have attained it."

Mr. Walpole followed next in defense of the novel:

"There has come a certain amount of confusion to the debate owing to the difficulty in deciding what is the spirit of the age. There are, I think, two little figures which go hand in hand. One eternal, but the other sprite was born yesterday and dies to-morrow. This last tiny fellow is the immediate present, but it takes the two together to make up the spirit of the age. It is no use, I think, to quote lists of dramatists and novelists, for one can find excellent work by both. Mr. Drinkwater has admitted that tho he has read some novels he has never bought one, so he can not sit in judgment on novels. On the other hand, I claim that I am a regular attendant at the theater. I can say on the strength of what I have seen in the theater of to-day that if this represents the spirit of the age, then heaven help that spirit. There is nothing tangible in the drama of to-day which truly characterizes the age, but surely there are novels, such as 'Dangerous Ages,' by Rose Macaulay, and 'Johanna Godden,' by Sheila K. Smith, that could never have been written in any other generation. How much easier it is for the novelist to catch the spirit o the age than it is for the dramatist. Drama always has been and always will be an ephemeral thing and in any case there are factors, such as the inquisitive and critical audience, the producer, the manager, and the weather outside, to prevent him from capturing the spirit of the age. The novel always has been and always would be the better mirror of the times."

The motion, we are told, on whatever grounds, was lost by eighty-three votes.

In spite of the vote, however, the *Morning Post* asks editorially whether any novelist has ever produced "such disturbances as Ibsen, Strindburg, Shaw or Brieux," or any novelist affected his own art as Ibsen did his. The questions are left unanswered and further comment tends to break down the impression of opposition at the sight of "theatrical managers turning more and more to novelists for their plays"—

"Indeed, it almost seems a rule that plays are accepted only from playwrights who have novels to their credit. The chances, therefore, are that if novels represent the spirit of the age, so do the plays, and that there is very little to choose between them in this respect. It is doubtful if this tendency to make the popular novelist the favored dramatist is to the advantage of either the drama or the novel, for the chances are that in most cases the motive which leads the novelist to write plays and the manager to accept them is commercial. The novelist hears of these handsome royalties which flow when a theater is playing to capacity, and the manager apparently attaches considerable importance to the safety and promise which attach themselves to a familiar name. Otherwise, it is hard to see how a writer could abandon the writing of a novel with its delightful sense of intimacy, of mastery, and of complete control, for the writing of a play where between the author and the final production intervene the producer, the actor, and, above all, the public. Mr. Walpole can say of his novels: 'Good or bad, they are my own, and alone I made them.' Can Mr. Drinkwater say the same of his plays?"

ARE OUR SCHOOL HISTORIES NOW TOO PRO-BRITISH?

IT WILL BE NEWS to most of us that Washington was not our first President. He is assigned second place by Mr. Abraham Wakeman who, describing himself as "a citizen," appeared before a committee of the Board of Education of New York City, with this startling declaration. "Washington was the first President under the Constitution," admits our citizen-critic, "but there was another President before him in 1786." "Why don't the school histories put the children straight on this?" Deponent does not name him, however. "Then they ought to mention Capt. John Underhill, who commanded our army of fifty men, was a strong advocate of woman's suffrage" and was expelled from Boston for flirting. The stage was set for objections to our histories on the grounds that they are "un-American and pro-British." The war found many of our school books pro-German and anti-British and revisions were hastily adopted to set us right. Now a campaign quite as rigorous seems to be under way to correct our alleged pro-British predilections. The New York *Herald*, reporting the meeting already mentioned, says:

"The hearing was marked by an acerbity which grew as the afternoon progressed and by a wide divergence of criticism regarding alleged facts set forth in the school books. Dr. William Irving Sirovish, vice-president of the Child Welfare Board, felt aggrieved that no mention was made in some of the school histories of the death of Nathan Hale, executed as a spy by the British during the Revolution. Abraham Wakeman, who said he appeared as a 'citizen,' was critical, on the contrary, because the histories had anything to say regarding Paul Revere.

"'Why do we teach children about Paul Revere?' Mr. Wakeman wanted to know. 'It's only because Longfellow made a hero out of him on account of his poetic name. It's twelve miles from Boston to Concord, and it took him from 10 o'clock to midnight to get there—that's only six miles an hour. And another thing,' went on Mr. Wakeman, 'George Washington wasn't the first President of the United States'—

"'I thought he was,' interrupted Frederick H. Paine, a

Brooklyn school superintendent who teaches history and is a member of the committee. . . .

"'The misstatements of history in the school books,' said the Rev. P. J. Cormican of Fordham University, 'are due to a systematic effort to "de-Americanize America" and ultimately to bring it back within the British Empire.' It was in this connection that the charge that Lord Northcliffe had spent $150,000,000 for propaganda purposes here was made and a statement by him in the London *Times* of July 4, 1919, was cited as proof that he had a carefully outlined plan of action. 'The Carnegie Foundation,' Father Cormican declared, 'pensioned superannuated college professors who had been active in "doing Carnegie's work" of endeavoring to get the United States back into the British Empire.

"'Our children are being poisoned, and if you poison the young it is only a question of time before our patriotism will be poisoned,' said he. 'The Sons and Daughters of the Revolution are engaged in the movement. They have been offering prizes for essays for years, ostensibly for patriotism, but really to propagate the views of Great Britain'."

Two histories published in 1919 are criticized as inaccurate, and the author of a preface to an American edition of Burke's "Conciliation with America" is attacked for his contention that the Revolutionary War was brought on by King George III. rather than by the British people. A new movement is inaugurated by the Knights of Columbus to "revive interest in the origins and progress of American history." Mr. John B. Kennedy, writing in the *New York Times Current History*, says:

"The object of the Knights of Columbus American history movement is not so much negative—the opposing of errors in history, and their correction—as the positive promotion of research into original sources of American history and the analysis of the results of this research distributed in millions of pamphlets throughout the country. The Knights have offered $7,500 in prizes to stimulate interest in the movement—$3,000 for professors of history, $2,000 for school superintendents and school teachers, $1,000 each for students in Mexico, Central and South America, and overseas, who have facilities for studying archives and American history relations, and $500 for students in colleges in the United States. It is estimated that with the completion and distribution of a cycle of some score of monographs, with the vast clerical and expert work that will be involved, the movement will involve an expenditure of approximately $1,000,000. . . .

"Headquarters for the commission have been established at 199 Massachusetts Avenue, Boston, where the campaign is directed to enroll 100,000 teachers and students in the movement, behind which the Knights of Columbus have thrown their organized strength.

"The breadth of the subjects to be studied, embracing the period from the discovery to the Pilgrim settlement, from the origin of Colonial Charters to the Arms Conference, indicates the possibilities of the movement as a stimulant to interest in the history of the Republic's strides to international greatness. The prominence and acknowledged scholarship of the men serving on the commission and the board of judges are a guaranty that every monograph judged by them and published by the organization will be authoritative."

Of this "rediscovery of America" by the Knights of Columbus, Mr. Kennedy says further in *America:*

"The pamphlets will then be combined in a book of American history, one-hundred-per-cent. proof, if an obsolescent term is permissible. We who are rather wearily amused at the stale pæans of Anglo-Saxon impulse, at Gallic enthusiasms, at Teuton boasts, at Hungarian rhapsodies, are thankful, to put it punfully, that the K. of C. are providing another record. They are setting out to rediscover American history. Godspeed them!"

MACBETH AGAIN IN A SINGLE SCENE

THE CRITICS LAUGHED "Macbeth" from the stage of our theater a year ago, mainly because they could not struggle with Mr. Jones's advanced ideas of scenery. His scenery consisted of a series of screens which suggested doorways and windows, and thus supplied hints of the outdoor and indoor scene of action for the piece. Something of the same thing has been done by a Russian sojourning in Geneva, where he gave "Macbeth" with a single setting, helped out by the "scene-changing" light which was described in our issue of December 10, as utilized by Pavlowa and the Greenwich Village Follies. Whether Mr. Pitoëff has been more successful than Mr. Jones is left for further experimenters to prove. The idea evidently does not intend to die at the hands of the critics. The London *Sphere* supplies us with the scene, and a brief comment thereon mainly derived from *L'Illustration* (Paris). The photograph here reproduced of course can not give any ideas of the variety of transformations to which the "skeleton" lends itself, but we can imagine the center of light shifting from one point of the stage to another, leaving the parts not needed for the given moment in obscurity. Taking the scene as a whole, we see the play skeletonized. We read further:

"MACBETH" IN CUBIC BUT NOT CUBISTIC SETTING.

The single scene available without change, save by lights for the entire play.

"For his recent production of 'Macbeth' at Geneva, M. Pitoëff, a well-known actor-manager, has devised an ingenious setting in which numerous changes of scene are effected by the distribution of lights and shadows, apparently somewhat on the lines of M. Samoiloff's method now used at the London Hippodrome.

"Describing M. Pitoëff's setting (here illustrated), a French writer says: 'Fully lit, it becomes part of a Gothic castle. Above the arch formed by the two stairways, on the left, is the entrance to a guard-room; the stair on the right disappears into gloom, suggesting invisible upper stories inhabited. Below the arch, opening downwards, is a lower hall, where people are seen only half-length. Finally, in the left foreground, begins a stair descending into the castle's mysterious depths.' M. Pitoëff's setting is 'cubic' in the geometrical sense, but has no affinity with 'Cubism.' He does not aim at sensation, or at a setting adaptable to every piece. A good setting, he thinks, must create an atmosphere, without losing itself in details that divert the spectator's attention from the play. He proposes to give 'Macbeth' in Paris. Last spring he produced 'Hamlet' at Geneva."

A DWINDLING CROP OF BAD BOYS

CANDIDATES FOR THE GALLOWS will be fewer in the next generation, believe some students of juvenile delinquency who base their hope on the promising results of children's courts, welfare societies, reformatories and the parole system. "Like every other school, the school of crimes can be perpetuated only by the kindergarten class," writes Willis Steele in the New York *Herald*, and of this "the prison commissions, the wardens of reformatories, tell a hopeful story. Bad boys are decreasing in number in the various institutions, and if the ratio existing between the populations of these places and the penal institutions means anything, it is that there are fewer bad boys growing up in the country than has been the case in the preceding score of years." Experience shows that habitual incorrigibility is in the majority of cases due to mental abnormality, and usually children who come under this heading require continued supervision and care and separate treatment. At the recent conference held at Jacksonville, Fla., George L. Sehon, of Kentucky, a member of the committee on juvenile delinquency, declared that he subscribed to the "optimistic belief that juvenile delinquency is not now on the increase. This note of hope and encouragement is sounded by a chorus of a majority of the men and women of this committee. It is echoed in the statistics offered by authorities in leading cities throughout the country." Contrary to popular belief, Charles E. Chute, secretary of the National Probation Association, said at the same convention that "no statistics have been produced anywhere showing a general crime increase. A Chicago crime commission makes the statement that there has been no crime wave in Chicago, but a marked decrease in major crimes during the last year. Statistics from the courts of forty-two of the largest cities in New York State show a decrease of about 10,000 in the total arraignments during 1920, as compared with 1919."

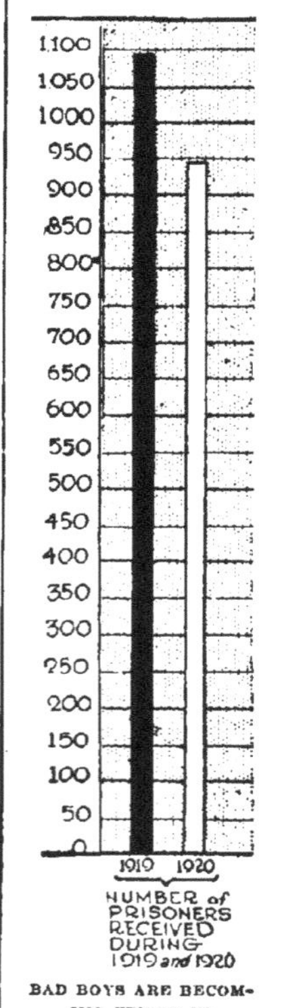

BAD BOYS ARE BECOMING FEWER IN NEW YORK

Never before, in the opinion of Dr. Frank L. Christian, superintendent of the New York State Reformatory at Elmira, have there been so many influences at work as there are at present for the conservation of youth. As quoted by the *Herald* writer, he declares: "I am optimistic for the future and believe that the delinquent youth of our land will respond to the efforts society is putting forth for their betterment." Seventy per cent. of the juvenile delinquents, male and female, from the ages of 16 to 30, placed under probation and having served out a period of surveillance, are never heard of again, states John S. Kennedy, President of the New York State Commission of Prisons. "This means that they have been saved to society. It also accounts for diminution in the population of the prisons." Many of the delinquent children are found to be inherently weak mentally, and at the last conference of prison commissions, says Mr. Kennedy, "the hard-boiled wardens who had sneered at psychiatry and its information admitted that there was something in it. I express myself too mildly; all are willing to try what can be accomplished with this new aid to reform." As he is further quoted in the *Herald* article, this authority states:

"Every student of criminology has learned almost at the outset of his studies that the most important single factor found associated with chronic criminalism is the abnormal mental condition of the criminal himself. Well authenticated facts are at hand to indicate that at least 50 per cent. of the inmates of prisons and reformatories exhibit mental abnormalities and are in need of much more specialized treatment than is afforded by the ordinary routine methods employed in the average penal institutions; that from 27 to 30 per cent. of such inmates are feeble-minded and only possess the intelligence of the average American child of 12 years or under.

"A start has been made by making the Napanoch institution [the State Institution for Defective Delinquents] a clearing house for Elmira and other institutions of a correctional purpose. Delinquents and criminals sentenced to the various penal and correctional institutions of this State will receive close study at the clearing house, with its medical clinic attachment, and when the method of reconstruction is determined upon they are then to be distributed to the various penal institutions according to the needs in each case.

"In the treatment of bad boys the object after all is so to reconstruct the personality of each one that he may be restored as promptly and as permanently as possible to his normal relation to society. A complete reformation is rarely accomplished within prison walls and much depends on after work. But the number of bad boys is steadily decreasing and the records of all institutions in which our commission is interested already show that the crop of 1921-22 will be agreeably less.

"The chief reason for this is, I repeat, because an effort along intelligent lines is now being made to discover the mental disease, deterioration or feeble-mindedness before they are sent to prison."

It has been established, we are told, that the incorrigible suffers from a physical or mental defect which probably explains his actions in the reformatory and his obduracy to discipline, and the problem in regard to the incorrigibles "is whether or not they shall be permitted to go back into the community and continue to be the menace they were before their commitment. The real question takes on a material aspect: is such a boy useful or useless; is he a danger and unfit for freedom; would his being at large interfere with the well-being of society?" Before answering, says the writer, it must be remembered that the true basis of incorrigibility is mental inferiority, and he goes on,

"Another bit of statistics not to be forgotten is this one: more than half of the bad boys released from institutions on parole have violated its conditions and have been recommitted. Unable as they are to compete successfully in the industrial world, unless parents or friends are active in their behalf, disaster quickly overtakes them. The incorrigibles cannot make their way alone and soon become the easy tools of crooks or schemers who may want them to hold the bag, or in some way act as accomplices in nefarious acts.

"But is this type of bad boy to be permanently incarcerated? One revolts at such a sentence for unfortunates and it is probable that the middle way is the right one. This looks to some form of permanent custody or custodial care. And with the development of the special training class, which is a new thing and only now being tried out, more and more incorrigibles may be saved."

DISARMING RELIGIOUS "JINGOES"

SECTARIAN DISARMAMENT is said to be as necessary in the religious world as physical disarmament is among the nations, for, in proportion to their numbers and influence in every denomination, the sects "embarrass and delay the progress of the kingdom of God." Like politics, Christianity has its "war party," "jingoes," "dollar diplomacy" and its "ecclesiastical Prussianism," writes Rev. Edgar De Witt Jones in *The Christian Century* (Undenominational), and as in the former field, so in the latter must effort be made to wipe out the divisive forces of jealousy and distrust. Being a "crude mixture of bigotry, prejudice, jealousy and intolerance," sectarianism may be characterized as one of the most disruptive forces in Christianity, but the writer, who is a Disciples minister in Detroit, thinks "it is too much to hope that it can be completely routed in any one or several generations." Limitation of sectarian armament, he holds, "is as much as can be expected at present." In common with many other surveyors of the field, this observer, who says he has practised what he preaches, declares that a reduction of unnecessary church building enterprises, with the consequent overlapping and duplication of activities, is imperative. As matters stand,

SOWING THE TARES.

—From the Sydney (Australia) *Bulletin*.

"Some portions of the country are wofully over-churched, other portions are without any church privileges at all. In 1911 in Colorado, one hundred thirty-three villages were found to be entirely without a Protestant church, over one hundred of them having no church of any sort. On the other hand, in a Pennsylvania village of four hundred fifty people there are six churches, each one struggling against heavy odds and presenting to the community an inadequate, a despairing, and an utterly discouraged spectacle. In a New England village of one hundred fifty inhabitants there are six churches. In another Eastern township, eighteen churches minister to a population of about a thousand. It was Dr. Earl Taylor who said—and he was in a position to know—'The great problem with the Protestant churches is not so much to get together as it is to keep apart—at least half a mile apart.' Says Professor Durant Drake: 'The needless multiplication of churches means half-filled pews, half-hearted enthusiasm, a generally dreary and depressing atmosphere in which it is difficult to cultivate an eager spirituality; it means division of forces . . . impaired prestige . . . diminished power to fight sin and wrong. . . .

"What a blessing it would be if communicants of churches could rid themselves of the idea that the only true church is the one to which they belong. There is no church that has fully apprehended Christian truth or that mirrors flawlessly the ideals of Jesus Christ. There are no 'Christians only' in the fullest sense of the term. Those who are Christian are Christian plus some practises that are not Christian and minus other practises that are Christian. God has not given to any one race, any one nation, any one religion, a monopoly on Truth, or elected any particular communion to be the custodian of orthodoxy, not even my own. . . .

"There is only one cure for the sectarian spirit, and that is love, even the love of Jesus Christ. Love is the only panacea."

CATHOLIC REVIVAL IN FRANCE.

THAT FRANCE, "THE PRODIGAL," has returned to the bosom of her Mother Church, is the view of various Catholic French writers, who look back on the first days of the Separation Law as an interval of nightmare. Then the crucifix was torn from the walls of courtroom and of schools, great numbers of French priests and nuns were obliged to seek asylum in foreign lands, many coming to America, and vociferous Socialist French legislators assured the world that France had chased religion out of the country for good and all. Now, after fifteen years of separation of Church and State, Viscount D'Avenel investigates the situation of the Church in seventy-six dioceses and finds a great reawakening of the faithful, whose practising number far exceeds that of thirty years ago. Just before the outbreak of the war there were signs of this revival, which was intensified by the exalted emotionalism of the war period. Moreover, there has been a rapid growth of certain Protestant denominations in France, during and since the war, of which note was made in these pages on November 5.

The Protestant churches now count about 1,000,000 adherents, and are said to be in flourishing condition. Under the Act of Separation Catholic Church property valued at about 600,000,000 francs was confiscated, the dioceses were deprived of seminaries, and the material situation of the priests appeared very uncertain. During several years, we are told, the number of vocations diminished, and the recruiting of clergy was insufficient. To-day, however, seminaries have been reestablished in practically all dioceses, and the number of vocations is large enough to promise a sufficient number of priests. Moreover, through the establishment of an inter-diocesan fund and by means of various fees, the salaries of the clergy formerly paid by the State are maintained, tho the clergy's resources are limited "to the strict minimum essential for living expenses."

As to the attitude of the people towards the Catholic Church, the writer notes that the number who are hostile or who profess other faiths form a minority. In one of the less devout dioceses, for instance, the bishop called a referendum at the time of the separation, and out of a population of 240,000 about 230,000 declared their desire to keep their churches and their priests. Only 10,000 answered in a negative or doubtful manner. In other dioceses, however, the religious attitude is said to be weaker. An examination of statistics for attendance at mass and communion shows that religious practises are more wide-spread in the country than in the cities. "At the present time, however, there is a general awakening, which is especially manifested in the cities by different works, by societies for young people, by increased attendance of men at mass." As summarized from articles in the *Revue des Deux Mondes* by the

National Catholic Welfare Council News Service for its American readers, the French writers' reports show that—

"This progress is proved by accurate figures. In 1851, Mgr. Dupanloup, Bishop of Orleans, stated that he was responsible to God for 350,000 souls, of whom barely 45,000 performed their religious duties. To-day, in that diocese, there are 100,000 Easter communions. The number of frequent, or pious communions, is fifteen times greater than formerly. In a diocese in Normandy with a population of 278,000 inhabitants, there are 120,900 Easter communions, that is to say, a proportion of 43 per cent.

"This proportion is higher than the average in France. M. d'Avenel established the average by classing the dioceses in three categories: 1st—those which may be classed as 'religious,' numbering 27, in which the majority of the women go to mass, and to communion at Easter and in which half of the men go to mass and one-fourth make the Easter communion; 2nd—those qualified as 'lukewarm,' 28 in number, in which the majority of the women go to mass, but where only half go to Easter communion, and where only one-third of the men go to mass and make their Easter communion in the proportion of 12 to 25 per cent; 3rd—18 dioceses classed as indifferent.

"In conclusion for the country as a whole—Paris and Alsace and Lorraine excepted—out of a population of 34,000,000 at least 10,000,000 are practical Catholics; 16,000,000 to 17,000,000 fulfil, in part at least, the duties imposed by the Church, and 7,000,000 to 8,000,000 only, among whom is a very small group openly hostile, live in indifference to religion of any kind, and, altho baptized, are Christians in name only. The result of fifteen years of separation in France therefore shows that not only has the country not become dechristianized, but it has made noticeable religious progress."

SAVING SAILORS FROM MORAL SHIPWRECK

A GREEN LIGHT FLASHING nightly out to sea bids Jack Tar a welcome to New York, and guides him to a friendly shelter where he can find a change from hard tack and scouse, drop into a warm bed, receive medical care if necessary, and find some of the other comforts of home he has missed since he became a transient of the sea. The Seaman's Church Institute of New York, finished just before the war at a cost of $1,225,000, has paid its way in the health and happiness of thousands of seamen, we are told, and in saving many others from moral shipwreck. It carried on business as usual during the industrial slump, and is still performing the difficult task of housing nearly a thousand seamen every night, providing doctors to care for their health, and amusements to occupy their leisure time. Furthermore, it is planning, we are told, greater things than have ever been done for seamen in any port of the world. The thirteen-story structure on South Street, near the water-front—a familiar landmark to sailors of every land and tongue—is not only a great seamen's hotel and club, where the sailor is safe from the perils and temptations of time ashore, writes Lillian Beynon Thomas in *The World's Markets* (New York); it is a seamen's community with practically everything the men need under one roof. "It gives the men of the sea what they desire, the opportunity to live safely and comfortably in respectable surroundings for a reasonable price." Shipwrecked men, submarined men, and other waifs of misfortune cast up by the sea came in such numbers during the war that often beds had to be made on the floor. A large room for games had to be turned into a dormitory because of the great demand, and has never been restored to its original use. At present 714 men sleep in the house. The man who wants a bed must book it before ten o'clock, tho a few are kept off the market for cases of emergency. During 1920, we are told, lodgings were furnished to 260,449 men, at a charge of from 30 cents to $1 a night, the former sum being for a bed in a dormitory, and the latter the rate for an officer's room. A safe place for the seaman's gear is provided, and in the baggage department last year 82,543 pieces were checked in.

To save them from the perils of the eating-places along the water-front, where those who prey on the sailor's loneliness and frailty gather every night, the Institute has established a restaurant and soda fountain where food and drinks are provided at the lowest prices; a savings department, which last year received $1,201,067 on deposit; a post-office, which will forward mail to any part of the world, or hold it six months if necessary, a missing men's bureau, the bulletin of which is posted in twenty-one countries; a "slop chest," or clothing store; laundry, shipping-office, barber shop and tailor shop. Nor is it forgotten, says the writer, that man does not live by bread alone. Returning from the long monotony of the sea, the sailor looks forward to having a good time ashore, and the Institute tries to give it to him. A concert hall is filled three evenings a week for music and motion pictures, and on Sunday evening there is "The Home Hour," when all get together and sing and talk, and listen to good music while they drink a cup of coffee and enjoy a doughnut. Of course, we are told,

"The work of the Institute is based on religion, but the forms of religion are not obtrusive. The Chapel of Our Saviour is in the building and services are held every Sunday. The men are never urged to attend; they are merely given the opportunity to go to church among men of their own kind, where they will not be conspicuous, whether drest in their best or in overalls. Many attend the services.

"There are two doctors in the building at all times who care for the health of the seamen in the house and those who go to them. There is a fully equipped clinic where the more serious cases are sent for examination. They are treated there if possible, or if they require extended care they are sent to the hospital, where they will receive just what they need. In the chaplain's office minor ills like cut fingers and bruises are cared for by the doctor who is there during business hours.

"The chaplain's office is the clearing house of the Institute. There the men go with all their troubles and perplexities. These are too varied to enumerate, but they are what is to be expected from men who are strangers in the port and are often hampered by not knowing the language. Last year 12,000 men appealed for advice or help of some kind, their requests covering a large arc of human needs. There were the men, not a small number, who wished to become citizens, and had no home but the Institute in this country, and no friends but those they met there. Some one had to go with them to testify as to their character. There were old men who desired to get into Snug Harbor, but were as helpless as children when it came to getting the evidence necessary to admit them. Days were spent looking over old records, and the difficulty may be imagined when it is remembered that sailors like to change their names. One man whose record was being sought could remember the names of twelve ships that he had been on, but as he had used ten different names his memory failed at its task of saying which name he used on each ship.

"Other men needed legal advice, while others were in domestic trouble and wanted help and counsel to enable them to see clearly, for when a man sees his wife and family only once or twice a year, suspicion and misunderstanding come easily. Then among the younger men there are often lonely ones who wish an opportunity to meet a nice girl, their lives too often bringing them into contact only with those whom they would prefer to shun. And there are always the careless and unfortunate who need money until they get a ship. The minds of the men are not neglected in this great seamen's community. Books and magazines are provided in the reading-rooms, and on the thirteenth floor there is a navigation and marine engineering and radio school that had an enrollment last year of 972 students. Of these 527 have successfully passed Government examinations and secured licenses."

Help is not limited to those ashore. From a high-powered radio station a-top the building messages flash out carrying medical advice to men at sea. Eighty per cent. of merchant ships do not carry a doctor, says the writer, and in case of sickness or accident aboard, the ship's officers have had to depend on their own resources. Now, however, the Seamen's Church Institute has arranged with the United States Public Health Service that when a call comes for KDKF, and the symptoms of the trouble are given, the Public Health Service doctor will diagnose the cases and give advice, which will be immediately sent back by radio.

Lightning Source UK Ltd.
Milton Keynes UK
UKHW031333131021
392145UK00007B/1307

CW00337350

Girona

Edición Published by Verlag	Triangle Postals S.L.
Texto Text Text	Antoni Puigverd
Versión castellana Translation Übersetzung	Antoni Puigverd Jina Monger Susanne Engler
Coordinación Coordination Koordination	Paz Marrodán
Concepto gráfico Design Gestaltung	America Sanchez scp.
Maquetación Layout Layout	Triangle Postals
Fotografias Photographs Fotografien	© Jordi Puig 69, 71, 73, 74, 75, 81 © Pere Vivas / Jordi Puig 69, 73, 74, 75 Derechos reservados © Cabildo de la Catedral de Girona 93 Con la colaboración de la Fundació del Cinema - Col·lecció Tomàs Mallol
Fotomecánica Colour separations Fototechnick	Tecnoart
Impresión Printed by Druck	Industrias Gráficas Viking S. A.
Papel Paper Papier	Creator Silk 150 gr/m², Torraspapel S. A.
Tapas Cover Buchdeckel	Cartón *Dorexpak*, Papelera Catalana S. A
Triangle Postals	Sant Lluís (Menorca) Tel. 971 15 04 51 Fax 971 15 18 36 e-mail: triangle@menorca.net Barcelona Tel./Fax 93 218 77 37 e-mail: paz@sendanet.es
Depósito Legal ISBN	B: 11.707-98 84-89815-31-3

Fotografías / Photographs / Fotografien
Jordi Puig

Texto / Text / Text
Antoni Puigverd

Edición / Published by / Verlag
Triangle Postals

◀
1 Patchwork
Patchwork
Patchwork

▲
2 Espectáculo inicial
At first sight
Schauspiel zu Beginn

◀
3 Casas del Onyar
Houses on the Onyar
Die Häuser am Onyar

▲
4 Escudo
Coat of arms
Wappenschild

▶▶
5 Eiffel en Girona
Eiffel in Girona
Eiffel in Girona

GIRONA

Antoni Puigverd

Cae sobre Girona el peso de la historia. Dos mil largos años que se condensan en su comprimido y espléndido cuerpo de piedra y que, sin embargo, no han dejado una impresión de cansancio o de vejez urbana. Fueron dos mil largos años repletos de dureza, de sufrimiento. Dos mil años de agónica resistencia que los románticos y los castizos consideraron heroica y que a los contemporáneos nos parecen inevitables y dolorosos signos de la crueldad de los tiempos.

Girona tuvo que resistir a lo largo de su historia muchas invasiones militares, cercos durísimos, bombardeos, incendios, inundaciones, hambrunas, sed y epidemias. La crueldad de la historia con esta ciudad ha sido enorme, insidiosa y difícil de entender a la luz de la actual bonanza. La ciudad tardó mucho en crecer. Las crueldades históricas la dejaron repetidamente maltrecha y anémica; cada esfuerzo por crecer fue decapitado en una nueva sangría. Sólo la llegada de la industrialización, durante el siglo XIX, permitió un cierto arranque demográfico. El perfil expansivo y la capitalidad regional que el visitante actual descubre son muy recientes. En los últimos decenios, efectivamente, y gracias a una fuerte inmigración, pero también a una concatenación de factores culturales, administrativos y comerciales, Girona se ha convertido en una ciudad bulliciosa, dinámica y atractiva que está superando sus antiguos achaques con una sorprendente alegría, con un excelente dinamismo, con una pasión que tiene mucho de mediterránea y que guarda con el trágico pasado una relación meramente estética.

Parece, pues, que la historia esté compensando a la ciudad por sus largos siglos de azote y desgracias. Lo cierto es que toda la tragedia que vivió la ciudad se está reconvirtiendo en belleza, tal como simbólicamente demuestra la transformación de la parte que queda en pie de las antiguas murallas: símbolo que fueron de los sufrimientos de antaño y ahora transformadas en amenos itinerarios turísticos, desde los cuales puede observarse cómo la ciudad se despereza creciendo hacia el exterior y recuperando, para el goce de sus ciudadanos y de sus visitantes, los signos del pasado, su alma más profunda.

Lo trágico cede, así, testigo a lo bello. De la misma manera que lo religioso cede a lo cultural. El componente religioso es, junto al militar, fundamental en la configuración histórica de la ciudad. Cualquier visitante puede captar, de un simple vistazo, la importancia de las edificaciones religiosas de Girona, entre las que destaca la catedral, cuya colosal nave es el mayor espacio gótico sin soporte columnario que existe. Aunque inicialmente Girona fue una triangular fortificación militar fundada por los romanos, lo cierto es que cuando el mundo romano desapareció, la ciudad resistió al desorden de los tiempos y a la crisis del mundo urbano merced a su condición de sede episcopal. El hecho de ser capital de una región eclesiástica le permitió sobrevivir en un contexto histórico en el que llegaron a desaparecer incluso ciudades de gran peso comercial y de rancia tradición greco-romana, como Ampurias.

Girona era la ciudad del obispo, una especialización que el paseante no necesita que le sea descrita, tal es la densidad de construcciones eclesiásticas que se acumulan en el apretado casco histórico; una especialización que conformó aun la estructura de la propiedad urbana medieval y llegó a caracterizar el clima cultural de la ciudad hasta muy entrado el siglo XX. Girona, en efecto, ha sido, a decir de muchos de sus comentaristas y glosadores, una ciudad "levítica". Canónigos, arciprestes, frailes y seminaristas, clérigos de todo tipo abundaron en sus calles y definieron el acento social y mental de una ciudad que tuvo larga fama de conservadora, discretísima y beata.

Súbitamente, sin embargo, la ciudad clerical, la capital levítica se transforma en capital artística, en patria cultural. La religiosidad, acorde con el espíritu liberal y secularizado de los tiempos actuales, ha abandonado los espacios urbanos y fructifica, de hacerlo, en los espacios íntimos de los creyentes. La influencia del obispo o de los clérigos, el peso de la doctrina católica, ya no puede medirse en términos sociales, sino en términos individuales. En virtud de este cambio social, el patrimonio católico, emblema de lo que fue durante siglos la ciudad, se está convirtiendo casi exclusivamente en patrimonio artístico, aunque ya la desamortización de bienes eclesiásticos provocó, durante el siglo XVIII, el abandono de muchos edificios que sufrieron una lamentable degradación a causa de forzados usos civiles o militares.

En la actualidad, los más emblemáticos edificios religiosos, comparten significación católica y artística. Éste es, naturalmente, el caso de la imponente catedral, de origen románico, nave gótica y fachada barroca; y también el de la colegiata de Sant Feliu (San Félix), de un gótico tardío, cuya torre en forma de inacabada "aguja de agujas" conforma, junto a la mole catedralicia, la estampa más típica de la ciudad. No es éste el espacio adecuado para ponderar los muchos valores artísticos que contienen estos dos grandes templos –valores que abarcan una muy amplia gama de épocas y estilos. No obstante, sería imperdonable no citar al menos los de mayor argumento: los importantes sarcófagos romanos, el Cristo yacente de alabastro (s. XIV) o la interesantísima capilla neoclásica de Sant Narcís, que se encuentran en la colegiata de Sant Feliu; y, en la catedral: el colosal e ingrávido espacio gótico, en el que la imponente monumentalidad de la piedra queda matizada por la suavidad de la luz que filtran las vidrieras policromas; la antiquísima ara del altar mayor (s. XI); la cátedra de piedra popularmente llamada de Carlomagno (s. XIV); los sarcófagos, retablos y ornamentaciones medievales; los bulliciosos retablos barrocos y, por encima de todo, los tres elementos esenciales que justifican una visita al anexo museo catedralicio: el claustro, de una elegancia arcaica y acogedora, desde donde se alza la magnífica torre llamada de Carlomagno correspondiente a la antigua iglesia románica; el célebre *tapiz de la Creación* (s. XI-XII), joya de este Museo, un bordado único que resume en fascinantes lanas de colores y mediante una curiosa mezcla de imágenes, la cosmovisión medieval de la vida y del tiempo; y el *Beatus,* un códice manuscrito (s. X) con extraordinarias miniaturas debidas a Emeterio y a Eude.

Mientras en la catedral y en la colegiata de Sant Feliu es posible compaginar la vivencia católica con la vivencia estrictamente cultural, en muchos otros edificios religiosos la reconversión ha sido completa: abandonada la significación religiosa, las piedras antiguas ya sólo remiten al simbolismo cultural propio del presente urbano. He aquí unos ejemplos: el precioso cenobio románico de Sant Pere de Galligants, sede del Museo Arqueológico (donde se conservan importantes estelas funerarias procedentes del antiguo cementerio judío); la deliciosa capilla de Sant Nicolau, muy cerca de Sant Pere, delicado espacio románico que acoge manifestaciones artísticas de vanguardia; el mismo palacio episcopal, adosado a la catedral, convertido, a instancias del obispado y de la mano de las administraciones públicas, en un importante museo de arte (el Md'A) que contiene, entre otras colecciones, una soberbia compilación de tallas y esculturas religiosas de los períodos románico y gótico; el centro cultural la Mercè, actual impulsor de la vida intelectual y sede de la escuela de arte, que ha transformado la antigua iglesia de los frailes mercedarios en un teatro-auditorio abierto tanto al clasicismo como a la vanguardia. De entre este conjunto de edificios religiosos reconvertidos al uso cultural destaca, finalmente, el convento de los dominicos, en la bellísima plaza de Sant Domènec, la mayor parte del cual ha sido reedificado, en una audaz revisión arquitectónica, como facultad de letras de la joven universidad (UdG); quedando todavía pendientes de restauración los espléndidos claustros y la iglesia de este mismo convento, que debe ser ya el último edificio medieval con sabor a ruina romántica que acoge la ciudad.

Este cambio de uso y de significación del patrimonio arquitectónico religioso tiene un curioso paralelismo en la operación de rescate de la antigua judería situada no muy lejos de la catedral, en lo más profundo del casco antiguo. En contra de lo que muchos creen, la judería, arquitectónicamente, no tiene origen hebreo. Al crearse la canónica catedralicia (s. IX), diversos clérigos trasladaron su residencia a la catedral, y los edificios que anteriormente habían ocupado fueron vendidos a unas familias hebreas procedentes de pueblos vecinos. Hay noticias de la existencia de esta judería ya en 1160. Hasta finales del siglo XV, en que los judíos fueron expulsados de la península, la de Girona fue, descontando la barcelonesa, una de las juderías más importantes de Cataluña por su extensión y dinamismo (unas 300 familias en el momento de su máximo esplendor), pero sobretodo por el prestigio de su escuela cabalística. El centro Bonastruc ça Porta, que reivindica el nombre del máximo pensador de esta escuela, pretende impulsar el conocimiento de la aportación intelectual de los judíos de Girona y a la vez promover el reconocimiento de las formas de vida y de la arquitectura íntima de este barrio de callejuelas húmedas y oscuras, donde parece haberse detenido el tiempo. El rescate de la judería es un signo más de la reconversión de un pasado doloroso (la judería fue repetidamente asaltada) en un presente cultural. Es otro signo, asimismo, de la reconversión de un ámbito religioso en ámbito de la reflexión, de la belleza artística y de la memoria cultural.

Si el patrimonio arquitectónico de origen religioso contribuye tan decisivamente a acentuar la apuesta cultural de la ciudad, es lógico que el patrimonio civil también responda a este modelo. Así, el magnífico edificio de la plaza de la catedral, conocido por *Pía Almoina* (s. XIV): un inmenso, espectacular y sobrio lienzo de piedra, amenizado solamente por algunas ventanas de grácil factura gótica, es ahora sede del Colegio de Arquitectos y fue sometido hace ya algún tiempo a una espectacular readaptación, precursora de muchas de las que posteriormente ha contemplado la ciudad. La apuesta por la síntesis entre modernidad y tradición arquitectónica, que se inició en Girona con la restauración de la Pía Almoina, puede parecer una opción puramente estética, aunque a veces tiene un sentido práctico. En todo caso es siempre respuesta a una pregunta imprescindible: ¿cómo salvar un edificio destrozado por la dejadez y el abandono? ¿Recreando lo perdido con criterio histórico o innovando con enfoque contemporáneo? Esta pregunta, que, naturalmente, no sólo en Girona se plantea, ha obtenido en esta ciudad distintas respuestas según el momento cultural en el que se inició el rescate del edificio. Así, en algunas iglesias (como la citada de Sant Pere de Galligants) y en algunos edificios civiles (*Fontana d'Or,* sede del Centro Cultural de la Caixa de Girona), la respuesta ha sido la recreación. Las restauraciones que ha impulsado la UdG (el ya comentado caso de Sant Domènec, por ejemplo), mucho más recientes, son respuestas más arriesgadas, acordes con la idea de síntesis entre pasado y futuro. El caso más relevante es, en este sentido, el del edificio Les Àligues de la plaza de Sant Domènec. Sede de la universidad en tiempo de los Austrias, había sufrido un proceso de degradación casi definitivo y ha sido recuperado como sede del rectorado de la nueva universidad. La recuperación ensambla voluminosas formas geométricas de cemento a las doradas piedras de la antigua fachada renacentista. Una mirada al patio interior, desde la portada renacentista, ofrece una de las mejores visiones de la síntesis: las paredes de la capilla del fondo han sido coronadas con vidrio y cemento y la combinación resultante es a la vez armónica y sorprendente, valiente y respetuosa, antigua y moderna.

En general, el casco antiguo de Girona está siendo renovado con esta ambición de síntesis. Y no me refiero sólo a los edificios singulares, ni tampoco exclusivamente al aspecto arquitectónico y urbanístico. Desde que la nueva Universidad ha optado por situar algunas de sus facultades y servicios a lo largo del casco antiguo, la recuperación (y revisión consecuente) de la Girona histórica ha avanzado a un buen ritmo. Ha sido, sin duda, el golpe de gracia al fatalismo de la decadencia que el ayuntamiento democrático y la sociedad civil han combatido a lo largo de los últimos años con entusiasmo. Y es que a lo largo de todo el siglo, los poetas que residieron en la ciudad, o la visitaron, crearon el mito de la Girona triste, ensimismada, húmeda, católica, arruinada. Una Girona fantasmagórica, perdida en su propio túnel, destilando sueños de piedra y niebla, lento naufragio de la historia, cansada monumentalidad, melancolía de la pérdida.

Romper con esta inercia decadente no era fácil, puesto que la ciudad, en la segunda mitad del siglo XIX, cuando son derribadas las murallas del llano, crece y se expande por todas partes: bien conectando con los antiguos núcleos vecinos (Santa Eugènia, Sant Daniel, la Rodona...), bien en forma de diversos ensanches más o menos confusos (Carrer Nou, Marqués de Camps, l'Havana Petita, la Creu, Sant Narcís, Palau Petit...), bien, como en los últimos años, mediante nuevas urbanizaciones privadas o públicas (altas, medias o bajas: Pedreres, Font de la Pólvora, Vilaroja, Montilivi, Palau, Montjuïc, Fontajau, Güell). Cada nueva expansión de la bulliciosa Girona contemporánea implicaba para el nucleo histórico una nueva confirmación de la decadencia. No bastaban los equipamientos culturales (Fontana d'Or, Colegio de Arquitectos, la Mercè, Md'A, Museo de Historia, Centre Bonastruc ça Porta), no bastaban las iniciativas lúdicas y comerciales de bares, tiendas o restaurantes. Para revitalizar el núcleo duro de la ciudad antigua, hacía falta el gran revulsivo de la Universidad. Gracias a ella, los jóvenes protagonizan, junto a los visitantes, el renacimiento de este viejo espacio tatuado por un laberinto de callejuelas y plazas intimistas y trufado de importantes edificios religiosos.
Se produce, por otro lado, una sinergia entre la vida universitaria, la iniciativa comercial, el esfuerzo cultural de las instituciones y la dinámica económica: se multiplican los bares y los restaurantes, aparecen comercios singulares o especializados, regresan las galerías de arte, conviven las tiendas de antiguedades y las de diseño, las agencias turísticas han incorporado la visita a la Girona antigua entre las principales de Cataluña y el mercado inmobiliario ha empezado a moverse en el sentido de recuperar partes del casco antiguo de legendaria marginación (el Pou Rodó, antiguo barrio de la prostitución). Lentamente, el mito de la Girona vieja, soñolienta y ensimismada deja paso al de la Girona culta, refinada y elegante. Los dos son mitos inexactos; el antiguo puede que produjera mejor literatura, pero cantaba a la ruina; el actual puede que sea menos espontáneo, pero favorece la recuperación. La vieja Europa del ocio cultural tiene en la Girona antigua una alumna aventajada.

Girona es naturalmente mucho más que el núcleo antiguo. Sin embargo, es inevitable recurrir al símbolo de las viejas piedras para definir la ciudad. Cansada y soñolienta o vigorizada por afeites contemporáneos, la piedra es protagonista de su actual renovación y también símbolo del pasado, memoria del origen: si los romanos construyeron el triangular asentamiento que fundó la ciudad es porque, en los promontorios sobre el río Onyar en donde alzaron la fortificación, la piedra numulítica se encontraba en abundancia. Una nueva urbanización no muy lejos de la muralla, lleva el nombre de Les Pedreres (las canteras) y son visibles, en los promontorios que dominan la ciudad, restos de antiguas extracciones de piedra. Son las personas que viven y han vivido en esta ciudad las que le han dado la impronta, naturalmente; pero las piedras son el testimonio de su paso.

No obstante, la piedra no es el único componente simbólico. También lo es el agua. Los romanos construyen su fortificación en una confluencia de ríos y torrentes: el Ter encara su último tramo y recoge, en un punto cercano al barrio de Sant Feliu, las aguas de dos torrentes, Galligants y Güell (actualmente desviado), y las del Onyar, un río extremista que arrastra normalmente un caudal muy débil, pero que ha sido causa de graves inundaciones. El Onyar, más que el Ter, es el río de la ciudad. En la franja derecha, entre el antiguo arenal y el promontorio, creció la ciudad antigua, romana o feudal correspondiente a la Girona más propiamente clerical. Cuando el rey catalán sacó a la venta los terrenos del arenal, adelgazando el cauce del Onyar, la población burguesa y artesana pudo ocupar esta parte de la ciudad que corresponde hoy al punto más bullicioso: la rambla y los estrechos y comerciales callejones, más o menos perpendiculares o paralelos a ella, que conectan con la plaza del *Vi* (vino), donde está el ayuntamiento y el teatro, y con la calle de *Ciutadans* (ciudadanos), que había sido la ruta principal de la ciudad y que conserva algunas casas nobles (entre ellas la ya citada Fontana d'Or).

La muralla de la ciudad modeló el lecho actual del río durante un tiempo. Más tarde, en el otoño de la edad media, esta frontera fue superada y creado el barrio del Mercadal, con la erección de diversos conventos que contaban con importantes huertas regadas por una acequia que, proveniente del Ter, todavía hoy desemboca en el Onyar. El agua de esta acequia, llamada Monar, fue decisiva en la configuración de la ciudad. En efecto, después de la desamortización, este espacio urbano cambió totalmente su fisonomía:

los conventos fueron destruidos y en su lugar apareció, gracias a la importante corriente de la acequia, la industria y el primer ensanche moderno de la ciudad. El barrio del Mercadal, que también había sido amurallado, marca la dimensión de la ciudad antigua. Con la vía del tren ya en uso, a principios del siglo XX, las murallas, que habían sido desbordadas por muchos arrabales, fueron eliminadas y substituidas por una gran avenida que significó el despegue de la ciudad contemporánea.

El agua del Onyar, primero como frontera y después como eje, define, pues, el popularismo burgués de la ciudad antigua, de la misma manera que la energía de la acequia (que ahora alimenta y embellece la parte central del tramo urbano del Onyar) abre el destino de la ciudad moderna. La convergencia de las aguas (las del Ter, que se está convirtiendo en eje de la ciudad futura, y las del Güell, Onyar y Galligants) es, por otro lado, causante de dos características climáticas de la ciudad: la humedad y la frecuencia de las nieblas, que fueron ingrediente de la leyenda de una Girona melancólica, otoñal y decadente a la que ya nos hemos referido.

Los puentes y pasadizos que cruzan el Onyar colaboran en el pintoresquismo típico de este eje fluvial: desde ellos, las visiones de la colosal monumentalidad de la catedral y de Sant Feliu son de un efectismo teatral. La reforma y coloración de las casas de la ribera del Onyar permite una estampa italianizante, casi florentina, y responde a la misma voluntad de renovar lo antiguo de que hablábamos al principio: una estetizante manera de depurar la historia. Lo que fueron casas humildes ahora son la base pintoresca y divertida sobre la que se alza el colosalismo artístico y religioso de la ciudad. Las casas del Onyar ofrecen, pues, una lectura alegre y bulliciosa del pasado: amenizan el rigor monumental y almibaran o desdramatizan el excesivo peso ideológico que el pasado impone a la ciudad contemporánea. Complemento ideal del divertimento de las casa del Onyar son los paseos comerciales paralelos a este tramo del río: la Rambla, que funciona como el gran salón de la vida social doméstica, con sus terrazas burguesas y su mercadillo sabatino de flores; y la calle de Santa Clara, en el lado contrario, que con su acentuado diseño y su refinamiento comercial, se ha convertido en avanzadilla del nuevo mito que presenta una Girona alegre, complacida, elegante y un poco vanidosa.

Entre la parte baja, la del eje del Onyar, que define una Girona burguesa y popular, y la parte alta, monumental y religiosa, existe un desnivel real y simbólico que salvan las calles empinadas y, muy especialmente, las escaleras. La geografía abstracta de Girona recuerda a los teatros griegos: una súbita gradería montañosa alzada sobre una ancha llanura.
Las escaleras son, por lo tanto, un ingrediente primordial de la ciudad antigua y ayudan de manera muy relevante a darle un aire escenográfico. Las hay humildes y entrañables, como las de *la Llebre* (de la liebre); húmedas y oscuras, de un ambiente cerrado y opresivo, como las de *Cúndaro* y *Sant Llorenç*. Algunas se alzan en un silencioso ambiente pétreo (*Escuela Pía*), otras, en elegante armonía, como las de *la Pera*. Aunque las más célebres son de un efectismo espacial extraordinario.
La impresionante escalinata de la catedral (alzándose en una plaza, que parece de diminutas dimensiones, para culminar en la visión ciclópea de la catedral) es uno de los mayores espectáculos pétreos que puedan observarse en ciudad alguna, muy especialmente si se desemboca en ella desde la estrechísima calle de la Força. La plaza de la Catedral con su singular escalera es uno de los espectáculos barrocos de la ciudad: un contraste impactante de espacios y volúmenes. La otra gran estampa barroca de Girona está en la cuesta (*pujada*) de Sant Domènec; allí, las escaleras se bifurcan teatralmente: una asciende con suavidad pasando por debajo de la fascinante arcada de un palacio renacentista (Palau d'Agullana), mientras que la principal sube decididamente hacia la gran fachada barroca de la iglesia de Sant Martí. El efecto es menos espectacular que el de la catedral, pero el juego barroco de contrastes es mucho más sutil, gracias, en parte, al dislocamiento de la perspectiva, ya que el palacio Agullana altera la limpia visión del templo.

Contiene Girona otros muchos aspectos de interés. En la ciudad antigua y, también, naturalmente, en la ciudad moderna. Bien es verdad, sin embargo, que los sucesivos ensanches modernos no hacen honor a la belleza que la historia, despojada de su dramatismo, ha legado a la ciudad. Y ello a pesar de los enormes y visibles esfuerzos de depuración y dignificación que se han realizado durante los últimos años. La Girona moderna es anodina y creció incomprensiblemente angosta, sin sentido, impulsada sólo por el voraz sentido de la especulación. Ahora es una ciudad limpia, ordenada y con buenos servicios. El esfuerzo del ayuntamiento democrático por dignificar y reunir los fragmentos dispersos de la ciudad es incuestionable. Girona, por demás, se ha convertido en una capital con gancho, que fagocita un importante territorio regional. Sin embargo, a pesar de los esfuerzos, en la ciudad moderna son escasos los puntos en que la gracia urbana se presenta con la fuerza del casco antiguo. Habría que destacar, en todo caso, lo que se salvó de la obra del arquitecto Masó (Farinera Teixidor, Casa de la Punxa) y el parque de la Devesa (dehesa) una impresionante arboleda situada en la ribera del Ter que fue, según la leyenda, plantada por los soldados de Napoleón. La zona del Ter, a la altura de la Devesa, se está configurando como nuevo eje: el palacio de ferias, la rotunda geometría del pabellón deportivo, el formidable nuevo puente sobre el río, el parque fluvial creado en esta zona y la espectacular entrada viaria a la ciudad conforman un nuevo y atractivo urbanismo de futuro. también en el campus de Montilivi (UdG) han aparecido signos de potente modernidad. Empieza en Girona, pues, a ser posible el entusiasmo del poeta J.V. Foix, que exclamaba: “Me exalta lo nuevo y me enamora lo viejo”. ❧

6 Estela hebraica
Hebrew stele
Hebräische Grabsäule

GIRONA

Antoni Puigverd

The weight of history hangs heavily over Girona. Two thousand long years of history are condensed within its splendid stone body, yet they have not left an impression of fatigue nor urban decrepitude. They were two thousand years of hardship and suffering, two thousand years of resistance which were qualified as heroic by both romantics and traditionalists, but today are observed as the inevitable and painful signs of the hardness of those times.

Throughout its history, Girona has had to face many military invasions, sieges, bombardments, fires, floods, famine, drought and epidemics. History has been enormously and insidiously cruel to this city, to an extent that is hard to comprehend in the light of its present day bonanza. The city was slow in growing, as each attempt at expansion was thwarted by these historic cruelties, leaving it weakened and damaged time and time again. Only the arrival of industrialisation in the 19th century allowed for a certain demographic growth. The expansive profile as regional capital, apparent to the contemporary visitor, is a product of recent times. During the last decades, thanks to significant immigration and, also, to a linking of cultural, administrative and commercial factors, Girona has been transformed into a vivacious, dynamic and attractive city that has overcome its ancestral mishaps with surprising goodwill, optimum energy, and with a passion that contains much of the Mediterranean spirit and maintains with the past a merely aesthetic relationship.

It would seem, therefore, that history is compensating the city for its many centuries of privation and misfortune. In fact, all the tragedies of the past are being transformed into beauty, as is symbolically represented by the conversion of the area at the foot of the old city walls (once emblems of past afflictions), and now agreeable leisure itineraries from where the city can be observed, growing outwards, fired by new energy, retrieving the landmarks of the past, its true soul, to the satisfaction of citizens and visitors alike.

Thus, tragedy makes way for beauty. Just as religion makes way for culture. The religious component is, along with the military factor, fundamental to the historic configuration of the city. Any visitor can perceive at first glance the importance of Girona's ecclesiastical buildings, among which the cathedral (whose colossal nave is the largest existing Gothic space without supporting columns), is the outstanding feature. Although, initially, Girona was a triangular military fortification, it was able to overcome the avatars of time after the fall of the Roman Empire owing to its condition of episcopal see. Being the capital of an ecclesiastical region enabled the city to survive the historic events that brought about the disappearance of sites of such importance as the well-established Greco-Roman city of Empúries.

Girona was the bishop's city, a qualification immediately apparent to all those who wander through the streets, such is the density of ecclesiastical monuments concentrated in the historic city centre; a qualification that even influenced the structure of medieval property and came to characterise the city's cultural climate until well into the 20th century. Girona has been, in fact, according to many of its chroniclers, a clerical city. Canons, archpriests, friars and seminarians, clergymen of all kinds have always abounded in the streets and have defined the social and philosophical profile of a city long considered conservative, discreet and devout.

Suddenly, however, the clergymens' city, the clerical capital, has been transformed into an artistic capital, a place of culture. Religiosity, in accordance with the liberal and secular spirit of the age, has moved away from urban centres and flourishes, as it may, within the intimate confines of its believers. The influence of the bishop or the clergy, the weight of Catholic doctrine, is no longer measured in terms of society, but in terms of the individual. In virtue of this change, the Catholic heritage, emblem of the city over the ages, is being converted almost exclusively into an artistic heritage, although the amortisation of church posessions gave rise, in the 18th century, to the neglect of many monuments which suffered much regrettable degradation due to enforced civil or military usage.

At the present time, the most symbolic religious buildings share both relgious and artistic significance. This is, naturally, the case of the imposing cathedral of Roman origin, Gothic nave and Baroque façade, and also the late-Gothic Sant Feliu collegiate, whose needle-shaped tower conforms, along with the cathedral, the city's most emblematic symbol. These pages are not the ideal place to ponder at length on the many artistic values confined within these two great temples - values which cover a wide range of periods and styles. It would, however, be unforgivable not to mention at least those of greatest artistic worth: the important Roman sarcophagus; the 14th century reclining alabaster Christ, or the neo-Classical chapel of Sant Narcís, found in the Sant Feliu collegiate and, within the cathedral, the monumental weightlessness of the nave where the imposing mass of stone is alleviated by the soft light filtered through the multicoloured glass; the ancient 11th century altar; the 15th century catedra stone (popularly known as the Carlomagno); the sarcophagi, altarpieces and medieval ornamentations; the riotous Baroque retables and, above all, the three essential elements that justify a visit to the adjoining musuem: the cloister, elegant, archaic and welcoming with the magnificent Carlomagno tower which belonged to the old Romanesque church; the famous *Tapestry of the Creation,* dating from the 11th-12th centuries, crowning jewel of the museum, (this unique work represents the medieval cosmovision of life and time by means of a curious mixture of images elaborated in fascinating coloured wools); and, finally, the *Beatus,* a 10th century codex manuscript with extraordinary miniatures by Emeterio and Eude.

Whereas, in the cathedral and the Sant Feliu collegiate, it is still possible to reconcile the experience of Catholic life with that of a strictly cultural nature, in many other religious buildings the reconversion has been complete, bringing with it the loss of religious significance so that the ancient stones now merely reflect the cultural symbolism proper to the present day. The following are some examples of this: the beautiful Romanesque monastery of Sant Pere de Galligants, seat of the archaeological museum (where important funeral steles found in the old Jewish cemetery are preserved); the delightful Sant Nicolau chapel, very near Sant Pere, a Romanesque recint where avant-garde works of art are now shown; the episcopal palace itself, adjoined to the cathedral and converted (on the instance of Bishop Camprodon and aided by public administration), into an important museum, (the *Md'A*) that houses, among other collections, a superb compilation of carvings and religious sculptures from the Romanesque and Gothic periods; the *la Merçè* cultural centre (current promotor of intellectual activities and seat of the art school) which has transformed the old church of the Mercedarian friars into a theatre-auditorium open to both classical and modern works. Within this ensemble of religious buildings converted for secular ends, the convent of the Dominicans finally stands out in the lovely plaça de Sant Domènec. It has been almost fully rebuilt under an audacious architectural revision as the arts faculty of the young university (*UdG*). While restoration of the splendid cloisters and the convent church are still pending, this is probably the last of the medieval buildings remaining in the city to still retain an air of romantic ruin.

This change of usage and meaning of the architectural heritage has a curious parallel in the rescue operation carried out in the old Jewish quarter, situated quite close to the cathedral in the depths of the old city. Despite widespread beliefs, the Jewish quarter, as far as it architecture is concerned, is not of Hebrew origin. When the community of cathedral canons was created in the 9th century, many clergymen moved their residence from the cathedral and the buildings they vacated were sold to Hebrew families from the neighbouring villages. Reports of the existence of this Jewish quarter can be found as far back as 1160 A.D. Until the end of the 15th century, when the Jews were expelled from the Iberian peninsula, their quarter in Girona was, after Barcelona, the largest of all Catalunya, partly due to its size and dynamism (about 300 families during its most splendid period), but, above all, owing to the prestige of its cabalistic school. The *Bonastruc ça Porta* centre, that takes its name from the greatest philosopher of this school, aims to promote knowledge of the intellectual apportation of Girona's Jews and, at the same time, the recognition of the way of life and architecture of this quarter of sinuous, dark alleways where time appears to have stood still for centuries.

The conservation of the Jewish quarter is yet another sign of the conversion of a painful past (it was frequently under siege), into an enlightened present. At the same time, it is also a sign of the conversion of a religious environment into an environment of reflection, artistic beauty and cultural memory.

If the architectural heritage of religious origin plays such a decisive role in accentuating the city's trends, it stands to reason that the secular heritage also forms a crucial part. Thus, the magnificent 14th century building in the cathedral square known as *Pia Almoina,* an immense, spectacular and superb creation of stone adorned by a few gracious, Gothic style windows, is now the seat of the Colegio de Arquitectos. The far-reaching renovation carried out on this building some time ago was precursor of many similar projects. The alliance between modern and traditional architecture, instigated in Girona with the *Pia Almoina* restoration, may appear as a purely aesthetic option, although, in some cases, it has its practical side. In any event, it is always the answer to a necessary question: how should we save a building which has been degraded by carelessness and neglect? To re-create what has been lost, should we follow historic criteria, or contemporary innovation?

These are universal dilemmas which, in this city, have received different answers at different times, depending upon the circumstances of the moment. For this reason, in some churches (such as the aforementioned Sant Pere de Galligants), and some secular buildings (*Fontana d'Or,* seat of the Centre Cultural de la Caixa de Girona), traditional rebuilding was the option chosen. The restoration work promoted, more recently, by the Universitat de Girona, (the case of Sant Domènec, for example), is of a more audacious nature, in accordance with the idea of alliance between past and future. The most relevant case is, in this sense, the *les Àligues* building in the plaça de Sant Domènec. Seat of the university at the time of the Austrias dynasty, it had suffered an almost definitive process of degradation and has been saved as the rectory of the new university. This reform brings together voluminous geometrical cement forms with the golden stones of the old Renaissance façade. A look into the interior patio, from the Renaissance portal, offers one of the best visions of this amalgamation:

NAVE 2

the walls of the far chapel have been crowned with glass and cement, and the resulting combination is harmonious yet surprising, daring yet respectful, ancient yet modern.

In general terms, the old centre of Girona is being renovated following these guidelines of alliance, and not only in its architectural or urban aspect. Since the new university opted to situate some of its faculties and facilities within the old city, the recuperation (and consequent revision) of historic Girona has advanced at a healthy pace. This has, without doubt, acted as a *coup de grâce* for the fatalism of decadence against which both the municipal authorities and local society have fought with a not always ready enthusiasm. Throughout history, both Girona's resident poets, and those who came to visit, created the legend of the sad city, engrossed in itelf, damp, devout and in ruins. A phantasmagoric Girona, lost within its own time-bend, exuding dreams of stones and mist, the slow moving disaster of history, weary monuments, the melancholy of loss.

To put a stop to this decadent inertia was no easy feat as the city, in the second half of the 19th century when the lower walls were demolished, grew and expanded in all directions. The old neighbouring villages of Santa Eugènia, Sant Daniel and la Rodona were absorbed by the city. Some of the streets, such as carrer Nou, Marqués de Camps, l'Havana petita, la Creu, Sant Narcís, Palau petit, were widened, and, more recently, new private and public developments have been built. Each new expansion of the dynamic, contemporary Girona implied a new confirmation of decadence on the city's historic nucleus. Cultural movements such as Fontana d'Or, Colegi d'Arquitectes, la Merçè, Md'A, Museu d'Història, Centre Bonastruc ça Porta, could not do enough, nor could the recreational and commercial iniciatives of bars, shops and restaurants. Only the great revolution brought about by the presence of the university sufficed to revitalise the hard core of the old city. Thanks to this, young people and visitors alike are the protagonists of the rebirth of this ancient ensemble with its labyrinth of narrow streets, secluded squares and abundant religious monuments. At the same time, a common front has been formed between academic life, commercial iniciative, the effort of cultural institutions and economic growth. More and more bars, restaurants, specialised or unusual shops are opened. Art galleries return, antique shops rub shoulders with designer stores, travel agents include the visit to old Girona among the most important of its kind in Catalunya, and the real estate market has taken the first steps towards reclaiming parts of the old city from its ancestral fate, an example of which is the Pou Rodó, the old red-light district. Slowly the legend of old Girona, a drowsy and melancholic city, makes way for the impression of the cultured, refined and elegant Girona of today. Both images are inexact; the old may have produced better literature, but it was destined for ruin: the new may be less spontaneous, but it stands in favour of regeneration. The old Europe of cultured leisure has, in Girona, an advantaged and studious pupil.

X

Girona, of course, is comprised of more than just the old city. To define it, however, one returns inevitably to the symbol of the old stones. Weary and spent, or envigorated by contemporary changes, the stone is protagonist of the current renovation and also an emblem of the past, a memory of origin. If the Romans built a triangular settlement when founding the city, it was because an abundance of nummulite stone was to be found on the promontories over the river Onyar where they erected the fortification. A new development not far from the city walls bears the name *les Pedreres* (the quarries), and, on the promontories that overlook the city, remains of ancient excavation sites may still be seen. The people who have lived, and live today, in this city have left their mark upon it, but the stones are witnesses to their footprints. Stone is not, however, the only symbolic component. Water is, too. The Romans, for defensive purposes, built their fortification on a strategically placed promontory at the confluence of rivers and streams. The river Ter reaches its final stretch and receives, at a point close to the Sant Feliu quarter, water from the Galligants and Güell streams (although the latter has now been diverted), and the Onyar, a river of extremes whose normally modest flow has been known to cause devastating floods. The Onyar, rather than the Ter, is the city's river. The right bank, between the sandbank and the promontory, is where the old city grew in both Roman and feudal times. When the Catalan king put the sandbank lands up for sale, thus reducing the flow of the Onyar, this part of the city was occupied by the bourgeoisie and craftsmen, and is now its liveliest area: the Rambla and the narrow, commercial streets that run perpendicular and parallel to it and connect with the *plaça del Ví*, site of the Town hall and theatre, and *carrer Ciutadans*, once the city's main thoroughfare where many noble mansions still stand today, among them the aforementioned Fontana d'Or.

The city walls modelled the course of the river for some time. Later, towards the end of the Middle Ages, this barrier was overcome and the Mercadal quarter was founded. Here, several convents were built, and their considerable vegetable gardens were watered by an irrigation channel that had its origin in the river Ter and today still flows into the Onyar. The water from this stream, the Monar, was decisive in the configuration of the city. In fact, after the desamortisation, this part of the town underwent drastic change: the convents were destroyed and, thanks to the important flow of the stream, industry and the first development of the city took place. The Mercadal quarter, that had also been walled, defines the limit of the old city. At the beginning of the 20th century, with trains already running, new suburbs had sprung up beyond the walls which were eliminated and substituted by a wide avenue whose creation gave rise to the contemporary city as we know it today.

The waters of the Onyar, first as a barrier and later as a focal point, therefore define the bourgeois character of the old city, just as the energy of the stream (that now waters and embellishes the Onyar's urban, central stretch), set in motion the destiny of the modern city. The conflux of the waters (the Ter, increasingly important to the city's future, and the Güell, Onyar and Galligants) is, on the other hand, the cause of the city's climatic characteristics: the dampness and the frequent mist, intrinsic ingredients of Girona's melancholy, autumnal and decadent reputation.

The bridges and catwalks that span the Onyar add to the picturesque image of the flowing river. From them, the views of the colossal monument of the cathedral and Sant Feliu have a theatrical effect. The reforms and multicoloured refurbishing of the riverside houses offer an Italianised, almost Florentine, appearance and follow the same criteria mentioned at the beginning: an aesthetic way of exonerating history. What were once humble dwellings now form the picturesque and amusing base upon which the city's artistic and religious greatness has been founded. The houses along the Onyar offer a lively and animated interpretation of the past: they alleviate the seriousness of the monuments and give relief to the excessive weight of piety imposed by the past on the modern city. An ideal complement to the colourful riverside houses are the commercial streets that run parallel to this stretch of the river: the Rambla, scenario of local social life with its terraces and Saturday flower market, and carrer Santa Clara on the other side, where the emphasis on design and commercial refinement have placed it at the forefront of the Girona of today – cheerful, satisfied, elegant and somewhat vain.

Between the lower part, along the banks of the Onyar (where popular middle class Girona is defined), and the higher part, steeped in religiosity and monuments, there exists a both symbolic and real difference of level which is overcome by steeply sloping streets and, particularly, flights of steps. Girona's abstract geography resembles that of a Greek theatre: an abrupt grandstand rising above the ample plain. The steps are, therefore, a primordial ingredient of the old city and go a long way in conferring this theatrical impression upon it. Some of them, such as the *de la Llebre* steps, are humble, damp and dark, and others are closed and oppressive as in the cases of *Cundaro* and *Sant Llorenç*. Some rise in a silent, stony atmosphere (*Escola Pia*), and others in elegant harmony, such as *la Pera*. The most renowned have an extraordinarily spacious effect. The impressive staircase of the cathedral, rising from a square of apparently diminutive proportions to culminate in the cyclopean image of the temple, is one of the greatest stone ensembles to be seen in any city, particularly when entering the square from the narrow *carrer de la Força*. The cathedral square, with its singular flight of steps is one of the city's leading Baroque spectacles: a stunning contrast between space and volume. Girona's other great Baroque hallmark is the *pujada de Sant Domènec* with its theatrically bifurcated steps. One flight rises gradually, passing beneath the fascinating arch of a Renaissance palace (Palau d'Agullana), while the principal flight rises decidedly towards the great Baroque façade of the church of Sant Martí. The effect here is less spectacular than at the cathedral, but the play on ornate contrasts is far more subtle thanks, in part, to the shift in perspective caused by the Agullana palace which partially impedes the view of the temple.

Within Girona, many other interesting aspects are to be found in both the old city and the new. It is true, however, that the successive modern developments do not do justice to the beauty which history, now undramatised, has bequeathed to the city. Despite the enormous and apparent efforts that have been made, and the steps that have been taken during the past few years, the growth of the new Girona is anodine and incomprehensibly constricted, without direction and anarchic, driven only by voracious speculation. Today it is a clean and orderly city with good services, proof of the unquestionable endeavours of the municipal authorities who have also done much to integrate the more disperse fragments of the city. At the same time, Girona has become an enticing city under whose spell the surrounding region has succumbed. Nevertheless, despite all these endeavours, few places in the modern town have achieved a degree of urban grace comparable to the old. As exceptions to this generalisation we would mention: what remains of the work of the architect Masó (Farinera Teixidor, Casa de la Punxa) and the Devesa area, an impressive woodland park which, according to tradition was planted by Napoleon's army. The area around the Ter as it passes the Devesa, is beginning to take shape as a new centre: the trade fair hall, the resounding geometry of the sports pavilion, the tremendous new bridge over the river, the fluvial park and the spectacular roadways into the city, comprise an attractive complex of futuristic urban planning. More signs of this vigorous modernity are also making their appearance at the Montilivi campus (UdG). Here, then, in Girona, we may share in the enthusiasm of the poet J.V. Foix when he exclaimed: "I am exalted by the new and enamoured of the old".

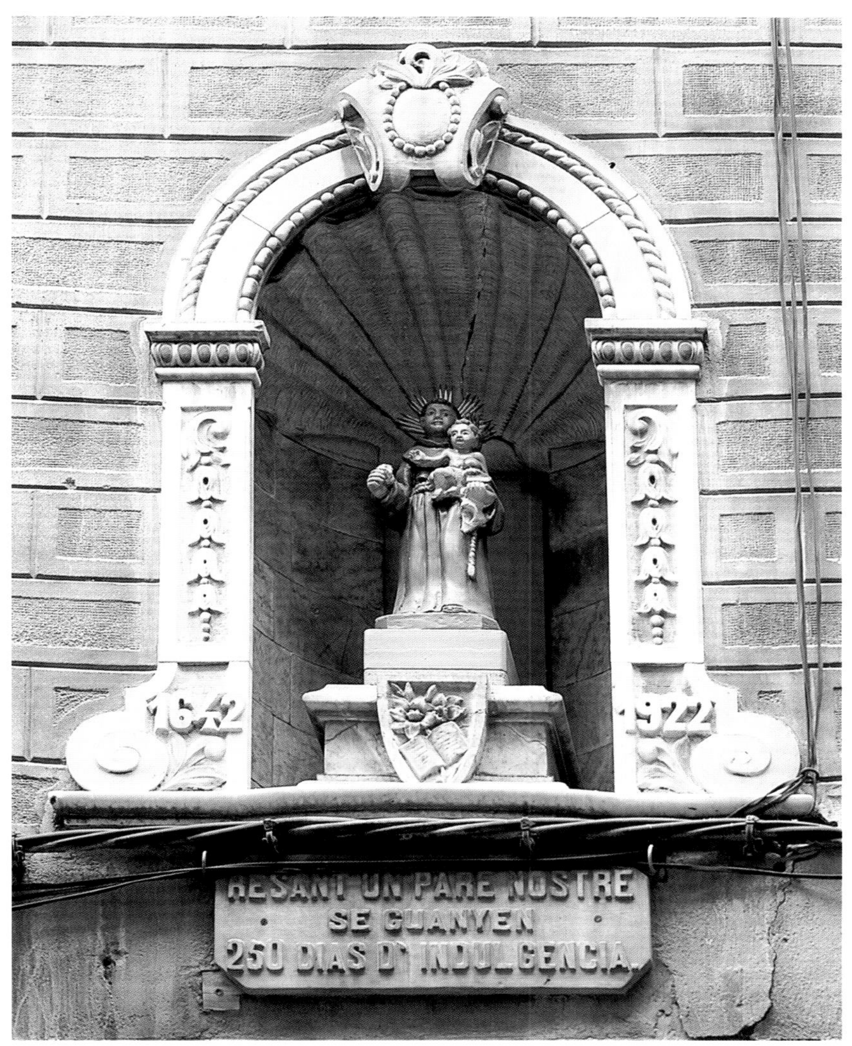

▲
7 Levítica
Levitical
Levitisch

GIRONA

Antoni Puigverd

Auf der Stadt Girona liegt das Gewicht ihrer Geschichte. Zweitausend Jahre sind in ihrem verdichteten und herrlichem Körper aus Stein zusammengefaßt, die dennoch nicht den Eindruck von Müdigkeit oder städtischen Altersbeschwerden hinterlassen haben. Zweitausend Jahre eines mit dem Tode ringenden Widerstandes, den die Romantiker und die Castizos (Spanier reiner Abkunft) als heldenhaft betrachteten und der uns Menschen der heutigen Zeit ein unvermeidliches und schmerzliches Zeichen für die Grausamkeit der Zeiten erscheint.

Girona mußte im Laufe seiner Geschichte vielen militärischen Invasionen, harten Belagerungen, Bombardements, Bränden, Überschwemmungen, Hungersnöten, Durst und ansteckenden Krankheiten widerstehen. Die Stadt wurde wiederholt übel zugerichtet; jeder Wachstumsversuch wurde durch einen neuen Aderlaß vereitelt. Nur der Beginn der Industrialisierung während des XIX. Jahrhunderts erlaubte einen leichten demographischen Anstieg. Girona präsentiert sich heutzutage dem Besucher als Hauptstadt einer Provinz mit expansivem Profil. Dank einer starken Einwanderung, aber auch einer Verkettung kultureller, administrativer und kommerzieller Faktoren hat sich Girona während der letzten Jahrzehnte tatsächlich in eine lebendige und attraktive Stadt verwandelt, die ihre alten Gebrechen mit einer erstaunlichen Heiterkeit und einer Leidenschaft überwindet, die sehr mediterran ist und die zu der tragischen Vergangenheit in einem rein ästhetischem Verhältnis steht.

Anscheinend hat die Geschichte die Stadt für die langen Jahrhunderte an Schicksalsschlägen und Unglück entschädigt. Die Tragödie wurde in Schönheit verwandelt. Symbol dafür ist die Umwandlung des am Fuße der alten Stadtmauer gelegenen Stadtteiles: Erinnerung an die Leiden der Vergangenheit und heutzutage eine Promenade anmutiger, touristischer Wege, von denen aus man zusehen kann, wie die Stadt nach Außen wächst und dabei zur Freude ihrer Anwohner und Besucher wieder zur Vergangenheit und ihrer tiefsten Seele zurückfindet.

Die Tragik wird so zum Zeugen der Schönheit. Das religiöse Element läßt dem kulturellen Element den Vorrang. Religion und Militär waren entscheidend für die historische Gestaltung der Stadt. Unter den religiösen Bauten sticht die Kathedrale mit ihrem riesigem Kirchenschiff hervor; es handelt sich dabei um den größten existierenden, gotischen Raum, der nicht von Säulen gestützt wird. Obwohl Girona ursprünglich eine dreieckige, militärische Festung war, die von den Römern gegründet wurde (auch wenn einige Historiker glauben, daß die Stadt um einiges älter ist und Beweise beibringen, daß der Ortsname keltischen Ursprungs ist), so ist eines sicher: Als die Welt der Römer verschwand, widerstand die Stadt der Verwirrung der Zeiten dank ihrer Stellung eines Bischofssitzes. So überlebte sie in einem historischen Kontext, in dem sogar große Städte mit einiger Bedeutung im Handel und einer alten griechisch-römischen Tradition wie Ampurias verschwanden.

Eine große Zahl kirchlicher Bauten drängen sich im historischen Zentrum der Stadt. Durch diese Spezialisierung auf die Religion wurde auch die Struktur des urbanen Eigentums im Mittelalter gestaltet und das kulturelle Klima der Stadt bis weit in das XX. Jahrhundert hinein charakterisiert. Girona war tatsächlich, wie es viele Kommentatoren und Geschichtsdeuter gesagt hatten, eine "klerikale" Stadt. Stiftsherren, Erzpriester, Ordensmönche und Seminaristen, Geistliche aller Klassen bevölkerten die Straßen und definierten den sozialen und geistigen Charakter einer Stadt, die lange im Rufe stand, konservativ, geistreich und fromm zu sein.

Heute ist Girona eine von der Kunst geprägte Stadt, eine kulturelle Heimat. Aufgrund des liberalen und verweltlichten Geistes der heutigen Zeit hat die Religiosität den städtischen Raum verlassen und gedeiht in den intimen Kreisen der Gläubigen. Der Einfluß des Bischofs oder des Klerus, das Gewicht der katholischen Lehre, kann nun nicht mehr in sozialen Maßstäben gemessen werden, sondern nur noch in individuellen. Aufgrund dieser sozialen Veränderung wird aus dem katholischen Erbe, Kennzeichen der Stadt durch Jahrhunderte, ein fast ausschließlich kulturelles Erbe. Allerdings verursachte die Säkularisierung von Kirchengut schon während des XVIII. Jahrhunderts die Verwahrlosung vieler Gebäude, die aufgrund erzwungener ziviler oder militärischer Nutzungen sehr abgenutzt wurden.

Heutzutage haben die wichtigsten religiösen Gebäude sowohl eine katholische als auch eine künstlerische Bedeutung. Das ist der Fall der beeindruckenden Kathedrale, die romanischen Ursprungs ist, während das Kirchenschiff gotisch und die Fassade barock ist; und der Stiftskirche von Sant Feliu, ein spätgotisches Bauwerk, deren nichtvollendeter Spitzturm zusammen mit der Kathedrale das typischste Wahrzeichen der Stadt darstellen. Das ist jetzt nicht der geeignetste Ort, um die vielen Kunstschätze verschiedener Epochen und Stilrichtungen, die diese beiden großen Kirchen enthalten, zu beschreiben. Doch muß man wenigstens die wichtigsten erwähnen: die berühmten römischen Sarkophage, der ruhende Christus aus Alabaster (XIV. Jahrhundert) oder die interessante, klassizistische Kapelle des Sant Narcís, die sich in der Stiftskirche von Sant Feliu befinden. Und in der Kathedrale: der riesige, schwerelose gotische Raum, in dem die beeindruckende Größe des Steines durch die Sanftheit des Lichtes, das sich durch die bunten Glasfenster filtert, nuanciert wird; der antike Altarstein des großen Altares (XI. Jahrhundert); die Steinkathedrale, die im Volksmund Carlomagno (Karl, der Große) genannt wird (XIV. Jahrhundert), die mittelalterlichen Sarkophage, Altargemälde und Verzierungen; die barocken Altargemälde, und vor allem die drei wichtigsten Elemente, die einen Besuch des an die Kathedrale angeschlossenen Museums rechtfertigen: der Kreuzgang mit seiner archaischen Eleganz, von dem aus sich der prächtige Turm erhebt, der so wie die romanische Kirche Carlosmagno genannt wird; der berühmte *Tapiç de la Creació* (Teppich der Schöpfung) (XI. - XII. Jahrhundert) mit einer einzigartigen Stickerei, die mit Garnen in wundervollen Farben und durch eine interessante Mischung von Bildern die mittelalterliche Weltanschauung darstellt; und der *Beatus,* eine handgeschriebene Vorschriftensammlung (X. Jahrhundert) mit ausserordentlichen Miniaturen von Emeterio und Eude.

Während man in der Kathedrale und in der Stiftskirche von Sant Feliu das katholische Erlebnis mit dem rein kulturellen verbinden kann, so ist dies in vielen anderen Gebäuden nicht mehr der Fall: Die religiöse Bedeutung ging verloren und die alten Steine drücken nur noch die kulturelle Symbolik der städtischen Gegenwart aus. Beispiele dafür sind das schöne romanische Kloster Sant Pere de Galligants, Sitz des archäologischen Museums (in dem wichtige Grabsäulen vom alten, jüdischen Friedhof aufbewahrt werden); die Kapelle Sant Nicolau in der Nähe von Sant Pere, ein wundervoller, romanischer Raum, in dem Kunst der Avantgarde untergebracht ist; der Bischofspalast selbst, der sich an die Kathedrale anlehnt und der aufgrund der Bitten des Bischofs Camprodon und durch die öffentliche Verwaltung in ein Museum verwandelt wurde (das *Md'A*), in dem unter anderem eine prachtvolle Sammlung von religiösen Bildhauerarbeiten und Skulpturen der romanischen und gotischen Periode enthalten ist; das Kulturzentrum *la Mercè,* gegenwärtiger Anreiz für das intellektuelle Leben und Sitz der Schule der Schönen Künste, der aus der alten Kirche der Mönche des Ordens der Mercè ein Theaterauditorium gemacht hat, offen sowohl für den Klassizismus als auch für die Avantgarde. Unter diesem Komplex von religiösen Bauten mit kultureller Nutzung sticht das Konvent der Dominikaner an dem Platz Sant Domènec hervor, dessen größter Teil in einer gewagten, architektonischen Revision als Fakultät der Geisteswissenschaften der jungen Universität (*UdG*) wiedererrichtet wurde. Noch nicht begonnen wurde die Restaurierung des bewundernswerten Kreuzganges und der Kirche dieses Konventes, der das letzte mittelalterliche Gebäude mit der Atmosphäre einer romanischer Ruine sein dürfte, das es noch in der Stadt gibt.

Dieser Wandel im Gebrauch und Bedeutung des religiösen, architektonischen Nachlasses zeigt einen interessanten Parallelismus zur Rettung des alten Judenviertels auf, das in der Nähe der Kathedrale mitten in der Altstadt liegt. Im Gegensatz zu der Meinung vieler ist das Judenviertel architektonisch nicht hebräischen Ursprungs. Als die Ordensregel der Kathedrale (IX. Jahrhundert) gegründet wurde, verlegten verschiedene Kleriker ihren Sitz in die Kathedrale, und die Gebäude, die sie vorher benutzt hatten, wurden an hebräische Familien aus den umliegenden Dörfern verkauft. Dieses Judenviertel wurde schon im Jahre 1160 erstmals erwähnt. Bis zur Vertreibung der Juden von der Iberischen Halbinsel Ende des XV. Jahrhunderts, war die jüdische Gemeinde von Girona aufgrund ihrer Größe und Dynamik (im Moment ihrer größten Bedeutung um die 300 Familien), aber vor allem wegen des Ruhmes ihrer kabbalistischen Schule, neben der von Barcelona eine der wichtigsten in ganz Katalonien. Das Zentrum Bonastruc ça Porta, das den Namen des größten Denkers dieser Schule wieder aufgreift, hat sich zum Ziel gesetzt, das Wissen über den intellektuellen Beitrag der Juden Gironas zu vertiefen und gleichzeitig die Erkundung der Lebensformen und der intimen Architektur dieses Viertels voller feuchter und dunkler Gassen, in denen scheinbar die Zeit angehalten hat, zu fördern. Die Rettung des Judenviertels ist ein anderes Symbol für die Umwandlung einer schmerzlichen Vergangenheit (das Judenviertel wurde wiederholt überfallen) in eine kulturelle Gegenwart. So ist es ebenfalls ein Symbol für die Umwandlung einer religiösen Umgebung in einen Ort der Meditation, der künstlerischen Schönheit und des kulturellen Zeugnisses.

Da der architektonische Nachlaß religiösen Ursprungs so entscheidend dazu beiträgt, den kulturellen Anspruch der Stadt herauszustellen, ist es logisch, daß der zivile Nachlaß auch diesem Modell entspricht. Ein Beispiel dafür ist das prächtige Gebäude Pia Almoina (XIV. Jahrhundert) am Platz der Kathedrale. Mit seiner riesigen, beeindruckenden und schlichten Fassadenfront aus Stein, nur durch einige Fenster von zierlicher, gotischer Gestalt verschönert, ist es heute Sitz der Berufsgenossenschaft der Architekten und wurde schon vor längerer Zeit einer aufsehenerregenden Umgestaltung unterworfen, die vielen darauffolgenden Umformungen von städtischen Bauten vorausgegangen ist. Das Konzept der Synthese zwischen der Modernität und der architektonischen Tradition, das in Girona mit der Restaurierung der Pia Almoina begann, kann als eine rein ästhetische Möglichkeit erscheinen, auch wenn sie manchmal einen praktischen Sinn hat. Auf jeden Fall ist es immer die Antwort auf die unvermeidliche Frage: Wie kann man ein Gebäude retten, das durch Nachlässigkeit und Besitzaufgabe zerstört ist? Soll man das Verlorene einem historischen Kriterium folgend wiederherstellen oder soll man mit einer zeitgenössischen Einstellung erneuern? Auf diese Frage, die sich natürlich nicht nur in Girona stellt, gab es in dieser Stadt verschiedene Antworten je nach dem kulturellen Moment, in dem mit der Rettung des Gebäudes begonnen wurde. So war bei einigen Kirchen (z. B. die Kirche von Sant Pere de Galligants) und einigen zivilen Gebäuden (Fontana d'Or, Sitz des Kulturzentrums der Caixa de Girona), die Antwort die Wiederherstellung. Die Restaurierungen, die von der Universität Girona veranlaßt wurden (z. B. Sant Domènec), wurden vor viel kürzerer Zeit durchgeführt und sind gewagtere Antworten, die die Idee der Synthese zwischen der Vergangenheit und der Zukunft aufgreifen. Das beste Beispiel dafür ist das Gebäude *les Àligues* auf dem Platz Sant Domènec. Zur Zeit der

Habsburger Sitz der Universität und danach fast vollständig verfallen, wurde das Gebäude als Sitz des Rektorates der neuen Universität wiederhergestellt. Dabei wurden voluminöse geometrische Formen aus Zement an die goldenen Steine der alten Renaissancefassade angefügt. Ein Blick in den Innenhof von dem Renaissanceportal aus läßt deutlich die Synthese erkennen: die Wände der Kapelle im Hintergrund wurden mit Glas und Zement bekränzt, die daraus resultierende Kombination ist gleichzeitig harmonisch und überraschend, mutig und rücksichtsvoll, alt und modern.

Die Altstadt von Girona wird im allgemeinen mit diesem Anspruch der Synthese restauriert, und zwar nicht nur im Hinblick auf einzelne Gebäude oder auf den architektonischen und urbanistischen Aspekt. Seitdem die neue Universität sich entschieden hat, einige ihrer Fakultäten und Dienstleistungen in der Altstadt anzusiedeln, hat die Wiederherstellung (und die darausfolgende Revision) des historischen Gironas große Fortschritte gemacht. Das beendet zweifellos die Dekadenz, gegen die die demokratische Stadtverwaltung und die bürgerliche Gesellschaft mit viel Enthusiasmus gekämpft haben. Tatsächlich haben dieses ganze Jahrhundert lang die in der Stadt lebenden oder besuchende Dichter den Mythos der melancholischen, feuchten, katholischen und zerstörten Stadt Girona geschaffen. Ein gespenstisches, verlorenes Girona, voller Träume aus Stein und Nebel, ein langsamer Schiffbruch der Geschichte, eine müde Monumentalität und Melancholie.

Es war nicht leicht, diese dekadente Stumpfheit zu durchbrechen, da die Stadt in der zweiten Hälfte des XIX. Jahrhunderts seit dem völligen Abbruch der Stadtmauern nach allen Richtungen wächst. Dabei werden zum einen die alten Nachbarorte (Santa Eugènia, Sant Daniel, la Rodona...) miteingeschlossen und zum anderen verschiedene mehr oder weniger konfuse Stadterweiterungen (Carrer Nou, Marqués de Camps, l'Havana Petita, la Creu, Sant Narcís, Palau Petit...) durchgeführt oder, wie in den letzten Jahren, neue private oder öffentliche Siedlungsgebiete verschiedener Kategorie wie Pedreres, Font de la Pólvora, Vilaroja, Montilivi, Palau, Montjuic, Fontajau, Güell geschaffen. Jede Erweiterung des lebhaften, zeitgenössischen Gironas bedeutete für das historische Zentrum eine neue Bestätigung seiner Dekadenz. Die kulturellen Einrichtungen (Fontana d'Or, Colegi d'Arquitectes, la Mercè, Md'A, Museu d'Història, Centre Bonastruc ça Porta) und die Initiativen der Gaststättenbetriebe und Geschäfte reichten nicht aus. Zur Wiederbelebung der Altstadt war die große Umwälzung der Universität notwendig. Ihr ist es zu verdanken, das die Jugend und die Besucher für die Wiedergeburt dieses Viertels mit seinem Labyrinth enger Gassen, intimer Plätze und wichtiger religiöser Bauten so wichtig waren. Andererseits tragen das universitäre Leben, die kommerziellen Initiativen, die kulturelle Anstrengung der Institutionen und die Dynamik der Wirtschaft zur Wiederbelebung bei. Die Zahl der Gaststättenbetriebe und interessanten Geschäfte steigt, es gibt Kunstgalerien, Antiquitätenläden und Designstudios, die Tourismusbranche hat den Besuch der Altstadt Gironas als eine der wichtigsten Altstädte Kataloniens in ihr Programm aufgenommen und der Immobilienmarkt versucht Teile der Altstadt vor der legendären Marginalisierung (El *Pou Rodó*, das alte Viertel der Prostitution) zu retten. Langsam verliert sich der Mythos des alten, verschlafenen und melancholischen Gironas, um für ein kultiviertes und elegantes Girona Platz zu machen. Beide Mythen sind ungenau; das alte Mythos hat vielleicht die bessere Literatur hervorgebracht, aber es handelte von der Zerstörung, und das neue Mythos ist weniger spontan, aber besser für die Wiederherstellung der Altstadt. Das Europa der kulturellen Freizeitgestaltung hat in dem antiken Girona eine begabte Schülerin gefunden.

Natürlich ist Girona viel mehr als nur sein alter Stadtkern. Trotzdem muß man für die Definition der Stadt auf das Symbol der antiken Steine zurückgreifen. Müde und verträumt oder belebt durch den zeitgenössischen Putz ist der Stein der Hauptdarsteller seiner Erneuerung und Symbol für die Vergangenheit: Die Römer erbauten die dreieckige Siedlung, die die Stadt gründete, deswegen, weil in den Vorgebirgen des Flusses Onyar, wo die Festung errichtet wurde, reichlich Gestein vorhanden war. Eine neue Siedlung in der Nähe der Stadtmauer trägt den Namen *Les Pedreres* (der Steinbruch) und in den Vorgebirgen kann man Reste der alten Steinbrüche entdecken. Natürlich wurde die Stadt von den Menschen, die dort leben und lebten, geprägt, aber die Steine sind das Zeugnis ihrer Spuren.

Der Stein ist jedoch nicht das einzige Symbol der Stadt. Auch das Wasser spielt eine wichtige Rolle. Die Römer erbauten ihre Festung in einem Vorgebirge, das strategisch günstig an dem Zusammenfluß von Flüssen und Wildbächen gelegen war: der Ter befindet sich in seinem letztem Abschnitt und nimmt in der Nähe des Viertels Sant Feliu das Wasser von zwei Wildbächen auf, dem Galligants und Güell (der heute umgeleitet ist), und das des Flusses Onyar, ein unberechenbarer Fluß, der normalerweise nur sehr wenig Wasser führt, aber der trotzdem schon schwere Überschwemmungen verursacht hat. Eher als der Ter ist der Onyar der Fluß der Stadt. Auf seiner rechten Seite wuchs die alte, römische oder feudale Stadt, die dem eher klerikalen Girona entsprach. Als der katalanische König die Gebiete der Sandfläche zum Verkauf anbot und das Flußbett des Onyar verschmälerte, konnte die bürgerliche und handwerkliche Bevölkerung diesen Teil der Stadt besiedeln; heute ist es der lebhafteste Stadtteil: die Rambla und die engen Gassen, die perpendikular oder parallel zur Rambla laufen und mit dem *Plaça del Vi* (Platz des Weines) verbinden, wo sich das Rathaus und das Theater befinden, und mit der *Carrer de Ciutadans* (Straße der Bürger), ehemalige Hauptstraße der Stadt mit einigen sehr edlen Bauten, (darunter das erwähnte Gebäude Fontana d'Or). Die Stadtmauer modellierte das heutige

Flußbett eine Zeitlang. Gegen Ende des Mittelalters wurde diese Barriere aufgehoben und das Viertel Mercadal gegründet, in dem sich verschiedene Konvente mit großen Gärten und einem vom Ter gespeisten Bewässerungsgraben befanden. Das Wasser dieses Bewässerungsgraben, der Monar heißt, war entscheidend für die Gestaltung der Stadt. Tatsächlich veränderte dieser Stadtteil nach der Aufhebung der lehensrechtlichen Bindung völlig sein Aussehen; die Konvente wurden zerstört und statt ihrer tauchten dank des beträchtlichen Wasserstroms des Monar die Industrie und die erste, moderne Stadterweiterung der Stadt auf. Das Viertel Mercadal, das auch eine Stadtmauer hatte, markiert die Abmessungen der Altstadt. Zu Beginn des XX. Jahrhunderts, als die Bahnstrecke befahren wurde, wurden die Stadtmauern, die schon durch viele Vorstädte durchbrochen worden waren, abgetragen und durch eine große Allee ersetzt, ein Symbol für den Beginn der zeitgenössischen Stadt.

Das Wasser des Onyar definiert zuerst als Grenze und dann als Achse die bürgerliche Volkstümlichkeit der Altstadt auf die gleiche Weise, wie die Energie des Bewässerungsgrabens (der jetzt den zentralen Teil des Abschnittes des Onyar, der durch die Stadt fließt, nährt und verschönert) die Zukunft der modernen Stadt bestimmt. Der Zusammenfluß der Gewässer (das Wasser des Ter, Achse der zukünftigen Stadt, und das Wasser des Güell, Onyar und Galligants) ist andererseits der Grund für die beiden klimatischen Kennzeichen der Stadt: Feuchtigkeit und häufiger Nebel, Teil der Legende des melancholischen und dekadenten Girona. Die Brücken, die den Onyar kreuzen, tragen zu dem malerischen Aussehen dieser Flußachse bei; von ihnen aus hat der Anblick der monumentalen Kathedrale von Sant Feliu einen theatralen Effekt. Die Renovierung und Farben der Häuser am Ufer des Onyar lassen einen nahezu italienischen Eindruck aufkommen, fast mit Florenz zu vergleichen, und auch hier wollte man das Alte erneuern; eine ästhetisierende Art, die Geschichte zu bereinigen. Das, was einst bescheidene Häuser waren, ist jetzt die pittoreske Grundlage für die die künstlerische und religiöse Großartigkeit der Stadt. Die Häuser am Onyar sind wie eine heitere Lektüre der Vergangenheit, sie gestalten die monumentale Strenge anmutig und entdramatisieren das exzessive ideologische Gewicht der Vergangenheit. Die ideale Ergänzung dieser Häuser am Onyar sind die Geschäftspromenaden, die parallel zu diesem Flußabschnitt verlaufen. Die Rambla, auf der sich das soziale Leben abspielt, mit ihren bürgerlichen Terrassen und dem Blumenmarkt am Samstag, und die elegante Straße Santa Clara auf der anderen Seite tragen zum Mythos vom heiteren, eleganten und ein wenig eitlem Girona bei.

Zwischen dem unteren Teil der Stadt am Onyar, der das bürgerliche und volkstümliche Girona bestimmt, und dem oberen Teil der Stadt, monumental und religiös, besteht eine Ungleichheit, die durch die engen Straßen und besonders durch die Treppen ausgeglichen wird. Die Geographie von Girona erinnert an griechische Theater: Ein Stufengang erhebt sich plötzlich über eine weite Ebene. Die Treppen sind ein wesentliches Element der alten Stadt und tragen in entscheidender Weise zu ihrem bühnenbildmäßigen Charakter bei. Es gibt bescheidene Treppen wie die *De la Llebre;* feuchte und dunkle, mit einer Stimmung von Eingeschlossensein wie die des *Cúndaro* und *Sant Llorenç.* Einige erheben sich in einer steinernen, schweigsamen Umgebung (*Escola Pia*), andere in eleganter Harmonie wie die *De la Pera*. Jedoch die berühmtesten unter ihnen haben eine ganz besondere räumliche Wirkung. Die beeindruckende Freitreppe zur Kathedrale, die von einem scheinbar ganz kleinen Platz aufsteigt, um dann in einem riesenhaften Anblick der Kathedrale ihren Höhepunkt zu finden, ist ein phantastisches, steinernes Schauspiel, ganz besonders, wenn man auf die Treppe von der engen Gasse La Força zukommt. Ein anderes großes, barockes Kennzeichen der Stadt befindet sich in der Pujada de Sant Domènec; hier teilen sich die Treppen theatralisch auf, eine steigt langsam an und verläuft unterhalb der Arkade des Renaissancepalastes (Palau d'Agullana) hindurch, während die andere zu der großen Barockfassade von der Kirche Sant Martí ansteigt. Der Effekt ist nicht ganz so spektakulär wie im Falle der Kathedrale, aber das barocke Spiel mit den Kontrasten ist viel subtiler, teilweise dank der Verschiebung der Perspektive, da der Palast Agullana die Sicht auf den Tempel verändert.

In Girona gibt es sowohl in der Altstadt als auch in der Neustadt viele andere interessante Aspekte. Doch leider machen die wiederholten Stadterweiterungen der Schönheit, die die Geschichte der Stadt verliehen hat, keine Ehre. Und trotz der sichtbaren Anstrengungen zur Verbesserung des Stadtbildes während der letzten Jahre ist das moderne Girona aufgrund der Spekulation nichtssagend und unverständlich eng gewachsen, eine ordentliche Stadt mit guten Dienstleistungen. Die Anstrengungen der demokratischen Stadtverwaltung, die verstreuten Fragmente der Stadt aufzubessern und zu vereinigen, können nicht in Zweifel gestellt werden. Girona hat sich zu einer anziehenden Hauptstadt entwickelt, die ein bedeutendes, regionales Territorium kontrolliert. Doch trotz dieser Anstrengungen gibt es in der modernen Stadt wenige Orte, in denen sich die urbane Schönheit so stark wie in der Altstadt präsentiert. Interessant ist, was von dem Werk des Architekten Masó erhalten blieb (Farinera Teixidor, Casa de la Punxa) und der Park La Devesa, eine beeindruckende Baumallee am Ufer des Ters, die der Legende nach von den Soldaten Napoleons gepflanzt wurde. Die Zone des Ters auf der Höhe des Parks Devesa wurde zu einer neuen Achse: der Messepalast, die runde Geometrie des Sportpalastes, die neue Brücke, der Park am Fluß und die spektakuläre Einfahrt in die Stadt sind interessante Aspekte des neuen Urbanismus. Auch auf dem Campus der Montilivi (UdG) gibt es neue, moderne Elemente. In Girona wird also der Enthusiasmus des Dichter J.V. Foix möglich, der sagte: "Mich begeistert das Neue und mich verzaubert das Alte". ❧

◀◀
8 Paseo de la muralla
Promenade on the city walls
Promenade an der Stadtmauer

◀
9 Escaleras
Staircases
Treppen

▲
10 Ambigüedad
Ambiguity
Zweideutigkeit

◀
11 Piedra amarilla
Yellow stone
Gelber Stein

▲
12 Puentes
Bridges
Brücken

GE-G
5659

◀
13 Cromatismo
Chromatism
Färbung

▲
14 Nobleza de la piedra
The nobleness of stone
Adel des Steines

▲
15 Espejos
Mirrors
Spiegel

▶
16 El trenet (el trenecillo)
The miniature railway
El trenet (der kleine Zug)

En Gerió
GI·VE
31695

▲
17 La Força
La Força
La Força

▶
18 Porches
Porches
Säulenhallen

19 Naturalidad
Naturalness
Natürlichkeit

20 Heroísmo
Heroism
Heldentum

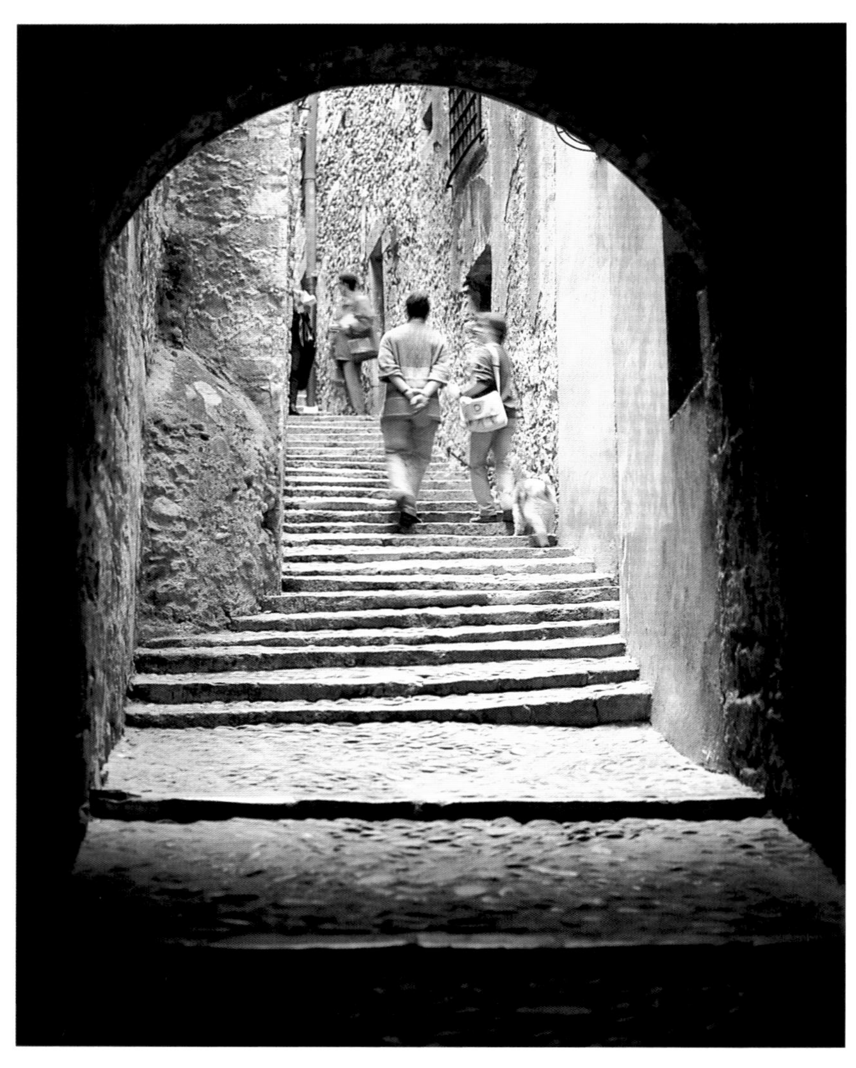

▲
21 Call (Judería)
Call (Jewry)
Call (Judenviertel)

▶
22 Densidad
Density
Dichte

OPTICA AGUSTI
Totes direccions
Centre Històric
Museus
NUCLI ZOOLOGIC
OK
SERVICE
BARRI VELL

TRETZE
CROISSANTERIA

CARRER
BONAVENTURA
CARRERAS I PERALTA
CARRER
DE LES
BALLESTERIES
Antiguitats IV Cantons
Antiguitats IV Cantons
CIS

◀◀
23 Quatre cantons (Cuatro caminos)
Quatre cantons (Crossroads)
Quatre cantons (Vier Wege)

◀
24 Pont de Pedra
Pont de Pedra
Pont de Pedra (Steinbrücke)

▲
25 Ambiente
Atmosphere
Atmosphäre

TEATRE

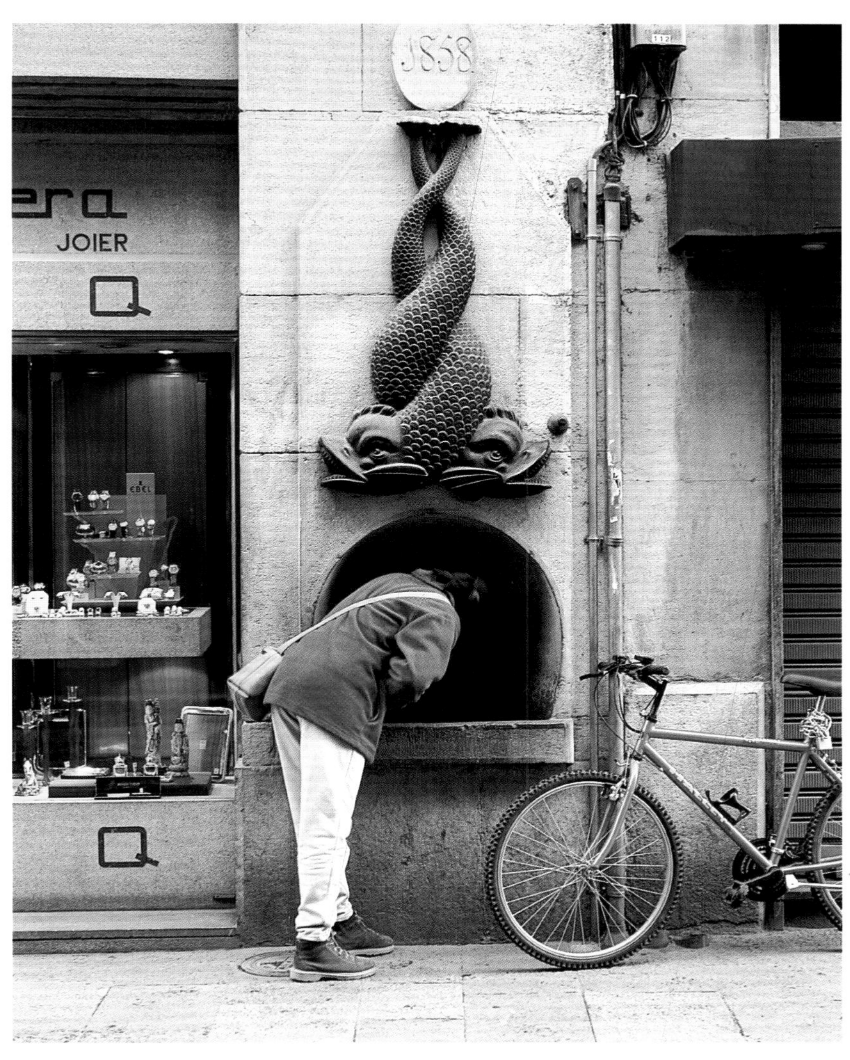

◀
26 Río de tilos
River of lindens
Der Fluß mit Lindenbäumen

▲
27 Agua
Water
Wasser

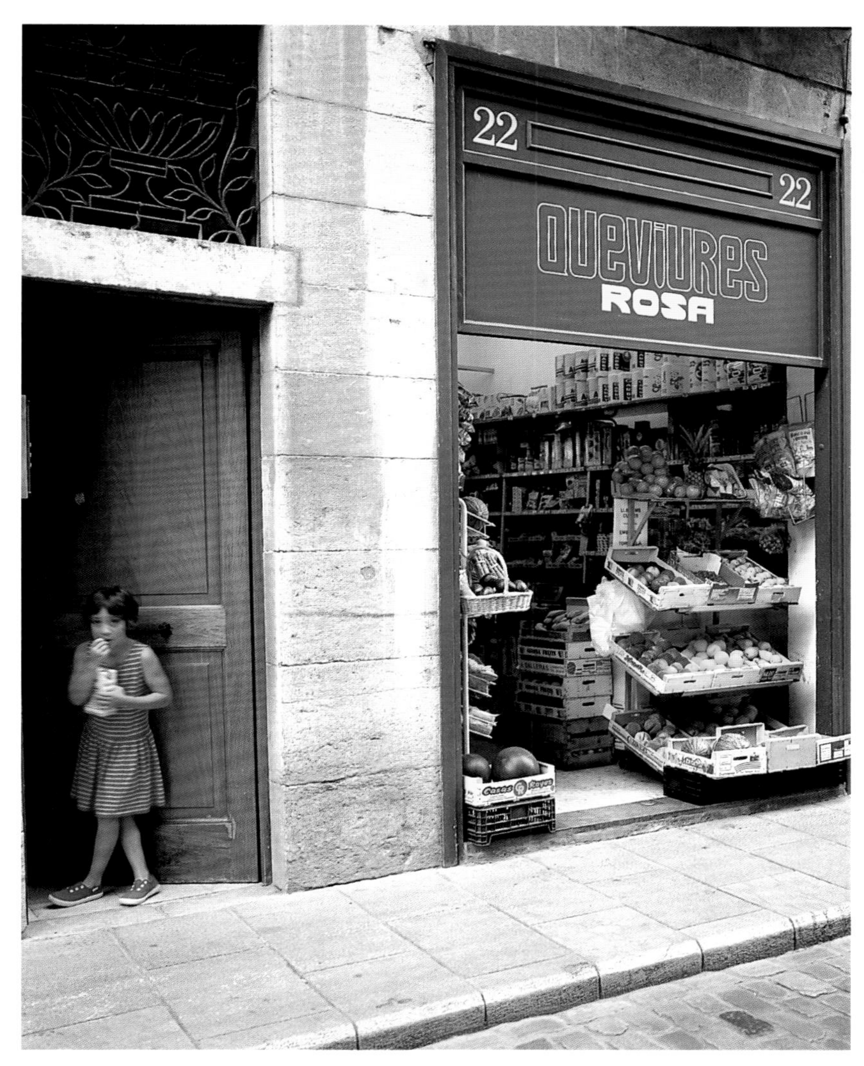

◀
28 Colores
Colours
Farben

▲
29 Colores (2)
Colours (2)
Farben (2)

▲
30 El culo de la leona
The lioness's bottom
Der Hintern der Löwin

▶
31 El agua que se va
Flowing water
Das Wasser, das weiterfließt

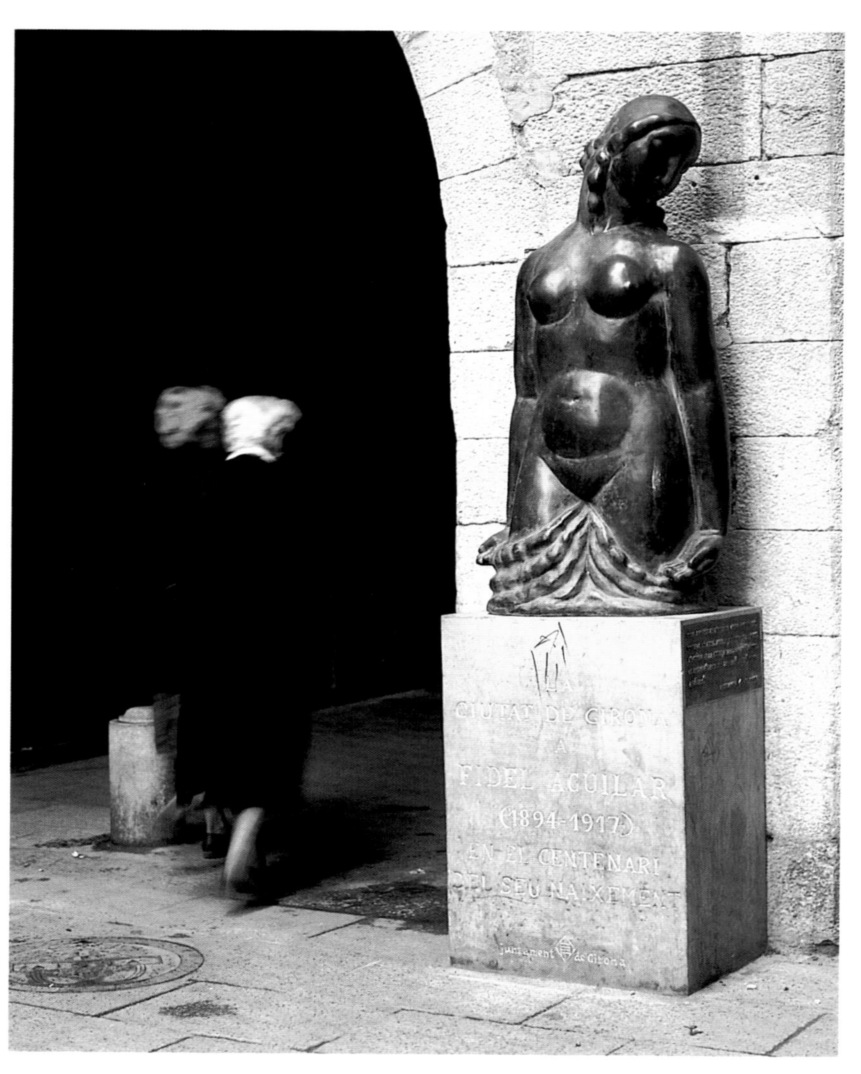

▲
32 Clásico
Classical
Klassisch

▶
33 Detalle
Detail
Detail

▲
34 Luces
Lights
Lichter

▶
35 Suma
Addition
Ergebnis

▲
36 Gaviotas
Seagulls
Möwen

▶
37 Decoración
Decoration
Dekoration

◀◀
38 Mediterráneos
Mediterranean
Mediterran

◀
39 Metáforas
Metaphors
Metaphern

▲
40 Secretos de familia
Secrets
Familiengeheimnisse

◀
41 Constancia gerundense
Constancy of Girona
Die Ausdauer Gironas

▲
42 Vejez
Age
Das Alter

◀
43 Simplicidad
Simplicity
Einfachheit

▲
44 Sant Narcís
Sant Narcís
Sant Narcís

▲
45 Verde
Greenery
Grün

▶
46 Devesa de otoño
Autumn in the Devesa
Devesa (Weideplatz) des Herbstes

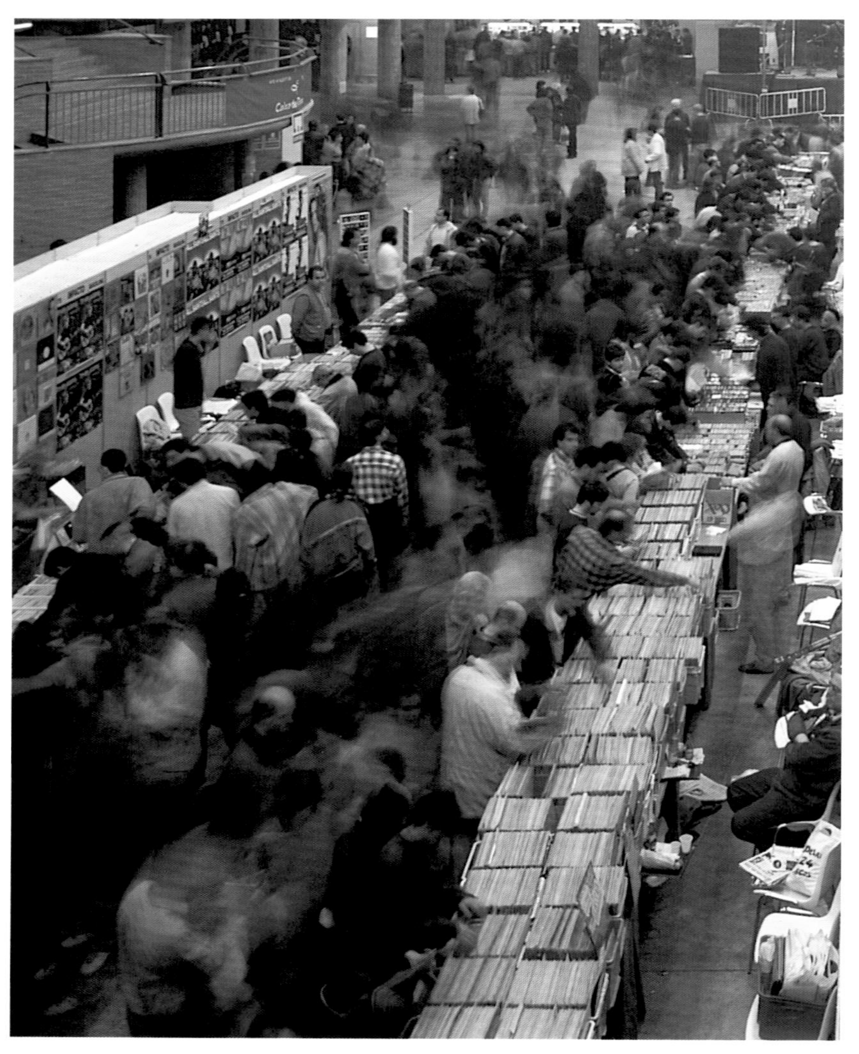

▲
47 Feria
Fairs
Messe

▶
48 Plátanos
Plane trees
Platanen

▲
49 Baloncesto
Basketball
Basketball

▶
50 Devesa verde
Green Devesa
Grüne Devesa

▲
51 Mercadillo
Street market
Markttag

▶
52 El Ter
The Ter
Der Fluß Ter

◀◀
53 Devesa de otoño (2)
Autumn in the Devesa (2)
Devesa (Weideplatz) des Herbstes. (2)

◀
54 Niebla
Mist
Nebel

▲
55 Geometría
Geometry
Geometrie

◀
56 Sant Feliu
Sant Feliu
Sant Feliu

▲
57 Catedral bancaria
Cathedral of banking
Bankkathedrale

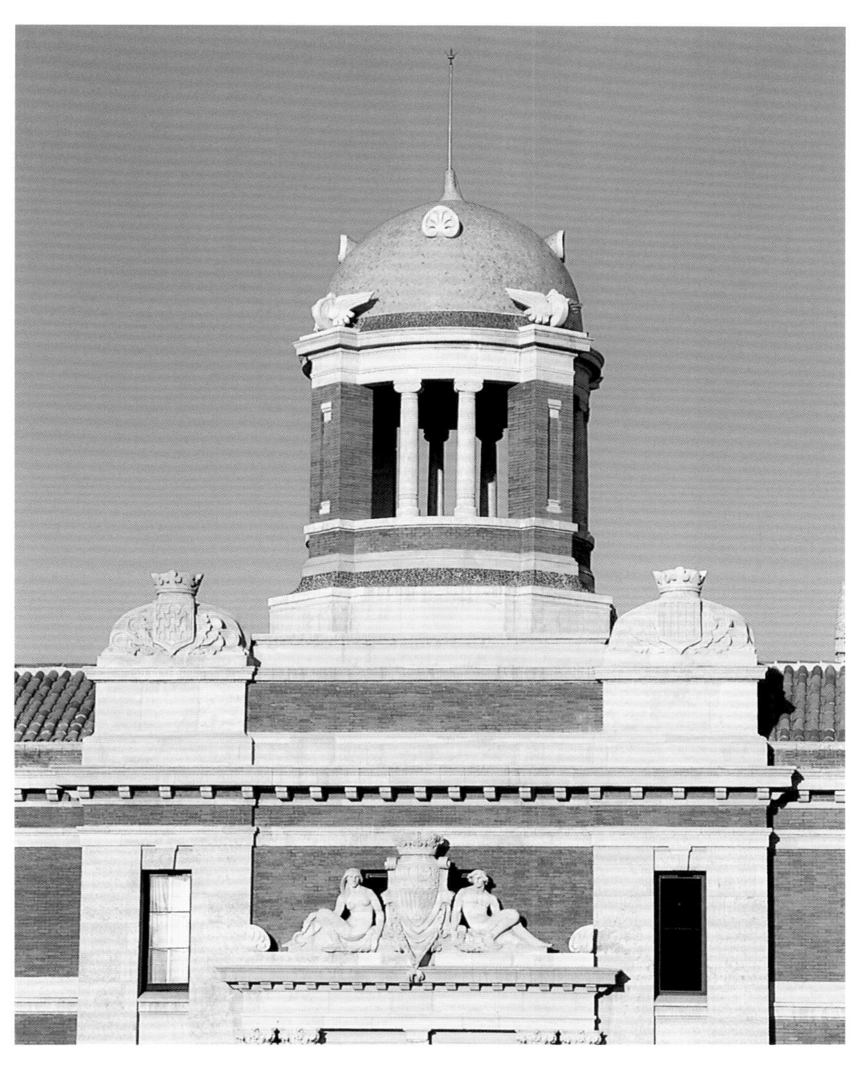

◀
58 Parque central
Parc Central
Parc Central

▲
59 Clasicismo
Classicism
Klassizismus

▲
60 Teatro
Theatre
Theater

▶
61 Modernismo
Modernisme
Modernisme

▲
62 Centro comercial
Commercial centre
Einkaufszone

▶
63 Montilivi
Montilivi
Montilivi

▶
64 Lo nuevo y lo viejo
Ancient and modern
Das Alte und das Neue

65 Supervivencia
Survival
Überleben

66 Masó
Masó
Masó

▲
67 Novecentismo
Noucentisme
Mode des neunzehnten Jahrhunderts

▶
68 Les Fires (las ferias)
Les Fires (the fairs)
Les Fires (Jahrmakt, Volksfest)

◀◀
69 Intimidad claustral
Cloister
Die Intimität des Kreuzganges

◀
70 Signo
Symbol
Sinnbild

▲
71 El vuelo de la piedra
Flight of stone
Der Flug des Steines

MARE

◀
74 El bordado más exquisito
Exquisite embroidery
Die feinste Stickerei

▲
75 Cosmovisión
Cosmovision
Weltanschauung

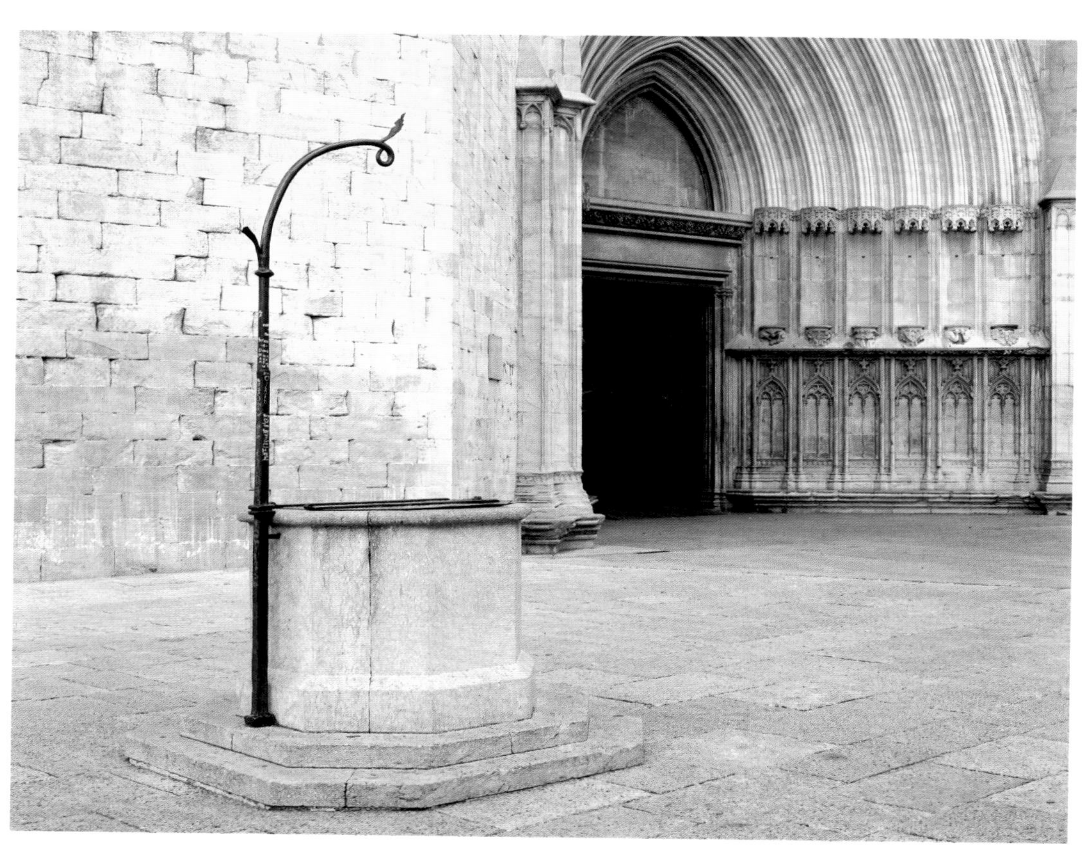

▲
76 Severidad
Severity
Strenge

▶
77 Md'A (Museu d'Art)
Md'A
Md'A

8

▲
78 Sepulcros
Sepulchres
Grabstätten

▶
79 Numulites
Fossils
Nummuliten

▲
80 Sugestión de las piedras
Insinuation of the stones
Einwirkung der Steine

▶
81 Mestizaje cultural
Cultural crossbreeding
Kulturelle Vermischung

▲
82 Divertimiento barroco
Baroque style
Barocker Zeitvertreib

▶
83 Carlomagno
Charlemagne
Charlemagne

◀◀
84 Tejados
Rooftops
Dächer

◀
85 Barroco
Baroque
Barock

▲
86 Gris
Grey
Grau

◀
87 Sant Pere
Sant Pere
Sant Pere

▲
88 La Mercè
La Mercè
La Mercè

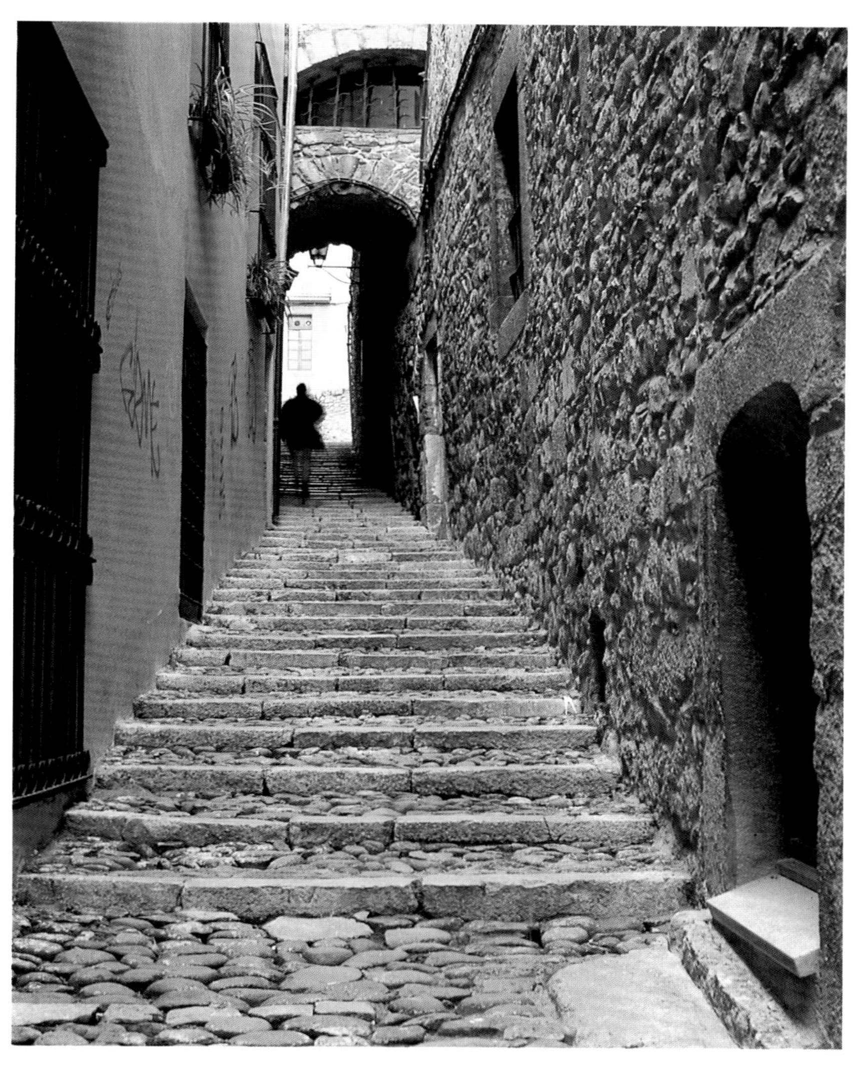

◀
89 Bonastruc
Bonastruc
Bonastruc

▲
90 El pasado, confidente
The confident past
Die Vergangenheit, vertraulich

▲
91 Farmacia barroca
Baroque pharmacy
Die barocke Apotheke

▶
92 Oro y óxidos
Gold and rust
Gold und Rost

Ext.
Opy
Sev.

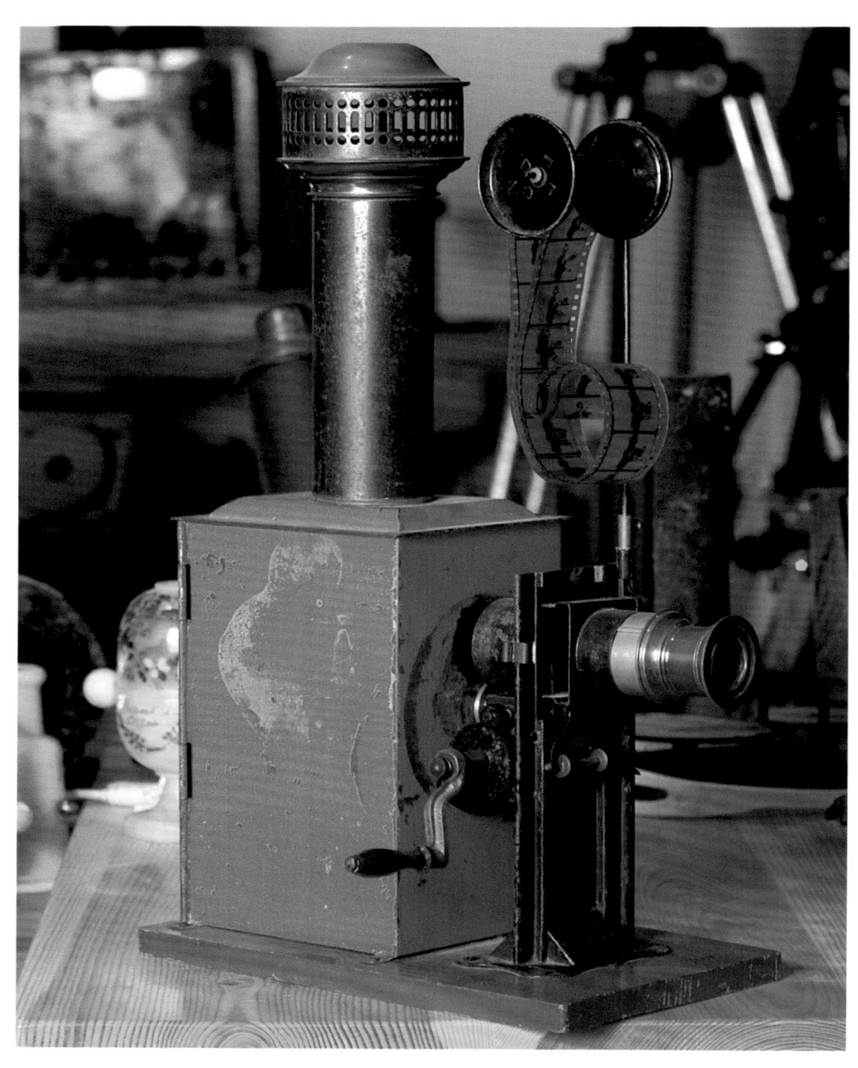

▲
93 Cine
Cinema
Kino

▶
94 Romana
Roman
Romanisch

CAL

95 Pedret
Pedret
Pedret

96 Artesanía
Craftsmanship
Kunsthandwerk

▲
97 “Espais”
“Espais”
“Espais”

▶
98 Habaneras
Havaneres
Havaneres

CALAMAR

PORTAL DEL
NATURALEZA Y VIDA

◀◀
99 Agua contradictoria
Contradictory water
Widersprüchliches Wasser

◀
100 Fetichismo
Fetishism
Fetischismus

▲
101 Infierno alegre
Merry inferno
Fröhliche Hölle

◀
102 Gigantes
Giants
Giganten

▲
103 La "marcha" de las piedras
The action and the stones
Ausgehen zwischen den Steinen

▶
104 Serpientes de la muerte
Serpents of death
Todesschlangen

	Castellano	English	Deutsch
	1 Patchwork El Onyar –un río mínimo, amenizado por los puentes y domesticado por una plaza– separa la ciudad nueva (contradictoria de volúmenes y colores como todas las ciudades modernas) de la ciudad vieja (de un tejido más denso, laberíntico).	Patchwork The Onyar, a small river enlivened by bridges and delimitated by a square, separates the new city (a contradiction of volumes and colours like most modern towns), from the old (dense and labyrinthine).	Patchwork Der Onyar, ein sehr kleiner Fluß, der durch die Brücken angenehm gestaltet und durch einen Platz besänftigt wird, trennt die neue Stadt (widersprüchlich in Volumen und Farben wie alle modernen Städte) von der Altstadt (aus einem dichteren und labyrinthischen Geflecht).
	2 Espectáculo inicial La entrada norte de Girona es un moderno nudo de comunicaciones que enmarca la postal más célebre de la ciudad antigua. El brillante dinamismo del nuevo urbanismo encaja espectacularmente con las solemnes construcciones góticas.	At first sight The northern entrance to the city is an ultramodern junction which frames old Girona's most renowned image. The new town is a dynamic contrast to the solemn Gothic buildings of the old.	Schauspiel zu Beginn Die nördliche Einfahrt nach Girona ist ein moderner Verkehrsknotenpunkt, der als Rahmen für die berühmteste Postkartenansicht der Altstadt dient. Der bemerkenswerte Dynamismus des neuen Urbanismus paßt ausgezeichnet zu den feierlichen, gotischen Bauten.
	3 Casas del Onyar La ciudad "gris y negra" es ahora patria del color: mediterránea y vitalista. Las casas del Onyar, de inspiración a la vez popular y florentina, dan la razón a Rafael Masó (Casa Masó, a la derecha), precursor de la modernidad arquitectónica.	Houses on the Onyar The "grey and black city" is now the home of colour, Mediterranean and vitalistic. These houses, of both popular and Florentine inspiration, pay homage to Rafael Masó (Casa Masó, on the right), precursor of architectural modernity.	Die Häuser am Onyar Die "graue und schwarze" Stadt ist heute die Heimat der Farben: mediterran und lebensfroh. Die Häuser am Onyar, die gleichzeitig volkstümlich und florentinisch inspiriert sind, geben Rafael Masó, dem Vorläufer der architektonischen Modernität recht (Casa Masó auf der rechten Seite).
	4 Escudo Detalle del escudo de Girona en la portada renacentista del edificio de Les Àligues (s. XVI). Un agua de piedra centra el escudo: síntesis, al mismo tiempo material y simbólica, de los elementos fundacionales de la ciudad.	Coat of arms Detail of Girona's coat of arms on the Renaissance porch of the 16th century Les Àligues building. Water and stone, material and symbolic synthesis of the founding elements of the city.	Wappenschild Detail des Wappenschildes von Girona auf dem Renaissanceportal der Gebäudes Les Àligues (XVI. Jahrhundert). Wasser und Stein: Synthese der Gründungselemente der Stadt, gleichzeitig Material und Symbolik.
	5 Eiffel en Girona Desde este puente, el último que queda de los que construyó la empresa del célebre autor de la Torre de París, se obtienen curiosas perspectivas de la coloreada fachada del Onyar y de los grandes edificios religiosos que la coronan.	Eiffel in Girona Unusual views of the colourful riverside façade of the Onyar and the great religious buildings which crown it may be observed from this bridge, the only one remaining which was built by the creator of the famous tower in Paris.	Eiffel in Girona Von dieser Brücke aus, der letzten, die von denen, die das Unternehmen des berühmten Erbauers des Eiffelturms in Paris konstruiert hat, übrig geblieben ist, hat man einen sehr interessanten Blick auf die bunte Fassade am Onyar und die großen religiösen Bauten, die sie krönen.

	6 Estela hebraica Procedentes de Montjuïc, donde se encontraba el cementerio medieval de los judíos gerundenses, las inscripciones funerarias (Museu Arqueològic) dan testimonio de la presencia, actualmente reivindicada, de una importante comunidad judía.	Hebrew stele From the medieval Jewish cemetery at Montjuïc, the funeral inscriptions (Museu Arqueologic), are evidence of the presence of an important Jewish community.	Hebräische Grabsäule Sie stammen vom Montjuïc, wo sich der mittelalterliche Friedhof der Juden Gironas befand und die Grabschriften (Museu Arqueològic) bezeugen die Existenz einer wichtigen jüdischen Gemeinschaft. Heutzutage wird diese Existenz wieder besonders unterstrichen.
	7 Levítica El tópico de la ciudad clerical tiene fundamento: la ciudad sobrevive a la caída del imperio romano porque es "ciudad episcopal". Detalle de religiosidad tradicional: "Rezando un padrenuestro se ganan 250 días de indulgencia".	Levitical Girona's clerical reputation is well-founded. Thanks to its position as episcopal see, the city survived beyond the fall of the Roman Empire. Religious detail: "250 days of indulgence are achieved by saying the Lord's Prayer".	Levitisch Der Gemeinplatz der klerikalen Stadt ist nicht unbegründet: die Stadt überlebt den Untergang des römischen Reiches aufgrund ihres Statuses einer "Bischofsstadt". Ein Detail der traditionellen Religiosität: "Wenn man ein Vaterunser betet, gewinnt man 250 Tage Ablaß."
	8 Paseo de la muralla Símbolo de los antiguos sufrimientos de la ciudad, la muralla es ahora un paseo elevado, originalísimo: un balcón abierto a todas la amenidades visuales.	Promenade on the city walls Symbol of ancestral afflictions, the city walls are now an original, elevated promenade: a balcony with agreeable views.	Promenade an der Stadtmauer Symbol der alten Leiden der Stadt ist die Stadtmauer heutzutage eine erhöhte, sehr originelle Promenade: Ein Balkon, der für alle visuellen Annehmlichkeiten offen ist.
	9 Escaleras Para salvar los desniveles radicales de los promontorios que caen sobre los ríos, la Girona vieja está llena de escaleras que intensifican el predominio de la piedra: la pura geometría de la piedra.	Staircases Owing to the differences of level, there are many flights of steps in the old city. Their presence intensifies the predominance of stone: the pure geometry of stone.	Treppen Um die sehr starken Höhenunterschiede des Vorgebirges, das sich an den Flüssen befindet, auszugleichen, ist das alte Girona voller Treppen, die die Vorherrschaft des Steines noch verstärken: die reine Geometrie des Steines.
	10 Ambigüedad Las caprichosas formas de esta calle dan noticia del alma ambigua de la ciudad: de piedra dura, pero también ondulante, esquiva, femenina.	Ambiguity The fanciful forms of this street bear witness to the components of the city's ambiguous soul: hard stone that is also undulating, bashful and feminine.	Zweideutigkeit Die bizarren Formen dieser Straße bezeugen die doppeldeutige Seele dieser Stadt: aus hartem Stein, aber auch sich windend, ausweichend, feminin.
	11 Piedra amarilla Entre las cuatro texturas que ha escogido el fotógrafo Jordi Puig para formar este *collage*, hay la de unos bloques de piedra amarilla y muy erosionada. Es la piedra que los romanos usaron para construir la primera muralla de la ciudad: estos son los sillares más antiguos, por tanto; los más cansados.	Yellow stone Some worn and ancient yellow stone appears between the four textures chosen by the photographer Jordi Puig for this *collage*. This is the stone used by the Romans in the building of the city walls and is, therefore, the oldest and most eroded.	Gelber Stein Unter den vier Stoffen, die der Fotograph Jordi Puig ausgesucht hat, um diese *Collage* zu formen, gibt es einige Blöcke aus gelben, stark erodiertem Stein. Es sind die Steine, die die Römer benutzt hatten, um die erste Stadtmauer zu erbauen; das sind die ältesten und damit müdesten Quadersteine.

12 Puentes

La mayoría de puentes son pasajes relativamente modernos, como éste "d'en Gómez" de inspiración modernista. Conectan partes de la ciudad que habían vivido de espaldas por culpa, más que del río, de la muralla.

Bridges

The majority of bridges are relatively new, such as the "d'en Gómez", of Modernist inspiration. They have brought together parts of the city previously separated by the walls rather than by the river.

Brücken

Die meisten der Brücken sind relativ moderne Übergänge, wie die "d'en Gómez", die modernistisch inspiriert ist. Sie verbinden Teile der Stadt miteinander, die vorher sich den Rücken zukehrten, daran war nicht so sehr der Fluß schuld, sondern die Stadtmauer.

13 Cromatismo

El color de un objeto contemporáneo, una Vespa, flamea magníficamente sobre la memoria pétrea de la ciudad antigua.

Chromatism

The blazing colour of a contemporary artefact stands out against the old city's heart of stone.

Färbung

Die Farbe eines zeitgenössischen Objektes, einer Vespa, flammt wundervoll vor dem steinernen Vermächtnis der Altstadt auf.

14 Nobleza de la piedra

La Fontana d'Or, en la calle Ciutadans, es una noble mansión restaurada como centro cultural de la Caixa de Girona. La nobleza actual no proviene ya de la sangre, sino de la cultura.

The nobleness of stone

The Fontana d'Or, a mansion on carrer Ciutadans, has been restored as the Centre Cultural Caixa de Girona. Today, culture, rather than ancestry, is the foundation of nobility.

Adel des Steines

Das Gebäude Fontana d'Or in der Straße Ciutadans ist ein edles, renoviertes Herrenhaus, umgestaltet zum Kulturzentrum der Caixa de Girona. Sein zeitgenössischer Adel stammt nun nicht mehr von seiner Herkunft, sondern von der Kultur her.

15 Espejos

Se abren nuevos espacios, como éste de la plaza Santaló. También la Girona moderna, nacida sin atractivos por culpa de la especulación, se restaura y maquilla. Delante del espejo: como un adolescente luchando contra el acné.

Mirrors

New open spaces such as the plaça Santaló have been created. Even modern Girona, the ungraceful fruit of speculation, is being restored and retouched. A look in the mirror: like an adolescent struggling with acne.

Spiegel

Es öffnen sich neue Räume, so wie der Platz Santaló. Auch das moderne Girona, das aufgrund der Spekulation als ein nicht sehr attraktiver Teil der Stadt entstanden ist, erneuert und verschönert sich. Vor dem Spiegel: Wie ein Jugendlicher, der gegen Akne kämpft.

16 El trenet (el trenecillo)

Tiene un punto de infantil alegría, nada dramática, el reencuentro de Girona con su pasado (tren turístico sobre el Pont de Pedra).

The miniature railway

From the Pont de Pedra bridge, Girona, with a touch of childish gaiety, undramatically rediscovers its past history.

El trenet (der kleine Zug)

Die Wiederbegegnung Gironas mit seiner Vergangenheit (touristischer Zug über die Pont de la Pedra) besitzt eine gewisse kindliche Freude, nichts dramatisches.

17 La Força

Conexión exterior y columna vertebral de la ciudad arcaica, la calle de la Força es, todavía hoy, la vía iniciática, oscura y sugestiva, que abre los secretos de la Girona antigua.

La Força

Exterior connection and backbone of the ancient city, the carrer de la Força is, even today, the dark and suggestive key to the secrets of old Girona.

La Força

Verbindung nach außen und Wirbelsäule der alten Stadt ist die Straße La Força, noch heute der dunkle und lockende Einstiegsweg, der die Geheimnisse des alten Gironas enthüllt.

18 Porches

De bóveda baja y pesado cuerpo, las arcadas son un ingrediente característico de la Girona vieja. No son esbeltas, sino acogedoras y oscuras como un claustro materno.

Porches

Low-vaulted and heavy, archways are a characteristic feature of old Girona. They are not svelte, but as dark and secure as a womb.

.

Säulenhallen

Mit niedrigen Gewölben und schwerem Körper sind die Arkaden ein charakteristisches Element des alten Gironas. Sie sind nicht elegant, sondern einladend und dunkel wie ein Mutterleib.

19 Naturalidad

Más vale no buscar la nota pintoresca. Hay muchos rincones de la ciudad antigua donde la belleza está perfectamente acomodada, sin ninguna pretensión, con naturalidad, en la butaca de las piedras.

Naturalness

There is no need to seek the picturesque note. In the old town there are many unpretentious corners where beauty sits comfortably in its stone armchair, naturally and without pretensions.

Natürlichkeit

Man sollte besser nicht die pittoreske Note suchen. Es gibt viele Winkel in der Altstadt, in denen die Schönheit perfekt, ehrgeizlos und natürlich im Parterresitz der Steine untergebracht ist.

20 Heroísmo

En la plaza de la Independencia, un grupo escultórico (s. XIX) conmemora la lucha contra el ejército napoleónico. Bares, restaurantes, cines y ferias de libros o de artesanía han convertido este espacio en eje de la diversión y la trivialidad.

Heroism

A 19th century sculpture, in the plaça de la Independència, commemorates the struggle against Napoleon's troops. This spot has been converted into a place of entertainment by the presence of bars restaurants, cinemas and book fairs.

Heldentum

Auf dem plaça de la Independencia (Platz der Unabhängigkeit) erinnert eine Skulpturengruppe (XIX. Jahrhundert) an den Kampf gegen das Heer Napoleons. Gaststätten, Restaurants, Kinos und Bücher- und Kunsthandwerksstände hab diesen Platz in einen Ort des Vergnügen und der Trivialität verwandelt.

21 Call (Judería)

Altas y estrechas paredes de piedra (de una piedra humilde: húmeda y troceada). Calles como pasadizos, bóvedas como puertas, escaleras interiores, luz oscura. En el silencio de los siglos, el debilísimo eco de lágrimas hebraicas.

Call (Jewry)

High and confing walls of stone, humble, damp and crumbling. Streets like corridors, vaults like doorways, interior stairways, tenebrous light. Amid the silence of centuries, the distant echo of Hebrew tears.

Call (Judenviertel)

Hohe und enge Steinwände (aus einem bescheidenen Stein: feucht und zerstückelt). Straßen als Durchgänge, Gewölbe als Tore, Innentreppen, dunkles Licht. In der Stille der Jahrhunderte, das schwache Echo hebräischer Tränen.

22 Densidad

Durante siglos, la ciudad vivió comprimida entre los promontorios y el río. Una placita de cemento sobre el arenal del Onyar recuerda la antigua estrechez en clave contemporánea.

Density

For centuries, the city was constricted between the promontories and the river. A cement square on the sand of the Onyar is a modern reminder of this ancestral limitation.

Dichte

Jahrhunderte lang lebte die Stadt zwischen den Vorgebirgen und dem Fluß eingequetscht. Ein kleiner Platz aus Zement auf der Sandfläche des Onyar erinnert an die ehemalige Enge in zeitgenössischer Verschlüsselung.

23 Quatre cantons (Cuatro caminos)

Durante la edad media, robando espacio al Onyar, creció la ciudad de los burgueses y de los artesanos. Ahora, esta llana y ondulante franja es el anillo comercial de la Girona histórica.

Crossroads

The city of the bourgeois and craftsmen reclaimed land from the Onyar during the Middle Ages and was thus able to expand. Today, this flat area is historic Girona's commercial ring.

Quatre cantons (Vier Wege)

Während des Mittelalters wuchs die Stadt der Bürger und Handwerker, in dem sie dem Onyar Platz raubte. Heute ist dieser flache und wellende Streifen das Geschäftsviertel des historischen Gironas.

24 Pont de Pedra

Las bóvedas bajas y pesadas de este puente conectan la ciudad vieja con la primera versión de la ciudad moderna. Debajo, las aguas del Onyar, generalmente quietas, exangües. Encima, la Girona de siempre.

Pont de Pedra

The low and weighty vaults of the bridge connect the old town with the first version of the modern city. Beneath, the usually tranquil and depleted waters of the Onyar. Above, eternal Girona.

Pont de Pedra (Steinbrücke)

Die niedrigen und schweren Gewölbe dieser Brücke verbinden die Altstadt mit der ersten Version der Neustadt. Darunter liegt das Wasser des Onyars, normalerweise ruhig und kraftlos. Darüber liegt Girona, wie es immer war.

25 Ambiente

En el punto donde confluyen el Pont de Pedra y la Rambla es donde habitualmente se produce el mayor hormigueo ciudadano.

Atmosphere

The point where the Pont de Pedra and the Rambla meet is the nerve centre of the city's activity.

Atmosphäre

Dort wo sich die Pont de Pedra und die Rambla vereinigen, trifft man fast immer auf das größte Menschengewimmel der Stadt.

26 Río de tilos

Sobre la antigua muralla del Onyar se construyeron las casas del río, ahora multicolores, que también dan a la Rambla: un paseo lleno de tilos que en la época de floración destilan un intenso perfume de dulce urbanidad.

River of lindens

Over the old wall of the Onyar, the now multicoloured houses were built. To their rear, they also overlook the Rambla, an avenue lined by linden trees whose blossom exudes a sweet, intense perfume.

Der Fluß mit Lindenbäumen

Auf der alten Stadtmauer am Onyar wurden die Häuser am Fluß errichtet, die auch eine Front zur Rambla haben und heute in bunten Farben angestrichen sind. Eine Lindenbaumallee, die während der Blütezeit den intensiven Duft von städtischer Süße ausströmen.

27 Agua

La Rambla desemboca en la calle de la Argentería, donde todavía abundan los joyeros; y donde una fuente ochocentista (la Font del Pou de la Cadena) subraya la mitología gerundense del agua.

Water

The Rambla leads into the carrer de l'Argenteria, where jewellers still abound and where a fountain (Font del Pou de la Cadena) illustrates Girona's aquatic mythology.

Wasser

Die Rambla mündet in die Straße de la Argentería ein, wo es immer noch sehr viele Juweliere gibt und wo ein Brunnen aus dem achtzehnten Jahrhundert (Font del Pou de la Cadena) die Mythologie Gironas vom Wasser unterstreicht.

28 Colores

El agua quieta del Onyar es un espejo donde los colores de las casas vacilan, tal vez incrédulos: no hace mucho que estas casas transmitían los grises y los blancos de la modestia.

Colours

The houses are mirrored in the tranquil waters of the Onyar, and seem surprised by their newly acquired colouring. Not so long ago, they were mere reflections of the greys and broken whites of modesty.

Farben

Das ruhige Wasser des Onyars ist ein Spiegel, in dem die Farben der Häuser schwanken, vielleicht mißtrauisch; vor nicht allzulanger Zeit zeigten diese Häuser die Grau- und Weißtöne der Bescheidenheit

29 Colores (2)

La vida es el color más dulce.

Colours (2)

Life is the sweetest colour of all.

Farben (2)

Das Leben ist die süßeste Farbe.

30 El culo de la leona

Según la tradición popular, "no es buen ciudadano de Girona quien no ha besado el culo de la leona". La imagen colocada en la plaza de Sant Feliu es una copia del original del s. XII que se conserva en el Museu d'Art.

The lioness's bottom

According to popular tradition, a person is not a true "gironin" if he or she has not kissed the lioness's bottom. The statue, in the plaça de Sant Feliu, is a copy of the 12th century original, now kept in the Museu d'Art.

Der Hintern der Löwin

Nach dem Volksglauben "ist man kein guter Bürger Gironas, wenn man nicht den Hintern der Löwin geküßt hat". Die Abbildung, die man auf dem Platz Sant Feliu aufgestellt hat, ist eine Kopie des Originales aus dem XII. Jahrhundert, die sich im Museu d'Art befindet.

31 El agua que se va

En la ribera del Ter, en el barrio del Pedret, los sauces llorones acompañan el trayecto del agua.

Flowing water

On the banks of the Ter, in the Pedret quarter, the weeping willows follow the course of the water.

Das Wasser, das weiterfließt

Am Ufer des Ter, im Viertel del Pedret, begleiten die Trauerweiden den Weg des Wassers.

32 Clásico

El escultor Fidel Aguilar, que a principios del s. XX recuperaba el clasicismo griego, murió muy joven. No hace mucho que la reproducción ampliada de una de sus obras ha sido colocada al principio de les Voltes d'en Rosés.

Classical

The sculptor Fidel Aguilar, who followed the Greek classic school at the beginning of the 20th century, died very young. Recently, an enlarged reproduction of one of his pieces has been installed at the beginning of the Voltes d'en Rosés.

Klassisch

Der Bildhauer Fidel Aguilar, der zu Beginn des XX. Jahrhunderts den griechischen Klassizismus wiedererneuerte, starb sehr jung. Vor nicht allzu langer Zeit wurde eine Nachbildung eines seiner Werke am Anfang der Straße Les Voltes d'en Rosés aufgestellt.

33 Detalle

Las colosales dimensiones de la catedral no excluyen los detalles menores, como esta forja de la puerta principal.

Detail

The colossal dimensions of the cathedral do not exclude minor details, such as this wrought iron on the main door.

Detail

Die riesigen Ausmasse der Kathedrale schließen nicht die kleineren Details wie diese Schmiedeeisenarbeit am Haupteingang aus.

34 Luces

La Rambla tiene un espacio solar, luminoso, festivo; y otro interior, de luz incierta, arcaica.

Lights

The Rambla has one sunny, luminous and festive aspect; and another, introspective, archaic, of hesitant light.

Lichter

Die Rambla besitzt einen Teil, der sonnig, hell und festlich ist und einen Innenraum mit unstetem, altertümlichen Licht.

35 Suma

El gusto por las formas contemporáneas subraya las formas antiguas.

Addition

The taste for contemporary forms places emphasis on the older forms.

Ergebnis

Die Vorliebe für die zeitgenössischen Formen unterstreicht die alten Formen.

36 Gaviotas

Las aves marinas han colonizado los ríos de Girona. Desde los puentes, a veces, el Onyar es una pista de baile, o de circo.

Seagulls

Seabirds have colonised Girona's rivers. The Onyar sometimes has the appearance of a dance floor, or circus.

Möwen

Die Meeresvögel haben die Flüsse Gironas kolonisiert. Die Brücken des Onyars sind für sie manchmal ein Tanzparkett oder eine Zirkusarena.

37 Decoración

Es difícil saber si es más decorativa o pintoresca la ropa tendida o las cerámicas incrustadas, como una joya, en la fachada de esta casa del Onyar.

Decoration

It is hard to say which is more decorative and picturesque: the laundry out to dry or the ceramics, encrusted like jewels, in the façade of this house on the Onyar.

Dekoration

Manchmal ist es schwer zu sagen, was dekorativer oder pittoresker ist: Die Wäsche, die an den Häusern des Onyars aufgehängt wurde oder die Keramik, die wie ein Schmuckstück in die Wand dieses Hauses eingelassen ist.

38 Mediterráneos

Criticada inicialmente, la reforma colorista de las casa del Onyar (dirigida por los artistas Ansesa y Faixó) es la bandera de la Girona contemporánea: un nuevo fundamento vitalista para la antigua severidad gótica.

Mediterranean

Although initially criticised, the colourist reform of the houses on the Onyar (carried out by Ansesa and Faixó), is the hallmark of contemporary Girona: a new and vital contrast to the old Gothic strictness.

Mediterran

Obwohl sie zu Anfang kritisiert wurde, ist die bunte Renovierung der Häuser am Onyar (die von den Künstlern Ansesa und Faixó geleitet wurde) das Aushängeschild des zeitgenössischen Gironas: ein neues, lebendiges Fundament für die alte, gotische Strenge.

39 Metáforas

La yedra que recubre la piedra: Girona romántica. El óxido de las hojas de los plátanos: Girona en otoño. La piedra humilde de la Girona anónima. Las grietas de la piedra donde se alimentan las raíces: Girona histórica, superviviente.

Metaphors

Ivy-covered stone: romantic Girona. The russet leaves of the plane trees: autumnal Girona. The humble stone of the anonymous side of Girona. Roots growing up through cracked stones: historic Girona, living on.

Metaphern

Der Efeu, der den Stein bedeckt: das romantische Girona. Die Rostfarbe der Blätter der Platanen. Girona im Herbst. Der bescheidene Stein des namenlosen Gironas. Die Risse in den Steinen, in denen sich die Wurzeln ernähren: das historische Girona, das überlebt hat.

40 Secretos de familia

Durante mucho tiempo, antes de la transformación contemporánea, la pasión de los gerundenses por la belleza era un secreto de jardines interiores.

Secrets

For many years, prior to the contemporary transformation, much of Girona's beauty was a guarded secret of the interior gardens.

Familiengeheimnisse

Vor der modernen Umgestaltung der Stadt war lange Zeit die Leidenschaft der Bewohner Gironas für die Schönheit ein Geheimnis der Gärten der Innenhöfe.

41 Constancia gerundense

La erosión de la piedra, la persistencia del agua.

The constancy of Girona

The erosion of stone, the persistance of water.

Die Ausdauer Gironas

Die Erosion des Steines, die Beharrlichkeit des Wassers.

42 Vejez

Hay una Girona antigua y rehabilitada: impresionante; pero también una Girona envejecida y menor: deliciosa.

Age

There is one, ancient and rehabilitated Girona, but also an aged, lesser Girona not bereft of charm.

Das Alter

Es gibt ein altes und wieder zu Ehren gekommenes Girona, beeindruckend, aber auch ein gealtertes und kleineres Girona, charmant.

43 Simplicidad

Los jardines interiores del barrio antiguo pueden visitarse durante la exposición primaveral de flores. Por lo general, son de una belleza improvisada, elemental, doméstica, sin retórica.

Simplicity

In the springtime, the interior gardens of the old town are an exhibition of flowers, generally of an impromtu nature, without retoric.

Einfachheit

Die Gärten der Innenhöfe der Altstadt können während der Blumenausstellung im Frühjahr besichtigt werden. Sie besitzen im allgemeinen eine improvisierte, primitive, häusliche Schönheit ohne Rhetorik.

44 Sant Narcís

La escultura de *Piculives* se refiere al ama de llaves de San Narciso, una ficción contemporánea sobre la leyenda del patrón de Girona. La relativización del discurso épico y religioso favorece la proliferación de ficciones: entre la historia, la ironía amable y el turismo.

Sant Narcís

The *Piculives* statue represents Sant Narcís's housekeeper; contemporary fiction based on the legend of Girona's patron saint. The relativisation of epic and religious history gives rise to a proliferation of fiction.

Sant Narcís

Die Skulptur von *Piculives* bezieht sich au die Haushälterin des Stadtheilingen Narz eine zeitgenössische Dichtung basieren auf der Legende. Durch das Relativiere der epischen und religiösen Factoren werden zwischen der Geschichte, der liebenswürdigen Ironie und dem Tourismu angesiedelte Dichtungen verbreitet.

45 Verde

El jardín interior del parque de la Devesa (dehesa): la habitación verde de la ciudad.

Greenery

The inner garden of Devesa (meadow) park: the city's green quarter.

Grün

Der Innengarten des Parks Devesa (Weideplatz): Das grüne Zimmer der Stadt.

46 Devesa de otoño

"Por entre los claros de los plátanos se veía la metamorfosis de las nubes y el encanto del cielo bajo –o del cielo tierno, blando, ligeramente azul" (Josep Pla).

(Josep Pla, *Girona,* Ediciones Destino)

Autumn in the Devesa.

"Through the clearings among the plane trees, the metamorphosis of the clouds could be seen, and the enchantment of the low sky, or the soft sky, tender, slightly blue". (Josep Pla)

Devesa (Weideplatz) des Herbstes

"Zwischen den Platanen konnte man die Metamorphose der Wolken und den Zauber des niedrigen Himmels entdecken – oder des sanften, zarten und hellblauen Himmels". (Josep Pla)

47 Feria

Alzado sobre el nuevo eje urbano del Ter, el palacio ferial, que recoge una larga tradición expositora, se ha convertido en un centro de iniciativas de gran repercusión, como la Feria del disco del coleccionista –un fenómeno social, más que económico.

Fairs

The trade fair hall, built along the Ter, is where the city's tradition as an exhibition centre is now perpetuated. Among others, the record collectors fair (a social, rather than economic event) is held here.

Messe

Der Messepalast, der über der neuen, urbanen Achse des Ter errichtet wurde, ist zu einem Zentrum für Initiativen mit großer Reichweite geworden, wie zum Beispiel die Messe für Plattensammler – ein eher soziales als wirtschaftliches Phänomen.

48 Plátanos

Quiere la leyenda que sean los soldados napoleónicos los fundadores de la Devesa, pero ya desde el siglo XV hay noticias de ella. La Devesa actual es un parque de árboles altísimos plantados a la orilla del Ter durante la segunda mitad del s. XIX;
el parque urbano más extenso del país.

Plane trees

Legend has it that the Devesa park was founded by Napoleon's soldiers, but, in fact, it can be traced back as far as the 15th century. Today it is a woodland of tall trees planted along the river during the second half of the 19th century. It is the largest city park in the country.

Platanen

Der Legende nach haben die Soldaten Napoleons den Park Devesa erschaffen, jedoch wurde er schon im XV. Jahrhundert erwähnt. Die augenblickliche Devesa ist ein Park mit hohen Bäumen, die am Ufer des Ter während der zweiten Hälfte des XIX. Jahrhunderts gepflanzt wurden; der größte Stadtpark des Landes.

49 Baloncesto

Cerca de la Devesa, delante del Ter y mirando a la ciudad antigua, el nuevo Pabellón deportivo. El Valvi Girona, el equipo de baloncesto local, es el embajador más popular de la ciudad contemporánea.

Basketball

The new sports pavilion stands near the Devesa, facing the Ter and the old city. Valvi Girona, the local basketball team is thecontemporary city's most popular ambassador.

Basketball

In der Nähe der Devesa, vor dem Ter und gegenüber der Altstadt, die neue Sporthalle. Das lokale Basketballteam, Valvi Girona, ist der bekannteste Botschafter der modernen Stadt.

50 Devesa verde

Si la belleza oxidada del otoño concentra el prestigio literario de la Devesa, su fresco verdor primaveral o veraniego concentra una frescura de pozo, benéfica, impagable.

Green Devesa

If the russet beauty of autumn epitomises the literary prestige of the Devesa, the fresh verdor of the Devesa in summer personifies the purity of a freshwater spring, beneficent and invaluable.

Grüne Devesa

Während die Schönheit des rostfarbenen Herbstes die literarische Berühmtheit der Devesa in sich vereinigt, konzentriert ihr frisches Grün des Frühjahres und Sommers die wohltuende und unbezahlbare Frische eines Brunnens.

51 Mercadillo

Bajo las altísimas hojas, casi góticas, de la Devesa, un festival de colores comestibles: las frutas y verduras del mercado.

Street market

Beneath the lofty, almost Gothic leaves of the Devesa, a festival of edible colours: the fruits and vegetables of the market.

Markttag

Unter den sehr hohen, fast gotischen Blättern der Devesa, ein Fest der eßbaren Farben: die Früchte und Gemüse des Marktes.

52 El Ter

Llega cansado, el Ter, a Girona, desangrado por los pantanos.
La ciudad, que vivía de espaldas a él, lo está convirtiendo en eje del futuro, y el parque de las riberas del Ter le ha devuelto la dignidad. Los gerundenses empiezan a aprender a contemplarlo.

The Ter

The river arrives wearily, depleted by the reservoirs. Girona, after practically ignoring it for centuries, is now converting the river into an intrinsic part of the city and the riverside park has reinstated some of its dignity.

Der Fluß Ter

Der Fluß Ter kommt müde, von den Stauseen entleert, in Girona an. Die Stadt, die bisher mit dem Rücken zu ihm lebte, verwandelt ihn nun in die Achse der Zukunft und der Park an seinem Ufer hat ihm seine Würde zurückgegeben. Die Einwohner Gironas beginnen langsam, ihn zu betrachten.

53 Devesa de otoño (2)

"...el suelo de las avenidas era un fraseo de hojas muertas, y los árboles, en el momento de iniciar la desnudez invernal, eran como una inmensa brasa fría, tocada por un resplandor de vinagre..." (Josep Pla)

(Josep Pla, *Girona*, Ediciones Destino)

Autumn in the Devesa (2)

"...the floor of the avenues was a murmur of dead leaves, and the trees, just at the onset of their winter nudity, were like an immense cold ember, touched by a resplendence of vinegar..." (Josep Pla)

Devesa (Weideplatz) des Herbstes. (2)

"...der Boden der Alleen war ein Geflecht aus toten Blättern, und die Bäume waren in dem Augenblick, in dem sie die winterliche Nacktheit begannen, wie eine enorme, erkaltete Glut, die von einem Schimmer von Essig berührt wurde..." (Josep Pla).

54 Niebla

La niebla es un tópico climático gerundense, una discreta cortina blanca que cae amablemente sobre los perfiles vulgares de la ciudad moderna.

Mist

In Girona, the mist is a climatic cliché, a discreet white curtain that falls mercifully over the vulgar outlines of the modern city.

Nebel

Der Nebel ist ein klimatischer Allgemeinplatz von Girona, ein diskreter, weißer Vorhang, der liebenswürdig über die gewöhnlichen Formen der modernen Stadt fällt.

55 Geometría

En los últimos años, mientras luchaba por recuperar los espacios antiguos, la ciudad ha visto crecer algunos notables espacios modernos. Edificio de los juzgados.

Geometry

During recent years, and coinciding with endeavours to recover old spaces, some new and notable modern buildings have been created. Court house.

Geometrie

Während die Stadt in den letzten Jahren um die Wiederherstellung der alten Stadtteile kämpfte, wuchsen auch einige bemerkenswerte neue Anlagen. Das Gerichtsgebäude.

56 Sant Feliu

O San Félix. Hermano menor o alegre compañero de la catedral en las estampas del típico perfil. Posible sede del *martyrium*, o sepulcro de sant Feliu, el mártir local; núcleo simbólico, por tanto, de la primitiva comunidad cristiana.

Sant Feliu

Sant Feliu, like a little brother or cheerful companion to the cathedral in the pictures of its typical silhouette. It is the possible site of the *martyrium* (sepulchre) of sant Feliu, the local martyr, and is therefore the symbolic centre of the primitive Christian community

Sant Feliu

Oder der Heilige Feliu. Der kleine Bruder oder der fröhliche Begleiter der Kathedrale auf den typischen Abbildungen. Möglicher Sitz des *Martyrium*, oder Grabstätte des Heiligen Felix, des lokalen Märtyrers; also ein symbolischer Kern der primitiven, christlichen Gemeinschaft.

57 Catedral bancaria

Uno de los espacios más admirados de la Girona contemporánea es el nuevo edificio del Banco de España (de los arquitectos Clotet y Paricio), situado delante de la gran plaza, también contemporánea, de la Constitución. El templo circular del dios de los tiempos modernos.

Cathedral of banking

One of Girona's most admired contemporary buildings is the new seat of the Banco de España (by Clotet and Paricio), situated in the modern plaça de la Constitució. The circular temple of the God of our times.

Bankkathedrale

Einer der meistbewundertsten Bauten des modernen Gironas ist das neue Gebäude der Bank von Spanien (Banco de España), an dem großen, ebenfalls zeitgenössischen Platzes Plaça de la Constitució gelegen. Der runde Tempel für den Gott der modernen Zeiten.

58 Parque central

Una de las señales abiertas en el territorio expansivo de la ciudad es la vía del tren, que, en la parte que limita con el barrio de Sant Narcís, ha permitido la construcción de una zona verde muy popular: el Parc Central (la raya obscura que centra la fotografía).

Parc Central

The railway is one of the expanding city's open scars which, as it borders the Sant Narcís quarter, has given rise to the creation of a popular green zone: the Parc Central, (the dark line in the centre of the photograph).

Parc Central

Eines der offenen Merkmale im expansivem Bereich der Stadt ist die Bahnlinie, die in dem Abschnitt, der das Viertel Sant Narcís begrenzt, die Konstruktion einer Grünzone mit dem volkstümlichen Namen Parc Central (der dunkle Streifen im Zentrum des Fotos) ermöglicht hat.

59 Clasicismo

El edificio novecentista de Correos hace chaflán con la plaza de la Independencia. Forman un espacio neoclásico tal vez poco inspirado, pero digno. Prácticamente el único punto de flexión entre la ciudad medieval o barroca y el presente futurista.

Classicism

The *noucentista* Post Office building stands on a corner of the plaça de la Independència, forming a worthy, if uninspired, Neoclassical image. This is practically the only point where the medieval, or Baroque city meets the futuristic present.

Klassizismus

Das Postgebäude im Stil des neunzehnten Jahrhunderts befindet sich an der Plaça de la Independencia. ein klassizistischer Bau mit vielleicht wenig Inspiration, aber viel Würde. Es handelt sich praktisch um den einzigen Annäherungspunkt zwischen der mittelalterlichen oder barocken Stadt und der futuristischen Gegenwart.

60 Teatro

La vida teatral de la zona de Girona es intensa y variada gracias a la existencia del Teatre de Salt, a la sala independiente La Planeta, a la Escuela El Galliner y al esplendoroso Teatre Municipal (s. XIX), que fue construido con gusto romántico y opulencia de estucados, terciopelos y pinturas.

Theatre

The splendid 19th century Teatre Municipal was built after the romantic style with opulent stuccowork, paintings and velvets, and forms (along with the Teatre de Salt, La Planeta and the El Galliner school), Girona's varied theatrical repertoire.

Theater

Das Theaterleben im Einzugsgebiet von Girona ist intensiv und vielseitig aufgrund der Existenz des Theaters Teatre de Salt, des unabhängigen Theaters La Planeta, der Schule El Galliner, und des prächtigen Teatre Municipal (XIX. Jahrhundert), das nach romantischem Geschmack mit üppigem Stuck, Samt und Malereien erbaut wurde.

61 Modernismo

Desgraciadamente no toda la obra del arquitecto Rafael Masó se ha conservado. La Farinera Teixidor (actualmente en restauración) revela, en las formas fantasiosas y en el uso de materiales, la influencia de Gaudí.

Modernisme

Unfortunately, not all the work of Rafael Masó (1880-1935) has been conserved. The Farinera Teixidor (currently being restored), reveals Gaudí's influence on the architect, both in its imaginative forms and the building materials used.

Modernisme

Leider ist nicht das gesamte Werk des Architekten Rafael Masó erhalten worden. Die Farinera Teixidor (die zur Zeit renoviert wird), läßt an den phantasievollen Formen und am Gebrauch der Materialien den Einfluß Gaudís erkennen.

62 Centro comercial

Las calles de la parte baja del barrio viejo se han restaurado con prudencia y forman un pequeño laberinto comercial. Cada calle tiene un acento particular, como si se renovase el recuerdo de los antiguos gremios.

Commercial centre

The streets of the lower part of the old city have been carefully restored and form a small commercial labyrinth. Each street has a particular emphasis, as if renewing the memory of the old guilds.

Einkaufszone

Die Straßen im unteren Teil der Altstadt sind mit Umsicht erneuert worden und formen ein kleines, kommerzielles Labyrinth. Jede Straße hat einen einzigartigen Akzent, so als ob die Erinnerung an die alten Innungen wiederhergestellt würde.

63 Montilivi

El Campus universitario de Montilivi concentra varias facultades. El conjunto arquitectónico resultante confirma visualmente el impulso de futuro que significa la UdG.

Montilivi

The Montilivi campus is the site of various faculties. The resulting architectural complex is visual confirmation of the university's role in the modernisation of the city.

Montilivi

Auf dem Campus der Universität Montilivi gibt es mehrere Fakultäten. Das sich daraus ergebende, architektonische Gesamtbild bestätigt visuell den Anreiz für die Zukunft, den die Universität von Girona gibt.

64 Lo nuevo y lo viejo

La remodelación (arquitectos Fuses y Viader) del edificio de Les Àligues, sede del rectorado de la UdG, es un sensacional ejemplo de fusión entre modernidad y antigüedad. Una síntesis simbólica que la Universidad encarna.

Ancient and modern

The transformation (by the architects Fuses and Viader) of the Àligues building, seat of the University rectory, is a sensational example of the fusion between ancient and modern styles symbolized by the university.

Das Alte und das Neue

Die Wiederherstellung (unter den Architekten Fuses und Viader) des Gebäudes Les Àligues, Sitz des Rektorates der UdG, ist ein sensationelles Beispiel für die Verschmelzung von Modernität und Altertümlichkeit. Eine symbolische Synthese verkörpert von der Universität.

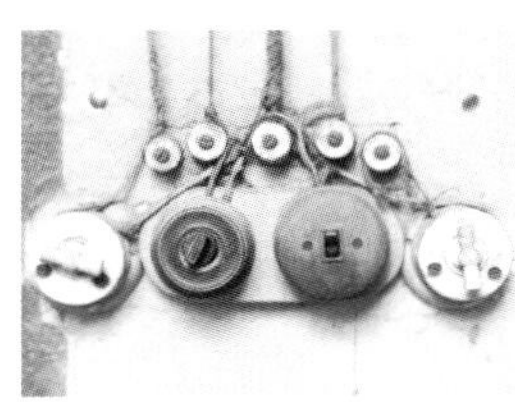

65 Supervivencia

Entre la antigüedad y la modernidad, prácticamente ya no hay lugar –en Girona como en toda Europa– para las variantes impuras. Por ello, estos desfasados interruptores eléctricos tienen un valor artístico: han sobrevivido.

Survival

Between antiquity and modernity, there is practically no room in Girona, or for that matter, anywhere in Europe, for unorthodox variations. These outdated switches have, therefore, an artistic value: they have survived.

Überleben

Zwischen der Altertümlichkeit und der Modernität gibt es weder in Girona noch in ganz Europa fast keinen Ort mehr für die unreinen Varianten. Deshalb haben diese überholten, elektrischen Schalter einen künstlerischen Wert; sie haben überlebt.

66 Masó

La restauración de la mansion medieval de los Salietti, en la calle Ciutadans, es también obra del arquitecto Masó, que puso la piedra, la cerámica, las vidrieras y el hierro al servicio de un idealismo gótico.

Masó

The restoration of the medieval Salietti mansion on carrer Ciutadans is also work of Masó. He put stone, glass and iron at the service of a Gothic idealogy.

Masó

Die Renovierung des mittelalterlichen Herrenhauses der Salietti in der Straße Ciutadans ist ebenfalls ein Werk des Architekten Masó, der den Stein, die Keramik, die Verglasungen und das Eisen in den Dienst eines gotischen Idealismus stellte.

67 Novecentismo

En la antigua zona de los gremios, la modernización ya se inició a caballo de los siglos XIX y XX. Esta farmacia de la plaza de las Castañas, por ejemplo, responde a las elegantes innovaciones del novecentismo.

Noucentisme

In the old area of the craftsmen, the modernisation of the ancient city was initiated at the turn of the century. This pharmacy, on the plaça de les Castanyes, follows the elegant innovations of the *noucentisme* movement.

Mode des neunzehnten Jahrhunderts

In dem alten Stadtteil der Innungen fing die Modernisierung schon im XIX. und XX. Jahrhundert an. Ein Beispiel für die eleganten Erneuerungen der Mode des neunzehnten Jahrhunderts ist die Apotheke am Plaça de les Castanyes.

68 Les Fires

Un mercado de arte, antigüedades y artesanía se extiende por todos los rincones del casco antiguo y de los ensanches más céntricos: es 29 de octubre, día de Sant Narcís, patrono de la ciudad. Les Fires (Las ferias), Girona hierve y los visitantes la ocupan.

Les Fires

An art, antiques and handicraft market occupies every corner of the old city on October 29th, Sant Narcis's Day, patron saint of the city. Girona, overrun by visitors, throbs with life.

Les Fires

Ein Markt für Kunstwerke, Antiquitäten und Kunsthandwerk erstreckt sich über alle Winkel der Altstadt und der zentral gelegensten Stadterweiterungen; es ist der 29. Oktober, der Tag von Sant Narcís, dem Stadtheiligen. Les Fires (Jahrmarkt, Volksfest), ein emsiges Treiben in Girona, überall sind die Besucher.

69 Intimidad claustral

Por más argumentos que se usen (las maravillosas escenas bíblicas de los capiteles, la arcaica presencia de la torre románica, la doble columnata), nada explica la prodigiosa belleza del claustro de la catedral: el silencio verde.

Cloister

Above and beyond the wonderful biblical scenes on the capitals, the archaic presence of the Romanesque tower and the double colonnade, the prodigious beauty of the cathedral cloister resides in its silent verdancy.

Die Intimität des Kreuzganges

Wieviel Gründe man auch anführt (die wundervollen, biblischen Szenen an den Kapitellen, die altertümliche Präsenz des romanischen Turmes, der doppelte Säulengang), nichts kann die außerordentliche Schönheit des Kreuzganges der Kathedrale erklären; die grüne Stille.

70 Signo

Un detalle anónimo de religiosidad popular. De una belleza oscura, primitiva, informa, tanto o más que la catedral, de la Girona del pasado.

Symbol

An anonymous detail of popular belief; obscure, primitive beauty, as eloquent as the cathedral itself about the Girona of the past.

Sinnbild

Eine anonyme Einzelheit der Religiosität des Volkes. Es besitzt eine dunkle und primitive Schönheit und zeugt genauso oder mehr als die Kathedrale von dem Girona der Vergangenheit.

71 El vuelo de la piedra

La catedral es una inmensa masa pétrea que vuela sobre la ciudad, como un saurio arcaico, indiferente y único.

Flight of stone

The cathedral, an immense stone mass, flies over the city like a prehistoric creature, indifferent and unique.

Der Flug des Steines

Die Kathedrale ist eine enorme Steinmasse, die über der Stadt schwebt, wie ein uraltes Saurier, gleichgültig und einzigartig.

72 La escalinata

Es bastante más que un dinámico y atrevido preámbulo de la catedral. Cuando los visitantes la ocupan, se convierte en un plató; cuando está vacía sugiere el movimiento y la desmesura del arte.

Stairway

More than just a dynamic and audacious approach to the cathedral, when crowded with visitors, the staircase becomes a stage; when empty, it suggests the movement and extravagance of art.

Der Treppengang

Er ist viel mehr als nur ein dynamisches und gewagtes Vorspiel zur Kathedrale. Wenn die Besucher sich auf ihm befinden, verwandelt er sich in eine Filmkulisse, wenn er leer ist, deutet er Bewegung und die Maßlosigkeit der Kunst an.

73 Prodigiosa nave

La nave única de la catedral, la más ancha entre las góticas, provoca –tal como ha descrito Narcís-Jordi Aragó– una impresión "de singular potencia y de ingravidez al mismo tiempo". La luz de las deliciosas vidrieras de época endulza la formidable expansión de la piedra.

Prodigous nave

The Gothic cathedral nave, the largest of its kind, evokes (according to Narcís-Jordi Aragó), a simultaneous impression "of singular power and weightlessness". Light from the delightful stained-glass windows comes to brighten the formidable expansion of stone.

Außerordentliches Kirchenschiff

Das einzigartige Kirchenschiff der Kathedrale, das breiteste dieser Art, ruft laut Narcís-Jordi Aragó einen "Eindruck von einzigartiger Macht und gleichzeitiger Schwerelosigkeit hervor". Das Licht der zarten Glasfenster versüßt die ungeheure Ausdehnung der Steine.

74 El bordado más exquisito

Una deliciosa figura del célebre Tapiz de la Creación. El detallismo fotográfico permite observar los preciosos hilos del bordado, joya única del arte medieval (siglos XI-XII) que se conserva en el Museu de la Catedral.

Exquisite embroidery

A delightful figure from the famous Tapis de la Creaciò. Photographic detail reveals the beautiful threads of the embroidery, unique gem of medieval art (11th-12th centuries), kept in the Museu de la Catedral.

Die feinste Stickerei

Eine wundervolle Figur des berühmten Tapiç de la Creaciò. Die Fotografie läßt die wertvollen Fäden der Stickerei erkennen, ein einzigartiges Schmuckstück der mittelalterlichen Kunst (XI.-XII. Jahrhundert), das im Museum der Kathedrale aufbewahrt wird.

75 Cosmovisión

El Tapiz de la Creación –que por sí solo justifica una visita a Girona– representa, a través de una fascinante combinación de figuras y símbolos, la visión medieval de la vida y el tiempo.

Cosmovision

The Tapestry of the Creation – in itself a reason to visit Girona – illustrates the medieval conception of life and time by means of a fascinating combination of figures and symbols.

Weltanschauung

Der Tapiç de la Creaciò – nur um ihn zu sehen, lohnt schon ein Besuch in Girona – stellt in einer faszinierenden Kombination von Figuren und Symbolen die mittelalterliche Vision des Lebens und der Zeit dar.

76 Severidad

La Porta dels Apòstols (Puerta de los Apóstoles), salida lateral de la catedral, es de origen gótico, pero no fue acabada hasta 1975. A pesar de esto, el espacio tiene una rara solemnidad: un patio de piedra, con escalones de piedra, definido por la piedra gris y severa del entorno.

Severity

The Porta dels Apóstols, side entrance to the cathedral, is of Gothic origin, but completeed in 1975. Despite this, it has an air of rare solemnity: a stone patio, with stone steps, defined by the severe grey stone of the surroundings.

Strenge

Die Porta dels Apòstols, der Seitenausgang der Kathedrale, ist gotischen Ursprungs, wurde jedoch erst im Jahre 1975 fertiggestellt. Trotzdem hat dieser Raum eine seltene Feierlichkeit; ein Innenhof aus Steinen mit steinernen Stufen, der von den grauen und strengen Steinen der Umgebung bestimmt wird.

77 Md'A

El Museu d'Art, situado en el Palacio Episcopal acoge una importantísima colección de tallas y retablos medievales y una excelente muestra de la historia del arte gerundense; pero es, sobre todo, una institución viva, uno de los pulmones culturales de la ciudad.

Md'A

The art museum, in the Palau Episcopal, is home to an important collection of carvings and altarpieces and an excellent exhibition of Girona's artistic heritage; but, above all, it is a lively institution and one of the city's cultural driving forces.

Md'A

Das Museu d'Art im Bischofspalast enthält eine wichtige Sammlung von mittelalterlichen Bildhauerarbeiten und Altargemälden und eine sehr gute Ausstellung über die Kunstgeschichte von Girona. Vor allem ist dieses Museum jedoch eine lebendige Einrichtung, eine der kulturellen Antriebsstätten der Stadt.

78 Sepulcros

Este bellísimo sepulcro romano está adosado a la pared lateral de la iglesia de Sant Feliu, una iglesia que atesora lápidas valiosísimas: el sarcófago gótico de Sant Narcís, o los sarcófagos romanos, que provenían de los mejores talleres del Imperio, de un refinamiento excepcional.

Sepulchres

This beautiful Romanesque sepulchre is adjoined to the side wall of the church of Sant Feliu where other valuable stones are kept: the Gothic sarcophagus of Sant Narcís, for example, or the Roman sarcophagi made in one of the Empire's finest workshops and particularly refined.

Grabstätten

Diese wunderschöne, romanische Grabstätte befindet sich an der Seitenwar der Kirche Sant Feliu, eine Kirche, die wertvollste Grabsteine hortet; den gotischen Sarkophag des Sant Narcís ode die romanischen Sarkophage, die aus den besten Werkstätten des Reiches stammter und außerordentlich schön gearbeitet sinc

79 Numulites

En esta erosionada columna de la catedral son perfectamente visibles los pequeños moluscos fosilizados que forman la piedra numulítica: la clásica piedra gris de Girona. Una piedra con alma.

Fossils

Small fossilized crustaceans are clearly visible in this eroded cathedral column, forming the grey, nummilite stone, so typical of Girona. Stone with a soul.

Nummuliten

In dieser erodierten Säule der Kathedrale kann man perfekt die kleinen, versteinerten Weichtiere erkennen, die das Nummulitgestein bilden; der klassische, graue Stein von Girona. Ein Stein mit Seele.

80 Sugestión de las piedras

En ninguna parte como en algunos rincones de los Baños árabes para captar, sin connotaciones religiosas, atmósferas pasadas.

Insinuation of the stones

The Arab baths, like nowhere else, exude an atmosphere of the past, devoid of religious connotations.

Einwirkung der Steine

Es gibt keinen besseren Ort als einige Winkel der arabischen Bäder, um ohne religiöse Konnotationen vergangene Stimmungen einzufangen.

81 Mestizaje cultural

Los Baños árabes son, en realidad, románicos. Pero ciertamente incorporan muchas influencias: un edificio románico que reproduce las instalaciones termales romanas según un modelo árabe.

Cultural crossbreeding

The Arab baths are, in fact, Romanesque, but encompass many cultural influences: a Romanesque building reproducing Roman thermae after an Arab model.

Kulturelle Vermischung

Die arabischen Bäder sind in Wirklichkeit romanisch. Aber ganz sicher beinhalten sie verschiedene Einflüsse; ein romanisches Gebäude, das die römischen Badeanlagen nach einem arabischen Modell reproduziert.

82 Divertimiento barroco

El arco renacentista del Palacio de Agullana permite la espectacular bifurcación de las escaleras de la cuesta de Sant Domènec. El palacio rompe, además, la perspectiva de la fachada de Sant Martí, que corona la escalera principal. Belleza barroca: ingenio, divertimiento, utilidad.

Baroque style

The Renaissance arch of the Palau d'Agullana allows for the spectacular bifurcation of the Pujada de Sant Domènec stairs. The palace also alters the perspective of the façade of the Sant Martí church, at the top of the main flight. Baroque beauty: inventive, beguiling, practical.

Barocker Zeitvertreib

Der Renaissancegewölbebogen des Palau de Agullana erlaubt die einzigartige Verzweigung der Treppen der Pujada de Sant Domènec. Außerdem unterbricht der Palast die Perspektive der Fassade von Sant Martí, die die Haupttreppe krönt. Barocke Schönheit: Kunstwerk, Zeitvertreib, Nützlichkeit.

83 Carlomagno

El río Galligants se escurre por el ameno valle de Sant Daniel y, antes de confluir con el Ter, crea un espacio fértil y sombrío desde donde se alza, inexpugnable, el perfil más arcaico de la catedral con la torre románica llamada de Carlomagno.

Charlemagne

The river Galligants flows through the pleasant Sant Daniel valley and, before joining the Ter, creates a fertile and shady area where the city's most archaic building stands: the Romanesque Charlemagne tower.

Charlemagne

Der Fluß Galligants durchläuft das liebliche Tal Sant Daniel und bevor er in den Ter mündet, schafft er eine fruchtbare und schattige Zone, von der sich, uneinnehmbar, die altertümlichste Ansicht der Kathedrale erhebt; der romanische Turm, der Charlemagne genannt wird.

84 Tejados

Desde cualquier punto elevado de la Girona antigua, un mar de tejados: discretas olas de color de arcilla.

Rooftops

From any vantage point within old Girona, a sea of rooftops, discreet waves, the colour of clay.

Dächer

Von jedem erhöhten Punkt des alten Gironas aus, ein Meer von Dächern; diskrete Wellen in der Farbe von Ziegelerde.

85 Barroco

La Girona antigua es medieval pero también barroca, llena de contrastes formales: la plaza de la Catedral, por ejemplo, tensada por una desmesurada escalinata y por la enorme masa de la catedral.

Baroque

Old Girona is medieval, but also Baroque, full of contrasts. For example, the plaça de la Catedral, with its disproportionate stairway and the huge bulk of the cathedral.

Barock

Das alte Girona ist mittelalterlich, aber auch barock, voller formaler Kontraste: der Kathedralenplatz zum Beispiel, der von einem riesigen Treppengang und der wuchtigen Masse der Kathedrale gestrafft wird.

86 Gris

Desde Sant Feliu se llega a la catedral por el Portal de Sobreportes, que es la entrada al primitivo recinto fortificado fundado por los romanos. Tan sólo una señal de tráfico altera la radical uniformidad del gris histórico.

Grey

From Sant Feliu, the Portal de Sobreportes (entrance to the original Roman fortification), leads to the cathedral. Only a road sign interrupts the historic grey uniformity.

Grau

Von Sant Feliu zur Kathedrale kommt man durch das Portal de Sobreportes, das der Eingang zur ursprünglichen, von den Römern gegründeten Festung ist. Nur ein Verkehrssignal unterbricht die radikale Einheitlichkeit des historischen Graus

87 Sant Pere

Bestiario fabuloso, motivos florales, inspiración clásica y oriental: fantasía y refinamiento artístico en los capiteles de Sant Pere de Galligants, ahora reconvertido en museo arqueológico.

Sant Pere

The fabulous bestiary, floral motifs, classical and oriental inspiration: fantasy and artistic refinement on the cloister capitals in the monastery of Sant Pere de Galligants, today the Museu Arqueologic.

Sant Pere

Fabelhaftes Bestiarium, Blumenmotive, klassische und orientalische Inspiration; Phantasie und künstlerische Verfeinerung in den Kapitellen von Sant Pere de Galligants, das heute zum archäologischen Museum umgeformt ist.

88 La Mercè

Escuela de arte, Auditorio y ámbito de un apretado programa de humanidades, el Centre Cultural La Mercè ocupa el antiguo convento de los mercedarios y se ha convertido en el eje que conecta la universidad con la sociedad gerundense.

La Mercè

The Centre Cultural La Mercè is an art school, auditorium and scene of a busy humanities programme which has become the connecting element between the university and society.

La Mercè

Kunsthochschule, Auditorium und Umfeld für ein gedrängtes Programm der humanistischen Bildung. Das Kulturzentrum La Mercè befindet sich in dem ehemaligen Kloster der Mönche der Mercè und ist heutzutage die Achse, die die Universität mit der Gesellschaft Gironas verbindet.

89 Bonastruc

El máximo pensador de la escuela cabalística de Girona fue Bonastruc ça Porta; el centro cultural que reivindica su nombre pretende impulsar el reconocimiento de la aportación intelectual de los hebreos gerundenses.

Bonastruc

Bonastruc ça Porta was the greatest philosopher of Girona's cabalistic school. The cultural centre which bears his name seeks to promote recognition of the intellectual apportation of Girona's Jews.

Bonastruc

Der wichtigste Denker der kabbalistischen Schule Gironas war Bonastruc ça Porta; das Kulturzentrum, das seinen Namen trägt, versucht die Anerkennung des intellektuellen Beitrag der Hebräer Gironas zu fördern.

90 El pasado, confidente

Varias calles de la judería, en escalera como ésta de Cúndaro, avanzan entre estrecheces, como túneles. El pasado parece aquí haberse detenido y es más sugestivo que una confidencia.

The confident past

Various streets of the Jewry, in the form of stairways (such as the Cundaro), advance narrowly, like tunnels. The past is omnipresent here, as insinuating as a whisper.

Die Vergangenheit, vertraulich

Verschiedene Straßen in Form einer Treppe wie die Straße Cúndaro dringen zwischen der Enge wie Tunnel vor. Hier scheint die Vergangenheit angehalten zu haben und suggestiver als eine Vertraulichkeit zu sein

91 Farmacia barroca

El edificio del Hospital de Santa Caterina, todavía en uso como centro sanitario, acoge, además de una excelente portada, una farmacia histórica que contiene la más importante colección catalana de tarros de boticario (siglos XVII y XVIII).

Baroque pharmacy

The Hospital de Santa Caterina, still in use as a medical centre, boasts a splendid portal and an historic pharmacy containing the finest collection of 17th and 18th century apothecary jars in Catalunya.

Die barocke Apotheke

In dem Gebäude des Hospital de Santa Caterina, das heute noch als ein Gesundheitszentrum genutzt wird, befindet sich außer eines wundervollen Eingangstores eine historische Apotheke die die wichtigste Sammlung Katalonien an Apothekertiegeln (XVII. und XIII. Jahrhundert) enthält.

92 Oro y óxidos

Detalle de la farmacia de Santa Caterina. Durante años, el otoño, que aporta a las hojas de la Devesa estos mismos colores, fue el emblema poético de la belleza decadente de la ciudad. Ahora, en cambio, se imponen colores más vivos, otros símbolos.

Gold and rust

Detail of the Santa Caterina pharmacy. For years, autumn was the poetic emblem of the city, bringing these same colours to the leaves of the Devesa. Now, new, brighter colours and other symbols are the order of the day.

Gold und Rost

Ein Detail der Apotheke von Santa Caterina. Während vieler Jahre war der Herbst, der die Blätter der Devesa in diesen Farben färbt, das poetische Sinnbild der dekadenten Schönheit der Stadt. Jetzt jedoch setzen sich lebendigere Farben und andere Sinnbilder durch.

93 Cine

El equipamiento cultural más nuevo es el Museu del Cinema, construido a partir de la colección Tomàs Mallol de aparatos cinematográficos antiguos, una colección única e insólita que complementa la intensa cinefilia ciudadana.

Cinema

The Museu del Cinema is the city's newest cultural institution, created around the unique Tomàs Mallol collection of antique cimematographic apparatus.

Kino

Die neuste, kulturelle Einrichtung ist das Museu del Cinema (Kinomuseum), das ausgehend von der Sammlung Tomàs Mallol alter kinematographischer Apparate eingerichtet wurde; eine Sammlung, die einzigartig und ungewöhnlich ist und die Begeisterung der Bürger für das Kino ergänzt.

94 Romana

Estos mosaicos romanos conservados en el Museu d'Història, otro importante equipamiento cultural, dan testimonio del origen romano de *Gerunda*: una fortificación triangular construida hacia el año 76 A.C. por el general romano Cnaeus Pompeius Magnus.

Roman

These Roman mosaics conserved in the Museu d'Història, another important cultural centre, are witnesses to the Roman origin of *Gerunda*: a triangular fortification, built circa 76 B.C., by General Cnaeus Pompeius Magnus.

Romanisch

Diese romanischen Mosaike, die sich im Museu d'Història, einer anderen wichtigen, kulturellen Einrichtung, befinden, zeugen von dem römischen Ursprung von Gerunda; eine dreieckige Festung, die etwa im Jahre 76 v. Chr. von dem römischen General Cnaeus Pompeius Magnus erbaut wurde.

95 Pedret

Convertido actualmente en una zona de ocio, con una gran concentración de bares, pubs y restaurantes, el barrio de Pedret, que fuera de la muralla sigue el curso del Ter, tenía un colorido popular que este artesano superviviente ejemplifica.

Pedret

Now a busy area of bars, pubs and restaurants, the Pedret quarter, which follows the course of the Ter, has always had a popular character, as exemplified by this surviving craftsman.

Pedret

Heutzutage ein Stadtteil für die Freizeitgestaltung, mit einer Vielzahl von Gaststätten, Pubs und Restaurants, besaß das Viertel Pedret, das außerhalb der Stadtmauer dem Verlauf des Ters folgt, eine volkstümliche Färbung, wie dieser noch überlebende Kunsthandwerker verdeutlicht.

96 Artesanía

Todos estos instrumentos del tonelero de Pedret, hijos de una vieja tradición, aún están vivos; conservan la naturalidad de las cosas de siempre. Si sobreviven, lo hacen al margen de la cirugía estética y de los maquillajes de la modernidad.

Craftsmanship

These barrelmaker's tools, with the simplicity of objects born of ancient tradition, survive today despite the plastic surgery and makeup of modernity.

Kunsthandwerk

All diese Werkzeuge des Böttchers von Pedret, Nachfolger einer alten Tradition, sind immer noch lebendig; sie bewahren die Natürlichkeit der althergebrachten Gegenstände. Wenn sie überleben, tun sie es am Rande der Schönheitschirurgie und der Schminke der Modernität

97 Espais

El Centre d'Art Contemporani Espais, situado en el ensanche moderno de la ciudad, apuesta por las manifestaciones más radicales del arte de vanguardia y ayuda a equilibrar el peso cultural del pasado.

Espais

The Centre d'Art Contemporàni Espais, in the new part of the city, is site of exhibitions of the most radical avant-garde art, counterbalance to the cultural weight of the past.

Espais

Das Centre d'Art Contemporani (Zentrum für zeitgenössische Kunst) Espais, das sich in der modernen Stadterweiterung befindet, setzt auf die radikaleren Manifestationen der Kunst der Avantgarde und hilft, das kulturelle Gewicht der Vergangenheit auszugleichen

98 Habaneras

La escenográfica escalinata de la catedral ha sido, desde siempre, escenario de grandes encuentros litúrgicos. Y lo continua siendo: por Semana Santa culminan en ella las procesiones, aunque tampoco le son extraños los espectáculos laicos, como la anual cantada de habaneras de Les Fires.

Havaneres

Since time immemorial, the cathedral staircase has been the scene of important religious gatherings, notably the Holy Week processions. But secular events also have their place here, such as the *havaneres* recital during Les Fires.

Havaneres

Eine bühnenbildartige Freitreppe der Kathedrale war schon seit je her Schauplatz großer, liturgischer Treffen. Während der Osterwoche ist sie Schauplatz der Prozessionen, aber auch weltliche Darbietungen sind ihr nicht fremd, wie zum Beispiel die jährliche Aufführung von Habaneras während des Volksfestes *Havaneres*

99 Agua contradictoria

El Onyar es un río de caudal humilde, discretísimo. Sin embargo, durante las lluvias del otoño puede llegar a ser furioso e implacable. Por ello entra en la ciudad domesticado con un vestido de cemento.

Contradictory water

The Onyar is a discreet and humble river. During the autumn rains, however, it can become furious and relentless. For this reason, its entry into the city is contained by cement.

Widersprüchliches Wasser

Der Onyar ist ein Fluß mit einem bescheidenem und sehr zurückhaltendem Flußbett. Dennoch kann er im Herbst, wenn es viel regnet, wütend und unerbittlich werden. Deshalb fließt er durch ein Zementgewand gebändigt in die Stadt hinein.

100 Fetichismo

A medio camino de la obsesión y de la diversión, el coleccionismo de postales y de libros antiguos. El pasado recuperado como un fetiche.

Fetishism

Halfway between obsession and diversion, the collecting of old books and postcards is a way of reliving the past.

Fetischismus

Auf halbem Wege zwischen der Besessenheit und dem Zeitvertreib liegt die Sammelleidenschaft für Postkarten und alte Bücher. Die in Form eines Fetischs wiedererlangte Vergangenheit.

101 Infierno alegre

La magia festiva del fuego, que recupera formas antiguas del folklore catalán, se ha convertido en ingrediente esencial de las fiestas urbanas. Pólvora, fuego y disfraces transforman la ciudad en un infierno mediterráneo.

Merry inferno

The magical festival of fire, with its connotations of ancient Catalan folklore, is an intrinsic part of the city's festivities. Gunpowder, fire and fancy dress transform the city into a Mediterranean inferno.

Fröhliche Hölle

Die festliche Magie des Feuers, die alte Formen der katalanischen Folklore wiedererlangt, ist zu einem Hauptbestandteil der Stadtfeste geworden. Pulver, Feuer und Verkleidungen machen die Stadt zu einer mittelalterlichen Hölle.

102 Gigantes

La Trobada de Gegants (encuentro de gigantes) es uno de los espectáculos de participación popular más característicos de Les Fires. Si el *correfoc* (correfuegos) es juvenil, la concentración de gigantes tiene un aire de candor doméstico, infantil.

Giants

The Trobada de Gegants is one of the most characteristic events of Les Fires. If the *correfoc* is youthful in spirit, the parade of the giants has an air of childlike naiveté.

Giganten

Die Trobada de Gegants (das Treffen der Giganten) ist eines der charakteristischste Schauspiele während der Fires, an dem viele Bürger Gironas teilnehmen. Währer der *correfoc* (Umzug mit feuerspeienden Ungeheuern) ein Vergnügen für die Jugendlichen ist, ist das Treffen der Giganten eher gezähmt, eher für die Kind

103 La "marcha" de las piedras

Impulsores de la renovación del casco antiguo: los bares, los restaurantes, las galerías de arte y los comercios. Pero sobre todo los bares, los cafés, los pubs. Las piedras antiguas también combinan con el jazz, el rock, el hielo y los alcoholes.

The action and the stones

Bars, restaurants, art galleries and shops are the driving force behind the renovation of the old city, but particularly the bars cafés and pubs. The ancient stones have learnt to coexist with jazz, rock, ice cubes and alcohol.

Ausgehen zwischen den Steinen

Impuls für die Erneuerung der Altstadt: Gaststätten, Restaurants, Kunstgalerien und Geschäfte. Aber vor allem die Gaststätten, Cafés und Pubs. Die alten Steinen werden auch mit dem Jazz, dem Rock, dem Eis und dem Alkohol kombiniert.

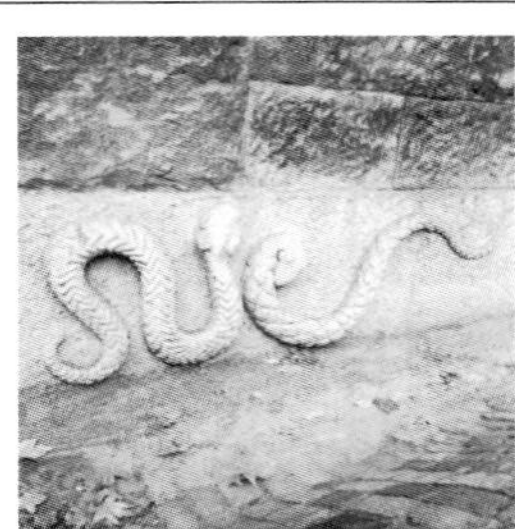

104 Serpientes de la muerte

El cementerio de Vila-roja, inaugurado en 1829, fue parcialmente reformado por Rafael Masó, quien diseñó el muro novecentista (1909) de piedra y cerámica, en la cual hizo esculpir estas serpientes fascinantes.

Serpents of death

The Vila-roja cemetery, inaugurated in 1829, was partially refurbished by Rafael Masó. He designed the noucentista (1909) stone and ceramic wall with these fascinating sculptured snakes.

Todesschlangen

Der Friedhof von Vila-roja, der im Jahre 1829 eingeweiht wurde, wurde teilweise von Rafael Masó renoviert, der die Mauer aus Stein und Keramik im Stile des neunzehnten Jahrhunderts (1909) erschuf, in die diese faszinierenden Schlangen gemeißelt sind.